Critical acclaim for

OPERATIONS MANAGEMENT

Third edition

The third edition of this terrific textbook maintains the very high standard set by its two predecessors. It succeeds by explaining the many individual aspects of the subject without ever losing sight of the bigger, integrated picture. In keeping with the trend towards global operations this updated version places more emphasis on the topic of supply chain management with the complexities of modern practice, via numerous cases and vignettes taken from different types of both service and manufacturing organizations. These examples are chosen so as to illustrate operations in various countries in Europe and indeed right around the world.

DR GEOFF BUXLEY
Bowater School of Management and Marketing, Deakin University, Australia

I can honestly say that each edition gets better and better. The original features of a clear framework, numerous practical examples and cases, and a good balance between manufacturing and service have been maintained, with the addition of new material on key topics. For example, in this edition, there is good coverage of the Internet and knowledge management, changes that are having significant effects on operations but which are ignored by many authors. Not only do my colleagues and I appreciate the clarity and relevance of the book for teaching purposes, but my students also like it, citing it as one of the most readable, up-to-date and well-referenced texts that they use. A textbook that is popular with both staff and students deserves increasingly wide recognition.

DR RUTH BOADEN
School of Management, UMIST

This is *the* book for management teaching and training. It is a text with real management perspective and a real focus on Operations. It covers many areas and applications beyond manufacturing and production planning and control. Every area of the production system and its context are dealt with. Hence it is of great value for those who will be active in and manage operations as well as those who will deal with and take decisions about operations. Both the student and the practising manager will learn from the text since it gives the concepts and the issues as well as the practical tools to manage operations. The book is especially suitable for teaching and executive development in business schools since it presents the central role of operations in the whole organization and conveys the knowledge every manager regardless of his/her profession should have about operations.

DR CHRISTER KARLSSON
Professor of Industrial Production, Stockholm School of Economics

In the 3rd edition of *Operations Management*, Nigel Slack and his colleagues have recognized the increasing importance of service operations by adopting a more generic approach to much of their material. This is especially evident in the substantially revised chapters on 'process technology' and 'supply chain management'.

DR DAVID BENNETT
Professor of Technology Management, Aston Business School, Birmingham

The Slack *et al.* text is the best operations management textbook on the market. Its clear structure, comprehensive coverage and wealth of practical examples make it ideal for MBA and executive programmes, as well as traditional undergraduate courses.

DR ANDY NEELY
Professor Operations Strategy and Performance, Cranfield School of Management

This is the only textbook that fully explores the meaning of operations management.

DR PÄR ÅHLSTRÖM
Centre for Innovation and Operations Management, Stockholm School of Economics

Pearson
Education

We work with leading authors to develop the
strongest educational materials in operations management,
bringing cutting-edge thinking and best learning
practice to a global market.

Under a range of well-known imprints, including
Financial Times Prentice Hall, we craft high quality print and
electronic publications which help readers to understand
and apply their content, whether studying or at work.

To find out more about the complete range of our
publishing please visit us on the World Wide Web at:
www.pearsoneduc.com

OPERATIONS MANAGEMENT

Third edition

Nigel Slack

Stuart Chambers

Robert Johnston

An imprint of **Pearson Education**

Harlow, England · London · New York · Reading, Massachusetts · San Francisco · Toronto · Don Mills, Ontario · Sydney
Tokyo · Singapore · Hong Kong · Seoul · Taipei · Cape Town · Madrid · Mexico City · Amsterdam · Munich · Paris · Milan

Pearson Education Limited
Edinburgh Gate
Harlow
Essex CM20 2JE
England

and Associated Companies around the World

Visit us on the World Wide Web at:
www.pearsoneduc.com

———————————————

First published under the Pitman Publishing imprint 1995
Second edition (Pitman Publishing) 1998
Third edition 2001

ISBN 0273-64657-5

British Library Cataloguing-in-Publication Data
A catalogue record for this book can be obtained from the British Library

Library of Congress Cataloging-in-Publication Data
Available from the publisher

10 9 8 7 6 5 4 3 2 1
05 04 03 02 01

Typeset by 30 in 9/12pt Stone Serif
Printed and bound by Rotolito Lombarda, Italy

Contents

Part One
INTRODUCTION

Part Two
DESIGN

Preface

Introduction

Operations management is *important*. It is concerned with creating the products and services upon which we all depend. And creating products and services is the very reason for any organization's existence, whether that organization be large or small, manufacturing or service, for profit or not for profit. Thankfully, most companies have now come to understand the importance of operations. One survey of chief executive officers[1] showed 43 per cent of them citing operations as the most important area of employee know-how. Also there is evidence that organizations are spending increasing amounts of money on improving their operations. The figure below shows what companies are spending with consultancy firms worldwide in the different management areas. Operations management is the largest segment of the market. This is probably because organizations have realized that effective operations management gives the potential to improve revenues and, at the same time, enables goods and services to be produced more efficiently. It is this combination of higher revenues and lower costs which is understandably important to any organization.

Operations management is also *exciting*. It is at the centre of so many of the changes affecting the business world – changes in customer preference, changes in supply networks brought about by internet-based technologies, changes in what we want to do at work, how we want to work, where we want to work, and so on. There has rarely been a time when operations management was more topical or more at the heart of business and cultural shifts.

Finally, operations management is *challenging*. Promoting the creativity which will allow organizations to respond to so many changes is becoming the prime task of operations managers. It is they who must find the solutions to technological and environmental challenges, the pressures to be socially responsible, the increasing globalization of markets and the difficult-to-define areas of knowledge management.

The consultancy services market: percentage of world revenues of 40 largest firms

Financial (6)
Marketing/sales (2)
Organizational design (11)
Operations and process management (31)
Benefits/ actuarial (16)
Corporate strategy (17)
IT strategy (17)

Source: *The Economist*, 22 March 1997

The aim of this book

The aim of this book is to provide a clear, well structured and interesting treatment of operations management as it applies to a variety of businesses and organizations. The text provides both a logical path through the activities of operations management and an understanding of their strategic context.

More specifically, this text aims to be:

- *Strategic* in its perspective of operations management's contribution to the organization's long-term success. We are unambiguous in treating the operations function as being central to competitiveness.

---

[1] Hall, R. (1992) 'The Strategic Analysis of Intangible Resources', *The Strategic Management Journal*, vol 13, p. 142.

- *Conceptual* in the way it explains the reasons why operations managers need to take decisions. Although some quantitative techniques are included, their primary aim is to illustrate the underlying principles of operations decisions.
- *Comprehensive* in its coverage of the significant ideas and issues which are relevant to most types of operation.
- *Practical* in that the issues and difficulties in making operations management decisions *in practice* are discussed. Generally, the treatment reflects actual operations practice, illustrated in the case exercises and 'boxes' which explore the approaches taken by actual companies.
- *International* in the examples which are used. Out of over 110 descriptions of operations practice, around a third are from continental Europe, a third from the UK and a third are general or from elsewhere in the world.
- *Balanced* in its treatment. This means we treat service operations with the same level of seriousness as manufacturing operations and, where possible, we have included both service and manufacturing examples to illustrate a point.

● Who should use this book?

This book is intended to provide an introduction to operations management for all students who wish to understand the nature and activities of operations management; for example:

- *Undergraduates* on business studies, technical or joint degrees should find it sufficiently structured to provide an understandable route through the subject (no prior knowledge of the area is assumed).
- *MBA students* should find that its practical discussions of operations management activities enhance their own experience.
- *Postgraduate students* on other specialist masters degrees should find that it provides them with a well-grounded and, at times, critical approach to the subject.

● Distinctive features

Clear structure

As before we have chosen to structure the book on a model of operations management which distinguishes between design, planning and control, and improvement. In addition, we both start and finish the book by treating the strategic aspects of the subject.

Illustrations-based

Operations management is a practical subject and cannot be taught satisfactorily in a purely theoretical manner. Because of this we have used both abstracted examples and 'boxed' examples which explain some issues faced by real operations.

Worked examples

Operations management is largely a qualitative subject but does include consideration of some quantitative techniques. When these are included, we have often illustrated them by means of 'worked examples' to demonstrate how a technique can be used.

Critical commentaries

Not everyone agrees about what is the best approach to the various topics and issues with operations management. This is why we have, at certain points in the text, included a 'critical commentary'. These are alternative views to the one being expressed in the main flow of the text. They do not necessarily represent our view, but they are worth debating.

Summary answers to key questions

Each chapter is summarized in the form of a list of bullet points. These extract the essential points which answer the key question posed at the beginning of each chapter.

Case exercises

Every chapter includes at least one case exercise which is a short case study suitable for class discussion. The cases are usually short enough to serve as illustrations, which can be referred to in class, but have sufficient content also to serve as the basis of case sessions.

Selected further reading

Every chapter ends with a list of further reading which takes the topics covered in the chapter further, or treats some important related issues.

Instructor's manual

A completely new instructor's manual is available to lecturers adopting this textbook. It includes short commentaries on each chapter which can be used as student handouts, as well as selected OHP masters which are also available on a Powerpoint disk.

Website

A very much expanded and enhanced range of support materials is available to lecturers and students on the Pearson Education website.

● New for the third edition

The second edition proved to be even more successful than the first, and again we would like to thank everyone who helped us make it such a success. Although we have not made any radical changes to the structure in this edition, regular users of the book will notice some significant changes.

- The book is now in full colour throughout. This has allowed us to position the colour illustrations and boxes more appropriately in the text, as well as including some further illustrations.
- There has been some repositioning of material, but not to the extent that it disturbs the essential flow of the topics covered in the book.
- The idea of the worked examples has been much extended to cover all the quantitative-based techniques described in the book.
- Critical commentaries have been introduced which we hope will encourage debate around some of the more contentious operations management issues.
- Several of the popular boxed examples have been updated or adapted, and some are totally new.
- Some additional material is included, most notably in the chapter on operations strategy (Chapter 3), the chapter on supply chain planning and control (Chapter 13) and in the final chapter on operations challenges.

A Companion Web Site accompanies
Operations Management, 3/e by Slack *et al.*

Visit the *Operations Management* Companion Web Site at http://www.booksites.net/slack to find valuable teaching and learning material including:

For students:
- Study material designed to help you improve your results
- Links to valuable resources on the web
- Extra self-assessment questions
- Search for specific information on the site

For lecturers:
- A syllabus manager that will build and host a course web page
- A downloadable version of the full instructor's manual
- Downloadable OHP masters
- Extra case material to download

Also: This regularly maintained site also has search functions.

About the authors

Nigel Slack is the A E Higgs Professor of Manufacturing Policy and Strategy at Warwick University. Previously he was Professor of Manufacturing Strategy and Lucas Professor of Manufacturing Systems Engineering at Brunel University, University Lecturer in Management Studies at Oxford University and Fellow in Operations Management at Templeton College, Oxford.

He worked initially as an industrial apprentice in the hand-tool industry and then as a production engineer and production manager in light engineering. He holds a Bachelor's degree in Engineering and Master's and Doctor's degrees in Management. He is also a chartered engineer. He is the author of several publications in the operations management area, including *The Manufacturing Advantage*, published by Mercury Business Books, 1991, and *Making Management Decisions* (with Steve Cooke) now in its second edition, 1991, published by Prentice Hall, and more recently, *Service Superiority* (with Robert Johnston), published in 1993 by EUROMA and *Cases in Operations Management* (with Robert Johnston, Alan Harrison, Stuart Chambers and Christine Harland) second edition published by Financial Times Pitman Publishing in 1997. His research is in the operations and manufacturing flexibility and operations strategy areas.

Stuart Chambers has been a lecturer at Warwick Business School since 1988. He began his career as an undergraduate apprentice at Rolls Royce Aerospace, graduating in mechanical engineering, and then worked in production and general management with companies including Tube Investments and the Marley Tile Company. In his mid-thirties and seeking a career change, he studied for an MBA, and then took up a three-year contract as a researcher in manufacturing strategy. This work enabled him to help executives develop the analyses, concepts and practical solutions required for them to develop manufacturing strategies. Several of the case studies prepared from this work have been published in an American textbook on manufacturing strategy.

In addition to lecturing on a range of operations courses at the Business School and in industry, Stuart is continuing his research in the manufacturing strategy field. His research interests also include service quality management in leisure and catering businesses. He undertakes consultancy in a diverse range of industries and is co-author of several operations management books.

Robert Johnston is Professor of Operations Management at Warwick Business School and Associate Dean, responsible for finance and resources. He is the founding editor of the *International Journal of Service Industry Management* and he also serves on the editorial board of the *Journal of Operations Management* and the *International Journal of Tourism and Hospitality Research*. Before moving to academia Dr Johnston held several line management and senior management posts in a number of service organizations in both the public and private sectors. He continues to maintain close and active links with many large and small organizations through his research, management training and consultancy activities. As a specialist in service operations, his research interests include service design, service recovery, performance measurement and service quality. He is the author or co-author of many books, as well as chapters in other texts, numerous papers and case studies.

Foreword

by Rupert Gasser

Executive Vice President, Nestlé S.A.

It is always a pleasure, and satisfying to introduce a book which is serious and of high quality. The text by Nigel Slack and his team on *Operations Management* meets both these criteria, certainly as I measure it against the reality of the largest food company in the world – Nestlé.

Nestlé's network of functions is orchestrated and managed across the entire globe, the final objective of which is to get products to the consumer on time, at reasonable cost, giving good value for money. It is not only the size of Nestlé, with business operations in about 500 factories all over the world and its diversity of products, which is impressive, but also its rate of growth. It has doubled its turnover about every decade. There are on average about six factories or distribution centres under construction at any one time. Its R&D operation supplies new products and technology innovation; Marketing, Sales and Distribution operations bring high quality products to consumers of the industrialized world, as well as to villages in the tropical forests of South America and Africa. Optimization of the effectiveness of these functions, in all their complexity, is the responsibility of our Operations Managers. Their key responsibilities are, of course, to help maintain or improve our competitive edge, to apply consistently and systematically the experience and lessons learned each day in the running of the operation, to maximize the return on our assets, to help effectively to introduce new technologies, to integrate and to drive costs out of the supply chains. It is the Operations Manager's direct responsibility to involve and motivate people and to get the best potential out of them. The Operations Manager continuously has to fight waste and, more importantly, ensure that we maintain our consistently high level of quality. We are right at the heart of any large company when we talk about operations, therefore it is crucial for all managers – and all aspiring managers – to understand the importance and the contribution of operations management.

Operations Management reflects this admirably. Its emphasis on the central contribution which Operations Managers play in ensuring competitiveness is exactly the message which all students of management should grasp. Also, its international perspective shows how the subject is relevant to all types of operations in all parts of the world.

Nigel Slack and his team have written a lively and interesting text on what I believe to be a valuable subject. I am convinced that this book will contribute to operations management being taken seriously by all of tomorrow's managers.

R. Gasser

RUPERT GASSER

Acknowledgements

Again, in preparing the third edition of this book, the authors unashamedly exploited their friends and 'picked the brains' of their colleagues. We express our gratitude to all who helped us in this and previous editions, especially, Professor Sven Åke Hörte of Lulea University of Technology, Pär Åhlström of Stockholm School of Economics, Colin Armistead of Bournemouth University, David Barnes of The Open University, David Bennett of Aston University, John Bessant of Brighton University, Ruth Boaden of the University of Manchester Institute of Science and Technology, Peter Burcher of Aston University, Geoff Buxey of Deakin University, John K Christiansen of Copenhagen Business School, Sarah Caffyn of Brighton University, Philippa Collins of Heriot-Watt University, Henrique Correa of FGV, Saõ Paulo, Doug Davies of University of Technology, Sydney, Tony Dromgoole of the Irish Management Institute, Dr J.A.C de Haan, Job de Haan of Tilburg University, David Evans of Middlesex University, Paul Forrester of Keele University, Keith Goffin of Cranfield University, Ian Graham of Edinburgh University, Alan Harle of Sunderland University, Norma Harrison of Macquarie University, Catherine Hart of Loughborough Business School, Chris Hillam of Sunderland University, Ian Holden of Bristol Business School, Brian Jefferies of West Herts College, Tom Kegan of Bell College of Technology, Hamilton, Peter Long of Sheffield Hallam University, John Maguire of the University of Sunderland, Charles Marais of the University of Pretoria, Harvey Maylor of Bath University, John Meredith Smith of EAP, Oxford, Michael Milgate of Macquarie University, Keith Moreton of Staffordshire University, Adrian Morris of Sunderland University, Alastair Nicholson of London Business School, John Pal of Manchester Metropolitan University, Peter Race of Henley College, Ian Sadler of Victoria University, Amrik Sohal of Monash University, Alex Skedd of Northumbria Business School, Martin Spring of UMIST, Roy Staughton of University of Bath, R. Stratton of Nottingham Trent University, Mike Sweeney of Cranfield University, Dr Nelson Tang of the University of Leicester, David Twigg of Brighton University, Helen Valentine of the University of the West of England, Professor Roland van Dierdonck of the University of Ghent, Dirk Pieter van Donk of the University of Groningen and Peter Worthington.

Our academic colleagues in the Operations Management Group at Warwick Business School also helped, both by contributing ideas and by creating a lively and stimulating work environment. Our thanks go to Joy Batchelor, Hilary Bates, Alan Betts, Simon Croom, Mike Giannakis, Michael Lewis, Mike Shulver, Rhian Silvestro, Bridget Sullivan-Taylor, Ram Venuprasad, Paul Walley and Adrian Watt.

We are also grateful to many friends, colleagues and company contacts. In particular thanks for help with this edition goes to Cormak Campbell and his expert colleagues at ODEE for help beyond the call of duty, Shirley Johnston for case writing help, Ian Cobold for web help, Carole Driver for being Carole, and Richard Carleton for lots. Also special thanks go to Marc Palacio Balmer of Torres Wines, Barbara Fairclough of Jaeger, David Garman of TDG, Terry Kind of CV Clothing, Hans Mayer and Tyko Persson of Nestlé, Peter Norris and Mark Fisher of NatWest Bank, Bill Shardlow of Coats Viyella, John Tyley of Lloyds TSB, and Parminder Singh of Shimla Pinks.

During the writing of the first edition we were assisted, kept cheerful and encouraged by Fiona Rennie (now of PA Consulting). We still remember her contributions with affection. Mary Walton is secretary to our group at Warwick Business School. Her continued efforts at keeping us organized (or as organized as we are capable of being) are always appreciated, but never more so than when we were engaged on 'the book'.

During the preparation of this edition the world of academic publishing took another step towards consolidation when Financial Times Management, Addison Wesley Longman and Prentice Hall merged to form Pearson Education. Nonetheless we were lucky to receive continuing professional and friendly assistance from a great publishing team. Especial thanks to Penelope Woolf, Alison Kirk, Stuart Hay, Bridget Allen, Laura Graham, Suki Cheyne, David Harrison, Katarina Amcoff, Julie Knight, Marlene Olsavsky and Claire Cameron. John Yates is still with Pearson Education and looked after us for a while; he was wise enough to move and head up another part of the business before things became hectic, but we thank him for his help and advice.

Our erstwhile colleagues Dr Christine Harland and Professor Alan Harrison both have moved on to greater things. We wish them well and offer our sincere thanks for all their contributions to the first two editions.

Finally, every word of all three editions, and much more besides was word-processed by Angela Slack. She typed and retyped several versions of both manuscripts, made sense of our writing, spelling, eccentric word-processing styles and creative punctuation. It was, yet again, an heroic effort, which she undertook with (relatively) little complaint. To Angela – our thanks.

How to use this book

All academic textbooks in business management are, to some extent, simplifications of the messy reality which is actual organizational life. Any book has to separate topics, in order to study them, which in reality are closely related. For example, technology choice impacts on job design which in turn impacts on quality control; yet we have treated these topics individually. The first hint therefore in using this book effectively is to *look out for all the links between the individual topics*. Similarly with the sequence of topics, although the chapters follow a logical structure, they need not be studied in this order. With the exceptions of Chapters 1, 4, 10 and 18 which form introductions to each part of the book, every chapter is, more or less, self-contained. Therefore study the chapters in whatever sequence is appropriate to your course or your individual interests. But because each part has an introductory chapter, those students who wish to start with a brief 'overview' of the subject may wish first to study Chapters 1, 4, 10 and 18 and the chapter summaries of selected chapters. The same applies to revision – *study the introductory chapters and summary answers to key questions*.

The book makes full use of the many practical examples and illustrations which can be found in all operations. Many of these were provided by our contacts in companies, but many also come from journals, magazines and newspapers. So if you want to understand the importance of operations management in everyday business life *look for examples and illustrations of operations management decisions and activities in newspapers and magazines*. There are also examples which you can observe every day. Whenever you use a shop, eat a meal in a restaurant, borrow a book from the library or ride on public transport, *consider the operations management issues of all the operations for which you are a customer.*

The case exercises and discussion questions are there to provide an opportunity for you to think further about the ideas discussed in the chapters. Discussion questions should be used to test out your understanding of the specific points and issues discussed in the chapter. *If you cannot answer these you should revisit the relevant parts of the chapter.* The case exercises at the end of each chapter will require some more thought. *Use the questions at the end of each case exercise to guide you through the logic of analysing the issue treated in the case.* When you have done this individually *try to discuss your analysis with other course members*. Most important of all, every time you analyse one of the case exercises (or any other case or example in operations management) start off your analysis with the two fundamental questions:

- how is this organization trying to compete (or satisfy its strategic objectives if a not-for-profit organization)?, and,
- what can the operation do to help the organization compete more effectively?

Plan of the book

PART ONE – INTRODUCTION		
Chapter 1 Operations management	**Chapter 2** The strategic role and objectives of operations	**Chapter 3** Operations strategy

PART TWO – DESIGN		
Chapter 4 Design in operations management	**Chapter 5** The design of products and services	**Chapter 6** Design of the operations network
Chapter 7 Layout and flow	**Chapter 8** Process technology	**Chapter 9** Job design and work organization

PART THREE – PLANNING AND CONTROL		
Chapter 10 The nature of planning and control	**Chapter 11** Capacity planning and control	**Chapter 12** Inventory planning and control
Chapter 13 Supply chain planning and control	**Chapter 14** MRP	**Chapter 15** Just-in-time planning and control
Chapter 16 Project planning and control		**Chapter 17** Quality planning and control

PART FOUR – IMPROVEMENT		
Chapter 18 Operations improvement	**Chapter 19** Failure prevention and recovery	**Chapter 20** Total quality management

PART FIVE – THE OPERATIONS CHALLENGE
Chapter 21 The operations challenge

Part One

INTRODUCTION

This part of the book introduces the idea of the operations function in different types of organization. It identifies the common set of objectives to which operations managers aspire in order to serve their customers, and it explains how operations strategy influences the activities of operations managers.

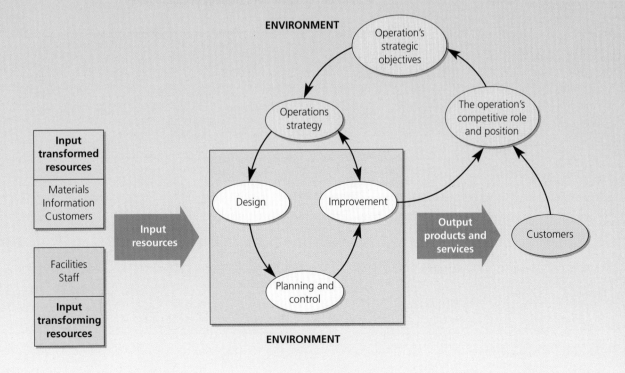

Key operations questions

Chapter 1
Operations management

- What is operations management?
- What are the similarities between all operations?
- How are operations different from each other?
- What responsibilities do operations managers have?

Chapter 2
The strategic role and objectives of operations

- What role should the operations function play in achieving strategic success?
- What are the performance objectives of operations and what are the internal and external benefits which derive from excelling in each of them?

Chapter 3
Operations strategy

- What is strategy?
- What is the difference between a 'top-down' and a 'bottom-up' view of operations strategy?
- What is the difference between a 'market requirements' and an 'operations resources' view of operations strategy?
- How can an operations strategy be put together?

Operations management

Introduction

Operations management is about the way organizations produce goods and services. Everything you wear, eat, sit on, use, read or knock about on the sports field comes to you courtesy of the operations managers who organized its production. Every book you borrow from the library, every treatment you receive at the hospital, every service you expect in the shops and every lecture you attend at university – all have been produced. While the people who supervised their production' may not always be called operations managers, that is what they really are. And that is what this book is concerned with – the tasks, issues and decisions of those operations managers who have made the services and products on which we all depend. In this introductory chapter we will examine the overall nature of operations management and the activities of operations managers. The model which is developed to explain the subject is shown in Figure 1.1.

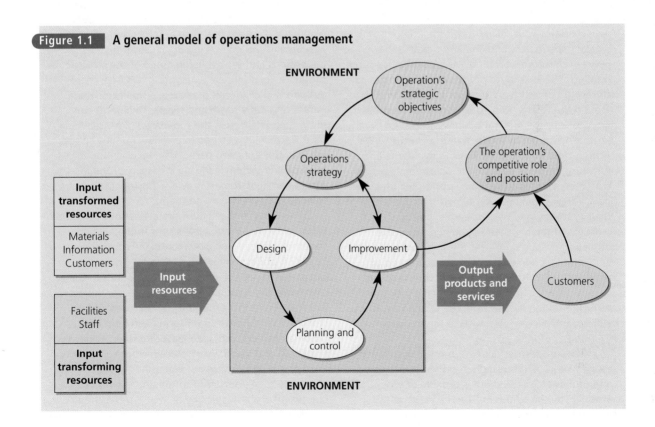

Figure 1.1 **A general model of operations management**

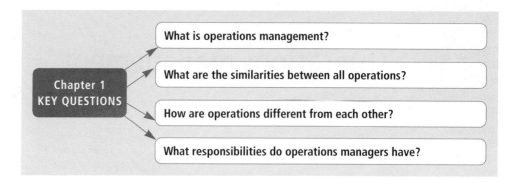

**Chapter 1
KEY QUESTIONS**

What is operations management?

What are the similarities between all operations?

How are operations different from each other?

What responsibilities do operations managers have?

Effective operations management

Operations management, above all else, is a practical subject which deals with real issues. So let us start our examination of the subject with a practical example of an organization which, starting out in Europe, is now known for the originality of its operations throughout the world.

IKEA[1]

IKEA is a furniture retailer with a difference. With around 100 giant stores operating in over 15 countries worldwide it has managed to develop its own special way of selling furniture. IKEA customers typically spend between one-and-a-half and two hours in the store – far longer than in rival furniture retailers. This is because of the way it organizes its stores – all of which are more or less the same all around the world. IKEA's philosophy for its stores goes back to the original business, started in southern Sweden by Ingvar Kamprad in the 1950s. At that time Mr Kamprad was successfully selling furniture, through a catalogue operation. Because customers wanted to see some of his furniture, he built a showroom in Stockholm. Not in the centre of the city where land was expensive, but on the outskirts of town. Instead of buying expensive display stands, he simply set the furniture out as it would be in a domestic setting. Also, instead of moving the furniture from the warehouse to the showroom area, he asked customers to pick the furniture up themselves from the warehouse. This almost 'anti-service' approach to service is the foundation of IKEA's stores today.

IKEA's furniture is 'value for money' with a wide range of choice. It is usually designed to be stored and sold as a 'flat pack' but is capable of easy assembly by the customer. The stores are all designed around the same self-service concept – that finding the store, parking, moving through the store itself, and ordering and picking up goods should be simple, smooth and problem-free. At the entrance to each store are large notice-boards which proclaim IKEA's philosophy and provide advice to shoppers who have not used the store before. Catalogues are available at this point showing illustrations, dimensions and the available range of the store's products. For shoppers with young children, there is a supervised children's play area, a small cinema, a parent and baby room and toilets, so parents can leave their children in the supervised play area for a time. Each child is attired in a yellow numbered top while in this area and parents are recalled via the loudspeaker system if the child has any problems. Alternatively customers may also borrow pushchairs to keep their children with them.

Some parts of the showroom are set out in 'room settings' while others show, for example, all beds together, so that customers can make comparisons. The IKEA philosophy is not to 'hassle' customers, but rather to let them make up their minds in their own time. If a customer does want advice, there are information points around the showroom where staff, in their bright red uniforms, can help and guide customers, provide measuring rules, paper for sketching and so on. Every piece of furniture carries a ticket which indicates its dimensions, price, materials used, country of origin and the other colours in which it is available. It also has a code number which indicates the location in the warehouse from where it can be collected. The tickets on larger items ask customers to go to the information desks for assistance. After viewing the showroom, customers pass into the 'free-service' area where smaller items are displayed on shelves. These can be picked directly off the display shelves by customers and put into yellow shoulder bags or trolleys. Customers then pass through the self-service warehouse where they can pick up the items they viewed in the showroom. Finally, the customers pay at the checkouts, each of which is constructed with a ramped conveyor belt which moves the customer's purchases up to the checkout staff. At the exit area there are information and service points, and often a 'Swedish Shop' with Swedish foodstuffs. A large loading area allows customers to bring their cars from the car park and load their purchases. Customers may also rent or buy a roof rack.

Questions

1 How is the IKEA operations design different from that of most furniture retail operations?

2 What do you think might be the major problems in running an operation like IKEA?

3 What do you identify as the 'operations function' within IKEA? How is this different from the 'sales function'?

So why is IKEA able to survive and succeed? It certainly understands its market and how it can serve the needs of its customers. Furthermore, its products must be regarded by its customers as representing outstanding value for money. At least as important, however, is the way it organizes the delivery of its services within its stores. This is the responsibility of the company's operations management – *the people who manage its store operations*. There are other large furniture retailers operating out of large (although not always quite as large) stores. Nor is IKEA the first furniture business to promote 'Nordic' design. Where IKEA scores is in the novelty and effectiveness of its operation management, who have responsibility for the staff who help customers, keep the warehouse supplied and maintain the facilities, and those who design, plan, control and constantly improve the way things are done. They are also responsible for the buildings, the computers and checkouts, the warehouses and transportation systems. Figure 1.2 illustrates just some of the activities which IKEA's operations management will need to address.

Figure 1.2 **Some operations management activities at IKEA**

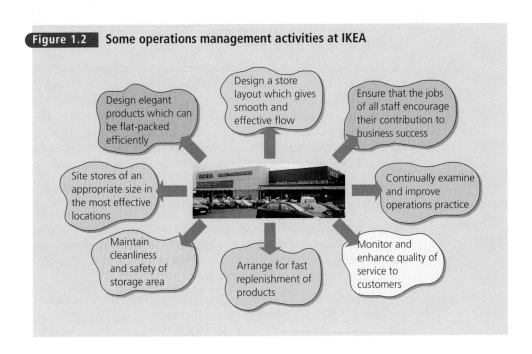

Now is the point to establish some definitions.

- The *operations function* of the organization is the arrangement of those resources which are devoted to the production and delivery of its products and services. Every organization has an operations function because every organization produces some type of products and/or services. However, not all types of organization will necessarily call the operations function by this name, as we will discuss later.

  Note in addition that we also use the shorter terms 'the operation' or 'operations' and, at times, the 'operations system' interchangeably with the 'operations function'.
- *Operations managers* are the staff of the organization who have particular responsibility for managing some, or all, of the resources which comprise the operations function. Again in some organizations the operations manager could be called by some other name. For example, he or she might be called the 'fleet manager' in a distribution company, the 'administrative manager' in a hospital, or the 'store manager' in a supermarket.
- *Operations management* is the term that is used for the activities, decisions and responsibilities of operations managers.

As we have seen in the case of IKEA, if the operations function is to be effective it must use its resources efficiently and produce goods and services in a way that satisfies its customers. In addition, it must be creative, innovative and energetic in introducing novel and improved ways of producing goods and services. If the operation can do these things it will provide the organization with the means to survive in the long term, because it gives the organization a competitive advantage over its commercial rivals. An alternative way of putting this in a not-for-profit organization is that an effective operation gives the means to fulfil the organization's long-term strategic goals.

Operations in the organization

The operations function is central to the organization because it produces the goods and services which are its reason for existing, but it is neither the only, nor necessarily the most important, function. It is, however, one of the three *core functions* of any organization. These are:

- the marketing (including sales) function – which is responsible for *communicating* the organization's products and services to its markets in order to generate customer requests for service;
- the product/service development function – which is responsible for *creating* new and modified products and services in order to generate future customer requests for service;
- the operations function – which is responsible for *fulfilling* customer requests for service throughout the production and delivery of products and services.

In addition, there are the *support functions* which enable the core functions to operate effectively. These include, for example:

- the accounting and finance function – which provides the information to help economic decision-making and manages the financial resources of the organization.
- the human resources function – which recruits and develops the organization's staff as well as looking after their welfare.

Remember that different organizations will call their various functions by different names and will have a different set of support functions. Almost all organizations, however, will have the three core functions, because all organizations have a fundamental need to sell their services, satisfy their customers, and create the means to satisfy customers in the future. Table 1.1 shows the activities of the three core functions for a sample of operations.

Table 1.1 The activities of core functions in some organizations

Core functional activities	Internet service provider (ISP)	Fast food chain	Charity	Furniture manufacturer
Marketing and sales	Promote services to users and get registrations Sell advertising space	Advertise on TV Devise promotional materials	Develop funding contracts Mail out appeals for donations	Advertise in magazines Determine pricing policy Sell to stores
Product/service development	Devise new services and commission new information content	Design hamburgers, pizzas, etc. Design decor for restaurants	Develop new appeals campaigns Design new assistance programmes	Design new furniture Coordinate with fashionable colours
Operations	Maintain hardware, software and content Implement new links and services	Make burgers, pizzas etc. Serve customers Clear away Maintain equipment	Give service to the beneficiaries of the charity	Make components Assemble furniture

It is important to stress, however, that functional names, boundaries and responsibilities vary between organizations; and also that there is no clear division either between the three core functions or between core and support functions. In fact many of the interesting problems in management (and the opportunities for improvement) lie at the overlapping boundaries between functions. This leads to some confusion over where

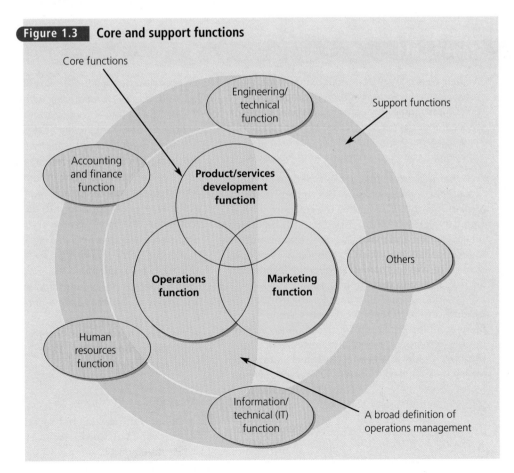

Figure 1.3   Core and support functions

Core functions

Engineering/ technical function

Support functions

Accounting and finance function

Product/services development function

Others

Operations function

Marketing function

Human resources function

Information/ technical (IT) function

A broad definition of operations management

the boundaries of the operations function should be. In this book we incline towards a relatively broad definition of operations (*see* Fig. 1.3). We treat much of the product/service development, engineering/technical and IT activities and some of the personnel, marketing, and accounting and finance activities as coming within the sphere of operations management. Most significantly, we treat the core operations function as comprising all the activities necessary for day-to-day customer request fulfilment. This includes sourcing products and services from suppliers and transporting products and services to customers. Therefore, what in some organizations are the separate functions of 'purchasing' and 'distribution' are, to us, a core part of operations management.

Operations management in small organizations

Theoretically, operations management is the same set of activities whatever the size of the organization in which it practices. However, in practice, managing operations in a small or medium size organization has its own set of problems. Large companies may have the resources to dedicate individuals to specific organizational roles but smaller companies often cannot. This means that people may have to do different jobs as the need arises. The box on Stagepoint illustrates this. Such an informal structure can allow the company to respond quickly as opportunities or problems present themselves. But decision making can also become confused as individual's roles overlap. Small companies may have exactly the same operations management issues as large ones but they can be more difficult to isolate from the mass of other issues in the organization. Figure 1.4 illustrates some of the operations management issues faced by Richard Carleton of Stagepoint.

Stagepoint[2]

'We may be a small company but many of our customers are big industrial firms or production companies and they expect as professional a level of service from us as from any other of their suppliers. They also expect us to give advice, provide our services anywhere in the world and never let them down.'

Richard Carleton, one of the three directors of Stagepoint, a theatrical services company in the Midlands of the UK, founded the company with a friend in 1995 when he decided to ditch his career as an accountant and make his hobby into his business. In fact, Stagepoint, which now employs 12 people, consists of two companies: Stagepoint Technical Services hires and sells lighting, sound, special effects and staging equipment for theatrical productions, conferences and events, while Stagepoint Productions offers a complete creative design, 'visualization' and installation service for theatres, venues and events. Customers range from large international companies who want an event like a sales conference organizing on the Riviera, to local amateur dramatic societies.

'One of the reasons we have been so successful is that we always try to offer a higher quality of service than our competitors. All equipment is checked and cleaned before it is hired out and we are willing to respond quickly when a customer is in trouble. Basically, we try and run an effective and responsive operation, while at the same time offering a high level of creativity in our set designs. But, although the way we manage our operation is vital, we don't always think in terms of operations management, marketing and finance as separate activities. You cannot afford to do that in small companies. To some extent everybody has to be prepared to do anything. In a typical day I might spend some time selling a job to a prospective client, help to install equipment in the National Exhibition Centre which is nearby, and find out why a client is late in paying us. At the same time I might be trying to sort out why one of our trucks has been held up at the Czech border when the equipment needs installing by the next day. It's very different from being an accountant!'

Questions

1 What is the overlap between operations, marketing and product/service development at stagepoint?

Figure 1.4   Some operations management issues at Stagepoint

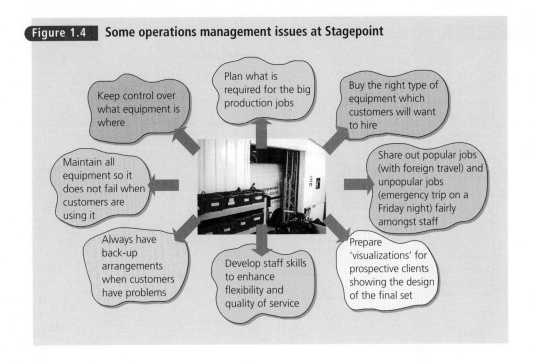

Keep control over what equipment is where

Plan what is required for the big production jobs

Buy the right type of equipment which customers will want to hire

Maintain all equipment so it does not fail when customers are using it

Share out popular jobs (with foreign travel) and unpopular jobs (emergency trip on a Friday night) fairly amongst staff

Always have back-up arrangements when customers have problems

Develop staff skills to enhance flexibility and quality of service

Prepare 'visualizations' for prospective clients showing the design of the final set

● Operations management in not-for-profit organizations

Terms such as *competitive advantage*, *markets* and *business*, which are used in this book are usually associated with companies in the for-profit sector. So, is operations management relevant to organizations whose purpose is not primarily to earn profits? Are the issues associated with managing the operations of, say, an animal welfare charity, hospital, research organization or government department the same as those in profit-making institutions? Certainly the strategic objectives of not-for-profit organizations may be more complex and involve a mixture of political, economic, social or environmental objectives. Because of this there may be a greater chance of operations decisions being made under conditions of conflicting objectives. So, for example, it is the operations staff in a children's welfare department who have to face the conflict between the cost of providing extra social workers and the risk of a child not receiving adequate protection. But essentially not-for-profit operations are the same as for-profit ones. They transform input resources into output products and services and they have to make the same set of decisions as do for-profit organizations – how to produce their products and services, invest in technology, contract out some of their activities, devise performance measures, improve their operations performance and so on. The vast majority of the topics covered in this book have relevance to all types of organization, including non-profit, even if some terms and ideas may have to be adapted.

The transformation process model

All operations produce goods and services by devising processes which transform or change the state or condition of something to produce *outputs*. Figure 1.5 shows this general *transformation process model* which is used to describe the nature of operations. Put simply, operations processes take in a set of input resources which are then used to transform something, or are transformed themselves, into outputs of goods and services which satisfy customer needs.

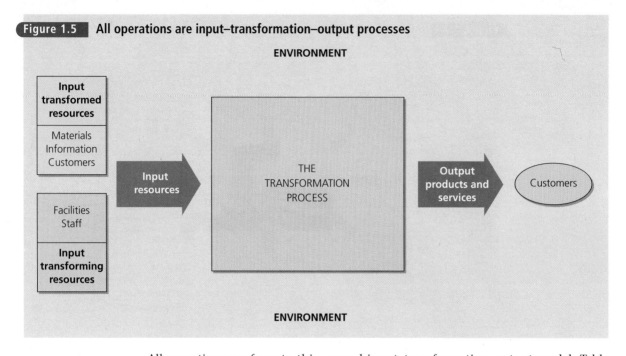

Figure 1.5 All operations are input–transformation–output processes

All operations conform to this general input–transformation–output model. Table 1.2 illustrates how a wide range of operations can be described in this way. However, there are differences between different operations. If you stand far enough away from, say, a hospital or a motor vehicle plant, they might look the same. Each is likely to be a large building into which staff enter and deliveries take place. But move closer and clear differences do start to emerge. For a start, one is a manufacturing operation producing largely physical goods, and one is a service operation which produces changes in the physiological condition, feelings and behaviour of patients. The nature of the processes which each building contains will also be different. The motor vehicle plant contains metal cutting and forming machinery and assembly processes, whereas the hospital contains diagnostic, care and therapeutic processes. Perhaps the most important difference between the two operations, however, is the nature of their inputs. Both have 'staff' and 'facilities' as inputs to the operation but they act upon very different things. The motor vehicle plant uses its staff and facilities to transform steel, plastic, cloth, tyres and other materials. They make them into vehicles which are eventually delivered to customers. The staff and technology in the hospital, on the other hand, transform the customers themselves. The patients form part of the input to, and the output from, the operation – it is they who are being 'processed'. This has important implications for how the operation needs to be managed.

● Inputs to the transformation process

The inputs to an operation can be conveniently classified as either:

- transformed resources – the resources that are treated, transformed or converted; or
- transforming resources – the resources that act upon the transformed resources.

Transformed resources
The transformed resources which operations take in are usually a mixture of the following:

- materials
- information
- customers.

Table 1.2 Some operations described in terms of input–transformation–output processes

Operation	Input resources	Transformation process	Outputs
Airline	Aircraft Pilots and air crew Ground crew Passengers and freight	Move passengers and freight around the world	Transported passengers and freight
Department store	Goods for sale Staff sales Computerized registers Customers	Display goods Give sales advice Sell goods	Customers and goods assembled together
Printer	Printers and designers Printing presses Paper, ink, etc.	Design Print Bind	Designed and printed material
Police	Police officers Computer systems Information Public (law-abiding and criminals)	Prevent crime Solve crime Apprehend criminals	Lawful society Public with feeling of security
Frozen food manufacturer	Fresh food Operators Food-processing equipment Freezers	Food preparation Freeze	Frozen food

Often one of these is dominant in an operation. For example, a bank devotes part of its energies to producing printed statements of accounts for its customers. In doing so, it is *processing materials* and acting as a printer, but no one would claim that a bank and a printer are the same type of operation. The bank also *processes customers*. It gives them advice regarding their financial affairs, cashes their cheques, deposits their cash, and has direct contact with them. However, most of the bank's activities are concerned with *processing information* about its customers' financial affairs. As customers, we may be unhappy with badly printed statements and we may be more unhappy if we are not treated appropriately in the bank. If the bank makes errors in our financial transactions, however, we suffer in a far more fundamental way. This is not to say that materials processing or customer processing is unimportant to the bank. On the contrary, it must be good at these things to keep its customers happy. Error-free, fast and efficient information processing, though, is its central objective.

Table 1.3 gives examples of operations with their dominant transformed resources.

Transforming resources

There are two types which form the 'building blocks' of all operations:

● facilities – the buildings, equipment, plant and process technology of the operation;
● staff – those who operate, maintain, plan and manage the operation. (Note we use the term 'staff' to describe all the people in the operation, at any level.)

Of course the exact nature of both facilities and staff will differ between operations. To a five-star hotel, its facilities consist mainly of buildings, furniture and fittings. To a nuclear-powered aircraft carrier, its facilities are the nuclear generator, turbines, and sophisticated electronic detection equipment. One operation has relatively 'low-

Table 1.3 Dominant transformed materials of various operations

Predominantly materials processors	Predominantly information processors	Predominantly customer processors
All manufacturing operations	Accountants	Hairdressers
Mining and extraction companies	Bank headquarters	Hotels
Retail operations	Market research company	Hospitals
Warehouses	Financial analysts	Mass rapid transports
Postal services	News service	Theatres
Container shipping line	University research unit	Theme parks
Trucking companies	Archives Telecoms company	Dentists

technology' facilities and one 'high-technology' facilities, but both are important to the operation concerned. A five-star hotel would be just as ineffective with worn and broken furniture as an aircraft carrier would be with inoperative electronics.

The nature of staff will also differ between operations. The majority of staff employed in a factory assembling domestic refrigerators do not need a particularly high level of technical skill. In contrast, the majority of staff employed by an accounting company are likely to be highly skilled in their own particular 'technical' skill (accounting). Yet although skills vary, all staff have a contribution to make to the effectiveness of their operation. An assembly worker who consistently misassembles refrigerators will dissatisfy customers and increase costs just as surely as an accountant who cannot add up.

Operations will also vary in their balance between facilities and staff resources. So, for example, a computer chip manufacturing company, such as Intel, will have a considerable quantity of money invested in its physical facilities. A single chip fabrication plant generally costs in excess of $1 billion. Not surprisingly, operations managers in this industry spend a lot of their time designing, siting, maintaining and generally managing the performance of their facilities. Conversely, a management consultancy firm, such as Andersen Consulting, depends entirely on the quality and characteristics of its staff for its future success. Here operations management is largely concerned with the recruitment, development and deployment of skilled consultants and the management of the knowledge which they possess. Of course, good staff are important in chip manufacture, and good buildings and information technology are important in management consulting. But the balance is different and so are the concerns of each company's operations management.

● The transformation process

The purpose of the transformation process in operations is closely connected with the nature of its transformed input resources.

Materials processing

Operations which process materials could do so to transform their *physical properties* (shape or composition, for example). Most manufacturing operations are like this. Other operations process materials to change their *location* (parcel delivery companies, for example). Some, like retail operations, do so to change the *possession* of the materials. Finally, some operations *store* materials, such as warehouses.

Information processing

Operations which process information could do so to transform their *informational properties* (that is the purpose or form of the information); accountants do this. Some change the *possession* of the information, for example market research companies.

Some *store* the information, for example archives and libraries. Finally, some operations change the *location* of the information, such as telecommunication companies.

Customer processing

Operations which process customers might change their *physical properties* in a similar way to materials processors: for example, hairdressers or cosmetic surgeons. Some *store* (or more politely *accommodate*) customers: hotels, for example. Airlines, mass rapid transport systems and bus companies transform the *location* of their customers, while hospitals transform their *physiological state*. Finally, some customer-processing operations are concerned with transforming their *psychological state*, for example most entertainment services such as music, theatre, television, radio and theme parks. Table 1.4 summarizes these various types of transformation processes.

● Outputs from the transformation process

The outputs from (and purpose of) transformation processes are products and services, which are generally seen as being different, in several ways.

Tangibility

Products are usually tangible: for example, you can physically touch a television set or a newspaper. Services are usually intangible. You cannot touch consultancy advice or a haircut (although you can often see or feel the results of these services).

Table 1.4 Different types of transformation processes

	Physical properties	Informational properties	Possession	Location	Storage/ accommodation	Physiological state	Psychological state
Materials processors	All manufacturing operations Mining and extraction		Retail operations	Postal services Freight distribution Port operations	Warehouses		
Information processors		Bank HQs Accountants Architects	Financial analysts Market research companies Universities Consultants News services	Telecoms company	Library archives		
Customer processors	Hairdressers Plastic surgeons			Public transport Taxis	Hotels	Hospitals Other health care	Education Psychoanalysts Theatres Theme parks

Storability

Partly because of their tangibility, products can also be stored, at least for a short time after their production. Services, on the other hand, are usually non-storable: for example, the service of 'accommodation in an hotel room for tonight' will perish if it is not sold before tonight – accommodation in the same room tomorrow is a different service.

Transportability

Another consequence of tangibility is the ability to transport goods. Automobiles, machine tools and video cameras can all be moved. However, if services are intangible, they may be difficult to transport. Health services, for example, cannot be exported as such (though the means of producing health services can).

Simultaneity

The other main distinction between products and services concerns the timing of their production. Products are nearly always produced prior to the customer receiving (or even seeing) them. For example, the CD you just bought was produced well before you bought it. Services, however, are often produced simultaneously with their consumption. The service which the shop provided in selling you the CD happened at the same time as you 'consumed' the service by buying it.

Customer contact

Separate production and consumption implies that customers have a low contact level with the operations which produce products. You may have bought and consumed bread for most of your life, but have you seen the inside of a bakery? Services which are produced and consumed simultaneously must involve a higher level of contact between the customer and the operation.

Quality

Finally, because generally customers do not see the production of products, they will judge the quality of the operation which produced them on the evidence of the products themselves. Even if we disagree as to the quality of our new personal computer, we can measure its capabilities in a reasonably objective manner. But in services the customer judges not only the outcome of the service, but also the aspects of the way in which it was produced. For example, in purchasing a new pair of shoes you might be perfectly satisfied that the shoes were in stock and that you were promptly served. Yet if the shop assistant was discourteous, you would not consider the service to be of a high quality. Other customers, on the other hand, might be less sensitive than you in judging the service.

Most operations produce both products and services

Some operations produce just goods and some produce just services, but most operations produce a mixture of the two. Figure 1.6 shows a number of operations positioned in a spectrum from 'pure' goods producers to 'pure' service producers. Crude oil producers are concerned almost exclusively with the product which comes from their oil wells. So are aluminium smelters, but they might also produce some services such as technical advice. Services produced in these circumstances are called *facilitating services*. To an even greater extent, machine tool manufacturers produce facilitating services such as technical advice, applications engineering services and training. The services produced by a restaurant are an essential part of what the customer is paying for. It is both a manufacturing operation which produces food and a provider of service in the advice, ambience and service of the food. A computer systems services company may produce software 'products', but primarily it is providing a service to its customers, with *facilitating products*. Certainly, a management consultancy, although it produces reports and documents, would see itself as a service provider which uses facilitating goods. Finally, some pure services do not produce products at all. A psychotherapy clinic, for example, provides therapeutic treatment for its customers without any facilitating goods.

Services and products are merging

Increasingly the distinction between services and products is both difficult to define and not particularly useful. Information and communications technologies are even overcoming some of the consequences of the intangibility of services. Internet-based

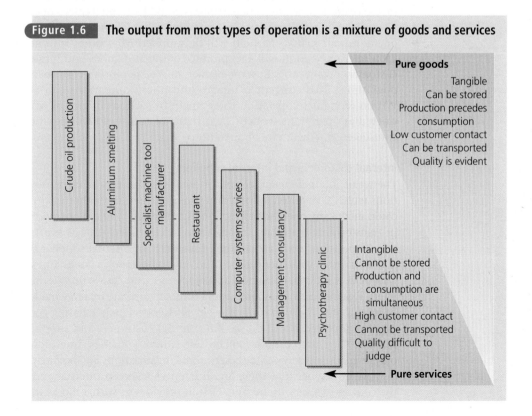

Figure 1.6 **The output from most types of operation is a mixture of goods and services**

retailers, for example, are increasingly 'transporting' a larger proportion of their services into customers' homes. Even the official statistics compiled by governments have difficulty in separating products and services. Software sold on a disk is classified as a product. The same software sold over the internet is a service. Some authorities see the essential purpose of all businesses, and therefore operations processes, as being to 'service customers'. Therefore, they argue, all operations are service providers who may produce products as a means of serving their customers. Our approach in this book is close to this. We treat operations management as being relevant to all organizations whether they see themselves as manufacturers or service providers.

● The process hierarchy

The transformation process model can also be used within operations. Look inside most operations and they will be made up of several units or departments, which themselves act as smaller versions of the whole operation of which they form a part.

For example, a television programme and video production company has inputs of production, technical and administrative staff, cameras, lighting, sound and recording equipment, studio space, props, video tape, and so on. It transforms these into finished programmes and promotional videos, etc. Within this overall operation, however, there are many smaller operations. For example, there will be, amongst others:

- workshops which manufacture the sets, scenery and props for the productions;
- marketing and sales staff who liaise with potential customers, test out programme ideas and give information and advice to programme makers;
- an engineering maintenance and repair department which cares for, modifies and designs technical equipment;
- production units which organize and shoot the programmes and videos;
- the finance and costing department which estimates the likely cost of future projects and controls operational budgets.

The whole television programme and video production operation could be termed a macro operation, while its departments could be termed micro operations (see Fig. 1.7). These micro operations have inputs, some of which will come from outside the macro operation but many of which will be supplied from other internal micro operations. Each micro operation will also produce outputs of goods and services for the benefit of customers. Again though, some of each micro operation's customers will be other micro operations. This concept of macro and micro operations can be extended further. Within each micro operation there might be sections or groups which can also be considered as operations in their own right. In this way any operations function can be considered as a hierarchy of operations.

Internal customers and internal suppliers

The terms internal customer and internal supplier can be used to describe micro operations which take outputs from, and give inputs to, any other micro operations. Thus we could model any operations function as a network of micro operations which are engaged in transforming materials, information or customers (that is staff) for each other, each micro operation being at the same time both an internal supplier of goods and services and an internal customer for the other micro operation's goods and services. However, we cannot treat internal customers and suppliers exactly as we do external customers and suppliers. External customers and suppliers usually operate in a free market. If an organization believes that in the long run it can get a better deal by purchasing goods and services from another supplier, it will do so. But internal customers and suppliers are not in a 'free market'. They often cannot look outside either to purchase input resources or to sell their output goods and services (although some organizations are moving this way).

If we remember that there are differences between internal and external customers, the concept is a very useful one. First, it provides us with a model to analyse the internal

Figure 1.7

Figure 1.7 **All macro operations are made up of many micro operations**

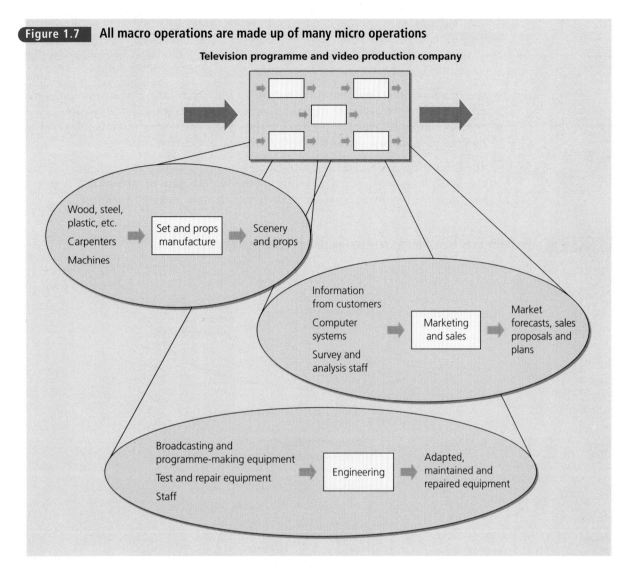

Television programme and video production company

Wood, steel, plastic, etc.
Carpenters
Machines
→ Set and props manufacture → Scenery and props

Information from customers
Computer systems
Survey and analysis staff
→ Marketing and sales → Market forecasts, sales proposals and plans

Broadcasting and programme-making equipment
Test and repair equipment
Staff
→ Engineering → Adapted, maintained and repaired equipment

activities of an operation. If the macro operation is not working as it should, we can trace the problem back along the internal network of customers and suppliers. Second, it is a useful reminder to all parts of the operation that, by treating their internal customers with the same degree of care that they exercise on their external customers, the effectiveness of the whole operation can be improved. This idea is one of the foundations of total quality management, covered in Chapter 20.

All parts of the organization are operations

If micro operations act in a similar way to the macro operation, then many of the issues, methods and techniques which we treat in this book have some meaning for each unit, section, group or individual within the organization. For example, the marketing function of an organization can be viewed as a transformation process. It has inputs of market information, staff, computers, and so on. Its staff then transform the information into such outputs as marketing plans, advertising campaigns and sales force organizations. In other words, all functions can be viewed as operations themselves. They are there to provide goods or (more usually) services to the other parts of the organization. Each function will have its 'technical' knowledge. In marketing, this is the expertise in designing and shaping marketing plans; in finance, it is the technical knowledge of financial reporting. Yet each will also have an operations role of producing plans, policies, reports and services.

The implications of this are important. It means that every manager in all parts of an organization is to some extent an operations manager. All managers need to organize their resource inputs effectively so as to produce goods and services. It also means that we must distinguish between two meanings of 'operations':

- *operations as a function*, meaning the part of the organization which produces the products and services for the organization's external customers;
- *operations as an activity*, meaning any transformation of input resources in order to produce products and services, for either internal or external customers.

The first meaning of 'operations' is the most commonly used, and the one we shall use in this book. It is always worth remembering the second usage of 'operations', however. Figure 1.8 shows the three core functions as transformation process 'operations'.

Figure 1.8 **The three core functions as transformation process 'operations'**

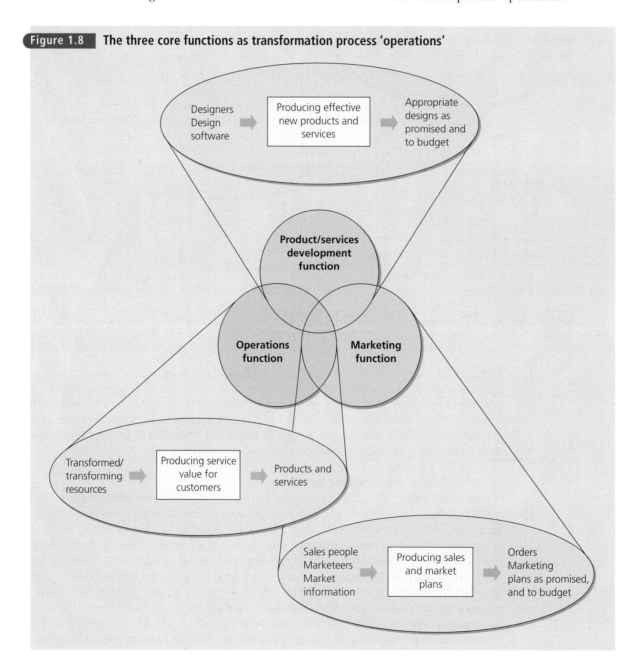

Business processes

Breaking a whole operation down into its constituent micro operations helps to demonstrate that operations management applies to all parts of the organization, both core and support functions, and helps us to focus on local improvement. But stand back from the macro operation and examine the connections between the micro operations. Each micro operation will contribute some part to 'producing' several of the products and services with which the organization attempts to satisfy the needs of its customers. For example, the television programme and video production company, described previously, might satisfy its customers' needs by 'producing' several products and services. Each of these, to different extents, involves the micro operations within the company. So, preparing quotations (estimates of the time and cost involved in potential projects) needs the contributions of the marketing and sales micro operation and the finance and costing micro operation more than the others. Providing technical support (which involves designing systems for, and advising, other media companies) mainly involves the engineering micro operation, but does also need some contribution from the others. Figure 1.9 illustrates the contribution of each micro operation to each product or service. No particular sequence is implied by Figure 1.9. The contributions of each micro operation will not all occur in the same order. In fact the flow of information, materials or customers between micro operations might be complex, involving delays and recycling.

These collections of contributions from each micro operation which fulfil customer needs are called 'end-to-end' business processes and often cut across conventional

Figure 1.9 Example of how each micro operation contributes to the business processes which fulfil external customer needs

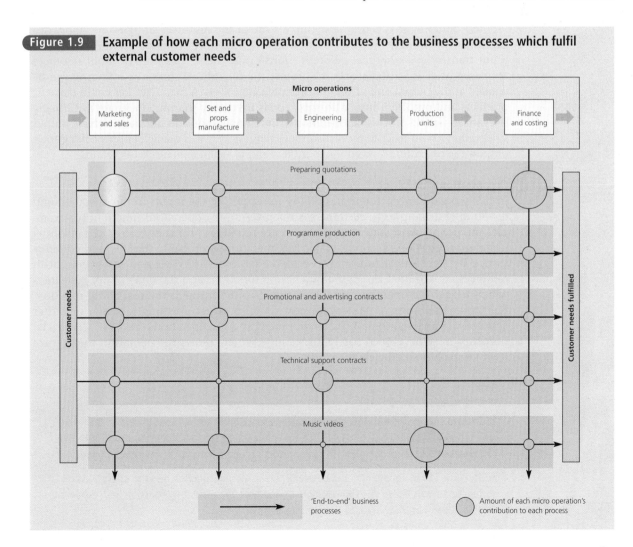

organizational boundaries. Reorganizing (or 're-engineering') layouts and organizational responsibilities around these business processes is the philosophy behind business process re-engineering (BPR) which is discussed further in Chapter 18.

● Buffering the operation

The turbulent environment in which most organizations do business means that the operations function is having to adjust continually to changing circumstances. For example, a food-processing operation might not be able to predict exactly when some foods will be harvested (bad weather might totally disrupt the supply to a factory for weeks). Demand could also be prone to disruption. Unpredictable changes in the weather, a 'health scare' story in the press, and so on, can all introduce turbulence. One way in which operations managers try to minimize 'environmental' disruption is by buffering or insulating the operations function from the external environment. It can be done in two ways:[4]

- *physical buffering* – designing an inventory or stock of resources either at the input side of the transformation process or at the output side;
- *organizational buffering* – allocating the responsibilities of the various functions in the organization so that the operations function is protected from the external environment by other functions.

Physical buffering

Physical buffering involves building up a store of the resources so that any supply disruptions will (initially at least) be absorbed by the store. The operation is storing its input transformed resources before it 'transforms' them. The store of input resources are being used as 'buffer stocks' to protect the operation. Similarly, buffering can be applied at the output end of the transformation process. A manufacturer could make its products and put them into a finished goods inventory (output stocks are not usually relevant to people-processing operations). Often operations do not need to have output stocks; they could react to each customer's request as it was made. Yet by stocking their output, the operation is given much more stability when demand is uncertain.

Organizational buffering

In many organizations the responsibility for acquiring the inputs to the operation and distributing its outputs to customers is not given to the operations function. For example, the people who staff the operation are recruited and trained by the personnel function; the process technology for the operation is probably selected and commissioned by a technical function; the materials, parts, services and other bought-in resources are acquired through a purchasing function; and the orders from customers which trigger the operation into activity will come through the marketing function. The other functions of the organization are, in effect, forming a barrier or buffer between the uncertainties of the environment and the operations function. These relationships have developed partly for stability which allows the operation to organize itself for maximum efficiency.

● CRITICAL COMMENTARY

The whole concept of buffering the operations function is not without its critics. Buffering may promote stability but, partly due to the influence of Japanese operations practice,[5] we can now see several problems with over-protecting operations from their environment:

- The time lag of communicating between the insulating function and the operations function slows down decision-making. By the time the insulating function has responded, operations has 'moved on to the next problem'.

- Operations which never interact with the environment never develop an understanding of the environment (e.g. labour or technological markets) which would help them exploit new developments.

- Operations managers are not required to take responsibility for their actions. There is always another function to blame.

- Physical buffering often involves tolerating large stocks of input or output resources. These are both expensive (*see* Chapter 12, Inventory planning and control) and prevent the operation improving (*see* Chapter 15, Just-in-time planning and control).

- Physical buffering in customer-processing operations means making the customer wait for service, which in turn could lead to customer dissatisfaction.

For all of these reasons, it is better gradually to expose the operations function to its environment. Only then will it learn to develop the necessary flexibility to respond to and understand what is really happening with its customers and suppliers.

Types of operations

Although all operations are similar in that they all transform input resources into output products and services, they do differ in four important respects:

- the volume of their output;
- the variety of their output;
- the variation in the demand for their output;
- the degree of 'visibility' which customers have of the production of the product or service (also called the degree of customer contact).

The volume dimension

Let us take a familiar example – the production and sale of the internationally ubiquitous hamburger. The epitome of high-volume hamburger production is McDonald's, which serves millions of burgers around the world every day. Volume has important implications for the way McDonald's operations are organized. Look behind the counter and the first thing you notice is the *repeatability* of the tasks people are doing. Because tasks are repeated frequently it makes sense to *specialize*: one person assigned to cooking the burgers, another assembling the buns, another serving, and so on. This leads to the *systemization* of the work where standard procedures are set down in a manual, with instructions on how each part of the job should be carried out. Also, because tasks are systematized and repeated, it is worthwhile developing specialized fryers and ovens. The most important implication of high volume, though, is that it gives *low unit costs*; the fixed costs of the operation, such as heating and rent, are spread over a large number of products or services.

Now consider a small local cafeteria serving a few 'short order' dishes. The range of items on the menu may be similar to the larger operation, but the volume will be far lower. Therefore the degree of repetition will also be far lower. Furthermore, the number of staff will be lower (possibly only one person) and therefore individual staff are likely to perform a wider range of tasks. This may be more rewarding for the staff, but less open to systemization. Fewer burgers cooked also makes it less feasible to invest in specialized equipment. For all of these reasons it follows that the cost per burger served is likely to be higher (even if the price is comparable).

Dealing with infinite variety – two examples

The Bombay Tiffin Box Suppliers Association (TBSA) operates a service to transport home-cooked food from workers' homes to office locations in downtown Bombay. Workers from residential districts must ride commuter trains some 30–40 km to work. Typically, they are conservative diners, and are also constrained by strong cultural taboos on food handling by caste, which discourage eating out. TBSA arranges for food to be picked up in the morning in a regulation tin 'tiffin' box, deposited at the office at lunch time, and returned to the home in the afternoon. TBSA takes advantage of public transport to carry the tins, usually using otherwise under-utilized capacity on commuter trains in the mid-morning and afternoon. Different colours and markings are used to indicate to the (sometimes illiterate) TBSA workers the process route for each tin.

Standardized shipping containers

For as long as ships have navigated the seas, ports have had to handle an infinite variety of cargoes with widely different contents, sizes and weights, and, whilst in transit or in storage, protect them from weather and pilferage. Then the transportation industries, in conjunction with the International Standards Organization (ISO), developed a standard shipping container design. Almost overnight the problems of security and weather protection were solved. Anyone wanting to ship goods in volume only had to seal them into a container and they could be signed over to the shipping company. Ports could standardize handling equipment and dispense with warehouses (containers could be stacked in the rain if required). Railways and trucking companies could develop trailers to accommodate the new containers. Such was the success of the new design that very soon specialist containers were developed which still conformed to the ISO standard module sizes. For example, refrigerated containers provide temperature-controlled environments for perishable goods.

Standard tiffin boxes being transported from home to office

Questions

1 What are the common features of these two examples?
2 What other examples of standardization in transport operations can you think of?

The variety dimension

A taxi company offers a high-variety service. It may confine its services to the transportation of people and their luggage, but it is prepared to pick you up from almost anywhere and drop you off almost anywhere. It may even (at a price) take you by a route of your choice. In order to do this it must be relatively *flexible*. Drivers must have a good knowledge of the area, and communication between the base and the taxis must be effective. The variety on offer by the service does allow it to match its services closely to its customers' needs. However, this does come at a price. The cost per kilometre travelled will be higher for a taxi than for a less customized form of transport such as a bus service.

Although both serve, more or less, the same customers with the same needs by providing transport over relatively short distances (say, less than 20 km), the taxi service has, in theory, an infinite number of routes to offer its customers, while the bus service has a few well-defined routes. The buses travel these routes according to a set schedule, published well in advance and adhered to in a routine manner. If all goes to schedule, little, if any, flexibility is required from the operation. All is standardized and regular. More significantly, the lack of change and disruption in the day-to-day running of the operation results in relatively low costs compared with using a taxi for the same journey.

The Henry Ford of ophthalmology[6]

High-volume operations can be found in some surprising places – even surgery. Not all surgery conforms to our preconceptions of the individual 'super-craftsperson', aided by his or her back-up team, performing the whole operation from first incision to final stitch. Many surgical procedures are, in fact, fairly routine. There can be few examples, however, of surgery being made quite as routine as in the Russian clinics of eye surgeon, Svyatoslav Fyodorov.

He has been called the 'Henry Ford of ophthalmology', and his methods are indeed closer to the automobile assembly plant than the conventional operating theatre. The surgical procedure in which he specializes is a revolutionary treatment for myopia (short-sightedness) called radial keratotomy. In the treatment the curvature of the cornea is corrected surgically – still a controversial procedure among some in the profession, but very successful for Fyodorov. From his Moscow headquarters he controls nine clinics throughout Russia.

The source of his fame is not the treatment as such – other eye surgeons around the world perform similar procedures – but the way he organizes the business of the surgery itself. Eight patients lie on moving tables arranged like the spokes of a wheel around its central axis, with only their eyes uncovered.

Six surgeons, each with his or her 'station', are positioned around the rim of the wheel so that they can access the patients' eyes. After the surgeons have completed their own particular portion of the whole procedure, the wheel indexes round to take patients to the next stage of their treatment. The surgeons check to make sure that the previous stage of the operation was performed correctly and then go on to perform their own task. Each surgeon's activity is monitored on TV screens overhead and the surgeons talk to each other through miniature microphones and headsets.

The result of this mass production approach to surgery according to Fyodorov is not only far cheaper unit costs (he and his staff are paid for each patient treated, so they are all exceptionally wealthy as a result) but also a better success rate than that obtained in conventional surgery.

Questions

1 Compare this approach to eye surgery with a more conventional approach.

2 What do you think are the advantages and disadvantages of this approach to eye surgery?

● The variation dimension

Consider the demand pattern for a successful summer holiday resort hotel. Not surprisingly, more customers want to stay in summer vacation times than in the middle of winter. At the height of 'the season' the hotel could possibly accommodate twice its capacity if it had the space. Off-season demand, however, could be a small fraction of its capacity; it might even consider closing down in very quiet periods. The implication of such a marked variation in demand levels is that the operation must change its capacity in some way. It might, for example, hire extra staff for the summer period only. But in flexing its activities the hotel must try to predict the level of demand it is likely to receive. If it gets this wrong and adjusts its capacity below the actual demand level, it will lose business. All of these factors have the effect of increasing the hotel's costs. Recruitment costs, overtime costs and under-utilization of its rooms all make for a relatively high cost per guest operation compared with an hotel of a similar standard with level demand.

Conversely, an hotel which is close to both a major road network and a tourist attraction might be patronized by business travellers during the week and by tourists at weekends and holiday periods. Its demand is therefore relatively level. Under these circumstances the hotel can plan its activities well in advance. Staff can be scheduled, food can be bought and rooms can be cleaned in a *routine* and *predictable* manner. This results in a high utilization of resources. Not surprisingly, the unit costs of this hotel are likely to be lower than those of the comparable hotel with a highly variable demand pattern.

● The visibility dimension

Visibility is a slightly more difficult dimension of operations to envisage. It means how much of the operation's activities its customers experience, or how much the operation is 'exposed' to its customers. Obviously customer-processing operations have more of their activities visible to their customers than most material-processing operations. But even customer-processing operations exercise some choice as to how visible they wish their operations to be. For example, in clothes retailing, an organization could decide to operate as a chain of conventional shops. Alternatively, it could decide not to have any shops at all but rather to run an internet-based operation.

The 'bricks and mortar' shop operation is a high-visibility operation insomuch as its customers experience most of its 'value-adding' activities. Customers in this type of operation have a relatively *short waiting tolerance*. They will walk out if not served in a reasonable time. They might also judge the operation by their perceptions of it rather than always by objective criteria. If they perceive that a member of the operation's staff is discourteous to them, they are likely to be dissatisfied (even if the staff member meant no discourtesy), so high-visibility operations require staff with good customer contact skills. Customers could also request goods which clearly would not be sold in such a shop, but because the customers are actually in the operation they can ask what they like! This is called *high received variety*, and will occur even if the variety of service for which the operation is designed is low. This does not make it easy for high-visibility operations to achieve high productivity of resources, with the consequence that they tend to be relatively high-cost operations.

Contrast the clothes shop with the internet-based retailer. It is not a pure low-contact operation; it still has to communicate with its customers through its website. It may even be interactive in quoting real-time availability of items. As with the 'bricks and mortar' shop, customers will react badly to slow, poorly designed or faulty sites But overall the operation has far lower visibility. Most of the process is more 'factory-like'. The *time lag* between the order being placed and the items ordered by the customer being retrieved and dispatched does not have to be minutes as in the shop, but can be hours or even days. This allows the tasks of finding the items, packing and dispatching them to be *standardized* by organizing staff, who need no *customer contact skills*, so as to achieve *high staff utilization*. The internet-based organization can also centralize its operation on one (physical) site, whereas the 'bricks and mortar' shop, because of its high-contact nature, necessarily needs many shops close to centres of demand. For all these reasons the catalogue operation will have lower costs than the shop chain.

Mixed high- and low-visibility operations

Some operations have both high- and low-visibility micro operations within the same macro operation. This serves to emphasize the difference which the degree of customer contact makes. Take an airport as an example: some of its activities are totally 'visible' to its customers (ticketing staff dealing with the queues of travellers; the information desk answering people's queries; caterers serving meals and drinks; and passport control and security staff checking documentation and baggage). These staff operate in what is termed a *front-office* environment. Other parts of the airport have relatively little, if any, customer 'visibility' (the baggage handlers; the overnight freight operations staff; the ground crew putting meals on board and refreshing the aircraft; the cleaners preparing them for their next flight; the cooks and the administrators). We rarely see these staff; they perform the vital but low customer contact tasks, in what is termed the *back-office* part of the operation. Many operations have a mixture of front-office, high-visibility and back-office, low-visibility micro operations.

The implications of the four Vs of operations

All four dimensions have implications for the cost of creating the products or services. Put simply, high volume, low variety, low variation and low customer contact all help to keep processing costs down. Conversely, low volume, high variety, high variation and high customer contact generally carry some kind of cost penalty for the operation. This is why the volume dimension is drawn with its 'low' end at the left, unlike the other dimensions, to keep all the 'low cost' implications on the right. Figure 1.10 summarizes the implications of such positioning.

To some extent the position of an operation in the four dimensions is determined by the demand of the market it is serving. However, most operations have some discretion in moving themselves on the dimensions. Look at the different positions on the visibility dimension which banks have adopted. At one time, using branch tellers was the only way

Some parts of a bank are high-visibility operations, such as the branch on the left above, others are lower-visibility operations whose workers never 'see' a customer (although they may talk to them on the telephone) such as the back-office operation (above right)

Figure 1.10 A typology of operations

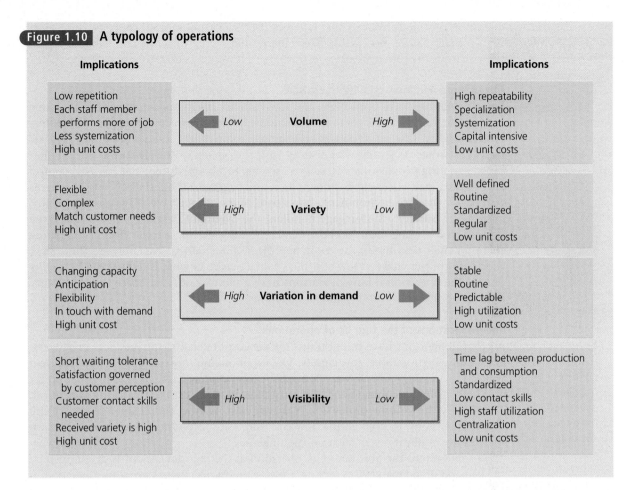

Implications   **Implications**

Low repetition / Each staff member performs more of job / Less systemization / High unit costs	**← Low Volume High →**	High repeatability / Specialization / Systemization / Capital intensive / Low unit costs
Flexible / Complex / Match customer needs / High unit cost	**← High Variety Low →**	Well defined / Routine / Standardized / Regular / Low unit costs
Changing capacity / Anticipation / Flexibility / In touch with demand / High unit cost	**← High Variation in demand Low →**	Stable / Routine / Predictable / High utilization / Low unit costs
Short waiting tolerance / Satisfaction governed by customer perception / Customer contact skills needed / Received variety is high / High unit cost	**← High Visibility Low →**	Time lag between production and consumption / Standardized / Low contact skills / High staff utilization / Centralization / Low unit costs

customers could contact a bank. The other services have been developed by banks to create different markets. For almost any type of industry one can identify operations which inhabit different parts of the four dimensions and which are therefore implicitly competing for business in different ways. Figure 1.11 illustrates the different positions on the dimensions of the Formule 1 hotel chain (*see* the box on Formule 1) and a very different type of hotel. An island resort hotel in the Caribbean, for example, provides the same

Figure 1.11 Profiles of two operations

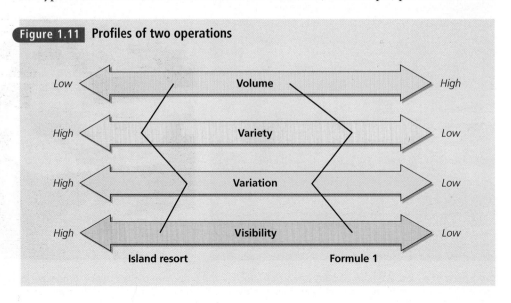

Providing budget-priced hotel accommodation which is also modern, comfortable, hygienic and of consistent quality seems to be almost a contradiction. Hotels, after all, are outstanding examples of high-contact services – they are both staff-intensive and have to cope with the variety demanded by customers, each with a variety of needs and expectations. Is it then impossible to run a highly successful chain of affordable hotels without the crippling costs of high customer contact? Not for Formule 1, a subsidiary of the French Accor group, whose chain of budget hotels stretches throughout Europe and South Africa. They manage to offer outstanding value by adopting two principles not always associated with hotel operations – standardization and an innovative use of technology.

Formule 1 hotels are usually located close to industrial trading estates, by trunk roads, junctions and close to cities, in order to be visible and accessible for prospective customers. The hotels themselves, which are instantly recognizable and made from state-of-the-art volumetric prefabrications, come in five sizes – 50, 64, 73, 80 and 98 rooms. The prefabricated units are arranged in various configurations to suit the characteristics of each individual site. Figure 1.12 shows some configurations. All rooms are nine square metres in area, and are designed to be attractive, functional, comfortable and soundproof. Most important, they are designed to be easy to clean and maintain. All have the same fittings, including a double bed, an additional bunk-type bed, a wash basin, a storage area, a working table with seat, a wardrobe and a television set.

The reception of a Formule 1 hotel is staffed only from 6.30 am to 10.00 am and from 5.00 pm to 10.00 pm. Outside these times an automatic machine sells rooms to credit card users, providing access to the hotel, dispensing a security code for the room and even printing out a receipt. Technology is also evident in the washrooms. Showers and toilets are automatically cleaned after each use by using nozzles and heating elements to spray the room with a disinfectant solution and dry it before it is used again.

To keep things even simpler, Formule 1 hotels do not include a restaurant as they are usually located near existing restaurants. However, a continental breakfast is available, usually between 6.30 am and 10.00 am, and of course on a 'self-service' basis!

Questions

1 What is the role of technology in allowing Formule 1 to keep its costs low?

2 How does the concept of 'standardization' help Formule 1 to keep its costs down?

Figure 1.12 Some configurations of Formule 1 pre-manufactured room units

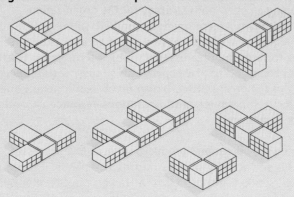

basic service as any other hotel. However, it could very well be of a small, intimate nature with relatively few customers (some hotel resorts of this type cater for only 10 or 20 guests at a time). Its variety of services is almost infinite in the sense that customers can make individual requests in terms of food and entertainment. Variation might be very high, with the resort closing in the off-season. Finally, customer contact, and therefore visibility, in order to ascertain customers' requirements and provide for them, is likely to be very high. All of which is very different from Formule 1, where volume is high (although not as high as in a large city-centre hotel), variety of service is strictly limited, and business and holiday customers use the hotel at different times, which limits variation. Most notably, though, customer contact is kept to a minimum. The island resort hotel has very high levels of service but provides them at a high cost (and therefore a high price). Conversely, Formule 1 has arranged its operation in such a way as to minimize its costs.

The activities of operations management

Operations managers have some responsibility for all the activities in the organization which contribute to the effective production of goods and services. Here, we divide these responsibilities into:

- *direct responsibility* for the activities which produce and deliver products and services;
- *indirect responsibility* for the activities of other functions of the organization;
- *broad responsibility* to respond to the emerging challenges for operations management in the future.

● The direct responsibilities of operations management

The exact nature of the operations function's direct responsibilities will, to some extent, depend on the way the organization has chosen to define the boundaries of its operations function. There are some general classes of activities, however, which apply to all types of operation no matter how functional boundaries have been drawn.

Understanding the operation's strategic objectives

The first responsibility of any operations management team is to understand what it is trying to achieve. This means developing a clear vision of how the operation should help the organization achieve its long-term goals. It also means translating the organization's goals into their implications for the operation's performance objectives, quality, speed, dependability, flexibility and cost. All these issues are discussed in Chapter 2.

Developing an operations strategy for the organization

Operations management involves hundreds of minute-by-minute decisions. So it is vital that operations managers have a set of general principles which can guide decision-making towards the organization's longer-term goals. This is an operations strategy. It involves being able to place operations strategy within the general strategy, i.e. decision-making of the organization. It also involves reconciling the often conflicting pressures of market requirements and operations resource capabilities. Chapter 3 deals with operations strategy.

Designing the operation's products, services and processes

Design is the activity of determining the physical form, shape and composition of products, services and processes. Although direct responsibility for the design of products and services might not be part of the operations function in some organizations, it is crucial to the operation's other activities. Therefore we examine the design process in general in Chapter 4 and the design of products and services in particular in Chapter 5. But the transformation process itself also has to be designed. At the most strategic level, this means designing the whole network of operations which provide inputs to the operations function and deliver its output to customers. This is treated in Chapter 6. At a more immediate level, operations managers need to design their process layouts and the flow of transformed resources through the operation, an issue treated in Chapter 7. Closely connected are the two main transforming resources in any operation – process technology and people. The design issues relating to process technology and job design are examined in Chapters 8 and 9, respectively.

Planning and controlling the operation

Planning and control is the activity of deciding what the operations resources should be doing, then making sure that they really are doing it. Chapter 10 explains the nature of planning and control activities, while the planning and control of capacity so as to meet fluctuating demand levels is treated in Chapter 11. The planning and control of the flow of the transformed resources through the operation are treated in Chapter 12, which deals with inventory management, and Chapter 13, which deals with 'supply chain' management. Some specific approaches to planning and control have been developed for particular circumstances. For example, materials requirements planning (MRP) is treated as part of Chapter 14, just-in-time (JIT) planning and control is described in Chapter 15, while Chapter 16 treats planning and control in project operations. Finally, Chapter 17 treats the management of the quality of products and services.

Improving the performance of the operation

The continuing responsibility of all operations managers is to improve the performance of their operation. Failure to improve at least as fast as competitors (in for-profit organizations) or at the rate of customers' rising expectations (in all organizations) is to condemn the operations function always to fall short of what the organization should expect from it. Chapter 18 describes how the process of improvement can be organized within the operation. The other side of making operations better is stopping them going wrong in the first place. Chapter 19 deals with how failures are prevented in operations, and how the operation can recover when failure does occur. Finally, powerful improvement ideas of total quality management (TQM) are covered in Chapter 20.

● The indirect responsibilities of operations management

Many decisions taken outside the operations function still can have an effect on operations activities. For example, developing advertising plans is quite clearly in the marketing domain, but it may have a significant impact on operations by affecting overall demand levels and the exact mix of products and services which customers will want. In these circumstances the responsibility of operations management is to explore the possible consequences of the advertising plans with the marketing function. It should understand their impact on the operation, make clear to marketing what the operation can and cannot do in response to any change in demand, and work together with marketing to find ways of allowing them to meet, or manage, market needs while also allowing the operation to run efficiently and effectively.

It is working together with the other parts of the organization which forms the most important indirect responsibilities of operations management. Not that 'indirect' means that these responsibilities are unimportant. On the contrary, it is a fundamental of modern organizational principles that functional boundaries should not hinder efficient internal processes. So developing and improving the relationships between operations and the other functions of the firm should be central to operations' contribution to overall performance.

Figure 1.13 illustrates some of the responsibility relationships between the operations and other functions. While the flow of information between the functions is not

Figure 1.13 **Some interfunctional relationships between the operations function and other core and support functions**

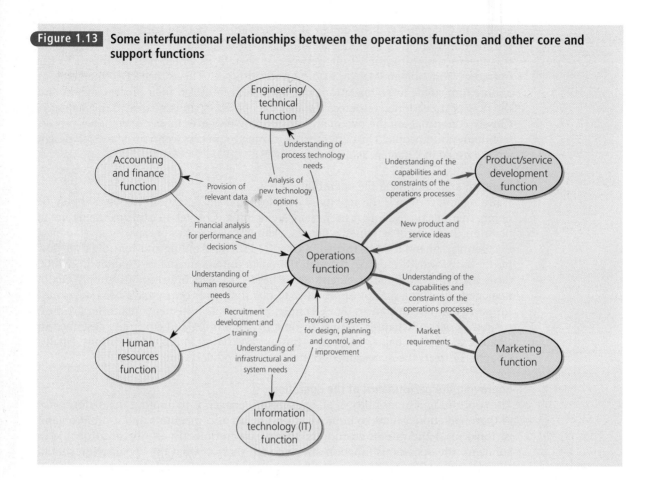

comprehensive, it does give an idea of the nature of each relationship. However, note that the support functions have a different relationship with operations than the other core functions. Operations management's responsibility to support functions is primarily to make sure that they understand operations' needs and help them to satisfy these needs. The operations function is clearly the internal customer. The relationship with the other two core functions is more equal – less of 'this is what we want' and more 'this is what we can do currently – how do we reconcile this with broader business needs?'

● The broad responsibilities of operations management

Both the direct and indirect responsibilities of operations management are largely focused on those concerns which are of clear and immediate benefit to the organization itself. But increasingly it is recognized that all businesses, including their operations managers, have a set of broader responsibilities. Some of these are to the longer-term interests of the business, some are to the environment in which the business operates and some to the well-being of the people who the business employs. All businesses will interpret these broader responsibilities in different ways. Here we identify six that are of general relevance to operations managers and which are already important issues in the early twenty-first century.

- *Globalization* – the world is a smaller place; very few operations do not either source from or sell to foreign markets. How do operations managers cope with this expanded set of opportunities?
- *Environmental protection* – operations managers cannot avoid responsibility for their organization's environmental performance. It is often operational failures which are at the root of pollution disasters and operations decisions (such as product design)

The Body Shop formulates and manufactures skin- and hair-care products, but perhaps it is best known for its highly successful shops which brim with brightly coloured lotions, soaps, shampoos and oils. It is also renowned for its positive approach to environmentally conscious operations. The company has led the field in green operations by using only minimal and simple packaging, encouraging the recycling and refilling of containers, by not testing products on animals, by using natural materials wherever possible, and by having explicit social policies. Although not without its critics, Body Shop argues that it wanted to prove that it is possible to develop a profitable business and at the same time maintain a respect for the environment, the communities where its operations have an impact, its employees and its customers. This philosophy affects its operations management policies in a number of ways:

- *Socially responsible purchasing*. At one time wooden foot rollers were purchased from a company in Frankfurt. The company now sources them from a workshop which it set up in an Indian village to provide employment and training for the older children in an orphanage. Ignoring the lower costs, the company paid the same price to the workshop, the revenue being used to help the village to improve its education, health and nutritional standards. Six similar workshops have now been established in India.

- *Using renewable sources*. The company took a lead in encouraging a Nepalese paper factory to switch from clearing the local forest for its raw materials to using renewable sources such as banana skins.
- *Social location*. The company bought an abandoned factory in a deprived area of Glasgow and converted it into a soap factory which now makes over 25 million bars, sold throughout the world. As well as bringing much needed employment to the area, a quarter of the profit is returned for community projects.
- *Re-using*. The company provides a refill service in all its shops where empty plastic bottles can be refilled in return for a reduction on the purchase price. Over two million bottles are refilled every year in the UK alone.
- *Recycling waste*. Most synthetic polymers which can be recycled need to be sorted prior to recycling. The company has a standard labelling scheme which identifies the type of plastic used on each of its packages. This makes the sorting process, and therefore recycling, easier.

Questions

1 How do you think Body Shop's environmental policy relates to its overall business strategy?

2 What do you think are the dilemmas posed by the decisions described above for the company's operations managers?

can impact on longer-term environmental issues. So how can environmental responsibility be balanced against economic factors?

- *Social responsibility* – the way in which an operation is managed has a significant impact on the individuals who work for it, the individuals who work for its suppliers (and sometimes its customers), the groups who represent employees' interests and the local community in which the operation is located. How can operations be managed to be responsible employers and good neighbours?
- *Technology awareness* – technology has always been a central part of operations management's concerns (process technology issues, for example, are treated in Chapter 8). However, in times of particularly fast changing technologies, operations managers have a responsibility to understand the implications of technologies which may seem to be unrelated to their activities. How many operations in 1995, for example, understood the full impact that internet technologies would have on almost all types of operation?
- *Knowledge management* – increasingly it is recognized that the key resource in businesses is the knowledge they contain. Knowledge is gained through experience, experience through activity, and activity (doing things) is what operations management is about. This is why operations managers have a particular responsibility to build the organization's stock of knowledge through the learning processes which should accompany its ongoing activities.

All of these broad responsibilities represent considerable challenges to modern operations managers, in addition to the more obvious challenges of improving the way they produce and deliver products and services. All of them will be touched on throughout the book and we will return to them in the last chapter.

The model of operations management

We can now combine two ideas to develop the model of operations management which will be used throughout this book. The first is the input–transformation–output model and the second is the categorization of operations management's activity areas. Figure 1.14 shows how these two ideas go together.

The model now shows two interconnected loops of activities. The bottom one more or less corresponds to what is usually seen as operations management, and the top one to what is seen as operations strategy. This book concentrates on the former but tries to cover enough of the latter to allow the reader to make strategic sense of the operations manager's job.

Figure 1.14 A general model of operations management and operations strategy

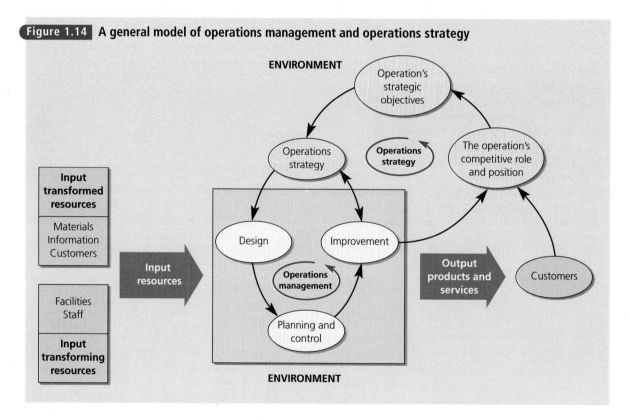

What is operations management?

● Operations management is the term used for the activities, decisions and responsibilities of operations managers who manage the production and delivery of products and services.

● It is one of the core functions of any business, although it may not be called operations management in some industries.

● The span of responsibility varies between companies, but will usually overlap to some extent with the other functions.

● Operations management can also be viewed as that part of any function's or manager's responsibility which involves producing the internal products and services within the organization, as opposed to the strictly technical decisions which they take within their functions.

What are the similarities between all operations?

● All operations can be modelled as a process which transforms inputs into outputs.

● All have inputs of transforming resources which are usually divided into 'facilities' and 'staff'. All also have transformed resources which are some mixture of materials, information and customers.

● All operations transform inputs into outputs by acting on some aspect of their physical properties, informational properties, possession, location, storage or accommodation, physiological state or psychological state.

● All operations produce some mixture of tangible goods or products and less tangible services. Few operations produce only products or only services.

● All operations can be divided into micro operations which form a network of internal customer–supplier relationships within the operation.

● All operations can be viewed as a set of business processes which often cut across functionally based micro operations.

How are operations different from each other?

● Operations differ in terms of the volume of their outputs. High volume is usually associated with low cost.

● All operations differ in terms of the variety of outputs they produce. Low variety is usually associated with low cost.

● All operations vary in terms of the variation in demand with which they have to cope. Low variation is usually associated with low cost.

● All operations vary in terms of the degree of 'visibility' or customer contact they have. Low customer 'visibility' is usually associated with low cost.

What responsibilities do operations managers have?

● They translate the strategic direction of an organization into operational action.

● They design the operation, not only the products and services themselves, but the systems or processes which produce them.

● They plan and control the activities of the operation by deciding when and where activities will take place, and detecting and responding to any deviations from plans.

● They improve the performance of the operation with reference to its strategic objectives, through some combination of major and minor improvement activities.

● Indirect responsibilities include working closely with other functional areas of the business.

● Broad responsibilities include understanding the impact on the operation of globalization, environmental responsibility, social responsibility, new technologies and knowledge management.

A business trip to Brussels

My flight to Stockholm would be late landing. The pilot told us that we were in a 'stack' of planes circling above the snow clouds that were giving Brussels its first taste of winter. Air traffic control had closed the runways for a short period at dawn, and the early morning flights from all around Europe were now being allocated new landing slots along with the long-haul jumbos from the Far East and the US. After a 20-minute delay, we descended bumpily through the clouds, and landed on a recently cleared runway. Even then there was a further 'hold' on a taxiway; we were told that the de-icing of the apron was being completed so that planes could proceed to their allocated stands and airbridges. All around the airport I could see the scurrying flashing beacons of the snow-clearing vehicles, the catering suppliers' vans, the aviation fuel trucks, the baggage trailers, buses transporting crews and passengers, security police cars, and an assortment of other vehicles all going purposefully about their work. Brussels airport always looks busy, with over 10 million passengers a year, but this morning the complexity and scale of the operations were particularly evident.

Finally, about an hour late, we pulled up to the gate, the engines were turned off, and we disembarked into an icy-cold airbridge, leaving behind a particularly untidy plane strewn with litter from a full cabin of restless passengers. We passed the team of cleaners and maintenance staff waiting just outside. 'They will have a hard time this morning; more mess to clear and probably less time than usual to do it, as the airline will want a quick turnaround to get back on to schedule,' I commented to my colleagues. We could just hear the sounds of frantic activities going on below the plane: baggage and cargo being unloaded, catering vehicles arriving, fuel being loaded, and technicians checking over the engines and control surfaces – everyone trying to get their work completed quickly and correctly, not least so that they could get back indoors out of the biting cold wind!

From the airbridge we walked past the crowded seating areas, where plane-sized groups were gathering anxiously awaiting the signal from the gate staff to board their much delayed flights. Then on to the moving walkways, conveyed leisurely past other departure lounges, equally overfilled with passengers. Anxious to get ahead of the crowd, we took to a running pace past the rows of cafés, bars and shops, hoping to avoid the usual morning queue for Passport Control. I should have remembered the old saying 'more haste, less speed' because my next journey was to the First Aid room! I had apparently slipped on some spilt coffee that had not been cleaned up in the haste of the morning, and had fallen awkwardly, straining my ankle and breaking my duty-free brandy. 'At least they would clean the floor after that,' I thought, sadly.

Suitably patched up, I hobbled with my colleagues and joined the long queue for Passport Control, and eventually through to Baggage Reclaim. Even with the excellent new baggage-handling systems in Brussels, the passengers usually get there first, but the accident had changed all that! Scanning the video screens, we found no reference to our flight arrival; the remaining bags from our flight had apparently already been removed from the carousel and were stored in an adjacent office. After a simple signing ceremony, we were reunited with our belongings, and hastened (slowly in my case) to the taxi rank. Our hopes of a quick ride to the city were dispelled when we saw the long queue in the icy wind, so we made our way to the station below, where a dedicated 'City Express' train departs every 20 minutes for the *Gare de Nord* and *Gare Centrale*. We just missed one!

After a busy and successful day at our Brussels office, a taxi was called, and we were back at the airport in the thick of the evening rush hour. The departures check-in area is the upper floor of a vast new terminal extension, and is very orderly and well equipped. Facing you on entry from the taxi drop-off point is a huge electronic display which lists all departures scheduled for the next few hours and showing the appropriate check-in desk number for each flight. The speed of the check-in systems has been improved dramatically, so there was no queue at our desk, and the three of us were issued with boarding passes in only a couple of minutes. Our baggage sped away on conveyors down to the new sorting hall two storeys below. Brochures explain that the new terminal extension was designed to make it possible to go from check-in to final boarding in only 20 minutes, which has involved investment in a state-of-the-art automated baggage-handling system. On my last visit, following traffic delays on the way to the airport, I found that this system works, but I doubt that it would if everyone arrived only 20 minutes before departure! It is no wonder that they advise checking in one hour before; it also gives passengers much more time to spend money in the duty-free shops, restaurants and bars!

By this time, my injured leg had swollen up and was throbbing painfully. This seemed to be a routine situation for the check-in staff, who arranged for a wheelchair and attendant to take me through Border Control and security checks. While my colleagues travelled down to the departures hall by escalator, I took the slower route by lift, meeting just outside the duty-free shops where the attendant left them to take care of me. We had some time to spare, so we replenished the brandy, bought some Belgian chocolates and headed for a café-bar. While Brussels is renowned for its excellent cuisine, we didn't expect to find high standards of food in the quick-service environment of an airport, but we were wrong! The delicious aromas of freshly prepared food attracted our custom, and we weren't disappointed. After a welcome glass of speciality raspberry-flavoured beer to round off the meal, we headed for the airline's executive lounge.

The view across the airfield was not promising! After a bright, crisp day, more snow-laden clouds had arrived and a chill wind cut across the tarmac. De-icing crews were working on the parked aircraft and others were treating the runways, taking quick action between the aircraft movements. Concerned that we might be delayed and miss our connection at Oslo, we checked with the staff at the airline's flight information desk. After some phoning, they confirmed that, although there could be some delays, Oslo had arranged to hold connecting

flights, as many passengers originated from Brussels. Their professional and friendly advice made us feel much more at ease, and they even offered to allow us to send fax or phone messages to our destination. They couldn't have been more helpful.

Announcements of the minor delays were made over the speaker system, but it wasn't long before we were directed to the departure lounge and were preparing to board. Outside, around the aircraft in the gloom, the baggage trucks were pulling away and the giant push-off tractor was being connected up to the nose-wheel. Ten minutes later, we were at the end of the runway, ready for take-off.

'Today must have been a very busy one for everyone involved in keeping the airport open,' I thought, 'but perhaps every day has its own challenges in such a complex operation.'

Questions

1 Identify all the micro operations and their activities which are mentioned.

2 Classify them in accordance with the structure in Table 1.4.

3 Which of these micro operations were most affected by the severe weather?

4 Approximately how many different organizations are involved in delivering the goods and services described in this report? What are the implications of this?

Discussion questions

(All chapters have discussion questions. Some of them can be answered by reading the chapter. Others will require some general knowledge of business activity and some might require an element of investigation.)

1 The port of Rotterdam is the largest port in the world. It provides a vital link between sea-based transportation of cargo and inland transport into Europe such as rail, road and inland waterways. List the transformation processes which you think the port's operations managers have to run, and identify their inputs and outputs.

2 Describe the operations of the following organizations using the transformation model. Carefully identify the transforming resources, transformed resources, the type of transformation process and the outputs from the transformation process for:
   – an international airport
   – a supermarket
   – a high-volume car plant.

3 What mixture of goods and services is produced by the following operations:
   – Airbus Industrie
   – The Channel Tunnel
   – Marks & Spencer
   – Federal Express parcel service
   – Volvo motor cars
   – Novotel hotels?

4 Why is operations management relevant to managers in other organization functions?

5 Explain the difference between micro and macro operations. Describe some of the micro operations in a university and discuss the relationships between their internal customers and suppliers.

6 Talk with an operations manager from a local organization and find out what he (or she) says or does and how he or she works with the organization's marketing, financial, personnel and purchasing functions.

7 Draw the hierarchy of operations for a small manufacturing company.

8 What are the main differences between internal and external customers?

9 Discuss the advantages and disadvantages of buffering an operation from the environment. Illustrate your answer with an organization of your choice.

10 How do you think a blood transfusion service operation buffers itself against environmental uncertainty?

11 Describe the relative volume, variety, variation and customer contact for the following organizations:
   – a theme park
   – a bread bakery
   – a dentist.

12 Explain the advantages and disadvantages to an operation of reducing its volume, variety and 'visibility'. How could a university change volume, variety and 'visibility' in order to reduce its costs?

13 What do you think would be the main design, planning and control, and improvement activities in a large airport such as London Heathrow?

14 Over recent years there has been a resurgence of interest in operations management in universities but especially in business. Why do you think this is?

Notes on chapter

1 Sources: Thornhill, J. (1992) 'Hard Sell on the High Street', *Financial Times*, May 16. Horovitz, J. and Jurgens Panak, M. (1992) *Total Customer Satisfaction*, Pitman Publishing. Walley, P. and Hart, K. (1993) IKEA (UK) Ltd, Loughborough University Business School, company website (2000).

2 We are grateful to Stagepoint for their assistance.

3 Source: 'Hayek's Watch Works', *World Link*, July 1994.

4 A number of authors have commented on the way the operations function is protected from the environment. For example, Thompson, J.D. (1967) *Organizations in Action*, McGraw-Hill, originally commented on organization buffering, while Wild, R. (1977) *Concepts for Operations Management*, John Wiley, extended the ideas to physical buffering.

5 One of the most articulate proponents of how an organization can be more responsive to environmental influence is Richard Schonburger. *See*, for example, *Building a Chain of Customers*, Hutchinson Business Books, 1990.

6 Sources: Pean, P. (1989) 'How to Get Rich on Perestroika', *Fortune*, 8 May, pp 95–6, and 'Vision Factory', *National Geographic*, Nov 1993.

7 Sources: Groupe Accor published accounts 1992, *Formule 1, The Most Affordable Hotel Chain*, company information brochure. Sharon Dannelley (1993) 'Groupe Accor', *Warwick Business School Report*.

8 Sources: Franssen, M. (1993) 'Beyond Profits', *Business Quarterly*, Autumn. Hopfenbeck, W. (1992) *The Green Management Revolution*, Prentice Hall.

Selected further reading

Adams, E.E. and Ebert, R.J. (1992) *Production and Operations Management* (5th edn), Prentice Hall.

Albrecht, K. and Bradford, L.J. (1990) *The Service Advantage*, Dow Jones Irwin.

Andrews, C.G. (1982) 'The Critical Importance of Production and Operations Management', *Academy of Management Review*, Vol 7, Jan.

Armistead, C.G. (ed) (1994) *The Future of Services Management*, Kogan Page.

Bowen, D.E., Chase, R.B., Cummings, T.G. and Associates (1990) *Service Management Effectiveness*, Jossey-Bass.

Chase, R.B., Aquilano, N.J. and Jacobs, F.R. (1998) *Production and Operations Management: Manufacturing and Services* (8th edn), Unwin/McGraw-Hill.

Flaherty, M.T. (1996) *Global Operations Management*, McGraw-Hill.

Gaither, N. and Frazier, G. (1999) *Production and Operations Management* (8th edn), South-Western College Publishing, Cincinnati.

Gronroos, C. (1990) *Service Management and Marketing*, Lexington Books.

Heizer, J. and Render, B. (1999) *Operations Management* (5th edn), Prentice Hall, New Jersey.

Hill, T. (1991) *Production/Operations Management* (2nd edn), Prentice Hall.

Johnston, R., Chambers, S., Harland, C., Harrison, A. and Slack, N. (1997) *Cases in Operations Management* (2nd edn), Pitman Publishing.

Keen, P.G.W. (1997) *The Process Edge: Creating Value where it Counts*, Harvard Business School Press.

Krajewski, L.J. and Ritzman, I.P. (1991) *Operations Management* (4th edn), Addison-Wesley.

Melnyk, S.A. and Denzler, D.R. (1996) *Operations Management: A Value Driven Approach*, Unwin/McGraw-Hill.

Ould, M.A. (1995) *Business Processes*, John Wiley.

Schonberger, R. (1990) *Building a Chain of Customers*, Hutchinson Business Books.

Slack, N. (ed) (1997)*The Blackwell Encyclopedic Dictionary of Operations Management*, Blackwell Business, Oxford.

Starr, M.K. (1996) *Operations Management: A Systems Approach*, Boyd and Fraser Publishing.

Voss, C. and Johnston, R. (1996) *Service in Britain: How do we Measure Up?*, Severn Trent.

Wild, R. (1989) *Production and Operations Management* (4th edn), Cassell.

Womack, J.P. and Jones, D.T. (1996) *Lean Thinking: Banish Waste and Create Wealth in your Corporation*, Simon and Schuster.

The strategic role and objectives of operations

Introduction

If any operation wants to understand its contribution to the organization of which it is a part, it must answer two questions. First, what is the *role* of the operations function – that is, what part is it expected to play within the business? Second, what are the specific *performance objectives* against which the business can assess the contribution of the operation to its strategic aspirations? Both these issues are vitally important to any operation. Without an appreciation of its role within the business, the people who manage the operation can never be sure that they really are contributing to the long-term success of the business. At a more practical level, it is impossible to know whether an operation is succeeding or not if the specific performance objectives against which its success is measured are not clearly spelt out. This chapter deals with both these issues. On our general model of operations management they are represented by the areas marked on Figure 2.1.

Figure 2.1 **This chapter covers the role and strategic objectives of operations management**

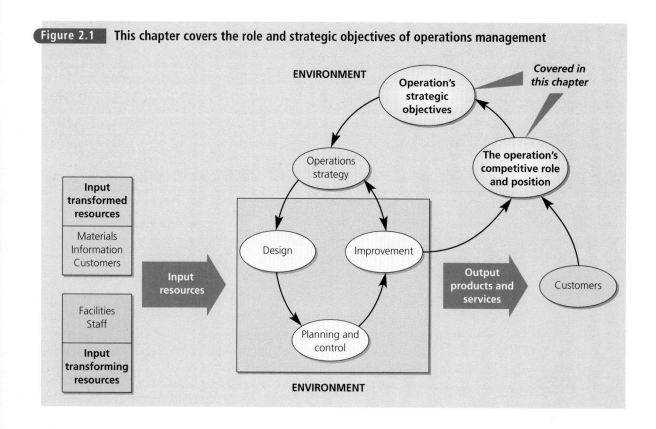

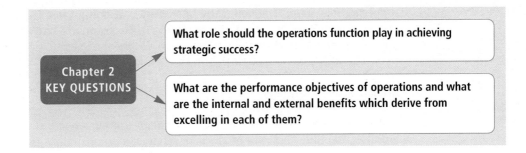

Chapter 2 KEY QUESTIONS

What role should the operations function play in achieving strategic success?

What are the performance objectives of operations and what are the internal and external benefits which derive from excelling in each of them?

The role of the operations function

By the role of the operations function we mean something beyond its obvious responsibilities and tasks in the company. We mean the underlying rationale of the function – the very reason that the function exists.

Why should any business go to the bother of having an operations function? Many organizations have the option of contracting out the production of their services and goods to become 'virtual' organizations. They could simply pay some other business to provide what their operations function currently does for them. This then prompts the further question 'What does the operations function have to do in order to justify its continued existence within the business?' This is what we mean by its role. Three roles seem to be particularly important for the operations function:

- as the *implementer* of business strategy;
- as a *support* to business strategy;
- as the *driver* of business strategy.

Implementing business strategy

One role of the operations part of the business is to implement strategy. Most companies will have some kind of strategy but it is the operation which puts it into practice. You cannot, after all, touch a strategy; you cannot even see it; all you can see is how the operation behaves in practice. For example, if an airline has a strategy of attracting a higher proportion of business-class travellers, it is the operations part of each function which has the task of 'operationalizing' the strategy. Its marketing 'operation' must organize appropriate promotions and pricing activities. The personnel 'operation' needs to train its cabin and ground staff to achieve higher levels of customer service. Most significantly, its operations function will have to supervise the refitting of the aircraft, organize express ticketing, baggage-handling and waiting facilities, and design special food, beverages and entertainment for the cabin service. The implication of this role for the operations function is very significant. It means that even the most original and brilliant strategy can be rendered totally ineffective by an inept operations function.

Supporting business strategy

Another role is to support strategy.[1] That is, it must develop its resources to provide the capabilities which are needed to allow the organization to achieve its strategic goals. For example, if a manufacturer of personal computers has decided to compete by being the first in the market with every available new product innovation, then its operations function needs to be capable of coping with the changes which constant innovation will bring. It must develop or purchase processes which are flexible enough to manufacture novel parts and products. It must organize and train its staff to understand the way products are changing and put in place the necessary changes to the operation. It must develop relationships with its suppliers which help them respond quickly when supplying new parts. The better the operation is at doing these things, the more support it is giving to the company's strategy. If the company had adopted a different business strategy, its operations function would have needed to adopt different objectives. This idea is developed further in the next chapter.

Driving business strategy

The third role of the operations part of the business is to drive strategy by giving it a long-term competitive edge. Badly made products, sloppy service, slow delivery, broken promises, too little choice of products or services or an operations cost base which is too high will sink any company in the long term. Conversely, any business which makes its products and/or services better, faster, on-time, in greater variety and less expensively than its competition has the best advantage any company could desire. More importantly, an operation which has developed the capabilities to cope with whatever the market requires in the future is providing the organization with the means for its future success. So both short-term and longer-term success can come directly from the operations function. An operations function which is providing both long- and short-term advantage is 'driving' business strategy by being the ultimate custodian of competiveness.

TNT – the worldwide transportation group   CWS

To illustrate the three roles of the operations function, examine the case of the transportation company, TNT.

TNT is the European market leader in global express distribution, logistics and international mail. It provides regional services in Europe, North and South America and Australasia and also global services which transport freight to almost any destination. The Amsterdam-based group employs 100 000 people around the world. TNT's main businesses are general freight, express freight by road and air, and specialist services including bulk cartage, materials handling, car carrying, refrigerated transport, industrial waste disposal, contract distribution and logistics support. The group is also directly involved in passenger and freight airline operations, aircraft leasing, tourism and leisure resort management.

The group's most familiar international face is its TNT Skypack International Express range of services which mail and courier packages, letters and parcels to around 190 countries. The Express Courier service uses a global online computer network, linking all parts of its operation for real-time communication of data and immediate access to vital shipment information. The TNT Skytrak information system also services the customer from point of request for collection of a shipment, through driver dispatch, operational routing and tracking, to proof of delivery. The Mailfast's Premium Letter Service offers expedited mailing for businesses by using the mailing network to inject mail direct into destination post offices or to hand deliver in major business centres. The Registered Mail Service offers signed receipt of delivery. The Express Post Service is designed to compete with post office accelerated services.

The long-term aim of the group is to provide a comprehensive range of transportation services around the world, with services to suit a wide variety of customer needs in all major regions of the world. Individually the group's different services compete in different ways. In courier services, price is less important than such factors as variety of service options (next day, overnight, two days, etc.) and dependable delivery. Mailfast focuses on ease of use and quality of service at the collection and delivery stages. Express Post competes on speed of delivery and price. The heavier freight end of the group's range is highly price-competitive but customers are willing to sign up for long-term contracts.

The three roles of the operations function in a company such as TNT could be interpreted as follows:

- *Implementing business strategy*. The group as a whole is moving towards being a fully comprehensive integrated supplier of its services worldwide. Operations must be able to evaluate alternative methods of achieving this and implement whatever investment in aircraft, vehicles, staff and systems is necessary.

- *Supporting business strategy*. Operations must provide dependable delivery for all services with other performance objectives suitable for the nature of competition. Cost especially must be kept low in the heavy freight and Express Post services. Quality of service is particularly important in the courier and Mailfast services. Speed of delivery is vital for the Express Post.

The resources devoted to each of these services should be developed to emphasize the key aspects of competitiveness for each service.

- *Driving business strategy.* Operations should move towards providing the capability to exceed competitors' performance and customers' expectations, initially in the more important aspects of competitiveness, and eventually in all aspects of performance. This means providing a more dependable, higher quality, faster, more flexible and cheaper service than any competitor.

Questions

1 How do the various services described above appear to differ from an operations point of view? (Start by identifying the different performance objectives which each service should have.)

2 What do you think are the problems in offering these different services using the same set of operations resources?

Judging the operation's contribution

The ability of any operation to play these roles within the organization can be judged by considering the organizational aims or aspirations of the operations function. Professors Hayes and Wheelwright of Harvard University,[2] with later contributions from Professor Chase of the University of Southern California,[3] have developed what they call the '*Four-Stage Model*' which can be used to evaluate the competitive role and contribution of the operations function of any type of company. The model traces the progression of the operations function from what is the largely negative role of stage 1 operations to it becoming the central element of competitive strategy in excellent stage 4 operations.

Stage 1: Internal neutrality

This is the very poorest level of contribution by the operations function. The other functions regard it as holding them back from competing effectively. The operations function is inward-looking and at best reactive with very little positive to contribute towards competitive success. Its goal is to be ignored. At least then it isn't holding the company back in any way. Certainly the rest of the organization would not look to operations as the source of any originality, flair or competitive drive. Its ambition is to be 'internally neutral', a position it attempts to achieve not by anything positive but by avoiding the bigger mistakes. Even good organizations can be let down by their operations function and the resulting publicity can be damaging (*see* Fig. 2.2).

Stage 2: External neutrality

The first step of breaking out of stage 1 is for the operations function to begin comparing itself with similar companies or organizations in the outside market. This may not immediately take it to the 'first division' of companies in the market, but at least it is measuring itself against its competitors' performance and trying to be 'appropriate', by adopting 'best practice' from them. By taking the best ideas and norms of performance from the rest of its industry, it is trying to be 'externally neutral'.

Stage 3: Internally supportive

Stage 3 operations have probably reached the 'first division' in their market. They may not be better than their competitors on every aspect of operations performance but they are broadly up with the best. Yet, stage 3 operations still aspire to be clearly and unambiguously the very best in the market. They achieve this by gaining a clear view of the company's competitive or strategic goals and developing 'appropriate' operations resources to excel in the areas in which the company needs to compete effectively. The operation is trying to be 'internally supportive' by providing a credible operations strategy.

Stage 4: Externally supportive

Stage 3 used to be taken as the limit of the operations function's contribution. Yet Hayes and Wheelwright capture the growing importance of operations management by suggesting a further stage – stage 4.

Korean Air navigation equipment failed

by Juliette Jowit, Transport Correspondent

Vital navigation equipment failed moments before last month's Korean Air Boeing 747 crash near Stansted airport despite attempts by engineers on the ground to fix it before take-off, an official interim report into the accident revealed last night

The crash on the night of December 22 killed the four Korean Air crew and narrowly missed nearby houses.

The problem with the altitude director indicator, which tells crews the exact position of the aircraft at night and in cloud, was discovered on the previous flight by the cargo jet.

An avionics engineering from based maintenance

Boeing Boeing Gone

Failures to co-ordinate its price operations, a botched attempt to out come of its activities and badly handled relations have all contributed to Boeings re problems. Industry expert Richard Selby Boeing were re

France takes Coca-Cola off shelves

FRENCH distribution chains yesterday removed from sales 50m cans of Coca-Cola, Fanta and Sprite, as the French authorities reported that 80 people had fallen ill after drinking Coca-Cola products.

Production problems are understood to have resulted in the possible contamination.

Faulty bolt fear for Boeings

FROM GRACE BRADBERRY IN LOS ANGELES

Hundreds of Boeing 767 aircraft – the same model as the Air Egypt plane that crashed a week ago, killing all 217 people aboard – could be flying with faulty tail bolts.

The Boeing Co. says the bolts, which hold the vertical tail to the fuselage, are not likely to pose a safety threat because of the jet's structure. However, the company is considering issuing a service bulletin warning operators of the problem.

News of this latest problem

yesterday revealed news of the faulty tail bolt, it is not clear whether the suspect bolts could be in planes built as far back as 1989 – the year in which Air Egypt's 767-300 was delivered.

Late la grounded which is a the tail bolt Seven othe still at the since had l moved and

to audit Boeing's tool-calibration procedures.

The problem first came to light when a carrier – thought to be American Airlines – con -ducted a major

Rat in the aisle forces BA to cancel flight out of Africa

FROM INIGO GILMORE IN JOHANNESBURG

More than 200 British Airways passengers were stranded in Johannesburg yesterday when their overnight flight to London was cancelled after a stewardess spotted what she thought was a rat running down the aisle.

The rat – or possibly mouse – was seen while the aircraft was being cleaned after it had arrived in Johannesburg from Gaborone, the capital of neighbouring Botswana. British Airways said yesterday

grounds that the aircraft h to be fumigated and techni checks carried out in case rodent had chewed throu any wiring. "As always passengers are the first pri ty," a BA statement said

The BA statement s "Whenever possible, pa gers with onward connec were rebooked on flights. Other passengers accomm

Rats, mice and

Bacs to front

BANK of Scotland customers had an unexpected bonus at the end of last year. Because of an error in Bacs, the auto-mated clearing system, 90,000 cheques paid in by customers were credited twice man for the bank the error, which are of the large number going through the sy rectified almost imm However, it does not b for the bank's protract paign to take over Nat during which the S bank has been claimin have superior systems.

Operations failure behind Leeson disaster

Nick Leeson, the Barings trader who brought the company down, could never have done it with better operational procedures. "The failure

Sources (from the top): Financial Times, Sunday Business, The Sunday Times, The Sunday Times, The Times, Financial Times, The Wall St Journal

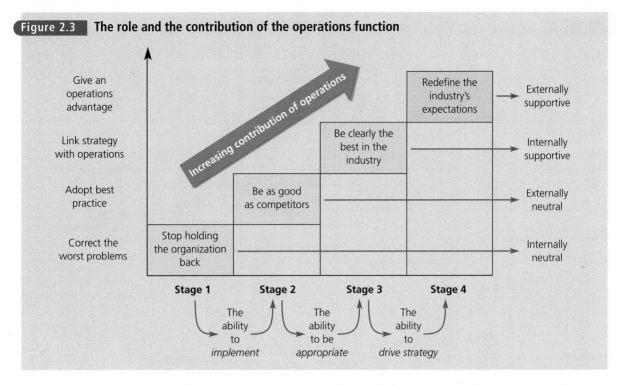

Figure 2.3 The role and the contribution of the operations function

The difference between stages 3 and 4 is subtle, but nevertheless important. A stage 4 company is one which sees the operations function as providing the foundation for its competitive success. Operations looks to the long term. It forecasts likely changes in markets and supply, and it develops operations-based capabilities which will be required to compete in future market conditions. The operations function is becoming central to strategy-making. Stage 4 operations are creative and proactive. They are likely to be innovative and capable of adaptation as markets change. Essentially they are trying to be 'one step ahead' of competitors in the way that they create products and services and organize their operations – what Hayes and Wheelwright call being 'externally supportive'.

Figure 2.3 brings together the two concepts of the *role* and the *contribution* of the operations function. Moving from stage 1 to stage 2 requires operations to overcome its problems of implementing existing strategies. The move from stage 2 to stage 3 requires operations actively to develop its resources so that they are appropriate for long-term strategy. Moving up to stage 4 requires operations to be driving strategy through its contribution to competitive superiority.

Operations performance objectives

At a strategic level, a useful classification of the performance objectives which any operation might pursue can be gained from identifying the operation's *stakeholders*. Stakeholders are the people and groups of people who have an interest in the operation and who may be influenced by, or influence, the operation's activities. Some stakeholders are internal, for example the operation's employees; others are external, for example society or community groups, and a company's shareholders. Some external stakeholders have a direct commercial relationship with the organization, for example the suppliers to the operation and the customers who receive its products and services. Figure 2.4 illustrates some main stakeholder groups together with some of the aspects of operations performance in which they will be interested. Return to the TNT box (p.40). Such a company is clearly concerned to satisfy its customers' requirements for fast and dependable services at reasonable prices, as well as helping its own suppliers (a whole range of

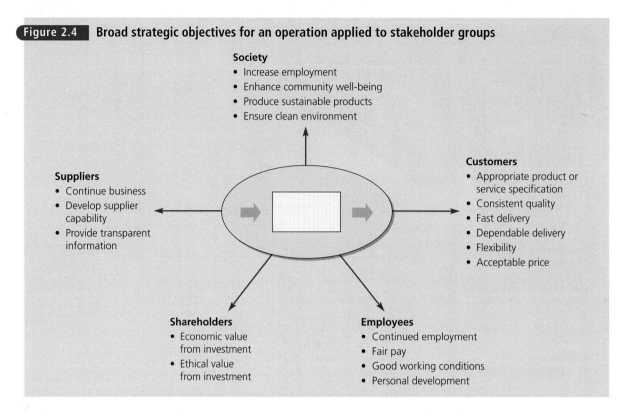

Figure 2.4 Broad strategic objectives for an operation applied to stakeholder groups

Society
- Increase employment
- Enhance community well-being
- Produce sustainable products
- Ensure clean environment

Suppliers
- Continue business
- Develop supplier capability
- Provide transparent information

Customers
- Appropriate product or service specification
- Consistent quality
- Fast delivery
- Dependable delivery
- Flexibility
- Acceptable price

Shareholders
- Economic value from investment
- Ethical value from investment

Employees
- Continued employment
- Fair pay
- Good working conditions
- Personal development

organizations, from those who print packets to those who clean the offices) to improve the services they offer. Similarly, it is concerned to ensure the long-term economic value delivered to the people and institutions who have bought shares in the company. But the company also has a responsibility to ensure that its own employees are well treated and that society at large is not negatively affected by the operation's activities – the company's vehicles must be well maintained so as not to pollute the environment; it must try to minimize the wastage of materials or energy; it must ensure that its operations do not disrupt the life and well-being of those who live nearby, and so on.

In many not-for-profit operations, these stakeholder groups can overlap. So, a government department may be both the 'shareholder' of a public service agency and its main customer. Similarly, groups within society may also be the customers for a charitable operation, or voluntary workers in a charity may be employees, shareholders and customers all at once. However, in any kind of organization, it is a responsibility of the operations function to understand the (sometimes conflicting) objectives of its stakeholders and set it objectives accordingly.

● The five performance objectives

The broad objectives which operations must pursue to satisfy stakeholders form the backdrop to all operations decision-making. However, at an operational level, we require a more tightly defined set of objectives. These are the five basic 'performance objectives' and they apply to all types of operation.

Imagine that you are an operations manager in any kind of business – a hospital administrator, for example, or a production manager at a car plant, the operations manager for a city bus company or the manager of a large supermarket. What kind of things are you likely to want to do in order to contribute to competitiveness?

- You would want to *do things right*; that is, you would not want to make mistakes, and would want to satisfy your customers by providing error-free goods and services which are 'fit for their purpose'. This is giving a *quality advantage* to your company's customers.

- You would want to *do things fast*, minimizing the time between a customer asking for goods or services and the customer receiving them in full, thus increasing the availability of your goods and services and giving your customers a *speed advantage*.
- You would want to *do things on time*, so as to keep the delivery promises you have made to your customers. If the operation can do this, it is giving a *dependability advantage* to its customers.
- You would want to be able to *change what you do*; that is, being able to vary or adapt the operation's activities to cope with unexpected circumstances or to give customers individual treatment. Hence the range of goods and services which you produce has to be wide enough to deal with all customer possibilities. Either way, being able to change far enough and fast enough to meet customer requirements gives a *flexibility advantage* to your customers.
- You would want to *do things cheaply*; that is, produce goods and services at a cost which enables them to be priced appropriately for the market while still allowing for a return to the organization; or, in a not-for-profit organization, give good value to the taxpayers or whoever is funding the operation. When the organization is managing to do this, it is giving a *cost advantage* to its customers.

The next part of this chapter examines these five performance objectives in more detail by looking at what they mean for the four different operations previously mentioned: a general hospital, an automobile factory, a city bus company and a supermarket chain.

● The quality objective

Quality means 'doing things right', but the things which the operation needs to do right will vary according to the kind of operation (*see* Fig. 2.5). For example, in the hospital, quality could mean making sure that patients get the most appropriate treatment, that the treatment is carried out in a medically correct manner, that patients are kept clearly informed as to what is happening and also are consulted if there are alternative forms of treatment. It would also include such things as ensuring that the hospital is clean, hygienic and tidy and that the staff are well informed and courteous towards patients. In the automobile factory, quality means that the car is made to its specifications and is

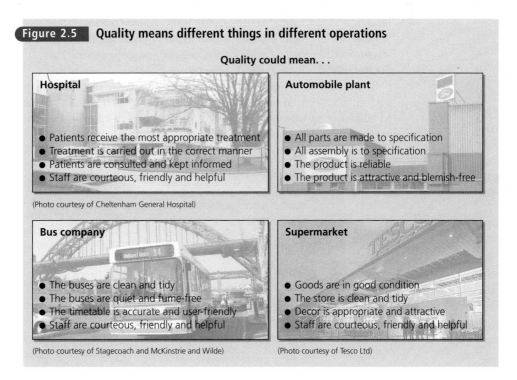

Figure 2.5 **Quality means different things in different operations**

Quality could mean. . .

Hospital
- Patients receive the most appropriate treatment
- Treatment is carried out in the correct manner
- Patients are consulted and kept informed
- Staff are courteous, friendly and helpful

(Photo courtesy of Cheltenham General Hospital)

Automobile plant
- All parts are made to specification
- All assembly is to specification
- The product is reliable
- The product is attractive and blemish-free

Bus company
- The buses are clean and tidy
- The buses are quiet and fume-free
- The timetable is accurate and user-friendly
- Staff are courteous, friendly and helpful

(Photo courtesy of Stagecoach and McKinstrie and Wilde)

Supermarket
- Goods are in good condition
- The store is clean and tidy
- Decor is appropriate and attractive
- Staff are courteous, friendly and helpful

(Photo courtesy of Tesco Ltd)

reliable. All parts are assembled correctly and all extras and documents are present and in the right place. Visually the car should look attractive and be blemish- and scratch-free. In a city bus company, quality means that the buses are clean, quiet and do not emit unpleasant fumes. It also means that timetables and other published information relating to the bus service are accurate and usable. Finally, it means that the bus staff are courteous and helpful to passengers. For the manager of the supermarket, quality means that the goods it sells are in good condition, that the store is clean and tidy, that the decor is attractive and that the staff are helpful and courteous.

Put this way, it is not surprising that all operations regard quality as a particularly important objective. In some ways quality is the most visible part of what an operation does. Furthermore, it is something that a customer finds relatively easy to judge about the operation. Is the product or service as it is supposed to be? Is it right or is it wrong? There is something fundamental about quality. Because of this, it is clearly a major influence on customer satisfaction or dissatisfaction. Good-quality products and services mean high customer satisfaction and therefore the likelihood that the customer will return (*see* box on Jaguar). Conversely, poor quality reduces the chances of a customer coming back for more.

Quality inside the operation

Good quality performance in an operation not only leads to external customer satisfaction, but makes life easier inside the operation as well. Satisfying internal customers can be as important as satisfying external customers.

Quality reduces costs

The fewer mistakes each micro operation or unit makes in the operation, the less time it will need to spend correcting these mistakes and the less confusion and irritation will be spread. For example, if a supermarket's regional warehouse sends the wrong goods to the supermarket, it will mean staff time, and therefore cost, being used to sort out the problem.

Quality increases dependability

Increased costs are not the only consequence of poor quality, however. At the supermarket it could also mean that goods run out on the supermarket shelves with a resulting loss of revenue to the operation and irritation to the external customers. Sorting the problem out could also distract the supermarket management from giving attention to the other parts of the supermarket operation. This in turn could result in further mistakes being made.

The important point here is that the performance objective of quality (like the other performance objectives, as we shall see) has both an external aspect to it, which leads to customer satisfaction, and an internal aspect, which leads to a stable and efficient organization.

Jaguar regains its reputation

Originally called the Swallow Side Car Company, Jaguar Cars was founded in 1922 and became famous for its luxury and sports cars. In 1990, Jaguar was taken over by Ford and is now a wholly owned subsidiary. At the time of the Ford takeover, Jaguar's quality performance was something of a paradox. Aesthetically and in terms of on-the-road performance the cars were often highly regarded, especially by a hard core of enthusiasts. Yet even they could not ignore Jaguar's reputation for making cars which were, in comparison to its rivals, of exceptionally poor reliability. Plagued by under-investment and a conservative technical-led, rather than customer-led, culture, the company's old plants were struggling to achieve even acceptable levels of conformance quality. At this time, the JD Power survey of customer satisfaction of cars imported to the US ranked only one car (the Yugo) lower than Jaguar.

Photo courtesy of Jaguar

in' and a general productivity bonus introduced which encouraged flexible working. Other shop floor initiatives included the introduction of multi-skilled teams, total productive maintenance (*see* Chapter 19), continuous improvement teams (*see* Chapter 18) and benchmarking against the best in the business (*see* Chapter 18). The success of this quality improvement programme was dramatic. It encouraged Ford to invest in new Jaguar models and also had a significant impact on customer satisfaction. The same surveys which once put Jaguar at the bottom of the league now rank it in the very top group of luxury car makers.

All this changed through the 1990s. The company invested heavily in training, especially in quality techniques such as statistical process control (*see* Chapter 17). Piecework was abolished, as was 'clocking

> **Questions**
>
> **1** What does 'quality' mean for a motor vehicle manufacturer such as Jaguar?
>
> **2** How did the changes which Jaguar made to its operations practice affect the quality of its products?

● The speed objective

Speed is concerned with how long customers have to wait to receive their products or services (*see* Fig. 2.6). For example, in the hospital it means that patients in the Accident and Emergency department are seen and treated quickly before they suffer any further distress. It also means that the patients with less urgent needs do not have to suffer a long waiting list. For the automobile factory, speed means that the time between a dealer ordering a particular car for one of its customers and the car being

---

Figure 2.6   **Speed means different things in different operations**

Speed could mean. . .

Hospital

- The time between requiring treatment and receiving treatment kept to a minimum
- The time for test results, X-rays, etc. to be returned kept to a minimum

(Photo courtesy of Cheltenham General Hospital)

Automobile plant

- The time between dealers requesting a vehicle of a particular specification and receiving it kept to a minimum
- The time to deliver spares to service centres kept to a minimum

Bus company

- The time between a customer setting out on the journey and reaching his or her destination kept to a minimum

(Photo courtesy of Stagecoach and McKinstrie and Wilde)

Supermarket

- The time taken for the total transaction of going to the supermarket, making the purchases and returning kept to a minimum
- The immediate availability of goods

(Photo courtesy of Tesco Ltd)

Speed and dependability are particularly important for roadside assistance services. Here a Royal Automobile Club of Victoria (RACV) patrol assists a motorist in Melbourne. RACV's communications and control systems have made it one of the most effective roadside assistance operations

delivered from the factory is as short as possible. For the city bus company, speed literally means how fast the operation can get customers from A to B. For the supermarket manager, speed means how fast customers can get to the store, park their cars, select their purchases, get through the checkout, return to their cars, and arrive back home.

The main benefit to the operation's (external) customers of speedy delivery of goods and services lies in the way it enhances the operation's offering to the customer. Quite simply, for most goods and services, the faster a customer can have the product or service, the more likely he or she is to buy it.

Speed inside the operation

Inside the operation, speed is also important. Fast response to external customers is greatly helped by speedy decision-making and speedy movement of materials and information inside the operation. Internal speed can have further benefits, however.[4]

Speed reduces inventories

Take, for example, the automobile plant. The steel which is used to make the vehicle's door panels is first delivered to the press shop where it is pressed into shape. It is then transported to the painting area where it is coated for colour and protection. After this it is moved to the assembly line where it is fitted to the automobile. This is a simple three-stage manufacturing process, but in practice each door panel does not flow smoothly from one stage to the next. If you follow one product through the process, its journey can take a surprisingly long time. First, the steel is delivered as part of a far larger batch, containing enough steel to make possibly several hundred products. Eventually it is taken to the press area where it is pressed into shape, and again waits until it is transported to the paint area. It then waits until it can be painted, only to wait once more until it is transported to the assembly line. Yet again it waits by the trackside until it is eventually fitted to the automobile.

The door panel's journey through the factory was far longer than the time needed to actually make and fit the product, and was also composed mainly of waiting time. When hundreds of products are moving through the plant every day, this waiting time results in large stocks (or inventories) of parts and products. If, on the other hand, the waiting can be reduced (say by moving and processing the parts in smaller batches), the parts will move faster through the plant and as a result the amount of inventories between each stage of the process will be reduced. This idea has some very important implications which will be explored in Chapter 15 on lean operations.

Speed reduces risks

Forecasting tomorrow's events is far less of a risk than forecasting next year's. The further ahead companies forecast, the more likely they are to get it wrong. This has important implications for the throughput speed of any operation. Consider the automobile plant again. If the total time for the door panel to complete its journey through the plant is six weeks, door panels are being processed through their first operation six weeks before they reach their final destination. The quantity of door panels being processed will be determined by the forecasts for demand six weeks ahead. Almost certainly the plant at any time will be making the wrong number of door panels because the forecast for six weeks ahead will be wrong.

Alternatively, consider the risk of making the wrong number of door panels if, instead of six weeks, they take only one week to move through the plant. Now the door panels being processed through their first stage are intended to meet demand only one week ahead. Under these circumstances it is far more likely that the number and type of door panels being processed are the number and type which eventually will be needed.

When speed means life or death[5]

Of all the operations which have to respond quickly to customer demand, few have more need of speed than the emergency services. In responding to road accidents especially, every second is critical. The treatment you receive during the first hour after your accident (what is called the 'golden hour') can determine whether you survive and fully recover or not. Making full use of the golden hour means speeding up three elements of the total time to treatment – the time it takes for the emergency services to find out about the accident, the time it takes them to travel to the scene of the accident, and the time it takes to get the casualty to appropriate treatment.

Alerting the emergency services immediately to an accident is the idea behind Mercedes-Benz's new TeleAid (Telematic Alarm Identification on Demand), offered initially to drivers of their s-class cars in Germany. As soon as the vehicle's air bag is triggered, an on-board micro computer reports through the mobile phone network to a control centre (drivers can also trigger the system manually if not too badly hurt). The on-board satellite facility then allows the vehicle to be precisely located, and the type of vehicle and owner identified (if special medication is needed).

Getting to the accident quickly is the next hurdle. Often the fastest method is by helicopter. For example, in London, the Helicopter Emergency Medical Service (HEMS) initially operated from an airfield to the south of the city; later it moved to a specially constructed helipad on the roof of the Royal London Hospital. This relocation halved the average journey time of eight minutes. Now many of the rescues are only a couple of minutes' flying time back to the hospital – an important factor when speed saves lives. Typically, the HEMS attends four or five incidents a day, although eight is not unusual. However, it is not always possible to land the helicopter safely at night (because of possible overhead wires and other hazards) so conventional ambulances will always be needed, both to get paramedics quickly to accident victims and to speed them to hospital. One increasingly common method of ensuring that ambulances arrive quickly at the accident site is to position them, not at hospitals, but close to where accidents are likely to occur. Computer analysis of previous accident data helps to select the ambulance's waiting position, and global positioning systems help controllers to mobilize the nearest unit.

Questions

1 Draw a chart which illustrates the stages between an accident occurring and full treatment being made available.

2 What are the key issues (both those mentioned above and any others you can think of) which determine the time taken at each stage?

● The dependability objective

Dependability means doing things in time for customers to receive their goods or services when they were promised (see Fig. 2.7). A hospital with a high standard of dependability would not cancel operations or any other appointments made with its patients. It would always, for example, deliver the results of tests and X-ray investigations on time and keep to schedule on its immunization programmes. A dependable automobile plant will deliver cars and spare parts to the car dealers exactly as promised. A dependable city bus company will always keep to its published timetable, picking up passengers at every point on the journey precisely on schedule. Furthermore, there will be seats available for the passengers who are there to catch the bus. A dependable supermarket chain has predictable opening hours. It will never run out of stock of any of the items which it has led its customers to expect to be in stock.

Customers might only judge the dependability of an operation after the product or service has been delivered. Initially this may not affect the likelihood that customers will select the service – they have already 'consumed' it. Over time, however, dependability can override all other criteria. No matter how cheap a bus service is, or how fast it is advertised as being, if the service is always late (or unpredictably early) or the buses are always full, then potential passengers will be better off calling a taxi.

Dependability inside the operation

Inside the operation dependability has a similar effect. Internal customers will judge each other's performance partly by how reliable the other micro operations are in delivering material or information on time. Operations where internal dependability is high are more effective than those which are not, for a number of reasons.

Dependability saves time

Take, for example, the maintenance and repair centre for the city bus company. The manager will always have a plan of the centre's activities each day for a period ahead. Probably this plan will have been drawn up to keep the centre's facilities as fully utilized as possible while ensuring that the bus fleet always has enough clean and serviced

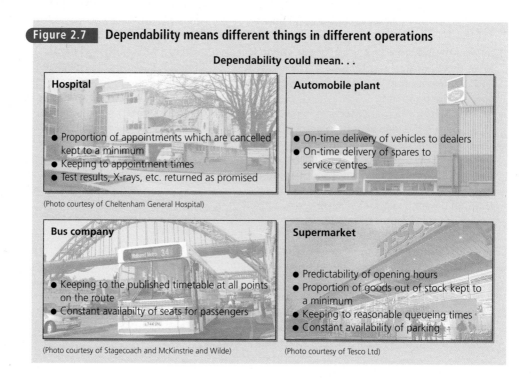

Figure 2.7 **Dependability means different things in different operations**

Dependability could mean. . .

Hospital
- Proportion of appointments which are cancelled kept to a minimum
- Keeping to appointment times
- Test results, X-rays, etc. returned as promised

(Photo courtesy of Cheltenham General Hospital)

Automobile plant
- On-time delivery of vehicles to dealers
- On-time delivery of spares to service centres

Bus company
- Keeping to the published timetable at all points on the route
- Constant availabilty of seats for passengers

(Photo courtesy of Stagecoach and McKinstrie and Wilde)

Supermarket
- Predictability of opening hours
- Proportion of goods out of stock kept to a minimum
- Keeping to reasonable queueing times
- Constant availability of parking

(Photo courtesy of Tesco Ltd)

vehicles to match demand at any time. If the centre runs out of some crucial spare parts which are needed to repair two of the buses which are booked in for servicing that day, the manager of the centre will need to spend time trying to arrange a special delivery of the required parts. It is unlikely that the resources which had been reserved to service the buses will be able to be used as productively as they would have been without this disruption. More seriously, the fleet will be short of two buses until they can be repaired. The fleet operations manager will have to spend time rescheduling the services to minimize the disruption to customers. Entirely due to the one failure of dependability of supply, a significant part of the operation's time will have been occupied trying to cope with the disruption.

Dependability saves money

Ineffective use of time will translate into extra cost. The spare parts might cost more to be delivered at short notice. The maintenance staff will expect to be paid even when there is not a bus to work on. Similarly, the fixed costs of the operation, such as heating and rent, will not reduce because the two buses are not being serviced. The rescheduling of buses to routes will probably mean that some routes have inappropriately sized buses and some services could have to be cancelled. This will result in empty bus seats (if too large a bus has to be used) or a loss of revenue (if potential passengers are not transported).

Dependability gives stability

The disruption caused to operations by a lack of dependability goes beyond time and cost. It affects the 'quality' of the operation's time. If everything in an operation is perfectly dependable, and has been for some time, a level of trust will have built up between the different parts of the operation. There will be no 'surprises' and everything will be predictable. Under such circumstances, each part of the operation can concentrate on improving its own area of responsibility without having its attention continually diverted by a lack of dependable service from the other parts.

● The flexibility objective[6]

Flexibility means being able to change the operation in some way. This may mean changing what the operation does, how it is doing it, or when it is doing it. Specifically, customers will need the operation to change so that it can provide four types of requirement:

- *product/service flexibility* – different products and services;
- *mix flexibility* – a wide range or mix of products and services;
- *volume flexibility* – different quantities or volumes of products and services;
- *delivery flexibility* – different delivery times.

Figure 2.8 gives examples of what these different types of flexibility mean to the four different operations.

Product/service flexibility

Product/service flexibility is the operation's ability to introduce new products and services. In the hospital this could mean introducing new surgical techniques or new medical record information. In the automobile plant it means the ability to adapt its manufacturing resources so that it can launch new models. To the city bus company it means introducing new routes or special excursion services, while to the supermarket it means introducing new lines on its shelves, novel promotions or new payment services.

Mix flexibility

Mix flexibility means being able to provide a wide range or mix of products and services. Most operations produce more than one product or service. In addition, most operations do not make their products or services in high enough volumes to dedicate

Figure 2.8 **Flexibility means different things in different operations**

Flexibility could mean. . .

Hospital

- Product/service flexibility – the introduction of new types of treatment
- Mix flexibility – a wide range of available treatments
- Volume flexibility – the ability to adjust the number of patients treated
- Delivery flexibility – the ability to reschedule appointments

(Photo courtesy of Cheltenham General Hospital)

Automobile plant

- Product/service flexibility – the introduction of new models
- Mix flexibility – a wide range of options available
- Volume flexibility – the ability to adjust the number of vehicles manufactured
- Delivery flexibility – the ability to reschedule manufacturing priorities

Bus company

- Product/service flexibility – the introduction of new routes or excursions
- Mix flexibility – a large number of locations served
- Volume flexibility – the ability to adjust the frequency of services
- Delivery flexibility – the ability to reschedule trips

(Photo courtesy of Stagecoach and McKinstrie and Wilde)

Supermarket

- Product/service flexibility – the introduction of new goods or promotions
- Mix flexibility – a wide range of goods stocked
- Volume flexibility – the ability to adjust the number of customers served
- Delivery flexibility – the ability to obtain out-of-stock items (very occasionally)

(Photo courtesy of Tesco Ltd)

Flexibility and dependability in the newsroom[7]

CWS

Television news is big business. Satellite and cable, as well as developments in terrestrial transmission, have all helped to boost the popularity of 24-hour news services. But news perishes fast. A daily newspaper delivered one day late is practically worthless. This is why broadcasting organizations like the BBC have to ensure that up-to-date news is delivered on time, every time. The BBC's ability to achieve high levels of dependability is made possible by the technology employed in news gathering and editing. At one time news editors would have to schedule a video-taped report to start its countdown five seconds prior to its broadcasting time. With new technology the video can be started from a freeze-frame and will broadcast the instant the command to play is given. The team has faith in the dependability of the process. In addition, technology allows them the flexibility to achieve dependability, even when news stories break just before transmission. In the hours before scheduled transmission, journalists

Photo courtesy of BBC

and editors prepare an 'inventory' of news items stored electronically. The presenter will prepare his or her commentary on the Autocue and each item will be timed to the second. If the team needs to make a short-term adjustment to the planned schedule, the news studio's technology allows the editors to take broadcasts live from journalists at their locations, on satellite 'takes', directly into the programme. Editors can even type news reports directly onto the Autocue for the presenter to read as they are typed – nerve-racking, but it keeps the programme on time.

Questions

1 What do the five performance objectives mean for an operation such as the BBC's newsroom?

2 How do these performance objectives influence each other?

all parts of their activities exclusively to a single product or service. This means that most parts of any operation will have to process more than one type of product or service and so will at times need to change from doing one activity to doing another. For example, some parts of a hospital need to provide a relatively wide range of services. The Accident and Emergency department has to provide immediate treatment for the wide range of complaints from which its patients suffer. The General Surgery department also has a similarly wide range of complaints to treat. The staff, technology and organization of these departments need to be flexible enough to cope with this variety. Other departments in the hospital will require less flexibility because they provide a comparatively narrow range of services. The X-ray department, for example, is expected only to provide radiographic services. In the automobile plant, flexibility is needed to provide all the range of options which customers are able to choose when buying their cars. The city bus company needs to provide a wide enough variety of routes to satisfy demand between its more popular areas of the city. To the supermarket, mix flexibility means being able to stock a wide range of products on its shelves.

Volume flexibility

Volume flexibility is the ability of the operation to change its level of output or activity. All operations will need to change their level of activity because all operations to some extent have to cope with fluctuating demand for their products and services. Of course, all operations could theoretically ignore these fluctuations in demand, dispense with all volume flexibility and keep their activity levels constant. However, this totally 'inflexible' option can have serious consequences on customer service, operating costs or both. (Chapter 11 on capacity management will deal with this.)

The hospital will need to be flexible enough to provide an appropriate level of service as demand varies throughout the day as well as over the week and the year. In addition, it will need to cope with the occasional unpredictable demand for its services such as when a major road accident occurs. In a similar way, the demand for automobiles will vary throughout the year and the automobile factory will need to adjust its output accordingly. The city bus company will also need to change its activity levels throughout the day as demand varies. In the supermarket, flexibility again means coping with a variety of activity levels as demand varies throughout the day.

Delivery flexibility

Delivery flexibility is the ability to change the timing of the delivery of the service. Usually this means the operation providing goods or services earlier than anticipated, although it may mean delaying delivery.

In the hospital, delivery flexibility means rescheduling a patient's treatment. A maternity ward, for example, needs to have high delivery flexibility (in both senses!) to deal with a patient's premature labour. The automobile plant might occasionally have to rush a particular product through the plant to meet the special needs of a customer (although this might cause expensive disruption to the plant's schedules). The city bus company would be even more unlikely to reschedule its regular services so as to change their delivery times, but might have to do this for its excursion services. Similarly, the supermarket might not generally want to change the regular delivery schedules to its stores but, in exceptional circumstances, to placate a dissatisfied customer, for example, it might bring forward the delivery of an out-of-stock item.

Flexibility inside the operation

Developing a flexible operation can also have advantages to the internal customers within the operation.

Flexibility speeds up response

Being able to give fast service often depends on the operation being flexible. For example, if the hospital has to cope with a sudden influx of patients from a road accident, it clearly needs to deal with injuries quickly. Under such circumstances a flexible hospital which can speedily transfer extra skilled staff and equipment to the Accident and Emergency department will provide the fast service which the patients need.

Flexibility saves time

In many parts of the hospital, staff have to treat a wide variety of complaints. Fractures, cuts or drug overdoses do not come in batches. Each patient is an individual with individual needs. The hospital staff cannot take time to 'get into the routine' of treating a particular complaint; they must have the flexibility to adapt quickly. They must also have sufficiently flexible facilities and equipment so that time is not wasted waiting for equipment to be brought to the patient. The time of the hospital's resources is being saved because they are flexible in 'changing over' from one task to the next. (*See* also the box on Godiva Chocolatier for an example of how flexibility can save time.)

Flexibility maintains dependability

Internal flexibility can also help to keep the operation on schedule when unexpected events disrupt the operation's plans. For example, if the sudden influx of patients to the hospital also results in emergency surgery being performed, the emergency patients will almost certainly displace other routine operations. The patients who were expecting to undergo their routine operations will have been admitted and probably prepared for their operations. Cancelling their operations is likely to cause them distress and probably considerable inconvenience. A flexible hospital might be able to minimize the disruption by possibly having reserved operating theatres for such an emergency, and being able to bring in medical staff quickly who are 'on call'.

Flexibility at Godiva Chocolatier[8]

The world-famous chocolate maker, Godiva Chocolatier, is situated right in the heart of Brussels, Europe's centre of quality chocolate manufacturing. Godiva is a relatively small producer which makes more than 100 different chocolates and packs them in a vast range of cartons and bulk packs. Over the last 10 years, the company has invested to achieve improvements in productivity through automation, but at the same time to ensure that flexibility is built in at every stage of production. There are two basic methods of production used at Godiva: *enrobing* and *moulding*.

Enrobed products begin as extruded strips of hard fillings such as marzipan, which are cut into short

pieces and passed through a machine which coats them in liquid chocolate. The enrobing department operates by linking together the various pieces of equipment (extruders, guillotines, depositors, enrobers, decorators, etc.) in different sequences and combinations to suit the individual product designs. Sometimes, where the volumes justify the effort involved in repositioning them, this is done by using moveable conveyors to make the link between the machines. Otherwise, the products are transferred around as required in plastic trays, allowing the equipment (and the skilled staff) to be decoupled and thereby to work at different speeds and times. Only small tanks of liquid chocolate are used at the enrobing machines so that changeovers can be fast. Typically it takes only 20 minutes to disconnect the tank and clean out the enrobing machine prior to starting another colour. Because of the wide variety of products, planning is complex, with the sequence of products being critical to productivity and quality. Normally, it is considered uneconomic to produce less than 300 kg of a particular colour of chocolate, but where possible, longer runs of different products with the same chocolate coating are planned, so that the colour change can be carried out at the end of the day's production.

Most *moulded products* are produced on a new and complicated 80 metre long production line, which was designed to handle almost the full range of moulded products. It can mould all three colours with a 20 minute changeover of the liquid chocolate. These are normally done only at the end of a day's production. Moulds can be changed without stopping the line using a simple operator-assisted device. Filling the shells with creams, fondants, etc. is carried out using computer-controlled depositing machines. Three of these depositors are available, allowing one or two to be in use while the third is moved aside for cleaning, programming and setting-up with the next batch of filling. It is possible, therefore, to change product in under one minute, and to use two depositors simultaneously for products where nuts or cherries

are to be incorporated in the middle of creams. After demoulding, the chocolates can be routed to an automatic individual wrapping machine, but most are conveyed directly to a packing robot which picks and places the products on blister packs for bulk sales to shops, or on flat plastic trays for transfer to the assortment packing lines.

The most flexible part of the operation is the *assortment packing* section. Here, the finished chocolates are packed according to the appropriate mix and positions in the various retail cartons. These pass along a conveyor where each individual chocolate is added to the pack by hand. Although it is technically possible for this to be done by a robot, Godiva engineers have found that people are less expensive and can also continuously inspect the quality of every chocolate packed. Many of the staff are also very adept at adding value-added features to the packaging, such as ribbons, bows and labels.

Source: By kind permission of Godiva SA

Questions

1 Why is flexibility so important to a company like Godiva?

2 What does the company appear to have done to enhance its flexibility?

● The cost objective

Cost is the last objective to be covered, although not because it is the least important. To the companies which compete directly on price, cost will clearly be their major operations objective. The lower the cost of producing their goods and services, the lower can be the price to their customers. Even those companies which compete on things other than price, however, will be interested in keeping their costs low. Every euro or dollar removed from an operation's cost base is a further euro or dollar added to its profits. Not surprisingly, low cost is a universally attractive objective.

The ways in which operations management can influence cost will depend largely on where the operation costs are incurred. Put simply, the operation will spend its money on:

● *staff costs* (the money spent on employing people);
● *facilities, technology and equipment costs* (the money spent on buying, caring for, operating and replacing the operation's 'hardware');
● *material costs* (the money spent on the materials consumed or transformed in the operation).

Figure 2.9 shows typical cost breakdowns for the hospital, car plant, supermarket and bus company.

Although comparing the cost structure of different operations is not always straightforward, and depends on how costs are categorized, some general points can be made.

Many of the hospital's costs are fixed and will change little for small changes in the number of patients it treats. Its facilities such as beds, operating theatres and laboratories

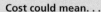

Figure 2.9   Cost means different things in different operations

Cost could mean. . .

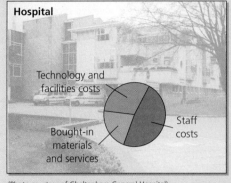

Hospital

- Technology and facilities costs
- Staff costs
- Bought-in materials and services

(Photo courtesy of Cheltenham General Hospital)

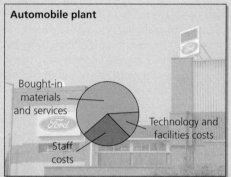

Automobile plant

- Bought-in materials and services
- Technology and facilities costs
- Staff costs

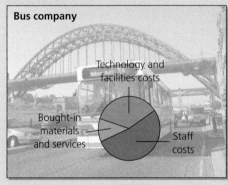

Bus company

- Technology and facilities costs
- Bought-in materials and services
- Staff costs

(Photo courtesy of Stagecoach and McKinstrie and Wilde)

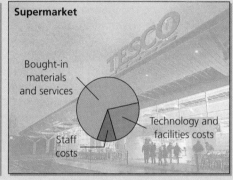

Supermarket

- Bought-in materials and services
- Technology and facilities costs
- Staff costs

(Photo courtesy of Tesco Ltd)

are expensive, as are some of its highly skilled staff. Some of the hospital's costs will be payments to outside suppliers of drugs, medical supplies and externally sourced services such as cleaning, but probably not as high a proportion as in the car factory. The car factory's payment for materials and other supplies will by far outweigh all its other costs put together. Conversely, the city bus company will pay very little for its supplies, fuel being one of its main bought-in items. At the other extreme, the supermarket's costs are dominated by the cost of buying its supplies. In spite of its high 'material' costs, however, an individual supermarket can do little if anything to affect the cost of goods it sells. All purchasing decisions will probably be made at company headquarters. The individual supermarket will be more concerned with the utilization of its main asset, the building itself, and its staff.

Cost is affected by the other performance objectives

So far we have described the meaning and effects of quality, speed, dependability and flexibility for the operations function. In doing so, we have distinguished between the value of each performance objective to external customers and, inside the operation, to internal customers. Each of the various performance objectives has several internal effects, but all of them affect cost:

- High-quality operations do not waste time or effort having to re-do things, nor are their internal customers inconvenienced by flawed service.
- Fast operations reduce the level of in-process inventory between micro operations, as well as reducing administrative overheads.
- Dependable operations do not spring any unwelcome surprises on their internal customers. They can be relied on to deliver exactly as planned. This eliminates wasteful disruption and allows the other micro operations to operate efficiently.

Performance objectives have both external and internal effects. Internally, cost is influenced by the other performance objectives

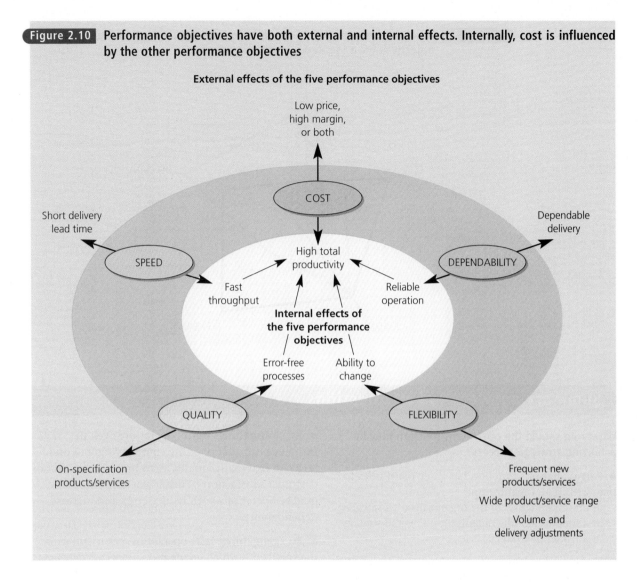

External effects of the five performance objectives

Low price, high margin, or both

COST

Short delivery lead time

SPEED

Dependable delivery

DEPENDABILITY

High total productivity

Fast throughput

Reliable operation

Internal effects of the five performance objectives

Error-free processes

Ability to change

QUALITY

FLEXIBILITY

On-specification products/services

Frequent new products/services

Wide product/service range

Volume and delivery adjustments

- Flexible operations adapt to changing circumstances quickly and without disrupting the rest of the operation. Flexible micro operations can also change over between tasks quickly and without wasting time and capacity.

Inside the operation, therefore, one important way to improve cost performance is to improve the performance of the other operations objectives (*see* Fig. 2.10).

The polar representation of performance objectives

A useful way of representing the relative importance of performance objectives for a product or service is shown in Figure 2.11. This is called the polar representation because the scales which represent the importance of each performance objective have the same origin. A line describes the relative importance of each performance objective. The closer the line is to the common origin, the less important is the performance objective to the operation. Two services are shown, a taxi and a bus service. Each essentially provides the same basic service, but with different objectives. The differences between the two services are clearly shown by the diagram.

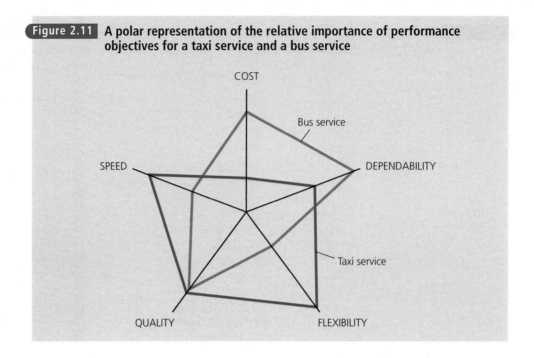

Figure 2.11 A polar representation of the relative importance of performance objectives for a taxi service and a bus service

Summary answers to key questions

What role should the operations function play in achieving strategic success?

● Any operations function has three main roles to play within an organization:
– as an implementer of the organization's strategies;
– as a supporter of the organization's overall strategy;
– as a leader of strategy.

● The extent to which an operations function fulfils these roles, together with its aspirations, can be used to judge the operations function's contribution to the organization. Hayes and Wheelwright provide a four-stage model for doing this.

What are the performance objectives of operations and what are the internal and external benefits which derive from excelling in each of them?

● At a strategic level, performance objectives relate to the interests of the operation's stakeholders. These relate to the company's responsibility to customers, suppliers, shareholders, employees and society in general.

● By 'doing things right', operations seek to influence the quality of the company's goods and services. Externally, quality is an important aspect of customer satisfaction or dissatisfaction. Internally, quality operations both reduce costs and increase dependability.

● By 'doing things fast', operations seek to influence the speed with which goods and services are delivered. Externally, speed is an important aspect of customer service. Internally, speed both reduces inventories by decreasing internal throughput time and reduces risks by delaying the commitment of resources.

● By 'doing things on time', operations seek to influence the dependability of the delivery of goods and services. Externally, dependability is an important aspect of customer service. Internally, dependability within operations increases operational reliability, thus saving the time and money that would otherwise be taken up in solving reliability problems and also giving stability to the operation.

- By 'changing what they do', operations seek to influence the flexibility with which the company produces goods and services. Externally, flexibility can:
  - produce new products and services (product/service flexibility);
  - produce a wide range or mix of products and services (mix flexibility);
  - produce different quantities or volumes of products and services (volume flexibility);
  - produce products and services at different times (delivery flexibility).

Internally, flexibility can help speed up response times, save time wasted in changeovers, and maintain dependability.

- By 'doing things cheaply', operations seek to influence the cost of the company's goods and services. Externally, low costs allow organizations to reduce their price in order to gain higher volumes or, alternatively, increase their profitability on existing volume levels. Internally, cost performance is helped by good performance in the other performance objectives.

CASE EXERCISE

Operations objectives at the Penang Mutiara[9]

There are many luxurious hotels in the South-East Asia region but few can compare with the Penang Mutiara, a 440 room top-of-the-market hotel which nestles in the lush greenery of Malaysia's Indian Ocean Coast. Owned by Pernas–OUE of Malaysia and managed by Singapore Mandarin International Hotels, the hotel's General Manager is Wernie Eisen, a Swiss hotelier who has managed luxury hotels all over the world.

He is under no illusions about the importance of running an effective operation.

'Managing a hotel of this size is an immensely complicated task,' he says. *'Our customers have every right to be demanding. They expect first-class service and that's what we have to give them. If we have any problems with managing this operation, the customer sees them immediately and that's the biggest incentive for us to take operations performance seriously.*

'Our quality of service just has to be impeccable. First of all this means dealing with the basics. For example, our staff must be courteous at all times and yet also friendly towards our guests. And of course they must have the knowledge to be able to answer guests' questions. The building and equipment – in fact all the hardware of the operation – must support the luxury atmosphere which we have created in the hotel. Stylish design and top-class materials not only create the right impression but, if we choose them carefully, are also durable so the hotel still looks good over the years. Most of all, though, quality is about anticipating our guests' needs, thinking ahead so you can identify what will delight or irritate a guest.'

The hotel tries to anticipate guests' needs in a number of ways. For example, if guests have been to the hotel before, staff avoid their having to repeat the information they gave on the previous visit. Reception staff simply check to see if guests have stayed before, retrieve the information and take them straight to their room without irritating delays. Quality of service also means helping guests sort out their own problems. If the airline loses a guest's luggage en route to the hotel, for example, he or she will arrive at the hotel understandably irritated.

'The fact that it is not us who have irritated them is not really the issue. It is our job to make them feel better.'

Speed, in terms of fast response to customers' requests is something else that is important.

'A guest just should not be kept waiting. If a guest has a request, he or she has that request now so it needs to be sorted out now. This is not always easy but we do our best. For example, if every guest in the hotel tonight decided to call room service and request a meal instead of going to the restaurants, our room service department would obviously be grossly overloaded and customers would have to wait an unacceptably long time before the meals were brought up to their rooms. We cope with this by keeping a close watch on how demand for room service is building up. If we think it's going to get above the level where response time to customers would become unacceptably long, we will call in staff from other restaurants in the hotel. Of course, to do this we have to make sure that our staff are multi-skilled. In fact we have a policy of making sure that restaurant staff can always do more than one job. It's this kind of

flexibility which allows us to maintain fast response to the customer.'

Likewise, Wernie regards dependability as a fundamental principle of a well-managed hotel.

'We must always keep our promises. For example, rooms must be ready on time and accounts must be ready for presentation when a guest departs; the guests expect a dependable service and anything less than full dependability is a legitimate cause for dissatisfaction.'

It is on the grand occasions, however, when dependability is particularly important in the hotel. When staging a banquet, for example, everything has to be on time. Drinks, food, entertainment have to be available exactly as planned. Any deviation from the plan will very soon be noticed by customers.

'It is largely a matter of planning the details and anticipating what could go wrong,' says Wernie. *'Once we've done the planning we can anticipate possible problems and plan how to cope with them, or better still, prevent them from occurring in the first place.'*

Flexibility means a number of things to the hotel. First of all it means that they should be able to meet a guest's requests.

'We never like to say NO!' says Wernie. *'For example, if a guest asks for some Camembert cheese and we don't have it in stock, we will make sure that someone goes to the supermarket and tries to get it. If, in spite of our best efforts, we can't get any we will negotiate an alternative solution with the guest. This has an important side-effect – it greatly helps us to maintain the motivation of our staff. We are constantly being asked to do the seemingly impossible – yet we do it, and our staff think it's great. We all like to be part of an organization which is capable of achieving the very difficult, if not the impossible.'*

Flexibility in the hotel also means the ability to cope with the seasonal fluctuations in demand. They achieve this partly by using temporary part-time staff. In the back-office parts of the hotel this isn't a major problem. In the laundry, for example, it is relatively easy to put on an extra shift in busy periods by increasing staffing levels. However, this is more of a problem in the parts of the hotel that have direct contact with the customer.

'New temporary staff can't be expected to have the same customer contact skills as our more regular staff. Our

solution to this is to keep the temporary staff as far in the background as we possibly can and make sure that our skilled, well-trained staff are the ones who usually interact with the customer. So, for example, a waiter who would normally take orders, service the food, and take away the dirty plates would in peak times restrict his or her activities to taking orders and serving the food. The less skilled part of the job, taking away the plates, could be left to temporary staff.'

As far as cost is concerned, around 60 per cent of the hotel's total operating expenses go on food and beverages, so one obvious way of keeping costs down is by making sure that food is not wasted. Energy costs, at 6 per cent of total operating costs, are also a potential source of saving. However, although cost savings are welcome, the hotel is very careful never to compromise the quality of its service in order to cut costs. Wernie's view is quite clear:

'It is impeccable customer service which gives us our competitive advantage, not price. Good service means that our guests return again and again. At times, around half our guests are people who have been before. The more guests we have, the higher is our utilization of rooms and restaurants, and this is what really keeps cost per guest down and profitability reasonable. So in the end we've come full circle: it's the quality of our service which keeps our volumes high and our costs low.'

Questions

1 Describe how you think Wernie will:

  (a) make sure that the way he manages the hotel is *appropriate* to the way it competes for business;

  (b) *implement* any change in strategy;

  (c) develop his operation so that *it drives* the long-term strategy of the hotel.

2 What questions might Wernie ask to judge whether his operation is a stage 1, stage 2, stage 3 or stage 4 operation on Hayes and Wheelwright's scale of excellence?

3 The case describes how quality, speed, dependability, flexibility and cost impact on the hotel's external customers. Explain how each of these performance objectives might have internal benefits.

Discussion questions

1 For the following organizations, explain how their operations functions can support business strategy, implement business strategy and drive business strategy:
   – a fast-food restaurant
   – a film-processing service
   – an oil refinery.

2 Explain the seeming paradox of the operations function, which is concerned with day-to-day operational decisions, while having a central role to play in achieving long-term strategic success.

3 Describe how the operations function of a car hire company might perform as it progressed from being a stage 1 to a stage 4 operation (using Hayes and Wheelwright's terms).

4 Illustrate the concept of a stage 4 company by explaining how a stage 4 operations function within the following organizations could contribute to their long-term competitive success:
   – a salted snack manufacturer
   – an airline
   – a parcel delivery service
   – an hotel.

5 Discuss what constitutes quality, speed, dependability and flexibility in the following operations:
   – a university library
   – a university sports centre
   – a university restaurant
   – an operations management course.

   (Try asking the managers of these operations!)

6 Describe the different types of flexibility that might be found in each of the following operations:
   – a university
   – a factory making tennis racquets
   – a rail network.

7 For each of the following organizations explain what is meant by, and discuss the relative importance of, quality, speed, dependability and flexibility:
   – a high-volume car producer
   – a hairdresser
   – a package collection and distribution service (e.g. UPS or Federal Express).

8 Many organizations see the role of operations as getting on with the job of making products or serving customers. Discuss the implications of this view of the operations function.

9 Using an example of your own choice, describe how the cost of the operation might be affected by changing the levels of performance of quality, speed, dependability and flexibility.

10 There are many different fast-food restaurants throughout the world (McDonalds, Burger King, etc.). Discuss some of the stakeholder objectives for this type of operation. Are there any conflicts between the objectives of the different stakeholders which you can identify?

11 Many retail banks are reducing the size of their branch network and moving over to other forms of service delivery such as internet and telephone banking. Discuss the implications of these trends in terms of both broad stakeholder objectives and the specific operations objectives of quality, speed, dependability, flexibility and cost.

12 The 'forensic science' service of a European country has traditionally been organized to provide separate forensic science laboratories for each police force around the country. In order to save costs, the government has decided to centralize this service in one large central facility close to the country's capital. What do you think are the external advantages and disadvantages of this to the stakeholders of the operation? What do you think are the internal implications to the new centralized operation that will provide this service?

Notes on chapter

1 This idea was first popularized by Wickham Skinner at Harvard University. *See* Skinner, W. (1985) *Manufacturing: The Formidable Competitive Weapon*, John Wiley.

2 Hayes, R.H. and Wheelwright, S.C. (1984) *Restoring our Competitive Edge*, John Wiley.

3 Chase, R. and Hayes, R.H. (1991) 'Beefing up Service Firms', *Sloan Management Review*, Fall.

4 For a much more detailed discussion of the speed objective, *see* Stalk, G. and Hout, T.M. (1990) *Competing Against Time*, Free Press.

5 Sources: 'Angels with an Audi', *The Audi Magazine*, Summer 1994. 'Smart Car will Call Police in a Crash', *The Sunday Times*, 23 Feb 1997.

6 For a further discussion of the flexibility objective, *see* Slack, N. (1989) 'Focus on Flexibility' *in* Wild, R. (ed)

International Handbook of Production/Operations Management, Cassell.

7 Source: Discussions with the News Team at the BBC.

8 Source: The management of Godiva Chocolatier.

9 We are grateful to Wernie Eisen and the management of the Penang Mutiara for permission to use this example.

Selected further reading

Azzone, G., Bertelé, U. and Masella, C. (1991) 'The Design of Performance Measures for Time Based Companies', *International Journal of Operations and Production Management*, Vol 11, No 3.

Bhattacharya, A.K., Jina, J. and Walton, A.D. (1996) 'Product Market Turbulence and Time Compression: Three Dimensions of an Integrated Approach to Manufacturing Systems Design', *International Journal of Operations and Production Management*, Vol 16, No 9.

Blenkinsop, A. and Burns, N. (1992) 'Performance Measurement Revisited', *International Journal of Operations and Production Management*, Vol 12, No 10.

Chase, R. and Hayes, R.H. (1991) 'Beefing up Operations in Service Firms', *Sloan Management Review*, Fall, pp 15–26.

Chyr, F. (1996) 'The Effect of Varying Set-up Costs', *International Journal of Operations and Production Management*, Vol 16, No 3.

De Meyer, A. and Fedows, K. (1990) 'The Influence of Manufacturing Improvement Programmes on Performance', *International Journal of Operations and Production Management*, Vol 10, No 2.

Donaldson, T. and Preston, L.G. (1995) 'The Stakeholder Theory of the Corporation', *Academy of Management Review*, Vol 20, No 2.

Feitzinger, E. and Lee, H.L. (1997) 'Mass Customization and Hewlett-Packard: The Power of Postponement', *Harvard Business Review*, Vol 75, No 1.

Gupta, Y.P., Lonial, S.C. and Mangold, W.G. (1991) 'An Examination of the Relationship between Manufacturing Strategy and Marketing Objectives', *International Journal of Operations and Production Management*, Vol 11, No 10.

Hayes, R.H. and Wheelwright, S.C. (1984) *Restoring Our Competitive Edge*, John Wiley, Chap 14.

Hill, T. (1993) *Manufacturing Strategy* (2nd edn), Macmillan.

Kritchanchai, D. and MacCarthy, B.L. (1999) 'Responsiveness of the Order Fulfilment Process', *International Journal of Production and Operations Management*, Vol 19, No 8.

Matson, J.B. and McFarlane, D.C. (1999) 'Assessing the Responsiveness of Existing Production Operations', *International Journal of Production and Operations Management*, Vol 19, No 8.

New, C. (1992) 'World-Class Manufacturing versus Strategic Trade-offs', *International Journal of Operations and Production Management*, Vol 12, No 4.

Pine, B.J. (1993) *Mass Customization*, Harvard Business School Press.

Shaw, W.N., Clarkson, A.H. and Stone, M.A. (1992) 'The Competitive Characteristics of Scottish Manufacturing Companies', *International Journal of Operations and Production Management*, Vol 12, No 6.

Slack, N. (1991) *The Manufacturing Advantage*, Mercury Business Books.

Stalk, G. and Webber, A.M. (1993) 'Japan's Dark Side of Time', *Harvard Business Review*, Vol 71, No 4.

Operations strategy

Introduction

No organization can plan in detail every aspect of its current or future actions, but all organizations can benefit from some idea of where they are heading and how they could get there. Put another way, all organizations need some strategic direction. It is just the same with the operations function. Once the operations function has understood its role in the business and after it has articulated the performance objectives which define its contribution to strategy, it needs to formulate a set of general principles which will guide its decision-making. This is the operations strategy of the company. Yet the concept of 'strategy' itself is not straightforward; neither is operations strategy. This chapter considers four perspectives, each of which goes partway to illustrating the forces which shape the content of operations strategy. It also presents two approaches to the process of formulating operations strategies in practice. Figure 3.1 shows the position of the ideas described in this chapter in the general model of operations management.

Figure 3.1 **This chapter examines operations strategy**

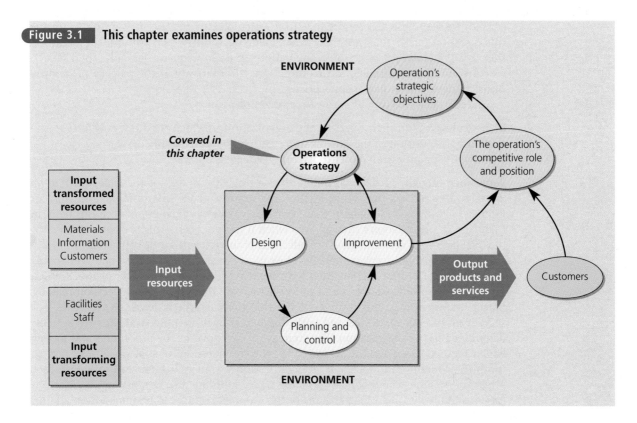

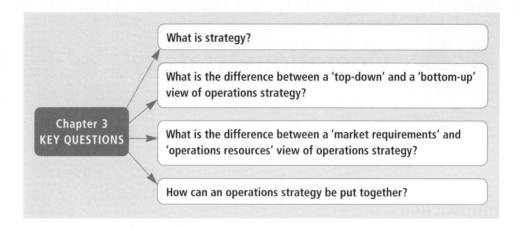

What is strategy?

What is the difference between a 'top-down' and a 'bottom-up' view of operations strategy?

What is the difference between a 'market requirements' and 'operations resources' view of operations strategy?

How can an operations strategy be put together?

Chapter 3
KEY QUESTIONS

What is strategy?

Before dealing with operations strategy it is necessary to consider what we mean by the term 'strategy'. Unfortunately there is little agreement amongst either practitioners or academics. Some authors on the subject even believe that to attempt a single definition of strategy would be misleading. Certainly it is possible, and often helpful, to take different and alternative perspectives on what we mean by strategy. While it is not within the scope of this book to do this to strategic management generally, later we examine operations strategy from different perspectives. As far as the term 'strategy' is concerned, we assume when an organization articulates its strategy it is going to pursue this direction rather than another. It has made decisions which commit the organization to a particular set of actions. The pattern of its subsequent decisions then reflects its continuing commitment to this direction. Alternatively, if the pattern of its decisions changes, this indicates some change in its strategic direction.

Strategic decisions usually mean those decisions which:[1]

● are widespread in their effect on the organization to which the strategy refers;
● define the position of the organization relative to its environment;
● move the organization closer to its long-term goals.

Remember, though, a 'strategy' is more than a single decision; it is the *total pattern of the decisions* and actions that position the organization in its environment and that are intended to achieve its long-term goals. Defining strategy as a pattern of decisions helps us to discuss an organization's strategy even when it has not been explicitly stated. Observing the total pattern of decisions gives an indication of the actual strategic behaviour.

When companies develop strategies they must consider two separate but overlapping sets of issues. The first is concerned with what is known as the *content* of the strategy. These are the specific strategies and actions which are the subject of the decision-making; that is, the *what* questions of strategy, the things about which decisions are made. The second set of issues is concerned with the *process* of how these strategies are actually determined in the organization. The strategy process governs the procedures and models which are used to make strategic decisions – the *how* questions of strategy.

Both the content and process of an organization's strategy overlap and influence each other. For example, the process of deciding where to locate new capacity can be relatively formal and involve quantified analysis of the economic returns to be gained from alternative location options. The process for designing an organization's reporting strategy, however, is less clear. Subtle changes in organizational structure may have significant implications which can only be assessed through widespread consultation and negotiation. In both cases, content will influence process. However, provided that we keep the interrelationship between process and content in mind, each aspect can be considered separately.

● Operations strategy

Operations strategy concerns the pattern of strategic decisions and actions which set the role, objectives and activities of the operation. As with any type of strategy, we can consider its content and process separately. Here we treat content and process as follows:

- The *content* of operations strategy comprises the specific decisions and actions which set the operations role, objectives and activities.
- The *process* of operations strategy is the method that is used to make the specific 'content' decisions.

The content of operations strategy

Operations strategy is clearly part of an organization's total strategy, but most authors on the subject have slightly different views and definitions.[2] Some of these authors are represented in the further reading to this chapter. Between them, four perspectives on operations strategy emerge:[3]

- Operation strategy is a top-down reflection of what the whole group or business wants to do.
- Operations strategy is a bottom-up activity where operations improvements cumulatively build strategy.
- Operations strategy involves translating market requirements into operations decisions.
- Operations strategy involves exploiting the capabilities of operations resources in chosen markets.

None of these four perspectives alone gives the full picture of what operations strategy is. But together they provide some idea of the pressures which go to form the content of operations strategy. We will treat each in turn (*see* Fig. 3.2).

● The 'top-down' perspective

A large, diversified corporation will need a strategy to position itself in its global, economic, political and social environment. This will consist of decisions about what types of business the group wants to be in, what parts of the world it wants to operate in, how to allocate its cash between its various businesses, and so on. Decisions such as these form the *corporate strategy* of the corporation. Each business unit within the corporate group will also need to put together its own business strategy which sets out its individual mission and objectives. This *business strategy* guides the business in relation to its customers, markets and competitors, and also the strategy of the corporate group of which it is a part. Similarly, within the business, *functional strategies* need to consider what part each function should play in contributing to the strategic objectives of the business. The operations, marketing, product/service development and other functions will all need to consider how best they should organize themselves to support the business's objectives.

So one perspective on operations strategy is that it should take its place in this hierarchy of strategies. Its main influence, therefore, will be whatever the business sees as its strategic direction. For example, a company which prints packaging for consumer products decides to expand rapidly. It figures that, in the long-term, the companies with significant market share will survive, while the small players will not. Its business objectives therefore stress volume growth, even above short-term profitability or return on investment. The implication for operations strategy is that it needs to invest in extra capacity (factories, equipment and labour) even if it means some excess capacity. It also needs to establish new factories in all parts of its market to offer relatively fast delivery.

The four perspectives on operations strategy

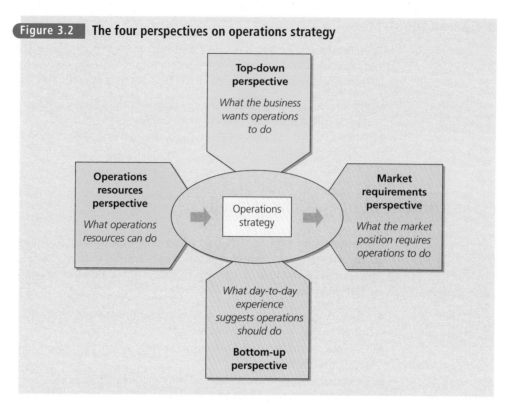

Top-down perspective

What the business wants operations to do

Operations resources perspective

What operations resources can do

Operations strategy

Market requirements perspective

What the market position requires operations to do

What day-to-day experience suggests operations should do

Bottom-up perspective

The important point here is that different business objectives would probably result in a very different operations strategy. The role of operations is therefore largely one of implementing or 'operationalizing' business strategy. Figure 3.3 illustrates this strategic hierarchy, with some of the decisions at each level and the main influences on the strategic decisions.

Photo courtesy of Tesco Ltd

It is the experience at an operational level (in this case how customers react to waiting) which can influence company strategy (for example, by switching to a 'no more than one in front' policy for the whole company)

Figure 3.3 **The top-down perspective of operations strategy**

Corporate strategy decisions
- What business to be in, i.e. how diversified to be?
- What businesses to acquire and what to divest?
- How to allocate cash to different businesses?
- How to manage the relationships between different businesses?

Business strategy decisions
- Defining the mission of the business
- Defining the strategic objectives of the business such as:
  - growth targets
  - return on investment
  - profitability targets
  - cash generation
- Setting the way that the business wishes to compete in its markets

Functional strategy decisions
- What role to play in contributing to the strategic objectives of the business?
- How to translate business and competitive objectives into functional objectives?
- How to manage the function's resources so as to achieve functional objectives?
- What performance improvement priorities to establish?

● The 'bottom-up' perspective

The 'top-down' perspective provides an orthodox view of how functional strategies *should* be put together. But in fact the relationship between the levels in the strategy hierarchy is more complex than this. Although it is a convenient way of thinking about strategy, this hierarchical model is not intended to represent the way strategies are always formulated. When any group is reviewing its corporate strategy, it will also take into account the circumstances, experiences and capabilities of the various businesses that form the group. Similarly, businesses, when reviewing their strategies, will consult the individual functions within the business about their constraints and capabilities. They may also incorporate the ideas which come from each function's day-to-day experience.

Therefore an alternative view to the top-down perspective is that many strategic ideas emerge over time from operational experience. Sometimes companies move in a particular strategic direction because the ongoing experience of providing products and services to customers at an operational level convinces them that it is the right thing to do. There may be no high-level decisions examining alternative strategic options and choosing the one which provides the best way forward. Instead, a general consensus emerges from the operational level of the organization. The 'high level' strategic decision-making, if it occurs at all, may confirm the consensus and provide the resources to make it happen effectively.

Suppose the delivery company described previously succeeds in its expansion plants. However, in doing so it finds that having surplus capacity and a distributed network of factories allows it to offer an exceptionally fast service to customers. It also finds that some customers are willing to pay considerably higher prices for such a responsive service. Its experiences lead the company to set up a separate division dedicated to providing fast, high-margin printing services to those customers willing to pay. The strategic objectives of this new division are not concerned with high-volume growth but high profitability.

This idea of strategy being shaped by operational level experience over time is sometimes called the concept of *emergent strategies*.[4] Strategy is gradually shaped over time and based on real-life experience rather than theoretical positioning. Indeed, strategies are often formed in a relatively unstructured and fragmented manner to reflect the fact that the future is at least partially unknown and unpredictable (*see* Fig. 3.4).

This view of operations strategy is perhaps more descriptive of how things really happen, but at first glance it seems less useful in providing a guide for specific decision-making. Yet while emergent strategies are less easy to categorize, the principle governing a bottom-up perspective is clear: shape the operation's objectives and action, at least partly, by the knowledge it gains from its day-to-day activities. The key virtues required for shaping strategy from the bottom up are an ability to learn from experience and a philosophy of continual and incremental improvement.

● The market requirements perspective

One of the obvious objectives for any organization is to satisfy the market it is attempting to serve. No operation that continually fails to serve its markets adequately is likely to survive in the long term. And although understanding markets is usually thought of as the domain of the marketing function, a market perspective is also of importance to operations management. Without an understanding of what markets require, it is

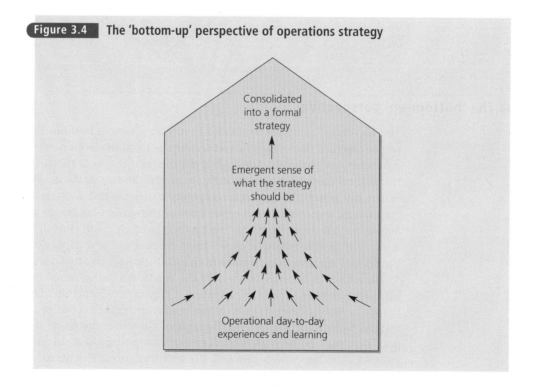

Figure 3.4 The 'bottom-up' perspective of operations strategy

CWS

The rules of clothes retailing in the fast-growing markets around Hong Kong, Taiwan and Singapore used to be clear. Up-market shops sold high-quality products and gave good service. Cheaper clothes were piled high and sold by sales assistants who were more concerned with taking the cash than smiling at customers. Jimmy Lai, founder of Giordano Holdings, changed all that. Although he originally set up to sell expensive clothes, Mr Lai saw that unpredictable quality and low levels of service offered an opportunity in the casual clothes market. His experience indicated that giving value and service, together with low prices, would generate a better profit than existing retailers were getting. His methods were radical. Overnight he raised the wages of his salespeople by between 30 and 40 per cent, all employees were told they would receive at least 60 hours of training a year and new staff would be allocated a 'big brother' or 'big sister' from among experienced staff to help them develop their service quality skills. Even more startling by the standards of his competitors, Mr Lai brought in a 'no-questions asked' exchange policy irrespective of how long ago the garment had been purchased. Staff were trained to talk to customers and seek their opinion on products and the type of service they would like. This information would be immediately fed back to the company's designers for incorporation into their new products. Within a few years of his change in policy, Mr Lai had seen dramatic growth in both profits and turnover to a position where

Exterior of a Giordano shop in Hong Kong

Photo courtesy of Roy Johnston

Giordano achieved the highest sales per square metre of almost any retailer in Hong Kong.

Questions

1 In what way did Mr Lai's experiences change the market position of his Giordano operation?

2 What are the advantages of sales staff talking to the customers?

impossible to ensure that operations is achieving the right mix and level in its performance objectives (quality, speed, dependability, flexibility and cost).

Priority of performance objectives

Chapter 2 described and illustrated the five performance objectives. But it is in the market perspective that performance objectives *should* have priority. In fact, the relative priority of performance objectives for this or any other operation is often influenced by two particular factors:

● the specific needs of the organization's customer groups;
● the activities of the organization's competitors.

Both these factors can be combined in terms of the stage of the product life cycle at which the product or service stands (*see* Fig. 3.5).

Customer influence on performance objectives

Operations seek to satisfy customers through developing their five performance objectives. For example, if customers particularly value low-priced products or services, the operation will place emphasis on its cost performance. If customers insist on error-free products or services, the operation will concentrate on its quality performance. A customer emphasis on fast delivery will make speed important to the operation, while a customer emphasis on reliable delivery will make dependability important. If customers

Figure 3.5 **The market requirements perspective of operations strategy**

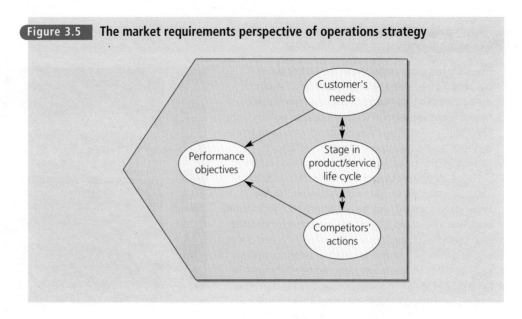

expect very innovative products and services, the operation must provide a high degree of flexibility in order to get its innovations to its customers before its rivals. Similarly, if a wide range of products and services are demanded by customers, the operation will need to be flexible enough to provide the necessary variety without excessive cost.

These factors which define the customers' requirements are called competitive factors.[5] Figure 3.6 shows the relationship between some of the more common competitive factors and the operation's performance objectives. This list is not exhaustive. Many other factors could be important. The important point is that the priority of each performance objective is influenced by the competitive factors particularly valued by customers. Some organizations put considerable effort into bringing an 'image' of their customers' needs into the operation. The box on Kwik-Fit illustrates this.

Figure 3.6 **Different competitive factors imply different performance objectives**

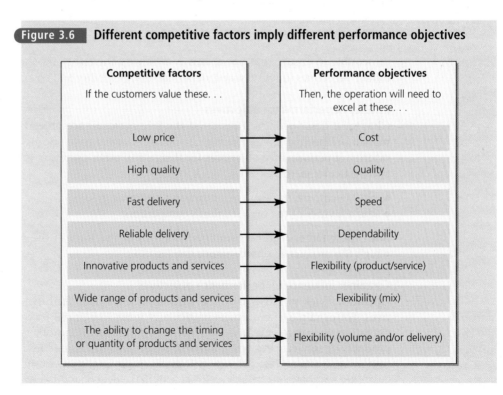

Kwik-Fit customers' needs[6]

In an industry not always known for the integrity of its companies, Kwik-Fit has carved out a reputation for service which combines low cost with fast and trustworthy service. Founded in 1971, the company is one of the largest automotive parts repair and replacement firms in the world, with around 2000 service points across Europe. The service dilemma of the company is how to satisfy (or even delight) customers who do not want to be in a repair shop at all.

Customers have not planned to have a breakdown; they are making a distress purchase and can often be suspicious of the company. They may believe that it is in the company's interest to recommend an expensive repair or replacement, even when it is not necessary. Customers want to be able to trust the diagnosis and advice they receive, get served as fast and with as little hassle as possible, have their problem solved and not be charged an excessive amount.

These competitive factors have shaped the company's operations performance objectives. It sums up its operations strategy as 'a quality of service which will give 100 per cent customer

Photo courtesy of Kwik-fit Ltd

satisfaction' – an objective which is captured by the notices that decorate the walls of Kwik-Fit centres.

Question

How do customer needs and competitor actions influence the major performance objectives of a Kwik-Fit centre?

I AM YOUR CUSTOMER

I am your customer. Satisfy my wants, add personal attention and a friendly touch, and I will become a walking advertisement for your products and services. Ignore my wants, show carelessness, inattention and poor manners, and I will simply cease to exist, as far as you are concerned.

I am sophisticated. Much more so than I was a few years ago. My needs are more complex. I have grown accustomed to better things. I have money to spend. I am an egotist. I am sensitive; I am proud. My ego needs the nourishment of a friendly, personal greeting from you. It is important to me that you appreciate my business. After all, when I buy your products and services, my money is feeding you.

I am a perfectionist. I want the best I can get for the money I spend. When I criticize your products or services – and I will, to anyone who will listen, when I am dissatisfied – then take heed. The source of my discontent lies in something you or the products you sell have failed to do. Find that source and eliminate it or you will lose my business and that of my friends as well.

I am fickle. Other businessmen continually beckon me with offers of 'more' for my money. To keep my business, you must offer something better than they. I am your customer now, but you must prove to me again and again that I have made a wise choice in selecting you, your products and services above all others.

Order-winning and qualifying objectives

A particularly useful way of determining the relative importance of competitive factors is to distinguish between 'order-winning' and 'qualifying' factors.[7]

Order-winning factors are those things which directly and significantly contribute to winning business. They are regarded by customers as key reasons for purchasing the product or service. Raising performance in an order-winning factor will either result in more business or improve the chances of gaining more business. *Qualifying factors* may not be the major competitive determinants of success, but are important in another way. They are those aspects of competitiveness where the operation's performance has to be above a particular level just to be considered by the customer. Performance below this 'qualifying' level of performance will possibly disqualify the company from being considered by many customers. But any further improvement above the qualifying level is unlikely to gain the company much competitive benefit.

To order-winning and qualifying factors can be added less important factors which are neither order-winning nor qualifying. They do not influence customers in any significant way. They are worth mentioning here only because they may be of importance in other parts of the operation's activities.

Figure 3.7 shows the difference between order-winning, qualifying and less important factors in terms of their utility or worth to the competitiveness of the organization. The curves illustrate the relative amount of competitiveness (or attractiveness to customers) as the operation's performance at the factor varies. Order-winning factors show a steady and significant increase in their contribution to competitiveness as the operation gets better at providing them. Qualifying factors are 'givens'; they are expected by customers and can severely disadvantage the competitive position of the operation if it cannot raise its performance above the qualifying level. Less important objectives have little impact on customers no matter how well the operation performs in them.

Different customer needs imply different objectives

If, as is likely, an operation produces goods or services for more than one customer group, it will need to determine the order-winning, qualifying and less important competitive factors for each group. For example, Table 3.1 shows two 'product' groups in the banking industry.[8] Here the distinction is drawn between the customers who are looking for banking services for their private and domestic needs (current accounts, overdraft facilities, savings accounts, mortgage loans, etc.) and those corporate customers who need banking services for their (often large) organizations. These latter services would include such things as letters of credit, cash transfer services and commercial loans.

Competitor influence on performance objectives

Customers are not the only influence on the priority of performance objectives. Competitor activity may also be important. If, for example, a home delivery pizza operation competes by guaranteeing a fast delivery to customers in its area, it is concentrating on delivery speed, because that is what it believes its customers want. However, if a rival pizza shop offers equally fast delivery together with an extended range of pizza toppings, the operation could respond by extending its own range. Its priorities might shift from speed towards developing the flexibility to offer a sufficiently wide range of products to match its competitor.

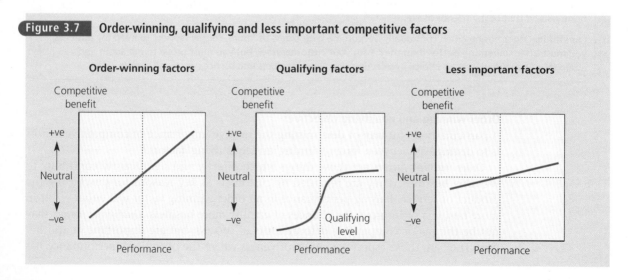

Figure 3.7 Order-winning, qualifying and less important competitive factors

Table 3.1 Different banking services require different performance objectives

	Retail banking	Corporate banking
Products	Personal financial services such as loans and credit cards	Special services for corporate customers
Customers	Individuals	Businesses
Product range	Medium but standardized, little need for special terms	Very wide range, many need to be customized
Design changes	Occasional	Continual
Delivery	Fast decisions	Dependable service
Quality	Means error-free transactions	Means close relationships
Volume per service type	Most services are high volume	Most services are low volume
Profit margins	Most are low to medium, some high	Medium to high

Competitive factors		
Order winners	Price Accessibility Speed	Customization Quality of service Reliability
Qualifiers	Quality Range	Speed Price
Less important		Accessibility

Internal performance objectives	Cost Speed Quality	Flexibility Quality Dependability

Not that an organization will always match its competitors' moves. The pizza operation could have responded to its competitor's extended product range by shifting its priorities to some totally different competitive factor. For example, instead of extending its own range, it could have chosen to shorten its delivery times even more, so as to capitalize on its experience of fast delivery. Alternatively, it could have chosen an entirely new competitive direction such as cutting its prices. Figure 3.8 illustrates this.

The main point here is that, even without any direct change in the preferences of its customers, an organization may have to change the way it competes and therefore the priority of its performance objectives. Alternatively, an organization might choose to compete in a different way to its rivals in order to distinguish itself from its competitors (*see* the box on Ryanair).

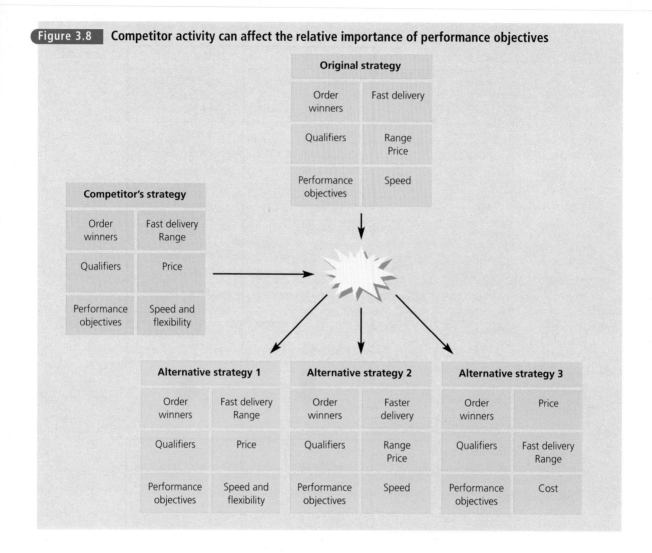

Figure 3.8 Competitor activity can affect the relative importance of performance objectives

The product/service life cycle[9] influence on performance objectives

One way of generalizing the behaviour of both customers and competitors is to link it to the life cycle of the products or services that the operation is producing. The exact form of product/service life cycles will vary, but generally they are shown as the sales volume passing through four stages – introduction, growth, maturity and decline. The important implication of this for operations management is that products and services will require operations strategies in each stage of their life cycle (*see* Fig. 3.9).

Introduction stage

When a product or service is first introduced, it is likely to be offering something new in terms of its design or performance. Few competitors will be offering the same product or service, and because the needs of customers are not perfectly understood, the design of the product or service could frequently change. Given the market uncertainty, the operations management of the company needs to develop the flexibility to cope with these changes and the quality to maintain product/service performance.

Growth stage

As the volume of products or services grows, competitors start to develop their own products and services. In the growing market, standardized designs emerge.

Photo courtesy of Ryanair

Ryanair is today one of Europe's largest and most successful low-cost airlines (LCAs). Operating its low-fare, no-frills formula, its over 1000 employees and growing fleet of Boeing 737 aircraft provide services between over 30 cities around Europe. Operating from its Dublin headquarters, it carries around six million passengers every year.

But Ryanair was not always so successful. Entering the market in early 1985, its early aim was to provide an alternative low-cost service between Ireland and London to the two market leaders, British Airways and Aer Lingus. Ryanair chose this route because it was expanding in both the business and leisure sectors. However, the airline business is marked by economies of scale and Ryanair, then with a small fleet of all old-fashioned aircraft, was no match for its larger competitors. The first six years of Ryanair's operation resulted in a IR£20 million loss. In 1991, Ryanair decided to rework its strategy. Inspired by the most successful LCA, Southwest Airlines in the United States, it adopted what has become the operations strategy formula for LCAs. First, the service offered is 'no frills', there are no free snacks or drinks served and no pre-booked seat allocation. This saves material (peanuts, drinks etc.) and labour (nothing to be served) costs. Second, turnaround time at airports is kept to a minimum. This is achieved partly because there are

no meals to be loaded onto the aircraft and partly through improved employee productivity. Third, all the aircraft in the fleet are identical. This gives savings through standardization of parts, maintenance and servicing. It also means large orders to a single aircraft supplier and therefore the opportunity to negotiate prices down. Fourth, the company will often use secondary airports who charge lower landing and service fees. Finally, the cost of selling its services is reduced where possible. Although Ryanair is one of the few LCAs in Europe which still uses travel agents, it has also developed its own low-cost internet booking service.

Questions

1 What seem to be the major reasons why Ryanair is so successful?

2 What threats to its success could Ryanair face in the future?

Standardization is helpful in that it allows the operation to supply the rapidly growing market. Keeping up with demand could prove to be the main operations preoccupation. Rapid and dependable response to demand will help to keep demand buoyant while ensuring that the company keeps its share of the market as competition starts to increase. Also, increasing competition means that quality levels must be maintained.

Maturity stage

Eventually demand starts to level off. Some early competitors will have left the market and the industry will probably be dominated by a few larger companies. The designs of the products or services will be standardized and competition will probably emphasize price or value for money, although individual companies might try to prevent this by attempting to differentiate themselves in some way. So operations will be expected to get the costs down in order to maintain profits or to allow price cutting, or both. Because of this, cost and productivity issues, together with dependable supply, are likely to be the operation's main concerns.

	Introduction	Growth	Maturity	Decline
	Product/service first introduced to market	Product/service gains market acceptance	Market needs start to be fulfilled	Market needs largely met
Volume	Slow growth in sales	Rapid growth in sales volume	Sales slow down and level off	Sales decline
Customers	Innovators	Early adopters	Bulk of market	Laggards
Competitors	Few/none	Increasing number	Stable number	Declining number
Variety of product/service designs	Possible high customization or frequent design changes	Increasingly standardized	Emerging dominant types	Possible move to commodity standardization
Likely order winners	Product/service characteristics, performance or novelty	Availability of quality products/services	Low price Dependable supply	Low price
Likely qualifiers	Quality Range	Price Range	Range Quality	Dependable supply
Dominant operations performance objectives	Flexibile Quality	Speed Dependability Quality	Cost Dependability	Cost

Recycling strategy at Veka UPVC windows[11]

Although customers and competitors are the main drivers of market pressures, other factors can affect even a 'mature' product. The legislative environment, for example, may create new pressures and opportunities. Germany's tough environmental laws, for example, limit disposal of waste in landfill sites. The final disposal of end-of-life products is severely constrained, encouraging disassembly into component materials which can then be re-used.

UPVC windows have been used in Germany for several decades, and many are now being replaced. At one time some 100 000 windows were deposited in landfill sites in Germany, but legislation curtailed this. Veka, the world's largest producer of UPVC

windows, recognized the potential impact of this legislation on the entire business and set about the development and design of a recycling process for discarded windows. The new DM 30 million plant, constructed in Behringen, shreds complete windows into fragments which are then sorted into the re-usable component materials of glass, metals, rubber and UPVC. The latter is used by Veka itself in new products, completing the cycle of materials; less than 3 per cent of the materials go to waste.

Veka's environmentally friendly operations strategy has not only been a logical response to a changing legislative environment, but has also created a new competitive advantage. Purchasers of new windows could not fail to be impressed with the product and processes which allow valuable materials to be recycled. In addition, Veka has also gained a sustained source of cheap materials, insulating itself from the fluctuating price of new plastic.

Questions

1 What have been the major pressures on Veka which caused it to change its operations strategy?

2 What opportunities for the operation do you think were created by the move to recycling?

Decline stage

After time, sales will decline and competitors will start dropping out of the market. To the companies left there might be a residual market, but if capacity in the industry lags demand, the market will continue to be dominated by price competition. Operations objectives will therefore still be dominated by cost.

The operations resources perspective

The fourth and final perspective we shall take on operations strategy is based on a particularly influential theory of business strategy – the resource-based view (RBV) of the firm.[12] Put simply, the RBV holds that firms with an 'above average' strategic performance are likely to have gained their sustainable competitive advantage because of the core competences (or capabilities) of their resources. This means that the way an organization inherits, or acquires, or develops its operations resources will, over the long term, have a significant impact on its strategic success. Furthermore, the impact of its 'operations resource' capabilities will be at least as great, if not greater, than that which it gets from its market position. So understanding and developing the capabilities of operations resources, although often neglected, is a particularly important perspective on operations strategy.

Figure 3.10 illustrates the operations resource perspective of operations strategy. Both the operation's resources and processes embody the operation's capabilities, consideration of which is important in shaping structural and infrastructural decisions (explained later).

Resource constraints and capabilities

No organization can merely choose which part of the market it wants to be in without considering its ability to produce products and services in a way that will satisfy that market.[13] In other words, the constraints imposed by its operations must be taken into account. For example, a small translation company offers general translation services to a wide range of

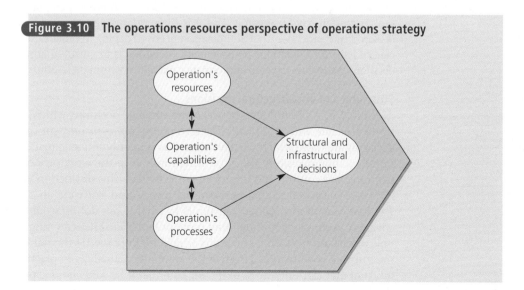

Figure 3.10 The operations resources perspective of operations strategy

customers who wish documents such as sales brochures to be translated into another language. A small company, it operates an informal network of part-time translators who enable the company to offer translation into or from most of the major languages in the world. Some of the company's largest customers want to purchase their sales brochures on a 'one-stop shop' basis and have asked the translation company whether it is willing to offer a full service, organizing the design and production, as well as the translation, of export brochures. This is a very profitable market opportunity, however the company does not have the resources, financial or physical, to take it up. From a market perspective, it is good business; from an operations resource perspective, it is not feasible.

However, the operations resource perspective is not always so negative. This perspective may identify *constraints* to satisfying some markets but it can also identify *capabilities* which can be exploited in other markets. For example, the same translation company has recently employed two new translators who are particularly skilled at website development. To exploit this, the company decides to offer a new service whereby customers can transfer documents to the company electronically, which can then be translated quickly. This new service is a 'fast response' service which has been designed specifically to exploit the capabilities within the operations resources. Here the company has chosen to be driven by its resource capabilities rather than the obvious market opportunities.

Operations resources and processes

An operations resource perspective must start with an understanding of the resource capabilities and constraints within the operation. It must answer the simple questions, what do we have, and what can we do? An obvious starting point here is to examine the transforming and transformed resource inputs to the operation. These, after all, are the 'building blocks' of the operation. However, merely listing the type of *resources* an operation has does not give a complete picture of what it can do. Trying to understand an operation by listing its resources alone is like trying to understand an automobile by listing its component parts. To describe it more fully, we need to describe how the component parts form the internal mechanisms of the motor car. Within the operation, the equivalent of these mechanisms are its *processes*. Yet, even for an automobile, a technical explanation of its mechanisms still does not convey everything about its style or 'personality'. Something more is needed to describe these. In the same way, an operation is not just the sum of its processes. In addition, the operation has some *intangible resources*.

An operation's intangible resources include such things as:

- its relationship with supplies and the reputation it has with its customers;
- its knowledge of and experience in handling its process technologies;
- the way its staff can work together in new product and service development.

These intangible resources may not be as evident within an operation, but they are important and often have real value. And it is these intangible resources, as well as the tangible resources and processes, that an operation needs to deploy in order to satisfy its markets. The central issue for operations management, therefore, is to ensure that its pattern of strategic decisions really does develop appropriate capabilities within its resources and processes.

Structural and infrastructural decisions

A distinction is often drawn between the strategic decisions which determine an operation's *structure* and those which determine its *infrastructure*. An operation's structural decisions are those which we have classed as primarily influencing design activities, while infrastructural decisions are those which influence the workforce organization and the planning and control, and improvement activities. This distinction in operations strategy has been compared to that between 'hardware' and 'software' in a computer system.[14] The hardware of a computer sets limits to what it can do. In a similar way, investing in advanced technology and building more or better facilities can raise the potential of any type of operation. Within the limits which are imposed by the hardware of a computer, the software governs how effective the computer actually is in practice. The most powerful computer can only work to its full potential if its software is capable of exploiting its potential. The same principle applies with operations. The best and most costly facilities and technology will only be effective if the operation also has an appropriate infrastructure which governs the way it will work on a day-to-day basis.

Table 3.2 illustrates both structural and infrastructural decision areas, arranged to correspond approximately to the chapter headings used in this book. The table also shows some typical questions which each strategic decision area should be addressing.

Table 3.2 Structural and infrastructural strategic decision areas

Structural strategic decisions	*Typical questions which the strategy should help to answer*
New product/service development strategy	Should the operation be developing its own novel product or service ideas or following the lead of others?
	How should the operation decide which products or services to develop and how to manage the development process?
Vertical integration strategy	Should the operation expand by acquiring its suppliers or its customers?
	If the former, what suppliers should it acquire?
	If the latter, what customers should it acquire?
	What balance of capabilities should it develop along its network of operations?
Facilities strategy	What number of geographically separate sites should the operation have?
	Where should the operations facilities be located?
	What activities and capacity should be allocated to each plant?
Technology strategy	What broad types of technology should the operation be using?
	Should it be at the leading edge of technology or wait until the technology is established?
	What technology should the operation be developing internally and what should it be buying in?
Infrastructural strategic decisions	*Typical questions which the strategy should help to answer*
Workforce and organization strategy	What role should the people who staff the operation play in its management?
	How should responsibility for the activities of the operations function be allocated between different groups in the operation?
	What skills should be developed in the staff of the operation?
Capacity adjustment strategy	How should the operation forecast and monitor the demand for its products and services?
	How should the operation adjust its activity levels in response to demand fluctuations?
Supplier development strategy	How should the operation choose its suppliers?
	How should it develop its relationship with its suppliers?
	How should it monitor its suppliers' performance?
Inventory strategy	How should the operation decide how much inventory to have and where it is to be located?
	How should the operation control the size and composition of its inventories?

Continued overleaf

Table 3.2 Continued

Infrastructural strategic decisions	Typical questions which the strategy should help to answer
Planning and control systems strategy	What system should the operation use to plan its activities?
	How should the operation decide the resources to be allocated to its various activities?
Improvement strategy	How should the operation's performance be measured?
	How should the operation decide whether its performance is satisfactory?
	How should the operation ensure that its performance is reflected in its improvement priorities?
	Who should be involved in the improvement process?
	How fast should the operation expect improvement in performance to be?
	How should the improvement process be managed?
Failure prevention and recovery strategy	How should the operation maintain its resources so as to prevent failure?
	How should the operation plan to cope with a failure if one occurs?

● The operations strategy matrix

The final two perspectives on operations strategy are particularly important. Most of the debate in organizations around operations strategy concerns the reconciliation of their market's requirements with their operation's resources. These two perspectives can be

Figure 3.11 The operations strategy matrix

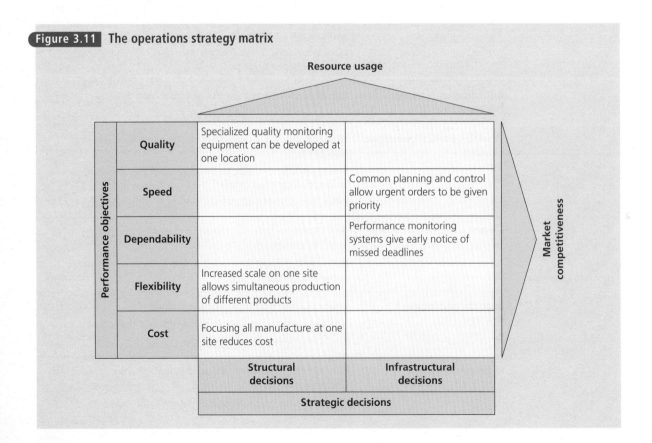

Jeans are one of the most commonly worn types of clothing around the world. Not surprisingly, the thread which holds them together has to be strong and of high quality. Coats Thread is a major manufacturer of jeans thread, supplying product to companies such as Levi-Strauss and Vanity Fair (who manufacture Lee and Wrangler brands). The manufacturer of jeans thread involves spinning the polycotton corespun thread, formulating and mixing the dyes, dyeing the thread in batches, lubricating and winding the thread onto smaller reels and shipping these to many jeans factories around Europe. Up until recently Coats sold product on a country-by-country basis, with up to five of its plants each producing jeans thread for customers all over Europe. Now all of Coats' jeans thread for its European markets is made at a single plant, Newton Mearns in Scotland. All orders and deliveries are also dealt with by a single integrated supply chain planning and control system. This has led to significant advantages for both Coats and their customers. The Scottish plant could focus on the manufacturing and marketing skills necessary to sell into this market and their customers had a single point of contact when they wanted to discuss supply issues.

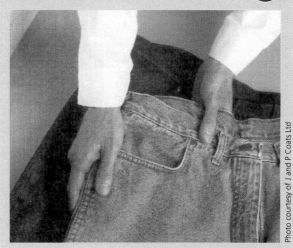

Photo courtesy of J and P Coats Ltd

Good thread helps ensure good quality finished products

Questions

1 What do you think are the main competitive issues in selling thread to jeans manufacturers?

2 What, therefore, will be the main issues for Coats' operations management?

brought together to form an *operations strategy matrix*. Figure 3.11 shows one such matrix (it can take different forms depending on how performance objectives and strategic decisions are classified) for the example described in the box 'A focus on jeans'. The matrix emphasizes the intersections between *what* is required by the market and *how* the operation tries to achieve this through the choices it makes in its strategic decision-making.

Notice that in Figure 3.11 not every intersection is filled in. This is because not every intersection is equally important. Some are particularly critical and one of the key tasks of operations strategy is deciding which intersection warrants particular attention. This task is treated by operations strategy process models, two of which are described next.

The process of operations strategy

The 'process' of operations strategy refers to the procedures which are, or can be, used to formulate those operations strategies which the organization should adopt. Most consultancy companies have developed their own frameworks, as have several academics. Two well-known procedures are briefly described here to give the flavour of how operations strategies are formulated in practice.

● The Hill methodology[15]

One of the first approaches to operations strategy formulation (although once again its development is largely connected with manufacturing operations) is the 'Hill methodology'. It is illustrated in Figure 3.12. Here the model is adapted to the terminology used in

Figure 3.12	The Hill methodology of operations strategy formulation

Step 1	Step 2	Step 3	Step 4	Step 5
Corporate objectives	Marketing strategy	How do products or services win orders?	Operations strategy	
			Process choice	Infrastructure
• Growth rates • Profitability • Return on net assets • Cash flow • Financial 'gearing'	• Product/service markets and segments • Range of products/ services • Mix of specifications • Volumes • Standardization or customization • Rate of innovation	• Price • Quality • Delivery speed • Delivery dependability • Product/service range • Product/service design • Brand image • Supporting services	• Process technology • Trade-offs embodied in process • Role of inventory • Capacity, size, timing, location	• Functional support • Operations planning and control systems • Work structuring • Payment systems • Organizational structure

Source: Based on Hill, T. (1993) *Manufacturing Strategy* (2nd edn), MacMillan

this book. It follows the well-tried approach of providing a connection between different levels of strategy-making. It is essentially a five-step procedure. Step 1 involves understanding the long-term corporate objectives of the organization so that the eventual operations strategy can be seen in terms of its contribution to these corporate objectives. Step 2 involves understanding how the marketing strategy of the organization has been developed to achieve corporate objectives. This step, in effect, identifies the product/service markets which the operations strategy must satisfy, as well as identifying the product or service characteristics, such as range, mix and volume, which the operation will be required to provide. Step 3 translates marketing strategy into what we called earlier 'competitive factors'. Hill goes on to divide the factors that win business into order-winners and qualifiers. Step 4 is what Hill calls 'process choice'. This is similar to the volume/variety analysis which we will treat in the next chapter. Its purpose is to define a set of structural characteristics of the operation which are consistent with each other and appropriate for the way the company wishes to compete. Step 5 involves a similar process, but this time with the infrastructural features of the operation.

This methodology is not intended to imply a simple sequential movement from step 1 to step 5, although during the formulation process the emphasis does move in this direction. Rather, it sees the process as iterative, whereby operations managers cycle between an understanding of the long-term strategic requirements of the operation and the specific resource developments which are required to support strategy. In this iterative process, the identification of competitive factors in step 3 is seen as critical. It is at this stage where any mismatches between what the organization's strategy requires and what its operation can provide become evident.

● The Platts–Gregory procedure[16]

Another influential process is that developed by Ken Platts and Professor Mike Gregory of Cambridge University. The procedure has three stages. Stage 1 involves developing an

Figure 3.13 Uses of profiling in the Platts–Gregory procedure

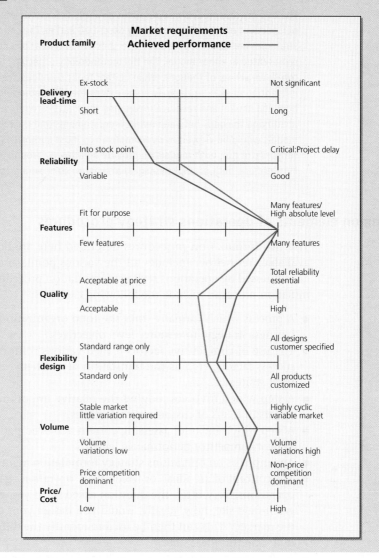

understanding of the market position of the organization. This is done by assessing the opportunities and threats within the competitive environment. More specifically, it also involves identifying the factors which are required by the market and compares these to the level of achieved performance (in terms of the operation being able to satisfy the market). This is an important part of the Platts–Gregory procedure and is different in emphasis from the Hill methodology described previously. Whereas the Hill methodology places its main emphasis on an operations strategy being developed from the customers' view of competitive factors, this procedure explicitly makes the comparison between what the market wants and how the operation performs. The procedure uses 'profiles' of market requirements and achieved performance to show up the gaps which the operations strategy must address. Figure 3.13 illustrates the use of these profiles.[17]

Stage 2 of the procedure involves assessing the capabilities of the operation. Its purpose is to identify current operations practice and assess the extent to which this practice helps to achieve the type of performance that was indicated as being important in stage 1.

Stage 3 concerns the development of new operations strategies. This stage involves reviewing the various options which are available to the organization and selecting those which best satisfy the criteria identified in the two previous stages.

● Common elements of operations strategy procedures

The two formulation procedures described here are broadly representative of those available. Yet neither includes all the various points and issues which, taken together, are addressed by operations strategy formulation procedures. Typically, many of the formulation processes include the following elements:

- A process which formally links the total organization strategic objectives (usually a business strategy) to resource level objectives.
- The use of competitive factors (called various things such as order winners, critical success factors, etc.) as the translation device between business strategy and operations strategy.
- A step which involves judging the relative importance of the various competitive factors in terms of customers' preferences.
- A step which includes assessing current achieved performance, usually as compared against competitor performance levels.
- An emphasis on operations strategy formulation as an iterative process.
- The concept of an 'ideal' or 'green field' operation against which to compare current operations. Very often the question asked is: 'If you were starting from scratch on a green-field site, how, ideally, would you design your operation to meet the needs of the market?' This can then be used to identify the differences between current operations and this ideal state.
- A 'gap-based' approach. This is a well-tried approach in all strategy formulation which involves comparing what is required of the operation by the marketplace against the levels of performance the operation is currently achieving.

What is strategy?

● Strategy is the total pattern of decisions and actions that position the organization in its environment and that are intended to achieve its long-term goals.

● A strategy has content and process. The content of a strategy concerns the specific decisions which are taken to achieve specific objectives. The process of a strategy is the procedure which is used within a business to formulate its strategy.

What is the difference between a 'top-down' and a 'bottom-up' view of operations strategy?

● The 'top-down' perspective views strategic decisions at a number of levels. Corporate strategy sets the objectives for the different businesses which make up a group of businesses. Business strategy sets the objectives for each individual business and how it positions itself in its marketplace. Functional strategies set the objectives for each function's contribution to its business strategy. In this sense, we use the term operations strategy as a functional strategy which deals with the parts of the organization that create goods and services.

● The 'bottom-up' view of operations strategy sees overall strategy as emerging from day-to-day operational experience.

What is the difference between a 'market requirements' and an 'operations resource' view of operations strategy?

● A 'market requirements' perspective of operations strategy sees the main role of operations as satisfying markets. Operations performance objectives and operations decisions should be primarily influenced by a combination of customers' needs and competitors' actions. Both of these may be summarized in terms of the product/service life cycle.

● The 'operations resource' perspective of operations strategy is based on the resource-based view (RBV) of the firm and sees the operation's core competences (or capabilities) as being the main influence on operations strategy. Operations capabilities are developed partly through the strategic decisions taken by the operation. Strategic decision areas in operations are usually divided into structural and infrastructural decisions. Structural decisions are those which define an operation's shape and form. Infrastructural decisions are those which influence the systems and procedures that determine how the operation will work in practice.

How can an operations strategy be put together?

● There are many different procedures which are used by companies, consultancies and academics to formulate operations strategies. The two we describe in this chapter are the Hill methodology and the Platts–Gregory procedure. The Hill methodology is based on the idea of making connections between different levels of strategy-making, from corporate objectives through marketing strategy, operations objectives and structural and infrastructural decisions. The Platts–Gregory procedure is based on identifying the gaps between, on the one hand, what the market requires from an operation and, on the other, how the operation is performing against market requirements.

Long Ridge Gliding Club[18]

Long Ridge Gliding Club is based at an old military airfield on the crest of a ridge about 400 metres above sea level. The facilities are simple but comfortable. A bar and basic catering services are provided, and inexpensive bunkrooms are available for course members and club members wishing to stay overnight. The club has a current membership of nearly 300 pilots, who range in ability from novice to expert. The club has essentially two different types of customers: club members and casual flyers who come for one-off trial flights, holiday courses and corporate events.

The club has six paid employees: a full-time flying manager, a club steward, two part-time office secretaries, a part-time mechanic and a cleaner. In the summer months the club employs a winch driver (for launching the gliders) and two flying instructors. Throughout the whole year, essential tasks such as getting the club gliders out of the hangar, staffing the winches, bringing back gliders and providing look-out cover are undertaken on a voluntary basis by club members. It takes a minimum of five experienced people (club members) to be able to launch one glider. The club's five qualified instructors, two of whom are paid during the summer, provide instruction in two-seater gliders for club members and casual flyers.

When club members fly they are expected to arrive by 9.30 am and be prepared to stay all day helping other club members and any casual flyers get airborne, whilst they wait their turn to fly. On a typical summer's day there might be 10 club members and four casual flyers. Club members would each expect to have three flights during a normal day, with durations of around two to 40 minutes per flight depending on conditions. But they are quite understanding when weather conditions change and they do not get a flight. When the more experienced pilots take to the air, using their own gliders, they can cover some considerable distance, about 300 kilometres, landing back at the club's grass airstrip some three or four hours later. Club members are charged a £5 winch fee each time they take to the air, plus 35p per minute they are in the air if they are using one of the club's six gliders.

The club's brochure encourages members of the public to:

'Experience the friendly atmosphere and excellent facilities and enjoy the thrill of soaring above Long Ridge's dramatic scenery. For just £28 you could soon be in the air. Phone now or just turn up and our knowledgeable staff will be happy to advise you. We have a team of professional instructors dedicated to make this a really memorable experience.'

The club offers trial flights, which are popular as birthday or Christmas presents, evening courses which include a light meal at the club's bar and one day flying courses, although any length of course can be arranged to suit the needs of individuals or groups. Income from casual flyers is small compared with membership income and the club views casual flying as a 'loss leader' to generate club memberships, which are £200 per annum.

Members of the public are encouraged to book trial flights in advance during the week, although at weekends they can just turn up and fly on a first-come, first-served basis. Trial flights and courses are dealt with by the club's administration, which is run from a cabin close to the car park and is staffed most weekday mornings from 9.00 am to 1.00 pm. An answerphone takes messages at other times. The launch point is out of sight, 1.5 kilometres from the cabin, although club members can let themselves onto the airfield and drive there. At the launch point the casual flyers might have to stand and wait for some time until a club member has time to find out what they want. Even when a flight has been pre-booked, casual flyers may then be kept waiting, on the exposed and often windy airfield, for up to two hours before their flight, depending on how many club members are present. Occasionally they will turn up for a pre-booked trial flight and will be turned away because there are not enough club members present to get a glider into the air. The casual flyers are encouraged to help out with the routine tasks but often seem reluctant to do so. After their flight they are left to find their own way back to their cars.

The club chairman is under some pressure from members to end trial flights. Although they provide a very useful source of income for the hard-pressed club (over 700 were sold in the previous year), only a handful had been converted into club memberships.

Questions

1 Evaluate the service to club members and casual flyers by completing a table similar to Table 3.1 (p.73).

2 Chart the five performance objectives to show the differing expectations of club members and casual flyers and compare these with the actual service delivered.

3 What advice would you give to the chairman?

Discussion questions

1 Explain the difference between corporate strategy, business strategy and functional strategy. Illustrate for the Disney Corporation.

2 Describe what you think is the business strategy for your university (you might like to have this confirmed). Describe what you think might be the strategies of some of the micro operations, such as the library, catering, student union and grounds maintenance. You might like to compare your views with those of the managers of some of these operations.

3 Illustrate how the four perspectives would operate in a 'not-for-profit' organization such as a charity which provides hostel accommodation and other welfare services to the homeless.

4 Explain how an individual branch of a large supermarket chain can:
(a) contribute directly to the strategic aims of the whole company;
(b) help other parts of the company to contribute.

5 Take the example of a prison and describe the specific needs of the different groups of customers (prisoners, society and the victims). For each customer, identify what you think will be the key operations performance objectives and discuss any conflicts between them.

6 Identify what you think might be the order-winning, qualifying and less important objectives for a music store selling compact discs. Discuss how the organization might go about changing its operation by focusing on the less important objectives to give itself an advantage in the marketplace.

7 Read the box on Kwik-Fit in the first part of this chapter
(a) What do you think are the main structural and infrastructural decision areas which would constitute an operations strategy for Kwik-Fit?
(b) You now have a list of performance objectives and a list of decision areas. Which decision areas do you think are particularly important in influencing each performance objective? (For example, you might think that quality will be particularly influenced by workforce and organization strategy.)

8 Assuming that video cassette recorders (VCRs) are in the maturity stage of their life cycle, how might the main performance objectives of a VCR manufacturer have changed over the life of the product type so far?

9 For organizations providing the following products or services, what do you think would be their order-winning factors and qualifying factors:
  – estate agency services
  – school textbooks
  – basic aluminium extrusions
  – accountancy services
  – industrial washing machines?

10 'When a company is introducing a totally novel product or service, it is competing exclusively on the technical specification of that product or service. The operations function therefore has no significant role to play.' Discuss.

11 Many Japanese manufacturers have based their success on products which were regarded as well into their 'mature' stage, such as automobiles and televisions. How did they manage to revitalize the markets for these products and what part did operations management play in this?

12 'A Rolls Royce motor car will always cost more than a Skoda.' Does this mean that manufacturing cost is unimportant to Rolls Royce?

13 Draw up a list of structural and infrastructural decisions for the following operations:
  – a TV rental company
  – a ship repair facility
  – Disneyland Paris
  – a national train network.

14 Sketch out what you think an 'operations strategy matrix' would look like for a convenience store.

Notes on chapter

1 There are many good books on strategy. For example, *see* Johnson, G. and Scholes, K. (1998) *Exploring Business Strategy* (4th edn), Prentice Hall; also *see* deWit, B. and Meyer, R. (1998) *Strategy: Process, Content, and Context*, International Thomson Business Press.

2 For a thorough review of the literature relating to operations strategy, *see* Anderson, J.C., Cleveland, G. and Schroeder, R. (1989) 'Operations Strategy – a Literature Review', *Journal of Operations Management*, Vol 8, No 2.

3 For a more thorough explanation, *see* Slack, N. and Lewis, M. (2001) *Operations Strategy*, Financial Times Prentice Hall.

4 Mintzberg, H. and Waters, J.A. (1995) 'Of Strategies: Deliberate and Emergent', *Strategic Management Journal*, July/Sept.

5 Also called critical success factors by some authors.

6 Gabb, A. (1992) 'Making Kwik Fit Fitter', *Management Today*, Mar.; and company information.

7 Hill, T. (1993) *Manufacturing Strategy* (2nd edn), Macmillan.

8 Adapted from Lim, B.K. (1993) 'Gaining Competitive Advantage from Operations in a Bank', Internal document, University of Warwick.

9 There are many treatments of the product life cycle. *See*, for example, Doyle, P. (1976) 'The Realities of the Product Life Cycle', *Quarterly Review of Marketing*, Summer; and Kotler, P. (1991) *Marketing Management*, Prentice Hall International.

10 Source: Venuprasad, R. (2000) 'The Strategies of Low Cost Airlines in Europe', Internal report, University of Warwick.

11 Gibson, M. (1994) 'Veka Opens Window on Recycling', *The European*, 26 Aug–1 Sept.

12 There is a vast literature which describes the resource-based view of the firm. For example, *see* Barney, J. (1991) 'The Resource-Based Model of the Firm: Origins, Implications and Prospect', *Journal of Management*, Vol 17, No 1; or Teece, D.J. and Pisano, G. (1994) 'The Dynamic Capabilities of Firms: An Introduction', *Industrial and Corporate Change*, Vol 3, No 3.

13 A point made initially by Skinner. Skinner, W. (1985) *Manufacturing: The Formidable Competitive Weapon*, John Wiley.

14 Hayes, R.H. and Wheelwright, S.C. (1984) *Restoring our Competitive Edge*, John Wiley.

15 Hill, T. (1993) *Manufacturing Strategy* (2nd edn), Macmillan.

16 Platts, K.W. and Gregory, M.J. (1990) 'Manufacturing Audit in the Process of Strategy Formulation', *International Journal of Operations and Production Management*, Vol 10, No 9. Also, for a very full explanation of all the steps in this procedure, *see* *Competitive Manufacturing*, The Department of Trade and Industry and IFS Publications, Kempston, UK (1988).

17 This profiling method is based on New, C.C. (1987) *UK Manufacturing: The Challenge of Transformation*, Cranfield School of Management.

18 This case was prepared by Shirley Johnston, 2000.

Selected further reading

Baden-Fuller, C. and Pitt, M. (1996) *Strategic Innovation*, Routledge.

Berry, W.L. and Hill, T. (1992) 'Linking Systems to Strategy', *International Journal of Operations and Production Management*, Vol 12, No 10.

Croom-Morgan, S. (1994) 'Managing External Resources: Strategic Positioning and Organizational Capability' *in* Platts, K.W., Gregory, M.J. and Neely, A.D. (eds) *Operations Strategy and Performance, European Operations Management Association*, Cambridge University.

Hamel, G. and Prahalad, C.K. (1993) 'Strategy as Stretch and Leverage', *Harvard Business Review*, Vol 71, Nos 2 & 3.

Hayes, R.H. and Pisano, G.P. (1994) 'Beyond World Class: The New Manufacturing Strategy', *Harvard Business Review*, Vol 72, No 1.

Hayes, R.H. and Wheelwright, S.C. (1984) *Restoring our Competitive Edge*, John Wiley, Chap 2.

Hayes, R.H., Pisano, G.P. and Upton, D.M. (1996) *Strategic Operations*, Free Press.

Hayes, R.H., Wheelwright, S.C. and Clarke, K.B. (1988) *Dynamic Manufacturing*, Free Press, Chaps 1 and 2.

Hill, T. (1993) *Manufacturing Strategy* (2nd edn), Macmillan, Chaps 2 and 3.

Lindberg, P. (1990) 'Strategic Manufacturing Management: A Proactive Approach', *International Journal of Operations and Production Management*, Vol 10, No 2.

Lindberg, P. and Trygg, L. (1991) 'Manufacturing Strategy in the Value System', *International Journal of Operations and Production Management*, Vol 11, No 3.

Lindberg, P., Voss, C.A. and Blackmon, K.L. (eds) (1998) *International Manufacturing Strategies*, Kluwer Academic Publishers.

New, C. (1992) 'World Class Manufacturing Versus Strategic Trade-offs', *International Journal of Operations and Production Management*, Vol 12, No 4.

Nicholson, T.A.J. (1991) 'Strategy and the Shop Floor: A One-Way Initiative?', *International Journal of Operations and Production Management*, Vol 11, No 3.

Ould, M.A. (1995) *Business Processes*, John Wiley.

Prahalad, C.K. and Hamel, G. (1990) 'The Core Competence of the Corporation', *Harvard Business Review*, Vol 68, No 3.

Samson, D. (1991) *Manufacturing and Operations Strategy*, Prentice Hall, Chap 1.

Slack, N. (1991) *The Manufacturing Advantage*, Mercury Business Books.

Slack, N. (2001) *Operations Strategy*, Financial Times Prentice Hall.

Sweeney, M.T. (1991) 'Towards a Unified Theory of Strategic Manufacturing Management', *International Journal of Operations and Production Management*, Vol 11, No 8.

Voss, C.A. (1992) *Manufacturing Strategy*, Chapman and Hall, Part 4.

Womack, J.P. and Jones, D.T. (1996) *Lean Thinking: Banish Waste and Create Wealth in your Corporation*, Simon and Schuster.

Woodcock, D.J. (1989) 'Measuring Strategic Control and Improvement in Manufacturing', *International Journal of Operations and Production Management*, Vol 9, No 5.

Part Two

DESIGN

This part of the book looks at the design of products and services as well as the design of the processes which produce them. At the most strategic level, process design means designing the network of operations which gets products and services to the customer. At a more operational level, process design means the physical arrangement of the operation's facilities, technology and people.

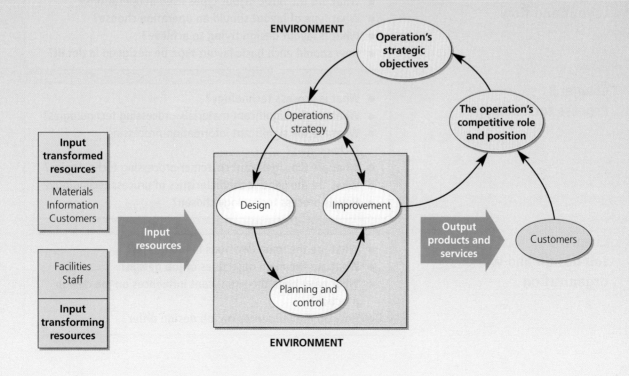

Key operations questions

Chapter 4
Design in operations management

- What is the design in operations management?
- What objectives should the design activity have?
- How can design decisions be made?
- How does the design activity differ in different types of operation?
- What are 'process types'?

Chapter 5
The design of products and services

- Why is good product and service design important?
- What are the stages in product and service design?
- Why should product and service design and process design be considered interactively?
- How should interactive design be managed?

Chapter 6
Design of the operations network

- Why should an organization take a total supply network perspective?
- What is involved in configuring a supply network?
- Where should an operation be located?
- How much capacity should an operation plan to have?

Chapter 7
Layout and flow

- What are the basic layout types used in operations?
- What type of layout should an operation choose?
- What is layout design trying to achieve?
- How should each basic layout type be designed in detail?

Chapter 8
Process technology

- What is process technology?
- What are the significant materials-processing technologies?
- What are the significant information-processing technologies?
- What are the significant customer-processing technologies?
- What are the generic characteristics of process technology?
- How is process technology chosen?

Chapter 9
Job design and work organization

- What are the main decisions in job design?
- What are the main objectives of job design?
- What have been the significant influences on job design practice?
- How do the influences on job design differ?

4 Design in operations management

Introduction

The most widely held image of a designer is of someone who is concerned with the looks of a product – a fashion designer or a motor car designer, for example. But the design activity is much broader than that. In fact, all operations managers are designers. The purchase of every machine or piece of equipment which is bought is a design decision because it affects the physical shape and nature of the operation. Similarly, every time a machine or piece of equipment is moved, or a member of staff's responsibility is changed, the design of the operation is changed. Operations managers also have an important influence on the 'technical' design of the *products and services*

they produce, by providing much of the information necessary for their design as well as providing the systems which produce them. This is why operations managers cannot afford to be ignorant of the basic principles of design, no matter whether it is a product, service or process that is being designed. This chapter serves as an introduction to Part Two of this book, which treats all the main issues concerned with the design activity in operations management. This includes *both* the design of products and services *and* the design of the processes which create them. Figure 4.1 shows the issues covered in Part Two and how they relate to each other.

Figure 4.1 **The design activities in operations management covered in Part Two**

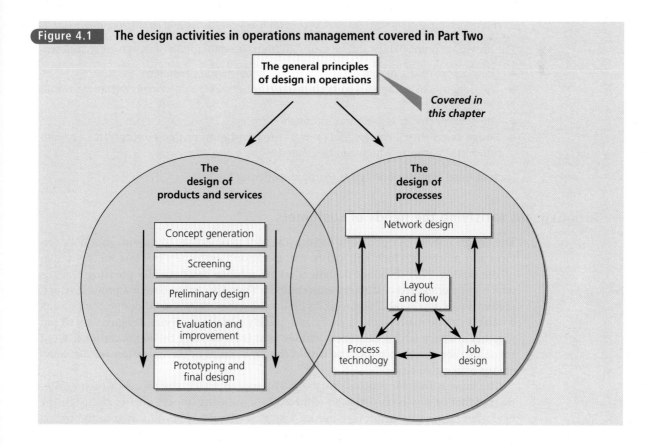

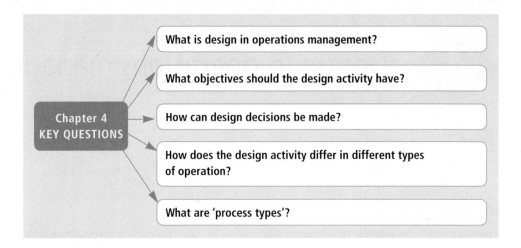

What is design?

There is no universally recognized definition of 'design'. Our view of the meaning of design is neatly captured by the following quotation:

'In my definition, design is the conceptual process by which some functional requirement of people, individually or en masse, is satisfied through the use of a product or of a system which derives from the physical translation of the concept. As examples of individual products which satisfy a public or a market need there is the motor car, the television set and the radio, the fridge and the dishwasher, shoes and socks and baby nappies but also the painting, the sculpture, the musical score and the other manifold realized expressionism of the artist, etc.; and as to systems there is the telephone and the railway, the motorway and the supermarket, the orchestra, the provision of utilities (gas, water and electricity), and so on.'[1]

The important points which can be extracted from this description of design are as follows:

- The purpose of the design activity is to *satisfy the needs of customers*.
- The design activity applies to both *products* (or *services*) and *systems* (what we would call *processes*).
- The design activity is itself a *transformation process*.
- Design starts with a *concept* and ends in the translation of that concept into a *specification* of something which can be created.

Each of these aspects of design is worth considering further.

● Design means satisfying the needs of customers

The design activity in operations has one overriding objective: to provide products, services and processes which will satisfy the operation's customers (*see* box on the design of the Boeing 777). Product designers try to achieve aesthetically pleasing designs which meet or exceed customers' expectations. They also try to design a product which performs well and is reliable during its lifetime. Further, they should design the product so that it can be manufactured easily and quickly. Similarly, service designers try to put together a service which customers will see as at least meeting their expectations. Yet at the same time the service must be within the capabilities of the operation and be delivered at reasonable cost.

The same is true for process designers. The way in which the process which creates the product or service is designed will have a significant impact on the ability of the operation to meet its customers' needs. A process which has been located in the wrong

Failure to understand the needs of customers and work these thoroughly into the design can cause problems which only emerge after the product or service is in use. This can be especially true when designers are motivated solely by the exciting possibilities offered by a new technology. For example, many of the so-called 'intelligent buildings' which incorporated extensive information technology suffered initial teething problems. One building incorporated 'intelligent blinds' on its windows. These were supposed to go up and down in response to the amount of sunlight falling on the windows. The outside lighting was sampled every seven minutes. On a sunny day the blinds were supposed to remain down and when it was cloudy they would stay up to let in more light. Unfortunately, when the sun passed behind a small cloud the blinds could go up and stay there for seven minutes. On intermittently cloudy days the blinds would be forever going up and down, to the considerable annoyance of staff, especially those with computer screens. The problem was eventually 'solved' when staff piled books on the bottom of the blinds until the motors blew up. Another building had conference rooms where the lights were activated by sensors in the ceiling which reacted to movement and heat. The lights went on automatically when people entered the room. Unfortunately this was the only mechanism by which the lights went on and off, so if someone wanted to show slides, everyone in the room had to sit still until the lights went out.

Questions

1 Why were each of the systems described in this box regarded as a failure?

2 How would you have ensured that the mistakes made by the designers of these systems could not have occurred?

3 Was it just incompetence that led the designers to install these systems or were they falling into a fairly predictable design trap?

place, which has insufficient capacity, which is arranged in a jumbled and confused layout, which is given inappropriate technology, or which is staffed with unskilled people cannot satisfy customers because it cannot perform efficiently or effectively (*see* box on troublesome technology). Table 4.1 illustrates how each performance objective of an operation is affected by the design of products and services and the design of the process which creates them.

Boeing brings its customers on board[3]

Arguably the most innovative new passenger aircraft to enter service over the last few years was the Boeing 777, a new twin-engined aircraft, in the 300-plus seats category, to compete with established models from McDonnell and Airbus. The existence of established competitor products is important. When Boeing developed the 747 'Jumbo' jet aircraft, it had no direct competitors. The company's customers either wanted the product or they didn't. Not so for the 777; Boeing knew that it must consider its customers' requirements. The company had to take a new course – to understand its customers' needs and then to transform that knowledge into an aircraft that could best meet those needs.

Boeing has always maintained close involvement with its customers, but this project called for a new depth of listening and understanding. Initially, eight large potential customers (including British Airways, Japan Airlines and Qantas) were invited to participate in creating the design concepts. It soon became clear that the customers did have important requirements, the most vital of which was that the aircraft should be around 25 per cent wider than the 767. In fact Boeing had originally hoped to lengthen the 767 fuselage to give the extra capacity, so avoiding some of the costs involved in a completely new fuselage. The customers also wanted much more flexibility in the configuration of the passenger space. Conventionally, cabin space had been divided up into sections, separated by fixed galleys and toilets at predetermined positions, fixing the ratio of passenger capacities of each class. However, the airlines all indicated that they wanted to be able to configure the cabin to their own requirements. Finally, the airlines insisted that the new design should be free of the usual level of minor, but irritating, faults which had bugged the early operations of some of the other aircraft.

Boeing did meet its customers' requirements and even improved upon them in some ways. They achieved this by using design/build teams (a concept similar to the interactive design principle described in Chapter 5), and by a particularly powerful computer-aided design (CAD) system (CAD is described in Chapter 5). Customers were closely involved right from the start of the design. They even came up with some good suggestions. For

example, one airline suggested a new layout for the rear galley which allowed an extra 12 seats to be included in the aircraft.

> **Questions**
>
> 1 What problems do you think might be associated with bringing customers together in the way that Boeing did?
>
> 2 Why do you think that Boeing's customers wanted the flexibility to configure passenger space?

Table 4.1 The impact of product/service and process design on performance objectives

Performance objective	Influence of good product/service design	Influence of good process design
Quality	Can eliminate potential fail points and 'error-prone' aspects of the product or service	Can provide the appropriate resources which are capable of producing the product or service to its design specifications
Speed	Can specify products which can be made quickly (for example, using modular design principles) or services which avoid unnecessary delays	Can move materials, information or customers through each stage of the process without delays
Dependability	Can help to make each stage of the process predictable by requiring standardized, predictable processes	Can provide technology and staff who are themselves dependable
Flexibility	Can allow for variations which allow a range of products or services to be offered to customers	Can provide resources which can be changed quickly so as to create a range of products or services
Cost	Can reduce the costs of each component part which goes into the product or service and also can reduce the cost of putting them together	Can ensure high utilization of resources and therefore efficient and low-cost processes

● Product/service design and process design are interrelated

Often we will treat the design of products and services, on the one hand, and the design of the processes which make them, on the other, as though they were separate activities. Yet they are clearly interrelated. It would be foolish to commit an organization to the detailed design of any product or service without some consideration of how it is to be produced. Small changes in the design of products and services can have profound implications for the way the operation eventually has to produce them. Similarly, the design of a process can constrain the freedom of product and service designers to operate as they would wish (see Fig. 4.2).

This holds good whether the operation is producing products or services. However, the overlap between the two activities is generally greater in operations which produce services. After all, many services involve the customer in being part of the transformation process. The nature and form of the service, as far as the customer sees it, cannot be separated from the process to which the customer is subjected.

The difficulties of overlapping the two activities of product and process design have

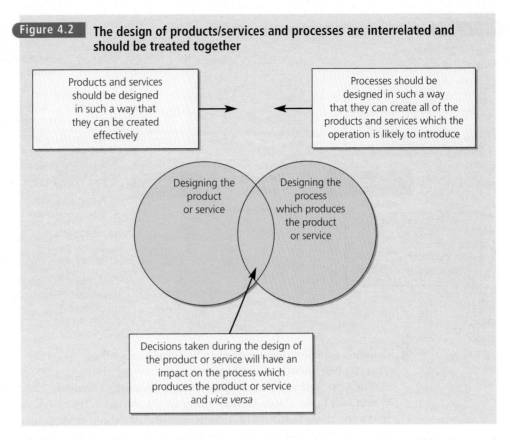

Figure 4.2 The design of products/services and processes are interrelated and should be treated together

Products and services should be designed in such a way that they can be created effectively

Processes should be designed in such a way that they can create all of the products and services which the operation is likely to introduce

Designing the product or service

Designing the process which produces the product or service

Decisions taken during the design of the product or service will have an impact on the process which produces the product or service and *vice versa*

implications for the way in which the design activity is organized, as will be discussed in Chapter 5. Certainly, when product designers also have to make or use the things which they design, it can concentrate their minds on what is important. For example, in the early days of flight, the engineers who designed the aircraft were also the test pilots who took them out on their first flight. For this reason, if no other, safety was a significant objective in the design activity.

The design activity is itself a transformation process

Producing designs for products, services or the processes which create them is itself a transformation process which conforms to the input–transformation–output model described in Chapter 1 and therefore has to be managed. Figure 4.3 illustrates the design activity as an input–transformation–output diagram. The transformed resource inputs will consist mainly of information in the form of market forecasts, market preferences, technical data, and so on. Transforming resource inputs includes administrative, clerical and technical staff, design equipment such as computer-aided design (CAD) systems (*see* Chapter 5) and perhaps development and testing equipment.

We can describe the objectives of the design activity in the same way as we do any transformation process. All operations satisfy customers by producing their services and goods according to customers' desires for quality, speed, dependability, flexibility and cost. In the same way, the design activity attempts to produce designs to the same objectives.

The design activity moves from a concept to a specification

Fully specified designs, which totally define every part or activity, do not spring fully formed from the designer's imagination. A design starts as a more general, ill-defined, even vague idea of what might be an appropriate solution to a felt need. Over time this original idea, or 'concept', is refined and made progressively more detailed until it

Figure 4.3 **Design is itself a transformation process**

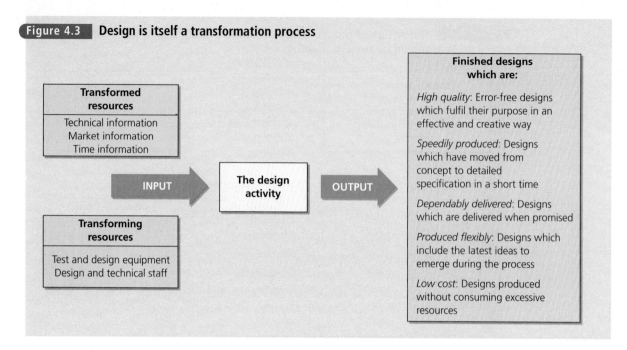

contains sufficient information to be turned into an actual product, service or process. This has two important implications.

The first is that at each stage design decisions cut down the number of options which will be available further along in the design activity. For example, deciding to make the outside casing of a camera case from aluminium rather than plastic limits later decisions, such as the overall size and shape of the case, the way the body is jointed together and the way in which the outer layer is bonded onto the case. This means that the uncertainty surrounding the design reduces as the number of alternative designs being considered decreases. In fact the design activity can be considered as one of progressively reducing the uncertainty regarding a product, service or process. Figure 4.4 shows what is sometimes called the design funnel, depicting the progressive reduction of design options from many to one.

Figure 4.4 **The design funnel – progressively reducing the number of possibilities until the final design is reached**

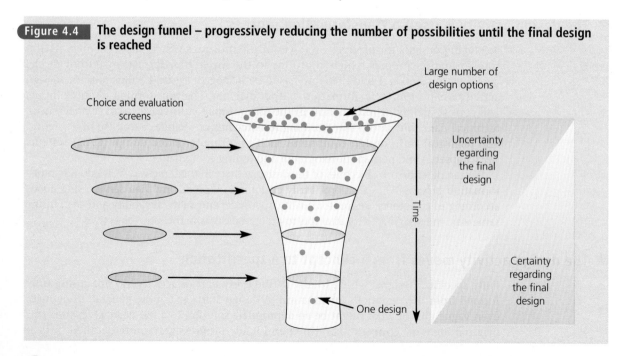

The second consequence of the progression from concept to detailed specification concerns the cost of changing one's mind on some detail of the design. In most stages of design the cost of changing a decision is bound to incur some sort of rethinking and recalculation of costs. Early on in the design activity, before too many fundamental decisions have been made, the costs of change are relatively low. Relatively quickly, however, as the design progresses, the interrelated and cumulative decisions already made become increasingly expensive to change.

● CRITICAL COMMENTARY

Not everyone agrees with the concept of the design funnel. For some it is just too neat and ordered an idea to reflect accurately the creativity, arguments and chaos that sometimes characterize the design activity. First, they argue, managers do not start out with an infinite number of options. No one could process that amount of information – and anyway, designers often have some set solutions in their mind, looking for an opportunity to be used. Second, the number of options being considered often *increases* as time goes by. This may actually be a good thing, especially if the activity was unimaginatively specified in the first place. Third, the real process of design often involves cycling back, often many times, as potential design solutions raise fresh questions or become dead ends. In summary, the idea of the design funnel does not describe what actually happens in the design activity. Nor does it necessarily even describe what *should* happen.

Creativity and design options

The final quality of the single design solutions emerging at the end of the design funnel will depend on how the process of reducing the options is managed and also on the quality of the initial set of options. Both these issues are influenced by the creativity of the designers involved in the design activity. Increasingly, creativity is seen as an essential ingredient not just in the design of products and services, but also in the design of operations processes. Partly because of the fast-changing nature of many industries, a lack of creativity (and consequently of innovation) is seen as a major risk.

'It has never been a better time to be an industry revolutionary. Conversely, it has never been a more dangerous time to be complacent .... The dividing line between being a leader and being a laggard is today measured in months or a few days, and not in decades.'[4]

Some organisations are recognising the increasing gains from creativity and innovation. This is especially true of the growing number of technology-based companies. According to one European survey, the number of technology-based companies that depend on high levels of creativity and innovation rose by nearly 50 per cent between 1994 and 1999. However, this trend is not uniform. Generally, small and small–medium sized companies find it more difficult to be innovative in the design process than do larger organizations.[5]

Of course, creativity can be expensive. By its nature it involves exploring sometimes unlikely possibilities. Many of these will die as they are proved to be inappropriate. Yet, to some extent, the process of creativity depends on these many seemingly wasted investigations. As Art Fry, the inventor of 3M's Post-it note products, said:

'You have to kiss a lot of frogs to find the prince. But remember, one prince can pay for a lot of frogs'.

Balancing creativity with evaluation

Creativity is a vital ingredient in effective design, but it must be balanced by the more systematic process of evaluation. Evaluation in design means assessing the worth or value of each design option, so that a choice can be made between them. This involves assessing each option against a number of *design criteria*. While the criteria used in any particular design exercise will depend on the nature and circumstances of the exercise, it is useful to think in terms of three broad categories of design criteria:

- The *feasibility* of the design option – can we do it?
- The *acceptability* of the design option – do we want to do it?
- The *vulnerability* of each design option – do we want to take the risk?

Figure 4.5 illustrates this classification of design criteria.

Key questions to assess the feasibility of a design option include:

- Do we have the skills (quality of resources) to cope with this option?
- Do we have the organizational capacity (quantity of resources) to cope with this option?
- Do we have the financial resources to cope with this option?

Key questions to assess the acceptability of a design option are:

- Does the option satisfy the performance criteria which the design is trying to achieve? (These will differ for different designs.)
- Does the option give a satisfactory financial return?

Key questions to assess the vulnerability of a design option include:

- Do we understand the full consequences of adopting the option?
- Being pessimistic, what could go wrong if we adopt the option? What would be the consequences of everything going wrong? (This is called the 'downside risk' of an option.)

● Simulation in design

Design involves making decisions in advance of the real product, service or process being created, and so the designer is often not totally sure of the consequences of his or her decisions. For example, a running shoe designer might make a decision about the construction of the shoe, or an architect about the layout of a public building, based on previous experience and basic theories. To increase their own confidence in their design decision, however, they will probably try to *simulate* how the product and the layout would work in practice. In some ways simulation is one of the most fundamental approaches to decision-making. Children play games and 'pretend' so as to extend their experience of novel situations; likewise, managers can gain insights and explore possibilities through the formalized 'pretending' involved in using simulation models. Simulation explores the consequences of decision-making rather than directly advising on the decision itself – it is a *predictive* rather than an *optimizing* technique.

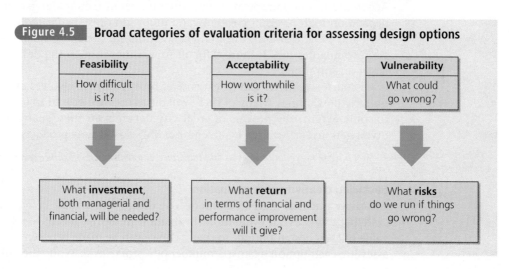

Figure 4.5 **Broad categories of evaluation criteria for assessing design options**

Feasibility	Acceptability	Vulnerability
How difficult is it?	How worthwhile is it?	What could go wrong?
What **investment**, both managerial and financial, will be needed?	What **return** in terms of financial and performance improvement will it give?	What **risks** do we run if things go wrong?

The simulation 'model' itself can take many forms. In the case of the running shoe design, the 'model' might be almost identical to the intended product, except that a 'one-off' prototype shoe would have been made rather than one produced on the actual manufacturing system which would be used for the eventual product. The prototype shoe would then be flexed many millions of times to simulate prolonged wear. In the case of the public building, the architect could devise a computer-based 'model' which would simulate the movement of people through the building according to the probability distribution which describes their random arrival and movement. This could then be used to predict where the layout might become overcrowded or where extra space might be reduced.

Simulation is especially useful in the design of very complex operations processes. For example, a typical use was a computer simulation which was used to redesign a North African shipping port. The model helped the designers to gain an understanding of how the detailed design of the docks and berths for the ships would affect the utilization and turnaround time of the ships depositing and picking up their cargoes at the port. The simulation led to a design which resulted in substantial savings to the World Bank who were involved in the funding of the project.[6]

The virtual reality of design

Photo courtesy of Silicon Graphics

Using a Silicon Graphics Reality Centre for operations design

Virtual reality, once seen solely as a high-technology arcade entertainment medium, has established itself as a powerful, three-dimensional professional design tool, with applications including architecture, car design and the planning of delicate surgical operations. It gives designers a much clearer concept of the relative positions of the individual elements than is possible with static, two-dimensional representations. Perhaps even more importantly, it also allows others, in particular the non-technically trained user, to visualize and suggest modifications to the design before any work is done on the physical entity concerned. An architect can allow a client to roam around the virtual building, walking along corridors and entering rooms at will. PERA, the European consultancy, R&D and technology transfer company, uses a 'virtual reality centre' to help its clients visualize the implications of their operations designs. Powered by a Silicon Graphics Onyx Infinite Reality supercomputer, the world's most powerful graphics supercomputer, the centre offers visualizations of real-time data.

'VR offers significant benefits in industrial applications, from market testing and design to training and maintenance planning. The virtual reality centre bridges the gap between software vendors and potential users by delivering tailored applications to address specific needs,' says Gary Eves, Business Manager at PERA.

For example, Barclaycard, the bank card company, has employed reality centre technology to let some of its 2500 staff in Northampton walk through and help design its new offices. Barclaycard staff could view the new building as it would look, with groups of staff encouraged to give feedback on the design of the offices including floor layout and accessibility.

Questions

1 What are the advantages of 'visualizing' operations before they are constructed?

2 PERA's virtual reality centre cost £2 million using the latest Silicon Graphics technology. How do you think it justified such an investment?

● Environmentally sensitive design

With the issues of environmental protection becoming more important, designers are increasingly having to take account of 'green' issues in their work. In many developed countries, legislation has already provided some basic standards which restrict the use of toxic materials, limit discharges to air and water, and protect employees and the public from immediate and long-term harm. Most of these constraints affect both the design and operation of *processes* and the design of the products themselves.

Volvo's environmental priority strategies (EPS) system[7]

There are many ways in which the life-cycle analysis approach can be used to evaluate environmental data so that it can be used to guide product designers in the use of different materials. One such tool has been developed by Volvo, the Swedish motor manufacturer, in conjunction with the Federation of Swedish Industries and the Swedish Environmental Research Institute. It uses 'environmental indices' calculated for specific materials as follows:

Environmental index = *scope* × *distribution* × *frequency or intensity* × *durability* × *contribution* × *remediability*

where:

scope = general impression of the environmental impact
distribution = extent of affected area
frequency or intensity = regularity or intensity of the problem in the affected area
durability = permanency of the effects
contribution = significance of 1 kg of the emission of the substance in relation to the total effect
remediability = relative cost to reduce the emission by 1 kg

The 'environmental load unit' (ELU) per kg of any substance can then be calculated as the product of the index and the amount of substance released into the environment.

Questions

1 What do you think are the general problems in trying to quantify the environmental impact of design?

2 What seems to you to be the major weakness of the particular approach presented here?

Interest has focused on some fundamental issues:

- *The sources of materials* used in a product. (Will it damage rainforests? Will it use up scarce minerals? Will it exploit the poor or use child labour?)
- *Quantities and sources of energy* consumed in the process. (Do plastic beverage bottles use more energy than glass ones? Should waste heat be recovered and used in fish farming?)

- *The amounts and type of waste material* that are created in the manufacturing processes. (Can this waste be recycled efficiently, or must it be burnt or buried in landfill sites? Will the waste have a long-term impact on the environment as it decomposes and escapes?)
- *The life of the product itself.* It is argued that if a product has a useful life of, say, 20 years, it will consume fewer resources than one that only lasts five years, which must therefore be replaced four times in the same period. However, the long-life product may require more initial inputs, and may prove to be inefficient in the latter part of its use, when the latest products use less energy or maintenance to run.
- *The end-of-life of the product.* (Will the redundant product be difficult to dispose of in an environmentally friendly way? Could it be recycled or used as a source of energy? Could it still be useful in third-world conditions? Could it be used to benefit the environment, such as old cars being used to make artificial reefs for sea life?)

Designers are faced with complex trade-offs between these factors, although it is not always easy to obtain all the information that is needed to make the 'best' choices. For example, it is relatively straightforward to design a long-life product, using strong material, over-designed components, ample corrosion protection, and so on. But its production might use more materials and energy and it could create more waste on disposal. To help make more rational decisions in the design process, some industries are experimenting with *life cycle analysis*. This technique analyses all the production inputs, the life-cycle use of the product and its final disposal, in terms of total energy used (and more recently, of all the emitted wastes such as carbon dioxide, sulphurous and nitrous gases, organic solvents, solid waste, etc.). The inputs and wastes are evaluated at *every* stage in its creation, beginning with the extraction or farming of the basic raw materials.

Computer screen image of the simulated plant

Actual completed plant

Photo courtesy of CAD Centre Ltd

Simulation is used in design to access the feasibility of the construction and the day-to-day running of the operation as well as its environment impact. Simulated operations can be almost indistinguishable from the real thing

The volume–variety effect on design

Although, so far, we have discussed those aspects of design which apply to all types of operations, there are differences between the design activity in, say, an architects' practice and that in an electricity utility. The most significant factor is the difference between their volume and variety characteristics.

In Chapter 1 we saw how operations can range from producing a very high volume of products or services (for example, a food canning factory) to a very low volume (for example, major project consulting engineers). We also saw how operations can range from producing a very low variety of products or services (for example, in an electricity utility) to a very high variety (as, for example, in an architects' practice). Usually the two dimensions of volume and variety go together. Low-volume operations often have a high variety of products and services, and high-volume operations often have a narrow variety of products and services. Thus there is a continuum from low volume–high variety through to high volume–low variety, on which we can position operations.

If you have had the opportunity to study operations, even at a superficial level, you may have noticed that different operations, perhaps within the same industry, have adopted different approaches to the design of their products, services and processes. Not all the retail operations you use, for example, are organized in the same way, or even look the same. Even within a single operation, different approaches to designing products, services and processes can be found. Many manufacturing plants will have a large area, organized on a 'mass-production' basis, in which it makes its high-volume 'best selling' products. In another part of the plant it may also have an area where it makes a wide variety of products in much smaller volumes. Both the design of each set of products and the design of the process which makes them are likely to be different. Similarly, in a medical service, compare the approach taken during mass medical treatments, such as large-scale immunization programmes, with that taken for a transplant operation where the treatment is designed specifically to meet the needs of one person. These differences go well beyond their differing technologies, or the different processing requirements of the products or services. They are explained by the fact that no one way of arranging resources is best for all types of operation in all circumstances. The differences are explained largely by the different *volume–variety positions* of the operations.

● Volume and variety affect all aspects of design

The volume–variety position of an operation has implications for almost every aspect of its design activities (*see* Table 4.2).

Table 4.2 The impact of the volume–variety position of an operation on different aspects of its design activities

Volume	Variety	Design emphasis in the operation	Product/service standardization	Location	Flow	Process technology	Staff skills
Low	High	Product/service design	Low	Can be decentralized	Intermittent	General purpose	Task
↓	↓	↓	↓	↓	↓	↓	↓
High	Low	Process design	High	Usually centralized	Continuous	Dedicated	System

Consider again the two operations discussed previously at the extremes of the volume–variety spectrum – the architects' practice and the electricity utility. The architects' high variety means that its services have little standardization. Some elements of the service will be common – all new designs will need a proposal to put before the client, an internal schedule of activities, plans, and so on – but the details of these will vary from job to job. This variety of activities also means that whatever technology the operation possesses (for example, computer-aided design systems) will need to be sufficiently general purpose to cope with all types of job. The flow of information within the operation will depend on the state of the projects being designed, the circumstances of clients and the overall level of activity in the operation. It will certainly not be regular; rather it will flow in an intermittent manner. The individual task skills of the architects themselves are likely to be more valued by the practice than the skill involved in running the operation itself.

The electricity utility, on the other hand, exhibits almost the mirror-image characteristics of the architects' practice. Volume is high, variety is virtually non-existent since electricity is almost a totally standardized product. The generators – its process technology – cannot be used to do much else but make electricity, which it does more or less continuously. No individual craft skills are needed directly to make electricity (although they will be needed to maintain the generators) but the skills of managing the 'electricity generating system', so as to provide continuous supply at the lowest feasible cost, are considerable.

Standardization and modularization

Operations sometimes attempt to overcome the cost penalties of high variety by standardizing their products, services or processes. This allows them to restrict variety to that which has real value for the end customer. In effect, standardization is a way of moving operations down the volume–variety scale in Table 4.2. Often it is the operation's outputs which are standardized. Examples of this are fast-food restaurants, discount supermarkets or telephone-based insurance companies. A danger facing established operations is that they allow variety to grow excessively. They are then faced with the task of *variety reduction*, often by assessing the real profit or contribution of each product or service. Many organizations have significantly improved their profitability by careful variety reduction. In order to overcome loss of business, customers may be offered alternative products or services which provide similar value.

The standardization of inputs to an operation can also reduce complexity and therefore costs. Standardizing components, for example, in a manufactured product can simplify purchasing, manufacturing and servicing tasks. Likewise, standardizing the format of information inputs to a process can be achieved by using appropriately designed forms or screen formats.

Modularization

The use of modular design principles involves designing standardized 'sub-components' of a product or service which can be put together in different ways. It is possible to create wide choice through the fully interchangeable assembly of various combinations of a smaller number of standard sub-assemblies; computers are designed in this way, for example. These standardized modules, or sub-assemblies, can be produced in higher volume, thereby reducing their cost. Similarly, the package holiday industry can assemble holidays to meet a specific customer requirement, from pre-designed and purchased air travel, accommodation, insurance, and so on. In education also there is an increasing use of modular courses which allow 'customers' choice but permit each module to have economical volumes of students.

The design of processes – process types

The position of an operation on the volume–variety continuum shapes the general approach it takes to managing its processes. These 'general approaches' to managing processes are called *process types*. Different terms are used to identify process types in manufacturing and service industries.

In manufacturing, these process types are (in order of increasing volume and decreasing variety):

- project processes
- jobbing processes
- batch processes
- mass processes
- continuous processes.

In service operations there is less consensus on the terms of the process type. The terms we use here are (again in order of increasing volume and decreasing variety):[8]

- professional services
- service shops
- mass services.

Process types in manufacturing

Each process type in manufacturing implies a different way of organizing operations' activities with different volume and variety characteristics (*see* Fig. 4.6).

Project processes

Project processes are those which deal with discrete, usually highly customized products. Often the timescale of making the product or service is relatively long, as is the interval between the completion of each product or service. So low volume and high

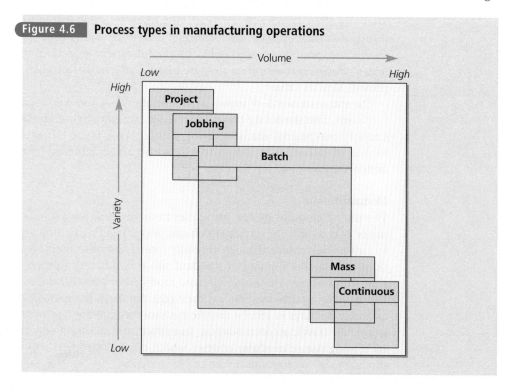

Figure 4.6 **Process types in manufacturing operations**

variety are characteristics of project processes. The activities involved in making the product can be ill-defined and uncertain, sometimes changing during the production process itself. Examples of project processes include shipbuilding, most construction companies, movie production companies, building the Channel Tunnel, large fabrication operations such as those manufacturing turbo generators, drilling oil wells and installing a computer system. The essence of project processes is that each job has a well-defined start and finish, the time interval between starting different jobs is relatively long and the transforming resources which make the product will probably have been organized especially for each product.

Jobbing processes

Jobbing processes also deal with very high variety and low volumes. Whereas in project processes each product has resources devoted more or less exclusively to it, in jobbing processes each product has to share the operation's resources with many others. The resources of the operation will process a series of products but, although all the products will require the same kind of attention, each will differ in its exact needs. Examples of jobbing processes include many precision engineers such as specialist toolmakers, furniture restorers, bespoke tailors, and the printer who produces tickets for the local social event. Jobbing processes produce more and usually smaller items than project processes but, like project processes, the degree of repetition is low. Most jobs will probably be 'one-offs'.

Batch processes

Batch processes can often look like jobbing processes, but batch does not have quite the degree of variety associated with jobbing. As the name implies, each time batch

Van der Lande smoothes the flow

When Packard Bell designed their new assembly centre in Angers, France, they did not want to stock any finished PCs. The key to achieving this came from Van der Lande, the Dutch materials handling equipment specialist. PC manufacture and testing can be complex. It involves a large number of hardware and software components, the specific choice of parts depending on the customers' specification. After assembly, the relevant operating and application software is installed and tested for reliability. If a computer is found not to comply fully with the high quality standards, it is automatically transported to the rectification station. After repair the products are reintroduced to the production process. In this way, potential loss of material as well as time is reduced to a minimum. Finally, manuals and documentation are added, after which the product is packed and dispatched. Throughout the assembly system, 'tracking and tracing' technology allows any part of the product to be monitored and steered through the entire production process. This allows any configuration to be produced in any order. All instructions required by each worker in the assembly system are presented on computer terminals which allow operators to view all assembly data and monitor test results as they happen.

Photo courtesy of Van der Lande

Operators have all the information they need at their individual assembly and test stations

Questions

1 How would you classify this manufacturing process?

2 Does it lie on the diagonal in Figure 4.8?

processes produce a product they produce more than one. So each part of the operation has periods when it is repeating itself, at least while the 'batch' is being processed. The size of the batch could be just two or three, in which case the batch process would differ little from jobbing, especially if each batch is a totally novel product. Conversely, if the batches are large, and especially if the products are familiar to the operation, batch processes can be fairly repetitive. Because of this, the batch type of process can be found over a wider range of volume and variety levels than other process types. Examples of batch processes include machine tool manufacturing, the production of some special gourmet frozen foods, the manufacture of most of the component parts which go into mass-produced assemblies such as automobiles, and the production of most clothing.

Mass processes

Mass processes are those which produce goods in high volume and relatively narrow variety – narrow, that is, in terms of the fundamentals of the product design. An automobile plant, for example, might produce several thousand variants of car if every option of engine size, colour, extra equipment, etc. is taken into account. Yet essentially it is a mass operation because the different variants of its product do not affect the basic process of production. The activities in the automobile plant, like all mass operations, are essentially repetitive and largely predictable. Examples of mass processes include the automobile plant, most consumer durable manufacturers such as a television plant, most food processes such as a frozen pizza manufacturer, a beer bottling plant and CD production.

Continuous processes

Continuous processes are one step beyond mass processes insomuch as they operate at even higher volume and often have even lower variety. They also usually operate for far longer periods of time. Sometimes they are literally continuous in that their products are inseparable, being produced in an endless flow. They may even be continuous in that the operation must supply the products without a break. Continuous processes are often associated with relatively inflexible, capital-intensive technologies with highly predictable flow. Examples of continuous processes include petrochemical refineries, electricity utilities, steel making and some paper making.

● Process types in service operations

As with manufacturing operations, each process type in service operations implies a different way of organizing the operation to cope with different volume–variety characteristics (*see* Fig. 4.7).

Professional services

Professional services are defined as high-contact organizations where customers spend a considerable time in the service process. Such services provide high levels of customization, the service process being highly adaptable in order to meet individual customer needs. A great deal of staff time is spent in the front office and contact staff are given considerable discretion in servicing customers. The amount of time and attention provided for each customer probably means that the ratio of staff to customers is high. Professional services tend to be people-based rather than equipment-based, with emphasis placed on the process (how the service is delivered) rather than the 'product' (what is delivered). Professional services include management consultants, lawyers' practices, architects, doctors' surgeries, auditors, health and safety inspectors and some computer field service operations.

A typical example would be Andersen Consulting, which sells the problem-solving expertise of its skilled staff to tackle clients' problems. Typically, the problem will first be discussed with clients and the boundaries of the project defined. Each 'product' is different. The project manager's role is to create a project team with the appropriate mix of skills to tackle the problem. A high proportion of work takes place at the client's premises, with frequent contact between members of the project team and the client.

At the other extreme are mass services.

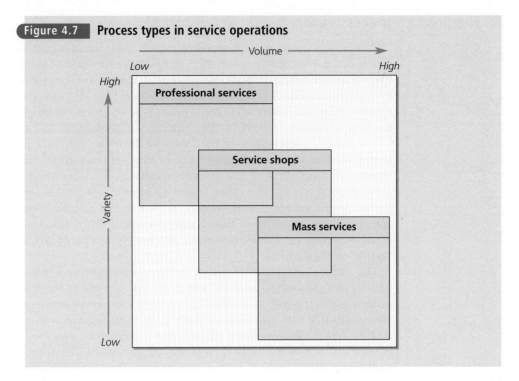

Figure 4.7   Process types in service operations

Volume

Low · High

Variety

High

Professional services

Service shops

Mass services

Low

Mass services

Mass services have many customer transactions, involving limited contact time and little customization. Such services are often predominantly equipment-based and 'product' oriented, with most value added in the back office and relatively little judgement applied by front-office staff. The mainly non-professional staff are likely to have a closely defined division of labour and to follow set procedures. Mass services include supermarkets, a national rail network, an airport, telecommunications service, library, television station, the police service and the enquiry desk at a utility.

For example, rail services such as Virgin Trains in the UK or SNCF in France all move a large number of passengers with a variety of rolling stock on an immense infrastructure of railways. Passengers pick a journey from the range offered. The rail company ticket-office staff can advise passengers on the quickest or cheapest way to get from A to B, but they cannot 'customize' the service by putting on a special train for them.

Service shops

Service shops are characterized by levels of customer contact, customization, volumes of customers and staff discretion, which position them between the extremes of professional and mass services. Service is provided via mixes of front- and back-office activities, people and equipment, and of product/process emphasis. Service shops include banks, high street shops, holiday tour operators, car rental companies, schools, most restaurants, hotels and travel agents.

For example, the Multibroadcast rental organization in the UK offers both rental and retail sales of home electronic products. Its range of products is displayed in its front-office outlets, while back-office operations looks after purchasing and administration. The front-office staff are not there solely to take money; they have some technical training and can advise customers during the process of selling the product. Essentially the customer is buying a fairly standardized product but will be influenced by the process of the sale which can be customized in the sense that the individual customer's needs are diagnosed and, within the limits of the operation's product range, met.

● The product–process matrix

Making comparisons along a spectrum which goes, for example, from shipbuilding at one extreme to electricity generation at the other has limited value. No one grumbles that yachts are so much more expensive than electricity. The real point is that in both manufacturing and service operations, because the different process types overlap, organizations often have a choice of what type of process to employ. This choice will have consequences to the operation, especially in terms of its cost and flexibility.

The classic representation of how cost and flexibility vary with process choice comes from Professors Hayes and Wheelwright of Harvard University.[9] They represent process choices on a matrix with the volume–variety as one dimension, and what we have called process types as the other. Figure 4.8 shows their matrix adapted to fit with the terminology used here. Most operations stick to the 'natural' diagonal of the matrix, and few, if any, are found in the extreme corners of the matrix. However, because there is some overlap between the various process types, operations might be positioned slightly off the diagonal.

The diagonal of the matrix shown in Figure 4.8 represents a 'natural' lowest cost position for an operation. Operations which are on the right of the 'natural' diagonal have processes which would normally be associated with lower volumes and higher variety. This means that their processes are likely to be more flexible than seems to be warranted by their actual volume–variety position. Put another way, they are not taking advantage of their ability to standardize their processes. Because of this, their costs are likely to be higher than they would be with a process that was closer to the diagonal. Conversely, operations that are on the left of the diagonal have adopted processes which would normally be used in a higher volume and lower variety situation. Their processes will therefore be 'over-standardized' and probably too inflexible for their volume–variety position. This lack of flexibility can also lead to high costs because the process will not be able to change from one activity to another as efficiently as a more flexible process.

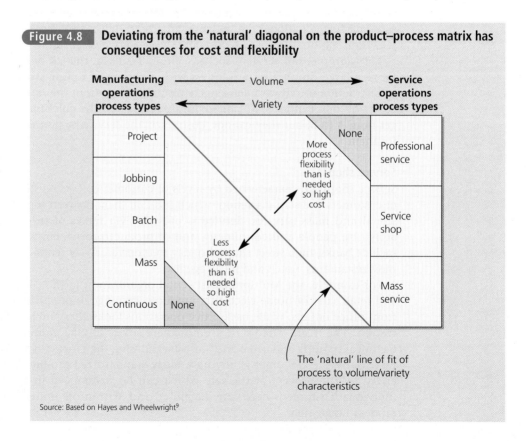

Figure 4.8 Deviating from the 'natural' diagonal on the product–process matrix has consequences for cost and flexibility

Source: Based on Hayes and Wheelwright[9]

Design – the structure of Part Two

The various aspects of the design activity in operations management are treated in the remaining five chapters of Part Two. All these aspects are shown in Figure 4.1 at the beginning of this chapter.

The design of products and services is a prerequisite (Chapter 5)

Notwithstanding our emphasis on the desirability of overlapping the design of products and services and the design of the processes which create them, some understanding of the product or service must be the starting point for all design considerations in operations management. This is why we begin our detailed examination of design with the *design of products and services* in Chapter 5. It will look at some of the basic design principles which we have covered in this chapter and apply them to the various stages which form the product/service design activity. These stages take the designer from the original concept for the product or service through to its final detailed specification.

Process design starts with the whole network (Chapter 6)

With an outline of what the products and services should look like, an operation can start to design the processes which will have to create them. At its most strategic level this means considering the whole network of operations which together produce and deliver products and services to the customers. From the perspective of a single operation within the network, design decisions will include how much of the network the operation wants to own (its vertical integration), where to place its sites (its location), and how large to make each site (its capacity). Chapter 6, *Design of the operations network*, covers all these design decisions.

Designing the operations layout defines its flow (Chapter 7)

The location decision is also significant within each individual site in the total operations network. At this level the decisions concerning where to locate machines, equipment, facilities and people relative to each other is usually termed the operation's layout. Layout decisions are particularly important because they determine the pattern of flow through the operation. Chapter 7, *Layout and flow*, deals with these decisions.

Technology plays a key role (Chapter 8)

Location of the machines and equipment within the operation will determine the pattern of its flow, but the nature of its technology will determine its capability. Although operations managers do not always need to know all the detailed science that lies behind the technologies they use, it is necessary to understand the implications of using alternative technologies. Chapter 8, *Process technology*, describes some of the more significant technologies which process materials, information and customers.

People make the processes work (Chapter 9)

Even after the products and services have been designed, the network configured, each site's layout determined and the process technology chosen, the operation cannot work until it is staffed. The people in any operation are the catalyst which makes the whole operation come alive. While the subject of this text is not human resources management as such, it is important to understand how the staff in the operation interact with its physical design. Chapter 9, *Job design and work organization*, examines how different approaches to designing people's jobs in operations influence the performance of the operation as a whole.

Summary answers to key questions

What is design in operations management?

- Design is the activity which shapes the physical form and purpose of both products and services and the processes which produce them. It is an activity which starts with a concept and ends in the translation of that concept into a specification of something which can be created.

- The overall purpose of the design activity is to meet the needs of customers, whether through the design of the products or services themselves, or through the design of the processes which will produce them.

What objectives should the design activity have?

- The design activity can be viewed as a transformation process in the same way as any other operation. It can therefore be judged in terms of its quality, speed, dependability, flexibility and cost.

- These objectives are more likely to be satisfied if the complementary activities of product or service design and process design are coordinated in some way.

- The design activity must also take account of environmental issues. These include examination of the source and suitability of materials, the sources and quantities of energy consumed, the amount and type of waste material, the life of the product itself, and the end-of-life state of the product.

How can design decisions be made?

- Design is a multi-stage process which moves from concept through to detailed specification.

- At each stage it is important to understand the design options and evaluate these in terms of their feasibility, acceptability and vulnerability.

- As the design activity progresses through its stages, uncertainty regarding the finished design is reduced. This makes it increasingly difficult to change previous decisions.

How does the design activity differ in different types of operation?

- The key characteristics of an operation which determine the nature of its design activity are the volume and variety of its output.

- An operation's position on the volume–variety continuum influences many aspects of its design activity, including the emphasis which is placed on either product/service design or process design, the location policy it chooses, the standardization of its products and services, its choice of process technology, the nature of its layout and flow, and the staff skills it requires.

What are 'process types'?

- Process types are general approaches to managing the transformation process and they depend on the volume and variety of an operation's output.

- In manufacturing, these process types are (in order of increasing volume and decreasing variety) project, jobbing, batch, mass and continuous processes.

- In service operations, although there is less consensus on the terminology, the terms often used (again in order of increasing volume and decreasing variety) are professional services, service shops and mass services.

Verenigde Bloemenveiling Aalsmeer (VBA) (United Flower Auctions), Aalsmeer, Holland

Standard 'trolleys' waiting in the 'sellers' section'

Photo courtesy of VBA

VBA is the largest flower auction operation in the world. It comprises two main parts. The first is the sellers' area known as the 'auction section' where flowers are received, held in cooled storage areas and auctioned. The second is the 'buyers' section' where around 300 buyers, exporters and wholesalers rent space to prepare flowers for shipment. Trucks leave Aalsmeer every working day with destinations (including airports) throughout Europe. On a typical day there are about 10 000 people working at the centre (1800 of whom work directly for VBA), together handling 17 million cut flowers and two million plants. This large and complex operation is held together by its information processing technology.

Flowers are extremely perishable, so dealing with them in such large quantities makes the speed, accuracy and dependability of the operation critical. During the evening and overnight, flowers are brought into the operation in standard containers which are subsequently handled in standard wheeled cages (there are over 124 000 of these 'trolleys' in circulation – *see* picture). Each lot of flowers is assigned a reference number, a quality inspection is made by VBA staff, and a description is entered on the 'delivery forms' attached to each

trolley. The trolleys are then held in cold storage until they are collected for the auctioning process the following morning.

The auction takes place every weekday in five separate halls, specialized by category of flower or plant. The largest flower auction hall has tiered desks for up to 500 buyers, each linked to the auction computer. Each buyer has an uninterrupted view of the flowers (which are automatically conveyed through the auction halls in their trolleys), and of the four auction price 'clocks' behind the auctioneers. Buyers can then choose the clock of their choice at any time using a selection switch. The auctioneer in charge of each clock may give brief information on the quality of a particular lot, relayed to the appropriate bidders' desk speakers, but most of the important information about the flowers is shown automatically on the clocks' displays (see picture). Flowers are sold by 'Dutch auction', whereby the clock, scaled 100 to 1 at its rim, is started by the auctioneer and moves rapidly downwards. The first bidder to press his desk button stops the clock and becomes the buyer of that lot. This type of bidding is particularly suitable for automation because only one bid needs to be recorded for each transaction. All the details are

An auction hall in the 'buyers' section' showing the auction clocks

recorded by computer and printed out on a 'distribution voucher' which is attached to the appropriate trolley. The whole bidding process, including the processing of the information, takes only a few seconds. The lots are then distributed on the trolleys to the appropriate packing or loading areas. For each buyer, the VBA computer prints an invoice for all the purchases made, which must be settled daily by bank letter of credit or by cash drawn at one of the four banks adjacent to the cashier's office.

The high levels of computerization and automation of material flow allow VBA to operate with very low costs (about 5 per cent of turnover), at high speed and dependability. Each of the 13 clocks handles about 1000 transactions per hour. Almost all business takes place between 7.00 am and

10.00 am so that fresh flowers can be in the shops as early as possible – by lunchtime in Holland, by early afternoon in London, Paris and Berlin, and by early morning the next day in New York.

Questions

1 Which of the five operations performance objectives (quality, speed, dependability, flexibility and cost) are the most important to build into the design of VBA's process, and why?

2 How does process technology help this operation to achieve its objectives?

3 Sketch the flow of flowers in the VBA operation. What do you think are the critical points in this flow?

Discussion questions

1 Explain how the good design of the products or services and processes of the following operations can support the five performance objectives:
   – a washing-machine manufacturer
   – a computer software house specializing in accountancy packages
   – a concert.

2 Why do you think product design and process design have been separate activities in many manufacturing organizations? Explain why this is changing.

3 Describe the activity of designing a new product or service of your choice in terms of the transformed and transforming resources, the activity and the outputs.

4 Discuss with someone who is involved in designing new products or services the problems involved.

5 The university catering manager is contemplating adding a take-away burger bar to the portfolio of outlets. Explain how the idea can be assessed.

6 Explain how the 'idea' of design might apply to the design of a 'home banking' service.

7 Explain the importance of the volume–variety dimension as a way of understanding operations and their approach to design.

8 Describe how the five performance objectives vary between:
   – a burger bar and a high-class restaurant
   – a high-volume car producer and a classic car restorer
   – a corner grocery store and a supermarket.

9 What do you think would be the key design issues to be faced when setting up a hairdressing salon?

10 Explain the relationship between variety and volume and describe why you are unlikely to find many high volume–high variety and low volume–low variety operations.

11 NYKKT are a high-quality consumer durable manufacturer of electronic sound and DVD equipment for the home market. Their engineers have devised a new DVD player which contains more features than any competitor product in the market. What problems do you think the users of such a product might have, and how can their views be taken into account during the design of the product?

12 What do you think are the differences between the design decisions faced by (a) a small up-market real estate agent selling exclusive properties to a small clientele, and (b) a new mass-market internet-based real estate agency?

13 An enterprising final year student at your university has set up an internet-based dating agency. What questions might you ask in order to evaluate the feasibility, acceptability and vulnerability inherent in the design of his or her website?

Notes on chapter

1 Sir Monty Finneston (1987) Address to the Department of Education and Science Conference, Loughborough University, UK, quoted *in* Norman, E., Riley J., Urry, S. and Whitacker, M. (1990) *Advanced Design and Technology*, Longman.

2 Source: *The Times*, 16 July 1993.

3 Sources: Wheatley, M. (1993/94) 'Boeing, Boeing', *Business Life*, Dec/Jan.

4 Garry Hamel, Chairman, Strategos (1998).

5 Source: *Community Innovations Survey*, EU, May (1999).

6 Most textbooks on financial analysis will describe the return on investment (ROI) criterion. For example, *see*

Cooke, S. and Slack, N. (1991) *Making Management Decisions* (2nd edn), Prentice Hall.

7 Horkeby, I. (1993) 'Environmentally Compatible Product and Process Development', *NAE Workshop on Corporate Environmental Stewardship*, 10–13 Aug, Woods Hole, Massachusetts, USA.

8 Fitzgerald, L., Johnston, R., Brignall, S., Silvestro, R. and Voss, C. (1991) *Performance Measurement in Service Industries*, CIMA.

9 Hayes, R.H. and Wheelwright, S.C. (1984) *Restoring our Competitive Edge*, John Wiley.

Selected further reading

Abernathy, W.J. (1976) 'Production Process Structure and Technological Change', *Design Sciences*, Vol 7, No 4.

Barker, T.B. (1994) *Quality by Experimental Design*, Marcel Dekker, New York.

Baxter, M. (1995) *Product Design*, Chapman and Hall.

Chaharbaghi, K. (1990) 'Using Simulation to Solve Design and Operational Problems', *International Journal of Operations and Production Management*, Vol 10, No 9.

Cooke, S. and Slack, N. (1991) *Making Management Decisions* (2nd edn), Prentice Hall.

Cross, N. (1984) *Developments in Design Methodology*, John Wiley.

Cross, N. (1989) *Engineering Design Methods*, John Wiley.

de Bono, E. (1970) *Lateral Thinking – A Textbook of Creativity*, Ward Lock Educational.

Design Council (1999) 'Are you Ready Now?: Design in the New Economy', *Design in Business*, Design Council.

Design Council (1999) 'Facts, Figures and Quotable Quotes', *Design in Britain* 2000.

Fox, J. (1993) *Quality Through Design: The Key to Successful Product Delivery*, McGraw-Hill.

Lorenz, C. (1990) *The Design Dimension*, Blackwell.

Love, D. and Barton, J. (1996) 'Evaluation of Design Decisions Through CIM and Simulation', *Integration Manufacturing Systems*, Vol 7, No 4.

Ramaswamy, R. (1996) *Design and Management of Service Processes*, Addison-Wesley Longman.

Rippinnes, H. (1999) 'Visualising success', *Manufacturing Engineering*, April.

Shostack, G.L. (1982) 'How to Design a Service', *European Journal of Marketing*, Vol 16, No 1.

Sparke, P. (1986) *An Introduction to Design and Culture in the Twentieth Century*, Allen and Unwin.

Walker, D. and Cross, N. (1983) *An Introduction to Design*, Open University Press.

Walsh, V., Roy, R., Bruce, M. and Potter, S. (1992) *Winning By Design, Technology, Product Design and International Competitiveness*, Blackwell.

Webb, A. (1994) *Managing Innovative Projects*, Chapman and Hall.

The design of products and services

Introduction

Products and services are usually the first thing which customers see of a company, so in addition to the intrinsic merit of its product and service designs, it is also the continual development of designs and the creation of totally new designs which help to shape an organization's competitive position. Operations managers do not always have the direct responsibility for product and service design, but they always have an indirect responsibility to provide the information and advice upon which successful product or service development depends. Figure 5.1 shows where this chapter fits into the overall operations design model. Remember, though, that there is an overlap between product/service design and process design, especially in the design of services.

Figure 5.1 **The design activities in operations management covered in this chapter**

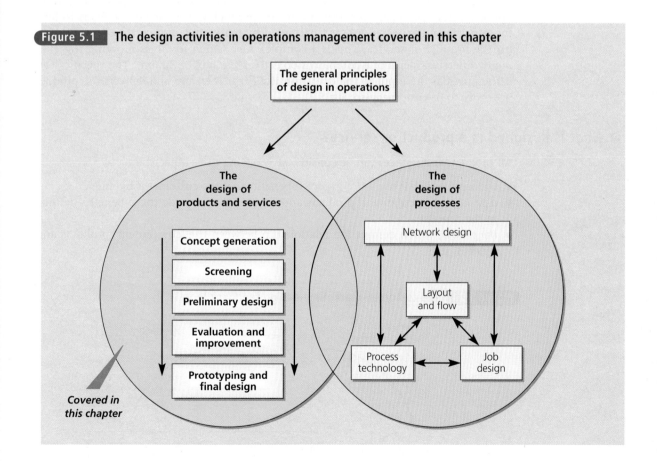

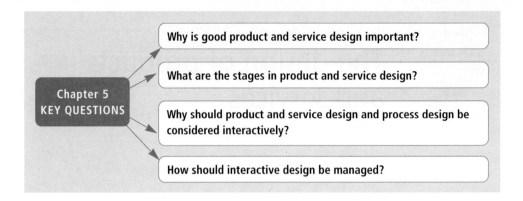

Chapter 5
KEY QUESTIONS

Why is good product and service design important?

What are the stages in product and service design?

Why should product and service design and process design be considered interactively?

How should interactive design be managed?

The competitive advantage of good design

The objective of designing products and services is to satisfy customers by meeting their actual or anticipated needs and expectations. This, in turn, enhances the competitiveness of the organization. Product and service design, therefore, can be seen as starting and ending with the customer. First, the task of marketing is to gather information from customers (and sometimes non-customers) in order to understand and identify their needs and expectations, and also to look for possible market opportunities. Following this, the task of the product and service designers is to take those needs and expectations, as interpreted by marketing, and create a specification for the product or service. This is a complex task which involves bringing together many different aspects of a company's objectives (*see* box on Braun). The specification is then used as the input to the operation itself which creates and delivers the product or service to its customers (*see* Fig. 5.2).

● What is designed in a product or service?

All products and services can be considered as having three aspects:

- *a concept*, which is the set of expected benefits that the customer is buying;
- *a package* of 'component' products and services that provide those benefits defined in the concept;
- *the process*, which defines the relationship between the 'component' products and services.

| Figure 5.2 | The customer–marketing–design feedback loop |

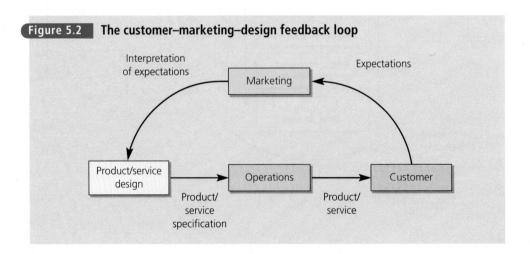

Design principles at Braun AG and the new Braun Multimix[1]

Braun, the leading European manufacturer of small appliances, is renowned for the innovative and functional designs of its products (over 60 per cent of the company's sales are of products which were launched within the last five years). The company has 150 of its products in the permanent collection of the Centre Pompidou in Paris and has 40 products on exhibition at the New York Museum of Modern Art. But Braun's design principles go beyond the aesthetic. Its designers follow their 'Ten principles of good design'. We will describe the design of the Braun Multimix, the design brief of which was 'to combine three specialist kitchen appliances (blender, food processor, kitchen machine) in such a way that the new single product performs at least as well in each of the applications as the best equivalent specialized product'.

Braun's 10 industrial design principles applied to the Multimix

1 *Usefulness*. The functionality of a product is the central reason for its existence. It was decided to align the motor, gearing and attachments in a single vertical direction (competitive products have horizontal motor and vertical attachments, requiring a complex gearbox). The 'form' of the product then follows its 'function'.

2 *Quality*. Braun designers emphasize four aspects of quality. First, its *versatility* provides a full range of tasks required in cooking: mixing, blending, kneading and chopping. Second, the high mechanical efficiency of the appliance and the seven speed settings provide *high performance* across the range of tasks. Third, many unique *safety features* have been included to prevent contact with moving parts and to prevent accidents. Fourth, the application of *advanced process technology* has enabled many integrated elements to be incorporated in a single moulding. A complex production moulding tool was developed to produce two housings in one injection moulding step.

3 *Ease of use*. Great emphasis was placed on 'human engineering' to ensure that the Multimix is convenient, comfortable to use and easy to clean.

4 *Simplicity*. Braun engineers believe in achieving maximum results with minimum means: what is relevant is stressed, what is superfluous is omitted.

5 *Clarity*. Particular emphasis is placed on eliminating the need for complex instructions: the Multimix controls 'speak for themselves'. For example, insertion of the attachments automatically sets the appropriate speed range of the drive.

6 *Order*. All details of a product should have a logical, meaningful place with nothing arbitrary or coincidental.

7 *Naturalness*. Braun designers strive to avoid any forced, contrived, or artificial decorative elements. Braun refers to a principle of 'understatement and modesty'.

8 *Aesthetics*. Although aesthetic quality is not a primary objective of the Braun designers during the development process, it is achieved through attention to detail and the quest for order and naturalness.

9 *Innovation*. Braun is committed to achieving long-lasting appeal in its designs, so innovations are carefully developed and brought together for new appliances such as the Multimix.

10 *Truthfulness*. A principle followed by Braun is that 'only honest design can be good design', so any attempt to play on people's emotions and weaknesses is avoided.

Questions

1 Braun is proud of its success in aesthetic design. What benefit do you think this gives the company with the domestic appliance buying public?

2 Braun's ten industrial design principles are applied above to a domestic appliance. How do you think they might change if they were applied to an industrial product such as a machine tool?

3 Pick a service with which you are familiar in an educational operation (such as your university, school or college) and evaluate it against Braun's ten principles. Which of these ten principles do you think were the most useful in making your evaluation?

● Customers buy 'concepts'

When customers make a purchase, they are not simply buying a product or service; they are buying a set of expected benefits to meet their needs and expectations. This is known as the concept of the product or service. For example, when customers buy a washing machine, they are purchasing a set of expected benefits which might include:

- an attractive metal box,
- that will fit in a conventional kitchen space,
- and will provide the means of cleaning clothes,
- over a long period of time,
- in the comfort of the customer's own home.

Similarly, a restaurant meal is purchased to provide us with more than the satisfaction of filling our stomachs. The expected benefits of the purchase include:

- an attractive environment,
- in which to consume a well cooked and presented meal,
- in a relaxing atmosphere.

In both cases the set of expected benefits is referred to as the *product* or *service concept* – that is, the overall intention of the product or service as seen from the customer's perspective. The concept is not a statement of the physical bits and pieces that we buy; rather it is the way that the customers, and hopefully also the organization, its staff and shareholders, perceive the benefits of the product or service.

The design of the British Airways first-class seating arrangement was the result of a fundamental re-think of the concept of first-class air travel

Photo courtesy of British Airways

● Concepts comprise a package of products and services

Normally the word product implies a tangible physical object, such as a washing machine or a watch, and the word 'service' implies a more intangible experience, such as an evening at a restaurant or a nightclub. In fact, as we discussed in Chapter 1, most, if not all, operations produce a combination of products *and* services. The restaurant meal includes:

Design is important, even in the most commonplace products. Here are two contrasting examples of how design can affect the humble glass bottle.

Exploding beer bottles

Even a beer bottle can become a killer when badly designed. In China one of the world's largest beer producers, with an annual output of around 50 billion bottles – thousands are injured or blinded every year by exploding beer bottles. Although official statistics show about 20 fatalities from beer bottle explosions every year, other estimates put the figure as high as 100. The problem lies in the design of the bottle which creates points of weakness in the material and allows the bottom to fly off as pressure rises inside. Bottled beer that is exported has to conform to different and more rigorous standards. Even so, they are supposed to be taken out of circulation after two years.

Delivering a better design

Doorstep delivery on a daily basis is still the means by which most milk is sold in the UK. Traditionally this has been in returnable glass bottles, still the most environmentally friendly packaging for milk. For 30 years the design of the standard milk bottle remained unchanged. Yet the design was far from perfect. Its parallel sides were not always easy to grip securely when wet. Consumer research showed that poor 'gripability' was a major concern for many customers. Also, when transported by crate, in the traditionally electric-powered milk delivery vehicle, they made a noise which was not altogether welcome early in the morning. The new bottle has a slight shoulder moulded into its shape which makes it easier and safer to handle. This new shape also means that the bottle sits 'tighter' in its crate – quieter as well as safer. As a further improvement, a snap-on plastic cap is supplied to customers so that the milk can be stored on its side.

- products such as 'food' and 'drink';
- services such as 'the delivery of the food to the table' and 'the attentions of the waiter or waitress'.

Similarly, the purchase of the washing machine includes:

- the product, that is 'the washing machine itself';
- services such as 'warranties', 'after-sales services' and 'the services of the person selling the machine'.

This collection of products and services is usually referred to as the *package* that customers buy. Some of the products or services in the package are *core*, that is they are fundamental to the purchase and could not be removed without destroying the nature of the package. Other parts will serve to enhance the core. These are *supporting* goods and services. In the case of the washing machine, the attractive box and guarantees are supporting goods and services. The core good is the machine itself. At the restaurant, the meal itself is the core. Its provision and preparation are important but not absolutely necessary (in some restaurants you might serve and even cook the meal yourself).

By changing the core, or adding or subtracting supporting goods and services, organizations can provide different packages, and in so doing design quite different products or services. For instance, a washing machine could be built to a smaller size, supporting a concept of a machine for the 'smaller kitchen'. Alternatively, it could be provided without after-sales support and guarantees as an 'economical purchase'. The restaurant may just provide you with the food but you may have to collect it yourself – the 'self-service' concept. Alternatively, you may even have to select the raw food yourself and cook it on burners at your own table.

The relationship between components defines the processes

The package of components which makes up a product, service or process are the 'ingredients' of the design. To make them into a final design they need to be connected in some way by having the relationship between them formalized. So, in the restaurant it is necessary to map the sequence of activities which customers will experience (entry, seating, menu, drinks orders, etc.). Also, the other processes essential to the service need to be defined, such as food preparation (ordering, receiving, quality check, washing, etc.) and menu design (customer data, chef's team meeting, printer selection, etc.). Each of these processes is an arrangement which defines the relationship between each 'component' activity. In the same way, the washing machine's package of components is connected formally by their positioning relative to each other. Their relationships define how each part of the machine operates.

In each case, the process inherent in the design of the product or service is the mechanism by which it is able to perform its function and fulfil the original concept. Often this 'mechanism' is literally how moving parts relate to each other, whether they be the moving parts of the washing machine or the 'moving' activities in the restaurant. Sometimes nothing actually moves – the process is in the connection of the component parts, as in the design of an electronic circuit. At other times it is the relative positioning of the component parts, as in the outer casing of the washing machine, which it is necessary to define (to determine the aesthetic appearance of the product). Always, though, it is the relationship between components in the design package which is being decided.

Dyson appliances sweep ahead

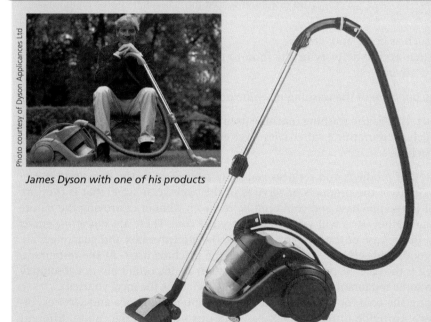

James Dyson with one of his products

James Dyson (pictured above) has revolutionized the vacuum cleaner industry. His approach to the design, manufacture and servicing of domestic appliances has brought him to the point where sales have eclipsed those of his main competitors. It all began when Dyson became frustrated with the performance of his own vacuum cleaner.

'The bag in the cleaner was empty, but the pores were clogged. A similar thing had been happening to the air filter in the spray-finishing room of a company where I had been working. We finally found the solution to the problem – a cyclone tower which removed the particles by centrifugal force.'

He started experimenting with the same idea applied to the domestic vacuum cleaner. Five thousand prototypes later he had a working design, since praised for its 'uniqueness and functionality'. However, existing vacuum cleaner manufacturers were not as impressed – two rejected the design outright. So Dyson set up his own factory which now outsells those two rivals by a margin of over 2 to 1. The aesthetics and functionality of the design help to keep sales growing in spite of a higher retail price. He also emphasizes customer service. Dyson will pick up a broken machine from a customer's home, repair it and deliver it back within a few days. He hires mainly young graduates who have 'fresh ideas, enthusiasm and energy'.

'Good design,' he says, 'is about looking at everyday things with new eyes and working out how they can be made better. It's about challenging existing technology.'

The production line at Dyson Appliances Ltd

Questions

1 What do you think makes 'good design' in markets such as the domestic appliances market?
2 Why do you think the two major vacuum cleaner manufacturers rejected Dyson's ideas?
3 How do you think Dyson's approaches to product design, service and manufacturing help each other?

The stages of design – from concept to specification

The outcome of the activity of design is a fully detailed specification of the product or service. The specification will require the collection of information which fully defines the product or service, namely:

● its overall concept (specifying the form, function and overall purpose of the design and the benefits it will provide);
● its package (specifying the collection of individual component products and services which are required to provide and support the concept);
● the process by which the design will fulfil its concept (the relationship between the component products and services, which forms the 'mechanism' of the design).

To get to this point, the design activity must pass through several stages. These form an approximate sequence, although in practice designers will often recycle or backtrack

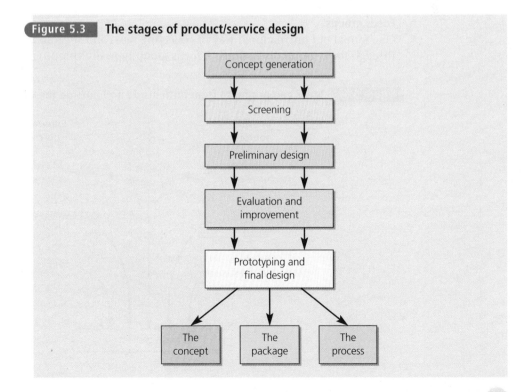

Figure 5.3 **The stages of product/service design**

through the stages. We will describe them in the order in which they usually occur, as shown in Figure 5.3.

The *concept generation stage* starts with an idea for a product or service. These ideas need to be formalized by translating them into a product or service concept. The concepts are then *screened* by different parts of the organization to try to ensure that, in broad terms, they will be a sensible addition to its product/service portfolio. The outcome of these first two stages is an agreed and acceptable product/service concept. The agreed concept has then to be turned into a *preliminary design* of the package and the process. This preliminary design then goes through a stage of *evaluation and improvement* to see if the concept can be served better, more cheaply or more easily. An agreed design can then be subjected to *prototyping and final design*. The outcome of this stage is a fully developed specification of the product or service.

Concept generation

The ideas for new product or service concepts can come from sources outside the organization, such as customers or competitors, and from sources within the organization, such as staff (for example, from sales staff and front-of-house staff) or from the R&D department (*see* Fig. 5.4).

● Ideas from customers

Marketing is responsible for keeping an eye and ear on the marketplace in order to identify new opportunities and possible products or services that might be appropriate. There are many market research tools for gathering data from customers in a formal and structured way, including questionnaires and interviews. These techniques, however, usually tend to be structured in such a way as only to test out ideas or check products or services against predetermined criteria. Listening to the customer, in a less structured way, is sometimes seen as a better means of generating new ideas.[3]

Focus groups
One formal but unstructured way of collecting ideas and suggestions from customers is through focus group discussions. A focus group typically comprises seven to 10 partici-

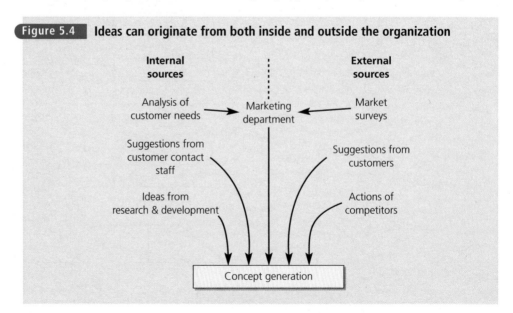

Figure 5.4   **Ideas can originate from both inside and outside the organization**

Sasco Overhead Projection Systems

Market research to understand the performance of products and services from a user's point of view is an important stage in design. Here, Sasco extensively researched their overhead projectors and identified the need to make controls clearer and easier to use. The use of focus groups and a value engineering exercise resulted in the new product above which incorporates all customers' suggestions at a significantly lower cost

pants who are unfamiliar with each other but who have been selected because they have certain characteristics in common that relate to the particular topic of the focus group.[4] Participants are invited to 'discuss' or 'share ideas with others'. The concept researcher tries to create a permissive environment that nurtures different perceptions and points of view, without pressurizing participants. The group discussion is conducted several times with similar types of participants in order to identify trends and patterns in perceptions. Careful and systematic analysis of the discussions provides clues and insights into product or service opportunities.

Listening to customers

Many ideas may come from customers on a day-to-day basis. They may write to complain about a particular product or service, or make suggestions for its improvement. Ideas may also come in the form of suggestions to staff during the purchase of the product or delivery of the service. Unfortunately, some staff may not see the passing on of this information as an important role; there may not even be the mechanisms in place to facilitate it. Although some organizations do have implicit mechanisms to capture ideas in a structured and formal way, few have internal mechanisms for passing on good ideas from customers.

● Ideas from competitor activity

Many organizations keep a sharp eye on the activities of their competitors. A new idea translated into a saleable concept, package and process may give a competitor an edge in the marketplace, even if it is only a temporary one. Competing organizations will then have to decide to follow the actions of the competitor with a similar product or service, or alternatively to come up with a somewhat different idea that may minimize or even reverse the competitor's lead.

Ideas from staff

Just one step away from the customers are the people who have to deal directly with them. The contact worker in a service organization or the salesperson in a product-oriented organization could meet customers every day. These staff may have good ideas about what customers like and do not like. They may have gathered suggestions from customers or have ideas of their own as to how products or services could be developed to meet the needs of their customers more effectively, or how a gap could be filled in the product or service range.

Ideas from research and development

One formal function found in many product-based organizations (but as yet few service-based organizations) is research and development (R&D). As its name implies, its role is twofold. Research usually means attempting to develop new knowledge and ideas in order to solve a particular problem or to grasp an opportunity. Development is the attempt to try to utilize and operationalize the ideas that come from research. In this chapter we are mainly concerned with the 'development' part of R&D – for example, exploiting new ideas that might be afforded by new materials such as thermoplastics or new technologies such as satellite communications. Different industries rely on R&D for their new product or service ideas to different extents.

Reverse engineering

'Reverse engineering' is taking apart a product to understand how a competing organization has made it. Closely analysing exactly what constitutes a competitor's design and how the product has been produced can help to isolate the key features of the design which are worth emulating. As a result, a company may amend and incorporate the key features in some way. Alternatively, it might apply to use, under licence, the part of the product that seems to be providing the difference. One example is the so-called 'widget' that is incorporated into the bottom of some canned beers. This device releases gas on opening to create a creamy head on the beer, thus giving the texture and appearance of draught beer. It is a design idea which was soon incorporated into many canned beers after its initial introduction.

Some aspects of services may be more difficult to reverse engineer (especially back-office services) as they are less transparent to competitors. However, by consumer testing a service, it may be possible to make educated guesses about how it has been created. Many service organizations employ 'testers' to check out the services provided by competitors. Just as supermarkets regularly check the prices displayed by rival supermarkets, so too do they investigate new services, such as delivery services, cash-back options, telephone ordering and packing services to see if they might be suitable for development or reproduction.

From idea to concept

Ideas are not the same as concepts. In fact, ideas need to be transformed into concepts so that they can be evaluated and then 'operationalized' by the organization. Concepts are different from ideas in that they are clear statements that both encapsulate the idea and indicate the overall form, function, purpose and benefits of the idea. The concept should be simple to communicate so that everyone in the organization can understand it, make it and sell it. Figure 5.5 illustrates two examples of how ideas have been enriched to become concepts. The broad idea of an adventure holiday is further defined to include its duration, purpose, residential nature and target market. The inexpensive telephone idea is defined in terms of its price, functionality and physical appearance.

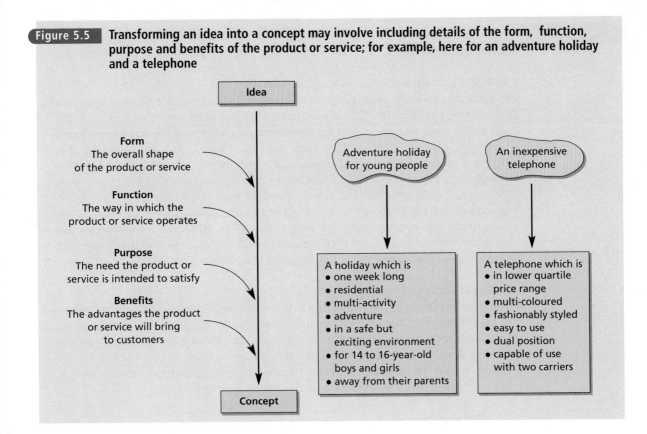

Figure 5.5 Transforming an idea into a concept may involve including details of the form, function, purpose and benefits of the product or service; for example, here for an adventure holiday and a telephone

Idea

Form
The overall shape of the product or service

Function
The way in which the product or service operates

Purpose
The need the product or service is intended to satisfy

Benefits
The advantages the product or service will bring to customers

Concept

Adventure holiday for young people

A holiday which is
- one week long
- residential
- multi-activity
- adventure
- in a safe but exciting environment
- for 14 to 16-year-old boys and girls
- away from their parents

An inexpensive telephone

A telephone which is
- in lower quartile price range
- multi-coloured
- fashionably styled
- easy to use
- dual position
- capable of use with two carriers

Concept screening

Not all concepts which are generated will necessarily be capable of further development into products and services. Designers need to be selective as to which concepts they progress to the point of designing the preliminary aspects of the package and processes. The purpose of the concept-screening stage is to take the flow of concepts emerging from the organization and evaluate them for their feasibility, acceptability and 'vulnerability' or risk (*see* Chapter 4). Concepts may have to pass through many different screens, and several functions might be involved (for example, marketing, operations and finance). Table 5.1 gives typical feasibility, acceptability and vulnerability questions for each of these three functional filters.

Table 5.1 Some typical evaluation questions for marketing, operations and finance

Evaluation criteria	Marketing	Operations	Finance
Feasibility	Is the market likely to be big enough?	Do we have the capabilities to produce it?	Do we have access to sufficient finance to develop and launch it?
Acceptability	How much market share could it gain?	How much will we have to reorganize our activities to produce it?	How much financial return will there be on our investment?
Vulnerability	What is the risk of it failing in the marketplace?	What is the risk of us being unable to product it acceptably?	How much money could we lose if things do not go to plan?

Figure 5.6 illustrates how screening might be applied for the telephone example described previously.

Competitor analysis

In this case, five competitor products have been chosen and evaluated against a number of criteria (their handling characteristics, their aesthetic styling, their robustness of construction, and the ease with which they can be fixed in different positions). However, each of these criteria is not of equal importance. In this case, styling is given a weight of four times, and handling two times, that of robustness and fixing. Each of the competitor products is evaluated by giving it a score out of 10 (where 1 indicates poor performance and 10 indicates exceptionally good performance). An indication of overall product performance can then be obtained by calculating the weighted total for each product (i.e. the score for each criterion multiplied by the weight and then summed across the row). In addition to product performance, the price of each competitor product is also obtained.

Price–performance targeting

The information from the competitor analysis now allows each competitor product to be evaluated on a price–performance graph as illustrated. This not only allows for comparison between competitor products, but more importantly allows the product designers to identify the target area for the new telephone. In Figure 5.6 it has been decided to design a product for a £30 'price point' but having performance characteristics superior to anything in the close price range.

Financial analysis

The company is now in a position to check the financial feasibility of the proposed new product. This is done in two ways: first, a 'top-down' or *price minus* approach is used to work backwards from the selling price. Typically, the retailer's margin and distribution margin are taken off the selling price in order to determine the price at which the telephone manufacturer must be able to sell the product, in order to meet the proposed selling price. Subtracting the retailer's margin and the distribution margin from the final selling price indicates that the telephone manufacturing company must be able to sell the product for £30 – £15 – £4 = £11, if the product is to be sold at its price point.

The other approach to costing, the 'bottom-up' or *cost plus* approach, can then be used. This involves starting from zero and adding the manufacturing costs: in this case, material costs plus parts manufacturing costs plus assembly costs. This indicates that the cost of producing the telephone will be £5 + £2.50 + £2 = £9.50. This leaves a manufacturer's profit of £1.50. The issue for the company then is whether this profit is sufficient to give it a return on its investment in such things as design costs, extra manufacturing equipment and market launch costs. If not, then it must reconsider its target area on the price–performance graph and/or revisit its assumptions of how it is going to make the product. This may mean changing the design in order to reduce material costs or parts manufacturing costs or assembly costs.

Figure 5.6 **Analysis of competitor products or services allows the desired price–performance area to be targeted which, in turn, enables intial financial analysis**

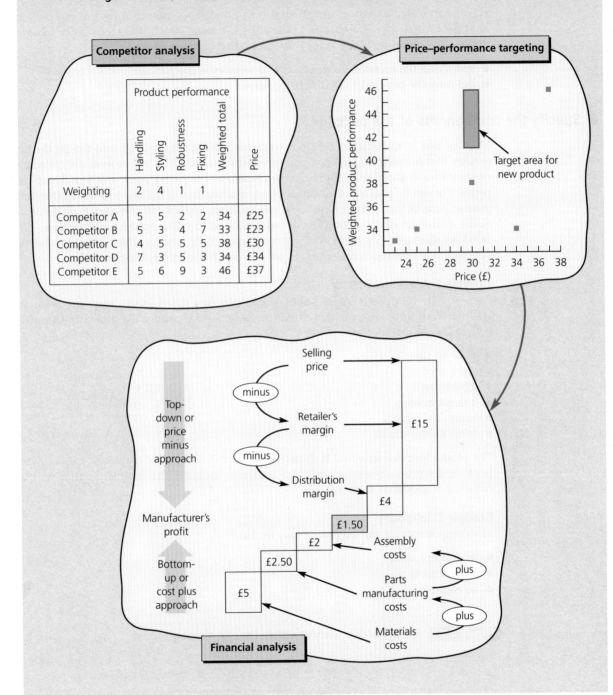

Preliminary design

Having generated a product or service concept that is acceptable to the various parts of an organization, an organization tackles the next stage, which is to create a preliminary design. The objective of this stage is to have a first attempt at:

- specifying the component products and services in the *package*;
- defining the *processes* to create the package.

● Specify the components of the package

The first task in this stage of design is to define exactly what will go into the product or service: that is, specifying the components of the package. This will require the collection of information about such things as the *constituent component parts* which make up the product or service package, *the product/service structure*, that is the order in which the component parts of the package have to be put together, and the *bill of materials* (BOM), that is the quantities of each component part required to make up the total package. The BOM, in particular, is a method of defining products or services which is used widely in other areas of operations management activity (*see*, for example, Chapter 14).

Example 1: Adventure holiday
Each activity on the adventure holiday can be broken down in this way. For example, the materials and equipment needed for each child to undertake the rifle-shooting activity might include:

- a .22 air rifle
- some shot
- a backboard
- a target holder
- some card targets
- some model targets

The product/service structure is shown in Figure 5.7. The bill of materials, which incorporates the product/service structure and also includes the quantities that will be required, is shown in Table 5.2.

Example 2: Telephone
The components for the telephone may include:

- a handset casing
- a base casing
- an earpiece

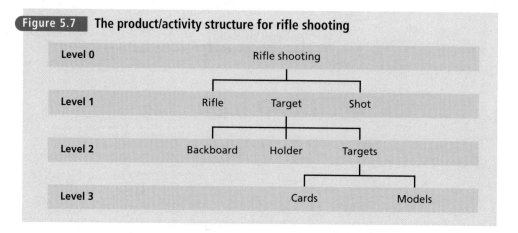

| Figure 5.7 | **The product/activity structure for rifle shooting** |

Level 0 — Rifle shooting
Level 1 — Rifle, Target, Shot
Level 2 — Backboard, Holder, Targets
Level 3 — Cards, Models

Table 5.2 Bill of materials for the rifle-shooting activity

Level 0	Level 1	Level 2	Level 3	Quantity
Rifle-shooting activity				
	Rifle			1
	Shot			50
	Target			
		Blackboard		1
		Holder		1
		Targets		
			Cards	10
			Models	5

- a mouthpiece
- a cord
- an input lead
- electronic circuitry
- a plug.

The product structure shows how these components fit together to make the telephone (*see* Fig. 5.8). The bill of materials, which incorporates the product/service structure and also includes the quantities which will be required, is shown in Table 5.3.

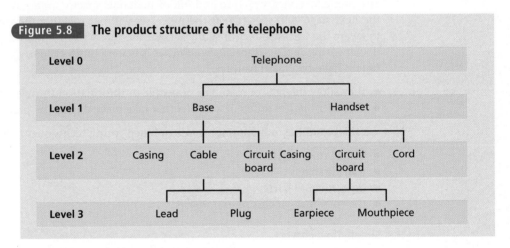

Figure 5.8   The product structure of the telephone

Table 5.3 Bill of materials for the telephone

Level 0	Level 1	Level 2	Level 3	Quantity
Telephone				
	Base			1
		Casing		1
		Cable		1
			Lead	1
			Plug	1
		Circuit board		1
	Handset			1
		Casing		1
		Circuit board		1
			Earpiece	1
			Mouthpiece	1
		Cord		1

Photo courtesy of Jaguar

At some stages in the design process, new products and services are kept secret so as not to detract from their market launch. This is why the vehicle on the left is disguised during testing. At other times, companies may deliberately wish to expose their design ideas to public comment. The 'concept car' on the right, is a design exercise which 'tests out' the designers' ideas

● Define the processes to create the package

The product/service structure and bill of materials specify *what* has to be put together; the next stage is to specify *how* the processes will put together the various components to create the final product or service. There are many techniques which can be used for documenting processes (or *blueprinting*, as it is sometimes called). However, all the techniques have two main features:[5]

- they show the *flow* of materials or people or information through the operation;
- they identify the different *activities* that take place during the process.

We shall examine four common types of blueprinting techniques here:

- simple flow charts
- routing sheets
- flow process charts
- the customer-processing framework.

Simple flow charts
Simple flow charts are used to identify the main elements of a process. They frequently include symbols which originated in computer flow charting and which identify the key decisions in the process and the implications of each decision. Figure 5.9 shows a flow chart which indicates the flow of information in the customer enquiries bureau of an electricity utility company.

Routing sheets
Routing sheets (also known as operations process charts) provide more information about the activities involved in the process, including a description of the activity and the tools or equipment needed. Part of a routing sheet for the assembly of the telephone is shown in Figure 5.10.

Flow process chart
The most commonly used chart for documenting processes in operations management is the flow process chart. This type of chart, as well as documenting the flow and the

130 Part Two • Design

Figure 5.9 **Information flow chart for the customer enquiries bureau of a utility company**

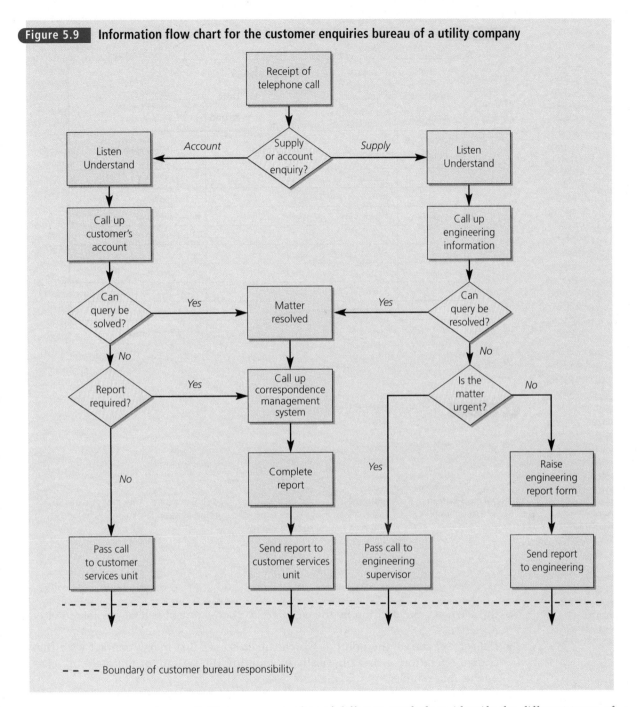

various activities, uses a number of different symbols to identify the different types of activities (*see* Fig. 5.11).

Flow process charts permit a more detailed design and evaluation of a design. Figure 5.12 shows part of a flow process chart for one day on an adventure holiday.

Customer-processing framework

The customer-processing framework[6] is a charting method devised specifically for customer flows. It identifies some of the key activities that may occur in 'processing' customers through an operation, including:

Figure 5.10 Routing sheet for the telephone

Route sheet

Item ....Telephone h1209....   **Date** ....1 / 5 / 97....

Item No. ....# 1209 (h)....   **Issued by** ....

Operation number	Operation description	Equipment
1	Assemble earpiece and mouthpiece	Jig #24/35A
2	Fix to lower casing	Jig #24/122
3	Insert and fix cord	Wire stripper (type #22)
		and screwholder/driver
4	Assemble upper casing	– –
5	Align and seal	Jig #24/490 and polysege
6	Light and vibration test	Qualitest 12 (main #488)
		and vibration board

Figure 5.11 Flow process chart sysmbols

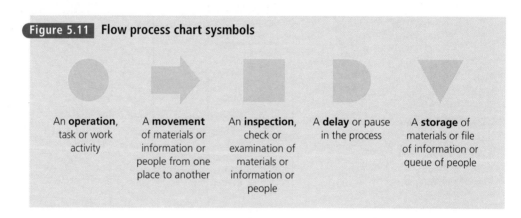

An **operation**, task or work activity

A **movement** of materials or information or people from one place to another

An **inspection**, check or examination of materials or information or people

A **delay** or pause in the process

A **storage** of materials or file of information or queue of people

- the *selection* – the decision by the customer to choose one of several possible service operations;
- the *point of entry* – the point at which the customer first makes contact with the chosen operation, either physically by entering the system, or remotely by telephone, for example;
- the *response time* – the time a customer has to wait for the system to respond;
- the *point of impact* – the moment at which the service worker starts to deal with the customer;
- the *delivery* – the part of the process which delivers the core service to the customer;
- the *point of departure* – the point at which the customer leaves the service process;
- the *follow-up* – the activities of the service staff to check on the customer after the completion of the service.

Figure 5.13 illustrates these key stages in the design of a hospital's Accident and Emergency department. When examined in more detail, most service operations comprise several customer-processing sequences which may be in series and/or in parallel with each other. The number of processes and the interrelationships between them are indications of the scale and complexity of the operations task.

Figure 5.12 **Flow process chart for one day on an adventure holiday**

Flow process chart

| Activity | A day on the adventure holiday | | Location | Perinong |

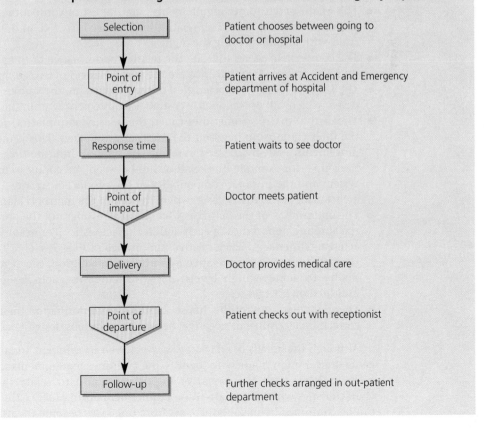

	Description of element					
1	Get up	●	➡	D	■	▽
2	Go to washroom	●	➡	D	■	▽
3	Wash, brush teeth	●	➡	D	■	▽
4	Return to bedroom	●	➡	D	■	▽
5	Dress	●	➡	D	■	▽
6	Go to dining room	●	➡	D	■	▽
7	Await serving	●	➡	D	■	▽
8	Eat	●	➡	D	■	▽
9	Go to rifle range	●	➡	D	■	▽
10	Await instructor and equipment	●	➡	D	■	▽
11	Check equipment	●	➡	D	■	▽
12	Rifle shooting	●	➡	D	■	▽

Figure 5.13 **Key stages as shown on a customer-processing framework diagram for a patient receiving treatment in an Accident and Emergency department**

| Selection | Patient chooses between going to doctor or hospital |

| Point of entry | Patient arrives at Accident and Emergency department of hospital |

| Response time | Patient waits to see doctor |

| Point of impact | Doctor meets patient |

| Delivery | Doctor provides medical care |

| Point of departure | Patient checks out with receptionist |

| Follow-up | Further checks arranged in out-patient department |

Design evaluation and improvement

The purpose of this stage in the design activity is to take the preliminary design and see if it can be improved before the product or service is tested in the market. There are a number of techniques that can be employed at this stage to evaluate and improve the preliminary design. Here we treat three which have proved particularly useful:

- Quality function deployment (QFD)
- Value engineering (VE)
- Taguchi methods.

● Quality function deployment

The key purpose of quality function deployment is to try to ensure that the eventual design of a product or service actually meets the needs of its customers. Customers may not have been considered explicitly since the concept generation stage, and therefore it is appropriate to check that what is being proposed for the design of the product or service will meet their needs.

Quality function deployment (QFD) is a technique that was developed in Japan at Mitsubishi's Kobe shipyard and used extensively by Toyota, the motor vehicle manufacturer, and its suppliers. It is also known as the 'house of quality' (because of its shape) and the 'voice of the customer' (because of its purpose). The technique tries to capture *what* the customer needs and *how* it might be achieved.[7]

Figure 5.14 shows an example of quality function deployment being used in the design of a new information system product.[8] The QFD matrix is a formal articulation of how the company sees the relationship between the requirements of the customer (the *whats*) and the design characteristics of the new product (the *hows*). The matrix contains various sections, as explained below:

- The *whats*, or 'customer requirements', are the list of competitive factors which customers find significant. Their relative importance is scored, in this case on a 10-point scale, with *accurate* scoring the highest.
- The competitive scores indicate the relative performance of the product, in this case on a 1 to 5 scale. Also indicated are the performances of two competitor products.
- The *hows*, or 'design characteristics' of the product, are the various 'dimensions' of the design which will operationalize customer requirements within the product or service.
- The central matrix (sometimes called the relationship matrix) represents a view of the interrelationship between the *whats* and the *hows*. This is often based on value judgements made by the design team. The symbols indicate the strength of the relationship – for example, the relationship between the ability to link remotely to the system and the intranet compatibility of the product is strong. All the relationships are studied, but in many cases, where the cell of the matrix is blank, there is none.
- The bottom box of the matrix is a technical assessment of the product. This contains the absolute importance of each design characteristic. [For example, the design characteristic 'interfaces' has a relative importance of $(9 \times 5) + (1 \times 9) = 54$]. This is also translated into a ranked relative importance. In addition, the degree of technical difficulty to achieve high levels of performance in each design characteristic is indicated on a 1 to 5 scale.
- The triangular 'roof' of the 'house' captures any information the team has about the correlations (positive or negative) between the various design characteristics.

Although the details of QFD may vary between its different variants, the principle is generally common, namely to identify the customer requirements for a product or service (together with their relative importance) and to relate them to the design characteristics which translate those requirements into practice. In fact, this principle can be continued by making the *hows* from one stage become the *whats* of the next (*see*

Figure 5.14 A QFD matrix for an information system product

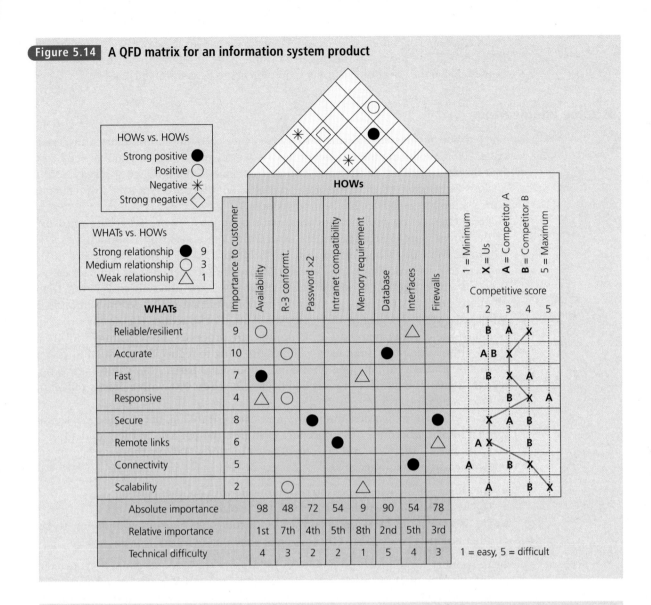

HOWs vs. HOWs
- Strong positive ●
- Positive ○
- Negative ✳
- Strong negative ◇

WHATs vs. HOWs
- Strong relationship ● 9
- Medium relationship ○ 3
- Weak relationship △ 1

WHATs	Importance to customer	Availability	R-3 conformt.	Password x2	Intranet compatibility	Memory requirement	Database	Interfaces	Firewalls	Competitive score
Reliable/resilient	9	○						△		B A X
Accurate	10		○				●			A B X
Fast	7	●				△				B X A
Responsive	4	△	○							B X A
Secure	8			●					●	X A B
Remote links	6				●			△		A X B
Connectivity	5							●		A B X
Scalability	2		○			△				A B X
Absolute importance		98	48	72	54	9	90	54	78	
Relative importance		1st	7th	4th	5th	8th	2nd	5th	3rd	
Technical difficulty		4	3	2	2	1	5	4	3	1 = easy, 5 = difficult

Competitive score legend:
1 = Minimum
X = Us
A = Competitor A
B = Competitor B
5 = Maximum

Figure 5.15 QFD matrices can be linked with the 'hows' of one matrix forming the 'whats' of the next

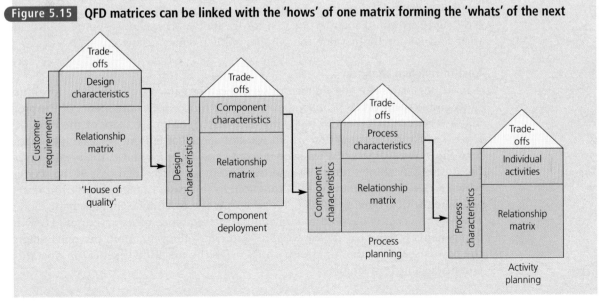

Fig. 5.15). Some experienced users of QFD have up to four linked matrices in this way. If engineering or process trade-offs need to be made at a later stage, the interrelated houses enable the effect on customer requirements to be determined.

Value engineering

The purpose of value engineering is to try to reduce costs, and prevent any unnecessary costs, before producing the product or service. Simply put, it tries to eliminate any costs that do not contribute to the value and performance of the product or service. (Value analysis is the name given to the same process when it is concerned with cost reduction after the product or service has been introduced.)

Value-engineering programmes are usually conducted by project teams consisting of designers, purchasing specialists, operations managers and financial analysts. Pareto analysis (*see* Chapters 12 and 18) is often used to identify the parts of the package that are worthy of most attention. The chosen elements of the package are then subject to rigorous scrutiny. The team analyses the function and cost of those elements and tries to find any similar components that could do the same job at lower cost. More specifically, the team would attempt to reduce the number of components, use cheaper materials and simplify the processes. For example, Motorola, the electronics manufacturer, used value engineering to reduce the production cost of its mobile phones. Initially one phone had about 3200 parts. After value engineering its new model, the number of parts had been reduced to 400, with a drastic reduction in processing time also.

Value engineering requires innovative and critical thinking, but it is also carried out using a formal procedure. The procedure examines the purpose of the product or service, its basic functions and its secondary functions. Taking the example of the telephone used previously:

- The *purpose* of the telephone is to communicate with another person.
- The *basic functions* are to hear and speak to the other person.
- The *secondary functions* are to connect with the other person's equipment, to key other numbers and to store other people's telephone numbers.

Team members would then propose ways to improve the secondary functions by combining, revising or eliminating them. For example, the earpiece and mouthpiece could be incorporated into the base casing, eliminating the need for a handset, or the circuitry and dial pad could be incorporated into the handset, eliminating the need for a base. All ideas would then be checked for feasibility, acceptability, vulnerability and their contribution to the value and purpose of the product or service.

Cost-to-function analyses

A revealing analysis of any product or service can be gained by examining how much of its cost is spent on its primary and secondary functions. Components of the product or service which seem to be taking up a disproportionate share of the total cost when related to their function would warrant special attention. For example, Figure 5.16 shows the features of a washing machine and Table 5.4 shows the breakdown of the washing machine's functions and the percentage of the total cost of the product which is devoted to achieving each function. In this case, 77.09 per cent of its cost is associated with achieving its basic function.[9] As the machine is an automatic model, much of the cost is devoted to controlling the sequence of its activities. After the components which provide the washing and controlling function, the remainder of the cost is spent on the functions which make the machine practical in operation and marketable to customers.

Figure 5.16 **Main components of an automatic washing machine**

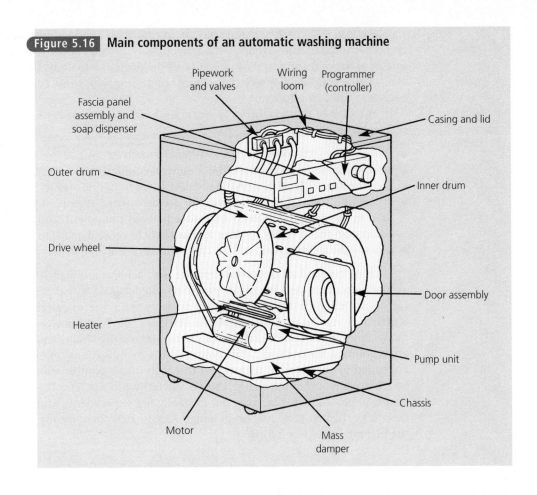

Table 5.4 **The functional breakdown of a washing machine**

Function	% of cost	Cumulative % of costs			
Control operations	24.41	24.41			
Provide or restrain motion	28.48	52.82	The washing function	A practical machine	A marketable product
Distribute water	11.09	63.91			
Retain water	8.89	72.80			
Heat water	4.29	77.09			
Provide protection	10.07	87.16			
Position parts	6.67	93.82			
Look attractive	6.18	100.00			

● Taguchi methods

The main purpose of Taguchi methods, as advocated by Genichi Taguchi,[10] is to test the robustness of a design. The basis of the idea is that the product or service should still perform in extreme conditions. A telephone, for example, should still work even when it has been knocked onto the floor. Although one does not expect customers to knock a telephone to the floor, this does happen, and so the need to build strength into the casing should be considered in its design.

Likewise, a pizza parlour should be able to cope with a sudden rush of customers and an hotel should be able to cope with early arrivals. Product and service designers therefore need to brainstorm to try to identify all the possible situations that might arise and check that the product or service is capable of dealing with those that are deemed to be necessary and cost-effective.

In the case of the adventure holiday, for example, the designers need to plan for such contingencies as:

- foul weather – the need for bad weather alternatives;
- equipment failure – the provision of enough equipment to cover for maintenance;
- staff shortages – flexible working to allow cover from one area to another;
- accidents – the ability to deal with an accident without jeopardizing the other children in the group, with easily accessible first-aid equipment, and using facilities and equipment that are easy to clean and unlikely to cause damage to children;
- illness – the ability to deal with ill children who are unable to take part in an activity.

The job of the product or service designer is to achieve a design which can cope with all these uncertainties. The major problem designers face is that the number of design factors which they could vary to try to cope with the uncertainties, when taken together, is very large. For example, in designing the telephone casing there could be many thousands of combinations of casing size, casing shape, casing thickness, materials, jointing methods, etc. Performing all the investigations (or experiments, as they are called in the Taguchi technique) to try to find a combination of design factors which gives an optimum design can be a lengthy process. The Taguchi procedure is a statistical procedure for carrying out relatively few experiments while still being able to determine the best combination of design factors. Here 'best' means the lowest cost and the highest degree of uniformity.

Prototyping and final design

The next stage in the design activity is to turn the improved design into a prototype so that it can be tested. It may be too risky to go into full production of the telephone, or the holiday, before testing it out, so it is usually more appropriate to create a prototype.

Product prototypes may include card or clay models and computer simulations, for example. Service prototypes may include computer simulations but also the actual implementation of the service on a pilot basis. Many retailing organizations pilot new products and services in a small number of stores in order to test customers' reaction to them.

● Virtual prototyping

Increasingly, it is possible to store the data that defines a product or service in a digital format on computer systems, which allows this 'virtual prototype' to be tested in much the same way as a physical prototype. This is a familiar idea in some industries such as magazine publishing, where images and text can be rearranged and subjected to scrutiny prior to them existing in any physical form. This allows them to be amended right up to the point of production without incurring high costs. Now this same principle is applied to the prototype stage in the design of three-dimensional physical products and services. Virtual reality-based simulations allow businesses to test new products and services as well as visualize and plan the processes that will produce them. Individual component parts can be positioned together virtually and tested for fit or interference. Even virtual workers can be introduced into the prototyping system to check for ease of assembly or operation.

● Computer-aided design (CAD)

CAD systems provide the computer-aided ability to create and modify product drawings. These systems allow conventionally used shapes (called entities), such as points, lines, arcs, circles and text, to be added to a computer-based representation of the product. Once incorporated into the design, these entities can be copied, moved about, rotated through angles, magnified or deleted. The system can usually also 'zoom in and out' to reveal different levels of detail. The designs thus created can be saved in the memory of the system and retrieved for later use. This enables a library of standardized drawings of parts and components to be built up. Not only can this dramatically increase the productivity of the process but it also aids the standardization of parts in the design activity.

The simplest CAD systems model only in two dimensions in a similar way to a conventional engineering 'blueprint'. More sophisticated systems can model products in three dimensions. They may do this either by representing the edges and corners of the shape (known as a wire-frame model) or by representing it as a full solid model. The advantage of wire-frame modelling is that it demands considerably less computer power because an object is represented only by its outline. However, for complex objects, wire-frame models can be confusing.

The advantages of CAD

The most obvious advantage of CAD systems is that their ability to store and retrieve design data quickly, as well as their ability to manipulate design details, can considerably increase the productivity of the design activity. In addition to this, however, because changes can be made rapidly to designs, CAD systems can considerably enhance the flexibility of the design activity, enabling modifications to be made much more rapidly. Further, the use of standardized libraries of shapes and entities can reduce the possibility of errors in the design. Perhaps most significantly, though, CAD can be seen as a prototyping device as well as a drafting device, especially when combined with the virtual prototyping approach described earlier. In effect the designer is modelling the design in order to assess its suitability prior to full production.

Photo courtesy of Land Rover

Computer-aided design (CAD) technology is now used in the design of many products and services

The benefits of interactive design

Earlier we made the point that in practice it is a mistake to separate the design of products and services from the design of the processes which will produce them. Operations managers should have some involvement from the initial evaluation of the concept right through to the production of the product or service and its introduction to the market. Merging the design of products/services and the processes which create them is sometimes called *interactive design*.

The benefits of interactive design lie in the elapsed time taken for the whole design activity, from concept through to market introduction. This is often called the design's *time to market* (TTM). The argument in favour of reducing time to market is that doing so gives increased competitive advantage. For example, if it takes a company five years to develop a product from concept to market, with a given set of resources, it can introduce a new product only once every five years. If its rival can develop products in three years, it can introduce its new product, together with its (presumably) improved performance, once every three years. This means that the rival company does not have to make such radical improvements in performance each time it introduces a new product, because it is introducing its new products more frequently. In other words, shorter TTM means that companies get more opportunities to improve the performance of their products or services.

If the development process takes longer than expected (or even worse, longer than competitors') two effects are likely to show. The first is that the costs of development will increase. Having to use development resources, such as designers, technicians, subcontractors, and so on, for a longer development period usually increases the costs of development. Perhaps more seriously, the late introduction of the product or service will delay the revenue from its sale (and possibly reduce the total revenue substantially if competitors have already got to the market with their own products or services). The net effect of this could be not only a considerable reduction in sales but also reduced profitability – an outcome which could considerably extend the time before the company breaks even on its investment in the new product or service. This is illustrated in Figure 5.17.

A number of factors have been suggested which can significantly reduce time to market for a product or service, including the following:

● simultaneous development of the various stages in the overall process;
● an early resolution of design conflict and uncertainty;
● an organizational structure which reflects the development project.

● Simultaneous development

Earlier in the chapter we described the design process as essentially a set of individual, predetermined stages. Sometimes one stage is completed before the next one commences. This step-by-step, or *sequential*, approach has traditionally been the typical form of product/service development. It has some advantages. It is easy to manage and control design projects organized in this way, since each stage is clearly defined. In addition, each stage is completed before the next stage is begun, so each stage can focus its skills and expertise on a limited set of tasks. The main problem of the sequential approach is that it is both time-consuming and costly. When each stage is separate, with a clearly defined set of tasks, any difficulties encountered during the design at one stage might necessitate the design being halted while responsibility moves back to the previous stage. This sequential approach is shown in Figure 5.18(a).

Often there is really little need to wait until the absolute finalization of one stage before starting the next. For example, perhaps while generating the concept, the evaluation activity of screening and selection could be started. It is likely that some concepts could be judged as 'non-starters' relatively early on in the process of idea generation.

Figure 5.17 **Delay in the time to market of new products and services not only reduces and delays revenues, it also increases the costs of development. The combination of both these effects usually delays the financial break-even point far more than the delay in the time to market**

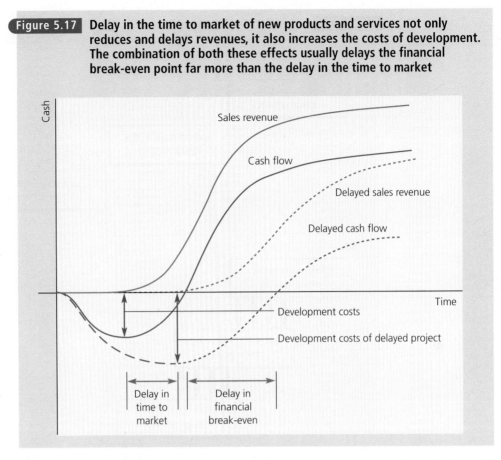

Similarly, during the screening stage, it is likely that some aspects of the design will become obvious before the phase is finally complete. Therefore, the preliminary work on these parts of the design could be commenced at that point. This principle can be taken right through all the stages, one stage commencing before the previous one has finished, so there is *simultaneous* or *concurrent* work on the stages (*see* Fig. 5.18(b)).

We can link this idea with the idea of uncertainty reduction which was discussed in the last chapter. There, we made the point that uncertainty reduces as the design progresses. This also applies to each stage of the design. If this is so then there must be some degree of certainty which the next stage can take as its starting point prior to the end of the previous stage. In other words, designers can be continually reacting to a series of decisions and clues which are given to them by the designers working on the preceding stage. However, this can only work if there is effective communication between each pair of stages.

Simultaneous engineering

What we have called simultaneous development is often called simultaneous (or concurrent) engineering in manufacturing operations. Although there is no single universally accepted definition of simultaneous engineering, most organizations' views are reasonably similar. For example, the following quotations give an idea of how the term is understood:

> '*Simultaneous engineering means that people who design or manufacture products work under the same targets and the same sense of values to tackle the same problems enthusiastically from the early phases. The targets here are the reduction of lead time, design for manufacturing, product development and development of advanced production technologies. The common measure of value is the satisfaction of customers, which is one of the corporate philosophies of the entire company.*'[11]

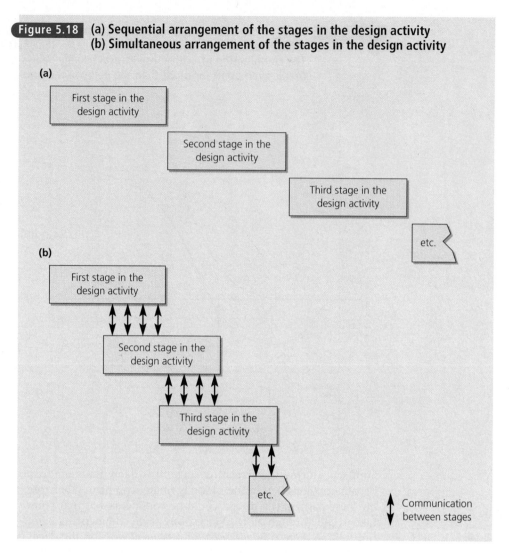

Figure 5.18 (a) Sequential arrangement of the stages in the design activity
(b) Simultaneous arrangement of the stages in the design activity

'Simultaneous engineering attempts to optimize the design of the product and manufacturing process to achieve reduced lead times and improve quality and cost by the integration of design and manufacturing activities and by maximizing parallelism in working practices.'[12]

● Early conflict resolution

Characterizing the design activity as a whole series of decisions is a useful way of thinking about design. However, a decision, once made, need not totally and utterly commit the organization. For example, if a design team is designing a new vacuum cleaner, the decision to adopt a particular style and type of electric motor might have seemed sensible at the time the decision was made but might have to be changed later, in the light of new information. It could be that a new electric motor becomes available which is clearly superior to the one initially selected. Under those circumstances the designers might very well want to change their decision.

There are other, more avoidable, reasons for designers changing their minds during the design activity, however. Perhaps one of the initial design decisions was made without sufficient discussion among those in the organization who have a valid contribution to make. It may even be that when the decision was made there was insufficient agreement to formalize it, and the design team decided to carry on without formally making the decision. Yet subsequent decisions might be made as though the decision

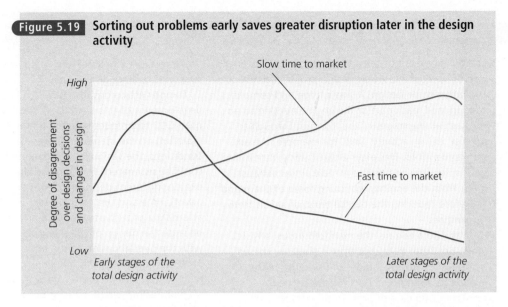

Figure 5.19 Sorting out problems early saves greater disruption later in the design activity

had been formalized. For example, suppose the company could not agree on the correct size of electric motor to put into its vacuum cleaner. It might well carry on with the rest of the design work while further discussions and investigations take place on what kind of electric motor to incorporate in the design. Yet much of the rest of the product's design is likely to depend on the choice of the electric motor. The plastic housings, the bearings, the sizes of various apertures, and so on, could all be affected by this decision. Failure to resolve these conflicts and/or decisions early on in the process can prolong the degree of uncertainty in the total design activity. In addition, if a decision is made (even implicitly) and then changed later on in the process, the costs of that change can be very large (as was discussed in Chapter 4).

However, if the design team manages to resolve conflict early in the design activity, this will reduce the degree of uncertainty within the project and reduce the extra cost and, most significantly, time associated with either managing this uncertainty or changing decisions already made. Figure 5.19 illustrates two patterns of design changes through the life of the total design, which imply different time-to-market performances.

● Project-based organization structures

The total process of developing concepts through to market will almost certainly involve personnel from several different areas of the organization. To continue the vacuum cleaner example, it is likely that the vacuum cleaner company would involve staff from its research and development department, engineering, production management, marketing and finance. All these different functions will have some part to play in making the decisions which will shape the final design. Yet any design project will also have an existence of its own. It will have a project name, an individual manager or group of staff who are championing the project, a budget and, hopefully, a clear strategic purpose in the organization. The organizational question is which of these two ideas – the various organizational functions which contribute to the design or the design project itself – should dominate the way in which the design activity is managed?

Before answering this, it is useful to look at the range of organizational structures which are available – from pure functional to pure project forms. In a pure functional organization, all staff associated with the design project are based unambiguously in their functional groups. There is no project-based group at all. They may be working full-time on the project but all communication and liaison are carried out through their functional manager. The project exists because of agreement between these functional managers.

The development of the 1.6 Zeta engine by Ford was one of its most important design projects for years. Like any engine design, it was a huge and complex task. Indeed, each part of the engine needed to go through all the stages of the 'concept through to market' design activity. Take, for example, the air intake manifold. This plays a particularly important part in the engine because it recirculates exhaust gases from the engine, reburning some of them and therefore reducing the overall emission levels from the engine.

In the Zeta engine, the manifold (unusually) is made not from metal but from a glass-reinforced nylon resin. The advantages of using this material include its strength, impact resistance, heat resistance and ease of processing. However, there were many design problems to sort out, including noise and vibration, the dimensional stability of the product and the ability of the material to stand up to the very high temperatures involved.

The design of the engine manifold took almost three years and was organized using all the interactive design principles. First of all, the various stages in the design were compressed and run in parallel (what Ford calls 'concurrent engineering'). Secondly, the various fundamental design problems were sorted out right at the beginning of the process. Third, a design team was put together involving not only various personnel from the Ford Motor Company but also the more significant suppliers. Those involved included design representatives from the Du Pont chemical company who were supplying the material, Dunlop who were to perform the moulding operation, and several specialist suppliers including Dowty who were designing the seals, Elring who were involved in

gasket design, Elm Steel who were involved with supplying tubing, and so on.

Design technology also played a large part in the development of this product. For example, Du Pont used CAD techniques to study the effects of engine vibration on the manifold. By simulating engine conditions, the various stress levels in the manifold could be estimated. This allowed the team to explore different design solutions without having to devote time and cost to manufacturing too many alternative prototypes – particularly important because the design of the manifold had to fit in with the overall design of the engine itself. Prototype manifolds were needed to supply the main engine design team who were wanting to start engine testing several months before the end of the manifold design process.

By involving its suppliers, by using them to resolve the considerable technical problems early on in the project, and by solving the technical problems in an interactive and simultaneous manner, the team managed to get a highly complex and very novel product designed to fit into the overall engine project more quickly, more cheaply and more dependably than it could otherwise have done.

Questions

1 In developing this product, Ford put together a team of suppliers. Do you think it would do the same for every single supplier of every part in every product? If not, how should it choose which suppliers, which parts and which products to subject to this sort of treatment?

2 Should Ford have included its suppliers' suppliers as well?

At the other extreme, all the individual members of staff from each function who are involved in the project could be moved out of their functions and perhaps even physically relocated to a 'task force' dedicated solely to the project. The task force could be led by a project manager who might hold all the budget allocated to the design project. Not all members of the task force necessarily have to stay in the team throughout the development period, but a substantial core might see the project through from start to finish. Some members of a design team may even be from other companies, as in the team which developed the inlet manifold for the Ford Zeta engine (*see* box).

In between these two extremes there are various types of 'matrix' organization with varying emphasis on these two aspects of the organization (*see* Fig. 5.20).

Although the 'task force' type of organization, especially for small projects, can sometimes be a little cumbersome, it seems to be generally agreed that, for substantial projects at least, it is more effective at reducing overall time to market.[14]

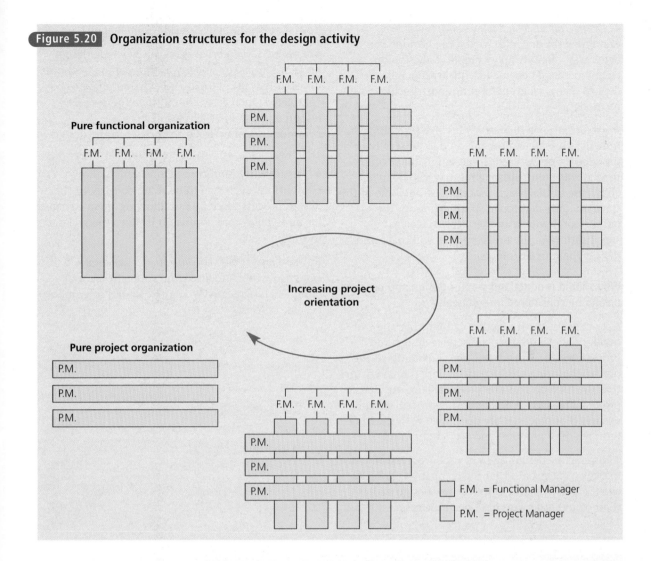

Figure 5.20 Organization structures for the design activity

Pure functional organization

F.M. F.M. F.M. F.M.

F.M. F.M. F.M. F.M.

P.M.
P.M.
P.M.

F.M. F.M. F.M. F.M.

P.M.
P.M.
P.M.

Increasing project
orientation

Pure project organization

P.M.
P.M.
P.M.

F.M. F.M. F.M. F.M.

P.M.
P.M.
P.M.

F.M. F.M. F.M. F.M.

P.M.
P.M.
P.M.

☐ F.M. = Functional Manager

☐ P.M. = Project Manager

Summary answers to key questions

Why is good product and service design important?

● Good product and service design translates customer needs into the shape and form of the product or service and by doing this specifies the required capabilities of the operation.

● This translation process includes formalizing three particularly important issues for operations managers: the concept, package and relationships implied by the design.

● Many companies have found that good aesthetic and functional design enhances profitability.

What are the stages in product and service design?

● *Concept generation* transforms an idea for a product or service into a concept which indicates the form, function, purpose and benefits of the idea.

● *Screening* the concept involves examining its acceptability in broad terms to ensure that it is a sensible addition to the company's product or service portfolio. Market, financial and operations evaluations must all be carried out during the screening process.

● *Preliminary design* involves the identification of all the component parts of the product or service and the way they fit together. Typical tools used during this phase include activity/product structures, bills of materials and flow charts.

- *Design evaluation and improvement* involve re-examining the design to see if it can be done in a better way, more cheaply or more easily. Typical techniques used here include quality function deploy- ment, value engineering and Taguchi methods.

- *Prototyping and final design* involve providing the final details which allow the product or service to be produced. Computer-aided design (CAD) is often used at this point, although it may also be used elsewhere in the design process. The outcome of this stage is a fully developed specification for the package of products and services, as well as a specification for the processes that will make and deliver them to customers.

Why should product and service design and process design be considered interactively?

- Looking at them together can improve the quality of both product and service design and process design. Considering the constraints of the operation during product and service design ensures that the final designs are 'producable'. Considering product and service design during process design ensures that processes are developed with the long-term needs of products and services in mind.

- Interactive design helps to produce a fast time to market. This ensures that the company will 'break even' on its investment in the new design earlier than would otherwise have been the case.

How should interactive design be managed?

- Employ *simultaneous development* where design decisions are taken as early as they can be, without necessarily waiting for a whole design phase to be completed. Such early commitment of design resources must also include effective communication between the phases in the design activity.

- Ensure early *conflict resolution* which allows contentious decisions to be resolved early in the design process, thereby not allowing them to cause far more delay and confusion if they emerge later in the process.

- Use a *project-based organizational structure* which can ensure that a focused and coherent team of designers is dedicated to a single design or group of design projects.

CASE EXERCISE

British Airways London Eye (A)

The British Airways London Eye is the world's largest observation wheel and one of the UK's most spectacular tourist attractions. It is over twice the height of the famous Prater Wheel in Vienna, but also has three key design differences compared with any such conventional Ferris wheel: firstly, the passenger capsules are fully enclosed and air-conditioned; secondly, they are positioned on the outside of the wheel structure and do not hang down; and thirdly, the entire structure is supported on an A-frame from one side only, so that it can be cantilevered out over the River Thames.

The 32 passenger capsules, fixed on the perimeter of the 135 metre diameter rim, each hold 25 people. The wheel rotates continuously, so entry requires customers to step into the capsules which are moving at 0.26 metres per second, which is a quarter of normal walking speed. One complete 360 degree rotation takes 30 minutes, at the end of which the doors open and passengers disembark. Boarding and disembarkation are separated on the specially designed platform which is built out over the river.

The attraction is operated on behalf of British Airways by the Tussauds Group, and it is their only attraction to use a 'timed admissions booking system' (TABS) for both individual and group bookings. This allocates requests for 'flights' on the basis of half-hour time slots. At the time of writing, the BA London Eye is open every day except Christmas Day. Admission is from 10.00 am to 9.30 pm (for the 9.30 – 10.00 pm slot) in the summer, from the beginning of April to mid-September. For the rest of the year, the winter season, admission begins at 10.00 am, and last admissions are for the 5.30 – 6.00 pm slot. Prices were set initially at £7.45 for adults, £4.95 for children and £5.85 for senior citizens. There is a 10 per cent discount for groups of 10 or more, plus one free flight for every 16 paid admissions. There is a charge for credit card pre-booking of £0.50 per person, and these tickets must be collected from the adjacent ticketing office, where purchases can be made in person. Prices were set to rise by £0.50 for the period June to December 2000.

The BA London Eye forecasts anticipated that 2.2 million passengers would fly the London Eye in 2000, excluding January, which was reserved for final testing and admission of invited guests only. An early press release told journalists that the London Eye would rotate an average of 6000 revolutions per year.

Information on the project of constructing the BA London Eye is included in Chapter 16, and further details are available on the internet at www.ba-londoneye.com.

Questions

1 What do you think were the main design issues during the design of the London Eye?

2 Calculate the hourly, weekly and annual design capacity of the London Eye, based on the planned operating time. How does this compare with the maximum theoretical design capacity if it operated 24 hours a day? How accurate is the annual number of revolutions mentioned in the press release?

3 Based on passenger numbers, what is the anticipated capacity utilization in the first year of operation? Explain why this is less than 100 per cent?

4 Stating your assumptions, estimate the revenue (£) that might be earned by the BA London Eye in its first year, based on the forecast passenger numbers. What might have to be done to increase the yield in subsequent years? What information should be collected during 2000 by the operators (the Tussauds Group) which would help develop a yield management strategy to maximize revenue and profits? Would these be consistent with the marketing objectives of the sponsor, British Airways?

CASE EXERCISE

The Royal Mint

A unique manufacturing operation in the UK is the Royal Mint at Llantrisant in South Wales. The Royal Mint is designated as an Executive Agency responsible to the Treasury of HM Government. The Chancellor of the Exchequer is appointed (*ex officio*) as Master of the Mint. Its objective is to provide the Government with coinage at a competitive price. The Royal Mint has the capacity to handle all of the UK business and still be able to bid for contracts from those countries who do not have their own minting operation. It serves over 60 countries in any one year and produces in excess of three billion coins annually. Its manufacturing requirement ranges from high volumes of standard coinage to individual service medals or commemorative coins.

In the UK, the Treasury contracts with the Royal Mint on an annual basis for the likely requirements for coins in the following 12 months, and the Treasury is also responsible for decisions on any changes to the coinage. The last coin that was introduced was the new, smaller 10p coin; this involved an issue of over one billion new coins and

the withdrawal of all the old coins from circulation. This represents one of the largest single projects undertaken and a massive logistics exercise to coordinate the movement of the coins. The Mint meets every three months with executives from the UK clearing banks to discuss their requirements for currency in the shorter term. These estimates are then updated at weekly planning meetings. The Mint would like to work to a 'just-in-time' schedule, but because of the nature of the product and the implications of the money not being available, they are obliged to keep a predetermined safety stock to cover any shortfalls.

As in any manufacturing operation, the unit cost of the product is a critical factor in measuring performance, and in the case of the Royal Mint, there is a unique cost ceiling, in that their cost base must always be less than the face value of the coins being produced. Therefore, this mass manufacturing process must focus on monitoring its operating costs. The issue of payment for the product is an interesting concept within the 'minting' industry

▶

and in the UK. The clearing banks pay the face value of the coins to the Treasury and the annual contract agreement with the Royal Mint is based on the Treasury agreeing to cover a fixed percentage of their fixed costs and the variable cost of each unit then purchased over the year. The Royal Mint can then invoice the Treasury for the currency produced.

The coins are costed in terms of pounds per thousand pieces. Of that cost, approximately 40–50 per cent comprises the raw material cost, with the next 20–40 per cent coming from the production process which transforms that raw metal into a blank coin. The actual stamping of the die onto the coin and the simultaneous milling of the edges form an almost insignificant part of the overall process cost, mainly due to the vast economies of scale at this stage. The efficiency of the stamping process is nominally determined by the life expectancy of the die, and the research at the Mint is involved in initiatives to improve the materials being used in both the coins and dies to extend this period of use. The coining machines used in the manufacturing process are flexible in that they can run to produce any of the UK and most overseas coins without long changeover periods, and orders vary from 1000 million coins for a large country to an order of 5000 for a small island. The machines are able to operate at speeds of up to 750 coins per minute and therefore the nature of a 5000 coin run is very costly, but all the same still viable.

One issue has been the threat of the intrinsic raw metal cost exceeding the face value of the coin: something which has been most prevalent in those countries facing high inflation and which leads to coinage being withdrawn from circulation by those wishing to capitalize on the returns available from the base material. In the UK, the smaller denominations were reaching that point and the Mint had to change the composition of the 2p and 1p coins to a steel core with an electroplated copper outer layer. This reduced the unit cost of the coin and also added to its expected lifetime because it used a less expensive base metal. This new format of coin represents the biggest change in the manufacturing process of coins to occur over the past few years and the pioneering of the electroplating technique, whereby a mild steel core is electroplated with copper, nickel or brass, resulted in a process which will aid the conservation of materials. The reduction in costs is also being achieved without a noticeable reduction in the recognized value of the coin. Another consequence of the electroplating procedure is that the coins have magnetic properties due to the presence of a mild steel core and this has caused initial problems for vending machine manufacturers.

Source: Reproduced by kind permission of the Royal Mint

Questions

1 What is the 'concept' of the Mint's products?

2 Explain the criteria which the Mint will need to take into account when it designs new coinage.

3 How might the concept of simultaneous design be applied in the design of coinage?

Discussion questions

1 Describe what you think might be the concept, package and the main processes involved in creating or providing the following:
   – a high-performance car
   – an airline flight
   – a visit to the dentist
   – an operations management textbook.

2 Using your knowledge as a customer of a university library, try to generate three new ways in which library services could be provided to you. Discuss the acceptability, feasibility and viability of each.

3 Take apart a simple product, such as a pen or an old cassette. Explain how it might have been put together (reverse engineering) and see if you can improve on its design.

4 Explain the difference between an idea and a concept. A hairdresser is considering opening up on campus. Develop this idea into what you think might be an acceptable, feasible and viable concept.

5 Look carefully at an item of furniture you have and create a product structure and bill of materials for it. Don't forget the nails, different types of screws and glue.

6 Draw an information flow chart describing the decision processes involved in a decision you frequently have to make, such as what to do in an evening. Evaluate the complexity and completeness of the chart.

7 Draw a process flow chart describing your last visit to see the doctor. How do you think the process could be improved?

8 Blueprinting, in one form or another, is a key tool for analysing, designing and developing products and services. Why do you think this is so?

9 Apply quality function deployment to a drawing pin and assess how well it appears to meet your perceived needs.

10 Explain what is meant by 'interactive design' and discuss the benefits for those organizations that employ it.

11 Why is it difficult or inappropriate to separate out the design of a product or service from the process of creating it?

12 Read again the box on Braun's Multimix design at the beginning of this chapter and answer the following questions:

(a) To what extent do the 'Braun design principles' appear to incorporate elements of:
   – design for manufacture
   – standardization
   – simultaneous engineering
   – quality function deployment?
(b) Which performance objectives are the most important for Braun?
(c) Braun has chosen to undertake most of its manufacturing in Europe, and much of it in Germany. What are the implications of this policy for the design of the company's products?

13 How might the concept of interactive design be applied to an internet-based retailer of MP3 downloads?

14 How could the QFD technique be applied to a conference centre or hotel?

Notes on chapter

1 Source: Presentation speech by Hartmut Stroth, Director of Communication at Braun AG, Mar 1994.
2 Source: 'Exploding Beer Bottles Kill Hundreds', *The Times*, 15 July 1999.
3 Peters, T. and Waterman, R. (1982) *In Search of Excellence*, Harper & Row, New York.
4 For more information on focus groups *see*, for example, Krueger, K.A. (1988) *Focus Groups*, Sage Publications.
5 Quinn, J.B. and Gagnon, C.E. (1986) 'Will Services Follow Manufacturing into Decline?', *Harvard Business Review*, Vol 64, No 6, pp 95–103.
6 Johnston, R. (1987) 'A Framework for Developing a Quality Strategy in a Customer Processing Operation', *International Journal of Quality and Reliability Management*, Vol 4, No 4, pp 35–44.
7 For more information on QFD for products and services *see*, for example:
Behara, R.S. and Chase, R.B. (1993) 'Service Quality Deployment: Quality Service by Design' *in* Sarin, R.V. (ed) *Perspectives in Operations Management: Essays in Honor of Elwood S. Buffa*, Kluwer Academic Publishers.
Evans, J.R. and Lindsay, W.M. (1993) *The Management and Control of Quality* (2nd edn), West.

Fitzsimmons, J.A. and Fitzsimmons, M.J. (1994) *Service Management for Competitive Advantage*, McGraw-Hill.
Meredith, J.R. (1992) *The Management of Operations* (4th edn), John Wiley.
8 Based on Cambridge, M. (1992) 'Quality Function Deployment', *Quality and Corporate Affairs Business Improvement Series*, 92/03 ICL, Dec.
9 This example is used by kind permission of Allan Webb, from Webb, A. (1994) *Managing Innovative Projects*, Chapman and Hall.
10 Taguchi, G. and Clausing, D. (1990) 'Robust Quality', *Harvard Business Review*, Vol 68, No 1, pp 65–75.
11 Yamazoe, T. (1990) 'Simultaneous Engineering: A Nissan Perspective' *in The Proceedings of the First International Conference on Simultaneous Engineering*, London, pp 73–80.
12 Broughton, T. (1990) 'Simultaneous Engineering in Aero Gas Turbine Design and Manufacture' *in The Proceedings of the First International Conference on Simultaneous Engineering*, London, pp 25–36.
13 Costanzo, L. (1992) 'Working as One', *Engineering*, Nov.
14 Hayes, R.H., Wheelwright, S.C. and Clarke, K.B. (1988) *Dynamic Manufacturing*, The Free Press.

Selected further reading

Albrecht, K. and Bradford, L.J. (1990) *The Service Advantage*, Dow Jones Irwin.

Baxter, M. (1995) *Product Design*, Chapman and Hall.

Bitner, M.J. (1992) 'Servicescapes: The Impact of Physical Surroundings on Customers and Employees', *Journal of Marketing*, Vol 56, April, pp 57–71.

Chase, R.B. (1991) 'The Service Factory: A Future Vision', *International Journal of Service Industry Management*, Vol 2, No 3, pp 60–70.

Clausing, D.P. (1994) *Total Quality Development*, ASME Press, New York.

Cohen, L. (1995) *Quality Function Deployment*, Addison-Wesley Longman.

Dean, J.H and Susman, G.I. (1984) 'Organizing for Manufacturable Design', *Harvard Business Review*, Vol 62, No 1, pp 28–36.

Groover, M.P. and Zimmers, E.W. (1984) CAD/CAM *Computer-Aided Design and Manufacturing*, Prentice Hall.

Heskett, J.L., Sasser, W.E. and Hart, C.W.L. (1990) *Service Breakthroughs: Changing the Rules of the Game*, The Free Press.

Kingman-Brundage, J. (1989) 'The ABCs of Service System Blueprinting' *in* Bitner, M.J. and Crosby, L. (eds) *Designing a Winning Service Strategy*, American Marketing Association. Also to be found *in* Lovelock, C.H. (1992) *Managing Services* (2nd edn), Prentice Hall International.

Shostack, G.L. (1984) 'Designing Services that Deliver', *Harvard Business Review*, Vol 62, No 1, pp 133–9.

Shostack, G.L. (1987) 'Service Positioning Through Structural Change', *Journal of Marketing*, Vol 51, Jan, pp 34–43.

Stuart, F.I. and Tax, S.S. (1996) 'Planning for Service Quality: An Integrative Approach', *International Journal of Service Industry Mangement*, Vol 7, No 4.

Thomas, R.J. (1995) *New Product Success Stories*, John Wiley.

Whitney, D.E. (1988) 'Manufacturing by Design', *Harvard Business Review*, Vol 66, No 1, pp 83–91.

6 Design of the operations network

Introduction

No operation, or part of an operation, exists in isolation. Every operation is part of a larger and interconnected network of other operations. This network will include suppliers and customers. It will also include suppliers' suppliers and customers' customers, and so on. At a strategic level, operations managers are involved in 'designing' the shape and form of the network in which their operation is set.

These network design decisions start with setting the strategic objectives for an operation's position in its network. This helps the operation to decide how it wants to influence the overall shape of its network, the location of each operation, and how it should manage its overall capacity within the network. This chapter treats all these strategic design decisions in the context of operations networks (*see* Fig. 6.1).

Figure 6.1 **The design activities in operations management covered in this chapter**

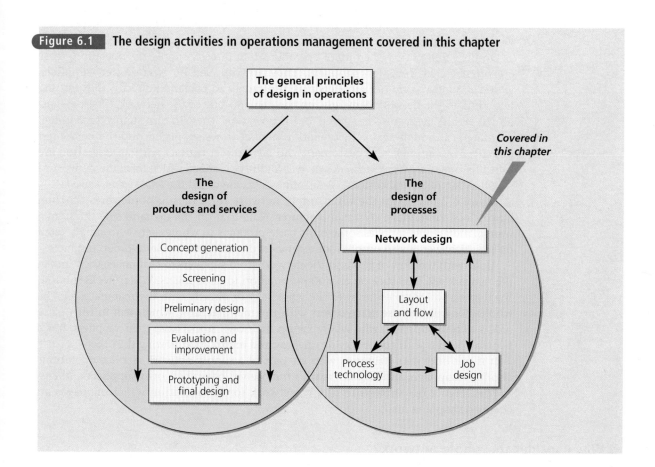

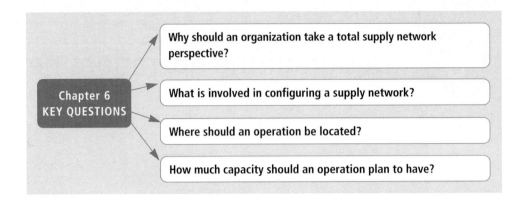

Chapter 6
KEY QUESTIONS

Why should an organization take a total supply network perspective?

What is involved in configuring a supply network?

Where should an operation be located?

How much capacity should an operation plan to have?

The network perspective

We begin our treatment of transformation processes design by setting the operation in the context of all the other operations with which it interacts, some of which are its suppliers and its customers. Materials, parts, other information, ideas and sometimes people all flow through the network of customer–supplier relationships formed by all these operations. On its *supply side* an operation has its suppliers of parts, or information, or services. These suppliers themselves have their own suppliers who in turn could also have suppliers, and so on. On the *demand side* the operation has customers. These customers might not be the final consumers of the operation's products or services; they might have their own set of customers.

On the supply side is a group of operations that directly supply the operation; these are often called 'first-tier' suppliers. They are supplied by 'second-tier' suppliers. However, some second-tier suppliers may also supply an operation directly, thus missing out a link in the network. Similarly, on the demand side of the network, 'first-tier' customers are the main customer group for the operation. These in turn supply 'second-tier' customers, although again the operation may at times supply second-tier customers directly. The suppliers and customers who have direct contact with an operation are called its *immediate supply network*, whereas all the operations which form the network of suppliers' suppliers and customers' customers, etc., are called the *total supply network*.

Figure 6.2 illustrates the total supply network for a plastic homewares (kitchen bowls, food containers, etc.) manufacturer. Note that on the demand side the homeware manufacturer supplies some of its basic products to wholesalers who supply retail outlets. However, it also supplies some retailers directly with 'made-to-order' products.

Along with the flow of goods in the network from suppliers to customers, each link in the network will feed back orders and information to its suppliers. When stocks run low, the retailers will place orders with the wholesaler or directly with the manufacturer. The wholesaler will likewise place orders with the manufacturer, which will in turn place orders with its suppliers, who will replenish their own stocks from their suppliers. It is a two-way process with goods flowing one way and information flowing the other.

It is not only manufacturers who are part of a supply network. Service operations also have suppliers and customers who themselves have their own suppliers and customers. Figure 6.3 shows the supply network for an operation which manages an enclosed shopping mall.

● Why consider the whole network?

At its most strategic level, the design activity of operations management must include the whole of the network of which an operation is a part. There are three important reasons for this:[1]

Figure 6.2 **Operations network for a plastic homewares manufacturer**

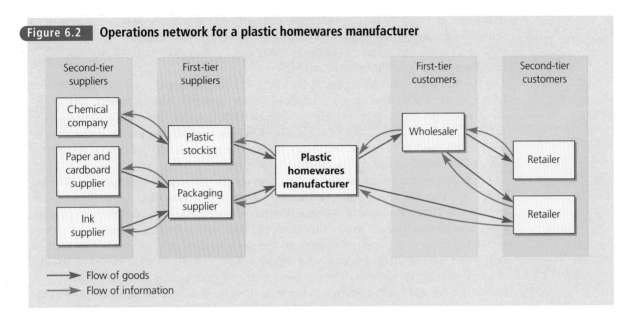

Figure 6.3 **Operations network for a shopping mall**

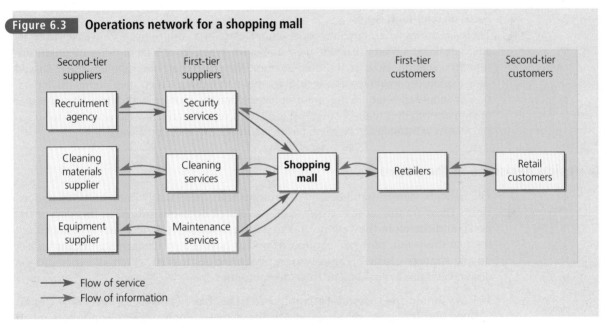

- It helps a company to understand how it can compete effectively.
- It helps to identify particularly significant links in the network.
- It helps the company to focus on its long-term position in the network.

Understanding competitiveness

Immediate customers and immediate suppliers, quite understandably, are the main concern to competitively minded companies. Yet sometimes they need to look beyond these immediate contacts to understand why customers and suppliers act as they do. Any operation has only two options if it wants to understand its ultimate customers' needs at the end of the network. It can rely on all the intermediate customers and customers' customers, etc., which form the links in the network between the company and its end customers. Alternatively, it can take on the responsibility itself for understanding how customer–supplier relationships transmit competitive requirements through the network. Increasingly, organizations are taking the latter course. Relying on one's immediate network is seen as putting too much faith in someone else's judgement of things which are central to an organization's own competitive health.

Identifying significant links in the network

The key to understanding supply networks lies in identifying the parts of the network which contribute to those performance objectives valued by end customers. Any analysis of networks must start, therefore, by understanding the 'downstream' end of the network. After this, the parts of the network which contribute most to end-customer service will need to be identified. Every link in the network will contribute something but not all contributions will be equally significant.

For example, the important end customers for domestic plumbing parts and appliances are the installers and service companies who deal directly with domestic consumers. They are supplied by 'stock holders' who compete on a combination of price, range and above all a high availability of supply. That means having all parts in stock and delivering them fast. Suppliers of parts to the stock holders can best contribute to their customers' competitiveness partly by offering a short delivery lead time but mainly through dependable delivery. The key players in this example are the stock holders. The best way of winning end-customer business in this case is to give the stock holder prompt delivery which helps keep costs down while providing high availability of parts.

Focus on long-term issues

There are times when circumstances render parts of a supply network weaker than its adjacent links. A major machine breakdown, for example, or a labour dispute might disrupt an operation. How then should its immediate customers and suppliers react? Should they exploit the weakness as a legitimate move to enhance their own competitive position or should they ignore the opportunity, tolerate the problems, and hope the customer or supplier will eventually recover?[2] A long-term supply network view would be to weigh the relative advantages to be gained from assisting or replacing the weak link.

● Design decisions in the network

The network view is useful because it prompts three particularly important design decisions. These are the most strategic of all the design decisions treated in this part of the book, and therefore they are not taken very frequently. It is necessary to understand them at this point, however, because, as well as having a particularly significant impact on the strategy of the organization, they set the context in which all other process design decisions are made. The three decisions are:

1 How should the network be configured? This has two aspects. First, how can an operation influence the shape which the network might take? Second, how much of the network should the operation own? This latter issue is called the *vertical integration* decision.

2 Where should each part of the network owned by the company be located? If the homewares company builds a new factory, should it be close to its suppliers or close to its customers, or somewhere in between? How should the shopping mall company choose a particular location for its mall? These decisions are called *operations location* decisions.

3 What physical capacity should each part of the network owned by the company have at any point in time? How large should the homeware factory be? If it expands, should it do so in large capacity steps or small ones? Should it make sure that it always has more capacity than anticipated demand or less? These decisions are called *long-term capacity management* decisions.

In Chapter 13, we will cover the more operational day-to-day issues of managing operations networks. In this chapter we deal with these three related strategic decisions.

Configuring the network

● Changing the shape of the network

Even when an operation does not directly own, or even control, other operations in its network, it may still wish to use its influence in order to change the shape of the network. This involves attempting to manage network behaviour by reconfiguring the network so as to change the scope of the activities performed in each operation and the nature of the relationships between them. Reconfiguring a supply network sometimes involves parts of the operation being merged – not necessarily in the sense of a change of ownership of any parts of an operation, but rather in the way responsibility is allocated for carrying out activities.

The most common example of network reconfiguration has come in the attempts made over the last few years by many companies to reduce the number of suppliers with whom they have direct contact. The complexity of dealing with many hundreds of suppliers may both be expensive for an operation and (sometimes more important) prevent the operation from developing a close relationship with a supplier. It is not easy to be close to hundreds of different suppliers. This has led many companies to reconfigure their supply side network to make it simpler and more orderly (*see* Fig. 6.4).

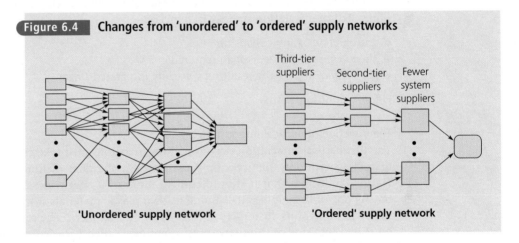

| Figure 6.4 | Changes from 'unordered' to 'ordered' supply networks |

'Unordered' supply network   'Ordered' supply network

Automotive system suppliers[3]

Take a look at the front part of a car – just the very front part, the bit with the bumper, radiator grill, fog lights, side-lights, badge and so on. At one time each of these components came from different specialist suppliers. Now the whole of this 'module' may come from one 'system supplier'. Traditional car makers are getting smaller and are relying on systems suppliers such as TRW in the US, Bosch in Germany, and Magna in Canada to provide them with whole chunks of car. Some of these system suppliers are global players who rival the car makers themselves in scope and reach. Typical among these is Magna. Based in Canada, it has more than 40 000 employees throughout the US, Canada, Mexico, Brazil and China, making everything from bumper/grill sub-assemblies for Honda, General Motors and Daimler-Chrysler, instrument panels for the Jaguar XK8 and metal-body exteriors for the BMW Z3 sports car. Magna, like the other system suppliers, has benefited from this shift in car maker supply strategy. Cost pressures have forced car makers to let their suppliers take more responsibility for engineering and pre-assembly. This also means them working with fewer suppliers. For example, in Ford's European operations, the old Escort model took parts from around 700 direct suppliers, while the newer Focus model uses only 210. Future models may have under 100 direct suppliers. Having fewer direct suppliers also makes joint development easier. For example, Volvo, who place a heavy emphasis on passenger safety, paired up with one supplier (Autoliv) to develop safety systems incorporating side air bags. In return for their support, Volvo got exclusive rights to use the systems for the first year. A smaller number of system suppliers also makes it easier to update components. While a car maker may not find it economic to change its seating systems more than once every seven or eight years, a specialist supplier could have several alternative types of seat in parallel development at any one time.

Question

What are the implications for companies reducing the number of their direct suppliers, both for the suppliers and for their customers?

● Vertical integration

Vertical integration is the extent to which an organization owns the network of which it is a part. In its strategic sense, it involves an organization assessing the wisdom of acquiring suppliers or customers. At the level of individual products or services, it means the operation deciding whether to make a particular individual component or to perform a particular service itself, or alternatively buy it in from a supplier.

Professors Hayes and Wheelwright of Harvard Business School[4] define an organization's vertical integration strategy in terms of:

- the *direction* of any expansion;
- the *extent* of the process span required;
- the *balance* among the resulting vertically integrated stages.

Figure 6.5 illustrates this.

The direction of vertical integration

The first vertical integration decision an organization must take concerns the *direction* of any ownership in the network. If the plastic homewares manufacturer illustrated in Figure 6.2 decides that it should control more of its network, should it expand by buying one of its suppliers (becoming its own plastic materials stockist, for instance) or by buying one of its customers (a wholesaler or a retailer)? The strategy of expanding on the supply side of the network is sometimes called *backward* or *'upstream' vertical integration*, and expanding on the demand side is sometimes called *forward* or *'downstream' vertical integration*.

Figure 6.5 **The direction, span and balance of vertical integration**

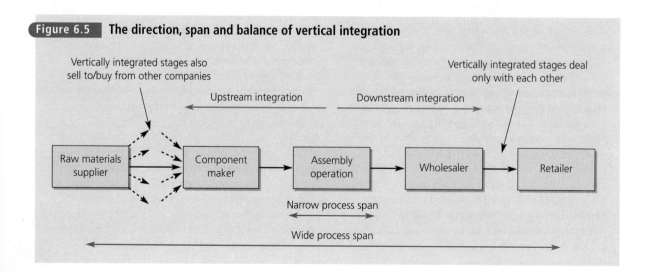

The extent of vertical integration

Having established its direction of expansion, an organization must then decide how far it wishes to take the extent of its vertical integration. Some organizations deliberately choose not to integrate far, if at all, from their original part of the network. For example, the shopping mall company illustrated in Figure 6.3 might decide that it wishes to concentrate solely on the management of its existing properties and the location, financing and building of new properties. It does not want to become a retailer in its own malls, nor does it want to employ security, maintenance or cleaning staff. Rather, it is content to specialize in what it knows best and 'buy in' all the services which are needed to run the malls.

Alternatively, some organizations choose to become very vertically integrated. Take a large international aluminium company, for example. It may be involved with smelting the minerals which produce aluminium (as well as recycling used aluminium products) to produce its basic ingots. It may also have operations which roll the ingots into sheet form. Separate operations may then roll the sheet further to produce aluminium foil which can be made into aluminium containers (for take-away food or home freezing) at yet another operation.

In choosing suppliers in some countries, businesses have to ensure that the working conditions of work and employment practices of the supplying company meet with its policies on ethical supply

The balance among stages

The final vertical integration decision is not strictly about the ownership of the network; it concerns the capacity and, to some extent, the operating behaviour of each stage in the network. The *balance* of the part of the network owned by an organization is the amount of the capacity at each stage in the network which is devoted to supplying the next stage. So a totally balanced network relationship is one where one stage produces only for the next stage in the network and totally satisfies its requirements. Less than full balance in the stages allows each stage to sell its output to other companies or to buy in some of its supplies from other companies.

Fully balanced networks have the virtue of simplicity and also allow each stage to focus on the requirements of the next stage along in the network. Having to supply other organizations, perhaps with slightly different requirements, might serve to distract from what is needed by their (owned) primary customer. However, a totally self-sufficient network is sometimes not feasible, nor is it necessarily desirable.

● The effects of vertical integration

The benefits and limitations of vertical integration are complex, and organizations in different circumstances with different objectives are likely to take different decisions. Yet the vertical integration question which all organizations must answer is relatively simple, even if the decision itself is not: 'Do the advantages which vertical integration gives an organization in a particular set of circumstances match the performance objectives which it requires in order to compete more effectively in its markets?' For example, if the main performance objectives for an operation are dependable delivery and meeting short-term changes in customers' delivery requirements, the key question should be: 'How does vertical integration enhance dependability and delivery flexibility?'

Answering these questions means judging two sets of opposing factors – those which give the *potential to improve performance*, and those which *work against this potential being realized*.

Vertical integration affects quality

The potential quality benefits of vertical integration derive from the closeness of the operation to its customers and its suppliers. The origins of any quality problems are usually easier to trace through 'in-house' operations than through outside suppliers. Acting against this is the danger that in-house operations, which are freed from the discipline of a true commercial relationship, will have less incentive to cooperate in quality improvement if there is no real possibility of their losing the business of their captive customers.

Vertical integration affects speed

Vertically integrated operations can mean a closer synchronization of schedules which speeds up the throughput of materials and information along the network. In addition, being close to suppliers and customers can help to reduce the risk of creating products or services for which demand never materializes. These potential advantages can be eroded if guaranteed 'in-house' demand means that the 'in-house' customers get low priority compared with 'proper' outside customers who can take their business elsewhere.

Vertical integration affects dependability

Improved communications along a vertically integrated network can also result in more dependable delivery promises. Even when internal hold-ups mean that deliveries will be missed, in-house suppliers might be more likely to give notice of the problem so that it can be communicated to the customer. All of which again assumes that the relationship between vertically integrated links in the network will indeed receive a high priority rather than being overlooked in favour of customers who can trade with competitors if they are not satisfied with the service they receive.

Vertical integration affects flexibility

Vertical integration gives the potential to guide technological developments as well as deny them to competitors. Forward vertical integration gives the flexibility potential for products and services to be developed specifically and more precisely to customer needs. The danger is that, if management attention is spread too thinly along a vertically integrated network, opportunities to exploit structural links are missed through dissipation of attention. As far as *volume and delivery flexibility* are concerned, the ownership of suppliers can give the potential to dictate volume changes to match downstream fluctuations, as well as helping to expedite specific orders through the network. Against this there can be a reluctance to inflict volume changes on in-house suppliers and customers. It is sometimes easier to be commercially realistic with independent companies.

Vertical integration affects costs

Vertically integrated operations can provide the potential for sharing some costs: research and development or logistics, for example. Over the longer term vertical integration can also allow capacity, and therefore capacity utilization, to be balanced. Perhaps more significantly, if margins are high in supplier operations, it allows integrated companies to capture the profits which would otherwise be lost, and to reduce the costs of bought-in parts or services. This assumes that other customers of a newly acquired supplier will be content to continue doing business with it. If they are not, demand could fall and therefore unit costs increase. Even if demand does remain at the same level, there is the question of whether a management now concerned with more separate businesses will be as concerned with keeping costs low as one which is concentrating on keeping its customers.

The location of capacity

After deciding on the overall shape of its operations network through vertical integration decisions, an organization must choose the location of each operation. Location is the geographical positioning of an operation relative to the input resources, other operations or customers with which it interacts. Not all operations can logically justify their location. Some are where they are for historical reasons. Yet even the operations that are 'there because they're there' are implicitly making a decision not to move. Presumably their assumption is that the cost and disruption involved in changing location would outweigh any potential benefits of a new location.

● The importance of location

It was reputedly Lord Sieff, the boss of Marks & Spencer, the UK-based retail organization, who said,

> *'There are three important things in retailing – location, location and location.'*

Any retailing operation knows exactly what he meant. Get the location wrong and it can have a significant impact on profits. In retailing, a difference in location of a few metres can make the difference between profit and loss. The location decision is also important in other types of operation. For example, mislocating a fire service station can slow down the average journey time of the fire crews in getting to the fires; locating a factory where there is difficulty attracting labour with appropriate skills will affect the effectiveness of the factory's operations, and so on. In other words, location decisions will usually have an effect on an operation's costs as well as its ability to serve its customers (and therefore its revenues). The other reason why location decisions are important is that, once taken, they are difficult to undo. The costs of moving an operation from one site to another can be hugely expensive and the risks of inconveniencing customers very high. No operation wants to move very often.

● Reasons for location decisions

There are two categories of stimuli which cause organizations to make location decisions:

- changes in *demand* for goods and services;
- changes in *supply* of inputs to the operation.

Location decisions prompted by demand changes are often due to increases or decreases in the aggregated volume of demand. For example, increased demand for a clothing manufacturer's products may necessitate more capacity. The company could either expand its existing site or, alternatively, if the site cannot accommodate a larger facility, it could choose a larger site in another location. A third option would be to keep its existing plant and find a second location for an additional plant. Two of these options will involve a location decision.

High-contact customer-processing operations often do not have the choice of expanding on the same site to meet rising demand. For example, if a company which offers a one-hour photo-processing service is so successful that it wants to expand its activities, enlarging its existing site would only bring in marginally more business. The company offers a local, and therefore convenient, service. Part of the way it competes is by having a location close to its customers. Finding a new location for an additional operation is probably its only option for expansion.

Changes in the cost, or availability, of the supply of inputs to the operation is the other reason for making the location decision. For example, a mining or oil company will need to relocate as the minerals it is extracting become depleted. A manufacturing company might choose to relocate its operations to a part of the world where labour costs are low, because the equivalent resources (people) in its original location have become rela-

---

Disneyland Paris[5]

CWS

For the Walt Disney Corporation, the decision to invest in Disneyland Paris was one of the most important location decisions it had ever made. The decision was in two parts. First, should Disney open one of its famous theme parks in Europe at all? Second, if so, where in Europe should it be located?

The decision to locate in Europe was influenced partly by its experiences in Japan. Tokyo Disneyland, which opened in 1983, had been a tremendous success from the start. In Europe, however, there was already a well-established market in holidays to Florida which took in Disney and other theme parks. For holiday-makers in the UK especially, Florida was only slightly more expensive than travelling to what was then called Euro Disney, with the added benefit of better weather. There was also a difference between the Japanese view of the themes of the Disney experience and the European view. Many of the Disney stories are based on European legends. *'Why'*, said some critics, *'build a fake castle on a continent full of real castles? Why build a theme park on a continent which is already a theme park?'*

If any doubts troubled Disney, it overcame them. Its next decision was where in Europe to build the park. At least two sites were considered – one in Spain and one in France. The advantage of France was that it was a far more central location. The demography of Europe means that by locating its theme park 30 kilometres east of Paris, it is within relatively easy travelling distance of literally millions of potential customers. Spain is geographically less convenient. There was also an existing transport infrastructure in this part of France, which was made even better by the French government as an

inducement. The French government also offered Disney numerous other financial inducements.

Spain, geographically more isolated and reputedly unable to match the French government's inducements, had the critical advantage, however, of better and more predictable weather. What perhaps was not forecast at the time was the initial hostility of the French media to what some regarded as cultural imperialism. The project was called a *'cultural Chernobyl'*, and described by one French critic as *'a horror made of cardboard, plastic and appalling colours; a construction of hardened chewing gum and idiotic folklore taken straight out of comic books written for obese Americans'*. Initally there were also, reportedly, some cultural issues in the recruitment and training of staff (or 'cast' as Disney calls them). Not all the European (largely French) staff were as amenable to the strict dress and behaviour codes as were their equivalents in Disney's US locations.

Questions

1 Summarize what you see as the major factors influencing the Walt Disney Corporation's decision to locate near Paris.

2 What difficulties do you think the Disney Corporation must have faced in the early days of running Disneyland Paris?

3 When transferring a service operation of this type between national or regional cultures, how might the design of the operation need to change?

tively expensive. Sometimes it is the price of land which prompts a move. For example, a company might choose to move its office headquarters because the value of the land it occupies is considerably more than an alternative, equally good, location. Selling the site and moving could generate considerable funds for the company.

● The objectives of the location decision

The aim of the location decision is to achieve an appropriate balance between three related objectives:

- the *spatially variable costs* of the operation (spatially variable means that something changes with geographical location);
- the *service* the operation is able to provide to its customers;
- the *revenue* potential of the operation.

In for-profit organizations the last two objectives are related. The assumption is that the better the service the operation can provide to its customers, the better will be its potential to attract custom and therefore generate revenue. In not-for-profit organizations, revenue potential might not be a relevant objective and so cost and customer service are often taken as the twin objectives of location.

In making decisions about where to locate an operation, operations managers are concerned with minimizing spatially variable costs and maximizing revenue/customer service. Location affects both of these but not equally for all types of operation. For example, with most products, customers may not care very much where they were made. Location is unlikely to affect the operation's revenues significantly. However, the costs of the operation will probably be very greatly affected by location. Services, on the other hand, often have both costs and revenues affected by location.

The location decision for any operation is determined by the relative strength of supply-side and demand-side factors (*see* Fig. 6.6).

● Supply-side influences

Labour costs

The costs of employing people with particular skills can vary between different areas in any country, but are likely to be a far more significant factor when international com-

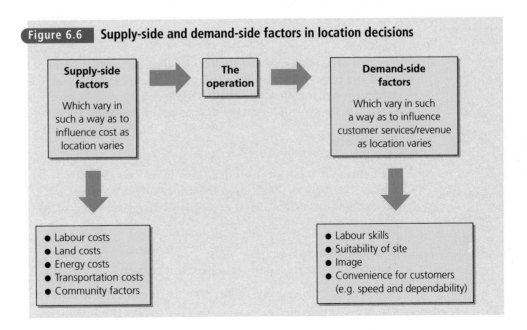

Figure 6.6 Supply-side and demand-side factors in location decisions

Supply-side factors	The operation	Demand-side factors
Which vary in such a way as to influence cost as location varies		Which vary in such a way as to influence customer services/revenue as location varies

- Labour costs
- Land costs
- Energy costs
- Transportation costs
- Community factors

- Labour skills
- Suitability of site
- Image
- Convenience for customers (e.g. speed and dependability)

parisons are made. For example, Figure 6.7 shows the labour costs for a number of countries. These costs include both direct wage costs and non-wage costs. The latter include employment taxes, social security costs, holiday payments and any welfare provision. The costs are expressed in two ways. The hourly cost is what firms have to pay workers on average per hour. However, the unit cost is an indication of the labour cost per unit of production. This includes the effects both of productivity differences between countries and of differing currency exchange rates. Exchange rate variation can cause unit costs to change dramatically over time. Yet in spite of this, labour costs exert a major influence on the location decision, especially in some industries such as clothing, where labour costs as a proportion of total costs are relatively high.

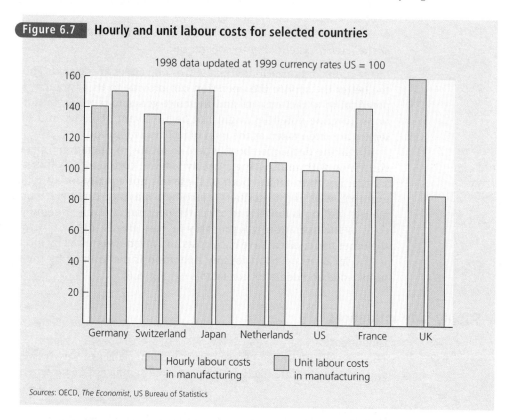

Figure 6.7 **Hourly and unit labour costs for selected countries**

Sources: OECD, *The Economist*, US Bureau of Statistics

Land costs

The cost of acquiring the site itself is sometimes a relevant factor in choosing a location. Land and rental costs vary between countries and cities. At a more local level, land costs are also important. A retail operation, when choosing 'high street' sites, will pay a particular level of rent only if it believes it can generate a certain level of revenue from the site.

Energy costs

Operations which use large amounts of energy, such as aluminium smelters, can be influenced in their location decisions by the availability of relatively inexpensive energy. This may be direct, as in the availability of hydroelectric generation in an area, for example, or indirect, such as low-cost coal which can be used to generate inexpensive electricity.

Transportation costs

Transportation costs can be considered in two parts:

(a) the cost of transporting inputs from their source to the site of the operation;
(b) the cost of transporting goods from the site to customers.

Nissan wins a new model

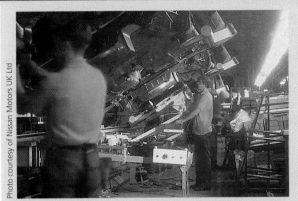

Final assembly, Nissan Primera, Sunderland Plant, UK

times and the number of reject components from its suppliers significantly from an already low level. It also included a programme to help suppliers enhance their own product development skills. People development activities within the plant embraced improved career development, job rotation to give variety at work and ergonomically inspired changes to job designs on the shop floor. All this helped push performance up to Japanese averages in many areas – unusual for a European plant. The next initiative (called Next 21) is aiming to bring all of Nissan's European operations up to the best Japanese performance levels.

In the global automobile industry, multinational car manufacturers think very carefully before choosing where to spend the money needed to build new models. Cost factors, local taxes, proximity to markets and expansion opportunities are all issues which influence such decisions. But just as important is each plant's track record of operations improvement. It was (at least partly) its excellent operations performance that secured Nissan's Sunderland plant in the UK its new model, which started production in 2000. The Sunderland plant's improvement programme had, over four years, reduced delivery

Questions

1 The improvement initiative which helped to win the Sunderland plant its new model was called NX96, a four-year programme which started in 1992. The new model did not start production until 2000. Why do you think it takes eight years for initiatives like this to come to fruition?

2 What did Nissan do to help its suppliers? Why do you think it is so important to put time and effort into developing a good supply base?

Whereas almost all operations are concerned to some extent with (a), not all operations transport goods to customers; rather, customers come to them (for example, hotels) and so they are not concerned with (b). Even for operations that do transport their goods to customers (most manufacturers, for example), we consider transportation as a supply-side factor because as location changes, transportation costs also change.

Proximity to sources of *supply* dominates the location decision where the cost of transporting input materials is high or difficult. Food processing and other agricultural-based activities, for example, are often carried out close to growing areas. Conversely, transportation to *customers* dominates location decisions where this is expensive or difficult. Civil engineering projects, for example, are constructed mainly where they will be needed.

Community factors

Community factors are those influences on an operation's costs which derive from the social, political and economic environment of its site. These include:

- local tax rates
- capital movement restrictions
- government financial assistance
- government planning assistance
- political stability
- local attitudes to 'inward investment'
- language

- local amenities (schools, theatres, shops, etc.)
- availability of support services
- history of labour relations and behaviour
- environmental restrictions and waste disposal
- planning procedures and restrictions.

Community factors can have a direct impact on the profitability of an organization. Local tax rates, for example, not surprisingly, play an important part in the location decisions of international companies. Others, such as the language spoken in the area, may not seem to have many cost consequences but can, in practice, prove very important (*see* box on Japanese inward investment).

Why Japan invested in the UK[6]

The 1990s saw many hundreds of Japanese companies setting up operations in Europe. Manufacturing companies particularly have recognized the importance of developing a foothold in the huge European market to avoid having to add European Union import duties to the cost of their products. The largest number of these companies have chosen to locate in the UK.

Some large early arrivals, such as Nissan, were attracted to the UK by generous government-funded financial support and tax concessions in regional development areas. They recognized that although potential employees did not necessarily have the skills needed to make their products, they were willing to be trained and did not come with any 'bad habits' picked up from similar employment. Later arrivals had much fewer direct financial incentives, but saw the other advantages gained by the early arrivals. In some areas, such as Telford and Milton Keynes, a critical mass of Japanese companies developed, creating a flow of good publicity back to Japan and encouraging further interest in these locations. This success was reinforced by a growth in support infrastructure, such as Japanese schools, social activities, and even food retailing to help the expatriate families feel at home.

Another important factor was language. Many Japanese manufacturing companies are accustomed to trading and producing in the US, and so the English language is the first foreign language of most business people. Drawings of products and processes, instruction sheets and computer programs were often immediately available for use without further translation for the UK. This meant a lower risk of misunderstandings and mistranslation, smoothing communications between the new plant and head office in Japan.

It also became apparent that both the quality and cost of labour were important reasons to locate in the UK. While many large indigenous manufacturing companies had been criticizing the educational standard of the workforce, Japanese companies took great care to select employees who were keen to learn, adaptable, willing to work hard and able to create improvements. Some companies were able to quote exceptionally high levels of productivity and quality performance in the UK, as an example to their Japanese workforce. Others began to export products from the UK to Japan. At the same time, the total cost of labour in the UK was relatively low, both due to hourly wage rates significantly below those typically paid in some other European Union countries, and also because of low indirect labour costs. Other significant reasons for a choice of the UK have been the relatively low rate of corporation tax, good communication links with most parts of the world, and a stable political and social system.

The development planning process is (as in most advanced economies) cumbersome, but at least it is transparent and difficulties of bribery and protection do not usually arise.

There are also other underlying factors which cannot be discounted: the UK is renowned for its excellent golf courses; spacious housing is available in the countryside near industrial development areas; and London is known for its excellent shopping and leisure facilities. The climate, although not the kindest in Europe, is temperate and the rainfall is not unlike that in Japan.

Questions

1 Summarize what you see as being the major factors which favoured the UK in attracting inward investment from Japan.

2 Nissan, Toyota and Honda all now have plants in the UK. What factors do you think will influence whether these plants expand or not?

Demand-side influences

Labour skills

The abilities of a local labour force can have an effect on customer reaction to the products or services which the operation produces. For example, 'science parks' are usually located close to universities because they hope to attract companies who are interested in using the skills available at the university.

The suitability of the site itself

Different sites are likely to have different intrinsic characteristics which can affect an operation's ability to serve customers and generate revenue. For example, the location of a luxury resort hotel which offers up-market holiday accommodation (such as the one described in the case exercise in Chapter 2) is very largely dependent on the intrinsic characteristics of the site. Located next to the beach, surrounded by waving palm trees and overlooking a picturesque bay, the hotel is very attractive to its customers. Move it a few kilometres away into the centre of an industrial estate and it rapidly loses its attraction.

Image of the location

Some locations are firmly associated in customers' minds with a particular image. Suits from Savile Row (the centre of the up-market bespoke tailoring district in London) may be no better than high-quality suits made elsewhere but, by locating its operation there, a tailor has probably enhanced its reputation and therefore its revenue. The product and fashion design houses of Milan and the financial services in the City of London also enjoy a reputation shaped partly by that of their location.

Convenience for customers

Of all the demand-side factors, this is, for many operations, the most important. Locating a general hospital, for instance, in the middle of the countryside may have many advantages for its staff, and even perhaps for its costs, but it clearly would be very inconvenient to its customers. Those visiting the hospital would need to travel long distances. Those being attended to in an emergency would have to wait longer than necessary to be brought in for admission. Because of this, general hospitals are located close to centres of demand. Similarly with other public services, location has a significant effect on the ability of the operation to serve its customers effectively. Likewise with restaurants, stores, banks, petrol filling stations and many other high customer contact operations, location determines the effort to which customers have to go in order to use the operation.

Levels of the location decision

The location decision is usually presented at three levels:

- choosing the region/country in which to locate the operation;
- choosing the area of the country or region;
- choosing the specific site within the area.

Choosing the region or country

Increasingly the location decision in many larger companies is taken with the whole world offering possible locations. While it has always been possible to manufacture in one part of the world in order to sell in another, until recently non-manufacturing operations were assumed to be confined to their home market. But no longer; the operational skills (as well as the brand image) of many service operations are transferable across national boundaries. Companies such as Novotel hotels, McDonald's restaurants,

Benetton clothing shops and Arthur Andersen (the accountants) make location decisions on an international stage. Similarly, information-processing operations can now locate outside their immediate home base, thanks to sophisticated telecommunications networks. If a bank sees a cost advantage in locating part of its back-office operation in a part of the world where the 'cost per transaction' is lower, it can do so. The keyboard operators, computer service managers and computer programmers of Stockholm, Frankfurt and London are now often competing directly with those in Delhi, Kuala Lumpur and Seoul.

Choosing an area within the country or region

Once an organization has decided in which country it wishes to locate, it will then need to choose an area of the country. Many of the factors which went into deciding the country will also play a part in deciding the area. Political stability and language might be less of an issue. Land prices, the local labour force, infrastructural development and community factors can play an important part, however.

Choosing a site

The choice of a site within an area is a different type of decision from those taken at the two 'higher' levels. Usually the number of alternatives is far smaller. At any time there may be just one available site, and the decision is whether to take it or not. If not, the search for an acceptable site will continue. The factors used to accept or reject a site are usually concerned with the characteristics of the specific site and its immediate surroundings. For example, the shape of the site and its soil composition can limit the nature of any buildings erected there. The access to any site by road or rail, so that materials and goods can be shipped conveniently in and out, is also likely to be important. Similarly, the availability of utilities, drains and waste-disposal facilities will need to be taken into account. Room for expansion might also be an issue, so the ability to lease or buy land close by or adjacent to the site could be important.

● Location techniques

Although operations managers must exercise considerable judgement in the choice of alternative locations, there are some systematic and quantitative techniques which can help the decision process. We describe two here – the weighted-score method and the centre-of-gravity method.

Weighted-score method

The procedure involves, first of all, identifying the criteria which will be used to evaluate the various locations. Second, it involves establishing the relative importance of each criterion and giving weighting factors to them. Third, it means rating each location according to each criterion. The scale of the score is arbitrary. In our example we shall use 0 to 100, where 0 represents the worst possible score and 100 the best.

Worked example

An Irish company which prints and makes specialist packaging materials for the pharmaceutical industry has decided to build a new factory somewhere in the Benelux countries so as to provide a speedy service for its customers in continental Europe. In order to choose a site it has decided to evaluate all options against a number of criteria, as follows:

- the cost of the site;
- the rate of local property taxation;
- the availability of suitable skills in the local labour force;

- the site's access to the motorway network;
- the site's access to the airport;
- the potential of the site for future expansion.

After consultation with its property agents the company identifies three sites which seem to be broadly acceptable. These are known as sites A, B and C. The company also investigates each site and draws up the weighted-score table shown in Table 6.1. It is important to remember that the scores shown in Table 6.1 are those which the manager has given as an indication of how each site meets the company's needs specifically. Nothing is necessarily being implied regarding any intrinsic worth of the locations. Likewise, the weightings are an indication of how important the company finds each criterion in the circumstances it finds itself. The 'value' of a site for each criterion is then calculated by multiplying its score by the weightings for each criterion.

Table 6.1 Weighted-score method for the three sites

| | | Scores | | |
| | | Sites | | |
Criteria	Importance weighting	A	B	C
Cost of the site	4	80	65	60
Local taxes	2	20	50	80
Skills availability	1	80	60	40
Access to motorways	1	50	60	40
Access to airport	1	20	60	70
Potential for expansion	1	75	40	55
Total weighted scores		585	580	605*

*Preferred option

For location A, its score for the 'cost-of-site' criterion is 80 and the weighting of this criterion is 4, so its value is $80 \times 4 = 320$. All these values are then summed for each site to obtain its total weighted score.

Table 6.1 indicates that location C has the highest total weighted score and therefore would be the preferred choice. It is interesting to note, however, that location C has the lowest score on what is, by the company's own choice, the most important criterion – cost of the site. The high total weighted score which location C achieves in other criteria, however, outweighs this deficiency. If, on examination of this table, a company cannot accept what appears to be an inconsistency, then either the weights which have been given to each criterion, or the scores that have been allocated, do not truly reflect the company's preference.

The centre-of-gravity method

The centre-of-gravity method is used to find a location which minimizes transportation costs. It is based on the idea that all possible locations have a 'value' which is the sum of all transportation costs to and from that location. The best location, the one which minimizes costs, is represented by what in a physical analogy would be the weighted centre of gravity of all points to and from which goods are transported. So, for example, in Figure 6.8 two suppliers, each sending 20 tonnes of parts per month to a factory, are located at points A and B. The factory must then assemble these parts and send them to one customer located at point C. Since point C receives twice as many tonnes as points A and B (transportation cost is assumed to be directly related to the tonnes of goods shipped) then it has twice the weighting of points A or B. The lowest transportation cost location for the factory is at the centre of gravity of a (weightless) board where the two suppliers' and one customer's locations are represented to scale and have weights equivalent to the weightings of the number of tonnes they send or receive.

Figure 6.8 **The centre-of-gravity method**

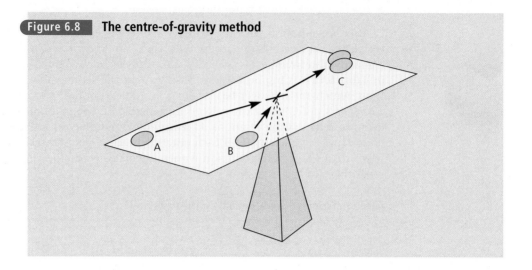

Worked example | A company which operates four out-of-town garden centres has decided to keep all its stocks of products in a single warehouse. Each garden centre, instead of keeping large stocks of products, will fax its orders to the warehouse staff who will then deliver replenishment stocks to each garden centre as necessary.

Figure 6.9 **Centre-of-gravity location for the garden centre warehouse**

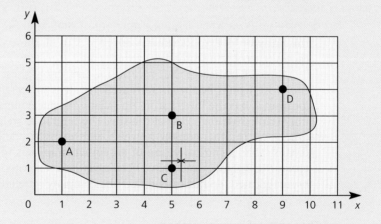

The location of each garden centre is shown on the map in Figure 6.9. A reference grid is superimposed over the map. The centre-of-gravity coordinates of the lowest cost location for the warehouse, $\bar{x}$ and $\bar{y}$, are given by the formulae:

$$\bar{x} = \frac{\sum x_i V_i}{\sum V_i}$$

and

$$\bar{y} = \frac{\sum y_i V_i}{\sum V_i}$$

where

x_i = the x coordinate of source or destination i
y_i = the y coordinate of source or destination i
V_i = the amount to be shipped to or from source or destination i.

Each of the garden centres is of a different size and has different sales volumes. In terms of the number of truck loads of products sold each week, Table 6.2 shows the sales of the four centres.

Table 6.2 The weekly demand levels (in truck loads) at each of the four garden centres

	Sales per week (truck loads)
Garden centre A	5
Garden centre B	10
Garden centre C	12
Garden centre D	8
Total	35

In this case

$$\bar{x} = \frac{(1 \times 5) + (5 \times 10) + (5 \times 12) + (9 \times 8)}{35}$$

$$= 5.34$$

and

$$\bar{y} = \frac{(2 \times 5) + (3 \times 10) + (1 \times 12) + (4 \times 8)}{35}$$

$$= 1.14$$

So the minimum cost location for the warehouse is at point (5.34, 1.14) as shown in Figure 6.9. That is, at least, theoretically. In practice, the optimum location might also be influenced by other factors such as the transportation network. So if the optimum location was at a point with poor access to a suitable road or at some other unsuitable location (in a residential area or the middle of a lake, for example) then the chosen location will need to be adjusted. The technique does go some way, however, towards providing an indication of the area in which the company should be looking for sites for its warehouse.

Four location decisions[7]

In practice, companies are driven by a whole variety of motives when they make their location decisions. Here are four which illustrate a diversity of operations objectives.

● In 1994 the Ford Motor Company embarked on one of its most radical reorganizations on a worldwide scale. Part of its plan was to establish five vehicle programme centres (VPCs). Each VPC was to take responsibility for the design of a particular type of vehicle worldwide. The idea of forming these five VPCs was to avoid costly duplication of design and development effort. For example, the Ford Escort launched in the early 1990s had been developed separately for the US and European markets. Although both cars were of almost the same dimensions and aimed at very similar parts of their respective markets, entirely unrelated versions were built in the US and Europe. Ford figured that locating all design and development of each class of vehicle in one place would prevent this kind of waste. The location of its five VPCs was based on which part of its organization had the greater experience and expertise. For example, the European VPC would take worldwide responsibility for the design, development and engineering of all of Ford's small and medium front-wheel-drive cars. North America by contrast had the greater experience in larger cars, trucks, higher displacement engines and automatic transmission.

- The Polish government has been engaged in its strategy of returning formerly state-owned industries into private hands. One industry in particular has attracted considerable interest and investment from Western companies. The country's car- and truck-making capacity was the focus of attention from such car giants as Fiat, PSA (Peugeot and Citroen), Ford, Volvo, General Motors, Mercedes-Benz and Volkswagen. The cause of all this interest was only partially due to Poland's lower manufacturing costs (anyway, exports from Poland were sometimes restricted: for example, the European Union allowed only a certain number of models to be imported free of its 30 per cent customs duty). The car companies were playing a longer game. They had in mind the potential growth in the East European market in the medium to long term. When Fiat bought 90 per cent of the former state-held FSM car maker based in Bielsko-Biola in southern Poland, it was not only investing in the experience and under-utilized resources of the company, it was seeing its investment as a longer-term gateway to other East European markets.

- When Hyundai moved its personal computer operations to America, its market share had shifted from 5 per cent in the late 80s down to 1.5 per cent in the 90s. It seems, therefore, an unusual decision to move to a country with higher labour and accommodation costs. In fact,

Hyundai reckoned that the increased costs were more than offset by savings in time and inventories. When it manufactured in Korea its goods used to take two months to reach the US, after which its sales operations used to hold the stocks for around three months of sales. After the move, the amount of stock was reduced to less than a third and responsiveness to market trends was enhanced by being far closer to the market itself. Also, product development time, which had been between 12 and 18 months, was reduced to five months after the move.

- In 1994 the domestic appliance manufacturer Hoover (owned by the American Maytag Corporation) closed its French vacuum cleaner manufacturing operation and relocated production to its Scottish plant. The decision was primarily influenced by cost of manufacture. The company had figured that, to remain competitive in its global business, all vacuum cleaner production for Europe should be concentrated on a single plant in order to gain economies of scale. Hoover's workers in Scotland were also paid lower wages than their French counterparts. Furthermore, non-wage costs such as health insurance were a much lower percentage of overall costs in Britain than they were in France. Reportedly, the company also believed that the workforce in its Scottish plant had demonstrated more flexibility in adapting to new working methods, which would help it to keep manufacturing costs down in the future.

Questions

1 For each of these four location decisions, rank what you think are the main factors which influenced the location decision.

2 What do you think the companies described in each of these four location decisions were trying to improve and why?

3 In the decision by the Ford Motor Company to establish vehicle programme centres, do you think the factors influencing the location of design centres are different from those that influence the location of manufacturing operations?

Long-term capacity management

After the vertical integration of the operation's network and the location of its various operations have been decided, the next set of decisions concerns the size or capacity of each part of the network. Here we shall treat capacity in a general long-term sense. The specific issues involved in measuring and adjusting capacity in the medium and short terms are examined in Chapter 11.

● The optimum capacity level

Most organizations need to decide on the size (in terms of capacity) of each of their facilities. An air-conditioning unit company, for example, might operate plants each of which has a capacity (at normal product mix) of 800 units per week. At activity levels below this, the average cost of producing each unit will increase because the fixed costs of the factory are being covered by fewer units produced. The total production costs of the factory have some elements which are fixed – they will be incurred irrespective of how much, or little, the factory produces. Other costs are variable – they are the costs incurred by the factory for each unit it produces. Between them, the fixed and variable costs comprise the total cost at any output level. Dividing this cost by the output level itself will give the theoretical average cost of producing units at that output rate. This is the green line shown as the theoretical unit cost curve for the 800-unit plant in Figure 6.10. However, the actual average cost curve may be different from this line for a number of reasons:

- All fixed costs are not incurred at one time as the factory starts to operate. Rather they occur at many points (called fixed cost 'breaks') as volume increases. This makes the theoretically smooth average cost curve more discontinuous.
- Production levels may be increased above the theoretical capacity of the plant, by using prolonged overtime, for example, or temporarily sub-contracting some parts of the work.
- There may be less obvious cost penalties of operating the plant at levels close to or above its nominal capacity. For example, long periods of overtime may reduce productivity levels as well as costing more in extra payments to staff; operating plant for long periods with reduced maintenance time may increase the chances of breakdown, and so on. This usually means that average costs start to increase after a point which will often be lower than the theoretical capacity of the plant.

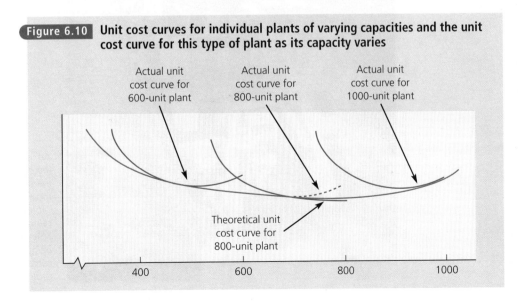

Figure 6.10 Unit cost curves for individual plants of varying capacities and the unit cost curve for this type of plant as its capacity varies

The blue dotted line in Figure 6.10 shows this effect. The two other blue lines show similar curves for a 600-unit plant and a 1000-unit plant. Figure 6.10 also shows that a similar relationship occurs between the average cost curves for plants of increasing size. As the nominal capacity of the plants increases, the lowest cost points at first reduce. There are two main reasons for this:

- The fixed costs of an operation do not increase proportionately as its capacity increases. An 800-unit plant has less than twice the fixed costs of a 400-unit plant.
- The capital costs of building the plant do not increase proportionately to its capacity. An 800-unit plant costs less to build than twice the cost of a 400-unit plant.

These two factors, taken together, are often referred to as *economies of scale*. However, above a certain size, the lowest cost point may increase. In Figure 6.10 this happens with plants above 800 units capacity. This occurs because of what are called the *diseconomies of scale*, two of which are particularly important:

- Transportation costs can be high for large operations. For example, if a manufacturer supplies the whole of its European market from one major plant in Denmark, all supplies may have to be brought in from several countries to the single plant and all products shipped from there throughout Europe.
- Complexity costs increase as size increases. The communications and coordination effort necessary to manage an operation tends to increase faster than capacity. Although not seen as a direct cost, this can nevertheless be very significant.

An increase in the use of internet technologies has made it necessary to increase the capacity of the cables which carry telecommunications traffic. This cable laying ship is being used to lay new cables and higher capacity cables

Scale of capacity and the demand–capacity balance

Large units of capacity also have some disadvantages when the capacity of the operation is being changed to match changing demand. For example, suppose that the air-conditioning unit manufacturer forecasts demand increase over the next three years, as shown in Figure 6.11, to level off at around 2400 units a week. If the company seeks to satisfy all demand by building three plants, each of 800 units capacity, the company will have substantial amounts of over-capacity for much of the period when demand is increasing. Over-capacity means low capacity utilization, which in turn means higher unit costs. If the company builds smaller plants, say 400-unit plants, there will still be over-capacity but to a lesser extent, which means higher capacity utilization and possibly lower costs.

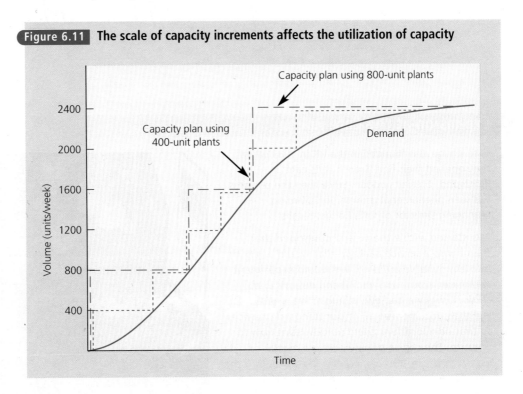

Figure 6.11   **The scale of capacity increments affects the utilization of capacity**

● Balancing capacity

So far we have confined our discussion of capacity to the assumption that a single operation is internally homogeneous. Yet, as we discussed in Chapter 1, all operations are made up of micro operations, and each micro operation will itself have its own capacity. So, for example, the 800-unit capacity air-conditioning plant not only assembles the products but probably also manufactures most of the parts from which they are made. If so, the capacity of the parts manufacturing section of the factory must be capable of producing parts at a rate sufficient for the assembly department to produce units at a rate of 800 per week, if the output of the whole factory is not to be reduced. Similarly, further down the network of internal operations, the air-conditioning units are moved to the warehouse after assembly, where they are packed in cases, stored and loaded onto trucks as needed. The company's fleet of trucks then distributes them to its customers.

This is a four-stage network of operations: parts manufacturing feeds assembly which feeds the warehouse which feeds the distribution operation. For the network to operate efficiently, all its stages must have the same capacity. If they have different capacities, the capacity of the network as a whole will be limited to the capacity of its slowest link. This can be visualized as a series of pipes of different diameters through which liquid is flowing. The throughput rate of the whole system will be limited by the pipe with the smallest diameter. Figure 6.12 illustrates this for the air-conditioning unit manufacturer. In this case the warehouse is what is called the *bottleneck* in the supply network.

Figure 6.12 **When capacity at each stage is not balanced, the capacity of the total system is limited by that of the bottleneck stage**

Assembly capacity = 800 units/week

Distribution capacity = 820 units/week

Parts manufacturing capacity = 850 units/week

Warehouse capacity = 700 units/week

Expansion at the Café Rouge · CWS

Café Rouge was founded in the UK in 1989 when they opened their first 'French-style café' in Richmond, Greater London. Since then the business has seen phenomenal growth. Jo Cumming, Managing Director of Café Rouge, recalls:

'We started with a theme and developed that theme into a service package that would easily fit into any suitable building. We would experiment with café layouts and with menu designs and choices until we had everything as we wanted it. We then documented all of our standard practices so that new locations could quickly learn how to operate. The choice of new sites is a matter of assessing the potential market and considering the structural constraints of any potential properties. Some areas have a better profile of regular restaurant users than others. Also, we needed to locate reasonably close to other restaurants. Our learning curve was quite rapid and now we can recognize whether or not a site will be appropriate and have also got the period from moving in to opening up down to less than two weeks. The restaurant staff are trained in other cafés and the furniture and fittings are all standardized, so it is really just a matter of adding the final touches and we're in and running. We also have to make sure that we can keep up with the rapid pace of expansion. Opening a new site needs both financial and management resources.

Photo courtesy of Café Rouge

Diners enjoy individual service at Café Rouge locations, all of which have a similar layout and appearance

We put a lot of effort into working out the cash flow and workload implications of each step in our expansion.'

Questions

1 What seem to be the main expansion-related issues for Café Rouge?

2 Why do they like to locate close to other restaurants?

● The timing of capacity change

Changing the capacity of an operation is not just a matter of deciding on the best size of a capacity increment. The operation also needs to decide when to bring 'on-stream' new capacity. For example, Figure 6.13 shows the forecast demand for the new air-conditioning unit. The company has decided to build 400-unit-per-week plants in order to meet the growth in demand for its new product. In deciding *when* the new plants are to be introduced the company must choose a position somewhere between two extreme strategies:

● *capacity leads demand* – timing the introduction of capacity in such a way that there is always sufficient capacity to meet forecast demand;
● *capacity lags demand* – timing the introduction of capacity so that demand is always equal to or greater than capacity.

Figure 6.13 shows these two extreme strategies, although in practice the company is likely to choose a position somewhere between the two. Each strategy has its own advantages and disadvantages. These are shown in Table 6.3. The actual approach taken by any company will depend on how it views these advantages and disadvantages. For example, if the company's access to funds for capital expenditure is limited, it is likely to find the delayed capital expenditure requirement of the capacity-lagging strategy relatively attractive.

'Smoothing' with inventory

The strategy on the continuum between pure leading and pure lagging strategies can be implemented so that no inventories are accumulated. All demand in one period is satisfied (or not) by the activity of the operation in the same period. Indeed, for customer-processing operations there is no alternative to this. An hotel cannot satisfy demand in one year by using rooms which were vacant the previous year. For some materials- and information-processing operations, however, the output from the operation which is not required in one period can be stored for use in the next period. The

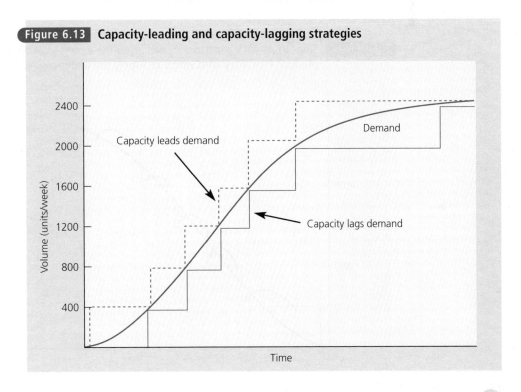

Figure 6.13 Capacity-leading and capacity-lagging strategies

Table 6.3 The arguments for and against pure leading and pure lagging strategies of capacity timing

Advantages	Disadvantages
Capacity-leading strategies	
Always sufficient capacity to meet demand, therefore revenue is maximized and customers satisfied	Utilization of the plants is always relatively low, therefore costs will be high
Most of the time there is a 'capacity cushion' which can absorb extra demand if forecasts are pessimistic	Risks of even greater (or even permanent) over-capacity if demand does not reach forecast levels
Any critical start-up problems with new plants are less likely to affect supply to customers	Capital spending on plant early
Capacity-lagging strategies	
Always sufficient demand to keep the plants working at full capacity, therefore unit costs are minimized	Insufficient capacity to meet demand fully, therefore reduced revenue and dissatisfied customers
Over-capacity problems are minimized if forecasts are optimistic	No ability to exploit short-term increases in demand
Capital spending on the plants is delayed	Under-supply position even worse if there are start-up problems with the new plants

economies of using inventories are fully explored in Chapter 12. Here we confine ourselves to noting that inventories can be used to obtain the advantages of both capacity leading and capacity lagging.

Figure 6.14 shows how this can be done. Capacity is introduced such that demand can always be met by a combination of production and inventories, and capacity is, with the occasional exception, fully utilized.

Figure 6.14 Smoothing with inventory means using the excess capacity of one period to produce inventory with which to supply the under-capacity of another period

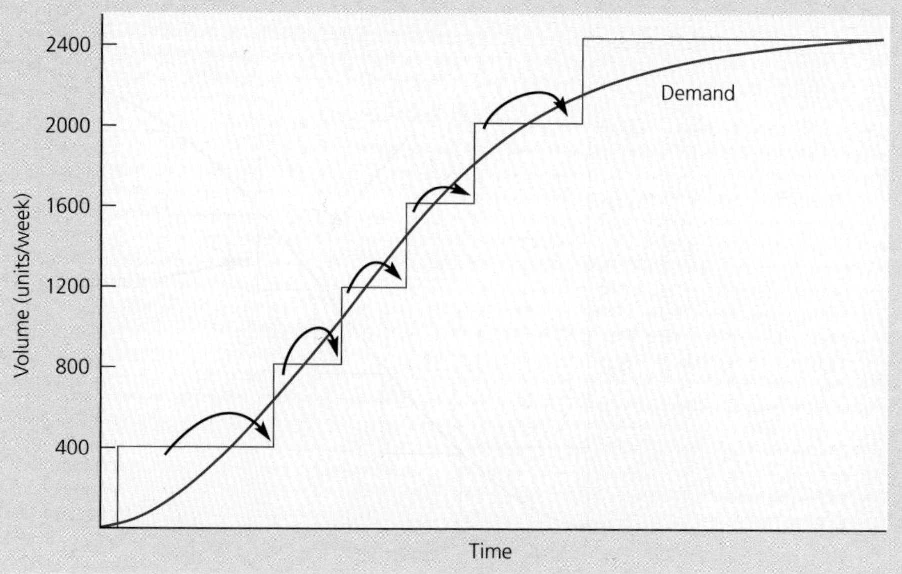

This may seem like an ideal state. Demand is always met and so revenue is maximized. Capacity is usually fully utilized and so costs are minimized. There is a price to pay, however, and that is the cost of carrying the inventories. Not only will these have to be funded (*see* Chapter 12) but the risks of obsolescence and deterioration of stock are introduced. Table 6.4 summarizes the advantages and disadvantages of the 'smoothing-with-inventory' strategy.

Table 6.4 The advantages and disadvantages of a smoothing-with-inventory strategy

Advantages	Disadvantages
All demand is satisfied, therefore customers are satisfied and revenue is maximized	The cost of inventories in terms of working capital requirements can be high. This is especially serious at a time when the company requires funds for its capital expansion
Utilization of capacity is high and therefore costs are low	Risks of product deterioration and obsolescence
Very short-term surges in demand can be met from inventories	

● Break-even analysis of capacity expansion

An alternative view of capacity expansion can be gained by examining the cost implications of adding increments of capacity on a break-even basis. Figure 6.15 shows how increasing capacity can move an operation from profitability to loss. Each additional unit of capacity results in a *fixed-cost break*, that is a further lump of expenditure which will have to be incurred before any further activity can be undertaken in the operation.

The operation is therefore unlikely to be profitable at very low levels of output. Eventually, assuming that prices are greater than marginal costs, revenue will exceed total costs. However, the level of profitability at the point where the output level is equal to the capacity of the operation may not be sufficient to absorb all the extra fixed costs of a further increment in capacity. This could make the operation unprofitable in some stages of its expansion.

Figure 6.15 **Repeated incurring of fixed costs can raise total costs above revenue**

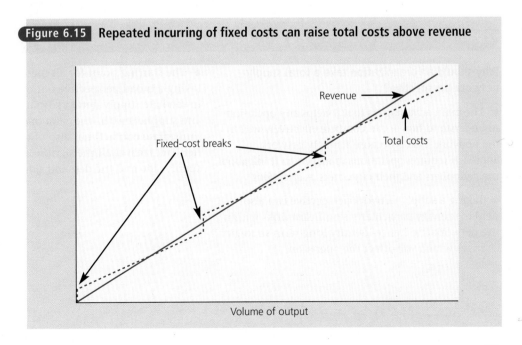

A specialist graphics company is investing in a new machine which enables it to make high-quality prints for its clients. Demand for these prints is forecast to be around 100 000 units in year 1 and 220 000 units in year 2. The maximum capacity of each machine the company will buy to process these prints is 100 000 units per year. They have a fixed cost of €200 000 per year and a variable cost of processing of €1 per unit. The company believe they will be able to charge €4 per unit for producing the prints.

Question

What profit are they likely to make in the first and second years?

$$
\begin{aligned}
\text{Year 1 demand} &= 100\,000 \text{ units; therefore company will need one machine}\\
\text{Cost of manufacturing} &= \text{fixed cost for one machine} + \text{variable cost} \times 100\,000\\
&= €200\,000 + (€1 \times 100\,000)\\
&= €300\,000\\
\text{Revenue} &= \text{demand} \times \text{price}\\
&= 100\,000 \times €4\\
&= €400\,000\\
\text{Therefore profit} &= €400\,000 - €300\,000\\
&= €100\,000
\end{aligned}
$$

$$
\begin{aligned}
\text{Year 2 demand} &= 220\,000; \text{therefore company will need three machines}\\
\text{Cost of manufacturing} &= \text{fixed cost for three machines} + \text{variable cost} \times 220\,000\\
&= (3 \times €200\,000) + (€1 \times 220\,000)\\
&= €820\,000\\
\text{Revenue} &= \text{demand} \times \text{price}\\
&= 220\,000 \times €4\\
&= €880\,000\\
\text{Therefore profit} &= €880\,000 - €820\,000\\
&= €60\,000
\end{aligned}
$$

Note – the profit in the second year will be lower because of the extra fixed costs associated with the investment in the two extra machines.

Summary answers to key questions

Why should an organization take a total supply network perspective?

● The main advantage is that it helps any operation to understand how it can compete effectively within the network. This is because a supply network approach requires operations managers to think about their suppliers and their customers *as operations*.

● Taking a supply network perspective can also help to identify particularly significant links within the network and hence identify long-term strategic changes which will affect the operation.

● The starting point for all these advantages is taking a broad perspective not only of the immediate supply network (that is the customers and suppliers with whom an operation has immediate contact) but also of the total supply network (that is all the significant operations on the supply side and the demand side of an operation).

What is involved in configuring a supply network?

● There are two main issues involved in configuring the supply network. The first concerns the overall shape of the supply network. The second concerns the nature and extent of *vertical integration*.

● Changing the shape of the supply network often involves reducing the number of suppliers to the operation so as to develop closer relationships.

● Vertical integration concerns the nature of the ownership of the operations within a supply network. The direction of vertical integration refers to whether an organization wants to own operations on its supply side or demand side (backwards or forwards integration). The extent of vertical integration relates to whether an organization wants to own a wide span of the stage in the supply network. The nature of the relationship between organizations in the network refers to whether operations can trade with only their vertically integrated partners or, alternatively, with any other organizations.

Where should an operation be located?

● An existing operation will relocate only if the costs and disruption of moving are less than the benefits it believes it will gain from its new location.

● The stimuli which act on an organization during the location decision can be divided into supply-side and demand-side influences. Supply-side influences are the factors such as labour, land and utility costs which change as location changes. Demand-side influences include such things as the image of the location, its convenience for customers and the suitability of the site itself.

● All of the factors above can be applied (to different degrees) at three levels: the choice of a country or region; the choice of an area within a country or region; and the choice of the specific site itself.

How much capacity should an operation plan to have?

● The amount of capacity an organization will have depends on its view of current and future demand. It is when its view of future demand is different from current demand that this issue becomes important.

● When an organization has to cope with changing demand, a number of capacity decisions need to be taken. These include choosing the optimum capacity for each site, balancing the various capacity levels of the operation in the network, and timing the changes in the capacity of each part of the network.

● Important influences on these decisions include the concepts of economy and diseconomy of scale, supply flexibility if demand is different from that forecast, and the profitability and cash-flow implications of capacity timing changes.

Delta Synthetic Fibres[8]

DSF is a small but technically successful company in the man-made fibre industry. The company is heavily dependent on the sales of Britlene, a product it developed itself, which accounted in 1996 for some 95 per cent of total sales.

Britlene is used mainly in heavy-duty clothing, although small quantities are used to produce industrial goods such as tyre cord and industrial belting. Its main properties are very high wear resistance, thermal and electrical insulation.

In 1996 the company developed a new product, Britlon. Britlon had all the properties of Britlene but was superior in its heat-resistant qualities. It was hoped that this additional property would open up new clothing uses (e.g. a substitute for mineral wool clothing, added to night-wear to improve its inflammability) and new industrial uses in thermal and electrical insulation.

By late 1996 the major technical and engineering problems associated with bulk production of Britlon seemed to have been solved and the company set up a working party to put forward proposals on how the new product should be phased into the company's activities.

The basic production method of Britlene and Britlon is similar to that of most man-made fibres. To make a man-made fibre, an oil-based organic chemical is polymerized (a process of joining several molecules into a long chain) in conditions of intense pressure and heat, often by the addition of a suitable catalyst. This polymerization takes place in large autoclaves (an industrial pressure cooker). The polymer is then extruded (forced through a nozzle like the rose of a garden watering can), rapidly cooled and then either spun onto cones or collected in bales.

The raw materials for Britlene and Britlon are produced at Teesside in the UK.

Britlene facilities

Britlene is produced at three factories in the UK: Teesside, Bradford and Dumfries. The largest site is Teesside with three plants. There is one plant at each of the other two sites.

All five production plants have a design capacity of 5.5 million kg per year of Britlene. However, after allowing for maintenance and an annual shutdown, expected output is 5 million kg per year.

Each plant operates on a 24-hours-per-day, seven-days-per-week basis.

Proposed Britlon facilities

Britlon's production process is very similar to that used for Britlene, but a totally new type of polymerization unit is needed prior to the extrusion stage.

DSF approached Alpen Engineering Company, an international chemical plant construction company, for help on a large-scale plant design of the new unit. Together they produced and tested an acceptable design.

Acquiring Britlon capacity

There are two ways of acquiring Britlon capacity. DSF could convert a Britlene plant, or it could construct an entirely new plant.

For a conversion, the new polymer unit would need to be constructed first. When complete it would be connected to the extrusion unit which would require minor conversion. At least two years would be needed either to build a new Britlon plant or to convert an old Britlene plant to Britlon production.

The company Chief Executive Officer was quoted as saying:

'The creation of an entirely new site would increase the complexities of multi-site operation to an unacceptable level. Conversely, the complete closure of one of the three existing sites is, I consider, a waste of the manpower and physical resources that we have invested in that location. I believe expansion could take place at one, two or all of the existing sites.'

Only on Teesside is there higher than average general unemployment, but the unemployment rate for skilled and semi-skilled workers is quite low at all sites. Demand for skilled labour on Teesside is from two giant companies, both of whom are expanding in that area; at Dumfries and Bradford there is little or no competition.

Demand

Demand forecasts for the two products are shown in Table 6.5. They show that, although Britlene sales will probably fall rapidly once Britlon is introduced, there is likely to be a residual level of sales of the older product.

Table 6.5 Forecast sales for Britlene and Britlon (millions of kg per year)

Potential sales	Britlene	Britlon
1996 (actual)	24.7	–
1997	22	–
1998	20	–
1999	17	3 (assuming availability)
2000	13	16
2001	11	27
2002	10	29

Questions

1 What order schedule would you propose for conversions and new plant?

2 In which locations would you make these capacity changes?

3 What criteria have you used to make your recommendations?

4 What do you see as the main dangers facing DSF as it changes its capacity over the next five or six years?

Discussion questions

1 Talk to an operations manager and then construct a diagram depicting the organization's supply network. How is the performance of suppliers monitored?

2 Why should operations managers be concerned with the whole network? Illustrate your answer using an organization of your own choice.

3 Explain what is meant by vertical integration. Explain how and why upstream and downstream integration might be used by a Mediterranean-based sailing holiday company.

4 Most organizations could, if they wished, choose to reduce the extent of their vertical integration. For the following operations, which activities do you think the organization could sub-contract out if it wished to focus more on its primary activity of serving customers:
   – a public library
   – a sports complex
   – a fast-food restaurant
   – a bank?

5 Oil companies are some of the most integrated companies in the world. For a large oil company, such as BP or Shell, draw the supply network from raw materials through to the end customers. Which of the activities you have drawn in the network do you think a company like Shell is involved in? Why do you think such companies are so vertically integrated?

6 An aluminium extrusion company, part of a large integrated aluminium company, has traditionally been engaged in extruding aluminium sections for use in the construction of double-glazed windows. However, the fashion in double-glazed windows has recently moved from aluminium towards a combination of aluminium and UPVC (a polymer). Currently all the aluminium which the extrusion company buys in comes from other parts of the integrated company. Do you think the extrusion company should continue to extrude aluminium sections and provide demand for the other parts of the company, in spite of the changes in its own markets? Alternatively, should the company pursue its own interests and begin extruding aluminium/UPVC combined sections, which it would appear the market wants?

7 A research company has decided to set up a new laboratory in Australia to provide analysis services for mineral extraction companies. Table 6.6 shows the three locations it is considering and the criteria which it is using to make the decision. If the first two factors are twice as important as the rest, which location do you think is most suitable for the new laboratory?

Table 6.6 Scoring for three locations (scores out of 100)

Factor	Perth	Sydney	Darwin
Closeness to customers	80	50	90
Closeness to universities	70	90	20
Attractiveness of city	70	90	50
Climate	60	80	60
Schools	70	80	60
Housing costs	60	20	100
Availability of sites	70	50	100

8 A Hong Kong company specializing in the manufacture of garden furniture has decided to establish a distribution centre in Europe. The possible locations are Birmingham, Amsterdam and Belgrade. Several criteria have been scored out of 100 (see Table 6.7).

Table 6.7 Scoring for three locations

Factor	Birmingham	Amsterdam	Belgrade
Cost of land	60	50	80
Distribution costs	15	70	60
Expected annual labour turnover	30	30	70
Housing availability	60	20	75
Market access	50	60	55
Expansion possibilities	70	20	80

The Managing Director considers the cost of land and the distribution costs to be three times as important as labour turnover and housing availability, and twice as important as the market access and expansion possibilities. Which location should the company adopt?

9 Join with a colleague and assess the location of two or three competing services, for example, supermarkets, dentists or car repair garages. Undertake your assessment individually then compare your results and identify and try to reconcile the differences in ratings and criteria. Are there any other performance criteria that compensate for any organization's poor location?

10 The Vegocream Corporation has decided to extend its operations from North America to Europe. The company retails its extensive range of vegetable-flavoured ice-creams through its high street outlets, where it caters for sit-down customers as well as take-away business. What decisions do you think the Vegocream company will have to take in planning its locations strategy? Draw up a series of questions which you think might be useful to the company when it decides whether to take up the lease on a particular site.

11 Location is always considered of particular importance in retail operations. Why do you think this is so?

12 A company which assembles garden furniture obtains its components from three suppliers. Supplier A provides all the boxes and packaging material; supplier B provides all metal components; and supplier C provides all plastic components. Supplier A sends one truck load of the materials per week to the factory and is located at the position (1,1) on a grid reference which covers the local area. Supplier B sends four truck loads of components per week to the factory and is located at point (2,3) on the grid. Supplier C sends three truck loads of components per week to the factory and is located at point (4,3) on the grid. After assembly, all the products are sent to a warehouse which is located at point (5,1) on the grid. Assuming there is little or no waste generated in the process, where should the company locate its factory so as to minimize transportation costs? Assume that transportation costs are directly proportional to the number of truck loads of parts, or finished goods, transported per week.

13 In what ways does the advent of internet-based delivery of services change the service location decision?

14 What is meant by capacity? What input and output measures of capacity might be used for the following operations, and explain which one is more likely to be used:
 – car plant
 – bus company
 – water company
 – chiropodist?

15 The forecast demand for a new product over the next seven periods is as shown in Table 6.8. The company is deciding the timing of its capacity expansion and contraction strategy. If the company has decided to build plants with a capacity of 15 000 units per period, when would you recommend the company commissions, or takes out of commission, its plants, assuming that:
 (a) it adopts a capacity-leading strategy;
 (b) it adopts a capacity-lagging strategy?

Table 6.8 Forecast demand

Period	Demand
1	10 000
2	30 000
3	50 000
4	60 000
5	64 000
6	62 000
7	55 000

16 A solicitor, although not as yet working as much as he would like, wishes to treble the size of his practice over the next five years. Explain how this might be achieved and the advantages and disadvantages of leading or lagging demand.

17 Why should the timing of capacity expansion affect the profitability of a company and its cash flow? Do you think the strategy which maximizes profitability also gives the best cash-flow performance?

Notes on chapter

1 Jones, C. (1990) 'Cross-boundary Supply Chain Management', *Professional Engineer*, Vol 3, No 5.
2 Jones, C. (1990), *op. cit.*
3 Source: Zwick, S. (1999) 'World Cars', *Time Magazine*, Feb 22.
4 Hayes, R.H. and Wheelwright, S.C. (1994) *Restoring our Competitive Edge*, John Wiley.
5 Sources: 'Unlucky or Unwise?', *Financial Times*, 13 Nov 1993; and Loveman, G. 'Euro Disney: The First 100 Days', *Harvard Business School Case Study 5-093-013*.
6 Sources: Pitman, J. (1994) 'Land of the Rising Sun Casts a Long Shadow', *The Times*, 7 Sept 1994; and Garner, R. (1990) 'Why Toyota Chose Derby', *Financial Times*, 5 June 1990.
7 Sources: 'Ford Revamp Leads Europe in the Driving Seat for Small Cars', *The European*, 29 April 1994; 'Car Giant Makes Poland their Gateway to the East', *The European*, 29 April 1994; 'Gone West', *The Economist*, 11 July 1992.
8 This case is based on an original case 'Doman Synthetic Fibres' by Peter Jones of Sheffield Hallam University, UK

Selected further reading

Bartlett, C. and Ghoshal, S. (1989) *Managing Across Borders*, Harvard Business School Press.

Blackstone, W.H. Jr (1989) *Capacity Management*, South Western.

Craig, C.S. *et al.* (1984) 'Models of the Retail Location Process', *Journal of Retailing*, Vol 60, No 1.

Ferdows, K. (1997) 'Making the Most of Foreign Factories', *Harvard Business Review*, March–April.

Financial Times (1999) 'Business Locations in Europe', *Financial Times Survey*, 4 Oct 1999.

Fuller, J.B., O'Connor, J. and Rawlinson, R. (1993) 'Tailored Logistics: The Next Advantage', *Harvard Business Review*, Vol 71, No 3.

Ghosh, A. and Craig, C.S. (1983) 'Formulating Retail Location Strategy in a Changing Environment', *Journal of Marketing*, Vol 47, Summer.

Goldhar, J.D. and Jelenek, M. (1983) 'Plan for Economies of Scope', *Harvard Business Review*, Vol 61, No 6.

Hammesfahr, R.D.J., Hope, J.A. and Ardalan, A. (1993) 'Strategic Planning for Production Capacity', *International Journal of Operations and Production Management*, Vol 13, No 5.

Hayes, R.H. and Wheelwright, S.C. (1984) *Restoring our Competitive Edge*, John Wiley.

Heinz, P. (1993) *Mutual Competitive Advantage*, Financial Times/Pitman Publishing.

Jarillo, J.C. (1993) *Strategic Networks: Creating the Borderless Organisation*, Butterworth-Heinemann.

Kanter, R.M. (1991) 'Transcending Business Boundaries, 12 000 World Managers You Change', *Harvard Business Review*, Vol 69, No 3.

Lamming, R. (1993) *Beyond Partnership: Strategies for Innovation and Lean Supply*, Prentice Hall.

Manne, A.S. (1967) *Investments for Capacity Expansion*, George Allen and Unwin.

Poirier, C.C and Reiter, S.E. (1996) *Supply Chain Optimisation*, Berrett-Koehler.

Porter, M.E. (1998) 'Clusters and the New Economy of Competition', *Harvard Business Review*, Vol 76, No 6.

Quinn, J.B. (1999) 'Strategic Outsourcing: Leveraging Knowledge Capabilities', *Sloan Management Review*, Summer.

Sasser, W.E. (1976) 'Match Supply and Demand in Service Industries', *Harvard Business Review*, Vol 54, No 6.

Schmenner, R.W. (1982) *Making Business Location Decisions*, Prentice Hall.

Schniederjans, M.J. (1998) '*International Facility Location and Acquisition Analysis*', Quorum Books, New York.

Sugiura, H. (1990) 'How Honda Localises its Global Strategy', *Sloan Management Review*, Fall.

Layout and flow

Introduction

The layout of an operation is concerned with the physical location of its transforming resources. Put simply, layout is deciding where to put all the facilities, machines, equipment and staff in the operation. Layout is one of the most obvious characteristics of an operation. It is the thing most of us would first notice on entering an operation for the first time, because it determines its 'shape' and appearance. It also determines the way in which the transformed resources – the materials, information and customers – flow through the operation. Relatively small changes in the position of a machine in a factory, or goods in a supermarket, or changing rooms in a sports centre can affect the flow of materials or people through the operation. This, in turn, can affect the costs and general effectiveness of the operation. Figure 7.1 shows the facilities layout activity in the overall model of design in operations.

| Figure 7.1 | The design activities in operations management covered in this chapter |

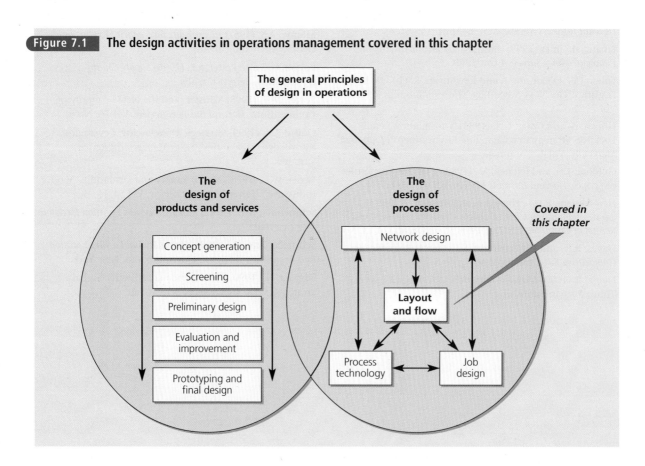

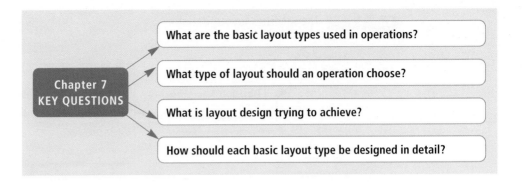

| Chapter 7 KEY QUESTIONS |

What are the basic layout types used in operations?

What type of layout should an operation choose?

What is layout design trying to achieve?

How should each basic layout type be designed in detail?

The layout procedure

There are some practical reasons why the layout decision is an important one in most operations:

- Layout is often a lengthy and difficult task because of the physical size of the transforming resources being moved.
- The re-layout of an existing operation can disrupt its smooth running, leading to customer dissatisfaction or lost production.
- If the layout (with hindsight) is wrong, it can lead to over-long or confused flow patterns, inventory of materials, customer queues building up in the operation, customers being inconvenienced, long process times, inflexible operations, unpredictable flow and high cost.

In effect there is a double pressure on the layout decision. Changing a layout can be difficult and expensive to execute, so operations managers are reluctant to do it too often. At the same time they have to get it right. The consequences of any misjudgements in an operation's layout will have a considerable, and usually long-term, effect on the operation.

Designing the layout of an operation, like any design activity, must start with an appreciation of the operation's strategic objectives. However, this is only the starting point of what is a multi-stage process which leads to the final physical layout of the operation (*see* Fig. 7.2).

● Select the process type

The concept of *process type* is often confused with that of layout. We described the decision of which process to adopt in Chapter 4. The process types shown in Figure 7.2 are broad approaches to the organization of the operations processes and activities. *Layout* is a narrower concept, but in many ways is the physical manifestation of a process type. Largely, it is the volume–variety characteristics of the operation which dictate its process type. There is often some overlap, however, between the process types which can be used for a given volume–variety position. In cases where more than one process type is possible, the relative importance of the operation's performance objectives can influence the decision. Broadly speaking, the more important the cost objective is to the operation, the more likely it is to adopt the process type closer to the high volume–low variety end of the process-type spectrum.

● Select the basic layout

After the process type has been selected, the *basic layout* type needs to be selected. The basic layout type is the general form of the arrangement of the facilities in the operation.

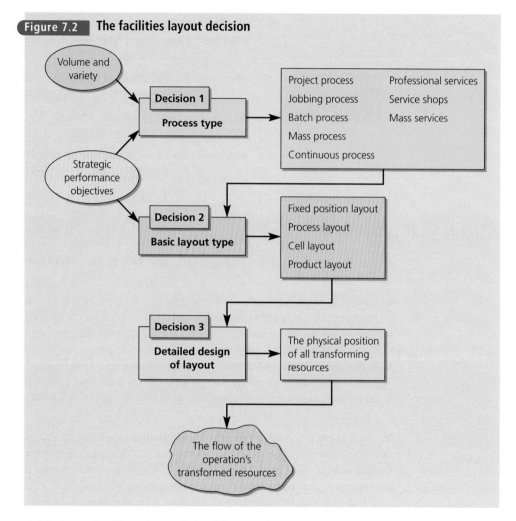

Figure 7.2 The facilities layout decision

Most practical layouts are derived from only four *basic layout types*:

- fixed-position layout
- process layout
- cell layout
- product layout.

The relationship between process type and basic layout type is not totally deterministic. One process type does not necessarily imply one particular basic layout. As Table 7.1 indicates, each process type could adopt a different basic layout type.

● Selecting the detailed design of the layout

Although the choice of a basic layout type governs the general way in which facilities are arranged relative to each other, it does not precisely define the exact position of each individual part of the operation. The final stage in the layout activity is to move towards this fully specified design of the layout. There are many techniques which help to do this, some of which are described later in the chapter.

Table 7.1 The relationship between process types and basic layout types

Manufacturing process types	Basic layout types	Service process types
Project processes / Jobbing processes	Fixed-position layout	Professional services
Batch processes	Process layout	Service shops
	Cell layout	
Mass processes / Continuous processes	Product layout	Mass services

The basic layout types

● Fixed-position layout

Fixed-position layout is in some ways a contradiction in terms, since the transformed resources do not move between the transforming resources. Instead of materials, information or customers flowing through an operation, the recipient of the processing is stationary and the equipment, machinery, plant and people who do the processing move as necessary. The reasons for this could be that the product or the recipient of the service is too large to be moved conveniently, or it might be too delicate to move, or perhaps it could object to being moved; for example:

- *Motorway construction* – the product is too large to move.
- *Open-heart surgery* – patients are too delicate to move.
- *High-class service restaurant* – customers would object to being moved to where food is prepared.
- *Shipbuilding* – the product is too large to move.
- *Mainframe computer maintenance* – the product is too big and probably also too delicate to move, and the customer might object to bringing it in for repair.

A construction site is typical of a fixed-position layout in that there is a limited amount of space which must be allocated to the various transforming resources. The main problem in designing this layout will be to allocate areas of the site to the various contractors so that:

- they have adequate space for their needs;
- they can receive and store their deliveries of materials;
- all contractors can have access to the part of the project on which they are working without interfering with each other's movements;
- the total movement of contractors and their vehicles and materials is minimized as far as possible.

In practice, the effectiveness of a fixed-position layout such as this will be tied up with the scheduling of access to the site and the reliability of deliveries. On most sites

Even some products which are themselves mobile are assembled on a fixed-position basis – these railway locomotives, for example

there is not room to allocate permanent space to every contractor who will, at some time, need access. Only the larger, more important or longer-term contractors are likely to warrant permanent space. Other contractors will take up space on a temporary basis. This leaves the layout vulnerable to any disruptions to the planning and control of the project (some of these issues are discussed in detail in Chapter 16).

● Process layout

Process layout is so called because the needs and convenience of the transforming resources which constitute the processes in the operation dominate the layout decision. In process layout, similar processes (or processes with similar needs) are located together. The reason can be that it is convenient for the operation to group them together, or that the utilization of transforming resources is improved. This means that when products, information or customers flow through the operation, they will take a route from process to process according to their needs. Different products or customers will have different needs and therefore take different routes through the operation. For this reason the flow pattern in the operation might be very complex.

Examples of process layouts include:

● *Hospital* – some processes (e.g. X-ray machines and laboratories) are required by several types of patient; some processes (e.g. general wards) can achieve high staff and bed utilization.

● *Machining the parts which go into aircraft engines* – some processes (e.g. heat treatment) need specialist support (heat and fume extraction); some processes (e.g. machining centres) require the same technical support from specialist setter–operators; some processes (e.g. grinding machines) get high machine utilization as all parts which need grinding pass through a single grinding section.

- *Supermarket* – some processes, such as the area holding tinned vegetables, are convenient to restock if grouped together. Some, such as the area holding frozen vegetables, need the common technology of freezer cabinets. Others, such as the areas holding fresh vegetables, might be together because that way they can be made to look attractive to customers (vegetables on market stalls, for example).

Fixed-position layout at Alstom combined-cycle generators[1] CWS

Alstom is one of the world's largest manufacturers of power generation and traction machinery. A growing area of its business is in the project management, manufacturing and construction of combined-cycle gas-turbine electricity generation stations. A typical project, illustrated in Figure 7.3, is an enormous undertaking, extending over at least three years. Most of the equipment is made-to-order, very large and heavy, and manufactured to very high specification and conformance.

Almost all aspects of the site construction of a power station involve fixed-position layouts. Components and raw materials, such as concrete and steel, are brought to the point of use and are progressively incorporated into the work. Cranes, building machinery and all the specialist equipment needed for the tasks are brought to site, along with the skilled employees and contractors who each

undertake specific tasks on the project.

Once most of this work is completed, the mechanical and electrical items are delivered to the site, according to a carefully prepared schedule. Some of these arrive as complete units, others as modules or kits of parts to be built up on site in their fixed positions. For example, one part of the steam turbine is made and assembled at the factory, again using a fixed-position layout, and then transported in one piece to site. A similar approach is used for the generator stator assembly which is built up on a frame in the factory.

At one time it was normal for the whole turbine/generator to be fully assembled in a fixed position in the factory; it was then dismantled and taken to site for reassembly. This was because many of the parts had to be adjusted to fit together perfectly, and so pre-assembly was used to ensure

| Figure 7.3 | **Products like this one are manufactured in a fixed-position layout** |

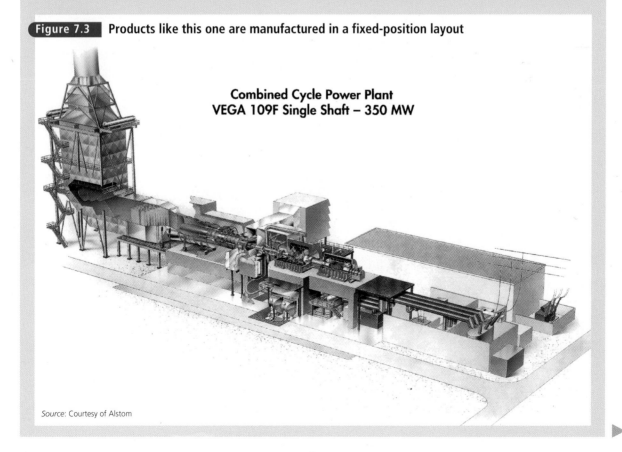

**Combined Cycle Power Plant
VEGA 109F Single Shaft – 350 MW**

Source: Courtesy of Alstom

that everything was correct before delivery. Now, however, improvements in design and manufacturing technologies have enabled the company to make these large components much more accurately, so that much more assembly can be done once only at the exact position required on site. This has also helped the company respond to market pressures which require much shorter lead times and lower prices.

Questions

1 Although the products described in this box are assembled in place using a fixed-position layout, they are not exactly one-offs. The company must have installed many of these type of machines. Do you think the nature of the layout for the installation is the same every time it installs a generator? If not, what factors at each site are likely to influence the layout?

2 Increasingly, parts of these products are assembled in the factory and transported to the site. What advantage do you think this gives the company?

Figure 7.4 shows a process layout in a business school library. The various 'processes' – reference books, enquiry desk, journals, and so on – are located in different parts of the operation. The customer is free to move between the processes depending on his or her requirements. The figure also shows the route taken by one customer on one visit to the library. If the routes taken by all the customers who visited the library were superimposed on the plan, the pattern of the traffic between the various parts of the operation

Figure 7.4 **An example of a process layout in a library showing the path of just one customer**

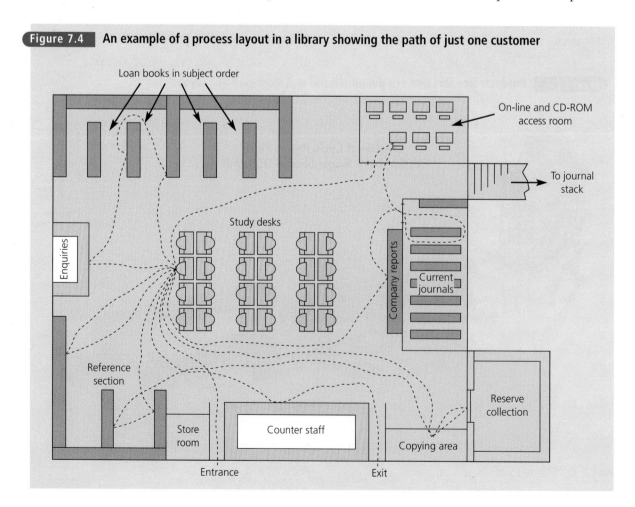

would be revealed. The density of this traffic flow is an important piece of information in the detailed design of this type of layout, as we shall see later in this chapter. The main point to understand at this stage is that changing the location of the various processes in the library will change the pattern of flow for the library as a whole.

● Cell layout

A cell layout is one where the transformed resources entering the operation are preselected (or preselect themselves) to move to one part of the operation (or cell) in which all the transforming resources, to meet their immediate processing needs, are located. The cell itself may be arranged in either a process or product (*see* next section) layout. After being processed in the cell, the transformed resources may go on to another cell. In effect, cell layout is an attempt to bring some order to the complexity of flow which characterizes process layout.

Examples of cell layouts include:

- *Some computer component manufacture* – the processing and assembly of some types of computer parts may need a special area dedicated to the manufacturing of parts for one particular customer who has special requirements such as particularly high quality levels.
- *'Lunch' products area in a supermarket* – some customers use the supermarket just to purchase sandwiches, savoury snacks, cool drinks, yoghurt, etc. for their lunch. These products are often located close together so that customers who are just buying lunch do not have to search around the store.
- *Maternity unit in a hospital* – customers needing maternity attention are a well-defined group who can be treated together and who are unlikely to need the other facilities of the hospital at the same time that they need the maternity unit.

Although the idea of cell layout is often associated with manufacturing operations, the same principle can be, and is, used in services. In Figure 7.5 the ground floor of a department store is shown, comprising displays of various types of goods in different parts of the store. In this sense the predominant layout of the store is a process layout. Each display area can be considered a separate process devoted to selling a particular class of goods – shoes, clothes, books, and so on. The exception is the sports shop. This area is a shop-within-a-shop area which is devoted to many goods which have a common sporting theme. For example, it will stock sports clothes, sports shoes, sports bags, sports magazines, sports books and videos, sports equipment and gifts and sports energy drinks. Within the 'cell' there are all the 'processes' which are also located elsewhere in the store. They have been located in the 'cell' not because they are similar goods (shoes, books and drinks would not usually be located together) but because they are needed to satisfy the needs of a particular type of customer. The store management calculates that enough customers come to the store to buy 'sports goods' in particular (rather than shoes, clothes, books etc.) to devote an area specifically for them. The store is also aware that someone coming to the store with the intention of purchasing some sports shoes might also be persuaded to buy other sports goods if they are placed in the same area.

● Product layout

Product layout involves locating the transforming resources entirely for the convenience of the transformed resources. Each product, piece of information or customer follows a prearranged route in which the sequence of activities that are required matches the sequence in which the processes have been located. The transformed resources 'flow' along a 'line' of processes. This is why this type of layout is sometimes called 'flow' or 'line' layout. The flow of products, information or customers in product layout is clear, predictable and therefore relatively easy to control. In fact, in

Figure 7.5 The ground floor plan of a department store showing the sports goods shop-within-a-shop retail 'cell'

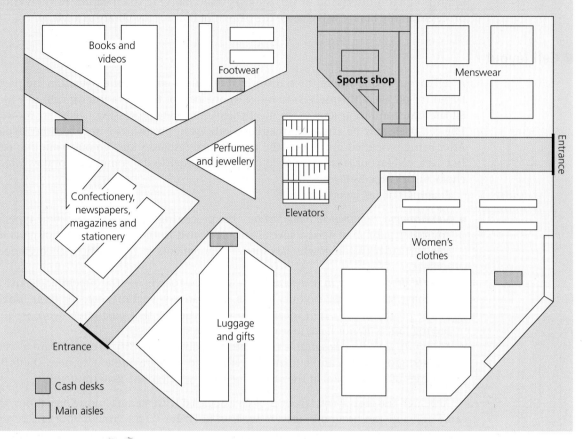

- Books and videos
- Footwear
- Sports shop
- Menswear
- Perfumes and jewellery
- Confectionery, newspapers, magazines and stationery
- Elevators
- Entrance
- Women's clothes
- Luggage and gifts
- Entrance
- ▭ Cash desks
- ▭ Main aisles

Layout of Delhaize De Leeuw supermarket in Ouderghem, Belgium[2]

The Delhaize Group operates over 400 retail outlets in Belgium, of which there are around 100 local Delhaize De Leeuw supermarkets. Delhaize supermarkets compete both by choices of location, which are convenient for frequent shoppers, and by the quality of the products and service. To remain profitable every Delhaize manager must maximize the revenue and contribution per square metre but must also minimize the costs of operating the store, in terms of material handling and checkout productivity, for example.

The Ouderghem supermarket has a somewhat unusual layout, having two entry points and two exit points. In common with most supermarket designs, the checkouts are positioned near the outside wall, but during most of the day only a few are used. Newspapers are sold near the checkout queues, so that customers can catch up with the news while waiting. Checkout operators face into the store, towards the queue, to emphasize the

need to work quickly when there is a queue. The store has 10 checkouts – a very large number for a store of only 1500 square metres. This is because there is a large peak of sales in the early evening, and long queues at the checkout would be unacceptable.

Delhaize uses relatively wide aisles between the shelves, to ensure good flows of trolleys, but this has been at the expense of reduced shelf space which would allow a wider range of products to be stocked. The actual location of all the products is a critical decision, directly affecting the convenience to customers, their level of spontaneous purchases, and the costs of filling the shelves. The overall layout of the supermarket has separate, clearly marked self-service areas for packaged food, drinks, fruit and vegetables, and household items. The served delicatessen area (which sells products with above-average margins) is positioned centrally so that most shoppers must pass it. The displays of fruit and vegetables are located adjacent to the main entrance, as a signal of freshness and wholesomeness, providing an attractive and welcoming point of entry.

High-turnover, 'essential', known-value items such as rice, pasta, sugar and oil are positioned centrally and visibly, so that they are easy to find. Profitable, fast-moving items are displayed at eye level, both to help the customer and to make restocking easier for the employees. Conversely, low-margin and low-turnover items are placed low down. Bulky or heavy products, such as packs of beer, are located near the storage area to facilitate restocking. Frozen foods are located at the ends of aisles, near the checkouts, so that

they can be purchased last. In some supermarkets, these positions are only used for promotions, as customers move slower around the ends of aisles and the goods on display can be seen from most directions.

Questions

1 What is the basic layout type used by this supermarket?

2 Are the objectives in designing a supermarket layout broadly similar to the objectives in designing a high-variety manufacturing operation? If not, what is the difference?

some customer-processing service operations, a product layout is adopted partly to help control the flow of customers through the operation. Predominantly, though, it is the standardized requirements of the product or service which lead to operations choosing product layouts.

Examples of product layout include:

- *Automobile assembly* – almost all variants of the same model require the same sequence of processes.
- *Mass-immunization programme* – all customers require the same sequence of clerical, medical and counselling activities.
- *Self-service cafeteria* – generally the sequence of customer requirements (starter, main course, dessert, drink) is common to all customers, but layout also helps control customer flow.

Figure 7.6 shows the sequence of processes in a paper-making operation. Such an operation would use product layout. The flow of materials through the operation is both evident and regular. Gone are the complexities of flow which characterized process layouts, and to a lesser extent cell layouts, and although different types of paper are produced in this operation, all types have the same processing requirements. First, the wood chips are combined with chemicals, water and steam in the 'cooking' process to form the 'pulp'. The pulp is then put through a cleaning process before being refined to help the fibres lock together. The mixing process combines the refined pulp

Figure 7.6 The sequence of processes in paper-making; each process will be laid out in the same sequence

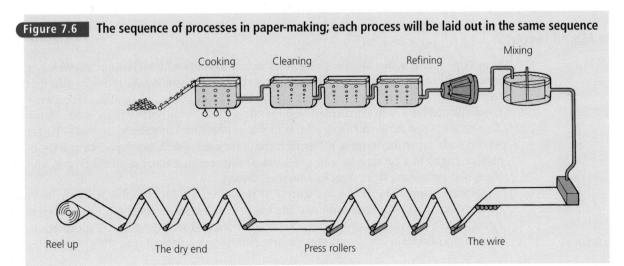

Figure 7.7   **An army induction centre which uses a product layout**

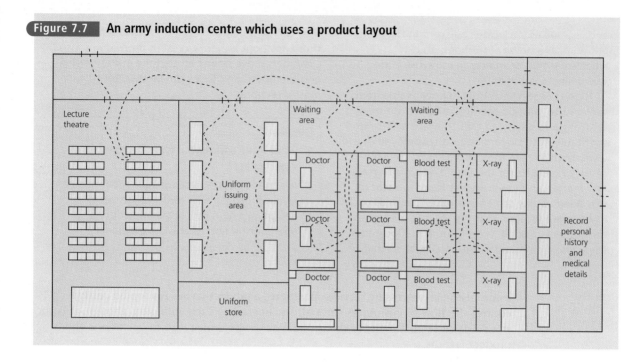

with more water, fillers, chemicals and dyes, after which it is spread on a fine flexible wire or plastic mesh. This is shaken from side to side as it moves along to lock the fibres into the sheet of paper and to drain away the water. The press rollers squeeze more water out of the paper and press the fibres closer together. The drying process continues to reduce the water level in the paper before, finally, it is wound onto large reels.[3]

It makes sense, then, to locate these processes in the order that they are required by the product and to let materials flow along in a predictable manner. In fact this particular example of product layout is an extreme one in some ways, because for the first part of its manufacture the paper is in a semi-liquid form. It would be physically difficult to handle the product in any way other than causing it to 'flow' between processes. Nevertheless, other products which have a common sequence of processes, such as televisions, freezers, air-conditioning units, and so on, are also manufactured using product layouts.

Service operations can also adopt a product layout if the 'processing' needs of customers or information have a common sequence. For example, recruits, on joining the armed forces, are likely to be 'processed' through an induction programme organized on a product-layout basis. Figure 7.7 shows the layout of an army induction unit.

● Mixed layouts

Many operations either design themselves hybrid layouts which combine elements of some or all of the basic layout types, or use the 'pure' basic layout types in different parts of the operation. For example, a hospital would normally be arranged on process-layout principles – each department representing a particular type of process (the X-ray department, the surgical theatres, the blood-processing laboratory, and so on). Yet within each department, quite different layouts are used. The X-ray department is probably arranged in a process layout, the surgical theatres in a fixed-position layout, and the blood-processing laboratory in a product layout.

Another example is shown in Figure 7.8. Here a restaurant complex is shown with three different types of restaurant and the kitchen which serves them all. The kitchen is arranged in a process layout, with the various processes (food storage, food preparation, cooking processes, etc.) grouped together. Different foods will take different routes

The grand piano assembly line at Yamaha

The Yamaha Corporation of Japan, founded in 1887, has grown to become the world's largest manufacturer of musical instruments, as well as producing a whole variety of other goods, from semiconductors and robots through to sporting goods and furniture, In recent years it has developed a reputation for product diversification, an understanding of new markets and, especially, innovative manufacturing methods. For example, it was one of the first piano manufacturers to make up-market grand pianos using assembly line techniques (the picture shows grand pianos being assembled in the same way as motor vehicles). Traditionally, grand pianos (as opposed to the less expensive and better selling vertical pianos) were made using individual build methods which relied on craft skills. The main advantage of this was that skilled workers could accommodate individual variations in the (often inconsistent) materials from which the piano is made. Each individual piano would be constructed around the idiosyncrasies of the material to make a product unique in its tone and tuning. Not so with Yamaha, who, although making some of the highest quality pianos in the world, emphasize consistency and reliability, as well as richness of tone.

Question

In the picture a white piano is moving down the assembly line with the black ones. Do you think this will pose any problems for managing this assembly line?

between the processes, depending on their processing requirements. The traditional service restaurant is arranged in a fixed-position layout. The customers stay at their tables while the food is brought to (and sometimes cooked at) the tables. The buffet restaurant is arranged in a cell-type layout with each buffet area having all the processes (dishes) necessary to serve customers with their starter, main course or dessert. In this case, customers who intend to partake of all three courses will need to be processed through all three cells before the completion of the service. Finally, in the cafeteria restaurant, all customers take the same route when being served with their meal. They may not take the opportunity to be served with every dish but they move through the same sequence of processes.

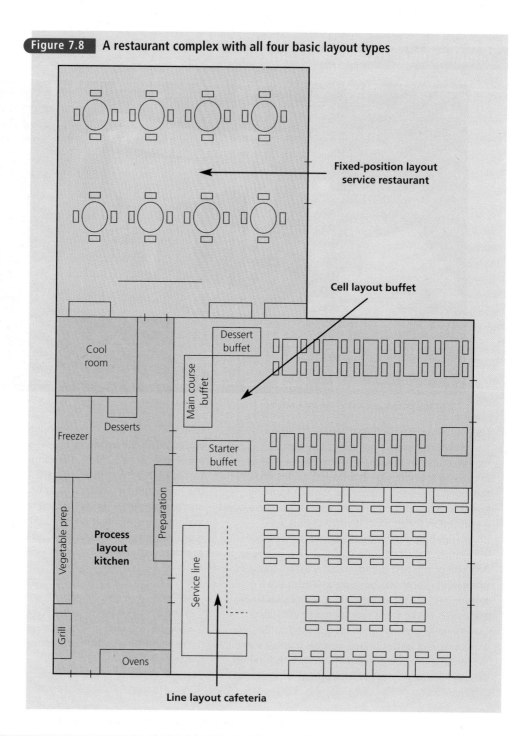

Figure 7.8 A restaurant complex with all four basic layout types

Fixed-position layout service restaurant

Cell layout buffet

Line layout cafeteria

Cool room

Dessert buffet

Main course buffet

Freezer

Desserts

Starter buffet

Vegetable prep

Preparation

Process layout kitchen

Service line

Grill

Ovens

Chocolate and customers flow through Cadbury's[4]

Flow of chocolate

In the famous Cadbury's chocolate factory at Bournville, on the outskirts of Birmingham, UK, chocolate products are manufactured to a high degree of consistency and efficiency. Production processes are based on a *product layout*. This has allowed Cadbury's engineers to develop and procure machinery to meet the technical and capacity requirements of each stage of the process. Consider, for example, the production of Cadbury's Dairy Milk bars. First, the standard liquid chocolate is prepared from cocoa beans, fresh milk and sugar using specialized equipment, connected together with pipes and conveyors. These processes operate continuously, day and night, to ensure consistency of both the chocolate itself and the rate of output. Next, the liquid is pumped through heated pipework to the moulding department, where it is automatically dispensed into a moving line of precision-made plastic moulds which form the chocolate bars and vibrate them to remove any trapped air bubbles. The moulds are continuously conveyed into a large refrigerator, allowing sufficient time for the chocolate to harden. The next stage inverts the moulds and shakes out the moulded bars. These then pass directly to a set of highly automated wrapping and packing machines, from where they go to the warehouse.

Flow of customers

In 1990, the company opened a large visitor centre called 'Cadbury World' alongside the factory (linked to a viewing area which looks onto the packaging area described above). Cadbury World is a permanent exhibition devoted entirely to chocolate and the part Cadbury has played in its fascinating history. Because most of the attractions are indoors, with limited circulation space, the main exhibition and demonstration areas are designed to allow a smooth flow of customers, where possible avoiding bottlenecks and delays. The design is also a 'product' layout with a single route for all customers.

Entry to the Exhibition Area is by timed ticket, to ensure a constant flow of input customers, who are free to walk around at their preferred speed, but are constrained to keep to the single track through the sequence of displays. On leaving this section, they are directed upstairs to the Chocolate Packaging Plant, where a guide escorts standard-sized batches of customers to the appropriate positions where they can see the packing processes and a video presentation. The groups are then led down to and around the Demonstration Area, where skilled employees demonstrate small-scale production of handmade chocolates. Finally, visitors are free to roam unaccompanied through a long, winding path of the remaining exhibits.

Cadbury has chosen to use the product layout design for both the production of chocolates and the processing of its visitors. In both cases, volumes are large and the variety offered is limited. Sufficient demand exists for each standard 'product', and the operations objective is to achieve consistent high quality at low cost. Neither operation has much volume flexibility, and both are expensive to change.

> **Question**
>
> Both customers and chocolate in the Cadbury's operation do seem to conform to a product-type layout. Does this mean that both operations have the same objectives?

● Volume–variety and layout type

The importance of flow to an operation will depend on its volume and variety characteristics. When volume is very low and variety is relatively high, 'flow' is not a major issue. For example, in telecommunications satellite manufacture, a fixed-position layout is likely to be appropriate because each product is different and because products 'flow' through the operation very infrequently. Under these conditions it is just not worth arranging facilities to minimize the flow of parts through the operation.

With somewhat higher volume and lower variety, the flow of the transformed resources becomes an issue which any layout must address. If the variety is still high, however, an entirely flow-dominated arrangement is difficult because products or customers will have different flow patterns. For example, the library in Figure 7.4 will arrange its different categories of books and its other services partly to minimize the average distance its customers have to 'flow' through the operation. Because its customers' needs vary, however, the library at best will arrange its layout to satisfy a majority of its customers but perhaps inconvenience a minority. When the variety of products or services reduces to the point where a distinct 'category' with similar requirements becomes evident but variety is still not small, cell layout could become appropriate, as in the sports goods cell in Figure 7.5. When the variety of products or services is relatively small and volume is high, the flow of materials, information or customers can become regularized and a product-based layout is likely to be appropriate, as in an assembly plant.

Examining these examples of the different basic layout types, we can see the different effects of volume and variety (*see* Fig. 7.9). Increasing volume increases the *importance* of flow, whereas reducing variety increases the *feasibility* of a layout based on evident and regular flow.

● Selecting a layout type

The decision of which layout type to adopt rarely, if ever, involves choosing between all four basic types. The volume–variety characteristics of the operation will, to a large extent, narrow the choice down to one or two options. Yet, as is implied in Figure 7.9, the spans of volumes and varieties encompassed by each layout type do overlap. The decision as to which layout type to adopt will be influenced by an understanding of their relative advantages and disadvantages.

Table 7.2 shows some of the more significant advantages and disadvantages associated with each layout type. It should be stressed, however, that the type of operation will influence their relative importance. For example, a high-volume television manufacturer may find the low-cost characteristics of a product layout attractive, but an amusement theme park may adopt the same layout type primarily because of the way it 'controls' customer flow. There may also be other ways of achieving flow objectives. The Eurohub terminal at Birmingham Airport switches the direction of flow by using technology to change customer routes.

Of all the characteristics of the various layout types, perhaps the most generally significant are the unit cost implications of layout choice. This is best understood by distinguishing between the fixed and variable cost elements of adopting each layout type. For any particular product or service, the fixed costs of physically constructing a fixed-position layout are relatively small compared with any other way of producing the same product or service. However, the variable costs of producing each individual product or service are relatively high compared to the alternative layout types. Fixed

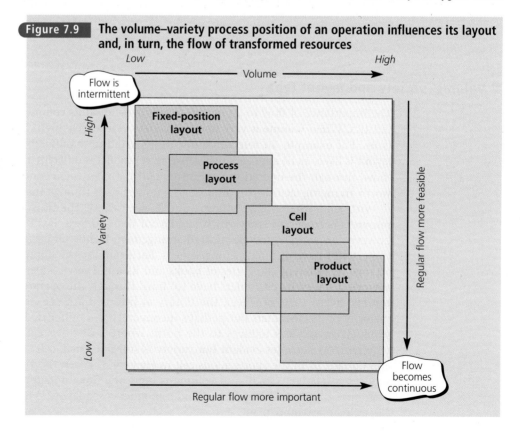

Figure 7.9 The volume–variety process position of an operation influences its layout and, in turn, the flow of transformed resources

Table 7.2 The advantages and disadvantages of the basic layout types

	Advantages	*Disadvantages*
Fixed-position	Very high mix and product flexibility	Very high unit costs
	Product or customer not moved or disturbed	Scheduling of space and activities can be difficult
	High variety of tasks for staff	Can mean much movement of plant and staff
Process	High mix and product flexibility	Low facilities utilization
	Relatively robust if in the case of disruptions	Can have very high work-in-progress or customer queueing
	Relatively easy supervision of equipment or plant	Complex flow can be difficult to control
Cell	Can give a good compromise between cost and flexibility for relatively high-variety operations	Can be costly to rearrange existing layout
		Can need more plant and equipment
	Fast throughput	Can give lower plant utilization
	Group work can result in good motivation	
Product	Low unit costs for high volume	Can have low mix flexibility
	Gives opportunities for specialization of equipment	Not very robust if there is disruption
	Materials or customer movement is convenient	Work can be very repetitive

Figure 7.10 (a) The basic layout types have different fixed and variable cost characteristics which seem to determine which one to use. (b) In practice the uncertainty about the exact fixed and variable costs of each layout means the decision can rarely be made on cost alone

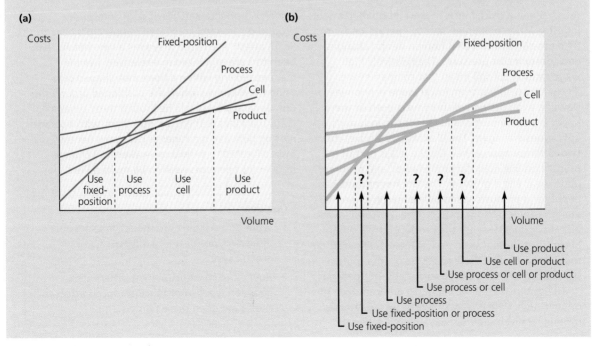

costs then tend to increase as one moves from fixed-position, through process and cell, to product layout. Variable costs per product or service tend to decrease, however. The total costs for each layout type will depend on the volume of products or services produced and are shown in Figure 7.10(a). This seems to show that for any volume there is a lowest-cost basic layout.

However, in practice, the cost analysis of layout selection is rarely as clear as this. The exact cost of operating the layout is difficult to forecast and will probably depend on many often difficult to predict factors. Rather than use lines to represent the cost of layout as volume increases, broad bands, within which the real cost is likely to lie, are probably more appropriate (*see* Fig. 7.10(b)). The discrimination between the different layout types is now far less clear. There are ranges of volume for which any of two or three layout types might provide the lowest operating cost. The less certainty there is over the costs, the broader the cost 'bands' will be, and the less clear the choice will be. The probable costs of adopting a particular layout need to be set in the broader context of advantages and disadvantages in Table 7.2.

Teams and lines in the garment industry

Photo courtesy of Terry King, CV Clothing

Line production of underwear and nightwear

Photo courtesy of Terry King, CV Clothing

Cell production of fashion clothes

Job design is a crucial issue in the European garment industry. Most companies have to operate under the twin pressures of seasonal fashion design changes and constant cost pressures. The relatively high wage rates in Europe mean that companies are always under threat from lower wage economies. Devising a job design which answers both of these needs is a continuing challenge for the industry's operations managers. The illustrations (above) show two different approaches. On the left is part of a production line manufacturing ladies' and childrens' underwear and nightwear. The line has around 30 people and products spend only a matter of seconds at each (single person) station. After performing the task, each operator puts the product into 'work-in-progress' stores between each stage. Usually staff do their own task, but there are three or four multi-skilled 'floaters' who can cover for absent operators.

The picture on the right shows a different type of organization. Here a team of five or six operators is making relatively high-fashion ladieswear – more complex products. Batches of garments, once produced, are rarely repeated so operators have to 'learn afresh' each time they start a new batch. The operators are organized in a relatively flexible manner, moving within a horseshoe-shaped cell, using the machines which are positioned around the cell. Generally there will be around three times as many machines as there are operators, with operators moving between machines as necessary. Because the tasks allocated to individual workers will change frequently, operators need to be multi-skilled.

Questions

1 What do you think are the advantages and disadvantages of the two types of work organization?

2 How would product/market differences between types of product produced affect the choice between these two systems?

Detailed design of the layout

Once the basic layout type has been decided, the next step is to decide the detailed design of the layout. Detailed design is the act of operationalizing the broad principles which were implicit in the choice of the basic layout type.

The output from the detailed design stage of layout is:

- the precise location of all facilities, plant, equipment and staff which constitute the 'work centres' of the operation;
- the space to be devoted to each work centre;
- the tasks which will be undertaken by each work centre.

● What makes a good layout?

Before considering the various methods used in the detailed design of layouts, it is useful to consider the objectives of the activity. To a certain extent the objectives will depend on circumstances, but there are some general objectives which are relevant to all operations:[5]

- *Inherent safety*. All processes which might constitute a danger to either staff or customers should not be accessible to the unauthorized. Fire exits should be clearly marked with uninhibited access. Pathways should be clearly defined and not cluttered.
- *Length of flow*. The flow of materials, information or customers should be channelled by the layout so as to be appropriate for the objectives of the operation. In many operations this means minimizing the distance travelled by transformed resources. This is not always the case, however: supermarkets, for example, might wish to make sure that customers pass particular goods on their way round the store.
- *Clarity of flow*. All flow of materials and customers should be well signposted, clear and evident to staff and customers alike. For example, manufacturing operations usually have clearly marked gangways. Service operations often rely on signposted routes, such as in hospitals which often have different coloured lines painted on the floor to indicate the routes to various departments.
- *Staff comfort*. Staff should be located away from noisy or unpleasant parts of the operation. The layout should provide for a well-ventilated, well-lit and, where possible, pleasant working environment.
- *Management coordination*. Supervision and communication should be assisted by the location of staff and communication devices.
- *Accessibility*. All machines, plant or equipment should be accessible to a degree which is sufficient for proper cleaning and maintenance.
- *Use of space*. All layouts should achieve an appropriate use of the total space available in the operation (including height as well as floor space). This usually means minimizing the space used for a particular purpose, but sometimes can mean achieving an impression of spacious luxury, as in the entrance lobby of a high-class hotel.
- *Long-term flexibility*. Layouts need to be changed periodically as the needs of the operation change. A good layout will have been devised with the possible future needs of the operation in mind. For example, if demand is likely to increase for a product or service, has the layout been designed to accommodate any future expansion?

● Detailed design in fixed-position layout

In fixed-position arrangements the location of resources will be determined, not on the basis of the flow of transformed resources, but on the convenience of transforming resources themselves. The objective of the detailed design of fixed-position layouts is to achieve a layout for the operation which allows all the transforming resources to maximize their contribution to the transformation process by allowing them to provide an effective 'service' to the transformed resources. The detailed layout of some fixed-position layouts, such as building sites, can become very complicated, especially if the planned schedule of activities is changed frequently. Imagine the chaos on a construction site if heavy trucks continually (and noisily) drove past the site office, delivery trucks for one contractor had to cross other contractors' areas to get to where they were storing their own materials, and the staff who spent most time at the building itself were located furthest away from it. Although there are techniques which help to locate resources on fixed position layouts, they are not widely used. One technique, called 'resource location analysis', evaluates the effects of locating the various transforming resources at all available locations on the site by using details of the site itself and the way the resources interact with each other.

Detailed design in process layout

The detailed design of process layouts is marked by the complexity, which is also the main flow characteristic, of this type of layout. Chief among the factors which lead to this complexity is the very large number of different options. For example, in the very simplest case of just two work centres, there are only two ways of arranging these *relative to each other*. But there are six ways of arranging three centres and 120 ways of arranging five centres.

The relationship is a factorial one. For N centres there are factorial N ($N!$) different ways of arranging the centres, where:

$$N! = N \times (N - 1) \times (N - 2) \times ... \quad (1)$$

So for a relatively simple process layout with, say, 20 work centres, there are $20! = 2.433 \times 10^{18}$ ways of arranging the operation.

It is partly because of this *combinatorial complexity* of process layouts that optimal solutions are difficult to achieve in practice. Most process layouts are designed by a combination of intuition, common sense, and systematic trial and error.

The information for process layouts

Before starting the process of detailed design in process layouts there are some essential pieces of information which the designer needs:

- the area required by each work centre;
- the constraints on the shape of the area allocated to each work centre;
- the degree and direction of flow between each work centre (for example, number of journeys, number of loads or cost of flow per distance travelled);
- the desirability of work centres being close together or close to some fixed point in the layout.

The last two pieces of information are particularly important because both influence directly the consequences of locating work centres relative to each other.

The degree and direction of flow are usually shown on a *flow record chart* like that shown in Figure 7.11(a) which records in this case the number of loads transported between departments. There are many ways in which this information could be gathered. For example, in some manufacturing operations, flow data can be derived from routing information for products and the demand for those products. Where flow is more random, as in a library for example, the information could be collected by observing the routes taken by customers over a typical period of time. If the direction of the flow between work centres makes little difference to the layout, the information can be collapsed as shown in Figure 7.11(b), an alternative form of which is shown in Figure 7.11(c).

In some operations there are significant differences in the costs of moving materials or customers between different work centres. For example, in Figure 7.11(d) the unit cost of transporting a load between the five work centres is shown. Here the unit cost of moving

Figure 7.11 | Collecting information in process layout

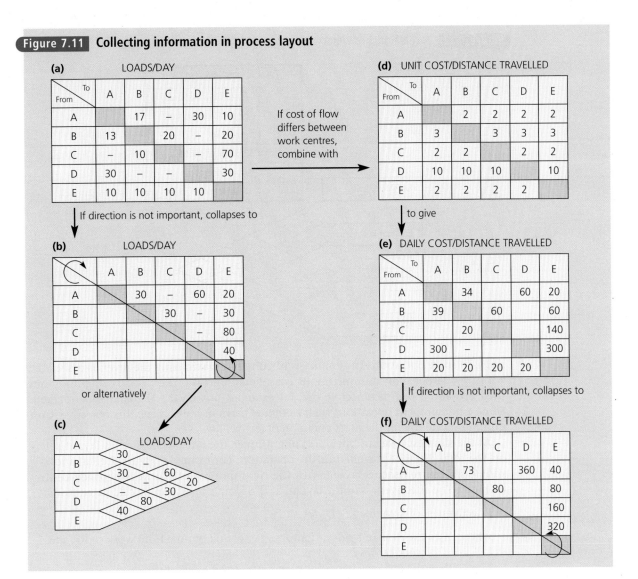

loads from work centre B is slightly higher than that from most other departments. There could be many reasons for this, for example because the products are particularly delicate after being processed at work centre B and need careful handling, or because they need to maintain temperature after being heat-treated and before they are processed further. Combining the unit cost and flow data gives the cost per distance travelled data shown in Figure 7.11(e). This has been collapsed as before into Figure 7.11(f).

An alternative qualitative method of indicating the relative importance of the relationship between work centres is the *relationship chart*. A relationship chart indicates the desirability of pairs of work centres being close to each other. Figure 7.12 shows the relationship chart for a testing laboratory. It is particularly important that some departments are close together, for example Electronic testing and Metrology. Other departments must be kept as far as possible from each other, for example Metrology and Impact testing.

The objectives of process layout

In most examples of process layout, the prime objective is to minimize the costs to the operation which are associated with the flow of transformed resources through the operation. So, for example, a furniture manufacturer would locate work centres in the factory so as to minimize the need to transport components. Similarly, a hospital would locate its departments to minimize the movement of its patients (and perhaps

Figure 7.12 A relationship chart

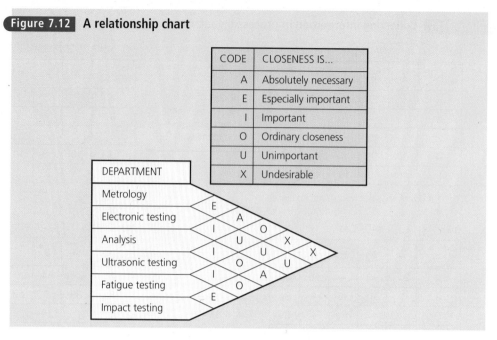

staff). In some operations the emphasis is shifted to maximizing the revenue associated with flow rather than minimizing its cost. Retail operations especially might lay out their operations to this objective (*see*, for example, box on the Delhaize supermarket). Some entertainment operations such as theme parks may also have this objective. Cost minimization is by far the most common objective, however.

At the simplest level an operation might judge the effectiveness of its layout solely on the total distance travelled in the operation. For example, Figure 7.13(a) shows a simple six-centre process layout with the total number of journeys between centres each day. The effectiveness of the layout, at this simple level, can be calculated from:

$$\text{Effectiveness of layout} = \Sigma F_{ij}\, D_{ij} \text{ for all } i \neq j$$

where F_{ij} = the flow in loads or journeys per period of time from work centre i to work centre j
         D_{ij} = the distance between work centre i and work centre j.

The lower the effectiveness score, the better the layout.

Figure 7.13 **(a) and (b) The objective of most process layouts is to minimize the cost associated with movement in the operation, sometimes simplified to minimizing the total distance travelled**

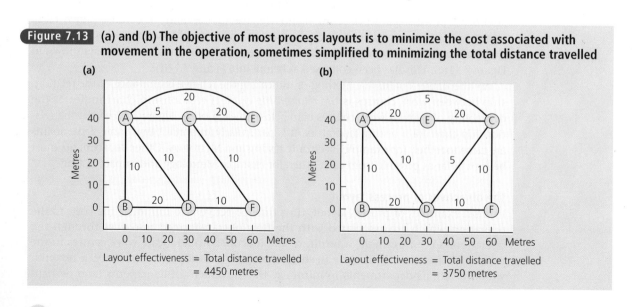

In this example the total of the number of journeys multiplied by the distance for each pair of departments where there is some flow is 4450 metres. This measure will indicate whether changes to the layout improve its effectiveness (at least in the narrow terms defined here). For example, if centres C and E are exchanged as in Figure 7.13(b) the effectiveness measure becomes 3750, showing that the new layout now has reduced the total distance travelled in the operation.

The calculations above assume that all journeys are the same in that their cost to the operation is the same. In some operations this is not so, however. For example, in the hospital some journeys involving healthy staff and relatively fit patients would have little importance compared with other journeys where very sick patients need to be moved from the operating theatres to intensive-care wards.

In these cases it might be worthwhile to incorporate a cost (or difficulty) element into the measure of layout effectiveness which is being minimized:

Effectiveness of layout = $\sum F_{ij} D_{ij} C_{ij}$ for all $i \neq j$

where C_{ij} = the cost per distance travelled of making a journey between departments i and j.

The general process layout design method

The general approach to determining the location of work centres in a process layout is as follows:

Step 1 Collect information relating to the work centres and the flow between them.

Step 2 Draw up a schematic layout showing the work centres and the flow between them, putting the work centres with the greatest flow closest to each other.

Step 3 Adjust the schematic layout to take into account the constraints of the area into which the layout must fit.

Step 4 Draw the layout showing the actual work centre areas and distances which materials or customers must travel. Calculate the effectiveness measure of the layout either as total distance travelled or as the cost of movement.

Step 5 Check to see if exchanging any two work centres will reduce the total distance travelled or the cost of movement. If so, make the exchange and return to step 4. If not, make this the final layout.

Worked example

Rotterdam Educational Group

As an example of a process layout, we can consider Rotterdam Educational Group (REG), a company which commissions, designs and manufactures education packs for distance-learning courses and training. It has leased a new building with an area of 1800 square metres, into which it needs to fit 11 'departments'. Prior to moving into the new building it has conducted an exercise to find the average number of trips taken by its staff between the 11 departments. Although some trips are a little more significant than others (because of the loads carried by staff) it has been decided that all trips will be treated as being of equal value.

Step 1 – Collect information

The areas required by each department together with the average daily number of trips between departments are shown in the flow chart in Figure 7.14. In this example the direction of flow is not relevant and very low flow rates (less than five trips per day) have not been included.

Figure 7.14 Flow information for Rotterdam Educational Group

DEPARTMENT	AREA (m²)	CODE
Reception	85	A
Meeting room	160	B
Layout and design	100	C
Editorial	225	D
Printing	200	E
Cutting	75	F
Receiving and shipping	200	G
Binding	120	H
Video production	160	I
Packing	200	J
Audio production	100	K

Flow values (from-to matrix): 40, 120, 100, 15, 80, 8, 30, 12, 40, 55, 70, 10, 5, 40, 100, 80, 25, 15, 20

Dimensions of the building = 30 metres × 60 metres

Step 2 – Draw schematic layout

Figure 7.15 shows the first schematic arrangement of departments. The thickest lines represent high flow rates between 70 and 120 trips per day; the medium lines are used for flow rates between 20 and 69 trips per day; and the thinnest lines for flow rates between 5 and 19 trips per day. The objective here is to arrange the work centres so that those with the thick lines are closest together. The higher the flow rate, the shorter the line should be.

Figure 7.15 Schematic layout placing centres with high traffic levels close to each other

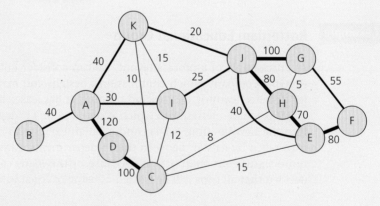

Step 3 – Adjust the schematic layout

If departments were arranged exactly as shown in Figure 7.15, the building which housed them would be of an irregular, and therefore high-cost, shape. The layout needs adjusting to take into account the shape of the building. Figure 7.16 shows the departments arranged in a more ordered fashion which corresponds to the dimensions of the building.

Figure 7.16 Schematic layout adjusted to fit building geometry

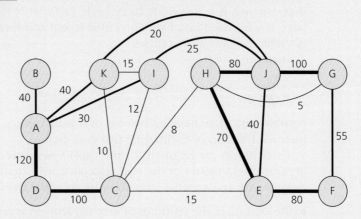

Step 4 – Draw the layout

Figure 7.17 shows the departments arranged with the actual dimensions of the building and occupying areas which approximate to their required areas. Although the distances between the centroids of departments have changed from Figure 7.16 to accommodate their physical shape, their relative positions are the same. It is at this stage that a quantitative expression of the cost of movement associated with this relative layout can be calculated.

Step 5 – Check by exchanging

The layout in Figure 7.17 seems to be reasonably effective but it is usually worthwhile to check for improvement by exchanging pairs of departments to see if any reduction in total flow can be obtained. For example, departments H and J might be exchanged, and the total distance travelled calculated again to see if any reduction has been achieved.

Figure 7.17 Final layout of building

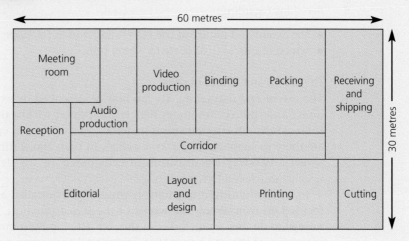

Computer-aided process layout design

The combinatorial complexity of process layout has led to the development of several heuristic procedures to aid the design process. Heuristic procedures use what have been described as 'shortcuts in the reasoning process' and 'rules of thumb' in the search for a reasonable solution. They do not search for an optimal solution (though they might find one by chance) but rather attempt to derive a good suboptimal solution.

One such computer-based heuristic procedure is called CRAFT (Computerized Relative Allocation of Facilities Technique).[6] The reasoning behind this procedure is that, whereas it is infeasible to evaluate factorial N ($N!$) different layouts when N is large, it is feasible to start with an initial layout and then evaluate all the different ways of exchanging two work centres.

There are

$$\frac{N!}{2!\,(N-2)!}$$

possible ways of exchanging two out of N work centres. So for a 20 work centre layout, there are 190 ways of exchanging two work centres.

Three inputs are required for the CRAFT heuristic: a matrix of the flow between departments; a matrix of the cost associated with transportation between each of the departments; and a spatial array showing an initial layout. From these:

- the location of the centroids of each department is calculated;
- the flow matrix is weighted by the cost matrix, and this weighted flow matrix is multiplied by the distances between departments to obtain the total transportation costs of the initial layout;
- the model then calculates the cost consequence of exchanging every possible pair of departments.

The exchange giving the most improvement is then fixed, and the whole cycle is repeated with the updated cost flow matrix. These iterations are repeated until no further improvement is made by exchanging two departments. Figure 7.18 shows the initial layout, which was an input to the model, and the final layout generated by the model.

● Detailed design in cell layout

Cells are a compromise between the flexibility of process layout and the simplicity of product layout (treated next). For example, Figure 7.19 shows how a process layout has been divided into four cells, each of which has the resources to process a 'family' of parts. In doing this the operations management has implicitly taken two interrelated decisions regarding:

- the extent and nature of the cells it has chosen to adopt;
- which resources to allocate to which cells.

The extent and nature of cells

The extent and nature of cells can best be described by examining the amount of the direct and indirect resources which are located within the cell. Direct resources are those which directly transform material, information or customers. Indirect resources are there to support the direct resources in their transformation activities. Figure 7.20 shows a two-way classification of cells based on the degree of direct and indirect resources included in the cell.

In the bottom-right quadrant is what might be called a 'pure' cell. Its activities are focused on completing the whole of the transformation, and all the direct resources needed to do this are included in the cell. The top-right quadrant represents the logical extension of the cell concept to include all the support and administrative indirect resources needed for the cell to 'stand alone'. These large 'cells' are sometimes referred to as the 'plant-within-a-plant' concept. Similarly, a maternity unit could, if it contains all its support resources, also stand alone. The bottom-left quadrant represents the type of cell where resources are placed together because they are frequently needed in the same part of total transformation. For example, two machines which are always used one after the other could be put together. Similarly, a large library, although it probably

Figure 7.18 — (a) Initial layout array for the CRAFT heuristic. (b) Final layout after four iterations of the CRAFT heuristic

(a)

```
                   Location pattern                 Iteration 0

      1  2  3  4  5  6  7  8  9 10 11 12 13 14 15 16 17 18 19 20
 1    A  A  A  A  A  A  B  B  B  B  C  C  C  C  C  C  C  D  D  D
 2    A              A  B        B  C                    D     D
 3    A              A  B        B  C              C  D     D
 4    A  A  A  A  A  A  B        B  C              C  D     D
 5    E  E  E  E  E  E  B  B  B  B  C  C  C  C  C  C  C  D  D  D
 6    E              E  F  F  F  F  F  G  G  G  G  G  G  G  G  G
 7    E              E  F              F  G                 G
 8    E  E  E  E  E  E  E  F  F  F  F  F  G                 G
 9    H  H  H  I  I  I  I  I  I  I  I  I  I  G              G
10    H     H  I                    I  G                    G
11    H     H  I                 I  I  I  G  G  G  G  G  G  G  G
12    H     H  I              I  J  J  J  J  J  J  K  K  K  K  K  K
13    H     H  I              I  J              J  K           K
14    H  H  H  I  I  I  I  I  I  I  J  J  J  J  J  J  K  K  K  K  K  K
```

Total cost 11 711.24   Est cost reduction 0

(b)

```
                   Location pattern                 Iteration 4

      1  2  3  4  5  6  7  8  9 10 11 12 13 14 15 16 17 18 19 20
 1    E  E  E  E  E  E  B  B  B  B  C  C  C  C  C  C  C  J  J  J
 2    E              E  B        B  C                    J     J
 3    E              E  B        B  C              C  J     J
 4    E  E  E  E  E  E  B        B  C              C  J     J
 5    A  A  A  A  A  A  B  B  B  B  C  C  C  C  C  C  C  J  J  J
 6    A              A  D  D  D  D  D  G  G  G  G  G  G  G  G  G
 7    A              A  D              D  G                 G
 8    A  A  A  A  A  A  D  D  D  D  D  G                    G
 9    K  K  K  I  I  I  I  I  I  I  I  I  I  G              G
10    K     K  I                    I  G                    G
11    K     K  I                 I  I  I  G  G  G  G  G  G  G  G
12    K     K  I              I  F  F  F  F  F  F  H  H  H  H  H  H
13    K     K  I              I  F              F  H           H
14    K  K  K  I  I  I  I  I  I  I  F  F  F  F  F  F  H  H  H  H  H  H
```

Total cost 11 238.43   Est cost reduction 472.81

Move A to E
Move D to F
Move K to H
Move F to J

has a copy machine area, could also locate a copy machine in the reference area for users to make copies if required. Finally, the top-left quadrant represents cells which some would dispute deserve the name. They only have the direct resources to apply to part of the total process, and in this way they might seem to be little different from a conventional work centre or department in a process layout. The difference is that they include all or most of the indirect resources they need. Again, they might theoretically be capable of 'standing alone' outside the rest of the operation. A specialist heat treatment cell in a manufacturing operation might contain all the specialist maintenance and supervisory and technical indirect staff to provide a complete technical and manufacturing service to the rest of the plant. The internal audit section of a bank might also need to contain its own technical and administrative support – this time perhaps to maintain its independence from the rest of the operation which it is auditing.

Allocating resources to cells

The detailed design of cellular layouts is difficult, partly because the idea of a cell is itself a compromise between process and product layout. With process layout we focus on the location of the various processes in the operation. With product layout

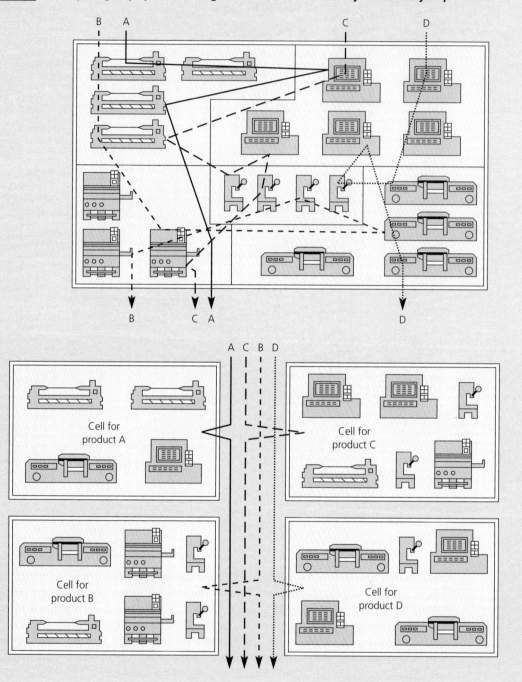

(treated next) we focus on the requirements of the 'product' – cell layout needs to consider the needs of both.

Sometimes, in order to simplify the task, it is useful to concentrate on either the process or product aspects of cell layout. If cell designers choose to concentrate on processes, they could use *cluster analysis* to find which processes group naturally together. This involves examining each type of process and asking which other types of processes a product or part using that process is also likely to need. For example, in furniture manufacture, if all the parts which need holes drilling in them also need countersinking, then whatever the cell arrangement finally decided upon, drilling and countersinking machines will need to go

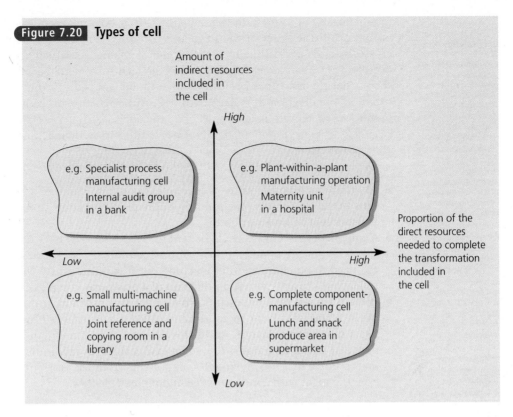

Figure 7.20 Types of cell

Amount of indirect resources included in the cell

High

e.g. Specialist process manufacturing cell

Internal audit group in a bank

e.g. Plant-within-a-plant manufacturing operation

Maternity unit in a hospital

Low — High

Proportion of the direct resources needed to complete the transformation included in the cell

e.g. Small multi-machine manufacturing cell

Joint reference and copying room in a library

e.g. Complete component-manufacturing cell

Lunch and snack produce area in supermarket

Low

together in the same cells. Alternatively, if the operation chooses to concentrate on its products to design its cell formation, they would probably use one of the *parts family coding and classification systems*. These systems use multi-digit codes for each part or product. The codes indicate the characteristics of the product such as shape, size, material and any other factors which define its processing requirements. There are several systems commercially available, for example the Brisch system from the UK, the Opitz system from Germany and MICLASS from the Netherlands.

Production flow analysis[7]

Perhaps the most popular approach to allocating tasks and machines to cells is production flow analysis (PFA), which examines both product requirements and process grouping simultaneously. In Figure 7.21(a) a manufacturing operation has grouped the components it makes into eight families – for example, the components in family 1

Figure 7.21 (a) and (b) Using production flow analysis to allocate machines to cells

(a)

Component families

Machines	1	2	3	4	5	6	7	8
1						X		X
2	X			X			X	
3		X			X			X
4			X			X		X
5	X			X			X	
6		X						X
7			X			X		
8		X			X			X

(b)

Component families

Machines	3	6	8	5	2	4	1	7
4	X	X	X					
1		X	X			Cell A		
6	X		X					
3			X	X	X	Cell B		
8				X	X			
2						X	X	X
5				Cell C		X	X	X
7							X	X

require machines 2 and 5. In this state the matrix does not seem to exhibit any natural groupings. If the order of the rows and columns is changed, however, to move the crosses as close as possible to the diagonal of the matrix which goes from top left to bottom right, then a clearer pattern emerges. This is illustrated in Figure 7.21(b) and shows that the machines could conveniently be grouped together in three cells, indicated on the diagram as cells A, B and C. Although this procedure is a particularly useful way to allocate machines to cells, the analysis is rarely totally clean. This is the case here where component family 8 needs processing by machine 3 which has been allocated to cell B.

Generally there are three ways of dealing with this, none of them totally satisfactory:

- Another machine the same as machine 3 could be purchased and put into cell A. This would clearly solve the problem but requires investing capital in a new machine which might be under-utilized.
- Components in family 8 could be sent to cell B after they have been processed in cell A (or even in the middle of their processing route if necessary). This solution avoids the need to purchase another machine but it conflicts partly with the basic idea of cell layout – to achieve a simplification of a previously complex flow.
- If there are several components which have this problem, it might be necessary to devise a special cell for them (usually called a *remainder cell*) which will almost be like a mini-process layout. Again this does not conform strictly to the simplicity of pure cell layout and also can involve extra capital expenditure. The remainder cell does remove the 'inconvenient' components from the rest of the operation, however, leaving it with a more ordered and predictable flow.

Detailed design in product layout

It may seem that there is little detailed design necessary in product layout because it involves arranging the transforming resources of the operation to fit the sequence required by the product or service. However, although the requirements of the product or service do indeed dominate product layout design, there are still many detailed design decisions to be taken. The nature of the design decision also changes a little. In other types of layout, the decision is 'where to place what'. In product layout it is concerned more with 'what to place where', insomuch as locations are frequently decided upon and then work tasks are allocated to the location. For example, it may have been decided that four stations are needed to make briefcases on an assembly-line basis. The decision is then which of the tasks that go into making the briefcase should be allocated to which of the four stations.

This design decision is called the *line-balancing* decision and is only one (although sometimes the most difficult) of the decisions involved in the detailed design of product layouts. These decisions are as follows:

- What cycle time is needed?
- How many stages are needed?
- How should the task-time variation be dealt with?
- How should the layout be balanced?
- How should the stages be arranged?

The cycle time of product layouts

The cycle time of a product layout is the time between completed products, pieces of information or customers emerging from the operation. Cycle time is a vital factor in the design of product layouts and has a significant influence on most of the other detailed design decisions. It is calculated by considering the likely demand for the products or services over a period and the amount of production time available in that period.

In mechanically 'paced' lines, such as this one, where pasta is being packed, the balancing of the line may be dictated largely by the requirements of the process technology

Worked example

Suppose the regional back-office operation of a large bank is designing an operation which will process its mortgage applications. The number of applications to be processed is 160 per week and the time available to process the applications is 40 hours per week.

$$\text{Cycle time for the layout} = \frac{\text{time available}}{\text{number to be processed}}$$

$$= \frac{40}{160} = \frac{1}{4} \text{ hours}$$

$$= 15 \text{ minutes}$$

So the bank's layout must be capable of processing a completed application once every 15 minutes.

The number of stages

The next decision in the detailed design of a product layout concerns the number of stages in the layout. In practice this can be anything between one and several hundred, depending partly on the cycle time required and the total quantity of work involved in producing the product or service. This latter piece of information is called the *total work content* of the product or service. The larger the total work content and the smaller the required cycle time, the more stages will be necessary.

Worked example

Suppose the bank in the previous example calculated that the average total work content of processing a mortgage application is 60 minutes. The number of stages needed to produce a processed application every 15 minutes can be calculated as follows:

$$\text{Number of stages} = \frac{\text{total work content}}{\text{required cycle time}}$$

$$= \frac{60 \text{ minutes}}{15 \text{ minutes}}$$

$$= 4 \text{ stages}$$

If this figure had not emerged as a whole number it would have been necessary to round it up to the next largest whole number. It is difficult (although not always impossible) to hire fractions of people to staff the stages.

Task-time variation

Thus far we could imagine a line of four stages, each contributing a quarter of the total work content of processing the mortgage, and passing the documentation on to the next stage every 15 minutes. In practice, of course, the flow would not be so regular. Each station's allocation of work might on average take 15 minutes, but almost certainly the time will vary each time a mortgage application is processed. This is a general characteristic of all repetitive processing (and indeed of all work performed by humans) and can be caused by a number of different factors:

- Each product or service being processed along the line might be different – for example, different models of automobile going down the same line.
- Products or services, although essentially the same, might require slightly different treatment. For instance, in the mortgage-processing example, the time some tasks require will vary depending on the personal circumstances of the person applying for the loan.
- There are usually slight variations in the physical coordination and effort on the part of the person performing the task.

This variation can introduce irregularity into the flow along the line, which in turn can lead to both periodic queues at the stages and lost processing time. It may even prove necessary to introduce more resources into the operation to compensate for the loss of efficiency resulting from worktime variation.

Balancing worktime allocation

Perhaps the most problematic of all the detailed design decisions in product layout is that of ensuring the equal allocation of tasks to each stage in the line. This process is called *line balancing*. In the mortgage-processing example we have assumed that the 15 minutes of work content are allocated equally to the four stations. This is nearly always impossible to achieve in practice and some imbalance in the work allocation between stages results. Inevitably this will raise the effective cycle time of the line. If it becomes greater than the required cycle time, it may be necessary to devote extra resources, in the shape of a further stage, to compensate for the imbalance. The effectiveness of the line-balancing activity is measured by what is called *balancing loss*. This is the time wasted through the unequal allocation of work as a percentage of the total time invested in processing the product or service.

Balancing techniques[8]

As in the other basic layout types, there are a number of techniques available to help in the line-balancing task. Again, in practice, the most useful and most used 'techniques' are the simple heuristic approaches. Foremost among the latter is the *precedence diagram*. This is a representation of the ordering of the elements which comprise the total work content of the product or service. Each element is represented by a circle. The circles are connected by arrows which signify the ordering of the elements. Two rules apply when constructing the diagram:

- the circles which represent the elements are drawn as far to the left as possible;
- none of the arrows which show the precedence of the elements should be vertical.

The precedence diagram, either using circles and arrows or transposed into tabular form, is the most common starting point for most balancing techniques. We do not treat the more complex of these techniques here but it is useful to describe the general approach to balancing product layouts.

In Figure 7.22 the work allocations in a four-stage line are illustrated. The total amount of time invested in producing each product or service is four times the cycle time because, for every unit produced, all four stages have been working for the cycle time. When the work is equally allocated between the stages, the total time invested in each product or service produced is $4 \times 2.5 = 10$ minutes. However, when work is unequally allocated, as illustrated, the time invested is $3.0 \times 4 = 12$ minutes, i.e. 2.0 minutes of time, 16.67 per cent of the total, is wasted.

Figure 7.22 **Balancing loss is that proportion of the time invested in processing the product or service which is not used productively**

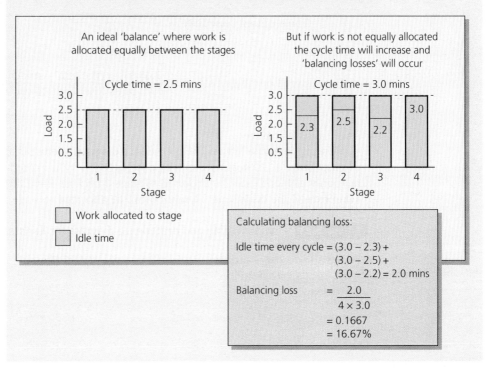

This general approach is to allocate elements from the precedence diagram to the first stage, starting from the left, in order of the columns until the work allocated to the stage is as close to, but less than, the cycle time. When that stage is as full of work as is possible without exceeding the cycle time, move on to the next stage, and so on until all the work elements are allocated. The key issue is how to select an element to be allocated to a stage when more than one element could be chosen. Two heuristic rules have been found to be particularly useful in deciding this:

● Simply choose the largest that will 'fit' into the time remaining at the stage.
● Choose the element with the most 'followers': that is the highest number of elements which can only be allocated when that element has been allocated.

Arranging the stages

Our assumption so far has been that all the stages necessary to fulfil the requirements of the layout will be arranged in a sequential 'single line'. Yet this need not necessarily be so. Return to the mortgage-processing example, which requires four stages working on the task to maintain a cycle time of one processed application every 15 minutes. The conventional arrangement of the four stages would be to lay them out in one line, each stage having 15 minutes' worth of work. However, nominally, the same output rate could also be achieved by arranging the four stages as two shorter lines, each of

Karlstad Kakes

Consider Karlstad Kakes (KK), a manufacturer of speciality cakes, which has recently obtained a contract to supply a major supermarket chain with a speciality cake in the shape of a space rocket. It has been decided that the volumes required by the supermarket warrant a special production line to perform the finishing, decorating and packing of the cake. This line would have to carry out the elements shown in Figure 7.23, which also shows the precedence diagram for the total job. The initial order from the supermarket is for 5000 cakes a week and the number of hours worked by the factory is 40 per week. From this:

$$\text{The required cycle time} = \frac{40 \text{ hrs} \times 60 \text{ mins}}{5000}$$

$$= 0.48 \text{ mins}$$

$$\text{The required number of stages} = \frac{1.68 \text{ mins (the total work content)}}{0.48 \text{ mins (the required cycle time)}}$$

$$= 3.5 \text{ stages}$$

This means four stages.

Working from the left on the precedence diagram, elements a and b can be allocated to stage 1. Allocating element c to stage 1 would exceed the cycle time. In fact, only element c can be allocated to stage 2 because including element d would again exceed the cycle time. Element d can be allocated to stage 3. Either element e

Figure 7.23 **Element listing and precedence diagram for Karlstad Kakes**

Element (a)	– De-tin and trim	0.12 mins
Element (b)	– Reshape with off-cuts	0.30 mins
Element (c)	– Clad in almond fondant	0.36 mins
Element (d)	– Clad in white fondant	0.25 mins
Element (e)	– Decorate, red icing	0.17 mins
Element (f)	– Decorate, green icing	0.05 mins
Element (g)	– Decorate, blue icing	0.10 mins
Element (h)	– Affix transfers	0.08 mins
Element (i)	– Transfer to base and pack	0.25 mins

Total work content = 1.68 mins

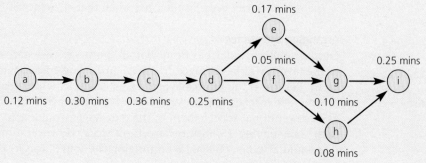

or element f can also be allocated to stage 3, but not both or the cycle time would be exceeded. Following the 'largest element' heuristic rule, element e is chosen. The remaining elements then are allocated to stage 4. Figure 7.24 shows the final allocation and the balancing loss of the line.

Figure 7.24 **Allocation of elements to stages and balancing loss for Karlstad Kakes**

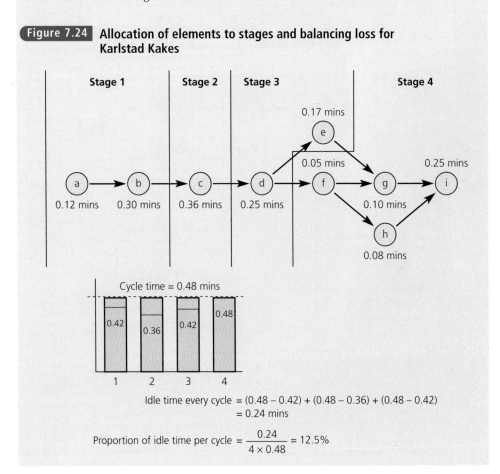

Idle time every cycle $= (0.48 - 0.42) + (0.48 - 0.36) + (0.48 - 0.42)$
$$= 0.24 \text{ mins}$$

Proportion of idle time per cycle $= \dfrac{0.24}{4 \times 0.48} = 12.5\%$

two stages with 30 minutes' worth of work each. Alternatively, following this logic to its ultimate conclusion, the stages could be arranged as four parallel stages, each responsible for the whole work content. Figure 7.25 shows these options.

This may be a simplified example, but it represents a genuine issue. Should the layout be arranged as a single 'long thin' line, as several 'short fat' parallel lines, or somewhere in between? (Note that 'long' means the number of stages and 'fat' means the amount of work allocated to each stage.) In any particular situation there are usually technical constraints which limit either how 'long and thin' or how 'short and fat' the layout can be, but there is usually a range of possible options within which a choice needs to be made. The advantages of each extreme of the long thin to short fat spectrum are very different and help to explain why different arrangements are adopted.

The advantages of the long thin arrangement
These include:

- *Controlled flow of materials or customers* – which is easy to manage.
- *Simple materials handling* – especially if a product being manufactured is heavy, large or difficult to move.
- *Lower capital requirements*. If a specialist piece of equipment is needed for one element in the job, only one piece of equipment would need to be purchased; on short fat arrangements every stage would need one.

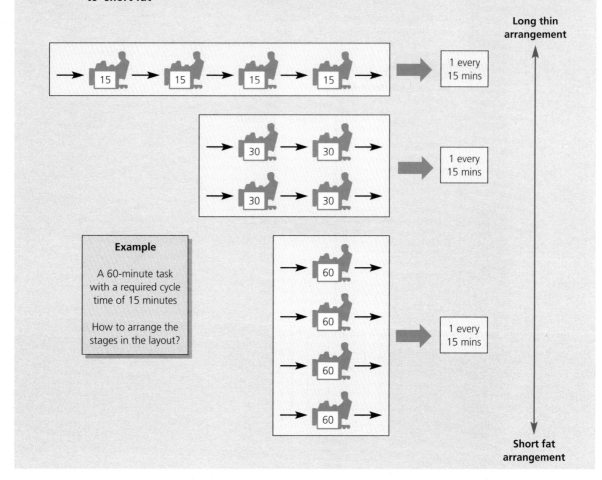

- *More efficient operation*. If each stage is only performing a small part of the total job, the person at the stage will have a higher proportion of direct productive work as opposed to the non-productive parts of the job, such as picking up tools and materials.

This latter point is particularly important and is fully explained in Chapter 9 when we discuss job design.

The advantages of the short fat arrangement
These include:

- *Higher mix flexibility*. If the layout needs to process several types of product or service, each stage or line could specialize in different types.
- *Higher volume flexibility*. As volume varies, stages can simply be closed down or started up as required; long thin arrangements would need rebalancing each time the cycle time changed.
- *Higher robustness*. If one stage breaks down or ceases operation in some way, the other parallel stages are unaffected; a long thin arrangement would cease operating completely.
- *Less monotonous work*. In the mortgage example, the staff in the short fat arrangement are repeating their tasks only every hour; in the long thin arrangement it is every 15 minutes.

Again, this latter point is particularly important and is treated further in Chapter 9.

The shape of the line

If it is decided to adopt an arrangement which involves some sequential flow between stages arranged in series, a further decision concerns the shape of the line. Partly inspired by the experience of Japanese manufacturers, many manufacturing operations are adopting the practice of curving line arrangements into U-shaped or 'serpentine' arrangements (*see* Fig. 7.26). U shapes are usually used for shorter lines and serpentines for longer lines. Richard Schonberger, the expert on Japanese manufacturing, sees several advantages in this:[9]

- *Staffing flexibility and balance.* The U shape enables one person to tend several work stations – adjacent or across the U – without much walking. This opens up options for balancing work among the people: when demand grows, more labour can be added until every station has an operator.
- *Rework.* When the line bends around itself, it is easy to return bad work to an earlier station for rework without either fuss or much distance travelled.
- *Handling.* From a centre position within the U, a handler (human, vehicle, crane or robot) can deliver materials and handle tools conveniently.
- *Passage.* Long straight lines interfere with cross travel in the rest of the operation. It is annoying when shelving in a supermarket is too long. People protest when a superhighway cuts a neighbourhood in half. It is the same with flow lines.
- *Teamwork.* A semicircle even looks like a team.

Figure 7.26   The arrangement of stages

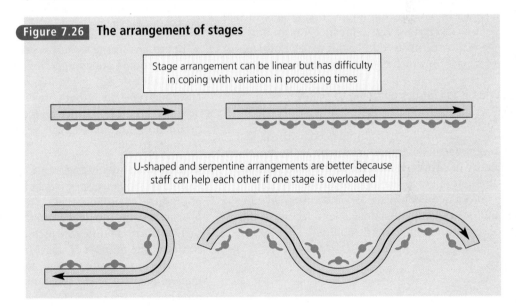

Stage arrangement can be linear but has difficulty in coping with variation in processing times

U-shaped and serpentine arrangements are better because staff can help each other if one stage is overloaded

Summary answers to key questions

What are the basic layout types used in operations?

- There are four basic layout types:
  - fixed-position layout
  - process layout
  - cell layout
  - product layout.

What type of layout should an operation choose?

- Partly this is influenced by the nature of the process type, which in turn depends on the volume–variety characteristics of the operation.

- Partly also the decision will depend on the objectives of the operation. Cost and flexibility are particularly affected by the layout decision.

- The fixed and variable costs implied by each layout differ such that, in theory, one particular layout will have the minimum costs for a particular volume level. However, in practice, uncertainty over the real costs involved in layout make it difficult to be precise on which is the minimum-cost layout.

What is layout design trying to achieve?

- In addition to the conventional operations objectives which will be influenced by the layout design, factors of importance include the length and clarity of customer, material or information flow; inherent safety to staff and/or customers; staff comfort; accessibility to staff and customers; the ability to coordinate management decisions; the use of space; and long-term flexibility.

How should each basic layout type be designed in detail?

- Obviously this very much depends on the basic layout type chosen.

- In fixed-position layout the materials or people being transformed do not move but the transforming resources move around them. Techniques are rarely used in this type of layout, but some, such as resource location analysis, bring a systematic approach to minimizing the costs and inconvenience of flow at a fixed-position location.

- In process layout all similar transforming resources are grouped together in the operation. The detailed design task is usually (although not always) to minimize the distance travelled by the transformed resources through the operation. Either manual or computer-based methods can be used to devise the detailed design.

- In cell layout the resources needed for a particular class of product are grouped together in some way. The detailed design task is to group the products or customer types such that convenient cells can be designed around their needs. Techniques such as production flow analysis can be used to allocate products to cells.

- In product layout, the transforming resources are located in sequence specifically for the convenience of products or product types. The detailed design of product layouts includes a number of decisions, such as the cycle time to which the design must conform, the number of stages in the operation, the way tasks are allocated to the stages in the line, and the arrangement of the stages in the line. The cycle time of each part of the design, together with the number of stages, is a function of where the design lies on the 'long thin' to 'short fat' spectrum of arrangements. This position affects costs, flexibility, robustness and staff attitude to work. The allocation of tasks to stages is called line balancing, which can be performed either manually or through computer-based algorithms.

Weldon Hand Tools

Weldon Hand Tools, one of the most successful of the European hand tool manufacturers, decided to move into the 'woodworking' tools market. Previously its products had been confined to car maintenance, home decorating and general hand tools. One of the first products which it decided to manufacture was a general-purpose 'smoothing plane', a tool which smooths and shapes wood. Its product designers devised a suitable design and the company's work measurement engineers estimated the time it would take (in standard minutes) to perform each element in the assembly process. The marketing department also estimated the likely demand (for the whole European market) for the new product. Its sales forecast is shown in Table 7.3.

Table 7.3 Sales forecast for smoothing plane

Time period	Volume
Year 1	
1st quarter	98 000 units
2nd quarter	140 000 units
3rd quarter	140 000 units
4th quarter	170 000 units
Year 2	
1st quarter	140 000 units
2nd quarter	170 000 units
3rd quarter	200 000 units
4th quarter	230 000 units

The marketing department was not totally confident of its forecast, however.

'A substantial proportion of demand is likely to be export sales, which we find difficult to predict. But whatever demand does turn out to be, we will have to react quickly to meet it. The more we enter these parts of the market, the more we are into impulse buying and the more sales we lose if we don't supply.'

This plane was likely to be the first of several similar planes. A further model had already been approved for launch about one year after this, and two or three further models were in the planning stage. All the planes were similar, merely varying in length and width.

Designing the manufacturing operation

It has been decided to assemble all planes at one of the company's smaller factory sites where a whole workshop is unused. Within the workshop there is plenty of room for expansion if demand proves higher than forecast. All machining and finishing of parts would be performed at the main factory and the parts shipped to the smaller site where they would be assembled at the available workshop.

An idea of the assembly task can be gained from the partially exploded view of the product (*see* Fig. 7.27). Table 7.4 gives the 'standard time' for each element of the assembly task. Some of the tasks are described as 'fly press' operations. A fly press is a relatively simple tool, about a metre high, which has two weights mounted onto a screw thread. When the two weights are rotated they give momentum to the downward action of the screw thread which

Table 7.4 Standard times for each element of assembly task in standard minutes (SM)

Fly press operations	
Assemble poke S/A (LH poke, RH poke, poke bush)	0.12 S.M. (standard minutes)
Fit poke S/A to frog (poke, S/A, poke pin, frog)	0.10 S.M.
Rivet adjusting lever to frog (adjust lever, rivet, frog)	0.15 S.M.
Press adjusting nut screw to frog (frog, adjusting nut screw)	0.08 S.M.
TOTAL PRESS OPERATIONS	0.45 S.M.
Bench operations	
Fit adjusting nut to frog	0.15 S.M.
Fit frog screw to frog	0.05 S.M.
FROG S/A COMPLETE	
Fit knob to base	0.15 S.M.
Fit handle to base	0.17 S.M.
Fit frog S/A to base	0.15 S.M.
Assemble blade S/A	0.08 S.M.
Assemble blade S/A, clamp and label to base and adjust	0.20 S.M.
PLANE COMPLETE	
TOTAL FOR PRESS AND ASSEMBLY OPERATIONS	1.40 S.M.
Make up box, wrap plane, pack and stock	0.20 S.M.
TOTAL WORK TIME FOR ASSEMBLY AREA	1.60 S.M.

S/A = sub assembly

applies a downward force. This force is used for simple bending, riveting or force-fitting operations. A fly press is not an expensive or sophisticated piece of technology.

Costs and pricing

The standard costing system at the company involves adding a 150 per cent overhead charge to the direct labour cost of manufacturing the product, and the product would retail for the equivalent of around £25 in Europe where most retailers will sell this type of product for about 70–120 per cent more than they buy it from the manufacturer.

Questions

1 How many staff should the company employ?
2 What type of facilities and technology will the company need to buy in order to assemble this product?
3 Design a layout for the assembly operation (to include the fly press work) including the tasks to be performed at each part of the system.
4 How would the layout need to be adjusted as demand for this and similar products builds up?

Figure 7.27 **Partially exploded view of the new plane**

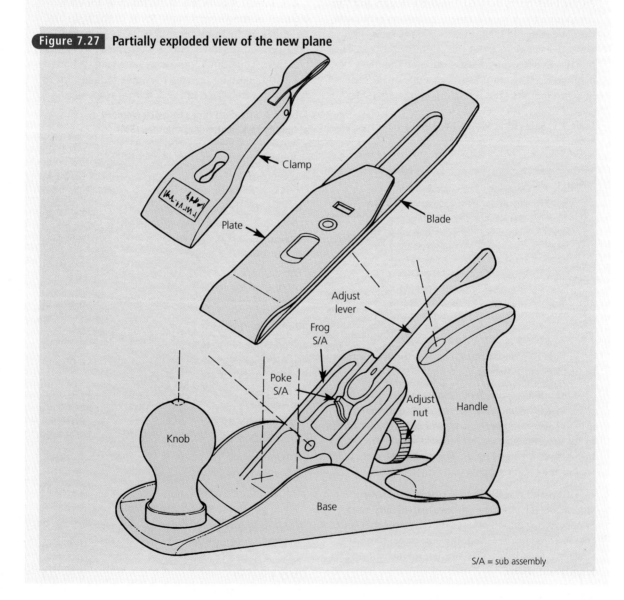

S/A = sub assembly

1 Identify the type of layout that might be adopted by the following organizations, explaining the reasoning behind your choice:

   – a ski resort
   – a dairy farm
   – a tree surgeon
   – a bakery
   – a bank.

   Discuss the implications of variety and volume on flow.

2 Sketch the layout of your local shop, coffee bar or sports hall reception area. Observe the area and draw onto your sketch the movements of people through the area over a sufficient period of time to get over 20 observations. Assess the flow in terms of volume, variety and type of layout.

3 A tractor manufacturer, making a wide range of tractors to customer specification, is considering changing its layout from product to process. Discuss the implications of so doing.

4 Identify the main stages in the construction of a house from laying services and foundations to plastering and decorating. If each of these tasks were to be carried out by different sub-contractors, describe the potential layout problems.

5 (a) Visit a supermarket in your area. Try to get an appointment to talk with the manager to discuss the layout design issues.
   (b) Compare the design of your supermarket with that of the Delhaize store described in the box. List and tabulate the main similarities and differences, and try to understand the reasons for these differences.
   (c) What do you think, therefore, are the main criteria considered in the design of a supermarket layout?
   (d) What competitive or environmental changes may result in the need to change store layouts in the future? Will these apply to all supermarkets, or only certain ones, such as town centre stores?

6 The flow of materials through eight departments is shown in Table 7.5.

   Assuming that the direction of the flow of materials is not important, construct a relationship chart, a schematic layout and a suggested layout, given that each department is the same size and the eight departments should be arranged four along each side of a corridor.

Table 7.5 Flow of materials

	D1	D2	D3	D4	D5	D6	D7	D8
D1	\	30						
D2	10	\	15	20				
D3		5	\	12	2		15	
D4		6		\	10	20		
D5				8	\	8	10	12
D6	3				2	\	30	
D7	3					13	\	2
D8				10	6		15	\

7 The university's students union is going to rearrange the layout of its lounge. It has been noticed that different groups of students use the two bars and four machines in the room in different ways, as shown in Table 7.6. The union would like to group the facilities in twos. Which groupings would you suggest, given that the sandwich bar and drinks bar are at opposite ends of the room and cannot be moved?

Table 7.6 Students' use of union facilities

Facility	Student type					
	1	2	3	4	5	6
Cola machine			X	X		X
Drinks bar		X	X			
Hot drinks machine	X		X		X	
Cigarette machine		X	X			
Sandwich bar	X				X	
Chocolate machine				X		X

8 Table 7.7 shows 12 work elements that constitute the total work content of an assembly task. Using the information about duration times and precedences in the table, draw a precedence diagram and design an assembly line to produce as near as possible, but no less than, three items per hour. Calculate the balancing loss for the line.

9 Visit an assembly factory and look at the shape of the line. Find out why the line is the shape that it is.

10 A bicycle plant currently has a straight 20-stage assembly line with raw materials coming in at one side of the factory and the finished bikes going out at the other. Assess the implications of moving to a U-shaped line.

Table 7.7 Work content of assembly line

Element number	Duration (mins)	Preceding element(s)
1	4	–
2	7	–
3	5	1
4	6	1,2
5	4	2
6	3	2
7	4	3
8	6	4,5
9	5	5,6
10	4	9
11	6	8,10
12	6	7,11

11 Observe the preparation of a meal in a kitchen (you can do this yourself, or watch someone else do it). Chart the movement around the kitchen and suggest ways in which the layout of the kitchen might be improved.

12 Identify two service operations which use a 'product-based' layout. Discuss the implications of this for the organization and for the customer.

13 Select an organization of your choice and subject its layout to an evaluation based on the list provided in the section 'what makes a good layout?' in this chapter.

Notes on chapter

1 Source: Discussions with Alstom staff.
2 Source: Interviews with company staff.
3 Source: (1991) *Paper and the Environment*, Arjo Wiggins Fine Papers, used with permission.
4 Sources: Interviews with company staff and Johnston, R., Chambers, S., Harland, C., Harrison, A. and Slack, N. (1997) *Cases in Operations Management* (2nd edn), Pitman Publishing.
5 This list kindly supplied by Paul Walley of Warwick University Business School, UK.
6 Armour, G.C. and Buffa, E.S. (1963) 'A Heuristic Algorithm and Simulation Approach to the Relative Location of Facilities', *Management Science*, Vol 9, No 2.
7 Burbidge, J.L. (1978) *The Principles of Production Control* (4th edn), Macdonald and Evans.
8 There are many different methods of balancing. See, for example, Kilbridge, K. and Wester, L. (1961) 'A Heuristic Method of Assembly Line Balancing', *Journal of Industrial Engineering*, Vol 57, No 4; or Steyn, P.G. (1977) 'Scheduling Multi-Model Production Lines', *Business Management*, Vol 8, No 1.
9 Schonberger, R. (1990) *Building a Chain of Customers*, Hutchinson Business Books.

Selected further reading

Brandon, J.A. (1996) *Cellular Manufacturing: Integrated Tehnology and Management*, John Wiley, New York

Francis, R.L. and White, J.A. (1987) *Facility Layout and Location: An Analytical Approach*, Prentice Hall.

Gaither, N., Frazier, B.V. and Wei, J.C. (1990) 'From Job Shops to Manufacturing Cells', *Production and Inventory Management Journal*, Vol 31, No 4.

Green, T.J. and Sadowski, R.P. (1984) 'A Review of Cellular Manufacturing Assumptions and Advantages and Design Techniques', *Journal of Operations Management*, Vol 4, No 2.

Gunther, R.E., Johnson, G.D. and Peterson, R.S. (1983) 'Currently Practiced Formulations of The Assembly Line Balance Problem', *Journal of Operations Management*, Vol 3, No 3.

Hyer, N.L. and Wemmerlov, U. (1984) 'Group Technology and Productivity', *Harvard Business Review*, Vol 62, No 4.

Karlsson, C. (1996) 'Radically New Production Systems', *International Journal of Operations and Production Management*, Vol 16, No 11.

Malas, G.H. (1990) 'Assembly Line Balancing – Let's Remove the Mystery', *Journal of Industrial Engineering*, May.

Mellor, R.D. and Gau K.Y. (1996) 'The Facility Layout Problem: Recent and Emerging Trends and Perspectives', *Journal of Manufacturing Systems*, Vol 29, No 5.

Miller, J.G. and Vollmann, T.E. (1985) 'The Hidden Factory', *Harvard Business Review*, Vol 63, No 5.

Prickett, P. (1994) 'Cell-based Manufacturing Systems: Design and Implementation', *International Journal of Operations and Production Management*, Vol 14, No 2.

Schuler, R.S., Writzman, L.P. and Davis, V.L. (1981) 'Merging Prescriptive and Behavioural Approaches for Office Layout', *Journal of Operations Management*, Vol 1, No 3.

Shafer, S.M. and Meredith, J.R. (1993) 'An Empirically Based Simulation Study of Functional Versus Cellular Layouts with Operations Overlapping', *International Journal of Operations and Production Management*, Vol 13, No 2.

Shambu, G., Suresh, N.C. and Pegels, C.C. (1996) 'Performance Evaluation of Cellular Manufacturing Systems', *International Journal of Operations and Production Management*, Vol 16, No 8.

Sule, V.E. (1988) *Manufacturing Facilities – Location Planning and Design*, PWS-Kent.

Winarchick, C. and Caldwel, R.D. (1997) 'Physical Interactive Simulation: A Hands-on Approach to Facilities Improvements', *IIE Solutions*, Vol 29, No 5.

Wu, B. (1994), *Manufacturing System Design and Analysis* (2nd edn), Chapman and Hall.

Process technology

Introduction

All operations use some kind of process technology. Whether its process technology is a humble word processor or the most complex and sophisticated of automated factories, the operation will have chosen to use the technology because it hopes to get some kind of advantage from it. Sometimes a process technology helps the operation address a clear market need; at other times the technology becomes available and an operation chooses to adopt it in the expectation that it can exploit its potential in some, as yet unspecified, way. Whatever the motivation, however, all operations managers need to understand what emerging technologies can do, in broad terms how they do it, what advantages the technology can give and what constraints it might impose on the operation. This is the purpose of this chapter. Figure 8.1 shows how the issues covered in this chapter relate to the overall model of design of operations.

Figure 8.1 ◼ **The design activities in operations management covered in this chapter**

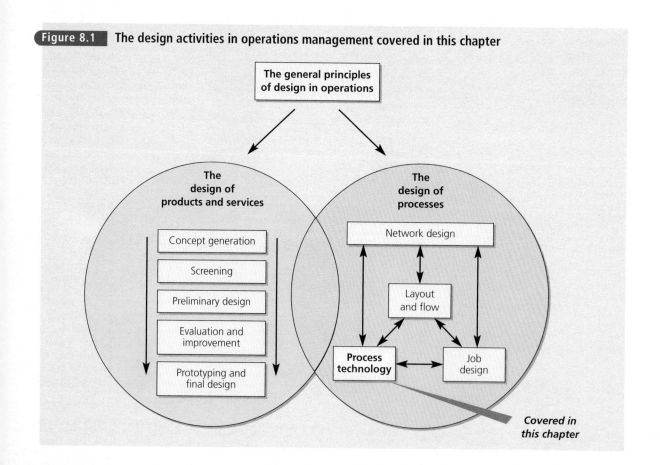

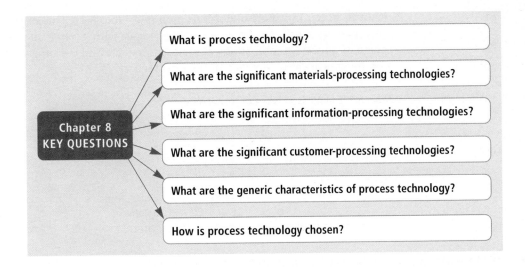

	What is process technology?
	What are the significant materials-processing technologies?
Chapter 8 KEY QUESTIONS	What are the significant information-processing technologies?
	What are the significant customer-processing technologies?
	What are the generic characteristics of process technology?
	How is process technology chosen?

What is process technology?

Process technologies are the machines, equipment and devices which help the operation transform materials and information and customers in order to add value and fulfil the operation's strategic objectives. All operations use technology, from the cheap and flexible telephone to very expensive and dedicated machinery, such as integrated mail processors (IMPs). These are machines used by postal sorting offices which can scan and sort more than 30 000 letters and cards an hour, at a cost of around two million euros each. In this chapter, we discuss *process* technology – the machines and devices that *create* and/or *deliver* the goods and services – as opposed to *product* technology. Mechanical milking machines, for example, perform the task of several farmhands by milking and feeding the cows, in order to provide the raw milk for the next stage in the process (*see* box on milking machines). Body scanners in hospitals provide a service that could not be performed by humans, using magnetic forces to create a picture of soft body tissue. Large entertainment complexes such as Disney World use flight simulation technologies to create the thrill of space travel. This technology often involves the whole room, which is mounted on moveable hydraulic struts that can move the room and all the people in it. This movement, combined with widescreen projection, can provide a very realistic experience. Using technology in this way is one of the latest in a long history of achievements from what the Disney Corporation call its 'imagineers', whose role is to engineer the experience for their customers. Communication devices such as fax machines, mobile telephones, satellite-based global positioning systems (GPS) and the internet are other processing technologies which create and/or deliver goods and services to customers.

In manufacturing, the process technologies are the machine tools, often computer-controlled, which shape the metal, mount electronic components onto circuit boards and assemble all the components into a television, video player or tumble dryer.

Some technology is peripheral to the actual creation of goods and services but plays a key role in *facilitating* the process that creates and delivers the goods and services. For example, the computer systems which run planning and control activities, accounting systems and stock control systems can be used to help managers and operators control and improve the processes.

In the next section we examine some of the process technologies that have a particular significance for operations managers. These have been categorized as materials-processing (as in manufacturing operations or warehouses), information-processing (as in financial services, for example) or customer-processing technologies (as in retail, medical, hotel, transport operations etc.) (*see* Table 8.1). This distinction is only for convenience, because many newer technologies with greater information-processing capability process combinations of materials, people and customers. These 'integrating' technologies are also described in the next section.

Table 8.1 Examples of types of technology

	Material processing	Information processing	Customer processing
Examples of process technology	Integrated mail processing	Telecommunication systems	Milking machines
	Machine tools	Global positioning systems	Body scanners

Operations management and process technology

Operations managers are continually involved in the management of process technology. To do this effectively, they should be able to:

- articulate how technology could improve the operation's effectiveness;
- be involved in the choice of the technology itself;
- manage the installation and adoption of the technology so that it does not interfere with ongoing operations activities;
- integrate the technology into the rest of the operation;
- monitor its performance continually;
- upgrade or replace the technology when necessary.

Operations managers do not need to be experts in engineering, computing, biology, electronics or whatever constitutes the core science of the technology. They do, however, need to know enough about the principles behind the technology to be comfortable in evaluating some technical information, capable of dealing with experts in the technology and confident enough to ask relevant questions, such as:

- What does the technology do which is different from other similar technologies?
- How does it do it? That is, what particular characteristics of the technology are used to perform its function?
- What benefits does using the technology give to the operation?
- What constraints does using the technology place on the operation?

Customers are not always human[1]

The first milking machines were introduced to grateful farmers over 100 years ago. Until recently, however, they could not operate without a human hand to attach the devices to the cows. This problem has been overcome by a consortium in the Netherlands which includes the Dutch government and several private firms. They hope that the 'robot milkmaid' will do away with the farmers' early morning ritual of milking. Each machine can milk between 60 and 100 cows a day and 'processes' the cows through a number of stages. Computer-controlled gates activated by transmitters around the cows' necks allow the cows to enter. The machine then checks their health, connects them to the milking machine and feeds them while they are being milked. If illness is detected in any cow, or if the machine for some reason fails to connect the milking cups to the cow after five attempts, automatic gates divert it into special pens where the farmer can inspect it later. Finally, the machine ushers the cows out of the system. It also self-cleans periodically and can detect and reject any impure milk. Rather than herding all the cows in a 'batch' to the milking machine twice a day, the system relies on the cows being able to find their own way to the machine. Cows, it would appear, are creatures of habit. Once they have been shown the way to the machine a few times, they go there of their own volition because they know that it will relieve the discomfort in their udders, which grow heavier as they fill up. The cows may make the journey to the machine three or more times per day (*see* Fig. 8.2).

Farmers also appear to be as much creatures of habit as their cows, however. Mr Riekes Uneken of Assen, the Dutch farmer who bought the very first robot milking machine, admitted:

'I have a bleeper if things go wrong. But I still like to get up early in the morning. I just like to see what goes on.'

Questions

1 What advantages do you think the technology described above gives?

2 Do you think the cows mind?

3 Why do you think the farmer still goes to watch the process?

Figure 8.2 **Cows are also customers**

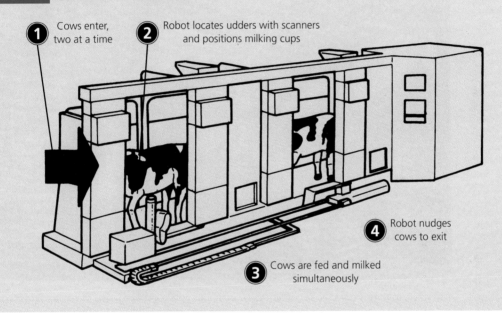

① Cows enter, two at a time

② Robot locates udders with scanners and positions milking cups

③ Cows are fed and milked simultaneously

④ Robot nudges cows to exit

Materials-processing technology

Technological advances have meant that the ways in which metals, plastics, fabric and other materials are processed have improved over time. However, here, it is not the specific materials-forming technologies with which we are concerned. Rather, it is the immediate technological context in which they are used.

● Computer numerically controlled machine tools

Computer numerically controlled (CNC) machines hold a set of coded instructions on computers attached to the machine. These have taken the place of the operator who would previously have controlled the machine by hand. This replacement gives more accuracy, precision and repeatability to the process. It can also give better productivity, partly through the elimination of possible operator error, partly because computer control can work to optimum cutting patterns, and partly because of the substitution of expensive, skilled labour.

Most early CNC machine tools did little more than the conventional machine tools they replaced. Later technologies developed in two ways. First, they increased their degrees of freedom. Very simple machine tools, such as a drilling machine, might have only one degree of freedom – up and down. Others, such as a lathe, which turns cylindrical shapes, have two – in and out and along the piece being shaped. Machining centres usually have three or more (where the cutting head tilts) degrees of freedom, which allow them to shape more complex parts. The second development was the ability to store magazines of different cutting tools within the machine. When the programme calls for it, the old tool is replaced in the magazine and the new tool is put into the cutting head. Together, these two developments increased the variety and complexity of what could be produced.

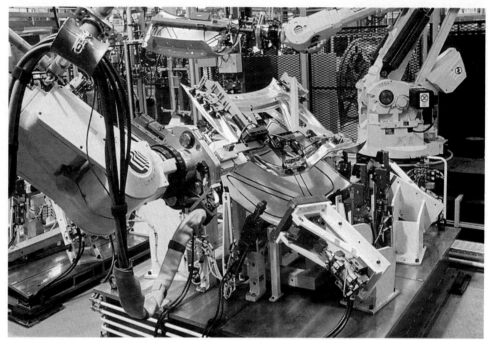

Photo courtesy of Jaguar

Part of a car body is clamped together in precision 'jigs' while a robot welds its components together

Robotics

A robot can be defined as:[2]

> *'an automatic position-controlled reprogrammable multi-function manipulator having several degrees of freedom capable of handling materials, parts, tools or specialized devices through variable programmed motions for the performance of a variety of tasks … It often has the appearance of one or several arms ending in a wrist. Its control unit uses a memorizing device and sometimes it can use sensing and adaptation appliances that take account of the environment and circumstances. These multi-purpose machines are generally designed to carry out repetitive functions and can be adapted to other functions without permanent alternation of the equipment.'*

In terms of their application, robots can be classified as follows:[3]

- *Handling robots.* The workpiece is handled by the robot, for example, for loading and unloading of workpieces.
- *Process robots.* The tool is gripped by the robot, for example, in various types of metal working operations, joining of materials, surface treatment, etc.
- *Assembly robots.* Robots are used in the assembly of parts into components and complete products.

More recent robots can also include some limited sensory feedback through vision control and touch control. However, although the sophistication of robotic movement is increasing, their abilities are still more limited than popular images of robot-driven factories suggest. In fact, most robots are, in practice, used for mundane operations such as welding, paint spraying, stacking pallets, grinding/deburring, packing, loading and unloading machines. In these tasks, the attribute of the robots which is being exploited is their ability to perform repetitive, monotonous and sometimes hazardous tasks for long periods, without variation and without complaining (*see* the box on robot use at Ecco and Scania, and the box on radioactive robots).

Robots Take over some of the repetitive work at Ecco Shoes and at Scania Trucks[4]

Ecco, a Danish shoe company, produces over seven million shoes each year and has invested in extensive robot facilities in the manufacturing operation, primarily to improve its quality consistency. Initial manufacturing stages are still processed by hand.

The soft leather upper is cut and sewn together in the Indian and Indonesian factories before being shipped to the more automated plants for completion. A robot is used to cut a 5 mm track around the leather upper which is then transferred

| Figure 8.3 | **Robots used in small parts assembly** |

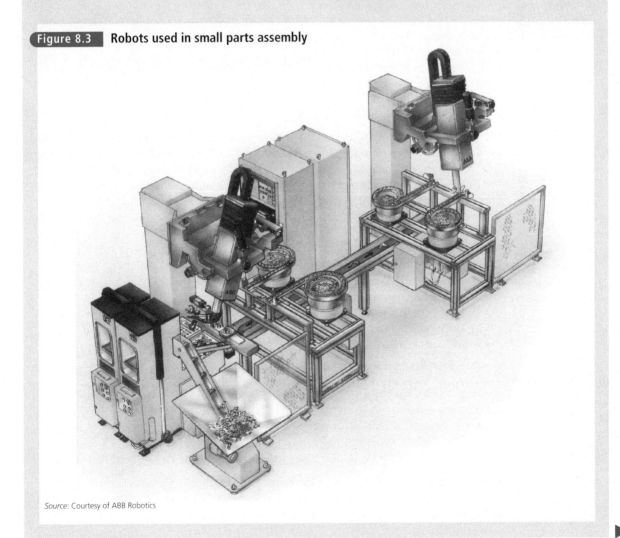

Source: Courtesy of ABB Robotics

by a second robot to the sole-forming machine where the leather upper is moulded onto a flexible sole. A third robot is employed to cut away any excess material from the sole, without damaging the upper. Each robot is programmed to operate according to the recognized size and model of the shoe being processed. Ecco operations managers believe that the working environment is much improved by using robots for the more physically demanding or boring tasks, as well as giving increased productivity and enhancing quality.

The Swedish truck group Scania decided to build a new painting facility for its axle factory at Falun. The decision to use robotics in the paint shop was based on their ability to meet precise customer requirements for paint type, colour and specification. The robots are easily and quickly changed over and adaptable to new products. Two operators can run the whole system from a control room, where computer screens depict the movements and settings for each of the robots. The robot first prepares and cleans the parts, then dries off the moisture by blowing compressed air into the cavities and remaining holes; the parts are then primed and

finally painted, again all by robots. The axle parts on Scania trucks are shaped differently, which means that the spray guns on the painting system need to be adjusted continually during the process. There is an integrated computer control system which co-ordinates all of these adjustments, controlling the amount of paint being sprayed and thus reducing spillage (both an environmental and cost benefit). Essentially, the main feature of the robots is their flexibility. Scania is confident that it can adapt the systems as necessary to suit its precise needs in the future. The use of robots has also improved the working conditions of the employees and has assisted in reducing waste and solvent emissions.

Questions

1 In Ecco's shoe factories, why are some manufacturing stages performed by hand and some by robots?

2 What are the advantages of using robot technology to paint axles at the Scania plant?

● Automated guided vehicles (AGVs)

For every activity in a manufacturing process which adds value to the product by physically transferring it, there is usually one which moves or stores the material. Although they are often unavoidable, such activities add no value to the material. It is not surprising then that operations managers seek ways of automating them. Automated guided vehicles (AGVs) are one class of technology which does this. AGVs are small, independently powered vehicles which move materials to and from value-adding operations. They are often guided by cables buried in the floor of the operation and receive instructions from a central computer. AGVs can help promote just-in-time delivery of parts between stages in the production process (*see* Chapter 15 for a discussion of just-in-time principles) and can be used as mobile workstations; for example, truck engines can be assembled on AGVs, which move between assembly stations. AGVs are sometimes used to move materials in non-manufacturing operations. Warehousing is the obvious example, but they are also used in libraries to move books, in offices to move mail and even in hospitals to transport samples.

● Flexible manufacturing systems

Flexible manufacturing systems (FMSs) bring together several technologies into a coherent system. A FMS can be defined as 'a computer-controlled configuration of semi-independent workstations connected by automated material handling and machine loading'. This definition gives an indication of the component parts of FMSs:

- NC 'workstations', either machine tools or more sophisticated work centres, which perform the 'machining' operations;
- loading/unloading facilities, often robots which move parts to and from the workstations;

Photo courtesy of Yo! Sushi

Yo! Sushi are sushi restaurants with a difference. With an accent on style, they also employ technology to create their unique atmosphere. Prepared dishes are circulated around the sitting area on a moving conveyor. Customers simply take what they want as they pass by. Tables have personal metred beer taps but also a one metre high automated moving trolley, which stocked with drinks glides gently through the eating area inciting customers to 'stop me if you wish'

- transport/materials-handling facilities which move the parts between workstations (these may be AGVs or conveyor systems or, if distances are short, robots);
- a central computer control system which controls and coordinates the activities in the system.

Radioactive robots[5]

Decommissioning spent nuclear power stations is an agonizingly slow process which in many countries will take well over 100 years to complete. It is also a delicate and potentially dangerous process for those involved. This is why robots are used where possible to move, dismantle and manipulate hazardous radioactive material. Robots are also used for controlled-circuit television inspections as well as the pumping and removal of radioactive sludge. For example, at BNFL's Windscale Plant, remote-controlled robotic crushers are being used to dismantle the plant's pile chimneys, and in nearby Sellafield a floating robot is draining and dismantling a tank of highly active liquid waste.

> **Question**
>
> Robots are used in this example because of the hazardous environment in which the tasks take place. What other examples can you think of where the safety of operators is the major motivation for investment in robot technology?

A FMS is more than a single technology as such. It has integrated the single technologies into a system that has the potential to be greater than the sum of its parts. In effect, a FMS is a self-contained 'micro operation' which is capable of manufacturing a whole component from start to finish. Furthermore, the flexibility of each of the individual technologies combine to make a FMS (at least in theory) a supremely versatile manufacturing technology. A sequence of products, each different but within the capability 'envelope' of the system, could be processed in the system in any order and without changeover delays between each product. The 'envelope of capability' concept is important here. Any collection of machines within a FMS must have some finite limits on the size and shape of the materials it can process. The implication of this is that a FMS is best suited to manufacturing applications where the designs of parts are basically similar yet whose batch sizes can be small (perhaps as small as one).

● CRITICAL COMMENTARY

The flexibility advantage of FMSs is often less than it seems. It is true that, compared with any previous attempts to automate manufacturing processes, FMSs are flexible. Previously, 'hard' automation required the instructions to the machine to be fixed in its hardware. Any change required the machine itself to be physically reconfigured. The new manufacturing technologies such as FMSs hold their instructions in the form of software which can be changed very easily. But is this the real point? FMSs may be more flexible than any previous automated manufacturing technologies, but often they are not more flexible than the manufacturing systems which they replace. The fairly high-variety, fairly low-volume operations where FMSs seem to be most appropriate would previously have used stand-alone machine tools arranged in either a process or a cell layout (*see* Chapter 7 for a description of these layouts). Such a manufacturing system is extremely flexible in terms of the variety of components it can process, certainly more flexible than any FMS. Perhaps this is why in practice most FMSs are used for applications where the range of parts is not particularly wide.

The advantages of FMSs

One kind of flexibility at which FMSs do excel is what we called in Chapter 2 product flexibility, that is, the ability to introduce changes to product designs. The integrated control and programmable flexibility of FMSs make this a relatively straightforward task. However, most of the reported benefits seem to come from other performance objectives.

A survey of firms who adopted FMSs, reported by Professor John Bessant of Brighton University, identified the following benefits:[6]

- *Lead-time and throughput (factory door-to-door) time reduction* of between 60 and 70 per cent.
- *Inventory savings (especially of work in progress) and smoother flow of material* through the factory with less queueing and build-up of material waiting for machining.
- *Increased utilization* (in batch manufacturing there is a relatively low level of utilization of equipment, since so much time is spent waiting for products to be put on machines). Reported improvements ranged from 200 to 400 per cent.
- *Reduced set-up times* (closely linked to improved utilization). Improvements of between 50 and 90 per cent were reported.
- *Reduced number of machines or operations* (derived from the physical integration of operations into fewer, more complex machines).
- *Increased quality* (not wholly attributed to the technology); improvements ranged from 20 to 90 per cent.

Other reported benefits include space savings, reduced dependence on sub-contractors, skill saving, increased responsiveness to customers (speed and quality of service), facilitation of more rapid production innovation cycles and improved prototyping capability.

● Volume and variety characteristics

The technologies described here differ in their flexibility capabilities and economics and will therefore each be appropriate for different parts of the volume–variety continuum. Figure 8.4 positions the technologies on the volume–variety matrix we introduced in Chapter 4.

The volume–variety characteristics of manufacturing technologies

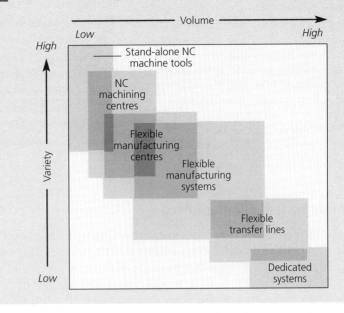

The positions illustrated in Figure 8.4 are not intended to be prescriptive, just indicative of what is sensible under current conditions of cost and technological development. Furthermore, the area occupied by FMS technology has increased, and is likely to increase further, as FMSs really do become more flexible while retaining the cost advantages of integration and automation.

FMS at Yamazaki Mazak

The Japanese tool manufacturers, Yamazaki, have, in their European factory, one of the most advanced machine tool manufacturing operations in Europe. Their four FMS systems allow overnight unstaffed production and so allow the company to make the most from its investment. Of course, the Yamazaki products are built by Yamazaki FMS systems (*see* picture). With a wide range of over 60 products, individual volumes are small. Because of this, the company wanted an operation that would be so flexible it would not matter in which order items were processed. High utilization would be maintained by having very fast set-ups, which would also reduce the need for large batches. The operation can make individual pieces to suit the tight production schedules. This enables the company to offer typical order lead-times of only four weeks, in comparison with competitors' lead-times of eight or more weeks for similar products. All component workpieces are loaded into fixtures mounted on special pallets. The operators prepare enough work to enable the system to run overnight unsupervised. At the centre of the FMS is a host computer which schedules and controls the

FMS installation at Yamazaki Mazak's European plant

Photo courtesy of Yamazaki Machinery UK Ltd

activity of each machining centre and the materials-handling devices. The computer predetermines the pallet locations and, as the machining centres become free, an automatic pick/load device will select the next workpiece from the waiting queue and will place it into the available machine. Each machine is capable of handling almost any of the components so that bottlenecks do not develop at any point in the system. Spare tools used for the machining centres are stored in a central tool bank at the ends of the area and are transported to the required machine by a holding device on a highway which runs above the machining centres. At the end of the shift, the incoming operator can consult the computer for a printout of the tools that may need to be replaced in the tool bank. Many of the materials are delivered from the warehouse to the factory by AGVs, which pick up the items when requested by the central scheduling system.

Questions

1 What seem to be the benefits of Yamazaki's investment in its highly automated plant?

2 What do you think are the main problems with unstaffed overnight operation, and what has Yamazaki done to avoid them?

3 What type of flexibility does Yamazaki's FMS give them?

Computer-integrated manufacturing

The integration of the separate developments in manufacturing technology exemplified by FMSs can be taken further. FMSs integrate those activities which are concerned directly with the transformation process but need not necessarily include the other activities such as design, scheduling and so on which are necessary for parts to be manufactured. These other activities, which are themselves computer-based, can be integrated with the direct materials-processing technologies. This wider integration is known as computer-integrated manufacturing (CIM). It can be defined as 'the integration of computer-based monitoring and control of all aspects of the manufacturing process, drawing on a common database and communicating via some form of computer network', although the term CIM is now frequently used to indicate far less ambitious forms of integrated manufacturing.[7]

Figure 8.5 illustrates how manufacturing technologies can be described as being progressively more integrated states of more basic technologies. The first stage is the integration between areas of activity to produce such combined technologies as CAD/CAM and FMS. Second, the integration of all the internal activities produces the broad definition of CIM. Finally, integration of the organization's CIM activity with other functions, and perhaps even suppliers and customers, approaches what has been termed the computer-integrated enterprise (CIE).

Human-centred CIM

Some argue that, by taking a purely technical perspective on developing integrated manufacturing systems, process technologies are neglecting the skills of the people who staff them. Rather than design CIM systems to technical criteria and then consider how people are to fit into them, it is argued that a 'parallel design' approach should be adopted. This would allow users of a CIM system to shape its design before the format of the system is finally fixed. This encourages users to integrate their skills and contribution with the technological elements of the system. Table 8.2 illustrates how 'pure' human-centred systems might differ from purely technology-centred systems.

Technology summaries

It is useful to summarize some of the materials-processing technologies we have discussed in terms of the four questions which we identified at the beginning of this chapter (*see* Table 8.3):

- What does the technology do?
- How does it do it?
- What advantages does it give?
- What constraints does it impose?

Figure 8.5 **Increasing integration of manufacturing technologies**

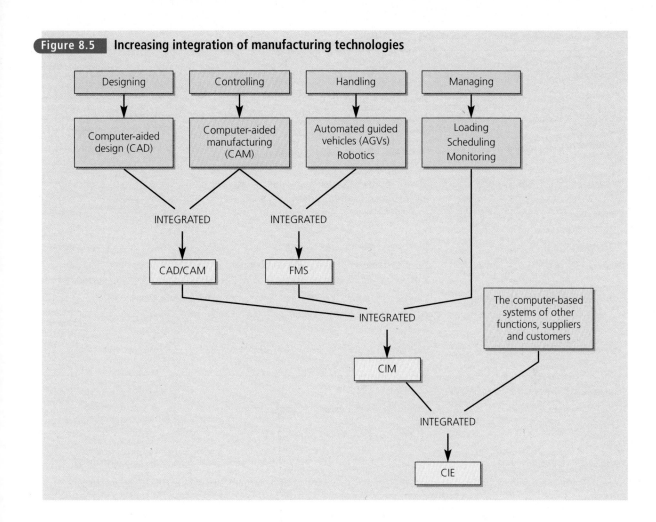

Table 8.2 A comparison of technology-centred and human-centred AMT systems design

Design choice point	Technology-centred systems	Human-centred systems
Allocation of function	Operator carries out only those functions that cannot be automated	Operator allocates functions depending upon particular circumstances and judgement during production
Systems architecture	Centralized control system, with production machines controlled at highest possible level	Decentralized control system, with machines controlled at lowest possible level
Control characteristics	User actions paced and regulated by directives stored in machine	User discretion and control maximized; the technology does not dictate work methods
Information characteristics	System status data presented only to management; restricted access for shop-floor users	System status data available at all machines; facilitation of cross-functional communication
Allocation of responsibilities	Work controlled by functional specialists	Work controlled by multi-skilled shop-floor users

Source: Adapted from Corbett, J.M. (1992) 'Working at the Interface' *in* Adler, P.S. and Winograd, T.A. (eds) *Usability*, Oxford University Press

Table 8.3 Summary of materials-processing technologies

NC (and CNC) machine tools

What does it do?	Performs the same types of metal cutting and forming operations which have always been done, but with control provided by a computer
How does it do it?	Preprogrammed instructions are read from a disk, tape or paper tape by a computer which activates the physical controls in the machine tool
What advantages does it give?	Precision, accuracy, optimum use of cutting tools which maximizes their life, and higher labour productivity
What constraints does it impose?	Higher capital cost than manual technology. Needs skilled staff to preprogramme the instructions for the controlling computer

Industrial robots

What does it do?	Moves and manipulates products, parts or tools
How does it do it?	Through a programmable and computer-controlled (sometimes multi-jointed) arm with an effector end piece which will depend on the task being performed
What advantages does it give?	Can be used where conditions are hazardous or uncomfortable for humans, or where tasks are highly repetitive. Performs repetitive tasks at lower cost than using humans and gives greater accuracy and repeatability
What constraints does it impose?	Cannot perform tasks which require delicate sensory feedback or sophisticated judgement

Automated guided vehicles (AGVs)

What does it do?	Moves materials between operations
How does it do it?	Independently powered vehicles guided by buried cables and controlled by computer
What advantages does it give?	Independent movement, flexibility of routing and long-term flexibility of use
What constraints does it impose?	Capital cost considerably higher than alternative (conveyor) systems

Flexible manufacturing systems (FMSs)

What does it do?	Completely manufactures a range of components (occasionally whole simple products) without significant human intervention during the processing
How does it do it?	By integrating programmable technologies such as machine tools, materials-handling devices and robots through centralized computer control
What advantages does it give?	Faster throughput times, higher utilization of capital equipment, lower work-in-progress inventories, more consistent quality, higher long-term product flexibility
What constraints does it impose?	Very high capital costs with uncertain payback, needs programming skills, and can be vulnerable to tool breakage (which can stop the whole system)

Computer-integrated manufacturing (CIM)

What does it do?	Coordinates the whole process of manufacturing and manufactures a part, component or product
How does it do it?	Connects and integrates the information technology which forms the foundation of design technology (CAD), manufacturing technology (FMC or FMS), materials handling (AGVs or robots) and the immediate management of these activities (scheduling, loading, monitoring)
What advantages does it give?	Fast throughput times, flexibility when compared with other previous 'hard' technologies, the potential for largely unsupervised manufacture
What constraints does it impose?	Extremely high capital costs, formidable technical problems of communications between the different parts of the system, and some vulnerability to failure and breakdown

Information-processing technology

Information-processing technologies include any devices which collect, manipulate, store or distribute information. Most of these we class under the general heading of 'computer-based technologies', the most common single type of technology within operations. The presence of computer-based technology in nearly all types of operation and the sheer pace of technical improvement make information processing technology particularly significant. Often organizational and operational issues are the main constraints in applying information technology because managers are unsure how best to use the potential in the technology. The following quotation gives some idea of how fast information technology has changed:[8]

> 'The rate of progress in information technology has been so great that if comparable advances had been made in the automotive industry, you could buy a Jaguar that would travel at the speed of sound, go 600 miles on a thimble of gas and cost only $2!'

● Centralized and decentralized information processing

All computers used for management purposes (as opposed to process control) were, at one time, large and centralized. It was simply the most economical way of buying processing power. The different parts of the organization originally accessed the computer in 'batch mode'. Each of the separate transactions associated with a particular activity would not be processed as they were originated. Instead they would be collected together or 'batched' until the scheduled processing time. With increasing use of computer-based technology, centralized computers became viewed as cumbersome for some applications. At the same time the cost and power of mid-range computers reached the point where it was economically feasible for different parts of the operation to have their own dedicated computer. Those 'minicomputers' could be placed under the direct control of the staff who would use them. Applications software could be designed specifically for their needs, and transactions processed when and how they thought appropriate. This is the distributed processing concept. The obvious problem with such an arrangement was that, in bringing computing power closer to its users, coordinating all the various processing activities became more complex. The answer to the problem was for the distributed minicomputers to exchange information. This eventually led to the concept of the network.

Local area networks (LANs)

The need to retain the clear advantages of distributed processing while retaining the control and communication benefits of centralized computing focused attention on the mechanism of communications itself – that is, the network which connects the distributed processing power. Combine the concept of the network with smaller and cheaper personal computers (PCs) and the concept of the local area network (LAN) emerges.

A LAN is a communications network which operates over a limited distance, usually within an operation. Connected to the network are devices such as PCs, display screens, printers, interfaces and minicomputers. Information (data, text and sometimes video) is exchanged between the devices along the network. The network itself can be formed from optical fibres, coaxial cable or simple telephone-type wiring, depending on the speed and volume of information which is being exchanged. The most common type of LAN connects the PCs in a workgroup or several departments and allows all staff to share common access to data files, other devices such as printers, and links to outside networks such as telephone lines.

The great advantage of LANs (and their larger cousins, wide area networks [WANs]) is their greater flexibility when compared with other more cumbersome forms of distributed processing. In particular, advantages include the following:[9]

- *Incremental growth.* New devices can be added to the network as they are required or become available.
- *Redundancy.* Robustness can be built into the system by keeping spare machines and duplicate files.
- *Location flexibility.* Workstations and peripherals can be located where needed and relocated with relatively little disruption when necessary.
- *Operational autonomy.* Both the control and the administration of hardware and software can be assigned to those staff who use them.

Photo courtesy of British Airways

Airlines now invest substantial amounts of money in in-flight communications and entertainment. In addition to multi-channel video entertainment, phone and other communication links to business contacts, hotels, car hire companies, etc. are often provided for business class passengers.

● Telecommunications and information technology

Computer-based technologies in business use have always been based on digital principles, that is, converting information into a binary form using 0s and 1s. Telecommunications, on the other hand, were originally based on analogue technology. The digitization of telecommunications transmissions (including digital compression techniques, which allow information to be squeezed into a smaller 'space' so that more can be sent using a given amount of transmission capacity), together with the use of high-capacity optical fibre networks, brought new possibilities. The technologies of computing and telecommunications in effect merged. Digital telecommunication lines could carry both voice and non-voice (text, data, etc.) traffic at the same time, so separate sites of the same organization, or separate operations, could lease lines for their exclusive use. Alternatively, separate operations could use one of the public integrated services digital networks (ISDNs).

The effect on telecommunications companies of these developments has been far-reaching. Figure 8.6 shows the increase in the new types of services they can offer, most of which are the result of digital technologies.

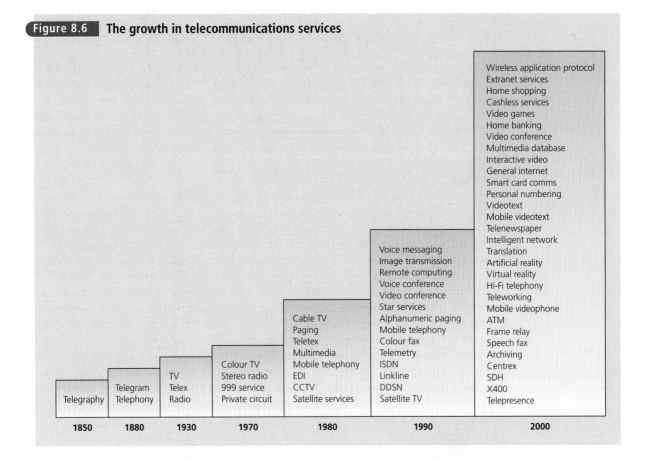

Figure 8.6 The growth in telecommunications services

1850	1880	1930	1970	1980	1990	2000
Telegraphy	Telegram Telephony	TV Telex Radio	Colour TV Stereo radio 999 service Private circuit	Cable TV Paging Teletex Multimedia Mobile telephony EDI CCTV Satellite services	Voice messaging Image transmission Remote computing Voice conference Video conference Star services Alphanumeric paging Mobile telephony Colour fax Telemetry ISDN Linkline DDSN Satellite TV	Wireless application protocol Extranet services Home shopping Cashless services Video games Home banking Video conference Multimedia database Interactive video General internet Smart card comms Personal numbering Videotext Mobile videotext Telenewspaper Intelligent network Translation Artificial reality Virtual reality Hi-Fi telephony Teleworking Mobile videophone ATM Frame relay Speech fax Archiving Centrex SDH X400 Telepresence

The internet

Undoubtedly the most significant technology to impact on operations management in the last few years has been the internet. In effect, the internet is a 'network of networks'. It is used to link computer networks with other computer networks. Its origins lie in the development of LANs in the '70s and '80s (and later, WANs). However, because they used different types of computer, LANs usually found it difficult to talk to each other. Nor did WANs use the same language as LANs. The breakthrough came with the development of a technique called 'packet switching'. This enabled many messages to be sent to different locations at the same time conveniently and allowed individual networks to communicate. In practical terms, though, most of us think of the internet as the provider of services such as the ability to browse the World Wide Web.

The World Wide Web

Until 1993, the internet was used primarily by universities and some businesses to exchange messages and files. Then the World Wide Web (WWW or Web) dramatically changed our view. The Web was developed by CERN in Switzerland and MIT in the United States to provide a 'distributed hypermedia/hypertext' system. Information on the Web was organized into pages which contained text and graphics. Elements of the page were identified as links which allowed users to transfer to another page of information, which in turn had hypertext links to other pages, and so on.

The exact impact of the WWW, and internet technologies generally, on operations management is already significant, and is likely to become more so. This is what has become known as the 'e-business revolution'. E-business is the application of internet technologies to business processes. It became possible because of what is the essential internet capability – the ability of any computer to talk to another.

Extranets

Extranets link organizations together through secure business networks using internet technology. They are used primarily for various aspects of supply chain management (*see* Chapter 13). They tend to be cheaper to set up and cheaper to maintain than the commercial trading networks which preceded them. For example, details of orders placed with suppliers, orders received from customers, payments to suppliers and payments received from customers can all be transmitted through the extranet. Banks and other financial institutions can also be incorporated into these networks. The use of networks in this way is often called electronic data interchange (EDI).

E-business

The use of internet-based technology, either to support existing business processes or to create entirely new business opportunities, has come to be known as e-business. The most obvious impact has been on those operations and business processes that are concerned with the buying and selling activity (e-commerce). The internet provided a whole new channel for communicating with customers. The advantage of internet selling was that it increased both *reach* (the number of customers who could be reached and the number of items they could be presented with) and *richness* (the amount of detail which could be provided concerning both the items on sale and customers' behaviour in buying them). Traditionally, selling involved a trade-off between reach and richness. The internet effectively overcame this trade-off.

However, the internet had equally powerful implications for the ongoing provision of services. Figure 8.7 illustrates the relative cost to a retail bank of providing its services using different channels of communication. With cost savings of this magnitude, internet-based services have become the preferred medium for many operations.[10]

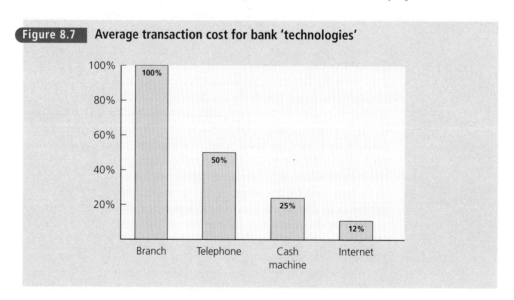

Figure 8.7 Average transaction cost for bank 'technologies'

Technology and the retail revolution[11]

Not everyone predicts a golden future for internet retailing. The sociologist Professor Laurie Taylor believes that hi-tech shopping is doomed unless it pays more attention to people's psychological needs. *'People welcome advice,'* he says, *'especially when buying such items as clothes, electrical goods and home decoration where they feel they need guidance*. 'Retailers must try to bring back conversation into shopping: *'Banishing customers to the remote and impersonal bank teller machines was* a huge mistake,' he says, 'because banks lost all those wonderful human contacts as well as the chance to sell customers life insurance and pensions.'

This may also limit the potential of selling through the internet. *'The most successful businesses sell books and CDs where people know exactly what they want to buy and the product goes through the letterbox.'* Businesses where customers are less sure about what they want to buy and where products cannot be delivered through the mail may not be the best candidates for technology-based selling.

the
"there are three keys to retail success: location, location, location" solution

Can a website really rival a storefront on the Ku'damm, Avenue Montaigne or Oxford Street? It can when it's built around IBM's CommercePoint. Our experts can help you open up a real shop on the Internet. One with actual till-ringing sales and millions of affluent potential customers.

People aren't just browsing. They're buying.

We've already helped some of the world's leading companies to make millions by selling their goods and services on the web. Airlines, clothing companies and camera shops are finding new customers at minimal costs.

Virtual shops. Not virtual shoplifters.

IBM Net.Commerce protects you and your customers. We've worked with major credit card organisations to set tough new security standards for payment transactions. Doesn't opening up on the Internet sound like a smart move? Visit us at www.ibminfo.com/uk4/ or call us on 0800 675 675 (quoting EW1).

IBM
Solutions for a small planet

Advertisement courtesy of IBM United Kingdom Limited and Ogilvy & Mather

In this advertisement, IBM, one of the largest and most experienced information systems providers, questions the relevance of the retail industry's preoccupation with location

● Management information systems (MISs)

Most of our discussion so far has concerned the arrangement of information-processing technologies – what computers and similar devices can do, and how they are connected to each other. Within the configuration of the physical system, however, what is important is the way in which information moves, is changed, is manipulated and presented so that it can be used in managing an organization. These systems are management information systems (MISs). Operations managers make considerable use of MISs, especially in their planning and control activities. Systems which are concerned with inventory management, the timing and scheduling of activities, demand forecasting, order processing, quality management and many other activities are an integral part of many operations managers' working lives, and are referred to in the planning and control chapters of Part Three.

Decision support systems (DSSs)

A decision support system is one which provides information with the direct objective of aiding or supporting managerial decision-making. It does this by storing relevant information, processing it and presenting it in such a way as to be appropriate to the decision being made. In this way, it supports managers by helping them to understand the nature of decisions and their consequences, but it does not actually make the decision itself. Often DSSs are used for 'what if' analyses which explore the (often financial) consequences of changing operations practice. For example, suppose a synthetic fibre manufacturer (such as Delta Synthetic Fibres which was discussed as a case example in Chapter 6) is considering adding extra capacity for a new product, as well as converting its existing capacity to manufacture the new product. A typical DSS would have at its disposal the full manufacturing costs associated with making each product at all the company's alternative locations, the costs involved with transporting products to worldwide markets, the costs and lead-times involved in the construction and conversion of capacity, and so on. It would then allow managers to enter alternative decisions regarding the location, size and timing of capacity change and show the results in terms of such measures as capacity utilization, inventory levels, profitability and cash flow.

Electronic benefit transfer[12]

Even social programmes around the world are being revolutionized through the use of technology. For example, electronic benefit transfer (EBT) is making pension books and welfare cheques obsolete. Countries as diverse as South Africa, Italy, Finland and Namibia are all starting to use cash-dispensing machines to issue state pensions. Pensioners simply use a government-issued card and a personal identity number (PIN) to obtain their cash. A similar system, shortly to be widespread in the United States, can issue food stamps and other welfare payments to poor families through the card. One such system enables welfare recipients to swipe their cards through a terminal at the retail checkout, enter their PIN number, and the cost of their food is automatically deducted from their entitlement and added to the retailer's account.

> **Question**
>
> List what you see as being the major advantages and problems as social programmes become more dependent on the type of technology described above.

Expert systems (ESs)

Expert systems take the idea of DSSs one stage further in that they attempt to 'solve' problems that would normally be solved by humans. An ES exhibits (within a specified area) a sufficient degree of expertise to mimic human problem-solving. The key part of an ES is its 'inference engine' which performs the reasoning or formal logic on the rules that have been defined as governing the decision. These rules are called the 'knowledge base' of the ES (which is why ESs are also called knowledge-based systems).

There have been many attempts to utilize the idea of an ES in operations management. Table 8.4 illustrates some of the decision areas and questions which have been treated. However, although authorities agree that ESs will become far more important in the future of operations management, not all applications so far have been totally successful. The problems which have been encountered include the following:

- Most expert systems can treat only narrow problems rather than the more realistic issues of integration and conflict between problem areas of the operation.
- Putting even some of an operations manager's expertise into a knowledge base is very expensive in terms of time and processing power.
- Like all information-based systems, it is rendered impotent if the data it is working with is wrong or inaccurate.

Table 8.4 Examples of the application of expert systems in operations management[13]

Decision area	Typical issues	Some current applications
Capacity planning	What is a reasonable size for a facility? What is the workforce size for our operation system?	PEP, CAPLAN
Facility location	Where is the best geographic site to locate the operation?	FADES
Facility layout	How should we arrange equipment in our facility site?	CRAFT, CORELAP, WORKPLACE DESIGNER
Aggregate planning	What should be the output rates and staffing levels for this quarter?	PATRIARCH, CAPLANLITE
Product design	Does the design of the product fit the firm's capability to produce it?	XCON, CDX
Scheduling	Which customers or jobs should receive top priority?	ISIS, MARS
Quality management	How do we best achieve our quality goals? Is the process capable of meeting the specifications?	PL DEFT
Inventory control	How much inventory do we need in our store? How should we control it?	IVAN, LOGIX, RIM
Maintenance	Where do we have a problem in our equipment? What kind of measures should we take to control or remove this problem?	DELTA/CATS

● Technology summaries

Again, it is useful to summarize the information-processing technologies in terms of our operations questions (*see* Table 8.5).

Table 8.5 Summary of information-processing technologies

Local area networks (LANs)	
What does it do?	Allows decentralized information processors such as personal computers to communicate with each other and with shared devices over a limited distance
How does it do it?	Through a hard-wired network and shared communication protocols
What advantages does it give?	Flexibility, easy access to other users, shared databases and applications software
What constraints does it impose?	The cost of installing the network can initially be high

Internet	
What does it do?	Links LANs and WANs to provide an integrated network
How does it do it?	Packet switching which allows many messages to be sent simultaneously
What advantages does it give?	Allows access to the World Wide Web (WWW), the distributed hypermedia/ hypertext system. This has significant implications for most, if not all, operations management tasks
What constraints does it impose?	A fast-developing medium with potential for 'information overload'

Extranet	
What does it do	Allows companies to exchange secure information electronically
How does it do it?	By connecting through the internet, allowing customers, suppliers and banks to exchange trading information
What advantages does it give?	Allows applications such as electronic data interchange (EDI)
What constraints does it impose?	The initial cost of setting up the network can be high and system skills are necessary to integrate EDI into internal systems. This can be especially daunting for small suppliers

Decision support systems (DSSs)	
What does it do?	Provides information to assist decision-making
How does it do it?	Uses data storage, models and presentation formats to structure information and present consequences of decisions
What advantages does it give?	Speed and sophistication of decision-making
What constraints does it impose?	Can be expensive to set up and can lead to 'over-analysis'. Also dependent on quality of data and models

Expert systems (ESs)	
What does it do?	Makes operational decisions
How does it do it?	By mimicking human decision-making using data, knowledge bases and an inference engine
What advantages does it give?	Takes some routine decision-making out of human hands, saving time and giving consistency
What constraints does it impose?	Expensive to model human decision-making and can only treat narrow problems

Customer-processing technology

Traditionally, customer-processing operations have been seen as 'low-technology' when compared with materials-processing operations. The assumption is that manufacturing needs machines while services rely on people. To some extent this is understandable – visit most factories and their technology is often very evident. For example, there is no mistaking the centrality of a steel producer's process technology to its business. However, process technology is very much in evidence in customer processing. For any airline flight, for example, airline reservation technology, check-in technology and even the aircraft itself all play vital parts in the delivery of the service. The personal element is undoubtedly important – the aircraft could not fly without the pilot, nor could a meal be served at one's seat without the cabin attendants. However, in some cases, the human element has been removed altogether, or significantly reduced. For example, the Formule 1 hotel chain described in Chapter 1 uses 'check-in' machines at its front entrance to take payment and issue pass keys when the hotel is unattended. As with many types of customer-processing technology, the objective is to give an acceptable level of service while significantly reducing costs to the operation.

There are essentially two types of customer-processing technologies, those that you interact with yourself and those that are operated by an intermediary. When booking an hotel room, airline seat or theatre performance, for example, you can either make the reservation yourself by interacting with the reservation computer via the internet or have an intermediary do it for you (a secretary, personal assistant or travel agent).

Many banking transactions are carried out by customers 'trained' to operate a range of technologies, all of which have lower operational costs than face-to-face transactions

● Technology involving customer interaction

Cars, direct dial telephones, internet bookings and purchases, fitness equipment and automatic teller machines (ATMs – cash machines) are all examples of technology with which the customer interacts directly. In these cases, customers are 'driving' the technology to create the service for themselves (*see* Fig. 8.8). On an airline flight, for example, the passenger may choose to use the aircraft's entertainment facilities. This is likely to be an individual screen and headphones which can be used to view movies or listen to audio entertainment. The passenger might even make use of telecommunications equipment at the seat to book hotels or rent a car. In these cases, the customer takes control of the technology.

Sometimes the customer may take a more passive role, such as being a 'passenger' in an aircraft, mass transport systems, moving walkways and lifts, cinemas and theme parks. This technology guides customers rather than the other way around. In all these cases, customers are interacting with the technology, but the technology 'processes' the customers and also controls them by constraining their actions in some way. The

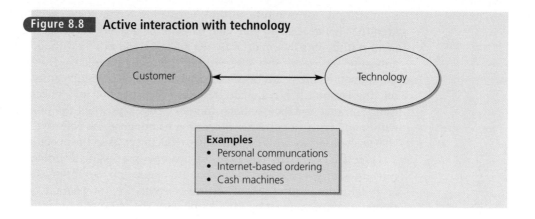

Figure 8.8 Active interaction with technology

Customer ↔ Technology

Examples
- Personal communcations
- Internet-based ordering
- Cash machines

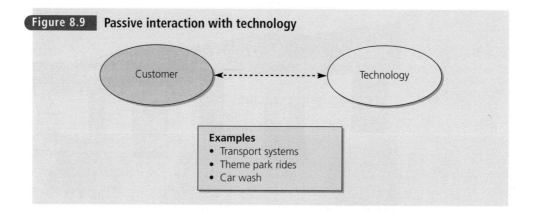

Figure 8.9 Passive interaction with technology

Customer ⇠⇢ Technology

Examples
- Transport systems
- Theme park rides
- Car wash

technology helps to reduce the variety in the operation. Figure 8.9 illustrates this class of technology in terms of customers, staff and technology.

Sometimes customers may not be aware of the technology, and while not actually hidden from them, it may be 'invisible' or 'transparent'. The technology is 'aware' of customers but not the other way round; for example, security monitoring technologies in shopping malls or at national frontier customs areas. The objective of these 'hidden' technologies is for staff to track customers' movements or transactions in an unobtrusive way. Supermarkets, for example, can use bar-code scanner technologies to track the movement of customers around the store and indicate the relationship between the customers and their propensity to buy particular products – for example, do customers who buy frozen fish also tend to buy frozen potato products? Suppose a retailer wanted to sell soft toys by displaying them next to children's clothes. Bar-code data scanners at the checkout could indicate that these two types of product were purchased by the same customers more often when they were placed next to each other. This would confirm the store's display decision. The same technology could, for example, issue a customer with a discount voucher for a product only if the customer had bought a rival brand. Figure 8.10 illustrates the nature of the relationship in this type of technology. Credit card companies and airlines also use this approach to target their marketing or frequent-flyer privileges.

● Interaction with technology through an intermediary

When the customers of an airline check in at the airport, they collect their boarding passes. They may choose to do this at an automatic ticketing machine or they may

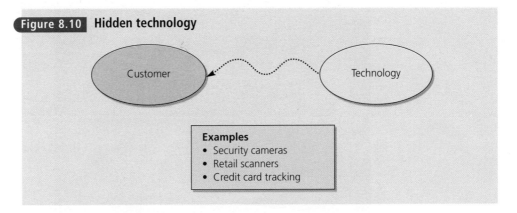

Figure 8.10 Hidden technology

choose an intermediary. The intermediary may be the travel agent or the airline staff at check-in. The benefits to the customer are a more flexible service, whereas an automated system may not accept requests for special meals or allocate seats. An intermediary dealing with the complex airline systems may be able to do this. In such cases, the customer does not directly use the technology: the staff member does that on behalf of the customer. The customer may 'navigate'[14] or guide the process but does not 'drive' it. The technology may even be arranged to help customers navigate the process. For example, some airlines have a screen with the seat layout of the aircraft facing the customer, showing which seats are still available. But this is an aid to the customer, who has no direct contact as such (*see* Fig. 8.11).

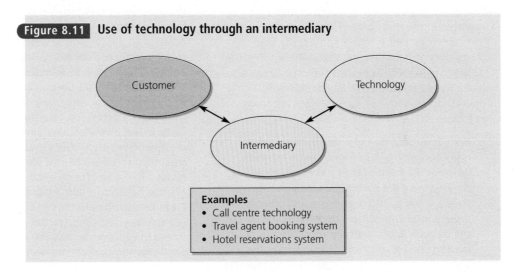

Figure 8.11 Use of technology through an intermediary

Other examples of this kind of technology are the reservations systems in hotels or theatres, the customer support enquiry lines used by utilities, the package tracking systems in parcel delivery services, and holiday booking systems in travel agents.

The main concern in the development of these types of technology, be they aircraft or medical robots, is the safety of the customer. By definition, this class of technology is processing customers and is outside of their control. The technology must therefore have the potential to do harm to the customer. This is why aircraft and most other transport technologies are governed by strict governmental regulations. Similarly with medical technologies – the pace of progress in robot surgery, for example, is relatively slow, not because of technological constraints, but because surgeons cannot take risks with their patients' lives.

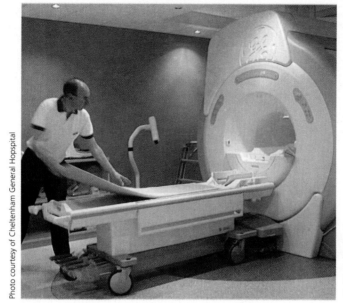

Photo courtesy of Cheltenham General Hopspital

Many medical technologies, such as this scanner, are very expensive and therefore need to be kept busy to maintain high utilization

Technology in medicine[15]

The technological breakthroughs in medical care reported in the press often focus on those dramatic 'miracle cures' which have undoubtedly improved the quality of medical care. Yet a whole collection of changes in medical process technology has also had a huge impact on the way health care operations manage themselves. Here are some examples.

- Even in surgery, that ultimate in human skill, robot technology is becoming more common. Whereas the hand of the most experienced surgeon trembles slightly, a robot arm is totally steady. Some applications move instruments around inside the patient under the direction of the surgeon. More radically, robots can now be used to remove soft tissue. For example, the PROBOT technology developed at Guy's Hospital in London has been specially developed for prostate surgery. Guided by an ultrasonic scanner (which, usefully, can see through flesh) the robot can scan the area to be operated on and convert its readings into a three-dimensional image. In this way, the human surgeon can identify the tissue to be removed, which is then done with an electronic probe. The human surgeon, however, is in control throughout the procedure.

- It is a routine familiar in hospital wards throughout the world. At more or less the same time each day, a doctor progresses from bed to bed doing his or her 'ward rounds' to check up on

the progress of each patient. Conventionally, before this happens the doctor would consult the notes of all the patients as a reminder of their recent history and condition. This might take anything from 30 to 60 minutes. In some hospitals, though, this time has been virtually eliminated through the use of radio-connected laptop computers. Doctors just take their laptops to the bedside and access information through the radio receiver. If necessary, they can update and change treatment regimes instantly without having to revisit their office. Just as important, the system enables patients to take a hand in their own care. Preferences and opinions can be recorded immediately and added to the central database where they can be accessed by other doctors, physiotherapists, dieticians or social workers.

- It is called telemedicine and it is challenging one of the most fundamental assumptions of medical treatment – that medical staff need to be physically present to examine a patient. Connected to the patients through a television screen, keyboard and camera, a nurse can talk to them and enter their replies into the communications computer as they speak. Using simple electronic instruments, patients can also measure their own pulse rate and take their own temperature while on camera. The proponents of telemedicine claim a number of advantages. The system can make use of decision support diagnostic systems, which give accurate and consistent diagnoses; patients having convenient access to medical advice can make fewer visits to the hospital; and, most significantly, nurses can see up to 15 patients in four hours, whereas, visiting them in their home, they can see only five or six patients a day. Even when the costs of the technology are taken into account, telemedicine can represent a significant cost saving, especially in rural or remote areas.

- The computer screen can also be used to educate and reassure patients without any access to medical staff. For example, multimedia 'MediBooks' are used at St Thomas's hospital in London to help patients understand their own condition. Using large-format, colour-touch screens, patients can be guided through various aspects of their condition on a CD-ROM packed with narrative animations and diagrams.

Question

From an operations management point of view, what are the major advantages and what are the major problems likely to result from each of the technologies described above?

Customer training

If customers are to have direct contact with technology, they must have some idea of how to operate it. Where customers have an active interaction with technology, the limitations of their understanding of the technology can be the main constraint on its use. For example, even some domestic technology such as video recorders cannot be used to their full potential by most owners. Other 'customer-driven' technologies can face the same problem, with the important addition that if customers cannot use technologies such as ATMs, there are serious commercial consequences for a bank's customer service. Staff in manufacturing operations may require several years of training before they are given control of the technology they operate. Service operations rarely have the same opportunity for customer training.

Walley and Amin[16] suggest that the ability of the operation to train its customers in the use of its technology depends on a number of factors.

The complexity of the service

If services are complex to operate, higher levels of training will be needed to ensure correct use of the technology. Alternatively, the need for customer training can be reduced if operational complexity is minimized. In some cases, the training is delivered by potential customers watching experienced customers performing the task correctly. For example, the technologies in theme parks and fast-food outlets rely on customers copying the behaviour of others.

Repetition of the service

The frequency with which a technology is used is an important factor in two ways. First, if a service has to invest in customer training for the technology, then the payback for this investment will be greater if the customer uses the technology frequently. The greater the repetition, the more worthwhile the investment becomes. Second, customers may, over time, forget how to use the technology. Regular repetition will reinforce the training. Conversely, if customers do not use the technology for a long period, they may require retraining.

Low variety of focus

Training will be easier if the customer is presented with a low variety of tasks. For example, vending machines tend to concentrate on one category of product, so that the sequence of tasks required to operate the technology remains consistent.

● Technology summaries

While there is far less consensus on how customer-processing technologies can be classified than there is with other types of technology, we include in Table 8.6 some of the technologies mentioned above to illustrate their general characteristics.

Table 8.6 Summary of customer-processing technologies

In-flight entertainment	
What does it do?	Provides a range of entertainment services, film, TV, radio and news programmes to entertain the passenger during a long flight
How does it do it?	Through personalized terminals at the passenger's seat linked to a central processor
What advantages does it give?	Gives the passengers something to keep themselves busy and reduces the role of the cabin attendants
What constraints does it impose?	High initial costs and need to continually update the material and programme choices as competitors develop them further
Moving walkways	
What does it do?	Transports large numbers of customers over short distances
How does it do it?	Simple moving belts driven from under the floor
What advantages does it give?	Eases long journeys (particularly through airports) for passengers and improves aircraft punctuality by speeding the flow of passengers through the terminals
What constraints does it impose?	Initial costs plus fixed nature of the installation, i.e. cannot move to areas of sudden high demand
Bar code scanners	
What does it do?	Tracks items, for example, usage, costs, movement
How does it do it?	Links individual items to central information processing
What advantages does it give?	Fast and easy detailed information about items
What constraints does it impose?	Requires wide-scale usage and acceptance of bar-coding and common conventions
Airline check-in	
What does it do?	Allocates passengers to aircraft and seats, identifies luggage movements
How does it do it?	By connecting the check-in agent to the central processing unit
What advantages does it give?	Controls movement of passengers and their baggage, allocates people to seats
What constraints does it impose?	High initial costs
Electronic point of sale technology (EPOS)	
What does it do?	Assists cashier and purchasing functions
How does it do it?	Scans item bar codes, checks prices, adds prices and reduces stock levels with central processor
What advantages does it give?	Fast processing of items for the customers and real-time information on store inventory and stock movements
What constraints does it impose?	High set-up costs; given the number of items involved, errors may be difficult to trace

Integrating technologies

Some technologies, usually centred around information processing, process a combination of material, customers and information (*see* Fig. 8.12).

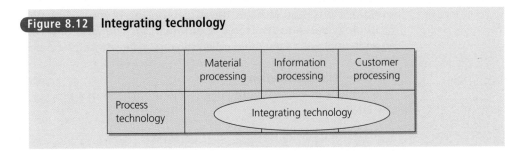

Figure 8.12 **Integrating technology**

Electronic point of sale (EPOS) technology, for example, processes shoppers, groceries and information. The electronic till (with the assistance of an intermediary – the cashier) processes the customers by adding up their purchases, processing their credit card and providing a receipt which details all of the purchases and their prices. In some stores, an additional banking service, 'cash-back', is provided. EPOS also processes the materials from unsold items to sold items, and through its information retrieval and storage capabilities linked to a central processor, it updates stock records and creates purchase orders to replenish stocks approaching re-order levels. Further, EPOS provides information for operations control systems and financial systems, such as information on slow moving items, out-of-stock items, cashier speed, and store turnover and profitability.

Some internet sites may also integrate all three types of technologies. For example, a customer may at first interact with a company's website to obtain information about a new shirt or a CD. Having selected the item and provided credit card details, the technology interacts with the organization's materials-processing technologies to create picking sheets and a routing slip, or in the case of music it may automatically find the CD or selected tracks and transfer them digitally directly to the customer's computer. The distinctions between the things that are being processed – material, customers or information – start to become blurred and, indeed, less important. Other examples include airline check-in, electronic benefit transfer (*see* box) and applications in medicine (*see* 'Technology in medicine' box).

The dimensions of technology

So far, at least one thing should be clear – process technology comes in many different forms. This makes it difficult to generalize across technologies which are used for such a wide variety of purposes. All operations make choices regarding their technology, however, and there are always alternative ways of configuring any technology. Exploring these alternatives involves thinking on three dimensions:

- the degree of automation of the technology;
- the scale of the technology;
- the degree of integration of the technology.

The degree of automation of the technology

No technology operates totally without human intervention. To some extent, they all need human intervention some of the time. It may be minimal – for example, the periodic maintenance interventions in a petrochemical refinery, or occasional reprogramming of a computer control system. Conversely, the staff member who operates the technology may be the entire 'brains' of the process – for example, the operator working a precision lathe or the surgeon using keyhole surgery techniques. Process technology varies in its degree of automation. The ratio of technological to human effort it employs is sometimes called the *capital intensity* of the process technology.

The benefits of automation

Two benefits of increasing the degree of automation in a process technology are usually cited:

- It saves direct labour costs.
- It reduces variability in the operation.

Automation is usually justified on the former, but it is sometimes the latter which is more significant. Nevertheless, it is worth examining what type of labour can be saved through automation in any particular case.

Direct labour can often be saved, but that does not mean that the net effect is an overall cost saving. Operations managers need to consider the following points before automating for cost savings alone:

- Can the technology perform the task better or safer than a human (not just faster, although this can obviously be important, but better in a broader sense)? Can the technology make fewer mistakes, change over from one task to the next faster and more reliably, or respond to breakdowns effectively?
- What support activities, such as maintenance or programming, does the technology need in order to function effectively? What will be the effect on indirect costs (not just the extra people and skills which might be necessary, but also the effect of increased complexity of support activities)?
- Can the technology cope with new product or service possibilities as effectively as less automated alternatives? This is a difficult question because no one will know exactly what the operation will need to produce in the future. Nevertheless, it is an important question; automation represents a risk as well as an opportunity.
- What is the potential for human creativity and problem-solving to improve the machines' performance? Is it worth getting rid of human potential along with its cost?

Methodology before technology

Automated technologies in many operations have provided the potential for improved performance, but there is a danger. Technology can be seen as a panacea for all the operation's ills, a 'technology fix' which avoids more fundamental problems. If the methods and processes are themselves flawed, technology will just speed up the problems, not solve them. Those companies that have attempted the difficult task of separating the benefits that come directly from investment in automated technology from those that come from improved methodology have reported some surprising results. Paradoxically, capital investment often makes it necessary to consider the organization of the operation as a whole, which in turn prompts improvements that are independent of the technology for which it is preparing the way. For example, the following are extracts from surveys of companies that have installed flexible manufacturing systems (FMSs):

> ' ... *on average 40 per cent of the benefits predicted for an FMS are in fact achievable, or have been achieved, before the FMS is delivered. This is because the planning process itself*

has highlighted existing custom and practice which ... can be put right without major investment.'[17]

'(We) frequently receive estimates that approximately half of the benefits of FMS were derived from managerial and work-based organizational change.'[18]

' ... companies who operate FMS, and who have presumably undergone some formal evaluation process, tend to concentrate their efforts more than other manufacturing firms on improving product quality, shortening lead times and set-up times and integrating information and control systems.'[19]

This does not mean that investing in capital-intensive automated equipment is a waste of time; rather, that there are considerable benefits to be gained from rethinking the overall 'methodology' of the operation, whether or not the investment in technology is subsequently made. Perhaps the right order should be first to improve the methods of the operation and only then to put in automated technology where it is needed.

The scale of the technology

Operations often need to decide between acquiring one large-scale unit of technology or several smaller ones. For example, the duplicating department of a large office complex may decide to invest in a single, very large, fast copier, or alternatively in several smaller, slower copiers. An airline may purchase one or two wide-bodied aircraft or a larger number of smaller aircraft. A manufacturer may design its operation around a single large-capacity machine or several smaller machines. No matter what the technology, there is usually some discretion as to how large a piece of plant it is wise to acquire. The economies of the technology itself will influence the decision. Some process technologies, such as intercontinental aircraft, petrochemical refineries or steel-making plants, benefit from scale and so tend to come in large-capacity increments. Others, like personal computers or ATMs, for example, are efficient when operating on a small scale.

The advantages of large-scale technologies are similar to those of large-capacity increments discussed in Chapter 6 and are summarized in Table 8.7.

Table 8.7 Advantages of large-scale and small-scale technologies

Advantages of large-scale technology	Advantages of small-scale technology
Economies of scale can lead to lower cost per product or service delivered	Good mix flexibility – each unit of technology can be engaged in different activities
Lower capital costs per unit of capacity	High robustness against failure
Can incorporate support and control elements in the technology (e.g. 'rest room' facilities in larger buses)	Lower obsolescence risk
Can pool work for better utilization (e.g. batch processing in centralized computer systems)	Can be located closer to where the technology is needed

Many of the advantages of large-scale technologies are associated with the cost advantages they can bring. However, nimbleness and flexibility can be virtues of smaller-scale technology. Mix flexibility (*see* Chapter 2), in particular, is enhanced. For example, four small machines can between them produce four different products simultaneously (albeit slowly), whereas a single large machine with four times the output can produce one product four times faster. Small-scale technologies are also more robust. Suppose the choice is between three small machines and two larger ones. In the first case, if one machine breaks down, a third of the capacity is lost, but in the second, capacity is halved. It is also easier to take advantage of technology improvement with small-scale technology. Buying a small machine just equal to current needs allows the operation to buy the latest technology when demand increases.

● The degree of integration of the technology

Integration means the linking together of previously separated activities within a single piece of technology or system. This issue has arisen at points earlier in this chapter. For example, the technological development represented by local area networks (LANs) is largely that of integration. Similarly, the development of advanced manufacturing technologies is the result of microprocessor-based integration.

Integration, synchronization and speed

The benefits of integration come directly from the effects of combining several separate technology units into one simple synchronized whole. First, there is fast throughput of information or materials. For example, in a FMS there is no inter-machine decision-making over which job has priority. Second, and as a consequence of throughput speed, inventory of materials or information will be lower – it can't accumulate when there are no 'gaps' between activities. Third, flow is simple and predictable. It is easier to keep track of parts when they pass through fewer stages, or information when it is automatically distributed to all parts of an information network. Integrated technology can be more expensive, however. For example, in manufacturing, even simple materials-handling linkages are costly. Furthermore, the more integrated the technology, the higher the level of skill that may be required to maintain it. When failures do occur, the whole integrated system is likely to go down. In one sense, this makes integrated plant more vulnerable.

Choice of technology

Understanding process technologies and being able to characterize their different dimensions are essential skills for all operations managers. Only then can they manage process technology's contribution to operations effectiveness. But the most common technology-related decision in which operations managers will be involved is the choice between alternative technologies, or alternative variants of the same technology. Like many 'design' decisions, technology choice is a relatively long-term issue. It can have a significant effect on the operation's strategic capability. Therefore, in order to make technology choices, it is useful to return to two of the perspectives we took on operations strategy in Chapter 3. There, we distinguished between the *market requirements* perspective, which emphasizes the importance of satisfying customer needs, and the *operations resource* perspective, which emphasizes the importance of building the intrinsic capabilities of operations resources.

Both these perspectives provide useful views of technology choice. In addition, the more conventional financial perspective is clearly important. Together, these three perspectives provide useful questions which can form the basis for technology evaluation:

- What effect does the proposed technology have on the operation's ability to service its markets?
- How does the proposed technology help to build the operation's resource capabilities?
- What are the financial consequences of investing in the technology?

● Market requirements evaluation

In Chapters 2 and 3, we identified the five *performance objectives* as the mechanism used by operations management to 'translate' market requirements into operations objectives. So a sensible approach to evaluating the impact of any process technology on an operation's ability to serve its markets is to assess how it affects the quality, speed, dependability, flexibility and cost performance of the operation.

Technology can have an impact on each performance objective. For example, consider a warehouse that stores spare parts which it packs and distributes to its customers. It is considering investing in a new 'retrieval and packing' system which converts sales orders into 'retrieval lists' and uses materials-handling equipment to automatically pick up the goods from its shelves and bring them to the packing area. The market requirements evaluation for this warehouse might be as follows:

- *Quality*. The impact on quality could be the fact that the computerized system is not prone to human error, which may previously have resulted in the wrong part being picked off the shelves.
- *Speed*. The new system may be able to retrieve items from the shelves faster than human operators can do safely.
- *Dependability*. This will depend on how reliable the new system is. If it is less likely to break down than the operators in the old system were likely to be absent (through illness etc.), then the new system may improve dependability of service.
- *Flexibility*. New service flexibility is not likely to be as good as the previous manual system. For example, there will be a physical limit to the size of products able to be retrieved by the automatic system, whereas people are capable of adapting to doing new things in new ways. Mix flexibility will also be poorer than was previously the case, for the same reason. Volume (and perhaps delivery) flexibility, however, could be better. The new system can work for longer hours when demand is higher than expected or deadlines are changed.
- *Cost*. The new system is certain to require fewer direct operatives to staff the warehouse, but will need extra engineering and maintenance support. Overall, however, lower labour costs are likely.

● Operations resource evaluation

Acquiring new resources, especially process technology, will impact on the intrinsic constraints and capabilities of the operation. By constraints we mean the things it will find difficult to do because of the acquisition of the technology. By capabilities we mean the things which the operation can now do because of the technology. Note that constraints and capabilities are not what the operation *does* necessarily do, but what it *can* do. In other words, this operation's resource evaluation is an assessment of the potential that the organization is acquiring through its process technology. Let us return to the warehouse example described previously.

Constraints

The main constraints imposed by the new process technology for the warehouse probably lie in its inability to cope with products of very different sizes, or a rapidly changing mix of products stored within the warehouse. While this may not be a serious problem for the current requirements of the company's markets, it does impose some rigidity in terms of the markets which the company might wish to pursue in the future.

Capabilities

The new technology could enable the company to link its sales order processing information systems directly to its warehouse management systems. This could be seen as the first step to a fully integrated supply chain management system which would oversee all demand and supply management for the company. Thus the new technology will provide an opportunity for the company to learn how such systems might work. Key questions here might be concerned with whether the new technology can be expanded in this way. If so, this will mean that the knowledge the company gains in managing this new technology can be exploited in the future.

● Financial evaluation

Assessing the financial value of investing in process technology is in itself a specialized subject. And while it is not the purpose of this book to delve into the details of financial analysis, it is important to highlight one important issue that is central to financial evaluation: while the benefits of investing in new technology can be spread over many years into the future, the costs associated with investing in the technology usually occur up front. So we have to consider the *time value of money*. Simply, this means that receiving €1000 now is better than receiving €1000 in a year's time. Receiving €1000 now enables us to invest the money so that it will be worth more than the €1000 we receive in a year's time. Alternatively, reversing the logic, we can ask ourselves how much would have to be invested now to receive €1000 in one year's time. This amount (lower than €1000) is called the *net present value* of receiving €1000 in one year's time.

For example, suppose current interest rates are 10 per cent per annum; then the amount we would have to invest to receive €1000 in one year's time is

$$€1000 \times \frac{1}{1.10} = €909.10$$

So the present value of €1000 in one year's time, *discounted for the fact that we do not have it immediately*, is €909.10. In two years' time, the amount we would have to invest to receive €1000 is:

$$€1000 \times \frac{1}{(1.10)} \times \frac{1}{(1.10)} = €1000 \times \frac{1}{(1.10)^2} = €826.50$$

The rate of interest assumed (10 per cent in our case) is known as the *discount rate*. More generally, the present value of €x in n years' time, at a discount rate of r per cent, is:

$$€ \frac{x}{(1 + r/100)} n$$

Worked example The warehouse which we have been using as an example has been subjected to a costing and cost savings exercise. The capital cost of purchasing and installing the new technology can be spread over three years, and from the first year of its effective operation, overall operations cost savings will be made. Combining the cash that the company will have to spend and the savings that it will make, the cash flow year by year is shown in Table 8.8.

Table 8.8 Cash flows for the warehouse process technology

Year	0	1	2	3	4	5	6	7
Cash flow (E000s)	−300	30	50	400	400	400	400	0
Present value (discounted at 10%)	−300	27.27	41.3	300.53	273.21	248.37	225.79	0

However, these cash flows have to be discounted in order to assess their 'present value'. Here the company is using a discount rate of 10 per cent. This is also shown in Table 8.8. The effective life of this technology is assumed to be six years:

The total cash flow (sum of all the cash flows) = €1.38 million

However the net present value (NPV) = €816 500

This is considered to be acceptable by the company.

Summary answers to key questions

What is process technology?

● Process technology is the collection of machines, equipment or devices that help operations to transform their materials, information or customers.

● Operations managers do not need to know the technical details of all technologies, but they do need to know the answers to the following questions: What does it do? How does it do it? What advantages does it give? What constraints does it impose?

What are the significant materials-processing technologies?

● Technologies which have had a particular impact include numerically controlled machine tools, robots, automated guided vehicles, flexible manufacturing systems and computer-integrated manufacturing systems.

● Each of these technologies can be seen as implying a different extent of integration between the four basic elements of designing, controlling, handling and managing materials.

What are the significant information-processing technologies?

● Significant technologies include local area networks (LANS) and wide area networks (WANS), electronic data interchange (EDI), the internet, and the World Wide Web and extranets. Of particular importance are the latter technologies, which include the integration of computing and telecommunications technology.

● Within these information technologies are such developments as management information systems, decision support systems and expert systems.

What are the significant customer-processing technologies?

● There are no universally agreed classifications of customer-processing technologies, such as there are with materials- and information-processing technologies.

● The way we classify technologies here is through the nature of the interaction between customers, staff and the technology itself. Using this classification, technologies can be categorized into those with direct customer interaction and those which are operated by an intermediary.

What are the generic characteristics of process technology?

● All technologies can be conceptualized on three dimensions: the degree of automation of the technology, the scale of the technology, and the degree of integration of the technology.

How is process technology chosen?

● Process technology can be assessed by judging it on three dimensions – market requirements, operations resources and financial evaluation.

● Market requirements evaluation includes assessing the impact that the process technology will have on the operation's performance objectives (quality, speed, dependability, flexibility and cost).

● Operations resource assessment involves judging the constraints and capabilities which will be imposed by the process technology.

● Financial evaluation involves the use of some of the more common eva luation approaches, such as net present value (NPV).

Rochem Ltd

Dr Rhodes was losing his temper.

'It should be a simple enough decision. There are only two alternatives. You are only being asked to choose a machine!'

The Management Committee looked abashed. Rochem Ltd was one of the largest independent companies supplying the food-processing industry. Its initial success had come with a food preservative used mainly for meat-based products and marketed under the name of 'Lerentyl'. Other products were subsequently developed in the food colouring and food container coating fields, so that now Lerentyl accounted for only 25 per cent of total company sales, which were now slightly over £10 million.

The decision

The problem over which there was such controversy related to the replacement of one of the process units used; to manufacture Lerentyl. Only two such units were used; both were 'Chemling' machines. It was the older of the two Chemling units which was giving trouble. High breakdown figures, with erratic quality levels, meant that output level requirements were only just being reached. The problem was: should the company replace the ageing Chemling with a new Chemling, or should it buy the only other plant on the market capable of the required process, the 'AFU' unit? The Chief Chemist's staff had drawn up a comparison of the two units, shown in Table 8.9.

The body considering the problem was the newly formed Management Committee. The committee consisted of the four senior managers in the firm: the Chief Chemist and the Marketing Manager, who had been with the firm since its beginning, together with the Production Manager and the Accountant, both of whom had joined the company only six months before.

What follows is a condensed version of the information presented by each manager to the committee, together with their attitudes to the decision.

The Marketing Manager

The current market for this type of preservative had reached a size of some £5 million, of which Rochem Ltd supplied approximately 48 per cent. There had, of late, been significant changes in the market – in particular, many of the users of preservatives were now able to buy products similar to Lerentyl. The result had been the evolution of a much more price-sensitive market than had previously been the case. Further market projections were somewhat uncertain. It was clear that the total market would not shrink (in volume terms) and best estimates suggested a market of perhaps £6 million within the next three or four years (at current prices). However, there were some people in the industry who believed that the present market only represented the tip of the iceberg.

Although the food preservative market had advanced by a series of technical innovations, 'real' changes in the basic product were now few and far between. Lerentyl was sold in either solid powder or liquid form, depending on the particular needs of the customer. Prices tended to be related to the weight of chemical used, however. Thus, for example, the current average market price was

Table 8.9 A comparison of the two alternative machines

	CHEMLING	AFU
Capital cost	£590 000	£880 000
Processing costs	Fixed: £15 000/month Variable: £750/kg	Fixed: £40 000/month Variable: £600/kg
Design capacity	105 kg/month 98 ± 0.7% purity	140 kg/month 99.5 ± 0.2% purity
Quality	Manual testing	Automatic testing
Maintenance	Adequate but needs servicing	Not known – probably good
After-sales services	Very good	Not known – unlikely to be good
Delivery	Three months	Immediate

approximately £1050 per kg. There were, of course, wide variations depending on order size, etc.

'At the moment I am mainly interested in getting the right quantity and quality of Lerentyl each month and although Production has never let me down yet, I'm worried that unless we get a reliable new unit quickly, it soon will. The AFU machine could be on line in a few weeks, giving better quality too. Furthermore, if demand does increase (but I'm not saying it will), the AFU will give us the extra capacity. I will admit that we are not trying to increase our share of the preservative market as yet. We see our priority as establishing our other products first. When that's achieved, we will go back to concentrating on the preservative side of things.'

The Chief Chemist

The Chief Chemist was an old friend of John Rhodes and together they had been largely responsible for every product innovation. At the moment, the major part of his budget was devoted to modifying basic Lerentyl so that it could be used for more acidic food products such as fruit. This was not proving easy and as yet nothing had come of the research, although the Chief Chemist remained optimistic.

'If we succeed in modifying Lerentyl the market opportunities will be doubled overnight and we will need the extra capacity. I know we would be taking a risk by going for the AFU machine, but our company has grown by gambling on our research findings, and we must continue to show faith. Also the AFU technology is the way all similar technologies will be in the future. We have to start learning how to exploit it sooner or later.'

The Production Manager

The Lerentyl Department was virtually self-contained as a production unit. In fact, it was physically separate, located in a building a few yards detached from the rest of the plant. Production requirements for Lerentyl were currently at a steady rate of 190 kg per month. The six technicians who staffed the machines were the only technicians in Rochem who did all their own minor repairs and full quality control. The reason for this was largely historical since, when the firm started, the product was experimental and qualified technicians were needed to operate the plant. Four of the six had been with the firm almost from its beginning.

'It's all right for Dave and Eric (Marketing Manager and Chief Chemist) to talk about a big expansion of Lerentyl

sales; they don't have to cope with all the problems if it doesn't happen. The fixed costs of the AFU unit are nearly three times those of the Chemling. Just think what that will do to my budget at low volumes of output. As I understand it, there is absolutely no evidence to show a large upswing in Lerentyl. No, the whole idea (of the AFU plant) is just too risky. Not only is there the risk. I don't think it is generally understood what the consequences of the AFU would mean. We would need twice the variety of spares for a start. But what really worries me is the staff's reaction. As fully qualified technicians they regard themselves as the elite of the firm; so they should, they are paid practically the same as I am! If we get the AFU plant, all their most interesting work, like the testing and the maintenance, will disappear or be greatly reduced. They will finish up as highly paid process workers.'

The Accountant

The company had financed nearly all its recent capital investment from its own retained profits, but would be taking out short-term loans the following year for the first time for several years.

'At the moment, I don't think it wise to invest extra capital we can't afford in an attempt to give us extra capacity we don't need. This year will be an expensive one for the company. We are already committed to considerably increased expenditure on promotion of our other products and capital investment in other parts of the firm, and Dr Rhodes is not in favour of excessive funding from outside the firm. I accept that there might eventually be an upsurge in Lerentyl demand but, if it does come, it probably won't be this year and it will be far bigger than the AFU can cope with anyway, so we might as well have three Chemling plants at that time.'

Questions

1 How do the two alternative process technologies (Chemling and AFU) differ in terms of their scale and automation? What are the implications of this for Rochem?

2 Remind yourself of the distinction between feasibility, acceptability and vulnerability, discussed in Chapter 4. Evaluate both technologies using these criteria.

3 What would you recommend the company should do?

Discussion questions

1   Identify as many applications of automation as you can in the following operations:
    – a hospital
    – an airline
    – a university
    – a chain of hotels
    – retail banking
    – farming and agriculture.

2   Many universities and colleges around the world are under increasing pressure to reduce the cost per student of their activities. How do you think technology could help operations such as universities to keep their costs down but their quality of education high?

3   In the popular press, there have been many stories about the 'fully automated factory', sometimes known as the 'dark factory' because it does not need any human intervention (who would switch the lights on?). What do you think might be some of the major problems in trying to achieve this goal of the fully automated factory? In what kind of manufacturing do you think we are first likely to see the extensive use of full automation?

4   Identify some technologies you use in day-to-day life. Assess the value of them by thinking what it would be like to be without them. Can you identify which ones are product/service technologies and which are process technologies?

5   Assess the differences between a fax machine and a telephone in terms of their operational capabilities.

6   Discuss the relationship between product/service and process technology for a product or service with which you are familiar.

7   The human-centred CIM philosophy aims to retain the advantages of computer-integrated manufacturing while also allowing humans to interact with such systems, so as to fulfil their own job aspirations and needs. Do you think this is just idealism or, alternatively, the only way to achieve the best of the mechanized and human worlds?

8   Discuss the advantages and disadvantages of centralized and decentralized information processing for air traffic controllers.

9   What benefits could EDI bring to a university?

10 What do you think would have to be done to make internet-based technology attractive to those who currently do not use it?

11 Describe the following technologies that might be found at an airport in terms of the customer–staff–technology interactions:
    – X-ray machines for customers at an airport
    – airbridges connecting walkways to the aircraft
    – air traffic control system
    – scanners that check the destination bar codes on luggage
    – automatic ticket machines.

12 The vast majority of services offered by retail banks could be provided entirely automatically. Automatic teller machines, automated depositing facilities, internet services and the full range of voice-activated and person-to-person home banking services all raise the possibility of a bank where customers never have face-to-face communication with the staff. What factors do you think influence retail banks when they are deciding how far to automate their various services?

13 Robot-type technology is starting to play a part in some medical surgical procedures. What would it take before you were willing to subject yourself to a robot doctor?

14 Visit your local or university library and write a report on how technology could be applied to enhance the efficiency and effectiveness of the operation. What do you think might be the biggest problems if the library attempted to operate on an entirely automated basis?

15 Airlines are already discussing with aircraft manufacturers the possibility of the development of an aircraft carrying 600–700 passengers. The desire for such large aircraft comes from the increased demand for air travel, especially on some routes. Generally, it is cheaper and faster to run one large aircraft than two of half the size. In principle, current technology could allow the development of aircraft which carry around 1000 passengers. What do you think might limit the use of technology to develop such large aircraft?

16 A high street bank is considering providing an internet banking service. What do you think are the main issues that the bank will have to consider in terms of getting customers to use this service?

17 Some Japanese manufacturers prefer to employ simple and unsophisticated technologies rather than large-scale fully integrated technologies. Why do you think this is so?

18 One problem with technology that is open to all members of the public to use, for example cash machines (ATMs), is that it could be open to fraud or misinterpretation. For example, some bank customers have complained that they did not make the transactions at cash machines which have shown up on their accounts. How do you think the technology might be developed to overcome this problem?

19 Using the criteria in the technology summaries, choose three technologies (one each of materials processing, information processing and customer processing) and evaluate them.

Notes on chapter

1 Brown, D. (1993) 'Mechanical Milkman Allows Farmer a Lie In', *The Daily Telegraph*, 11 Sept.
2 Economic Commission for Europe (1985) *Production and Use of Industrial Robots*, UN Economic Commission for Europe, ENC/ENG.ATV/15.
3 Edquist, C. and Jacobsson, S. (1988) *Flexible Automation*, Blackwell.
4 Source: *ABB Robotics Review*, No 2, 1993 and company literature, kindly supplied by ABB.
5 Source: 'When Robots do the Really Dangerous Jobs', *The Times*, 14 Aug 1996.
6 Bessant, J. (1991) *Managing Advanced Manufacturing Technology*, Blackwell.
7 Boaden, R. and Dale, B. (1986) 'What is Computer Integrated Manufacturing?', *International Journal of Operations and Production Management*, Vol 6, No 3.
8 Source: Tobias R.L., Henry Ford II Scholar Award Lecture, Cranfield School of Management, 1992.
9 Gunton, T. (1990) *Inside Information Technology*, Prentice Hall.
10 Source: Booz Allen and Hamilton data quoted in de Jacquelot, P. (1999) 'Ups and Downs of Internet Banking', *Connections*, Issue 1, Financial Times.
11 'Electronic Shopping Ignores Our Needs', *The Times*, 5 March 1997; 'Revolution Sweeps Through Cashpoints', *The Sunday Times*, 18 Aug 1996.
12 'Bar Coding the Poor', *The Economist*, 25 Jan 1997.
13 Adapted from Jayaraman, V. and Srivastara, R. (1996) 'Expert Systems in Production and Operations Management', *International Journal of Operations and Production Management*, Vol 16, No 12.
14 Walley, P. and Amin, V. (1994) 'Automation in a Customer Contact Environment', *International Journal of Operations and Production Management*, Vol 14, No 5, pp 86–100.
15 Sources: 'Know your Ailment Without Taking up the Doctor's Time', *The Times*, 24 Apr 1996; 'Big Sister is Watching You', *The Economist*, 11 Jan 1997; 'How Doctors Improved their Bedside Manners', *The Times*, 11 Sept 1996; 'Robodoc', *The Economist*, 15 June 1996.
16 Walley, P. and Amin, V., *op. cit.*
17 Bessant, J., *op. cit.*
18 Dempsey, P. (1983) 'New Corporate Perspectives on FMS', *FMS Conference Proceedings*, IFS.
19 Tombak, M. and De Meyer, A. (1986) 'How the Managerial Attitudes of Firms with FMS Differ from Other Manufacturing Firms', *INSEAD Working Paper*, No 86/15.

Selected further reading

Adler, T.S. and Winograd, T.A. (1992) *Usability, Turning Technology in Tools*, Oxford University Press.

Avishai, B. (1989) 'A CEO's Common Sense of CIM: An Interview with J.Tracy O'Rourke', *Harvard Business Review*, Vol 67, No 1.

Ayres, R. (1992) 'CIM: A Challenge to Technology Management', *International Journal of Technology Management*, Vol 7, No 2.

Benders, J., DeHaan, J. and Bennett, D. (eds) (1995) *The Symbiosis of Work and Technology*, Taylor and Francis.

Bennett, D., Forrester, P. and Hassard, J. (1992) 'Market-driven Strategies and the Design of Flexible Production Systems: Evidence from the Electronics Industry', *International Journal of Operations and Production Management*, Vol 12, No 2.

Bessant, J. (1991) *Managing Advanced Manufacturing Technology, The Challenge of the Fifth Wave*, NCC, Blackwell.

Carr, N.G. (2000) 'Hypermediation: "Commerce and Clickstream"', *Harvard Business Review*, January–February.

Delene, L.M. and Lyte, D.M. (1989) 'Interactive Service Operations: The Relationships Among Information, Technology and Exchange Transactions on the Quality of the Customer-Contact Interface', *International Journal of Operations and Production Management*, Vol 9, No 5.

Evans, P. & Thomas S.W. (1999) 'Getting Real About Virtual Commerce', *Harvard Business Review*, November–December.

Goldhar, J.D. and Jelinek, M. (1983) 'Plan for Economies of Scope', *Harvard Business Review*, Vol 61, No 6.

Gunton, T. (1990) *Inside Information Technology, A Practical Guide to Management Issues*, Prentice Hall.

Harrison, M. (1990) *Advanced Manufacturing Technology Management*, Pitman Publishing.

Kaplan, R.S. (1986) 'Must CIM be Justified by Faith Alone?', *Harvard Business Review*, Vol 64, No 2.

Karlsson, C. (1992) 'Knowledge and Material Flow in Future Industrial Networks', *International Journal of Operations and Production Management*, Vol 12, No 7/8.

Lindburg, P. (1992) 'The Management of Uncertainty in AMT Implementation: The Case of FMS', *International Journal of Operations and Production Management*, Vol 12, No 7/8.

Monroe, J. (1989) 'Strategic Use of Technology', *California Management Review*, Summer.

Rhodes, D. (1989) 'CIM and the Integration of Users, Vendors and Educators', *International Journal of Operations and Production Management*, Vol 9, No 2.

Skinner, W. (1984) 'Operations Technology: Blind Spot in Strategic Management', *Interfaces*, Vol 14, No 1.

Zorkoczy, P. (1993) *Information Technology: An Introduction* (3rd edn), Pitman Publishing.

Job design and work organization

Introduction

Operations management is often presented as a subject the main focus of which is on technology, systems, procedures and facilities – in other words the non-human parts of the organization. This is not true of course. On the contrary, the manner in which an organization's human resources are managed has a profound impact on the effectiveness of its operations function. In this chapter we look especially at the elements of human resource management which are traditionally seen as being directly within the sphere of operations management. These are the activities which influence the relationship between people, the technology they use, and the work methods employed by the operation. This is usually called job design. Figure 9.1 shows how job design fits into the overall model of design.

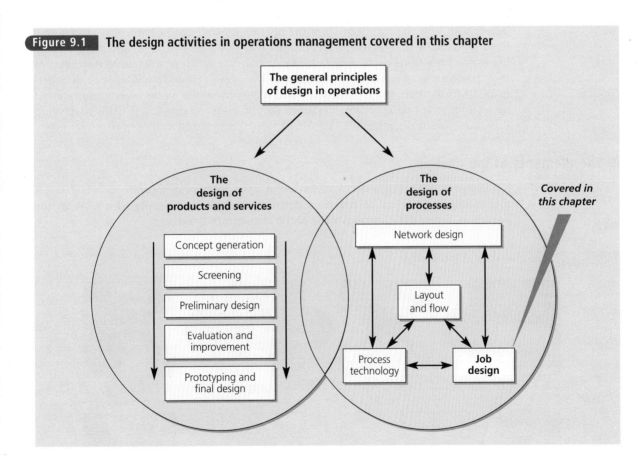

Figure 9.1 The design activities in operations management covered in this chapter

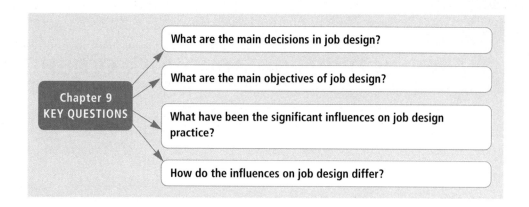

Chapter 9
KEY QUESTIONS

What are the main decisions in job design?

What are the main objectives of job design?

What have been the significant influences on job design practice?

How do the influences on job design differ?

The design of jobs

To say that an organization's human resources are its greatest asset is something of a cliché. Yet it is worth reminding ourselves of the importance of human resources, especially in the operations function, where most 'human resources' are to be found. It follows that it is operations managers who are most involved in the leadership, development and organization of human resources. In fact the influence of operations management on the organization's staff is not limited to how their jobs are designed. (Nor is the coverage of this book: Chapters 18 and 20, for example, are concerned largely with how the contribution of the operation's staff can be harnessed.) Job design has a particularly pivotal role. It defines the way in which people go about their working lives. It positions their expectations of what is required of them, and it influences their perceptions of how they contribute to the organization. It defines their activities in relation to their work colleagues and it channels the flows of communication between different parts of the operation. But, of most importance, it helps to develop the culture of the organization – its shared values, beliefs and assumptions.

● The elements of job design

Job design is not a single decision. Rather, it has a number of separate, yet related elements which, when taken together, define the jobs of the people who work in the operation. Figure 9.2 illustrates some of the elements of job design.

Figure 9.2   The elements of job design

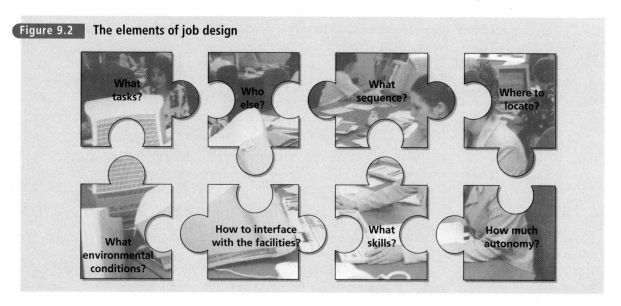

What tasks are to be allocated to each person in the operation?

Producing goods and services involves a whole range of different tasks which need to be divided between the people who staff the operation. Different approaches to job design will lead to different task allocations. For example, one company might choose to confine each staff member to repeating the same type of task to encourage simplicity and efficiency. Another might choose to allocate a wide variety of tasks to each staff member so as to reduce monotony.

What sequence of tasks is to be established as the approved manner to do the job?

Sometimes the sequence of tasks is dictated by the design of the product or service. For example, an operator working on an automobile assembly line must put the wheels in place before putting on the wheel nuts. Sometimes sequence is part of the job design. Paying for goods at a supermarket involves a sequence of taking your cash or card, asking you to sign the authorization, returning your card, etc., which minimizes mistakes.

Where is the job to be located within the operation?

Some jobs can be performed quite satisfactorily in more than one place. For example, a maintenance worker in a large hospital could be located centrally along with all other maintenance workers. Alternatively, he or she could be assigned responsibility for just one part of the hospital and located in that part.

Who else should be involved in the job?

It may be that instead of allocating a well-defined set of tasks to each person in the operation, a larger set of tasks is allocated to a group of people. The group then might choose a flexible task-sharing, or a task-rotation, pattern of working. If so, the size of the group and its interactions with other groups and individuals must be decided.

How are the facilities and equipment associated within the job to be used?

Very few jobs do not involve some interaction with tools, equipment, machines or facilities. Inappropriately positioned computer screens, badly designed controls and ill-fitting desks are all failures to consider the interfaces between people and the 'hardware' of their job.

What environmental conditions should be established in the workplace?

The conditions under which jobs are performed can have just as significant an impact on people's effectiveness, comfort and safety as the intrinsic details of the tasks themselves.

How much autonomy is to be included in the job?

There is a difference between allocating tasks to an individual and encouraging autonomy in the way the job is performed. For example, a retail operation might decide that the staff in a section of the shop should be allocated the tasks of reordering stock when it runs low, displaying the goods, organizing their own meal breaks, and so on.

What skills are to be developed in staff?

Different decisions in the elements of job design described here all have implications for the skills and capabilities which people will need to perform their jobs effectively.

● Approaches to job design practice

There are several approaches which can be taken to job design. Over the years, different approaches have been particularly influential at different times. None of these approaches is mutually exclusive as such, but they do represent different philosophies or, at least, emphasize different aspects of job design. Chronologically, the approaches are as shown in Figure 9.3. It should be stressed, however, that these approaches did not replace each

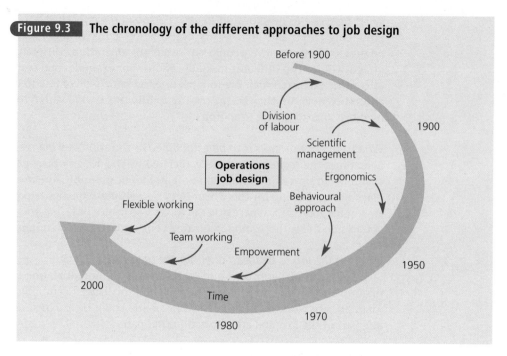

Figure 9.3 The chronology of the different approaches to job design

Before 1900

Division of labour

Operations job design

Scientific management

1900

Ergonomics

Behavioural approach

Flexible working

Team working

Empowerment

1950

2000

Time

1970

1980

other. The influence of all of them is still evident in the way jobs are designed today. Rather each added a new 'layer' or perspective to the job design activity.

Division of labour

The division of labour becomes an issue in job design as soon as an operation is large enough to warrant the employment of more than one person. For example, a single tailor will measure clients, select the cloth, cut the cloth, sew the pieces together, fit the clothes to the customer, try to elicit further business, and so on. As soon as business increases such that two or more people are needed to staff the business, the possibility of specialization arises. For example, if volume warrants three people, they could divide the total set of tasks so that one person serves in the shop and measures customers, the second person cuts out the material and the third person sews the clothes.

This idea is called the division of labour – dividing the total task down into smaller parts, each of which is accomplished by a single person. It was first formalized as a concept by the economist Adam Smith in his *Wealth of Nations* in 1746.[1] Perhaps the epitome of the division of labour is the assembly line, where products move along a single path and are built up by operators continually repeating a single task.[2] This may seem an outdated image, yet it is still the predominant model of job design in most mass-produced products and in some mass-produced services (fast food, for example). This is because, in spite of its drawbacks, there are some *real advantages* in division-of-labour principles:

● *It promotes faster learning.* It is obviously easier to learn how to do a relatively short and simple task than a long and complex one. This means that new members of staff can be quickly trained and assigned to their tasks when they are short and simple.
● *Automation becomes easier.* Dividing a total task into small parts raises the possibility of automating some of those small tasks. Substituting technology for labour is considerably easier for short and simple tasks than for long and complex ones.
● *Reduced non-productive work.* This is probably the most important benefit of division of labour. In large, complex tasks the proportion of time spent picking up tools and

materials, putting them down again and generally finding, positioning and searching can be very high indeed. For example one person assembling a whole motor car engine would take two or three hours and involve much searching for parts, positioning, and so on. Around half the person's time would be spent on these reaching, positioning, finding tasks (called non-productive elements of work). Now consider how a motor car engine is actually made in practice. The total job is probably divided into 20 or 30 separate stages, each staffed by a person who carries out only a proportion of the total. Specialist equipment and materials-handling devices can be devised to help them carry out their job more efficiently. Furthermore, there is relatively little finding, positioning and reaching involved in this simplified task. Non-productive work can be considerably reduced, perhaps to under 10 per cent, which would be very significant to the costs of the operation.

However, it soon became evident that there are also *serious drawbacks* to highly divided jobs:

- *Monotony*. The shorter the task, the more often operators will need to repeat it. Repeating the same task, for example every 30 seconds, eight hours a day and five days a week, can hardly be called a fulfilling job. As well as any ethical objections, there are other, more obviously practical objections to jobs which induce such boredom. These include the increased likelihood of absenteeism and staff turnover, the increased likelihood of error and even the deliberate sabotage of the job.
- *Physical injury*. The continued repetition of a very narrow range of movements can, in extreme cases, lead to physical injury. The over-use of some parts of the body (especially the arms, hands and wrists) can result in pain and a reduction in physical capability. This is sometimes called repetitive strain injury (RSI).
- *Low flexibility*. Dividing a task up into many small parts often gives the job design a rigidity which is difficult to change under changing circumstances. For example, if an assembly line has been designed to make one particular product but then has to change to manufacture a quite different product, the whole line will need redesigning. This will probably involve changing every operator's set of tasks, which can be a long and difficult procedure.
- *Poor robustness*. Highly divided jobs imply materials (or information) passing between several stages. If one of these stages is not working correctly, for example because some equipment is faulty, the whole operation is affected. On the other hand, if each person is performing the whole of the job, any problems will only affect that one person's output.

Scientific management

The term 'scientific management' became established in 1911 with the publication of the book of the same name by Fredrick Winslow Taylor (this whole approach to job design is sometimes referred to, pejoratively, as 'Taylorism'). In this work he identified what he saw as the basic tenets of scientific management:[3]

- All aspects of work should be investigated on a scientific basis to establish the laws, rules and formulae governing the best methods of working.
- Such an investigative approach to the study of work is necessary to establish what constitutes a 'fair day's work'.
- Workers should be selected, trained and developed methodically to perform their tasks.
- Managers should act as the planners of the work (analysing jobs and standardizing the best method of doing the job) while workers should be responsible for carrying out the jobs to the standards laid down.

- Cooperation should be achieved between management and workers based on the 'maximum prosperity' of both.

Two separate, but related, fields of study emerged. One, *method study*, concentrates on determining the methods and activities which should be included in jobs. The other, *work measurement*, is concerned with measuring the time that should be taken for performing jobs. Together, these two fields are often referred to as *work study* (*see* Fig. 9.4). Work measurement and method study are discussed later in this chapter.

The important thing to remember about scientific management is that it is not particularly 'scientific' as such, although it certainly does take an 'investigative' approach to improving operations. Perhaps a better term for it would be 'systematic management'.

For example, a tale is told of Frank Gilbreth (the founder of method study) addressing a scientific conference with a paper entitled 'The Best Way to Get Dressed in a Morning'. In his presentation, he rather bemused the scientific audience by analysing the 'best' way of buttoning up one's waistcoat in the morning. Among his conclusions was that waistcoats should always be buttoned from the bottom upwards. This would enable the man getting dressed to straighten his tie in the same motion. Buttoning from the top downwards would mean that the hands would have to be raised again (a wasted motion) to straighten the tie. What his scientific audience felt about these conclusions is not on record, but think of this example if you want to understand scientific management and method study in particular. First of all, he is quite right. Method study and the other techniques of scientific management may often be without any intellectual or scientific validation, but by and large they work in their own terms. Second, Gilbreth reached his conclusion by a systematic and critical analysis of what motions were necessary to do the job. Again, these are characteristics of scientific management – detailed analysis and painstakingly systematic examination. Third (and possibly most important), the results are relatively trivial. A great deal of effort was put into reaching a conclusion that was unlikely to have any earth-shattering consequences. Indeed, one of the criticisms of scientific management, as developed in the early part of the twentieth century, is that it concentrated on relatively limited, and sometimes trivial, objectives.

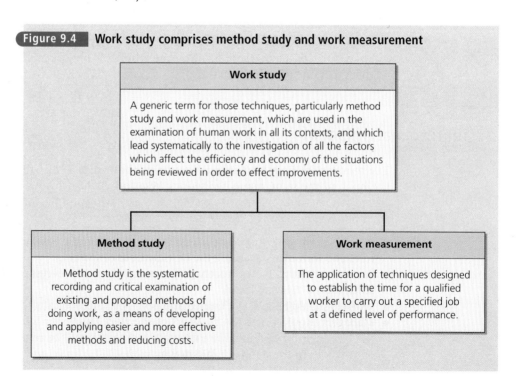

Figure 9.4 Work study comprises method study and work measurement

Work study

A generic term for those techniques, particularly method study and work measurement, which are used in the examination of human work in all its contexts, and which lead systematically to the investigation of all the factors which affect the efficiency and economy of the situations being reviewed in order to effect improvements.

Method study

Method study is the systematic recording and critical examination of existing and proposed methods of doing work, as a means of developing and applying easier and more effective methods and reducing costs.

Work measurement

The application of techniques designed to establish the time for a qualified worker to carry out a specified job at a defined level of performance.

Even in 1915, criticisms of the scientific management approach were being voiced.[4] In a submission to the United States Commission on Industrial Relations, scientific management is described as:

● being in 'spirit and essence a cunningly devised speeding up and sweating system';

● intensifying the 'modern tendency towards specialization of the work and the task';

● condemning 'the worker to a monotonous routine';

● putting 'into the hands of employers an immense mass of information and methods that may be used unscrupulously to the detriment of workers';

● tending to 'transfer to the management all the traditional knowledge, the judgement and skills of workers';

● greatly intensifying 'unnecessary managerial dictation and discipline';

● tending to 'emphasize quantity of product at the expense of quality'.

Two themes evident in this early criticism do warrant closer attention. The first is that scientific management inevitably results in standardization of highly divided jobs and thus reinforces the negative effects of excessive division of labour previously mentioned. Second, scientific management formalizes the separation of the judgemental, planning and skilled tasks, which are done by 'management', from the routine, standardized and low-skill tasks, which are left for 'operators'. Such a separation, at the very least, deprives the majority of staff of an opportunity to contribute in a meaningful way to their jobs (and, incidentally, deprives the organization of their contribution). Both of these themes in the criticisms of scientific management lead to the same point: that the jobs designed under strict scientific management principles lead to low motivation among staff, frustration at the lack of control over their work, and alienation from the job.

Before dismissing the whole of the work done by the followers of scientific management, it is worth making two points:

● More recent applications of *some* of the principles of scientific management claim to have overcome, at least partly, the objections to it by moving responsibility for the use of its methods and procedures from 'management' to the staff who are being studied. (The box on how scientific management principles were used at the NUMMI plant illustrates this.)

● Some of the methods and techniques of scientific management, as opposed to its philosophy (especially those which come under the general heading of 'method study'), can in practice prove useful in critically re-examining job designs. It is the practicality of these techniques which possibly explains why they are still influential in job design almost a century after their inception.

● Method study

The method study approach involves systematically following six steps:

1 Select the work to be studied.
2 Record all the relevant facts of the present method.
3 Examine those facts critically and in sequence.
4 Develop the most practical, economic and effective method.
5 Install the new method.
6 Maintain the method by periodically checking it in use.

In practically all parts of the world, Japanese motor manufacturers are producing their cars to rigorously high standards of quality and cost by using 'Japanese' production methods. For example, a plant in Freemont, California, a joint venture between General Motors (GM) and Toyota, uses a plant which GM had previously closed in 1982. Through the '70s and early '80s the quality of products produced in the Freemont plant was extremely poor, even by the relatively low standards of the time. Productivity was among the lowest of any GM plant in the United States, absenteeism was running at around 20 per cent, labour relations in the plant had earned a national reputation for militancy and wildcat strikes, and alcohol and drug abuse was a problem both inside the plant and out.

Soon after GM had closed the plant, it began discussions with Toyota about the possibility of a joint venture. Agreement was reached in 1983 to produce a Japanese-designed car, sold under the GM name, but manufactured using Toyota's methods of production. The NUMMI plant, as it was now called, was formally opened in 1984. Over the next two years the plant built up production levels, progressively hiring more workers, about 85 per cent of whom had worked in the plant before GM had closed it.

The performance of the NUMMI plant could hardly have contrasted more with that of the old GM-run factory. By the end of 1986 the plant's productivity was more than twice as high as when it was run by GM, and higher than any other GM factory. Indeed, productivity was almost as high as Toyota's Takoaka plant in Japan, in spite of the fact that NUMMI's workforce was new to Toyota's production methods. Quality also improved dramatically. Audits showed that quality levels were almost as high as Takoaka's and certainly higher than any other GM plant. Absenteeism had dropped from over 20 per cent in the old GM-run plant to between three and four per cent.

Among the reasons for the success of the NUMMI plant are clearer organizational goals, a selective approach to recruiting, single status and dress codes for everyone in the factory, even the pride of working on a better designed product. However, the new plant and its management did not abandon the techniques of scientific management which the previous plant's regime had supposedly used. The philosophy of job standardization was still rigorously applied – if anything, more rigorously than in the past. Every job in the plant is carefully analysed using method study principles to achieve maximum efficiency and quality. Jobs are timed, using stop watches, and the detail of jobs questioned critically.

Yet whereas before, the company's industrial engineers were in charge of applying method-study techniques, now it is the operators (or team members as they are called) themselves who perform the analysis of their own jobs. Team members time each other, using stop watches, and analyse the sequence of tasks in each job. They look for alternative ways of doing the job which improve safety and efficiency and can be sustained at a reasonable pace throughout the day. Each team will then take its improved job proposals and compare them with those developed by the comparable team doing the same job on a different shift. The resulting new job specification is then recorded and becomes the standard work definition for all staff performing that job.

NUMMI's claim is that the standardization of tasks results in less variability in task performance, which has in turn led to several further benefits:

- Safety and work-related stress injuries improve because potentially dangerous or harmful elements have been removed from the job.
- Productivity improves because wasted elements of the job have been eliminated.
- Quality standards improve because potential 'fail points' in the job have been analysed out.
- Flexibility improves and job rotation is easier because standards are clearer and all staff understand the intrinsic structure of their jobs.

One team leader compared the way in which the industrial engineers in the old plant had designed jobs with the way it was done under the NUMMI regime.

'I don't think the industrial engineers were dumb. They were just ignorant. Anyone can watch someone else doing a job and come up with improvement suggestions ... and it's even easier to come up with the ideal procedure if you don't even bother to watch the worker at work, but just do it from your office ... almost anything can look good that way. Even when we do our own analysis in our teams some of the silliest ideas can slip through before we actually try them out. ... there's a lot of things that enter into a good job design ... the person actually doing the job is the only one who can see all factors.'

Questions

1 What do you see as the main differences between traditional work study as described in the text and the way in which NUMMI operates it?

2 What other aspects of job design seem to be put into practice at NUMMI?

Step 1 – Selecting the work to be studied

Most operations have many hundreds and possibly thousands of discrete jobs and activities which could be subjected to study. The first stage in method study is to select those jobs to be studied which will give the most return on the investment of the time spent studying them. This means it is unlikely that it will be worth studying activities which, for example, may soon be discontinued or are only performed occasionally. On the other hand, the types of job which should be studied as a matter of priority are those which, for example, seem to offer the greatest scope for improvement, or which are causing bottlenecks, delays or problems in the operation.

Step 2 – Recording the present method

There are many different recording techniques used in method study. Most of them:

- record the sequence of activities in the job;
- record the time interrelationship of the activities in the job; or
- record the path of movement of some part of the job.

Perhaps the most commonly used recording technique in method study is the flow process chart which was discussed in Chapter 5.

Note that we are here recording the present method of doing the job. It may seem strange to devote so much time and effort to recording what is currently happening when, after all, the objective of method study is to devise a better method. The rationale for this is, first of all, that recording the present method can give a far greater insight into the job itself, and this can lead to new ways of doing it. Second, recording the present method is a good starting point from which to evaluate it critically and therefore improve it. In this last point the assumption is that it is easier to improve the method by starting from the current method and then criticizing it in detail than by starting with a 'blank sheet of paper'.

Step 3 – Examining the facts

This is probably the most important stage in method study and the idea here is to examine the current method thoroughly and critically. This is often done by using the so-called 'questioning technique'. This technique attempts to expose the reasons behind existing methods in order to detect weaknesses in their rationale and therefore develop alternative methods.

Questions are asked regarding:

- *The purpose of each element:*
    What is done?
    Why is it done?
    What else could be done?
    What should be done?
- *The place in which each element is done:*
    Where is it done?
    Why is it done there?
    Where else could it be done?
    Where should it be done?

This may suggest a combination of certain activities or operations.

- *The sequence in which the elements are done:*
  - When is it done?
  - Why is it done then?
  - When should it be done?
  - This may suggest a change in the sequence of the operation.
- *The person who does the element:*
  - Who does it?
  - Why does that person do it?
  - Who else could do it?
  - Who should do it?
  - This may suggest a combination and/or change in sequence.
- *The means by which each element is done:*
  - How is it done?
  - Why is it done in that way?
  - How else could it be done?
  - How should it be done?

Following this approach may appear somewhat detailed and tedious, yet it is fundamental to the method study philosophy – everything must be critically examined. Understanding the natural tendency to be less than rigorous at this stage, some organizations use pro forma questionnaires, asking each of these questions and leaving space for formal replies and/or justifications, which the job designer is required to complete.

Step 4 – Developing a new method

The previous critical examination of current methods has by this stage probably indicated some changes and improvements. This step involves taking these ideas further in an attempt to:

- eliminate parts of the activity altogether;
- combine elements together;
- change the sequence of events so as to improve the efficiency of the job; or
- simplify the activity to reduce the work content.

A useful aid during this process is a checklist such as the 'Revised principles of motion economy'. Table 9.1 illustrates these.

Table 9.1 The principles of motion economy

Using the human body the way it works best	1 Work should be arranged so that a natural rhythm can become automatic.
	2 Consider the symmetry of the body; for example, the motions of the arms should be:
	– simultaneous; and
	– opposite and symmetrical.
	3 The full capabilities of the human body should be employed; for example:
	– Neither hand should ever be idle.
	– Work should be distributed to parts of the body in line with their ability.
	– The safe 'design limits' of the body should be observed.
	4 Arms and hands as weights are subject to the physical laws and energy should be conserved; for example:
	– Momentum should work for the body and not against it.
	– The smooth, continuous arc of ballistic motions is most efficient.
	– The distance of movements should be minimized.
	5 Tasks should be simplified; for example:
	– Eye contacts should be few and grouped together.
	– Unnecessary actions, delays and idle time should be eliminated.
	– The degree of required precision and control should be minimized.
	– The number of individual motions should be minimized along with the number of muscle groups involved.

Table 9.1 Continued

Arranging the workplace to assist performance	1	There should be a defined place for all tools and materials.
	2	Tools, materials and controls should be located close to the point of use.
	3	Tools, materials and controls should be located to permit the best sequence and path of motions.
	4	The workplace should be fitted both to the tasks and to human capabilities.
Using mechancial devices to reduce human effort	1	Vices and clamps should hold the work precisely where needed.
	2	Guides should assist in positioning the work without close operator attention.
	3	Controls and foot-operated devices can relieve the hands of work.
	4	Mechanical devices can multiply human abilities.
	5	Mechanical systems should be fitted to human use.

Source: Adapted from Barnes, Frank C. (1983) 'Principles of Motion Economy: Revisited, Reviewed, and Restored', *Proceedings of the Southern Management Association Annual Meeting* (Atlanta, GA 1983), p 298

Steps 5 and 6 – Install the new method and regularly maintain it

The method study approach to the installation of new work practices concentrates largely on 'project managing' the installation process (*see* Chapter 16 for a full description of project management). It also emphasizes the need to monitor regularly the effectiveness of job designs after they have been installed. Although not originally intended as some kind of 'continuous improvement' philosophy (rather it was to make sure that conditions had not changed to make the method anything less than optimal for its purpose), it can be used as an opportunity to rethink and improve methods on a continuous basis.

Most assembly jobs in car factories are designed on 'division of labour' and 'scientific management' principles, but ergonomic considerations influence the positioning of products at workstations, and increasingly team-working is used

Method study at Intel

Although dating from the scientific management period, method study has undergone something of a revival in the last few years. In non-manufacturing operations especially, the method study approach of systematically challenging methods of work is proving an effective approach to improvement. For example, Figure 9.5 shows the flow process chart which Intel Corporation, the computer chip

Figure 9.5 The flow process chart for processing expense reports at Intel

Flow process chart						
Activity	**Processing expense reports**		Location		Accounts Dept	
	Description of element	●	➡	D	■	▼
1	Report arrives at accounts payable desk					
2	Wait for processing					
3	Check expenses report					
4	Stamp and date report					
5	Send cash to receipt desk					
6	Wait for processing					
7	Check to see if advance payment has been made					
8	Send to accounts receivable desk					
9	Wait for processing					
10	Check employee's past account					
11	Send to accounts payable desk					
12	Attach payment voucher to report					
13	Log report					
14	Check items against company guidelines					
15	Wait for batching					
16	Collect reports into batch					
17	Batch goes to audit desk					
18	Wait for processing					
19	Batch of reports logged					
20	Check payment vouchers					
21	Reports go to batch control					
22	Control number applied to batch					
23	Copies of reports to filing					
24	Reports filed					
25	Copies of payment voucher to keyboard					
26	Cheque					
	Totals	7	8	5	5	1

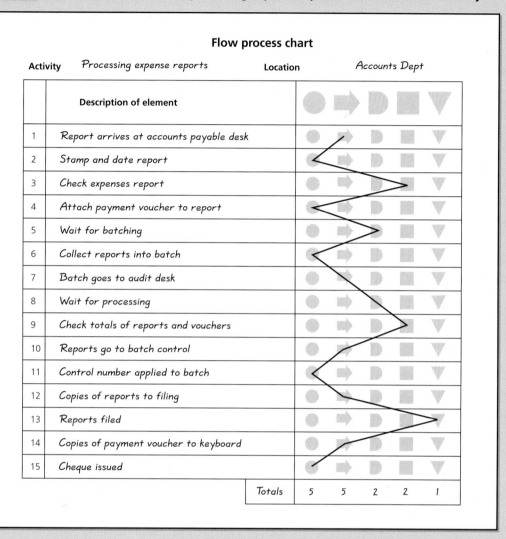

Flow process chart

Activity	Processing expense reports	Location	Accounts Dept				
	Description of element		●	➡	D	■	▼
1	Report arrives at accounts payable desk						
2	Stamp and date report						
3	Check expenses report						
4	Attach payment voucher to report						
5	Wait for batching						
6	Collect reports into batch						
7	Batch goes to audit desk						
8	Wait for processing						
9	Check totals of reports and vouchers						
10	Reports go to batch control						
11	Control number applied to batch						
12	Copies of reports to filing						
13	Reports filed						
14	Copies of payment voucher to keyboard						
15	Cheque issued						
		Totals	5	5	2	2	1

company, drew to describe its method of processing expense reports (claims forms).

After critically examining its existing method of processing these reports, the company developed a new method which cut the number of elements from 26 down to 15 (*see* Fig. 9.6). The accounts payable desk's activities were combined with the cash-receipt's activities of checking employees' past expense accounts (elements 8, 10 and 11) which also eliminated elements 5 and 7. After consideration, it was decided to eliminate the activity of checking items against company guidelines, because it seemed '*... more trouble than it was worth*'. Also, logging the batches was deemed unnecessary. All this combination and elimination of activities had the effect of removing several 'delays' from the process. The end result was a much simplified process which reduced the staff time needed to do the job by 28 per cent and considerably speeded up the whole process.

Questions

1 This box describes how Intel used a flow process chart. What was the nature of the improvement it effected by doing this?

2 Do you think it was necessary to draw this chart in order to make the improvement?

3 What do you think are the limitations of using charts like this for improvement?

Work measurement and performance measurement

Work measurement is the process of establishing the time for a *'qualified worker'*, at a *'defined level of performance'*, to carry out a *'specified job'*. Although not a precise definition, generally it is agreed that a *specified job* is one for which specifications have been established to define most aspects of the job.

A *qualified worker* is one who is accepted as having the necessary physical attributes, intelligence, skill, education and knowledge to perform the task to satisfactory standards of safety, quality and quantity.

Standard performance is defined as:

the rate of output which qualified workers will achieve without over-exertion as an average over the working day provided they are motivated to apply themselves to their work.

Basic times

Terminology is important in work measurement. When a *qualified worker* is working on a *specified job* at *standard performance*, the time he or she takes to perform the job is called the *basic time* for the job. Basic times are useful because they are the 'building blocks' of time estimation. With the basic times for a range of different tasks, an operations manager can construct a time estimate for any longer activity which is made up of the tasks.

Standard times

The *standard time* for a job is an extension of the basic time and has a different use. Whereas the basic time for a job is a piece of information which can be used as the first step in estimating the time to perform a job under a wide range of conditions, standard time refers to the time *allowed* for the job under specific circumstances. This is because standard time includes *allowances* which reflect the rest and relaxation allowed because of the conditions under which the job is performed.

So the standard time for each element consists principally of two parts (although in some cases extra allowances may be applicable):

- *basic time* – the time taken by a qualified worker, doing a specified job at standard performance;
- *allowance* – this is added to the basic time to allow for rest, relaxation and personal needs.

Most of the techniques of work measurement involve the breaking down of the job to be studied into *elements*. For each of these elements, separate *standard times* are then determined. The standard time of the job as a whole is then the sum of all the standard times of is constituent elements.

Time study

Time study is a work measurement technique for recording the times and rate of working for the elements of a specified job, carried out under specified conditions, and for analysing the data so as to obtain the time necessary for the carrying out of the job at a defined level of performance.

The technique takes three steps to derive the basic times for the elements of the job:

- observing and measuring the time taken to perform each element of the job;
- adjusting, or 'normalizing', each observed time;
- averaging the adjusted times to derive the basic time for the element.

Step 1 – Observing, measuring and rating

A job is observed through several cycles. Each time an element is performed, it is timed using a stopwatch. Simultaneously with the observation of time, a rating of the perceived performance of the person doing the job is recorded.

The *rating* of observed times is defined as:

the process of assessing the worker's rate of working relative to the observer's concept of the rate corresponding to standard performance. The observer may take into account, separately or in combination, one or more factors necessary to carrying out the job, such as speed of movement, effort, dexterity, consistency, etc.

There are several ways of recording the observer's rating. The most common is on a scale which uses a rating of 100 to represent standard performance. If an observer rates a particular observation of the time to perform an element at 100, the time observed is the actual time which anyone working at standard performance would take.

Step 2 – Adjusting the observed times

The adjustment to normalize the observed time is:

$$\frac{\text{observed rating}}{\text{standard rating}}$$

where standard rating is 100 on the common rating scale we are using here. For example, if the observed time is 0.71 minutes and the observed rating is 90, then:

$$\text{Basic time} = \frac{0.71 \times 90}{100} = 0.64 \text{ mins}$$

Step 3 – Average the basic times

In spite of the adjustments made to the observed times through the rating mechanism, each separately calculated basic time will not be the same. This is not necessarily a function of inaccurate rating, or even the vagueness of the rating procedure itself; it is a natural phenomenon of the time taken to perform tasks. Any human activity cannot be repeated in *exactly* the same time on every occasion.

Figure 9.7 shows how the data from a study can be used to give average basic times for each element in the job. These are the basic times which are used to derive the standard time for the job. It also shows how the standard time is calculated by including the allowances (low in this example) for each element.

● CRITICAL COMMENTARY

The criticisms aimed at work measurement are many and various. Amongst the most common are the following:

- All the ideas on which the concept of a standard time is based are impossible to define precisely. How can one possibly give clarity to the definition of qualified workers, or specified jobs, or especially a defined level of performance?

- Even if one attempts to follow these definitions, all that results is an excessively rigid job definition. Most modern jobs require some element of flexibility, which is difficult to achieve alongside rigidly defined jobs.

- Using stopwatches to time human beings is both degrading and usually counterproductive. At best it is intrusive, at worst it makes people into 'objects for study'.

- The rating procedure implicit in time study is subjective and usually arbitrary. It has no basis other than the opinion of the person carrying out the study.

- Time study, especially, is very easy to manipulate. It is possible for employers to 'work back' from a time which is 'required' to achieve a particular cost. Also, experienced staff can 'put on an act' to fool the person recording the times.

Figure 9.7 **Time study of a packing task – standard time for the whole task calculated**

Job _Pack 20 x pt. # 73/2A_ ......   Location _Packing Dept._ ....   Observer _FWT_ ....

Element		Observation										Average basic time	Allowances	Element standard time
		1	2	3	4	5	6	7	8	9	10			
Make box	Observed time	0.71	0.71	0.71	0.69	0.75	0.68	0.70	0.72	0.70	0.68			
	Rating	90	90	90	90	80	90	90	90	90	90			
	Basic time	0.64	0.64	0.63	0.62	0.60	0.61	0.63	0.65	0.63	0.61	0.626	10%	0.689
Pack x 20	Observed time	1.30	1.32	1.25	1.33	1.33	1.28	1.32	1.32	1.30	1.30			
	Rating	90	90	100	90	90	90	90	90	90	90			
	Basic time	1.17	1.19	1.25	1.20	1.20	1.15	1.19	1.19	1.17	1.17	1.168	12%	1.308
Seal and secure	Observed time	0.53	0.55	0.55	0.56	0.53	0.53	0.60	0.55	0.49	0.51			
	Rating	90	90	90	90	90	90	85	90	100	100			
	Basic time	0.48	0.50	0.50	0.50	0.48	0.48	0.51	0.50	0.49	0.51	0.495	10%	0.545
Assemble outer,	Observed time	1.12	1.21	1.20	1.25	1.41	1.27	1.11	1.15	1.20	1.23			
fix and label	Rating	100	90	90	90	90	90	100	100	90	90			
	Basic time	1.12	1.09	1.08	1.13	1.27	1.14	1.11	1.15	1.08	1.21	1.138	12%	1.275

Raw standard time		3.817
Allowances for total job	5%	0.191
Standard time for job		4.01 SM

Notwithstanding the weak theoretical basis of work measurement, understanding the work-time consequences is clearly an important part of job design. The advantage of structured and systematic work measurement is that it gives a common currency for the evaluation and comparison of all types of work.

Worked example

Two work teams in the Monrovian Embassy have been allocated the task of processing visa applications. Team A processes applications from Europe, Africa and the Middle East. Team B processes applications from North and South America, Asia and Australasia. Team A has chosen to organize itself in such a way that each of its three team members processes an application from start to finish. The four members of Team B have chosen to split themselves into two sub-teams. Two open the letters and carry out the checks for a criminal record (no one who has been convicted of any crime other than a motoring offence can enter Monrovia), while the other two team members check for financial security (only people with more than Monrovian $1000 may enter the country).

The head of consular affairs is keen to find out if one of these methods of organizing the teams is more efficient than the other. The problem is that the mix of applications differs region by region. Team A typically processes around two business applications to every one tourist application. Team B processes around one business application to every two tourist applications.

A study revealed the following data:

Average standard time to process a business visa   =   63 standard minutes

Average time to process a tourist visa   =   55 standard minutes

Average weekly output from Team A is:

85.2   Business visas
39.5   Tourist visas

Average weekly output from Team B is:

53.5   Business visas
100.7 Tourist visas

All team members work a 40-hour week.

The efficiency of each team can be calculated by comparing the actual output in standard minutes and the time worked in minutes.

So Team A processes:

$$(85.2 \times 63) + (39.5 \times 55) = 7540.1 \text{ standard minutes of work}$$

$$\text{in } 3 \times 40 \times 60 \text{ minutes} = 7200 \text{ minutes}$$

So its efficiency $= \dfrac{7540.1}{7200} \times 100 = 104.72\%$

Team B processes:

$$(53.5 \times 63) + (100.7 \times 55) = 8909 \text{ standard minutes of work}$$

$$\text{in } 4 \times 40 \times 60 \text{ minutes} = 9600 \text{ minutes}$$

So its efficiency $= \dfrac{8909}{9600} \times 100 = 92.8\%$

The initial evidence therefore seems to suggest that the way Team A has organized itself is more efficient.

Ergonomics

Ergonomics is concerned primarily with the physiological aspects of job design – that is, with the human body and how it fits into its surroundings. This involves two aspects: first how the person interfaces with the physical aspect of his or her workplace, where the 'workplace' includes tables, chairs, desks, machines, computers, and so on; second, how a person interfaces with environmental conditions in his or her immediate working area. By this we mean the temperature, lighting, noise environment, and so on. Ergonomics is sometimes referred to as 'human factors engineering' or just 'human factors'. Both of these aspects are linked by two common ideas:

● There must be a fit between people and the jobs they do. To achieve this fit there are only two alternatives. Either the job can be made to fit the people who are doing it, or, alternatively, the people can be made (or perhaps less radically, recruited) to fit the job. Ergonomics addresses the former alternative.
● It is important to take a 'scientific' approach to job design, for example collecting data to indicate how people react under different job design conditions and trying to find the best set of conditions for comfort and performance.

● Ergonomic workplace design

In many operations, new demands, technologies and work methods have refocused attention on the way people interface with the physical parts of their jobs. This is especially noticeable in office and information-related work because of the predominance of computer, keyboard and screen-based 'interfaces'.

Understanding how workplaces affect performance, fatigue, physical strain and injury is all part of the ergonomics approach to job design.

Anthropometric aspects

Many ergonomic improvements are primarily concerned with what are called the anthropometric aspects of jobs – that is, the aspects related to people's size, shape and other physical abilities. The design of an assembly task, for example, should be governed partly by the size and strength of the operators who do the job. The data which ergonomists use when doing this is called *anthropometric data*. Table 9.2 gives an example of this type of data.

Note that because we all vary in our size and capabilities, ergonomists are particularly interested in our range of capabilities – usually expressed in percentile terms as in Table 9.2. Figure 9.8 illustrates this idea. This shows the idea of size (in this case height) variation. Only 5 per cent of the population are smaller than the person on the extreme left (5th percentile), whereas 95 per cent of the population are smaller than the person on the extreme right (95th percentile). When this principle is applied to other dimensions of the body, for example arm length, it can be used to design work areas. Figure 9.8 shows the normal and maximum work areas derived from anthropometric data. It would be inadvisable, for example, to place frequently used components or tools outside the maximum work area derived from the 5th percentile dimensions of human reach.

Neurological aspects

Ergonomics is also concerned with the way in which people's sensory capabilities are engaged in their jobs. These so-called neurological aspects of job design include the sight, feel, sound and perhaps even smell which the workplace displays in order to give information to an operator, and the way in which an operator can transmit instructions back to the workplace. The part of the 'workplace' in which we are interested is usually some type of process technology or machine, and the interface between the operator and machine involves *displays* of information from the machine to the operator and the manipulation of *controls* by the operator in communicating with the machine.

Table 9.2 An example of anthropometric data – US civilian body dimensions, female/male in cm for ages 20 to 60 years

	Percentiles			Standard deviation
	5th	*50th*	*95th*	
Stature (height)	149.5/161.8	160.5/173.6	171.3/184.4	6.6/6.9
Eye height	138.3/151.1	148.9/162.4	159.3/172.7	6.4/6.6
Shoulder height	121.1/132.3	131.1/142.8	141.9/152.4	6.3/6.1
Elbow height	93.6/100.0	101.2/109.9	108.8/119.0	4.6/5.8
Height, sitting	78.6/84.2	85.0/90.6	90.7/96.7	3.5/3.7
Eye height, sitting	67.5/72.6	73.3/78.6	78.5/84.4	3.3/3.6
Shoulder height, sitting	49.2/52.7	55.7/59.4	61.7/65.8	3.8/4.0
Elbow rest height, sitting	18.1/19.0	23.3/24.3	28.1/29.4	2.9/3.0
Knee height, sitting	45.2/49.3	49.8/54.3	54.4/59.3	2.7/2.9
Back of knee height, sitting	35.5/39.2	39.8/44.2	44.3/48.8	2.6/2.8
Thigh clearance height, sitting	10.6/11.4	13.7/14.4	17.5/17.7	1.8/1.7

Source: Adapted from Kroemer, K.H.E. (1983) 'Engineering Anthropometry: Work Space and Equipment to Fit the User' *in* Osborne, D.J. and Gruneberg, M.M. (eds) *The Physical Environment at Work*, John Wiley.

Figure 9.8 **The use of anthropometric data in job design**

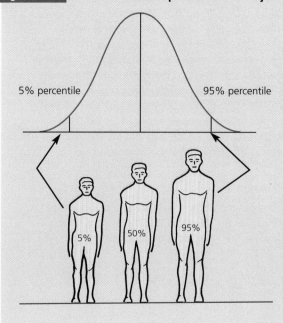

5% percentile   95% percentile

5%   50%   95%

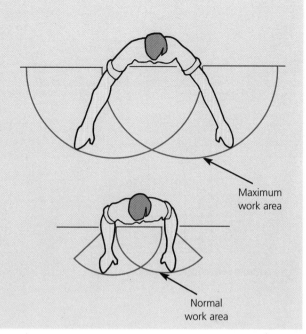

Maximum work area

Normal work area

Ergonomics makes work safer at the Royal Mail

CWS

Ergonomic trials of the Royal Mail container

Photo courtesy of Fraser Chambers, Royal Mail

Mail has traditionally been transported in strong cloth mailbags. When the Royal Mail (a part of the UK Post Office) decided to rethink these activities in order to reduce effort and increase productivity, it called in its Ergonomics Design Group, who undertook a study. The handling of mailbags was a particular issue because it often involved staff lifting weights which were heavier than the recommended ergonomic standards. If an item is to be lifted from the floor to chest height, it passes through the 10, 20 and 25 kg zones, and so should not be heavier than 10 kg. Furthermore, these recommendations are for tasks that occur less than once per minute, and are reduced by up to 80 per cent if they are repeated more than 12 times per minute. Clearly, the existing method of handling mailbags would

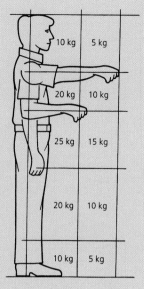

10 kg 5 kg

20 kg 10 kg

25 kg 15 kg

20 kg 10 kg

10 kg 5 kg

Acceptable forces/weights used in lifting

have to be re-thought. After extensive research, a special 250 kg Royal Mail container was designed.

Trial containers were introduced, allowing potential problems to be identified and improvements made. The final design of container (see the picture) was introduced only after trials which evaluated its performance under working conditions. As well as providing a safer working method, it allowed significant improvements in labour efficiency because of the greater number of items in each movement.

Question

Why do you think it is necessary for organizations like the Royal Mail to have limits on the loads to be lifted as illustrated on the left?

● Ergonomic environmental design

The immediate environment in which jobs take place can influence the way they are performed. Working conditions which are too hot or too cold, insufficiently illuminated or glaringly bright, excessively noisy or irritatingly silent will all influence the way jobs are carried out. Ergonomics is also concerned with this aspect of job design. Perhaps one point to note is the boost which this aspect of ergonomics received from the introduction of occupational health and safety legislation which controls environmental conditions in workplaces throughout the world. A thorough understanding of this aspect of ergonomics is necessary to work within the guidelines of such legislation.

Working temperature

Predicting the reactions of individuals to working temperature is not straightforward. Individuals vary in the way their performance and comfort vary with temperature. Furthermore, most of us judging 'temperature' will also be influenced by other factors such as humidity and air movement. Nevertheless, some general points regarding working temperatures provide guidance to job designers:[6]

● Comfortable temperature range will depend on the type of work being carried out, lighter work requiring higher temperatures than heavier work.
● The effectiveness of people at performing vigilance tasks reduces at temperatures above about 29°C; the equivalent temperature for people performing light manual tasks is a little lower.
● The chances of accidents occurring increase at temperatures which are above or below the comfortable range for the work involved.

Illumination levels

The intensity of lighting required to perform any job satisfactorily will depend on the nature of the job. Some jobs which involve extremely delicate and precise movement, surgery for example, require very high levels of illumination. Other, less delicate jobs do not require such high levels. Table 9.3 shows the recommended illumination levels (measured in lux) for a range of activities.

Table 9.3 Examples of recommended lighting levels for various activities[7]

Activity	Illuminance (lx)
Normal activities in the home, general lighting	50
Furnace rooms in glass factory	150
General office work	500
Motor vehicle assembly	500
Proofreading	750
Colour matching in paint factory	1 000
Electronic assembly	1 000
Close inspection of knitwear	1 500
Engineering testing inspection using small instruments	3 000
Watchmaking and fine jewellery manufacture	3 000
Surgery, local lighting	10 000–50 000

Noise levels

The damaging effects of excessive noise levels are perhaps easier to understand than some other environmental factors. Noise-induced hearing loss is a well-documented consequence of working environments where noise is not kept below safe limits. The noise levels of various activities are shown in Table 9.4. When reading this list, bear in mind that the recommended (and often legal) maximum noise level to which people can be subjected over the working day is 90 decibels (dB) in the UK (although in some parts of the world the legal level is lower than this). Also bear in mind that the decibels unit of noise is based on a logarithmic scale, which means that noise intensity doubles about every 3 dB.

Table 9.4 Noise levels for various activities

Noise	Decibels (dB)
Quiet speech	40
Light traffic at 25 metres	50
Large busy office	60
Busy street, heavy traffic	70
Pneumatic drill at 20 metres	80
Textile factory	90
Circular saw – close work	100
Riveting machine – close work	110
Jet aircraft taking off at 100 metres	120

In addition to the damaging effects of high levels of noise, it can also affect work performance at far lower levels – for example, on tasks requiring attention and judgement:[8]

- Intermittent and unpredictable noises are more disruptive than steady-state noise at the same level.
- High-frequency noise (above about 2000 Hz) usually produces more interference with performance than low-frequency noise.
- Noise is more likely to affect the error rate (quality) of work rather than the rate of working.

Ergonomics in the office

As the number of people working in offices (or office-like workplaces) has increased, ergonomic principles have been applied increasingly to this type of work. At the same time, legislation has been moving to cover office technology such as computer screens

Figure 9.9   **Ergonimics in the office environment**

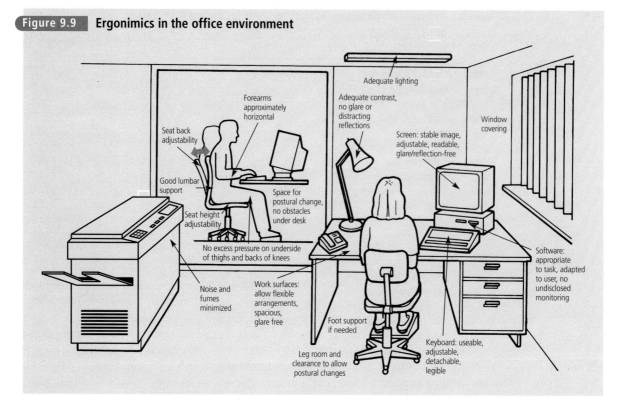

and keyboards. For example, European Union directives on working with display screen equipment require organizations to:[9]

● assess all workstations to reduce the risks inherent in their use;
● make sure that all workstations meet specific requirements;
● plan work times to all breaks and changes in activity;
● provide information and training for users;
● test the eyesight of users if they request it.

Figure 9.9 illustrates some of the ergonomic factors which should be taken into account when designing office jobs.

Behavioural approaches to job design

The ideas and concepts concerning motivation theory contribute to the behavioural approach to job design. Jobs which are designed purely on division of labour, scientific management or even purely ergonomic principles can alienate the people performing them. Job design should also take into account the desire of individuals to fulfil their needs for self-esteem and personal development. This achieves two important objectives of job design. First, it provides jobs which have an intrinsically higher quality of working life – an ethically desirable end in itself. Second, because of the higher levels of motivation it engenders, it is instrumental in achieving better performance for the operation, in terms of both the quality and the quantity of output.[10]

Whereas previous approaches to job design assumed a more or less direct connection between the characteristics of the job and people's performance at that job, the behavioural approach to job design implicitly adopted a different model. This assumed an intervening variable of the person's motivation for performing the job. Now the approach to job design would involve two stages: first, exploring how the various characteristics of the job affect people's motivation; second, exploring how individuals' motivation towards the job affects their performance at that job. To reduce alienation and increase personal motivation the job should:

- allow people to feel personally responsible for an identifiable and meaningful portion of the work;
- provide a set of tasks which are intrinsically meaningful or worthwhile;
- provide feedback about performance effectiveness.

Typical of the models which underlie this approach to job design is that by Hackman and Oldham shown in Figure 9.10.[11] Here a number of 'techniques' of job design are recommended in order to affect particular core 'characteristics' of the job. These core characteristics of the job are held to influence various positive 'mental states' towards the job. In turn, these are assumed to give certain performance outcomes.

In Figure 9.10 some of the 'techniques' (which Hackman and Oldham originally called 'implementing concepts') need a little further explanation:

- Combining tasks means increasing the number of separate elements or activities allocated to individuals.
- Forming natural work units means putting together activities which make a coherent (preferably also a continuing) whole.
- Establishing client relationships means that staff make contact with their internal customers (see Chapter 1) directly rather than exclusively through their supervisors.
- Vertical loading means including 'indirect' activities (such as the maintenance, scheduling and general management of the job) in the tasks allocated to the individual.
- Opening feedback channels means ensuring not only that internal customers feed back perceptions of performance directly to staff, but also that staff are provided with information regarding their overall performance.

Hackman and Oldham also indicate how these techniques of job design shape the core characteristics of the resulting job, and further, how the core characteristics influence the 'mental states' of the person doing the job. By 'mental states' they mean the attitude of individuals towards their jobs – specifically, how meaningful they find the job, how much responsibility and control they feel they have over the way the job is done, and how much they understand about the results of their efforts. High levels of all these mental states, it is held, positively influence people's performance at their job in terms of their motivation, quality of work, satisfaction with their work, turnover and absenteeism.

Figure 9.10 **A typical 'behavioural' job design model**

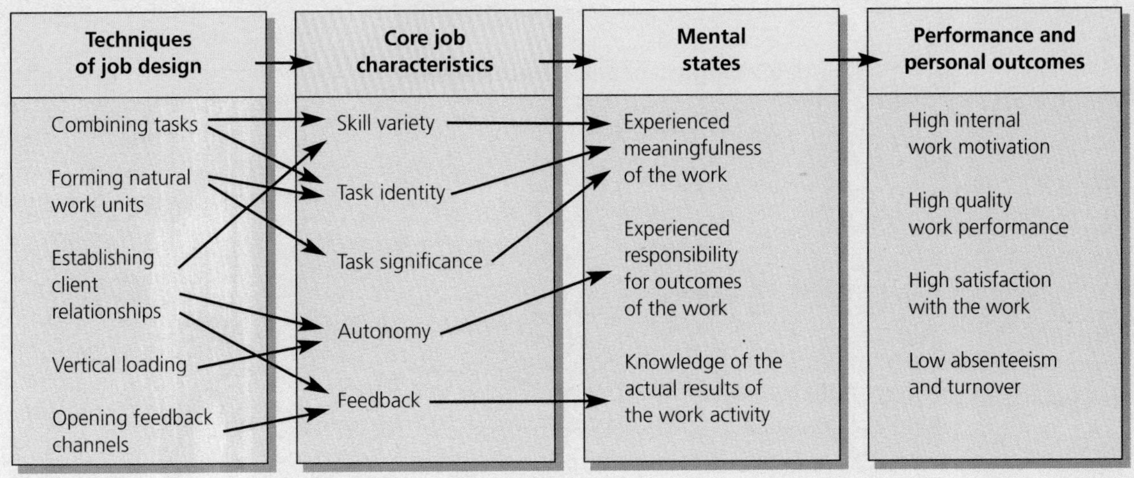

Job rotation

If increasing the number of related tasks in the job is constrained in some way, for example by the technology of the process, one approach may be to rotate jobs. This means moving individuals periodically between different sets of tasks to provide some variety in their activities. When successful, job rotation can increase skill flexibility and make a small contribution to reducing monotony. However, it is not viewed as universally beneficial either by management (because it can disrupt the smooth flow of work) or by the people performing the jobs (because it can interfere with their rhythm of work).

Job enlargement

The most obvious method of achieving at least some of the objectives of behavioural job design is by allocating a larger number of tasks to individuals (what Hackman and Oldham called *combining* tasks). If these extra tasks are broadly of the same type as those in the original job, the change is called *job enlargement*. This may not involve more demanding or fulfilling tasks, but it may provide a more complete and therefore slightly more meaningful job. If nothing else, people performing an enlarged job will not repeat themselves as often, which could make the job marginally less monotonous.

So, for example, suppose that the manufacture of a product has traditionally been split up on an assembly-line basis into 10 equal and sequential jobs. If that job is then redesigned so as to form two parallel assembly lines of five people, the output from the system as a whole would be maintained but each operator would have twice the number of tasks to perform. This is job enlargement. Operators repeat themselves less frequently and presumably the variety of tasks is greater, although no further responsibility or autonomy is necessarily given to each operator.

Job enrichment

Job enrichment, like job enlargement, increases the number of tasks which are allocated to jobs. However, it means allocating extra tasks which involve more decision-making, greater autonomy and therefore greater control over the job. For example, the extra tasks could include the maintenance of, and adjustments to, any process technology used, the planning and control of activities within the job, or the monitoring of quality levels. The effect is both to reduce repetition in the job and to increase the autonomy and personal development opportunities in the job. So, in the assembly-line example, each operator, as well as being allocated a job which is twice as long as that previously performed, could also be allocated responsibility for carrying out routine maintenance and such tasks as record-keeping and managing the supply of materials. As a result, both the autonomy and decision-making responsibility of the job have been increased.

> **Figure 9.11** **Job enlargement and job enrichment**

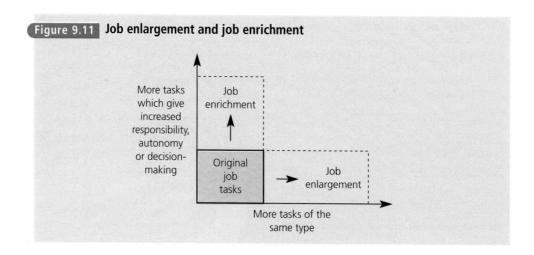

One way of understanding the difference between job enlargement and job enrichment is by thinking of changing jobs on what are sometimes termed horizontal dimensions of job design and vertical dimensions of job design. Figure 9.11 illustrates the difference between horizontal and vertical changes. Broadly, horizontal changes are those which extend the variety of *similar* tasks assigned to a particular job. Vertical job changes are those which add responsibilities, decision-making or autonomy to the job. Job enlargement implies movement only in the horizontal scale, whereas job enrichment certainly implies movement on the vertical scale and perhaps on both scales.

Empowerment

Empowerment is an extension of the *autonomy* job characteristic prominent in the behavioural approach to job design. However, it is usually taken to mean more than autonomy. Whereas autonomy means giving staff the *ability* to change how they do their jobs, empowerment means giving staff the *authority* to make changes to the job itself, as well as how it is performed. This can be designed into jobs to different degrees – 'suggestion involvement', 'job involvement', or 'high involvement':[12]

- *Suggestion involvement* is not really empowerment in its true form but does 'empower' staff to contribute their suggestions for how the operation might be improved. However, staff do not have the autonomy to implement changes to their jobs. High-volume operations, such as fast-food restaurants or the NUMMI car plant in the earlier box, may choose not to dilute their highly standardized task methods, yet they do want staff to be involved in how these methods are implemented.
- *Job involvement* goes much further and empowers staff to redesign their jobs. However, again there must be some limits to the way each individual makes changes which could impact on other staff and on the performance of the operations as a whole.
- *High involvement* means including all staff in the strategic direction and performance of the whole organization. This is the most radical type of empowerment and there are few examples. However, the degree to which individual staff of an operation contribute towards, and take responsibility for, overall strategy can be seen as a variable of job design. For example, a professional service such as a group of consulting engineers (who design large engineering projects) might very well move in this direction. It may be partly to motivate all its staff. It may be partly to ensure that the operation can capture everyone's potentially useful ideas.

The *benefits* of empowerment are generally seen as including the following:

- faster online responses to customer needs;
- faster online responses to dissatisfied customers;
- employees feel better about their jobs;
- employees will interact with customers with more enthusiasm;
- empowered employees can be a useful source of service;
- it promotes 'word-of-mouth' advertising and customer retention.

However, there are *costs* associated with empowerment:

- larger selection and training costs;
- slower or inconsistent training;
- violation of equity of service and perceived fair play;
- 'give-aways' and bad decisions made by employees.

A number of key factors will determine whether the benefits outweigh the costs of empowerment. These factors are contained in Table 9.5. The closer an individual job design requirement is to the right of the continuum, the more likely it is that an empowerment approach should be adopted.

Table 9.5 The contingencies of empowerment

Factor	Non-empowerment approach	Empowerment approach
Basic business strategy	Low cost, high volume	Differentiation, customized, personalized
Links with customer	Transaction, short time period	Relationship, long time period
Technology	Routine, simple	Non-routine, complex
Business environment	Predictable, few surprises	Unpredictable, many surprises
Types of people	Autocratic managers, employees with low growth needs, low social needs, and weak interpersonal skills	Democratic managers, employees with high growth needs, high social needs and strong interpersonal skills

Source: Adapted from Bowen, D. and Lawler, E. (1992) 'Empowerment', *Sloan Management Review*, Spring

Team–working and job design

A development in job design which is closely linked to the empowerment concept is that of team-based work organization (sometimes called self-managed work teams). This is where staff, often with overlapping skills, collectively perform a defined task and have a high degree of discretion over how they actually perform the task. The team would typically control such things as task allocation between members, scheduling work, quality measurement and improvement, and sometimes the hiring of staff.

To some extent most work has always been a group-based activity. The concept of teamwork, however, is more prescriptive and assumes a shared set of objectives and responsibilities. Groups are described as teams when the virtues of working together are being emphasized, such as the ability to make use of the various skills within the team.

● Teams are more common

Some of the developments within operations management over the last 15 years have added to the importance of team-based working. Perhaps the most commonly found type of team is the *quality improvement team*. Usually a group of workers (rarely more than 10) get together to either solve problems or generally improve processes in their

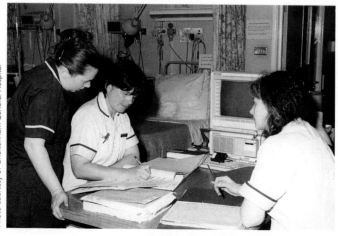

Nurse are often organized in teams who share responsibility for a group of patients. Here members of a nursing team discuss the treatment of patients

immediate work areas. (Chapter 20 on total quality management discusses this further.) Quality improvement teams are usually formed from the individuals who work in one particular area. Another kind of team is the *improvement task force*. This is a team where individuals are brought together, perhaps from different parts of the organization, in order to tackle a single specific problem. They are essentially short-term in nature, being disbanded after the task is complete. In some ways these are similar to *project management teams*, who together manage a project from beginning to end. In certain industries, such as construction, where most operations activity is composed of a series of discrete projects, project teams may be the dominant way of working. *Customer* (or *supplier*) *teams* are formed to liaise directly with external or internal customers (or suppliers). Their purpose is to improve relationships along internal or external supply chains (*see* Chapter 13 on supply chain management).

Teams as an organizational device

Teams may also be used to compensate for other organizational changes such as the move towards flatter organizational structures. When organizations have fewer managerial levels, each manager will have a wider span of activities to control. Teams which are capable of autonomous decision-making have a clear advantage in these circumstances. Effective decision-making, however, may require a very broad mix of skills within the team. For example, the computer equipment maker Hewlett-Packard brings together very different specialisms within single teams. These may include marketing managers, engineers, lawyers, technical writers, purchasing managers and shop-floor workers.

The benefits of teamwork can be summarized as:

- improving productivity through enhanced motivation and flexibility;
- improving quality and encouraging innovation;
- increasing satisfaction by allowing individuals to contribute more effectively;
- making it easier to implement technological changes in the workplace because teams are willing to share the challenges this brings.

CRITICAL COMMENTARY

Teamwork is not only difficult to implement successfully, but it can also place undue stress on the individuals who form the teams. Some teams are formed because more radical solutions, such as total reorganization, are being avoided. Teams cannot compensate for badly designed organizational processes; nor can they substitute for management's responsibility to define how decisions should be made. Often teams are asked to make decisions but are given insufficient responsibility to carry them out. In other cases, teams may provide results but at a price. The Swedish car maker Volvo introduced self-governing teams in the 70s and 80s which improved motivation and morale but eventually proved prohibitively expensive. Perhaps most seriously, teamwork is criticized for substituting one sort of pressure for another. Although teams may be autonomous, this does not mean they are stress-free. Top-down managerial control is often replaced by excessive peer pressure which is in some ways more insidious.

Flexible working

The nature of most jobs has changed significantly over the last 25 years. New technologies, more dynamic marketplaces, more demanding customers and a changed understanding of how individuals can contribute to competitive success have all had their impact. Also changing is our understanding of how home life, work and social life need to be balanced. Alternative forms of organization and alternative attitudes to work are being sought which allow, and encourage, a degree of flexibility in working practice which matches the need for flexibility in the marketplace. Whereas once most people had a single trade or profession and stuck to it throughout their lives, now careers may change, possibly more than once. Again, this reflects the flexibility required by dynamic markets, but also the idea that individuals may want to 'refresh' their working lives by changing careers.

● Types of flexible working

From an operations management perspective, three aspects of flexible working are significant:

- skills flexibility
- time flexibility
- location flexibility.

Skills flexibility

Given that both the nature and level of demand for many services and products are uncertain, a flexible workforce that can adapt itself to several tasks is clearly a major advantage. If staff can move across several different jobs, they can be deployed (or deploy themselves) in whatever activity is in demand at the time. This may be a short-term issue. So, for example, members of staff at a supermarket may be moved from warehouse activities to shelf replenishment in the store to the checkout, depending on what is needed at the time. In the longer-term sense, multi-skilling means being able to migrate individuals from one skill set to another as longer-term demand trends become obvious. So, for example, an engineer who at one time maintained complex equipment by visiting the sties where such equipment was installed may now perform most of his or her activities by using remote computer diagnostics and 'helpline' assistance. This requires the same basic knowledge of the equipment but a whole new set of diagnostic and customer relationship skills.

Other trends in operations management also call for increased skill flexibility. For example, the just-in-time (JIT) philosophies described in Chapter 15 often require enhanced flexibility. If bottlenecks occur in a production process, JIT allows few buffer stocks to compensate for irregularities of work flow. Under these circumstances, staff may be required to transfer to different parts of the production process to keep work flowing. Similarly, JIT requires fast changeover of equipment from performing one task to another. This may require individual members of staff to join the changeover team as and when they are required.

The implication of such job flexibility is that a greater emphasis must be placed on training, learning and knowledge management. Defining what knowledge and experience are required to perform particular tasks and translating these into training activities are clearly prerequisites for effective multi-skilling. Following on from this, the nature of remuneration systems is changing. Rather than basing pay on output, payment systems now often relate pay to the range of skills possessed by an individual.

Time flexibility

Not every individual wants to work full-time. Many people, often because of family responsibilities, only want to work for part of their time, sometimes only during specific parts of the day or week (because of childcare responsibilities, etc.). Likewise, employers may not require the same number of staff at all times. They may, for example, need extra staff only at periods of heavy demand. To some extent, skills flexibility may allow them to transfer staff to where demand is occurring; for example, the supermarket which transfers its staff from shelf replenishment to checkout work at busy periods. However, in addition, it may be necessary to vary the absolute number of staff on duty at any time.

Bringing both the supply of staff and the demand for their work together is the objective of 'flexible time' or 'flexi-time' working systems. These may define a *core* working time for each individual member of staff and allow other times to be accumulated flexibly. Other schemes include *annual hours* schemes, one solution to the capacity management issue described in Chapter 11.

Location flexibility – teleworking

The sectoral balance of employment has also changed. The service sector in most developed economies now accounts for between 70 and 80 per cent of all employment. Even within the manufacturing sector, the proportion of people with indirect jobs (those not directly engaged in making products) has also increased significantly. One result of all this is that the number of jobs which are not 'location-specific' has increased. Location-specific means that a job must take place in one fixed location. So a shop worker must work in a shop and an assembly line worker must work on the assembly line. But many jobs could be performed at any location where there are communication links to the rest of the organization. The realization of this has given rise to what is known as *teleworking*, which is also known as using 'alternative workplaces' (AW), 'flexible working', 'home working' (misleadingly narrow) and creating the 'virtual office'.

Degrees of teleworking

Not everyone who has the opportunity to telework will require, or even want, the same degree of separation from their work office. Professors Davenport and Pearlson[13] have identified five stages on a continuum of alternative work arrangements:

- *Occasional telecommuting* – this is probably still the most common form, where people have fixed offices but occasionally work at home. Information technology workers, academics and designers may work in this way.
- *'Hotelling'* – this is an arrangement where individuals often visit the office, yet, because they are not always present, they do not require fixed office space. Rather, they can reserve an office cubicle ('hotel room') in which they can work. Professional service staff, such as consultants, may use this approach.
- *Home working* – probably have no office as such (although they may 'hotel' occasionally) but they may have a small office or office space at home. Much of their work may be performed on the internet or telephone. For example, customer service workers or telemarketing personnel could fall into this category.
- *Fully mobile* – at the extreme level, staff may not even have home offices. Instead they spend their time with customers or suppliers, or travelling between them. They rely on mobile communications technology. Field sales staff and customer service staff may fall into this category.

The degree of communications technology required varies with different degrees of teleworking. Occasional telecommuting needs only a simple computer with e-mail connections. Fully mobile working may potentially require far more sophisticated wireless applications. But, as the technology demands of teleworking increase, so the space requirements of staff decrease. Indeed, much of the justification for teleworking is based on the (sometimes dramatically) reduced level of office space required.

● CRITICAL COMMENTARY

There is always a big difference between what is technically possible and what is organizationally feasible. None of the types of teleworking described above is without its problems. In particular, those types that deny individuals the chance to meet with colleagues often face difficulties. Problems can include the following:

▶

- *Lack of socialization* – offices are social places where people can adopt the culture of an organization as well as learn from each other. It is naïve to think that all knowledge can be codified and learnt formally at a distance.

- *Effectiveness of communication* – a large part of the essential communication we have with our colleagues is unplanned and face-to-face. It happens on 'chance meet' occasions, yet it is important in spreading contextual information as well as establishing specific pieces of information necessary to the job.

- *Problem-solving* – it is still often more efficient and effective informally to ask a colleague for help in resolving problems than formally to frame a request using communications technology.

- *It is lonely* – isolation amongst teleworkers is a real problem. For many of us, the workplace provides the main focus for social interaction. A computer screen is no substitute.

BA at Waterside

Waterside is British Airway's new state-of-the-art complex and training centre, designed by architect Niels Torp and based on the SAS Headquarters on the outskirts of Stockholm, which he designed some years earlier. The complex comprises six buildings arranged along a common spine called 'the Street'. They all have their own outward facing courtyards and are linked by the Street which creates a 'mall' or 'village' atmosphere with trees and fountains, coffee shops and restaurants surrounded by glass-walled offices, walkways and lifts.

British Airways Waterside building incorporates many ideas which encourage flexibility and provide an attractive working environment

Photo courtesy of British Airways

Waterside brings together, for the first time, cabin crew and customer service staff (the 'uniforms') with product developers, strategists and sales staff (the 'suits') in open-plan offices which are spacious and airy. Even the Chief Executive shares his office area with two other directors, and the wedge under the door to the area confirms their open-door policy. All the furniture and equipment in the buildings is the same, so office moves are simple. Many desks are shared and these 'hot desks' can be booked by staff as and when required. PIN numbers provide access to the telephone networks and personal follow-me style telephone numbers, and, like the computer links, they can be accessed from any desk. Likewise, small cordless phones can be taken and used around the building, minimizing previously large mobile phone bills. Other more transient staff – sales staff, for example – are provided with 'touch-down points' where they can use a phone or computer or plug in their own laptop. Even more efficient use of space has come from the creation of 'club' areas where employees can work informally in a lounge setting. Duty rotas and training manuals are all computerized and accessible throughout the building.

Waterside creates a relaxed atmosphere which encourages interaction, communication and teamwork. Hours of work are flexible, with employees judged on their output rather than attendance. According to the company:

'Staff should enjoy the experience of being here, whether they are in the building all of the time or call in once a week. It is an informal environment, very modern and very transparent. People can see and meet others who work in different

departments. In the old building, it was different. People worked in their own rooms and had their own space. If you went to visit them it was like going onto someone else's territory. The way we operate here is not only more transparent it is more efficient.'

Control versus commitment

It is important to stress again that, although we have presented them in the chronological order of their emergence, the various approaches have not replaced each other. The principles of division of labour are still influential today and take their place along with ideas concerning empowerment and all the other approaches. However, there are clear differences between the approaches, both in the methods and 'techniques' which they adopt to design jobs and, more importantly, in their underlying aims and philosophies. The most obvious difference between approaches is the relative emphasis they place on the need for management to *control* the job, and the desire to engage the *commitment* of the staff performing the job.

Figure 9.12 shows how the balance between control and commitment has moved with the emergence of each approach to job design. Division of labour is totally concerned with controlling the work done by staff. Management control over the job allows it to be reduced, routinized and thereby made more efficient. Scientific management in its original form might also be regarded as concerned exclusively with

Figure 9.12 **The different approaches to job design: each implies a different balance between control and commitment**

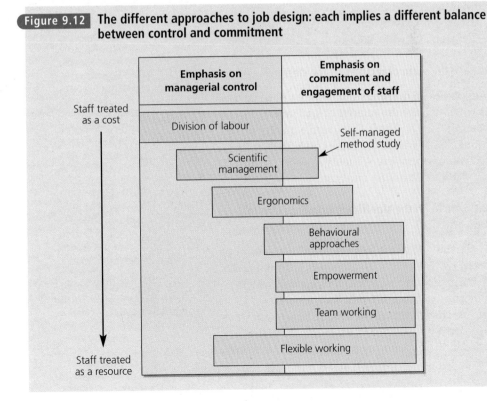

controlling the way the job is performed. Again, it is argued that control is necessary to find the 'best' method of doing the job. However, the recent developments in method study could be seen as moving the use of scientific management techniques more into the hands of staff, and thereby increasing its concern with staff commitment. Ergonomics, by being concerned with the way staff respond to physical and environmental conditions, can be considered to be, at least partly, attempting to influence their commitment. However, ergonomics is concerned with staff's physiological responses as much as, if not more than, their psychological responses.

Behavioural approaches to job design focus far more on the commitment of staff to their jobs, and indeed place staff engagement and motivation as the central theme of job design. Finally, empowerment not only highlights the commitment of staff but also transfers to them at least part of the control of their jobs. Paradoxically, this moves the emphasis back to control, but now it is individual or group control rather than 'managerial' control.

Likewise team-based working emphasizes both commitment and group control. Flexible working is more difficult to characterize in this way. It certainly offers the potential for individuals to reconcile some aspects of home and work life. Yet the technology on which some teleworking depends can exercise an insidious control over working activities.

Summary answers to key questions

What are the main decisions in job design?

● Job design involves deciding what tasks to allocate to each person in the organization, and in what sequence to perform them, where to locate the job, who else should be involved in it, how people should interact with their workplace and their immediate work environment, what autonomy to give the staff and what skills to develop in the staff.

What are the main objectives of job design?

● All job design decisions should attempt to devise jobs which engage the interest of staff, are inherently safe, and give a reasonable quality of working life, as well as the more conventional objectives of operations – quality, speed, dependability, flexibility and cost.

What have been the significant influences on job design practice?

● Historically, the first influence was the concept of division of labour. This involves taking a total task and dividing it into separate parts, each of which can be allocated to a different individual to perform. The advantages of this are largely concerned with reducing costs. However, highly divided jobs are monotonous and, in their extreme form, contribute to physical injury.

● Scientific management took some of the ideas of division of labour but applied them more systematically. The area of work study (divided into method study and work measurement) is most often associated with scientific management. Although scientific management in its original form has fallen out of favour, new forms in which staff themselves perform method study analyses have been successfully applied more recently.

● Ergonomics is concerned primarily with the physiological aspects of job design. This includes the study of how the human body fits into its workplace and of how humans react to their immediate environment, especially its heating, lighting and noise characteristics.

● Behavioural models of job design are more concerned with individuals' reactions to, and attitudes to, their job. It is argued that jobs which are designed to fulfil people's need for self-esteem and personal development are more likely to achieve satisfactory work performance.

● The empowerment principle of job design has concentrated on increasing the autonomy which individuals have to shape the nature of their own jobs.

- Team-working can both put together a required mixture of skills and allow decisions to be made by the people who have to manage the results.

- Flexible working involves individuals in being able to change the nature of their jobs, the time which they spend at their jobs and the location in which jobs are performed. While only applicable to certain jobs, flexible working may have a significant impact.

How do the influences on job design differ?

- The major difference lies in the relative balance between the two concepts of *control* of the job and the commitment of the staff performing the job. The chronological progression of influences on job design from division of labour through to empowerment is broadly in line with the movement from an emphasis on managerial control to an emphasis on the commitment and engagement of staff.

CASE EXERCISE

South West Cross Bank

Towards the end of the 1990s, much of the European retail banking industry was facing unprecedented levels of competition. This was partly the result of excess capacity (many towns had four or more bank branches within 100 metres of each other) and partly triggered by the presence of aggressive new entrants, including insurance companies and other retailers, such as supermarkets. Many of the new retail banks concentrated on a few simple financial products such as current accounts, deposit accounts and mortgages, in contrast to most conventional banks, which offered hundreds or even thousands of different products. At the same time, new delivery systems such as telephone and internet banking were being introduced.

South West Cross Bank (SWX) had not performed well, and was in the lower quartile of the big banks in Europe. However, it did have a strong retail brand image, high market shares in some sectors (such as small business loans), and a reliable but unspectacular profit record. But it was perceived to be late in recognizing the importance of developing its operations. Many large banks had been much quicker to install the latest information systems, allowing automation of many routine activities. Several competitors had experimented with centralization and/or regionalization of routine operations, such as telephony and correspondence, that had previously been carried out in the branches. This had freed up staff time for selling financial products, and at the same time had introduced efficiencies that could never have been achieved at branch level. Some banks, however, had paid a price. Not all customers were satisfied by the changes, and some banks had received bad publicity.

This letter to a national newspaper was typical:

'My bank recently introduced, without warning, a bizarre system whereby a customer cannot telephone his branch manager, or write to him and expect him to receive the letter and reply to it. A London customer now has to ring a number in Wales, where a call will be diverted to some central point which deals with general inquiries, balances, standing orders, statements, etc. If the customer writes to his branch manager, he does not see the letter and it frequently seems to disappear. When the customer does not receive a reply, he has no idea whom to ring to check up. In other words, there is no one point of contact within the bank. This appalling treatment is being meted out to all customers of however long standing. Everyone I know is complaining bitterly about it.'

The appended editor's comment was:

'Everyone I know is complaining too! I sympathize wholeheartedly and have commented about it before in this paper. In an attempt to cut costs, all the big banks have introduced customer service call centres to deal with routine enquiries, frequently with automated recorded messages which require you to punch in numbers to access information on your account. These are known in the industry as "factories".'

As a late implementer of operational change, SWX had the advantage of being able to learn from competitors' mistakes. It decided that radical change was required to make the retail operation more efficient in driving down costs and more effective in improving customer service quality. These were to be achieved simultaneously, using the latest 'state-of-the-art' equipment.

SWX embarked on one of the most extensive operational change programmes ever conducted in the European banking industry. The project, budgeted at around three billion euros, was planned to roll out over two years and would redesign almost every process in the retail bank division. Most processes that had previously been carried out at branches were to be transferred to large, specialized processing centres, allowing head-count reductions and space saving at every branch. Valuable back-office space could then be sold or rented to other businesses, whilst more space could be devoted to front-office, customer-facing activities. Branch staff had previously been involved both with dealing with customers, and with a wide variety of back-office tasks. These included cheque processing, cash balancing, answering phone calls from branch customers, letter writing, setting up direct debits and other payment processes. One long-serving branch employee, Christina Kusonski, summed up her feelings about the proposed changes.

'With the expected halving of the branch staff numbers, those of us who have been asked to stay will see major changes to our jobs. We currently have to do a variety of tasks, including some boring ones like cheque processing. But these routine jobs only last for around half an hour, and then we can do something else, as directed by the Assistant Manager. Every day is different, because the mix of work changes and we work with different people when they need help. For example, Fridays are usually busy on the cash desk, with people drawing money for the weekend. On Mondays we get more cheques paid in and more phone calls too. Under the new system, there will be hardly any back-room jobs, so we will be "on show" from morning to night. We won't be able to have a chat out of sight of the customers like before when we were doing some routine office jobs! And the pressure will be on being nice to the customers, and taking every opportunity to sell them insurance, or some other product. And what about lunchtime when so many customers come in? Almost everyone used to come to serve at the counter, but now there won't be anyone to call forward! To be honest, I'm not looking forward to it at all, and I only hope the customers are very patient and loyal to our bank. Our manager has given us a number of briefings, and has assured us that we are his selected team, but I am not convinced. Each of us will be responsible for serving just one customer at a time, so I can't see how we will be working as an empowered work team as he described! Actually, I think it will be a worse job – we will be very isolated from each other, and constantly under pressure. I will give it a try, but if my fears come true, I will apply to work in the new call centre down the road. There are more than 300 staff

there and they work in close teams of 10. It has already got a reputation as a good place to work … the latest telephone equipment, a nice office, and managers who are listening to suggestions from teams and individuals. I don't think there is much future for us in the branches!'

That evening, at a social event in the local pub, Christina met a former colleague, Silvia Lowener, who had been the first to leave the branch three weeks earlier. She now travelled daily to the new cheque processing centre (CPC) some 20 km away. Inevitably, they soon began talking about work, and Silvia was full of enthusiasm for the new job:

'At first I found the job rather boring, but at least we don't get any problems with customers; they could not get anywhere near the place! We work in teams, and I am in the data entry department, where we read digital images (electronic photographs) of the cheques and key in the amount shown. We are only keying the ones which the automated optical character recognition (OCR) system has not been able to read, which includes many with terrible handwriting. Most of the work comes in from the retail branches from lunchtime onwards, so we are all on afternoon or evening shifts. I work six hours, from 4 o'clock in the afternoon. I am in a team of eight and our workstations are on an octagonal layout facing in, so we can see each other. The team leader is one of the eight and is responsible for our output and quality performance, which can be compared with other teams here and the other CPCs. When working, we are required to key 12 000 characters per hour, which is around 3000 cheques, so we have to concentrate hard! We all have a 15-minute break every two hours; some of the staff go for a smoke, whilst others socialize over a coffee. We meet as a team for 10 minutes at the beginning of every shift. We are encouraged to join process improvement teams, both in our own areas and covering the whole process. We have already made lots of good suggestions for improvements, but most involve re-programming, so there are long delays in getting the changes we want. I think we will also soon run out of things to do!'

'We are near the end of the process here. The polythene-wrapped parcels of cheques are delivered periodically from the branches by a security firm, the bar codes are scanned and the parcels are check-weighed and signed for, in the Reception Department. They are then accumulated in a wheeled trolley until it is full. The trolley is then wheeled through to the Preparation Room where the parcels are cut open and the bundles of cheques are extracted. Individuals then sort through them, looking for and extracting any metal staples, rubber bands and perforations at the edges, all of which can cause blockages in the OCR machines. When this has been done, the bundles of cheques are vibrated in a

special "joddle" machine to align two edges in preparation for feeding the OCRs. The prepared bundles are placed in trays and then on shelved trolleys to be moved, when full, to the OCR machine room, where they wait in a queue until an operative prepares them (further joddling!) for the machine. The first "capture pass" through the machine records the image and print encodes the cheques for subsequent identification. The digital image is either successfully read by the computer or passed to us for manual keying. Once this is done, and the batch balances (credits and debits must match exactly), the cheques are then re-fed into the machines. This second pass sorts by the origination bank in preparation for clearing in London. Sorted cheques are packed (by bank), taken to the Reception Department and then taken by courier to London.'

Questions

1 How would these changes affect the job of a branch manager? What new skills would be required?

2 What would the effect be on the job design of branch employees in terms of the elements of the 'behavioural' design model?

3 Compare the extent to which empowerment is feasible and desirable at a branch and at a CPC.

4 Prepare a process flow chart for the cheque processing operation. How many of the steps are value-adding?

Discussion questions

1 Imagine that you and four friends have to prepare and serve a five-course meal for 20 people. Identify and describe the main elements that will be involved in designing the jobs involved.

2 Explain how the design of a job which involves making overhead transparencies for university lecturers might affect the performance of the person doing the job.

3 Explain the difference between division of labour and scientific management.

4 Get together with a few colleagues and undertake a method study of an operation: for example, the loading and unloading of a local car ferry, a small catering operation or a gardening task. What improvements could you make and how acceptable might they be to the operators involved?

5 Draw a process chart for the following tasks:
   – loading paper into a printer
   – changing the tyre on a car
   – making a cup of coffee.

6 Assess the workplace design of your lecture theatre.

7 Explain why some operations managers might be concerned about implementing job rotation, enrichment and enlargement.

8 Explain how empowerment differs from the behavioural approaches.

9 How might empowerment differ between professional and mass-service organizations? Illustrate your answer with references to organizations of your choice.

Notes on chapter

1 For a discussion of the origins of the division of labour, *see* Wild, R. (1972) *Mass Production Management*, John Wiley.

2 Ford, H. with Crowther, S. (1924) *My Life and Works* (rev. edn), Heinemann.

3 Taylor, F.W. (1947) *Scientific Management* (edn published by Harper and Row, New York).

4 Hoxie, R.F. (1915) *Scientific Management and Labour*, D. Appleton.

5 Source: Adler, P.S. (1933) 'Time and Motion Regained', *Harvard Business Review*, Vol 11, No 1.

6 Kobrick, J.L. and Fine, B.J. (1983) 'Climate and Human Performance' in Osborne, D.J. and Gruneberg, M.M. (eds) *The Physical Environment and Work*, John Wiley.

7 *Illuminating Engineering Society*, IES Code for Interior Lighting, 1977.

8 Environmental Protection Agency (US)(1974), 'Information on Levels of Environmental Noise Requisite to Protect Public Health and Welfare with Adequate Margin of Safety', EPA.

9 There are other recommendations similar to those published in the European Union Directive; they broadly agree on what is good practice.

10 Hackman, J.R. and Lawler, E.E. (1971) 'Employee Reaction to Job Characteristics', *Journal of Applied Psychology*, Vol 55, pp 259–86.

11 Hackman, J.R. and Oldham, G. (1975) 'A New Strategy for Job Enrichment', *California Management Review*, Vol 17, No 3.

12 Bowen, D. and Lawler, E. (1992) 'Empowerment', *Sloan Management Review*, Spring.

13 Davenport, T.H. and Pearlson, K. (1998) 'Two Cheers for the Virtual Office', *Sloan Management Review*, Summer.

Selected further reading

Apgar, M. (1998) 'The Alternative Workplace: Changing Where and How People Work', *Harvard Business Review*, May–June.

Argyris, C. (1998) 'Empowerment: The Emperor's New Clothes', *Harvard Business Review*, May–June.

Bailey, J. (1983) *Job Design and Work Organisation*, Prentice Hall.

Berggren, C. (1992) *The Volvo Experience, Alternatives to Lean Production in the Swedish Auto Industry*, Macmillan.

Clegg, C.W. and Corbett, J.M. (1987) 'Research and Development in "Humanising" Advanced Manufacturing Technology' *in* Wall, T.D., Clegg, C.W. and Kemp, N.J. (eds) *The Human Side of Advanced Manufacturing Technology*, John Wiley.

Corlett, N., Wilson, J. and Manencia, F. (eds) (1986) *Ergonomics of Working Posture*, Taylor and Francis.

Cunningham, J.B. and Eberle, T. (1990) 'A Guide to Job Enrichment and Redesign', *Personnel*, Feb.

Fisher, K.K. (1993) *Leading Self-Directed Workteams*, McGraw-Hill.

Hackman, R.J. and Oldham, G. (1980) *Work Redesign*, Addison-Wesley.

Herzberg, F. (1987) 'One More Time: How Do You Motivate Employees?' (with retrospective commentary), *Harvard Business Review*, Vol 65, No 5.

Katzenbach, J.R. and Smith, D.K. (1993) *The Wisdom of Teams: Creating the High Performance Organisation*, Harvard Business School Press.

Main, J. (1982) 'Battling your own Bureaucracy' *in Working Smarter*, by the Editors of *Fortune*, New York, Viking Press, Prentice Hall, pp 88–9.

Malone, T.W. (1997) 'Is Empowerment Just a Fad?', *Sloan Management Review*, Winter.

Osborne, D.J. (1995), *Ergonomics at Work* (3rd edn), John Wiley.

Rubenowitz, S. (1992) 'The Role of Management in Production Units with Autonomous Work Groups', *International Journal of Operations and Production Management*, Vol 12, No 7/8.

Scarborough, H. and Corbet, M. (1992) *Technology and Organisation*, Routledge.

Talbot, K.D. (1999) 'The Virtual Company', *Engineering Management Journal*, April.

Part Three

PLANNING AND CONTROL

The physical design of an operation should have provided the fixed resources which are capable of satisfying customers' demands. Planning and control are concerned with operating those resources on a day-to-day basis and ensuring availability of materials and other variable resources in order to supply the goods and services which fulfil customers' demands. This part of the book will look at several different aspects of planning and control, including some of the specialist approaches which are used in particular types of operations.

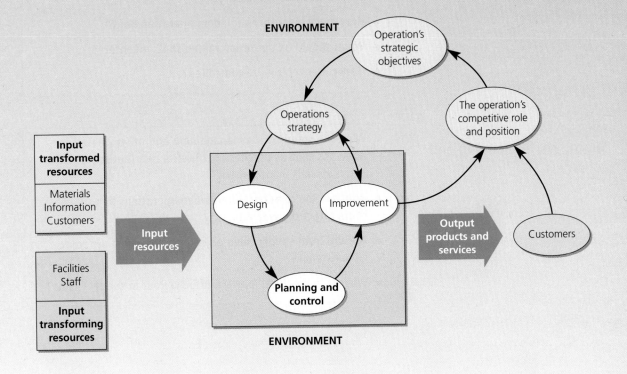

Chapter 10
The nature of planning and control

- What is planning and control?
- What is the difference between planning and control?
- How does the nature of demand affect planning and control?
- What is involved in planning and control?

Chapter 11
Capacity planning and control

- What is capacity planning and control?
- How is capacity measured?
- What are the ways of coping with demand fluctuation?
- How can operations plan their capacity level?
- How can operations control their capacity level?

Chapter 12
Inventory planning and control

- What is inventory?
- Why is inventory necessary?
- How much inventory should an operation hold?
- When should an operation replenish its inventory?
- How can inventory be controlled?

Chapter 13
Supply chain planning and control

- What are supply chain management and other related activities such as purchasing, physical distribution, logistics and materials management?
- How can the relationship between operations in a supply chain affect the way it works?
- Are different supply chain objectives needed in different circumstances?
- What is the 'natural' pattern of behaviour in supply chains?

**Chapter 14
MRP**

- What is MRP?
- What is the process involved in MRP planning and control?
- What are the main elements of an MRP system?
- What is 'closed loop' MRP?
- What are MRP II and Enterprise Resource Planning (ERP)?

**Chapter 15
Just-in-time planning and
control**

- What is JIT and how is it different from traditional operations practice?
- What are the main elements of JIT philosophy?
- What are the techniques of JIT?
- How can JIT be used for planning and control?
- Can JIT be used in service operations?
- Can JIT and MRP coexist?

**Chapter 16
Project planning and control**

- What is a project and what is project management?
- Why is it important to understand the environment in which a project takes place?
- How are specific projects defined?
- What is project planning and why is it important?
- What techniques can be used for project planning?
- What is project control and how is it done?

**Chapter 17
Quality planning and control**

- How can quality be defined?
- How can quality problems be diagnosed?
- What steps lead towards conformance to specification?
- How can statistical process control help quality planning and control?
- How can acceptance sampling help quality planning and control?

CHAPTER

10

The nature of planning and control

Introduction

Within the constraints imposed by its design, an operation has to be run on an ongoing basis. This is what 'planning and control' is concerned with – managing the ongoing activities of the operation so as to satisfy customer demand. All operations require plans and require controlling, although the degree of formality and detail may vary. Some operations are more difficult to plan than others. Those where there is a high level of unpredictability can be particularly difficult to plan. Some operations are more difficult to control than others. Those which have high customer contact may be difficult to control because of the immediate nature of their operations and the variability that customers may impose on the operation. This chapter introduces and provides an overview of some of the principles and methods of planning and control. Some of these, such as MRP (materials requirements planning) and JIT (just-in-time), have been developed into more extensive concepts and these are examined in separate chapters. Similarly, there are separate specialist tools to plan and control in project environments and a separate chapter is devoted to this area. In all cases, however, the different aspects of planning and control can be viewed as representing the reconciliation of supply with demand (*see* Fig. 10.1).

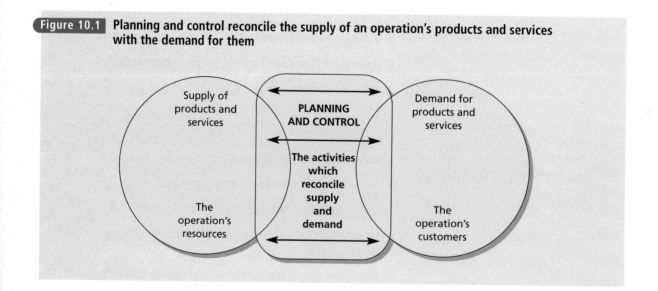

Figure 10.1 Planning and control reconcile the supply of an operation's products and services with the demand for them

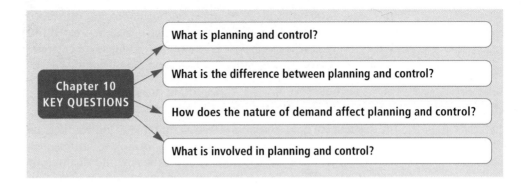

Chapter 10
KEY QUESTIONS

What is planning and control?

What is the difference between planning and control?

How does the nature of demand affect planning and control?

What is involved in planning and control?

What is planning and control?

The previous part of this book examined the design activities of operations management. These design activities determine the form and nature of the system and the resources it contains, and although they will affect the ongoing management of operations processes, they are not themselves concerned with the day-to-day running of the process. That is the purpose of planning and control – to ensure that the operation's processes run effectively and efficiently and produce products and services as required by customers.

Consider, for example, the way in which routine surgery is organized in a hospital. When a patient arrives and is admitted to the hospital, much of the planning for the surgery will already have happened. The operating theatre will have been reserved, and the doctors and nurses who staff the operating theatre will have been provided with all the information regarding the patient's condition. Appropriate preoperative and postoperative care will have been organized. All this will involve staff and facilities in different parts of the hospital. All must be given the same information and their activities coordinated. Soon after the patient arrives, he or she will be checked to make sure that the condition is as expected (in much the same way as material is inspected on arrival in a factory). Blood, if required, will be cross-matched and reserved, and any medication will be made ready (in the same way that all the different materials are brought together in a factory). Any last-minute changes may require some degree of replanning. For example, if the patient shows unexpected symptoms, observation may be necessary before the surgery can take place. Not only will this affect the patient's own treatment, but other patients' treatment may also have to be rescheduled (in the same way as machines will need rescheduling if a job is delayed in a factory). All these activities of scheduling, coordination and organization are concerned with the planning and control of the hospital.

● Reconciling supply with demand

In Chapter 3, when discussing operations strategy, we discussed operations' strategic objectives in terms of the reconciliation between market requirements and operations resources. Planning and control can be seen in the same way. On the one hand, the resources of the operation have the general capability to supply to customers, but as yet they have not been given the instructions on how to do so. On the other hand, we have a set of both general and specific demands from actual and potential customers. Planning and control activities provide the systems, procedures and decisions which bring these two entities together. This model of planning and control as the reconciling activity between supply and demand is one that we shall use throughout this part of the book. Different aspects of supply and demand, and different circumstances under which supply and demand must be reconciled, will be treated in the various chapters. But in every case, the purpose is the same – to make a connection between the two, which will trigger the operation into satisfying its customers.

● The difference between planning and control

In this text we have chosen to treat planning and control together. This is because the division between planning and control is not clear, either in theory or in practice. However, there are some general features that help to distinguish between the two. A plan is a formalization of what is intended to happen at some time in the future. But a plan does not guarantee that an event will actually happen. Rather it is a statement of intention. Although plans are based on expectations, during their implementation things do not always happen as expected. Customers change their minds about what they want and when they want it. Suppliers may not always deliver on time, machines may fail, or staff may be absent through illness. Control is the process of coping with changes in these variables. It may mean that plans need to be redrawn in the short term. It may also mean that an 'intervention' will need to be made in the operation to bring it back 'on track' – for example, finding a new supplier who can deliver quickly, repairing the machine which failed, or moving staff from another part of the operation to cover for the absentees. Control makes the adjustments which allow the operation to achieve the objectives that the plan has set, even when the assumptions on which the plan was based do not hold true.

We can define a plan as setting the intention for what is supposed to happen, and control as the driving through of the plan, monitoring what actually happens and making changes as necessary.

Long-, medium- and short-term planning and control

The nature of planning and control activities changes over time. In the very long term, operations managers make plans concerning what they intend to do, what resources they need, and what objectives they hope to achieve. The emphasis is on planning rather than control, because there is little to control as such. They will use forecasts of likely demand which are described in aggregated terms. For example, a hospital will make plans for '2000 patients' without necessarily going into the details of the individual needs of those 2000 patients. Similarly, the resources will be planned in an aggregated form. The hospital might plan to have 100 nurses and 20 doctors but again without deciding on the specific attributes of the staff. In carrying out their planning activities, the operations managers will be concerned mainly to achieve financial targets. Budgets will be put in place which identify the costs and revenue targets which it is intended to achieve.

Medium-term planning and control is concerned with planning in more detail (and replanning if necessary). It looks ahead to assess the overall demand which the operation must meet in a partially disaggregated manner. By this time, for example, the hospital must distinguish between different types of demand. The number of patients coming as accident and emergency cases will need to be distinguished from those requiring routine operations. Similarly, resources will be set at a more disaggregated level. For example, different categories of staff will have been identified and broad staffing levels in each category set. Just as important, contingencies will have been put in place which allow for slight deviations from the plans. These contingencies will act as 'reserve' resources and make planning and control easier in the short term.

In short-term planning and control, many of the resources will have been set and it will be difficult to make large-scale changes in resourcing. However, short-term interventions are possible if things are not going to plan. By this time, demand will be assessed on a totally disaggregated basis. The hospital will be treating all types of surgi-

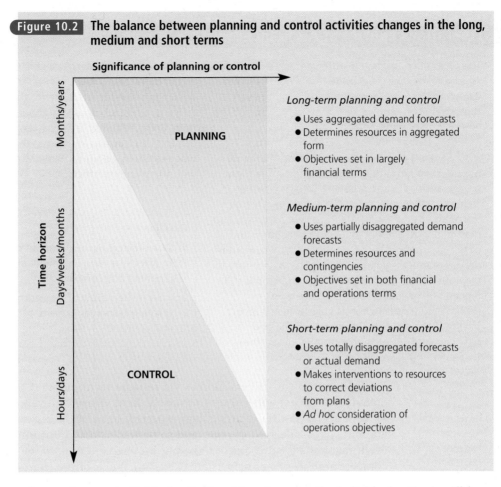

Figure 10.2 The balance between planning and control activities changes in the long, medium and short terms

Significance of planning or control

PLANNING

CONTROL

Time horizon

Months/years

Days/weeks/months

Hours/days

Long-term planning and control
- Uses aggregated demand forecasts
- Determines resources in aggregated form
- Objectives set in largely financial terms

Medium-term planning and control
- Uses partially disaggregated demand forecasts
- Determines resources and contingencies
- Objectives set in both financial and operations terms

Short-term planning and control
- Uses totally disaggregated forecasts or actual demand
- Makes interventions to resources to correct deviations from plans
- *Ad hoc* consideration of operations objectives

cal procedures as individual activities. More importantly, individual patients will have been identified by name, and specific time slots booked for their treatment. In making short-term interventions and changes to the plan, operations managers will be attempting to balance the quality, speed, dependability, flexibility and costs of their operation on an *ad hoc* basis. It is unlikely that they will have the time to carry out detailed calculations of the effects of their short-term planning and control decisions on all these objectives, but a general understanding of priorities will form the background to their decision-making.

Figure 10.2 shows how the control aspects of planning and control increase in significance closer to the date of the event.

The nature of supply and demand

If planning and control is the process of reconciling demand with supply, then the nature of the decisions taken to plan and control an operation will depend on both the nature of demand and the nature of supply in that operation. In this next section, we examine some differences in demand and supply which can affect the way in which operations managers plan and control their activities.

Uncertainty in supply

Some operations are reasonably predictable and usually run to plan. In these situations, the need for control is minimal. For example, cable TV services provide programmes to

The difficulties associated with planning a schedule which involves the worldwide resources of a major airline such as Air France and ensuring that every flight leaves on time make this operation one of the most complex planning and control tasks.

Eighty flight planners work 24-hour shifts in Air France's flight planning office at Roissy Charles de Gaulle. Their job is to establish the optimum flight routes, anticipate any problems such as weather changes, and minimize fuel consumption. Overall the goals of the flight planning activity are first, and most important, safety followed by economy and passenger comfort. Increasingly powerful computer programs process the mountain of data necessary to plan the flights, but in the end many decisions still rely on human judgement. Even the most sophisticated expert systems only serve as support for the flight planners. For flights within and between Air France's 12 geographic zones, they construct a flight plan that will form the basis of the actual flight only a few hours later. All planning documents need to be ready for the flight crew who arrive two hours before the scheduled departure time. Being responsible for passenger safety and comfort, the captain always has the final say and, when satisfied, co-signs the flight plan together with the planning officer.

Questions

1 What factors in the nature of demand are likely to affect the long-, medium- and short-term planning and control activities at Air France?

2 How is the supply of transformed and transforming resources likely to affect planning and control?

a schedule into subscribers' homes via reliable technology. It is rare that the programme plan is not adhered to. Conversely, local village carnivals rarely work to plan. Processions take longer to arrive than expected, some of the acts scheduled in the programme may be delayed *en route*, and some traders may not turn up on the day. The event requires a good compere to keep it moving and to keep the crowd amused. The compere and his or her helpers are exercising much of the short-term control that is used to minimize customer dissatisfaction.

Dependable supply requires availability of all transformed and transforming resources. If any are absent, it is unlikely that supply can occur. So, when trying to understand uncertainty in supply, it is important to understand the uncertainty of each input resource which governs supply.

Uncertainty in demand

For some operations, demand is fairly predictable. In a school, for example, once classes are fixed and the term or semester has started, a teacher knows how many pupils are in the class. When planning how many handouts are required, the demand is predictable. Absentees can have their handouts on return, so this variable does not affect demand. However, this is medium- and short-term planning and control for the school. Prior to the start of the year, the head teacher may not know exactly how many new pupils will be joining the school and how many existing pupils will leave the area or move to another school. Therefore, in the long term, the head teacher has to predict this demand to determine resources such as staff, books and computers for which commitment must be made in advance.

In other operations, demand is unpredictable even in the short term. A fast-food outlet inside a shopping centre does not know how many people will arrive, when they will arrive and what they will order. It is possible to predict certain patterns, such as an increase in demand over the lunch and tea-time periods, but a sudden rainstorm that drives shoppers indoors into the centre could significantly and unpredictably increase demand in the very short term. Demand for fast-moving consumer goods such as packets of biscuits varies enormously depending on television advertising campaigns – a successful campaign can have an impact the following day, which can cause demand to soar to 10 times its normal selling pattern. While some extra stocks could be provided to supermarkets in advance of the campaign, the size of the reaction is not easy to predict.

● Dependent and independent demand

Knowing what demands customers are going to place on an operation is never totally certain. However, some operations can predict demand with more certainty than others. For example, consider an operation providing professional decorating and refurbishment services which has as its customers a number of large hotel chains. Most of these customers plan the refurbishment and decoration of their hotels months or even years in advance. Because of this, the decoration company can itself plan its activities in advance. Its own demand is dependent upon the relatively predictable activities of its customers. By contrast, a small painter and decorator serves the domestic and small business market. Some business also comes from house construction companies, but only when their own painters and decorators are fully occupied. In this case, demand on the painting and decorating company is relatively unpredictable. To some extent, there is a random element in demand which is virtually independent of any factors obvious to the company.

Dependent demand, then, is demand which is relatively predictable because it is dependent upon some factor which is known. For example, the manager who is in charge of ensuring that there are sufficient tyres in an automobile factory will not treat the demand for tyres as a totally random variable. He or she will not be totally surprised by the exact quantity of tyres which are required by the plant every day. The process of demand forecasting is relatively straightforward. It will consist of examining the manufacturing schedules in the car plant and deriving the demand for tyres from these. If 200 cars are to be manufactured on a particular day, then it is simple to calculate that 1000 tyres will be demanded by the car plant (each car has five tyres) – demand is dependent on a known factor, the number of cars to be manufactured. Because of this, the tyres can be ordered from the tyre manufacturer to a delivery schedule which is closely in line with the demand for tyres from the plant (*see* Fig. 10.3). In fact, the demand for every part of the car plant will be derived from the assembly schedule for the finished cars. Manufacturing instructions and purchasing requests will all be dependent upon this figure. Other operations will act in a dependent demand manner because of the nature of the service or product which they provide. For example, a jobbing dressmaker will not buy fabric and patterns and make up dresses in many different sizes just in case someone comes along and wants to buy one. Nor will a high-class restaurant begin to cook food just in case a customer arrives

Figure 10.3 **The demand for tyres in a car plant is dependent on the manufacturing schedule of the cars**

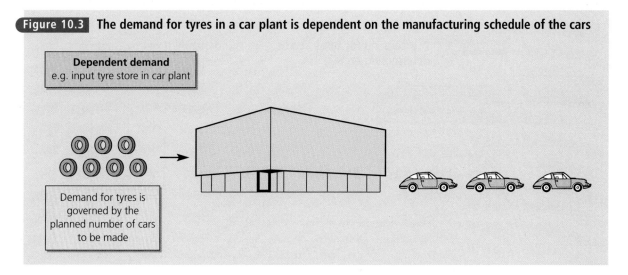

and requests it. In both these cases, a combination of risk and the perishability of the product or service prevents the operation from starting to create the goods or services until it has a firm order.

Dependent demand planning and control concentrates on the consequences of the demand within the operation. Materials requirements planning, which is treated in Chapter 14, is one such dependent demand approach.

Some operations have little choice but to take decisions on how they will supply demand without having any firm forward visibility of customer orders. For example, customers do not have to inform a supermarket when they are arriving and what they will buy. The supermarket takes its planning and control decisions based on its experience and understanding of the market, independent of what may actually happen. They run the risk of being out of stock of items when demand does not match their expectations. For example, the Ace Tyre Company, which operates a drive-in tyre replacement service, will need to manage a stock of tyres. In that sense it is exactly the same task that faced the manager of tyre stocks in the car plant. However, demand is very different for Ace Tyres. It cannot predict either the volume or the specific needs of customers. It must make decisions on how many and what type of tyres to stock, based on demand forecasts and in the light of the risks it is prepared to run of being out of stock. This is the nature of *independent demand planning and control*. It makes 'best guesses' concerning future demand, attempts to put the resources in place which can satisfy this demand, and attempts to respond quickly if actual demand does not match the forecast (*see* Fig. 10.4). Inventory planning and control, treated in Chapter 12, is typical of independent demand planning and control.

● Responding to demand

Dependent and independent demand concepts are closely related to how the operation chooses to respond to demand. In conditions of dependent demand, an operation will only start the process of producing goods or services when it needs to. Each order triggers the planning and control activities to organize their production. For example, a specialist house builder might only start the process of planning and controlling the construction of a house when requested to do so by the customer. The builder might not even have the resources to start building before the order is received. The material that will be necessary to build the house will be purchased only when the timing and nature of the house are certain. The staff and the construction equipment might also be 'purchased' only when the nature of demand is clear. In a similar way, a specialist conference organizer will start planning for an event only when specifically requested to do so by the clients. A venue will be booked, speakers organized, meals arranged and the delegates contacted

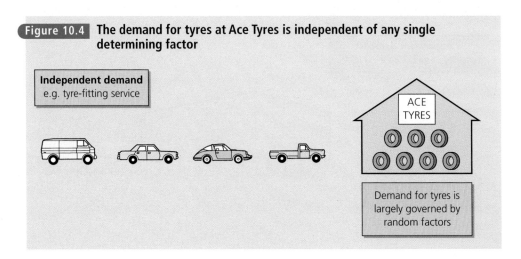

Figure 10.4 **The demand for tyres at Ace Tyres is independent of any single determining factor**

Independent demand
e.g. tyre-fitting service

ACE TYRES

Demand for tyres is largely governed by random factors

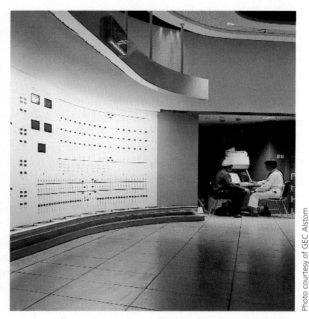

Power station generator units   Part of a power station's central control room

A power station is controlled using highly automated systems. This plant has a single operator controlling four of the eight generator units during normal operation. The control systems are designed with 'redundancy' built in so that control is maintained even if some parts of the system malfunction. The central control room has been ergonomically designed with the supervisory operator workstations at the centre. Around this central hub are positioned the unit control desks, which communicate with the units. The plant is also provided with computerized facilities to monitor and predict the plant condition, including efficiency, environmental conditions, life expectancy, etc. An on-site plant simulator helps operator training and the development of optimum plant operating procedures

only when the nature of the service is clear. The planning and control necessary for this kind of operation can be called *resource-to-order* planning and control.[2]

Other operations might be sufficiently confident of the nature of demand, if not its volume and timing, to keep 'in stock' most of the resources it requires to satisfy its customers. Certainly it will keep its transforming resources, if not its transformed resources. However, it would still make the actual product or service only to a firm customer order. For example, a housebuilder who has standard designs might choose to build each house only when a customer places a firm order. Because the design of the house is relatively standard, suppliers of materials will have been identified, even if the building operation does not keep the items in stock itself. The equivalent in the conference business would be a conference centre which has its own 'stored' permanent resources (the building, staff, etc.) but only starts planning a conference when it has a firm booking. In both cases, the operations would need *make-to-order* planning and control.

Some operations produce goods or services ahead of any firm orders 'to stock'. For example, some builders will construct predesigned standard houses or apartments ahead of any firm demand for them. This will be done either because it is less expensive to do so or because it is difficult to create the goods or services on a one-off basis (it is difficult to make each apartment only when a customer chooses to buy one). If demand is high, customers may place requests for houses before they are started or during their construction. In this case, the customer will form a backlog of demand and must wait. The builder is also taking the risk, however, of holding a stock of unsold houses if buyers do not come along before they are finished. In fact, it is difficult for small builders to operate in this way, but less so for (say) a bottled cola manufacturer or other mass producer. The equivalent in the conference market would be a conference centre which schedules a series of events and conferences, programmed in advance and open to individual customers to book into or even turn up on the day. Cinemas and theatres usually work in this manner. Their performances are produced and supplied irrespective of the level of actual demand. Operations of this type will require make-to-stock planning and control.

● *P:D* ratios[3]

Another way of characterizing the graduation between resource-to-order planning and control and make-to-stock planning and control is by contrasting the total length of time customers have to wait between asking for the product or service and receiving it, demand time, D, and the total throughput time, P. Throughput time is how long the operation takes to obtain the resources, and produce and deliver the product or service.

P and *D* times depend on the operation

In a typical make-to-stock operation such as those making consumer durables, demand time, D, is the sum of the times for transmitting the order to the company's warehouse or stock point, picking and packing the order and physically transporting it to the customer – the 'deliver' cycle. Behind this visible order cycle, however, lie other cycles. Reduction in the finished goods stock will eventually trigger the decision to manufacture a replenishment batch. This cycle – the 'make' cycle – involves scheduling work to the various stages in the manufacturing process. Physically this involves withdrawing materials and parts from input inventories and processing them through the various stages of the manufacturing route. Behind the 'make' cycle lies the 'purchase' cycle – the time for replenishment of the input stocks – involving transmitting the order to suppliers and awaiting their delivery.

So, for this type of manufacturing, the 'demand' time which the customer sees is very short compared with the total 'throughput' cycle. Contrast this with a resource-to-order operation. Here, D is the same as P. Both include the 'purchase', 'make' and 'delivery' cycles. The make-to-order operation lies in between these two (*see* Fig. 10.5).

Some operations are hybrids. Take, for example, a manufacturer of industrial couplings whose product range is far wider than the range of components it makes, because it can configure components in many different ways. Given its wide range of finished products, the company does not hold them as inventories. Instead it makes most of its components 'to stock' and then assembles its products (a relatively short process) 'to order'. This is shown in Figure 10.6. Not all the company's products are made in this way, however. Some are demanded so infrequently that it makes them entirely to order as 'specials'. Most operations will operate with different *P:D* ratios for different classes of product or service.

P:D ratios indicate the degree of speculation

In the company previously described, reducing total throughput time P will have varying effects on the time the customer has to wait for demand to be filled. For many of its 'specials', P and D are virtually the same – the customer waits from the material being ordered, through all stages in the production process and for delivery. Speeding up any part of P will reduce customer's waiting time, D. On the other hand, customers purchasing standard 'assemble-to-order' products would only see reduced D time if the 'assemble' and 'deliver' parts of P were reduced and savings in times were passed on to the customer.

In Figure 10.5, D is always shown as being smaller than P, which is the case for most companies. How much smaller D is than P is important because it indicates the proportion of the operation's activities which are speculative, that is, carried out on the expectation of eventually receiving a firm order for the work. The larger P is compared with D, the higher the proportion of speculative activity in the operation and the greater the risk the operation carries. The speculative element in the operation is not there only because P is greater than D, however; it is there because P is greater than D

Figure 10.5 **P and D for the different types of planning and control**

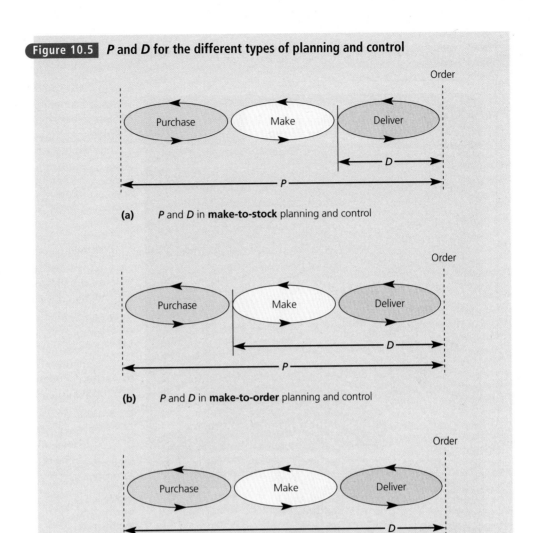

(a) P and D in **make-to-stock** planning and control

(b) P and D in **make-to-order** planning and control

(c) P and D in **resource-to-order** planning and control

and demand cannot be forecast perfectly. With exact or close to exact forecasts, risk would be non-existent or very low, no matter how much bigger P was than D. Expressed another way: when P and D are equal, no matter how inaccurate the forecasts are, speculation is eliminated because everything is made to a firm order (although bad forecasting will lead to other problems). Reducing the P:D ratio becomes, in effect, a way of taking some of the risk out of operations planning and control.

Figure 10.6 **P and D in make-to-stock, assemble-to-order planning and control**

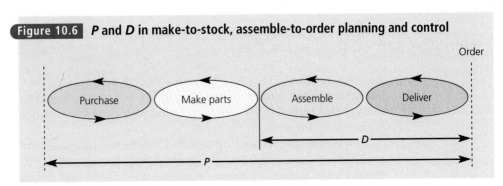

Photo courtesy of Hewlett-Packard and Publicis

In this advertisement for Hewlett-Packard computers, an analogy is made between the way we ask for variations on standard products when we buy a meal (in this case a BLT – bacon, lettuce and tomato sandwich) and the way we cannot always do the same for more complex products.

Questions

1 Why is this type of customization important for competitiveness?

2 Why does offering customers product variety in products such as motor cars and computers create problems for the operation which makes them?

3 What do you think H-P might have done to help it overcome the problems posed by product variety?

Planning and control activities

Planning and control requires the reconciliation of supply and demand in terms of volumes, timing and quality. In this chapter we will focus on volume and timing because most of this part of the book is concerned with these issues. Chapter 17 will deal with quality planning and control.

To reconcile volume and timing, four overlapping activities are performed: loading, sequencing, scheduling, and monitoring and control (*see* Fig. 10.7). Some caution is needed when using these terms. Different organizations may use them in different ways,

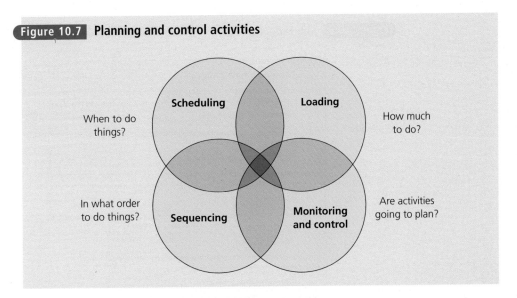

Figure 10.7 Planning and control activities

Scheduling — When to do things?

Loading — How much to do?

Sequencing — In what order to do things?

Monitoring and control — Are activities going to plan?

and even textbooks in the area may adopt different definitions. For example, some authorities term what we have called planning and control as 'operations scheduling'. Ultimately, though, the terminology of planning and control, although confusing, is less important than understanding the basic ideas described in the remainder of this chapter.

Loading

Loading is the amount of work that is allocated to a work centre. For example, a machine on the shop floor of a manufacturing business is available, in theory, 168 hours a week. However, this does not necessarily mean that 168 hours of work can be loaded onto that machine. Figure 10.8 shows what erodes this available time. For some periods the machine cannot be worked; for example, it may not be available on statutory holidays and weekends. Therefore, the load put onto the machine must take this into account. Of the time that the machine is available for work, some tasks other than producing output must be performed, which further reduces available time. For example, time may be lost while changing over from making one component to another. In addition, the machine may need cleaning between operations before another can be started. These lost times must also be taken into account when a plan is formed of how much work can be loaded onto the machine. If the machine breaks down, it will not be available. If there is machine reliability data available, this must also be taken into account. There are two main approaches to loading operations – finite and infinite loading.

Finite loading

Finite loading is an approach which only allocates work to a work centre (a person, a machine, or perhaps a group of people or machines) up to a set limit. This limit is the estimate of capacity for the work centre (based on the times available for loading). Work over and above this capacity is not accepted. Figure 10.9 shows that the load on the work centre is not allowed to exceed the capacity limit. Finite loading is particularly relevant for operations where:

- *it is possible to limit the load* – for example, it is possible to run an appointment system for a general medical practice or a hairdresser;
- *it is necessary to limit the load* – for example, for safety reasons only a finite number of people and weight of luggage are allowed on aircraft;
- *the cost of limiting the load is not prohibitive* – for example, the cost of maintaining a finite order book at a specialist sports car manufacturer does not adversely affect demand, and may even enhance it.

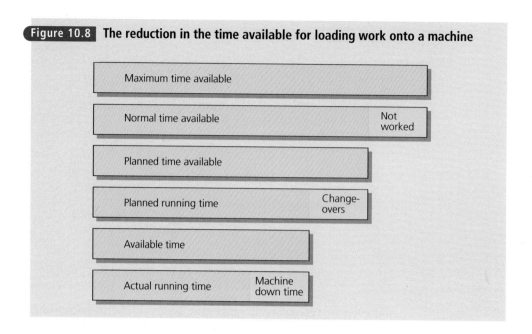

Figure 10.8 The reduction in the time available for loading work onto a machine

Maximum time available

Normal time available | Not worked

Planned time available

Planned running time | Change-overs

Available time

Actual running time | Machine down time

Infinite loading

Infinite loading is an approach to loading work which does not limit accepting work, but instead tries to cope with it. Figure 10.10 illustrates a loading pattern where capacity constraints have not been used to limit loading. Infinite loading is relevant for operations where:

- *it is not possible to limit the load* – for example, an accident and emergency department in a hospital should not turn away arrivals needing attention;
- *it is not necessary to limit the load* – for example, fast-food outlets are designed to flex capacity up and down to cope with varying arrival rates of customers. During busy periods, customers accept that they must queue for some time before being served. Unless this is extreme, the customers might not go elsewhere;
- *the cost of limiting the load is prohibitive* – for example, if a retail bank turned away customers at the door because a set amount were inside, customers would feel less than happy with the service.

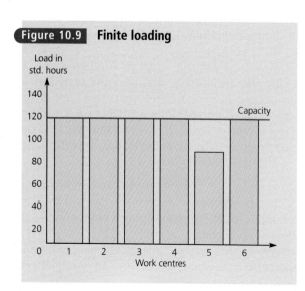

Figure 10.9 Finite loading

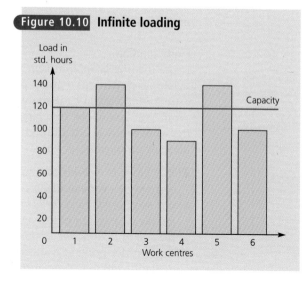

Figure 10.10 Infinite loading

In complex planning and control activities where there are multiple stages, each with different capacities and with a varying mix arriving at the facilities, such as a machine shop in an engineering company, the constraints imposed by finite loading make loading calculations complex and not worth the considerable computational power which would be needed.

● Sequencing

Whether the approach to loading is finite or infinite, when work arrives, decisions must be taken on the order in which the work will be tackled. This activity is termed sequencing.

The priorities given to work in an operation are often determined by some predefined set of rules. Some of these sequencing rules are relatively complex. They require several types of information but can be useful when sequencing jobs through a complex arrangement of work centres. Others are more straightforward. Some of these are summarized below.

Physical constraints

The physical nature of the materials being processed may determine the priority of work. For example, in an operation using paints or dyes, lighter shades will be sequenced before darker shades. On completion of each batch, the colour is slightly darkened for the next batch. This is because darkness of colour can only be added to and not removed from the colour mix. Similarly, the physical nature of the equipment used may determine sequence. For example, in the paper industry, the cutting equipment is set to the width of paper required. It is easier and faster to move the cutting equipment to an adjacent size (up or down) than it is to reset the machine to a very different size.

Sometimes the mix of work arriving at a part of an operation may determine the priority given to jobs. For example, when fabric is cut to a required size and shape in garment manufacture, the surplus fabric would be wasted if not used for another product. Therefore, jobs that physically fit together may be scheduled together to reduce waste.

Customer priority

Operations will sometimes allow an important or aggrieved customer, or item, to be 'processed' prior to others, irrespective of the order of arrival of the customer or item. This approach is typically used by operations whose customer base is skewed, containing a mass of small customers and a few large, very important customers. Some banks, for example, give priority to important customers. Similarly, in hotels, complaining customers will be treated as a priority because their complaint may have an adverse effect on the perceptions of other customers. More seriously, the emergency services often have to use their judgement in prioritizing the urgency of requests for service. For example, Figure 10.11 shows the priority system used by a police force. Here the operators receiving emergency and other calls are trained to grade the calls into one of five categories. The response by the police is then organized to match the level of priority. The triage system in hospitals operates in a similar way (*see* box).

Sequencing work by customer priority may mean that 'large volume' customers receive a very high level of service, but that service to many other customers is eroded. This may lower the average performance of the operation if existing work flows are disrupted for important customers. It can also erode the quality and productivity of the operation, making it less efficient overall.

Figure 10.11 The call grading system for a police force

NORTHAMPTONSHIRE POLICE
INCIDENT GRADING
From 1st April 2000

Grade One Incidents require immediate deployment and are subject to current KPI response targets.

Grade One Incidents are where: a) there is a threat to life b) crime is in progress or offender is still in the vicinity c) traffic accidents involving personal injury or where position of vehicles is likely to cause serious danger to other road users.

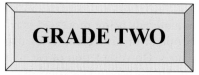

Grade Two Incidents require immediate allocation. Responding resources will attend immediately or as soon as practicable.

Grade Two Incidents are incidents that do not fit the criteria for Grade One, but the individual circumstances of the incident, or the vulnerable nature of the victim/caller require prompt police attendance to resolve the situation, preserve evidence or reassure the caller/victim.

Grade Two Incidents would not usually warrant the use of blue lights and sirens.

Grade Three Incidents do not require an immediate attendance and include all incidents where deployment can be delayed for more than a few minutes and those that can be allocated by way of appointment.

It is vitally important that the caller is fully aware of the grade allocated to the incident, and where possible given an estimated time for police attendance at the incident.

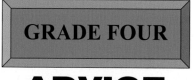

Grade Four Incidents require no deployment but are recorded for the information of an individual officer, sector, or for general information.

(Courtesy of Northamptonshire Police)

Due date (DD)

Prioritizing by due date means that work is sequenced according to when it is 'due' for delivery, irrespective of the size of each job or the importance of each customer. For example, a support service in an office block, such as a reprographic unit, will often ask when photocopies are required, and then sequence the work according to that due date. Due date sequencing usually improves the delivery reliability of an operation and improves average delivery speed. However, it may not provide optimal productivity, as a more efficient sequencing of work may reduce total costs. However, it can be flexible when new, urgent work arrives at the work centre.

One of the hospital environments that is most difficult to schedule is the Accident and Emergency department, where patients arrive at random, without any prior warning, throughout the day. It is up to the hospital's reception and the medical staff to devise very rapidly a schedule which meets most of the necessary criteria. In particular, patients who arrive having had very serious accidents, or presenting symptoms of a serious illness, need to be attended to urgently. Therefore, the hospital will schedule these cases first. Less urgent cases – perhaps patients who are in some discomfort, but whose injuries or illnesses are not life-threatening – will have to wait until the urgent cases are treated. Routine non-urgent cases will have the lowest priority of all. In many circumstances, these patients will have to wait for the longest time, which may be many hours, especially if the hospital is busy. Sometimes these non-urgent cases may even be turned away if the hospital is too busy with more important cases.

In situations where hospitals expect sudden influxes of patients, they have developed what is known as a triage system, whereby medical staff hurriedly sort through the patients who have arrived to determine which category of urgency each patient fits into. In this way a suitable schedule for the various treatments can be devised in a short period of time.

Questions

1 Why do you think that the triage system is effective in controlling operations in Accident and Emergency departments?

2 Are there any dangers in this approach?

Last in first out (LIFO)

Last in first out (LIFO) is a method of sequencing usually selected for practical reasons. For example, unloading an elevator is more convenient on a LIFO basis, as there is only one entrance and exit. However, it is not an equitable approach. Patients at hospital clinics may be infuriated if they see medical records added to a pile in the sequence of arriving patients, which means that, if the doctor takes the records from the top of the pile first, patients are served in reverse order of when they arrived. LIFO has a very adverse effect on delivery speed and reliability. The sequence is not determined for reasons of quality, flexibility or cost, and therefore none of these performance objectives is well served by this method.

First in first out (FIFO)

Some operations serve customers in exactly the sequence they arrive in, on a first in first out (FIFO) basis. This rule is also sometimes called 'first come, first served' (FCFS). For example, the UK passport offices receive post and put it in a pile according to the

Photo courtesy of Coats Thread

Sometimes sequencing is dictated by the technical characteristics of the process. For example, this thread is being dyed in batches which are separated from light colours to dark to minimize the risk of contamination between batches

day on which it arrived. They work through the post, opening it in sequence, then processing the passport applications as they come to them. Queues in theme parks may be designed so that one long queue snakes around the lobby area until the row of counters is reached. When customers reach the front of the queue, they are served at the next free counter.

In high-contact operations, arrival time may be viewed by customers in the system as a fair way of sequencing, thereby minimizing customer complaints and enhancing service performance. However, because there is no consideration of urgency or due date, some customers' needs may not be served as well as others. Delivery speed and delivery reliability, therefore, may not be at their highest. It is also difficult to be flexible in a system where this prioritization is visible to customers. If the 'queue' is not physically visible, it may be more possible to exercise some flexibility, allowing some work to queue-jump without other customers being aware of it happening.

Longest operation time first (LOT)

Under certain circumstances, operations may feel obliged to sequence their longest jobs first. This has the advantage of occupying the work centres within the operation for long periods. Relatively small jobs progressing through an operation will take up time at each work centre which will need to change over from one job to the next. Where staff are under some incentive to keep utilization high, such a sequencing rule might seem particularly attractive. However, although utilization may be high (and therefore cost relatively low), this rule does not take into account delivery speed, delivery reliability or flexibility. Indeed, it may work directly against these performance objectives.

Shortest operation time first (SOT)

Most operations at some stage become cash constrained. In these situations, the sequencing rules may be adjusted to tackle short jobs first. These jobs can then be invoiced and payment received to ease cash-flow problems. Larger jobs that take more time will not enable the business to invoice as quickly. This has an effect of improving delivery performance, if the unit of measurement of delivery is jobs. However, it may adversely affect total productivity and can damage service to larger customers.

Judging sequencing rules

All five performance objectives, or some variant of them, could be used to judge the effectiveness of sequencing rules. However, the objectives of dependability, speed and cost are particularly important. So, for example, the following performance objectives are often used:

- meeting 'due date' promised to customer (dependability);
- minimizing the time the job spends in the process, also known as 'flow time' (speed);
- minimizing work-in-progress inventory (an element of cost);
- minimizing idle time of work centres (another element of cost).

Worked example   Steve Smith is a website designer in a business school. Returning from his annual two-day vacation (he finished all outstanding jobs before he left), five design jobs are given to him upon arrival at work. He gives them the codes A to E. Steven has to decide in which sequence to undertake the jobs. He wants both to minimize the average time the jobs are tied up in his office and, if possible, to meet the deadlines (delivery times) allocated to each job.

His first thought is to do the jobs in the order they were given to him, i.e. first in first out (FIFO):

Sequencing rule – first in first out (FIFO)

Sequence of jobs	Process time (days)	Start time	Finish time	Due date	Lateness (days)
A	5	0	5	6	0
B	3	5	8	5	3
C	6	8	14	8	6
D	2	14	16	7	9
E	1	16	17	3	14
	Total time in process	60		Total lateness	32
	Average time in process (total/5)	12		Average lateness (total/5)	6.4

Alarmed by the average lateness, he tries the due date (DD) rule:

Sequencing rule – due date (DD)

Sequence of jobs	Process time (days)	Start time	Finish time	Due date	Lateness (days)
E	1	0	1	3	0
B	3	1	4	5	0
A	5	4	9	6	3
D	2	9	11	7	4
C	6	11	17	8	9
	Total time in process	42		Total lateness	16
	Average time in process (total/5)	8.4		Average lateness (total/5)	3.2

Better! But Steve tries out the shortest operation time (SOT) rule:

Sequencing rule – shortest operation time (SOT)

Sequence of jobs	Process time (days)	Start time	Finish time	Due date	Lateness (days)
E	1	0	1	3	0
D	2	1	3	7	0
B	3	3	6	5	1
A	5	6	11	6	5
C	6	11	17	8	9
	Total time in process	38		Total lateness	16
	Average time in process (total/5)	7.6		Average lateness (total/5)	3.2

This gives the same degree of average lateness but with a lower average time in the process. Steve decides to use the SOT rule.

Comparing the results from the three sequencing rules described in the worked example together with the two other sequencing rules described earlier and applied to the same problem, gives the results summarized in Table 10.1.

In this case the shortest operation time (SOT) rule resulted in both the best average time in process and the best (or least bad) in terms of average lateness. Although different rules will perform differently depending on the circumstances of the sequencing problem, in practice the SOT rule generally performs well.

Table 10.1 Comparison of five sequencing decision rules

Rule	Average time in process (days)	Average lateness (days)
FIFO	12	6.4
DD	8.4	3.2
SOT	7.6	3.2
LIFO	8.4	3.8
LOT	12.8	7.4

Johnson's Rule[5]

Johnson's Rule applies to the sequencing of *n* jobs through two work centres. Figure 10.12 illustrates its use. In this case, a printer has to print and bind six jobs. The times for processing each job through the first (printing) and second (binding) work centres are shown in the figure. The rule is simple. First look for the smallest processing time. If that time is associated with the first work centre (printing in this case) then schedule that job first, or as near first as possible. If the next smallest time is associated with the second work centre then sequence that job last or as near last as possible. Once a job has been sequenced, delete it from the list. Carry on allocating jobs until the list is complete. In this particular case, the smallest processing time is 35 minutes for printing job B. Because this is at the first process (printing), job B is assigned first position in the schedule. The next smallest processing time is 40 minutes for binding (job D). Because this is at the second process (binding), it is sequenced last. The next lowest processing time, after jobs B and D have been struck off the list, is 46 minutes for binding job A. Because this is at the second work centre, it is sequenced as near last as possible, which in this case is fifth. This process continues until all the jobs have been sequenced. It results in a schedule for the two processes which is also shown in Figure 10.12.

Figure 10.12 **The application of Johnson's Rule for scheduling *n* jobs through two work centres**

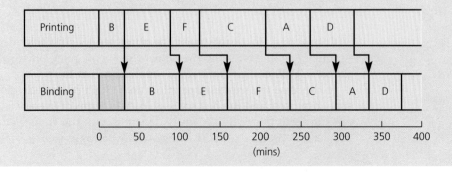

● Scheduling

Having determined the sequence that work is to be tackled in, some operations require a detailed timetable showing at what time or date jobs should start and when they should end – this is a schedule. Schedules are familiar statements of volume and timing in many consumer environments. For example, a bus schedule shows that more buses are put on routes at more frequent intervals during rush-hour periods. The bus schedule shows the time each bus is due to arrive at each stage of the route. Schedules of work are used in operations where some planning is required to ensure that customer demand is met. Other operations, such as rapid-response service operations where customers arrive in an unplanned way, cannot schedule the operation in a short-term sense. They can only respond at the time demand is placed upon them.

The complexity of scheduling[6]

The scheduling activity is one of the most complex tasks in operations management. First, schedulers must deal with several different types of resource simultaneously. Machines will have different capabilities and capacities; staff will have different skills. More importantly, the number of possible schedules increases rapidly as the number of activities and processes increases. For example, suppose one machine has five different jobs to process. Any of the five jobs could be processed first and, following that, any one of the remaining four jobs, and so on. This means that there are:

$5 \times 4 \times 3 \times 2 = 120$ different schedules possible

More generally, for n jobs there are $n!$ (factorial n) different ways of scheduling the jobs through a single process.

We can now consider what impact there would be if, in the same situation, there was more than one type of machine. If we were trying to minimize the number of setups on two machines, there is no reason why the sequence on machine 1 would be the same as the sequence on machine 2. If we consider the two sequencing tasks to be independent of each other, for two machines there would be

$120 \times 120 = 14\,400$ possible schedules of the two machines and five jobs.

A general formula can be devised to calculate the number of possible schedules in any given situation, as follows:

Number of possible schedules = $(n!)m$

where n is the number of jobs and m is the number of machines.

If we relate this to a real situation, where there may be 100 jobs going through 30 machines, in a route which takes each individual job through five different machines, then we can see that the scheduling task rapidly becomes very complicated. Within this vast number of schedules there are many acceptable options as to which are appropriate routes and sequences for any set of jobs. Even where a product is manufactured repeatedly, there may be a number of different routes which that product could take. However, most of the schedules that are possible in theory will not be workable in practice and these can be rapidly eliminated.

The scheduling task has to be repeated on a very frequent basis to allow for market variations and product mix changes. Remember that even minor product mix changes may cause the capacity constraints within the facility to change very dramatically over a comparatively short period of time; hence bottleneck operations may move about the factory quite quickly.

Forward and backward scheduling

Forward scheduling involves starting work as soon as it arrives. Backward scheduling involves starting jobs at the last possible moment to prevent them from being late. For example, assume that it takes six hours for a contract laundry to wash, dry and press a batch of overalls. If the work is collected at 8.00 am and is due to be picked up at 4.00 pm, there are more than six hours available to do it. Table 10.2 shows the different start times of each job, depending on whether they are forward or backward scheduled.

Table 10.2 The effects of forward and backward scheduling

Task	Duration	Start time (backwards)	Start time (forwards)
Press	1 hour	3.00 pm	1.00 pm
Dry	2 hours	1.00 pm	11.00 am
Wash	3 hours	10.00 am	8.00 am

The choice of backward or forward scheduling depends largely upon the circumstances. Table 10.3 lists some advantages and disadvantages of the two approaches. In theory, both materials requirements planning (MRP, *see* Chapter 14) and just-in-time planning (JIT, *see* Chapter 15) use backward scheduling, only starting work when it is required. In practice, however, users of MRP have tended to allow too long for each task to be completed, and therefore each task is not started at the latest possible time. In comparison, JIT is started, as the name suggests, just in time.

Table 10.3 Advantages of forward and backward scheduling

Advantages of forward scheduling	Advantages of backward scheduling
High labour utilization – workers always start work to keep busy	Lower material costs – materials are not used until they have to be, therefore delaying added value until the last moment
Flexible – the time slack in the system allows unexpected work to be loaded	Less exposed to risk in case of schedule change by the customer
	Tends to focus the operation on customer due dates

Gantt charts

The most common method of scheduling is by use of the Gantt chart. This is a simple device which represents time as a bar, or channel, on a chart. Often the charts themselves are made up of long plastic channels into which coloured pieces of paper can be slotted to indicate what is happening with a job or a work centre. The start and finish times for activities can be indicated on the chart and sometimes the actual progress of the job is also indicated. Figures 10.13 and 10.14 illustrate two Gantt charts for a small specialist furniture manufacturer. Figure 10.13 is a job progress Gantt chart, indicating when each job is scheduled to start and finish as well as the degree of completion of the job. Also indicated on the chart is the current time. In this case the table has been completed already, even though it was not scheduled to be completed until the end of the next day. On the other hand, the shelves are behind schedule. The manufacturer of the kitchen units is not scheduled to start for another day.

Figure 10.14 illustrates another Gantt chart which may be used by this company. This time it indicates the activities which are taking place at each work centre. Here we can see that the shelves seem to be held up in the wood preparation work centre.

The advantages of Gantt charts are that they provide a simple visual representation both of what should be happening and of what actually is happening in the operation. Furthermore, they can be used to 'test out' alternative schedules. Especially when using moveable pieces of paper, it is a simple task to represent alternative schedules (even if it

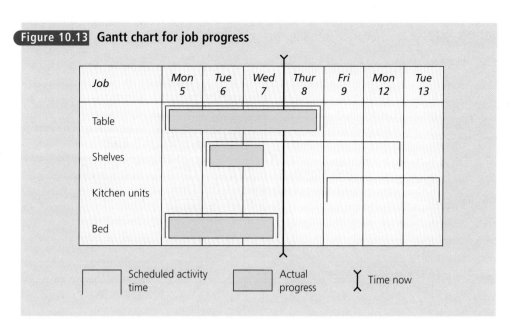

Figure 10.13 Gantt chart for job progress

Figure 10.14 Gantt chart for work centres

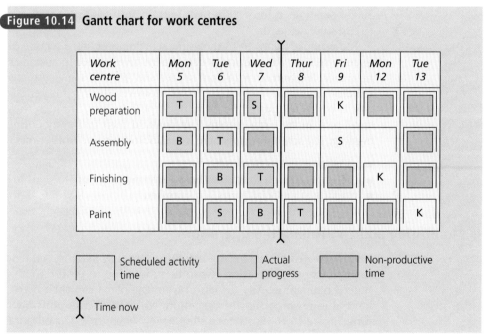

is a far from simple task to find a schedule which fits all the resources satisfactorily). Of course, the Gantt chart is in no way an optimizing tool. It merely facilitates the development of alternative schedules by communicating them effectively.

Scheduling work patterns

Where the dominant resource in an operation is its staff, then the schedule of work times effectively determines the capacity of the operation itself. The main task of scheduling, therefore, is to make sure that sufficient numbers of people are working at any point in time to provide a capacity appropriate for the level of demand at that point in time. Operations such as postal delivery services, telephone operators, policing services, holiday couriers, shop workers and hospital staff will all need to schedule the working hours of their staff with demand in mind. This is a direct consequence of these operations having relatively high customer contact (we introduced this idea in Chapter 1).

Figure 10.15 Shift scheduling in a home-banking enquiry service

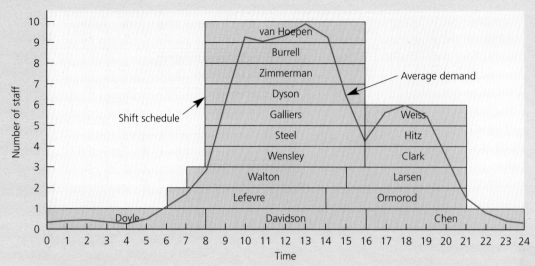

Such operations cannot store their outputs in inventories and so must respond directly to customer demand.

For example, Figure 10.15 shows the scheduling of shifts for one part of a home-banking enquiry service. This particular department gives advice to customers on home loans and insurance. It advertises a 24-hour service and, indeed, some customers do make use of the enquiry service throughout the night. However, during this period, demand is relatively low. It builds up during the morning to peak halfway through the day. There is another small peak in the early evening, but demand then falls away during the later part of the evening. The scheduling task here is to allocate start and finish times to staff such that:

● capacity matches demand;
● the length of each shift is neither excessively long nor too short to be attractive to staff;
● working at unsocial hours is minimized.

● Monitoring and controlling the operation

Having created a plan for the operation through loading, sequencing and scheduling, each part of the operation has to be monitored to ensure that planned activities are indeed happening. Any deviation from the plans can then be rectified through some kind of intervention in the operation, which itself will probably involve some replanning. Figure 10.16 illustrates a simple view of control. The output from a work centre is monitored and compared with the plan which indicates what the work centre is supposed to be doing. Deviations from this plan are taken into account through a replanning activity and the necessary interventions made to the work centre which will (hopefully) ensure that the new plan is carried out. Eventually, however, some further deviation from planned activity will be detected and the cycle is repeated.

Push and pull control

One element of control, then, is periodic intervention into the activities of the operation. An important decision is how this intervention takes place. The key distinction is between intervention signals which *push* work through the processes within the operation and those which *pull* work only when it is required. In a push system of control, activities are scheduled by means of a central system and completed in line with central instructions, such as an MRP system (*see* Chapter 14). Each work centre pushes out work without considering whether the succeeding work centre can make use of it. Work centres

Figure 10.16 **A simple model of control**

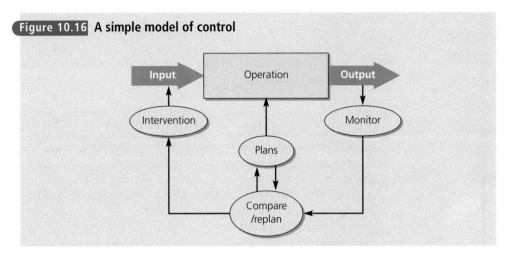

are coordinated by means of the central operations planning and control system. In practice, however, there are many reasons why actual conditions differ from those planned. As a consequence, idle time, inventory and queues often characterize push systems.

In a pull system of control, the pace and specification of what is done are set by the 'customer' workstation, which 'pulls' work from the preceding (supplier) workstation. The customer acts as the only 'trigger' for movement. If a request is not passed back from the customer to the supplier, the supplier cannot produce anything or move any materials. A request from a customer not only triggers production at the supplying stage, but also prompts the supplying stage to request a further delivery from its own suppliers. In this way, demand is transmitted back through the stages from the original point of demand by the original customer.

The inventory consequences of push and pull

Understanding the differing principles of push and pull is important because they have different effects in terms of their propensities to accumulate inventory in the operation. Pull systems are far less likely to result in inventory build-up and are therefore favoured by JIT operations (*see* Chapter 15). To understand why this is so, consider an analogy: the 'gravity' analogy is illustrated in Figure 10.17. Here a push system is represented by an operation, each stage of which is on a lower level than the previous stage. When

Figure 10.17 **Push versus pull: the gravity analogy**

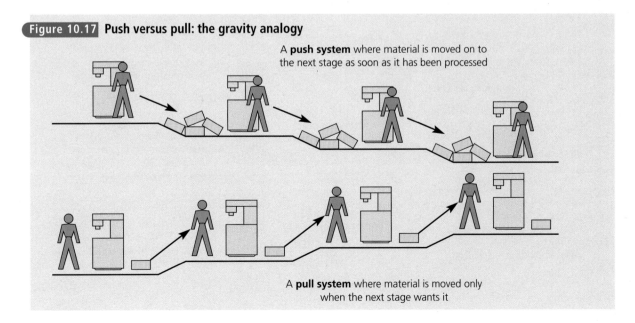

A **push system** where material is moved on to the next stage as soon as it has been processed

A **pull system** where material is moved only when the next stage wants it

parts are processed by each stage, it pushes them down the slope to the next stage. Any delay or problem at that stage will result in the parts accumulating as inventory. In the pull system, parts cannot naturally flow uphill, so they can only progress if the next stage along deliberately pulls them forward. Under these circumstances, inventory cannot accumulate as easily.

● CRITICAL COMMENTARY

This way of looking at control is very much a simplification of a far more messy reality. It is based on a model used to understand mechanical systems such as car engines. But anyone who has worked in real organizations knows that they are not machines. They are social systems, full of complex and ambiguous interactions. Simple models such as these assume that operations objectives are always clear and agreed, yet organizations are political entities where different and often conflicting objectives compete. Local government operations, for example, are overtly political. Furthermore, the outputs from operations are not always easily measured. A university may be able to measure the number and qualifications of its students, for example, but it cannot measure the full impact of its education on their future happiness. Also, even if it is possible to work out an appropriate intervention to bring an operation back into 'control' , most operations cannot perfectly predict what effect the intervention will have. Even the largest of burger bar chains does not know *exactly* how a new shift allocation system will affect performance. Also, some operations never do the same thing more than once anyway. Most of the work done by construction operations are one-offs. If every output is different, how can 'controllers' ever know what is supposed to happen? Their plans themselves are mere speculation.

Figure 10.18 **How easy is an operation to control?**

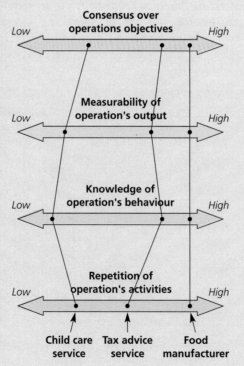

Control in some operations can mean split second decisions, as in funnelling incoming aircraft by air control staff into landing slots. The case exercise at the end of the chapter highlights some of the issues in this control task

The degree of difficulty in controlling operations

The simple monitoring control model in Figure 10.18 helps us to understand the basic functions of the monitoring and control activity. But, as the critical commentary box says, it is a simplification. Some simple technology-dominated processes may approximate to it, but many other operations do not. In fact, the specific criticisms cited in the critical commentary box provide a useful set of questions which can be used to assess the degree of difficulty associated with control of any operation:[7]

- Is there consensus over what the operation's objectives should be?
- How well can the output from the operation be measured?
- Are the effects of interventions into the operation predictable?
- Are the operation's activities largely repetitive?

Figure 10.18 illustrates how these four questions can form dimensions of 'controllability'. It shows three different operations. The food processing operation is relatively straightforward to control, while the child care service is particularly difficult. The tax advice service is somewhere in between.

The volume–variety effect on planning and control

In Chapter 4 we identified that many of the detailed design decisions in operations management were significantly affected by the volume–variety position of an operation. This is also true of the planning and control activities. Operations which produce a high variety of products or services in relatively low volume will clearly have customers who require a different set of factors and use processes which have a different set of needs from those operations which create standardized products or services in high volume (*see* Table 10.4).

Table 10.4 The volume–variety effects on planning and control

Volume	Variety	Customer responsiveness	Planning horizon	Major planning decision	Control decisions	Robustness
Low ↓ High	High ↓ Low	Slow ↓ Fast	Short ↓ Long	Timing ↓ Volume	Detailed ↓ Aggregated	High ↓ Low

Again, let us take the two operations that were discussed in Chapter 4, which occupy the two extremes of the volume–variety spectrum – an architects' practice and an electricity utility. The architects' high variety means that their services will have little or no standardization. This means that they cannot produce their designs in advance of customers requesting them. Because of this, the time it will take to respond to customers' requests will be relatively slow. Indeed, their customers will understand this and expect to be consulted extensively as to their needs. Thus the *P:D* ratio of the operation will be 1 or very close to 1. The details and requirements of each job will emerge only as each individual building is designed to the client's requirements. This means that planning occurs on a relatively short-term basis. The architects are unlikely to be able to plan several years ahead because they do not know what jobs they will be doing at that time. The individual decisions which are taken in the planning process will usually concern the timing of activities and events – for example, when a design is to be delivered, when building should start, when each individual architect will be needed to work on the design, and so on. Most of the control decisions will be at a relatively detailed level. A small delay in calculating one part of the design could have very significant implications in many other parts of the job. In general, the planning and control of the operation cannot be totally routinized; rather, it will need managing on an individual project basis. Finally, the robustness of the operation (that is, its vulnerability to serious disruption if one part of the operation breaks down) will be relatively high. There are probably plenty of other things to get on with if an architect is prevented from progressing one part of the job.

The electricity utility, on the other hand, will exhibit very different planning and control characteristics. Volume is high, production is continuous, and variety is virtually non-existent. Customers expect an extremely fast response to their request for the product. In effect, they expect instant 'delivery' whenever they plug in an appliance. The planning horizon in electricity generation can be very long. Major decisions regarding the capacity of power stations are made many years in advance. Even the fluctuations in demand over a typical day can be forecast to a certain extent in advance. Popular television programmes can affect minute-by-minute demand and these are scheduled weeks or months ahead. The weather, which also affects demand, is less prone to being forecast, but can to some extent be predicted. The individual planning decisions made by the electricity utility will centre not around the timing of output, but rather around the volume of output. Control decisions will not be concerned with the detailed intricacies of the operation's output, because the product is more or less homogeneous. Rather, control will concern aggregated measures of output such as the total kilowatts of electricity generated. Finally, the robustness of the operation is very low, insomuch as, if the generator fails, the operation's capability of supplying electricity from that part of the operation also fails (*see* Table 10.4).

The WIZARD system at Avis

It is possible to rent cars at almost every major airport and city centre in the world, and there is invariably intense competition to attract and keep customers. Since the hire companies all offer similar ranges of relatively new vehicles, and the reliability of these cars is taken for granted by most customers, competition is generally on service and/or price. The most critical service factor is the availability of the desired category (size and specification) of car, and the speed with which all the hire contract paperwork can be completed, so that the customer is not unnecessarily delayed. This depends on the effectiveness of the hire company's planning and control system. One of the most important Avis sites in Belgium is the operation at Brussels National Airport at Zaventem, which deals predominantly with business customers, and hires out up to 200 cars on a busy day. Avis's advertisement, targeted at the business market, emphasizes its ability to process customers quickly and efficiently. The objective is to complete the transaction in less than two minutes and this is facilitated by Avis's well-developed computer system, known as WIZARD, which handles all reservations, preparation of hire contracts at the service desks, inventory management and invoicing systems. WIZARD is a globally integrated system, with over 15 000 terminals in Avis branches worldwide, allowing international reservations to be made with accuracy and certainty, and helping to maximize the utilization of vehicles throughout the network.

Regular customer surveys and analyses of actual demand patterns are carried out to determine the customers' preferences in terms of type and category of vehicles, providing a guide to the Belgian fleet composition, which is managed from the central 'clearing house' at Machelen. Because each of the Belgian branch offices has access to a pool of cars held at Machelen, their local buffer stock requirements can be minimized. The requirements for the movement of car inventory between branches and between countries is centralized in this way, allowing the branches to concentrate on the task of providing good customer service. Each regular business customer has a unique reference number in WIZARD, allowing reservations to be made and rental contracts to be completed quickly, with only three pieces of information: the customer's number, the type of car required, and the duration of the hire. This type of transaction is usually completed in under two minutes, after which the customer goes directly to the car park and collects the car.

Questions

1 What do you see as the main planning and control tasks of the Wizard system?

2 How would you evaluate the effectiveness of the planning and control activity at Avis?

Summary answers to key questions

What is planning and control?

● Planning and control is the reconciliation of the potential of the operation to supply products and services, and the demands of its customers on the operation. It is the set of day-to-day activities that run the operation on an ongoing basis.

What is the difference between planning and control?

● A plan is a formalization of what is intended to happen at some time in the future. Control is the process of coping with changes to the plan and the operation to which it relates.

- Although planning and control are theoretically separable, they are usually treated together.

- The balance between planning and control changes over time. Planning dominates in the long term and is usually done on an aggregated basis. At the other extreme, in the short term, control usually operates within the resource constraints of the operation but makes interventions into the operation in order to cope with short-term changes in circumstances.

How does the nature of demand affect planning and control?

- The degree of uncertainty in demand affects the balance between planning and control. The greater the uncertainty, the more difficult it is to plan, and greater emphasis must be placed on control.

- This idea of uncertainty is linked with the concepts of dependent and independent demand. Dependent demand is relatively predictable because it is dependent on some known factor. Independent demand is less predictable because it depends on the chances of the market or customer behaviour.

- The different ways of responding to demand can be characterized by differences in the *P:D* ratio of the operation. The *P:D* ratio is the ratio of total throughput time of goods or services to demand time.

What is involved in planning and control?

- In planning and controlling the volume and timing of activity in operations, four distinct activities are necessary:
  - loading, which dictates the amount of work that is allocated to each part of the operation;
  - sequencing, which decides the order in which work is tackled within the operation;
  - scheduling, which determines the detailed timetable of activities and when activities are started and finished;
  - monitoring and control, which involve detecting what is happening in the operation, replanning if necessary, and intervening in order to impose new plans. Two important types are 'pull' and 'push' control. Pull control is a system whereby demand is triggered by requests from a work centre's (internal) customer. Push control is a centralized system whereby control (and sometimes planning) decisions are issued to work centres which are then required to perform the task and supply the next workstation. In manufacturing, 'pull' schedules generally have far lower inventory levels than 'push' schedules.

- The ease with which control can be maintained varies between operations.

- The volume–variety position of an operation has an effect on the nature of its planning and control. Customer responsiveness, the planning horizon, the major planning decisions, the control decision and the robustness of planning and control are especially affected by volume and variety.

CASE EXERCISE

Two multiplex cinemas: Kinepolis Cinema in Brussels, Belgium, and UCI Cinema in Solihull, Birmingham, UK

Kinepolis Cinema in Brussels, Belgium

Kinepolis is thought to be the largest cinema complex in the world, with 28 screens, a total of 8000 seats, and four showings of each film every day. It dominates the cinema market in the area, attracting around a 60 per cent share of attendances. One of the reasons for its success is that it is equipped with a full range of the latest projection technology (large screens, THX sound, Dolby stereo, Cinema Digital sound and Imax). Kinepolis is located on the outskirts of Brussels in Bruparck next to the Heizel Stadium and the famous Atomium, a

journey of about 15 minutes by car or by the metro public transport system. Although the majority of customers come by car, there is usually ample parking space either in the cinema's own car park or at the adjacent Bruparck facilities.

All the film performances are scheduled to start at the same times every day: 4 pm, 6 pm, 8 pm and 10.30 pm. Since the majority of the visitors arrive within 30 minutes of the start of the film, during busy periods queues can often build up considerably at the 18 ticket desks: 10 in the large, airport-style foyer and eight at the rear entrance. Above the desks there are TV monitors which display the menu of the films, classification and the remaining availability of seats for each. It takes three monitors to provide the whole menu!

Each desk has a networked computer terminal and a ticket printer. For each customer, a screen code is first entered to identify and confirm seat availability of the requested film. Then the number of seats required is entered, and the tickets are printed, but these do not allocate specific seat positions. The operator then takes payment by cash or credit card and issues the tickets. These operations take an average of 19.5 seconds, and a further 5 seconds is needed for the next customer to move forward and start the cycle again. In this way, the peak capacity is approximately 150 transactions per desk per hour – 2700 per hour using all the desks. Since an average transaction involves the sale of approximately 1.7 tickets, the ticketing process can satisfy an input of 4500 customers per hour, which is sufficient for most normal levels of demand; queuing times rarely exceed five minutes. The ticketing capacity would clearly be under strain if demand approached the full seating capacity of the centre.

UCI Cinema in Solihull, Birmingham, UK

This UCI (United Cinemas International) cinema has been open since 1989 and has eight screens. It was built on a premium site, on a business park close to the busy motorway network at the very centre of England. Almost all the customers come by car, and go to the cinema's own private car park, where there are usually adequate spaces; but there is occasionally considerable congestion at the entry/exit just before the start of popular films.

The cinema incorporates many 'state-of-the-art' features, including the high-quality THX sound system, fully computerized ticketing and a video games arcade off the main hall. There are two sets of giant TV screens in the entrance hall, giving notice of future attractions. In total the eight screens can seat 1840 people; the sizes (seating) of the screens vary, and thus the cinema management can allocate the more popular films to the larger screens and use the smaller screens for the more minority showings.

The film titles are selected for the cinema by Head Office, but local management has responsibility for the scheduling of the showings on each screen. Contracts from the distributors govern the number of showings each day, but the detailed schedule is at the discretion of the cinema management. The starting times of the eight films at UCI are usually staggered by 10 minutes, with the most popular film in each category (for example, adults only) being scheduled to run first. Because the films are of different durations, and since the manager must try to maximize the utilization of the seating, the scheduling task is complex and critical to the financial performance of the site.

The ticket office staff are continually aware of the remaining capacity of each screen through their terminals. There are up to four ticket desks open at any one time. The target time per overall transaction is 20 seconds; thus the maximum throughput is 12 sales per minute, or 720 per hour. The average number of ticket sales per transaction is 1.8, and therefore the maximum seat sales per hour is 1300 – easily within maximum expected demand levels. All tickets indicate specific seat positions, and these are allocated on a first-come-first-served basis. A central pre-booking facility is now offered by the UCI group, where customers can call a UK freephone number and order their tickets by credit card, for collection at their local cinema. Although there is a small charge for this service, the view is that the convenience will attract more users to purchase their tickets in this way and thus reduce the numbers queueing to pay for tickets on the night.

UCI's mission statement emphasizes the need to provide clean and tidy premises, cheerful staff, adequate food facilities and, above all, a high-quality film and sound presentation. UCI believes that it provides the best cinema experience outside London.

Questions

1 What are the main differences between the two cinemas from the perspectives of the operations managers?

2 What are the advantages and disadvantages of the two different methods of scheduling the films onto the screens? How does each approach affect different types of customers?

3 Group exercise:

(a) Find out the running times and classification of eight popular films. Try to schedule these onto the UCI Solihull screens, taking account of what popularity you might expect at different times. You should allow at least 20 minutes for emptying and cleaning, 10 minutes for admitting the next audience, and 15 minutes for advertising, before the start of the film.

(b) Try to make an appointment to visit your local cinema to meet the manager. Compare the operations with those at Kinepolis and UCI, particularly in terms of scheduling.

Air traffic control: a world-class juggling act

Air traffic controllers have one of the most stressful jobs in the world. They are responsible for the lives of thousands of passengers who fly every day in and out of the world's airports. Over the last 15 years, the number of planes in the sky has doubled, leading to congestion at many airports and putting air traffic controllers under increasing pressure. The controllers battle to maintain 'separation standards' that set the distance between planes as they land and take-off. Sheer volume pushes the air traffic controllers' skills to the limit. Jim Courtney, an air traffic controller at LaGuardia Airport in New York, says: *'There are half a dozen moments of sheer terror in each year when you wish you did something else for a living.'*

New York – the world's busiest airspace

The busiest airspace in the world is above New York. Around 7500 planes arrive and depart each day at New York's three airports, John F. Kennedy, LaGuardia and Newark. The three airports form a triangle around New York and are just 15 miles from each other. This requires careful coordination of traffic patterns, approach and take-off routes, using predetermined invisible corridors in the sky to keep the planes away from each other. If the wind changes, all three airports work together to change the flight paths.

Sophisticated technology fitted to most of the bigger planes creates a safety zone around the aircraft so that when two aircraft get near to each other their computers negotiate which is going to take action to avoid the other and then alerts the pilot who changes course. Smaller aircraft, without radar, rely upon vision and the notion of 'little plane, big sky'.

During its passage into or out of an airport, each plane will pass through the hands of about eight different controllers. The airspace is divided into sectors controlled by different teams of air traffic controllers. Tower controllers at each airport control planes landing and taking off together with ground controllers who manage the movement of the planes on the ground around the airport. The TRACON (Terminal Radar Approach Control) controllers oversee the surrounding airspace. Each New York air traffic controller handles about 100 landings and take-offs an hour, about one every 45 seconds.

TRACON controllers

The 60 TRACON controllers manage different sectors of airspace, with planes being handed over from one controller to the next. Each controller handles about 15 planes at a time, yet they never see them. All they see is a blip on a two-dimensional radar screen, which shows their aircraft type, altitude, speed and destination. The aircraft, however, are in three-dimensional airspace, flying at different altitudes and in various directions. The job of the approach controllers is to funnel planes from different directions into an orderly queue before handing each one over to the tower controllers for landing.

Tower controllers

The tower controllers are responsible for coordinating landing and taking off. Newark is New York's busiest airport. During the early morning rush periods, there can be 40 planes an hour coming into land, with about 60 wanting to take-off. As a result there can be queues of up to 25 planes waiting to depart.

At LaGuardia, there are two runways that cross each other, one used for take-off and the other for landing. At peak times, air traffic controllers have to 'shoot the gap' – to get planes to take off in between the stream of landing aircraft, sometimes less than 60 seconds apart. Allowing planes to start their take-off as other planes are landing, using 'anticipated separation', keeps traffic moving and helps deal with increasing volumes of traffic. At peak times, controllers have to shoot the gap 80 times an hour.

Most airports handle a mixture of large and small planes, and tower controllers need to be able to calculate safe take-off intervals in an instant. They have to take into account aircraft type and capabilities in order to ensure that appropriate separations can be kept. The faster planes need to be given more space in front of them than the slower planes. Wake turbulence – mini-hurricanes which trail downstream of a plane's wing tips – is another major factor in determining how closely planes can follow each other. The larger the plane and the slower the plane, the greater the turbulence.

Besides the usual 'large' planes, controllers have to manage the small aircraft, business helicopters, traffic spotter planes and the many sightseeing planes flying over Manhattan, or up the Hudson towards the Statue of Liberty. The tower controllers have to control the movement of over 2000 helicopters and light aircraft that fly through New York's airspace every day, being sure to keep them out of the airspace around each airport used by the arriving and departing aircraft.

Ground controllers

As an aircraft lands, it is handed over to the ground controllers who are responsible for navigating it through the maze of interconnecting taxiways found at most international airports. Some airport layouts mean that planes, having landed, have to cross over the runway where other planes are taking off in order to get to the terminal. All this needs careful coordination by the ground controllers.

Some pilots may be unfamiliar with airport layouts and need careful coaxing. Worse still is poor visibility, fog or low cloud. At Kennedy airport, the ground radar does not show aircraft type, so the controllers have to rely upon memory and constant checking of aircraft position by radio to ensure they know where each aircraft is at any time.

Stress

Dealing continually with so many aircraft movements means that controllers have but a split second to analyse and react to every situation, yet they need to be right 100 per cent of the time. Any small error or lapse in concentration can have catastrophic consequences. They can't afford to lose

track of a single aircraft, because it may stray into someone else's air space and into the path of another aircraft. If the computer projects that two planes are about to fly closer than three miles, the Conflict Alert buzzer sounds and the controllers have just seconds to make the right decision and then transmit it to the pilots. Sometimes problems arise in the planes themselves, such as an aircraft running short of fuel. Emergency landing procedures cover such eventualities. At Kennedy airport, they have about one such incident each day. As one controller remarked: *'It's like an enhanced video game, except you only have one life.'*

Questions

1 What does 'planning and control' mean to air traffic controllers?

2 What are the differing problems faced by TRACON, tower and ground controllers?

3 What sequencing rules do you think the tower controllers use?

Discussion questions

1 Identify the ways in which planning and control activity could reconcile supply and demand in the following operations:
   - an ambulance service
   - a medical centre
   - a pizza manufacturing company
   - a national rail service
   - a psychotherapy clinic
   - a bespoke tailor.

2 What is the difference between dependent and independent demand?

3 To what extent is demand dependent or independent in the following types of operation:
   - a manufacturer of nuclear-powered submarines
   - a specialist catering company
   - a fast-food hamburger restaurant
   - a specialist packaging manufacturer who supplies a computer manufacturer
   - a television production company?

4 How does scheduling affect the five performance objectives of operations management?

5 How might a police force schedule its officers so as to match its capacity to demand?

6 If you were a tutor at a local university, which sequencing rule would you use to determine the order in which you saw your students? What do you think are the advantages and disadvantages of each sequencing rule in this particular situation?

7 A painter of fake masterpieces has been commissioned to paint and frame five different paintings. Each of the paintings requires a different, but ornate, frame. The painter wishes to execute this commission as quickly as possible and has estimated the times for painting and framing the paintings as follows:

   Van Gogh   painting 2 hours; framing $4\frac{1}{2}$ hours
   Monet   painting 3 hours; framing $3\frac{1}{2}$ hours
   Pollock   painting 10 minutes; framing 1 hour
   Renoir   painting 4 hours; framing 2 hours
   Picasso   painting $1\frac{1}{2}$ hours; framing $4\frac{1}{2}$ hours

   The painter has employed a specialist framer to join him on this enterprise. In what order should the pair tackle the paintings?

8 In this chapter, a description was given of the planning and control of a concert. How do you think these planning and control activities would change if the organization promoting the concert gave the same concert every week of the year?

9 Visit a local automotive service centre which carries out servicing and repairs on cars and find out the following:

(a) What is their approach to prioritizing jobs?

(b) What is the typical utilization of some of their equipment?

(c) How do they cope when a job takes longer than they expect?

10 What is the main difference between planning and controlling a hospital where the majority of surgical procedures are routine operations, and planning and controlling a hospital which has a very high level of accident and emergency work?

Notes on chapter

1   Source: Jean Farman (1999) 'Les Coulisses du Vol', Air France.

2   For an interesting discussion of how these categories of planning and control can be modelled *see* Wild, R. (1988) *Production and Operations Management*, Cassell.

3   The concept of *P:D* ratios comes originally from Shingo, S. (1981) *Study of Toyota Production Systems*, Japan Management Association; and was extended by Mather, K. (1988) *Competitive Manufacturing*, Prentice Hall.

4   Source: Walley, P. and Slack, N. (1994) MBA Course Notes, Warwick University, UK.

5   Johnson, S.M. (1954) 'Optimal Two-stage and Three-stage Production Schedules', *Naval Logistics Quarterly*, Vol 1, No 1.

6   We are grateful to our colleague Paul Walley for this section.

7   These are described in Betts, A. and Slack, N. (1999) 'Control, Knowledge and Learning in Process Development', *Internal Report*, University of Warwick Business School. The original four dimensions are based on Hofstede, G. (1981) 'Management Control in Public and Not For Profit Activities', *Accounting Organisation and Society*, Vol 6, No 3.

Selected further reading

Ashby, J.R. and Uzsoy, R. (1995) 'Scheduling and Order Release in a Single-Stage Production System', *Journal of Manufacturing Systems*, Vol 14, No 4.

Baker, K.R. (1984) *Introduction to Sequencing and Scheduling*, John Wiley.

Basset, G. and Todd, R. (1994) 'The SPT Priority Sequence Rule', *International Journal of Operations and Production Management*, Vol 14, No 12.

Browne, J.J. (1979) 'Simplified Scheduling of Routine Work Hours and Days Off', *Industrial Engineering*, Dec.

Conway, R.W. (1965) 'Priority Despatching and Job Lateness in a Job Shop', *Journal of Industrial Engineering*, Vol 16, No 4.

Fry, T.D. and Philipoom, P.R. (1989) 'A Despatching Rule for Allowing Trade-offs Between Inventory and Customer Satisfaction', *International Journal of Operations and Production Management*, Vol 9, No 7.

Goldratt, E.Y. and Cox, J. (1984) *The Goal*, North River Press.

Kanet, J.K. and Hayya, J.C. (1982) 'Priority Despatching with Operation Due Dates in a Job Shop', *Journal of Operations Management*, Vol 2, No 3.

Sule, D.R. (1997) *Industrial Scheduling*, PWSs Publishing Company.

11 Capacity planning and control

Introduction

Providing the capability to satisfy current and future demand is a fundamental responsibility of operations management. An appropriate balance between capacity and demand can generate high profits and satisfied customers, whereas getting the balance 'wrong' can be potentially disastrous. Yet although planning for, and controlling, capacity is a major responsibility of operations managers, it should also involve other functional managers. There are three reasons for this. The first is that capacity decisions have a company-wide impact. The second is that all the other functions provide vital inputs to the planning process. The third is that each business function will usually have to plan and control the capacity of its own 'micro operations' to match that of the main operations function.

What we have called here *capacity planning and control* is also sometimes referred to as *aggregate planning and control*. This is because, at the 'highest level' of the planning and control process, demand and capacity calculations are usually performed on an aggregated basis which does not discriminate between the different products and services that an operation might produce. The essence of the task is to reconcile, at a general and aggregated level, the supply of capacity with the level of demand which it must satisfy (*see* Fig. 11.1).

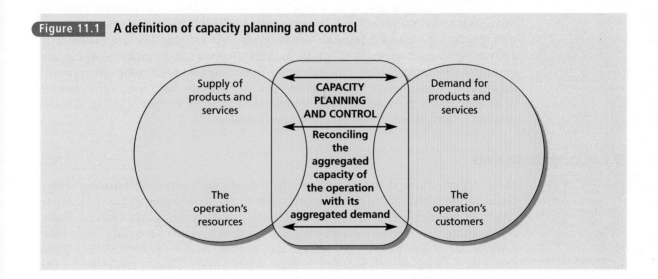

Figure 11.1 **A definition of capacity planning and control**

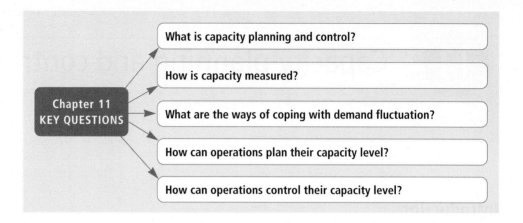

	What is capacity planning and control?
Chapter 11 KEY QUESTIONS	How is capacity measured?
	What are the ways of coping with demand fluctuation?
	How can operations plan their capacity level?
	How can operations control their capacity level?

What is capacity?

The most common use of the word 'capacity' is in the static, physical sense of the fixed *volume* of a container, or the space in a building. This meaning of the word is also sometimes used by operations managers. For example, a pharmaceutical manufacturer may invest in new 1000-litre capacity reactor vessels, a property company purchases a 500-vehicle capacity city-centre car park, and a 'multiplex' cinema is built with 10 screens and a total capacity of 2500 seats. Although these capacity measures describe the *scale* of these operations, they do not reflect the processing capacities of these investments. To do this we must incorporate a *time* dimension appropriate to the use of assets. So the pharmaceutical company will be concerned with the level of output that can be achieved using the 1000-litre reactor vessel. If a batch of standard products can be produced every hour, the planned processing capacity could be as high as 24 000 litres per day. If the reaction takes four hours, and two hours are used for cleaning between batches, the vessel may only produce 4000 litres per day. Similarly, the car park may be fully occupied by office workers during the working day, 'processing' only 500 cars per day. Alternatively, it may be used for shoppers staying on average only one hour, and theatre-goers occupying spaces for three hours in the evening. The processing capacity would then be up to 5000 cars per day. Thus the definition of the capacity of an operation is the *maximum level of value-added activity over a period of time* that the process can achieve under normal operating conditions.

● Capacity constraints

Many organizations operate at below their maximum processing capacity, either because there is insufficient demand completely to 'fill' their capacity, or as a deliberate policy, so that the operation can respond quickly to every new order. Often, though, organizations find themselves with some parts of their operation operating below their capacity while other parts are at their capacity 'ceiling'. It is the parts of the operation that are operating at their capacity 'ceiling' which are the *capacity constraint* for the whole operation.

The concept of one micro operation acting as the 'bottleneck' constraint on capacity was introduced in Chapter 6. Depending on the nature of demand, different parts of an operation might be pushed to their capacity ceiling and act as a constraint on the total operation. For example, a retail superstore might offer a gift-wrapping service which at normal times can cope with all requests for its services without delaying customers unduly. At Christmas, however, the demand for gift wrapping might increase proportionally far more than the overall increase in custom for the store as a whole. Unless extra resources are provided to increase the capacity of this micro operation, it could constrain the capacity of the whole store.

Planning and controlling capacity

Capacity planning and control is the task of setting the effective capacity of the operation so that it can respond to the demands placed upon it. This usually means deciding how the operation should react to fluctuations in demand. We have faced this issue before in Chapter 6 where we examined long-term changes in demand and the alternative capacity strategies for dealing with the changes. These strategies were concerned with introducing (or deleting) major increments of physical capacity. We called this task *long-term capacity strategy*. In this chapter we are treating the shorter timescale where capacity decisions are being made largely within the constraints of the physical capacity limits set by the operation's long-term capacity strategy.

Medium- and short-term capacity

Having established long-term capacity, operations managers must decide how to adjust the capacity of the operation in the *medium term*. This usually involves an assessment of the demand forecasts over a period of 2–18 months ahead, during which time planned output can be varied, for example, by changing the number of hours the equipment is used. In practice, however, few forecasts are accurate, and most operations also need to respond to changes in demand which occur over a shorter timescale. Hotels and restaurants have unexpected and apparently random changes in demand from night to night, but also know from experience that certain days are on average busier than others. So operations managers also have to make *short-term capacity adjustments*, which enable them to flex output for a short period, either on a predicted basis (for example, bank checkouts are always busy at lunchtimes) or at short notice (for example, a sunny warm day at a theme park).

Aggregate demand and capacity

The important characteristic of capacity planning and control, as we are treating it here, is that it is concerned with setting capacity levels over the medium and short terms in aggregated terms. That is, it is making overall, broad capacity decisions, but is not concerned with all of the detail of the individual products and services offered. Thus aggregate plans assume that the mix of different products and services will remain relatively constant during the planning period. Figure 11.2 shows how four operations might aggregate their capacity and demand levels.

The objectives of capacity planning and control

The decisions taken by operations managers in devising their capacity plans will affect several different aspects of performance:

- *Costs* will be affected by the balance between capacity and demand (or output level if that is different). Capacity levels in excess of demand could mean under-utilization of capacity and therefore high unit cost.
- *Revenues* will also be affected by the balance between capacity and demand, but in the opposite way. Capacity levels equal to or higher than demand at any point in time will ensure that all demand is satisfied and no revenue lost.
- *Working capital* will be affected if an operation decides to build up finished goods inventory prior to demand. This might allow demand to be satisfied, but the organization will have to fund the inventory until it can be sold.
- *Quality* of goods or services might be affected by a capacity plan which involved large fluctuations in capacity levels, by hiring temporary staff for example. The new

Figure 11.2 Examples of aggregation in capacity and demand measurement

Hotel

Room nights per month

Ignores the number of guests in each room and their individual requirements

Woollen knitwear factory

Units per month

Ignores size, colour and style variations

Aluminium producer

Tonnes per month

Ignores types of alloy, gauge and batch size variations

Retail store

Revenue per month

Ignores variation in spend, number of items and gross margin of items, per customer transaction

staff and the disruption to the routine working of the operation could increase the probability of errors being made.

- *Speed* of response to customer demand could be enhanced, either by the build-up of inventories (allowing customers to be satisfied directly from the inventory rather than having to wait for items to be manufactured) or by the deliberate provision of surplus capacity to avoid queueing.
- *Dependability* of supply will also be affected by how close demand levels are to capacity. The closer demand gets to the operation's capacity ceiling, the less able it is to cope with any unexpected disruptions and the less dependable its deliveries of goods and services could be.
- *Flexibility*, especially volume flexibility, will be enhanced by surplus capacity. If demand and capacity are in balance, the operation will not be able to respond to any unexpected increase in demand.

The steps of capacity planning and control

The sequence of capacity planning and control decisions which need to be taken by operations managers is illustrated in Figure 11.3. Typically, operations managers are faced with a forecast of demand which is unlikely to be either certain or constant. They will also have some idea of their own ability to meet this demand. Nevertheless, before any further decisions are taken, they must have quantitative data on both capacity and demand. So the first step will be to *measure the aggregate demand and capacity* levels for the planning period. The second step will be to *identify the alternative capacity plans* which could be adopted in response to the demand fluctuations. The third step will be to *choose the most appropriate capacity plan* for their circumstances.

Measuring demand and capacity

● Forecasting demand fluctuations

In most organizations, demand forecasting is the responsibility of the sales and/or marketing departments. However, it is a major input into the capacity planning and control decision, which is usually an operations management responsibility. After all, without an estimate of future demand it is not possible to plan effectively for future

Figure 11.3 The steps in capacity planning and control

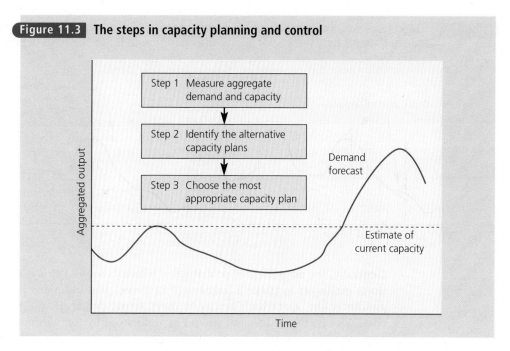

events, only to react to them. It is therefore important for operations managers to understand the basis and rationale for these demand forecasts. As far as capacity planning and control is concerned, there are three requirements from a demand forecast.

It is expressed in terms which are useful for capacity planning and control

If forecasts are expressed only in money terms and give no indication of the demands that will be placed on an operation's capacity, they will need to be translated into realistic expectations of demand, expressed in the same units as the capacity (for example, machine hours per year, operatives required, space, etc.).

It is as accurate as possible

In capacity planning and control, the accuracy of a forecast is important because, whereas demand can change instantaneously, there is a lag between deciding to change capacity and the change taking effect. Thus many operations managers are faced with a dilemma. In order to attempt to meet demand, they must often decide output in advance, based on a forecast which might change before the demand occurs, or worse, prove not to reflect actual demand at all.

It gives an indication of relative uncertainty

Decisions to operate extra hours and recruit extra staff are usually based on forecast levels of demand, which could in practice differ considerably from actual demand, leading to unnecessary costs or unsatisfactory customer service. For example, Figure 11.4 shows the average demand levels of a supermarket throughout one day in terms of the number of customers entering the store. Demand is initially slow but then builds up to a lunchtime rush. After this, demand slows, only to build up again for the early evening rush, and it finally falls again at the end of trading. The supermarket manager can use this forecast to adjust (say) checkout capacity throughout the day. But although this may be an accurate average demand forecast, no single day will exactly conform to this pattern. Of equal importance is an estimate of how much actual demand could differ from the average. This can be found by examining demand statistics to build up a distribution of demand at each point in the day. The importance of this is that the manager now has an understanding of when it will be important to have reserve staff, perhaps filling shelves, but on call to staff the checkouts should demand warrant it.

Figure 11.4 **Good forecasts are essential for effective capacity planning, but so is an understanding of demand uncertainty because it allows the operation to judge the risks to service level**

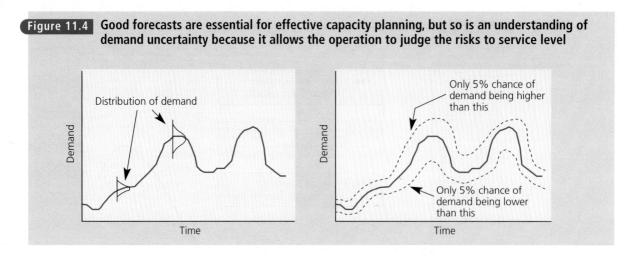

Generally, the advantage of probabilistic forecasts such as this is that it allows operations managers to make a judgement between possible plans that would virtually guarantee the operation's ability to meet actual demand, and plans that minimize costs. Ideally, this judgement should be influenced by the nature of the way the business wins orders: price-sensitive markets may require a risk-avoiding cost minimization plan that does not always satisfy peak demand, whereas markets that value responsiveness and service quality may justify a more generous provision of operational capacity.

Seasonality of demand

In many organizations, capacity planning and control is concerned largely with coping with seasonal demand fluctuations. Almost all products and services have some *seasonality of demand* and some also have *seasonality of supply*, usually where the inputs are seasonal agricultural products – for example, in processing frozen vegetables. These fluctuations in demand or supply may be reasonably forecastable, but some are usually also affected by unexpected variations in the weather and by changing economic conditions. Figure 11.5 gives some examples of seasonality.

Consider the four organizations previously referred to in Figure 11.2. Their demand patterns are shown in Figure 11.6. The woollen knitwear business and the city hotel

Figure 11.5 **Many types of operation have to cope with seasonal demand**

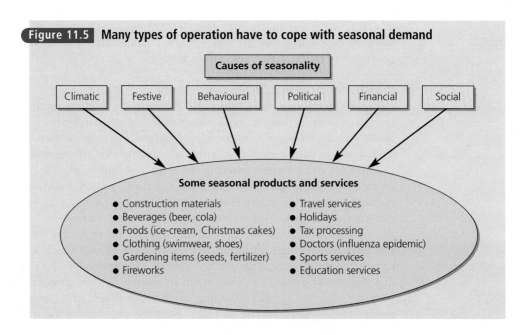

Figure 11.6 **Aggregate demand fluctuations for four organizations**

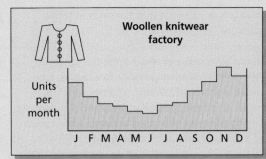

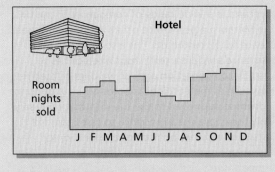

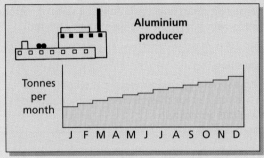

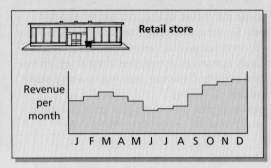

both have seasonal sales demand patterns, but for different reasons: the woollen knitwear business because of climatic patterns (cold winters, warm summers) and the hotel because of demand from business people, who take vacations from work at Christmas and in the summer. The retail supermarket is a little less seasonal, but is affected by pre-vacation peaks and reduced sales during vacation periods. The aluminium producer shows virtually no seasonality, but is showing a steady growth in sales over the forecast period.

Weekly and daily demand fluctuations

Seasonality of demand occurs over a year, but similar predictable variations in demand can also occur for some products and services on a shorter cycle. We have already illustrated the daily demand pattern of a supermarket in Figure 11.4, but it will also be subjected to predictable demand fluctuations over a week. Demand might be low on Monday and Tuesday, build up during the latter part of the week and reach a peak on Friday and Saturday. Banks, public offices, telephone sales organizations and electricity utilities all have weekly and daily, or even hourly, demand patterns which require capacity adjustment. The extent to which an operation will have to cope with very short-term demand fluctuations is partly determined by how long its customers are prepared to wait for their products or services. An operation whose customers are incapable of, or unwilling to, wait will have to plan for very short-term demand fluctuations. Emergency services, for example, will need to understand the hourly variation in the demand for their services and plan capacity accordingly.

● Measuring capacity

The main problem with measuring capacity is the complexity of most operations. Only when the operation is highly standardized and repetitive is capacity easy to define unambiguously. So if a television factory produces only one basic model, the weekly

Producing while the sun shines

It has long been obvious that the sales of some products are profoundly affected by the weather. Sunglasses, sunscreen, waterproof clothing and ice-cream are all obvious examples. Yet the range of operations interested in weather forecasting has expanded significantly. Energy utilities, soft drink producers and fresh food producers and retailers are all keen to purchase the latest weather forecasts. But so are operations such as banking call centres and mobile phone operators. It would appear that the demand for telephone banking falls dramatically when the sun shines, as does the use of mobile phones. Similarly, insurance companies have found it wise to sell their products when the weather is poor and likely customers are trapped indoors rather than relaxing outside in the sun, refusing to worry about the future.

Because of this, meteorological services around the world now sell increasingly sophisticated forecasts to a wide range of companies. In the UK, the Meteorological Office offers an internet-based service for its customers. It is also used to help insurance specialists price insurance policies to provide compensation against weather-related risk. However, as meteorologists point out, it is up to the individual businesses to use the information wisely. Only they have the experience to assess the full impact of weather on their operation. So, for example, supermarkets know that a rise in temperature will impact on the sales of cottage cheese (whereas, unaccountably, the sales of cottage cheese with pineapple chunks are not affected).

> **Question**
>
> How should a business work out what it is prepared to pay for these increasingly sophisticated weather forecasts?

capacity could be described as 2000 Model A televisions. A government office may have the capacity to print and post 500 000 tax forms per week. A fast ride at a theme park might be designed to process batches of 60 people every three minutes – a capacity to transform 1200 people per hour. In each case, the *output* is the most appropriate measure of capacity, because the output from the operation does not vary in its nature. For many operations, however, the definition of capacity is not so obvious. When a much wider range of outputs places varying demands on the process, for instance, output measures of capacity are less useful. Here *input* measures are frequently used to define capacity. Almost every type of operation could use a mixture of both input and output measures, but in practice, most choose to use one or the other (*see* Table 11.1).

Table 11.1 Input and output capacity measures for different operations

Operation	Input measure of capacity	Output measure of capacity
Air-conditioner plant	Machine hours available	**Number of units per week**
Hospital	**Beds available**	Number of patients treated per week
Theatre	**Number of seats**	Number of customers entertained per week
University	**Number of students**	Students graduated per year
Retail store	**Sales floor area**	Number of items sold per day
Airline	**Number of seats available on the sector**	Number of passengers per week
Electricity company	Generator size	**Megawatts of electricity generated**
Brewery	Volume of fermentation tanks	**Litres per week**

(Note: The most commonly used measure is shown in **bold**.)

Capacity depends on activity mix

The hospital measures its capacity in terms of its resources, partly because there is not a clear relationship between the number of beds it has and the number of patients it treats. If all its patients required relatively minor treatment with only short stays in hospital, it could treat many people per week. Alternatively, if most of its patients required long periods of observation or recuperation, it could treat far fewer. Output depends on the mix of activities in which the hospital is engaged and, because most hospitals perform many different types of activities, output is difficult to predict. Certainly it is difficult to compare directly the capacity of hospitals which have very different activities.

Worked example   Suppose an air-conditioner factory produces three different models of air-conditioner unit: the deluxe, the standard and the economy. The deluxe model can be assembled in 1.5 hours, the standard in 1 hour and the economy in 0.75 hours. The assembly area in the factory has 800 staff hours of assembly time available each week.

If demand for deluxe, standard and economy units is in the ratio 2:3:2, the time needed to assemble 2 + 3 + 2 = 7 units is:

$$(2 \times 1.5) + (3 \times 1) + (2 \times 0.75) = 7.5 \text{ hours}$$

The number of units produced per week is:

$$\frac{800}{7.5} \times 7 = 746.7 \text{ units}$$

If demand changes to a ratio of deluxe, economy, standard units of 1:2:4, the time needed to assemble 1 + 2 + 4 = 7 units is:

$$(1 \times 1.5) + (2 \times 1) + (4 \times 0.75) = 6.5 \text{ hours}$$

Now the number of units produced per week is:

$$\frac{800}{6.5} \times 7 = 861.5 \text{ units}$$

Design capacity and effective capacity

The theoretical capacity of an operation – the capacity which its technical designers had in mind when they commissioned the operation – cannot always be achieved in practice. For example, a company coating photographic paper will have several coating lines which deposit thin layers of chemicals onto rolls of paper at high speed. Each line will be capable of running at a particular speed. Multiplying the maximum coating speed by the operating time of the plant gives the *theoretical design capacity* of the line. But in reality the line cannot be run continuously at its maximum rate. Different products will have different coating requirements, so the line will need to be stopped while it is changed over. Maintenance will need to be performed on the line, which will take out further productive time. Technical scheduling difficulties might mean further lost time. Not all of these losses are the operations manager's fault; they have occurred because of the market and technical demands on the operation. The actual capacity which remains, after such losses are accounted for, is called the *effective capacity* of operation. Not that these causes of reduction in capacity will be the only losses in the operation. Such factors as quality problems, machine breakdowns, absenteeism and other avoidable problems will all take their toll. This means that the *actual output* of the line will be even lower than the effective capacity. The ratio of the output actually achieved by an operation to its design capacity, and the ratio of output to effective capacity are called, respectively, the *utilization* and the *efficiency* of the plant:

$$\text{Utilization} = \frac{\text{actual output}}{\text{design capacity}}$$

$$\text{Efficiency} = \frac{\text{actual output}}{\text{effective capacity}}$$

Worked example

Suppose the photographic paper manufacturer has a coating line with a design capacity of 200 square metres per minute, and the line is operated on a 24-hour day, 7 days per week (168 hours per week) basis.

Design capacity is $200 \times 60 \times 24 \times 7 = 2.016$ million square metres per week. The records for a week's production show the following lost production time:

1	Product changeovers (set-ups)	20 hrs
2	Regular preventative maintenance	16 hrs
3	No work scheduled	8 hrs
4	Quality sampling checks	8 hrs
5	Shift change times	7 hrs
6	Maintenance breakdown	18 hrs
7	Quality failure investigation	20 hrs
8	Coating material stockouts	8 hrs
9	Labour shortages	6 hrs
10	Waiting for paper rolls	6 hrs

During this week the actual output was only 582 000 square metres.

The first five categories of lost production occur as a consequence of reasonably unavoidable, planned occurrences and amount to a total of 59 hours. The last five categories are unplanned, and avoidable, losses and amount to 58 hours.

Measured in hours of production, and illustrated in Figure 11.7:

Design capacity = 168 hours per week

Effective capacity = $168 - 59 = 109$ hrs

Figure 11.7 Utilization and efficiency

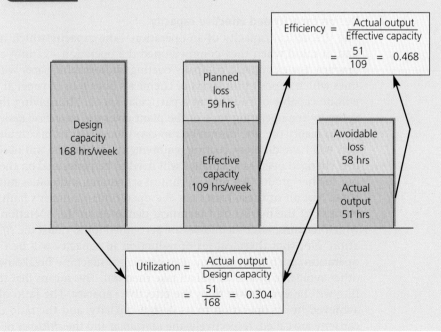

$$\text{Actual output} \quad = \quad 168 - 59 - 58 = 51 \text{ hrs}$$

$$\text{Utilization} \quad = \quad \frac{\text{actual output}}{\text{design capacity}} = \frac{51 \text{ hrs}}{168 \text{ hrs}} = 0.304$$

$$\text{Efficiency} \quad = \quad \frac{\text{actual output}}{\text{effective capacity}} = \frac{51 \text{ hrs}}{109 \text{ hrs}} = 0.468$$

Overall equipment effectiveness[1]

The overall equipment effectiveness (OEE) measure is an increasingly popular method of judging the effectiveness of individual pieces of operations equipment. It is based on three aspects of performance:

- *the speed*, or throughput rate, of the equipment (its cycle time);
- *the quality* of the product or service it produces;
- *the time* that it is available to operate.

For equipment to operate effectively, it needs to achieve high levels of performance against all three of these dimensions. Viewed in isolation, these metrics are important indicators of plant performance, but they do not give a complete picture of the machine's *overall* effectiveness. This can only be understood by looking at the combined effect of the three measures, calculated by multiplying the three individual metrics together. All these losses to the OEE performance can be expressed in terms of units of time – the design cycle time to produce one good part. So, a reject of one part has an equivalent time loss. In effect, this means that an OEE represents the valuable operating time as a percentage of the design capacity.

Worked example

If a machine operates at 80 cycles per minute but has a design speed of 100 cycles per minute, its performance rate is 80 per cent. Similarly, if it produces 90 good parts out of every 100 made, it has a quality rate of 90 per cent. If we plan to run (load) the equipment for 8 hours but it breaks down for 2, its availability is 75 per cent.

In this example, a 90 per cent quality rate combines with an 80 per cent performance rate and a 75 per cent availability to produce an overall OEE performance of 54 per cent ($0.9 \times 0.8 \times 0.75$).

Utilization as a measure of operations performance

For many businesses, utilization is one of the key measures of the performance of the operation. Many organizations require high utilization levels before they will authorize investment in additional capacity. Utilization may be known by different names in different industries, for example:

- the 'room occupancy level' in hotels;
- the 'load factor' for aircraft seats;
- 'uptime' in some factories.

Unfortunately, as a measure of an operation's performance, it can be misleading. Low utilization could be a result of low demand, frequent breakdowns of the plant, or running out of materials. Hence, it is measuring the performance of many parts of the business rather than operations alone. Nor is seeking high utilization always desirable. In batch-type operations, in particular, an emphasis on high utilization can result in the build-up of in-process inventories. This is discussed further in Chapter 15 on just-in-time planning and control. High utilization can also adversely affect the customer if it reduces the speed and volume flexibility of the overall operation. Popular, high-

The 'supply' of news coming into a newsroom is partly predictable (government statements, fixed sporting fixtures, etc.) but partly unpredictable (crime stories, natural disasters, etc.). Yet 'demand', in terms of filling a predetermined number of minutes of news broadcast time, is (usually) fixed. Here, a newsroom editor processes news stories and stores them in a digital inventory, ready to be used at the scheduled time

utilization ATMs at banks will frequently be accompanied by long queues. High runway utilization at airports during the morning and evening commuter rush results in aircraft 'stacking' which wastes fuel and delays passengers.

The alternative capacity plans

With an understanding of both demand and capacity, the next step is to consider the alternative methods of responding to demand fluctuations. There are three 'pure' options available for coping with such variation:

- Ignore the fluctuations and keep activity levels constant (*level capacity plan*).
- Adjust capacity to reflect the fluctuations in demand (*chase demand plan*).
- Attempt to change demand to fit capacity availability (*demand management*).

In practice, most organizations will use a mixture of all of these 'pure' plans, although often one plan might dominate.

● Level capacity plan

In a level capacity plan, the processing capacity is set at a uniform level throughout the planning period, regardless of the fluctuations in forecast demand. This means that the same number of staff operate the same processes and should therefore be capable of producing the same aggregate output in each period. Where non-perishable materials are processed, but not immediately sold, they can be transferred to finished goods inventory in anticipation of sales at a later time. Thus this plan is feasible (but not necessarily desirable) for our examples of the woollen knitwear company and the aluminium producer (*see* Fig. 11.9).

Seasonal salads[2]

Lettuce is an all-year-round ingredient for most salads, but both the harvesting of the crop and its demand are seasonal. Lettuces are perishable and must be kept in cold stores and transported in refrigerated vehicles. Even then the product only stays fresh for a maximum of a week. In most north European countries, demand continues throughout the winter at around half the summer levels, but outdoor crops cannot be grown during the winter months. Glasshouse cultivation is possible but expensive.

One of Europe's largest lettuce growers is G's Fresh Salads, based in the UK. Their supermarket customers require fresh produce to be delivered 364 days a year, but because of the limitations of the English growing season, the company has developed other sources of supply in Europe. It acquired a farm and packhouse in the Murcia region of south-eastern Spain, which provides the bulk of salad crops during the winter, transported daily to the UK by a fleet of refrigerated trucks. Further top-up produce is imported by air from around the world.

Sales forecasts are agreed with the individual supermarkets well in advance, allowing the planting and growing programmes to be matched to the anticipated level of sales. However, the programme is only a rough guide. The supermarkets may change their orders right up to the afternoon of the preceding day. Weather is a dominant factor. First, it determines supply – how well the crop grows and how easy it is to harvest. Second, it influences sales – cold, wet periods during the summer discourage the eating of salads, whereas hot spells boost demand greatly.

Figure 11. 8 illustrates this. The iceberg lettuce sales programme is shown, and compared with the actual English-grown and Spanish-grown sales. The fluctuating nature of the actual sales is the result of a combination of weather-related availability and supermarket demand. These do not always match. When demand is higher than expected, the picking rigs and their crews continue to work into the middle of night, under floodlights. Another capacity problem is the operation's staffing levels. It relies on temporary seasonal harvesting and packing staff to supplement the full-time employees for both the English and Spanish seasons. Since most of the crop is transported to the UK in bulk, a large permanent staff is maintained for packing and distribution in the UK. The majority of the Spanish workforce is temporary, with only a small number retained during the extremely hot summer to grow and harvest other crops such as melons.

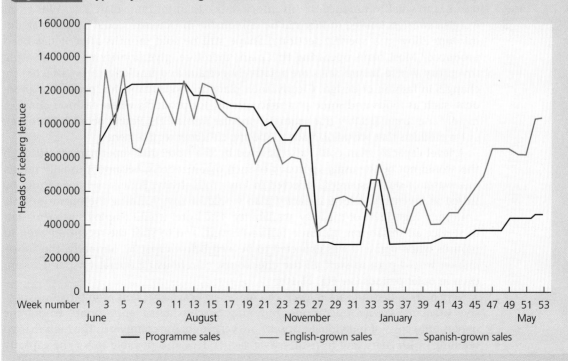

Figure 11.8 Typical year's iceberg lettuce sales

The specialist lettuce harvesting machines (the 'rigs') are shipped over to Spain every year at the end of the English season, so that the company can achieve maximum utilization from all this expensive capital equipment. These rigs not only enable very high productivity of the pickers, but also ensure the best possible conditions for quality packing and rapid transportation to the cold stores.

Questions

1 What approach(es) does the company seem to take to its capacity management?

2 What are the consequences of getting its planting and harvesting programmes wrong?

Figure 11.9 **Level capacity plans which use anticipation inventory to supply future demand**

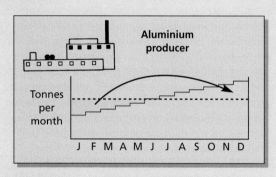 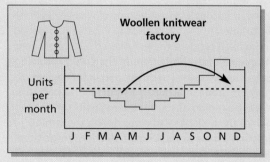

☐ Inventory built up in anticipation of future demand

Level capacity plans of this type can achieve the objectives of stable employment patterns, high process utilization, and usually also high productivity with low unit costs. Unfortunately, they can also create considerable inventory which has to be financed and stored. Perhaps the biggest problem, however, is that decisions have to be taken as to what to produce for inventory rather than for immediate sale. Will green woollen sweaters knitted in July still be fashionable in October? Could a particular aluminium alloy in a specific sectional shape still be sold months after it has been produced? Most firms operating this plan, therefore, give priority to only creating inventory where future sales are relatively certain and unlikely to be affected by changes in fashion or design. Clearly, such plans are not suitable for 'perishable' products, such as foods and some pharmaceuticals, for products where fashion changes rapidly and unpredictably (for example, popular music CDs, young people's clothing), or for products that are tailor-made to specific customer requirements.

A level capacity plan could also be used by the hotel and supermarket, although this would not be the usual approach of such organizations, because it usually results in a waste of staff resources, reflected in low productivity. Because service cannot be stored as inventory, a level capacity plan would involve running the operation at a uniformly high level of capacity availability. The hotel would employ sufficient staff to service all the rooms, to run a full restaurant, and to staff the reception even in months when demand was expected to be well below capacity. Similarly, the supermarket would plan to staff all the checkouts, warehousing operations, and so on, even in quiet periods (*see* Fig. 11.10).

Very high under-utilization levels can make level capacity plans prohibitively expensive in many service operations, but may be considered appropriate where the opportunity costs of individual lost sales are very high: for example, in the high-margin retailing of jewellery and in (real) estate agents. It is also possible to set the capacity somewhat below the forecast peak demand level in order to reduce the degree of under-

Figure 11.10 Level capacity plans with under-utilization of capacity

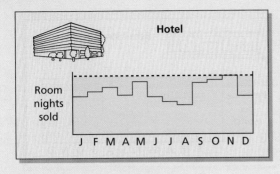

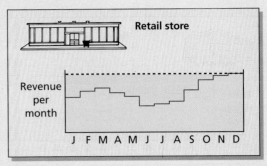

☐ Capacity under-utilized

utilization. However, in the periods where demand is expected to exceed planned capacity, customer service may deteriorate. Customers may have to queue for long periods or may be 'processed' faster and less sensitively. While this is obviously far from ideal, the benefits to the organization of stability and productivity may outweigh the disadvantages of upsetting some customers.

● Chase demand plan

The opposite of a level capacity plan is one which attempts to match capacity closely to the varying levels of forecast demand. This is much more difficult to achieve than a level capacity plan, as different numbers of staff, different working hours, and even different amounts of equipment may be necessary in each period. For this reason, pure chase demand plans are unlikely to appeal to operations which manufacture standard, non-perishable products. Also, where manufacturing operations are particularly capital-intensive, the chase demand policy would require a level of physical capacity, all of which would only be used occasionally. It is for this reason that such a plan is less likely to be appropriate for the aluminium producer than for the woollen garment manufacturer (*see* Fig. 11.11). A pure chase demand plan is more usually adopted by operations which cannot store their output, such as customer-processing operations or manufacturers of perishable products. It avoids the wasteful provision of excess staff that occurs with a level capacity plan, and yet should satisfy customer demand

Figure 11.11 Chase demand capacity plans with changes in capacity which reflect changes in demand

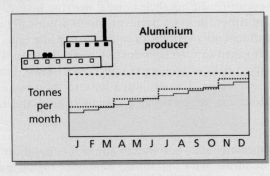

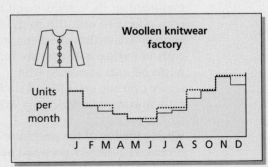

·············· Capacity throughout the year

- - - - - - - Processing equipment capacity limit

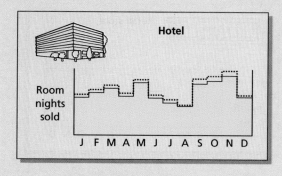

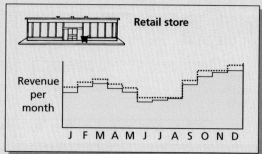

.... Capacity throughout the year

throughout the planned period. Where output can be stored, the chase demand policy might be adopted in order to minimize or eliminate finished goods inventory.

Sometimes it is difficult to achieve very large variations in capacity from period to period. If the changes in forecast demand are as large as those in the hotel example (*see* Fig. 11.12), significantly different levels of staffing will be required throughout the year. This would mean employing part-time and temporary staff, requiring permanent employees to work longer hours, or even bringing in contract labour. The operations managers will then have the difficult task of ensuring that quality standards and safety procedures are still adhered to, and that the customer service levels are maintained.

Methods of adjusting capacity

The chase demand approach requires that capacity is adjusted by some means. There are a number of different methods for achieving this, although they may not all be feasible for all types of operation. Some of these methods are listed below.

Overtime and idle time

Often the quickest and most convenient method of adjusting capacity is by varying the number of productive hours worked by the staff in the operation. When demand is higher than nominal capacity, the working day may be extended, and when demand is lower than nominal capacity the amount of time spent by staff on productive work can be reduced. In the latter case, it may be possible for staff to engage in some other activity such as cleaning or maintenance. This method is only useful if the timing of the extra productive capacity matches that of the demand. For example, there is little to be gained in asking a retail operation's staff to work extra hours in the evening if all the extra demand is occurring during their normal working period. The costs associated with this method are either the extra payment which is normally necessary to secure the agreement of staff to work overtime, or in the case of idle time, the costs of paying staff who are not engaged in direct productive work. Further, there might be costs associated with the fixed costs of keeping the operation heated, lit and secure over the extra period staff are working. There is also a limit to the amount of extra working time which any workforce can deliver before productivity levels decrease.

Varying the size of the workforce

If capacity is largely governed by workforce size, one way to adjust it is to adjust the size of the workforce. This is done by hiring extra staff during periods of high demand and laying them off as demand falls. However, there are cost and ethical implications to be taken into account before adopting such a method. The costs of hiring extra staff include those associated with recruitment, as well as the costs of low productivity while new staff go through the learning curve. The costs of lay-off may include possible severance payments, but might also include the loss of morale in the operation and loss of goodwill in the local labour market. At a micro operation level, one method of coping with peaks in demand in one area of an operation is to build sufficient flexibility into job design and job demarcation so that staff can transfer across from less busy parts of the operation. For example, the French hotel chain Novotel has trained some of its kitchen staff to escort customers from the reception area up to their rooms. The peak times for registering new customers coincide with the least busy times in the kitchen and restaurant areas.

Using part-time staff

A variation on the previous strategy is to recruit staff on a part-time basis, that is, for less than the normal working day. This method is extensively used in service operations such as supermarkets and fast-food restaurants but is also used by some manufacturers to staff an evening shift after the normal working day. However, if the fixed costs of employment for each employee, irrespective of how long he or she works, are high then using this method may not be worthwhile.

Sub-contracting

In periods of high demand, an operation might buy capacity from other organizations. This might enable the operation to meet its own demand without the extra expense of investing in capacity which will not be needed after the peak in demand has passed. Again, there are costs associated with this method. The most obvious one is that sub-contracting can be very expensive. The sub-contractor will also want to make sufficient margin out of the business. A sub-contractor may not be as motivated to deliver on time or to the desired levels of quality. Finally, there is the risk that the sub-contractors might themselves decide to enter the same market.

> ● **CRITICAL COMMENTARY**
>
> To many, the idea of fluctuating the workforce to match demand, either by using part-time staff or by hiring and firing, is more than just controversial. It is regarded as unethical. It is any business's responsibility, they argue, to engage in a set of activities which are capable of sustaining employment at a steady level. Hiring and firing merely for seasonal fluctuations, which can be predicted in advance, is treating human beings in a totally unacceptable manner. Even hiring people on a short-term contract, in practice, leads to them being offered poorer conditions of service and leads to a state of permanent anxiety as to whether they will keep their jobs. On a more practical note, it is pointed out that, in an increasingly global business world where companies may have sites in different countries, those countries that allow hiring and firing are more likely to have their plants 'downsized' than those where legislation makes this difficult.

● Manage demand

Stable and uniform demand could allow an organization to reduce costs *and* improve service; capacity could be better utilized and profit potential could be enhanced. Many organizations have recognized these benefits and attempt to 'manage demand' in various ways. The objective is to transfer customer demand from peak periods to quiet periods. This is usually beyond the immediate responsibility of operations managers, being the responsibility of marketing and/or sales functions. The primary role of the operations manager is, therefore, to identify and evaluate the benefits of demand management and to ensure that the resulting changes in demand can be satisfactorily met by the operations system. One method of managing demand is to *change demand*; more radical policies may create *alternative products or services* to fill capacity in quiet periods.

Change demand

The most obvious mechanism to change demand is through price. Although this is probably the most widely applied approach in demand management, it is less common for products than for services. For example, some city hotels offer low-cost 'city break' vacation packages in the months when fewer business visitors are expected. Skiing and camping holidays are cheapest at the beginning and end of the season and are particularly expensive during school vacations. Discounts are given by photo-processing firms during winter periods, but never around summer holidays. Ice-cream is 'on offer' in many supermarkets during the winter. The objective is invariably to stimulate off-peak demand and to constrain peak demand, in order to smooth demand as much as possible. Organizations can also attempt to increase demand in low periods by appropriate advertising. For example, turkey growers in the UK and the USA make vigorous attempts to promote their products at times other than Christmas and Thanksgiving.

Working by the year[3]

One method of fluctuating capacity as demand varies throughout the year without many of the costs associated with overtime or hiring temporary staff is called the Annual Hours Work Plan. This involves staff contracting to work a set number of hours per year rather than a set number of hours per week. The advantage of this is that the amount of staff time available to an organization can be varied throughout the year to reflect the real state of demand. For example, Figure 11.13 shows the total number of hours worked by staff in a photo-processing company throughout the year.

Annual hours plans can also be useful when supply varies throughout the year. For example, a UK cheese factory of Express Foods, like all cheese factories, must cope with processing very different quantities of milk at different times of the year. In spring and during early summer, cows produce large quantities of milk, but in late summer and autumn the supply of milk slows to a trickle. Before the introduction of annualized hours, the factory had relied on overtime and hiring temporary workers during the busy season. Now the staff are contracted to work a set number of hours a year

Figure 11.13   **The use of annualized hours to reflect seasonal demand**

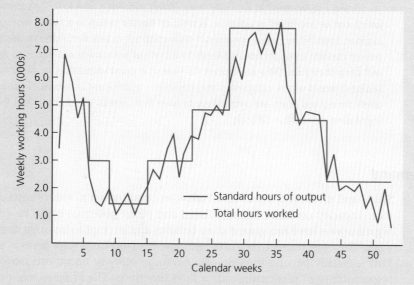

Source: From Lynch, P. (1991) 'Making Time for Productivity', *Personnel Management*, March, reproduced with permission.

with rotas agreed more than a year in advance and after consultation with the union. This means that at the end of July staff broadly know what days and hours they will be working up to September of the following year. If an emergency should arise, the company can call in people from a group of 'super crew' who work more flexible hours in return for higher pay but can do any job in the factory.

However, not all experiments with annualized hours have been as successful as that at Express Foods. In cases where demand is very unpredictable, staff can be asked to come in to work at very short notice. This can cause considerable disruption to social and family life. For example, at one news-broadcasting company, the scheme caused some initial problems. Some journalists and camera crew who went to cover a foreign crisis found that they had worked so many hours, they were asked to take the whole of one month off to compensate. Since they had no holiday plans, many would have preferred to work.

> **Question**
>
> What do you see as being the major advantages and disadvantages to both the company and the staff of adopting the Annual Hours Work Plan?

Alternative products and services

Sometimes, a more radical approach is required to fill periods of low demand. Organizations can develop new outputs which can be produced on the existing processes, but which have different demand patterns throughout the year. Most universities fill their accommodation and lecture theatres with conferences and company meetings during vacations. Ski resorts provide organized mountain activity holidays in the summer. Charter planes that shuttle Canadians from Toronto to Florida in the winter ply the Toronto–Europe routes in the summer. Some garden tractor companies in the US now make snow movers in the autumn and winter. The apparent benefits of filling capacity in this way must be weighed against the risks of damaging the core product or service, and the operation must be fully capable of serving both markets. Some universities have been criticized for providing sub-standard, badly decorated accommodation which met the needs of impecunious undergraduates, but which failed to impress executives at a trade conference.

● Mixed plans

Each of the three 'pure' plans is applied only where its advantages strongly outweigh its disadvantages. For many organizations, however, these 'pure' approaches do not match their required combination of competitive and operational objectives. Most operations managers are required simultaneously to reduce costs and inventory, to minimize capital investment, and yet to provide a responsive and customer-oriented approach at all times. For this reason, most organizations choose to follow a mixture of the three approaches. This can be best illustrated by the woollen knitwear company example (*see* Fig. 11.14). Here some of the peak demand has been brought forward by the company offering discounts to selected retail customers (manage demand plan). Capacity has also been adjusted at two points in the year to reflect the broad changes in demand (chase demand plan). Yet the adjustment in capacity is not sufficient to avoid totally the build-up of inventories (level capacity plan).

● Yield management

In operations which have relatively fixed capacities, such as airlines and hotels, it is important to use the capacity of the operation for generating revenue to its full potential. One approach used by such operations is called *yield management*.[4] This is really a collection of methods, some of which we have already discussed, which can be used to

Getting the message[5]

Companies which traditionally operate in seasonal markets can demonstrate some considerable ingenuity in their attempts to develop counter-seasonal products. One of the most successful industries in this respect has been the greetings card industry. Mother's Day, Father's Day Hallowe'en, Valentine's Day and other occasions have all been promoted as times to send (and buy) appropriately designed cards. Now, having run out of occasions to promote, greetings card manufacturers have moved on to 'non-occasion' cards, which can be sent at any time. These have the considerable advantage of being less seasonal, thus making the companies' seasonality less marked.

Hallmark Cards, the market leader in North America, has been the pioneer in developing non-occasion cards. Their cards include those intended to be sent from a parent to a child with messages such as 'Would a hug help?', 'Sorry I made you feel bad', and 'You're perfectly wonderful – it's your room that's a mess'. Other cards deal with more serious adult themes such as friendship ('You're more than a friend, you're just like family') or even alcoholism ('This is hard to say, but I think you're a much neater person when you're not drinking'). Whatever else these products may be, they are not seasonal!

Questions

1 What seem to be the advantages and disadvantages of the strategy adopted by Hallmark Cards?

2 What else could it do to cope with demand fluctuations?

ensure that an operation maximizes its potential to generate profit. Yield management is especially useful where:

- capacity is relatively fixed;
- the market can be fairly clearly segmented;
- the service cannot be stored in any way;
- the services are sold in advance;
- the marginal cost of making a sale is relatively low.

Figure 11.14 **A mixed capacity plan for the woollen knitwear factory**

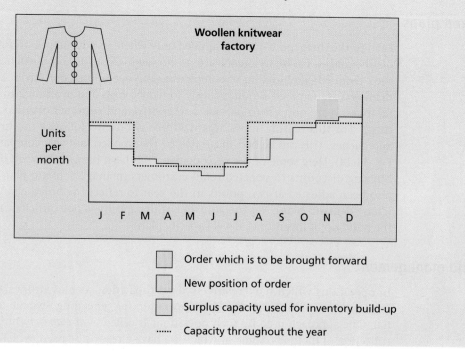

Order which is to be brought forward

New position of order

Surplus capacity used for inventory build-up

...... Capacity throughout the year

Airlines, for example, fit all these criteria. They adopt a collection of methods to try to maximize the yield (i.e. profit) from their capacity. These include the following:

- *Over-booking capacity*. Not every passenger who has booked a place on a flight will actually show up for the flight. If the airline did not fill this seat it would lose the revenue from it. Because of this, airlines regularly book more passengers onto flights than the capacity of the aircraft can cope with. If they over-book by the exact number of passengers who fail to show up, they have maximized their revenue under the circumstances. Of course, if more passengers show up than they expect, the airline will have a number of upset passengers to deal with (although they may be able to offer financial inducements for the passengers to take another flight). If they fail to over-book sufficiently, they will have empty seats. By studying past data on flight demand, airlines try to balance the risks of over-booking and under-booking.
- *Price discounting*. At quiet times, when demand is unlikely to fill capacity, airlines will also sell heavily discounted tickets to agents who then themselves take the risk of finding customers for them. In effect, this is using the price mechanism to affect demand.
- *Varying service types*. Discounting and other methods of affecting demand are also adjusted depending on the demand for particular types of service. For example, the relative demand for first-, business-, and economy-class seats varies throughout the year. There is no point discounting tickets in a class for which demand will be high. Yield management also tries to adjust the availability of the different classes of seat to reflect their demand. They will also vary the number of seats available in each class by upgrading or even changing the configuration of airline seats (*see* box in Chapter 4 on the new Boeing 777, p. 93).

Choosing a capacity planning and control approach

Before an operation can decide which of the capacity plans to adopt, it must be aware of the consequences of adopting each plan in its own set of circumstances. Two methods are particularly useful in helping to assess the consequences of adopting particular capacity plans:

- cumulative representations of demand and capacity;
- queueing theory.

Cumulative representations

Figure 11.15 shows the forecast aggregated demand for a chocolate factory which makes confectionery products. Demand for its products in the shops is greatest at Christmas. To meet this demand and allow time for the products to work their way through the distribution system, the factory must supply a demand which peaks in September, as shown. One method of assessing whether a particular level of capacity can satisfy the demand would be to calculate the degree of over-capacity below the graph which represents the capacity levels (areas A and C) and the degree of under-capacity above the graph (area B). If the total over-capacity is greater than the total under-capacity for a particular level of capacity, then that capacity could be regarded as adequate to satisfy demand fully, the assumption being that inventory has been accumulated in the periods of over-capacity.

However, there are two problems with this approach. The first is that each month shown in Figure 11.15 may not have the same amount of productive time. Some months (August, for example) may contain vacation periods which reduce the availability of capacity. The second problem is that a capacity level which seems adequate

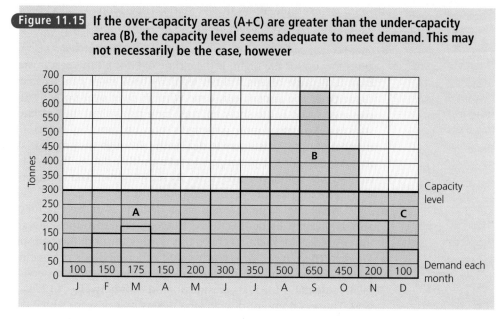

Figure 11.15 If the over-capacity areas (A+C) are greater than the under-capacity area (B), the capacity level seems adequate to meet demand. This may not necessarily be the case, however

may only be able to supply products *after* the demand for them has occurred. For example, if the period of under-capacity occurred at the beginning of the year, no inventory could have accumulated to meet demand. A far superior way of assessing capacity plans is first to plot demand on a *cumulative* basis. This is shown as the thicker line in Figure 11.16.

The cumulative representation of demand immediately reveals more information. First, it shows that although total demand peaks in September, because of the restricted number of available productive days, the peak demand per productive day occurs a month earlier in August. Second, it shows that the fluctuation in demand over the year is even greater than it seemed. The ratio of monthly peak demand to monthly lowest demand is 6.5:1, but the ratio of peak to lowest demand per productive day is 10:1. Demand per productive day is more relevant to operations managers, because productive days represent the time element of capacity.

The most useful consequence of plotting demand on a cumulative basis is that, by plotting capacity on the same graph, the feasibility and consequences of a capacity plan can be assessed. Figure 11.16 also shows a level capacity plan which produces at a rate of 14.03 tonnes per productive day. This meets cumulative demand by the end of the year. It would also pass our earlier test of total over-capacity being the same or greater than under-capacity.

However, if one of the aims of the plan is to supply demand when it occurs, the plan is inadequate. Up to around day 168, the line representing cumulative production is above that representing cumulative demand. This means that at any time during this period, more product has been produced by the factory than has been demanded from it. In fact the vertical distance between the two lines is the level of inventory at that point in time. So by day 80, 1122 tonnes have been produced but only 575 tonnes have been demanded. The surplus of production above demand, or inventory, is therefore 547 tonnes. When the cumulative demand line lies above the cumulative production line, the reverse is true. The vertical distance between the two lines now indicates the shortage, or lack of supply. So by day 198, 3025 tonnes have been demanded but only 2778 tonnes produced. The shortage is therefore 247 tonnes.

For any capacity plan to meet demand as it occurs, its cumulative production line must always lie above the cumulative demand line. This makes it a straightforward task to judge the adequacy of a plan, simply by looking at its cumulative representation. An impression of the inventory implications can also be gained from a cumulative repre-

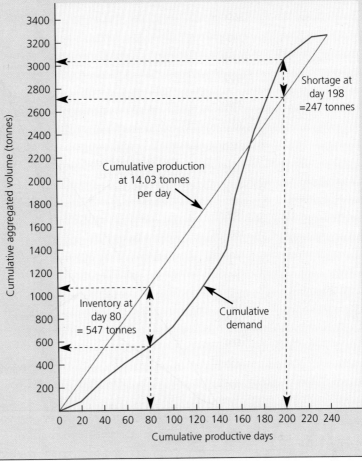

Figure 11.16 A level capacity plan which produces shortages in spite of meeting demand at the end of the year

	J	F	M	A	M	J	J	A	S	O	N	D
Demand (tonnes/month)	100	150	175	150	200	300	350	500	650	450	200	100
Productive days	20	18	21	21	22	22	21	10	21	22	21	18
Demand (tonnes/day)	5	8.33	8.33	7.14	9.52	13.64	16.67	50	30.95	20.46	9.52	5.56
Cumulative days	20	38	59	80	102	124	145	155	176	198	219	237
Cumulative demand	100	250	425	575	775	1075	1425	1925	2575	3025	3225	3325
Cumulative production (tonnes)	281	533	828	1122	1431	1740	2023	2175	2469	2778	3073	3325
Ending inventory (tonnes)	181	283	403	547	656	715	609	250	(106)	(247)	(150)	0

sentation by judging the area between the cumulative production and demand curves. This represents the amount of inventory carried over the period. Figure 11.17 illustrates an adequate level capacity plan for the chocolate manufacturer, together with the costs of carrying inventory. It is assumed that inventory costs £2 per tonne per day to keep in storage. The average inventory each month is taken to be the average of the beginning- and end-of-month inventory levels, and the inventory-carrying cost each month is the product of the average inventory, the inventory cost per day per tonne and the number of days in the month.

Comparing plans on a cumulative basis

Chase demand plans can also be illustrated on a cumulative representation. Rather than the cumulative production line having a constant gradient, it would have a varying gradient representing the production rate at any point in time. If a pure demand

Figure 11.17 A level capacity plan which meets demand at all times during the year

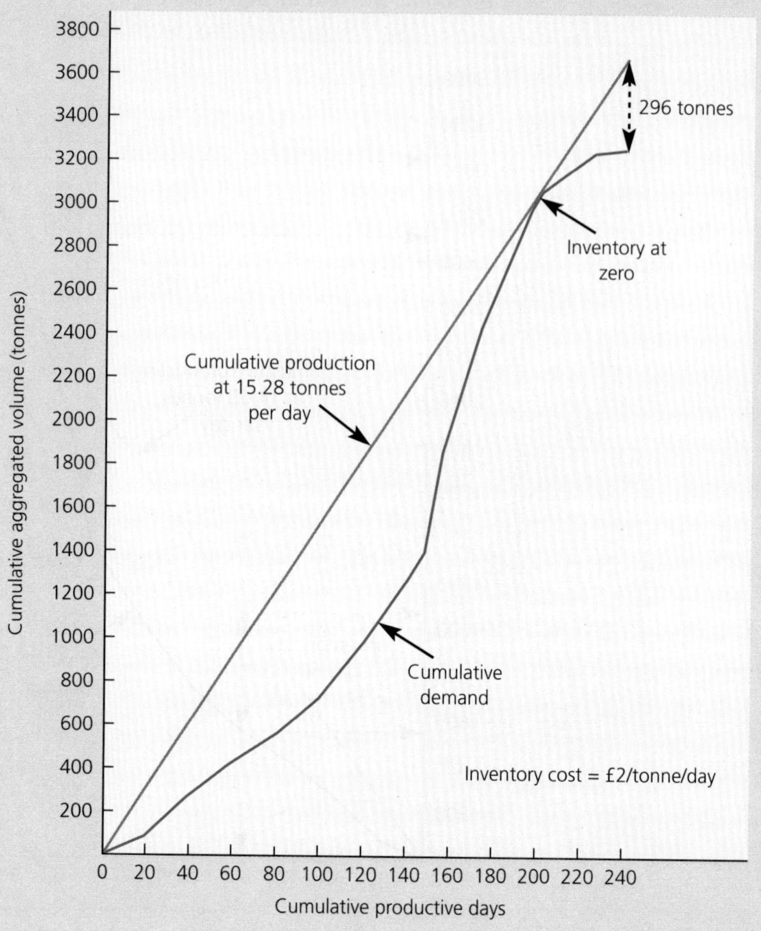

(Graph: Cumulative aggregated volume (tonnes) on the y-axis from 200 to 3800, Cumulative productive days on the x-axis from 0 to 240. Lines show "Cumulative production at 15.28 tonnes per day", "Cumulative demand", marked "Inventory at zero", "296 tonnes", and "Inventory cost = £2/tonne/day".)

	J	F	M	A	M	J	J	A	S	O	N	D
Demand (tonnes/month)	100	150	175	150	200	300	350	500	650	450	200	100
Productive days	20	18	21	21	22	22	21	10	21	22	21	18
Demand (tonnes/day)	5	8.33	8.33	7.14	9.52	13.64	16.67	50	30.95	20.46	9.52	5.56
Cumulative days	20	38	59	80	102	124	145	155	176	198	219	237
Cumulative demand	100	250	425	575	775	1075	1425	1925	2575	3025	3225	3325
Cumulative production (tonnes)	306	581	902	1222	1559	1895	2216	2368	2689	3025	3346	3621
Ending inventory (tonnes)	206	331	477	647	784	820	791	443	114	0	121	296
Average inventory (tonnes)	103	270	404	562	716	802	806	617	279	57	61	209
Inventory cost for month (£)	4120	9720	16968	23604	31504	35288	33852	12340	11718	2508	2562	7524

Total inventory cost for year = £191 608

chase plan was adopted, the cumulative production line would match the cumulative demand line. The gap between the two lines would be zero and hence inventory would be zero. Although this would eliminate inventory-carrying costs, as we discussed earlier, there would be costs associated with changing capacity levels. These *capacity change costs* are sometimes drawn as shown in Figure 11.18. The cost of a capacity change depends on the degree of change, the direction of the change, and the capacity level from which the change is being made. Usually, the marginal cost of making a capacity change increases with the size of the change. For example, if the chocolate manufacturer wishes to increase capacity by 5 per cent, this can be achieved by requesting its staff to work overtime – a simple, fast and relatively inexpensive option. If the change is 15 per cent, overtime cannot provide sufficient extra capacity and temporary staff

Coping with seasonality at Nestlé

Packing high-quality chocolate assortments

Any food manufacturer has to learn how to cope with seasonal fluctuations. Nestlé, the Swiss-based multinational, the largest food company in the world, has more experience than most. Either the supply of materials is seasonal (frozen vegetables) or demand is seasonal (ice-cream), or both (dried milk). The manufacturer of chocolate products is typical. Demand is driven partly by the weather – chocolate is less popular in summer – and partly by cultural factors – chocolate is a popular gift at Christmas and Easter in many countries. Nestlé plants use a combination of strategies to cope with these demand fluctuations. Some products can be stored in anticipation of seasonal peaks. However, there is a 'shelf-life' limit on storage time if Nestlé's high-quality standards are to be maintained. Off-peak sales volumes can also be influenced through the use of 'special offers' and product promotions. Within Nestlé's plant themselves, output rates can be fluctuated, although different ways of doing this may be appropriate at different stages in the process. The manufacture of the chocolate itself is constrained by the capacity limits of the process

technology, whereas in the packing of assortments, for example (*see* picture), extra staff can be hired at peak times. All this makes for a sensitive decision-making environment. If Nestlé managers get it wrong, either we run out of our favourite products or the company is left with surplus stock.

Some of Nestlé's popular chocolate products

Questions

1   What are the main 'trade-offs' which Nestlé managers have to get right in coping with the seasonality of their chocolate products?

2   What do you think are the differences between managing seasonality for the popular products illustrated to the left (known as 'count lines') and the up-market chocolate assortments shown being packed in the right-hand picture.

---

will need to be employed – a more expensive solution which also would take more time. Increases in capacity of above 15 per cent might only be achieved by sub-contracting some work out. This would be even more expensive. The cost of the change will also be affected by the point from which the change is being made, as well as the direction of the change. Usually, it is less expensive to change capacity towards what is regarded as the 'normal' capacity level than away from it.

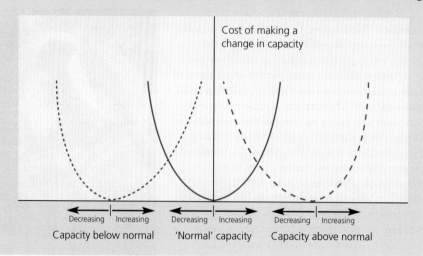

Figure 11.18 The costs of changing capacity will depend on the point from which the change is made, the degree of change and the direction of the change

Decreasing | Increasing   Decreasing | Increasing   Decreasing | Increasing
Capacity below normal   'Normal' capacity   Capacity above normal

Suppose the chocolate manufacturer, which has been operating the level capacity plan as shown in Figure 11.17, is unhappy with the inventory costs of this approach. It decides to explore two alternative plans, both involving some degree of demand chasing.

Plan 1

- Organize and staff the factory for a 'normal' capacity level of 8.7 tonnes per day.
- Produce at 8.7 tonnes per day for the first 124 days of the year, then increase capacity to 29 tonnes per day by heavy use of overtime, hiring temporary staff and some sub-contracting.
- Produce at 29 tonnes per day until day 194, then reduce capacity back to 8.7 tonnes per day for the rest of the year.

The costs of changing capacity by such a large amount (the ratio of peak to normal capacity is 3.33:1) are calculated by the company as being:

Cost of changing from 8.7 tonnes/day to 29 tonnes/day = £110 000
Cost of changing from 29 tonnes/day to 8.7 tonnes/day = £60 000

Plan 2

- Organize and staff the factory for a 'normal' capacity level of 12.4 tonnes per day.
- Produce at 12.4 tonnes per day for the first 150 days of the year, then increase capacity to 29 tonnes per day by overtime and hiring some temporary staff.
- Produce at 29 tonnes/day until day 190, then reduce capacity back to 12.4 tonnes per day for the rest of the year.

The costs of changing capacity in this plan are smaller because the degree of change is smaller (a peak to normal capacity ratio of 2.34:1), and they are calculated by the company as being:

Cost of changing from 12.4 tonnes/day to 29 tonnes/day = £35 000
Cost of changing from 29 tonnes/day to 12.4 tonnes/day = £15 000

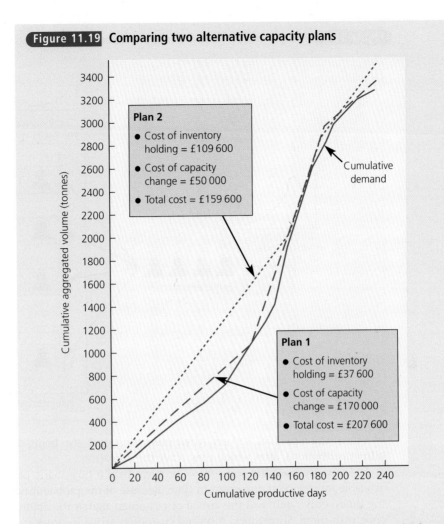

Figure 11.19 Comparing two alternative capacity plans

Plan 2
- Cost of inventory holding = £109 600
- Cost of capacity change = £50 000
- Total cost = £159 600

Cumulative demand

Plan 1
- Cost of inventory holding = £37 600
- Cost of capacity change = £170 000
- Total cost = £207 600

Cumulative aggregated volume (tonnes)

Cumulative productive days

Figure 11.19 illustrates both plans on a cumulative basis. Plan 1, which envisaged two drastic changes in capacity, has high capacity change costs but, because its production levels are close to demand levels, it has low inventory carrying costs. Plan 2 sacrifices some of the inventory cost advantage of Plan 1 but saves more in terms of capacity change costs.

Queueing theory

Cumulative representations of capacity plans are useful where the operation has the ability to store its finished goods as inventory. For operations which, by their nature, cannot store their output, such as most service operations, capacity planning and control presents a different set of problems.

Although service operations do, of course, make forecasts of their expected average level of demand, they cannot usually predict exactly when each individual customer or order will arrive. A distribution which describes the probability of customers arriving might be known, but not each individual arrival. This makes providing adequate capacity particularly difficult. Furthermore, as well as the arrival of customers being uncertain, the time that each customer will need in the operation might also be uncertain. Figure 11.20 shows the general form of this capacity issue. Customers arrive according to some probability distribution and wait to be processed (unless part of the operation is idle); when they have reached the front of the queue, they are processed

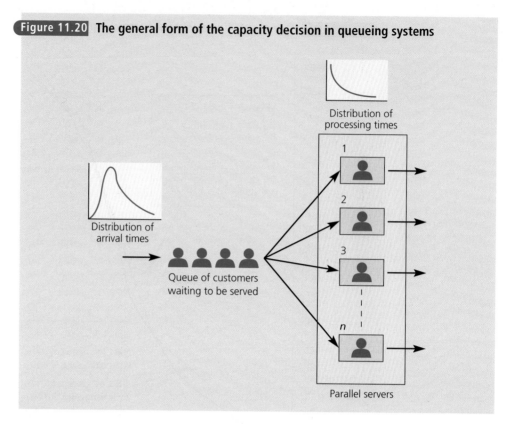

by one of the *n* parallel 'servers' (their processing time also being described by a probability distribution), after which they leave the operation.

The capacity planning and control problem here is how many parallel servers to have available for service at any point in time. Because of the probabilistic arrival and processing times, only rarely will the arrival of customers match the ability of the operation to cope with them. Sometimes, if several customers arrive in quick succession and require longer-than-average processing times, queues will build up in front of the operation. At other times, when customers arrive less frequently than average and also require shorter-than-average processing times, some of the servers in the system will be idle. So even when the average capacity (processing capability) of the operation matches the average demand (arrival rate) on the system, both queues and idle time will occur. There are many examples of this kind of system. Table 11.2 illustrates some of these.

If the operation has too few servers (that is, capacity is set at too low a level), queues will build up to a level where customers become dissatisfied with the time they are having to wait, although the utilization level of the servers will be high. If too many

Table 11.2 Examples of operations which have parallel processors

Operation	Arrivals	Processing capacity
Bank	Customers	Tellers
Supermarket	Shoppers	Checkouts
Hospital clinic	Patients	Doctors
Graphic artist	Commissions	Artists
Custom cake decorators	Orders	Cake decorators
Ambulance service	Emergencies	Ambulances with crews
Telephone switchboard	Calls	Telephonists
Maintenance department	Breakdowns	Maintenance staff

A waiting area in a bank which allows customers to wait in comfort with distractions such as magazines and a television

servers are in place (that is, capacity is set at too high a level), the time which customers can expect to wait will not be long but the utilization of the servers will be low. This is why the capacity planning and control problem for this type of operation is often presented as a trade-off between customer waiting time and system utilization. What is certainly important in making capacity decisions is being able to predict both of these factors for a given queueing system.

Analytical queueing models

Management scientists have developed formulae which can predict the steady-state behaviour of different types of queueing system. The type of system illustrated in Figure 11.20 is the most useful for capacity management purposes, but it is only one of several types of queueing system. Unfortunately, these formulae can be extremely complicated, especially for all but the most simple assumptions, and are beyond the scope of this book. In fact, computer programs are almost always now used to predict the behaviour of queueing systems. However, Figure 11.21 shows some curves, derived from queueing formulae, which give the relationship between the mean number of customers in the system (either queueing or being served) and the 'utilization factor' (which indicates the average proportion of their time which the servers spend processing customers) for various values of n, the number of parallel servers.

The curves in Figure 11.21 are calculated on the assumption that customers arrive in a random fashion. That is, the arrival of each customer is independent of that of the other customers. The number of arrivals per unit of time is assumed to be described by a Poisson distribution. Processing times are assumed to be described by a negative exponential distribution. Both these assumptions are made largely for mathematical convenience, but are usually quite appropriate for actual arrival and processing rates in many real systems. The final assumptions are that customers are sufficiently patient to stay in the queue once they have joined it, and are processed on a 'first come, first served' basis.

We shall use the following notation:

λ = mean arrival rate (customer arrivals per hour)
μ = mean service rate per busy server (capacity, in customers per hour)
ρ = traffic intensity (λ/μ)
n = number of servers
L_s = mean number of customers in the system

Figure 11.21 Queueing curves for a system with *n* parallel servers

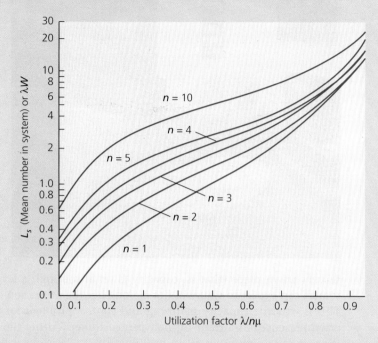

Source: Adapted from Fitzsimmons, J.A. and Fitzsimmons, M.J. (1994) *Service Management for Competitive Advantage*, McGraw-Hill. Copyright © McGraw-Hill, with permission.

Managing queues at Madame Tussaud's Scenerama, Amsterdam[6]

A short holiday in Amsterdam would not be complete without a visit to Madame Tussaud's Scenerama, located on four upper floors of the city's most prominent department store in Dam Square. With 600 000 visitors each year, this is the third most popular tourist attraction in Amsterdam, after the flower market and canal trips. On busy days in the summer, the centre can just manage to handle 5000 visitors. On a wet day in January, however, there may only be 300 visitors throughout the whole day. The centre is open for admission, seven days a week, from 10.00 am to 5.30 pm.

In the streets outside, orderly queues of expectant tourists snake along the pavement, looking in at the displays in the store windows. In this public open space, Tussaud's can do little to entertain the visitors, but entrepreneurial buskers and street artists are quick to capitalize on a captive market. On reaching the entrance lobby, individuals, families and groups purchase their admissions tickets. The lobby is in the shape of a large horseshoe, with the ticket sales booth in the centre. On winter days or at quiet spells, there will only be one sales assistant, but on busier days, visitors can

pay at either side of the ticket booth, to speed up the process. Having paid, the visitors assemble in the lobby outside the two lifts. While waiting in this area, a photographer wanders around offering to take photos of the visitors standing next to life-sized wax figures of famous people. They may also be entertained by living lookalikes of famous personalities who act as guides to groups of visitors in batches of around 25 customers (the capacity of each of the two lifts which takes visitors up to the facility). The lifts arrive every four minutes and customers simultaneously disembark forming one group of about 50, customers who stay together throughout the Scenerama section.

Source: By kind permission of Dr Willem Bijleveld, Director, Madame Tussaud Scenerama B.V., Amsterdam

Questions

1 Generally, what could Madame Tussaud's do to cope with its demand fluctuations?

2 What does the operation do to make queueing relatively painless? What else could it do?

$$L_q = \text{mean number of customers in queue} = L_s - \rho$$

$$W_s = \text{mean time customer spends in the system} = \frac{L_q}{\lambda} + \frac{1}{\mu}$$

$$W_q = \text{mean time customer spends in the queue} = \frac{L_q}{\lambda}$$

Worked example

A bank wishes to decide how many enquiry staff to schedule during the busy lunch period. Its investigations have revealed that, during this period, customers arrive at a rate of nine per hour and the enquiries which customers have during this period (checking on accounts, opening new accounts, arranging loans, etc.) take, on average, 15 minutes. The bank manager feels that four staff should be on duty during this period but wants to make sure that customers do not wait more than three minutes on average before they are served:

$$\lambda = \text{arrival rate} = 9 \text{ per hour}$$

$$\mu = \text{service rate} = \frac{1}{0.25} = 4 \text{ per hour}$$

$$n = 4 \text{ servers}$$

$$\text{Utilization factor} = \frac{1}{n\mu} = \frac{9}{4 \times 4}$$
$$= 0.5625$$

From Figure 11.21, for a utilization factor of 0.5626 and $n = 4$,

$$L_s = \text{mean number of customers in the system} = 2.56$$
$$L_q = \text{mean number of customers in the queue} = L_s - \rho$$

$$= 2.56 - \frac{9}{4} = 0.31$$

$$W_q = \text{mean queueing time} = \frac{L_q}{\lambda}$$

$$= \frac{0.31}{9} = 0.0344 \text{ hrs}$$

$$= 2.07 \text{ minutes}$$

So the manager can be assured that, with a capacity of four enquiry staff during the lunch period, the average time a customer will wait is less than three minutes.

● The dynamics of capacity planning and control

Our emphasis so far has been on the planning aspects of capacity management. In practice, the management of capacity is a far more dynamic process which involves controlling and reacting to *actual* demand and *actual* capacity as it occurs. The capacity control process can be seen as a sequence of partially reactive capacity decision processes as shown in Figure 11.22. At the beginning of each period, operations management considers its forecasts of demand, its understanding of current capacity and, if appropriate, how much inventory has been carried forward from the previous period. Based on all this information, it makes plans for the following period's capacity. During the next period, demand might or might not be as forecast and the actual capacity of the operation might or might not turn out as planned. But whatever the actual conditions during that period, at the beginning of the next period the same types of decisions must be made, in the light of the new circumstances.

The outlook matrix[7]

One of the main influences on operations managers, when they are making period-by-period capacity decisions, is their confidence in future demand matching future

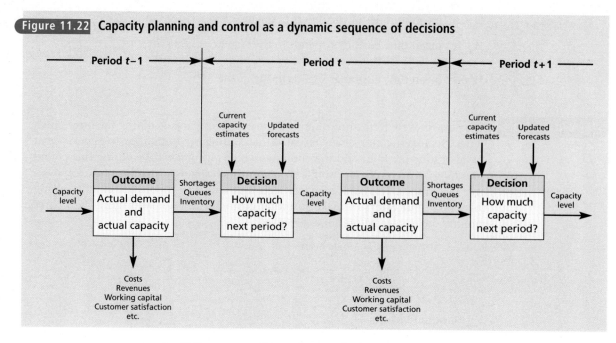

capacity. If they are confident that, in the long term, demand is likely to exceed current capacity then, irrespective of the current level of demand, they will be more likely to be tolerant of policies which could lead to short-term over-capacity. Conversely, if long-term demand looks poor, it will be necessary to start implementing policies that will reduce long-term capacity. Overlying this are the needs of current demand. Even if long-term demand looks poor, it might be necessary to increase capacity if there is a short-term requirement. Figure 11.23 gives examples of the types of methods which

Figure 11.23 The dynamics of capacity planning are governed partly by the combination of long-term and short-term outlook

		Short-term outlook	
	POOR Outlook < 1	NORMAL Outlook = 1	GOOD Outlook > 1
POOR Outlook < 1	Lay-off staff	Delay any action	Overtime Hire temporary staff
NORMAL Outlook = 1	Short-time Idle time	Do nothing	Overtime Hire temporary staff
GOOD Outlook > 1	Make for inventory Short-time	Hire and make for inventory Start to recruit	Hire staff

(Long-term outlook)

$$\text{Outlook} = \frac{\text{Forecast demand}}{\text{Forecast capacity}}$$

might be adopted for different combinations of long-term and short-term outlook. Here outlook is defined as:

$$\text{Outlook} = \frac{\text{forecast demand}}{\text{forecast capacity}}$$

Three broad states of outlook are identified for both the long and short term: 'poor' is when the ratio of forecast demand to forecast capacity is less than 1; 'normal' is when the ratio is approximately equal to 1; 'good' is when the ratio is greater than 1.

When both long-term outlook and short-term outlook are poor, there is relatively little choice but to reduce the capacity of the operation; capacity is not needed now, nor is it likely to be needed in the future. Staff lay-offs might be the only method of achieving this. When short-term outlook is normal, but long-term outlook is poor, current capacity needs to be maintained, though certainly not increased. Under these circumstances the operation is most likely to delay any decisions. Certainly it would not commit investments in capacity which are unlikely to be needed in the future. When short-term outlook is good in spite of long-term outlook being poor, the operation faces a dilemma. It does not want to make any permanent commitments to increase capacity because the extra capacity will not be needed in the future. However, it does need to meet current levels of demand. Under these circumstances the use of overtime or the recruitment of temporary staff might be the least permanent methods of achieving short-term capacity requirements.

When long-term outlook is normal and short-term outlook is poor, capacity needs to be temporarily reduced but not in such a way as to compromise longer-term requirements. The operation here is likely to tolerate a certain amount of unproductive or idle time, or might perhaps reduce the working hours of its staff temporarily. When both long-term outlook and short-term outlook are normal, no action is required. However, when short-term outlook is good, capacity will need to be increased but not in any permanent manner. Again, overtime and the use of temporary staff are likely to be appropriate methods.

When the long-term outlook is good, there will be a requirement to build up capacity in some way, irrespective of short-term circumstances. So, when the short-term outlook is poor, the operation will not want to do anything which compromises long-term capacity. It may even, if possible, use any short-term surplus capacity to build up inventory. It is also likely to do this when long-term outlook is good and the short-term outlook is normal. Here, though, it will need to start recruiting extra staff or working overtime if it wants to make products for inventory. Finally, when both long-term outlook and short-term outlook are good, capacity will need to be increased relatively quickly and probably in a permanent manner through hiring extra staff.

What is capacity planning and control?

● It is the way operations organize the level of value-added activity which they can achieve under normal operating conditions over a period of time.

● We usually distinguish between a long-, medium- and short-term capacity decision. This chapter has dealt with medium- and short-term capacity management where the capacity level of the organization is adjusted within the fixed physical limits which are set by long-term capacity decisions.

● This is sometimes called aggregate planning and control because it is necessary to aggregate the various types of output from an operation into one composite measure.

● Decisions made in capacity planning and control affect the ability to generate revenues and the extent of working capital required by the organization, as well as the normal operations objectives of quality, speed, dependability, flexibility and cost.

● Almost all operations have some kind of fluctuation in demand (or seasonality) caused by some combination of climatic, festive, behavioural, political, financial or social factors.

How is capacity measured?

● Either by the availability of its input resources or by the output which is produced.

● Which of these measures is used partly depends on how stable is the mix of outputs. If it is difficult to aggregate the different types of output from an operation, input measures are usually preferred.

● The usage of capacity is measured by the factors 'utilization' and 'efficiency'.

What are the ways of coping with demand fluctuation?

● Output can be kept level, in effect ignoring demand fluctuations. This will result in under-utilization of capacity where outputs cannot be stored, or the build-up of inventories where output can be stored.

● Output can chase demand by fluctuating the output level through some combination of overtime, varying the size of the workforce, using part-time staff and sub-contracting.

● Demand can be changed, either by influencing the market through such measures as advertising and promotion, or by developing alternative products with a counter-seasonal demand pattern.

● Most operations use a mix of all these three 'pure' strategies.

How can operations plan their capacity level?

● Representing demand and output in the form of cumulative representations allows the feasibility of alternative capacity plans to be assessed.

● In many operations, especially service operations, queueing theory can indicate the consequences of alternative capacity strategies.

How can operations control their capacity level?

● By considering the capacity decision as a dynamic decision which periodically updates the decisions and assumptions upon which decisions are based.

● By considering the major influences on which, periodically, capacity strategies are adopted. The 'outlook matrix' which compares long-term and short-term outlook for demand (against capacity) is one way of doing this.

Fine Country Fruit Cakes

September 1994 was a year to remember for Jean and Dave Fulbright! Their twin sons, Michael and Alan, then five years old, started school, and in the same month, Dave, a 29-year-old master baker at a large bakery, was made redundant. Jean, who had a part-time secretarial job with a local builder, saw this misfortune to be an unrepeatable opportunity. They had always wanted to work together, and it seemed to be a good chance to set up a small speciality business, based on Dave's skills and financed by his redundancy payments plus a small loan.

Traditionally, small local baking and confectionery businesses produce a wide range of breads, cakes, biscuits, etc., many on a daily basis. This involves a very early start (4 am), high complexity and considerable risk. Dave wanted a 'simpler' business that would involve relatively normal hours of work, for both himself and his wife. Neither wanted to be employers; the business would be run by just the two of them. Dave felt that his greatest satisfaction came from producing high-quality decorated fruit cakes, so together they decided that there was an opportunity to specialize in this product. Using an old family recipe, samples were made and packaged. 'Market research' was confined to taking these samples to various retail outlets in the area; the reaction was so enthusiastic, and the potential margin seemed so high, that by January 1993 they were in business. They rented a small modern factory near home, modestly equipped with weighing and preparation equipment, a large 15 kg food mixer, two small catering ovens, a small coolroom and sundry utensils. Talking to a friend in spring 1997, Dave recalled:

'In early 1995 we only made one size: beautiful 2 kg cakes, symmetrically decorated on top with a pattern of almonds, cherries, walnuts and ginger. We sold most to cafés and restaurants; their customers loved portions of them with their teas/coffees. Demand ran at about 150–200 cakes a month, which wasn't enough to make much of a living, but we had time to visit our customers and to try new outlets. Although sales were growing, it gradually became clear that we should be selling a smaller cake to retail shops for family purchasers – one which could be bought as a treat, or as a gift for friends. We introduced the 1 kg cake (with the same recipe) in July 1995. We had no problems selling these, and demand soon exceeded all our expectations. The delicatessens in the area heard about our products and soon sales of the 1 kg cake overtook those of the original 2 kg cake. Somehow, however, it's not been so easy running the business since then; we can only just cope every day making the cakes. Jean can go to get the children from school at about 3.30 pm (a neighbour takes them in the morning) but I rarely get back before 7.00 pm in the week; and we usually do our selling and prospecting for new customers on Saturdays. We certainly don't want to start production at weekends; we couldn't cope with that! Anyway, although we're making a reasonable profit now, I feel we could do a better job somehow. There were times last year (1996) when we had over-produced and we had to sell off some stock at a discount because of its age. Tests have shown that this recipe of rich fruit cakes lasts for up to 12 months, but for best flavour and texture, it should really be eaten within six months. The retailers demand at least three months of this, so I can't keep stock more than three months here at the factory. Anyway, I only have space for about 3000 kg in the coolroom, allowing for stock rotation.'

Jean's view of the business was somewhat different:

'I think we are chasing the wrong markets! The delicatessens demand big discounts and are always expecting us to deliver at short notice, particularly around Easter (March/April) and at Christmas (November/December) when the cakes are apparently popular gifts. I have found that craft shops and visitor centres of local tourist spots (such as castles and historic houses) can also sell our 1 kg cakes and, moreover, they don't expect much discount! We were really pleased with the level of orders from these outlets last summer, but we don't hear from them much during the winter. I really should go and take some more samples! I also feel we should open a factory shop where regular users could come and buy directly, but I am sure we would need to provide a bigger range of cakes. We could develop lots of different types in the two sizes – then we would get a lot more repeat business!'

Production

Preparation

In order to simplify weighing, mixing and baking, all production is done in nominal 10 kg batches of one size at a time. Thus a batch is either ten 1 kg cakes or five 2 kg cakes. For each batch, dried fruits (raisins, sultanas, currants, cherries, crystallized ginger, etc.) are weighed and cleaned as necessary, other ingredients are prepared and measured, and a

Table 11.3 Company records of sales 1995/96 and forecast sales for 1997

	1995	Jan	Feb	Mar	Apr	May	Jun	Jul	Aug	Sep	Oct	Nov	Dec	Total	1997 (Forecast)
1 kg cakes	900	80	200	600	320	120	80	120	80	240	480	800	1 600	4 720	6 000
2 kg cakes	1 950	160	340	300	240	140	160	240	160	180	260	300	400	2880	3 500
Total (kg)	4 800	400	880	1 200	800	400	400	600	400	600	1 000	1 400	2 400	10 480	13 000

cake mixture is made in the mixer. Tins are greased, and the mixture is weighed into each; the top surface is then decorated with carefully selected specimen dried fruits and nuts, and brushed with a glaze. This complete preparation stage takes almost exactly 30 minutes per batch for Dave and Jean working as a team, for either size of cake. Each batch is prepared just before the oven is ready to accept it, to avoid contamination and to maintain consistency of method, and hence of texture.

Baking

The ovens are turned on at 8.00 am and are ready by 8.30 when the first batch is loaded (which only takes a few minutes). A 10 kg batch of cakes fills one oven; baking time is three hours for the 1 kg cakes, four and a half hours for 2 kg cakes. When ready, the cakes are removed from the hot oven, which is ready for a further batch in a quarter of an hour. For convenience, Dave has always baked the 1 kg cakes in the oldest oven (Oven 1) to avoid having to carry 10 tins to Oven 2 which is further from the workbench. Each oven normally bakes only two batches per day. Dave thinks that the temperature control on Oven 1 is inaccurate which would be a particular problem for the larger size cakes!

Packing

Cakes are turned out onto racks to cool overnight. The next day, once the first batches are in the oven, the previous day's cakes are inspected, packed in a film, a decorative ribbon and an outer-wrap, and then labelled and dated. Packed cakes are then carried to the coolroom and stacked according to size. These processes take two people six minutes per cake (either size). The couple take one hour for lunch from 12.30 to 1.30 pm (when Oven 2 is ready to unload).

Planning

'The only times in 1996 that we changed production were in March, April, November and December when we increased 2 kg output only by 50 per cent (one extra

batch per day). I had to bake the 2 kg cakes in Oven 1 and the quality wasn't really so good, but none of our regular customers noticed! Even so, I had to work into the evenings all those months; it was a lot of work. All other months we have kept to the plan of two batches of each size each day (1 kg, followed by 2 kg, 1 kg, 2 kg) which helps us keep to a rhythm.'

Sales

Records were kept of monthly sales of each size during 1996 (Table 11.3). On 1st January 1996 there was an opening stock of 100 of each size of cake. Dave commented:

'I am worried that we won't be able to cope with demand in 1997, and that we will start giving bad service. Perhaps we should drop the idea of selling to the tourist spots, although the margins are very attractive. Clearly, we musn't upset the retailers who give us so much business.'

Questions

1 With the current method of working, what is the monthly and annual capacity of the business? Is the total weight (kg) of product a useful aggregate measure of capacity for this business? How does capacity compare with demand in 1996 and forecast demand in 1997?

2 Why did Dave have to sell stock at reduced prices in 1996? In which months do you think that happened, and explain clearly the reasons. Justify your answer with simple calculations.

3 Jean believes that they should try to get more business from craft shops and tourist centres. What advantages/disadvantages would this market have compared with the existing retail outlets?

4 What are the main differences in operations tasks of running the proposed retail shop? What are the implications of this for the owners?

5 What are the operational implications of making 10 varieties of cake, each in two sizes?

1 Explain what is meant by capacity planning and control and describe the implications of a capacity constraint in one of the micro operations of an organization of your own choice.

2 Discuss the implications of having too much or too little capacity for the following operations:
   – a national train network
   – a lecture room
   – a vineyard's grape-pressing equipment.

3 Discuss with an operation's manager the demand trends for the organization's products or services, covering the long, medium and short terms. Find out the periods over which the manager makes or uses forecasts and the problems resulting from any inaccuracies in those forecasts.

4 Identify several ways in which the following organizations might measure their capacity (discuss the relative merits of each and suggest the one you think each organization will use):
   – a city bus company
   – a dentist
   – a lift (elevator) maintenance company
   – a jobbing plumber.

5 A car battery manufacturer makes four types of car battery: compact, compact-heavy duty, standard and standard-heavy duty. Table 11.4 shows the number of batteries of each type currently produced to order for existing customers and the amount of time each battery spends with the acid-filling machine. The machine is capable of working up to 24 hours a day and needs no adjusting between battery types. The operations manager is under pressure to increase the utilization of the plant. The company has been approached by two new customers to supply batteries. Company A requires someone to supply them with between 80 and 100 batteries per day of various types. Company B requires 10 compact and 70 standard batteries a day, all heavy duty; however, delivery must be assured.

Table 11.4 Battery production

	Number produced per day	Time with acid filler (mins)
Compact	80	3
Compact HD	50	5
Standard	90	4
Standard HD	20	6

Assuming the acid-filling machine is the only capacity constraint, review the merits of each order.

6 Explain how utilization might be measured in the operations following and discuss the relative merits of using utilization and efficiency as measures of operations performance:
   – a doctor's surgery
   – a university lecture
   – an ice-cream manufacturer.

7 What factors do you think would affect the volume, timing and types of calls coming into a call centre run by a car insurance company which advertises in newspapers and on television?

8 Which do you think will be the main capacity plans, and how might they be implemented, for the following organizations:
   – a university
   – an Accident and Emergency ward at a hospital
   – a compact disc producer
   – a taxi service?

   (Explain the reasons for your choice.)

9 The management of an hotel on a popular Greek holiday island is concerned that its hotel is full between March and September, is about 80 per cent occupied in February, March and December and about 30 per cent occupied during the other months. Discuss ways in which it might try to move towards 100 per cent occupancy all the year round.

10 A computer bureau's telephone help desk is staffed by 10 people throughout the day. It is known that the bureau handles about 15 customers an hour and the average time it takes to deal with a problem is 10 minutes. The operations manager believes that customers will be aggrieved if they have to wait for more than two minutes for their calls to be answered. Comment on the situation.

11 The Speedy Cleaning Company operates a drive-in car valeting service. This comprises a number of cleaning bays where customers can drive in and use special cleaning equipment to valet their cars. On Saturday mornings the arrival rate averages five customers per hour. The arrival rate appears to conform to a Poisson distribution. The average time to clean a car is 10 minutes, with times being distributed according to a negative exponential distribution. How many bays should the company open to ensure that customers wait no longer than three minutes before being able to enter a bay?

12 The Dagenham Chow-Mein Pizza Company has a demand forecast for the next 12 months which is shown in Table 11.5.

The current workforce of 100 staff can produce 1000 cases of pizzas per month.

(a) Prepare a production plan which keeps the output level. How much warehouse space would the company need for this plan?

(b) Prepare a demand chase plan. What implications would this have for staffing levels, assuming that the maximum amount of overtime would result in production levels of only 10 per cent greater than normal working hours?

Table 11.5 Pizza demand forecast

Months	Demand (cases per month)
January	600
February	800
March	1000
April	1500
May	2000
June	1700
July	1200
August	1100
September	900
October	2500
November	3200
December	900

Notes on chapter

1 Thanks to Cormac Campbell, OEE Consulting Ltd.
2 Source: Interviews with company staff.
3 Sources: Lynch, P. (1991) 'Making Time for Productivity', *Personnel Management*, March; and Pickard, J. (1991) 'Annual Hours: A Year of Living Dangerously', *Personnel Management*, Aug.
4 Kimes, S. (1989) 'Yield Management: A Tool for Capacity-constrained Service Firms', *Journal of Operations Management*, Vol 8, No 4.
5 Source: *The Economist*, 10 Aug 1991.
6 Source: Discussions with company staff.
7 Based on Colley, J.L., Landell, R.D. and Fair, R.R. (1978) *Operations Planning and Control*, Holden Day.

Selected further reading

Bleuel, W.H. (1975) 'Management Science's Impact on Service Strategy', *Interfaces*, Vol 6, No 1.

Buxey, G. (1993) 'Production Planning and Scheduling for Seasonal Demand', *International Journal of Operations and Production Management*, Vol 13, No 7.

Chaiken, J.M. and Larson, R.C. (1972) 'Methods for Allocating Urban Emergency Units Survey', *Management Science*, Vol 19, No 4.

Coker, J.L. (1985) 'Analysing Production Switching Heuristics for Aggregate Planning Models via an Application', *Production and Inventory Management*, 4th Quarter.

Fitzsimmons, J.A. and Fitzsimmons, M.J. (1994) *Service Management for Competitive Advantage*, McGraw-Hill.

Gallagher, G.R. (1980) 'How to Develop a Realistic Master Schedule', *Management Review*, Apr.

Grassman, W.K. (1988) 'Finding the Right Number of Servers in Real-World Queueing Systems', *Interfaces*, Vol 8, No 2.

Holt, C., Modigliani, C.F. and Simon, H. (1955) 'A Linear Decision Rule for Production and Employment Scheduling', *Management Science*, Vol 2, No 2.

Lee, S.M. and Moore, L.J. (1974) 'A Practical Approach to Production Scheduling', *Production and Inventory Management*, 1st Quarter.

Lee, W.B. and Khumwala, B.M. (1974) 'Simulation Testing of Aggregate Production Planning Models in an Implementation Methodology', *Management Science*, Vol 20, No 6.

Mangiameli, P. and Krajewski, L. (1983) 'The Effects of Work Force Strategies on Manufacturing Operations', *Journal of Operations Management*, Vol 3, No 4.

Mapes, J. (1993) 'The Effect of Capacity Limitations on Safety Stock', *International Journal of Operations and Production Management*, Vol 13, No 10.

Northcraft, G.B. and Chase, R.B. (1985) 'Managing Service Demand at the Point of Delivery', *Academy of Management Review*, Vol 10, Jan.

Rothstein, M. (1985) 'Operations Research and the Airline Overbooking Problem', *Operations Research*, Vol 33, No 1.

Sasser, W.E. (1976) 'Match Supply and Demand in Service Industries', *Harvard Business Review*, Vol 54, No 6.

Vollmann, T.E., Berry, W.L. and Whybark, D.C. (1988) *Manufacturing Planning and Control Systems*, Irwin.

CHAPTER

12

Inventory planning and control

Introduction

Operations managers usually have an ambivalent attitude towards inventories. On the one hand, they are costly, tying up sometimes considerable amounts of working capital. They are also risky because items held in stock could deteriorate, become obsolete or just get lost, and, furthermore, they take up valuable space in the operation. On the other hand, they provide some security in a complex and uncertain environment. Knowing that you have the items in stock, should customers or production schedules demand them, is a comforting insurance against the unexpected. Certainly when a customer goes elsewhere because just one item is out of stock, or when a major project is waiting for just one small part, the value of inventories seems indisputable. This is the dilemma of inventory management: in spite of the cost and the other disadvantages associated with holding stocks, they do facilitate the smoothing of supply and demand. In fact they only exist because supply and demand are not in harmony with each other (*see* Fig. 12.1).

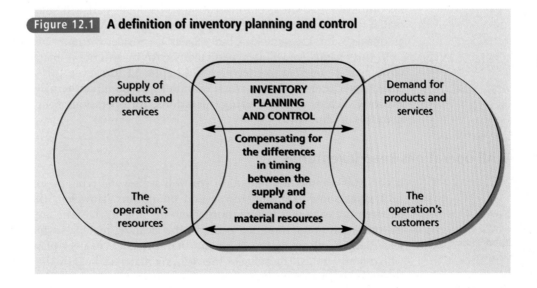

Figure 12.1 **A definition of inventory planning and control**

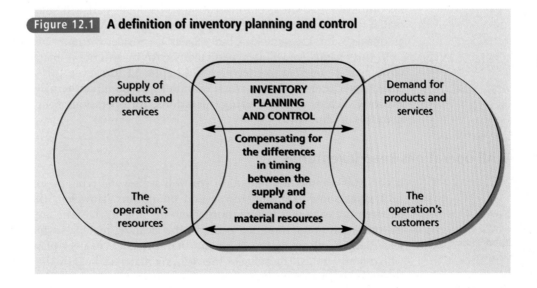

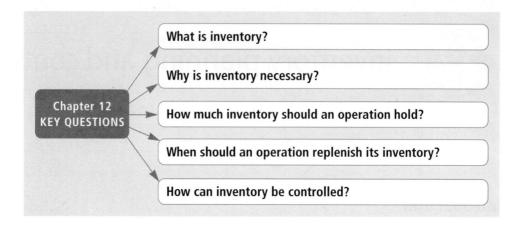

Chapter 12
KEY QUESTIONS

What is inventory?

Why is inventory necessary?

How much inventory should an operation hold?

When should an operation replenish its inventory?

How can inventory be controlled?

What is inventory?

Inventory, or 'stock' as it is more commonly called in some countries, is defined here as the *stored accumulation of material resources in a transformation system*. Sometimes inventory is also used to describe any stored resource. Thus, a bank would have a 'stock' of staff, a 'stock' of ATMs, even a 'stock' of retail branches. However, although these transforming resources are technically held as 'stocks', insomuch as they are not especially obtained every time a customer makes a request of the bank, they are not what we normally mean by the term 'stock' or 'inventory'. Usually we use the term to refer only to *transformed input resources*. So a manufacturing company will hold stocks of materials, a tax office will hold stocks of information and a theme park will hold stocks of customers (when it is customers who are being processed we normally refer to the 'stocks' of them as 'queues' – it is the same idea, but 'queues' is considered a more courteous term).

In this chapter we will deal particularly with inventories of materials. Inventories of customers are referred to elsewhere in Chapter 11. However, this does not imply that this chapter is only relevant when examining predominantly materials-processing operations such as manufacturing operations. All operations keep physical stocks of materials of some sort.

● All operations keep inventories

If you walk around any operation you will see several types of stored material. Table 12.1 gives some examples for several operations. However, there are differences between the examples of inventory given in Table 12.1. Some are relatively trivial to the operation in question: for example, the cleaning materials which are stored in the television factory are far less important than the stocks of steel, plastic and components which it also holds. The value of the cleaning materials held by the factory will be considerably less than the value of its steel, plastic and components. More importantly, the television plant would not stop if it ran out of cleaning materials, whereas if it ran out of any of its component parts, its activities would be severely disrupted. However, cleaning materials would be a far more important item of inventory for an industrial cleaning company, not only because it uses far more of this input, but also because its operation would stop if it ever ran out of them.

There is also a difference between how often the operations stock the items. Some of the examples of inventory are items which are stored just once within the operation. For example, food in an hotel is delivered to the hotel, stored and then used. In other operations, items are stored several times. For example, in a television factory a single piece of material is likely to progress through many different stages. Between each stage it has probably been stored as inventory.

Table 12.1 Examples of inventory held in operations

Operation	Examples of inventory held in operations
Hotel	Food items, drinks, toilet items, cleaning materials
Hospital	Wound dressings, disposable instruments, whole blood, food, drugs, cleaning materials
Retail store	Goods to be sold, wrapping materials
Warehouse	Goods being stored, packaging materials
Automotive parts distributor	Automotive parts in main depot, automotive parts at local distribution points
Television manufacturer	Components, raw materials, part-finished sub-assemblies, finished televisions, cleaning materials
Precious metals refiner	Material (gold, platinum, etc.) waiting to be processed, material partly processed, fully refined material

The value of inventories

Perhaps the most obvious difference between the operations in Table 12.1 is in the value of the inventories which they hold. In some, the value of inventory is relatively small compared with the costs of the total inputs to the operation. In others, it will be far higher, especially where storage is the prime purpose of the operation. For example, the value of the goods held in the warehouse is likely to be very high compared with its day-to-day expenditure on such things as labour, rent and running costs. Sometimes the value of the inventories can be so high that it is not even included in the organization's general financial accounts; this would be true, for example, of the precious metals refiner.[1]

Why inventory exists

No matter what is being stored as inventory, or where it is positioned in the operation, it will exist because there is a difference in the timing or rate of supply and demand. If the supply of any item occurred exactly when it was demanded, the item would never be stored. A common analogy is the water tank shown in Figure 12.2. If, over time, the rate of supply of water to the tank differs from the rate at which it is demanded, a tank of water (inventory) will be needed if supply is to be maintained. (More generally we use the process charting symbols (*see* Chapter 5) which are also shown in Fig. 12.2.) When the rate of supply exceeds the rate of demand, inventory increases; when the rate of demand exceeds the rate of supply, inventory decreases. The obvious point to make is that if an operation can make efforts to match supply and demand rates, it will also succeed in reducing its inventory levels. This important point is the basis of the just-in-time approach to inventory which we shall explore in more detail in Chapter 15.

Types of inventory[2]

The various reasons for an imbalance between the rates of supply and demand at different points in any operation lead to the different types of inventory. There are four of these: buffer inventory, cycle inventory, anticipation inventory and pipeline inventory.

Buffer inventory

Buffer inventory is also called safety inventory. Its purpose is to compensate for the uncertainties inherent in supply and demand. For example, a retail operation can never forecast demand perfectly, even when it has a good idea of the most likely demand

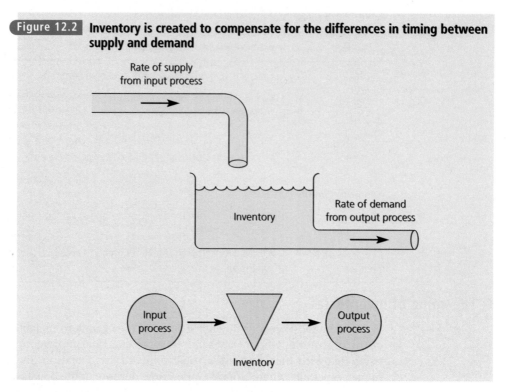

level. It will order goods from its suppliers such that there is always a certain amount of most items in stock. This minimum level of inventory is there to cover against the possibility that demand will be greater than expected during the time taken to deliver the goods. This is *buffer*, or *safety*, *inventory*. It compensates for the uncertainties in the process of the supply of goods into the store and that of the demand of goods from the store. Similarly, two stages in a production process might produce at exactly the same rate on average, but individual processing times might vary about the average.

Storing products can sometimes add value. The wine stored in oak barrels on the left is maturing for a finer flavour. The monitors on the right are undergoing a 'burn-in' period to detect any which are subjected to early-life' failure

Cycle inventory

Cycle inventory occurs because one or more stages in the operation cannot supply all the items it produces simultaneously. For example, suppose a baker makes three types of bread, each of which is equally popular with its customers. Because of the nature of the mixing and baking process, only one kind of bread can be produced at any time. The baker would have to produce each type of bread in batches (or 'lots' as they are sometimes known) as shown in Figure 12.3. The batches must be large enough to satisfy the demand for each kind of bread between the times when each batch is ready for sale. So even when demand is steady and predictable, there will always be some inventory to compensate for the irregular supply of each type of bread.

Anticipation inventory

We have already seen how anticipation inventory can be used in Chapter 11. Again, it was used to compensate for differences in the timing of supply and demand. There, rather than make chocolate only when it was needed, it was produced throughout the year ahead of demand and put into inventory until it was needed. *Anticipatory inventory* is most commonly used when demand fluctuations are significant but relatively predictable. It might also be used when supply variations are significant, such as in the canning of seasonal foods.

Pipeline inventory

Pipeline inventory exists because material cannot be transported instantaneously between the point of supply and the point of demand. If a retail store orders a consignment of items from one of its suppliers, the supplier will allocate the stock to the retail store in its own warehouse, pack it, load it onto its truck, transport it to its destination, and unload it into the retailer's inventory. From the time that stock is allocated (and therefore it is unavailable to any other customer) to the time it becomes available for the retail store, it is said to be *in the pipeline*. All stock thus in transit is pipeline inventory.

● The position of inventory

Not only are there several reasons for supply–demand imbalance, there could also be several points where such imbalance exists between different stages in the operation. Figure 12.4 illustrates different levels of complexity of inventory relationships within an operation. Perhaps the simplest level is the single-stage inventory system, such as a retail store, which will have only one stock of goods to manage. An automotive parts distribution operation will have a central depot and various local distribution points which contain inventories. In many manufacturers of standard items, there are three types of inventory. The *raw material and components store inventories* (sometimes called

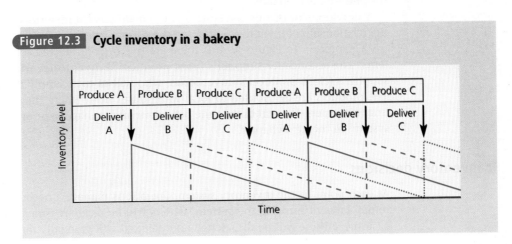

Figure 12.3 Cycle inventory in a bakery

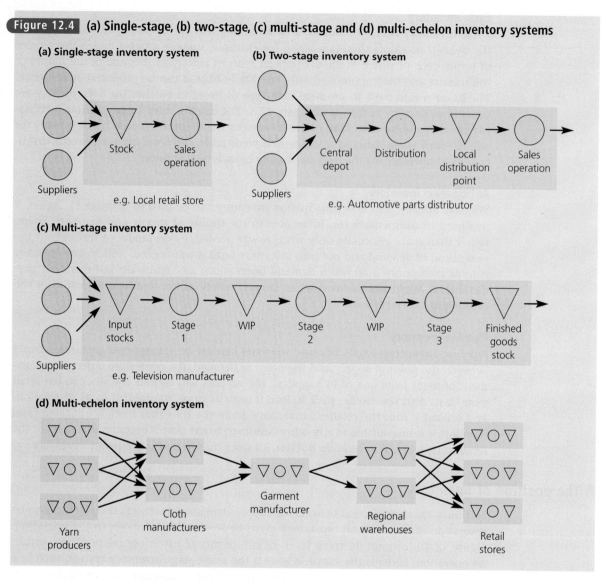

Figure 12.4 (a) Single-stage, (b) two-stage, (c) multi-stage and (d) multi-echelon inventory systems

(a) Single-stage inventory system

Suppliers → Stock → Sales operation

e.g. Local retail store

(b) Two-stage inventory system

Suppliers → Central depot → Distribution → Local distribution point → Sales operation

e.g. Automotive parts distributor

(c) Multi-stage inventory system

Suppliers → Input stocks → Stage 1 → WIP → Stage 2 → WIP → Stage 3 → Finished goods stock

e.g. Television manufacturer

(d) Multi-echelon inventory system

Yarn producers → Cloth manufacturers → Garment manufacturer → Regional warehouses → Retail stores

input inventories) receive goods from the operation's suppliers; the raw materials and components work their way through the various stages of the production process but spend considerable amounts of time as *work-in-progress* (WIP) before finally reaching the *finished goods inventory*.

A development of this last system is the *multi-echelon* inventory system. This maps the relationship of inventories between the various operations within a supply network (*see* Chapter 6). In Figure 12.4(d) there are five interconnected sets of inventory systems. The second-tier supplier's (yarn producer's) inventories will feed the first-tier supplier's (cloth producer's) inventories, who will in turn supply the main operation. The products are distributed to local warehouses from where they are shipped to the final customers. We will discuss the behaviour and management of such multi-echelon systems in the next chapter.

● Inventory decisions

At each point in the inventory system, operations managers need to manage the day-to-day tasks of running the system. Orders will be received from internal or external customers; these will be dispatched and demand will gradually deplete the inventory.

Orders will need to be placed for replenishment of the stocks, deliveries will arrive and require storing. In managing the system, operations managers are involved in three major types of decision:

- *How much to order*. Every time a replenishment order is placed, how big should it be (sometimes called the *volume decision*)?
- *When to order*. At what point in time, or at what level of stock, should the replenishment order be placed (sometimes called the *timing decision*)?
- *How to control the system*. What procedures and routines should be installed to help make these decisions? Should different priorities be allocated to different stock items? How should stock information be stored?

The remainder of this chapter deals with these three major decisions.

The volume decision – how much to order

To illustrate this decision consider a simple domestic situation. Probably the most common inventory we all deal with in our domestic lives is that of the food and provisions we keep in our apartment or house. In managing this inventory we implicitly make decisions on *order quantity*, that is how much to purchase at one time. In making this decision we are balancing two sets of costs: the costs associated with going out to purchase the food items and the costs associated with holding the stocks. One option would be to hold very little or no inventory of food and purchase each item only when it is needed. The advantage of this approach is that we would never have to raise the large amounts of money necessary to make major purchases, spending only when we needed to. However, such an approach would involve going out to purchase provisions three or four times a day. The costs in terms of our time and general inconvenience would probably make this a very unattractive proposition. At the very opposite extreme, we could make one journey to the local superstore every few months and purchase all the provisions we would need until our next visit. The advantage of this is that the time and costs incurred in making the purchase are incurred very infrequently. The major disadvantage is that we would have to pay out a very large amount of money each time the trip was made – money which could otherwise be in the bank and earning interest. A further disadvantage might be that the costs of storing such large quantities of food would also be expensive. We might have to invest in extra cupboard units and a very large freezer. Somewhere between these extremes there will lie an ordering strategy which will minimize the total costs and effort involved in the purchase of food.

Inventory costs
Exactly the same principles apply in commercial order-quantity decisions as in the domestic situation. In making a decision on how much to purchase, operations managers first try to identify the costs which will be affected by their decision. A number of costs are relevant:

1 *Cost of placing the order*. Every time an order is placed to replenish stock, a number of transactions are needed which incur costs to the company. These include the clerical tasks of preparing the order and all the documentation associated with it, arranging for the delivery to be made, arranging to pay the supplier for the delivery, and the general costs of keeping all the information which allows us to do this. If we are placing an order on part of our own operation, there are still likely to be the same types of transaction concerned with internal record-keeping, but there could also be a 'changeover' cost incurred by the part of the operation which is to supply the items and caused by the need to change from producing one type of item to another.

2 *Price discount costs*. In many industries suppliers offer discounts on the normal purchase price for large quantities; alternatively they might impose extra costs for small orders.

3 *Stock-out costs*. If we misjudge the order-quantity decision and our inventory runs out of stock, there will be costs to us incurred by failing to supply our customers. If the customers are external, they may take their business elsewhere; if internal, stock-outs could lead to idle time at the next process, inefficiencies and eventually, again, dissatisfied external customers.

4 *Working capital costs*. Soon after we place a replenishment order, suppliers will demand payment for their goods. Eventually, when we supply our own customers, we in turn will receive payment. However, there will probably be a lag between paying our suppliers and receiving payment from our customers. During this time we will have to fund the costs of however much we have in stock. This is called the *working capital* which we need to run the inventory. The costs associated with it are the interest we pay the bank for borrowing it, or the opportunity costs of not investing it elsewhere.

5 *Storage costs*. These are the costs associated with physically storing the goods. Renting, heating and lighting the warehouse can be expensive, especially when special conditions are required such as low-temperature or high-security storage.

6 *Obsolescence costs*. If we choose an ordering policy which involves very large order quantities, which will mean that stocked items spend a long time stored in inventory, there is a risk that the items might either become obsolete (in the case of a change in fashion, for example) or deteriorate with age (in the case of most foodstuffs, for example).

7 *Production inefficiency costs*. According to just-in-time philosophies, high inventory levels prevent us seeing the full extent of problems within the operation. This argument is fully explored in Chapter 15.

We can divide all these inventory-associated costs into two groups. The first three categories are costs which usually decrease as order size is increased. The other categories of cost usually increase as order size is increased.

Inventory profiles

An inventory profile is a visual representation of the inventory level over time. Figure 12.5 shows a simplified inventory profile for one particular stock item in a retail operation. Every time an order is placed, Q items are ordered. The replenishment order arrives in one batch instantaneously. Demand for the item is then steady and perfectly

For heavy and bulky items, such as builders' supplies above, the cost of the space needed for storage can be significant as a proportion of the value of the stock themselves

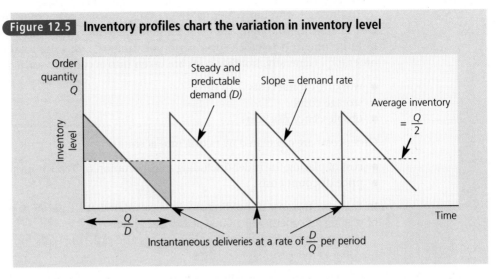

Figure 12.5 Inventory profiles chart the variation in inventory level

predictable at a rate of D units per month. When demand has depleted the stock of the items entirely, another order of Q items instantaneously arrives, and so on. Under these circumstances:

The average inventory $= \dfrac{Q}{2}$ (because the two shaded areas in Fig. 12.5 are equal)

The time interval between deliveries $= \dfrac{Q}{D}$

The frequency of deliveries = the reciprocal of the time interval $= \dfrac{D}{Q}$

The economic order quantity (EOQ) formula

The most common approach to deciding how much of any particular item to order when stock needs replenishing is called the economic order quantity (EOQ) approach. Essentially this approach attempts to find the best balance between the advantages and disadvantages of holding stock. For example, Figure 12.6 shows two alternative order-quantity policies for an item. Plan A, represented by the unbroken line, involves ordering in quantities of 400 at a time. Demand in this case is running at 1000 units per year. Plan B, represented by the dotted line, envisages smaller but more frequent replenishment orders. This time only 100 are ordered at a time, with orders being placed four times as often. However, the average inventory for plan B is one-quarter of that for plan A.

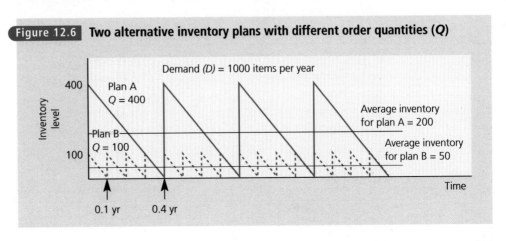

Figure 12.6 Two alternative inventory plans with different order quantities (*Q*)

To find out whether either of these plans, or some other plan, minimizes the total cost of stocking the item, we need some further information, namely the total cost of holding one unit in stock for a period of time (C_h) and the total costs of placing an order (C_o). Generally, holding costs are taken into account by including:

- working capital costs
- storage costs
- obsolescence risk costs.

Order costs are calculated by taking into account:

- cost of placing the order (including transportation of items from suppliers if relevant);
- price discount costs.

In this case the cost of holding stocks is calculated at £1 per item per year and the cost of placing an order is calculated at £20 per order.

We can now calculate total holding costs and ordering costs for any particular ordering plan as follows:

$$\text{Holding costs} = \text{holding cost/unit} \times \text{average inventory}$$

$$= C_h \times \frac{Q}{2}$$

$$\text{Ordering costs} = \text{ordering cost} \times \text{number of orders per period}$$

$$= C_o \times \frac{D}{Q}$$

So, total cost, $C_t = \dfrac{C_h Q}{2} + \dfrac{C_o D}{Q}$

We can now calculate the costs of adopting plans with different order quantities. These are illustrated in Table 12.2. As we would expect with low values of Q, holding costs are low but the costs of placing orders are high because orders have to be placed very frequently. As Q increases, the holding costs increase but the costs of placing orders decrease. Initially the decrease in ordering costs is greater than the increase in holding costs and the total cost falls. After a point, however, the decrease in ordering costs slows, whereas the increase in holding costs remains constant and the total cost starts

Table 12.2 Costs of adoption of plans with different order quantities

Demand (D) = 1000 units per year Order costs (C_o) = £20 per order		Holding costs (C_h) = £1 per item per year		
Order quantity (Q)	Holding costs $(0.5Q \times C_h)$	+ Order costs $((D/Q) \times C_o)$	=	Total costs
50	25	$20 \times 20 = 400$		425
100	50	$10 \times 20 = 200$		250
150	75	$6.7 \times 20 = 134$		209
200	100	$5 \times 20 = 100$		200*
250	125	$4 \times 20 = 80$		205
300	150	$3.3 \times 20 = 66$		216
350	175	$2.9 \times 20 = 58$		233
400	200	$2.5 \times 20 = 50$		250

* Minimum total cost.

Figure 12.7 Graphical representation of the economic order quantity

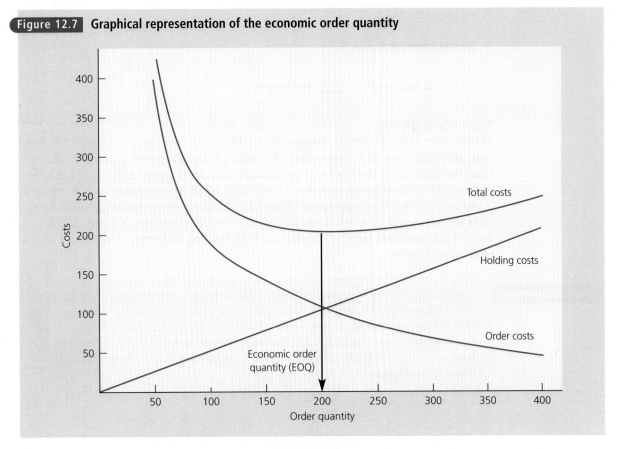

to increase. In this case the order quantity, Q, which minimizes the sum of holding and order costs, is 200. This 'optimum' order quantity is called the *economic order quantity* (*EOQ*). This is illustrated graphically in Figure 12.7.

A more elegant method of finding the EOQ is to derive its general expression. This can be done using simple differential calculus as follows. From before:

Total cost = holding cost + order cost

$$C_t = \frac{C_h Q}{2} + \frac{C_o D}{Q}$$

The rate of change of total cost is given by the first differential of C_t with respect to Q:

$$\frac{dC_t}{dQ} = \frac{C_h}{2} - \frac{C_o D}{Q^2}$$

The lowest cost will occur when $\frac{dC_t}{dQ} = 0$, that is:

$$0 = \frac{C_h}{2} - \frac{C_o D}{Q_o^2}$$

where $Q_o =$ the *EOQ*. Rearranging this expression gives:

$$Q_o = EOQ = \sqrt{\frac{2C_o D}{C_h}}$$

When using the *EOQ*:

$$\text{Time between orders} = \frac{EOQ}{D}$$

$$\text{Order frequency} = \frac{D}{EOQ} \text{ per period}$$

Sensitivity of the EOQ

Examination of the graphical representation of the total cost curve in Figure 12.7 shows that, although there is a single value of Q which minimizes total costs, any relatively small deviation from the EOQ will not increase total costs significantly. In other words, costs will be near-optimum provided a value of Q which is reasonably close to the EOQ is chosen. Put another way, small errors in estimating either holding costs or order costs will not result in a significant deviation from the EOQ. This is a particularly convenient phenomenon because, in practice, both holding and order costs are not easy to estimate accurately.

Worked example

A building materials stockist obtains its cement from a single supplier. Demand for cement is reasonably constant throughout the year. Last year the company sold 2000 tonnes of cement. It estimates the costs of placing an order at around £25 each time an order is placed, and charges inventory holding at 20 per cent of purchase cost. The company purchases cement at £60 per tonne. How much cement should the company order at a time?

$$EOQ \text{ for cement} = \sqrt{\frac{2C_o D}{C_h}}$$

$$= \sqrt{\frac{2 \times 25 \times 2000}{0.2 \times 60}}$$

$$= \sqrt{\frac{100\,000}{12}}$$

$$= 91.287 \text{ tonnes}$$

After calculating the EOQ the operations manager feels that placing an order for 91.287 tonnes *exactly* seems somewhat over-precise. Why not order a convenient 100 tonnes?

Total cost of ordering plan for Q = 91.287:

$$= \frac{C_h Q}{2} + \frac{C_o D}{Q}$$

$$= \frac{(0.2 \times 60) \times 91.287}{2} + \frac{25 \times 2000}{91.287}$$

$$= \text{£}1095.454$$

Total cost of ordering plan for Q = 100:

$$= \frac{(0.2 \times 60) \times 100}{2} + \frac{25 \times 2000}{100}$$

$$= \text{£}1100$$

The extra cost of ordering 100 tonnes at a time is £1100 − £1095.45 = £4.55. The operations manager therefore should feel confident in using the more convenient order quantity.

● Gradual replacement – the economic batch quantity (EBQ) model

Although the simple inventory profile shown in Figure 12.5 made some simplifying assumptions, it is broadly applicable in most situations where each replacement order arrives as a single delivery to the inventory point. In many cases, however, a replenishment order arrives over a time period rather than in one lot. A typical example of this is where an order is placed within the operation for a batch of parts to be produced on a machine. The machine will start to produce the parts and ship them in a more or less continuous stream into the inventory point. During the time that these units are being added to the inventory, demand is continuing to take place. Provided the rate at which parts are being made and put into the inventory (P) is higher than the rate at which demand is depleting the inventory (D) then the size of the inventory will increase. After the batch has been completed the machine will go on to produce some other part and demand will continue to deplete the inventory level. The resulting profile is shown in Figure 12.8. Such an inventory profile is typical of the inventories supplied by batches or 'lots' of items produced internally. For this reason the minimum-cost order quantity for this profile is called the *economic batch quantity* (EBQ). It is also sometimes known as the economic manufacturing quantity (EMQ) or the production order quantity (POQ). It is derived as follows:

$$\text{Maximum stock level} = M$$
$$\text{Slope of inventory build-up} = P - D$$

Also:

$$\text{Slope of inventory build-up} = M \div \frac{Q}{P}$$
$$= \frac{MP}{Q}$$

So,

$$\frac{MP}{Q} = P - D$$

$$M = \frac{Q(P-D)}{P}$$

$$\text{Average inventory level} = \frac{M}{2}$$

$$= \frac{Q(P-D)}{2P}$$

Figure 12.8 | **Inventory profile for gradual replacement of inventory**

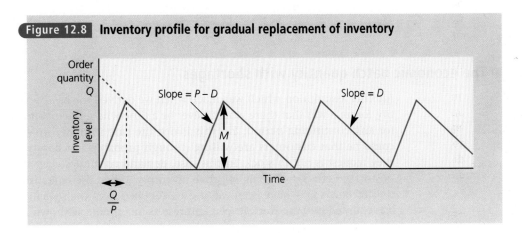

As before:

Total cost = holding cost + order cost

$$C_t = \frac{C_h Q (P - D)}{2P} + \frac{C_o D}{Q}$$

$$\frac{dC_t}{dQ} = \frac{C_h(P - D)}{2P} - \frac{C_o D}{Q^2}$$

Again, equating to zero and solving Q gives the minimum-cost order quantity EBQ:

$$EBQ = \sqrt{\frac{2C_o D}{C_h(1-(D/P))}}$$

Worked example

The manager of a bottle-filling plant which bottles soft drinks needs to decide how long a 'run' of each type of drink to ask the lines to process. Demand for each type of drink is reasonably constant at 80 000 per month (a month has 160 production hours). The bottling lines fill at a rate of 3000 bottles per hour but take an hour to change over between different drinks. The cost (of labour and lost production capacity) of each changeover has been calculated at £100 per hour. Stock-holding costs are counted at £0.1 per bottle per month.

$$D = 80\,000 \text{ per month}$$

$$= 500 \text{ per hour}$$

$$EBQ = \sqrt{\frac{2C_o D}{C_h(1-(D/P))}}$$

$$= \sqrt{\frac{2 \times 100 \times 80\,000}{0.1\,(1-(500/3000))}}$$

$$EBQ = 13\,856$$

The staff who operate the lines have devised a method of reducing the changeover time from 1 hour to 30 minutes. How would that change the EBQ?

$$\text{New } C_o = £50$$

$$\text{New } EBQ = \sqrt{\frac{2 \times 50 \times 80\,000}{0.1(1-(500/3000))}}$$

$$= 9798$$

● The economic batch quantity with shortages

Another assumption which was made when we derived the basic economic batch quantity formula was that there would never be a time where the inventory level fell to zero for any continuing period. Yet this is not the case in many inventory situations. It could be that customers are willing (though probably not happy) to wait if an item they request is not in stock. In this case, demand continues even though no items are in stock, in effect producing negative inventory. When the replenishment order arrives, the customers who have been waiting are supplied from the replenishment order before it is counted into the stock levels. This results in a profile as shown in Figure 12.9.

Figure 12.9 **Inventory plans allowing for shortages**

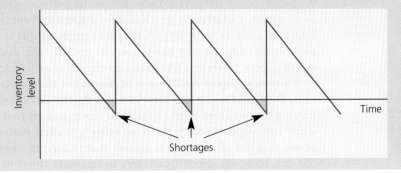

Deriving an expression for the EBQ in a similar manner gives,

$$EBQ = \sqrt{\frac{2DC_o}{C_h}} \ \sqrt{\frac{C_h + C_s}{C_s}}$$

where C_s = cost per unit of shortage per time period.

Worked example

Super Soups manufactures specialist gourmet frozen soups for the restaurant trade. All its soups used to sell at a reasonably steady rate of 700 litres per day. Recently the company adopted a policy of reducing the price by £1 per litre for every day a customer had to wait for delivery. Normally orders are delivered on the same day as ordering but if the soup is not in stock, customers have to wait until it is next manufactured. Keeping soup frozen is expensive and the company charges itself for storage at a rate of £0.16 per litre per day. It has also calculated that the cost of changing its production processes to make a different flavour is £100. The new policy was a success and increased demand for all its soups to 1000 litres per day. What effect should these changes have on its stock-ordering policy?

Previously:

$$D = 700 \text{ litres/day}$$

$$C_o = £100$$

$$C_h = £0.16 \text{ per day}$$

$$EOQ = \sqrt{\frac{2 \times 700 \times 100}{0.16}} = 935 \text{ litres}$$

Now:

$$C_s = £1 \text{ per litre per day}$$

From formula allowing shortages:

$$EOQ = \sqrt{\frac{2 \times 1000 \times 100}{0.16}} \times \sqrt{\frac{0.16 + 1}{1}}$$

$$= 1204$$

The economic order quantity needs to be increased from 935 litres per day to 1204 litres per day.

If customers won't wait – the news-seller problem

A special case of the inventory order-quantity decision refers to the situation where an order quantity of items is purchased for a specific event or time period, after which the items are unlikely to be sold. A simple example of this is the decision taken by a news-paper seller of how many newspapers to stock for the day. If the news-seller should run out of papers, customers will either go elsewhere or decide not to buy a paper that day.

If any newspapers are left over at the end of the day, the value of yesterday's news is zero. Demand for the newspapers varies day by day depending on who happens to be passing, the weather at the time, and the appeal of that day's news. In deciding how many newspapers to carry, the news-seller is in effect balancing the risk and consequence of running out of newspapers against that of having newspapers left over at the end of the day. To a certain extent, retailers and manufacturers in the fashion garment business, publishers and popular music CD producers all face the same problem. The method for determining the optimum order quantity is best illustrated through an example.

Worked example

A concert promoter needs to decide how many concert T-shirts to order emblazoned with the logo of the main act. The profit on each T-shirt sold at the concert is £5 and any unsold T-shirts are returned to the company that supplies them, but at a loss to the promoter of £3 per T-shirt. Demand is uncertain but is estimated to be between 200 and 1000. The probabilities of different demand are as follows:

Demand level	200	400	600	800
Probability	0.2	0.3	0.4	0.1

How many T-shirts should the promoter order? Table 12.3 shows the profit which the promoter would make for different order quantities and different levels of demand.

Table 12.3 Pay-off matrix for T-shirt order quantity (profit or loss in £s)

Demand level	200	400	600	800
Probability	0.2	0.3	0.4	0.1
Promoter orders 200	1000	1000	1000	1000
Promoter orders 400	400	2000	2000	2000
Promoter orders 600	−200	1400	3000	3000
Promoter orders 800	−800	800	2400	4000

We can now calculate the *expected* profit which the promoter will make for each order quantity by weighting the outcomes by their probability of occurring.

If the promoter orders 200 T-shirts:

$$\text{Expected profit} = 1000 \times 0.2 + 1000 \times 0.3 + 1000 \times 0.4 + 1000 \times 0.1$$
$$= £1000$$

If the promoter orders 400 T-shirts:

$$\text{Expected profit} = 400 \times 0.2 + 2000 \times 0.3 + 2000 \times 0.4 + 2000 \times 0.1$$
$$= £1680$$

If the promoter orders 600 T-shirts:

$$\text{Expected profit} = -200 \times 0.2 + 1400 \times 0.3 + 3000 \times 0.4 + 3000 \times 0.1$$
$$= £1880$$

If the promoter orders 800 T-shirts:

$$\text{Expected profit} = -800 \times 0.2 + 800 \times 0.3 + 2400 \times 0.4 + 4000 \times 0.1$$
$$= £1440$$

The order quantity which gives the maximum profit is 600 T-shirts, which results in a profit of £1880.

Criticism of the EOQ approach[3]

The approach to determining order quantity which involves optimizing costs of holding stock against costs of ordering stock, typified by the EOQ and EBQ models, has always been subject to criticisms. Originally these concerned the validity of some of the assumptions of the model; more recently they have involved the underlying rationale of the approach itself. We shall examine three classes of criticism concerning:

- the assumptions included in the models;
- the real costs of stock in operations;
- the use of the models as prescriptive devices.

Model assumptions

In order to keep EOQ-type models relatively straightforward, it was necessary to make assumptions concerning such things as the stability of demand, the existence of a fixed and identifiable ordering cost, the cost of stock-holding which can be expressed by a linear function, shortage costs which were identifiable, and so on. While these assumptions are rarely strictly true, most of them can approximate to reality. Furthermore, as we have pointed out before, the shape of the total cost curve has a relatively flat optimum point which means that small errors will not significantly affect the total cost of a near-optimum order quantity. However, at times the assumptions do pose severe limitations to the models. For example, the assumption of steady demand (or even demand which conforms to some known probability distribution) is untrue for a wide range of the operation's inventory problems. For example, a bookseller might be very happy to adopt an EOQ-type ordering policy for some of its products such as dictionaries and other reference books. However, estimating demand for some books is far more difficult. For some novels the probability distribution which describes likely demand is bimodal. If the book does not catch the public's imagination it will sell a reasonable number to customers who are familiar with the author; however, if it is well reviewed or other publicity surrounds it, the demand could be many times what it would otherwise be. An EOQ approach has difficulty in coping with such wild fluctuations in demand.

Other questions surround some of the assumptions made concerning the nature of stock-related costs. For example, placing an order with a supplier as part of a regular and multi-item order might be relatively inexpensive, whereas asking for a special one-off delivery of an item could prove far more costly. Similarly with stock-holding costs – although many companies make a standard percentage charge on the purchase price of stock items, this might not be appropriate over a wide range of stock-holding levels. The marginal costs of increasing stock-holding levels might be merely the cost of the working capital involved. On the other hand, it might necessitate the construction or lease of a whole new stock-holding facility such as a warehouse. Operations managers using an EOQ-type approach must check that the decisions implied by the use of the formulae do not exceed the limits within which the cost assumptions apply.

How costly is stock?

In Chapter 15 we fully explore the just-in-time approach to operations management which holds that inventories generally exert a malign influence in operations. We will postpone exploration of this idea until Chapter 15, but it is useful at this stage to examine the effect on an EOQ approach of regarding stock as being more costly. Increasing the slope of the holding cost line increases the level of total costs of any order quantity, but more significantly, shifts the minimum cost's optimum point substantially to the left, in favour of a lower economic order quantity. In other words, the less sanguine an operation is about holding stock, the more it should move towards smaller, more frequent ordering.

Using EOQ models as prescriptions

Perhaps the most fundamental criticism of the EOQ approach again comes from the Japanese-inspired JIT philosophies. The emphasis of EOQ is on trying to determine representative costs of ordering and stock holding and then optimizing order decisions in the light of these costs. Implicitly the costs are taken as fixed, in the sense that the task of operations managers is to find out what are the true costs rather than to change them in any way. EOQ is essentially a reactive approach. Some critics would argue that it fails to ask the right question. Rather than asking the EOQ question of 'What is the optimum order quantity?', operations managers should really be asking, 'How can I change the operation in some way so as to reduce the overall level of stocks it is necessary to hold in the operation?'. The EOQ approach may be a reasonable description of stock-holding costs but should not necessarily be taken as a strict prescription over what decisions to take.

For example, many organizations have made considerable efforts to reduce the effective cost of placing an order. Often they have done this by working to reduce changeover times on machines. This means that less time is taken changing over from one product to

Figure 12.10 If the true costs of stock holding are taken, the economic order quantity, the real EOQ, is much smaller

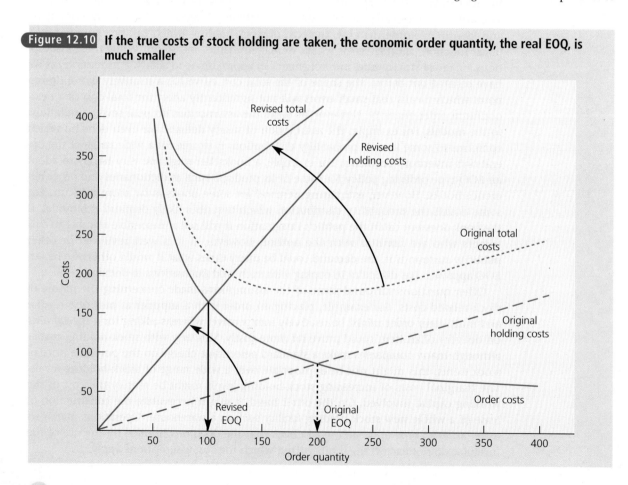

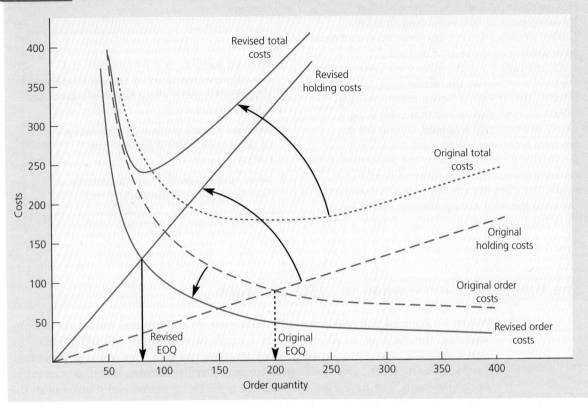

the other and therefore less operating capacity is lost, which in turn reduces the cost of the changeover. Under these circumstances, the order cost curve in the EOQ formula reduces and, in turn, reduces the effective economic order quantity. Figure 12.10 shows the EOQ formula represented graphically with increased holding costs (*see* the previous discussion). Figure 12.11 shows also the further effects of reduced order costs, the net effect of which is to shift the value of the EOQ even further to the left.

Should we reorder? – the Marks & Spencer approach[4]

A special case of the 'How much to order?' decision in inventory control is the 'Should we order any more at all?' decision. Retailers especially need continually to review the stocked lines they keep on the shelves. For example, Marks & Spencer (M & S) has a simple philosophy: if it sells, restock it quickly and avoid stock-outs; if it doesn't sell, get it off the shelves quickly and replace it with something which *will* sell. The M & S approach often means putting a new line on the shelves of a pilot store and watching customer reaction very closely. The store most often used for these trials is the company's Marble Arch store in London. Sometimes it is possible to make a restocking decision within a few hours – not surprising when the time-frame for stock rotation can be as little as a week.

For more routine stock control decisions the company uses an automatic stock-ordering system which it calls ASR (Assisted Stock Replenishment). This helps always to have the right stock of textile products in the store at the right time. The system, which is now installed in its flagship Marble Arch store, takes into account all goods bought at the till through the electronic point-of-sale (EPOS) system and automatically generates an order to replenish that item. The system anticipates orders for each item based on the previous week's sales and delivers in advance. The current day's sales are continually reviewed and any extra items required are delivered the next day. Orders arrive at the store from the local distribution centre at Neasden in North London. New orders are usually placed before 8.30 am and

85 per cent of these will arrive before close of business that day. The remainder arrives the following morning before opening time. The number of deliveries each day varies between 14 and 24 depending on the level of business.

On the sales floor, the main stock control tasks are to ensure that all the clothing rails are fully stocked, that the stock tickets reflect the sales information on display and that everything is neatly and correctly arranged. During the day the area supervisor watches the stock levels and the flow of customers around the displays in case any changes to stock location need to be made. The store has a policy of not bringing stock out onto the floor during opening hours; but in the case of fast-moving items, this can at times be unavoidable.

Questions

1 Why is it particularly important for retail operations such as Marks & Spencer to make judgements quickly about how well a product is likely to sell?

2 What do you see as the major advantages of using the electronic point-of-sale (EPOS) system?

3 What kind of inventory policy seems to operate in Marks & Spencer's stores?

The timing decision – when to place an order

When we assumed that orders arrived instantaneously and demand was steady and predictable, the decision on when to place a replenishment order was self-evident. An order would be placed as soon as the stock level reached zero. This would arrive instantaneously and prevent any stock-out occurring. If replenishment orders do not arrive instantaneously, but have a lag between the order being placed and it arriving in the inventory, we can calculate the timing of a replacement order as shown in Figure 12.12. The lead time for an order to arrive is in this case two weeks, so the re-order point (ROP) is the point at which stock will fall to zero minus the order lead time. Alternatively, we can define the point in terms of the level which the inventory will have reached when a replenishment order needs to be placed. In this case this occurs at a re-order level (ROL) of 200 items.

Figure 12.12 Re-order level (ROL) and re-order point (ROP) are derived from the order lead time and demand rate

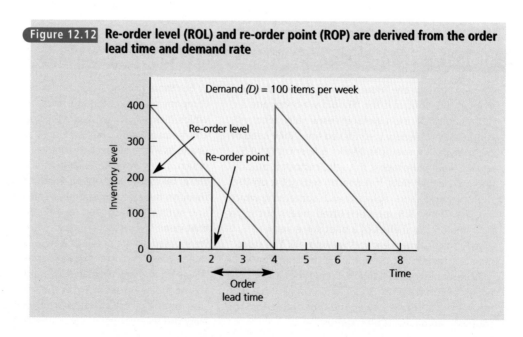

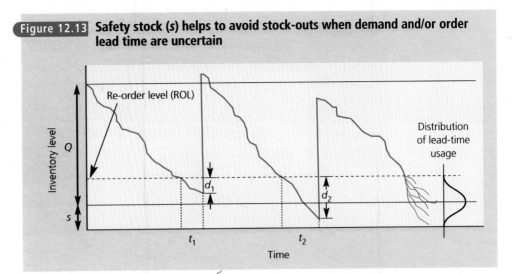

However, this assumes that both the demand and the order lead time are perfectly predictable. In most cases, of course, this is not so. Both demand and the order lead time are likely to vary to produce a profile which looks something like that in Figure 12.13. In these circumstances it is necessary to make the replenishment order somewhat earlier than would be the case in a purely deterministic situation. This will result in, on average, some stock still being in the inventory when the replenishment order arrives. This is buffer or safety stock (*s*). The earlier the replenishment order is placed, the higher will be the expected level of safety stock (*s*) when the replenishment order arrives. But because of the variability of both lead time (*t*) and demand rate (*d*), there will sometimes be a higher-than-average level of safety stock and sometimes lower. The main consideration in setting safety stock is not so much the average level of stock when a replenishment order arrives but rather the probability that the stock will not have run out before the replenishment order arrives.

The key statistic in calculating how much safety stock to allow is the probability distribution which shows the *lead-time usage*. The lead-time usage distribution is a combination of the distributions which describe lead-time variation and the demand rate during the lead time. If safety stock is set below the lower limit of this distribution then there will be shortages every single replenishment cycle. If safety stock is set above the upper limit of the distribution, there is no chance of stock-outs occurring. Usually, safety stock is set to give a predetermined likelihood that stock-outs will not occur. Figure 12.13 shows that, in this case, the first replenishment order arrived after t_1, resulting in a lead-time usage of d_1. The second replenishment order took longer, t_2, and demand rate was also higher, resulting in a lead-time usage of d_2. The third order cycle shows several possible inventory profiles for different conditions of lead-time usage and demand rate.

Worked example

A company which imports running shoes for sale in its sports shops can never be certain of how long, after placing an order, the delivery will take. Examination of previous orders reveals that out of 10 orders: one took one week, two took two weeks, four took three weeks, two took four weeks and one took five weeks. The rate of demand for the shoes also varies between 110 pairs per week and 140 pairs per week. There is a 0.2 probability of the demand rate being either 110 or 140 pairs per week, and a 0.3 chance of demand being either 120 or 130 pairs per week. The company needs to decide when it should place replenishment orders if the probability of a stock-out is to be less than 10 per cent.

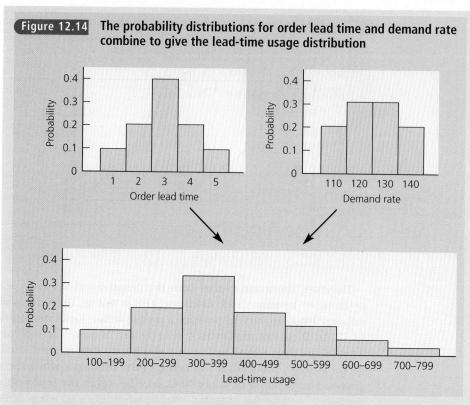

Figure 12.14 The probability distributions for order lead time and demand rate combine to give the lead-time usage distribution

Both lead time and the demand rate during the lead time will contribute to the lead-time usage. So the distributions which describe each will need to be combined. Figure 12.14 and Table 12.4 show how this can be done. Taking lead time to be either one, two, three, four or five weeks, and demand rate to be either 110, 120, 130 or 140 pairs per week, and also assuming the two variables to be independent, the distributions can be combined as shown in Table 12.4. Each element in the matrix shows a possible lead-time usage with the probability of its occurrence. So if the lead time is one week and the demand rate is 110 pairs per week, the actual lead-time usage will be $1 \times 110 = 110$ pairs. Since there is a 0.1 chance of the lead time being one week, and a 0.2 chance of demand rate being 110 pairs per week, the probability of both these events occurring is $0.1 \times 0.2 = 0.02$.

Table 12.4 Matrix of lead-time and demand-rate probabilities

			Lead-time probabilities				
			1 *0.1*	*2* *0.2*	*3* *0.4*	*4* *0.2*	*5* *0.1*
	110	0.2	110 (0.02)	220 (0.04)	330 (0.08)	440 (0.04)	550 (0.02)
	120	0.3	120 (0.03)	240 (0.06)	360 (0.12)	480 (0.06)	600 (0.03)
Demand-rate *probabilities*	130	0.3	130 (0.03)	260 (0.06)	390 (0.12)	520 (0.06)	650 (0.03)
	140	0.2	140 (0.02)	280 (0.04)	420 (0.08)	560 (0.04)	700 (0.02)

We can now classify the possible lead-time usages into histogram form. For example, summing the probabilities of all the lead-time usages which fall within the range 100–199 (all the first column) gives a combined probability of 0.1. Repeating this for subsequent intervals results in Table 12.5.

Table 12.5 Combined probabilities

Lead-time usage	100–199	200–299	300–399	400–499	500–599	600–699	700–799
Probability	0.1	0.2	0.32	0.18	0.12	0.06	0.02

This shows the probability of each possible range of lead-time usage occurring, but it is the cumulative probabilities that are needed to predict the likelihood of stock-out (*see* Table 12.6).

Table 12.6 Combined probabilities

Lead-time usage X	100	200	300	400	500	600	700	800
Probability of usage being greater than X	1.0	0.9	0.7	0.38	0.2	0.08	0.02	0

Setting the re-order level at 600 would mean that there is only a 0.08 chance of usage being greater than available inventory during the lead time, i.e. there is a less than 10 per cent chance of a stock-out occurring.

● Continuous and periodic review

The approach we have described to making the replenishment timing decision is often called the *continuous review approach*. This is because, to make the decision in this way, operations managers need to review the stock level of each item continuously and then place an order when the stock level reaches its re-order level. The virtue of this approach is that, although the timing of orders may be irregular (depending on the variation in demand rate), the order size (Q) is constant and can be set at the optimum economic order quantity. However, continually checking on inventory levels can be time-consuming, especially when there are many stock withdrawals compared with the average level of stock.

An alternative and far simpler approach, but one which sacrifices the use of a fixed (and therefore possibly optimum) order quantity, is called the *periodic review approach*. Here, rather than ordering at a predetermined re-order level, the periodic approach orders at a fixed and regular time interval. So the stock level of an item could be checked, for example, at the end of every month and a replenishment order placed to bring the stock up to a predetermined level. This level is calculated to cover demand between the replenishment order being placed and the following replenishment order arriving. Figure 12.15 illustrates the parameters for the periodic review approach.

At time T_1 in Figure 12.15 the inventory manager would examine the stock level and order sufficient to bring it up to some maximum, Q_m. However, that order of Q_1 items will not arrive until a further time of t_1 has passed, during which demand continues to deplete the stocks. Again, both demand and lead time are uncertain. The Q_1 items will arrive and bring the stock up to some level lower than Q_m (unless there has been no demand during t_1). Demand then continues until T_2, when again an order Q_2 is placed which is the difference between the current stock at T_2 and Q_m. This order arrives after t_2, by which time demand has depleted the stocks further. Thus the replenishment

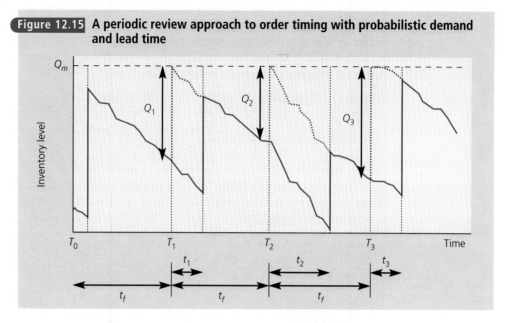

Figure 12.15 A periodic review approach to order timing with probabilistic demand and lead time

order placed at T_1 must be able to cover for the demand which occurs until T_2 and t_2. Safety stocks will need to be calculated, in a similar manner to before, based on the distribution of usage over this period.

The time interval

The interval between placing orders, t_1, is usually calculated on a deterministic basis, and derived from the EOQ. So, for example, if the demand for an item is 2000 per year, the cost of placing an order £25, and the cost of holding stock £0.5 per item per year:

$$\text{EOQ} = \sqrt{\frac{2C_oD}{C_h}} = \sqrt{\frac{2 \times 2000 \times 25}{0.5}} = 447$$

The optimum time interval between orders, t_f, is therefore:

$$t_f = \frac{EOQ}{D} = \frac{447}{2000} \text{ years}$$

$$= 2.68 \text{ months}$$

It may seem paradoxical to calculate the time interval assuming constant demand when demand is, in fact, uncertain. However, uncertainties in both demand and lead time can be allowed for by setting Q_m to allow for the desired probability of stock-out based on usage during the period t_f + lead time.

Two-bin and three-bin systems

Keeping track of inventory levels is especially important in continuous review approaches to re-ordering. A simple and obvious method of indicating when the re-order point has been reached is necessary, especially if there are a large number of items to be monitored. The two- and three-bin systems illustrated in Figure 12.16 are such methods. The simple two-bin system involves storing the re-order point quantity plus the safety inventory quantity in the second bin and using parts from the first bin. When the first bin empties, that is the signal to order the next re-order quantity. Sometimes the safety inventory is stored in a third bin (the three-bin system), so it is clear when demand is exceeding that which was expected.

Different 'bins' are not always necessary to operate this type of system. For example, a common practice in retail operations is to store the second 'bin' quantity upside-down behind or under the first 'bin' quantity. Orders are then placed when the upside-down items are reached.

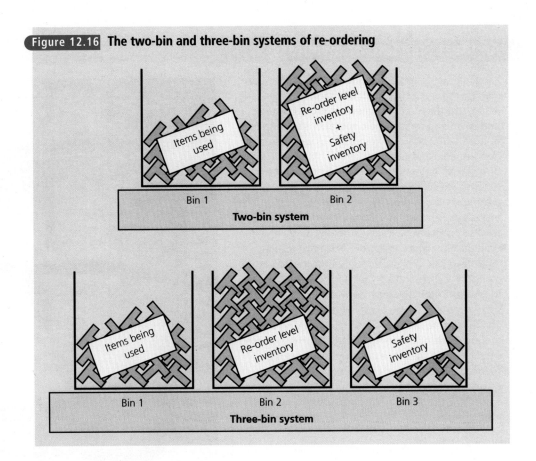

Figure 12.16 The two-bin and three-bin systems of re-ordering

Inventory analysis and control systems

The models we have described so far, even the ones which take a probabilistic view of demand and lead time, are still simplified compared with the complexity of real stock management. Coping with many thousands of stocked items, supplied by many hundreds of different suppliers, with possibly tens of thousands of individual customers, makes for a complex and dynamic operations task. In order to control such complexity, operations managers have to do two things. First, they have to discriminate between different stocked items, so that they can apply a degree of control to each item which is appropriate to its importance. Second, they need to invest in an information-processing system which can cope with their particular set of inventory control circumstances.

● Inventory priorities – the ABC system

In any inventory which contains more than one stocked item, some items will be more important to the organization than others. Some items, for example, might have a very high usage rate, so if they ran out many customers would be disappointed. Other items might be of particularly high value, so excessively high inventory levels would be particularly expensive. One common way of discriminating between different stock items is to rank them by the *value of their usage* (their usage rate multiplied by their individual value). Items with a particularly high value of usage are deemed to warrant careful control, whereas those with low usage values need not be controlled quite so rigorously. Generally, a relatively small proportion of the total items contained in an inventory will account for a large proportion of the

An Ideal Standard of inventory

Ideal Standard, part of American Standard Inc., are manufacturers of bathroom and sanitary wear. Like many manufacturers of consumer products, they must plan and control their operations so as to best utilize their production resources, as well as give a good standard of customer service. At one time the only way of doing this was thought to be by the use of large finished goods inventories. But since the advent of 'just-in-time' type principles, manufacturers such as Ideal Standard have managed to raise productivity, improve quality and dramatically reduce inventory. The programme which was put in place throughout American Standard Inc. was called 'Demand Flow Manufacturing'. All areas of inventory holding were scrutinized and driven down by reducing batch sizes and making to demand rather than making to stock. In some parts of the company, stock turns increased threefold and the money tied up in inventories reduced by over 75 per cent; productivity and quality have also improved significantly.

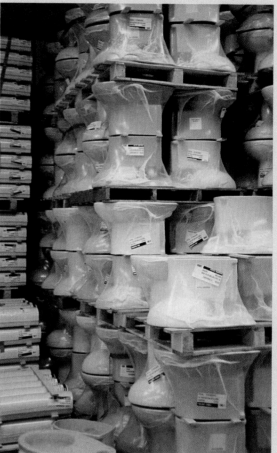

Photo courtesy of Ideal Standard

Even at reduced inventory levels, stocks can take up space

Questions

1 What do you think are the particular difficulties in inventory management at Ideal Standard?

2 What are the major changes in attitude necessary in moving from a make-to-stock to a make-to-order philosophy of planning and control?

Inventory management at Flame Electrical[5]

Inventory management in some operations is more than just a part of their responsibility; it is their very reason for being in business. Flame Electrical, South Africa's largest independent supplier and distributor of lamps, is such a business. It stocks over 2900 different types of lamp, which are sourced from 14 countries and distributed to customers throughout the country.

'In effect our customers are using us to manage their stocks of lighting sources for them,' says Jeff Schaffer, the Managing Director of Flame Electrical. *'They could, if they wanted to, hold their own stock but might not want to devote the time, space, money or effort to doing so. Using us they get the widest range of products to choose from, and an accurate, fast and dependable service.'*

Central to the company's ability to provide the service its customers expect is its computerized stock management system. The system holds information on all of Flame's customers, the type of lamps they may order, the quality and brand of lamps they prefer, the price to be charged and the location of each item in the warehouse. When a customer phones in to order, the computer system immediately accesses all this information, which is confirmed to the customer. This leaves only the quantity of each lamp required by the customer to be keyed in. The system then generates an instruction to the warehouse to pick up and dispatch the order. This instruction includes the shelf location of each item. The system even calculates the location of each item in the warehouse which will minimize the movement of stock for warehouse staff.

Orders for the replenishment of stocks in the warehouse are triggered by a re-order point system. The re-order point is set for each stocked item depending on the likely demand for the product during the order lead time (forecast from the equivalent period's orders the previous year), the order lead time for the item (which varies from 24 hours to four months) and the variability of the lead time (from previous experience). The size of the replenishment order depends on the lamp being ordered. Flame prefers most orders to be for a whole number of container loads (the shipping costs for part-container loads being more expensive). However, lower order quantities of small or expensive lamps may be used. The order quantity for each lamp is based on its demand, its value and the cost of transportation from the suppliers. However, all this can be overridden in an emergency. If a customer, such as a hospital, urgently needs a particular lamp which is not in stock, the company will even use a fast courier to fly the item in from overseas – all for the sake of maintaining its reputation for high service levels.

'We have to get the balance right,' says Jeff Schaffer. *'Excellent service is the foundation of our success. But we could not survive if we did not control stocks tightly. After all we are carrying the cost of every lamp in our warehouse until the customer eventually pays for it. If stock levels were too high we just could not operate profitably. It is for that reason that we go as far as to pay incentives to the relevant staff based on how well they keep our working capital and stocks under control.'*

Questions

1 Define what you think the five performance objectives (quality, speed, dependability, flexibility and cost) mean for an operation such as Flame Electrical.

2 What are the most important of these performance objectives for Flame Electrical?

3 What seems to influence the stock replenishment policy of Flame Electrical?

4 How does this differ from conventional economic order quantity theory?

---

total inventory value. This phenomenon is known as the *Pareto law* (after the person who described it), sometimes referred to as the 80/20 rule. It is called this because, typically, 80 per cent of an operation's inventory value is accounted for by only 20

Photo courtesy of ACE

Managing the receiving, storage, care and dispatch of goods in a warehouse such as this is a micro operation in its own right

per cent of all stocked item types. The Pareto law is also used elsewhere in operations management (*see*, for example, Chapter 18). Here the relationship can be used to classify the different types of items kept in an inventory by their usage value. This allows inventory managers to concentrate their efforts on controlling the more significant items of stock.

- *Class A items* are those 20 per cent or so of high-value items which account for around 80 per cent of the total stock value.
- *Class B items* are those of medium value, usually the next 30 per cent of items which account for around 10 per cent of the total value.

- *Class C items* are those low-value items which, although comprising around 50 per cent of the total types of items stocked, probably only account for around 10 per cent of the total value of stocked items.

Worked example Table 12.7 shows all the parts stored by an electrical wholesaler. The 20 different items stored vary in terms of both their usage per year and cost per item as shown. However, the wholesaler has ranked the stock items by their usage value per year. The total usage value per year is £5 569 000. From this it is possible to calculate the usage value per year of each item as a percentage of the total usage value, and from that a running cumulative total of the usage value as shown. The wholesaler can then plot the cumulative percentage of all stocked items against the cumulative percentage of their value. So, for example, the part with stock number A/703 is the highest value part and accounts for 25.14 per cent of the total inventory value. As a part, however, it is only one-twentieth or 5 per cent of the total number of items stocked. This item together with the next highest value item (D/012) account for only 10 per cent of the total number of items stocked, yet account for 47.37 per cent of the value of the stock, and so on.

This is shown graphically in Figure 12.17. Here the wholesaler has classified the first four part numbers as class A items and will monitor the usage and ordering of these items very closely. A few improvements in order quantities or safety stocks for these items could bring significant savings. Part numbers C/375 through to

Table 12.7 Warehouse items ranked by usage value

Stock no.	Usage (items/year)	Cost (£/item)	Usage value (£000/year)	% of total value	Cumulative % of total value
A/703	700	20.00	14 000	25.14	25.14
D/012	450	2.75	1238	22.23	47.37
A/135	1000	0.90	900	16.16	63.53
C/732	95	8.50	808	14.51	78.04
C/375	520	0.54	281	5.05	83.09
A/500	73	2.30	168	3.02	86.11
D/111	520	0.22	114	2.05	88.16
D/231	170	0.65	111	1.99	90.15
E/781	250	0.34	85	1.53	91.68
A/138	250	0.30	75	1.34	93.02
D/175	400	0.14	56	1.01	94.03
E/001	80	0.63	50	0.89	94.92
C/150	230	0.21	48	0.86	95.78
F/030	400	0.12	48	0.86	96.64
D/703	500	0.09	45	0.81	97.45
D/535	50	0.88	44	0.79	98.24
C/541	70	0.57	40	0.71	98.95
A/260	50	0.64	32	0.57	99.52
B/141	50	0.32	16	0.28	99.80
D/021	20	0.50	10	0.20	100.00
Total			5 569	100.00	

A/138 are to be treated as class B items with slightly less effort devoted to their control. All other items are classed as class C items whose stocking policy is reviewed only occasionally.

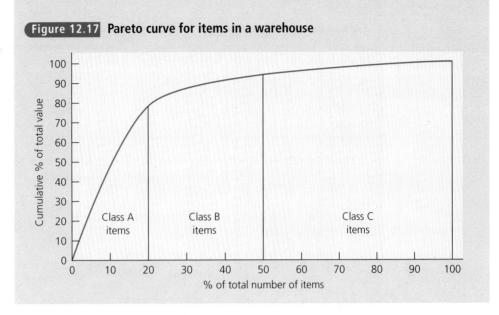

Figure 12.17 **Pareto curve for items in a warehouse**

Although annual usage and value are the two criteria most commonly used to determine a stock classification system, other criteria might also contribute towards classifying each item:

- *Consequence of stock-out*. High priority might be given to those items which would seriously delay or disrupt other operations if they were not in stock.
- *Uncertainty of supply*. Some items, although of low value, might warrant more attention if their supply is erratic or uncertain.
- *High obsolescence or deterioration risk*. Items which lose their value through obsolescence or deterioration might need extra attention and monitoring.

Some more complex stock classification systems might include these criteria by classifying on an A, B, C basis for each. For example, a part might be classed as A/B/A meaning it is an A category item by value, a class B item by consequence of stock-out and a class A item by obsolescence risk.

● Measuring inventory

In our example of ABC classifications we used the monetary value of the annual usage of each item as a measure of inventory usage. Monetary value can also be used to measure the absolute level of inventory at any point in time. This would involve taking the number of each item in stock, multiplying it by its value (usually the cost of purchasing the item) and summing the value of all the individual items stored. This is a useful measure of the investment which an operation has in its inventories but gives no indication of how large that investment is relative to the total throughput of the operation. To do this we must compare the total number of items in stock against their rate of usage. There are two ways of doing this. The first is to calculate the amount of time the inventory would last, subject to normal demand, if it were not replenished. This is sometimes called the number of weeks' (days', months', years' etc.) *cover* of the stock. The second method is to calculate how often the stock is used up in a period. This is called the *stock turn* or *turnover of stock* and is the reciprocal of the stock-cover figure mentioned earlier.

A small specialist wine importer holds stocks of three types of wine, Chateau A, Chateau B and Chateau C. Current stock levels are 500 cases of Chateau A, 300 cases of Chateau B, and 200 cases of Chateau C. Table 12.8 shows the number of each held in stock, their cost per item and the demand per year for each.

Table 12.8 Stock, cost and demand for three stocked items

Item	Average number in stock	Cost per item (£)	Annual demand
Chateau A	500	3.00	2000
Chateau B	300	4.00	1500
Chateau C	200	5.00	1000

The total value of stock $= \Sigma$(average stock level $\times$ cost per item)

$$= (500 \times 3) + (300 \times 4) + (200 \times 5)$$
$$= 3700$$

The amount of *stock cover* provided by each item stocked is as follows (assuming 50 sales weeks per year):

$$\text{Chateau A, stock cover} = \frac{\text{stock}}{\text{demand}} = \frac{500}{2000} \times 50 = 12.5 \text{ weeks}$$

$$\text{Chateau B, stock cover} = \frac{\text{stock}}{\text{demand}} = \frac{300}{1500} \times 50 = 10 \text{ weeks}$$

$$\text{Chateau C, stock cover} = \frac{\text{stock}}{\text{demand}} = \frac{200}{1000} \times 50 = 10 \text{ weeks}$$

The *stock turn* for each item is calculated as follows:

$$\text{Chateau A, stock turn} = \frac{\text{demand}}{\text{stock}} = \frac{2000}{500} = 4 \text{ times/year}$$

$$\text{Chateau B, stock turn} = \frac{\text{demand}}{\text{stock}} = \frac{1500}{300} = 5 \text{ times/year}$$

$$\text{Chateau C, stock turn} = \frac{\text{demand}}{\text{stock}} = \frac{1000}{200} = 5 \text{ times/year}$$

To find the average stock cover or stock turn for the total items in the inventory, the individual item measures can be weighted by their demand levels as a proportion of total demand (4500). Thus:

$$\text{Average stock cover} = \left(12.5 \times \frac{2000}{4500}\right) + \left(10 \times \frac{1500}{4500}\right) + \left(10 \times \frac{1000}{4500}\right)$$
$$= 11.11$$

$$\text{Average stock turn} = \left(4 \times \frac{2000}{4500}\right) + \left(5 \times \frac{1500}{4500}\right) + \left(5 \times \frac{1000}{4500}\right)$$
$$= 4.56$$

● Inventory information systems

Most inventories of any significant size are managed by computerized systems. The many relatively routine calculations involved in stock control lend themselves to computerized support. This is especially so since data capture has been made more convenient through the use of bar-code readers and the point-of-sale recording of sales

In September 1994 a plea was transmitted on the national news in the UK for blood donors to give blood urgently. The empty racks in the blood storage bank on the television screens graphically portrayed the urgency of the request. Momentarily the National Blood Service had lost its continuing battle to balance the supply of blood with demand.

Blood and by-products need to be stored under a variety of conditions. Red blood cells, used for surgical procedures and to correct anaemia, have to be stored at 4°C and have a shelf-life of 35 days. Platelets, extracted from donated blood and used to treat leukaemia and bone marrow transplants, have to be stored at 20–24°C and have a shelf-life of only five days, during which time they have to be constantly agitated. Frozen fresh plasma is used for liver transplants and for massive transfusion operations. It has to be stored at between –30 and –40°C and has a shelf-life of six months. In addition, blood can be categorized by two main systems or groups. The ABO group includes A, B, AB and O. The rhesus group includes Rh-positive and Rh-negative. In addition there are many less common and more complex types of blood, often relating to ethnic groups. Giving a patient the wrong type of blood can be fatal. However, group O negative can be given to emergency patients before blood tests have been made. Because of this, hospitals like to stock O negative. However, O negative represents only eight per cent of the population, whereas 12 per cent of blood issued is of this type.

Demand is affected significantly by accidents. One serious accident involving a cyclist used 750 units of blood, which completely exhausted the available supply (miraculously, he survived). Large-scale accidents usually generate a surge of offers from donors wishing to make immediate donations. There is also a more predictable seasonality to the donating of blood, however, with a low period during the summer vacation.

Unless blood is controlled carefully, it can easily go past its 'use-by date' and be wasted. For some patients the control of the age of stored blood is critical. For example, new-born babies, the elderly, and patients whose immune systems have been suppressed so that they do not reject transplanted organs are all prone to infection. Very fresh blood is therefore kept 'on hold' for these patients.

Questions

1 What are the factors which constitute inventory holding costs, order costs, and stock-out costs in a National Blood Service?

2 What makes this particular inventory planning and control example so complex?

3 How might the efficiency with which a National Blood Service controls its inventory affect its ability to collect blood?

---

transactions. Many commercial systems of stock control are available, although they tend to share certain common functions. These include the following:

Updating stock records

Every time a transaction takes place (such as the sale of an item, the movement of an item from a warehouse into a truck, or the delivery of an item into a warehouse) the position, status and possibly value of the stock will have changed. This information needs recording so that operations managers can determine their current inventory status at any time.

Generating orders

The two major decisions we have described previously, namely how much to order and when to order, can both be made by a computerized stock control system. The first decision, setting the value of how much to order (Q), is likely to be taken only at relatively infrequent intervals. The system will hold all the information which goes into the economic order quantity formula but might periodically check to see if demand or order lead times, or any of the other parameters, have changed significantly and recalculate Q accordingly. The decision on when to order, on the other hand, is a far more routine affair which computer systems make according to whatever decision rules operations managers have chosen to adopt: either continuous review or periodic review. Furthermore, the systems can automatically generate whatever documentation is required, or even transmit the re-ordering information electronically through an electronic data interchange (EDI) system. Chapter 8 explains how EDI systems work.

Generating inventory reports

Inventory control systems can generate regular reports of stock value for the different items stored, which can help management monitor its inventory control performance. Similarly, customer service performance, such as the number of stock-outs or the number of incomplete orders, can be regularly monitored. Some reports may be generated on an exception basis. That is, the report is only generated if some performance measure deviates from acceptable limits.

Forecasting

All inventory decisions are based on forecast future demand. The inventory control system can compare actual demand against forecast and adjust the forecast in the light of actual levels of demand. See Appendix 1.

Control systems of this type are treated in more detail in Chapter 14.

Summary answers to key questions

What is inventory?

● Inventory, or stock, is the stored accumulation of the transformed resources in an operation.

● Sometimes the words 'stock' and 'inventory' are also used to describe transforming resources, but the terms *stock control* and *inventory control* are nearly always used in connection with transformed resources.

● Almost all operations keep some kind of inventory, most usually of materials but also of information and customers (customer inventories are normally called queues).

Why is inventory necessary?

● Inventory occurs in operations because the timing of supply and the timing of demand do not always match. Inventories are needed, therefore, to smooth the differences between supply and demand.

● There are four main reasons for keeping inventory.
  – to cope with random or unexpected interruptions in supply or demand (buffer inventory);
  – to cope with an operation's inability to make all products simultaneously (cycle inventory);
  – to cope with planned fluctuations in supply or demand (anticipation inventory);
  – to cope with transportation delays in the supply network (pipeline inventory).

How much inventory should an operation hold?

● This depends on balancing the costs associated with holding stocks against the costs associated with placing an order. The main stock-holding costs are usually related to working capital, whereas the main order costs are usually associated with the transactions necessary to generate the information to place an order.

● The most common approach to determining the amount of inventory to order is the economic order quantity (EOQ) formula. The EOQ formula can be adapted to different types of inventory profile using different stock behaviour assumptions.

● The EOQ approach, however, has been subject to a number of criticisms regarding the true cost of holding stock, the real cost of placing an order, and the use of EOQ models as prescriptive devices.

When should an operation replenish its inventory?

● Partly this depends on the uncertainty of demand. Orders are usually timed to leave a certain level of average safety stock when the order arrives. The level of safety stock is influenced by the variability of both demand and the lead time of supply. These two variables are usually combined into a lead-time usage distribution.

● Using re-order level as a trigger for placing replenishment orders necessitates the continual review of inventory levels. This can be time-consuming and expensive. An alternative approach is to make replenishment orders of varying size but at fixed time periods.

How can inventory be controlled?

● The key issue here is how managers discriminate between the levels of control they apply to different stock items. The most common way of doing this is by what is known as the ABC classification of stock. This uses the Pareto principle to distinguish between the different values of, or significance placed on, types of stock.

● Inventory is usually managed through sophisticated computer-based information systems which have a number of functions: the updating of stock records, the generation of orders, the generation of inventory status reports and demand forecasts.

CASE EXERCISE

Pan-Europe Plastics (PEP)

Patrik Staaf, General Manager of the Swedish factory of Pan-European Plastics, had become increasingly concerned at the rising level of inventory in the Stockholm warehouse. Many of the products in the ever-widening range of consumer household items were physically large, requiring an enormous finished goods warehouse, but each product had to be available from stock for immediate delivery. Almost 1000 different products ('stock keeping units' or SKUs) had to be kept, although there were only 20 injection moulding machines to make them on. Patrik's factory was a typical batch production operation. Production schedules were prepared weekly by the Planning Office; this determined which products/moulds were to be used, at what time, on which machine, and the batch quantity of each colour of the product that was to be produced. For each production run, the factory operatives would therefore 'set up' a mould, a process taking an average of three hours. The product would then be moulded until a colour change or further mould change was required. The site accountant calculated that the average cost of a mould setup, per hour, was 1000 kr (kroner).

One important product was the standard baby bath, available only in white. Because of the relatively large size and cost of this product, Patrik decided to review the seemingly large production guideline ('batch rule') of 8640 units

per batch, which was always used by the Planning Office. The Swedish factory was responsible for all the company's production of this product, amounting to 108 000 baths per year. Demand was relatively stable and non-seasonal. Unit variable costs of production were 30 kr, and holding costs were estimated to be 20 per cent per year, which took account of finance charges and warehousing costs. The factory operated 24 hours per day, five day per week, for 50 weeks per year, and baby baths were made at the rate of one every 40 seconds (the cycle time).

Questions

1 Using the EBQ model, what batch size would you recommend for this product? How long will each batch take to produce, and how many batches per year will be made? Given the physical characteristics and cost of the product, do you have any reservations about your recommendations?

2 Following a setup reduction initiative, ways were found to reduce the setup time to 1.5 hours. However, the Group Controller reassessed holding costs at 40 per cent taking additional account of opportunity costs of capital. What effect would this have on the recommendations you would make to Patrik?

Plastix Plc

Plastix Plc is one of Europe's largest and most profitable manufacturers of plastic household durables. The Swedish factory makes a range of 300 products which are sold to wholesalers and large retailers throughout Europe. The company offers ex-stock delivery of all items, and dispatch within 24 hours of receipt of orders by a reputable international haulier; on this basis, customers expect to receive all their requirements within one week.

Concerned about the declining delivery reliability, increased levels of finished goods inventory, and falling productivity (apparently resulting from 'split-batches' where only part of a planned production batch is produced to overcome immediate shortages), the Managing Director, Laas-Uno Duman, employed consultants to undertake a complete review of operations. On 1 September 1996, a full physical inventory check was taken; a representative sample of 20 products is shown in Table 12.9.

Plastix uses batch-production, injection-moulding processes; typical setups (changeovers) take four hours, costing approximately £400. Because of current high demand for Plastix products, the backlog of work for planned stock replenishment currently averages eight weeks, and so all factory orders must be planned at least eight weeks in advance. Actual re-order quantities (*see* Table 12.9) are always established by the Estimating Department when each new product is designed and the manufacturing costs are established, based on Marketing's estimates of likely demand. However, in order to minimize the cost of setups, and to maximize capacity utilization, all products are now planned for a *minimum* production run of 20 hours,

Table 12.9 Details of a representative sample of 20 Plastix products

Product reference number*	Description	Unit manuf'g variable cost (£)	Last 12 mths' sales (000s)	Physical inventory 1 Sept 96 (000s)	Re-order quantity (000s)	Standard moulding rate** (items/hour)
016GH	Storage bin large	1.60	10	0	2	240
033KN	Bread bin + lid	2.40	60	8	2	200
041GH	10 litre bucket	0.50	2200	360	600	300
062GD	Grecian pot	3.00	40	15	5	180
080BR	Bathroom mirror	5.00	5	6	5	260
101KN	1 litre jug	0.60	100	20	10	600
126KN	Pack (10) bag clips	0.30	200	80	50	2000
143BB	Baby bath	2.50	50	1	2	120
169BB	Baby potty	1.50	60	0	2	180
188BQ	Barbecue table	10.80	10	8	5	120
232GD	Garden bird bath	2.00	2	6	2	200
261GH	Broom head	0.80	60	22	8	400
288LY	Pack (10) clothes pegs	1.00	10	17	50	1000
302BQ	Barbecue salad fork	0.20	5	12	2	400
351GH	Storage bin small	1.00	25	2	2	300
382KN	Round mixing bowl	0.50	800	25	80	650
421KN	Pasta jar	2.00	1	3	5	220
444GH	Wall hook	0.05	200	86	50	3000
472GH	Dustbin + lid	6.00	300	3	10	180
506BR	Soap holder	0.80	10	9	20	400

*   The reference number uses the following codes for ranges:

   BB = Babycare   BQ = Barbecue   BR = Bathroom
   GD = Garden   GH = General household KN = Kitchen
   LY = Laundry

**   Moulding rate is for the product as described (e.g. includes lids, or pack quantities).

with re-order levels based on the previous 13 weeks' average sales. About 20 per cent of the products (e.g. Barbecue Range and Garden Range) are very seasonal, with peak demand during April–August.

Storage bins sell particularly well from October to December. Monthly forecasts of sales value are prepared annually and reviewed quarterly; this analysis is by product range (e.g. Babycare, Gardenware) for budgeting, cash-flow forecasting and aggregate capacity planning. The Marketing Manager summarized the current position thus:

'Our coverage of the market has never been so comprehensive; we are able to offer a full range of household plastics in fashionable colours, which appeals to most European tastes. But we will not retain our newly developed markets unless we can give distributors confidence that we will supply all their orders within one week. Unfortunately, at the moment, many receive several deliveries for each order, spread over many weeks. This certainly increases their administrative and handling costs, and our haulage costs. And sometimes the shortfall is only some small, low-value items like clothes pegs!'

The factory operates on three shifts, Monday to Friday: 120 hours per week. Regular overtime, typically 16 hours on a Saturday, has been worked most of the last year. Sunday is never used for production, allowing access to machines for routine and major overhauls. Machines are laid out in groups so that each operator can be kept highly utilized, attending to at least four machines. Although the moulding processes run automatically, the operators are needed to ensure that inputs of raw materials and outputs of products continue to flow without problems. They are encouraged by an output-based bonus scheme which directly rewards the productivity of each operator. All machines are the same size to allow full interchangeability of the tooling, so any product can be made on any machine.

Christian Roos, the Manufacturing Director, gave more details about production:

'Because of the fast output rates of all the moulding machines, it is very easy to produce slightly faulty products at a very fast rate! Typical problems could be damaged or worn tooling causing poor surface finish (marks and scratches); or perhaps slightly bent or twisted products caused by incorrect adjustment of temperatures or pressures. The real problem is that our operators' perception of a fault may be different from that of the inspectors, particularly just after we have had a few customer complaints! The Quality Control Manager, Monique Ryan, reports directly to the MD. Her 14 inspectors (four per shift, two on Saturday mornings) are fully occupied taking random samples from each of our 30 moulding machines, checking them in the laboratory for critical variables and attributes. Recently the
reject rate has increased, yet we are also getting higher levels of complaints from the trade ... but that is probably to be expected as our products become more up-market and complicated. Fortunately, all faulty products can be ground up and made into garden pots, so we don't lose any of the expensive material. Monique has recently persuaded the MD to employ another inspector on each shift to try to reduce the quality problems, and I am sure that will help. I am worried, however, that the effect may be to make our delivery problems worse as even more batches are rejected or delayed while problems are rectified. Also further valuable factory and warehouse space is being allocated to Quality Control for their working and storage needs, which I really cannot afford to give up!

'At the moment our warehouse is full, with products stacked on the floor in every available corner, which makes it vulnerable to damage from passing forklifts and from double-handling. We have finally agreed to approve a £1 million warehouse extension to be constructed January – May 1997, which will give good payback as it will replace contract warehousing and associated transport which is costing us about 5 per cent of the manufacturing costs of the stored capital. The return on investment is well above our current 10 per cent cost of capital. There is no viable alternative, because if we run out of space, production will have to stop for a time. Some of our products occupy very large volumes of rack space!

'We all work hard to keep down manufacturing costs. Our Group Central Purchasing Department in Stockholm sources all our raw materials, and because of their purchasing power, we are able to get the lowest prices for all types of plastics. Recently they contracted a Hungarian company to supply polyethylene granules for the Industrial Products Division, and we are able to get this material at a saving of about 5 per cent. We will have to sample this material carefully, as it is likely to be more variable than UK-sourced material. Monique, the Quality Control Manager, is a polymer chemist, so she has agreed to do the tests herself every morning to save the cost and time involved in using an outside laboratory.'

Questions

1 Why is Plastix unable to deliver all its products within the target of one week, and what effects might that have on the distributors?

2 What internal problems result from the current planning and control policies? Categorize these broadly into categories of scheduling, capacity management and inventory management. Do these policies interact?

3 What recommendations would you make to Laas-Uno Duman?

4 How does the company's inventory management impact on its quality performance?

1 Describe and categorize the types of material inventories that might be found in the following organizations:
   – a theatre
   – a furniture retailer
   – a brewery
   – a city bus company.

2 Talk to an operations manager about the different types of inventory that the organization holds. Find out if there are different ways of planning and controlling some of the different types of inventory.

3 Get hold of the last few years' Annual Report and Accounts for a materials-processing organization of your choice. Calculate the organization's stock–turnover ratio and the proportion of inventory to current assets over the last few years. Try to explain what you think are the reasons for any trends you can identify and discuss the likely advantages and disadvantages for the organization concerned.

4 The Shocking Electricity Company uses 3000 metres of wire every month. The cost of placing an order for the wire has been calculated at £40 and the cost of stocking the wire is 5p per metre per year. In what quantities should the company order the wire? If it adopts an EOQ approach to ordering, what would be its annual inventory cost?

5 A university's printing department uses paper at the rate of 86 packets per day. A pack of paper costs £2 and the annual stock-holding cost is calculated at 10 per cent of the cost of the paper. If it costs £25 every time an order is placed and the department works 250 days in the year, what is the EOQ for the paper? If it takes three days between placing an order and receiving it, what is the re-order point at which an order should be placed?

6 The Pride of Scotland Butchers Limited has a haggis machine which can produce at a rate of 1000 haggises per day. Traditionally the company produces a day's worth of haggises which fully satisfies the demand for one week. The company sells its haggises throughout 50 weeks of the year. Each time the haggis machine is set up to produce a batch of haggises it costs £100. The haggises have to be kept in particularly cool and hygienic conditions and therefore it costs the company £0.5 per haggis per day to store stock. How much money is the company losing by producing 1000 haggises per week in one batch rather than adopting an EBQ policy (make any assumptions you believe reasonable)?

7 A company which has been using the EOQ formula to determine its order quantities has now found that demand has increased by 50 per cent since it last calculated the optimum order quantity. What adjustment will it have to make to its order quantity? What further adjustment will it have to make to its ordering quantity if its stock-holding costs increase by 50 per cent?

8 A university MBA programme keeps sweatshirts in stock for its students with the university's logo emblazoned on the front. On average it sells 200 of these sweatshirts every year. There is a fixed postage and packing charge of £5 every time it places an order. The cost of the sweatshirts is £15 and inventory is charged by the university at 30 per cent per year. How many sweatshirts should the university order at a time? The new programme director has responded to complaints from the students that the sweatshirts were out of stock last year by offering to pay £20 into the students' entertainment fund every time there is a stock-out. How would this affect the economic order quantity?

9 An ice-cream seller is required to purchase the ice-creams which are then kept in a cold box at the beginning of a sales day. The seller pays £0.20 for every ice-cream. Ice-creams are sold at £0.50 each but any ice-creams left at the end of the day cannot be returned and go to waste. The ice-cream seller classifies demand as either low, medium or high. Low demand is between 40 and 80 ice-creams, medium demand is between 80 and 120 ice-creams, and high demand is between 120 and 160 ice-creams. The probability of demand being low is 0.2, the probability of demand being medium is 0.5, and the probability of demand being high is 0.3. Approximately how many ice-creams would you advise the ice-cream seller to purchase every morning? If competition forces down the price the ice-cream seller can charge to £0.40, does this change the decision?

10 A furniture store sells tables which it obtains from a local furniture factory. Each time it places an order on the factory there is a delivery charge and general transaction cost of £60. The stock-holding cost is estimated to be £10 per table per year. Both demand and lead time vary according to the distribution in Table 12.11. Devise a re-order level policy for the furniture store if it is to have less than a 5 per cent probability of being out of stock in each order cycle.

Table 12.11 Lead-time usage of tables

Lead-time usage	Probability
600–650	0.2
650–700	0.2
700–750	0.3
750–800	0.2
800–850	0.05
850–900	0.05

11 Save all your food (and drink) bills over a two-week period (or otherwise make a note of such purchases) and conduct a Pareto analysis of the usage value of the items. How would you use this information to plan an inventory policy for your purchasing and storage of such items?

12 Identify 10 public companies from different industrial sectors and examine their published accounts (you can do this through the internet); calculate the value of their 'stock turn' ratios. What are the implications of the variations in this figure you will observe between the companies?

Notes on chapter

1 The 'stock to sales' ratio is a good indicator of the value of inventory in different businesses.
2 There are several different ways of classifying inventory. This is probably the most straightforward.
3 For further discussion on the limitations of the EOQ *see* Schonberger, R.J. and Knod, E.M. (1994) *Operations Management: Continuous Improvement* (5th edn), Irwin.
4 Sources: *The Economist*, 26 June 1993; Horovitz, J. and Jurgens Panak, M. (1992) *Total Customer Satisfaction*, FT/Pitman Publishing; and discussion with company staff.
5 We thank Jeff Schaffer for his help in supplying the information for this box.

Selected further reading

Adkins, A.C. Jr. (1984) 'EOQ in the Real World', *Production and Inventory Management*, Vol 25, No 4.

Austin, L.M. (1977) 'Project EOQ: A Success Story in Implementing Academic Research', *Interfaces*, Vol 7, Aug.

Flores, B.E. and Whybark, D.C. (1987) 'Implementing Multiple Criteria ABC Analysis', *Journal of Operations Management*, Vol 7, No 1.

Fogarty, D.W. and Blackstone, J.H. (1991) *Production and Inventory Management*, South-Western Publishing.

Greene, J.H. (1987) *Production and Inventory Control Handbook* (2nd edn), McGraw-Hill.

Hall, R. (1983) *Zero Inventories*, Dow Jones-Irwin.

Jessop, D. and Morrison, A. (1991) *Storage and Control of Stock*, Pitman Publishing.

Jinchiro, N. and Hall, R. (1983) 'Management Specs for Stockless Production', *Harvard Business Review*, Vol 61, No 3.

Lockyer, K.G. and Wynne, R.M. (1989) 'The Life Profile of Stock as a Control Measure', *International Journal of Operations and Production Management*, Vol 9, No 1.

Mapes, J. (1993) 'The Effect of Capacity Limitations on Safety Stock', *International Journal of Operations and Production Management*, Vol 13, No 10.

Mather, H. (1984) *How to Really Manage Inventories*, McGraw-Hill.

Newell, S., Swan, J. and Clarke, P. (1993) 'The Importance of User Design in the Adoption of New Information Technologies: The Example of Production and Inventory Control Systems', *International Journal of Operations and Production Management*, Vol 13, No 2.

Primrose, P.L. (1992) 'The Value of Inventory Savings', *International Journal of Operations and Production Management*, Vol 12, No 5.

Ronen, D. (1983) 'Inventory Service Measures – A Comparison of Measures', *International Journal of Operations and Production Management*, Vol 3, No 2.

Schonberger, R.J. and Schniederjans, M.J. (1984) 'Reinventing Inventory Control', *Interfaces*, Vol 14, No 3.

Silver, E.A. and Peterson, R. (1985) *Decision Systems for Inventory Management and Production Planning*, John Wiley.

Snyder, R.D. (1993) 'A Computerized System for Forecasting Spare Parts Sales: A Case Study', *International Journal of Operations and Production Management*, Vol 13, No 7.

Tersine, R.J. (1987) *Principles of Inventory and Materials Management* (2nd edn), North Holland.

Williams, K., Williams, J. and Haslam, C. (1989) 'Why Take the Stocks Out? Britain versus Japan', *International Journal of Operations and Production Management*, Vol 9, No 8.

Supply chain planning and control

Introduction

Historically operations managers have seen their main responsibility lying within their own operation. However, increasingly they now have to look beyond this traditional internal view if they want to manage their operations effectively. For example, in many industries, operations are becoming more focused on a narrower set of tasks. Consequently they need to purchase more of their services and materials from outside specialist suppliers. This, in turn, means that the way in which businesses manage the supply of products and services to their operations greatly increases in importance. Similarly, at the demand side of the business, the way in which the distribution chain which transports goods and services to customers is managed contributes to an operation's ability to serve its customers. Just as important, it can impact on total costs. This flow of materials and information through a business from the purchasing activity, through the operation and out to customers, by way of a distribution or service delivery activity, is what we described in Chapter 6 as the 'immediate' supply network or supply chain. Even beyond the immediate supply chain, there are often strategic benefits to be gained from managing the flow between customers' customers and suppliers' suppliers. Inter-company operations management of this nature is now more commonly termed *supply chain management*. In Chapter 6 we raised the strategic and structural issues of designing supply networks. In this chapter we are going to consider the more 'infrastructural' issues of planning and controlling the individual chains in the supply network. Figure 13.1 illustrates the supply–demand linkage treated in this chapter.

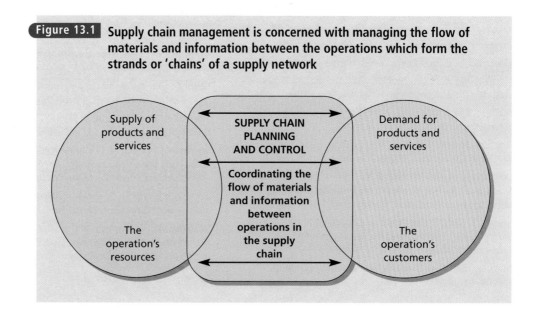

Figure 13.1 Supply chain management is concerned with managing the flow of materials and information between the operations which form the strands or 'chains' of a supply network

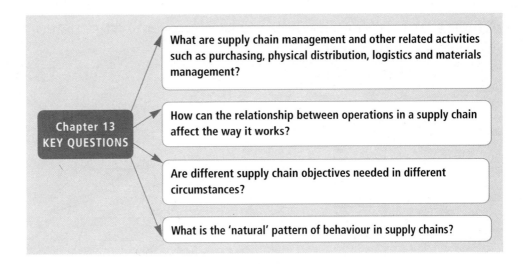

**Chapter 13
KEY QUESTIONS**

What are supply chain management and other related activities such as purchasing, physical distribution, logistics and materials management?

How can the relationship between operations in a supply chain affect the way it works?

Are different supply chain objectives needed in different circumstances?

What is the 'natural' pattern of behaviour in supply chains?

What is supply chain management?

In Chapter 6 we used the term 'supply network' to refer to all the operations that were linked together so as to provide goods and services through to the end customers. We also dealt with some of the structural issues involved in configuring supply networks, such as how much of the network to own, the shape the network should form, and the location and capacity of its constituent operations. In this chapter we are dealing with the 'ongoing' flow of goods and services through this network along individual channels or strands. In large organizations there can be many hundreds of strands of linked operations passing through the operation. These strands are more commonly referred to as supply chains. Many of the topics covered in this chapter on supply chain planning and control are relatively new. This means that some of the terms used to describe them are not universally applied. Furthermore, some of the concepts behind the terminology overlap in the sense that they refer to common parts of the total supply network. This is why it is useful first of all to distinguish between the different terms we shall use in this chapter. These are illustrated in Figure 13.2.

Supply chain management is the management of the interconnection of organizations which relate to each other through upstream and downstream linkages between the different processes that produce value in the form of products and services to the ultimate consumer. It is a holistic approach to managing across company boundaries. More to the point, it is becoming recognized that there are substantial benefits to be gained from managing a whole chain of operations so that they satisfy end customers. These benefits centre on the two key objectives of supply chain management: effectively satisfying customers and doing so efficiently.

A focus on satisfying end customers effectively

Because supply chain management includes all stages in the total flow of materials and information, it must eventually include consideration of the final customer. The final customer has the only 'real' currency in the supply chain. When a customer decides to make a purchase, he or she triggers action along the whole chain. All the businesses in the supply chain pass on portions of that end-customer's money to each other, each retaining a margin for the value it has added. However, although all the operations in the chain have the immediate objective of satisfying their own immediate customer, the purpose of supply chain management is to make sure that they have a full appreciation of how, together, they can satisfy the end customer. A key question for all

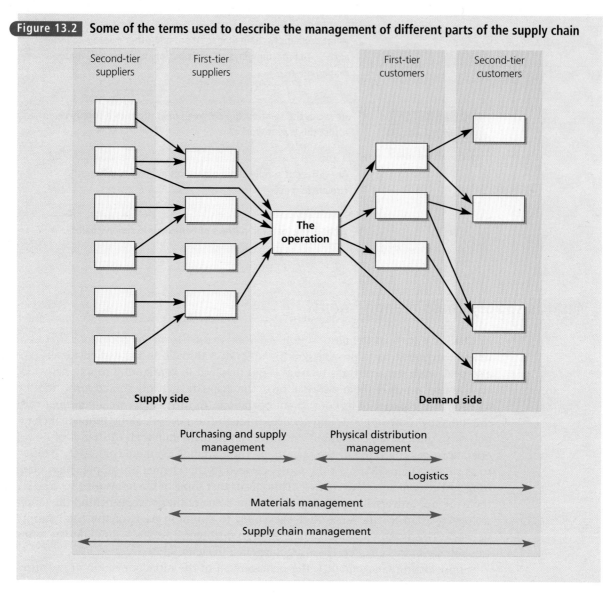

operations therefore is: '*What level of quality, speed, dependability and flexibility do I need to develop in my part of the chain in order to satisfy the end customer?*'

A focus on managing the chain efficiently

Taking an holistic approach to managing an entire supply chain opens up many opportunities for analysis and improvement. For example, in a supply chain for products with low profit margins, preventing too much inventory accumulation may be critical. In these circumstances, it is important to make sure that products move down the chain quickly rather than building up as inventory. Analysing the chain as a whole to find out where most of the time delays occur allows the supply chain manager to focus attention on those 'bottleneck' businesses in order to shorten throughput time. Often, analysing the whole supply chain can increase efficiency by allowing inventory only when it is needed, identifying bottlenecks, balancing capacity and generally coordinating the smooth flow of materials.

Effective supply chain planning and control is particularly important for operations which supply a wide range of products (many colours in several different types of paint) and whose customers could easily switch to another supplier

The component activities of supply chain management

From the perspective of a single operation in the chain (known as the focal operation), supply chain management can be seen as managing the operations that form its *supply side* and those that form its *demand side*:

- On the supply side, *purchasing and supply management* is a well-accepted term for the function that deals with the operation's interface with its supply markets.
- On the demand side, *physical distribution management* is again a well-accepted term for managing the activity of supplying immediate customers. *Logistics* is an extension of physical distribution management and usually refers to the management of materials and information flow from a business, down through a distribution channel, to end customers.
- *Materials management* is a more limited term than supply chain management and refers to the management of the flow of materials and information through the immediate supply chain, including purchasing, inventory management, stores management, operations planning and control and physical distribution management.[1]

Purchasing and supply management

At the supply end of the business, the purchasing function forms contracts with suppliers to buy in materials and services. Some of these materials and services are used directly in the production of the goods and services. Other materials and services are used to help run the business, for example, staff catering services or oil for machinery. These do not make up part of the finished goods or services but are still essential purchases for operations.

Purchasing activities

Purchasing managers provide a vital link between the operation itself and its suppliers. To be effective, they must understand the requirements of all the processes within the operation and also the capabilities of the suppliers (sometimes thousands in numbers) who could potentially provide products and services for the operation. Figure 13.3 shows a simplified sequence of events in the management of a typical supplier–operation interaction which the purchasing function must facilitate. First of all, the operation formally requests products or services. Purchasing should keep extensive

As the personal computer industry matured, and competition increasingly focused on the cost of its products, some companies decided to cut out a tier of their network and sell directly to customers rather than through retail outlets. This move into mail-order selling was prompted originally by the need to trim costs. With most manufacturers buying their components from the same group of suppliers, the potential for cost-cutting on the supply side of the network was limited. Furthermore, the nature of customers was changing. The growing number of sophisticated second- or third-time customers no longer needed quite the same degree of technical support from dealers. Cutting them out seemed a good move to Dell Computers, who initially became the most successful of the computer companies to bypass its demand-side supply chain and deal directly with its ultimate customers.

Yet Dell also found that reshaping its supply chain yielded benefits other than lower costs. Its (now direct) contact with customers meant that it could learn more about their needs and preferences

ahead of rival manufacturers. Realizing that this new-found potential needed to be exploited, Dell built computer-based information systems which could track every contact with customers, from their first enquiry through to details of every service and repair, thus building a service history for every machine. As well as helping to sell and service computers more effectively in the short term, this information base also led sales and support staff to pass better information back to product development teams.

Questions

1 Sketch what you think might be the structure of the supply chain for a personal computer manufacturer.

2 How did Dell Computers change this supply chain structure and what advantages did it gain? What else could a personal computer manufacturer do to restructure its supply chain?

information about potential suppliers and might be able to suggest alternative materials or services for consideration. The purchasing function prepares a formal request which can be sent to potential suppliers so that they can prepare quotations for the business. These requests might be sent to several suppliers if the products or services are either novel or have not been purchased for some time. The various quotations submitted by suppliers may be examined and, after negotiation, a 'preferred' supplier selected. The next important task for the purchasing function is to prepare a purchase order. The purchase order is important because it often forms the legal basis of the contractual relationship between the operation and its supplier. Again, the purchasing function needs to coordinate with the operation over the technical details of the purchase order. When the supplier receives the purchase order, it produces and delivers the products or services, usually directly to the operation. These then form the input into the operation's transformation process, but the operation should also inform purchasing of the arrival of the products or services and their condition on delivery.

Traditional objectives of the purchasing function

Most operations buy in a wide variety of materials and services, and typically the volume and value of these purchases are increasing as organizations concentrate on their 'core tasks'. Despite the variety of purchases that a firm makes, there are some underlying objectives of purchasing which are true for all materials and services bought. Purchased materials and services should:

- be of the right quality
- be delivered quickly if necessary
- be delivered at the right time and in full
- be able to be changed in terms of specification, delivery time or quantity (retain flexibility)
- be of the right price.

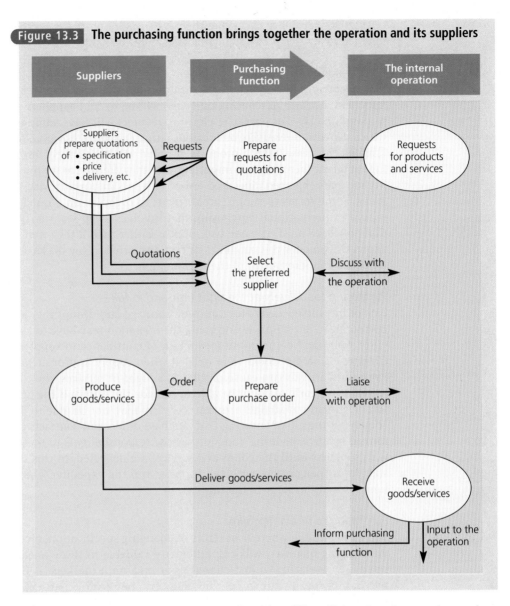

Figure 13.3 The purchasing function brings together the operation and its suppliers

In addition, the activity of purchasing should itself be *efficient*. In other words, purchasing should achieve the normal operations performance objectives – quality, speed, dependability, flexibility and cost.

Purchasing at the right quality

Traditionally, suppliers were not trusted to provide goods and services of the right quality. They were inspected to ensure that they conformed to the required specification. More recently, suppliers are being encouraged to ensure that they take responsibility themselves to provide a 'right-first-time' level of quality. Furthermore, they are required to certify to the purchasing company that quality levels have been met. This self-certification is based on a level of trust and confidence which has come about partly because purchasing organizations have invested time, money and effort into helping their suppliers reach the required quality levels. Supplier quality assurance (SQA) programmes monitor and improve levels of supplier quality, partly by assessing supplier capability in terms of their equipment, systems, procedures and training. Quality-conscious purchasing organizations such as aircraft manufacturers have always invested substantial effort in ensuring that suppliers are capable of meeting the right quality. Sometimes suppliers can self-certify their capability by having their systems and processes certified as conforming to internationally recognized standards such as ISO 9000 (discussed in Chapter 20).

Purchasing for fast delivery

In some organizations where competition is based on fast response or where demand is uncertain, a major purchasing objective will be to find suppliers who can themselves respond quickly. For example, clothing retailers will have some types of garment for which demand is relatively predictable. Other garments, however, will be more fashion-oriented. For these fashion products, demand will be relatively unpredictable. In choosing suppliers, therefore, it is important that they are able to supply quickly if demand is higher than expected. Speed of response is less important with the less fashionable items. Some forms of supply are difficult to organize on a quick response basis. For example, international purchasing that involves 'deep sea' transportation may mean that purchases must be made two months earlier than if they were bought locally. This allows the time for the purchases to be transported to the docks, loaded, shipped over, unloaded and transported to their destination.

Purchasing for delivery at the right time and in full

Late or incomplete deliveries can cause shortage and disrupt the smooth running of an operation. When supply is uncertain, the operation may have to keep inventories in an effort to try and compensate for its lack of confidence in supply. Remember how, in Chapter 12, safety stocks were needed when supply and/or demand were uncertain. Even early arrivals can cause problems. Bought-in services, such as cleaning services, which arrive early may not be able to provide the service if the operation is not ready for it. Similarly, materials arriving too early may not be able to be stored efficiently. Sometimes the job of ensuring that purchase orders and contracts are adhered to is performed by an 'expediting' function, whose responsibility is to track or 'progress' orders with suppliers until the goods and services are delivered. In this situation, purchasing staff form the contract with the supplier and the expediter 'chases' it. This chasing function adds no value to the transaction.

Purchasing to retain flexibility

Supply flexibility, whether in terms of changing specification, changing delivery time or changing quantity, will be particularly valuable to those operations which themselves are operating in fast-changing or uncertain markets. If flexibility is desired, purchasing staff might sometimes choose to buy from a particular source because of its future potential rather than its immediate direct benefits. For example, a purchasing department might be comparing two suppliers, A and B. Supplier A has submitted a quotation which is superior on price and delivery and, as far as they can tell, on quality as well. However, the purchasing department might suspect that supplier A will be inflexible with regard to changing the terms of the supply arrangement. They might also judge that supplier A does not have the capability to develop new products or services which they might require in the future. Supplier B, on the other hand, although its initial quotation might not match that of supplier A, might be judged to have more potential for improvement, or might possess the core capabilities of meeting future requirements.

Purchasing at the right price

The most obvious benefit of purchasing at the right price is that it can provide an operation with a cost advantage. Historically, this objective of purchasing has been emphasized in purchasing theory and practice. The performance of purchasing staff was even judged using cost savings as the main measure. The reason for this emphasis on 'the right cost' is understandable because purchasing can have a very significant impact on any operation's costs, and therefore profits.

To illustrate the impact that price-conscious purchasing can have on profits, consider a simple manufacturing operation with the following financial details:

Total sales	10 000 000
Purchased services and materials	£7 000 000
Salaries	£2 000 000
Overheads	£500 000

Therefore, profit = £500 000. Profits could be doubled to £1 million by any of the following:

- increase sales revenue by up to 100 per cent
- decrease salaries by 25 per cent
- decrease overheads by 100 per cent
- decrease purchase costs by 7.1 per cent.

A doubling of sales revenue does sometimes occur in very fast-growing markets, but this would be regarded by most sales and marketing managers as an exceedingly ambitious target. Decreasing the salaries bill by a quarter is likely to require substantial alternative investment – for example, in automation – or reflects a dramatic reduction in medium- to long-term sales. Similarly, a reduction in overheads by 100 per cent is unlikely to be possible over the short to medium term without compromising the business. However, reducing purchase costs by 7.1 per cent, although a challenging objective, is usually far more of a realistic option than the other actions.

The reason purchase price savings can have such a dramatic impact on total profitability is that purchase costs are such a large proportion of total costs. The higher purchase costs are as a proportion of total costs, the more profitability can be improved in this way. Figure 13.4 illustrates this.

Single- and multi-sourcing

An important decision facing most purchasing managers is whether to source each individual product or service from one or more than one supplier, known, respectively, as single-sourcing or multi-sourcing. Some of the advantages and disadvantages of single- and multi-sourcing are shown in Table 13.1.

It may seem as though companies who multi-source do so exclusively for their own short-term benefit. However, this is not always the case: multi-sourcing can have an altruistic motive, or at least one which brings benefits to both supplier and purchaser

---

Figure 13.4 The larger the level of material costs as a proportion of total costs, the greater the effect on profitability of a reduction in material costs

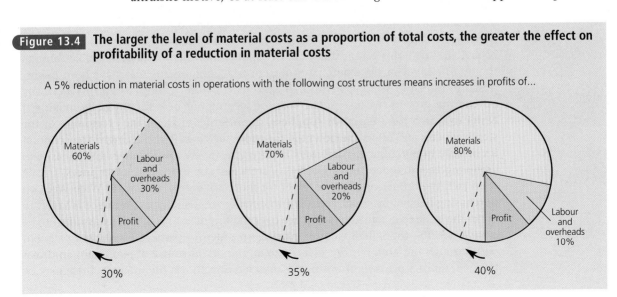

A 5% reduction in material costs in operations with the following cost structures means increases in profits of...

Table 13.1 Advantages and disadvantages of single- and multi-sourcing

	Single-sourcing	Multi-sourcing
Advantages	<ul><li>Potentially better quality because more SQA possibilities</li><li>Strong relationships which are more durable</li><li>Greater dependency encourages more commitment and effort</li><li>Better communication</li><li>Easier to cooperate on new product/service development</li><li>More scale economies</li><li>Higher confidentiality</li></ul>	<ul><li>Purchaser can drive price down by competitive tendering</li><li>Can switch sources in case of supply failure</li><li>Wide sources of knowledge and expertise to tap</li></ul>
Disadvantages	<ul><li>More vulnerable to disruption if a failure to supply occurs</li><li>Individual supplier more affected by volume fluctuations</li><li>Supplier might exert upward pressure on prices if no alternative supplier is available</li></ul>	<ul><li>Difficult to encourage commitment by supplier</li><li>Less easy to develop effective SQA</li><li>More effort needed to comminicate</li><li>Suppliers less likely to invest in new processes</li><li>More difficult to obtain scale economies</li></ul>

in the long term. For example, Robert Bosch GmbH, the German automotive components manufacturer and distributor, at one time required that sub-contractors do no more than 20 per cent of their total business with them.[3] This was to prevent suppliers becoming too dependent on them. The purchasing organization could then change volumes up and down without pushing the supplier into bankruptcy. However, despite these perceived advantages, there has been a trend for purchasing functions to reduce their supplier base in terms of numbers of companies supplying any one part or service. For example, Rank Xerox, the copier and document company, reduced its supply base from 5000 suppliers to a little more than 300 over a six-year period.[4]

Purchasing, the internet and e-commerce

For some years, electronic means have been used by businesses to confirm purchased orders and ensure payment to suppliers. The rapid development of the internet, however, opened up the potential for far more fundamental changes in purchasing behaviour. Partly this was as the result of supplier information made available through the internet. Previously, a purchaser of industrial components may have been predisposed to return to suppliers who had been used before. There was an inertia in the purchasing process because of the costs of seeking out new suppliers. By making it easier to search for alternative suppliers, the internet changes the economics of the search process and offers the potential for wider searches. It also changed the economics of scale in purchasing. Purchasers requiring relatively low volumes find it easier to group together in order to create orders of sufficient size to warrant lower prices.

In fact, the influence of the internet (or more accurately, the World Wide Web) on purchasing behaviour is not confined to *e-commerce*. Usually e-commerce is taken to mean the trade that actually takes place over the internet. This is usually assumed to be a buyer visiting the seller's website, placing an order for parts and making a payment (also through the site). But the web is also an important source of purchasing information. For every 1 per cent of business transacted directly via the internet, there may be

5 or 6 per cent of business which, at some point, involved the net, probably with potential buyers using it to compare prices or obtain technical information.

One increasingly common use of internet technology in purchasing (or e-procurement as it is sometimes known) is for large companies, or groups of companies, to link their e-commerce systems into a common 'exchange'. In their more sophisticated form, such an exchange may be linked into the purchasing companies' own information systems (see the discussion on ERP in Chapter 14). Many of the large automotive, engineering and petrochemical companies, for example, have adopted such an approach. Typical of these companies' motives are those put forward by Shell Services International, part of the petrochemical giant:[5]

> 'Procurement is an obvious first step in e-commerce. First, buying through the web is so slick and cheap compared to doing it almost any other way. Second, it allows you to aggregate, spend and ask: Why am I spending this money, or shouldn't I be getting a bigger discount? Third, it encourages new services like credit, insurance and accreditation to be built around it.'

● CRITICAL COMMENTARY

Not everyone is happy with e-procurement. Some see it as preventing the development of closer partnership-type relationships which, in the long run, could bring far greater returns. Some Japanese car makers, in particular, are wary of too much involvement in e-procurement. For example, while Toyota Motor, the world's third largest car marker, did join up with Ford, General Motors and Daimler Chrysler in a web-based trade exchange, it limits its purchases to trading in such items as bolts, nuts and basic office supplies. The main reason for its reluctance is that traditionally it has gained a competitive edge by building long-term relationships with its suppliers. This means establishing trust, getting an understanding of a trading partner's aspirations and not squeezing every last cent out of them in the short term (see the discussion on partnership relationships later). Taking this approach, e-procurement which is used primarily to drive down cost could do more harm than good.[6]

Keiretsu networks

A *keiretsu* is a Japanese term which is used to describe a coalition of companies who form a 'supplier network' to a (usually large) manufacturer. Often the large manufacturer will give financial support to these suppliers through loans, or even by taking equity stakes in the companies. Keiretsu members are expected to commit to providing excellent service, technical expertise and quality improvements to the manufacturer. In return, the manufacturer assures the coalition partners of long-term continuity of demand. In recent years, keiretsu have been criticized for being too cosy in their relationships. It is argued that without more open competition the coalition members become less innovative.

Global sourcing

One of the major supply chain developments of recent years has been the expansion in the proportion of products and (occasionally) services which businesses are willing to source from outside their home country. Traditionally, even companies who exported their goods and services all over the world (that is, they were international on their demand side) still sourced the majority of their supplies locally (that is, they were not international on their supply side). This has changed – companies are now increasingly willing to look further afield for their supplies. There are a number of reasons for this:

● The formation of trading blocks in different parts of the world has had the effect of lowering tariff barriers, at least within those blocks. For example, the single market developments within the European Union (EU), the North American Free Trade Agreement (NAFTA) and the South American Trade Group (MERCOSUR) have all made it easier to trade internationally within the regions.

- Transportation infrastructures are considerably more sophisticated and cheaper than they once were. Super-efficient port operations in Rotterdam and Singapore, for example, integrated road–rail systems, jointly developed auto route systems, and cheaper air freight have all reduced some of the cost barriers to international trade.
- Perhaps most significantly, far tougher world competition has forced companies to look to reducing their total costs. Given that in many industries bought-in items are the largest single part of operations costs, an obvious strategy is to source from wherever is cheapest. So, for example, much garment manufacture takes place where labour costs are relatively low.

There are of course problems with global sourcing. The risks of increased complexity and increased distance need managing carefully. In particular, the following issues are important:

- Suppliers who are a significant distance away need to transport their products across long distances. The risks of delays and hold-ups can be far greater than when sourcing locally.
- Negotiating with suppliers whose native language is different from one's own makes communication more difficult and can lead to misunderstandings over contract terms.
- It may not always be possible to investigate suppliers at long distance. Companies may inadvertently develop relationships with suppliers whose work practices are very much against its own ethical stance (the use of child labour, unsafe working practices, the use of bribes, etc.).

Consolidated value from GP

The GP Group is a global trading and shipping company based in Bangkok. A family firm, it was established 125 years ago in Burma and comprises over 20 companies worldwide, specializing (amongst many other things) in commodity trading, ship chartering and ship management. Kirit Shah, the Chief Executive Officer and owner of the Group, explains the size of their trading operations:

'We charter about 200 ships a year, so at any given time we have 20 or 30 ships somewhere in the chain between loading, sailing and discharging.'

One key capability of the Group is filling ships by consolidating cargoes. Mr Shah explains:

'We consolidate lots of small buyers into filling as large a vessel as possible. Let me give an example. Take soya bean meal for India. A typical Indian seller is capable of delivering between 500 and 1000 tons. However, the ship is going to load 20 000 tons, so we put together a dozen or so sellers and five to seven buyers at its destination. So what we have effectively done is consolidate a region's supply and consolidate a destination's demand. We manage this by having our own facilities at the port. We have our own warehousing, we have our own berths, and we carry it on our chartered ships. All the cargo is consolidated at our warehouse in the port and we

ship it only when it is ready in terms of quantity and quality. That way we have been able to control shipments better than other traders. It takes a great deal of planning to have a shipment ready by a certain date. From experience we know we have to "call forward" (give notice for) the goods from different sellers at different times. For some suppliers you have to call forward the goods 30 days, others 15 days or 10 days, depending on how well organized they are. We have to make sure the shipment goes on time because there are large penalties for lateness. This is not easy because we are dealing with originators and purchasers from around the world.'

The GP Group also helps suppliers in developing countries to meet the exacting standards imposed by many buyers.

'The quality of goods such as rice is set by the purchaser, usually in a developed country. However, it is very difficult for a poor farmer, 600 miles from a port, to meet those standards,' explains Mr Shah. 'So we try to help producers to do this. What typically happens in less developed countries is that sellers have to be very careful about how much they spend. As a result they have a tolerance for imperfection. But purchasers, such as a large Japanese food company, always want things 100 per cent right. So, for example, when packing the rice, the supplier may use 100-gram polypropylene bags when he should have used 110-gram bags, just to save 15 cents a ton. Instead of double stitching the bags he single stitches them, again saving 15 cents a ton. When printing the bags he did not use fast enough colours, so with multiple handling those marks are erased; once again he saved 15 cents. The problem is that a buyer would readily pay $300 for top quality rice. But for the same quality rice from India or Indonesia, Vietnam, parts of Africa or parts of the former Soviet Union, he will only pay $270, 10 per cent less. Why? Because although it is good rice, when he buys from India he buys a whole horde of uncertainties. Will the shipment be on time? Will every bag be perfect? The markings correct? The bags stitched correctly and the weight of each bag correct? These uncertainties add to my selling cost, so generally I have to sell at a discount. Also, I have to handle it more and spend more money at the destination putting things right. As a result the seller might get $30 a ton less for something on

which he had tried to save 50 cents.

'This is an area in which we believe our company helps. We charge our buyers $280 for the rice. Some buyers will pay this when they have experienced the product, our delivery and reliability, because we control the port and the warehouse and we have people in the chain supervising at various stages, which all costs a little money. But, they will pay us $10 above the market price. This allows me to pay $5 to my supplier not to take the shortcuts and it allows me to make $5. This is how I can add value to the supply chain.'

Questions

1 What are the important tasks which the GP Group has to get right if it wants to maintain the performance of its 'consolidating' business?

2 How does the GP Group add value to each stage of the rice supply?

Physical distribution management

On the demand side of the organization, products and services need to be 'communicated' or moved to the customer. In the case of manufacturing operations, this involves the physical transportation of the goods from the manufacturing operation to the customer. In the case of high customer contact services, the service is created in the presence of the customer. Here we limit ourselves to manufacturing operations that need physically to distribute their products to customers (and implicitly to those transportation operations, such as trucking companies, whose primary concern is physical distribution).

Managing regional warehouses and depots is a vital link in physical distribution management

Photo courtesy of ACE

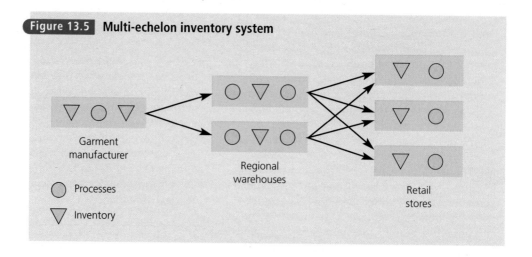

Figure 13.5 Multi-echelon inventory system

Garment manufacturer

Regional warehouses

Retail stores

○ Processes

▽ Inventory

Sometimes the term 'logistics' is used as being analogous to physical distribution management. Originally the term related to the movement and coordination of troops and military supplies. More recently, it has been used to describe physical distribution management beyond the immediate customer, through to the final customer in the chain.

Multi-echelon inventory systems

In Chapter 12 we identified some inventory systems as 'multi-echelon' systems. By this we meant that materials flowing through a system would be stored at different points, including points outside the operation, before reaching the customer. Figure 13.5 illustrates the demand-side part of the multi-echelon system we described in Chapter 12. In this case the garment manufacturer, after manufacturing the products, will store them in its own finished goods warehouse. From there they are transported to regional warehouses whose function is to serve as a distribution point for retail stores. When the retail stores require deliveries of garments, they will request them from their local warehouse who will arrange for the transportation of these garments to the retail store. The function of the warehouse is to provide an intermediate stage in the distribution system so that the manufacturer does not have to deal with every single customer. From the customers' point of view, it also means that they do not have to deal with a whole range of suppliers.

Warehouses can simplify routes and communications

To understand how warehouses can simplify physical distribution, consider Figure 13.6. Here a manufacturing operation which has three factories is supplying six customers. In the arrangement in Figure 13.6(a), each factory supplies each customer. This means that in total there are 18 routes (one between each pair of factory and customer). Each factory must have separate lines of communication with all six customers and each customer will need to communicate directly with each of the three factories. Now consider the arrangement in Figure 13.6(b). Two regional warehouses have been imposed between the factories and the customers. The three factories now distribute their products to the two regional warehouses from which their local customers are supplied. The total number of routes has been reduced from 18 to 12. Probably more significantly, each factory now has only to deal directly with two sources for its products instead of the previous six. Similarly, each customer now only has to deal with one supplier (its local warehouse) instead of six.

Physical distribution management and the internet

The potential offered by internet communications in physical distribution management has had two major effects. The first is to make information available more readily

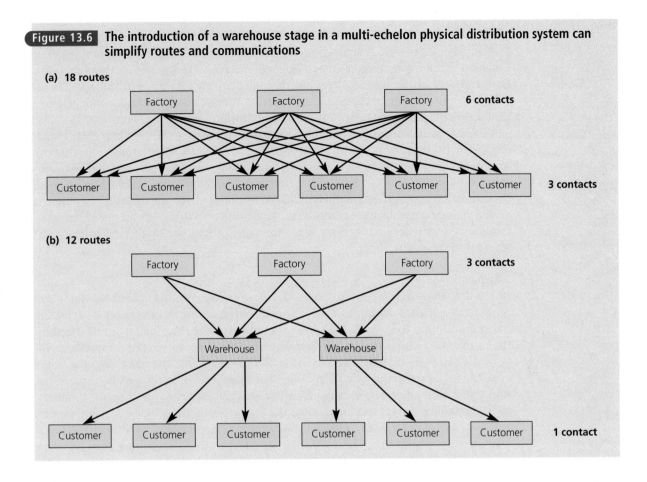

Figure 13.6 The introduction of a warehouse stage in a multi-echelon physical distribution system can simplify routes and communications

(a) 18 routes

Factory Factory Factory   **6 contacts**

Customer Customer Customer Customer Customer Customer **3 contacts**

(b) 12 routes

Factory Factory Factory **3 contacts**

Warehouse Warehouse

Customer Customer Customer Customer Customer Customer **1 contact**

along the distribution chain. This means that the transport companies, warehouses, suppliers and customers who make up the chain can share a knowledge of where goods are in the chain (and sometimes where they are going next). This allows the operations within the chain to coordinate their activities more readily. It also gives the potential for some significant cost savings. For example, an important issue for transportation companies is 'back-loading'. When the company is contracted to transport goods from A to B, its vehicles may have to return from B to A empty. Back-loading means finding a potential customer who wants their goods transported from B to A in the right time-frame. With the increase in information availability through the internet, the possibility of finding a back-load increases. Clearly, companies which can fill their vehicles on both the outward and return journeys will have significantly lower costs per distance travelled than those whose vehicles are empty for half the total journey.

The second impact of the internet has been in the 'business to consumer' (B2C, *see* the discussion on supply chain relationships later) part of the supply chain. While the last few years have seen an increase in the number of goods bought by consumers online, most goods still have to be physically transported to the customer. Often early e-retailers (or e-tailers) ran into major problems in the 'order fulfilment task' of actually supplying their customers. Partly this was because many traditional warehouse and distribution operations were not designed for e-commerce fulfilment. Supplying a 'bricks and mortar' retail operation requires relatively large vehicles to move relatively large quantities of goods on pallets from warehouses to shops. Distributing to customers who have bought goods online requires a large number of relatively small individual orders to be delivered, all of which may be different. Some traditional retailers who had moved part of their business online were faced with the dilemma of learning new physical distribution skills or subcontracting their distribution operations.

Materials management

The concept of materials management originated from purchasing functions that understood the importance of integrating materials flow and its supporting functions, both throughout the business and out to immediate customers. It includes the functions of purchasing, expediting, inventory management, stores management, production planning and control and physical distribution management.

Materials management was originally seen as a means of reducing 'total costs associated with the acquisition and management of materials'.[7] Different stages in the movement of materials through a multi-echelon system are typically buffered by inventory, as shown in Figure 13.7. Where materials management is not in place to integrate these different stages, they are often managed by different people, reporting to different senior managers within the organization. These different functions are managed separately, each with its own targets, each optimizing its own small part of the total materials flow system.

Merchandising

In retail operations, the purchasing task is frequently combined with the sales and physical distribution task into a role termed *merchandising*. A merchandiser typically has responsibility for organizing sales to retail customers, for the layout of the shop floor, inventory management and purchasing. This is because retail purchase operations have to be so closely linked to daily sales to ensure that the right mix of goods is available for customers to buy at any time. For example, fashion buyers have to understand what will sell and how garments will look when on display in their retail outlets. In food retailing, buyers specify in detail the packaging in terms of the printing process and materials, to ensure the product looks appealing when displayed in their stores. Daily trends of sales in some retail situations (typically food and fashion) can vary enormously. Replenishment of regularly stocked items has to be very quick to avoid empty shelves or rails. Electronic point-of-sale systems help the planning and control of fast-moving consumer goods; as items are registered as sold at the till, a replenishment signal is returned to the distribution centre to deliver replacements. To facilitate this link, many retail operations use bar coding to update the inventory situation and replenish shelves and rails.

Figure 13.7 Materials management integrates the management of the materials flow and its associated information flow

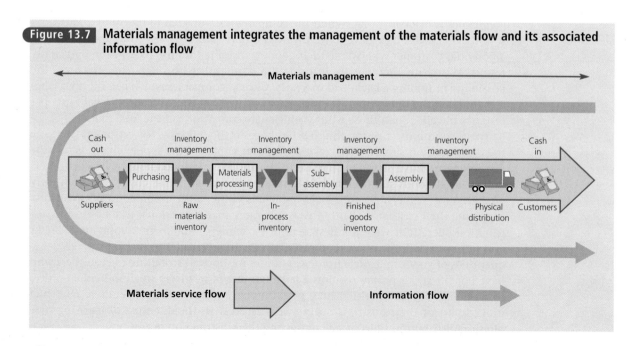

Types of relationships in supply chains

From the point of view of individual operations within a supply chain, one of the key issues is how they should manage their relationships with their immediate suppliers and customers. The behaviour of the supply chain as a whole is, after all, made up of the relationships which are formed between individual pairs of operations in the chain. It is important, therefore, to have some framework which helps us to understand the different ways in which supply chain relationships can be developed.

Business or consumer relationships?

The growth in e-commerce has established broad categorization of supply chain relationships. This happened because internet companies have tended to focus on one of four market sectors defined by who is supplying who. Figure 13.8 illustrates this categorization.

Figure 13.8 **The business/consumer relationship matrix[8]**

	Business	**Consumer**
Business	**B2B** *Relationship:* • Most common, all but the last link in the supply chain *E-commerce examples:* • EDI networks • Tesco information exchange	**B2C** *Relationship:* • Retail operations • Catalogue operations, etc *E-commerce examples:* • Internet retailers • Amazon.com, etc.
Consumer	**C2B** *Relationship:* • Consumer 'offer', business responds *E-commerce examples:* • Some airline ticket operators • Priceline.com, etc.	**C2C** *Relationship:* • Trading, 'swap' and auction transactions *E-commerce examples:* • Specialist 'collector' sites • Ebay.com, etc.

The distinction used in Figure 13.8 is whether the relationship is with the final link in the supply chain, involving the ultimate consumer, or whether it concerns one of the prior links in the supply chain, involving two commercial businesses. So, business to business (B2B) relationships are by far the most common in a supply chain context and include some of the e-procurement exchange networks discussed earlier. Business to consumer (B2C) relationships include both 'bricks and mortar' retailers and online retailers. Somewhat newer are the final two categories. Consumer to business (C2B) relationships involve consumers posting their needs on the web and stating the price they are willing to pay. Companies then decide whether to offer at that price. Customer to customer (C2C) relationships include the online exchange and auction services offered by some companies. In this chapter we deal almost exclusively with B2B relationships.

Types of business to business relationship

A convenient way of categorizing supply chain relationships is to examine the extent and nature of what a company chooses to buy in from suppliers. Two dimensions are particularly important – *what* the company chooses to outsource, and *who* it chooses to supply it.

In terms of what is outsourced, key questions are:

- How many activities are outsourced (from doing everything in-house at one extreme, to outsourcing everything at the other extreme)?
- How important are the activities outsourced (from outsourcing only trivial activities at one extreme, to outsourcing even core activities at the other extreme)?

In terms of who is chosen to supply products and services, again two question are important:

- How many suppliers will be used by the operation (from using many suppliers to perform the same set of activities at one extreme, through to only one supplier for each activity at the other extreme)?
- How close are the relationships (from 'arm's length' relationships at one extreme, through to close and intimate relationships at the other extreme)?

Figure 13.9 illustrates this way of characterizing relationships. It also identifies some of the more common types of relationship and shows some of the trends in how supply chain relationships have moved.[9]

Vertical integration

In Chapter 6 we identified the issues associated with vertical integration – that is, how much of the supply chain a company should own. Then we were dealing with the broad configuration of capacity, a very strategic design decision. Here we are more interested with slightly shorter-term decisions. On a day-to-day (or month by month) level the vertical integration decision is often characterized as the 'make-or-buy' (or for bought-in services, more accurately, 'do-or-buy') decision.

Make-or-buy decisions

When an operation decides to purchase products or services from a supplier, it is implicitly making the decision not to create those products or services itself. This may not always be a straightforward decision. In some cases the operation may be able to

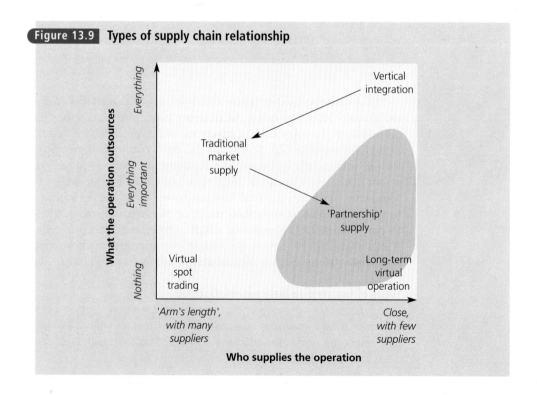

Figure 13.9 Types of supply chain relationship

produce parts or services in-house at a lower cost or at a higher quality than can suppliers. Yet in other cases, suppliers may be able to specialize in the production of certain parts or services and produce them more cheaply or at higher quality than can the operation itself. It is part of the responsibility of the purchasing function to investigate whether the operation is better served buying in products or services, or choosing to create them itself.

Often the major criterion used to decide whether to make or buy is financial. If a company can make a part or service in-house more cheaply than it can buy it, it is likely to do so, unless there are other overriding reasons for not doing so. However, the financial analysis involved is not always straightforward. The decision often needs to be based on the marginal cost of producing something in-house. The marginal cost is the extra cost that is incurred by the operation in creating the product or service. For example, if an operation already has the equipment and staff in place to make a particular product and there is spare capacity within the part of the operation which could make that product, then the extra, or marginal, cost of making the products in-house will be the variable costs associated with their manufacture. In other cases, an operation might make the decision on grounds other than cost. An increasingly popular rationale for buying in services, for example, is that they are not 'core' to the operation's main activity. Many companies are increasingly 'outsourcing' such services as transportation, cleaning, computing, catering and maintenance. Putting these services out to specialists allows an operation to concentrate on the things that directly win it business in the marketplace (*see* box on KLM Catering Services).

KLM Catering Services[10]

KLM Catering Services is the largest provider of aircraft catering and supply at Schiphol Airport near Amsterdam. Every day the company, which employs 1200 people, prepares around 30 000 meals and 'services' 200 flights for KLM and about 35 for other operators. It is now far more than just a food preparation operation; most of its activities involve organizing all onboard services, equipment, food and drinks, newspapers, towels, earphones, and so on.

KLM Catering Services places considerable emphasis on working in unison with cleaning staff, baggage handlers and maintenance crews to ensure that the aircraft are prepared quickly for departure (fast setups). Normally, no more than 40 minutes are allowed for all these activities, so complete preparation and a well-ordered sequence of working are essential. These requirements for speed and total dependability would be difficult enough to achieve in a stable environment, but there is a wide range of uncertainties to be managed. Although KLM Catering Services is advised of the likely numbers of passengers for each flight (forecasts are given 11 days, four days and 24 hours in advance), the actual minimum number of passengers for each class is only fixed six hours before take-off (although numbers can still be increased after this, due to late sales). The agreed menus are normally fixed for six-month

periods, but the actual requirements for each flight depend on the destination, the type of aircraft and the mix of passengers by ticket class. Finally, flight arrivals are sometimes delayed, putting pressure on everyone to reduce the turnaround time, and upsetting work schedules.

An additional problem is that, although KLM uses standardized items (such as food trolleys, cutlery, trays and disposables), other airlines have completely different requirements. The inventory of all this equipment is moved around with the planes. Some gets damaged or lost, and it can easily accumulate at a remote airport. If an aircraft arrives without a full inventory of equipment and other items, the company is obliged to fill the gaps from its local inventory, which amounts to over 15 000 different items.

Questions

1 Why would an airline use KLM Catering Services rather than organize its own onboard services?

2 What are the main operations objectives that KLM Catering Services must achieve in order to satisfy its customers?

3 Why is it important for airlines to reduce turnaround time when an aircraft lands?

Traditional market supply relationships

The very opposite of performing an operation in-house is to purchase goods and services from outside in a 'pure' market fashion, often seeking the 'best' supplier every time it is necessary to purchase. Each transaction effectively becomes a separate decision. The relationship between buyer and seller, therefore, can be very short-term. Once the goods or services are delivered and payment is made, there may be no further trading between the parties. The *advantages* of traditional market supplier relationships are usually seen as follows:

- They maintain competition between alternative suppliers. This promotes a constant drive between suppliers to provide best value.
- A supplier specializing in a small number of products or services (or perhaps just one), but supplying them to many customers, can gain natural economies of scale. This enables the supplier to offer the products and services at a lower price than would be obtained if customers performed the activities themselves on a smaller scale.
- There is inherent flexibility in outsourced supplies. If demand changes, customers can simply change the number and type of suppliers. This is a far faster and simpler alternative to having to redirect their internal activities.
- Innovations can be exploited no matter where they originate. Specialist suppliers are more likely to come up with innovative products and services which can be bought in faster and cheaper than would be the case if the company were itself trying to innovate.
- They help operations to concentrate on their core activities. One business cannot be good at everything. It is sensible therefore to concentrate on the important activities and outsource the rest.

There are, however, *disadvantages* in buying in a totally 'free market' manner:

- There may be supply uncertainties. Once an order has been placed, it is difficult to maintain control over how that order is fulfilled.
- Choosing who to buy from takes time and effort. Gathering sufficient information and making decisions continually are, in themselves, activities which need to be resourced.
- There are strategic risks in subcontracting activities to other businesses. An over-reliance on outsourcing can 'hollow out' the company, leaving it with no internal capabilities which it can exploit in its markets.

Short-term relationships may be used on a trial basis when new companies are being considered as more regular suppliers. Also, many purchases which are made by operations are one-off or very irregular. For example, the replacement of all the windows in a company's office block would typically involve this type of competitive-tendering market relationship, whereas the same firm might form a longer-term relationship with its supplier of cleaning services. In some public sector operations, purchasing is still based on short-term contracts. This is mainly because of the need to prove that public money is being spent as judiciously as possible. However, this short-term, price-oriented type of relationship can have a downside in terms of ongoing support and reliability. This may mean that a 'least cost' purchase decision actually involves a higher total cost to the purchasing organization over time.

Virtual operations

An extreme form of outsourcing operational activities is that of the *virtual operation*. Virtual operations do relatively little themselves, but rely on a network of suppliers who can provide products and services on demand. Often the network of suppliers used by virtual companies changes over time, sometimes dramatically. A network may be formed for only one project and then disbanded once that project ends. For example, some software and internet companies are virtual in the sense that they buy in all the services needed for a particular development. This may include not only the specific software development skills but also such things as project management, testing, applications prototyping, marketing, physical production, and so on. Much of the Hollywood film industry also operates in this way. A production company may buy and develop an idea for a movie, but it is created, edited and distributed by a loose network of agents, actors, technicians, studios and distribution companies.

The advantages of virtual operations are centred largely around the flexibility and speed with which they can operate and the fact that the risks of investing in production facilities are obviously far lower than in a conventional operation. The disadvantages come from the 'hollowing out' effect that we mentioned previously. Without any solid base of resources, a company may find it difficult to hold onto and develop a unique core of technical expertise. The resources used by virtual companies will almost certainly be available to competitors. In effect, the core competence of a virtual operation can only lie in the way it is able to manage its supply network.

● 'Partnership' supply relationships

Partnership relationships in supply chains are sometimes seen as a compromise between vertical integration on the one hand (owning the resources which supply you) and pure market relationships on the other (having only a transactional relationship with those who supply you). Although to some extent this is true, partnership relationships are not only a simple mixture of vertical integration and market trading, although they do attempt to achieve some of the closeness and coordination efficiencies of vertical integration, while at the same time attempting to achieve a relationship that has a constant incentive to improve. Partnership relationships are defined as:[11]

> '... relatively enduring inter-firm cooperative agreements, involving flows and linkages that use resources and/or governance structures from autonomous organizations, for the joint accomplishment of individual goals linked to the corporate mission of each sponsoring firm.'

What this means is that suppliers and customers are expected to cooperate, even to the extent of sharing skills and resources, to achieve joint benefits beyond those they could have achieved by acting alone. At the heart of the concept of partnership lies the issue of the *closeness* of the relationship. Partnerships are close relationships, the degree of which is influenced by a number of factors, as follows:

- *Sharing success.* An attitude of shared success means that both partners work together in order to increase the total amount of joint benefit they receive, rather than manoeuvring to maximize their own individual contribution.
- *Long-term expectations.* Partnership relationships imply relatively long-term commitments, but not necessarily permanent ones.
- *Multiple points of contact.* Communication between partners is not only through formal channels, but may take place between many individuals in both organizations.
- *Joint learning.* Partners in a relationship are committed to learn from each other's experience and perceptions of the other operations in the chain.
- *Few relationships.* Although partnership relationships do not necessarily imply single sourcing by customers, they do imply a commitment on the part of both parties to limit the number of customers or suppliers with whom they do business. It is difficult to maintain close relationships with many different trading partners.
- *Joint coordination of activities.* Because there are fewer relationships, it becomes possible jointly to coordinate activities such as the flow of materials or service, payment, and so on.
- *Information transparency.* An open and efficient information exchange is seen as a key element in partnerships because it helps to build confidence between the partners.
- *Joint problem solving.* Although partnerships do not always run smoothly, jointly approaching problems can increase closeness over time.

- *Trust.* This is probably the key element in partnership relationships. In this context, trust means the willingness of one party to relate to the other on the understanding that the relationship will be beneficial to both, even though that cannot be guaranteed. Trust is widely held to be both the key issue in successful partnerships, but also, by far, the most difficult element to develop and maintain.

Lean supply

Professor Lamming of Bath University has proposed a model of customer–supplier relationship which moves beyond simple partnership, which he calls 'lean supply'. He maintains that in partnership relationships, the supplier is still the junior partner; in lean supply the supplier and customer are equal partners. Table 13.2 illustrates some of the characteristics of lean supply.

In both partnership and lean relationships, boundaries may become 'blurred', which can create close connections between the two parties involved. However, the partners do not lose their own legal identity, as happens in merger or acquisition. They also retain their own culture and structure, and pursue their own strategies. Inevitably, how-

Table 13.2 Lamming's lean supply concept

Factor	Lean supply characteristics
Nature of competition	Global operation; local presence Based upon contribution to product technology Dependent upon alliances/collaboration
How suppliers are selected by customers	Early involvement of established supplier Joint efforts in target costing/value analysis Single and dual sourcing Supplier provides global benefits Re-sourcing as a last resort after attempts to improve
Exchange of information between supplier and customer	True transparency: costs, etc. Two-way: discussion of costs and volumes Technical and commercial information Electronic data interchange Kanban system for production deliveries (*see* Chapter 15)
Management of capacity	Regionally strategic investments discussed Synchronized capacity Flexibility to operate with fluctuations
Delivery practice	True just-in-time with kanban Local, long-distance and international JIT (*see* Chapter 15)
Dealing with price changes	Price reductions based upon cost reductions from order onwards: from joint efforts of supplier and customer
Attitude to quality	Supplier vetting schemes become redundant Mutual agreement on quality targets Continual interaction and kaizen (*see* Chapter 18) Perfect quality as goal

Source: Adapted from Lamming, R. (1993) *Beyond Partnership: Strategies for Innovation and Lean Supply*, Prentice Hall

The port of Rotterdam, the largest and busiest in the world, covers nearly 5000 hectares and has over 60 kilometres of dockside berths. Around 32 000 ships use the port each year, handling nearly 300 million tonnes of cargo. As well as being a vital link in the supply chains of countless organizations, the port also provides services to the transportation companies who ship goods through it. It is in this role – as provider of services – where it sees its future as developing 'partnership' arrangements with its major customers. Competition in the port business is fierce. Rotterdam is acutely aware of the intense competition from other large European ports such as Hamburg, Antwerp, Zeebrugge and Bremen. Forming partnerships with its customers is a response to such competitive pressures.

In order to focus on its customers' needs, the port has created dedicated areas of distinct competence which can support the needs of particular customers. One of these is the recently developed Fruit Port where most of the port's fruit, fruit juice and vegetable-related businesses are located, sharing the specially developed modern facilities and infrastructures. This development involves 70 hectares of new land, created by filling in redundant harbour basins. The internal logistics of the site have been redesigned to ensure rapid flows of these highly perishable products between vessels, storage facilities and land-based transport systems. The advantage of concentrating its fruit-related business in one part of the docks is that all the different operations that provide services related to fruit handling can now link together to ensure speed of handling of both produce and paperwork. The fruit port administration, forwarding agents, customs officers, inspection companies, traders, auctioneers at the fruit exchange, the managers of the temperature control warehouses and the distribution companies themselves are 'partners' who, by understanding each other's professional needs, form an effective link in their supply chain.

Questions

1 How is the port of Rotterdam trying to influence its relationship with its customers?

2 What do you think are the advantages and disadvantages of developing the Fruit Port?

ever, they reduce their freedom of action to some extent by strengthening their ties with the other organizations.

Relationships as 'exchange'

The relationships between the links of the supply chain are sometimes described in terms of the flows between the operations involved. These flows may be of transformed resources, such as materials, or of transforming resources, such as people or equipment. The term used to include all the different types of flow is *exchange*.

The different types of relationship and the main elements of exchange in the relationship are summarized in Figure 13.10.

Supply chain behaviour

Supply chains are dynamic systems. At any point of time, hundreds of activities and decisions are happening somewhere in the chain. Some of these will be as a result of deliberate policy by one or several operations in the chain. Others will be largely reactive – operations making local decisions which, in themselves, seem sensible but which may have negative effects on the chain as whole. In this final section of this chapter, we deal with supply chain behaviour by examining the performance of the chain as a whole. First, we shall examine how operations can manage supply chains in different ways depending on the requirements of their customers. Second, we shall look at how

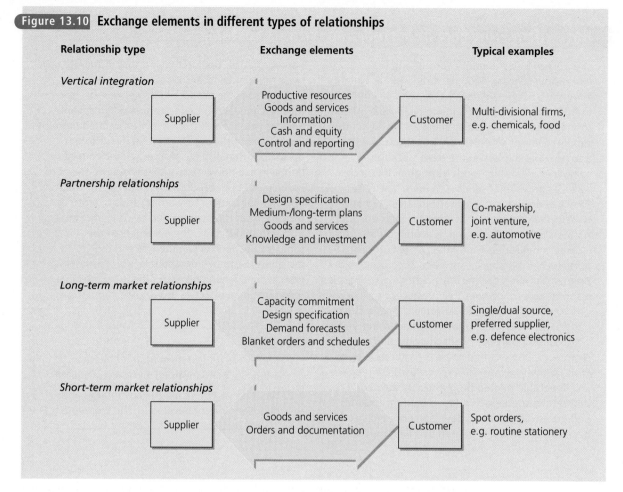

Figure 13.10 Exchange elements in different types of relationships

Relationship type	Exchange elements	Typical examples
Vertical integration	Productive resources / Goods and services / Information / Cash and equity / Control and reporting	Multi-divisional firms, e.g. chemicals, food
Partnership relationships	Design specification / Medium-/long-term plans / Goods and services / Knowledge and investment	Co-makership, joint venture, e.g. automotive
Long-term market relationships	Capacity commitment / Design specification / Demand forecasts / Blanket orders and schedules	Single/dual source, preferred supplier, e.g. defence electronics
Short-term market relationships	Goods and services / Orders and documentation	Spot orders, e.g. routine stationery

the natural dynamics of supply chain behaviour affect different parts of the chain. Finally we shall look at how companies try to improve supply chain performance.

● Supply chain policy

Supply chain policy is the way in which operations in a supply chain try to influence its behaviour to make it appropriate for the needs of end customers. This is not always easy, especially when a supply chain serves two sets of end customers.

For example, many manufacturers of automotive components serve two distinctly different groups of end customers. One group (the vehicle market) buys cars which contain their components; the other group (the spares market) buys spare parts for the repair of cars already in service. The latter group of customers is known as the 'after-market' for components. These two groups are shown in Figure 13.11.

The operations management implications of managing supply chains such as these which 'branch' to more than one end customer are significant. In this case, the competitive factors of importance to vehicle manufacturers are focused heavily towards achievement of quality and price. The volumes required by these customers are high and efforts are made by vehicle manufacturers to stabilize planning and control schedules so as to give some stability to the component manufacturers. This is a very different business from the other branch of the chain: the 'aftermarket'. The demands from here are for a much greater variety of parts, as they have to support vehicles up to 20 years old which are still on the road. Delivery speed is also very important. Repair and service of vehicles usually have to be carried out on the same day and, in most

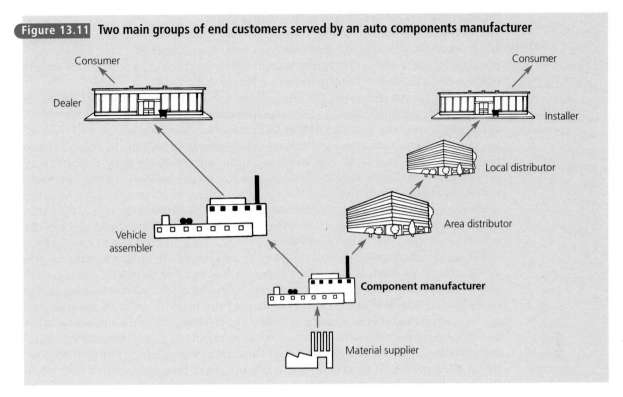

cases, the garage carrying out the repair does not know which parts are required until the vehicle is up on the ramp. Technical support and service from component manufacturers are high on the agenda of businesses in the aftermarket supply chains because they may not have the expertise to solve all of the repair problems they encounter.

This gives the component manufacturers who are trying to manage their supply chains some problems. In effect, they have two quite different supply chains which value different competitive factors. The way each link in the two supply chains is managed, the role of inventory, the planning and control priorities and price negotiations will all be different for each chain. Unfortunately, the components for both chains are probably made in the same operation. Unless this is carefully managed, or the operation split between the two chains, this can lead to conflicting objectives.

Even heavy products, such as these sports cars, may be transported by air freight if customers demand fast delivery

Different markets mean different supply chain policies

The question raised by the above example is: 'How should supply chains be managed when operations compete in different ways in different markets?' One answer, proposed by Professor Marshall Fisher of Warton Business School, is to organize the supply chains serving those individual markets in different ways.[13]

Fisher points out that many companies have seemingly similar products which, in fact, compete in different ways. Shoe manufacturers may produce classics which change little over the years, as well as fashions which last only one or two seasons. Chocolate manufacturers have stable lines which have been sold for 50 years, but also product 'specials' associated with an event or film release. These latter products may only sell for a matter of months. Demand for the former products will be relatively stable and predictable, but demand for the latter will be far more uncertain. Also, the profit margin commanded by the innovative product will probably be higher than that of the more functional product. However, the price (and therefore the margin) of the innovative product may drop rapidly once it has become unfashionable in the market.

The supply chain policies which are seen to be appropriate for functional products and innovative products are termed by Fisher *efficient supply chain policies* and *responsive supply chain policies*, respectively. Efficient supply chain policies include keeping inventories low, especially in the downstream parts of the network, so as to maintain fast throughput and reduce the amount of working capital tied up in the inventory. What inventory there is in the network is concentrated mainly in the manufacturing operation, where it can keep utilization high and therefore manufacturing costs low. Information must flow quickly up and down the chain from retail outlets back up to the manufacturer so that schedules can be given the maximum amount of time to adjust efficiently. The chain is then managed to make sure that products flow as quickly as possible down the chain to replenish what few stocks are kept downstream.

By contrast, responsive supply chain policy stresses high service levels and responsive supply to the end customer. The inventory in the network will be deployed as closely as possible to the customer. In this way, the chain can still supply even when dramatic changes occur in customer demand. Fast throughput from the upstream parts of the chain will still be needed to replenish downstream stocks. But those downstream stocks are needed to ensure high levels of availability to end customers. Figure 13.12 illustrates how the different supply chain policies match the different market requirements implied by functional and innovative products.

● Supply chain dynamics

It was demonstrated in the 1960s by Jay Forrester[14] that certain dynamics exist between firms in supply chains that cause errors, inaccuracies and volatility, and that these increase for operations further upstream in the supply chain. This effect (also known as the Forrester Effect) is analogous to the children's game of Chinese whispers. The first child whispers a message to the next child who, whether he or she has heard it clearly or not, whispers an interpretation to the next child, and so on. The more children the message passes between, the more distorted it tends to become. When the game finishes and the last child says out loud what the message is, the first child and all the intervening children are amused by the distortion of the original message.

The Forrester Effect is not caused by errors and distortions alone. In fact, the main cause is a perfectly understandable and rational desire by the different links in the supply chain to manage their production rates and inventory levels sensibly. To demonstrate this, examine the production rate and stock levels for the supply chain shown in Table 13.3. This is a four-stage supply chain where an original equipment manufacturer (OEM) is served by three tiers of suppliers. The demand from the OEM's market has been running at a rate of 100 items per period, but in period 2 demand reduces to 95 items per period. All stages in the supply chain work on the principle that

Figure 13.12 **Matching the operations resources in the supply chain with market requirements**

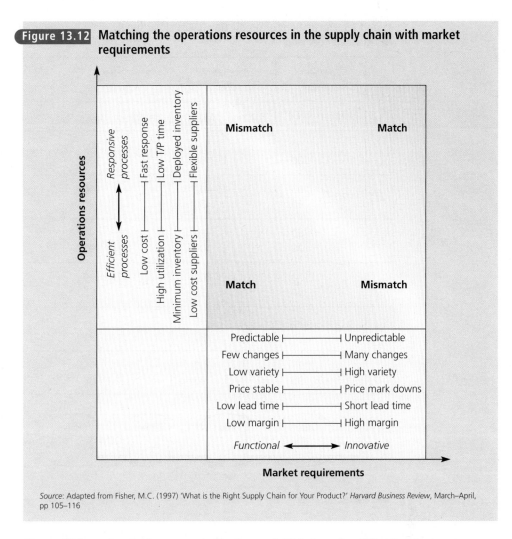

Source: Adapted from Fisher, M.C. (1997) 'What is the Right Supply Chain for Your Product?' *Harvard Business Review*, March–April, pp 105–116

they will keep in stock one period's demand. This is a simplification but not a gross one. Many operations gear their inventory levels to their demand rate. The column headed 'stock' for each level of supply shows the starting stock at the beginning of the period and the finish stock at the end of the period. At the beginning of period 2, the OEM has 100 units in stock (that being the rate of demand up to period 2). Demand in period 2 is 95 and so the OEM knows that it would need to produce sufficient items to finish up at the end of the period with 95 in stock (this being the new demand rate). To do this, it need only manufacture 90 items; these, together with five items taken out of the starting stock, will supply demand and leave a finished stock of 95 items. The beginning of period 3 finds the OEM with 95 items in stock. Demand is also 95 items and therefore its production rate to maintain a stock level of 95 will be 95 items per period. The original equipment manufacturer now operates at a steady rate of producing 95 items per period. Note, however, that a change in demand of only five items has produced a fluctuation of 10 items in the OEM's production rate.

Now carry this same logic through to the first-tier supplier. At the beginning of period 2, the second-tier supplier has 100 items in stock. The demand which it has to supply in period 2 is derived from the production rate of the OEM. This has dropped down to 90 in period 2. The first-tier supplier therefore has to produce sufficient to supply the demand of 90 items (or the equivalent) and leave one month's demand (now 90 items) as its finish stock. A production rate of 80 items per month will achieve this. It will therefore start period 3 with an opening stock of 90 items, but the demand from the OEM has now risen to 95 items. It therefore has to produce sufficient to fulfil

Table 13.3 Fluctuations of production levels along supply chain in response to small change in end-customer demand

Period	Third-tier supplier Prodn.	Stock	Second-tier supplier Prodn.	Stock	First-tier supplier Prodn.	Stock	Original equipment mfr Prodn.	Stock	Demand
1	100	100 / 100	100	100 / 100	100	100 / 100	100	100 / 100	100
2	20	100 / 60	60	100 / 80	80	100 / 90	90	100 / 95	95
3	180	60 / 120	120	80 / 100	100	90 / 95	95	95 / 95	95
4	60	120 / 90	90	100 / 95	95	95 / 95	95	95 / 95	95
5	100	90 / 95	95	95 / 95	95	95 / 95	95	95 / 95	95
6	95	95 / 95	95	95 / 95	95	95 / 95	95	95 / 95	95

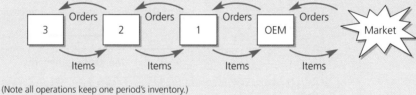

(Note all operations keep one period's inventory.)

this demand of 95 items and leave 95 items in stock. To do this, it must produce 100 items in period 3. After period 3 the first-tier supplier then resumes a steady state, producing 95 items per month. Note again, however, that the fluctuation has been even greater than that in the OEM's production rate, decreasing to 80 items a period, increasing to 100 items a period, and then achieving a steady rate of 95 items a period.

This logic can be extended right back to the third-tier supplier. If you do this, you will notice that the further back up the supply chain an operation is placed, the more drastic are the fluctuations caused by the relatively small change in demand from the final customer. In this simple case, the decision of how much to produce each month was governed by the following relationship:

Total available for sale in any period = total required in the same period

Starting stock + production rate = demand + closing stock

Starting stock + production rate = 2 × demand (because closing stock must be equal to demand)

Production rate = 2 × demand – starting stock

This relatively simple exercise does not include any time lag between a demand occurring in one part of the supply chain and it being transmitted to its supplier. In practice there will be such a lag, and this will make the fluctuations even more marked. Furthermore, the way different parts of the supply chain batch their manufacturing quantities can cause distortions which make production volumes fluctuate in upstream suppliers. Table 13.4 shows a simple example.

Table 13.4 Distortion of batching in the supply chain

Manufacturer	Area distributor	Local distributor	End customer
100	50	10	5
0	0	0	5
0	0	10	5
0	0	0	5
0	0	10	5
0	0	0	5
0	0	10	5
0	0	0	5
0	50	10	5
0	0	0	5
0	0	10	5

In Table 13.4 there is reasonably steady end-customer demand at a rate of five items per week. The end customer orders from a local distributor at this rate, and this local distributor, perhaps because of custom and practice, places bi-weekly orders with the area distributor – for this part, this is at a rate of 10 every two weeks. The area distributor delivers at this bi-weekly rate but, to replenish its stock, places monthly orders back to the manufacturer. In Table 13.4, this involves ordering 50 in the first month, none in the second and 50 in the third. The manufacturer actually makes them in economic batches of 100, and so therefore makes them only occasionally.

Supply chain improvement

Given the disruptive nature of the supply chain dynamics described previously, an important aspect of supply chain planning and control is the attempt by operations managers to improve supply chain performance. While the first step in doing this is to understand the nature of supply chain dynamics, there are several more proactive actions which operations can take. Most of these are concerned with coordinating the activities of the operations in the chain.

Efforts to coordinate supply chain activity can be described as falling into three categories: information-sharing, channel alignment and operational efficiency.[15]

Information-sharing

One of the reasons for the fluctuations in output described in the example earlier was that each operation in the chain reacted to the orders placed by its immediate customer. None of the operations had an overview of what was happening throughout the chain. If information had been available and shared throughout the chain, it is unlikely that such wild fluctuations would have occurred. It is sensible therefore to try to transmit information throughout the chain so that all the operations can monitor true demand, free of these distortions. So, for example, information regarding supply problems, or shortages, can be transmitted down the chain so that downstream customers can modify their schedules and sales plans accordingly.

One obvious improvement would be to make information on current demand downstream in the supply chain available to the operations upstream. Electronic point-of-sale (EPOS) systems used by many retailers attempt to do this. Sales data from checkouts or cash registers is consolidated and transmitted to the warehouses, transportation companies and supplier manufacturing operations that form its supply chain. Similarly, electronic data interchange (EDI) helps to share information (*see* the box on Tesco's information exchange). EDI can also affect the economic order quantities

The Benetton supply chain[16]

One of the best known examples of how an organization can use its supply chain to achieve a competitive advantage is the Benetton Group. Founded by the Benetton family in the 1960s, the company is now one of the largest garment retailers, with stores which bear its name located in almost all parts of the world. Part of the reason for its success has been the way it has organized both the supply side and the demand side of its supply chain.

Although Benetton does manufacture much of its production itself, on its supply side the company relies heavily on 'contractors'. Contractors are companies (many of which are owned, or part-owned, by Benetton employees) that provide services to the Benetton factories by knitting and assembling Benetton's garments. These contractors, in turn, use the services of sub-contractors to perform some of the manufacturing tasks. Benetton's manufacturing operations gain two advantages from this. First, its production costs for woollen items are significantly below some of its competitors because the small supply companies have lower costs themselves. Second, the arrangement allows Benetton to absorb fluctuation in demand by adjusting its supply arrangements, without itself feeling the full effect of demand fluctuations.

On the demand side of the chain, Benetton operates through a number of agents, each of whom is responsible for their own geographical area. These agents are responsible for developing the stores in their area. Indeed, many of the agents actually own some stores in their area. Products are shipped from Italy to the individual stores where they are often put directly onto the shelves. Benetton stores have always been designed with relatively limited storage space so that the garments (which, typically, are brightly coloured) can be stored in the shop itself, adding colour and ambience to the appearance of the store. Because there is such limited space for inventory in the stores, store owners require that deliveries of garments are fast and dependable. Benetton factories achieve this partly through their famous policy of manufacturing garments, where possible, in greggio, or in grey, and then dyeing them only when demand for particular colours is evident. This is a slightly more expensive process than knitting directly from coloured yarn, but their supply-side economies allow them to absorb the cost of this extra flexibility, which in turn allows them to achieve relatively fast deliveries to the stores.

Questions

1 Draw out the Benetton supply chain.

2 What are the major operations objectives of:
  (a) Benetton's retail operations;
  (b) the Benetton physical distribution operation;
  (c) the Benetton factory and its suppliers?

3 How well do these three interconnecting sets of operations fit together?

---

shipped between operations in the supply chain. In Chapter 12 we discussed how high ordering costs can result in large order quantities. If the effective cost of placing an order over an EDI network is small, batch sizes will reduce and therefore deliveries will become more frequent. The flow down the supply chain becomes more regular.

Channel alignment

Channel alignment means the adjustment of scheduling, material movements, stock levels, pricing and other sales strategies so as to bring all the operations in the chain into line with each other.

This goes beyond the provision of information. It means that the systems and methods of planning and control decision-making are harmonized through the chain. For example, even when using the same information, differences in forecasting methods or purchasing practices can lead to fluctuations in orders between operations in the chain. One way of avoiding this is to allow an upstream supplier to manage the inventories of its downstream customer. This is known as vendor-managed inventory (VMI) or continuous replenishment programme (CRP). So, for example, a packaging supplier could take responsibility for the stocks of packaging materials held by a food manufacturing customer. In turn, the food manufacturer takes responsibility for the stocks of its products which are held in its customer's, the supermarket's warehouses.

The Tesco Information Exchange[17]

Tesco is one of Europe's largest supermarket chains. During 2000, in an attempt to form closer partnerships with its suppliers, as well as improve the effectiveness of supply chain coordination into its stores, Tesco launched the Tesco Information Exchange (TIE). Developed in conjunction with GE Information Services, the TIE is an 'extranet' solution (i.e. it is based on internet technology) that allows Tesco and its suppliers to communicate trading information. It is linked to a number of Tesco's internal information systems in order to give suppliers access to relevant and up-to-date information. This includes EPOS data, sales tracking and an internal directory so suppliers can quickly and easily find the right person to talk to.

Although the system was trialled initially with Tesco's larger suppliers, such as Proctor and Gamble, Nestlé and Britvic, it was designed to be used by all suppliers, including the smallest.

Security is important to the TIE. Because it uses internet technology to ensure low cost access for its small suppliers, it is important to provide security through such devices as firewalls and passwords. Suppliers must also be confident that their own affairs are not visible to potential competitors. Suppliers only have access to data relevant to their own trading area. Figure 13.13 illustrates the TIE.

Information flows both ways in the system. Collaborative initiatives such as price discounts and other promotions can be planned jointly; tracking the progress of a sales promotion and evaluating its effectiveness can minimize stock outs and reduce production waste. It is this immediate visibility of data which helps with supply chain coordination. One experience by Proctor and Gamble, the consumer goods manufacturer, illustrates this:

'During the trial we spotted that the demand for one of our lines had reached 8000 units after two days, compared with an original forecast of 10 000 units for the whole week! As a result we were able to respond and increase depot stock at short notice. This resulted in a joint business gain of around £50 000 – and more importantly, we avoided disappointing some 15 000 shoppers'.

Figure 13.13   The Tesco Information Exchange

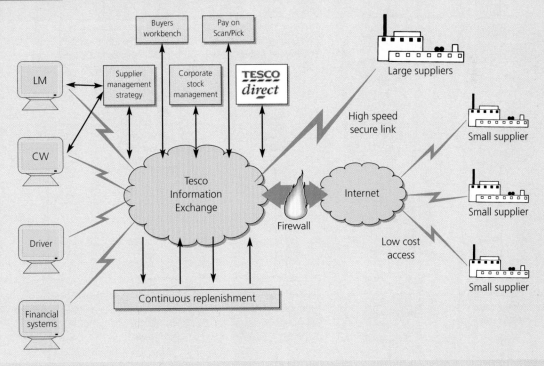

One important source of misalignment between operating practices of adjacent operations in a supply chain comes from the economics of transporting whole truckloads of products. So an individual supermarket or even central warehouse may not require a full truckload of every product in every sales period. Yet its suppliers, who may only produce one or a few types of product, naturally want to deliver their product only by the truckload. In other words, there is a mismatch between the volume–variety characteristics of the supplier (high volume, low variety) and those of its customer (low volume, high variety). Some customer–supplier agreements now attempt to ensure that every truckload of products delivered contains a mix of products from the supplier rather than a full truckload of the same product. Some supermarkets even use trucks with separate compartments at different temperatures so that they can transport products with different storage requirements in the same truck.

Operational efficiency

'Operational efficiency' means the efforts that each operation in the chain can make to reduce its own complexity, reduce the cost of doing business with other operations in the chain and increase throughput time. The cumulative effect of these individual activities is to simplify throughput in the whole chain.

For example, imagine a chain of operations whose performance level is relatively poor: quality defects are frequent, the lead time to order products and services is long, delivery is unreliable and so on. The behaviour of the chain would be a continual sequence of errors and effort wasted in replanning to compensate for the errors. Poor quality would mean extra and unplanned orders being placed, and unreliable delivery and slow delivery

---

Figure 13.14 **Supply chain time compression can both reduce costs and increase revenues[18]**

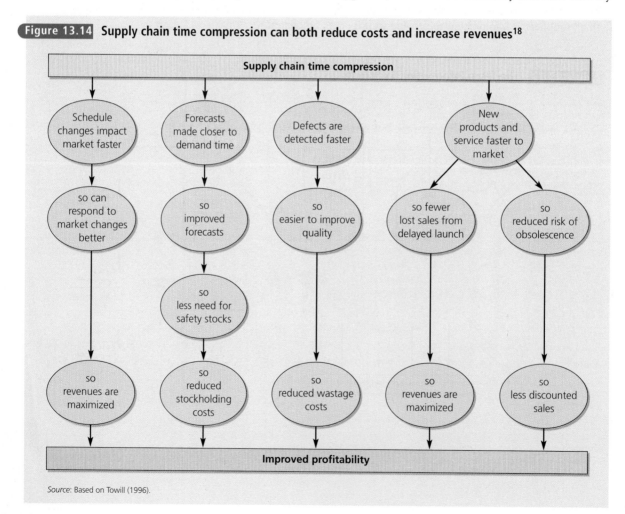

Source: Based on Towill (1996).

lead times would mean high safety stocks. Just as important, most operations managers' time would be spent coping with the inefficiency. By contrast, a chain whose operations had high levels of operations performance would be more predictable and have faster throughput, both of which would help to minimize supply chain fluctuations.

One of the most important approaches to improving the operational efficiency of supply chains is known as *time compression*. This means speeding up the flow of materials down the chain and the flow of information back up the chain. The supply chain dynamics effect we observed in Table 13.3 was due, in part, to the slowness of information moving back up the chain.

Many of the advantages of time compression in supply chains have been mentioned previously. The advantages of speed as an operations performance objective are discussed in Chapter 2. In a supply chain context, the advantages of speed are also discussed in Chapter 10 in terms of *P:D* ratios. Similarly, the discussion on just-in-time planning and control in Chapter 15 uses some of the same arguments. More specifically, Figure 13.14 illustrates the advantages of supply chain time compression in terms of its overall impact on profitability.

Summary answers to key questions

What are supply chain management and other related activities such as purchasing, physical distribution, logistics and materials management?

● Supply chain management is a broad concept which includes the management of the entire supply chain from the supplier of raw material to the end customer.

● Supply chain management is a strategy concept which includes the broad long-term consideration of the company's position in the supply network as well as the shorter term control of flow through the supply chain.

● Purchasing is concerned with the supply-side activities of an organization. It includes the formal preparation of requests to suppliers for a quotation, valuation of suppliers, the issuing of formal purchase orders, and monitoring of delivery.

● Physical distribution management is the management of the (often multi-echelon) inventory and transportation systems which link the operation with its customers. Decisions include the number and position of warehouses in the system and the mode of physical transport which needs to be adopted.

● Logistics includes the demand-side physical distribution of goods, often beyond the immediate customers, through the supply chain to the end customer.

● Materials management is an integrated concept which includes both purchasing activities and physical distribution activities.

How can the relationship between operations in a supply chain affect the way it works?

● Supply networks are made up of individual pairs of buyer–supplier relationships. The use of internet technology in these relationships has led to a categorization based on a distinction between business and consumer partners. Business to business (B2B) relationships are of the most interest in operations management terms. They can be characterized on two dimensions – what is outsourced to a supplier, and the number and closeness of the relationships.

● Make-or-buy decisions are an operational form of vertical integration. It means doing the activity within one organizational boundary and is the closest form of relationship.

● Traditional market supplier relationships are where a purchaser chooses suppliers on an individual periodic basis. No long-term relationship is usually implied by such 'transactional' relationships. In the short term, this can be the cheapest way of obtaining goods and services but it makes it difficult to build internal capabilities.

● Virtual operations are an extreme form of outsourcing where an operation does relatively little itself and subcontracts almost all its activities.

● Partnership supplier relationships involve customers forming long-term relationships with suppliers. In return for the stability of demand, suppliers are expected to commit to high levels of service. True partnerships are difficult to sustain and rely heavily on the degree of trust which is allowed to build up between partners.

Are different supply chain objectives needed in different circumstances?

- Often supply chains split at some point in order to serve two or more markets. If these markets are different in their requirements, the supply chain feeding the markets may be organized in different ways.

- Marshall Fisher distinguishes between functional markets and innovative markets. He argues that functional markets, which are relatively predictable, require efficient supply chains, whereas innovative markets, which are less predictable, require 'responsive' supply chains.

What is the 'natural' pattern of behaviour in supply chains?

- Supply chains exhibit a dynamic behaviour known as the Forrester Effect. This shows how small changes at the demand end of a supply chain are progressively amplified for operations further back in the chain.

- To reduce the Forrester Effect, operations can adopt some mixture of three coordination strategies:
  - information-sharing: the efficient distribution of information throughout the chain can reduce demand fluctuations along the chain by linking all operations to the source of demand;
  - channel alignment: this means adopting the same or similar decision-making processes throughout the chain to coordinate how and when decisions are made;
  - operational efficiency: this means eliminating sources of inefficiency or ineffectiveness in the chain; of particular importance is 'time compression', which attempts to increase the throughput speed of the operations in the chain.

CASE EXERCISE

Globalcast

Globalcast was one of the world's largest manufacturers of metal and plastic moulded components to almost every industry, including automotive, consumer durables, telecommunications, computers, power tools, etc. With over 100 manufacturing facilities, it operated on every continent, usually in areas of established or emerging industrialization. In Europe there were large factories in the UK, Germany, France, Spain and Italy, and smaller ones in Scandinavia, Austria, Turkey and Israel.

Every factory was considered to be a semi-autonomous profit centre and was headed up by a general manager. Each reported to a regional manager of one of the divisions (for example, Plastics Division). New business was generated both by national marketing and by word-of-mouth recommendations from existing customers, but most orders were for regular repeat business or for new designs from existing customers. The role of the small technical sales team at each factory was to follow up enquiries with technical advice visits to the customer, followed by the preparation of quotations. In many cases, Globalcast provided

design assistance to the customers. It was the role of the advisor to suggest ways of simplifying the overall design which would be cheaper for the customer, whilst being fast, easy and profitable to produce in the factory. Mould costs were calculated and quoted too, and in most cases the customer would pay for the moulds from the outset, retaining ownership. Globalcast organized the purchase of the moulds, costing up to £50 000 each, and could make a small profit on this activity.

In the late 1990s, the market started to change rapidly. First, major customers such as Hewlett Packard, Dell, Ford, GM and Black and Decker started building new factories in developing countries. These were being established both to exploit the benefits of lower wages and overheads, and as market-entry points for these rapidly developing economies. In most cases, however, large proportions of their output would serve existing markets throughout the world. Because Globalcast was one of the most important suppliers (only about five competitors had worldwide coverage), it was often encouraged by its customers to establish supply factories in the same regions, ideally on adjacent sites. Customers explained that business was, in part, being transferred to their new sites, and since Globalcast had been selected as a preferred supplier, it had the opportunity to benefit from ongoing business development and growth. Attractive forecasts were provided, but not guaranteed. 'Partnerships' would be established where Globalcast had the benefit of sole-supplier status to the customer's local plant.

The second change was the trend for customers' products to be of globally standard designs. This allowed buyers to purchase components for their many factories around the world, from virtually any approved supplier anywhere. Therefore they were in a powerful position to restrict the number of suppliers, as well as demanding a single global, low price. For Globalcast this provided a new set of problems; its costs had varied widely around the world, depending mainly on local labour and overhead costs. Selling prices had varied according to costs and local commercial conditions, but detailed costs of production had never been disclosed to customers. However, customers would now be able to 'shop around' and find the lowest Globalcast price for themselves. At the same time, each Globalcast general manager had tried to defend his or her business, even if that involved buying in the components from other company sites and adding a profit before selling to the customer. This was now becoming too obvious to large customers.

The third significant market trend was that customers increasingly wanted suppliers to do more assembly ('value-added') work. At its simplest, this could involve simply snapping together two parts. Alternatively, it could require complex purchasing, assembly and testing of major sub-assemblies. To do this, Globalcast would need to invest in assembly lines, testing equipment, storage, component and finished goods inventory, and systems to support purchasing and logistics. Specific approved suppliers were usually dictated by customers. Lead times from these global suppliers could be up to 12 weeks. Customers' initial delivery schedules were often stable and close to forecast levels, but could vary wildly as competitive forces affected customers' sales. But, overall, this type of work did appear commercially attractive, typically bringing in up to 10 times the revenue of a simple moulded part. The opportunity to become a 'first-tier' supplier to some of the world's leading manufacturers was hard to resist. Indeed, supplying global customers was the mainstay of the strategic plan for the new decade.

Questions

1 Using Lamming's lean supply concept model, evaluate the company's relationships with its large global customers. What does this imply about Globalcast's potential to support its customers' requirements in intensely price-sensitive global markets?

2 Would you describe Globalcast's strategic supply chain management decisions as more proactive or reactive, and why?

3 Are there other ways in which the company could organize itself to meet the challenges and market trends described in the case?

Discussion questions

1 If you were the owner of a small local retail shop, what criteria would you use to select suppliers for the goods which you wish to stock in your shop? Visit three shops which are local to you and ask the owners how they select their suppliers. In what way were their answers different from what you thought they might be?

2 What do you understand by the terms logistics, merchandising, materials management and supply chain management?

3 If you were drawing up a document to be sent out to potential suppliers of a new photocopying machine for your local library, what would you ask them to specify in their quotation?

4 How is vertical integration different from partnership purchasing?

5 A company is considering buying in leaflets to be included with the packaging of its products. Its own in-house printing department could produce the leaflets but not at the same level of quality which a specialist printer could supply. Nevertheless, the in-house printing department is keen to be given the job of printing the leaflets. The cost of printing the leaflets in-house is £10 per 1000 leaflets. This cost includes the cost of the paper and inks (£7), the cost of the energy used by the printing machines (£0.50) and a standard overhead charge calculated according to the time

the job would take (£2.50). The in-house printing department has sufficient capacity to print all the leaflets which will be required without any extra staff or machines. The company's purchasing department has several quotations from local printers, the cheapest of which is £8.50 per 1000 leaflets, although the printer made it clear that delivery times would be at least two weeks for each order because they have so much other business currently. How would you advise the company if it asked you whether it should buy in the leaflets or allow its own in-house printing unit to do the job?

6 If you were designing a system to evaluate the performance of a company's purchasing function, what criteria would you use?

7 Why do you think the use of expediters is less common than it once was? Do you think expediters could still play a useful role?

8 How is logistics different from materials management?

9 What do you think should be the main information which is exchanged between the purchasing function and other parts of the organization?

10 Under what circumstances do you think multi-sourcing would be advantageous?

Notes on chapter

1 Coyle, R.G. (1982) 'Assessing the Controllability of a Production Raw Material System', *IEEE Transactions*, SMC–12, Vol 6.

2 Dell, M. (1999) *Direct from Dell*, Harper Business, NY.

3 Sable, C., Herrigel, G., Kazis, R. and Deeg, R. (1987) 'How to Keep Mature Industries Innovative', *Technology Review*, Vol 90, No 3.

4 Morgan, I. (1987) 'The Purchasing Revolution', *McKinsey Quarterly*, Spring.

5 Source: Grad, C. (2000) 'A Network of Supplies to be woven into the web', *Financial Times*, 9th February.

6 Harney, A. (2000) 'Up close but impersonal', *Financial Times*, 10th March.

7 Lee, L. and Dobler, D.W. (1977) *Purchasing and Materials Management*, McGraw-Hill.

8 Source: Based on *The Economist* (2000) 'Shopping around the Web – A Survey of E-commerce', 26 February.

9 From Slack, N. and Lewis, M. (2001) *Operations Strategy*, Financial Times-Prentice Hall.

10 Source: KLM staff.

11 Parkhe, A. (1993) 'Strategic Alliance Structuring', *Academy of Management Journal*, Vol 36, pp 794–829.

12 Source: *Port of Rotterdam News*, 1994.

13 Fisher, M.L. (1997) 'What is the Right Supply Chain for Your Product', *Harvard Business Review*, March–April.

14 Forrester, J.W. (1961) *Industrial Dynamics*, MIT Press.

15 Lee, H.L., Padmanabhan, V., Whang, S. (1997) 'The Bull Whip Effect in Supply Chains', *Sloan Management Review*, Spring.

16 Benetton, A. (1984) Harvard Business School Case Study 6-985-014, and company literature.

17 Source: Company literature.

18 Towill, D.R. (1996) 'Time Compression and Supply Chain Management – A Guided Tour', *Supply Chain Management*, Vol 1, No 1.

Selected further reading

Bailey, P. and Farmer, D. (1994) *Purchasing Principles and Management* (7th edn), Pitman Publishing.

Blumenfeld, D.E., Burns, L.D., Daganzo, C.F., Frick, M.C. and Hall, R.W. (1987) 'Reducing Logistics Costs at General Motors', *Interfaces*, Vol 17, Jan–Feb.

Bund, J.B. (1985) 'Build Customer Relationships That Last', *Harvard Business Review*, Vol 63, No 6.

Burt, D.N. (1989) 'Managing Suppliers Up to Speed', *Harvard Business Review*, Vol 67, No 4.

Burt, D.N. and Soukup, W.R. (1985) 'Purchasing's Role in New Product Development', *Harvard Business Review*, Vol 63, No 5.

Carr, C.H. and Truesdale, T.A. (1992) 'Lessons From Nissan's British Suppliers', *International Journal of Operations and Production Management*, Vol 12, No 2.

Carter, J.R. and Narasimhan, R. (1990) 'Purchasing in the International Market Place: Implications for Operations', *Journal of Purchasing and Materials Management*, Summer.

Chadwick, T. and Rajagopal, S. (1995) *Strategic Supply Management*, Butterworth-Heinemann.

Child, J. and Faulkner, D. (1998) *Strategies of Cooperation: Managing Alliances, Networks and Joint Ventures*, Oxford University Press.

Cousins, P. D. (1992) 'Choosing the Right Partner', *Purchasing and Supply Management Journal*, March.

Cousins, P.D. (1992) 'Purchasing: The Professional Approach', *Purchasing and Supply Management Journal*, Sept.

Fisher, M.L. (1997) 'What is the Right Supply Chain for Your Product?', *Harvard Business Review*, Vol 75, No 2.

Fuller, J.B., O'Connor, J. and Rawlinson, R. (1993) 'Tailored Logistics: The Next Advantage', *Harvard Business Review*, Vol 71, No 3.

Harland, C.M., Lamming, R.C. and Cousins, P. (1999) 'Developing the Concept of Supply Strategy', *International Journal of Operations and Production Management*, Vol 19, No. 7.

Heinz, P. (1994) *Creating World Class Suppliers: Unlocking Mutual Competitive Advantage*, FT/Pitman Publishing.

Hines, P. and Rich, N. (1997) 'The Seven Value Stream Mapping Tools', *International Journal of Operations and Production Management*, Vol 17, No 1.

Jarillo, J.C. (1993) *Strategic Networks: Creating the Borderless Organisation*, Butterworth-Heinemann.

Lamming, R. (1993) *Beyond Partnership: Strategies for Innovation and Lean Supply*, Prentice Hall.

Lane, C. and Backmannn, R. (eds) (1998) *Trust Within and Between Organizations*, Oxford University Press, Oxford.

Macbeth, D.K., Baxter, L.F., Ferguson, N. and Neil, G.C. (1989) 'Not Purchasing but Supply Chain Management', *Purchasing and Supply Management Journal*, Nov.

Macbeth, D.K, and Ferguson, N. (1994) *Partnership Sourcing: An Integrated Supply Chain Approach*, Financial Times, Pitman.

Poirier, C.C. and Reiter, S.E. (1996) *Supply Chain Optimisation*, Berrett-Koehler.

Rackham, N., Friedman, L. and Ruff, R. (1996) *Getting Partnering Right*, McGraw-Hill.

Ramsay, J. and Wilson, I. (1990) 'Sourcing/Contracting Strategy Selection', *International Journal of Operations and Production Management*, Vol 10, No 8.

Womack, J.P., Jones, D.T. and Roos, D. (1990) *The Machine that Changed the World*, Rawson Associates.

14 MRP

Introduction

It is easy to become confused when trying to understand what MRP is. There are two different but related definitions of MRP – this chapter will define both of these and describe them. Both, however, share the same underlying theme – they help businesses plan and control their resource requirements with the aid of computer-based information systems. MRP can stand for both materials requirements planning or manufacturing resource planning. Over time, the concept of MRP has developed from an operations management-focused concept which helped in planning and controlling materials requirements to become, in recent years, a business system which helps to plan all business resource requirements. Typically, MRP is used in manufacturing businesses, although there are some examples of its application in non-manufacturing environments. Figure 14.1 shows the purpose of MRP in reconciling the supply and demand of resources.

Figure 14.1 **A definition of MRP**

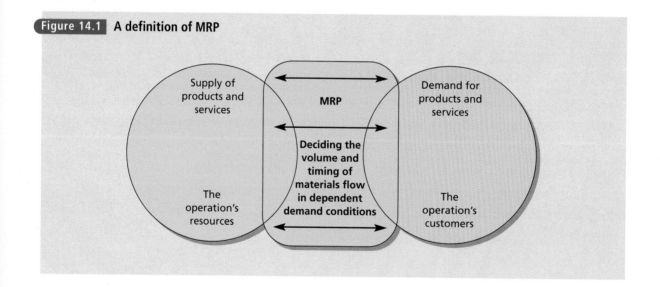

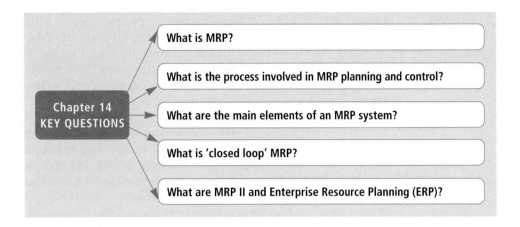

Chapter 14
KEY QUESTIONS

- What is MRP?
- What is the process involved in MRP planning and control?
- What are the main elements of an MRP system?
- What is 'closed loop' MRP?
- What are MRP II and Enterprise Resource Planning (ERP)?

What is MRP?

The original MRP dates back to the 1960s, when the letters stood for materials requirements planning (now called MRP One or MRP I). MRP I enables a company to calculate how many materials of particular types are required, and at what times they are required. To do this, it uses a sales order book which records known future orders and also a forecast of what sales orders the business is reasonably confident might be won. MRP then checks all the ingredients or components which are required to make these future orders and ensures they are ordered in time.

An easy way of thinking about this is to imagine that you have decided to hold a party in two weeks' time and expect about 40 people to attend. As well as some beer, wine and soft drinks, you decide to provide sandwiches and savoury snacks. Prior to shopping, you will probably do some simple calculations, estimating guests' preferences for red or white wine or beer and how much people are likely to drink and eat. You may already have some food and drink in the house which you will use, so you will take that into account when making your shopping list, reducing the list by these items. If any of your planned party food is to be cooked from a recipe, you may have to multiply up the ingredients to cater for 40 people; again you may already have some of these ingredients in stock. In addition to calculating how much of each item is required, you may also wish to take into account the fact that you will prepare some of the food the week before and freeze it, while you will leave the rest to either the day before or the day of the party. Therefore, you will need to decide when each item is required so that you can shop in time. In planning for your party, you will have been making a series of interrelated decisions about the volume (quantity) and timing of the materials which you need.

MRP is a system that helps companies make volume and timing calculations similar to these but on a much larger scale, and with a greater degree of complexity. Prior to the 1960s, companies did these types of calculations manually to ensure that they had the right materials available in their business at the right time. However, the advent of computers and their more widespread use in business from the 1960s onwards, provided the opportunity to perform these time-consuming, detailed calculations by computer quickly and relatively easily.

During the 1980s and 1990s, the system and the concept of materials requirements planning have expanded and been integrated with other parts of the business. This enlarged version of MRP is now known as manufacturing resource planning, or MRP II. MRP II enables companies to examine the engineering and financial implications of future demand on the business, as well as examining the materials requirements implications. Oliver Wight,[1] who with Joseph Orlicky[2] is considered to be the founder of modern MRP, described manufacturing resource planning as a 'total game plan' for a business. Using the party example, the wider implications of future demand can be seen: you may want to rig up a more powerful sound system borrowing a friend's speakers – you have to plan for this to ensure that, at the time of setting up the party, the equipment is available and you know what to do with it. Similarly, the party has financial implications. You may have to agree a temporary extension to your overdraft with your friendly bank manager or temporarily increase your credit card limit. Again, this requires some forward planning in terms of advanced telephone calls, as well as a prior calculation on your part of how much all this is going to cost, and therefore how much extra credit you require. Both these equipment and financial implications may vary if you increase the number of guests from 40 to 80. Similarly, if you postpone the party for a month, these arrangements will change.

Manufacturing businesses may make and sell several thousand different variations of end products to a customer base of several hundred regular customers as well as many hundreds of customers who order only irregularly. Many of these customers are also likely to vary their demand for the products. The implications of this are a bit like throwing 75 parties one week, 40 the next, 53 the following week, all for different groups of guests with different requirements who keep changing their minds about what they want to eat and drink. To make sure that the right food and drink are available at the right party at the right time, and that not too much money is spent, requires planning and control, not only of materials but also of cash, people and equipment. MRP II helps companies forward plan these types of decisions.

Materials requirements planning is still the heart of any MRP system (I or II) and therefore the majority of this chapter will be concerned with establishing the basic purpose and principles of MRP I.

What is required to run MRP I?

In order to perform the volume and timing calculations of the type just described, materials requirements planning systems (MRP I) typically require an operation to keep certain data records in computer files which, when the MRP I program is run, can be checked and updated. In order to understand the complexities of an MRP system, we must first understand these computer files and records.

Figure 14.2 shows the information required to perform MRP I and some of the outputs from it. Starting at the top of the figure, the first inputs to materials requirements planning are customer orders and forecast demand. The first are firm orders scheduled for some identified date in the future, while the second are realistic estimates of the quantity and timing of future orders. MRP performs its calculations based on the combination of these two parts of future demand. All other requirements calculated within the MRP process are derived from, and dependent on, these demands. Because of this, MRP is what we described in Chapter 10 as a dependent demand system. As a reminder, dependent demand is demand which is derived from some other decision taken within the operation, whereas independent demand systems are designed to operate where demand is outside the control of the operation.

● Demand management

Taken together, the management of customer orders and sales forecasts is termed 'demand management'. Demand management encompasses a set of processes which interface with the customer market. Depending on the business, these processes may include sales order entry, demand forecasting, order promising, customer service and physical distribution. For example, if you place an order with a mail-order catalogue

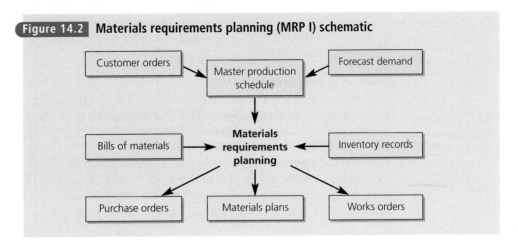

Figure 14.2 Materials requirements planning (MRP I) schematic

and ring up a week later to check why your purchase has not arrived, you will frequently be dealt with by a telesales customer service operator. This operator, looking at a computer screen, can access the details of your particular order and advise why there might have been a hold-up in delivery. In addition, he or she may be able to provide you with a delivery promise of when you should receive the item, and inform you what mode of delivery will be used (for example, if a courier will deliver it). The interaction with customers and the resulting requirements from that interaction trigger a chain reaction of operations requirements. To satisfy the customer, the item has to be picked from a warehouse; a stores operator must therefore be provided with the appropriate information to do that. A courier must also be booked for a particular time. This is why it is of vital importance to operations management that demand information is available and communicated effectively, so that plans can be made and resources organized.

We now need to consider some of the operations implications of managing demand, particularly relating to planning materials requirements. Chapter 11 considered these types of decisions at an aggregate level, but here we deal with the information at a more detailed level, specifically considering known demand, or orders, and forecast demand, as highlighted in Figure 14.3.

● Customer orders

Sales functions in most businesses typically manage a dynamic, changing order book made up of confirmed orders from customers. This order book may be a paper record in a smaller business, but is likely to be a computer file in medium-sized to large operations. Typically this order book would contain information about each customer order.

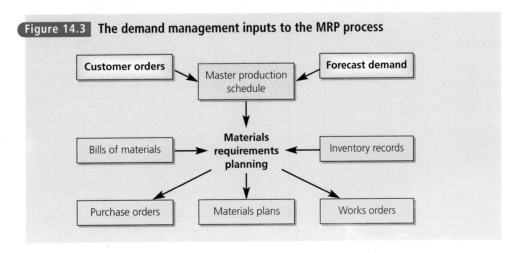

Figure 14.3 The demand management inputs to the MRP process

Of particular interest to the MRP I process of calculating materials requirements are the records of exactly what each customer has ordered, how many they have ordered and when they require delivery.

Variation of sales orders

Customers sometimes change their minds about what they require, after having placed their orders. Because customer service and flexibility are increasingly important competitive factors, having to change requirements is becoming a more common feature in most operations. Indeed, in business to business supply chain relationships it may be customers' customers who are the cause of the changing requirements. Considering that each of several hundred customers may make changes to their sales orders, not once, but possibly several times after the order has been placed, it is evident that managing the sales order book is a complex and dynamic process.

● Forecast demand

However sophisticated the forecasting process is in any business, using historical data to predict future trends, cycles or seasonality is always difficult. Driving a business using forecasts based on history has been compared to driving a car by looking only at the rear view mirror.[3] In spite of the difficulties, many businesses have no choice but to forecast ahead. To satisfy customers' demands for delivery speed, automotive manufacturers, for example, at the time a customer places an order, have already made estimates of the models, the engines and the colours they think will be sold. When a customer places the order, one of the models in the chosen colour with the right size of engine is already in production and is allocated to that customer. The customer can, at the time of ordering, choose from a wide range of options in terms of trim (such as upholstery and interior colours), audio systems and glass tinting, etc., all of which can be added to the main assembly, effectively giving the impression of customization. The manufacturer has to predict ahead the likely required mix of models and colours to manufacture and the likely mix of options to purchase and have available in inventory.

Combining orders and forecasts

A combination of known orders and forecasted orders is used to represent demand in many businesses. This should be the best estimate at any time of what reasonably could be expected to happen. In Figure 14.4 one of the most important features of demand management is evident: that is, the further ahead you look into the future, the less cer-

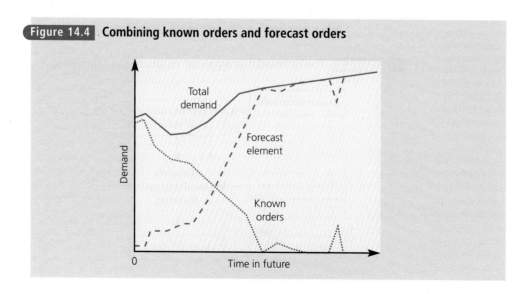

Figure 14.4 **Combining known orders and forecast orders**

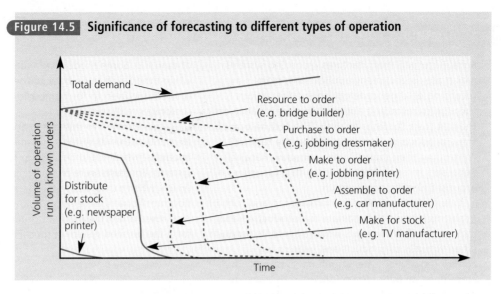

Figure 14.5 Significance of forecasting to different types of operation

Total demand

Resource to order
(e.g. bridge builder)

Purchase to order
(e.g. jobbing dressmaker)

Make to order
(e.g. jobbing printer)

Assemble to order
(e.g. car manufacturer)

Make for stock
(e.g. TV manufacturer)

Distribute
for stock
(e.g. newspaper
printer)

Volume of operation
run on known orders

Time

tainty there is about demand. Most businesses have knowledge in the short term about demand with regard to individual orders. However, few customers place orders well into the future. Based on history and on market information gained from field sales operatives, a forecast is put together to reflect likely demand. As orders come in, the forecast element of the demand profile should be reduced, giving the impression of the forecast being 'consumed' over time by firm orders.

Different types of operations have different profiles in terms of the mix of known orders and forecast orders. A make-to-order business, such as a jobbing printer, tends to have greater visibility of known orders over time than does a make-for-stock business, such as a consumer durables manufacturer. Purchase-to-order businesses do not order most of their raw materials until they receive a confirmed customer order. For example, a jobbing dressmaker would not order fabrics until it was sure that it had been awarded a contract. Other businesses not only cannot risk ordering materials, they also cannot place contracts for labour or equipment. These can be termed 'resource-to-order' businesses. For example, a civil engineering project manager would not order most of the materials for building a bridge until the tender had been won, but also would not be committed to labour and plant hire. At the opposite end of the spectrum, there are some operations that have very little order certainty at the time they take most of their decisions. For example, newspaper publishers distribute newspapers to retail outlets on a sale-or-return basis: that is, real demand is only evident to them after each day's trading has finished and they calculate how many papers were actually sold (*see* Fig. 14.5).

Many businesses have to operate with a varying combination of known orders and forecasts. For example, the week before Mother's Day, small local florists receive a large volume of orders for bouquets and flower arrangements. At other times of the year, a greater amount of their business is passing trade, which is affected by the weather and shopping patterns. Therefore different types of businesses have different degrees of confidence in demand at the time they take operations planning and control decisions, and their confidence may vary over time. From a planning and control perspective, the output from demand management is a prediction ahead over time of what customers will purchase. This information, be it known sales orders, forecast or a combination of both, is the major input to the master production schedule.

● Master production schedule

The master production schedule (MPS) is the most important planning and control schedule in a business, and forms the main input to materials requirements planning (*see* Fig. 14.6).

Racal Recorders manufactures recording systems which are used in many applications, from recording emergency telephone conversations through to recording automobile performance on the test track for later analysis. The technology of these products is sophisticated and the task of controlling their manufacture complex. Racal Recorders is the market leader with a turnover of around £30 million per annum.

One of its major production planning and control problems is how to coordinate the production and movement of all the parts which go into its products when virtually all products and systems are configured to meet the requirements of individual customers. An MRP system is needed to translate orders and forecasts into works instructions for purchasing and manufacturing parts, sub-assemblies and finished products. Its main problem was that after running the MRP process, the finished goods were put into stock to await customer orders. Yet the orders, when they came, never exactly matched what had been manufactured based on the forecast

of demand. Some products remained in storage while others had to go back to the workshops to be re-manufactured to form the configurations that customers really did want.

Racal's solution to this was to analyse the common elements within its systems and manufacture 'modules' which could be built up to make whole systems. Forecasts were prepared for the modules which, when manufactured, were kept on the shop floor until orders were firm. On the receipt of a confirmed order, the modules could be assembled to form the finished system as specified by the customer.

Questions

1 What exactly seems to be the problem with Racal's forecasting system?

2 What is the advantage, as far as planning and control is concerned, of forecasting demand at a 'modules' level?

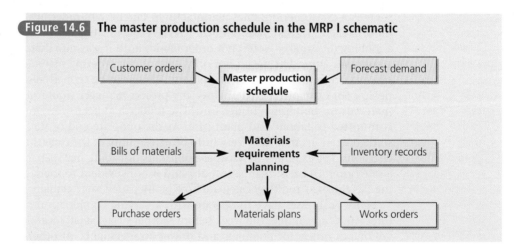

Figure 14.6 The master production schedule in the MRP I schematic

MPS in manufacturing

In manufacturing, the MPS contains a statement of the volume and timing of the end products to be made; this schedule drives the whole operation in terms of what is assembled, what is manufactured and what is bought. It is the basis of planning the utilization of labour and equipment and it determines the provisioning of materials and cash.

MPS in services

MPS can also be used in service organizations. For example, in a hospital theatre there is a master schedule which contains a statement of which operations are planned and when. This can be used to provision materials for the operations, such as the sterile instruments, blood and dressings. It also governs the scheduling of staff for operations, including anaesthetists, nurses and surgeons.

Figure 14.7 Inputs into the master production schedule

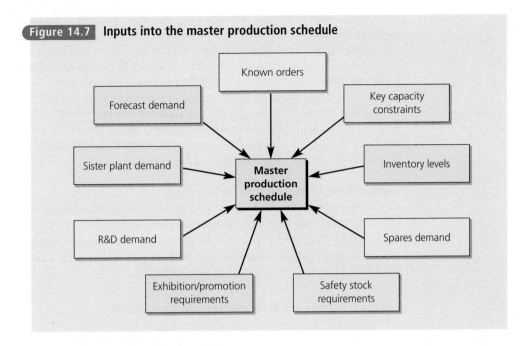

Sources of information for the MPS

It is important that all sources of demand are considered when the master production schedule is created. It is often the 'odds and ends' of requirements in a business that disrupt the entire planning system. For example, if a manufacturer of earth excavators plans an exhibition of its products and allows a project team to raid the stores so that it can build two pristine examples to be exhibited, this is likely to leave the factory short of parts. (If it doesn't, then the inventory was excess to requirements and should not have been there anyway.) Similarly, sister companies may be able to 'borrow' parts at short notice for their own purposes. If such practices are allowed, the planning and control system needs to take them into account. Figure 14.7 shows the inputs that may be taken into account in the creation of a master production schedule.

The master production schedule record

Master production schedules are time-phased records of each end product, which contain a statement of demand and currently available stock of each finished item. Using this information, the available inventory is projected ahead in time. When there is insufficient inventory to satisfy forward demand, order quantities are entered on the master schedule line.

Table 14.1 is a simplified example of part of a master production schedule for one item. The known sales orders and any forecast are combined to form 'Demand'. This is shown in the first row and can be seen to be gradually increasing. The second row, 'Available', shows how much inventory of this item is expected to be in stock at the

Table 14.1 Example of a master production schedule

					Week number				
		1	2	3	4	5	6	7	8	9
Demand		10	10	10	10	15	15	15	20	20
Available		20	10	0	0	0	0	0	0	0
MPS		0	0	10	10	15	15	15	20	20
On hand	30									

end of each weekly period. The opening inventory balance, 'On hand', is shown separately at the bottom of the record. Here, 30 of this part are currently in stock in week 0. The available figure of 20 in the first week is calculated by taking demand of 10 away from the on-hand inventory of 30. The third row is the master production schedule, or MPS; this shows how many finished items need to be completed and available in each week to satisfy demand. As there is adequate inventory already available in weeks 1 and 2, no plans are made to complete more in those weeks. However, in week 3, it is necessary for production to complete 10 of these items to satisfy projected demand; if production cannot complete 10 at this time, there is the possibility that customers will be put on back order (that is, they will be made to queue).

Chase or level master production schedules

In the example in Table 14.1, the MPS increases as demand increases and aims to keep available inventory at 0 – the master production schedule is 'chasing' demand. As we discussed in Chapter 11 on capacity planning and control, chasing demand involves adjusting the provision of resources, which may not always be desirable. An alternative level MPS for this situation is shown in Table 14.2.

Table 14.2 Example of a 'level' master production schedule

					Week number				
		1	2	3	4	5	6	7	8	9
Demand		10	10	10	10	15	15	15	20	20
Available		1	32	33	34	30	26	22	13	4
MPS		11	11	11	11	11	11	11	11	11
On hand	30									

Level scheduling involves averaging the amount required to be completed to smooth out peaks and troughs. Table 14.2 shows how this level schedule generates more inventory than the previous MPS. In this case, the average projected inventory of finished items over the nine-week period is 25 per week (that is, more than any one month's demand during this period). In the previous table, the average inventory was only 3.

Available to promise (ATP)

The master production schedule provides the information to the sales function on what can be promised to customers and when delivery can be promised. The sales function can load known sales orders against the master production schedule and keep track of what is available to promise (ATP) (*see* Table 14.3).

Table 14.3 Example of a level master production schedule including available to promise

					Week number				
		1	2	3	4	5	6	7	8	9
Demand		10	10	10	10	15	15	15	20	20
Sales orders		10	10	10	8	4				
Available		31	32	33	34	30	26	22	13	4
ATP		31	1	1	3	7	11	11	11	11
MPS		11	11	11	11	11	11	11	11	11
On hand	30									

Shimla Pinks is a small chain of gourmet Indian restaurants, specializing in high–quality authentic dishes. Although there is a fully qualified chef at each restaurant, some of the special sauces, on which the quality of the meal depends, are made at the chain's main restaurant and 'central kitchen' in Birmingham in the UK. To plan the 'production' of these sauces, Mrs Gurmit Kaur Pannum and Mr Rasphal Singh Sunner (right hand photo), two head chefs, work from their 'master production schedule' (estimate of demand) for each sauce for the next few days and with their secret bills of materials (the recipes for each sauce), they order and prepare all the individual components (ingredients) which go into the sauces. Although this is a service context, the process is, in essence, the same as any manufacturing MRP system

The ATP line in the master production schedule shows the maximum in any one week that is still available, against which sales orders can be loaded. If the sales function promises above that figure, it will not be able to keep its promise and the business will be viewed as unreliable by its customers. If sales orders are possible over and above this ATP figure, negotiation should take place with the master production scheduler to see if there is any possibility of satisfying these increased orders by adjusting the MPS. However, this must be run through the MRP process to see the resulting effects on resource requirements.

● The bill of materials

The master schedule drives the rest of the MRP process. Having established this top-level schedule, MRP performs calculations to work out the volume and timing of assemblies, sub-assemblies and materials required to meet this master schedule. To explain the process, an example product – a board game called 'Treasure Hunt' – will be used (see Fig. 14.8). This fictitious product is a boxed game which involves two to eight players tackling certain quests to find where treasure is buried on a board. To do this, adventure characters use a horse, an air balloon, a cart and other modes of transport to move around the board. Players take turns using two dice to determine their move. A set of instructions is provided with the game.

To be able to manufacture this game, Warwick Operations Games Inc. needs to understand what parts are required to go into each boxed game. If it wishes to use an MRP system to perform this task, it requires computer records of the ingredients or components that go into each item, much the same as a cook requires a list of ingredients to prepare a dish. These records are called bills of materials. The position of the bills of materials in the MRP schematic is shown in Figure 14.9.

Materials requirements planning programmes need to check the components or ingredients for each item that is to be made. Chapter 5 discussed design and introduced the idea of product structures. A bill of materials shows which parts and how many of them are required to go into which other parts. It is simplest to think about these as a

Figure 14.8 Treasure Hunt game

Figure 14.9 Bills of materials in the MRP schematic

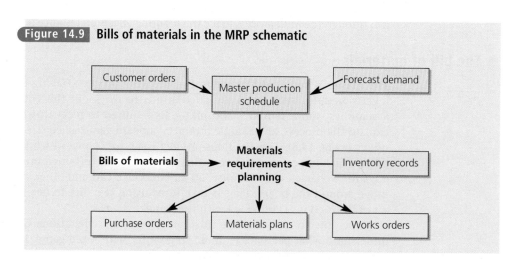

product structure initially (*see* Fig. 14.10). The product structure in Figure 14.10 is a simplified structure showing the parts required to make the game. It shows that to make one game you require the components of the game – board, dice, characters and quest cards – a set of rules and the packaging. The packaging comprises a printed cardboard box and, inside the base, an injection-moulded plastic inner tray. Since the game was launched, finance was provided for television advertising, so an additional sticker

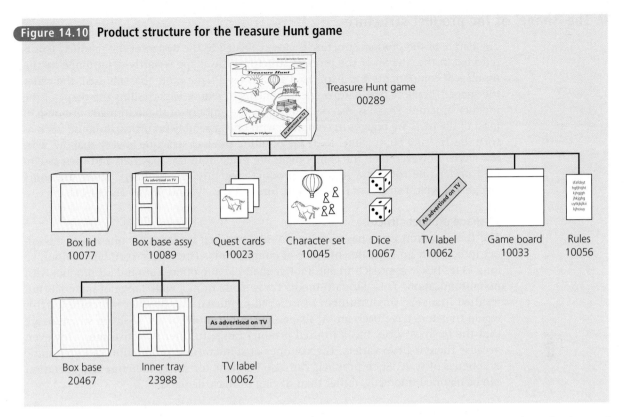

Figure 14.10 **Product structure for the Treasure Hunt game**

Treasure Hunt game
00289

Box lid
10077

Box base assy
10089

Quest cards
10023

Character set
10045

Dice
10067

TV label
10062

Game board
10033

Rules
10056

Box base
20467

Inner tray
23988

TV label
10062

stating 'As advertised on TV' is now stuck on the plastic inner tray and on the front of the complete box.

Levels of assembly

The product structure shows that some parts go into others, which, in turn, go into others. In MRP we term these levels of assembly. The finished product – the boxed game – is said to be at level 0. The parts and sub-assemblies that go into the boxed game are at level 1, the parts that go into the sub-assemblies are at level 2, and so on.

Features of MRP to note

There are several features of this product structure and of MRP generally that should be noted at this time:

- Multiples of some parts are required; this means that MRP has to know the required number of each part to be able to multiply up the requirements.
- The same part (the TV label, part number 10062) may be used in different parts of the product structure. In this example, the label is needed to make the box base assembly and also to complete the Treasure Hunt game. This means that MRP has to cope with this commonality of parts and, at some stage, aggregate the requirements to check how many labels in total are required.
- The product structure stops when it gets down to parts that are not made by this business; for example, another operation makes and supplies the plastic inner trays. This supplier needs to know the product structure for the trays – the weight of plastic granules and the colour of plastic which is required – but the game manufacturer's MRP system treats the plastic tray as a single, bought-in item. This is true even for complex modules or sub-assemblies, such as those bought in by computer manufacturers. Their product structure is not relevant to the in-house MRP, except in terms of the implications on the 'lead time' required to procure them.

The 'shape' of the product structure

The nature of the product structure is closely related to the design of the product. This is reflected in the 'shape' of the product structure. The shape is partly determined by the number of components and parts used at each level – the more that are used, the wider the shape. Therefore, standardizing components to reduce variety slims the shape of the product structure. Shape is also determined by the amount of the item made in-house. If most of the parts are bought in complete, with only assembly occurring in-house, such as with the Treasure Hunt game, then the resulting product structure is very shallow, with few levels. However, if all the components are made from raw materials and then assembled under one roof, the resulting product structure is very deep. There are some recognized typical shapes of product structure – 'A', 'T', 'V' and 'X' (*see* Fig. 14.11).

'A'-shape product structures

The Treasure Hunt game has a shallow 'A' shape in that there is only one finished product into which go a greater number of components. The Henry Ford 'any colour, so long as it's black' approach to automotive manufacture offered a standard product with no customization. This standard product was made from a wide range of materials but resulted in a very small number of finished products. The product structure for this would therefore have been an 'A' shape. The implications of an 'A'-shape structure are that the business only has a limited product range to offer the customer. However, because there is little variety, the volumes of standardized production can give some economies of scale. Such products can also be made for stock; therefore the operation can be planned smoothly, rather than having to chase demand.

'T'-shape product structures

A 'T'-shape product structure is typical of operations that have a small number of raw materials and a relatively standard process but which produce a very wide range of highly customized end products; an example of this is a label manufacturer producing personal name and address labels. Because the final part of the process is highly customized, it must therefore be performed to order. The earlier processes, however, are standard and can provide some economies of scale. The operations difficulties facing a company operating with a 'T' structure often relate to product flow. The part of the operation which makes to order is supplied by a continuous process. This can be difficult to manage because very different styles of operations management are required. The high-volume, low-variety part of the business is aiming for cost reduction and high utilization, whereas the high-variety, customized part of the business is aiming for delivery speed and service performance.

'V'-shape product structures

Similar to a 'T'-shape structure, but with less standardization of process, the 'V'-shape product structure is typical of the petrochemical industry. Here, a small number of raw materials are used to create a wide range of products and by-products, depending on

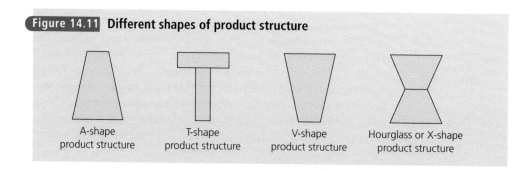

Figure 14.11 Different shapes of product structure

A-shape product structure   T-shape product structure   V-shape product structure   Hourglass or X-shape product structure

slight changes of mix of the input materials. Operations which have these types of products are driven by customer orders. Because of their reliance on a small number of raw materials, it is critical that these are reliably supplied. Failure of supply of one material can cause disruption of service to much of the customer base.

'X'-shape product structures

Some manufacturers have standardized their designs to consist of a small number of standard modules. For example, kitchen unit manufacturers make standardized bodies to which a wide range of doors and fittings can be attached. These standard modules are represented by the cross of the X. They are combined with a customized selection of features and options, giving a wide range of finished products. Automotive manufacturers typically use this 'X'-shape product structure. The same chassis assemblies, transmission assemblies, braking systems and engines are often used on a wide range of vehicles.

To some extent the 'X' shape provides the best of both worlds – customization and the impression of making to order at the final assembly stage, combined with the economies and stability of large-volume production in module manufacture. Companies with product structures of this shape tend to master schedule at the intersection of the X, rather than at the level of the ultimate finished product. The intersection represents a manageable number of items to plan and control.

● Single-level and indented bills of materials

Referring back to the simple product structure for the board game given earlier, it clearly would not be possible to represent bills of materials in full graphical form. They would simply be too unwieldy. In sophisticated engineering environments, there may be 15

Table 14.4 Single-level bills for board game

Part number: 00289

Description: Board game

Level: 0

Level	Part number	Description	Quantity
1	10089	Box base assy	1
1	10077	Box lid	1
1	10023	Quest cards set	1
1	10062	TV label	1
1	10045	Character set	1
1	10067	Die	2
1	10033	Game board	1
1	10056	Rules booklet	1

Part number: 10089

Description: Box base assy

Level: 1

Level	Part number	Description	Quantity
2	20467	Box base	1
2	10062	TV label	1
2	23988	Inner tray	1

levels of assembly and 5000 different parts within a finished product. MRP systems cope with this by using single-level bills of materials and indented bills of materials.

In single-level bills of materials, the details of the relationships between parts and sub-assemblies are stored as one single level at a time. For example, the single-level bills for the board game in the example provided previously are shown in Table 14.4. Each single-level bill of materials shows only the parts that go directly into it.

Most MRP systems store the relationships of parts to particular assemblies in this way, but they also usually have the capability of presenting them in the form of an indented bill of materials to show several levels at the same time. Table 14.5 shows the whole indented bill of materials for the board game. The term 'indented' refers to the indentation of the level of assembly, shown in the left-hand column.

Table 14.5 Indented bill of materials for board game

Part number: 00289
Description: Board game
Level: 0

Level	Part number	Description	Quantity
0	00289	Board game	1
.1	10077	Box lid	1
.1	10089	Box base assy	1
..2	20467	Box base	1
..2	10062	TV label	1
..2	23988	Inner tray	1
.1	10023	Quest cards set	1
.1	10045	Character set	1
.1	10067	Die	2
.1	10062	TV label	1
.1	10033	Game board	1
.1	10056	Rules booklet	1

Staedtler: Manufacturing and the use of MRP[5]

Staedtler is one of the world's premier manufacturers and suppliers of writing instruments, with an annual turnover in the region of over DM500 million, and employing almost 4000 people. The Staedtler range extends from standard, high-volume, consumer products such as pens, pencils, crayons and erasers, to highly specialized items designed for specific technical applications and for professional users. As the range has expanded, Staedtler has found that it can achieve very high-quality production by careful selection of raw materials and by using the latest precision manufacturing techniques. The technologies employed include wood and graphite processing, injection moulding and extrusion of plastics, and the fine engineering of metals. Modern automated assembly machines allow the low-cost, mass production of volume products such as ballpoint pens.

In managing the production of its complex range of over 6000 products, Staedtler has been aided by the use of a well-tried MRP system. Whereas some items, such as standard pencils, have a bill of materials with only a few levels, some of the more involved products require a breakdown of up to seven levels.

An example of a typical Staedtler bill of materials is shown in Table 14.6. This illustrates the different levels of production involved in manufacturing a '110-HB Tradition Pencil in Dozen Box' (level 0).

Table 14.6 The bill of materials for Staedtler's 'Tradition Pencil in Dozen Box'

Indented explosion		Sales unit	Parent/sales number	Parent description
		GS	110-HB	Tradition pencil in dozen box

Production level	Component quantity	Component unit	Component number	Component description
.1	12.000000	PC	V12TI	Tradition inners
.1	0.000600	PC	V12TF	Tradition shrinkwrap
.1	0.050000	PC	V12C	Tradition carton
.1	1.000000	GS	FTRAD	Pre-packing tradition pencils
..2	0.007000	KG	DLW	White dip lacquer
..2	0.020000	KG	DLB	Black dip lacquer
..2	0.023000	PC	GFT	Tradition gold foil
..2	1.000000	GS	PTRAD	Pre-finishing tradition pencils
...3	0.100000	KG	PLR	Red polishing lacquer
...3	0.030000	KG	SLB	Black stripe lacquer
...3	1.000000	GS	RTRAD	Pre-polishing tradition pencils
....4	0.050000	PC	CCP2	Wood slats – CCP
....4	0.000600	KG	RASKG	Wood glue
....4	1.000000	GS	STRAD	Tradition pencil slips

Units: PC = suppliers' unit; KG = kilogram; GS = gross of pencils.

Source: Reproduced by kind permission of Staedtler (UK) Ltd.

The top level on the bill (shown as .1) gives all the items involved in the final packaging, including the finished pencil itself – coded FTRAD. The next levels in the bill are all required in the production of pencils themselves, with level 2 being the materials required to label the pencils with the Staedtler name and paint for dipping to give the traditional 'dipped end' on the end of the pencil. At level 3 are the lacquers and paints required to coat the basic pencil, and finally level 4 details the raw materials, slats of wood, pencil lead slips and glue which are used in the initial production of the pencil.

The bills of materials for every end product are stored on the MRP system, as well as routing and standard times for the products through each manufacturing and assembly process. An inventory file is kept for every end item, at every level. The master production schedule is initially analysed to ensure that the weekly loadings on each work centre are realistic, and then the full MRP output is created, which schedules all the production requirements at each level. Once a production order has been completed and booked back onto the system, the inventory levels of all items mentioned on the bill of materials are deducted accordingly.

Questions

1 Draw the product structure implied by Table 14.6.

2 What do you think might be the major difficulties that a company like Staedtler faces in using MRP for its planning and control?

Planning bills of materials

Because each end product has its own, often large and detailed, bill of materials, it can become unwieldy to use these detailed bills for planning in the medium to long term. Instead, a smaller number of bills that represent an average product are used. For example, a particular model of car might have two-, three-, four- or five-door choices available. When planning across all models of cars made, the master production scheduler may use a 'super-bill' – a type of planning bill of materials – which lists the average numbers of components across a family of products. The average number of doors may be 3.5; obviously, no car of any model is made with 3.5 doors. However, the purpose of the planning bill is to allow longer-term forward planning to give a rough idea of how many doors (and other items) may be required in the future.

Inventory records

The bill of materials file therefore provides MRP with the base data on the ingredients or structure of products. Rather than simply taking these ingredients and multiplying them up in line with demand to determine the total materials requirements, MRP recognizes that some of the required items may already be in stock. This stock may be in the form of finished goods, work-in-progress or raw materials. It is necessary, starting at level 0 of each bill, to check how much inventory is available of each finished product, sub-assembly and component, and then to calculate what is termed the 'net' requirements – the extra requirements needed to supplement the inventory so that demand can be met. To do this, MRP requires that inventory records are kept (*see* Fig. 14.12).

There are three main files kept in MRP systems that help to manage inventory:

- the item master file
- the transaction file
- the location file.

The item master file

The key to all inventory records is usually a part number. Each part used in a manufacturing business has to be recognizable by one standard identification so that there is no confusion between people buying and supplying the part or using the part in the manufacturing process. Most manufacturers therefore assign a number to each part. Part numbers might be totally numeric or may be an alphanumeric combination of letters and numbers. Some companies have found it convenient to use mnemonics which help users to recognize which part is represented by a particular part number. Complex cross-checking numbering systems are often adopted to prevent an error being caused through, say, transposing two digits; credit card numbers use this type of cross-checking.

In addition to a part number, the item master file contains all the stable data on a part; this is often a computer screen of fields including the part description, the unit of measure (flour may be recorded in tonnes, washers in 1000s and engines in single discrete units) and a standard cost. Interestingly, the lead time to buy or make the part is

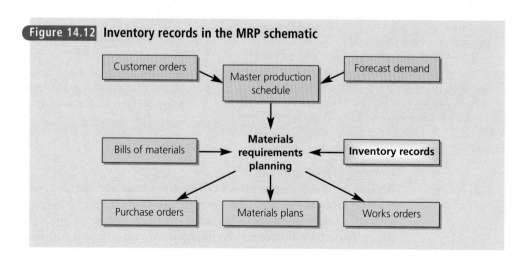

Figure 14.12 **Inventory records in the MRP schematic**

often treated as fixed data by virtue of the fact that it is located in the item master file. In fact, this may vary between suppliers and change at different times of the year and according to supply market conditions.

The transaction file

In order to take inventory levels into account, MRP needs to know the level of inventory of each part. The transaction file keeps a record of receipts into stock, issues from stock and a running balance. In the past, these transactions were entered onto the computer overnight or at periodic intervals; this caused problems in that the information was always lagging behind reality. MRP systems today run their inventory in real time. This means the transaction file is updated at the time a receipt or issue occurs. This has implications for the number of computer terminals required by the operation, their location and the number of people trained to use them. The benefits of real-time processing, however, far outweigh any increased cost of equipment and training.

The location file

The stores, or inventory points in the operation, need to be managed. Some stores operate a fixed location system so that a particular part can always be found at a particular location. However, companies that operate with a wide and changing range of inventory items find this system inefficient. Instead they operate a random location system where parts are located in the nearest available place. A random location system requires careful control, as the same item may be kept in several different locations at any one time. In addition to being more efficient on space utilization, a random location system can make it easier to ensure that stock physically 'turns over' by making a first-in-first-out principle easy to implement. When the computer generates picking lists instructing store operators (mechanical or human) to pick items from stock, it can ensure that the oldest stock is picked by sending the picker to the longest-standing location for an item.

Accuracy of the inventory files

As with the management of bills of materials, it is critical to an MRP system that inventory records are accurate and up to date. Mistakes do occur and inventory is pilfered or perishes, so inventory records will never reflect exactly what is physically in stock in a business. Because of this, perpetual physical inventory (PPI) checking is performed in many companies.

PPI involves continually checking that the physical inventory level and location of a part match the computer record. Where a difference is confirmed, the computer record is updated to reflect reality. Before the PPI process was well established in companies, stock was only checked annually to comply with end-of-year accounting procedures. The implications of inaccuracy of inventory records are shortages which lead to the rescheduling of production, with resulting inefficiencies and, possibly, failure to satisfy a customer order.

MRP calculations

So far we have examined all the information which is needed for operations to start the planning process. Although this information is a necessary prerequisite to MRP, it is not the 'heart' of the procedure. At its core, MRP is a systematic process of taking this planning information and calculating the volume and timing requirements which will satisfy demand. This next part of the chapter examines the way these calculations are performed, starting with what is probably the most important step, the netting process.

The MRP netting process

Figure 14.13 shows simplistically the process that MRP performs to calculate the volumes of materials required. MRP takes the master production schedule (the planned production schedule for each end item) and 'explodes', or examines the implications of, this schedule through the single-level bill of materials, checking how many sub-assemblies and parts are required. Before moving down the product structure to the next level, MRP checks how many of the required parts are already available in stock. It then generates 'works orders', or requests, for the net requirements of items that are made in-house. These net requirements then form the schedule which is exploded through the single-level bill of materials at the next level down. Again, available inventory of those items is checked; works orders are generated for the net requirements that are made in-house, as are purchase orders for the net requirements of items that are bought from suppliers. This process continues until the bottom of the product structure is reached.

Figure 14.14 uses our example of the board game to describe this part of the MRP process. Just considering the volume requirements at this moment, a top-level requirement for 10 board games does not automatically generate a works order to build 10. First the available inventory is checked. Because three board games are in stock, a works order to build seven board games is issued. MRP then checks the top, single-level bill for the board game and finds, among other parts, that one box base assembly (10089) is required per board game. MRP then checks how many box base assemblies are in stock and, finding two, generates a works order for the net requirement of five. Next the single-level bill of materials for the box base assembly is checked. This shows that one box base (20467), one inner tray (23988) and one TV label (10062) are required for each box base assembly. Again, the inventory is checked and, as there is one box base in stock, an order to purchase four more is generated. As there are more than enough TV labels and inner trays in stock, there is no need to raise a replenishment instruction.

Figure 14.13 The MRP netting process

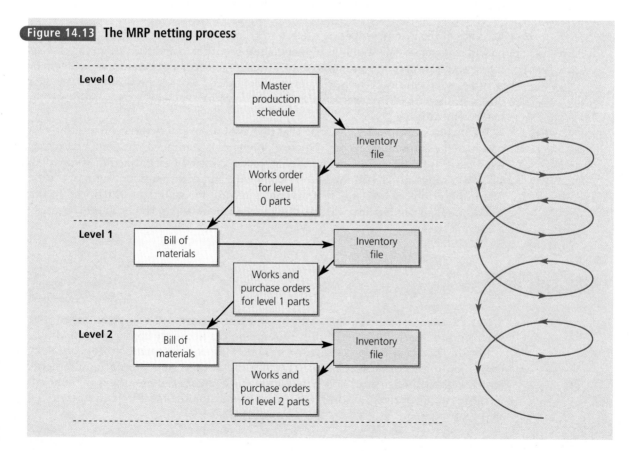

Figure 14.14 **Example of MRP netting process**

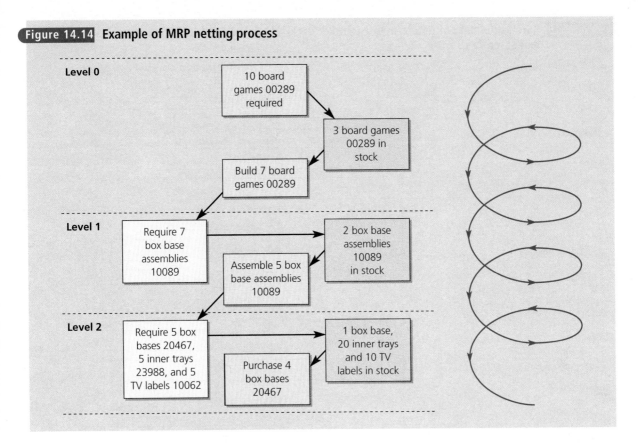

Back-scheduling

In addition to calculating the volume of materials required, MRP also considers when each of these parts is required, that is, the timing and scheduling of materials. It does this by a process called back-scheduling which takes into account the lead time at each level of assembly. Again using the example of the board game, assume that 10 board games are required to be finished by a notional planning day which we will term day 35. To determine when we need to start work on all the parts that make up the game, we need to know how much time to allow for each part of the process. These times are called lead times and are stored in MRP files for each part (*see* Table 14.7).

Table 14.7 Back-scheduling of requirements in MRP

Part no.	Description	Lead time (days)
00289	Board game	2
10077	Box lid	8
10089	Box base assy	4
20467	Box base	12
23988	Inner tray	29
10062	TV label	8
10023	Quest cards set	3
10045	Character set	3
10067	Die	5
10033	Game board	25
10056	Rules booklet	3

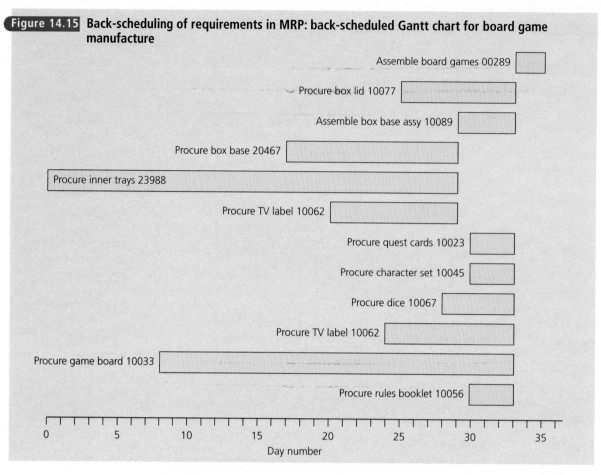

Figure 14.15 Back-scheduling of requirements in MRP: back-scheduled Gantt chart for board game manufacture

Now examine the Gantt chart shown in Figure 14.15 which includes the lead-time information. If it takes two days to carry out the final assembly, the sub-assemblies must be complete and available on the shop floor at the beginning of day 33. In this way, the programme is worked backwards to determine the tasks that have to be performed and the purchase orders that have to be placed. It can be seen in the example that to deliver the required board games on time, the inner trays must be purchased now.

Given the lead times in Table 14.7 and the inventory levels shown in Table 14.8, the MRP records shown in Figure 14.16 can be derived.

Table 14.8 Inventory of parts for board game

Part no.	Description	Inventory
00289	Board game	3
10077	Box lid	4
10089	Box base assy	2
20467	Box base	1
23988	Inner tray	20
10062	TV label	10
10023	Quest cards set	0
10045	Character set	0
10067	Die	0
10033	Game board	0
10056	Rules booklet	0

Figure 14.16 Extract of the MRP records for the board game

Treasure Hunt Game

Part number: 00289		1	2	3	4	5	6	7	8	9	10	11	12	13	14	15	16	17	18	19	20	21	22	23	24	25	26	27	28	29	30	31	32	33	34	35
Requirements (gross)																																				10
Scheduled receipts																																				
On hand inventory	3	3	3	3	3	3	3	3	3	3	3	3	3	3	3	3	3	3	3	3	3	3	3	3	3	3	3	3	3	3	3	3	3	3	3	0
Planned order release																																		7		

Box lid

Part number: 10077		1	2	3	4	5	6	7	8	9	10	11	12	13	14	15	16	17	18	19	20	21	22	23	24	25	26	27	28	29	30	31	32	33	34	35
Requirements (gross)																																		7		
Scheduled receipts																																				
On hand inventory	4	4	4	4	4	4	4	4	4	4	4	4	4	4	4	4	4	4	4	4	4	4	4	4	4	4	4	4	4	4	4	4	0	0	0
Planned order release																													5							

Box base assembly

Part number: 10089		1	2	3	4	5	6	7	8	9	10	11	12	13	14	15	16	17	18	19	20	21	22	23	24	25	26	27	28	29	30	31	32	33	34	35
Requirements (gross)																																		7		
Scheduled receipts																																				
On hand inventory	2	2	2	2	2	2	2	2	2	2	2	2	2	2	2	2	2	2	2	2	2	2	2	2	2	2	2	2	2	2	2	2	0	0	0
Planned order release																													5							

Box base

Part number: 20457		1	2	3	4	5	6	7	8	9	10	11	12	13	14	15	16	17	18	19	20	21	22	23	24	25	26	27	28	29	30	31	32	33	34	35
Requirements (gross)																														5						
Scheduled receipts																																				
On hand inventory	1	1	1	1	1	1	1	1	1	1	1	1	1	1	1	1	1	1	1	1	1	1	1	1	1	1	1	1	1	0	0	0	0	0	0
Planned order release																		4																	

Inner tray

Part number: 23988		1	2	3	4	5	6	7	8	9	10	11	12	13	14	15	16	17	18	19	20	21	22	23	24	25	26	27	28	29	30	31	32	33	34	35
Requirements (gross)																														5						
Scheduled receipts																																				
On hand inventory	20	20	20	20	20	20	20	20	20	20	20	20	20	20	20	20	20	20	20	20	20	20	20	20	20	20	20	20	15	15	15	15	15	15	15
Planned order release																																				

TV label

Part number: 10062		1	2	3	4	5	6	7	8	9	10	11	12	13	14	15	16	17	18	19	20	21	22	23	24	25	26	27	28	29	30	31	32	33	34	35
Requirements (gross)																														5				7		
Scheduled receipts																																				
On hand inventory	10	10	10	10	10	10	10	10	10	10	10	10	10	10	10	10	10	10	10	10	10	10	10	10	10	10	10	10	5	5	5	5	0	0	0
Planned order release																													2							

Quest cards set

Part number: 10023		1	2	3	4	5	6	7	8	9	10	11	12	13	14	15	16	17	18	19	20	21	22	23	24	25	26	27	28	29	30	31	32	33	34	35
Requirements (gross)																																		7		
Scheduled receipts																																				
On hand inventory	4	4	4	4	4	4	4	4	4	4	4	4	4	4	4	4	4	4	4	4	4	4	4	4	4	4	4	4	4	4	4	4	0	0	0
Planned order release																													3							

Character set

Part number: 10045		1	2	3	4	5	6	7	8	9	10	11	12	13	14	15	16	17	18	19	20	21	22	23	24	25	26	27	28	29	30	31	32	33	34	35
Requirements (gross)																																		7		
Scheduled receipts																																				
On hand inventory	0	0	0	0	0	0	0	0	0	0	0	0	0	0	0	0	0	0	0	0	0	0	0	0	0	0	0	0	0	0	0	0	0	0	0
Planned order release																														7						

Die

Part number: 10067		1	2	3	4	5	6	7	8	9	10	11	12	13	14	15	16	17	18	19	20	21	22	23	24	25	26	27	28	29	30	31	32	33	34	35
Requirements (gross)																																		14		
Scheduled receipts																																				
On hand inventory	0	0	0	0	0	0	0	0	0	0	0	0	0	0	0	0	0	0	0	0	0	0	0	0	0	0	0	0	0	0	0	0	0	0	0
Planned order release																														14						

Game board

Part number: 10033		1	2	3	4	5	6	7	8	9	10	11	12	13	14	15	16	17	18	19	20	21	22	23	24	25	26	27	28	29	30	31	32	33	34	35
Requirements (gross)																																		7		
Scheduled receipts																																				
On hand inventory	0	0	0	0	0	0	0	0	0	0	0	0	0	0	0	0	0	0	0	0	0	0	0	0	0	0	0	0	0	0	0	0	0	0	0
Planned order release						7																													

Rules booklet

Part number: 10023		1	2	3	4	5	6	7	8	9	10	11	12	13	14	15	16	17	18	19	20	21	22	23	24	25	26	27	28	29	30	31	32	33	34	35
Requirements (gross)																																		7		
Scheduled receipts																																				
On hand inventory	0	0	0	0	0	0	0	0	0	0	0	0	0	0	0	0	0	0	0	0	0	0	0	0	0	0	0	0	0	0	0	0	0	0	0
Planned order release																														7						

The gross requirements of each part at level 1 can be derived directly from the planned order release of the whole game. So at day 33, seven box lids, box base assemblies, TV labels, etc. are needed. Back-scheduling by the lead times for each level 1 item gives their planned order release time. Similarly, the level 2 items which are needed to produce the box base assembly are subject to the same procedure. Note that the TV label is both a level 1 and a level 2 item and has gross requirements originating from the planned order releases of both the game and the box base assembly.

In reality, some items can only be acquired in minimum-sized batches. Because of the time taken and costs involved to set up a machine, it may be seen to be efficient to run it for a reasonable size of batch. Similarly, some purchased items are bought in pack sizes or in order quantities of a size large enough to gain a volume discount, even though this means that more are bought than are needed. Another reason why some operations make or buy more than they immediately need is to give them a margin of safety in the event of unplanned variations in either demand or supply. All these issues of batch sizes and safety stocks are dealt with in Chapter 12.

Extensions to basic MRP

Several developments on the basic MRP idea have been made over the last few years. We briefly describe some of them here.

● Closed-loop MRP

When MRP was originally used in manufacturing, materials plans were launched at the beginning of the week, then a complete replanning exercise took place the following week, launching a new set of plans. This process was repeated weekly but there was no feedback loop to say whether a plan was achievable and whether it had actually been achieved. MRP systems which started to include feedback loops became known as 'closed-loop MRP' systems.

Closing the planning loop in MRP systems involves checking production plans against available resources. Therefore, capacity is checked throughout the process and, if the proposed plans are not achievable at any level, they are revised (*see* Fig. 14.17). All but the simplest MRP systems are now closed-loop systems. They use three planning routines to check production plans against the operation's resources.

Resource requirements plans (RRPs)
Resource requirements plans are static level plans which involve looking forward in the long term to predict the requirements for large structural parts of the operation, such as the numbers, locations and sizes of new plants. Because they are attempts at facilitating the long-term production plan by making arrangements to have the required resources available, they are sometimes termed 'infinite capacity plans', as they assume an almost infinite ability to step up production if demand warrants it.

Rough-cut capacity plans (RCCPs)
In the medium to short term, master production schedules have to use capacity which is available. The feedback loop at this level checks the MPS against known capacity bottlenecks and key resources only. If the MPS is not achievable, it should be adjusted. So, unlike the RRP, RCCP are 'finite capacity plans' because they have to operate within certain constraints.

Capacity requirements plans (CRPs)
On a day-to-day basis, works orders intended to be issued from the MRP will often have a variable effect on the loading of particular machines or individual workers. Capacity

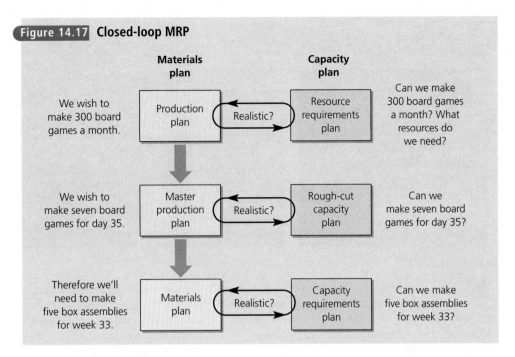

Figure 14.17 **Closed-loop MRP**

requirements plans (CRPs) project this load ahead. They are 'infinite capacity plans' insomuch as they do not take the capacity constraints of each machine or work area into account. If this load is lumpy it may be smoothed by replanning to a finite capacity or by allocating temporary resources to the area.

The closed-loop system of MRP can be further developed to drive very short-term plans, as is shown in Figure 14.18.

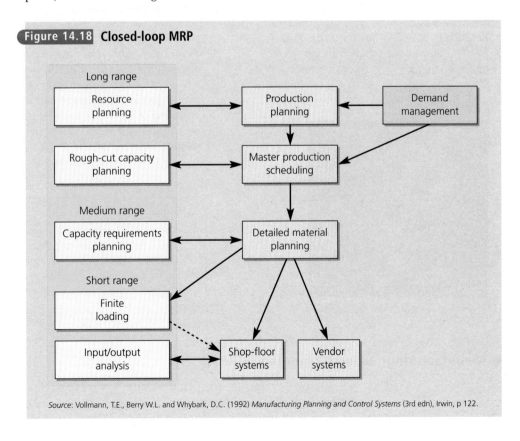

Figure 14.18 **Closed-loop MRP**

Source: Vollmann, T.E., Berry W.L. and Whybark, D.C. (1992) *Manufacturing Planning and Control Systems* (3rd edn), Irwin, p 122.

Customer service receiving orders ...   *... triggers the plant to schedule production ...*

Many businesses depend on their ability to perform a perpetual balancing act between supply and demand. Throw in too many orders and the plant becomes overloaded, with the threat of leaving customers dissatisfied. Manufacture too much product and the plant shifts the other way, tying up money and filling storage space with unsold stock. At ICI Chlor-Chemicals a process known as sales and operations planning (S&OP) works to ensure that the business keeps all the promises it makes to its customers. The S&OP process helps the business to order the raw materials and services it needs with accuracy, while also providing its plants with information as to which products to produce and in what quantity. The process has the power to plot the best plans and schedules for virtually any set of circumstances – planned or unplanned – in a way which will make

best use of all the company's resources. By running a financial model, it is possible to find a solution to unforeseen production problems by rescheduling production in way that keeps customers satisfied and avoids a potentially damaging impact on the bottom line. By providing accurate estimates of future demand, it helps the procurement process and reduces the amount of both raw materials and products that need to be held in stock. The interface with the S&OP programme is via intranet connections which allow customer service staff to view the production plans for the coming days and weeks. Every time customer service staff pick up the telephone to take a customer order, details of the relevant production plans are displayed automatically on screen to allow an instant and informed response. Receipts of raw materials trigger payments to the supplier, just as dispatches of finished product trigger the raising of an invoice to the customer. By providing more people with more information, S&OP helps the company's staff to take better decisions – for the benefit of the business and its customers.

... and even dispatch to the customer

Questions

1 What should a good planning and control system be able to do to help a complex operation such as ICI Chlor-Chemicals?

2 Why is the financial modelling part of S&OP useful?

Manufacturing resource planning (MRP II)

MRP I was essentially aimed at the planning and control of production and inventory in manufacturing businesses. However, the concepts have been extended to other areas of the business. This extended concept was termed MRP II by Oliver Wight, one of the founders of MRP. Wight[6] defined MRP II as:

a game plan for planning and monitoring all the resources of a manufacturing company: manufacturing, marketing, finance and engineering. Technically it involves using the closed-loop MRP system to generate the financial figures.

Without MRP II integrated systems, separate databases are held by different functions. For example, a product structure or bill of materials is held in engineering and also in materials management. If engineering changes are made to the design of products, both databases have to be updated. It is difficult to keep both databases entirely identical and discrepancies between them cause problems, which often are not apparent until a member of staff is supplied with the wrong parts to manufacture the product. Similarly, cost information from finance and accounting, which is used to perform management accounting tasks such as variance analysis against standard costs, needs to be reconciled with changes made elsewhere in the operation, such as changes in inventory holding or process methods.

MRP II is based on one integrated system containing a database which is accessed and used by the whole company according to individual functional requirements. However, despite its dependence on the information technologies which allow such integration, MRP II still depends on people-based decision-making to close the loop.

Optimized production technology (OPT)

Other concepts and systems have been developed which also recognize the importance of planning to known capacity constraints, rather than overloading part of the production system and failing to meet the plan. Perhaps the best known is the 'theory of constraints' (TOC) which has been developed to focus attention on the capacity constraints or bottleneck parts of the operation. By identifying the location of constraints, working to remove them, then looking for the next constraint, an operation is always focusing on the part that critically determines the pace of output.

The approach which uses this idea is called optimized production technology (OPT). Its development and the marketing of it as a proprietary software product were originated by Eliyahu Goldratt.[7]

OPT is a computer-based technique and tool which helps to schedule production systems to the pace dictated by the most heavily loaded resources, that is, bottlenecks. If the rate of activity in any part of the system exceeds that of the bottleneck, then items are being produced that cannot be used. If the rate of working falls below the pace at the bottleneck, then the entire system is under-utilized.

There are principles underlying OPT which demonstrate this focus on bottlenecks.

OPT principles

1 Balance flow, not capacity.
2 The level of utilization of a non-bottleneck is determined by some other constraint in the system, not by its own capacity.
3 Utilization and activation of a resource are not the same.
4 An hour lost at a bottleneck is an hour lost for ever out of the entire system.
5 An hour saved at a non-bottleneck is a mirage.
6 Bottlenecks govern both throughput and inventory in the system.
7 The transfer batch may not, and many times should not, equal the process batch.
8 The process batch should be variable, not fixed.
9 Lead times are the result of a schedule and cannot be predetermined.
10 Schedules should be established by looking at all constraints simultaneously.

OPT should not be viewed as a replacement to MRP; nor is it impossible to run both together. However, the philosophical underpinnings of OPT outlined above do show that it could conflict with the way that many businesses run their MRP systems in practice. While MRP as a concept does not prescribe fixed lead times or fixed batch sizes, many operations run MRP with these elements fixed for simplicity. However, demand, supply and the process within a manufacturing operation all present unplanned variations on a dynamic basis; therefore, bottlenecks are dynamic, changing their location and their severity. For this reason, lead times are rarely constant over time. Similarly, if bottlenecks determine schedules, batch sizes may alter throughout the plant depending on whether a work centre is a bottleneck or not.

OPT uses the terminology of 'drum, buffer, rope' to explain its planning and control approach. Using OPT, the bottleneck work centre becomes a 'drum', beating the pace for the rest of the factory. This 'drum beat' determines the schedules in non-bottleneck areas, pulling through work (the rope) in line with the bottleneck capacity, not the capacity of the work centre. A bottleneck should never be allowed to be working at less than full capacity; therefore, inventory buffers should be placed before it to ensure that it never runs out of work.

Some of the arguments for using OPT in MRP environments are that it helps to focus on critical constraints and that it reduces the need for very detailed planning of non-bottleneck areas, therefore cutting down computational time in MRP.

● Enterprise resource planning (ERP)

Enterprise resource planning is the latest, and probably the most significant, development of the basic MRP philosophy. It has spawned a huge industry devoted to developing the computer systems needed to drive it. The (now) large companies which have grown almost exclusively on the basis of providing ERP systems include SAP, PeopleSoft, Oracle and Baan.

At its most basic, the strength of MRP I lay always in the fact that it could explore the *consequences* of any changes to what an operation was required to do. So, if demand changed, the MRP system would calculate all the 'knock-on' effects and issue instructions accordingly. The same principle applies to ERP but on a much wider basis. ERP systems allow decisions and databases from all parts of the organization to be integrated so that the consequences of decisions in one part of the organization are reflected in the planning and control systems of the rest of the organization (*see* Fig. 14.19).

Figure 14.19 ERP integrates information from all parts of the organization

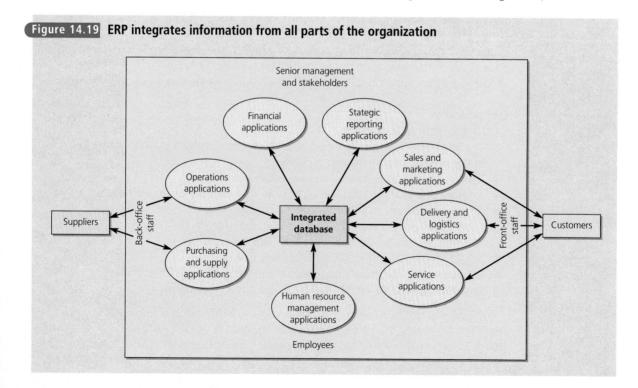

In fact, although the integration of several databases lies at the heart of ERP's power, it is nonetheless difficult to achieve in practice. This is why ERP installation can be particularly expensive. Attempting to get new systems and databases to talk to old (sometimes called *legacy*) systems can be very problematic. Not surprisingly, many companies choose to replace most, if not all, their existing systems with new ones. New common systems and relational databases help to ensure the smooth transfer of data between different parts of the organization.

In addition to the integration of systems, ERP usually includes other features which make it a powerful planning and control tool:

- It is based on a client/server architecture; that is, access to the information systems is open to anyone whose computer is linked to central computers.
- It can include decision support facilities (*see* Chapter 8) which enable operations decision makers to include the latest company information.
- It is often linked to external extranet systems, such as the electronic data interchange (EDI, *see* Chapter 13) systems, which are linked to the company's supply chain partners.
- It can be interfaced with standard applications programs which are in common use by most managers, such as spreadsheets etc.
- Often, ERP systems are able to operate on most common platforms such as Windows NT or Unix.

R/3 from SAP

By the start of the millennium, by far the biggest software company, whose success was based on ERP, was the German SAP company. Although founded 28 years before this, its latter success was almost entirely based on companies around the world being willing to invest large sums in order to plan their resources in an integrated manner. With 10 000 customers spread throughout 19 countries and around 30 per cent of the total market for ERP systems, the company was a very clear market leader in the field with its R/2 product. Many of the world's largest organizations, such as ABB, the European engineering conglomerate, Exxon, the worldwide petrochemical giant, and Microsoft, have invested in R/3. This is based on a three-tier client/server configuration with a network of databases forming the core of the system. The second tier surrounding the databases consists of a set of *application servers* which hold the basic logic flows and instructions for the applications. These communicate with the third layer, *front-end servers*, which are usually individual computers distributed on the shop floor or on manager's desks. The end result is a system which provides a comprehensive integration of most conventional business applications. R/3 divides these into four sections:

- *Manufacturing and logistics* – includes modules on materials management (based on the MRP logic), quality management, plant maintenance, production planning and control, project management, etc.
- *Sales and distribution* – includes modules for customer management, sales order management, product configuration management, distribution, export controls, shipping, transportation management, etc.
- *Financial accounting* – includes modules on accounts payable, accounts receivable, capital investment, etc.
- *Human resources* – contains modules on workforce scheduling, remuneration, hiring, payroll, benefits administration, personnel development, etc.

Why did companies invest in ERP?

If one accepts only some of the criticisms of ERP outlined in the critical commentary box overleaf, it does pose the question as to why companies have invested such large amounts of money in it. Partly it was the attraction of turning the company's information systems into a 'smooth running and integrated machine'. The prospect of such organizational efficiency is attractive to most managers, even if it does presuppose a very simplistic model of how organizations work in practice. After a while, although organizations could now see the formidable problems in ERP implementation, the investments were justified on the basis that, 'even if we gain no significant advantage by investing in ERP, we will be placed at a disadvantage by *not* investing in it because all our competitors are doing so'. There is probably some truth in this; sometimes businesses have to invest just to stand still.

Perhaps the most important justification, however, is the potential which ERP systems give the organization to link up with the outside world. For example, it is much easier for an operation to move into internet-based trading if it can integrate its external internet systems into its internal ERP systems.

Summary answers to key questions

What is MRP?

● MRP stands for materials requirements planning which is a dependent demand system that calculates materials requirements and production plans to satisfy known and forecast sales orders.

● MRP helps to make volume and timing calculations based on an idea of what will be necessary to supply demand in the future.

What is the process involved in MRP planning and control?

● MRP works from a master production schedule which summarizes the volume and timing of end products or services.

● The master production schedule is a slightly more detailed version of the aggregated capacity plans which are discussed in Chapter 11.

● Using the logic of the product or services bill of materials (BOM) and the inventory records of the operation, the production schedule is 'exploded' to determine how many sub-assemblies and parts are required, and when they are required in order to achieve the master production schedule.

- This process of exploding the master production schedule is called the MRP netting process. It is carried out throughout the different levels of the product structure.

- Within this process, 'back-scheduling' takes into account the lead time required to obtain parts at each level of the assembly.

What are the main elements of an MRP system?

- A demand management system must interface with customers in order to set the requirements for the master production schedule.

- The master production schedule is the central reference source for what the system is supposed to produce and when.

- Bills of materials and product structure information, together with lead times, enable the netting process to take place.

- Inventory records contain data which allows the MRP system to understand where stock is located, how many parts are in stock, and what issue and receipt transactions have occurred against any parts.

- The output from the materials requirements planning system comprises purchase orders, materials plans, and works orders which trigger the purchasing or manufacture of parts.

What is 'closed loop' MRP?

- Closed-loop MRP systems contain feedback loops which ensure that checks are made against capacity to see if plans are feasible.

What are MRP II and enterprise resource planning (ERP)?

- MRP II systems are a development of MRP. They integrate many processes that are related to MRP, but which are located outside the operation's function.

- Without MRP II, separate databases would be held for different functions.

- A system which performs roughly the same function as MRP II is optimized production technology (OPT). It is based on the theory of constraints, which has been developed to focus attention on capacity bottlenecks in the operation.

- ERP is possibly the most significant development to come from MRP. Now used by many different types of organization, it integrates the planning activities of operations, sales and marketing, finance and human resources.

CASE EXERCISE

Psycho Sports Ltd

Peter Townsend knew that he would have to make some decisions pretty soon. His sports goods manufacturing business, Psycho Sports, had grown so rapidly over the last two years that he would soon have to install some systematic procedures and routines to manage the business. His biggest problem was in manufacturing control. He had started making specialist high-quality table tennis bats but now made a wide range of sports products, including tennis balls, darts and protective equipment for various games. Furthermore, his customers, once limited to specialist sports shops, now included some of the major sports retail chains.

'We really do have to get control of our manufacturing. I keep getting told that we need what seems to be called an MRP system. I wasn't sure what this meant and so I have bought a specialist production control book from our local bookshop and read all about MRP principles. I

must admit, these academics seem to delight in making simple things complicated. And there is so much jargon associated with the technique, I feel more confused now than I did before.

'Perhaps the best way forward is for me to take a very simple example from my own production unit and see whether I can work things out manually. If I can follow the process through on paper then I will be far better equipped to decide what kind of computer-based system we should get, if any!'

Peter decided to take as his example one of his new products: a table tennis bat marketed under the name of the 'high-resolution' bat, but known within the manufacturing unit more prosaically as Part Number 5654. Figure 14.20 shows the product structure for this table tennis bat.

As can be seen from Figure 14.20, the table tennis bat is made up of two main assemblies: a handle

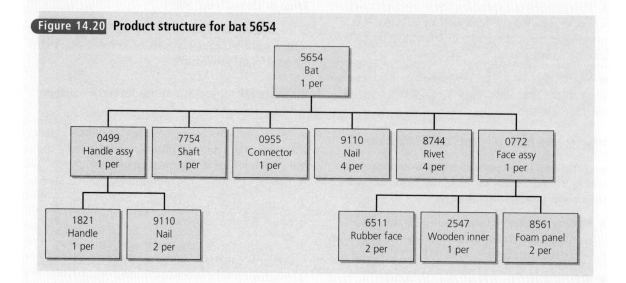

Figure 14.20 **Product structure for bat 5654**

assembly and a face assembly. In order to bring the two main assemblies together to form the finished bat, various fixings are required, such as nails, connectors, etc.

The gross requirements for this particular bat are shown below. The bat is not due to be launched until Week 13 (it is now Week 1), and sales forecasts have been made for the first 23 weeks of sales:

Weeks 13–21 inclusive, 100 per week
Weeks 22–29 inclusive, 150 per week
Weeks 30–35 inclusive, 200 per week

Peter also managed to obtain information on the current inventory levels of each of the parts which

made up the finished bat, together with cost data and lead times. He was surprised, however, how long it took him to obtain this information.

'It has taken me nearly two days to get hold of all the information I need. Different people held it, nowhere was it conveniently put together, and sometimes it was not even written down. To get the inventory data, I actually had to go down to the stores and count how many parts were in the boxes.'

The data Peter collected was as shown in Table 14.9.

Peter set himself six exercises which he knew he would have to master if he was to understand fully the basics of MRP.

Table 14.9 Inventory, cost and lead-time information for parts

Part no.	Description	Inventory	EQ	LT	Std cost
5645	Bat	0	500	2	12.00
0499	Handle assy	0	400	3	4.00
7754	Shaft	15	1000	5	1.00
0955	Connector	350	5000	4	0.02
9110	Nail	120	5000	4	0.01
8744	Rivet	3540	5000	4	0.01
0772	Face assy	0	250	4	5.00
1821	Handle	0	500	4	2.00
6511	Rubber face	0	2000	10	0.50
2547	Wooden inner	10	300	7	1.50
8561	Foam panel	0	1000	8	0.50

LT = lead time for ordering (in weeks); EQ = economic quantity for ordering; Std cost = standard cost in £.

Exercise 1

Draw up:
(a) the single-level bill of materials for each level of assembly;
(b) a complete indented bill of materials for all levels of assembly.

Exercise 2

(a) Create the materials requirements planning records for each part and sub-assembly in the bat.
(b) List any problems that the completed MRP records identify.
(c) What alternatives are there that the company could take to solve any problems? What are their relative merits?

Exercise 3

Based on the first two exercises, create another set of MRP records, this time allowing one week's safety lead time for each item: that is, ensuring the items are in stock the week prior to when they are required.

Exercise 4

Over the time period of the exercise, what effect would the imposition of a safety lead time have on average inventory value?

Exercise 5

If we decided that our first task was to reduce inventory costs by 15 per cent, what action would we recommend? What are the implications of our action?

Exercise 6

How might production in our business be smoothed?

Questions

1 Why did Peter have such problems getting to the relevant information?

2 Perform all the exercises which Peter set for himself. Do you think he should now fully understand MRP?

Discussion questions

1 What is the difference between MRP I and MRP II?

2 A manufacturer of electronic defence equipment uses an MRP system to control its production. At any time it has regular orders for its standard products, as well as specific orders for its specially adapted products. Occasionally also, one-off orders of standard products are received from foreign customers. Part of the company's competitive strategy is to offer a service which includes a full repair, spare parts supply and remanufacturing service to its customers. What elements will constitute the sources of demand which it must feed into its MRP system?

3 A company makes two types of mirror: the super-mirror has a golden frame, whereas the basic mirror has a plain black frame. Both mirrors are the same size. As well as the frame, the standard mirror piece and a backing piece are needed to manufacture each product. Both these last two items are exactly the same for both products. The lead time to manufacture either product is two weeks, while the lead time for the frame material is one week, for the mirror material (cut to size), three weeks, and for the backs, again cut to size, two weeks. Each mirror needs 2.5 metres of frame material. Neither product will be needed for 10 weeks when there will be an order to be filled for 200 of each type of mirror. In 11 weeks, a further 100 of these standard mirrors will be needed, and in 12 weeks 300 of the gold-framed mirrors will be needed. The next order will be in Week 14 when, again, 200 of each mirror will be needed. Currently, there is no inventory of any of the materials on hand. Using MRP procedures, derive a schedule which will meet the demand.

4 Draw up a product structure and indented bill of materials for a product described as follows. The main product A consists of one sub-assembly B and two sub-assemblies C. Sub-assembly B consists of one part D and two part Es. Sub-assembly C consists of one part E, one part F and two part Gs.

5 What different methods are available for a company to decide on how many of its parts to order at any time? What are the advantages and disadvantages of ordering whatever is required every single period?

6 What is meant by a closed-loop MRP system?

7 A company manufactures product A, which is made up of one unit of B and half a unit of C. Each unit of B is made up of one unit of D, two units of E, and one unit of F. Each unit of C needs half a unit of G

and three units of H. The lead times to manufacture all these components are as follows:

A	2 weeks	E	3 weeks
B	1 week	F	1 week
C	2 weeks	G	2 weeks
D	2 weeks	H	1 week

All these parts have 20 units in stock. It is required to make 100 units of A for delivery in seven weeks' time.

(a) Draw up a product structure and indented bill of materials for the product.

(b) Draw up a gross materials requirements plan for the manufacturer of the product.

(c) Construct a net materials requirements plan for the manufacturer of the product.

8 What would be the advantages and disadvantages for a hospital of adopting an ERP system such as SAP's R/3?

Notes on chapter

1 Wight, O. (1984) *Manufacturing Resource Planning: MRP II*, Oliver Wight Ltd.
2 Orlicky, J. (1975) *Materials Requirements Planning*, McGraw-Hill.
3 Kotler, P. (1991) *Marketing Management*, Prentice Hall.
4 Source: 'A Matter of Life and Death', *Manufacturing Today* (1993). Published by MSPL, an ICL company which installed Racal Recorders' MRP II system.
5 Source: Discussions with company staff at Staedtler.
6 Wight, O. (1984), *op. cit.*
7 Goldratt, E.M. and Cox, J. (1986) *The Goal*, North River Press.

Selected further reading

Burns, O.M., Turnipseed, D. and Riggs, W.E. (1991) 'Critical Success Factors in Manufacturing Resource Planning Implementation', *International Journal of Operations and Production Management*, Vol 11, No 4.

Buxey, G. (1993) 'Production Planning and Scheduling for Seasonal Demand', *International Journal of Operations and Production Management*, Vol 13, No 7.

Curran, T., Keller, G. and Ladd, A. (1998) *Business Blueprint: Understanding SAP's R/3 Reference Model*, Prentice Hall, NJ.

Davenport, T.H. (1998) 'Putting the Enterprise Into the Enterprise System', *Harvard Business Review*, July–August.

Financial Times (1999) 'Enterprise Resource Planning', *Financial Times Survey*, Wednesday, 15th December.

Jacobi, M.A. (1994) 'How to Unlock the Benefits of MRP II and Just-in-Time', *Hospital Maternity Management Quarterly*, Vol 15, No 4.

Luscombe, M. (1993) *MRP II: Integrating the Business*, Butterworth-Heinemann.

Orlicky, J. (1975) *Material Requirements Planning*, McGraw-Hill.

Porter, K., Little, D., Kenworthy, J. and Jarvis, P. (1996) 'Finite Capacity Scheduling Tools: Observations of Installations Offer Some Lessons', *Integrated Manufacturing Systems*, Vol 7, No 4.

Primrose, P.L. (1990) 'Selecting and Evaluating Cost Effective MRP and MRP II', *International Journal of Operations and Production Management*, Vol 10, No 1.

Shah, S. (1991) 'Optimum Order Cycles in MRP Form a Geometric Progression', *International Journal of Operations and Production Management*, Vol 11, No 5.

Soliman, F. and Youssef, M.A. (1998) 'The Role of SAP Software in Business Process Reengineering', *International Journal of Operations and Production Management*, Vol 18, No 9/10.

Vollmann, T.E., Berry, L. and Whybark, D.C. (1989) *Manufacturing Planning and Control Systems* (3rd edn), Irwin.

White, E.M., Anderson, J.C., Schroeder, R.G. and Tupy, S.E. (1982) 'A Study of the MRP Implementation Process', *Journal of Operations Management*, Vol 2, No 3.

Wight, O. (1982) *The Executive's Guide to Successful MRP II*, Prentice Hall.

Wight, O. (1984) *Manufacturing Resource Planning: MRP II*, Oliver Wight Ltd.

Wilson, F., Desmond, J. and Roberts, H. (1994) 'Success and Failure of MRP II Implementation', *British Journal of Management*, Vol 5.

Just-in-time planning and control

Introduction

Chapter 14 described MRP, one commonly used approach to operations planning and control. This chapter examines another approach which tackles the same issue but in a different way. This approach goes under the rather narrow name of 'just-in-time' (JIT). In this chapter, we will examine just-in-time (JIT) both as a philosophy and as a method of operations planning and control. This means that, for much of the chapter, we will take a relatively focused view of JIT, concentrating on its planning and control aspects, although in practice it has much wider implications for improving operations performance. In fact, many of the wider implications of JIT (often called 'lean' operations practice) underlie much of the material presented in this book. The JIT principles, which were a radical departure from traditional operations practice, have now themselves become the accepted wisdom in operations management. In effect, the chapter addresses the question: 'What is JIT, and how does it impact on operations planning and control?' Put another way, 'What are the implications of arranging for the delivery of goods (and sometimes services), literally, 'just-in-time' for them to be used by their internal or external customers?' Figure 15.1 illustrates the concept of JIT planning and control.

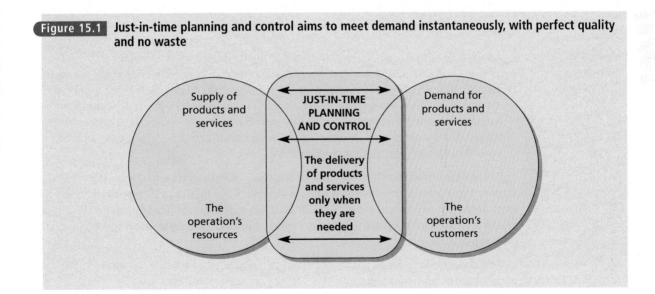

Figure 15.1 Just-in-time planning and control aims to meet demand instantaneously, with perfect quality and no waste

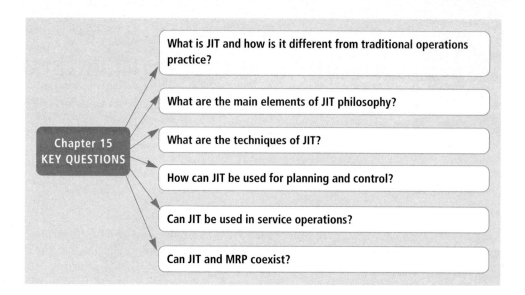

Chapter 15
KEY QUESTIONS

What is JIT and how is it different from traditional operations practice?

What are the main elements of JIT philosophy?

What are the techniques of JIT?

How can JIT be used for planning and control?

Can JIT be used in service operations?

Can JIT and MRP coexist?

What is just-in-time?

At its most basic, JIT can be taken literally – JIT means producing goods and services exactly when they are needed: not before they are needed so that they wait as inventory, nor after they are needed so that it is the customers who have to wait. In addition to this 'time-based' element of JIT we can add the requirements of quality and efficiency. A definition of JIT can then be taken as follows:[1]

> JIT aims to meet demand instantaneously, with perfect quality and no waste.

Alternatively, for those who prefer a fuller definition:[2]

> Just-in-time (JIT) is a disciplined approach to improving overall productivity and eliminating waste. It provides for the cost-effective production and delivery of only the necessary quantity of parts at the right quality, at the right time and place, while using a minimum amount of facilities, equipment, materials and human resources. JIT is dependent on the balance between the supplier's flexibility and the user's flexibility. It is accomplished through the application of elements which require total employee involvement and teamwork. A key philosophy of JIT is simplification.

Remember, though, that the first definition is a statement of aims. JIT will not achieve these aims immediately. Rather, it describes a state that a JIT approach helps to work towards. No definition of JIT fully conveys its full implications for operations practice, however. This is why so many different phrases and terms exist to describe JIT-type approaches, for example:

- lean operations
- continuous flow manufacture
- high value-added manufacture
- stockless production
- war on waste
- fast-throughput manufacturing
- short cycle time manufacturing.

The best way to understand how a JIT approach differs from more traditional approaches to manufacturing is to contrast the two simple manufacturing systems in Figure 15.2. The traditional approach assumes that each stage in the manufacturing process will place the parts it produces in an inventory which 'buffers' that stage from the next one downstream in the total process. The next stage down will then (eventually) take the parts from the inventory, process them, and pass them through to the next buffer inventory. These buffers are not there accidentally; they are there to insulate each stage from its neighbours. The buffers make each stage relatively independent so that if, for example, stage A stops producing for some reason (say a machine breakdown or parts shortage), stage B can continue working, at least for a time. Stage C can continue working for even longer because it has the contents of two buffers to get through before it runs out of work. The larger the buffer inventory, the greater is the degree of insulation between the stages, and therefore the less is the disruption caused when a problem occurs. This insulation has to be paid for in terms of inventory (working capital) and slow throughput times (slow customer response) but it does allow each stage to operate in an uninterrupted, and therefore efficient, manner.

The main argument against this traditional approach lies in the very conditions it seeks to promote, namely the insulation of the stages from one another. When a problem occurs at one stage, the problem will not immediately be apparent elsewhere in the system. The responsibility for solving the problem will be centred largely on the staff within that stage, and the consequences of the problem will be prevented from spreading to the whole system. However, contrast this position with that illustrated in the bottom system in Figure 15.2, which is an extreme form of JIT. Here parts are produced and then passed directly to the next stage 'just-in-time' for them to be processed. Problems at any stage have a very different effect in such a system. For example, now if stage A stops production, stage B will notice immediately and stage C very soon after. Stage A's problem is now quickly exposed to the whole system and the whole system is affected by the problem. One result of this is that the responsibility for solving the problem is no longer confined to the staff at stage A but is now shared by everyone. This considerably improves the chances of the problem being solved, if only because it is now too important to be ignored. In other words, by preventing inventory from accumulating between stages, the operation has increased the chances of the intrinsic efficiency of the plant being improved.

Although simplified, this highlights the differences between a traditional and a JIT approach. Although they both seek to encourage high efficiency in the operation, they

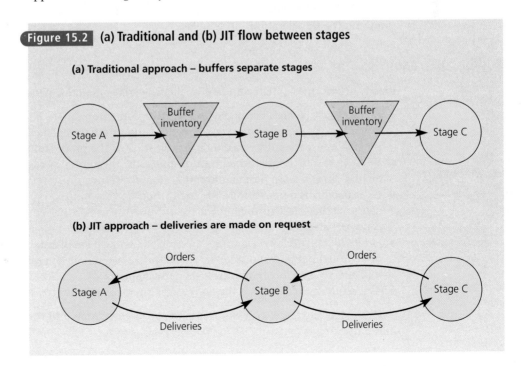

Figure 15.2 **(a) Traditional and (b) JIT flow between stages**

(a) Traditional approach – buffers separate stages

Stage A → Buffer inventory → Stage B → Buffer inventory → Stage C

(b) JIT approach – deliveries are made on request

Stage A — Orders / Deliveries — Stage B — Orders / Deliveries — Stage C

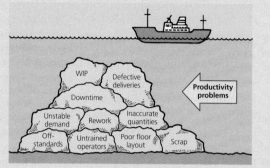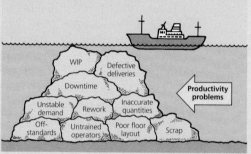

take different routes to doing so. Traditional approaches seek to encourage efficiency by protecting each part of the operation from disruption. Long, uninterrupted production runs are its ideal state. The JIT approach takes the opposite view. Exposure of the system (although not suddenly, as in our simplified example) to problems can both make them more evident and change the 'motivation structure' of the whole system towards solving the problems. JIT sees inventory as a 'blanket of obscurity' which lies over the production system and prevents problems being noticed. The idea of obscuring effects of inventory is often illustrated diagrammatically, as in Figure 15.3. The many problems of the operation are shown as rocks in a river bed which cannot be seen because of the depth of the water. The water in this analogy represents the inventory in the operation. Yet, even though the rocks cannot be seen, they slow the progress of the river's flow and cause turbulence. Gradually reducing the depth of the water (inventory) exposes the worst of the problems which can be resolved, after which the water is lowered further, exposing more problems, and so on.

The same argument can be used to characterize the relationship between the stages of production on a larger scale, where each stage is a 'macro' operation. Here stages A, B and C could be a supplier operation, a manufacturer and a customer's operation, respectively. At this level the two approaches are traditional 'mass production' operations and the JIT operation.

● What JIT requires

Ideally, JIT requires a high standard in all an operation's performance objectives:

- *Quality* must be high because disruption in production due to quality errors will slow down the throughput of materials, reduce the internal dependability of supply, and possibly cause inventory to build up if errors slow the production rate.
- *Speed*, in terms of fast throughput of materials, is essential if customer demand is to be met directly from production rather than from inventory.
- *Dependability* is a prerequisite for fast throughput, or put the opposite way, it is difficult to achieve fast throughput if the supply of parts or the reliability of equipment is not dependable.
- *Flexibility* is especially important in order to achieve small batch sizes and therefore fast throughput and short delivery lead times. We are referring here primarily to the mix and volume flexibilities described in Chapter 2.
- As a result of excellence in the above performance objectives, *cost* is reduced.

Ultimately the target cost is the sum of the raw materials and the value-adding activities only.

JIT and capacity utilization

Even in advanced JIT, operations achieving high standards in all performance objectives do demand some sacrifice. In JIT the main sacrifice is capacity utilization. Return to the production system shown in Figure 15.2. When production stoppages occur in the traditional system, the buffers allow each stage to continue working and thus achieve high capacity utilization. The high utilization does not necessarily make the system as a whole produce more parts. Often the extra production goes into the large buffer inventories. In the JIT system, any stoppage will affect the rest of the system, causing stoppages throughout the operation. This will necessarily lead to lower capacity utilization, at least in the short term. However, JIT proponents would argue that there is no point in producing output just for its own sake. Unless the output is useful and causes the operation as a whole to produce saleable products, there is no point in producing it anyway. In fact, producing just to keep utilization high is not only pointless, it is counter-productive, because the extra inventory produced merely serves to make improvements less likely. For a given level of demand, capacity requirements are often lower under JIT conditions. Figure 15.4 illustrates the two approaches to capacity utilization.

Figure 15.4 **The different views of capacity utilization in (a) traditional and (b) JIT approaches to operations**

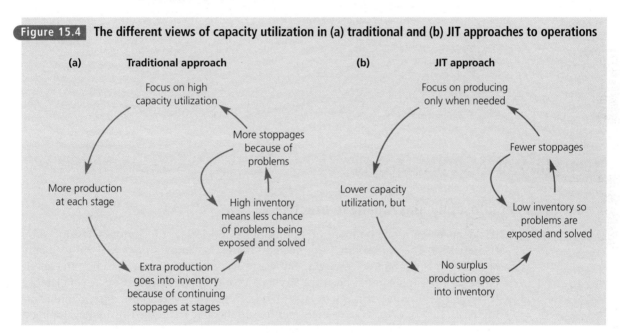

JIT – a philosophy and a set of techniques

To understand JIT it must be viewed on two levels. At its most general, JIT is often called a philosophy of manufacturing: that is, JIT gives a clear view which can be used to guide the actions of operations managers in many different activities and many different contexts. At the same time, JIT is a collection of several tools and techniques which promote the operational conditions that support its philosophy. Some of these tools and techniques are well known outside the JIT sphere and relate to activities covered in other chapters of this book. Other techniques relate specifically to the way production is planned and controlled under a JIT regime. This chapter summarizes JIT philosophy, draws together some of the techniques described elsewhere, and treats in more detail the planning and control aspects of JIT (*see* Fig. 15.5).

> **Figure 15.5** JIT is a philosophy, a set of techniques and a method of planning and control

JIT as a philosophy of operations

- Eliminate waste
- Involve everyone
- Continuous improvement

JIT as a set of techniques for managing operations

- Basic working practices
- Design for manufacture
- Operations focus
- Small simple machines
- Layout and flow
- TPM
- Set-up reduction
- Total people involvement
- Visibility
- JIT supply

JIT as a method of planning and control

- Pull scheduling
- Kanban control
- Levelled scheduling
- Mixed modelling
- Synchronization

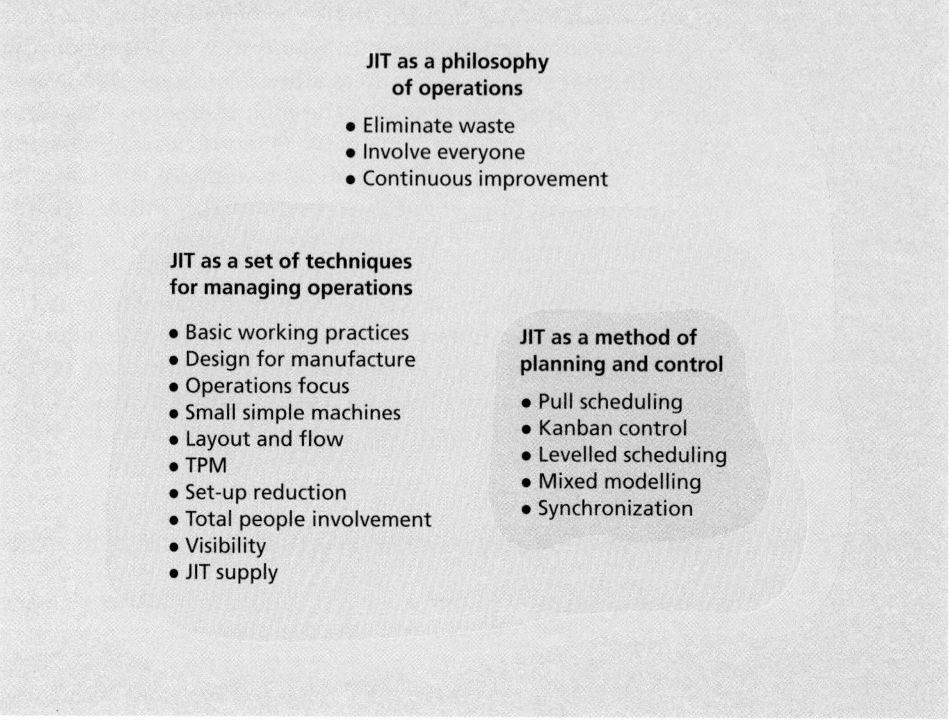

The philosophy of just-in-time

● Just-in-time philosophy and Japanese practice

JIT is the Western embodiment of a philosophy and series of techniques developed by the Japanese. The philosophy is founded on doing the simple things well, on gradually doing them better and on squeezing out waste every step of the way. Leading the development of JIT in Japan has been the Toyota Motor Company (*see* box on Toyota later in this chapter). Toyota's strategy in Japan has been progressively to interface manufacturing more closely with its customers and its suppliers. It has done this by developing a set of practices which has largely shaped what we now call JIT. Indeed some would argue that the origins of JIT lie within Toyota's reaction to the 'oil shock' of rising oil prices in the early 1970s.[3] The need for improved manufacturing efficiencies that this provoked spurred Toyota to accelerate its JIT ideas which were already forming. These developments by Toyota, and other Japanese manufacturers, were undoubtedly encouraged by the national cultural and economic circumstances. Japan's attitude towards waste ('make every grain of rice count'), together with its position as a crowded and virtually naturally resourceless country, produced ideal conditions in which to devise a manufacturing philosophy which emphasizes low waste and high added value. An alternative explanation of JIT's origins looks back to Japan's shipbuilding industry.[4] In the late 1950s and early 1960s, over-capacity among Japan's steelmakers meant that shipbuilders could demand deliveries of steel precisely when they wanted them. Because of this, the shipbuilders improved production methods so that they could reduce their steel inventories from about one month's worth to three days' worth. As the advantages of low stock-holding became apparent, the idea spread to other parts of Japanese industry.

Assembly lines such as this could not operate to today's high levels of quality and cost without just-in-time principles and techniques

The high dependency theory

One explanation of the JIT approach to operations management is called the high dependency theory.[5] It derives partly from the logic which we used earlier to describe the benefits of low buffer inventories. With high inventories insulating each stage in the production process, the dependency of the stages on one another was low. Take away the inventory and their mutual dependency increases. This is not the only example of high dependency in JIT (and Japanese practice generally). The JIT practice of empowering 'shop-floor' staff makes the organization dependent on their actions. The use of the internal customer concept (mentioned in Chapter 1 but explained further in Chapter 20) formalizes the dependence between all parts of the operation. The use of total productive maintenance (TPM, explained in Chapter 19) and the JIT-influenced supplier development policies (from Chapter 13) are also examples of dependency. Professors Nick Oliver and Barry Wilkinson sum up the dependency theory in the following way:[6]

> *Japanese systems of production, particularly JIT and total quality control, heighten the dependency of the organization on its agencies, or 'constituents', especially employees and supplying companies. This means … that the ability of the organization's constituents to exert leverage in their own interests is increased. The obvious implication is that it is imperative that such organizations take steps to counterbalance this by averting the possibility of such power being used …. In the light of the vulnerability of Japanese production systems to disruption and in the light of the high dependencies of the organization on its constituents, we suggest that such a system will only work successfully in a situation where organizations have either actively taken the appropriate measures to guard against disruption, or where social, economic and political conditions automatically provide safeguards.*

Just-in-time principles can be taken to an extreme. In the 1980s, in particular, when just-in-time ideas first started to have an impact on operations practice in the West, some authorities advocated the reduction of between-process inventories to zero. While in the long term this provides the ultimate in motivation for operations managers to ensure the efficiency and reliability of each process stage, it does not admit the possibility of some processes always being intrinsically less than totally reliable. An alternative view is to allow inventories (albeit small ones) around process stages with higher than average uncertainty. This at least allows some protection for the rest of the system. The same ideas apply to just-in-time delivery between factories. The Toyota Motor Corp., often seen as the epitomy of modern JIT, has suffered from its low inter-plant inventory policies. Both the Kobe earthquake and fires in supplier plants have caused production at Toyota's main factories to close down for several days because of a shortage of key parts. Even in the best-regulated manufacturing networks, one cannot always account for such events.

● The JIT philosophy of operations

Three key issues define the core of JIT philosophy: the elimination of waste, the involvement of staff in the operation, and the drive for continuous improvement.[7] We will look at each briefly in turn.

Eliminate waste

Waste can be defined as any activity which does not add value. For example, when Cummins Engineering, the engine manufacturer, began its JIT work, it carried out a study of how long it took for a number of products to work through the factory.[8] The study showed that, at best, an engine was only being worked on for 15 per cent of the time it was in the factory. At worst, this fell to 9 per cent, which meant that for 91 per cent of its time, the operation was adding cost to the engine, not adding value. Although already a relatively efficient manufacturer in Western terms, the results alerted Cummins to the enormous waste which still lay dormant in its operations, and which no performance measure then in use had exposed. Cummins shifted its objectives to reducing the wasteful activities and to enriching the value-added ones.[9]

Identifying waste is the first step towards eliminating it. Toyota identified seven types of waste, which have been found to apply in many different types of operations – both service and production – and which form the core of JIT philosophy.

- *Over-production.* Producing more than is immediately needed by the next process in the operation is the greatest source of waste according to Toyota.
- *Waiting time.* Machine efficiency and labour efficiency are two popular measures which are widely used to measure machine and labour waiting time, respectively. Less obvious is the amount of waiting time of materials, disguised by operators who are kept busy producing WIP which is not needed at the time.
- *Transport.* Moving materials around the plant, together with the double and triple handling of WIP, does not add value. Layout changes which bring processes closer together, improvements in transport methods and workplace organization can all reduce waste.
- *Process.* The process itself may be a source of waste. Some operations may only exist because of poor component design, or poor maintenance, and so could be eliminated.[10]
- *Inventory.* Under a JIT philosophy, all inventory becomes a target for elimination. However, it is only by tackling the causes of inventory that it can be reduced.
- *Motion.* An operator may look busy but sometimes no value is being added by the work. Simplification of work is a rich source of reduction in the waste of motion.

- *Defective goods.* Quality waste is often very significant in operations, even if actual measures of quality are limited. Total costs of quality are much greater than has traditionally been considered, and it is therefore more important to attack the causes of such costs. This is discussed further in Chapter 20.

The involvement of everyone

JIT philosophy is often put forward as a 'total' system. Its aim is to provide guidelines which embrace everyone and every process in the organization. An organization's culture is seen as being important in supporting these objectives through an emphasis on involving all of the organization's staff. This new culture is sometimes seen as synonymous with 'total quality' and is discussed in detail in Chapter 20.

This JIT approach to people management has also been called the 'respect-for-humans' system. It encourages (and often requires) team-based problem-solving, job enrichment (by including maintenance and setup tasks in operators' jobs), job rotation and multi-skilling. The intention is to encourage a high degree of personal responsibility, engagement and 'ownership' of the job.

● CRITICAL COMMENTARY

Not all commentators see JIT-influenced people-management practices as entirely positive. The JIT approach to people management can be viewed as patronizing. It may be, to some extent, less autocratic than some Japanese management practice dating from earlier times. However, it is certainly not in line with some of the job design philosophies which place a high emphasis on contribution and commitment, described in Chapter 9. Even in Japan the approach of JIT is not without its critics. Kamata wrote an autobiographical description of life as an employee at a Toyota plant called *Japan in the Passing Lane*.[11] His account speaks of 'the inhumanity and the unquestioning adherence' of working under such a system. Similar criticisms have been voiced by some trade union representatives.

Continuous improvement

JIT objectives are often expressed as ideals, such as our previous definition: 'to meet demand instantaneously with perfect quality and no waste'. While any organization's performance may be far removed from such ideals, a fundamental belief of JIT is that it is possible to get closer to them over time. Without such beliefs to drive progress, JIT proponents claim improvement is more likely to be transitory than continuous. This is why the concept of continuous improvement is such an important part of JIT philosophy. If the aims of JIT are set in terms of ideals which individual organizations may never fully achieve, then the emphasis must be on the way in which an organization moves closer to the ideal state. The Japanese word for continuous improvement is *kaizen*, and it is a key part of JIT philosophy. It is explained fully in Chapter 18.

JIT overcomes high labour costs [12]

One effect of an increasing global approach to business has been to highlight the relatively high labour costs which engineering manufacturing companies have to live with. This has led to two broad trends. The first is that many engineering companies are increasing the proportion of service in their product offerings. This can help to reduce the importance of manufacturing costs because customers are prepared to pay for the extra service value added. The second trend is to attempt to reduce manufacturing costs through JIT methods. Take two examples:

Jungheinrich is one of the world's biggest producers of lift trucks. Its products are found all over the world in factories, warehouses and anywhere that needs heavy objects moving short distances. The company's Hamburg factory makes over 30 000 lift trucks a year of around 10 000 varieties which are based on 10 basic platforms. JIT methods of manufacture allow the company to assemble each product in three hours. Only three or four years previously it would have taken 18 hours. Between 1998 and 2000 the company increased output from its Hamburg plant by 30 per cent, with 10 per cent fewer workers. Hans-Peter Schmohl, the company's CEO, attributes much of the company's success to improved links with its suppliers and smooth flow within the factory: 'To be competitive in this industry you need highly sophisticated logistics capabilities, plus a just-in-time culture.'

Komax is the world's largest maker of the machines that make wiring harnesses for automobiles. The company is based in Switzerland which, like Germany, has high labour costs. Yet, on sales of around $100m, it exports 99 per cent of its production. Again, this company doubled its sales while reducing the number of employees. Partly it succeeded in doing this because of a policy of outsourcing some of its manufacturing. But this could only work with JIT delivery. From requiring their suppliers to deliver every two months, the company organized them to deliver three times a week. This reduced inventories throughout the plant and speeded up throughput time.

JIT techniques

The 'engine room' of JIT is a collection of tools and techniques which are the means for cutting out waste. There are many techniques which could be termed 'JIT techniques' and they follow on naturally and logically from the overall JIT philosophy.

Basic working practices

'Basic working practices' form the basic preparation of the organization and its staff and are fundamental to implementing JIT.

Discipline
Work standards which are critical for the safety of company members and the environment, and for the quality of the product, must be followed by everyone all the time.

Flexibility
It should be possible to expand responsibilities to the extent of people's capabilities. This applies as equally to managers as it does to shop-floor personnel. Barriers to flexibility, such as grading structures and restrictive practices, should be removed.

Equality
Unfair and divisive personnel policies should be discarded. Many traditional organizations have divisive 'perks' for different grades of personnel: staff car parks and dining rooms, for example. Some companies are taking the egalitarian message further – to company uniforms, consistent pay structures which do not differentiate between full-time staff and hourly-rated staff, and open-plan offices.

Autonomy
Another principle is to delegate increasing responsibility to people involved in direct activities of the business, so that management's task becomes one of supporting the shop floor. Types of autonomy include the following:

- *Line stop authority.* If a quality problem arises, an assembly line operative has the authority to stop the line.
- *Materials scheduling.* Many routine aspects of materials scheduling can thereby be delegated away from the central production control system.

- *Data gathering.* Data relevant to shop-floor performance monitoring is gathered and used by shop-floor personnel.
- *Problem solving.* Shop-floor personnel get the first opportunity to solve problems that affect the work they do. Only if they need help from experts should that help be sought and provided.

Development of personnel
Over time, the aim is to create more company members who can support the rigours of being competitive.

Quality of working life (QWL)
This may include, for example, involvement in decision-making, security of employment, enjoyment and working area facilities.

Creativity
This is one of the indispensable elements of motivation. Most of us enjoy not just doing the job successfully, but also improving it for the next time.

In practice, it is difficult to achieve all the 'basic working practices' at the same time. There are trade-offs between discipline, autonomy and creativity, for example. It is best to consider these basic working practices as goals to be achieved.

Design for manufacture

Studies in automotive and aerospace companies have shown that design determines 70–80 per cent of production costs.[13] Design improvements can dramatically reduce product cost through changes in the number of components and sub-assemblies, and better use of materials and processing techniques. Often improvements of this magnitude would not be remotely possible by manufacturing efficiency improvements alone.

Operations focus

The concept behind operations focus is that simplicity, repetition and experience breed competence.[14] Focus within manufacturing is:

- learning to focus each plant on limited, manageable sets of products, technologies, volumes and markets;
- learning to structure basic manufacturing policies and supporting services so that they focus on one explicit manufacturing task instead of many implicit, inconsistent, conflicting tasks.

Small simple machines

The principle behind this technique is that several small machines are used instead of one large machine. Also 'home-grown', inexpensive equipment can be used to modify general-purpose machines so that they perform more reliably, are easy to maintain and produce better quality over time. This demands that in-house engineering skills are available and can be utilized to modify the machines so that new models can be introduced inexpensively. Small machines are also easily moved, so that layout flexibility is enhanced, and the risks of making errors in investment decisions are reduced because small machines usually require lower investment.

● Layout and flow

Layout techniques can be used to promote the smooth flow of materials, data and people in the operation. Flow is an important concept in JIT. Long process routes around a factory provide opportunities for inventory build-up, add no value to the products, and slow down the throughput time of products, all of which are contrary to JIT principles. Considerations for layout and flow are described in Chapter 7. The principles of layout which JIT particularly recommends are:

- placing workstations close together so that inventory cannot build up;
- placing workstations in such a way that all those that make up a particular part are in sight of each other, making flow transparent to all parts of the line;
- using U-shaped lines so that staff can move between workstations to balance capacity;
- adopting a cell-based layout (*see* Chapter 7).

● Total productive maintenance (TPM)

Total productive maintenance aims to eliminate the variability in operations processes caused by the effect of unplanned breakdowns. This is achieved by involving everyone in the search for maintenance improvements. Process owners are encouraged to assume ownership of their machines and to undertake routine maintenance and simple repair tasks. By so doing, maintenance specialists can then be freed to develop higher-order skills for improved maintenance systems. TPM is treated in more detail in Chapter 19.

Photo courtesy of BMW

Even massive press tools such as these which press out car body panels can be changed over relatively quickly thanks to fast changeover techniques like the in-line roller surfaces

● Setup reduction (SUR)

Setup time is defined as the time taken to change over the process from the previous batch to the first good piece of the next batch. Compare the time it takes you to change the tyre on your car with the time taken by a Formula 1 team. In SUR, setup times can be reduced by a variety of methods such as cutting out time taken to search for tools and equipment, the pre-preparation of tasks which delay changeovers, and the constant practice of setup routines. Often, relatively simple mechanical changes can reduce setup times considerably.

The other common approach to SUR is to convert work which was previously performed while the machine was stopped (called *internal* work) to work that is performed while the machine is running (called *external* work). There are three major methods of achieving the transfer of internal setup work to external work:[15]

- Pre-set tools so that a complete unit is fixed to the machine instead of having to be built up while the machine is stopped. Preferably, all adjustment should be carried out externally, so that the internal set-up is an assembly operation only.
- Attach the different tools or dyes to a standard fixture or jig. Again, this enables the internal setup to consist of a simple and standardized assembly operation.
- Make the loading and unloading of new tools and dyes easy. Using improved materials-handling devices, such as roller conveyor ball-mounted surface tables, can help greatly.

SUR is the means by which Cummins Engineering first convinced itself of the power of JIT. Setup time on the head face drill (a CNC machine tool on the block line) was 17 minutes. The operator team reduced this time to just eight seconds, and spent less than £100 in doing so. Within a few months, all setup times on the block line were down to less than five minutes. Batch sizes were cut from about 80 (two weeks' production) to one.[16]

Flexibility helps JIT at L'Oréal[17]

L'Oréal cosmetics is now the world's largest toiletries and cosmetics group, with a presence in over 140 different countries. In the UK, the 45 000 square metre purpose-built facility in mid-Wales produces 1300 product types in a spotlessly clean environment, which is akin to a pharmaceutical plant in terms of hygiene, safety and quality. The plant has 55 production lines and 45 different production processes, and the manufacturing systems employed are of a flexibility that allows them to run each of the 1300 product types every two months – that means over 150 different products each week. But the plant was not always as flexible as this. It has been forced to enhance its flexibility by the requirement to ship over 80 million items each year. The sheer logistics involved in purchasing, producing, storing and distributing the volume and variety of goods has led to its current focus on introducing JIT principles into the manufacturing process.

To help achieve its drive for flexibility and for JIT production, L'Oréal organized the site into three production centres, each autonomous and focused within technical families of products. Their processes and production lines are then further focused within product sub-divisions. Responsible for all the activities within his area, from pre-weighing to dispatch, is the Production Centre Manager, whose role also encompasses staff development, training and motivation. Within the focused production centres, improvement groups have been working on improving shop-floor flexibility, quality and efficiency. One of the projects reduced the setup times on the line which produces hair colourants from 2.5 hours to only eight minutes. These new changeover times mean that the company can now justify even smaller batches, and may give the company the flexibility to meet market needs just-in-time. Prior to the change in setup time, batch size was 30 000 units; now batches as small as 2000–3000 units can be produced cost-effectively.

Questions

1 What did L'Oréal do to help it organize the process of setup reduction?

2 What do you think L'Oréal gained from doing each of these things?

3 If we could halve all changeover times in the factory, what effect would this have on inventory?

● Total people involvement

Total people involvement[18] can be seen as an extension of 'basic working practices'. However, it sees staff taking on much more responsibility to use their abilities to the benefit of the company as a whole. They are trained, capable and motivated to take full responsibility for all aspects of the work they do. In turn, they are trusted to carry out these responsibilities with autonomy for their own work area. Staff are expected to participate in activities such as the following:

- the selection of new recruits;
- dealing directly with suppliers over schedules, quality issues and delivery information;
- the self-measurement of performance and improvement trends;
- spending improvement budgets (SP Tyres reputedly allocates 25 per cent of capital budgets to be spent by operators[19]);
- planning and reviewing work done each day through communication meetings;
- dealing directly with customer problems and requirements.

● Visibility

Problems, quality projects and operations checklists are made visible by displaying them so that they can be easily seen and understood by all staff. Visibility measures include:

- displayed performance measures in the workplace;
- coloured lights indicating stoppages;
- displayed SPC control charts (*see* Chapter 17);
- visible improvement techniques and checklists;
- a separate area displaying samples of own company products and competitors' products together with samples of good and defective products;
- visual control systems such as kanbans;
- open-plan workplace layouts.

● JIT supply

Just-in-time supply epitomizes the popular meaning of the term 'JIT' and conjures up the vision of parts arriving at the assembly process 'just-in-time'. Indeed, a misinterpretation of this view was first seized upon by some non-Japanese manufacturers, who often forced their suppliers to deliver just-in-time, while contributing little or nothing to improved logistics themselves. JIT supply is in fact a very rich area for improvement activity. In Chapter 13 we described 'partnerships', 'lean' relationships and 'integrated concepts' which are all based on JIT supply principles.

JIT planning and control

One of the sources of waste identified earlier was that caused by inventory timing. Poor inventory timing (parts arrive too early or too late) causes unpredictability in an operation. Inventory timing is governed by the two schools of thought which were described in Chapter 10: 'push' planning and control, and 'pull' planning and control. JIT planning and control is based on the principle of a 'pull system', while the MRP approach to planning and control, described in the previous chapter, is a 'push system'.

● Kanban control

The term *kanban* has sometimes been used as being equivalent to 'JIT planning and control' (which it is not) or even to the whole of JIT (which it most certainly is not). However, kanban control is one method of operationalizing a pull-based planning and control system. Kanban is the Japanese for card or signal. It is sometimes called the 'invisible conveyor' which controls the transfer of materials between the stages of an operation. In its simplest form, it is a card used by a customer stage to instruct its supplier stage to send more materials. Kanbans can also take other forms. In some Japanese companies, they are solid plastic markers or even coloured ping-pong balls, the different colours representing different parts. There are also different types of kanban:

- *The move or conveyance kanban.* A move kanban is used to signal to a previous stage that material can be withdrawn from inventory and transferred to a specific destination. This type of kanban would normally have details of the particular part's name and number, the place from which it should be taken, and the destination to which it is being delivered.
- *The production kanban.* This is a signal to a production process that it can start producing a part or item to be placed in an inventory. The information contained on this type of kanban usually includes the particular part's name and number, a description of the process itself, the materials required for the production of the part, and the destination to which the part or parts need to be sent when they are produced.
- *The vendor kanban.* These are used to signal to a supplier to send material or parts to a stage. In this way, it is similar to a move kanban but it is usually used with external suppliers.

Whichever kind of kanban is being used, the principle is always the same; that is, that the receipt of a kanban triggers the movement, production or supply of one unit or a standard container of units. If two kanbans are received, this triggers the movement, production or supply of two units or standard containers of units, and so on. The kanbans are the only means by which movement, production or supply can be authorized. This is true even when the kanban is not a card or object. Some companies use 'kanban squares'. These are marked spaces on the shop floor or bench which are drawn to fit one or more workpieces or containers. The existence of an empty square triggers production at the stage which supplies the square. Full squares mean that the preceding process must stop. Other variants include container-as-kanban (where the empty container acts as an instruction), verbal (simply shouting 'send some more'!), and colour-coded tokens (e.g. red = top priority, orange = moderate, green = normal).

There are two procedures which can govern the use of kanbans. These are known as the single-card system and the dual-card system. The single-card system is most often used because it is by far the simplest system to operate. It uses only move kanbans (or vendor kanbans when receiving supply of material from an outside source). The dual-card system uses both move and production kanbans.

The single-card system

Figure 15.6 shows the operation of a single-card kanban system. At each stage (only two stages are shown, A and B) there is a work centre and an area for holding inventory. All production and inventory are contained in standard containers, all of which contain exactly the same number of parts. When stage B requires some more parts to work on, it withdraws a standard container from the output stock point of stage A. After work centre B has used the parts in the container, it places the move kanban in a holding area and sends the empty container to the work centre at stage A. The arrival of the empty containers at stage A's work centre is the signal for production to take place at work centre A. The move kanban is taken from the holding box back to the output stock point of stage A. This acts as authorization for the collection of a further full container to be moved from the output stock of stage A through to the work centre at stage B. Two closed loops effectively control the flow of materials between the stages. The move kanban loop (illustrated by the thin arrows) keeps materials circulating between the stages, and the container loop (illustrated by the thicker arrows) connects the work centres with the stock point between them and circulates the containers, full from A to B and empty back from B to A.

The sequence of actions and the flow of kanbans may at first seem complicated. However, in practice their use provides a straightforward and transparent method of

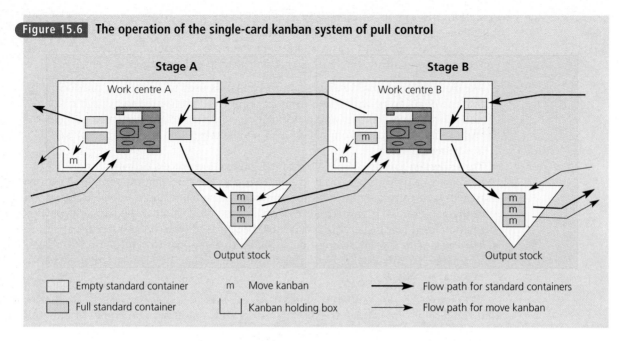

Figure 15.6 The operation of the single-card kanban system of pull control

calling for material only when it is needed and limiting the inventory which accumulates between stages. The number of kanbans put into the loops between the stages or between the stock points and the work centres is equal to the number of containers in the system and therefore the inventory which can accumulate. Taking a kanban out of the loop has the effect of reducing the inventory. In summary, the rules which govern the use of kanbans are as follows:

- Each container must have a kanban card, indicating part number and description, user and maker locations, and quantity.
- The parts are always pulled by the succeeding process (the customer or user).
- No parts are started without a kanban card.
- All containers contain exactly their stated number of parts.
- No defective parts may be sent to the succeeding process.
- The maker (supplier section) can only produce enough parts to make up what has been withdrawn.
- The number of kanbans should be reduced.
- The time period should be made shorter (months to weeks to days to hours).

These simple rules can be used to plan and control many other operations tasks. For example, spare parts benefit from the visibility and discipline that a kanban brings – so that instead of electric motors lying in an unsorted heap in a corner of a maintenance department, kanban control would allow working parts to be stored in exact locations in exact quantities. When one is required for repair, the kanban card could be used to place a replenishment order.

Levelled scheduling

Heijunka is the Japanese word for overall levelling of the production schedule so that mix and volume are even over time. For example, instead of producing 500 parts in one batch, which would cover the needs for the next three months, levelled scheduling would require the operation to make only one piece per hour regularly. The principle of levelled scheduling is straightforward but the requirements to put it into practice are quite severe, although the benefits resulting from it can be substantial. The move from conventional to levelled scheduling is illustrated in Figure 15.7. Conventionally, if a mix of products were required in a time period (usually a month), a batch size would be calculated for each product and the batches produced in some sequence. Figure 15.7(a) shows three products which are produced in a 20-day time period in a production unit.

Quantity of product A required = 3000
Quantity of product B required = 1000
Quantity of product C required = 1000

Batch size of product A = 600
Batch size of product B = 200
Batch size of product C = 200

Starting at day 1, the unit commences producing product A. During day 3, the batch of 600 As is finished and dispatched to the next stage. The batch of Bs is started but is not finished until day 4. The remainder of day 4 is spent making the batch of Cs and both batches are dispatched at the end of that day. The cycle then repeats itself. The consequence of using large batches is, first, that relatively large amounts of inventory accumulate within and between the units, and second, that most days are different from one another in terms of what they are expected to produce (in more complex circumstances, no two days would be the same).

Now suppose that the flexibility of the unit could be increased to the point where the batch sizes for the products were reduced to a quarter of their previous levels without loss of capacity (see Fig. 15.7b):

Batch size of product A = 150
Batch size of product B = 50
Batch size of product C = 50

Figure 15.7 **Levelled scheduling equalizes the mix of products made each day**

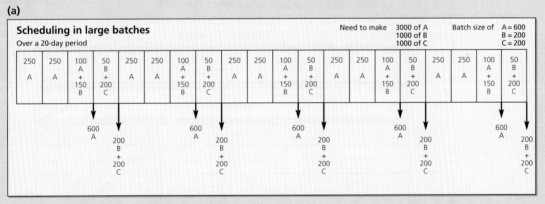

A batch of each product can now be completed in a single day, at the end of which the three batches are dispatched to their next stage. Smaller batches of inventory are moving between each stage, which will reduce the overall level of work-in-progress in the operation. Just as significant, however, is the effect on the regularity and rhythm of production at the unit. Now every day in the month is the same in terms of what needs to be produced. This makes planning and control of each stage in the operation much easier. For example, if on day 1 of the month the daily batch of As was finished by 11.00 am, and all the batches were successfully completed in the day, then the following day the unit will know that, if it again completes all the As by 11.00 am, it is on schedule. When every day is different, the simple question 'Are we on schedule to complete our production today?' requires some investigation before it can be answered. However, when every day is the same, everyone in the unit can tell whether production is on target by looking at the clock. Control becomes visible and transparent to all, and the advantages of regular, daily schedules can be passed to upstream suppliers.

● Mixed modelling

The principle of levelled scheduling can be taken further to give a repeated mix of parts. Suppose that the machines in the production unit can be made so flexible that they achieve the JIT ideal of a batch size of one. The sequence of individual products emerging from the unit could be reduced progressively as illustrated in Figure 15.8. This would produce a steady stream of each product flowing continuously from the unit.

However, the sequence of products does not always fall as conveniently as in Figure 15.8. The unit production times for each product are not usually identical and the ratios of required volumes are less convenient.

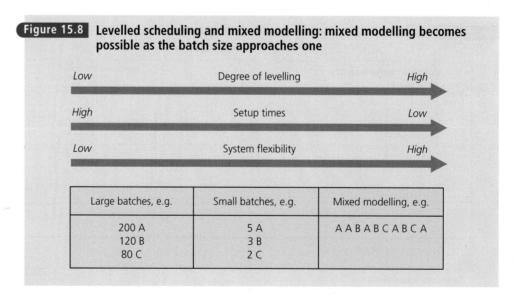

Figure 15.8 Levelled scheduling and mixed modelling: mixed modelling becomes possible as the batch size approaches one

Large batches, e.g.	Small batches, e.g.	Mixed modelling, e.g.
200 A 120 B 80 C	5 A 3 B 2 C	A A B A B C A B C A

● Synchronization

Many companies make a wide variety of parts and products, not all of them with sufficient regularity to warrant the full levelled scheduling treatment. Synchronization means the pacing of output at each stage in the production process to ensure the same flow characteristics for each part or product as it progresses through each stage. To do this, parts need to be classified according to the frequency with which they are demanded. One method of doing this distinguishes between runners, repeaters and strangers:[20]

- *Runners* are products or parts which are produced frequently, such as every week.
- *Repeaters* are products or parts which are produced regularly, but at longer time intervals.
- *Strangers* are products or parts which are produced at irregular and possibly unpredictable time intervals.

There are advantages in trying to reduce the variability of timing intervals for producing runners and repeaters. The aim is to synchronize processes concerned with parts and sub-assemblies for such products so that they appear to take place on a 'drum beat' pulse which governs material movements. It might even be better to slow down faster operations than to have them produce more than can be handled in the same time by the next process. In this way, output is made regular and predictable.

Worked example

Suppose the number of products required in the 20-day period are:

Product A = 1920
Product B = 1200
Product C = 960

Assuming an eight-hour day, the cycle time for each product – that is, the interval between the production of each of the same type of product (*see* Chapter 7 for a full explanation of cycle time) – is as follows:

Product A, cycle time $= 20 \times 8 \times 60/1920 = 5$ mins
Product B, cycle time $= 20 \times 8 \times 60/1200 = 18$ mins
Product C, cycle time $= 20 \times 8 \times 60/960 = 10$ mins

So, the production unit must produce:

1 unit of A every 5 minutes
1 unit of B every 8 minutes
1 unit of C every 10 minutes.

Put another way, by finding the common factor of 5, 8 and 10:

8 units of A every 40 minutes
5 units of B every 40 minutes
4 units of C every 40 minutes.

This means that a sequence which mixes eight units of A, five of B and four of C, and repeats itself every 40 minutes, will produce the required output. There will be many different ways of sequencing the products to achieve this mix, for example:

... BACABACABACABACAB ... repeated ... repeated

This sequence repeats itself every 40 minutes and produces the correct mix of products to satisfy the monthly requirements.

Toyota Production System

Toyota's version of JIT, which it calls the Toyota Production System (TPS), has been the driving force behind its advance into what has been called a 'truly great manufacturing company'. The 'two pillars' of TPS are (and have always been):

- *Just-in-time* – the rapid and coordinated movement of parts throughout the production system and supply chain to meet customer demand. JIT is operationalized by means of *heijunka* (levelling and smoothing the flow of materials), *kanban* (signalling to the preceding process that more parts are needed) and *nagare* (laying out processes to achieve smoother flow of parts throughout the production process).

- *Jidoka* – humanizing the interface between operator and machine. Toyota's philosophy is that the machine is there to serve the operator's purpose, while the operator should be free to exercise his/her judgement. Jidoka is operationalized by means of fail-safeing (*see* Chapter 19) or machine jidoka, line-stop authority or human jidoka, and visual control – at-a-glance status of production processes and visibility of process standards.

To Toyota the key control tool is its kanban system. The kanban is seen as serving three purposes:

- It is an instruction for the preceding process to send more.
- It is a visual control tool to show up areas of over-production and lack of synchronization.
- It is a tool for *kaizen* (continuous improvement). Toyota's rules state that 'the number of kanbans should be reduced over time'.

Toyota uses two of the basic types of kanban to support JIT pull scheduling: the 'production' kanban and the 'move' kanban. The production kanban authorizes the preceding process to make more parts. This kanban comes in two variants: the multi-process kanban for complex activities such as machining, and the single-process kanban for simple activities such as press work and casting. The move kanban shows the timing and quantity of parts involved when a process owner picks up a new supply of parts from a preceding process. This kanban also comes in two variants: internal (for internal suppliers) and external (for external suppliers).

Examples of the use of production and move kanbans are shown in Figure 15.9. The two-kanban system provides tight control, not only over production but also over movement. Kanbans replace works orders and routing cards with a simple, visual control system which enables routine material control to be delegated to process owners.

The number of parts per container is governed by factors such as part size and commonality between processes. Toyota believes that it is usually best that the number is divisible by 8 to facilitate hourly synchronization. This also means that the number of

---

Figure 15.9 Move kanbans and production kanbans at Toyota

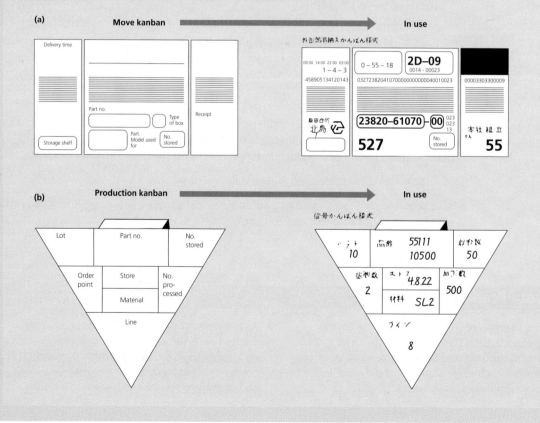

parts per container should be standardized where possible. The number of containers (hence the number of kanbans) is influenced by demand per hour, the lead time for the part and the number of parts per container. This is increased by a factor to allow for disruptions such as breakdowns and absenteeism. The number of kanbans should, of course, never be fixed, but subject to kaizen.

Major sub-assemblies like engines are not controlled by kanban. There are numerous different end options for such major sub-assemblies, and inventory would simply be generated if separate kanbans were used for each one. Engines are therefore controlled by a different method. They are sequenced by assembly line broadcasting. In this approach, the exact customer requirements for a vehicle are broken down to major components and communicated ('broadcast') to the relevant production section. The procedure, therefore, is to sequence control major sub-assemblies and to use kanbans for components and smaller sub-assemblies.

> **Questions**
>
> 1 List all the different techniques and practices which Toyota adopts. Which of these would you call just-in-time philosophies and which are just-in-time techniques?
>
> 2 How are operations objectives (quality, speed, dependability, flexibility, cost) influenced by the practices which Toyota adopts?

JIT in service operations

Many of the principles and techniques of just-in-time, although they have been described in the context of manufacturing operations, are also applicable to service settings. In fact, some of the philosophical underpinning to just-in-time can also be seen as having its equivalent in the service sector. Take, for example, our argument concerning the role of inventory in manufacturing systems. The comparison between manufacturing systems that held large stocks of inventory between stages and those that did not centred on the effect which inventory had on improvement and problem-solving. Exactly the same argument can be applied when, instead of queues of material (inventory), an operation has to deal with queues of customers. Table 15.1 shows how certain aspects of inventory are analogous to certain aspects of queues.

Table 15.1 Inventory and queues have similar characteristics

	Inventory (queues of material)	Queues (queues of people)
Cost	Ties up capital	Waste time
Space	Needs warehouse	Need waiting areas
Quality	Defects are hidden	Give negative impression
Decoupling	Makes stages independent	Promote division of labour and specialization
Utilization	Stages kept busy by work-in-progress	Servers kept busy by waiting customers
Coordination	Avoids having to synchronize flow	Avoid having to match supply and demand

Source: Adapted from Fitzsimmons, J.A. (1990) 'Making Continual Improvement: A Competitive Strategy for Service Firms' *in* Bowen, D.E., Chase, R.B., Cummings, T.G. and Associates (eds) *Service Management Effectiveness*, Jossey-Bass.

In this part of the chapter, we describe two service organizations which have benefited from applying some of the principles of just-in-time: the Little Chef restaurant chain and a hospital. You might also like to read the case exercise at the end of this chapter which gives a further example of JIT in a hospital setting.

JIT principles at Little Chef

The Little Chef roadside restaurant chain has over 350 sites located on busy roads around the UK. All restaurants trade from 7.00 am to 10.00 pm, 364 days a year, and offer an all-day menu supplemented by part-day menus and various seasonal promotions. Customers receive a table service of cooked-to-order meals. Target times are 30 minutes for a starter plus main course with an extra 10 minutes for a dessert. To achieve a high standard of customer service, it is necessary to forecast demand as accurately as possible and then to provide for sufficient resources (staff, food, etc.) to meet that demand. In practice, an all-year-round core of regular staff is maintained, supplemented by seasonal staff at peak periods. Staff planning is undertaken at three levels:

- *The quarterly manpower plan.* The main input to this plan is the forecast number of customers for each of the 12 weeks of the forecast period.
- *The weekly forecast.* The sales forecast from the quarterly plan is updated and broken down into daily sales.
- *The daily plans*, which allocate duties between staff.

All materials (food, cleaning items and crockery) are supplied from a single supplier. This helps to ensure that goods are up to a consistent standard. Each restaurant has three deliveries a week, typically Monday, Wednesday and Friday, with orders being placed the same morning. A weekly stock-take provides consumption of each item. The manager uses a locally determined re-order level combined with forecast daily sales to compute material orders. Most foods are delivered and stored frozen. Only salads and cured meats arrive date-coded, usually with four to five days' shelf-life after delivery. Bread and milk are delivered daily by local suppliers. Stock-holding amounts to about seven days at any one time.

Each restaurant has a 'menu manual', which specifies the ingredients, cooking procedures and presentation standards for every item on the menu. Orders are added to the cook's order pad, including the time when the waitress took the order. Orders are marked once cooking has started, and marked again when cooking has finished. The cooking process is simple. The cooking equipment is also simple – griddles, fryers and pre-programmed microwave ovens. Similarly, a housekeeping board enables, 'at a glance', staff to see jobs which need to be done. Standard cleaning products and methods are used throughout the company, and each cleaning task is broken down into 'how, what, when' elements. To help ensure that standards are maintained across the network, quality audits are conducted every three months by the local training officer.

Tasks fall into eight categories; there is usually enough flexibility to react on a daily basis to changing needs, however. The categories are:

- reception/cashier
- cooking/production
- beverage production
- sweet/salad production
- serving to tables
- relaying tables
- washing up
- cleaning/toilet checks.

Staff are cross-trained for greater flexibility (50 per cent of staff can cook). At quiet times, one person may perform more than one task. Facility flexibility is assisted by moveable tables and chairs so that parties of varying sizes can be accommodated.

Question

Although different from a manufacturing company, some of the principles which apply in the Little Chef case are similar to those used in a JIT manufacturer: What are they?

JIT and MRP

The wide acceptance of the JIT principles and techniques outlined in this chapter came in the 1980s, after many manufacturing operations had made use of the MRP-based systems described in Chapter 14. Furthermore, the operating philosophies of MRP and JIT do seem to be fundamentally opposed. JIT encourages a 'pull' system of planning and control, whereas MRP is a 'push' system. JIT has aims which are wider than the operations planning and control activity, whereas MRP is essentially a planning and control 'calculation mechanism'. Yet the two approaches can reinforce each other in the same operation, provided their respective advantages are preserved. This part of this chapter will address two important questions for operations managers:

- How can JIT and MRP be combined in the same operation?
- How do we choose whether to use an MRP-based approach, a JIT-based approach or a combined approach to planning and control?

Before treating these two questions, however, it is necessary to summarize the characteristics of each approach.

Key characteristics of MRP

- Although designed as a pull system (the master schedule provides the pull signal which drives the system), the way MRP is actually used internally is as a push system. Inventory is driven through each process in response to detailed, time-phased plans, calculated by part number.
- MRP uses orders derived from the master schedule as the unit of control. Therefore, achievement against schedule is a key control monitor.
- MRP systems usually need a complex, centralized computer-based organization to support the necessary hardware, software and systems. This can make the needs of the customer appear remote to staff whose responsibilities lie two or three levels down the organization structure.
- MRP is highly dependent on the accuracy of data derived from bills of materials, stock records, and so on.
- MRP systems assume a fixed operations environment, with fixed lead times which are used to calculate when materials should arrive at the next operation. However, loading conditions and other factors mean that lead times are, in reality, far from fixed. MRP systems find it extremely difficult to cope with variable lead times.
- MRP records take a long time to update. In theory, each transaction requires a full update of data records. In practice, it is more usual to batch the changes into weekly (or monthly) updates. Even sophisticated MRP systems, which allow net change features to be updated daily, are relatively insensitive to hour-by-hour changes.

Key characteristics of JIT

- The flow between each stage in the manufacturing process is 'pulled' by demand from the previous stage.
- The control of the pull between stages is accomplished by using simple cards, tokens or empty squares to trigger movements and production. This results in simple, visual and transparent control.
- Decision-making for operations control is largely decentralized; tactical decisions do not rely on computer-based information processing.
- JIT scheduling is 'rate-based' (calculated in terms of output of a part per unit of time) rather than volume-based (the absolute number of parts to be made in a given day or week).
- JIT assumes (and encourages) resource flexibility and minimized lead times.
- JIT planning and control concepts are only one part of a wider and explicit JIT philosophy of operations.

JIT and MRP similarities and differences

Examining key characteristics of each approach to planning and control provides an indication of how they can be used together. MRP seeks to meet projected customer demand by directing that parts and sub-assemblies are only produced as needed to meet that demand. As we noted in Chapter 14, MRP back-schedules demand for parts and sub-assemblies by using the bill of materials to calculate how many are needed and when they must be made. This is how MRP connects customer demand with the internal and external supply networks. The irony is that JIT planning and control has similar objectives. Pull scheduling aims to connect the new network of internal and external supply processes by means of invisible conveyors so that parts only move in response to coordinated and synchronized signals derived from end-customer demand.

Given the similarities in objectives, what are the differences? MRP is driven by the master production schedule, which identifies future end-item demand. It models a fixed lead-time environment, using the power of the computer to calculate how many of, and when, each part should be made. Its output is in the form of time-phased requirements plans that are centrally calculated and coordinated. But while MRP is based on ideals that are analogous to pull scheduling (only ordering parts to be made as needed), the way it is used is quite different. Parts are made in response to central instructions, regardless of whether the next process can take them or actually needs them at the time. Day-to-day disturbances, such as quality problems and inaccurate stock records, undermine MRP authority and make the plans unworkable at shop-floor level. While MRP is excellent at planning, it is weak at control.

On the other hand, JIT-style pull scheduling aims to meet demand instantaneously. This aim is achieved through simple, paperless control systems based on kanban. But in practice, as described in Chapter 10, the actual throughput time the system is capable of must be recognized. If the total throughput time (P) is less than the demand lead time (D), then JIT systems should be capable of meeting that demand. But if the $P:D$ ratio is greater than 1, some speculative production will be needed. And if demand is suddenly far greater than expected for certain products, the JIT system may be unable to cope. Pull scheduling is a reactive concept that works best when independent demand has been levelled and dependent demand synchronized. While JIT may be good at control, it is weak on planning.

Finally, MRP is better at dealing with complexity, as measured by numbers of parts and finished products. It can handle detailed parts requirements, even for products that are made infrequently and in low volumes ('strangers'). JIT pull scheduling is less capable of responding instantaneously to changes in demand as the part count, options and colours increase. Therefore, JIT production systems favour designs based on simpler product structures with high parts commonality. Such disciplines challenge needless complexity, so that more parts may be brought under pull-scheduling control.

Putting the relative advantages and disadvantages of JIT and MRP together suggests how the two approaches can be blended. Two blends are briefly described in the following sections.

● Separate systems for different products

Using the runners, repeaters, strangers terminology described earlier, pull scheduling using kanban can be used for 'runners' and 'repeaters'. MRP planning is used for supplier scheduling as described below. MRP control is then only necessary for strangers, for which works orders are issued to identify what must be done at each stage, and then the work itself is monitored to push materials through manufacturing stages.[21] The advantage of this is that by increasing responsiveness and reducing inventories, it makes it worthwhile to increase their number by design simplification.

As an example of the application of this approach, Professor Bill Berry describes a company where product structure analysis provided an understanding of how MRP and JIT could coexist.[22] A fork-lift truck manufacturer had always looked on itself as a jobbing system, with 240 000 possible end-product options, of which 20 000 were currently offered for sale and 8000 were master scheduled. The product range was divided up into five families, and detailed analysis of the bill of materials for each member of the product range in each family showed that, in the worst case, 50 per cent of the part numbers were common. (Strict rules were applied: in order to be classified as 'common', a part number

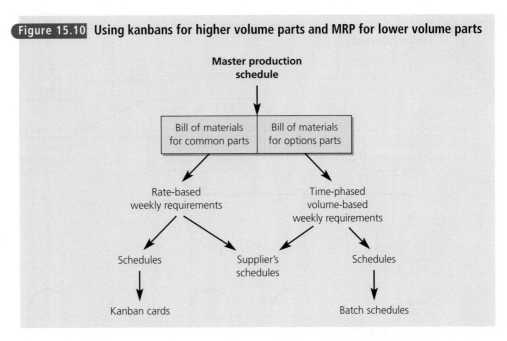

Figure 15.10 Using kanbans for higher volume parts and MRP for lower volume parts

had to be used in all family members.) The opportunity arose of using pull scheduling for the common parts without using time-phased MRP records. So common parts (runners and repeaters), both made-in and bought-out, could be controlled by rate-based weekly requirements. Irregularly made parts (strangers), on the other hand, would continue to be governed by time-based, weekly MRP. Figure 15.10 shows how the bill of materials could be redrawn in two parts: a common parts planned bill for runners and repeaters, and an options record for strangers. Further opportunities are then opened up to downsize the MRP system and to run it more frequently and more accurately, to control options more closely, and to rethink product designs to increase common parts.

MRP for overall control and JIT for internal control

MRP planning of supplier materials aims to ensure that sufficient parts are in the pipeline to enable them to be called up 'just-in-time'.[23] Figure 15.11 illustrates a simplified version of what may be achieved by the use of pull scheduling in manufacture supported by MRP materials procurement. The master production schedule (*see* Chapter 14) is broken down by means of MRP for supplier schedules (forecast future demand). Actual materials requirements for supplies are signalled by means of kanban to facilitate JIT delivery. Within the factory, all materials movements are governed by kanban loops between operations. The 'drum beat' for the factory is set by the factory assembly schedule.

A number of advantages over conventional MRP are claimed by combining the two systems in this way:

- There is no need for internal interstage works orders.
- In-process inventory need only be monitored between cells rather than for each activity.
- The bill of materials has fewer levels than in a conventional MRP system.
- Process-route information is simplified.
- Work-centre planning and control is simplified.
- Lead times and WIP are reduced.

When to use JIT, MRP and combined systems

Again it is the advantages and disadvantages of JIT and MRP which guide when to use 'pure' versions of the two, or one of the combined options. There are two ways of

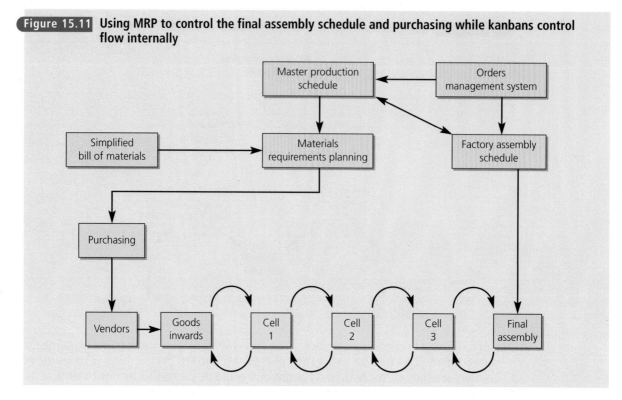

looking at this: one uses the system's ability to handle complexity as the main determinant of the decision, the other combines the volume and variety characteristics of the operation and the level of control required in order to make the choice.

The complexity determinant

Figure 15.12 distinguishes between the complexity of product structures and the complexity of the flow-path routings through which they must pass.[24] Simple product structures which have routings with high repeatability are prime candidates for pull control. JIT can easily cope with their relatively straightforward requirements. As structures and routings become more complex, so the power of the computer is needed in order to break down product structures and so assign orders to suppliers.

In many environments, it is possible to use pull scheduling for the control of most internal materials. Again, prime candidates for pull control are materials which are used regularly each week or each month. Their number can be increased by design standardization, as indicated by the direction of the arrow in Figure 15.12.

As structures and routings become even more complex, and parts usages become more irregular, so the opportunities for using pull scheduling decrease. Very complex structures require networking methods like PERT (program evaluation and review technique – *see* Chapter 16 on project planning and control) for planning and control. Such structures provide few opportunities for pull scheduling. However, even in this environment, a possible use for JIT is to limit the build-up of inventory, for example by means of kanban squares painted on the floor, so work cannot move to the next operation until a square is free.

The volume–variety and level of control determinants

Figure 15.13 again uses a matrix to determine the relative suitability of planning and control approaches. This time the dimensions are the type of production process and the level for which the control system is being designed.[25]

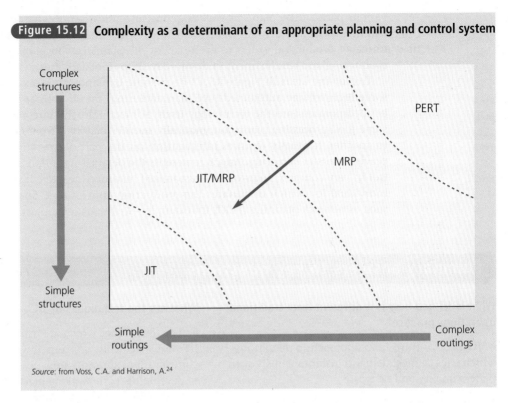

Figure 15.12 Complexity as a determinant of an appropriate planning and control system

Source: from Voss, C.A. and Harrison, A.[24]

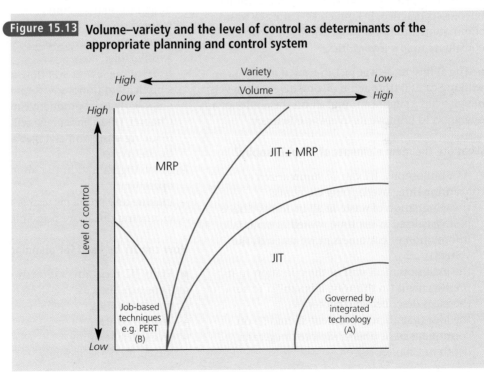

Figure 15.13 Volume–variety and the level of control as determinants of the appropriate planning and control system

The *type of production* uses the volume–variety characteristics we have used before. Taken together, they indicate the complexity of manufacturing. Variation in processing lead times, the number of alternative product routes, the complexity of product structures and the variety of product types can all be related to volume and variety.

The *level of control* indicates which set of production control tasks are being considered. High-level control involves broadly coordinating the flow of materials to the various parts of the plant, as well as giving an indication of what level of output they will be expected to achieve in future periods. Medium-level control is the detailed allocation of production orders to each part of the plant. Low-level control is the detailed monitoring and readjustment of day-to-day shop-floor activities.

Two of the areas in Figure 15.13 need some explanation. Area A indicates that, in some high-volume automated-type manufacturing, the shop-floor level of control may be incorporated into the technology itself. For example, the integrated technologies of some food-processing plants automatically transfer materials from one part of the plant to another. It usually requires intervention on the part of operations management to prevent transfer occurring. Area B represents the detailed shop-floor scheduling and control in very complex, high-variety customized manufacture. Here it is the nature of each individual job which dominates the production control task. Specialized techniques such as network planning (PERT, for example – *see* the next chapter) are usually needed.

Summary answers to key questions

What is JIT and how is it different from traditional operations practice?

● JIT (just-in-time) is an approach to operations which tries to meet demand instantaneously with perfect quality and no waste.

● It is an approach which differs from traditional operations practices insomuch as it stresses waste elimination and fast throughput, both of which contribute to low inventories.

● The ability to deliver just-in-time not only saves working capital (through reducing inventory levels) but also has a significant impact on the ability of an operation to improve its intrinsic efficiency.

What are the main elements of JIT philosophy?

● As a philosophy, JIT can be summarized as concerning three overlapping elements:
– the elimination of waste in all its forms (this is best visualized as the time wasted as materials, information or customers move through the system);
– the inclusion of all staff of the operation in its improvement (in this way, it is similar to some of the ideas described in Chapter 9);
– the idea that all improvement should be on a continuous basis (this is explored in greater depth in Chapter 18).

● A common feature of JIT philosophy is the progressive removal of (surplus) resources so as to enable the operation to learn how to manage without these resources.

What are the techniques of JIT?

● The techniques which are usually associated with JIT (not specifically concerned with planning and control; *see* next point) are:
– developing 'basic working practices' which support waste elimination and continuous improvement;
– design for manufacture;
– focused operations which reduce complexity;
– using simple, small machines which are robust and flexible;.
– rearranging layout and flow to enhance simplicity of flow;
– employing total productive maintenance (*see* Chapter 19) to encourage reliability;
– reducing setup and changeover times to enhance flexibility;
– involving all staff in the improvement of the operation;
– making any problems visible to all staff;
– extending the above principles to suppliers.

How can JIT be used for planning and control?

● Many JIT techniques directly concern planning and control, such as:
– pull scheduling
– kanban control
– levelled scheduling
– mixed-model scheduling
– synchronization of flow.

Can JIT be used in service operations?

● Many of the above techniques are directly applicable in service operations, although some translation is occasionally required.

Can JIT and MRP coexist?

● Although they may seem to be different approaches to planning and control, they can be combined in several ways to form a hybrid system.

● The way in which they can be combined depends on the complexity of product structures, the complexity of product routing, the volume–variety characteristics of the operation and the level of control required.

Just-in-time at Jimmy's[26]

St James's Hospital, affectionately known as 'Jimmy's', is Europe's largest teaching hospital. It employs around 4500 people to support the 90 000 in-patient treatments per year and over 450 000 total admissions. Under increasing pressure to reduce costs, to contain inventory and to improve service, the Supplies Department has recently undertaken a major analysis of its activities, helped by the consultancy division of Lucas Industries, the UK-based manufacturing company.

The initial review highlighted that Jimmy's had approximately 1500 suppliers of 15 000 different products at a total cost of £15 million. Traditionally, the Supplies Department ordered what the doctors asked for, with many cases of similar items supplied by six or more firms. Under a cross-functional task force, comprising both medical and supply staff, a major programme of supplier and product rationalization was undertaken, which also revealed many sources of waste. For example, the team found that wards used as many as 20 different types of gloves, some of which were expensive surgeons' gloves costing around £1 per pair, yet in almost all cases these could be replaced by fewer and cheaper (20 pence) alternatives. Similarly, anaesthetic items which were previously bought from six suppliers, were single-sourced. The savings in purchasing costs, inventory costs and general administration were enormous in themselves, but the higher-order volumes also helped the hospital negotiate for lower prices. Suppliers are also much more willing to deliver frequently in smaller quantities when they know that they are the sole supplier. Peter Beeston, the Supplies Manager, said:

'We've been driven by suppliers for years ... they would insist that we could only purchase in thousands, that we would have to wait weeks, or that they would only deliver on Wednesdays! Now, our selected suppliers know that if they perform well, we will assure them of a long-term commitment. I prefer to buy 80 per cent of our requirements from 20 or 30 suppliers, whereas previously, it involved over a hundred.'

The streamlining of the admissions process also proved fertile ground for improvement along JIT principles. For example, in the Urology Department, one-third of patients for non-urgent surgery found their appointments were being cancelled. One reason for this was that in the time between the consultant saying that an operation was required and the patient arriving at the operating theatre, there were 59 changes in responsibility for the process. The hospital reorganized the process to form a 'cell' of four people who were given complete responsibility for admissions to Urology. The cell was located next to the ward and made responsible for all record keeping, planning all operations, ensuring that beds were available as needed, and telling the patient when to arrive. As a result, the 59 handovers are now down to 13 and the process is faster, cheaper and more reliable.

Jimmy's also introduced a simple kanban system for some of its local inventory. In Ward 9's storeroom, for example, there are just two boxes of 10 mm syringes on the shelf. When the first is empty, the other is moved forward and the Ward Sister then orders another. The next stage will be to simplify the reordering: empty boxes will be posted outside the store, where codes will be periodically read by the Supplies Department, using a mobile data recorder.

The hospital's management are convinced of the benefits of their changes.

'Value for money, not cost cutting, is what this is all about. We are standardizing on buying quality products and now also have more influence on the buying decision ... from being previously functionally oriented with a number of buyers, we now concentrate on materials management for complete product ranges. The project has been an unmitigated success and although we are only just starting to see the benefits, I would expect savings in cost and in excess inventory to spiral! The report on Sterile Wound Care Packs shows the potential that our team has identified. The 'old' pack consisted of four pairs of plastic forceps, cotton wool balls and a plastic pot, which were used with or without additional gloves. This pack cost approximately 60 pence excluding the gloves. The "new" pack consists of a plastic pot, swabs, etc., and one pair of latex gloves only. This pack costs approximately 33 pence including gloves. Total target saving is approximately £20 000.'

Questions

1 List the elements in St James's new approach which could be seen as deriving from JIT principles of manufacturing.

2 What further ideas from JIT manufacturing do you think could be applied in a hospital setting such as St James's?

CASE EXERCISE

Boys and Boden (B&B)

'There **must** be a better way of running this place!' said Dean Hammond, recently recruited General Manager of B&B, as he finished a somewhat stressful conversation with a complaining customer, a large and loyal local building contractor.

'We had six weeks to make their special staircase, and we are still late. I'll have to persuade one of the joiners to work overtime this weekend to get everything ready for Monday. We never seem to get complaints about quality ... our men always do an excellent job, but there is usually a big backlog of work, so how can we set priorities? We could do the most profitable work first, or the work for our biggest customers, or the jobs which are most behind. In practice, we try to satisfy everyone as best we can, but inevitably someone's order will be late. On paper, each job should be quite profitable, since we build in a big allowance for waste, and for timber defects. And we know the work content of almost any task we would have to do, and this is the basis of our estimating system. But, overall, the department isn't very profitable in comparison to our other operations, and most problems seem to end up with higher-than-anticipated costs and late deliveries!'

Boys and Boden was a small, successful, privately owned timber and building materials merchant based in a small town. Over the years it had established its large Joinery Department, which made doors, windows, staircases and other timber products, all to the exact special requirements of the customers, comprising numerous local and regional builders. In addition, the joiners would cut and prepare special orders of timber, such as non-standard sections, and special profiles including old designs of skirting board, sometimes at very short notice while the customers waited. Typically, for joinery items, the customer provided simple dimensioned sketches of the required products. These were then passed to the central Estimating/Quotations Department which, in conjunction with the Joinery Manager, calculated costs and prepared a written quotation which was faxed to the customer. This first stage was normally completed within two/three days, but on occasions could take a week or more. On receipt of an order, the original sketches and estimating details were passed back to the Joinery Manager across the yard, who roughly scheduled them into his plan, allocating them to individual craftsmen as they became available. Most of the joiners were capable of making any product, and enjoyed the wide variety of challenging work.

The Joinery Department appeared congested and somewhat untidy, but everyone believed that this was acceptable and normal for job shops, since there was no single flow route for materials. Whatever the design of the item being made, or the quantity, it was normal for the joiner to select the required timber from the storage building across the yard. The timber was then prepared using a planer/thicknesser. After that, the joiner would use a variety of processes, depending on the product. The timber could be machined into different cross-sectional shapes, cut into component lengths using a radial arm saw, joints formed by hand tools, or using a mortise/tenon machine, and so on. Finally the products would be glued and assembled, sanded smooth by hand or machine, and treated with preservatives, stains or varnishes if required. All the large and more expensive machines were grouped together by type (for example, saws) or were single pieces of equipment shared by all 10 or so joiners. Dean described what one might observe on a random visit to the Joinery Department:

'One or two long staircases partly assembled, and crossing several work areas; large door frames on trestles being assembled; stacks of window components for a large contract being prepared and jointed, and so on. Off-cuts and wood shavings are scattered around the work area, but are cleared periodically when they get in the way or form a hazard. The joiners try to fit in with each other over the use of machinery, so are often working on several, part-finished items at once. Varnishing or staining has to be done when it's quiet – for example, evenings or weekends – or outside, to avoid dust contamination. Long off-cuts are stacked around the workshop, to be used up on any future occasion when these lengths or sections are required. However, it is often easier to take a new length of timber for each job, so the off-cuts do tend to build up over time. Unfortunately, everything I have described is getting worse as we get busier ... our sales are increasing so the system is getting more congested. The joiners are almost climbing over each other to do their work. Unfortunately, despite having more orders, the department has remained stubbornly unprofitable!

'Whilst analysing in detail the lack of profit, we were horrified to find that, for the majority of orders, the actual times booked by the joiners exceeded the estimated times by up to 50 per cent. Sometimes this was attributable to new, inexperienced joiners. Although fully trained and qualified, they might lack the experience needed to complete a complex job in the time an estimator would expect, but there had been no feedback of this to the individual. We put one of these men on doors only; having overcome his initial reluctance, he has become our enthusiastic "door expert", and gets closely involved in quotations too, so he always does his work within the time estimates! However, the main time losses were found to be the result of general delays caused by congestion, interference, double handling and rework to rectify in-process damage. Moreover, we found that a joiner walked an average of nearly 5 km a day, usually carrying around bits of wood.

'When I did my operations management course on my MBA, the professor described the application of cellular manufacturing and JIT. From what I can remember, the idea seemed to be to get better flow, reducing the times and distances in the process, and thus achieving quicker throughput times. That is just what we need, but these concepts were explained in the context of high-volume, repetitive production of bicycles, whereas everything we make are "one-offs". However, although we do make a lot of different staircases, they all use roughly the same process steps:

1 *Cutting timber to width and length*
2 *Sanding*
3 *Machining*
4 *Tenoning*
5 *Manual assembly (glue and wedges).*

'We have a lot of unused factory floor-space, so it would be relatively easy to set up a self-contained staircase cell. There is huge demand for special stairs in this region, but also a lot of competing small joinery businesses which can beat us on price and lead time. So we go to a lot of trouble quoting for stairs, but only win about 20 per cent of the business. If we got the cell idea to work, we could be more competitive on price and delivery, hence winning more orders. I know we will need a lot more volume to justify establishing the cell, so its really a case of "chicken and egg"!'

Questions

1 To what extent could (or should) Dean expect to apply the philosophies and techniques of JIT described in this chapter to the running of a staircase cell?

2 What are likely to be the main categories of costs and benefits in establishing the cell? Are there any non-financial benefits which should be taken into account?

3 At what stage, and how, should Dean sell his idea to the Joinery Manager and the workers?

4 How different would the cell work be to that in the main Joinery Department?

5 Should Dean differentiate the working environment by providing distinctive work-wear such as T-shirts and distinctively painted machines, in order to reinforce a cultural change?

6 What risks are associated with Dean's proposal?

Discussion questions

1 Explain your views on whether you think that JIT is a philosophy, a strategy or a selection of techniques.

2 Why does continuous improvement require a long-term view of the business? Discuss what is meant by an 'enabling company culture' in which continuous improvement can flourish.

3 How do make-to-order businesses avoid waste?

4 Why are work-in-progress and lead time related? How does this relationship affect a building society on a Saturday morning?

5 If you were aiming to develop your company into a JIT company, what would you look for in your suppliers?

6 Simplicity is often a theme associated with JIT companies. How does Little Chef incorporate this theme into its management of operations?

7 What are the deficiencies of the economic order quantity (EOQ) from a JIT point of view?

8 Explain how mixed modelling is used to develop a detailed operations schedule. How does this differ from a master schedule?

9 How can new technology be used to supply kanbans in a JIT operation?

10 Explain how JIT techniques can be used to support volume and mix flexibility in operations management.

11 Why is *jidoka* (line-stop authority) described as a 'cornerstone of the Toyota Production System'?

12 Explain the key differences between a 'traditional' approach and a JIT approach to manufacturing. Do these differences occur in service organizations?

13 Discuss the advantages and disadvantages of working just-in-time.

14 The elimination of waste is a core philosophy of JIT. What is meant by 'waste' and explain the origins and intentions of this approach?

15 Discuss the benefits of setup time reduction on each of the five operations performance objectives: cost, flexibility, quality, dependability and speed.

16 Explain the difference between 'push' and 'pull' planning and control. Why might different organizations choose such approaches?

17 Discuss how kanbans might be applied, and the form they might take, in a fast-food restaurant.

18 A manufacturer of printed circuit boards (PCBs) is currently producing them at a rate of one every three minutes from a four-part container. The overall efficiency of the system has been estimated to be 90 per cent and the existing setup times are 180 minutes per day. The management would like to develop a JIT system but with no more than three kanbans. To what level will setup times need to be reduced to achieve this?

19 Discuss the benefits of reducing batch quantities.

20 What do you think might be the advantages and disadvantages of employing 'jidoka' in service organizations. Illustrate your answer using an organization of your choice.

Notes on chapter

1 Bicheno, J. (1991) *Implementing Just-in-time*, IFS.
2 Voss, C.A. (1987) *in* Voss, C.A. (ed) *Just-in-time Manufacture*, IFS/Springer-Verlag.
3 Voss, C.A., *ibid*.
4 Schonberger, R. (1982) *Japanese Manufacturing Techniques*, The Free Press.
5 Oliver, N. and Wilkinson, B. (1988) *The Japanization of British Industry*, Basil Blackwell.
6 Oliver, N. and Wilkinson, B., *ibid*.
7 Harrison, A. (1992) *Just-in-time Manufacturing in Perspective*, Prentice Hall.
8 Lee, D.C. (1987) 'Set-up Time Reduction: Making JIT Work' *in* Voss, C.A. (ed), *Just-in-time Manufacture*, IFS/Springer-Verlag.
9 Quoted in Harrison, A., *op. cit.*
10 Quoted in Harrison, A., *op. cit.*
11 Kamata, S. (1983) *Japan in the Passing Lane: An Insider's Account of Life in a Japanese Auto Factory*, Allen and Unwin.
12 Source: Marsh, P. (1999) 'Just-in-time Culture Key for Europe', *Financial Times*, 18 October.
13 Whitney, D.E. (1990) 'Manufacturing by Design', *Harvard Business Review*, Vol 68, No 4.
14 Skinner, W. (1978) *Manufacturing in the Corporate Strategy*, John Wiley.
15 Yamashina, H. 'Reducing Set-up Times Makes your Company Flexible and More Competitive', unpublished, quoted in Harrison A., *op. cit.*
16 Harrison, A., *op. cit.*
17 Source: 'Behind the Face of Beauty – Manufacturing Flexibility for the Mass Market', *Europlus*, Jan 1994.

18 Hall, R. (1987) *Attaining Manufacturing Excellence*, Dow Jones/Irwin.

19 Harrison, A., *op. cit.*

20 Parnaby, J. (1988) 'A Systems Approach to the Implementation of JIT Methodologies in Lucas Industries', *International Journal of Production Research*, Vol 26, No 3.

21 Parnaby, J., *ibid.*

22 Berry, W.L., Talon, W.J. and Bol, W.J. (1988) *Production Structure Analysis for the Master Scheduling of Assemble-to-Order Products*, Working paper at the Centre for Manufacturing Excellence, Kenan Flagar School of Business, University of North Carolina.

23 Parnaby, J., *op. cit.*

24 Voss, C.A. and Harrison, A. (1987) 'Strategies for Implementing JIT' *in* Voss, C.A. (ed) *Just-in-time Manufacture*, IFS/Springer-Verlag.

25 Slack, N. (1991) *The Manufacturing Advantage*, Mercury Books.

26 Sources: *The Independent on Sunday*, 4 July 1993; *Update*, Issue 18, Aug 1993.

Selected further reading

Andersen Consulting (1992) *The Lean Enterprise Benchmarking Report*, Andersen Consulting/Cardiff Business School/Cambridge University.

Bicheno, J. (1991) *Implementing JIT*, IFS Publications.

Cheng, T.C.E. and Podolsky, S. (1996) *Just-in-time Manufacturing* (2nd edn), Chapman and Hall.

Fiedler, K., Galletly, J.E. and Bicheno, J. (1993) 'Expert Advice for JIT Implementation', *International Journal of Operations and Production Management*, Vol 13, No 6.

Goyal, S.K. and Deshmukh, S.G. (1992) 'A Critique of the Literature on Just-in-time Manufacturing', *International Journal of Operations and Production Management*, Vol 12, No 1.

Harrison, A.S. (1992) *Just-in-time Manufacturing in Perspective*, Prentice Hall.

Henricks, J.A (1994) 'Performance Measures for a JIT Manufacturer', *Industrial Engineering*, Vol 26, No 1.

Kidd, P.T. (1994) *Agile Manufacturing: Forging New Frontiers*, Addison-Wesley.

Marisako, S. (1992) *Prices, Quality and Trust*, Cambridge University Press.

Oliver, N., Delbridge, R. and Lowe, J. (1996) 'Lean Production Practices: International Comparisons in the Auto Components industry', *British Journal of Management*, Vol 7.

Oliver N. and Wilkinson, B. (1992) *The Japanization of British Industry* (2nd edn), Basil Blackwell.

Schniederjans, M.J. (1993) *Topics in Just-in-time Management*, Allyn & Bacon.

Schonberger, R.J. (1982) *Japanese Manufacturing Techniques: Nine Hidden Lessons in Simplicity*, The Free Press.

Schonberger, R.J. (1986) *World Class Manufacturing: The Lessons of Simplicity Applied*, The Free Press.

Schonberger, R.J (1996) *World Class Manufacturing: The Next Decade*, The Free Press.

Sohal, A.S., Ramsey, L. and Samson, D. (1993) 'JIT Manufacturing Industry: Analysis and a Method for Implementation', *International Journal of Operations and Production Management*, Vol 13, No 7.

Vollmann, T., Berry, W.L. and Whybark, D.C. (1992) *Manufacturing Planning and Control Systems* (3rd edn), Irwin.

Warnecke, H.J. and Huser, M. (1995) 'Lean Production', *International Journal of Production Economics*, Vol 41, No 1.

Whitson, D. (1997) 'Applying Just-in-time Systems in Health Care', *IIE Solution*, Vol 29, No 8.

Womack, J.P., Jones, D.T. and Roos, D. (1990) *The Machine that Changed the World*, Rawson Associates.

Womack, J.P. and Jones, D.T. (1996) *Lean Thinking: Banish Waste and Create Wealth in Your Corporation*, Simon and Schuster.

16 Project planning and control

Introduction

This chapter is concerned with the planning and control of operations that occupy the low volume–high variety end of the continuum which we introduced in Chapter 4. These 'project' operations are engaged in complex, often large-scale, activities with a defined beginning and end. The pioneers of planning and controlling project operations were the engineers and planners who worked on complex defence and construction projects. More recently, the methods they developed have been applied to projects as diverse as new product launches, education projects in the Third World and theatrical productions. Project planning and control is important because all managers will, at some point, get involved with managing projects. Many of these projects may be relatively small – a human resources manager planning a training course, for example. Some will be far larger, for example where the manager is part of a project team – such as an accountant providing cost information for a new marketing promotion. Whether large or small, however, the planning and control aspects of managing projects follow similar principles (*see* Fig. 16.1).

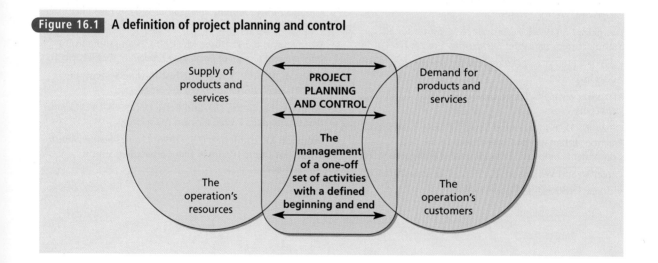

Figure 16.1 A definition of project planning and control

Supply of products and services

PROJECT PLANNING AND CONTROL

Demand for products and services

The operation's resources

The management of a one-off set of activities with a defined beginning and end

The operation's customers

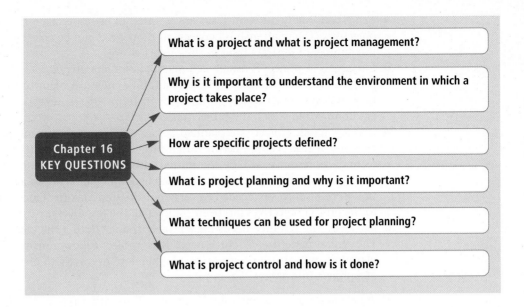

Chapter 16 KEY QUESTIONS

- What is a project and what is project management?
- Why is it important to understand the environment in which a project takes place?
- How are specific projects defined?
- What is project planning and why is it important?
- What techniques can be used for project planning?
- What is project control and how is it done?

What is a project?

A project is a set of activities with a defined start point and a defined end state, which pursues a defined goal and uses a defined set of resources. Although many small-scale operations management endeavours conform to this definition of a project, we will devote the majority of this chapter to examining the management of larger-scale projects. The assumption of 'large projects' when we discuss project management provides us with the opportunity to explore some of the special characteristics which come with large-scale activities. Large-scale (and therefore complex) undertakings consume a relatively large amount of resources, take a long time to complete and typically involve interactions between different parts of an organization. To plan and control a project, managers need to devise a model which both describes the project's complexity and extends it forward in time to make sure that the project will achieve its goals. The model of the project (its plan) can then be used to check progress as the real project proceeds (control of the project).

Projects come in many and various forms, including the following:

- an AIDS information campaign
- producing a television programme
- constructing the Channel Tunnel
- designing an aircraft
- putting on a one-week course in project management
- relocating a factory
- refurbishing an hotel
- installing a new information system
- cleaning up after an oil tanker spillage.

● The elements of a project

To a greater or lesser extent, all these projects have some elements in common, as follows:

- *An objective.* A definable end result, output or product which is typically defined in terms of the cost, the quality and timing of the output from the project activities.

- *Complexity.* Many different tasks are required to be undertaken to achieve a project's objectives. The relationship between all these tasks can be complex, especially when the number of separate tasks in the project is large.
- *Uniqueness.* A project is usually a 'one-off', not a repetitive undertaking. Even 'repeat' projects, such as the construction of another chemical plant to the same specification, will have distinctive differences in terms of resources used and the actual environment in which the project takes place.
- *Uncertainty.* All projects are planned before they are executed and therefore carry an element of risk. A 'blue sky' research project carries the risk that expensive, high-technology resources will be committed with no worthwhile outcome.
- *Temporary nature.* Projects have a defined beginning and end, so a temporary concentration of resources is needed to carry out the undertaking. Once their contribution to the project objectives has been completed, the resources are usually redeployed.
- *Life cycle.* The resource needs for a project change during the course of its life cycle. The typical pattern of resource needs for a project follow a predictable path. From a planning and control perspective, it is therefore necessary to divide up the life cycle of a project into *project phases*.

These elements serve to distinguish projects from other types of operation. They also serve to distinguish *projects* from *programmes*. A *programme*, such as a continuous improvement programme (*see* Chapter 18), has no defined end point. Rather it is an ongoing process of change. Projects, such as the Apollo 12 mission, may be individual sub-sections of an overall programme (the Lunar Apollo Programme in this case). Programme management overlays and integrates the individual projects.

Although the management of projects is associated with operations of the low volume–high variety type, this does not mean that only these types of operation will be concerned with projects. However, it is necessary for managers in all types of operation to understand the nature of project planning and control. Even if their prime operations rationale is not to create projects, they are likely to be either customers for them or suppliers to them at some time.

● A typology of projects

Figure 16.2 illustrates a typology for projects according to their *complexity* – in terms of size, value and the number of people involved in the project – and their *uncertainty* of achieving the project objectives of cost, time and quality.

The typology helps to give a rational presentation of the vast range of undertakings where project management principles can be applied.[1] It also gives a clue to the nature of the projects and the difficulties of managing them. Uncertainty particularly affects project planning, and complexity particularly affects project control.

Projects with *high uncertainty* are likely to be especially difficult to define and set realistic objectives for. If the exact details of a project are subject to change during the course of its execution, the planning process is particularly difficult. Resources may be committed, times may be agreed, but if the objectives of the project change or the environmental conditions change, or if some activity is delayed, then all the plans which were made prior to the changes will need to be redrawn. When uncertainty is high, the whole project planning process needs to be sufficiently flexible to cope with the consequences of change. For example, the implementation of a political treaty in the European Union is subject to the ratification of all the member governments. Politics being an uncertain business, any of the member countries might either fail to ratify the treaty or attempt to renegotiate it. The central planners at EU headquarters must therefore have contingency plans in place which indicate how they might have to change the 'project' to cope with any political changes. Table 16.1 illustrates the effects of uncertainty on project planning.

Figure 16.2 A typology of projects

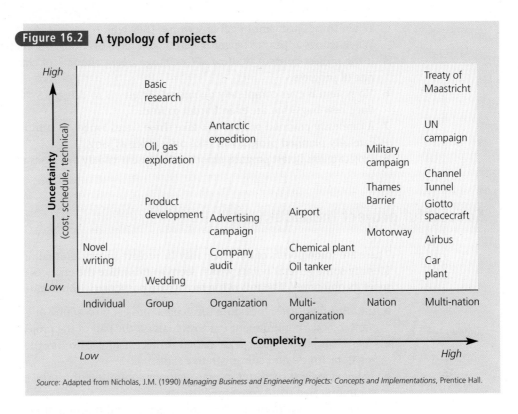

Source: Adapted from Nicholas, J.M. (1990) *Managing Business and Engineering Projects: Concepts and Implementations*, Prentice Hall.

Table 16.1 The effects of uncertainty on project planning

Aspect of project planning	Uncertainty	
	High	Low
Planning objectives	Evolving	Determined
Extent of planning	Ill defined	Clear
Outline of plan	Fuzzy	Defined

Projects with *high levels of complexity* need not necessarily be difficult to plan, although they might involve considerable effort; controlling them can be problematic, however. As projects become more detailed with many separate activities, resources and groups of people involved, the scope for things to go wrong increases. Furthermore, as the number of separate activities in a project increases, the ways in which they can impact on each other increases exponentially. This increases the effort involved in monitoring each activity. It also increases the chances of overlooking some part of the project which is deviating from the plan. Most significantly, it increases the 'knock-on' effect of any problem.

The (only partly joking) 'laws of project management' which were issued by the American Production and Inventory Control Society give a flavour of uncertain and complex projects:

1 No major project is ever installed on time, within budget, or with the same staff that started it. Yours will not be the first.
2 Projects progress quickly until they become 90 per cent complete, then they remain at 90 per cent complete for ever.
3 One advantage of fuzzy project objectives is that they let you avoid the embarrassment of estimating the corresponding costs.
4 When things are going well, something will go wrong.

When things just cannot get any worse, they will.

When things appear to be going better, you have overlooked something.

5 If the project content is allowed to change freely, the rate of change will exceed the rate of progress.

6 No system is ever completely debugged. Attempts to debug a system inevitably introduce new bugs that are even harder to find.

7 A carelessly planned project will take three times longer to complete than expected; a carefully planned project will take only twice as long.

8 Project teams detest progress reporting because it vividly manifests their lack of progress.

Successful project management

There are some points of commonality in project success and failure, which allow us to identify some general points which seem to minimize the chances of a project failing to meet its objectives. The following factors are particulary important:[2]

- *Clearly defined goals*: including the general project philosophy or general mission of the project, and a commitment to those goals on the part of the project team members.
- *Competent project manager*: a skilled project leader who has the necessary interpersonal, technical and administrative skills.
- *Top-management support*: top-management commitment for the project that has been communicated to all concerned parties.
- *Competent project team members*: the selection and training of project team members, who between them have the skills necessary to support the project.
- *Sufficient resource allocation*: resources, in the form of money, personnel, logistics, etc., which are available for the project in the required quantity.
- *Adequate communications channels*: sufficient information is available on project objectives, status, changes, organizational conditions and client's needs.
- *Control mechanisms*: the mechanisms which are in place to monitor actual events and recognize deviations from plan.
- *Feedback capabilities*: all parties concerned with the project are able to review the project's status and make suggestions and corrections.
- *Responsiveness to clients*: all potential users of the project are concerned with and are kept up to date on the project's status.
- *Troubleshooting mechanisms*: a system or set of procedures which can tackle problems when they arise, trace them back to their root cause and resolve them.
- *Project staff continuity*: the continued involvement of key project personnel through its life. Frequent turnover of staff can dissipate the team's acquired learning.

● Project managers

In order to coordinate the efforts of many people in different parts of the organization (and often outside it as well), all projects need a project manager. Many of a project manager's activities are concerned with managing human resources. The people working in the project team need a clear understanding of their roles in the (usually temporary) organization. Controlling an uncertain project environment requires the rapid exchange of relevant information with the project stakeholders, both within and outside the organization. People, equipment and other resources must be identified and allocated to the various tasks. Undertaking these tasks successfully makes the management of a project a particularly challenging operations activity. Five characteristics in particular are seen as important in an effective project manager:[3]

- background and experience which are consistent with the needs of the project;
- leadership and strategic expertise, in order to maintain an understanding of the overall project and its environment, while at the same time working on the details of the project;
- technical expertise in the area of the project in order to make sound technical decisions;
- interpersonal competence and the people skills to take on such roles as project champion, motivator, communicator, facilitator and politician;
- proven managerial ability in terms of a track record of getting things done.

The project planning and control process

Figure 16.3 proposes a project management model which is used as a framework for this chapter. The model categorizes project management activities into five stages, four of which are relevant to project planning and control:

Stage 1 Understanding the project environment – internal and external factors which may influence the project.

Stage 2 Defining the project – setting the objectives, scope and strategy for the project.

Stage 3 Project planning – deciding how the project will be executed.

Stage 4 Technical execution – performing the technical aspects of the project.

Stage 5 Project control – ensuring that the project is carried out according to plan.

We shall examine project planning and control under the headings of stages 1, 2, 3 and 5 – the project environment, project definition, project planning and project control. (Stage 4, the technical execution of the project, is determined by the specific technicalities of individual projects.) However, it is important to understand that the stages are not a simple sequential chain of steps; it is essentially an *iterative* process. Problems or changes which become evident in the control stage may require replanning and may even cause modifications to the original project definition.

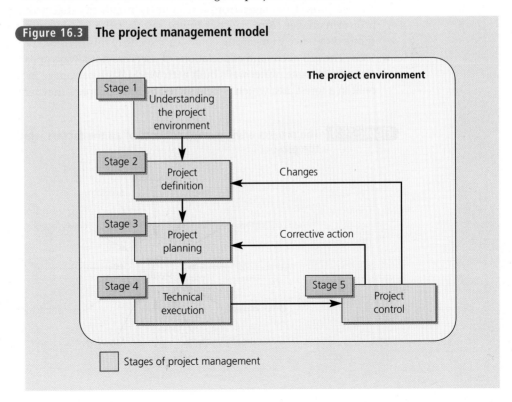

Figure 16.3 **The project management model**

● Stage 1 – Understanding the project environment

The project environment comprises all the factors which may affect the project during its life. It determines the setting and circumstances in which the project is executed. Examples of factors which may affect the environment are shown in Figure 16.4.

Example: An overseas education agency

The governments of many countries have agencies which organize the distribution of overseas aid by managing specific development projects in partnership with the host government. Such projects might include the building of schools, the design and development of a teacher education scheme, and the organization of a primary health education programme. Many environmental factors will affect the individual projects undertaken by an agency. The following are examples:

- *Geography.* Land-locked countries such as Afghanistan can be subject to serious shipment delays through neighbouring countries, which can extend activity times.
- *Finance.* Fluctuating commodity prices may impact on the ability of host governments to meet their resource commitments to a project.
- *Politics.* The political stance taken by the host government and the possibility of internal political dissent can influence the scale and timing of the project.
- *Local laws.* Local laws can vary considerably and influence the resources needed for a project. For example, in Francophone African countries, local labour law allows employees to take three days' absence when a close relative dies. With large families, this can cause serious disruptions to staff availability which must be allowed for at the planning stage.
- *National culture.* Developing an understanding of host country cultures is crucial to success in overseas projects. Even when a single language is being used by project managers, there can be differences in the meaning of words or phrases. People in some cultures may not be comfortable giving a direct response to some questions, so while a project manager from one country might say that 'work has not started', a project manager from another might say that the 'work is not yet complete'. The subtle difference in meaning could lead to costly misinterpretation.
- *Users.* The full needs and expectations of users are not always apparent to outside agencies. For example, water wells built with World Bank patronage in the Ivory Coast were built in a forest area which is held sacred by local people – they remain unused.

Figure 16.4 **The project environment consists of all the factors which can affect the project**

● Stage 2 – Project definition

Before starting the complex task of planning and executing a project, it is necessary to be as clear as possible about what is going to be done. This is not always straightforward. Some projects are simpler to define than others. Three different elements are needed to define a project:

- *its objectives:* the end state that project management is trying to achieve;
- *its scope:* the exact range of the responsibilities taken on by project management;
- *its strategy:* how project management is going to meet its objectives.

Project objectives

A project's objectives provide the overall direction for the project and help staff to focus on the rationale of the project and its expected results. Objectives help to provide a definition of the end point which can be used to monitor progress and identify when success has been achieved. However, judgement regarding the success of a project can depend on who is being asked. For example, a project to design and install a new production planning and control information system in a factory might be regarded as successful by the customer who commissioned the project (the Information Systems Department) but by the people who use the new system as less than successful (the production controllers). This is why it is useful to phrase the objectives of a project in *user terms*.

The hierarchy of objectives

The objectives of each part of the project must be related to its overall objective or goal. The goal to 'place an American on the moon this decade and to return him safely to earth' dictated the objectives of all the projects which contributed to achieving it. Within those projects (each of them major in their own right) the objectives of each sub-project will have been related to the project's objectives, and so on.

Objectives must be clear

Good objectives are those which are clear, measurable and, preferably, quantifiable. One method of clarifying objectives which has been found helpful is to break down project objectives into three categories – the purpose, the end results, and the success criteria. For example, a project which is expressed in general terms as 'improve process X' could be broken down into:

- *Purpose* – to prevent production from failing to meet output targets as forecast.
- *End result* – a report which identifies the causes of lost production, and which recommends how the target output can be met.
- *Success criteria* – the report should be completed by 30 June. The recommendation should enable output to reach at least 70 tonnes per year. Cost of the recommendations should not exceed €200 000.

Performance objectives in project management

Projects, like any other operations, can be judged in terms of the five performance objectives we outlined in Chapter 2 – quality, speed, dependability, flexibility and cost. However, flexibility is regarded as a 'given' in most projects which, by definition, are to some extent one-offs, and speed and dependability are compressed to one composite objective – 'time'. This results in what are known as the 'three objectives of project management' – cost, time and quality.

The relative importance of each objective will differ for different projects. Some aerospace projects, such as the development of a new aircraft, which impact on passenger safety, will place a very high emphasis on quality objectives. With other projects, for example a research project that is being funded by a fixed government grant, cost might predominate. Other projects emphasize time: for example, the organization of an open-air music festival has to happen on a particular date if the project is to meet its objectives. In each of these projects, although one objective might be particularly important, the other objectives can never be totally forgotten. Figure 16.5 shows the 'project objectives triangle' with these three types of project marked.[4]

The Channel Tunnel

During the construction of the Channel Tunnel

The £15 billion Channel Tunnel project was the largest construction project ever undertaken in Europe and the biggest single investment in transport anywhere in the world. The project, which was funded by the private sector, made provision for a 55-year concession for the owners to design, build and run the operation. The Eurotunnel Group (technically two holding companies, one French and one in the UK) awarded the contract to design and build the tunnel to TML (Trans-Manche Link), a consortium of 10 French and British construction companies. For the project managers it was a formidable undertaking. The sheer scale of the project was daunting in itself. The volume of rubble removed from the tunnel was three times greater than that of the Cheops Pyramid in Egypt. It increased the size of Britain by 90 acres, equivalent to 68 football fields. Two main railway tunnels, split by a service/access tunnel, each 7.6 metres in diameter, run 40 metres below the sea bed. In total there are in excess of 150 kilometres of tunnel. The whole project was never going to be a straightforward management task. During the early

negotiations, political uncertainty surrounded the commitment of both governments, and in the planning phase geological issues had to be investigated by a complex series of tests. Even the financing of the project was complex. It required investment by over 200 banks and finance houses, as well as over half a million shareholders. Furthermore, the technical problems posed by the drilling itself and, more importantly, in the commissioning of the tracks and systems within the tunnel needed to be overcome. Yet in spite of some delays and cost over-runs, the project ranks as one of the most impressive of the twentieth century.

Questions

1 What factors made the Channel Tunnel a particularly complex project and how might these have been dealt with?

2 What factors contributed to 'uncertainty' in the project and how might these factors have been dealt with?

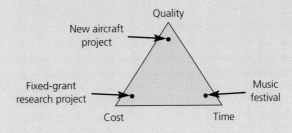

Figure 16.5 The project objectives triangle

Project scope

The scope of a project identifies its work content and its products or outcomes. It is essentially a boundary-setting exercise which attempts to define the dividing line between what each part of the project will do and what it won't do. Defining scope is particularly important for managing contractors because of the commercial and legal aspects of an outside contractor's relationship with the organization that is managing the project. A contractor's *scope of supply* will identify the boundaries within which the work must be done.

In general, defining the scope of a project or work package is helped by defining the following:

- *The parts of the organization which are affected*: for example, 'designing and installing an automated guided vehicle system in the warehouse up to the receiving bay'.
- *The time period involved*: for example, 'installation to begin no earlier than 15 January and to be completed no later than 2 March'.
- *The business processes involved*: for example, 'to interface with the current order retrieval system and stock location system'.
- *The resources to be used*: for example, 'to provide own power supply and limit the number of staff working on the installation to five at any one time'.
- *The contractor's responsibilities*: for example, 'to include all ancillary power and information supply systems, full maintenance schedules and initial training'.

The project specification

The scope of the project is formalized in the *project specification*, which is the written, pictorial and graphical information used to define the output, and the accompanying terms and conditions. Although written before the project starts, changes may have to be made to the scope which was originally specified. This is illustrated by the larger feedback loop in Figure 16.3. There are two broad categories of change which need to be considered: internal and external changes. *Internal changes* result from decisions by the project management to do things differently from the original specification. *External changes* occur when a customer has decided to change the specification. The difference between these two types of change in a commercial project can be very important. Often the company managing the project can demand payment for external changes, but not for internal changes.

Project strategy

The third part of a project's definition is the project strategy, which defines, in a general rather than a specific way, how the organization is going to achieve its project objectives and meet the related measures of performance. It does this in two ways. First, the project strategy should define the *phases* of the project. Phases break the project down into time-based sections. In the case of a software development project, the phases might be as follows:

- *Specification phase*: where customer requirements are specified, and a systems specification is drawn up.
- *Design phase*: where systems design and sub-system specifications are determined.
- *Implementation phase*: where modules are specified.
- *Module-testing phase*: where each module is tested separately.
- *Integration-testing phase*: where sub-systems and finally the complete system are tested.
- *Delivery phase*: where the system is handed over to the customer.

Second, the project strategy should set *milestones*, which are important events during the project's life at which specific reviews of time, cost and quality are made. At this stage the actual dates for each milestone are not necessarily determined. It is useful, however, to at least identify the significant milestones, either to define the boundary between phases or to help in discussions with the customer. For example, the milestones which are defined for the production of a television commercial campaign might be as follows:

Milestone 1 – overall concept agreed with client;
Milestone 2 – story-board outline prepared and agreed;
Milestone 3 – shooting fully planned and organized;
Milestone 4 – first portfolio presented to client;
Milestone 5 – final cut agreed with client.

Stage 3 – Project planning

The planning process fulfils four distinct purposes:

- It determines the cost and duration of the project. This enables major decisions to be made – such as the decision whether to go ahead with the project at the start.
- It determines the level of resources which will be needed.
- It helps to allocate work and to monitor progress. Planning must include the identification of who is responsible for what.
- It helps to assess the impact of any changes to the project.

Planning is not a one-off process. It may be repeated several times during the project's life as circumstances change. Nor is replanning a sign of project failure or mismanagement. In uncertain projects, in particular, it is a normal occurrence. In fact, later stage plans typically mean that more information is available, and that the project is becoming less uncertain. The process of project planning involves five steps (*see* Fig. 16.6).

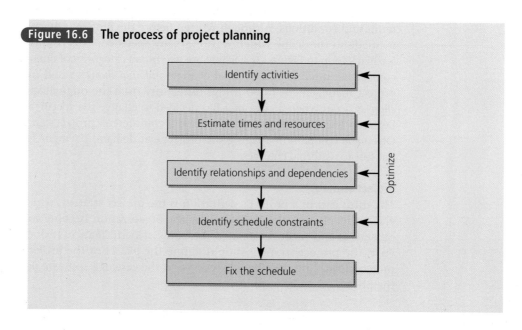

Figure 16.6 **The process of project planning**

Identify activities – the work breakdown structure

Most projects are too complex to be planned and controlled effectively unless they are first broken down into manageable portions. This is achieved by structuring the project into a 'family tree', along similar lines to the bill of materials (Chapter 14). But unlike the bill of materials, which specifies items, this specifies the major tasks or sub-projects. These in turn are divided up into smaller tasks until a defined, manageable series of tasks, called a *work package,* is arrived at. Each work package can be allocated its own objectives in terms of time, cost and quality. The output from this is called the *work breakdown structure* (WBS). The WBS brings clarity and definition to the project planning process. It shows 'how the jigsaw fits together'.[5] It also provides a framework for building up information for reporting purposes.

Example project

As a simple example to illustrate the application of each stage of the planning process, let us examine the following domestic project. The project definition is:

- *purpose:* to make breakfast in bed;
- *end result:* breakfast in bed of boiled egg, toast and orange juice;
- *success criteria:* plan uses minimum staff resources and time, and product is high quality (egg freshly boiled, warm toast, etc.);
- *scope:* project starts in kitchen at 6.00 am, and finishes in bedroom; needs one operator and normal kitchen equipment.

The work breakdown structure is based on the above definition and can be constructed as shown in Figure 16.7

Estimate times and resources

The next stage in planning is to identify the time and resource requirements of the work packages. Without some idea of how long each part of a project will take and how many resources it will need, it is impossible to define what should be happening at any time during the execution of the project. Estimates are just that, however – a systematic

The construction of Black Point, Hong Kong's first natural gas-fired station, was a major task for Alstom, the consortium leader for the project. The vast construction had to be managed so that it would be delivered to the customer, China Light and Power (CLP), on time, on specification and on budget. Managing such a large project, lasting several years, called for exceptional project management skills. These included coping with the environmental implications of the project (using simulation), managing the other contractors who had responsibility for the various parts of the project, and monitoring progress

Figure 16.7 **A work breakdown structure for a simple domestic project**

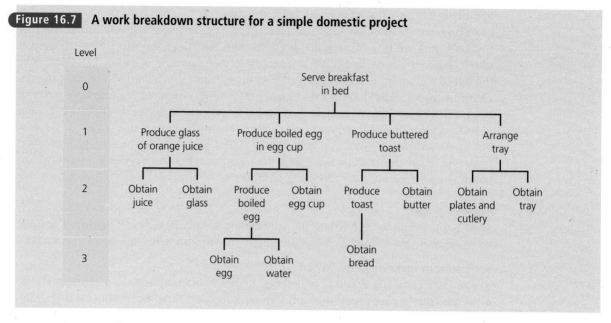

Level

0 — Serve breakfast in bed

1 — Produce glass of orange juice / Produce boiled egg in egg cup / Produce buttered toast / Arrange tray

2 — Obtain juice / Obtain glass / Produce boiled egg / Obtain egg cup / Produce toast / Obtain butter / Obtain plates and cutlery / Obtain tray

3 — Obtain egg / Obtain water / Obtain bread

best guess, not a perfect forecast of reality. Estimates may never be perfect but they can be made with some idea of how accurate they might be.

Example project

Returning to our very simple example 'breakfast-in-bed' project, the activities were identified and times estimated as in Table 16.2.

Table 16.2 Time and resources estimates for a 'breakfast-in-bed' project

Activity	Effort (person-min)	Duration (min)
Butter toast	1	1
Pour orange juice	1	1
Boil egg	0	4
Slice bread	1	1
Fill pan with water	1	1
Bring water to boil	0	3
Toast bread	0	2
Take loaded tray to bedroom	1	1
Fetch tray, plates, cutlery	1	1

While some of the estimates may appear generous, they take into account the time of day and the state of the operator.

Probabilistic estimates

The amount of uncertainty in a project has a major bearing on the level of confidence which can be placed on an estimate. The impact of uncertainty on estimating times leads some project managers to use a probability curve to describe the estimate. In practice, this is usually a positively skewed distribution, as in Figure 16.8. The greater the risk, the greater the range of the distribution. The natural tendency of some people is to produce *optimistic* estimates, but these will have a relatively low probability of being

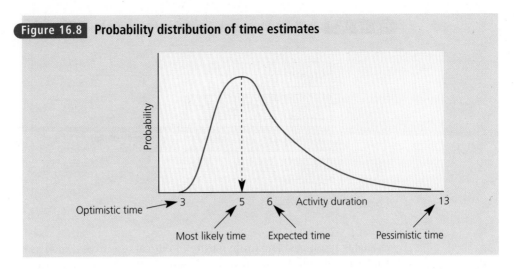

Figure 16.8 Probability distribution of time estimates

correct because they represent the time which would be taken if *everything* went well. *Most likely* estimates have the highest probability of proving correct. Finally, *pessimistic* estimates assume that almost everything which could go wrong does go wrong. Because of the skewed nature of the distribution, the expected time for the activity will not be the same as the most likely time.

Identify relationships and dependencies

All the activities which are identified as comprising a project will have some relationship with one another that will depend on the logic of the project. Some activities will, by necessity, need to be executed in a particular order. For example, in the construction of a house, the foundations must be prepared before the walls are built, which in turn must be completed before the roof is put in place. These activities have a *dependent* or *series* relationship. Other activities do not have any such dependence on each other. The rear garden of the house could probably be prepared totally independently of the garage being built. These two activities have an *independent* or *parallel* relationship.

Example project

Table 16.2 identified the activities for the breakfast preparation project. The list shows that some of the activities must necessarily follow others. For example, 'boil egg' cannot be carried out until 'fill pan with water' and 'bring water to boil' have been completed. Further logical analysis of the activities in the list shows that there are two major 'chains', where activities must be carried out in a definite sequence:

Slice bread – Toast bread – Butter toast
Fill pan with water – Bring water to boil – Boil egg

Both of these sequences must be completed before the activity 'take loaded tray to bedroom'. The remaining activities ('pour orange juice' and 'fetch tray, plates, cutlery') can be done at any time provided that they are completed before 'take loaded tray to bedroom'. An initial project plan might be as shown in Figure 16.9. Here, the activities have been represented as blocks of time in proportion to their estimated durations. From this, we can see that the 'project' can be completed in nine minutes. Some of the activities have spare time (called float) indicated by the dotted line. The sequence 'Fill pan – Boil water – Boil egg – Bedroom' has no float, and is called the *critical path* of the project. By implication, any activity which runs late in this sequence would cause the whole project to be delayed accordingly.

Identify schedule constraints

Once estimates have been made of the time and effort involved in each activity, and their dependencies identified, it is possible to compare project requirements with the

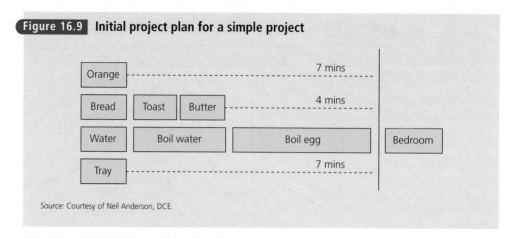

Figure 16.9 Initial project plan for a simple project

Source: Courtesy of Neil Anderson, DCE.

available resources. The finite nature of critical resources – such as special skills – means that they should be taken into account in the planning process. This often has the effect of highlighting the need for more detailed replanning. There are essentially two fundamental approaches:[6]

- *Resource-constrained.* Only the available resource levels are used in resource scheduling, and are never exceeded. As a result, the project completion may slip. Resource-limited scheduling is used, for example, when a project company has its own highly specialized assembly and test facilities.
- *Time-constrained.* The overriding priority is to complete the project within a given time. Once normally available resources have been used up, alternative ('threshold') resources are scheduled.

Example project

Returning to the breakfast-in-bed project, we can now consider the resource implications of the plan in Figure 16.9. Each of the four activities scheduled at the start (pour orange, cut bread, fill pan, fetch tray) consumes staff resources. Charting the required resources will give a resource profile as in Figure 16.10. There is clearly a resource-loading problem, because the project definition states that only one person is available. This is not an insuperable difficulty, however, because there is sufficient float to move some of the activities. A plan with levelled resources can be produced, as shown in Figure 16.11. All that has been necessary is to delay the toast preparation by one minute, and to use the elapsed time during the toasting and water-boiling processes to pour orange and fetch the tray.

Fix the schedule

Project planners should ideally have a number of alternatives to choose from. The one which best fits project objectives can then be chosen or developed. For example, it may be appropriate to examine both resource-limited and time-limited options. However, it is not always possible to examine several alternative schedules, especially in very large or very uncertain projects, as the computation could be prohibitive. However, modern computer-based project management software is making the search for the best schedule more feasible.

Example project

A further improvement to the plan can be made. Looking again at the project definition, the success criteria state that the product should be 'high quality'. In the plan shown in Figure 16.11, although the egg is freshly boiled, the toast might be cold. An 'optimized' plan which would provide hot toast would be to prepare the toast during the 'boil egg' activity. This plan is shown in Figure 16.12.

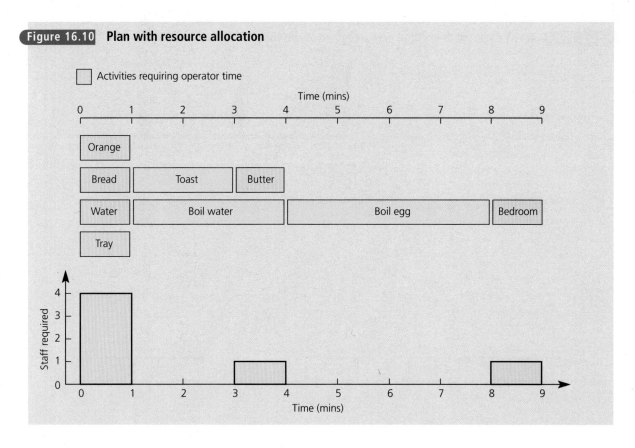

Figure 16.10 Plan with resource allocation

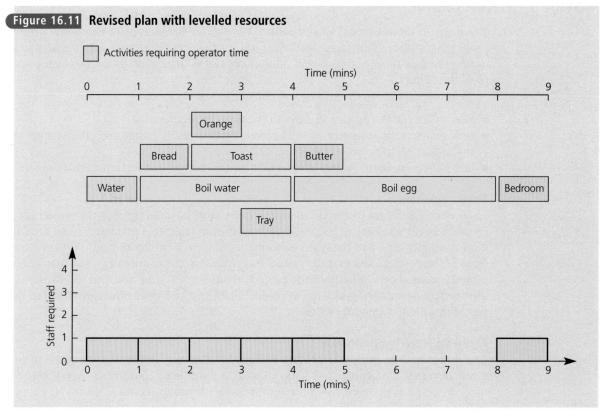

Figure 16.11 Revised plan with levelled resources

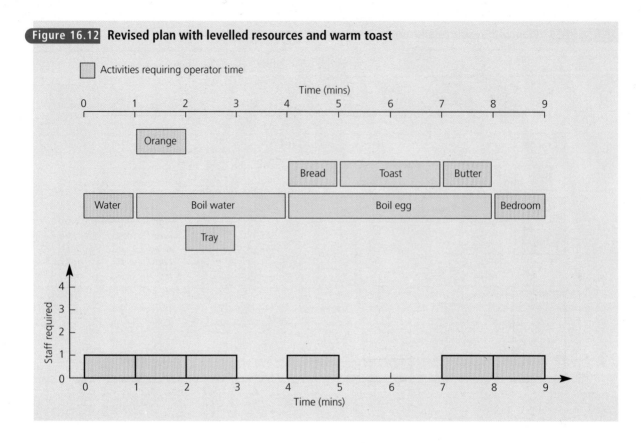

Figure 16.12 Revised plan with levelled resources and warm toast

● Stage 5 – Project control

The stages in project planning and control have so far all taken place before the actual project takes place. This stage deals with the management activities which take place during the execution of the project. Project control is the essential link between planning and doing.

The process of project control involves three sets of decisions:

- how to *monitor* the project in order to check on its progress;
- how to *assess the performance* of the project by comparing monitored observations of the project with the project plan;
- how to *intervene* in the project in order to make the changes that will bring it back to plan.

Project monitoring

Project managers have first to decide what they should be looking for as the project progresses. Usually a variety of measures are monitored. Table 16.3 illustrates some typical monitored measures and the main performance objectives which they affect. Note how some of these monitored measures affect mainly cost, some mainly time, but that when something affects the quality of the project, there are also time and cost implications. This is because quality problems in project planning and control usually have to be solved in a limited amount of time.

Assessing project performance

The monitored measures of project performance at any point in time need to be assessed so that project management can make a judgement concerning overall performance. A typical planned cost profile of a project through its life is shown in Figure 16.13. At the beginning of a project some activities can be started, but most activities will be dependant on finishing. Eventually, only a few activities will remain to be

Not all projects are very large scale but they still need careful planning and control if they are not to disrupt the operation and its customers. Failure to plan correctly for new water pipe installation can result in interrupted supply

Table 16.3 Monitored measures and their effect on project performance objectives

Monitored measure	Main performance objectives affected
Costs exceeding budget	Cost
Cash running low	Cost
Supplier price changes	Cost
Excessive overtime	Cost
Changes in project scope	Quality, time, cost
Technical performance poor	Quality, time, cost
Inspection failures	Quality, time, cost
Errors in information	Quality, time, cost
Waiting for resource delays	Time, cost
Supplier delays	Time, cost
Customer changes delivery date	Time, cost
Activities not started on time	Time.
Activities not finished on time	Time
Missed milestones	Time

completed. This pattern of a slow start followed by a faster pace with an eventual tail-off of activity holds true for almost all projects, which is why the rate of total expenditure follows an S-shaped pattern as shown in Figure 16.13, even when the cost curves for the individual activities are linear. It is against this curve that actual costs can be compared in order to check whether the project's costs are being incurred to plan. Figure 16.14 shows the planned and actual cost figures compared in this way. It shows that the project is incurring costs, on a cumulative basis, ahead of what was planned.

Earned-value control

The 'earned-value' method of project control assesses performance of the project by combining cost and time together. Rather than measure the progress of the project in days, it measures it in the value of the work done. A project which has a total value of

Figure 16.13 Typical S-shaped cost curve for the total project

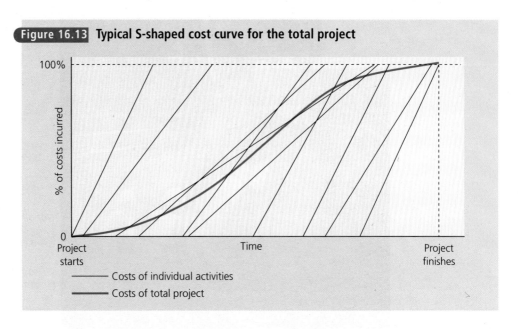

Figure 16.14 Comparing planned and actual expenditure

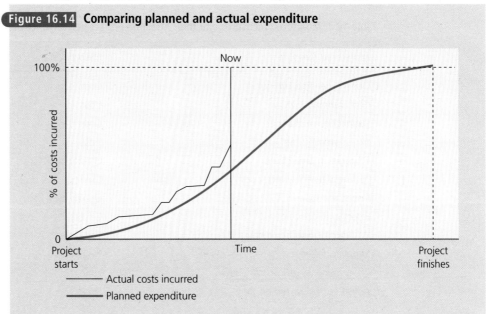

£100 000, therefore, would be half complete when the value of the activities which have actually been completed is £50 000. Figure 16.15 shows the progress of a project measured on an earned-value basis. It shows actual cost incurred against work completed. Because the work done is measured in monetary units, the line which represents the project plan will be at 45 degrees. That means that when £10 000 worth of work has been completed, the expenditure should have actually been £10 000, and so on. It actually shows that, at the end of three periods, this project has completed £50 000 worth of work when it should have completed £60 000 worth. Furthermore, the actual cost it has incurred is £65 000. These three figures each have terms to describe them:

- *The budgeted cost of work scheduled* (BCWS) is the amount of work which should have been completed by a particular time (£60 000 in our example).
- *The budgeted cost of work performed* (BCWP) is the actual amount of work which has been completed by a particular time (£50 000 in our example).

Figure 16.15 Comparing the planned and actual values of work completed in order to calculate cost and schedule variances

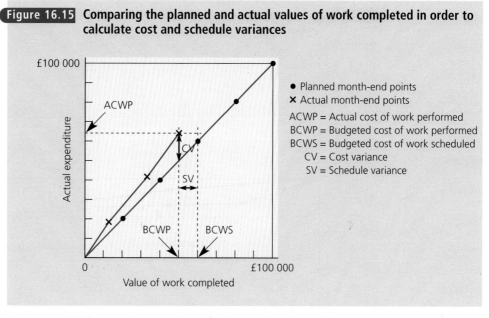

- *The actual cost of work performed* (ACWP) is the actual expenditure which has been spent on doing the work completed by a particular time (£65 000 in our example).

From these three figures two *variances*, which indicate the deviation from plan, can be derived.

Schedule variance (SV)   =   BCWP – BCWS
    In our example: SV   =   £50 000 – £60 000
                          =   – £10 000
    Cost variance (CV)   =   BCWP – ACWP
    In our example: CV   =   £50 000 – £65 000
                          =   – £15 000

Intervening to change the project

If the project is obviously out of control in the sense that its costs, quality levels or times are significantly different from those planned, then some kind of intervention is almost certainly likely to be required. The exact nature of the intervention will depend on the technical characteristics of the project, but it is likely to need the advice of all the people who would be affected. Given the interconnected nature of projects – a change to one part of the project will have knock-on effects elsewhere – this means that interventions often require wide consultation.

Sometimes intervention is needed even if the project looks to be proceeding according to plan. For example, Figure 16.16 shows the schedule and cost variances for a project, together with the 'allowable range' of variance. These are the tolerance limits between which the variance can move without it indicating that there is necessarily a problem. When the project managers look forward and project activities and cost into the future, however, they see that problems are very likely to arise. In this case it is the *trend* of performance which is being used to trigger intervention.

Figure 16.16 **Plotting cost and schedule variance over time and forecasting from the trend**

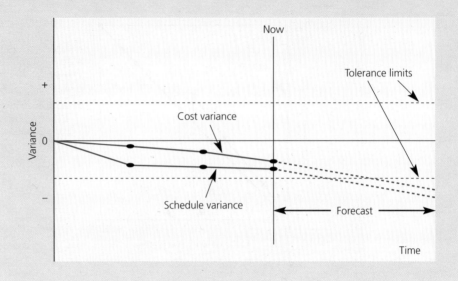

Virtual project management

CADCENTRE's Visuality group visualization system enables projects teams to check out and validate design proposals using interactive computer models

management experts who can integrate services extending from design and fabrication to maintenance and asset management. The working practices of these project management collaborators are also changing. Advanced computer-aided systems are helping to facilitate a new approach to major project design and management.

The picture opposite shows examples of this. Here, project teams are viewing computer models of an offshore structure using CADCENTRE plant design software and visualization system. This allows them to check out not only the original design but any modifications that have to be made during construction. More detailed CAD images can be used for more specific analysis.

The oil industry has always placed a high value on project management. Cost and time over-runs in the construction of offshore facilities or onshore refineries can mean the difference between profit and loss in the early years of most capital projects. The operating companies themselves are increasingly stepping back from hands-on engineering activities to focus more on their core business. They are relying on project

Questions

1 Why do you think a realistic picture of a completed project helps the process of project management?

2 Why are such visualizations becoming more important?

Network planning

The process of project planning and control is greatly aided by the use of techniques which help project managers to handle its complexity and time-based nature. The simplest of these techniques is the Gantt chart (or bar chart) which we introduced in Chapter 10. This spawned later techniques, most of which go under the collective name of *network analysis*. It is these which are now used, almost universally, to help plan and control all significant projects, but which can also prove helpful in smaller ventures. The two network analysis methods we will examine are the *critical path method* (CPM) or *analysis* (CPA) and *program evaluation and review technique* (PERT).

The length of the bar for each activity on a Gantt chart is directly proportional to the calendar time, and so indicates the relative duration of each activity. Progress against each activity is shown by the lower strips. The arrow which shows 'time now' indicates that all activities to the left should by now have been completed. Gantt charts are the simplest way to exhibit an overall project plan, because they have excellent visual impact and are easy to understand. They are also useful for communicating project plans and status to senior managers as well as for day-to-day project control.

Figure 16.17 **Implementing new logistics operation: Gantt chart**

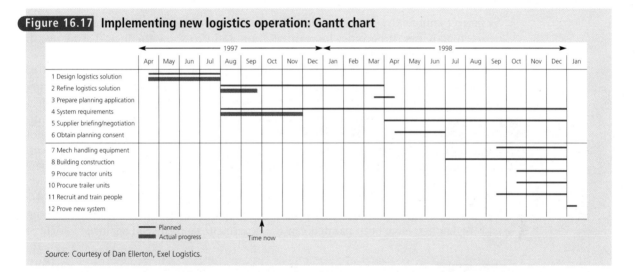

Source: Courtesy of Dan Ellerton, Exel Logistics.

Worked example

An example of a Gantt chart used to plan a project is shown in Figure 16.17. The chart is being used to plan and monitor the implementation of a new logistics operation. The new operation will involve the purchase of a fleet of trucks, the design of new routes and the building of a new distribution centre and associated handling equipment. The following major activities are planned:

1 *Design logistics solution*. Approximately three months' duration, given good data and direction from customer. (Key task is getting information from people who are not directly involved with the project.)
2 *Refine logistics solution*. An ongoing process which must be kept on track once an outline has been selected. (It must be completed before suppliers can be briefed.)
3 *Prepare planning application*. Needs four weeks. (Building specification must be ready first.)
4 *System requirements*. An ongoing process of integrating information systems. (All systems are available, but they must be integrated into overall project objectives.)

5 *Supplier briefing/negotiation.* New procedures need to be explained on an ongo-ing basis to all suppliers by the central coordination team.

6 *Obtain planning consent.* Statutory time is eight weeks, but experience suggests that 12 weeks is the norm.

7 *Mechanical handling equipment.* Lead time is currently 12 weeks for standard equipment, up to 16 weeks for specialist. (Have assumed standard. This activity includes design and layout of racking.)

8 *Building construction.* This would be six months for a 100 000 square foot build-ing. (Weather can have a major impact.)

9 *Tractor procurement.* Currently 10 to 12 weeks' lead time.

10 *Trailer procurement.* Eight weeks standard to 12 weeks for special requirements.

11 *Recruit and train.* Need to start recruitment of 100 staff three months before start-up. (Training to start two weeks before start-up.)

12 *Prove new system.* Two weeks are needed for system trials, proving and final training.

● Critical path method (CPM)

As project complexity increases, so it becomes necessary to identify the relationships between activities. It becomes increasingly important to show the logical sequence in which activities must take place.

Critical path method (CPM) models the project by clarifying the relationships between activities diagrammatically. The first way we can illustrate this is by using arrows to represent each activity in a project. For example, examine the simple project in Figure 16.18 which involves the decoration of an apartment. Six activities are identi-fied together with their relationships. The first, activity a, 'remove furniture', does not require any of the other activities to be completed before it can be started. However, activity b, 'prepare bedroom', cannot be started until activity a has been completed. The same applies to activity d, 'prepare the kitchen'. Similarly activity c, 'paint bedroom', cannot be started until activity b has been completed. Nor can activity e, 'paint the kitchen', be started until the kitchen has been prepared. Only when both the bedroom and the kitchen have been painted can the apartment be furnished again. The logic of

Figure 16.18 The activities, relationships, durations and arrow diagram for the project 'decorate apartment'

Activity	Immediate predecessors	Activity duration (in days)
a Remove furniture	None	1
b Prepare bedroom	a	2
c Paint bedroom	b	3
d Prepare kitchen	a	1
e Paint kitchen	d	2
f Replace furniture	c, e	1

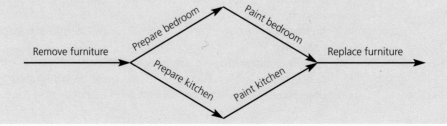

Figure 16.19 A network diagram for the project 'decorate apartment'

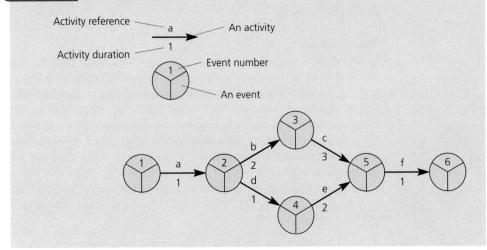

these relationships is shown as an arrow diagram, where each activity is represented by an arrow (the length of the arrows is not proportional to the duration of the activities).

This arrow diagram can be developed into a network diagram as shown in Figure 16.19. At the tail (start) and head (finish) of each *activity* (represented by an arrow) is a circle which represents an *event*. Events are moments in time which occur at the start or finish of an activity. They have no duration and are of a definite recognizable nature. Networks of this type are composed only of activities and events.

The rules for drawing this type of network diagram are fairly straightforward:

Rule 1 An event cannot be reached until all activities leading to it are complete. Event 5 in Figure 16.19 is not reached until activities c and e are complete.

Rule 2 No activity can start until its tail event is reached. In Figure 16.19 activity f cannot start until event 5 is reached.

Rule 3 No two activities can have the same head and tail events. In Figure 16.20 activities x and y cannot be drawn as first shown; they must be drawn using a *dummy activity*.

Figure 16.20 When dummy activities are necessary

(a) When two independent activities have the same head and tail event

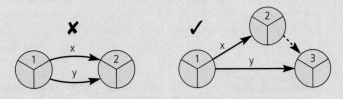

(b) When two independent chains of activities share a common event

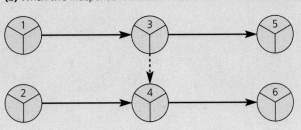

Dummy activities have no duration and are usually shown as a dotted line arrow. They are used either for clarity of drawing or to keep the logic of the diagram consistent with that of the project.

The critical path

In all network diagrams where the activities have some parallel relationships, there will be more than one sequence of activities which will lead from the start to the end of the project. These sequences of activities are called *paths* through the network. Each path will have a total duration which is the sum of all its activities. The path which has the longest sequence of activities is called the *critical path* of the network (note that it is possible to have more than one critical path if they share the same joint longest time). It is called the critical path because any delay in any of the activities on this path will delay the whole project.

In Figure 16.19, therefore, the critical path through the network is a, b, c, f, which is seven days long. This is the minimum duration of the whole project. By drawing the network diagram we can:

- identify which are the particularly important activities;
- calculate the duration of the whole project.

Calculating float

Earlier in the chapter we described the flexibility to change the timings of activities, which is inherent in various parts of a project, as *float*. We can use the network diagram to calculate this for each activity. The procedure is relatively simple:

1 Calculate the earliest and latest event times for each event. The earliest event time (EET) is the very earliest the event could possibly occur if all preceding activities are completed as early as possible. The latest event time (LET) is the latest time that the event could possibly take place without delaying the whole project.
2 Calculate the 'time window' within which an activity must take place. This is the time between the EET of its tail event and the LET of its head event.
3 Compare the actual duration of the activity with the time window within which it must take place. The difference between them is the float of the activity.

Consider again the simple network example. The critical path is the sequence of activities a, b, c, f. We can calculate the EET and LET for each event as shown in Figure 16.21. If activity a starts at time 0, the earliest it can finish is 1 because it is a one-day activity. If activity b is started immediately, it will finish at day 3 (EET of tail event + duration, 1 + 2). Activity c can then start at day 3 and because it is of three days' duration it will finish at day 6. Activity e also has event number 5 as its head event so we must also calculate the EET of activity e's tail event. This is determined by activity d. If activity d starts at day 1 (the earliest it can) it will finish at day 2. So the EET of event

Figure 16.21 **A network diagram for the project 'decorate apartment' with earliest and latest event times**

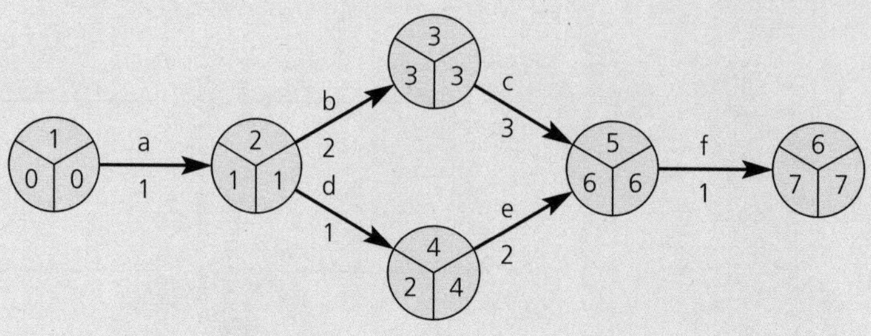

number 4 is day 2. If activity e is started immediately, it will then finish at day 4. Event number 5 cannot occur, however, until both e and c have finished, which will not be until day 6 (*see* rule 1 above). Activity f can then start and will finish at day 7.

The LETs can be calculated by using the reverse logic. If event number 6 *must* occur no later than day 7, the LET for event number 5 is day 6. Any later than this and the whole project will be delayed. Working back, if activity c must finish by day 6 it cannot start later than day 3, and if activity b must finish by day 3 it must start by day 1. Similarly, if activity e is to finish by day 6 it must start no later than day 4, and if activity d is to finish by day 4 it must start no later than day 3. Now we have two activities with event number 2 as their tail event, one of which needs to start by day 1 at the latest, the other by day 3 at the latest. The LET for event number 2, therefore, must be the smaller of the two. If it was delayed past this point, activity b, and therefore the whole project, would be delayed.

Activity on node networks

The network we have described so far uses arrows to represent activities and circles at the junctions or nodes of the arrows to represent events. This method is called the *activity on arrow* (AoA) method. An alternative method of drawing networks is the *activity on node* (AoN) method. In the AoN representation, activities are drawn as boxes, and arrows are used to define the relationships between them. There are three advantages to the AoN method:

- It is often easier to move from the basic logic of a project's relationships to a network diagram using AoN rather than using the AoA method.
- AoN diagrams do not need dummy activities to maintain the logic of relationships.
- Most of the computer packages which are used in project planning and control use an AoN format.

An AoN network of the 'apartment decorating' project is shown in Figure 16.22.

Figure 16.22 **Activity on node network diagram for project 'decorate apartment'**

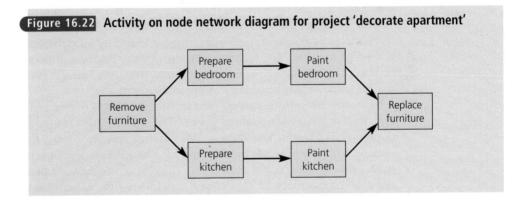

Example

Returning to the 'new logistics' operation described previously, an AoN network diagram is shown in Figure 16.23. In this example (as in most realistic examples) relationships are not always clear-cut. For example, 'Refine logistics' has been shown as impacting only on 'Supplier negotiation'. In practice, it would also impact on 'System requirements', and probably also on the design issues in activities 7 through 11. Such relationships could be shown on a lower-level network, which goes into more detail on such issues. The activity on system requirements is a sub-project in itself, and would require its own bar charts and logic diagrams for planning and monitoring.

Figure 16.23 New logistics operation: logic diagram

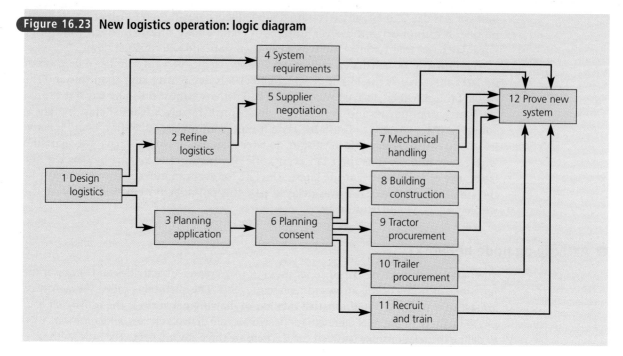

Time analysis

Figure 16.24 provides a full AoN network for the simple logic diagram in Figure 16.23. Activity numbers and abbreviated descriptions are as before.

The *earliest start times* for each activity are found by working from left to right across the network. Each start event can begin at $t = 0$. At a 'merge' event (where two or more activities come together, as at event 12), use the latest completion date of the various activities which lead into it. Earliest finish times of a 'burst' activity (such as activity 6, where five succeeding activities literally 'burst' out) are carried forward to form the earliest start dates of the succeeding activities (7 through 11).

The *latest start times* for each activity are found by working back from right to left across the network. The earliest start time for the final event on the network is often used as the latest start time for that event as well. At a 'merge' event (such as event 6), use the earliest completion date of the various activities.

First, we carry out a *forward pass* of the network (i.e. proceed from left to right). Activity 1 is given a start date of week 0. The earliest finish is then week 17, because the duration is 17 weeks. The earliest start date for activity 2 must then also be week 17. Activity 5 starts at 17 + 34, the duration for activity 2. Activity 4 is in parallel with activity 2, and can start at the same time. The rest of the forward pass is straight-forward until we reach activity 12. Here, seven activities merge, so we must use the highest earliest finish of the activities which lead into it as the earliest start time for activity 12. This is 91 (the earliest finish time for activity 4). Since the duration of activity 12 is two weeks, the earliest finish time for the whole network is 93 weeks.

Now we can carry out a *backward pass* by assuming that the latest finish time is also 93 weeks (the bottom right-hand box on activity 12). This means that there is no 'float', i.e. the difference between the earliest and latest start dates for this activity is zero. Hence, the latest start time is also week 91. This gets downdated into activities 7 through 11, which have week 91 as the latest finish time. The difference between week 91 and the various earliest finish times for these activities means that there is float on each one, that is that they can start much later than indicated by the earliest start dates. On the backward pass, activity 6 forms a merge event for activities 7 through 11. Take the lowest latest start time from these activities, i.e. week 67, as the latest finish time for

Figure 16.24 New logistics operation: precedence network

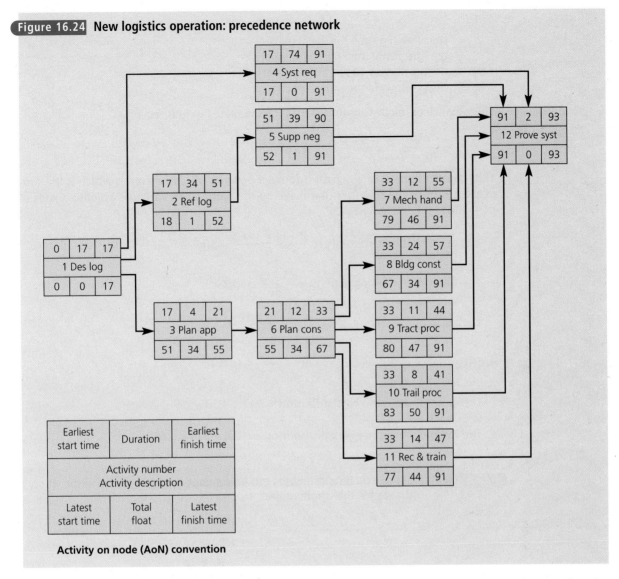

Activity on node (AoN) convention

activity 6. If all goes well, and the analysis is correct, there should also be zero float for activity 1. The *critical path* for the network is then the line which joins the activities with minimum float, i.e. activities 1, 4 and 12.

Program evaluation and review technique (PERT)

The program evaluation and review technique, or PERT as it is universally known, had its origins in planning and controlling major defence projects in the US Navy. PERT had its most spectacular gains in the highly uncertain environment of space and defence projects. The technique recognizes that activity durations and costs in project management are not deterministic (fixed), and that probability theory can be applied to estimates, as was shown in Figure 16.8.

In this type of network each activity duration is estimated on an optimistic, a most likely and a pessimistic basis, as shown in Figure 16.25. If it is assumed that these time estimates are consistent with a beta probability distribution, the mean and variance of the distribution can be estimated as follows:

$$t_e = \frac{t_o + 4t_l + t_p}{6}$$

where

t_e = the expected time for the activity
t_o = the optimistic time for the activity
t_l = the most likely time for the activity
t_p = the pessimistic time for the activity

The variance of the distribution (V) can be calculated as follows:

$$V = \frac{(t_p - t_o)^2}{6^2} = \frac{(t_p - t_o)^2}{36}$$

The time distribution of any path through a network will have a mean which is the sum of the means of the activities that make up the path, and a variance which is a sum of their variances. In Figure 16.25:

$$\text{The mean of the first activity} = \frac{2 + (4 \times 3) + 5}{6} = 3.17$$

$$\text{The variance of the first activity} = \frac{(5 - 2)^2}{36} = 0.25$$

$$\text{The mean of the second activity} = \frac{3 + (4 \times 4) + 7}{6} = 4.33$$

$$\text{The variance of the second activity} = \frac{(7 - 3)^2}{36} = 0.44$$

The mean of the network distribution = 3.17 + 4.33 = 7.5

The variance of the network distribution = 0.25 + 0.44 = 0.69

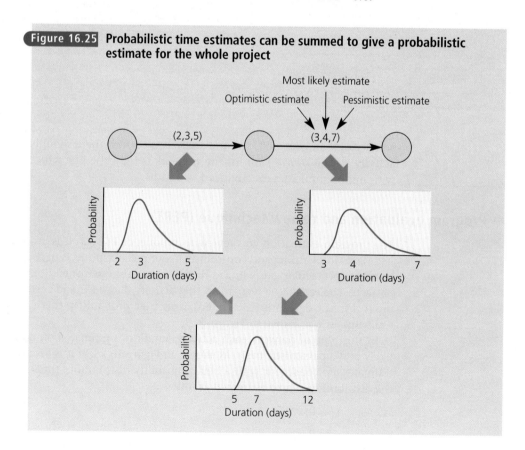

Figure 16.25 **Probabilistic time estimates can be summed to give a probabilistic estimate for the whole project**

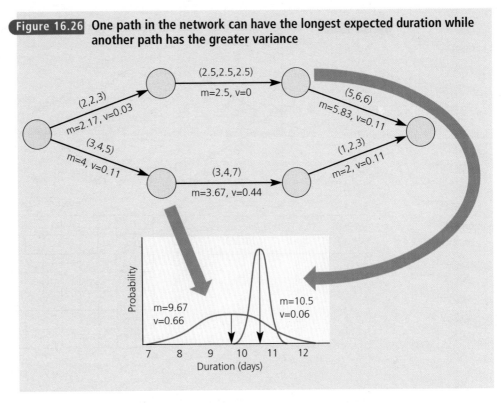

Figure 16.26 One path in the network can have the longest expected duration while another path has the greater variance

It is generally assumed that the whole path will be normally distributed.

The advantage of this extra information is that we can examine the 'riskiness' of each path through a network as well as its duration. For example, Figure 16.26 shows a simple two-path network. The top path is the critical one; the distribution of its duration is 10.5 with a variance of 0.06 (therefore a standard deviation of 0.245). The distribution of the non-critical path has a mean of 9.67 and a variance of 0.66 (therefore a standard deviation of 0.812). The implication of this is that there is a chance that the non-critical path could in reality be critical. Although we will not discuss the probability calculations here, it is possible to determine the probability of any sub-critical path turning out to be critical when the project actually takes place. However, on a practical level, even if the probability calculations are judged not to be worth the effort involved, it is useful to be able to make an approximate assessment of the riskiness of each part of a network.

● Introducing resource constraints

The logic which governs network relationships is primarily derived from the technical details of the project as we have described. However, the availability of resources may impose its own constraints, which can materially affect the relationships between activities. Figure 16.27 shows a simple two-path network with details of both the duration of each activity and the number of staff required to perform each activity. The total resource schedule is also shown. The three activities on the critical path, a, c, and e, have been programmed into the resource schedule first. The remaining activities all have some float and therefore have flexibility as to when they are performed.

The resource schedule in Figure 16.27 has the non-critical activities starting as soon as is possible. This results in a resource profile which varies from seven staff down to three. Even if seven staff are available, the project manager might want to even out the loading for organizational convenience. If the total number of staff available is less than seven, however, the project will need rescheduling. Suppose only five staff are available. It is still possible to complete the project in the same time, as shown in Figure 16.28.

Figure 16.27 Resource profile of a network assuming that all activities are started as soon as possible

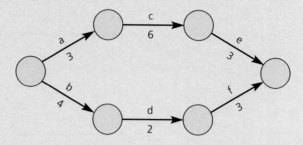

Activity	Duration (days)	Resources (staff)
a	3	4
b	4	3
c	6	2
d	2	3
e	3	3
f	3	2

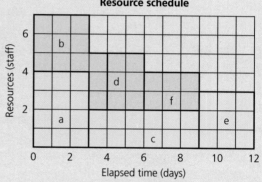

Figure 16.28 Resource profile of a network with non-critical activities delayed to fit resource constraints; in this case this effectively changes the network logic to make all activities critical

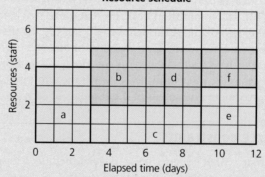

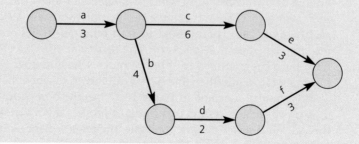

Activity b has been delayed until after activity a has finished. This results in a resource profile which varies only between four and five staff and is within the resourcing limit of five staff.

However, in order to achieve this it is necessary to *require* activity b to start only when activity a is completed. This is a logic constraint which, if it were included in the network, would change it as shown in Figure 16.28. In this network all activities are critical, as indeed one can see from the resource schedule.

Crashing networks

Crashing networks is the process of reducing time spans on critical path activities so that the project is completed in less time. Usually, crashing activities incurs extra cost. This can be as a result of:

- overtime working;
- additional resources, such as manpower;
- sub-contracting.

Figure 16.29 shows an example of crashing a simple network. For each activity the duration and normal cost are specified, together with the (reduced) duration and (increased) cost of crashing them. Not all activities are capable of being crashed; here activity e cannot be crashed. The critical path is the sequence of activities a, b, c, e. If the total project time is to be reduced, one of the activities on the critical path must be crashed. In order to decide which activity to crash, the 'cost slope' of each is calculated.

Figure 16.29 **Crashing activities to shorten project time becomes progessively more expensive**

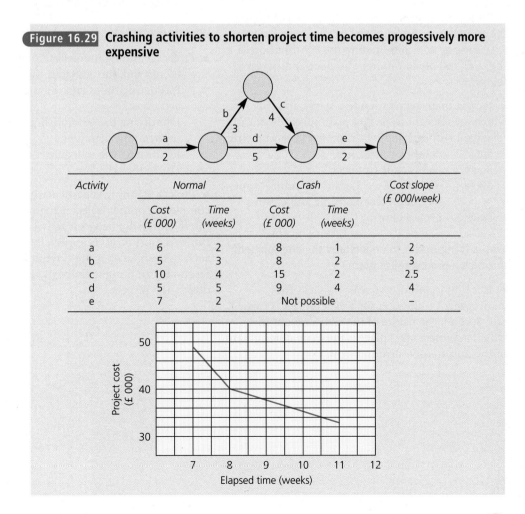

Activity	Normal		Crash		Cost slope (£ 000/week)
	Cost (£ 000)	Time (weeks)	Cost (£ 000)	Time (weeks)	
a	6	2	8	1	2
b	5	3	8	2	3
c	10	4	15	2	2.5
d	5	5	9	4	4
e	7	2	Not possible		–

This is the cost per time period of reducing durations. The most cost-effective way of shortening the whole project then is to crash the activity on the critical path which has the lowest cost slope. This is activity a, the crashing of which will cost an extra £2000 and will shorten the project by one week. After this, activity c can be crashed, saving a further two weeks and costing an extra £5000. At this point all the activities have become critical and further time savings can only be achieved by crashing two activities in parallel.

The shape of the time–cost curve in Figure 16.29 is entirely typical. Initial savings come relatively inexpensively if the activities with the lowest cost slope are chosen. Later in the crashing sequence the more expensive activities need to be crashed and eventually two or more paths become jointly critical. Inevitably by that point, savings in time can only come from crashing two or more activities on parallel paths.

Summary answers to key questions

What is a project and what is project management?

● A project is a set of activities with a defined start point and a defined end state, which pursues a defined goal and uses a defined set of resources.

● All projects can be characterized by their degree of complexity and the inherent uncertainty in the project.

● Project management is the process of managing the activities within a project by planning the work, executing it, and coordinating the contribution of the staff and organizations who have an interest in the project.

● Project management has five stages, four of which are relevant to project planning and control:
  Stage 1 – understanding the project environments;
  Stage 2 – defining the project;
  Stage 3 – planning the project;
  Stage 4 – technical execution of the project (not part of project planning and control);
  Stage 5 – project control.

Why is it important to understand the environment in which a project takes place?

● It is important for two reasons. First, the environment influences the way a project is carried out. Second, the nature of the environment in which a project takes place is the main determinant of the uncertainty surrounding it.

How are specific projects defined?

● Projects can be defined in terms of:
  – their objectives: the end state which project management is trying to achieve;
  – their scope: the exact range of the responsibilities taken on by project management;
  – their strategy: how project management is going to meet the project objectives.

What is project planning and why is it important?

● Project planning involves five stages.
  – Identifying the activities within a project;
  – Estimating times and resources for the activities;
  – Identifying the relationship and dependencies between the activities;
  – Identifying the schedule constraints;
  – Fixing the schedule.

● Project planning is particularly important where complexity of the project is high. The interrelationship between activities, resources and times in most projects, especially complex ones, is such that unless they are carefully planned, resources can become seriously overloaded at times during the project.

What techniques can be used for project planning?

● Network planning and Gantt charts are the most common techniques. The former (using either the activity-on-arrow or activity-on-node format) is particularly useful for assessing the total duration of a project and the degree of flexibility or float of the individual activities within the project.

● The most common method of network planning is called the critical path method (CPM).

● The logic inherent in a network diagram can be changed by resource constraints.

● Network planning models can also be used to assess the total cost of shortening a project where individual activities are shortened.

What is project control and how is it done?

● The process of project control involves three sets of decisions: how to monitor the project in order to check its progress, how to assess the performance of the project by comparing monitored observations to the project plan, and how to intervene in the project in order to make the changes which will bring it back to plan.

● Earned-value control assesses the performance of the project by combining cost and time. It involves plotting the actual expenditure on the project against the value of the work completed, both in the form of what was planned and what is actually happening. Both cost and schedule variances can then be detected.

CASE EXERCISE

Lemming Television

Lemming Television (LTV) is a television production company which specializes in making outside broadcast (OB) 'specials' for a variety of television networks. It was recently commissioned to make a series of 'summer roadshow' programmes which would be shot at locations around Europe during the spring and early summer and broadcast by the customer (a satellite broadcasting network) during the summer. The programmes would involve circus acts, displays, events and computer-graphic displays to entertain the crowds and popular entertainment acts and interviews which would be interspersed with contestant games. Managing the preparation for the series was the responsibility of the show's producer, Flo Brown. Flo, who had recently graduated with distinction from her MBA course, knew that she would need to keep a tight grip on the arrangements for the roadshow series. The shooting would start at the end of May and the final show would be recorded at the end of July. The shows would be broadcast between early July and late August, so any delay either in recording the material or in editing the programmes would cause considerable complications.

The company had known that it would be commissioned to make the programmes since December, but Flo had only been allocated the job in early February! Her first act was to list the various jobs which would have to be done before shooting could start. She then discussed each job with the part of the company which would carry it out, to try

to understand what decisions would need to be made before they could start on their jobs. The jobs which needed to be done prior to the start of the shooting are listed below together with some details.

The producer's responsibilities (as well as managing the whole project) included:

● *Scheduling the venues:* would take about two weeks to finalize and could be started straight away.
● *Defining the design concept:* would need discussions with the chief designer and would take about four weeks of considering alternative designs before finalizing the concept, but could be started straight away.
● *Specifying computer-graphic displays:* again in consultation with the chief designer, it would take about a week but could not be started until all the detailed planning had been finalized.

The design department's responsibility was:

● *Producing artwork for printed materials:* would take about three weeks but could be started only after completion of the detailed planning.

The programme planning department's responsibilities were:

● *Booking the venues:* a one-week job which could be started as soon as the venues had been decided by Flo.
● *Detailed planning:* the preparation of detailed plans and schedules, a two-week task which could

be started once the design concept had been finalized and the venues booked.

- *Printing the brochures:* an outside printer could be given this job as soon as the artwork for the printed materials had been prepared by the design department. The printer usually quoted a four-week delivery from receipt of the artwork.
- *Printing the display posters:* again depended on the preparation of the artwork but could be delivered within two weeks of the artwork being ready.
- *Ordering the roadshow vehicles:* several trailer trucks and ancillary vehicles were needed which could be ordered on completion of the detailed planning; delivery of the vehicles would take about six weeks.
- *Writing the graphic display software:* contracted out to a software house, it would take about four weeks but could only be started after the computer graphics had been specified by the producer and chief designer.
- *Final testing and rehearsals:* the programme planning department were finally responsible for getting the 'whole act together' immediately prior to shooting. Testing and rehearsals could only start once the brochures had been printed, the vehicles fully fitted out and customized and the promotion staff trained. Final tests and rehearsals should take around a week but, if things went wrong at any stage, could take longer.

The workshop's responsibility was:

- *Customizing and fitting out the vehicles:* after the vehicles are delivered and the artwork agreed and the computer-graphics software finished, the vehicles could be fitted out and customized for the shows; this would normally take around two weeks.

The personnel department was responsible for:

- *Recruiting the promotion (promo) staff:* these were the people (often 'resting' actors) who staffed the exhibits and entertained the crowds; they could be recruited as soon as the detailed planning was completed. Usually it took two weeks to recruit all the promo staff.
- *Training the promo staff:* once all promo staff had been recruited they would need training – a one-week task.

> **Questions**
>
> 1 Can Flo get the project together in time to start shooting on schedule?
>
> 2 Which are the jobs which she will have to manage particularly closely?
>
> 3 What general advice would you give her to help her to manage this project?

British Airways London Eye (B)

The British Airways (BA) London Eye is the world's largest observation wheel with a diameter of 135 metres, carrying 32 capsules of up to 25 people on a half-hour continuous ride above London. Its unique engineering design comprises a hub, rim and spokes construction similar to a giant bicycle wheel, supported on an arm cantilevered out over the Thames, just downstream of the Houses of Parliament. The air-conditioned capsules, featuring curved laminated glass, were to be fixed outside the rim, each requiring a motorized levelling system. The whole structure had to be designed to withstand high winds and to damp any natural-frequency resonance in the elegant and slender wheel structure. The extremely challenging technical complexity of the project can be appreciated when one considers the scale of the parts: the wheel rim weighs 800 tonnes, the hub and spindle are 330

tonnes, the cables (spokes) total 100 tonnes, and the legs are 400 tonnes. It was decided to manufacture the wheel in sections and assemble it horizontally on platforms in the river. The subsequent elevation of the whole wheel and leg assembly would attract worldwide press coverage, raising public awareness of London's latest tourist attraction which was to be completed for 31 December 1999, deriving the unofficial name 'The Millennium Wheel'.

The technical complexity and scale of the London Eye were mirrored by an equally difficult project management task. Although the original design had been conceived in 1994, and BA had become involved as the sponsor in 1996, real progress had been dogged by technical, safety, commercial and contractual difficulties. By August 1998, some of the original aesthetic design concepts had been compromised by the current engineering design, £5 million had been spent to date, and the opening date had been put back to Easter 2000! However, Bob Ayling, then the Chief Executive of BA, was adamant that the project had to be completed by the turn of the century.

In September 1998, Mace Ltd, a large firm of international consultants and the original project advisor to BA, was contracted to take full design and project management responsibility, with a brief to develop plans and processes to meet BA's end date. A new project team was formed comprising Mace, the original architect, the Tussauds Group (selected by BA as the operator of the completed attraction), marine engineers, independent checking engineers and major component manufacturing contractors. Much of the original compromised engineering design was rejected, but key long lead-time tasks were prioritized in the new design to allow early commencement of civil engineering works. The first two months of the project were used to resolve most of the outstanding technical and operational problems. Over the next few months, contracts were placed with manufacturers throughout Europe: for example, the French ski-lift contractor Poma would design and make the 32 capsules, the Dutch firm Hollandia was responsible for the rim segments, and so on. The overall budget, originally for around £11m, was reset to £20 million.

The main site works Gantt schedule was prepared, comprising 149 major site activities, grouped into work packages such as civil engineering works, river works (for example, piling and platforms), wheel assembly, capsule fixing, etc. Work was scheduled to begin in week 2 (11 January 1999) and to be completed in week 50. The Gantt chart identified the dependencies and the critical path. The rim segments were to arrive sequentially on barges from late May to mid-July. Task 89, scheduled for week 34 (23 August) was ' Up-end wheel', the critical and technically complex, crucial step of pulling the whole assembly upright. This was to be undertaken under the full scrutiny of the world's media!

Cumulative small delays in preparing the wheel assembly resulted in some programme slippage, and phase 1 of the lift (planned to tilt the wheel by 30 degrees) was actually first attempted late in week 36. On Friday 10 September, five of the anchor blockheads (which secured temporary stabilization cables to the rim) failed under unexpected lateral load, and the lift was stopped. Press releases explained the effect on the project...

'Other works are being rescheduled in an attempt to keep the programme on track. The construction and commissioning of components like the boarding platform, lighting, and assembly of the viewing capsules have been brought forward.'

The Mace project director, Tim Renwick, said: 'The floating crane equipment has been off-hired and no definite date has been given as to when it will be needed again. Although the wheel lift is critical, it has to be done safely.'

The BA spokesman added: 'We do not yet know the likely impact on completion ... we think the target date is still possible, but it is too early to say.'

The anchors had to be re-designed, made, shipped, fitted, connected to the cables and tested, culminating with final tests on Friday 8 October (week 40). The lift began on the Saturday at the rate of 35 cm every five minutes, and was completed in week 41.

On Monday 25 October, the structure was 'occupied' by 10 men from a Basque environmental group protesting against dam projects in the Itoitz valley in Spain and the Narmada valley in India. Eight were quickly removed and arrested, but two men, Bibi and Dany, remained at the top, spending one night in a mountaineers' tent at 135 metres, surrounded by protest banners. All work on the wheel assembly was stopped. A Mace spokesperson said: 'This is a civil construction site, not a high security building. Short of having dogs and barbed wire, there is little we could do!' The two protestors came down on Tuesday lunchtime, having delayed the work by two days.

Work proceeded through November and December, under the eagle eye of the press. Capsules were fitted, and the site was prepared for the visitors. Valuable time was made up by carefully selected 'crashing' of selected activities. The target of 31 December for the first party of important guests and prize-winners looked increasingly achievable, so invitations were sent out. By 9.00 am on 30 December, the commissioning team had completed all but the last 10 hours of their 500-hour safety testing and inspection work when disaster struck! The safety clutch on one capsule failed to release during a simulation of the fail-safe mechanism. This clutch is intended to release the capsule levelling mechanism in the event of a power failure to the capsule, allowing it to hang level under gravity. The failure had resulted in the automatic monitoring system shutting down of the whole system.

The 10-person project team met and decided to postpone the preview ride. The press release emphasized that safety was always the first priority.

The BA London Eye passed all tests in mid-January, and began taking paying customers in February. It is expected to serve 2.2 million customers in the first year, and is firmly established as a leading tourist attraction. The team was proud of what had been achieved, as explained by Tim Renwick:

'No-one had ever done anything like this before; it is unique and technically innovative. Our success has been the result of many things, not least the enthusiasm of the team. We needed to develop entirely new construction processes from scratch. We talked to the local community and got their buy-in to the project, despite the difficulties it presented them at times. We had to interface closely with the sponsor, BA, especially at times of difficulty. Whilst always having the target date in sight, we were never prepared to compromise safety.'

Website: www.ba-londoneye.com

Questions

1 How would you characterize this project using the 'typology of projects' described in the chapter?

2 What was the 'project environment' for this project?

3 What do you think the 'project definition' for the Millennium Wheel contained?

Discussion questions

1 Would professional services, such as a management consultancy project, benefit from the application of project management principles in the same way as would the manufacturer of a turbine generator set for a power station?

2 (a) Why is the concept of earliest and latest start times of value in project planning?

   (b) Draw up cumulative time–cost curves for the new logistics operation shown in Figure 16.17 and developed later in the chapter. Assume the total costs for each activity are as follows:

Activity 1	£34 000	Activity 7	£120 000
Activity 2	£68 000	Activity 8	£480 000
Activity 3	£12 000	Activity 9	£1.1m
Activity 4	£370 000	Activity 10	£400 000
Activity 5	£39 000	Activity 11	£42 000
Activity 6	nil cost	Activity 12	£20 000

   Money is consumed in a linear manner over time: that is, if one week has elapsed in a four-week activity, then one quarter of the cost has been incurred.

   (c) Show cumulative cost curves assuming that:
   – all work starts at the earliest start times;
   – all work starts at the latest start times.

3 Why is the critical path a helpful concept in project planning and control?

4 (a) If the network shown in Figure 16.24 had to be crashed to achieve a completion at week 80, which activities would need to have reduced durations?

   (b) What would be the implications for activity 4?

   (c) What would the cumulative time–cost curve now look like?

5 Identify possible differences between internal and external project performance reports.

6 Evaluate the job of the project manager.
   (a) Does project management tend to make people value short-term expediency in order to get the job done?
   (b) Why does the project manager tend to resist changes?
   (c) Is project management good training for general management?

7 Identify a number of projects with which you have been involved, for example 'project work' as part of the university course, moving house, preparing a large meal, organizing a foreign trip for several people, etc. Assess each of them in terms of their project elements and the complexity–uncertainty typology.

8 Using the list of projects identified in question 7, assess the success of each of them. Did any fail or not succeed as well as planned, and what do you think were the reasons for this? Compare your findings with the project management success factors.

9 Discuss the problems of managing a large-scale famine relief project.

10 Identify the key project planning phases for a major rock concert.

11 What criteria might you use to monitor a theatrical production?

12 The activities, their durations and precedences for designing, writing and installing a bespoke computer

Table 16.4 Bespoke computer database activities

Activity	Duration (weeks)	Activities that must be completed before it can start
1 Contract negotiation	1	–
2 Discussions with main users	2	1
3 Review of current documentation	5	1
4 Review of current systems	6	2
5 Systems analysis (a)	4	3, 4
6 Systems analysis (b)	7	5
7 Programming	12	5
8 Testing (prelim)	2	7
9 Existing system review report	1	3, 4
10 System proposal report	2	5, 9
11 Documentation preparation	19	5, 8
12 Implementation	7	7, 11
13 System test	3	12
14 Debugging	4	12
15 Manual preparation	5	11

database are shown in Table 16.4. Draw a Gantt chart for the operation and calculate the fastest time in which the operation might be completed.

13 Construct a network diagram which satisfies the following relationships:

A, B and C are the first activities of the project and can start simultaneously.
A and B precede D.
B precedes E, F and H.
F and C precede G.
E and H precede I and J.
C, D, F and J precede K.
K precedes L.
I, G and L are the terminal activities of the project.

14 A catering manager has been asked to organize a banquet for 100 guests. Table 16.5 shows the key activities, their durations and precedences. Identify the critical activities and prepare a Gantt chart showing all the activities and the float available for the non-critical activities.

15 Given the information in Table 16.6:
(a) What is the shortest time in which the project can be completed?
(b) What are the critical activities?
(c) What is the standard deviation of the critical path?
(d) What is the probability that the project will be completed in 20 weeks?

16 The chief surveyor of a firm that moves earth in preparation for the construction of roads has identified the activities, their durations and the

Table 16.5 Banquet activities

Activity		Duration (mins)	Preceding activities
A	Prepare ingredients	30	–
B	Clear/clean room	20	–
C	Prepare room and lay tables	20	B
D	Prepare dressings and cold dishes	20	A
E	Prepare meat, to oven	30	A
F	Meet and seat guests	50	C,D,E
G	Plate, dress and serve starter	70	C,D,E
H	Cook vegetables	30	C,E
I	Plate up puddings	20	C,E
J	Clear starter, serve main course	15	G,H
K	Clear main, serve pudding and coffee	15	J
L	Clear tables	20	K

Table 16.6 Project activities

Activity	Duration (weeks)			Preceding activities
	Optimistic	Most likely	Pessimistic	
A	1	2	3	–
B	3	5	11	A
C	5	7	9	A
D	5	7	12	B
E	1	2	3	C
F	7	9	11	C
G	2	3	4	D, E

Table 16.7 Road construction activites

Activity	Duration (days)	Preceding activities	No. of mechanical diggers required
A	5	–	3
B	10	–	5
C	1	–	4
D	8	B	2
E	10	B	3
F	9	B	1
G	3	A, D	5
H	7	A, D	4
I	4	F	9
J	3	F	7
K	5	C, J	1
L	8	H, E, I, K	2
M	4	C, J	10

number of mechanical diggers required for each stage of an operation to prepare a difficult stretch of motorway (*see* Table 16.7). The surveyor needs to know the minimum number of mechanical diggers required during the project.

Notes on chapter

1 Based on an idea by Nicholas, J.M. (1990) *Managing Business and Engineering Projects: Concepts and Implementation*, Prentice Hall.
2 Based on Pinto, J.K. and Slevin, D.P. (1987) 'Critical Success Factors in Successful Project Implementation', *IEEE Transactions on Engineering Management*, Vol 34, No 1.
3 Weiss, J.W. and Wysocki, R.K. (1992) *Five-Phase Project Management: A Practical Planning and Implementation Guide*, Addison-Wesley.
4 Barnes, M. (1985) 'Project Management Framework', *International Project Management Yearbook*, Butterworth Scientific.
5 Lock, D. (1996) *Project Management* (6th edn), Gower.
6 Lock, D. *ibid.*

Selected further reading

Baker, B.N. and Wileman, D.L. (1981) 'A Summary of Major Research Findings Regarding the Human Element in Project Management', *IEEE Engineering Management Review*, Vol 9, No 3.

Boddy, D. and Buchanan, D. (1992) *Take the Lead: Interpersonal Skills for Project Managers*, Prentice Hall.

Burke, R. (1993) *Project Management Planning and Control* (2nd edn), John Wiley.

Cammarano, J. (1997) 'Project Management: How to Make it Happen' *IEE Soulutions*, Vol 29, No 12.

Gilbreath, R.D. (1986) *Winning at Project Management*, John Wiley.

Harrison, F.L. (1981) *Advanced Project Management*, Gower.

Icmeli, O., Erenguc, S.S. and Zappe, C.J. (1993) 'Project Scheduling Problems: A Survey', *International Journal of Operations and Production Management*, Vol 13, No 11.

Littlefield, T.K. and Randolph, P.H. (1991) 'PERT Duration Times: Mathematical or MBO', *Interfaces*, Vol 21, No 6.

Lockyer, K. and Gordon, J. (1996) *Project Management and Project Network Techniques* (6th edn), Pitman Publishing.

Maylor, H. (1996) *Project Management*, Pitman Publishing.

Meredith, J.R. and Mantel, S. (1995) *Project Management: A Managerial Approach* (3rd edn), John Wiley.

Moder, J.J., Phillips, C.R. and Davis, E.W. (1983) *Project Management with CPM/PERT and Precedence Diagramming*, Van Nostrand Reinhold.

Morris, P.W. and Hough, G.H. (1987) *The Anatomy of Major Projects*, John Wiley.

Nicholas, J.M. (1990) *Managing Business and Engineering Projects: Concepts and Implementation*, Prentice Hall.

Obeng, E. (1993) *All Change: The Project Leaders' Secret Handbook*, Pitman Publishing.

O'Neal, K. (1987) 'Project Management Computer Software Buyers Guide', *Industrial Engineering*, Vol 9, No 1.

Randolph, W.A. and Posner, B.Z. (1988) 'What Every Project Manager Needs to Know About Project Management', *Sloan Management Review*, Vol 29, No 4.

Reinertson, D.G. and Smith, P.G. (1991) *Developing Products in Half the Time*, Van Nostrand Reinhold.

17 Quality planning and control

Introduction

Quality is the only one of the five 'operations performance criteria' to have its own dedicated chapter in this book (or two chapters if you include total quality management which is covered in Chapter 20). There are two reasons for this. First, in many organizations there is a separate and identifiable part of the operations function which is devoted exclusively to the management of quality. It is necessary, therefore, to examine the issues which concern staff in this area. Second, it is a current and key concern of many organizations. Business newspapers and management journals are dominated by articles on quality. It would appear that we have undergone a 'quality revolution'. Certainly there is a growing realization that high-quality goods and services can give an organization a considerable competitive edge. Good quality reduces the costs of rework, scrap and returns and, most importantly, generates satisfied customers. Some operations managers believe that, in the long run, quality is the most important single factor affecting an organization's performance relative to its competitors. Figure 17.1 illustrates the supply–demand relationship covered in this chapter.

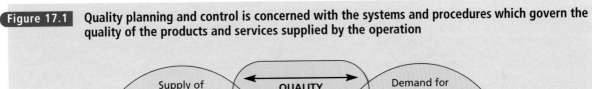

Figure 17.1 Quality planning and control is concerned with the systems and procedures which govern the quality of the products and services supplied by the operation

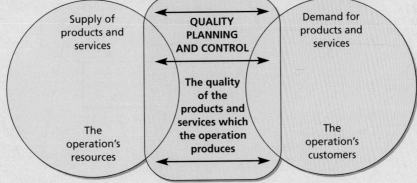

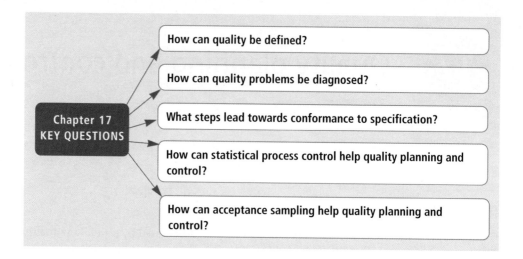

Chapter 17 **KEY QUESTIONS**	How can quality be defined?
	How can quality problems be diagnosed?
	What steps lead towards conformance to specification?
	How can statistical process control help quality planning and control?
	How can acceptance sampling help quality planning and control?

What is quality and why is it so important?

It is worth revisiting some of the arguments which were presented in Chapter 2 regarding the benefits of high quality. This will explain why quality is seen as being so important by most operations. Figure 17.2 illustrates the various ways in which quality

Figure 17.2 **Higher quality has a beneficial effect on both revenues and costs**

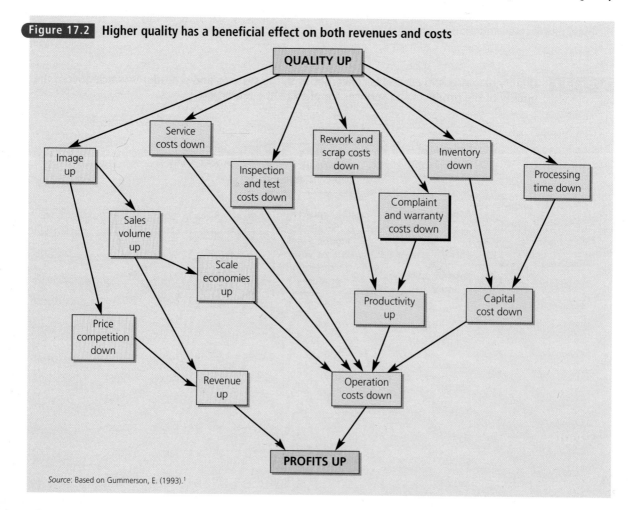

Source: Based on Gummerson, E. (1993).[1]

improvements can affect other aspects of operations performance.[1] Revenues can be increased by better sales and enhanced prices in the market. At the same time, costs can be brought down by improved efficiencies, productivity and the use of capital. A key task of the operations function must be to ensure that it provides quality goods and services to its internal and external customers. This is not necessarily straightforward. For example, there is no clear or agreed definition of what 'quality' means.

Professor David Garvin[2] has categorized many of the various definitions into 'five approaches' to quality: *the transcendent approach, the manufacturing-based approach, the user-based approach, the product-based approach* and *the value-based approach.*

The transcendent approach

The transcendent approach views quality as synonymous with *innate excellence*. A 'quality' car is a Rolls Royce. A 'quality' flight is one provided by Singapore Airlines. A 'quality' watch is a Rolex. Using this approach, quality is being defined as the absolute – the best possible, in terms of the product's or service's *specification*.

The manufacturing-based approach

The manufacturing-based approach is concerned with making products or providing services that are *free of errors* and that conform precisely to their design specification. A car which is less expensive than a Rolls Royce, or a Swatch watch or an economy flight, although not necessarily the 'best' available, is defined as a 'quality' product provided it has been built or delivered precisely to its design specification.

The user-based approach

The user-based approach is about making sure that the product or service is *fit for its purpose*. This definition demonstrates concern not only for its adherence to specification but also with the appropriateness of that specification for the customer. A watch that is manufactured precisely to its design specification yet falls to pieces after two days is clearly not 'fit for its purpose'. The cabin service on a night-time flight from Sydney to Stockholm may be designed to provide passengers with drinks every 15 minutes, meals every four hours and frequent announcements about the position of the plane. This quality specification may not be appropriate, however, for the customer whose main need is a good sleep.

The product-based approach

The product-based approach views quality as a precise and *measurable set of characteristics* that is required to satisfy the customer. A watch, for example, may be designed to run, without the need for servicing, for at least five years while keeping time correct to within five seconds.

The value-based approach

Finally, the value-based approach takes the manufacturing definition a stage further and defines quality in terms of *cost and price*. This approach contends that quality should be perceived in relation to price. A customer may well be willing to accept something of a lower specification quality, if the price is low. A simple and inexpensive watch may give good value by performing quite satisfactorily for a reasonable period of time. A passenger may be willing to fly from Singapore to Amsterdam with a four hour wait in Bangkok and endure cramped seating and mediocre meals in order to save hundreds of guilders over the cost of a direct flight.

● Quality – the operation's view

Here we try to reconcile some of these different views in our definition of quality:

Quality is consistent conformance to customers' expectations.

The use of the word 'conformance' implies that there is a need to meet a clear specification (the manufacturing approach); ensuring a product or service conforms to specification is a key operations task. 'Consistent' implies that conformance to specification is not an *ad hoc* event but that the materials, facilities and processes have been designed and then controlled to ensure that the product or service meets the specification using a set of measurable product or service characteristics (the product-based approach). The use of 'customers' expectations' attempts to combine the user- and value-based approaches.[3] It recognizes that the product or service must meet the expectations of customers, which may indeed be influenced by price.

The use of the word 'expectations' in this definition, rather than needs or wants, is important. 'Wants' would imply that anything the customer desires should be provided by the organization. 'Needs' implies only the meeting of a basic requirement. Take the example of a car. Our *need* might be for a mobile box that gets us from A to B. We might *want* a car that has the looks and acceleration of a sports car, with the carrying capacity of an estate, the ruggedness of a cross-country vehicle, and which comes to us at no cost. Our *expectation*, however, is that which we believe to be likely. We know that it is difficult to get sports performance with a large carrying capacity, and certainly not at zero cost.

● Quality – the customer's view

One problem with basing our definition of quality on customer expectations is that individual customer's expectations may be different. Past experiences, individual knowledge and history will all shape their expectations. Furthermore, customers, on receiving the product or service, may each *perceive* it in different ways. One person may perceive a long-haul flight as an exciting part of a holiday; the person on the next seat may see it as a necessary chore to get to a business meeting. One person may perceive a car as a status symbol; another may see it merely as an expensive means of getting from home to work. Quality needs to be understood from a customer's point of view because, to the customer, the quality of a particular product or service is whatever he or she perceives it to be. If the passengers on a skiing charter flight perceive it to be of good quality, despite long queues at check-in or cramped seating and poor meals, then the flight really is of good perceived quality. If customers believe that expensive German cars are of good quality despite short service intervals, expensive parts and poor fuel consumption, then the car really is of high perceived quality.[4]

Furthermore, in some situations, customers may be unable to judge the 'technical' operational specification of the service or product. They may then use surrogate measures as a basis for their perception of quality.[5] For example, after a visit to a dentist it might be difficult for a customer to judge the technical quality of the repair of a tooth except insofar as it does not give any more trouble. The customer may in reality judge, and therefore perceive, the quality of the repair in terms of such things as the dress and demeanour of the dentist and technician, the information that was provided, or the way in which it was provided.

● Reconciling the operation's and the customer's views of quality

The operation's view of quality is concerned with trying to meet customers' *expectations*. The customer's view of quality is what he or she *perceives* the product or service to be. To create a unified view, quality can be defined as the degree of fit between customers' expectations and their perception of the product or service.[6] Using this idea allows us to see the customers' view of quality of (and, therefore, satisfaction with) the product or service as the result of the customers comparing their expectations of the product or service with their perception of how it performs.

Jaeger excels at service

Photo courtesy of Jaeger

Jaeger store, Seoul, South Korea

Photo courtesy of Jaeger

Using the electronic point-of-sale tills with the 'special order' system

What is it that makes a company special enough to win The *Daily Telegraph* and British Telecom award for Customer Service? For Jaeger, the retailer of quality women's and menswear fashion garments, it is because they believe that:

'Service is about creating unique person-to-person shopping experiences. It's about adding quality people and quality service to a quality product in a major way. It's about getting personal. And the only means by which this can be truly achieved is to empower those closest to the customer to deliver great service.'

Putting this into practice includes many initiatives, often suggested by staff. These include 'mystery shopping' using actual customers, 'fast-reaction' systems to solve customers' problems, and branches collecting information on Customer Profile Cards. This information is the central point to generate better service tailored to individual service and stock requirements. This has led to initiatives such as early morning/late night shopping for individual customers, toys and videos for children, home shopping, and home deliveries at weekends. The use of complaint information was also improved and a 'no fuss' returns policy introduced. Any

member of staff can go to any length to satisfy customers. Examples include home deliveries on Sundays with birthday gifts, etc., birthday cards for customers, and advising on complementary products or alternatives from competing retailers. Responsive training ensures that details of garment properties or possible problems are sent to branches to maximize the advice provided to customers. Technology is also important. Electronic point-of-sale tills link to mainframe computers to give branches more direct information and stock control. Also a 'special order' system means that if an item is not in the shop, the system tracks available stock, requests it from any other Jaeger shop where available and ensures immediate delivery to the customer's home or nearest branch.

Questions

1 Jaeger sells high-quality formal and casual clothes. How do you think their operations objectives differ from a mass market casual clothing retail operation?

2 How does Jaeger's use of its human and techno-logical resources help it to achieve its objectives?

If the product or service experience was better than expected then the customer is satisfied and quality is perceived to be high. If the product or service was less than his or her expectations then quality is low and the customer may be dissatisfied. If the product or service matches expectations then the perceived quality of the product or service is seen to be acceptable. These relationships are summarized in Figure 17.3.

Both customers' expectations and perceptions are influenced by a number of factors, some of which cannot be controlled by the operation and some of which, to a certain extent, can be managed. Figure 17.4 shows some of the factors that will influence the gap between expectations and perceptions. This model of customer-perceived quality

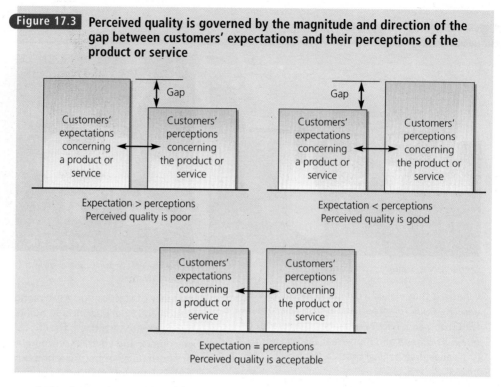

Figure 17.3 Perceived quality is governed by the magnitude and direction of the gap between customers' expectations and their perceptions of the product or service

can help us understand how operations can manage quality and identifies some of the problems in so doing.

The bottom part of the diagram represents the operation's 'domain' of quality and the top part the customer's 'domain'. These two domains meet in the actual product or service, which is provided by the organization and experienced by the customer. Within the operation's domain, management is responsible for designing the product or service and providing a specification of the quality to which the product or service has to be created. The specification of a car, for example, might include the surface finish of the body, its physical dimensions, reliability, and so on. Within the customer's domain, his or her expectations are shaped by such factors as previous experiences with the particular product or service, the marketing image provided by the organization and word-of-mouth information from other users. These expectations are internalized as a set of quality characteristics. A customer's expectations about the car, for example, may include its appearance, performance, luggage space, fuel consumption, leg room, and so on.

● Diagnosing quality problems[7]

The purpose of describing perceived quality as we have done in Figure 17.4 is so that we can use it to diagnose quality problems. If the perceived quality gap is such that customers' perceptions of the product or service fail to match their expectations of it, then the reason (or reasons) must lie in other gaps elsewhere in the model. Four other gaps could explain a perceived quality gap between customers' perceptions and expectations (see Fig. 17.5).

Gap 1: The customer's specification–operation's specification gap
Perceived quality could be poor because there may be a mismatch between the organization's own internal quality specification and the specification which is expected by the customer. For example, a car may be designed to need servicing every 10 000 kilometres but the customer may expect 15 000 kilometre service intervals. An airline may

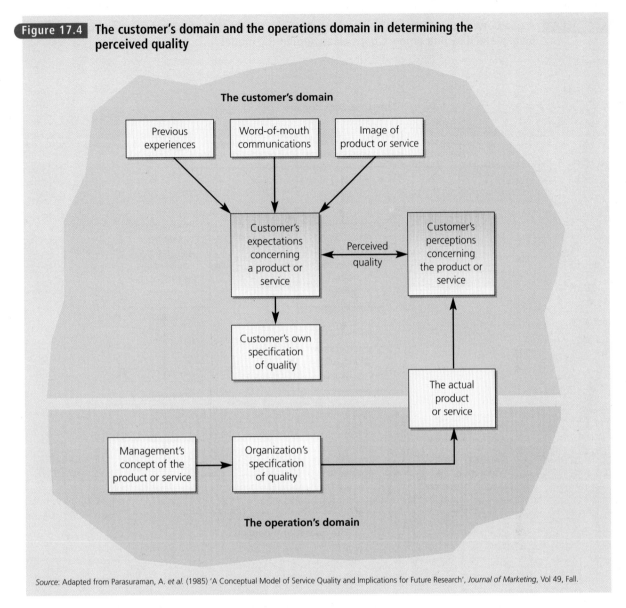

The customer's domain

Previous experiences

Word-of-mouth communications

Image of product or service

Customer's expectations concerning a product or service

Perceived quality

Customer's perceptions concerning the product or service

Customer's own specification of quality

The actual product or service

Management's concept of the product or service

Organization's specification of quality

The operation's domain

Source: Adapted from Parasuraman, A. *et al.* (1985) 'A Conceptual Model of Service Quality and Implications for Future Research', *Journal of Marketing*, Vol 49, Fall.

have a policy of charging for drinks during the flight whereas the customer's expectation may be that the drinks would be free.

Gap 2: The concept–specification gap

Perceived quality could be poor because there is a mismatch between the product or service concept (*see* Chapter 5) and the way the organization has specified the quality of the product or service internally. For example, the concept of a car might have been for an inexpensive, energy-efficient means of transportation, but the inclusion of a catalytic converter may have both added to its cost and made it less energy-efficient.

Gap 3: The quality specification–actual quality gap

Perceived quality could be poor because there is a mismatch between the actual quality of the service or product provided by the operation and its internal quality specification. This may be the result, for example, of an inappropriate or unachievable specification, or of poorly trained or inexperienced personnel, or because effective control systems are not in place to ensure the provision of defined levels of quality. For

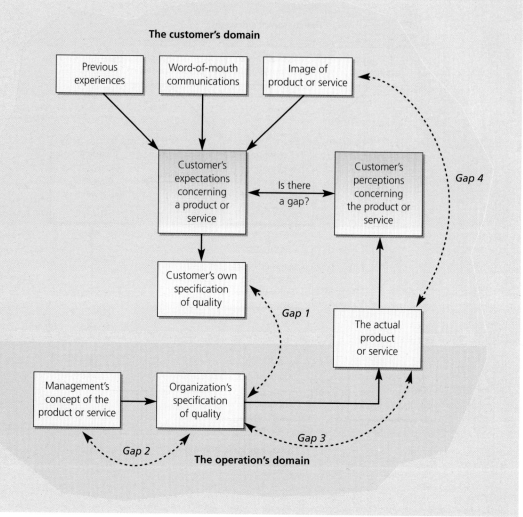

example, the internal quality specification for a car may be that the gap between its doors and body, when closed, must not exceed 7 mm. However, because of inadequate equipment, the gap in reality is 9 mm. A further example is where, despite an airline's policy of charging for drinks, some flight crews might provide free drinks, adding unexpected costs to the airline and influencing customers' expectations for the next flight, when they may be disappointed.

Gap 4: The actual quality–communicated image gap

Perceived quality could also be poor because there is a gap between the organization's external communications or market image and the actual quality of the service or product delivered to the customer. This may be the result of either the marketing function setting unachievable expectations in the minds of customers or operations not providing the level of quality expected by the customer. For example, an advertising campaign for an airline might show a cabin attendant offering to replace a customer's shirt on which food or drink has been spilt, whereas such a service may not in fact be available should this happen.

The organizational responsibility for closing the gaps

The existence of any one of these gaps is likely to result in a mismatch between expectations and perceptions and, consequently, in poor perceived quality. It is therefore important that managers take action to prevent quality gaps. Table 17.1 shows the actions which will be required to close each of the gaps and indicates the parts of the organization that bear the main responsibility for doing so.

Table 17.1 The organizational responsibility for closing quality gaps

Gap	Action required to ensure high perceived quality	Main organizational responsibility
Gap 1	Ensure that there is consistency between the internal quality specification of the product or service and the expectations of customers	Marketing Operations Product/service development
Gap 2	Ensure that the internal specification of the product or service meets its intended concept or design	Marketing Operations Product/service development
Gap 3	Ensure that the actual product or service conforms to its internally specified quality level	Operations
Gap 4	Ensure that the promises made to customers concerning the product or service can in reality be delivered by the operation	Marketing

Conformance to specification

Conformance to specification means producing a product or providing a service to its design specification. During the design of any product or service, its overall concept, purpose, package of components and the relationship between the components will have been specified (*see* Chapter 5). The model used to describe this activity in Chapter 5 was shown in Figure 5.2. We can extend this model to include the activities of ensuring that products and services are indeed made to conform with their specifications. This is the quality planning and control activity (*see* Fig. 17.6). Quality planning and control can be divided into six sequential steps:

Step 1   Define the quality characteristics of the product or service.
Step 2   Decide how to measure each quality characteristic.
Step 3   Set quality standards for each quality characteristic.
Step 4   Control quality against those standards.
Step 5   Find and correct causes of poor quality.
Step 6   Continue to make improvements.

This chapter will deal with steps 1 to 4. Steps 5 and 6 are dealt with in Chapters 18, 19 and 20.

Step 1 – Define the quality characteristics

Much of the 'quality' of a product or service will have been specified in its design. But not all the design details are useful in controlling quality. For example, the design of a television may specify that its outer cabinet is made with a particular veneer. Each television is not checked, however, to make sure that the cabinet is indeed made from that

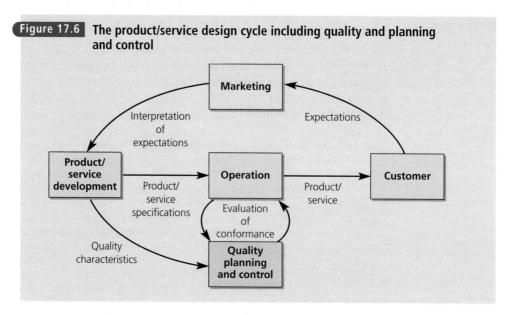

Figure 17.6 The product/service design cycle including quality and planning and control

particular veneer. Rather it is the *consequences* of the design specification which are examined – the appearance of the cabinet, for example.

These consequences for quality planning and control of the design are called the *quality characteristics* of the product or service. Table 17.2 shows a list of the quality characteristics which are generally useful, but the terms need a little further explanation.

Table 17.2 Quality characteristics for a motor car and an air journey

Quality characteristic	Car	Air journey
Functionality	Speed, acceleration, fuel consumption, ride quality, road-holding, etc.	Safety and duration of journey, onboard meals and drinks, car and hotel booking services
Appearance	Aesthetics, shape, finish, door gaps, etc.	Decor and cleanliness of aircraft, lounges and crew
Reliability	Mean time to failure	Keeping to the published flight times
Durability	Useful life (with repair)	Keeping up with trends in the industry
Recovery	Ease of repair	Resolution of service failures
Contact	Knowledge and courtesy of sales staff	Knowledge, courtesy and sensitivity of airline staff

Functionality means how well the product or service does its job. This includes its performance and features. *Appearance* refers to the sensory characteristics of the product or service: its aesthetic appeal, look, feel, sound and smell. *Reliability* is the consistency of the product's or service's performance over time, or the average time for which it performs within its tolerated band of performance. *Durability* means the total useful life of the product or service, assuming occasional repair or modification. *Recovery* means the ease with which problems with the product or service can be rectified or resolved. *Contact* refers to the nature of the person-to-person contact which might take place. For example, it could include the courtesy, empathy, sensitivity and knowledge of contact staff.

In the retail banking world the costs of poor quality are going up and at least some of these costs are self-inflicted. But now some banks are offering to pay cash to wronged customers for every mistake they make. Centrebank, the telephone-banking service of the Bank of Scotland, is one bank which is putting its money where its mouth is. It pays at least £10 to customers if the bank makes a mistake.

'We believe we have a good level of service already,' says the bank. *'We are not saying that we want to make mistakes, but we want to show customers that we are determined to offer good service.'*

One of the first quality schemes of this type originated at the Colorado National Bank of Denver. It used the slogan of 'putting its money where its mouth is' or PIMWIMI for short. Its strategy was straightforward: if 'quality' was actually guaranteed to customers, then the customer relationship would be strengthened. The programme had three main principles:

- The responsiveness, accuracy and courtesy of the service delivery would be guaranteed.
- Systems would be monitored for customer friendliness and front-line staff would be empowered to influence situations in which service quality could be improved.
- It would be easy for customers to express their opinions of the service, in order to gain feedback on progress.

Customers should not wait more than three minutes in a teller line, more than five minutes in Personal Banking, Personal Finance or Customer Assistance, and they should be received in a friendly manner, greeted by name and receive next-day turnaround on enquiries and personal loan applications, while expecting no less than 100 per cent accuracy throughout. The scheme called for the bank to:

'give a note from the President in the form of a $5 bill, every time a customer had cause for complaint, either due to system failure or staff behaviour'.

No problem was ever too small to be considered worthy of the $5 compensation – if it merited a moan or a mention of disappointment, then $5 was a small price to pay, to recover that customer's favour. The level of payoff remained at zero, however, well into the scheme.

Questions

1 What conditions do you think have to be obtained within an operation before a scheme of this type could be introduced?

2 What advantages do you think this kind of scheme gives, both from the customer's and from the operation's point of view?

3 What problems could it lead to?

● Step 2 – Decide how to measure each characteristic

These characteristics must be defined in such a way as to enable them to be measured and then controlled. This involves taking a very general quality characteristic such as 'appearance' and breaking it down, as far as one can, into its constituent elements. 'Appearance' is difficult to measure as such, but 'colour match', 'surface finish' and 'number of visible scratches' are all capable of being described in a more objective manner. They may even be quantifiable.

The process of disaggregating quality characteristics into their measurable sub-components, however, can result in the characteristics losing some of their meaning. For example, a quantified list of colour match, the 'smoothness' of the surface finish and the number of visible scratches do not convey everything about the appearance of a product. Customers will react to more factors than these: for example, the shape and character of a product. Many of the factors lost by disaggregating 'appearance' into its measurable parts are those which are embedded in the design of the product rather than the way it is produced.

Some of the quality characteristics of a product or service cannot themselves be measured at all. The 'courtesy' of airline staff, for example, has no objective quantified

Table 17.3 Variable and attribute measures for quality characteristics

Quality characteristic	Car		Airline journey	
	Variable	Attribute	Variable	Attribute
Functionality	Acceleration and braking characteristics from test bed	Is the ride quality satisfactory?	Number of journeys which actually arrived at the destination (i.e. didn't crash!)	Was the food acceptable?
Appearance	Number of blemishes visible on car	Is the colour to specification?	Number of seats not cleaned satisfactorily	Is the crew dressed smartly?
Reliability	Average time between faults	Is the reliability satisfactory?	Proportion of journeys which arrived on time	Were there any complaints?
Durability	Life of the car	Is the useful life as predicted?	Number of times service innovations lagged competitors	Generally, is the airline updating its services in a satisfactory manner?
Recovery	Time from fault discovered to fault repaired	Is the serviceability of the car acceptable?	Proportion of service failures resolved satisfactorily	Do customers feel that staff deal satisfactorily with complaints?
Contact	Level of help provided by sales staff (1 to 5 scale)	Did customers feel well served (yes or no)?	The extent to which customers feel well treated by staff (1 to 5 scale)	Did customers feel that the staff were helpful (yes or no)?

measure. Yet operations with high customer contact, such as airlines, place a great deal of importance on the need to ensure courtesy in their staff. In cases like this, the operation will have to attempt to measure customer *perceptions* of courtesy.

Variables and attributes

The measures used by operations to describe quality characteristics are of two types: *variables* and *attributes*. Variable measures are those that can be measured on a continuously variable scale (for example, length, diameter, weight or time). Attributes are those which are assessed by judgement and are dichotomous, i.e. have two states (for example, right or wrong, works or does not work, looks OK or not OK). Table 17.3 categorizes some of the measures which might be used for the quality characteristics of the car and the airline journey.

● Step 3 – Set quality standards

When operations managers have identified how any quality characteristic can be measured, they need a quality standard against which it can be checked, otherwise they will not know whether it indicates good or bad performance. For example, suppose that, on average, one passenger out of every 10 000 complains about the food. Should the airline regard that as good because it seems that 9999 passengers out of 10 000 are satisfied? Or should it regard it as bad because, if one passenger complains, there must be others who, although dissatisfied, did not bother to complain? Or, if that level of complaint is broadly similar to other airlines, should it regard its quality as just about satisfactory? While it might seem to be appropriate to have an absolute standard – that is, perfection – and indeed strive for it, to use perfection as an operational standard could be both demoralizing and expensive. Most manufactured products and delivered services are not 'perfect'. No car will last for ever. No airline could guarantee that there will always be seats available on its aircraft.

The quality standard is that level of quality which defines the boundary between acceptable and unacceptable. Such standards may well be constrained by operational factors such as the state of technology in the factory, and the cost limits of making the product. At the same time, however, they need to be appropriate to the expectations of customers. The quality standard for the reliability of a watch might be 10 maintenance-free years, for the availability of airline seats might be that seats should be available 95 per cent of the time, and so on.

Quality at Torres Wine

Mechanical harvesting

Fermentation towers

Back in 1870, Jaime Torres, having been forced to seek his fortune in Cuba when his elder brother inherited the family estates, returned to his native Catalonia. He founded the company which is now Spain's largest independently owned wine company with a turnover of around 17 million bottles of wine per year, together with around 6 million bottles of brandy. The (still family-owned) company's success is based firmly on the work it has put in to maintain the quality and consistency of its products. This starts with the vineyards themselves. Since the 1960s they have been experimenting with matching grape varieties to the individual microclimates in their estates, planting patterns which preserve water levels in the soil, and using environmentally friendly cultivation techniques such as the laser-guided plough, which eliminates the need for artificial chemical weed killers. Although much of the harvesting is still done by hand, mechanical harvesting (*see* picture) not only saves time and money, but also allows the fruit to be collected cool during the night and early morning, which further enhances quality. The trailers and tractors which transport the harvested grapes are unloaded into reception hoppers where precision controlled systems, coordinated by computer electronics, enable immediate assessment of the quality and

ripeness of grapes. The wines ferment in visually striking stainless steel towers (*see* picture). All these vats are equipped with cooling systems to ferment the grape juice at a controlled temperature, thus preserving its natural aromas. Torres' cellars, where the red wines are aged, extend through two kilometres of cool, dark, underground galleries that house more than 11 000 oak barrels. The use of new oak barrels for ageing the finest wines requires substantial investment, but it is an essential factor in obtaining the highest quality. The wine is then bottled in the company's on-site modern bottling plant, after which it is bottle-aged in the company's headquarters at nearby Vilafranca.

Questions

1 What constitutes quality for Torres' products?

2 Chart the various stages in wine-making and identify what influences quality at each stage.

3 What do you think Torres does, or can do, to pursue environmentally friendly production?

Step 4 – Control quality against those standards

After setting up appropriate standards the operation will then need to check that the products or services conform to those standards. There may well be times when products or services do not conform to those standards. Chapter 19 deals with the question of what operations can do when things do go wrong. Here we concern ourselves with how operations can try to ensure that it does things right, first time, every time. As far as operations managers are concerned, this involves three decisions:

1 Where in the operation should they check that it is conforming to standards?
2 Should they check every product or service or take a sample?
3 How should the checks be performed?

Where should the checks take place?

The key task for operations managers is to identify the critical control points at which the service, products or processes need to be checked to ensure that the product or services will conform to specification. There are three main places where checks may be carried out: at the start of the process, during the process and after the process.

At *the start of the process* the incoming transformed resources could be inspected to make sure that they are to the correct specification. For example, a car manufacturer may wish to check that the car headlights which are supplied to its production line are of the right specification. An airline might check that incoming food is satisfactory. A nightclub may wish to check that its incoming guests are dressed appropriately. A university will wish to screen applicants to try to ensure that they have a high chance of getting through the programme.

During the process checks may take place at any stage, or indeed all stages, but there are a number of particularly critical points in the process where inspection might be important (*see* box on Polaroid, which is a good example of this):[9]

- before a particularly costly part of the process;
- before a series of processes during which checking might be difficult;
- immediately after part of the process with a high defective rate or a fail point;
- before a part of the process that might conceal previous defects or problems;
- before a 'point of no return', after which rectification and recovery might be impossible;
- before potential damage or distress might be caused;
- before a change in functional responsibility.

Checks may also take place *after the process* itself to ensure that the product or service conforms to its specification or that customers are satisfied with the service they have received.

Check every product and service or take a sample?

Having decided the points at which the goods or services will be checked, the next decision is how many of the products or services to check. While it might seem ideal to check every single product being produced or every service being delivered, there are many good reasons why this might not be sensible:

- It might be dangerous to inspect the whole item or every constituent part. A doctor, for example, checks just a small sample of blood rather than taking all of a patient's blood because this would be life-threatening. The characteristics of this sample are taken to represent those of the rest of the patient's blood.
- The checking of every single product or every customer might destroy the product or interfere with the service. It would be inappropriate for a light bulb manufacturer to check the length of life of every single light bulb leaving the factory, as this would entail the destructive testing of each bulb. Likewise, it would not be appropriate for a head waiter to check whether his or her customers are enjoying the meal or having a good time every 30 seconds.

- Checking every product or service can be both time-consuming and costly. For example, it just might not be feasible to check every single item from a high-volume plastic moulding machine or to check the feelings of every single bus commuter in a major city every day.

Polaroid defeats the dark[10]

Many companies have some stage of production which, for some reason, it is more important to get right than others. The Polaroid factory at Dumbarton in Scotland is the largest film manufacturing plant in Europe, specializing in the production of instant film cartridges. In its process one of the most critical stages has to take place in the dark. Quality checks are important at all stages in the process but especially during the light-sensitive stage of the process.

'We have to be careful that the light-sensitive stage is reliable and that the quality of product we will get from that stage is predictable. Once the line is set up and running, there is a high level of disruption and downtime if we have to stop the line and open up the dark room. For small problems such as alignment, we can adjust the process and scrap only the small amount of the product which is produced in the meantime. In more drastic circumstances, we will stop the process and accept

the loss of the product currently in progress by opening the "dark stage".'

The critical nature of the 'dark stage' has focused the company's efforts on making sure that it is as error-free as possible. Error rates for this stage in the process are now small both in absolute terms and as a proportion of the total quality problems in the plant. This has been achieved through improving the design of the process technology, working closely with suppliers, matching key components prior to running the line, and providing back-up facilities.

Questions

1 Why is quality particularly important for a product such as Polaroid's film?

2 Why is an understanding of the process behaviour of film manufacture particularly important for Polaroid?

The use of 100 per cent checking, moreover, does not guarantee that all defects or problems will be identified, for a number of reasons:

- Making the checks may be inherently difficult. For example, although a doctor may undertake all the correct testing procedures to check for a particular disease, he or she may not necessarily be certain to diagnose it.
- Staff may become fatigued over a period of time, when inspecting repetitive items where it is easy to make mistakes. (For example, try counting the number of 'e's on this page. Count them again and see if you get the same score!)
- Quality measures may be unclear and staff making the checks may not know precisely what to look for. For example, how can an interviewer, making offers for university places, really tell whether a student will actually have the right attitude to group work or will be diligent?
- Wrong information may be given. For example, although all the customers in a restaurant may tell the head waiter, when asked, that 'everything is all right', they may actually have serious reservations about the food or their treatment.

Type I and type II errors

Using a sample to make a decision about the quality of products or services, although requiring less time than 100 per cent checking, does have its own inherent problems. Like any decision activity, we may get the decision wrong. Take the example of a pedestrian waiting to cross a street. He or she has two main decisions: whether to continue waiting or to cross. If there is a satisfactory break in the traffic and the pedestrian crosses then a correct decision has been made. Similarly, if that person continues to wait because the traffic is too dense then he or she has again made a correct decision. There are two types of incorrect decisions or errors, however. One incorrect decision would be if he or she decides to cross when there is not an adequate break in the traffic, resulting in an accident – this is referred to as a type I error. Another incorrect decision would occur if he or she decides not to cross even though there was an adequate gap in the traffic – this is called a type II error. In crossing the road, therefore, there are four outcomes, which are summarized in Table 17.4.

Table 17.4 Type I and type II errors for a pedestrian crossing the road

Decision	Road conditions	
	Unsafe	Safe
Cross	Type I error	Correct decision
Wait	Correct decision	Type II error

Type I errors are those which occur when a decision was made to do something and the situation did not warrant it. Type II errors are those which occur when nothing was done, yet a decision to do something should have been taken as the situation did indeed warrant it. For example, if a school's inspector checks the work of a sample of 20 out of 1000 pupils and all 20 of the pupils in the sample have failed, the inspector might draw the conclusion that all the pupils have failed. In fact, the sample just happened to contain 20 out of the 50 students who had failed the course. The inspector, by assuming a high fail rate would be making a type I error. Alternatively, if the inspector checked 20 pieces of work all of which were of a high standard, he or she might conclude that all the pupils' work was good despite having been given, or having chosen, the only pieces of good work in the whole school. This would be a type II error. Although these situations are not likely, they are possible. Therefore any sampling procedure has to be aware of these risks.

How should the checks be performed?

In practice most operations will use some form of sampling to check the quality of their products or services. The decision then is what kind of sample procedure to adopt. There are two different methods in common use for checking the quality of a sample product or service so as to make inferences about all the output from an operation. Both methods take into account the statistical risks involved in sampling.

Photo courtesy of Steve Bicknell

Visual quality inspection is still used, even in some complex products

Understanding the nature of type I and type II errors is an essential part of any surgeon's quality planning. Take the well-known appendectomy operation, for example. This is the removal of the appendix when it becomes infected or inflamed. Removal is necessary because of the risk of the appendix bursting and causing peritonitis, a potentially fatal poisoning of the blood. The surgical procedure itself is a relatively simple operation with expected good results but there is always a small risk associated with any invasive surgery needing a general anaesthetic. In addition, like any surgical procedure, it is expensive. The cost of the USA's approximately quarter-of-a-million appendectomies averages out to around $4500 per operation. Unfortunately, appendicitis is difficult to diagnose accurately. Using standard X-ray procedures a definite diagnosis can only be obtained about 10 per cent of the time. But now a new technique, developed in the Massachusetts General Hospital in Boston, claims to be able to identify 100 per cent of true appendicitis cases before surgery is carried out. The new technique (Focused Appendix Computed Tomography) uses spiral X-ray images together with a special dye. It scans only the relevant part of the body, so exposure to radiation is not as major an issue as with conventional X-ray techniques. The technique can also help in providing an alternative diagnosis when an appendectomy is not needed. Most significantly, the potential cost savings are very great. The test itself costs less than $250 which means that one single avoided surgery pays for around 20 tests.

Questions

1 How does this new test change the likelihood of type I and type II errors?

2 Why is this important?

The first, and by far the best known, is the procedure called *statistical process control* (SPC). SPC is concerned with sampling the process during the production of the goods or the delivery of service. Based on this sample, decisions are made as to whether the process is 'in control', that is, operating as it should be. The second method is called *acceptance sampling* and is more concerned with whether to regard an incoming or outgoing batch of materials or customers as acceptable or not. The rest of this chapter is concerned with these two quality planning and control methods.

Statistical process control (SPC)

Statistical process control (SPC) is concerned with checking a product or service during its creation. If there is reason to believe that there is a problem with the process, then it can be stopped (where this is possible and appropriate) and the problem can be identified and rectified. For example, an international airport may regularly ask a sample of customers if the cleanliness of its restaurants is satisfactory. If an unacceptable number of customers in one sample is found to be unhappy, airport managers may have to consider improving the procedures in place for cleaning tables. Similarly, a car manufacturer periodically will check whether a sample of door panels conforms to its standards so as to know whether the machinery which produces them is performing correctly. Again, if a sample suggests that there may be problems, then the machines may have to be stopped and the process checked.

Control charts

The significant value of SPC, however, is not just to make checks of a single sample but to monitor the results of many samples over a period of time. It does this by using *control charts*, to see if the process looks as though it is performing as it should, or alternatively if it is going out of control. If the process does seem to be going out of control, then steps can be taken *before* there is a problem.

Most operations chart their quality performance in some way. Figure 17.7, or something like it, could be found in almost any operation. The chart could, for example, represent the percentage of customers in a sample of 1000 who, each month, were dissatisfied with the restaurant's cleanliness. While the amount of dissatisfaction may be acceptably small, management should be concerned that it has been steadily increasing over time and may wish to investigate why this is so. In this case, the control chart is plotting an attribute measure of quality (satisfied or not).

Alternatively, the chart could just as easily represent the average impact resistance of samples of door panels selected each week (a variable measure). Again there is evidence of a clear trend. This time, though, the quality measure seems to be getting better. Yet this chart could be equally as disturbing to the car manufacturers as the airport's survey results were to the airport management. If the impact resistance is moving above the 'necessary' level, it could indicate that too much material is being used in the process. Certainly, if the reasons for the upward trend are unknown, the management of the operation should want to investigate the causes.

Looking for trends is an important use of control charts. If the trend suggests the process is getting steadily worse, then it will be worth investigating the process. If the trend is steadily improving, it may still be worthy of investigation to try to identify what is happening that is making the process better. This information might then be shared with other parts of the organization, or, on the other hand, the process might be stopped as the cause could be adding unnecessary expense to the operation.

● Variation in process quality

Common causes

The processes charted in Figure 17.7 showed an upwards trend. The trend was neither steady nor smooth, however. It varied, sometimes up, sometimes down. All processes vary to some extent. No machine will give precisely the same result each time it is used. All materials vary a little. The staff in the operation differ marginally in the way they perform each time they perform a task. Even the environment in which the processing takes place will vary. Given this, it is not surprising that the measure of quality

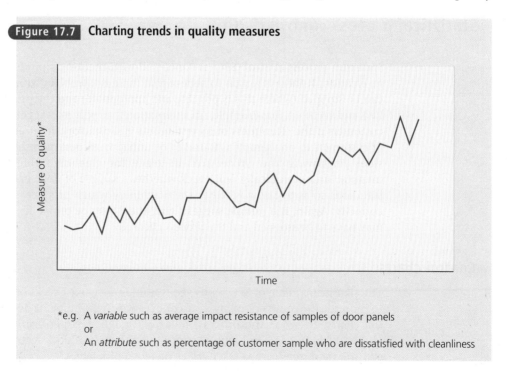

Figure 17.7 **Charting trends in quality measures**

*e.g. A *variable* such as average impact resistance of samples of door panels
or
An *attribute* such as percentage of customer sample who are dissatisfied with cleanliness

(whether attribute or variable) will also vary. Variations which derive from these *common causes* can never be entirely eliminated (although they can be reduced).

For example, if a machine is filling boxes with rice, it will not place *exactly* the same weight of rice in every box it fills; there will be some variation around an average weight. When the filling machine is in a stable condition (that is, no exceptional factors are influencing its behaviour) each box could be weighed and a histogram of the weights could be built up. Figure 17.8 shows how the histogram might develop. The first boxes weighed could lie anywhere within the natural variation of the process but are more likely to be close to the average weight (*see* Fig. 17.8a). As more boxes are weighed they clearly show the tendency to be close to the process average (*see* Fig. 17.8 b and c). After many boxes have been weighed they form a smoother distribution (Fig. 17.8d) which can be drawn as a histogram (Fig. 17.8e) which will approximate to the underlying process variation distribution (Fig. 17.8f).

Usually this type of variation can be described by a normal distribution with 99.7 per cent of the variation lying within ± 3 standard deviations.

In this case the weight of rice in the boxes is described by a distribution with a mean of 206 grams and a standard deviation of 2 grams. The obvious question for any operations manager would be: 'Is this variation in the process performance acceptable?' The answer will depend on the acceptable range of weights which can be tolerated by the operation. This range is called the *tolerance range*, or *specification range*. If the weight of rice in the box is too small then the organization might infringe labelling regulations; if it is too large, the organization is 'giving away' too much of its product for free.

Process capability

The *capability* of the process is a measure of the acceptability of the variation of the process. The simplest measure of capability (C_p) is given by the ratio of the specification range to the 'natural' variation of the process (i.e. ± 3 standard deviations):

$$C_p = \frac{\text{UTL} - \text{LTL}}{6s}$$

Figure 17.8 **The natural variation in the filling process can be described by a normal distribution**

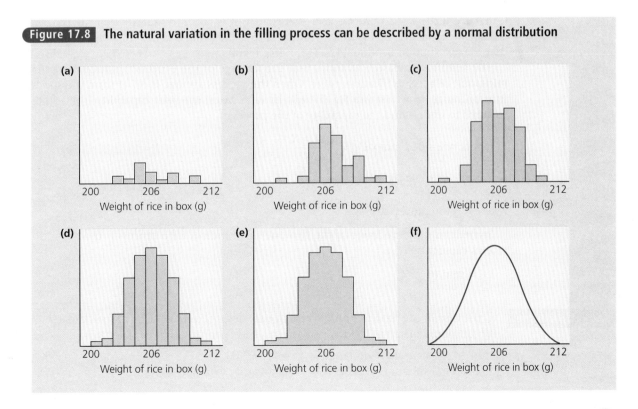

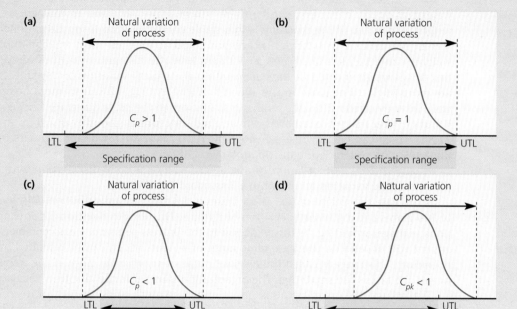

(a)
Natural variation of process
$C_p > 1$
LTL ←————————————→ UTL
Specification range

(b)
Natural variation of process
$C_p = 1$
LTL ←————————————→ UTL
Specification range

(c)
Natural variation of process
$C_p < 1$
LTL ←————————→ UTL
Specification range

(d)
Natural variation of process
$C_{pk} < 1$
LTL ←————————→ UTL
Specification range

LTL = Lower tolerance level
UTL = Upper tolerance level

where UTL = the upper tolerance limit
LTL = the lower tolerance limit
s = the standard deviation of the process variability.

Generally, if the C_p of a process is greater than 1, it is taken to indicate that the process is 'capable', and a C_p of less than 1 indicates that the process is not 'capable', assuming that the distribution is normal (*see* Fig. 17.9a, b and c).

The simple C_p measure assumes that the average of the process variation is at the mid-point of the specification range. Often the process average is offset from the specification range, however (*see* Fig. 17.9d). In such cases, *one-sided* capability indices are required to understand the capability of the process:

$$\text{Upper one-sided index } C_{pu} = \frac{\text{UTL} - X}{3s}$$

$$\text{Lower one-sided index } C_{pl} = \frac{X - \text{LTL}}{3s}$$

where X = the process average.

Sometimes only the lower of the two one-sided indices for a process is used to indicate its capability (C_{pk}):

$$C_{pk} = \min (C_{pu}, C_{pl})$$

Worked example

In the case of the process filling boxes of rice, described previously, process capability can be calculated as follows:

Specification range = 214 – 198 = 16 g
Natural variation of process = 6 × standard deviation
= 6 × 2 = 12 g

$$C_p = \text{process capability}$$
$$= \frac{\text{UTL} - \text{LTL}}{6s}$$
$$= \frac{214 - 198}{6 \times 2} = \frac{16}{12}$$
$$= 1.333$$

If the natural variation of the filling process changed to have a process average of 210 grams but the standard deviation of the process remained at 2 grams:

$$C_{\text{pu}} = \frac{214 - 210}{3 \times 2} = \frac{4}{6} = 0.666$$

$$C_{\text{pl}} = \frac{210 - 198}{3 \times 2} = \frac{12}{6} = 2.0$$

$$C_{\text{pk}} = \min (0.666, 2.0)$$
$$= 0.666$$

Assignable causes of variation

Not all variation in processes is the result of common causes. There may be something wrong with the process which is assignable to a particular and preventable cause. Machinery may have worn or been set up badly. An untrained member of staff may not be following the prescribed procedure for the process. The causes of such variation are called *assignable causes*. The question for operations management is whether the results from any particular sample, when plotted on the control chart, simply represent the variation due to common causes or due to some specific and correctable, *assignable* cause. Figure 17.10, for example, shows the control chart for the average impact resistance of

Motorola's six-sigma quality[12]

It is not often that the technical details of process capability become synonymous with a company's total quality programme, but that is what has happened for Motorola. Motorola is one of the world's largest industrial corporations making electronic components, semiconductors and communication systems, among other things. It employs over 100 000 people throughout the world at in excess of 50 sites. All the people in all the sites and many outside the company have now heard of Motorola's six-sigma quality objectives.

The foundations for six-sigma quality were laid some years ago when the company decided on its aim of 'total customer satisfaction'. According to Motorola this is only achieved when the product is delivered when promised, with no defects, the product does not experience any early-life failures, and the product does not fail excessively in service. To achieve this, Motorola initially focused on removing manufacturing defects. It soon came to realize, however, that many problems were caused by latent defects: that is, defects hidden within the design of its products. They may not show initially but eventually will cause failures in the field. The only way to eliminate these defects was to make sure that its design specifications were tight and its processes very capable indeed.

Motorola's six-sigma quality concept means that the natural variation of its processes (± 3 standard deviations) should be half their specification range. In other words, the specification range of any part of a product should be ±6 times the standard deviation of the process. The Greek letter sigma (σ) is often used to indicate the standard deviation of a process, hence the six-sigma label. A process capability (C_p) of 1 is represented by 'three sigma' quality. This implies a defect rate of 2.7 defects per 1000. Six-sigma quality is considerably more ambitious. It implies a defect rate of only 3.4 defects per *million*.

> **Questions**
>
> 1 What process capability is implied by Motorola's six-sigma target?
>
> 2 Do you think it is worth trying to achieve such high levels of conformance?

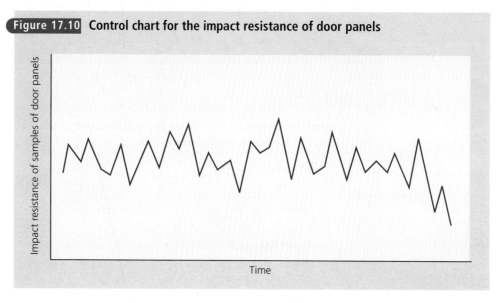

Figure 17.10 Control chart for the impact resistance of door panels

Impact resistance of samples of door panels

Time

samples of door panels taken over time. Like any process the results vary, but the last three points seem to be lower than usual. The question is whether this is natural variation or the symptom of some more serious cause. Is the variation the result of common causes or does it indicate assignable causes in the process?

To help make this decision, *control limits* can be added to the control chart which indicate the expected extent of 'common-cause' variation. If any points lie outside these control limits then the process can be deemed out of control in the sense that variation is likely to be due to assignable causes. These control limits could be set intuitively by examining past variation during a period when the process was thought to be free of any variation which could be due to assignable causes. For example, if the monthly survey of airport customers usually includes between 3 and 4 per cent of customers who are dissatisfied with the cleanliness of the airport's restaurants, an upper control limit could be set at 4 per cent complaints per month. If the actual proportion is ever 4 per cent or more then the situation is investigated.

Control limits can be set in a more statistically revealing manner, however, based on the probability that the mean of a particular sample will differ by more than a set amount from the mean of the population from which it is taken. For example, if the process which tests door panels had been measured to determine the normal distribution which represents its common-cause variation, then control limits can be based on this distribution. Figure 17.11 shows the same control chart as Figure 17.10 with the addition of control limits put at ±3 standard deviations (of the population of sample means) away from the mean of sample averages. It shows that the probability of the final point on the chart being influenced by an assignable cause is very high indeed. When the process is exhibiting behaviour which is outside its normal 'common-cause' range, it is said to be 'out of control'.

From this evidence alone, however, we cannot be absolutely certain that the process is out of control. There is a small but finite chance that the (seemingly out of limits) point is just one of the rare but natural results at the tail of the distribution which describes perfectly normal behaviour. Stopping the process under these circumstances would represent a type I error because the process is actually in control. Alternatively, ignoring a result which in reality is due to an assignable cause is a type II error (*see* Table 17.5).

Control limits are usually set at three standard deviations either side of the population mean. This would mean that there is only a 0.3 per cent chance of any sample mean falling outside these limits by chance causes (that is, a chance of a type I error

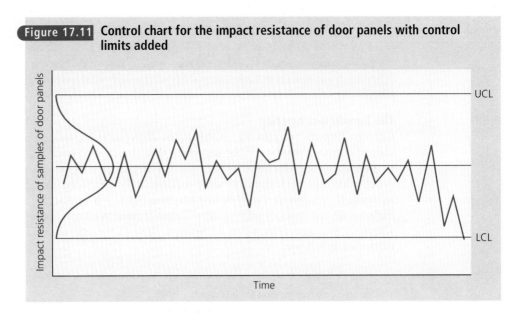

Figure 17.11 Control chart for the impact resistance of door panels with control limits added

Table 17.5 Type I and type II errors in SPC

Decision	Actual process state	
	In control	Out of control
Stop process	Type I error	Correct decision
Leave alone	Correct decision	Type II error

of 0.3 per cent). The control limits may be set at any distance from the population mean, but the closer the limits are to the population mean, the higher the likelihood of investigating and trying to rectify a process which is actually problem-free. If the control limits are set at two standard deviations, the chance of a type I error increases to about 5 per cent. If the limits are set at one standard deviation then the chance of a type I error increases to 32 per cent. When the control limits are placed at ±3 standard deviations away from the mean of the distribution which describes 'normal' variation in the process, they are called the *upper control limit* (UCL) and *lower control limit* (LCL).

● **CRITICAL COMMENTARY**

This approach to process control was how its statistically obsessed originators first described it more than half a century ago. Then, the key issue was only to decide whether a process was 'in control' or not. Now, we expect more from such techniques. We expect them to reflect common sense as well as statistical elegance, and we expect them to promote continuous operations improvement. This is why two particular criticisms have been levelled at the traditional approach to SPC (in fact, both criticisms are related).

The first is that SPC seems to assume that any values of process performance which lie within the control limits are equally acceptable, while any values outside the limits are not. However, surely a value close to the process average or 'target' value will be more acceptable than one only just within the control limits. For example, a service engineer arriving only 1 minute late is a far better 'performance' than one arriving 59 minutes late, even if the control limits are 'quoted time ± one hour'. Also, arriving 59 minutes late would be almost as bad as 61 minutes late! Second, trying to keep performance within control limits may indicate that the process is not deteriorating, but it does not help the process to improve. Rather than seeing the control limits of SPC as a fixed characteristic of a process, it would be better to view them as a reflection of how the process is being improved. Therefore we should expect any improving process to have progressively narrowing control limits.

The Taguchi loss function

Genichi Taguchi proposed a resolution of both the criticisms of SPC described in the critical commentary box.[13] He suggested that the central issue was the first problem – namely that the consequences of being 'off-target' (that is, deviating from the required process average performance) were inadequately described by simple control limits. Instead, he proposed a *quality loss function* (QLF) – a mathematical function which includes all the costs of poor quality. These include wastage, repair, inspection, service, warranty and generally, what he termed, 'loss to society' costs. This loss function is expressed as follows:

$$L = D^2 C$$

where $L =$ total loss to society costs
$D =$ deviation from target performance
$C =$ a constant

Figure 17.12 illustrates the difference between the conventional and Taguchi approaches to interpreting process variability. The more graduated approach of the QLF also answers the second problem raised in the critical commentary box. With losses increasing quadratically as performance deviates from target, there is a natural tendency to progressively reduce process variability. This is sometimes called a *target-oriented quality* philosophy.

Figure 17.12 **The conventional and Taguchi views of the cost of variability**

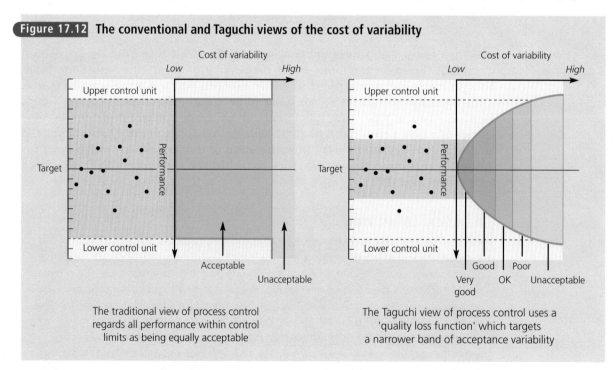

The traditional view of process control regards all performance within control limits as being equally acceptable

The Taguchi view of process control uses a 'quality loss function' which targets a narrower band of acceptance variability

● Control charts for attributes

Attributes have only two states – 'right' or 'wrong', for example – so the statistic calculated is the proportion of wrongs (*p*) in a sample. (This statistic follows a binomial distribution.) Control charts using *p* are called '*p*-charts'.

In calculating the limits, the population mean ($\bar{p}$) – the actual, normal or expected proportion of 'defectives' or wrongs to rights – may not be known. Who knows, for example, the actual number of city commuters who are dissatisfied with their journey time? In such cases the population mean can be estimated from the average of the proportion of 'defectives' ($\bar{p}$), from m samples each of n items, where m should be at least 30 and n should be at least 100:

$$\bar{p} = \frac{p^1 + p^2 + p^3 \dots p^n}{m}$$

One standard deviation can then be estimated from:

$$\sqrt{\frac{\bar{p}\,(1-\bar{p})}{n}}$$

The upper and lower control limits can then be set as:

UCL = $\bar{p}$ + 3 standard deviations

LCL = $\bar{p}$ − 3 standard deviations

Of course, the LCL cannot be negative, so when it is calculated to be so it should be rounded up to zero.

Worked example

A credit card company deals with many hundreds of thousands of transactions every week. One of its measures of the quality of service it gives its customers is the dependability with which it mails customers' monthly accounts. The quality standard it sets itself is that accounts should be mailed within two days of the 'nominal post date' which is specified to the customer. Every week the company samples 1000 customer accounts and records the percentage which were not mailed within the standard time. When the process is working normally, only 2 per cent of accounts are mailed outside the specified period, that is, 2 per cent are 'defective'.

Control limits for the process can be calculated as follows:

Mean proportion defective, $\bar{p}$ = 0.02

Sample size n = 1000

$$\text{Standard deviation } s = \sqrt{\frac{\bar{p}\,(1-\bar{p})}{n}}$$

$$= \sqrt{\frac{0.02\,(0.98)}{1000}}$$

$$= 0.0044$$

With the control limits at $\bar{p} \pm 3s$:

Upper control limit (UCL) = 0.02 + 3(0.0044) = 0.0332
= 3.32%

and lower control limit (LCL) = 0.02 − 3(0.0044) = 0.0068
= 0.68%

Figure 17.13 shows the company's control chart for this measure of quality over the last few weeks, together with the calculated control limits. It also shows that the process is in control.

Sometimes it is more convenient to plot the actual number of defects (c) rather than the proportion (or percentage) of defectives, on what is known as a c-chart. This is very similar to the p-chart but the sample size must be constant and the process mean and control limits are calculated using the following formulae:

$$\text{Process mean } \bar{c} = \frac{c_1 + c_2 + c_3 \ldots c_m}{m}$$

$$\text{Control limits} = \bar{c} \pm 3 \sqrt{\bar{c}}$$

where c = number of defects
        m = number of samples

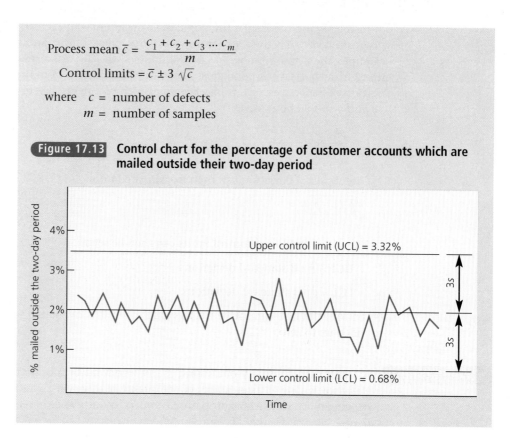

Figure 17.13 Control chart for the percentage of customer accounts which are mailed outside their two-day period

● Control chart for variables

The most commonly used type of control chart employed to control variables is the $\bar{X}$–R *chart*. In fact this is really two charts in one. One chart is used to control the sample average or mean ($\bar{X}$). The other is used to control the variation within the sample by measuring the range (R). The range is used because it is simpler to calculate than the standard deviation of the sample.

The means ($\bar{X}$) chart can pick up changes in the average output from the process being charted. Changes in the means chart would suggest that the process is drifting generally away from its supposed process average, although the variability inherent in the process may not have changed (*see* Fig. 17.14).

The range (R) chart plots the range of each sample, that is the difference between the largest and the smallest measurement in the samples. Monitoring sample range gives an indication of whether the variability of the process is changing, even when the process average remains constant (*see* Fig. 17.14).

Control limits for variables control chart

As with attributes control charts, a statistical description of how the process operates under normal conditions (when there are no assignable causes) can be used to calculate control limits. The first task in calculating the control limits is to estimate the grand average or population mean ($\bar{\bar{X}}$) and average range ($\bar{R}$) using m samples each of sample size n.

The population mean is estimated from the average of a large number (m) of sample means:

$$\bar{\bar{X}} = \frac{\bar{X}_1 + \bar{X}_2 + \ldots \bar{X}_m}{m}$$

Figure 17.14 The process mean or the process range (or both) can change over time

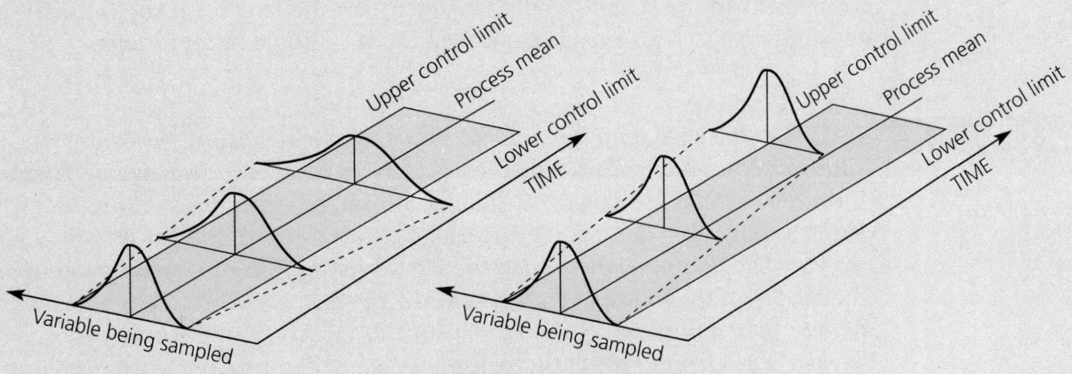

Upper control limit
Process mean
Lower control limit
TIME
Variable being sampled

Range changing over time
with process average constant

Upper control limit
Process mean
Lower control limit
TIME
Variable being sampled

Process average changing over
time with range constant

The average range is estimated from the ranges of the large number of samples:

$$\bar{R} = \frac{R_1 + R_2 + \dots R_m}{m}$$

The control limits for the sample means chart are:

Upper control limit (UCL) = $\bar{\bar{X}} + A_2\bar{R}$
Lower control limit (LCL) = $\bar{\bar{X}} - A_2\bar{R}$

The control limits for the range charts are:

Upper control limit (UCL) = $D_4\bar{R}$
Lower control limit (LCL) = $D_3\bar{R}$

The factors A_2, D_3 and D_4 vary with sample size and are shown in Table 17.6.

Table 17.6 Factors for the calculation of control limits

Sample size n	A_2	D_3	D_4
2	1.880	0	3.267
3	1.023	0	2.575
4	0.729	0	2.282
5	0.577	0	2.115
6	0.483	0	2.004
7	0.419	0.076	1.924
8	0.373	0.136	1.864
9	0.337	0.184	1.816
10	0.308	0.223	1.777
12	0.266	0.284	1.716
14	0.235	0.329	1.671
16	0.212	0.364	1.636
18	0.194	0.392	1.608
20	0.180	0.414	1.586
22	0.167	0.434	1.566
24	0.157	0.452	1.548

The LCL for the means chart may be negative (for example, temperature or profit may be less than zero) but it may not be negative for a range chart (or the smallest measurement in the sample would be larger than the largest). If the calculation indicates a negative LCL for a range chart then the LCL should be set to zero.

Worked example

GAM (Groupe As Maquillage) is a contract cosmetics company, based in France but with plants around Europe, which manufactures and packs cosmetics and perfumes for other companies. One of its plants, in Ireland, operates a filling line which automatically fills plastic bottles with skin cream and seals the bottles with a screw-top cap. The tightness with which the screw-top cap is fixed is an important part of the quality of the filling line process. If the cap is screwed on too tightly, there is a danger that it will crack; if screwed on too loosely it might come loose when packed. Either outcome could cause leakage of the product during its journey between the factory and the customer. The Irish plant had received some complaints of product leakage which it suspected was caused by inconsistent fixing of the screw-top caps on its filling line.

The 'tightness' of the screw tops could be measured by a simple test device which recorded the amount of turning force (torque) that was required to unfasten the tops. The company decided to take samples of the bottles coming out of the filling-line process, test them for their unfastening torque and plot the results on a control chart. Several samples of four bottles were taken during a period when the process was regarded as being in control. The following data were calculated from this exercise:

The grand average of all samples $\bar{\bar{X}} = 812$ g/cm^3
The average range of the sample $\bar{R} = 6$ g/cm^3

Control limits for the means ($\bar{X}$) chart were calculated as follows:

$$UCL = \bar{\bar{X}} + A_2 \bar{R}$$
$$= 812 + (A_2 \times 6)$$

From Table 17.6, we know, for a sample size of four, $A_2 = 0.729$. Thus:

$$UCL = 812 + (0.729 \times 6)$$
$$= 816.37$$

$$LCL = \bar{\bar{X}} - (A_2 \bar{R})$$
$$= 812 - (0.729 \times 6)$$
$$= 807.63$$

Control limits for the range chart (R) were calculated as follows:

$$UCL = D_4 \times \bar{R}$$
$$= 2.282 \times 6$$
$$= 13.69$$

$$LCL = D_3 \bar{R}$$
$$= 0 \times 6$$
$$= 0$$

After calculating these averages and limits for the control chart, the company regularly took samples of four bottles during production, recorded the measurements and plotted them as shown in Figure 17.15.

The control chart revealed that only with difficulty could the process average be kept in control. Occasional operator interventions were required. Also the process range was moving towards (and once breaking) the upper control limit. The process seemed to be becoming more variable. After investigation it was discovered that, because of faulty maintenance of the line, skin cream was occasionally contaminating the torque head (the part of the line which fitted the cap). This resulted in erratic tightening of the caps.

Figure 17.15 **The completed control form for GAM's torque machine showing the mean ($\bar{X}$) and range ($\bar{R}$) charts**

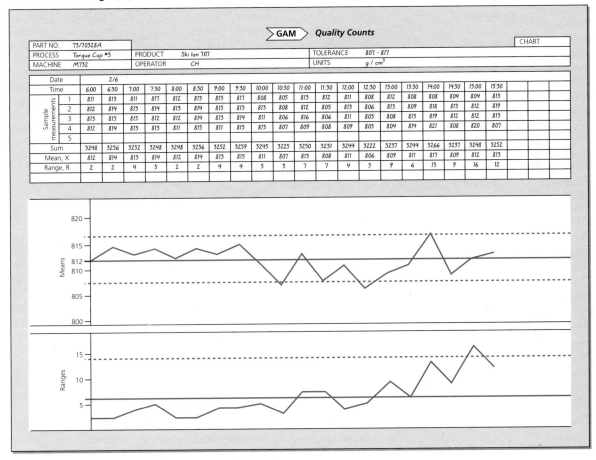

Interpreting control charts

Plots on a control chart which fall outside control limits are an obvious reason for believing that the process might be out of control, and therefore for investigating the process. This is not the only clue which could be revealed by a control chart, however. Figure 17.16 shows some other patterns which could be interpreted as behaviour sufficiently unusual to warrant investigation.

Process control, learning and knowledge

In recent years the role of process control, and SPC in particular, has changed. Increasingly, it is seen not just as a convenient method of keeping processes in control, but also as an activity which is fundamental to the acquisition of competitive

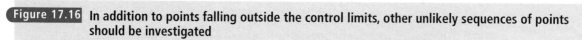

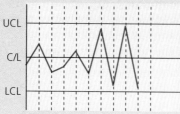

Figure 17.16 In addition to points falling outside the control limits, other unlikely sequences of points should be investigated

(a) Alternating behaviour – Investigate

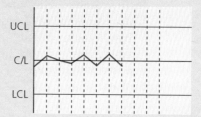

(d) Suspiciously average behaviour – Investigate

(b) Two points near control limit – Investigate

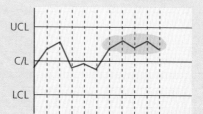

(e) Five points one side of centre line – Investigate

(c) Apparent trend in one direction – Investigate

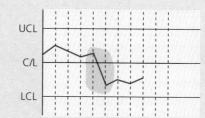

(f) Sudden change in level – Investigate

advantage. This is a remarkable shift in the status of SPC. Traditionally it was seen as one of the most *operational*, immediate and 'hands-on' operations management techniques. Yet it is now being connected with an operation's *strategic* capabilities.[14] This is how the logic of the argument goes:

1 SPC is based on the idea that process variability indicates whether a process is in control or not.
2 Processes are brought into *control* and improved by progressively reducing process variability. This involves eliminating the assignable causes of variation.
3 One cannot eliminate assignable causes of variation without gaining a better understanding of how the process operates. This involves *learning* about the process, where its nature is revealed at an increasingly detailed level.
4 This learning means that *process knowledge* is enhanced, which in turn means that operations managers are able to predict how the process will perform under different circumstances. It also means that the process has a greater capability to carry out its tasks at a higher level of performance.
5 This increased *process capability* is particularly difficult for competitors to copy. It cannot be bought 'off-the-shelf'. It only comes from time and effort being invested in controlling operations processes. Therefore, process capability leads to strategic advantage.

In this way, process control leads to learning which enhances process knowledge and builds difficult-to-imitate process capability.

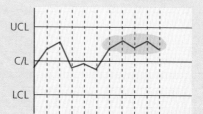

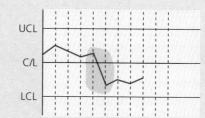

A team leader records process control data at Walkers Snack Foods

Photo courtesy of Walkers Ltd

products means booming sales and therefore continually increasing production volumes. Walkers uses a version of statistical process control, which they call 'control point management' (CPM), to maintain and improve their quality levels. The picture shows a team leader in the company's Doritos plant completing control chart sheets. The control points in the manufacturing process where process variables are measured are all specified for each production line. If any measurements fall outside the control limits, procedures in the form of decision trees help to guide the production technicians in bringing the process back within standard.

Walkers Snack Foods Limited, part of the worldwide Pepsico Company, operates in a highly competitive sector of the fast-moving consumer goods (FMCG) market. With increasingly discriminating customers, they need the competitive edge of high-quality manufacturing to help them retain customer satisfaction. This means that they must keep close control of all their manufacturing processes, a task which is especially difficult when success of your

Questions

1 What do you think are the characteristics of product quality for Walkers products which influence overall customer satisfaction? (Sample a packet and discuss this with friends!)

2 Why is it important that direct production staff, as opposed to managers or engineers, collect and analyse process data?

3 What purpose do the 'corrective' decision trees serve in controlling the process?

Acceptance sampling

Process control is usually the preferred method of controlling quality because quality is being 'built in' to the process rather than being inspected afterwards. However, sometimes it may be necessary to inspect batches of products or services either before or after a process. The purpose of acceptance sampling is to decide whether, on the basis of a sample, to accept or reject the whole batch. Examples include incoming component parts from a supplier, a batch of finished products, or a large number of examination scripts from an internal examiner. Acceptance sampling is usually carried out on attributes rather than variables. It uses the proportion of wrongs to rights, or defectives to acceptables.

Table 17.7 The risks inherent in acceptance sampling

	The batch actually is	
Decision	OK	Not OK
Reject batch	Type I error	Correct decision
Accept batch	Correct decision	Type II error

Again, in acceptance sampling, like process control, it is important to understand the risks inherent in using a sample to make a judgement about a far larger batch. Table 17.7 illustrates the risks of acceptance sampling in the form of type I and type II errors.

In acceptance sampling the type I risk is often referred to as the producer's risk because it is the risk that the operation rejects a batch that is actually of good quality. The type II risk is usually called the consumer's risk because it is the risk of accepting a batch that is actually poor and sending it to the consumer of the product or service.

Sampling plans

Acceptance sampling involves a sample being taken from a batch and a decision to accept or reject the batch being made by comparing the number of 'defects' found in the sample to a predetermined acceptable number. The sampling plan which describes this procedure is defined by two factors, n and c, where:

n = the sample size
c = the acceptance number of defects in the sample.

If x = number of defects actually found in the sample, a decision is made based on the following simple decision rule:

If $x \leq c$ then accept the whole batch.
If $x > c$ then reject the whole batch.

Unlike control charts it is not necessary for organizations to create their own acceptance plans. A set of tables called the Dodge–Romig Sampling Inspection Tables provides values for n and c for a given set of risks. The ability of this plan to discriminate between good batches and bad ones is based upon the binomial distribution and is described by an operating characteristic (OC) curve. The OC curve for a sampling plan

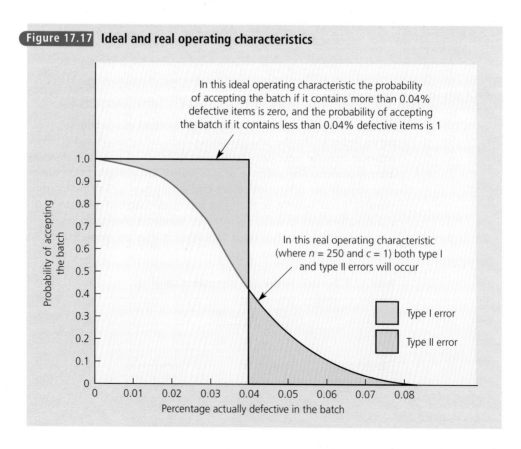

Figure 17.17 **Ideal and real operating characteristics**

In this ideal operating characteristic the probability of accepting the batch if it contains more than 0.04% defective items is zero, and the probability of accepting the batch if it contains less than 0.04% defective items is 1

In this real operating characteristic (where $n = 250$ and $c = 1$) both type I and type II errors will occur

Type I error
Type II error

Probability of accepting the batch

Percentage actually defective in the batch

shows the probability of accepting a batch as the actual percentage of defects varies. An ideal OC curve would look like the black line in Figure 17.17.

In this example the level of defects which is regarded as acceptable is 0.4 per cent and the sampling plan is perfect at discriminating between acceptable and unacceptable batches. The probability of accepting a batch whose actual level of defects is less than 0.4 per cent is 100 per cent and there is no chance of ever accepting a batch whose actual level of defects is more than 0.4 per cent. However, in practice, no procedure based on sampling, and therefore carrying risk, could ever deliver such an ideal curve. Only 100 per cent inspection using a perfect inspector could do so.

Any use of sampling will have to accept the existence of type I and type II errors. In Figure 17.17 the blue line shows a sampling plan for sampling 250 items ($n = 250$) and rejecting the batch if there is more than one defect ($c = 1$) in the sample. A batch is acceptable if it contains 0.4 per cent or fewer defects ($1/250 = 0.04$ per cent).

What is not known is the actual percentage of defective items in any one batch, and because the procedure relies on a sample, there will always be a probability of rejecting a good batch because the number of defects in the sample is two or more despite the batch in fact being acceptable (type I risk shown by the top shaded area). There is also a probability that in spite of accepting a batch (because the number of defects it contains is zero or one) the actual number of defects in the whole batch might be greater than 0.04 per cent (type II risk shown in the lower shaded area of Fig. 17.17). If the sizes of these risks are felt to be too great, the sample size can be increased, which will move the shape of the curve towards the ideal. However, this implies increased time and cost in inspecting the batch.

Creating an acceptance sampling plan

To create an appropriate sampling plan (that is, to decide the values of n and c) the levels of four factors need to be specified. These have been identified on the operating characteristic curve in Figure 17.18. These four factors are then fed into the Dodge–Romig tables to give the respective values for c and n. (Using these tables is

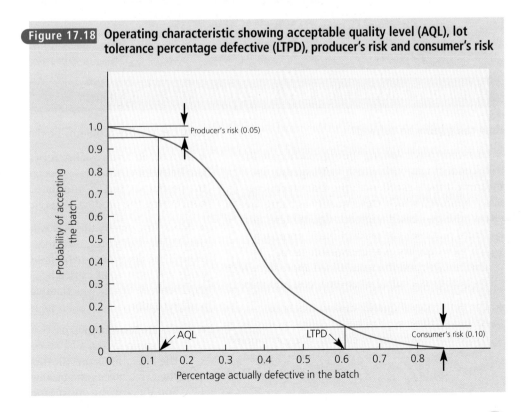

Figure 17.18 Operating characteristic showing acceptable quality level (AQL), lot tolerance percentage defective (LTPD), producer's risk and consumer's risk

beyond the scope of this book.) The four factors are type I error, type II error, acceptable quality level (AQL) and lot tolerance percentage defective (LTPD):

- *Type I error.* The usual value used for producer's risk (type I error) is often set with a probability of 0.05. This means that management is willing to take a 5 per cent chance that a batch of good quality will be rejected when it is actually acceptable. This also implies that there is a 95 per cent chance that a good-quality batch will be accepted.
- *Type II error.* The value for the consumer's risk (type II error) is often set with a probability of 0.1. This means that management is willing to risk at most a 10 per cent chance that a poor-quality batch will be accepted, implying that there is a 90 per cent chance that a poor-quality batch will actually be rejected.
- *AQL.* The acceptable quality level is the actual percentage of defects in a batch which the organization is willing to reject mistakenly (by chance) 5 per cent of the time (assuming a 0.05 type I error) when the batch is actually acceptable.
- *LTPD.* The lot tolerance percentage defective is the actual percentage of defects in a batch that management is willing to accept mistakenly 10 per cent of the time (assuming a 0.1 type II error).

● **CRITICAL COMMENTARY**

A frequently made criticism of acceptance sampling is that it assumes that some amount of defects and failure is acceptable to the organization, or its customers. By accepting the inevitability of failure and poor quality, it is argued, the operation will become 'lazy' at trying to eliminate the causes of bad quality. Rather than see quality as primarily something to be improved, acceptance sampling views it as being almost 'predetermined' by the characteristics of the process. The main task is to measure output and understand the risks involved, not to get to the root causes of poor quality. More recent approaches to quality management (such as TQM, *see* Chapter 20) suggest that 'right first time every time' is the only acceptable approach and that organizations should strive to produce zero defective items rather than some 'acceptable quality level'.

Summary answers to key questions

How can quality be defined?

- In several ways. Among the approaches are the transcendent approach which views quality as meaning 'innate excellence'; the manufacturing-based approach which views quality as being 'free of errors'; the user-based approach which views quality as 'fit for purpose'; the product-based approach which views quality as a 'measurable set of characteristics'; and the value-based approach which views quality as a balance between 'cost and price'.

- The definition of quality used in this book combines all these approaches to define quality as 'consistent conformance to customers' expectations'.

How can quality problems be diagnosed?

- At a broad level, quality is best modelled as the gap between customers' expectations concerning the product or service and their perceptions concerning the product or service.

- Modelling quality this way will allow the development of a diagnostic tool which is based around the perception–expectation gap. If such a gap exists it is likely to be caused by one or more of the gaps between factors which influence expectations and perceptions.

- There are four main gaps:
  - the gap between a customer's specification and the operation's specification;
  - the gap between the product or service concept and the way the organization has specified it;

- the gap between the way quality has been specified and the actual delivered quality;
- the gap between the actual delivered quality and the way the product or service has been described to the customer.

● It is the third gap (between the specification of quality and the actual quality delivered) which is of particular concern to operations managers.

What steps lead towards conformance to specification?

● There are six steps:
- define quality characteristics;
- decide how to measure each of the quality characteristics;
- set quality standards for each characteristic;
- control quality against these standards;
- find and correct the causes of poor quality;
- continue to make improvements.

● Most quality planning and control involves sampling the operations performance in some way. Sampling can give rise to erroneous judgements which are classed as either type I or type II errors. Type I errors involve making corrections where none are needed. Type II errors involve not making corrections where they are in fact needed.

How can statistical process control help quality planning and control?

● Statistical process control (SPC) involves using control charts to track the performance of one or more quality characteristics in the operation. The power of control charting lies in its ability to set control limits derived from the statistics of the natural variation of processes. These control limits are often set at ± 3 standard deviations of the natural variation of the process samples.

● Control charts can be used for either attributes or variables. An attribute is a quality characteristic which has two states (for example, right or wrong). A variable is one which can be measured on a continuously variable scale.

● Process control charts allow operations managers to distinguish between the 'normal' variation inherent in any process and the variations which could be caused by the process going out of control.

How can acceptance sampling help quality planning and control?

● Acceptance sampling helps managers to understand the risks they are taking when they make decisions about a whole batch of products on the basis of a sample taken from that batch. The risks of any particular sampling plan are shown on its operating characteristic (OC) curve.

● Some of the assumptions within acceptance sampling (most notably that a certain level of defects is 'acceptable') are not looked on favourably by proponents of total quality management (*see* Chapter 20).

Calling Sue

The idea of having a Personal Banking Consultant (PBC) seemed a great one at the time it was suggested. For a modest annual fee we would get a differentiated range of 'relationship' financial services designed for busy business people like us. These were listed in an attractive glossy 'membership' brochure and included: a larger overdraft facility with preferential interest rates, free annual travel insurance, a rewards point scheme, a 'gold' credit card with no credit limit, and our own PBC (Sue) and her personal assistant (Richard), who would be there to help whenever we needed them. Every other aspect would be as before, but our accounts would have to be transferred from our old branch in the south (where we lived until six years ago, but never bothered to move our accounts) to the north, where we now work. Having a remote bank branch had not been a problem until recently. If we needed anything done with any account, we simply had to ring the Assistant Manager in the south and he arranged it. But recently, a Southern West Region Office was established, and all phone calls were handled remotely, so it had become more difficult to maintain this personal relationship. Moreover, our business and private accounts were handled by separate people at different offices, using different telephone numbers. We were ready for a change!

Despite the attractions of the package described, we were hesitant to accept this generous offer. Changing all the cheque books, credit cards, standing orders, direct debit instructions, and anything else we had forgotten, including our personal and business accounts, seemed rather complex and time-consuming. We raised these concerns with the advisor who had been sent to sell us the idea, one dark December Monday.

'Oh, there will be absolutely no problem … we can deal with all that. All you and your wife will have to do today is to sign a few forms authorizing us to transfer the accounts, and one to agree to the new arrangements. Then leave the rest to us. There will be no problems, it's easy with all the technology we have today. You should get the new cheque books within seven days, and all balances will be transferred automatically by the computer'.

We signed up immediately – it looked a good scheme, and even the value of the free insurance alone would more than compensate for the annual membership fee.

The four cheque books for the two accounts arrived separately, over a three-day period, the last arriving on the Tuesday, nine days after the agreement. The business account cheques had an incorrectly spelt business name, and the current account cheques had my wife's initials reversed. At the same time we received (from Sue) a personalized welcoming pack and a professionally presented loose-leaf folder of information concerning the account and PBC services, which confirmed that the accounts were in operation. All this correspondence was correctly addressed and written in a friendly style, using our first names. I decided to call Sue about the spelling.

'I'm awfully sorry, sir, I'll order some new ones, and I will ask them to send them to you quickly. I know they've had a backlog due to computer problems at the card centre, but they can prioritize any PBC's cards. In the meantime, you can use your existing accounts, since they are linked to your new ones. I'll call you to confirm when this has been done. Again, may I apologize for any inconvenience you have experienced.'

One hour later she rang as promised, confirming her actions.

On the tenth day our credit cards arrived, correctly embossed with our names. However, these could not be used for cash withdrawals without personal identification numbers (PINs) and the cheques could not be used in UK retail outlets without cheque guarantee cards. The cheque guarantee card doubled as a cash card, for use at ATMs with another PIN number. Neither PIN number had arrived by the second Friday after our signing-up (11 days). I decided to call Sue, to see what was happening.

'Don't worry,' she said, confidently, *'The PINs always come a day or two after the cards, for security reasons, and you should get the guarantee cards about the same time.'*

By the following Friday lunchtime, returning from a week's business trip, we were getting concerned. Although our new cheque guarantee cards had arrived and were correct, our names on the envelope were again incorrect, which seemed odd and slightly disconcerting. We still had not received the new PIN numbers. I decided to call Sue, who apologized again, politely expressing her amazement at our dilemma, and asked me to hold while she checked the system. *'They have certainly been correctly issued on Monday'*, she said confidently, *'and have been sent … perhaps they have been lost in the post. I'll check with the card centre what we should do, and I'll call you back.'*

'You will have to be quick,' I retorted, *'We're just about to leave for a long weekend vacation, but you could call me on the mobile …'.*

Sue phoned two hours later and confirmed that because the PIN numbers had been mislaid, it would be necessary to re-issue the cards for security reasons. *'You should receive the replacement cards and PIN numbers within three days,'* she stated confidently. *'You should carry on using your original account's cards until then.'*

Her suggestion seemed okay at the time, but proved to be rather more of a problem than we had anticipated. On checking out of the hotel on Monday evening, we discovered that the existing credit card had expired, and the bill came to more than our existing cheque guarantee card limit. We settled the account with a combination of cheques and most of our remaining cash – an embarrassing end to a pleasant weekend.

In the post on Tuesday morning, we were surprised to receive two sets of PIN numbers, along with further cheque guarantee cards *and* credit cards. We went to the ATM with our new cards to draw out much needed cash, but the PINs weren't accepted. Careful examination of the packaging revealed that the PINs related to the original cards, not the replacements! We borrowed cash from a friend and called Sue!

By Friday, everything was working and we had received a correctly addressed letter of apology from the card issuing centre in Glasgow. An excellent bouquet of flowers was delivered that afternoon and Sue phoned to check we were now happy. She even called in to see us a week later, bringing some leather holders for cards and cheque books. We have had no more problems and generally the service is excellent. Sue has, however, confided that such problems are quite common (they apparently use a lot of agency staff in the processing centres, and mistakes are common).

But we can always call Sue.

Questions

1 What were the gaps between the customers' expectations and perceptions in the process described?

2 How were the customers' expectations influenced from the outset?

3 What aspects of the bank's service quality specification have been revealed to the customer? Are these reasonable for such an account?

4 Evaluate Sue's reaction to the problems at every stage. Was the bank's service recovery successful?

5 What costs have been created by these problems, and how do they compare with the underlying costs at the root cause of the problem?

CASE EXERCISE

Handles and Hinges (H&H) Ltd

H&H was established in Birmingham, England, in 1984 by two young entrepreneurs, Dave Philips and Chris Agnew, both experienced in the hardware trade. The business specialized in the 'designer' market for polished metal (brass or stainless steel) door handles, cupboard knobs, furniture fittings (mostly used in shop/office furniture) and hinges. By 1996, sales had grown to about £5 million per year. This success was based on H&H's reputation for high-quality, unique designs of both traditional and modern products, many of which were selected and specified by architects for large and prestigious projects such as new office developments in

London's Docklands. Dave, the Chief Executive Officer, with responsibility for sales, believed that most orders from construction companies were placed with H&H because they assumed they had no other choice once the H&H products had been specified. Larger companies would sometimes suggest to the architect that similar products were available at less than half the price. This advice was invariably ignored as the architect would be attracted by H&H's designs and quality, and would be reluctant to risk 'spoiling' multi-million pound projects for the sake of saving a few thousand pounds. Dave outlines the characteristics of the changing marketplace:

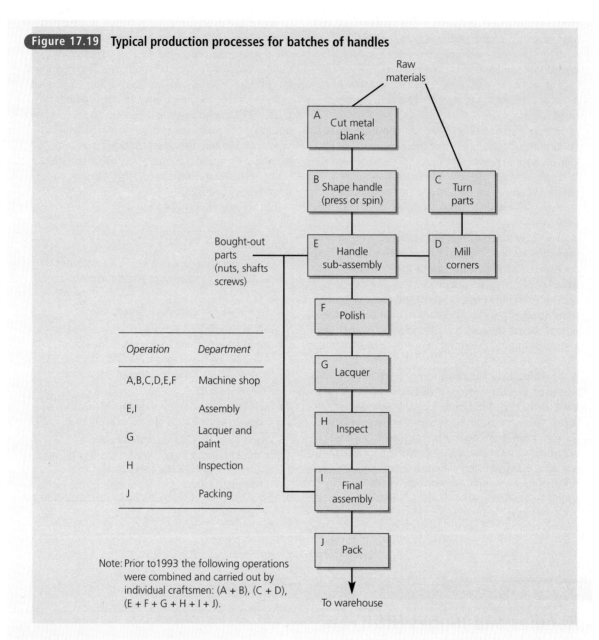

Figure 17.19 Typical production processes for batches of handles

Raw materials

A — Cut metal blank

B — Shape handle (press or spin)

C — Turn parts

Bought-out parts (nuts, shafts screws)

E — Handle sub-assembly

D — Mill corners

F — Polish

G — Lacquer

H — Inspect

I — Final assembly

J — Pack

To warehouse

Operation	Department
A,B,C,D,E,F	Machine shop
E,I	Assembly
G	Lacquer and paint
H	Inspection
J	Packing

Note: Prior to 1993 the following operations were combined and carried out by individual craftsmen: (A + B), (C + D), (E + F + G + H + I + J).

'Because of the recession in the construction industry, particularly in office building, we have, since 1990, expanded our direct sales to large UK hardware retail companies, which now account for about 40 per cent of our sales value, but only about 15 per cent of our gross profit. This segment is much more price-sensitive, so we must be able to manufacture good-quality, simple, standard products at low costs comparable to those of our competitors. Some of the reduced costs have been achieved by using thinner and cheaper materials similar to those used in our competitors' products. We have just received our first consignment of brass sheet from Poland with a saving of over 10 per cent in this case. We also had to re-organize to reduce our processing costs. Chris has done a great job of changing all production to modern batch methods (see Fig. 17.19). However, I am concerned that we are often late delivering to our UK retail customers, and this makes it difficult to keep good relationships and to get repeat orders. Fast delivery of relatively small quantities is required in the "retail segment", whereas the construction/contractors market allows very long production lead times. Dependable delivery is crucial to avoid completion delays, for which we have been held financially accountable on some occasions!

'When customers complain about delivery or about faulty products, we try to compensate them in some way to keep their business – for example, by credit notes or discounts on the next order. Our representatives each spend about one day a week dealing with the consequences of late deliveries, but on the positive side, a meeting with a client is an opportunity to get the next order. The hardware retail companies often require very quick delivery, which is often only achieved by switching production to the item which is required first.

'Really, I am more concerned about reports of quality problems; an increasing number of construction companies have complained to us about dented or scratched handles, but our production department assures us that they left the factory in good condition and must have been damaged on site; which is to be expected on a large construction site. The Quality Control Manager says, however, he cannot give an absolute guarantee that they were all OK, because we only do sampling of final production; if more than a few in a sample are found at final inspection to be sub-standard, the whole batch is rejected, reinspected, sorted and reworked. Using express courier transport and overtime in the factory, rework can usually be done in about a week, but invariably the contractors complain to the architect, perhaps because they dislike being told who to buy from. This can lead to lots of correspondence and meetings between H&H, the contractor and the architect, when we could be doing other things. This problem seems to have got worse in the last two years; often it's also difficult to agree if the product is sub-standard. It is frequently just a question of how shiny (or matt) the polish and lacquer finish is; at other times there are scratches in areas that really can't been seen in use. Often the customers are too fussy, anyway.'

Discussions with Chris (the Manufacturing Director) put a different perspective on the problem:

'The sales catalogue shows pictures of our products prepared for photography; special effects are used to give a bright polished finish but we actually use a matt finish. The samples used by Sales are specially made by experienced craftsmen to eliminate any scratching or minor faults; of course, we cannot always repeat that standard with the modern batch production methods.

'We were aware that the reorganization of production methods could lead to quality problems, so I introduced statistical control, a subject I studied extensively in a quantitative methods course at the local college. Our inspectors now take random samples of batches of components and measure important dimensions such as the diameter or length of brass handles, the thickness of the incoming materials, etc. Batches which fail are either rejected or reworked, and all material where we have

identified any fault at all is returned to the supplier, and our buyers routinely threaten to place orders elsewhere. I instructed the supervisors to inspect press tooling just before the start of each production batch to ensure that there are no surface faults, so I think it is unlikely that the dents and blemishes are caused in production. I must make a point of checking that this is happening. Anyway, our final inspection sampling has been changed to give an acceptable quality level (AQL) of 2 per cent whereas until recently it was only 5 per cent. We have had to increase the number of final inspectors by four at a cost of £15 000 each per annum, but all the management team agrees that with quality products we must be confident of the final quality before packing. We trained some of our best assemblers in SPC and made them full-time inspectors; the combination of their technical and statistical skills ensures that we have the right people for this job. We could not rely on our operators to do any dimensional checks; hardly any of them know how to measure using a metric rule, let alone a micrometer or vernier gauge. It is best to keep them concentrating on achieving correct output targets. I believe that most quality problems here must be caused by occasional operator carelessness.

'The batch method of production has given us much more control over operations. No longer do we have to rely on hard-to-recruit craftsmen who did everything slowly and unpredictably. Now we make the most of economic batches at each stage, benefiting from the economies of scale of longer runs and cheaper unskilled labour. With incentive bonuses based on effective performance against agreed standard times, all our people are working faster to achieve the company's goal of higher productivity. There is no doubt that our operations are now more productive than they've ever been. With high quality and low costs, we are now set for a major assault on the competition. We expect our profits to rise dramatically from the currently inadequate 1 per cent return on sales.'

Questions

1 How does the company compete in its market place, and what is the role of 'quality' in its competitive strategy?

2 Do you think that the company's use of statistical quality control is sensible?

3 Apply the gap model of quality diagnostics (Fig. 17.5) to the company.

Discussion questions

1 Describe and explain the differences between needs, wants and expectations that a customer might have for:
   - a tourist-class flight to America
   - a talking doll
   - an operations management course.

2 Define the quality characteristics for the following products and services and suggest ways in which each characteristic could be measured. Identify whether the characteristics are attributes or variables:
   - a restaurant meal
   - a washing machine
   - a taxi service.

3 Discuss the advantages and disadvantages of 100 per cent inspection. Comment on the appropriateness of 100 per cent inspection, and how it might be carried out, in the following examples:
   - the temperature of a restaurant meal
   - the appropriateness of a student for a first-class honours degree
   - the punctuality of a fleet of city buses
   - the results to be obtained from a packet of garden seeds.

4 Explain why, when 100 per cent inspection takes place, errors in the product or service may still get through to the customer. Illustrate your answer with a product and service of your own choice. What might be done to try to minimize such errors occurring?

5 A factory uses two machines to slice plastic extrusions. The specification range for the output of machine 1 is 16.7 to 17.3 cm, and is 22 to 26 cm for machine 2. The outputs of the machines are normally distributed around 17 and 24 cm, respectively, with standard deviations of 1.7 and 2.1 cm. The normal variation in the two machines is known to be 0.5 and 1.9 cm. The operations manager has the budget to upgrade one of the two machines this year. Which one would you recommend is replaced on the basis of its ability to do the job?

6 A manufacturer of printed circuit boards (PCBs) is concerned that the process is becoming out of control. The usual proportion of defective boards is

6 per cent which is thought to be better than the industry average. The manager has taken one sample a day for the last 10 days, with 100 boards in each sample. The results are shown below. Draw a control chart and comment on the process.

Sample no.	1	2	3	4	5	6	7	8	9	10
No. of defects	3	0	1	4	10	0	6	12	5	7

7 The regional manager of a national train network is considering giving guarantees to customers about the reliability of the trains arriving at the principal station in the region. The arrival times of 20 trains were checked each day over a period of several weeks when there were no known unusual circumstances. It was found that the trains were, on average, three minutes later than their scheduled time of arrival. The average range was 12 minutes. What advice would you give the manager?

8 Describe the advantages of using control charts to monitor processes. Discuss how appropriate they might be for the following activities:
   - complaint monitoring for a package holiday company
   - monitoring of marks for operations management examinations
   - engine failure in aircraft
   - supermarket checkout queues.

9 Once a day a company that specializes in ride-on lawn mowers undertakes a thorough check of a small sample of its products. There are five main checks covering the machine's appearance (measured in terms of the number of blemishes in the metalwork), its reliability (mean time between failures in hours), top speed (mph), fuel consumption (mpg) and noise levels (dB). Table 17.8 provides the UCLs, LCLs and averages for each factor and the results of the last 10 checks. Comment on whether or not you think any parts of the process need investigating and explain your reasons.

10 Explain what is meant by acceptance sampling. Compare this approach to quality control with the total quality management (TQM) approach explained in Chapter 20.

Table 17.8 Lawn mower sample checks

Factor	Appearance	Reliability	Speed	Fuel	Noise
UCL	5	190	10.5	45	3.4
Average	2	150	9	38	2.8
LCL	0	110	7.5	31	2.2
Sample					
1	2	112	8.6	41	3.0
2	1	161	8.4	38	2.9
3	2	120	8.7	43	2.6
4	2	182	8.8	35	2.8
5	1	115	9.0	32	2.9
6	2	173	9.6	41	2.7
7	4	143	9.1	34	3.0
8	4	180	9.2	33	2.3
9	4	119	9.8	33	2.3
10	4	175	9.5	32	2.5

Notes on chapter

1 Based on Gummesson, E. (1993) 'Service Productivity, Service Quality and Profitability', *Proceedings of the 8th International Conference of the Operations Management Association,* Warwick, UK.

2 Garvin, D. (1984) 'What Does "Product Quality" Really Mean?', *Sloan Management Review*, Fall.

3 Gummesson, E. *op. cit.*

4 Parasuraman, A., Zeithaml, V.A. and Berry, L.L. (1985) 'A Conceptual Model of Service Quality and Implications for Future Research', *Journal of Marketing*, Vol 49, Fall, pp 41–50; and Gummesson, E. (1987) 'Lip Service: A Neglected Area in Services Marketing', *Journal of Services Marketing*, Vol 1, No 1, pp 19–23.

5 Haywood-Farmer, J. and Nollet, J. (1991) *Services Plus: Effective Service Management*, Morin.

6 Berry, L.L. and Parasuraman, A. (1991) *Marketing Services: Competing Through Quality*, The Free Press.

7 Based on Parasuraman, A., *op. cit.*

8 Sources: 'Centrebank Says Sorry with Cash', *The Times*, 19 June 1994; and Browing, D.D. (1989) 'Put your Money Where your Mouth is', *Bank Marketing*, Vol 21, No 9.

9 Based on Wild, R. (1989) *Production and Operations Management*, Cassell.

10 Source: Discussion with company staff.

11 Source: 'Scan Avoids Needless Appendectomy', The *Sunday Times*, 23 Feb 1997.

12 Source: Discussions with company staff and company press releases.

13 For more details of the Taguchi approach, *see* Stuart, G. (1993) *Taguchi Methods: A Hands-on Approach*, Addison-Wesley

14 Based on Betts, A. and Slack, N. (2000) 'Control, Knowledge and Learning in Process Development', Warwick Operations Working Paper.

Selected further reading

Bounds, G., Yorks, L., Adams, M. and Ranney, G. (1994) *Beyond Quality Management: Towards the Emerging Paradigm*, McGraw-Hill.

Dale, B.G. (ed) (1994) *Managing Quality* (2nd edn), Prentice Hall.

Dale, B.G. and Oakland, J.S. (1994) *Quality Improvement Through Standards* (2nd edn), Stanley Thornes.

Dale, B.G. and Shaw, P. (1991) 'Statistical Process Control: An Examination of Some Common Queries', *International Journal of Production Economics*, Vol 22, No 1.

Dodge, H.F. and Romig, G.H. (1959) *Sampling Inspection Tables – Single and Double Sampling* (2nd edn), John Wiley.

Duncan, A.J. (1974) *Quality Control and Industrial Statistics*, Irwin.

Evans, J.R. and Lindsay, W.M. (1993) *The Management and Control of Quality* (2nd edn), West.

Garrity, S.M. (1993) *Basic Quality Improvement*, Prentice Hall International.

Garvin, D.A. (1988) *Managing Quality*, The Free Press.

Gupta, V.K. and Sagar, R. (1993) 'Total Quality Control Using PCs in an Engineering Company', *International Journal of Production Research*, Vol 31, No 1.

Kehoe, D.F. (1996) *The Fundamentals of Quality Management*, Chapman and Hall.

Montgomery, D.C. (1985) *Introduction to Statistical Quality Control,* John Wiley.

Montgomery, D.C. (1991) *Introduction to Statistical Quality Control* (2nd edn), John Wiley.

Mortimer, J. (ed) (1988) *Statistical Process Control – an ISF Executive Briefing*, IFS/Springer-Verlag.

Oakland, J.S. (1993) *Total Quality Management* (2nd edn), Butterworth-Heinemann.

Oakland, J.S. and Followell, R.F. (1990) *Statistical Process Control – A Practical Guide* (2nd edn), Heinemann.

Owen, M. (1993) *SPC and Business Improvement*, IFS.

Swenseth, S.R., Muralidhr, K. and Wilson, R.L. (1993) 'Planning for Continual Improvement in a Just-in-time Environment', *International Journal of Operations and Production Management*, Vol 13, No 6.

Zeithaml, V.A., Parasuraman, A. and Berry, L.L. (1990) *Delivering Quality Service: Balancing Customer Perceptions and Expectations*, The Free Press.

Part Four

IMPROVEMENT

Even the best operation will need to improve because the operation's competitors will also be improving. This part of the book looks at how managers can make their operation perform better, how they can stop it failing, and how they can bring their improvement activities together.

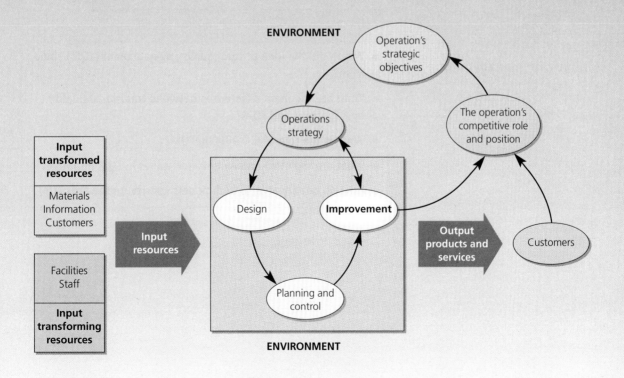

Key operations questions

Chapter 18
Operations improvement

- How can operations measure their performance in terms of the five performance objectives?
- How can operations managers prioritize improvement of performance objectives?
- What are the broad approaches to managing the rate of improvement?
- Where does business process re-engineering (BPR) fit into the improvement activity?
- What techniques can be used for improvement?

Chapter 19
Failure prevention and recovery

- Why do operations fail?
- How is failure measured?
- How can failure and potential failure be detected and analysed?
- How can operations improve their reliability?
- How should operations recover when failure does occur?

Chapter 20
Total quality management

- Where did the idea of total quality management (TQM) come from?
- What are the main differences between traditional quality management and TQM?
- What is the role of ISO 9000 in TQM?
- What are the main implementation issues in TQM initiatives?
- How do quality awards and models contribute towards TQM?

Operations improvement

Introduction

Even when an operation is designed and its activities planned and controlled, the operations manager's task is not finished. All operations, no matter how well managed, are capable of improvement. In fact in recent years the emphasis has shifted markedly towards making improvement one of the main responsibilities of operations managers. In this part of the book we choose to treat improvement activities in three stages. The first, in this chapter, looks at the approaches and techniques which can be adopted to improve the operation. The second, in Chapter 19, looks at improvement from another perspective, that is, how operations can prevent failure and how they can recover when they do suffer a failure. Finally, in Chapter 20, we look at how improvement activities can be supported through the total quality management (TQM) approach. These three stages are interrelated as shown in Figure 18.1.

Figure 18.1 Model of operations improvement showing the issues covered in this chapter

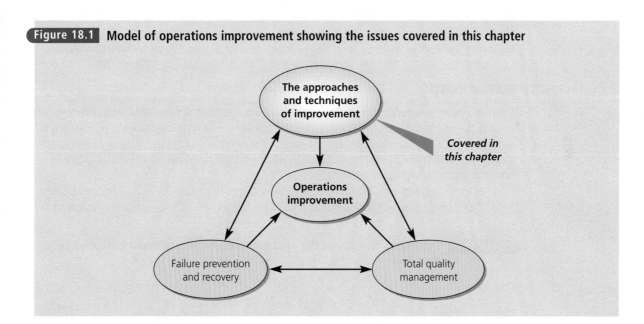

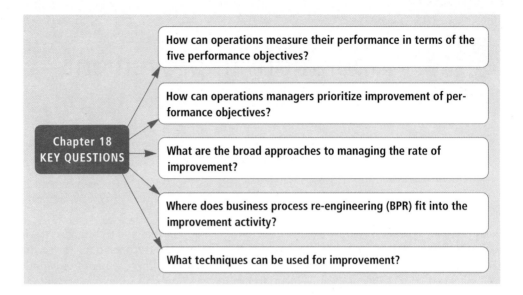

Chapter 18
KEY QUESTIONS

How can operations measure their performance in terms of the five performance objectives?

How can operations managers prioritize improvement of performance objectives?

What are the broad approaches to managing the rate of improvement?

Where does business process re-engineering (BPR) fit into the improvement activity?

What techniques can be used for improvement?

Measuring and improving performance

Before operations managers can devise their approach to the improvement of their operations, they need to know how good they are already. The urgency, direction and priorities of improvement will be determined partly by whether the current performance of an operation is judged to be good, bad or indifferent. All operations therefore need some kind of *performance measurement* as a prerequisite for improvement.

● Performance measurement

Performance measurement is the process of *quantifying action*, where measurement means the process of quantification and the performance of the operation is assumed to derive from actions taken by its management.[1] Performance here is defined as the degree to which an operation fulfils the five performance objectives at any point in time, in order to satisfy its customers.

The polar diagrams (which we introduced in Chapter 3) in Figure 18.2 illustrate this concept. The five performance objectives which we have used throughout this book can be

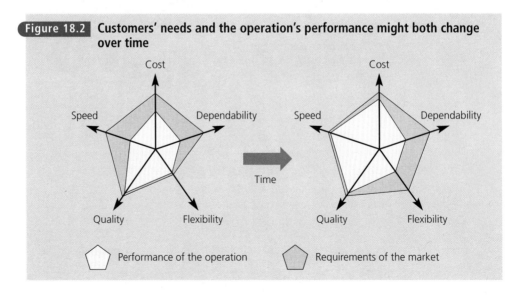

Figure 18.2 Customers' needs and the operation's performance might both change over time

regarded as the dimensions of overall performance which satisfy customers. The market's needs and expectations of each performance objective will vary (as we also discussed in Chapter 3). The extent to which an operation meets its market's needs will also vary, possibly only meeting them in some dimensions. In addition, market requirements and the operation's performance could also change over time. In Figure 18.2 the operation is originally almost meeting the requirements of the market as far as quality and flexibility are concerned, but is under-performing on its speed, dependability and cost. After some time has elapsed the operation has improved its speed and cost to match market requirements but its flexibility no longer matches market requirements, not because it has deteriorated in an absolute sense but because the requirements of the market have changed.

Performance measures

The five performance objectives – quality, speed, dependability, flexibility and cost – are really composites of many smaller measures. For example, an operation's cost is derived from many factors which could include the purchasing efficiency of the operation, the efficiency with which it converts materials, the productivity of its staff, the ratio of direct to indirect staff, and so on. All of these factors individually give a partial view of the operation's cost performance, and many of them overlap in terms of the information they include. Each of them does give a perspective on the cost performance of an opera-

Table 18.1 Some typical partial measures of performance

Performance objective	Some typical measures
Quality	Number of defects per unit Level of customer complaints Scrap level Warranty claims Mean time between failures Customer satisfaction score
Speed	Customer query time Order lead time Frequency of delivery Actual *versus* theoretical throughput time Cycle time
Dependability	Percentage of orders delivered late Average lateness of orders Proportion of products in stock Mean deviation from promised arrival Schedule adherence
Flexibility	Time needed to develop new products/services Range of products/services Machine change-over time Average batch size Time to increase activity rate Average capacity/maximum capacity Time to change schedules
Cost	Minimum delivery time/average delivery time Variance against budget Utilization of resources Labour productivity Added value Efficiency Cost per operation hour

tion, however, which could be useful either to identify areas for improvement or to monitor the extent of improvement. If an organization regards its 'cost' performance as unsatisfactory, therefore, disaggregating it into 'purchasing efficiency', 'operations efficiency', 'staff productivity', etc. might explain the root cause of the poor performance.

Table 18.1 shows some of the partial measures which can be used to judge an operation's performance.

Esther Toledo del Castillo[2]

Photo courtesy of Alstom España

The smooth running of trains like this depends on improvements in the services provided by Alstom Transporte SA

Esther Toledo del Castillo is the director of quality and environment at Alstom Transporte SA-Systems Maintenance, the Spanish transport services company – an autonomous unit within the transport services business group of Alstom, the engineering and transport group. It provides a whole range of services to railway operators, mainly in Spain, Portugal and South America. Although the company's history of pioneering quality management goes back to the 1960s, it was in the late 1990s that it received Spain's highest prize, the Príncipe Felipe Award. Such a reputation for quality is a valuable asset in an increasingly competitive market, says Ms Toledo del Castillo.

'We are continuoually looking for innovation in our contracts and the way we deliver our services because each of our customers wants us to give more or better service for a lower price. The continuous improvement of our processes is the only way to make our company more efficient.'

The company uses a defined set of criteria to identify particularly critical processes within its operations. Each process is allocated a 'process owner' by the company's quality steering committee. Because the company's sites are widely spread, it is important that excellence in process management practice is identified and the lessons learnt throughout the company. This is helped by the company's 'process excellence index' (EPI) which is an indicator of the way a process performs, particularly how it is designed, controlled and improved. The EPI score, which is expressed on a scale of 1 to 100, is calculated by the process owner and registered with the quality department.

'With one figure we know the state of a process in such a way that we can measure the cost, reliability and quality of each process so that we can compare performance. If you don't measure, you can't improve. And if you don't measure in the correct way, how can you know where you are?'

Employee recognition is also an important part of the company's improvement strategy. The company's suggestion scheme is designed to encourage staff to submit several linked ideas at one time. These can be evaluated and rated as a portfolio of suggestions from each employee. No individual suggestion is finally evaluated until it has been fully implemented. Where ideas are put forward by a team of employees, the score is divided between them, either equally or according to the wishes of the team itself. These employee policies are supported by the company's training schemes, many of which are designed to ensure all employees are customer-focused.

'Not everyone has direct contact with customers, so training is a way to get them all to think as a customer and handle customer enquiries and complaints. If people assume that the customer is wrong, it becomes difficult to make sure they are helped,' says Ms Toledo del Castillo.

Questions

1 What seem to be the key elements in this company's approach to improvement?

2 Do you think this approach is appropriate for all operations?

● Performance standards

After an operation has measured its performance by using a 'bundle' of partial measures, it needs to make a judgement as to whether its performance is good, bad or indifferent. There are several ways it can do this, each of which involves comparing the current achieved level of performance with some kind of standard. Four kinds of standard are commonly used.

Historical standards

Historical standards would mean comparing current performance against previous performance. For example, if an organization was delivering products to its customers four weeks after the customer initially requested them, its performance would be judged to be quite good if the previous year it was taking six weeks to deliver. Historical performance standards are effective when judging whether an operation is getting better or worse over time, but they give no indication as to whether performance should be regarded as satisfactory.

Target performance standards

Target performance standards are those which are set arbitrarily to reflect some level of performance which is regarded as appropriate or reasonable. For example, if, under the circumstances, it is regarded as reasonable for the previously mentioned operation to deliver within four weeks then the performance of an operation which actually did deliver in four weeks would be regarded as acceptable. The budgets which most large organizations prepare are examples of target performance standards.

Competitor performance standards

Competitor performance standards compare the achieved performance of the operation with that which is being achieved by one or more of the organization's competitors. For example, if the operation is delivering within four weeks but most of its competitors can deliver within three weeks then its performance would not be regarded as very good. The advantage of competitor-based performance standards is that they relate an operation's performance directly to its competitive ability in the marketplace. In terms of strategic performance improvement, competitive standards are the most useful. For some operations in the not-for-profit sector, this type of performance standard needs to be modified. Comparison against competitors might not even be possible. A police department, for example, would find it difficult to identify its 'competitors' but could compare its performance with that of similar police departments elsewhere.

Absolute performance standards

An absolute performance standard is one which is taken to its theoretical limits. For example, the quality standard of 'zero defects' or the inventory standard of 'zero inventories' are both absolute standards. These standards are perhaps never achievable in practice but they do allow an operation to calibrate itself against a theoretical limit. In the previous example, the product which was in fact delivered in four weeks to the customer might take only four hours to be made within the factory and delivered to the customer. In practice the operation will probably never achieve a four-hour delivery time, but the standard has illustrated how much the operation could theoretically improve.

● Benchmarking

One approach that some companies use to compare their operations with those of other companies, or other parts of its own company, is called *benchmarking*. Originally the term 'benchmark' derives from land surveying where a mark, cut in the rock, would act as a reference point. In 1979 the Xerox Corporation, the document and copying company, used the term 'competitive benchmarking' to describe a process:

World-class operations in a developing country

South African Breweries plc is currently the third largest brewing company in the world. SAB Limited, the domestic arm of the organization, embarked on a process of improving operations capabilities through the 1990s, which was founded on three 'best operating practices':

- *Process control* – operator-driven quality measurement, control and corrective action.
- *Process performance management* – improvement in yield and reduction of waste in all its forms: motion, materials handling, processing, waiting, over-production, correction and inventory.
- *Plant availability* – reliability-centred maintenance (*see* next chapter) with operators performing simple autonomous maintenance (including condition monitoring), with specialists being utilized for specialist tasks and coaching.

South Africa's unfortunate history resulted in an unusual mix of first- and third-world conditions in one country. It was ranked 47th out of 59 countries in the *1999 Global Competitiveness Report* published by the World Economic Forum. Of particular concern is the ranking for labour skills, where it was placed last. Historically, poor educational infrastructure had resulted in many South Africans being functionally illiterate. This obviously has huge ramifications for South African operations attempting to implement world-class operations on the shop floor. Attempts to improve the situation through part-time literacy training were of limited success, and it was realized that successful implementation of the changes envisaged would result in some job modification and, unfortunately, some staff losing their jobs. Following a joint management/union international benchmarking investigation, it was agreed that SAB needed to implement new world-class work practices in order to remain internationally competitive, but that negatively affected employees would need to be helped through the transition. A visit to ILO in Geneva resulted in SAB and the union

Photo courtesy of SAB

jointly instituting Project Noah – an initiative aimed at developing alternatives for redundant employees. The process involved ongoing formal administrative, business and psychological support for employees moving into alternative employment or entrepreneurial activities. Project Noah is now widely acknowledged as a great success, with past employees running a number of profitable SMEs, many involving the provision of non-core activities such as cleaning, building maintenance and catering services to other manufacturing organizations. The improvement programme has also enabled SAB to move towards world-class operations results, with the new work practices resulting in large improvements in production reliability and product quality.

> **Question**
>
> What are the particular challenges of implementing an improvement programme in a developing country?

used by the manufacturing function to revitalize itself by comparing the features, assemblies and components of its products with those of competitors.[3]

(*See* box on Rank Xerox's benchmarking process.) Since that time the term 'benchmarking' has widened its meaning in a number of ways:[4]

- It is no longer restricted only to the manufacturing operations but is also seen as being applicable to other functional areas such as purchasing and marketing.
- It is no longer confined only to manufacturing organizations but has been used in services such as hospitals and banks.

- It is no longer practised only by experts and consultants but can involve all staff in the organization.
- The term 'competitive' has been widened to mean more than just the direct comparison with competitors. It is now taken to mean benchmarking to gain competitive advantage (perhaps by comparison with, and learning from, non-competitive organizations).

Types of benchmarking

There are many different types of benchmarking (which are not necessarily mutually exclusive), some of which are listed below:

- *Internal benchmarking* is a comparison between operations or parts of operations which are within the same total organization. For example, a large motor vehicle manufacturer with several factories might choose to benchmark each factory against the others.

Xerox benchmarking[5]

CWS

Possibly the best-known pioneer of benchmarking in Europe is Rank Xerox, the document and imaging company, which created the original market for copiers. The virtual monopoly the company had in its sector almost became its undoing, however. Spurred by the threat from the emerging Japanese copier companies, an in-depth study within the company recognized that fundamental changes were needed. To understand how it should change, the company decided to evaluate itself externally – a process which became known as competitive benchmarking. The results of this study shocked the company. Its Japanese rivals were selling machines for about what it cost Xerox to make them. Nor could this be explained by differences in quality. The study found that, when compared with its Japanese rivals, the company had nine times more suppliers, was rejecting 10 times as many machines on the production line and taking twice as long to get products to market. Benchmarking also showed that productivity would need to grow 18 per cent per year over five years if it was to catch up with its rivals.

Rank Xerox sees benchmarking as helping it achieve two objectives. At a strategic level it helps set standards of performance, while at an operational level it helps the company understand the best practices and operations methods which can help it achieve its performance objectives. The benchmarking process developed by Rank Xerox has five phases (*see* Fig. 18.3).

Its experience of using this approach has led Xerox to a number of conclusions:

- The first phase, planning, is crucial to the success of the whole process. A good plan will

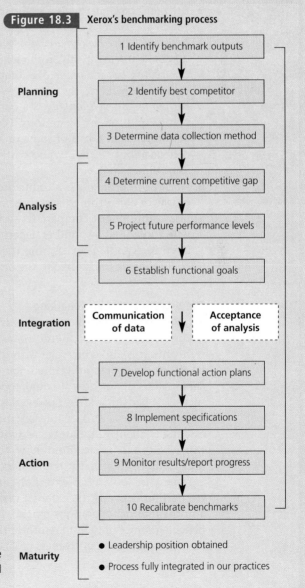

Figure 18.3 Xerox's benchmarking process

Planning
1 Identify benchmark outputs
2 Identify best competitor
3 Determine data collection method

Analysis
4 Determine current competitive gap
5 Project future performance levels

Integration
6 Establish functional goals

Communication of data → Acceptance of analysis

7 Develop functional action plans

Action
8 Implement specifications
9 Monitor results/report progress
10 Recalibrate benchmarks

Maturity
- Leadership position obtained
- Process fully integrated in our practices

identify a realistic objective for the benchmarking study, which is achievable and clearly aligned with business priorities.

- A prerequisite for benchmarking success is to understand thoroughly your own processes. Without this it is difficult to compare your processes against those of other companies.
- Look at what is already available. A lot of information is already in the public domain. Published accounts, journals, conferences and professional associations can all provide information which is useful for benchmarking purposes.

- Be sensitive in asking for information from other companies. The golden rule is: 'Don't ask any questions that we would not like to be asked ourselves.'

> **Questions**
>
> 1 What kind of information did Xerox discover in its benchmarking study?
>
> 2 Of the five performance objectives (quality, speed, dependability, flexibility, cost) which do you think are the most difficult to discover about your competitors' performance?

- *External benchmarking* is a comparison between an operation and other operations which are part of a different organization.
- *Non-competitive benchmarking* is benchmarking against external organizations which do not compete directly in the same markets.
- *Competitive benchmarking* is a comparison directly between competitors in the same, or similar, markets.
- *Performance benchmarking* is a comparison between the levels of achieved performance in different operations. For example, an operation might compare its own performance in terms of some or all of our performance objectives – quality, speed, dependability, flexibility and cost – against other organizations' performance in the same dimensions.
- *Practice benchmarking* is a comparison between an organization's operations practices, or way of doing things, and those adopted by another operation. For example, a large retail store might compare its systems and procedures for controlling stock levels with those used by another department store. The objective is usually to see whether anything can be learned from the practices adopted by other organizations, which could then be transferred to the organization's own operational practices.

The objectives of benchmarking

Benchmarking is partly concerned with being able to judge how well an operation is doing. It can be seen, therefore, as one approach to setting realistic performance standards. It is also concerned with searching out new ideas and practices which might be able to be copied or adapted. For example, a bank might learn some things from a supermarket about how it could cope with demand fluctuations during the day. The success of benchmarking, however, is largely due to more than its ability to set performance standards and enable organizations to copy one another. Benchmarking is essentially about stimulating creativity and providing a stimulus which enables operations better to understand how they should be serving their customers. Many organizations find that it is the process itself of looking at different parts of their own company or looking at external companies which allows them to understand the connection between the external market needs which an operation is trying to satisfy and the internal operations practices it is using to try to satisfy them. In other words, benchmarking can help to reinforce the idea of the direct contribution which an operation has to the competitiveness of its organization.

Improvement priorities[6]

In Chapter 3, when discussing the 'market requirements' perspective, we identified two major influences on the way in which operations decide which performance objectives require particular attention:

- the needs and preferences of customers;
- the performance and activities of competitors.

The consideration of customers' needs has particular significance in shaping the objectives of all operations. The fundamental purpose of operations is to create goods and services in such a way as to meet the needs of their customers. What customers find important, therefore, the operation should also regard as important. If customers for a particular product or service prefer low prices to wide range, then the operation should devote more energy to reducing its costs than to increasing the flexibility which enables it to provide a range of products or services. The needs and preferences of customers shape the *importance* of operations objectives within the operation.

The role of competitors is different from that of customers. Competitors are the points of comparison against which the operation can judge its performance. From a competitive viewpoint, as operations improve their performance, the improvement which matters most is that which takes the operation past the performance levels achieved by its competitors. The role of competitors then is in determining achieved *performance*.

Both importance and performance have to be brought together before any judgement can be made as to the relative priorities for improvement. Just because something is particularly important to its customers does not mean that an operation should necessarily give it immediate priority for improvement. It may be that the operation is already considerably better than its competitors at serving customers in this respect. Similarly, just because an operation is not very good at something when compared with its competitors' performance, it does not necessarily mean that it should be immediately improved. Customers may not particularly value this aspect of performance. Both importance and performance need to be viewed together to judge the prioritization of objectives.

Following the benchmarking rules

Some of the most successful examples of benchmarking have occurred when a number of companies cooperate in exchanging information about themselves. However, the potential for misunderstanding, misreporting or downright misinformation is high. Most organizations are understandably cautious about releasing information that will be of benefit to potential competitors without an equal pay-off. In order to impose some 'rules' into the process of identifying and learning from best practice, it is important for companies mutually to agree common 'protocols' relating to how companies should behave when exchanging information. The following protocol is that recommended by the American-based Productivity and Quality Center and gives a flavour of some of the issues which can help the mutual exchange of information:

1 Know and abide by the Benchmarking Code of Conduct.
2 Have basic knowledge of benchmarking and follow a benchmarking process.
3 Prior to initiating contact with potential benchmarking partners, determine what to benchmark, identify key performance variables to study, recognize superior performing companies, and complete a rigorous self-assessment.
4 Develop a questionnaire and interview guide, and share these in advance if requested.
5 Possess the authority to share and be willing to share information with benchmarking partners.
6 Work through a specified host and mutually agree on scheduling and meeting arrangements.

When the benchmarking process proceeds to a face-to-face visit, the following behaviours are encouraged:

- Provide meeting agenda in advance.
- Be professional, honest, courteous and prompt.
- Introduce all attendees and explain why they are present.
- Adhere to the agenda.
- Use language that is universal, not one's own jargon.
- Be sure that neither party is sharing proprietary information unless prior approval has been obtained by both parties from the proper authority.
- Share information about your own process, and, if asked, consider sharing study results.
- Offer to facilitate a future reciprocal visit.

- Conclude meetings and visits on schedule.
- Thank your benchmarking partner for sharing their process.

Questions

1 Much of the benchmarking protocol seems concerned with the planning that takes place before companies talk to each other directly. Why do you think this is so important?

2 Why do you think each of the face-to-face visit 'behaviours' is important?

Judging importance to customers

In Chapter 3 we introduced the idea of *order-winning, qualifying* and *less important competitive factors*.

Order-winning competitive factors are those which directly win business for the operation. *Qualifying competitive factors* are those which may not win extra business if the operation improves its performance, but can certainly lose business if performance falls below a particular point, known as the qualifying level. *Less important competitive factors*, as their name implies, are those which are relatively unimportant compared with the others.

In fact, to judge the relative importance of its competitive factors, an operation will usually need to use a slightly more discriminating scale. One way to do this is to take our three broad categories of competitive factors – order winning, qualifying and less important – and to divide each category into three further points representing strong, medium and weak positions. Figure 18.4 illustrates such a scale.

Judging performance against competitors

At its simplest, a competitive performance standard would consist merely of judging whether the achieved performance of an operation is better than, the same, or worse

Figure 18.4 **A nine-point scale of importance**

Order winner	Strong	1	Provides a crucial advantage
	Medium	2	Provides an important advantage
	Weak	3	Provides a useful advantage

Qualifier	Strong	4	Needs to be up to good industry standard
	Medium	5	Needs to be up to median industry standard
	Weak	6	Needs to be within close range of the rest of the industry

Less important	Strong	7	Not usually of importance but could become more so
	Medium	8	Very rarely considered by customers
	Weak	9	Never considered by customers

Figure 18.5 **A nine-point scale of performance**

Better than competitors			
	Strong	**1**	Considerably better than competitors
	Medium	**2**	Clearly better than competitors
	Weak	**3**	Marginally better than competitors

Same as competitors			
	Strong	**4**	Sometimes marginally better than competitors
	Medium	**5**	About the same as most competitors
	Weak	**6**	Slightly lower than the average of most competitors

Worse than competitors			
	Strong	**7**	Usually marginally worse than most competitors
	Medium	**8**	Usually worse than competitors
	Weak	**9**	Consistently worse than competitors

than that of its competitors. However, in much the same way as the nine-point importance scale was derived, we can derive a more discriminating nine-point performance scale, as shown in Figure 18.5.

The importance–performance matrix

The priority for improvement which each competitive factor should be given can be assessed from a comparison of their importance and performance. This can be shown on an importance–performance matrix which, as its name implies, positions each competitive factor according to its scores or ratings on these criteria. Figure 18.6 shows an importance–performance matrix divided into zones of improvement priority. The first zone boundary is the 'lower bound of acceptability' shown as line AB in Figure 18.6. This is the boundary between acceptable and unacceptable performance. When a competitive factor is rated as relatively unimportant (8 or 9 on the importance scale), this boundary will in practice be low. Most operations are prepared to tolerate performance levels which are 'in the same ball-park' as their competitors (even at the bottom end of the rating) for unimportant competitive factors. They only become concerned when performance levels are clearly below those of their competitors. Conversely, when judging competitive factors which are rated highly (1 or 2 on the importance scale) they will be markedly less sanguine at poor or mediocre levels of performance. Minimum levels of acceptability for these competitive factors will usually be at the lower end of the 'better than competitors' class. Below this minimum bound of acceptability (AB) there is clearly a need for improvement; above this line there is no immediate urgency for any improvement. However, not all competitive factors falling below the minimum line will be seen as having the same degree of improvement priority. A boundary approximately represented by line CD represents a distinction between an urgent priority zone and a less urgent improvement zone. Similarly, above the line AB, not all competitive factors are regarded as having the same priority. The line EF can be seen as the approximate boundary between performance levels which are regarded as 'good' or 'appropriate' on one hand and those regarded as 'too good' or 'excess' on the other. Segregating the matrix in this way results in four zones which imply very different priorities:

- *The 'appropriate' zone* – competitive factors in this area lie above the lower bound of acceptability and so should be considered satisfactory.
- *The 'improve' zone* – lying below the lower bound of acceptability, any factors in this zone must be candidates for improvement.

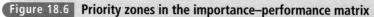

Figure 18.6 **Priority zones in the importance–performance matrix**

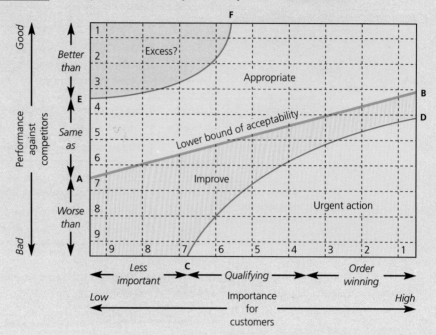

- *The 'urgent-action' zone* – these factors are important to customers but performance is below that of competitors. They must be considered as candidates for immediate improvement.
- *The 'excess?' zone* – factors in this area are 'high performing', but not important to customers. The question must be asked, therefore, whether the resources devoted to achieving such a performance could be used better elsewhere.

Worked example

EXL Laboratories is a subsidiary of an electronics company. It carries out research and development as well as technical problem-solving work for a wide range of companies, including companies in its own group. It is particularly keen to improve the level of service which it gives to its customers. However, it needs to decide which aspect of its performance to improve first. It has devised a list of the most important aspects of its service:

- *The quality of its technical solutions* – the perceived appropriateness by customers.
- *The quality of its communications with customers* – the frequency and usefulness of information.
- *The quality of post-project documentation* – the usefulness of the documentation which goes with the final report.
- *Delivery speed* – the time between customer request and the delivery of the final report.
- *Delivery dependability* – the ability to deliver on the promised date.
- *Delivery flexibility* – the ability to deliver the report on a revised date.
- *Specification flexibility* – the ability to change the nature of the investigation.
- *Price* – the total charge to the customer.

EXL assigns a score to each of these factors using the 1–9 scale described in Figure 18.4. This is shown in Figure 18.7.

EXL then turned their attention to judging the laboratory's performance against competitor organizations. Although they have benchmarked information for some

Rating 'importance to customers' and 'performance against competitors' on the nine-point scales for EXL Laboratories

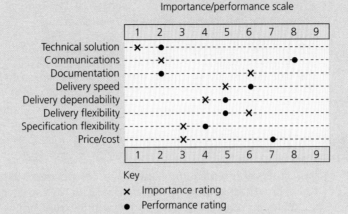

aspects of performance, they have to make estimates for the others. These are also shown in Figure 18.7.

EXL Laboratories plotted the importance and performance ratings it had given to each of its competitive factors on an importance–performance matrix. This is shown in Figure 18.8. It shows that the most important aspect of competitiveness – the ability to deliver sound technical solutions to its customers – falls comfortably within the appropriate zone. Specification flexibility and delivery flexibility are also in the appropriate zone, although only just. Both delivery speed and delivery dependability seem to be in need of improvement as each is below the minimum level of acceptability for their respective importance positions. However, two competitive factors, communications and cost/price, are clearly in need of immediate improvement. These two factors should

The importance–performance matrix for EXL Laboratories

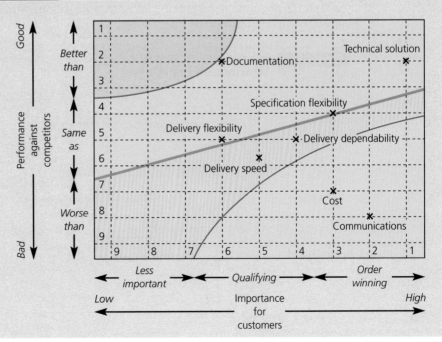

therefore be assigned the most urgent priority for improvement. The matrix also indicates that the company's documentation could almost be regarded as 'too good'.

The matrix may not reveal any total surprises. The competitive factors in the 'urgent-action' zone may be known to be in need of improvement already. However, the exercise is useful for two reasons:

- It helps to discriminate between many factors which may be in need of improvement.
- The exercise gives purpose and structure to the debate on improvement priorities.

Approaches to improvement

Once the priority of improvement has been determined, an operation must consider the approach or strategy it wishes to take to the improvement process. Two particular strategies represent different, and to some extent opposing, philosophies. These two strategies are *breakthrough improvement* and *continuous improvement*.

● Breakthrough improvement

Breakthrough improvement (or 'innovation'-based improvement as it is sometimes called) assumes that the main vehicle of improvement is major and dramatic change in the way the operation works. The introduction of a new, more efficient machine in a factory, the total redesign of a computer-based hotel reservation system, and the introduction of a new and better degree programme at a university are all examples of breakthrough improvement. The impact of these improvements is relatively sudden, abrupt and represents a step change in practice (and hopefully performance). Such improvements are rarely inexpensive, usually calling for high investment of capital, often disrupting the ongoing workings of the operation, and frequently involving changes in the product/service or process technology. The bold line in Figure 18.9 illustrates the pattern of performance with several breakthrough improvements.

The improvement pattern illustrated by the purple line in Figure 18.9 is regarded by some as being more representative of what really occurs when operations rely on pure breakthrough improvement.

Figure 18.9 **The intended and actual pattern of performance improvement with breakthrough improvement**

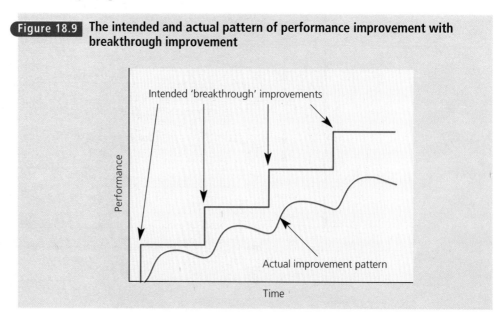

● Continuous improvement

Continuous improvement, as the name implies, adopts an approach to improving performance which assumes more and smaller incremental improvement steps. For example, modifying the way a product is fixed to a machine to reduce changeover time, simplifying the question sequence when taking a hotel reservation, and rescheduling the assignment completion dates on a university course so as to smooth the students' workload are all examples of incremental improvements. While there is no guarantee that such small steps towards better performance will be followed by other steps, the whole philosophy of continuous improvement attempts to ensure that they will be. Continuous improvement is not concerned with promoting small improvements *per se*. It does see small improvements, however, as having one significant advantage over large ones – they can be followed relatively painlessly by other small improvements (*see* Fig. 18.10).

Continuous improvement is also known as *kaizen*. Kaizen is a Japanese word, the definition of which is given by Masaaki Imai[7] (who has been one of the main proponents of continuous improvement) as follows:

> *Kaizen means improvement. Moreover, it means improvement in personal life, home life, social life and work life. When applied to the work place, kaizen means continuing improvement involving everyone – managers and workers alike.*

In continuous improvement it is not the *rate* of improvement which is important, it is the *momentum* of improvement. It does not matter if successive improvements are small; what does matter is that every month (or week, or quarter, or whatever period is appropriate) some kind of improvement has actually taken place.

Building a continuous improvement capability

The ability to improve on a continuous basis is not something which always comes naturally to operations managers and staff. There are specific abilities, behaviours and actions which need to be consciously developed if continuous improvement is to sustain over the long term. John Bessant and Sarah Caffyn, of Brighton University, distinguish between what they call 'organizational abilities' (the capacity or aptitude to adopt a particular approach to continuous improvement), 'constituent behaviours' (the routines of behaviour which staff adopt and which reinforce the approach to continuous improvement) and 'enablers' (the procedural devices or techniques used to progress the continuous improvement effort). They identify six generic organizational abilities, each with its own set of constituent behaviours. These are identified in Table 18.2. Examples of enablers are the improvement techniques described later in this chapter.

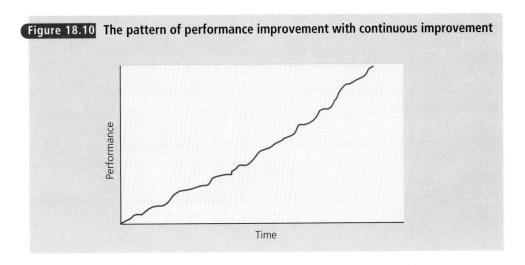

Figure 18.10 The pattern of performance improvement with continuous improvement

Table 18.2 Continuous improvement (CI) abilities and some associated behaviours[8]

Organizational ability	Constituent behaviours
Getting the CI habit Developing the ability to generate sustained involvement in CI	People use formal problem-finding and solving cycle
	People use simple tools and techniques
	People use simple measurement to shape the improvement process
	Individuals and/or groups initiate and carry through CI activities – they participate in the process
	Ideas are responded to in a timely fashion – either implemented or otherwise dealt with
	Managers support the CI process through allocation of resources
	Managers recognize in formal ways the contribution of employees to CI
	Managers lead by example, becoming actively involved in design and implementation of CI
	Managers support experiment by not punishing mistakes, but instead encouraging learning from them
Focusing on CI Generating and sustaining the ability to link CI activities to the strategic goals of the company	Individuals and groups use the organization's strategic objectives to prioritize improvements
	Everyone is able to explain what the operation's strategy and objectives are
	Individuals and groups assess their proposed changes against the operation's objectives
	Individuals and groups monitor/measure the results of their improvement activity
	CI activities are an integral part of the individual's or group's work, not a parallel activity
Spreading the word Generating the ability to move CI activity across organizational boundaries	People cooperate in cross-functional groups
	People understand and share an holistic view (process understanding and ownership)
	People are oriented towards internal and external customers in their CI activity
	Specific CI projects with outside agencies (customers, suppliers, etc.) take place
	Relevant CI activities involve representatives from different organizational levels
CI on the CI system Generating the ability to manage strategically the development of CI	The CI system is continually monitored and developed
	There is a cyclical planning process whereby the CI system is regularly reviewed and amended
	There is periodic review of the CI system in relation to the organization as a whole
	Senior management make available sufficient resources (time, money, personnel) to support the continuing development of the CI system
	The CI system itself is designed to fit within the current structure and infrastructure
	When a major organizational change is planned, its potential impact on the CI system is assessed
Walking the talk Generating the ability to articulate and demonstrate CI's values.	The 'management style' reflects commitment to CI values
	When something goes wrong, people at all levels look for reasons why, rather than blame individuals
	People at all levels demonstrate a shared belief in the value of small steps and that everyone can contribute, by themselves being actively involved in making and recognizing incremental improvements
Building the learning organization Generating the ability to learn through CI activity	Everyone learns from their experiences, both good and bad
	Individuals seeks out opportunities for learning/personal development
	Individuals and groups at all levels share their learning
	The organization captures and shares the learning of individuals and groups
	Managers accept and act on all the learning that takes place
	Organizational mechanisms are used to deploy what has been learned across the organization

The differences between breakthrough and continuous improvement

Breakthrough improvement places a high value on creative solutions. It encourages free thinking and individualism. It is a radical philosophy insomuch as it fosters an approach to improvement which does not accept many constraints on what is possible. 'Starting with a clean sheet of paper', 'going back to first principles' and 'completely rethinking the system' are all typical breakthrough improvement principles. Continuous improvement, on the other hand, is less ambitious, at least in the short term. It stresses adaptability, teamwork and attention to detail. It is not radical; rather it builds upon the wealth of accumulated experience within the operation itself, often relying primarily on the people who operate the system to improve it. One analogy which helps to understand the difference between breakthrough and continuous improvement is that of the sprint and the marathon. Breakthrough improvement is a series of explosive and impressive sprints. Continuous improvement, like marathon running, does not require the expertise and prowess required for sprinting; but it does require that the runner (or operations manager) keeps on going. Table 18.3 lists some of the differences between the two approaches.

Notwithstanding the fundamental differences between the two approaches, it is possible to combine the two, albeit at different times. Large and dramatic improvements can be implemented as and when they seem to promise significant improvement steps, but between such occasions the operation can continue making its quiet and less spectacular kaizen improvements (*see* Fig. 18.11).

The PDCA cycle

The concept of continuous improvement implies a literally never-ending process of repeatedly questioning and requestioning the detailed workings of an operation. The repeated and cyclical nature of continuous improvement is best summarized by what is called the PDCA cycle (or Deming wheel – named after the famous quality 'guru', W.E. Deming (*see* Chapter 20)). The PDCA cycle is the sequence of activities that are undertaken on a cyclical basis to improve activities (*see* Fig. 18.12).

Table 18.3 Some features of breakthrough and continuous improvement (based on Imai[9])

	Breakthrough improvement	*Continuous improvement*
Effect	Short-term but dramatic	Long-term and long-lasting but undramatic
Pace	Big steps	Small steps
Time-frame	Intermittent and non-incremental	Continuous and incremental
Change	Abrupt and volatile	Gradual and constant
Involvement	Select a few 'champions'	Everybody
Approach	Individualism, individual ideas and efforts	Collectivism, group efforts, systems approach
Stimulus	Technological breakthroughs, new inventions, new theories	Conventional know-how and state of the art
Risks	Concentrated – 'all eggs in one basket'	Spread – many projects simultaneously
Practical requirements	Requires large investment but little effort to maintain it	Requires little investment but great effort to maintain it
Effort orientation	Technology	People
Evaluation criteria	Results for profit	Process and efforts for better results

Figure 18.11 **The pattern of performance improvement with continuous improvement superimposed onto breakthrough improvement**

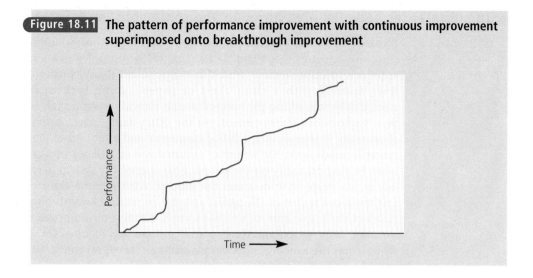

Figure 18.12 **The PDCA cycle is the basis of continuous improvement**

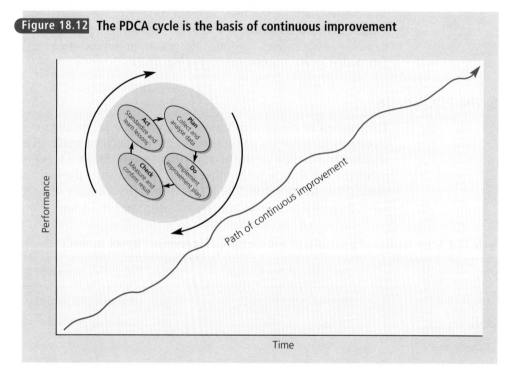

The cycle starts with the P (for plan) stage, which involves an examination of the current method or the problem area being studied. This involves collecting and analysing data so as to formulate a plan of action which is intended to improve performance. (The next section of this chapter explains some of the techniques which can be used to collect and analyse data in this stage.) Once a plan for improvement has been agreed, the next step is the D (for do) stage. This is the implementation stage during which the plan is tried out in the operation. This stage may itself involve a mini-PDCA cycle as the problems of implementation are resolved. Next comes the C (for check) stage where the new implemented solution is evaluated to see whether it has resulted in the expected performance improvement. Finally, at least for this cycle, comes the A (for act) stage. During this stage the change is consolidated or standardized if it has been successful. Alternatively, if the change has not been successful, the lessons learned from the 'trial' are formalized before the cycle starts again.

It is the last point about the PDCA cycle which is the most important – the cycle starts again. It is only by accepting that in a continuous improvement philosophy the PDCA cycle quite literally never stops that improvement becomes part of every person's job.

The business process re-engineering approach

Typical of the radical breakthrough way of tackling improvement is the 'business process re-engineering' (BPR) approach. BPR is a blend of a number of ideas which have been current in operations management for some time. Just-in-time concepts, process flow charting, critical examination in method study, operations network management and customer-focused operations all contribute to the BPR concept. It was the potential of information technologies to enable the fundamental redesign of processes, however, which acted as the catalyst in bringing these ideas together. BPR has been defined as:[10]

> the fundamental rethinking and radical redesign of business processes to achieve dramatic improvements in critical, contemporary measures of performance, such as cost, quality, service and speed.

Process *versus* functions

Underlying the BPR approach is the belief that operations should be organized around the total process which adds value for customers, rather than the functions or activities which perform the various stages of the value-adding activity. We have already pointed out the difference between a conventional micro operation organized around a specialist function, and a business process (Fig. 1.6 in Chapter 1 illustrated this idea). The core of BPR is a redefinition of the micro organizations within a total operation, to reflect the business processes which satisfy customer needs. Figure 18.13 illustrates this idea.

The principles of BPR

Even if BPR is not an entirely original idea, it can be seen as a useful collection of principles which embody the breakthrough approach. The main principles of BPR have been summarized as follows:[11]

- Rethink business processes in a cross-functional manner which organizes work around the natural flow of information (or materials or customers). This means organizing around outcomes of a process rather than the tasks which go into it.
- Strive for dramatic improvements in the performance by radically rethinking and redesigning the process.
- Have those who use the output from a process perform the process. Check to see if all internal customers can be their own supplier rather than depending on another function in the business to supply them (which takes longer and separates out the stages in the process).
- Put decision points where the work is performed. Do not separate those who do the work from those who control and manage the work. Control and action are just one more type of supplier–customer relationship which can be merged.

Example[12]

We can illustrate this idea of reorganizing (or re-engineering) around business processes through the following simple example. Figure 18.14(a) shows the traditional organization of a trading company which purchases consumer goods from several suppliers, stores them, and sells them on to retail outlets. At the heart of the operation is the warehouse which receives the goods, stores them, and packs and dispatches them when they are required by customers. Orders for more stock are placed by Purchasing which also takes charge of materials planning and stock control. Purchasing buys the goods based on a forecast which is prepared by Marketing, which takes advice from the Sales department which is processing customers' orders. When a customer does place an order, it is the

Figure 18.13 BPR advocates reorganizing (re-engineering) micro operations to reflect the natural customer-focused business processes

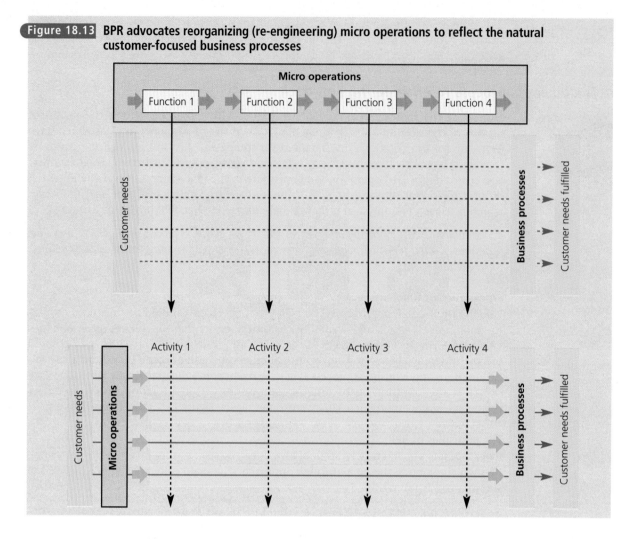

Sales department's job to instruct the warehouse to pack and dispatch the order and tell the Finance department to invoice the customer for the goods. So, traditionally, five departments (each a micro operation) have between them organized the flow of materials and information within the total operation. But at each interface between the departments there is the possibility of errors and miscommunication arising. Furthermore, *who is responsible for looking after the customer's needs?* Currently, three separate departments all have dealings with the customer. Similarly, *who is responsible for liaising with suppliers?* This time two departments have contact with suppliers.

Eventually the company reorganized around two essential business processes. The first process (called purchasing operations) dealt with everything concerning relationships with suppliers. It was this process's focused and unambiguous responsibility to develop good working relationships with suppliers. The other business process (called customer service operations) had total responsibility for satisfying customers' needs. This included speaking 'with one voice' to the customer.

Figure 18.14 **(a) Before and (b) after re-engineering a consumer goods trading company**

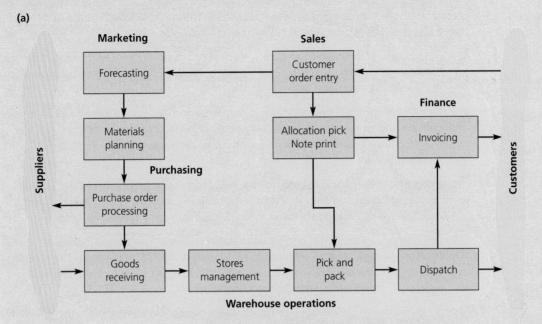

(a)

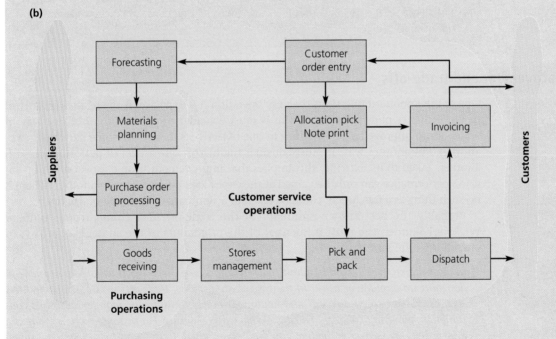

(b)

The whole idea of business process re-engineering has aroused considerable controversy. Most of its critics are academics, but some practical objections to BPR have also been raised. At a conceptual level, criticisms of BPR include the following:

● By its nature, BPR looks only at work activities rather than at the people who perform the work. Because of this, people become 'cogs in a machine'. BPR merely 'oils the wheels' of this destructive machine.

● As an approach BPR is imprecise. Its proponents cannot agree as to whether it has to be radical or can be implemented gradually, or exactly what a process is, or whether it has to be top-down or bottom-up, or on whether it has be supported by information technology or not.

● BPR is often treated as the latest management fad by some managers and as a cure-all for every problem. It is like, say the critics, attempting major surgery on every ailment, even those which would cure themselves naturally with some simple physiotherapy.

● BPR is merely an excuse for getting rid of staff. Companies that wish to 'downsize' (that is, reduce numbers of staff within an operation) are using BPR as an excuse. This puts the short-term interests of the shareholders of the company above either their longer-term interests or the interests of the company's employees.

● A combination of radical redesign together with downsizing can mean that the essential core of experience is lost from the operation. This leaves it vulnerable to any marked turbulence since it no longer has the knowledge and experience of how to cope with unexpected changes.

● Improvement and trade-offs

One of the important questions that any operation has to answer is the relative priority of its performance objectives. To do this it must consider the possibility that one way in which it can improve its performance in one objective is to sacrifice some performance in another. Put another way, it must consider trading off one aspect of performance with another. Taken to its extreme, this implies that improvement in one aspect of an operation's performance can only be gained at the expense of performance in another. 'There is no such thing as a free lunch' could be taken as a summary of the trade-off theory.

Probably the best-known summary of the trade-off idea comes from Professor Wickham Skinner, the most influential of the originators of the strategic approach to operations, who said:[13]

> ... most managers will readily admit that there are compromises or trade-offs to be made in designing an airplane or truck. In the case of an airplane, trade-offs would involve matters such as cruising speed, take-off and landing distances, initial cost, maintenance, fuel consumption, passenger comfort and cargo or passenger capacity. For instance, no one today can design a 500-passenger plane that can land on an aircraft carrier and also break the sound barrier. Much the same thing is true in ... [operations].

Yet this trade-off model of performance objectives has been challenged – many companies give 'the best of both worlds' to their customers. At one time, for example, a high-quality, reliable and error-free automobile was inevitably an expensive automobile. Now, with few exceptions, we expect even budget-priced automobiles to be reliable and almost free of any defects. Auto manufacturers found that not only could they reduce the number of defects on their vehicles without necessarily incurring extra costs, but they could actually reduce costs by reducing errors in manufacture. Put in terms of

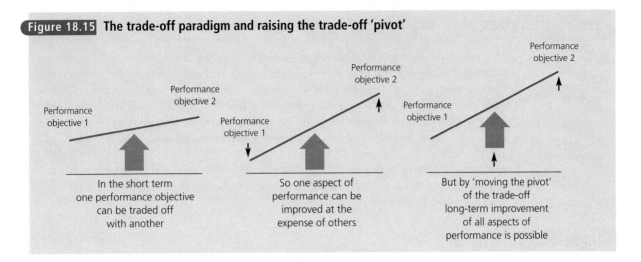

Figure 18.15 The trade-off paradigm and raising the trade-off 'pivot'

Performance objective 1

Performance objective 2

In the short term one performance objective can be traded off with another

Performance objective 2

Performance objective 1

So one aspect of performance can be improved at the expense of others

Performance objective 2

Performance objective 1

But by 'moving the pivot' of the trade-off long-term improvement of all aspects of performance is possible

the see-saw model in Figure 18.15, there are two ways to improve the position of one end of the lever. One is to depress the other end – in other words, improving one aspect of performance at the expense of another. But the other way is to raise the pivot of the see-saw. This would raise one end of the lever without depressing the other end. Alternatively, it could raise both ends. The 'pivot' in a real operation is the set of constraints which prevents both aspects of performance being improved simultaneously. Sometimes the constraints are technical, sometimes attitudinal. But the 'pivot' is stopping one aspect of performance improving without it reducing the performance of another. It should therefore be the prime target for any improvement process.

Reducing the trade-off

The approach which has been generally adopted in this book is that, although there are some situations where (especially in the short term) trade-offs between performance objectives have to be made, one of the main jobs of operations managers is to change whatever in the operation is causing one performance objective to deteriorate as another is improved. In fact, the 'pivot' of the trade-off is the main target of continuous improvement in operations.

Even trade-offs that seem to be inevitable can be reduced to some extent. For example, one of the decisions that any supermarket manager has to make is how many checkout positions to open at any time. If too many checkouts are opened then there will be times when the checkout staff do not have any customers to serve and will be idle. The customers, however, will have excellent service in terms of little or no waiting time. Conversely, if too few checkouts are opened, the staff will be working all the time but customers will have to wait in long queues. There seems to be a direct trade-off between staff utilization (and therefore cost) and customer waiting time (speed of service). Yet even the supermarket manager deciding how many checkouts to open can go some way to affecting the trade-off between customer waiting time and staff utilization. The manager might, for example, allocate a number of 'core' staff to operate the checkouts but also arrange for those other staff who are performing other jobs in the supermarket to be trained and 'on-call' should demand suddenly increase. If the manager on duty sees a build-up of customers at the checkouts, these other staff could quickly be used to staff checkouts. By devising a flexible system of staff allocation, the manager can both improve customer service and keep staff utilization high.

The techniques of improvement

All the techniques described in this book can be regarded as 'improvement' techniques insomuch as they attempt to improve some aspect of the performance of an operation. Some techniques are particularly useful for improving operations generally. For example, statistical process control (SPC) in Chapter 17 and failure mode and effect analysis (FMEA) in Chapter 19 could be used for almost any type of improvement project. In the remainder of this chapter we select some techniques which either have not been described elsewhere or need to be reintroduced in their role of helping operations improvement particularly. For example, flow charts were used in Chapter 5 as a design technique; later we will use essentially the same technique to generate improvements to existing operations.

Input–output analysis

A prerequisite for understanding any improvement opportunity is to understand the context in which the operation is set. This is the purpose of input–output analysis, which has three steps:

1 identifying the inputs and outputs from the process;
2 identifying the source of the inputs and the destination of the outputs;
3 clarifying the requirements of the internal customers who are served by the outputs from the process, and clarifying what requirements the process has for the internal suppliers who provide inputs to it.

Example: Kaston Pyral Services Ltd

Kaston Pyral Services Ltd (KPS) is the field service division of Kaston Pyral International, which manufactures and installs gas-fired heating systems. In the same group is KP Manufacturing, which makes the systems and spare parts, and KP Contracts, which installs the systems. Figure 18.16 shows an input–output diagram for KPS. The purpose is to reach an agreed understanding of the operational function of whichever part of the organization the problem is set in. It is not intended that input–output diagrams give any answers as such. They do, however, provide a useful 'way in' to improvement.

Flow charts

Input–output diagrams give a useful overview of the process context of improvement opportunities. A more detailed technique is the flow chart. Flow charts give a detailed understanding of parts of the process where some sort of flow occurs. They were briefly described in Chapter 5 in the context of new product and service design, but they have a far wider applicability. They record stages in the passage of information, products, labour or customers – in fact, anything which flows through the operation. They do this by requiring the decision-makers to identify each stage in the flow process as either:

- an *action* of some sort – recorded in a rectangular box; or
- a *question/decision* – recorded in a diamond-shaped box.

The purpose of this is to ensure that all the different stages in the flow processes are included in the improvement process, and that these stages are in some kind of logical sequence. The act of recording each stage in the process quickly shows up poorly organized flows. The technique can also clarify improvement opportunities and shed further light on the internal mechanics or workings of an operation. Finally, and probably most importantly, flow charts highlight problem areas where no procedure exists to cope with a particular set of circumstances.

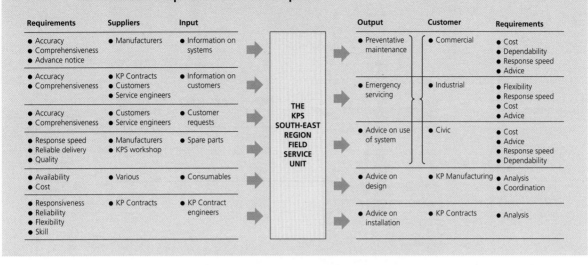

Figure 18.16 Full input–output diagram showing the suppliers and requirements of all inputs and the customers and requirements for all outputs

Example: Kaston Pyral Services Ltd (continued)

As part of its improvement programme the team at KPS is concerned that customers are not being served well when they phone in with minor queries over the operation of their heating systems. These queries are not usually concerned with serious problems, but often concern minor irritations which can be equally damaging to the customers' perception of KPS's service.

Figure 18.17 shows the flow diagram for this type of customer query.

The team found the chart illuminating. The procedure had never been formally laid out in this way before, and it showed up three areas where information was not being recorded. These are the three points marked with question marks on the flow chart in Figure 18.17. As a result of this investigation, it was decided to log all customer queries so that analysis could reveal further information on the nature of customer problems.

● Scatter diagrams

Scatter diagrams provide a quick and simple method of identifying whether there seems to be a connection between two sets of data: for example, the time at which you set off for work every morning and how long the journey to work takes. Plotting each journey on a graph which has departure time on one axis and journey time on the other could give an indication of whether departure time and journey time are related, and if so, how. Figure 18.18 shows the graph for one person's journeys. It would seem to show: (a) that there is a relationship between the two sets of data; (b) that the longest journeys were when departures were between 8.15 am and 8.22 am; and (c) that the journey is least predictable when departure is between 8.15 am and 8.30 am.

Scatter diagrams can be treated in a far more sophisticated manner by quantifying how strong is the relationship between the sets of data. But however sophisticated the approach, this type of graph only identifies the existence of a relationship, not necessarily the existence of a cause–effect relationship. If the scatter diagram shows a very strong connection between the sets of data, it is important evidence of a cause–effect relationship, but not proof positive. It could be coincidence!

Example: Kaston Pyral Services Ltd (continued)

The KPS improvement team had completed its first customer satisfaction survey. The survey asked customers to score the service they received from KPS in several ways. For

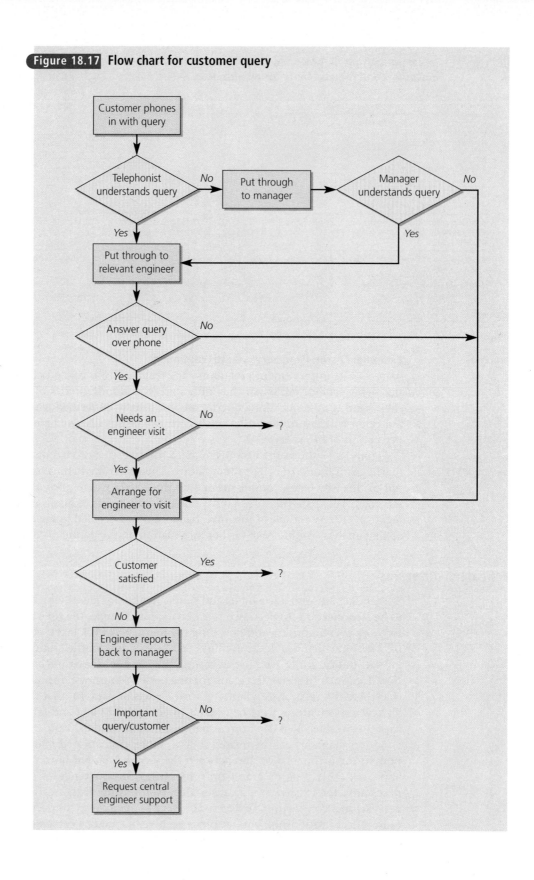

Figure 18.17 Flow chart for customer query

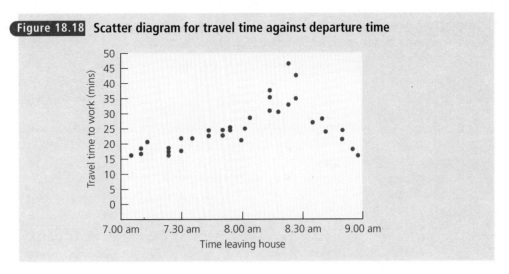

Figure 18.18 Scatter diagram for travel time against departure time

example, it asked customers to score services on a scale of one to 10 on promptness, friendliness, level of advice, etc. Scores were then summed to give a 'total satisfaction score' for each customer – the higher the score, the greater the satisfaction.

The spread of satisfaction scores puzzled the team, and they considered what factors might be causing such differences in the way their customers viewed them. Two factors were put forward to explain the differences:

● the number of times in the past year the customer had received a preventive maintenance visit;
● the number of times the customer had called for emergency service.

All this data was collected and plotted on scatter diagrams as shown in Figure 18.19. Figure 18.19(a) shows that there seems to be a clear relationship between a customer's satisfaction score and the number of times the customer was visited for regular servicing. The scatter diagram in Figure 18.19(b) is less clear. Although all customers who had very high satisfaction scores had made very few emergency calls, so had some customers with low satisfaction scores. As a result of this analysis, the team decided to survey customers' views on its emergency service.

Tightly controlled work activities, such as in call centres (left), can mitigate against staff involvement in continuous improvement (see the Lombard Direct case exercise at the end of the chapter)

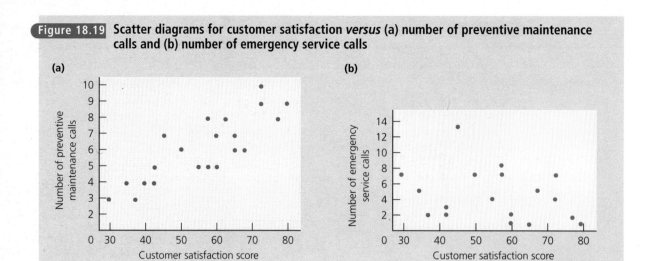

Figure 18.19 Scatter diagrams for customer satisfaction *versus* (a) number of preventive maintenance calls and (b) number of emergency service calls

Cause–effect diagrams

Cause–effect diagrams are a particularly effective method of helping to search for the root causes of problems. They do this by asking the what, when, where, how and why questions as before, but this time adding some possible 'answers' in an explicit way. They can also be used to identify areas where further data is needed. Cause–effect diagrams (which are also known as 'fish-bone' and 'Ishikawa' diagrams) have become extensively used in improvement programmes. Figure 18.20 shows the general form of the cause–effect diagram.

The procedure for drawing a cause–effect diagram is as follows:

Step 1 State the problem in the 'effect' box.

Step 2 Identify the main categories for possible causes of the problem. Although any categorization can be used for the main branches of the diagram, there are five categories which are commonly used: machinery; manpower; materials; methods and procedures; money.

Step 3 Use systematic fact-finding and group discussion to generate possible causes under these categories. Anything which may result in the effect that is being considered should be put down as a potential cause.

Step 4 Record all potential causes on the diagram under each category, and discuss each item in order to combine and clarify causes.

Some tips on using cause–effect diagrams

● Use separate diagrams for each problem. Do not confuse the issue by combining problems on a single diagram.
● Make sure diagrams are visible to everyone involved. Use large sheets of paper with plenty of space between items.

Figure 18.20 Cause–effect diagram

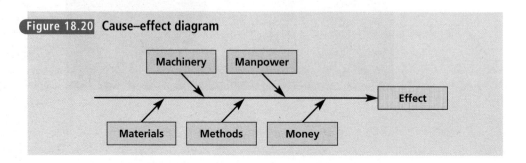

- Do not overload diagrams. Use separate diagrams for each major category on the cause–effect master diagram if necessary.
- Always be prepared to rework, take apart, refine and change categories.
- Take care not to use vague statements such as 'possible lack of'. Rather, describe what is actually happening that demonstrates the issues: for example, 'people are not filling out forms properly'.
- Circle causes which seem to be particularly significant.

Problem identification at Hewlett-Packard

Hewlett-Packard is proud of its reputation for high-quality products and services. Because of this it was especially concerned with the problems that it was having with its customers returning defective toner cartridges. About 2000 of these were being returned every month. The UK team suspected that not all the returns were actually the result of a faulty product, which is why the team decided to investigate the problem. The cause–effect diagram which they generated is shown in Figure 18.21.

Three major problems were identified. First, some users were not as familiar as they should have been with the correct method of loading the cartridge into the printer, or in being able to solve their own minor printing problems. Second, some of the dealers were also unaware of how to sort out minor problems. Third, there was clearly some abuse of Hewlett-Packard's 'no-questions-asked' returns policy. Empty toner cartridges were being sent to unauthorized refilling companies who would sell the refilled cartridges at reduced prices. Some cartridges were

being refilled up to five times and were understandably wearing out. Furthermore, the toner in the refilled cartridges was not up to Hewlett-Packard's high quality standards. The team went on to use the PDCA sequence of problem-solving and made suggestions which tightened up on their returns policy as well as improving the way in which customers were instructed on how to use the products. The results were impressive. Complaints in almost all areas shrank to a fraction of what they had been previously.

Questions

1 Take one branch of the decision tree shown in Figure 18.21 (for example, the materials branch) and expand on the possible reasons which are shown for the cartridge being returned.

2 What is your opinion of the alleged abuse of the 'no-questions-asked' returns policy adopted by Hewlett-Packard?

Figure 18.21 Cause–effect diagram for Hewlett-Packard's toner analysis

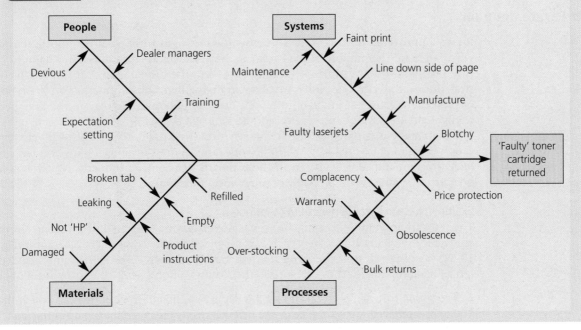

A team of nurses, administrators and doctors brainstorm improvements in patient care

Photo courtesy of Cheltenham General Hospital

Example: Kaston Pyral Services Ltd (continued)

The improvement team at KPS was working on a particular area which was proving a problem. Whenever service engineers were called out to perform emergency servicing for a customer, they took with them the spares and equipment which they thought would be necessary to repair the system. Although engineers could never be sure exactly what materials and equipment they would need for a job, they could guess what was likely to be needed and take a range of spares and equipment which would cover most eventualities. Too often, however, the engineers would find that they needed a spare or piece of equipment which they had not brought with them, and therefore they would have to return to the depot in order to collect it. Worse than that, very occasionally the required spare part would not be in stock, and so the customer would have to wait until it was brought from another part of the country. The cause–effect diagram for this particular problem, as drawn by the team, is shown in Figure 18.22.

● Pareto diagrams

In any improvement process, it is worthwhile distinguishing what is important and what is less so. The purpose of the Pareto analysis, which was introduced in Chapter 12, is to distinguish between the 'vital few' issues and the 'trivial many'. It is a relatively straightforward technique which involves arranging items of information on the types of problem or causes of problem into their order of importance. This can then be used to highlight areas where further decision-making will be useful.

Pareto analysis is based on the frequently occurring phenomenon of relatively few causes explaining the majority of effects. For example, most revenue for any company is likely to come from relatively few of the company's customers. Similarly, relatively few of a doctor's patients will probably occupy most of his time.

Example: Kaston Pyral Services Ltd (continued)

The KPS improvement team which was investigating unscheduled returns from emergency servicing (the issue which was described in the cause–effect diagram in Fig. 18.22) examined all occasions over the previous 12 months on which an unscheduled return had been made. They categorized the reasons for unscheduled returns as follows:

1 The wrong part had been taken to a job because, although the information which the engineer received was sound, he or she had incorrectly predicted the nature of the fault.

2 The wrong part had been taken to the job because there was insufficient information

Figure 18.22 Cause–effect diagram of unscheduled returns at KPS

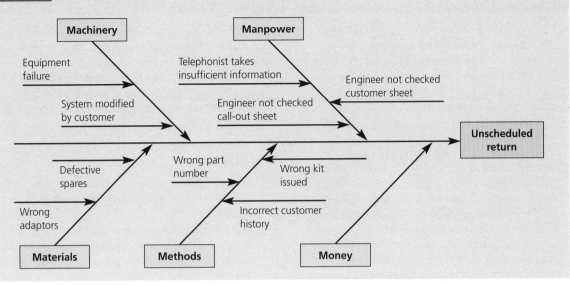

given when the call was taken.

3 The wrong part had been taken to the job because the system had been modified in some way not recorded on KPS's records.

4 The wrong part had been taken to the job because the part had been incorrectly issued to the engineer by stores.

5 No part had been taken because the relevant part was out of stock.

6 The wrong equipment had been taken for whatever reason.

7 Any other reason.

The relative frequency of occurrence of these causes is shown in Figure 18.23. About a third of all unscheduled returns were due to the first category, and more than half the returns were accounted for by the first and second categories together. It was decided that

Figure 18.23 Pareto diagram for causes of unscheduled returns

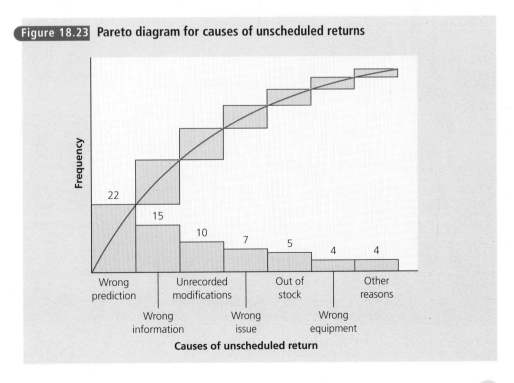

Customer service at Groupe Accor[14]

For over 10 years, Accor, the French hotel and restaurant group, has been developing self-managed improvement groups within its hotels. At one hotel reception desk, staff were concerned about the amount of time the desk was left unattended. To investigate this the staff began keeping track of the reasons they were spending time away from the desk and how long each absence kept them away. Everyone knew that reception desk staff often had to leave their post to help or give service to a guest. However, no one could agree what was the main cause of absence. Collecting the information was itself not easy because the staff had to keep records without affecting customer service. After three months the data was presented in the form of a Pareto diagram, which is shown in Figure 18.24. According to this, reception staff spent an average of 20 minutes away from their desk each shift. It came as

a surprise to reception staff and hotel management that making photocopies for guests was the main reason for absence. Fortunately, this was easily remedied by moving the photocopier to a room adjacent to the reception area, enabling staff to keep a check on the reception desk while they were making copies.

Questions

1 Do you think it was wise to spend so much time on examining this particular issue? Isn't it a trivial issue?

2 Should the Pareto diagram (Fig. 18.24) be used to reflect improvement priorities? In other words, was the group correct to put priority on avoiding absence through photocopying, and should its next priority be to look at absence because of the telefax service?

Figure 18.24 **Pareto diagram of staff time away from the reception desk**

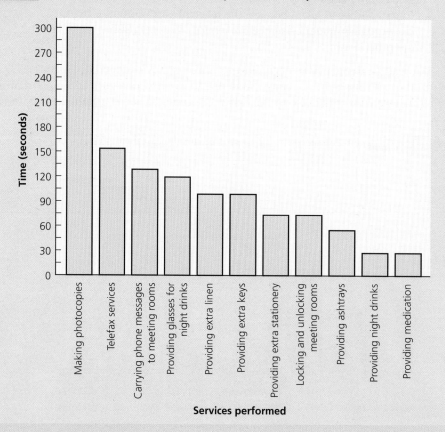

the problem could best be tackled by concentrating on how to get more information to the engineers which would enable them to predict the causes of failure accurately.

● Why–why analysis

We finish on another simple but effective technique for helping to understand the reasons for problems occurring. The technique starts by stating the problem and asking *why* that problem has occurred. Once the major reasons for the problem occurring have been identified, each of the major reasons is taken in turn and again the question is asked *why* those reasons have occurred, and so on. This procedure is continued until either a cause seems sufficiently self-contained to be addressed by itself or no more answers to the question 'Why?' can be generated.

Example: Kaston Pyral Services Ltd (continued)

Figure 18.25 illustrates the general structure of the why–why analysis for the KPS example discussed previously. In this example the major cause of unscheduled returns was the incorrect prediction of reasons for the customer's system failure. This is stated as the problem in the why–why analysis. The question is then asked, why was the failure wrongly predicted? Three answers are proposed: first, that the engineers were not trained correctly; second, that they had insufficient knowledge of the particular product installed in the customer's location; and third, that they had insufficient knowledge of the customer's particular system with its modifications. Each of these three reasons is taken in turn, and the questions are asked, why is there a lack of training, why is there a lack of product knowledge, and why is there a lack of customer knowledge? And so on.

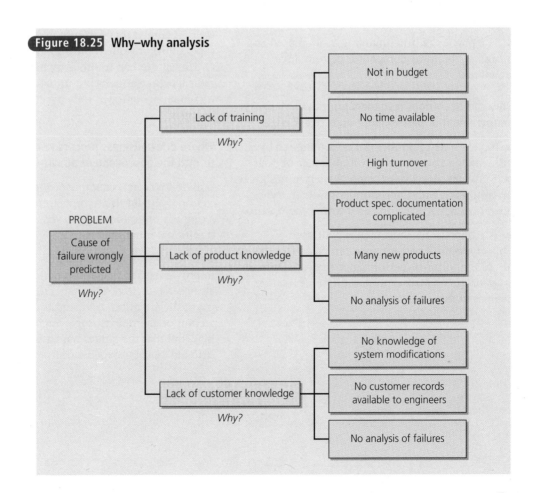

Figure 18.25 Why–why analysis

Summary answers to key questions

How can operations measure their performance in terms of the five performance objectives?

● It is unlikely that for any operation a single measure of performance will adequately reflect the whole of a performance objective. Usually operations have to collect a whole bundle of partial measures of performance.

● Each partial measure then has to be compared against some performance standard. There are four types of performance standard commonly used:
– historical standards, which compare performance now against performance sometime in the past;
– target performance standards, which compare current performance against some desired level of performance;
– competitor performance standards, which compare current performance against competitors' performance;
– absolute performance standards, which compare current performance against its theoretically perfect state.

● The process of benchmarking is often used as a means of obtaining competitor performance standards.

How can operations managers prioritize improvement of performance objectives?

● Improvement priorities can be determined by bringing together the relative importance of each performance objective or competitive factor as judged by customers, with the performance which the operation achieves as compared with its competitors.

● The operation's judgement about both importance and performance can be consolidated on an 'importance–performance matrix'. Different areas on this matrix represent different relative degrees of priority.

What are the broad approaches to managing the rate of improvement?

● An organization's approach to improving its operation can be characterized as lying somewhere between the two extremes of 'pure' breakthrough improvement and 'pure' continuous improvement.

● Breakthrough improvement, which is sometimes called innovation-based improvement, sees improvement as occurring in a few, infrequent but major and dramatic changes. Although such changes can be abrupt and volatile, they often incorporate radical new concepts or technologies which can shift the performance of the operation significantly.

● Continuous improvement assumes a series of never-ending, but smaller, incremental improvement steps. This type of improvement is sometimes called kaizen improvement. It is gradual and constant, often using collective group-based problem- solving. It does not focus on radical change but rather attempts to develop a built-in momentum of improvement.

● It is claimed that compromises between these two types of improvement philosophy are possible. Organizations can improve by having occasional radical breakthroughs but utilizing a more incremental approach in between these major changes.

Where does business process re-engineering (BPR) fit into the improvement activity?

● BPR is a typical example of the radical approach to improvement. It attempts to redesign operations along customer-focused processes rather than on the traditional functional basis.

● BPR has been responsible for some radical improvements in operations performance but it has also been criticized. The main criticisms are that it pays little attention to the rights of staff who are the victims of the 'downsizing' which often accompanies BPR, and that the radical nature of the changes can strip out valuable experience from the operation.

What techniques can be used for improvement?

● Many of the techniques described throughout this book could be considered improvement techniques, for example statistical process control (SPC).

● Techniques often seen as 'improvement techniques' are:
- input–output analysis, which attempts to clarify the nature of transformation in processes;
- flow charts, which attempt to describe the nature of information flow and decision-making within operations;
- scatter diagrams, which attempt to identify relationships and influences within processes;
- cause–effect diagrams, which structure the brainstorming that can help to reveal the root causes of problems;
- Pareto diagrams, which attempt to sort out the 'important few' causes from the 'trivial many' causes.

CASE EXERCISE

Lombard Direct

One of the most significant trends in the financial services industry has been the growth in telephone access. Many financial services, such as banks, have developed a more focused approach to personal customers through 24-hour telephone access. The concept of telephone-based financial services is not new. It was first launched successfully in 1985 by Första Sparbanken in Sweden with a service called Första Direckt. This has become a blueprint for several similar services.

Typical of these 'total access' services is that described below:

'You can call us 24 hours a day, 365 days a year. If you want to give us instructions to pay your gas bill on Christmas Day, that's fine. If you want to tell us to transfer money at 2.00 am, that's fine too. If you're on the other side of the world in a different time zone you can still call us ... [we are] ... more than just a convenient telephone banking service. Your own Personal Account Manager will offer you a highly individual approach to both your day-to-day finances and your long-term financial planning.'

Financial services have developed networks of call-centre operations to support such products. Call-centre staff are linked to sophisticated telephone and computer systems where up-to-date information and customer requests are instantly available so that customers can be dealt with promptly and efficiently. Part of this sector are the companies who offer loans and related services. Typical is Lombard Direct who must have one of the best-known telephone numbers in the UK: 0800 2 15000. This is based on their slogan 'loans from 800 to 15 000 pounds'. Lombard Direct is a subsidiary of Lombard Bank, part of the National Westminster Bank group. Unsecured loans over the telephone constitute about 90 per cent of the company's business, and other products include

insurance on loans, house, contents and motor insurance, savings and a credit card.

The main call centre, in Rotherham, West Yorkshire, is a 24-hour operation which operates every day of the year. The centre handles about two million calls a year. Monday is a typically busy day, when around 6000 calls are received. The call centre has around 200 'seats' or desks for their 'customer advisors' (CAs) and employs around 250 full-time equivalent staff, most of whom work part-time. When potential customers call to request a loan, they are asked a number of questions to rate their creditworthiness and then allocated into a band which reflects their 'credit rating'. This risk assessment affects the size of the borrowing allowed and the rate of interest to be charged.

Control to enabling culture

Sean Guilliam is the head of the call centre and has been working with the managers and team leaders to try to move from a 'control' culture to a more 'enabling' culture. Sean explains:

'We have a great atmosphere here, people really enjoy their work and we have lots of great events to build our team spirit and also develop the business. The problem is that despite these efforts the emphasis is still too much on control.'

One problem facing Sean was how he should use 'scripts'. Scripts are the set of questions and responses which CAs follow when they talk with customers and potential customers. They are often very carefully worded so as to avoid misunderstandings.

'We need to move away from the need to follow a set script in a strict way which allows no discretion and try to work with the customer to understand his or her needs and respond to them. We would also like to put ourselves

in the position of being able to offer more of our products, where appropriate. This is difficult to do when you are using a script which is devoted to loans. The script is a useful base of course. Indeed, there are several questions we are obliged to ask and information we have to provide to comply with the financial services laws. But there is a tendency to rely too heavily on the script. The problem is not people's willingness to improve but our systems which encourage them not to. For example, the CA's performance is partly assessed on tapes of their interactions with a customer. We call this "call analysis". If they are judged not to have followed the correct procedure, it is judged a "non-standard tape" and it will affect their pay, and possibly even their contract.

'We have five grades of performance, or "spot" levels, and CAs are reviewed every three months. Each level has a set of criteria based on six key measures. If someone attains a higher level for two consecutive assessments, they go up one spot level; if they perform less well over three periods they will go down. Going up a level can mean a significant increase in pay. Also CAs need to get to level 2 before we will offer them a permanent contract, although I believe that we need to remove this barrier and put everyone on permanent contracts from the start.

'We are making progress, however. Take, for example, our call analysis measure. In the past it was just used as a means of assessing people. Now it is a developmental tool. We have identified nine different skills we expect to see, including greeting callers (what we call the verbal handshake), the general approach to the conversation, gathering information, and so on. We now have descriptors for each of these skills, defining what constitutes excellent, very good and good performance, or

"an area for development". People can see exactly what we are trying to achieve. The call analysis framework tries to assess CAs but also encourages them to do the right things, such as use the caller's name, show interest in, and respect for, the customer, not ask for the same information twice, ensure that customers know all the costs involved and give customers time to make their decisions.

'Also we now refer to the script as a call guide and use about 30 cards in a simple "flip-open" type of photograph album to help the CAs. But yet when we get a new recruit, we still give them the cards and tell them to go home and learn them! The other issue is "cross-selling" other products. I compare loan conversions and insurance sales, for example. And, although we want a good ratio of insurance sales to loans, too high a ratio might mean that staff are doing too hard a sell. We don't want customers to be put off from using us again. The problem is in balancing flexibility with control, especially when a 1 per cent increase in insurance sales can contribute half a million to the bottom line.'

Questions

1 What do the five operations performance objectives (quality, speed, dependability, flexibility and cost) mean for call-centre operations such as Lombard's?

2 What do you think are the main operations management issues faced by call-centre managers?

3 What do you think might be the main obstacles facing Sean Guilliam in trying to improve CA performance?

Raydale Conference Centre

'Well, I suppose it's a mixed review: there are some things where we come out really well; on the other hand there are clearly areas where we need to improve.'

Alan Ray was speaking after the publication of an article in the *Conference Centre Journal*. Alan was the owner and General Manager of Raydale Conference Centre. He had bought the centre, which used to be a country house hotel, just over two years before and was broadly pleased with the business he had attracted so far. The centre had managed to

establish a presence in the fast growing and profitable conference market. His customers (usually large companies) would book some or all of his facilities for their sales conferences, training events and meetings. These events could be anything from one-day's duration through to two weeks'. Raydale Conference Centre, together with three others in the area, had been reviewed by the *Conference Centre Journal*, a summary of whose findings is shown in Table 18.4.

Table 18.4 Reviews of conference centres

Factor	Raydale	Miston	Hexley	Stannington
Price	Average	High	Average	Low
Size of menu	Excellent	Good	Good	Poor
Quality of food	Good	Excellent	Good	Acceptable
Quality of room	Very good	Good	Good	Good
Courtesy of staff	Very good	Good	Good	Poor
Flexibility to accommodate special needs	Poor	Very good	Good	Good
Documentation errors	Occasional	None	Very few	None
Special off-peak price discounts	No	Yes	Yes	Yes
Room availability	Good	Very good	Poor	Poor

Alan was more worried by some findings than others:

'Not everything is of equal importance, of course. In our part of the business probably the two things that customers value particularly are courtesy of staff, where we score very well, and the flexibility to accommodate their special needs, where we score very badly. I think there are two reasons for this. First of all, our conference rooms are relatively small and we have difficulty in accommodating very large groups. The other reason is, quite frankly, that some of our staff are not used to coping with the unexpected problems. Price is only slightly less important to our customers but we seem to score reasonably. What worries me more is that I know that our costs tend to be higher than those of our competitors. Given the level of business which we are doing, our profits are less than those being achieved by our competitors. Less important than price comes a middle-range of factors which, although not of prime importance to customers, will certainly irritate them if we are not up to standard. Room decor, room availability, the quality of our food and document errors all come into this category. I am particularly cross about the way they have reviewed

document errors. I suppose they talked to our customers and must have got one where we had made mistakes with their invoices or something. I'm sure a wider survey would have revealed us to be no worse than our rivals. Quite frankly, I am unconcerned about our performance in terms of the size of our menu or our ability to give special off-peak price discounts. In our type of market neither of those factors rates particularly highly with any customers.'

Questions

1 On what competitive factors would you advise Alan to concentrate if he wished to improve the competitive performance of his operation?

2 Do you think he is right to feel aggrieved by his operation's poor showing on the document errors factor?

3 Is he right to be unconcerned about the size of menu (that is, the range of different dishes offered on his standard menu) and his policy of not offering off-peak price discounts?

Discussion questions

1 A university library wishes to start a performance measurement programme which will enable it to judge the effectiveness with which it organizes its operations. The library loans books to students on both long-term and short-term loans, keeps an extensive stock of journals, will send off for specialist publications to specialist libraries and has an extensive online database facility. What measures of performance do you think it would be appropriate to use in this kind of operation and what type of performance standards should the library adopt?

2 Assess the overall performance of an operation that is familiar to you using a polar diagram. Overlap the operation's performance with what

you perceive to be the customers' needs and discuss any differences.

3 Using the five performance measures, list ways in which the performance of a university lecturer could be assessed.

4 Discuss with an operations manager how the performance of the operation is measured. Identify a range of measures and find out whether the targets used are based on historical, target performance, competitor performance or absolute performance standards.

5 List some of the micro operations of a humanitarian organization such as the International Red Cross, the Samaritans or United Nations High Commission for Refugees (UNHCR) and discuss the benefits of it benchmarking its operations. Which operations or micro operations might it be appropriate to benchmark against?

6 A university engineering department has chosen to benchmark itself against other university departments as the first step in an operations improvement process. What kinds of benchmarking do you think might be appropriate for the department and on what performance objectives do you think it should be focusing?

7 Identify the order winners, qualifiers and less important criteria for an organization of your own choice. Ask a colleague to assess the same organization and compare and discuss your results.

8 Choose an organization and compare it with a competing organization in terms of whether it is better than, the same as, or worse than the competitor. Ask a colleague to undertake the same evaluation and compare and discuss your results.

9 A bank is conducting a survey of all the customer complaints which it has received in its personal loan department. This department deals with the authorization of loans requested by the bank's customers, processes all the information concerning the loans and then sends documents to the customers. Table 18.5 classifies the type of complaints made by customers together with their frequency of occurrence.

Draw a Pareto diagram which describes the relative frequency of occurrence of different types of errors. Draw a cause–effect diagram which contains possible reasons for the most important category of error.

10 Explain the differences between breakthrough improvement and continuous improvement. Discuss the advantages and disadvantages of each.

11 List and describe 10 modifications that could be made to your course. What breakthrough improvements could be made?

12 Apply the PDCA cycle to your method of preparing for lectures. Describe each part of the cycle and assess the outcome.

13 Briefly explain what is meant by business process re-engineering. Why do you think that BPR is seen as a radical and somewhat formidable approach to improvement by many managers, including many operations managers?

14 Develop cause–effect diagrams for the following types of problem:
 – customers waiting too long for their calls to be answered when phoning to order from a mail-order catalogue store;
 – poor food in the company restaurant;
 – poor lecturing from teaching staff at a university;
 – customer complaints that the free plastic toy in their breakfast cereal packet is missing;
 – staff having to wait excessively long periods to gain access to the photocopier.

15 Construct a flow chart which identifies the different stages in a customer's complaint being processed in a large retail store. The chart should make sure the complaint is dealt with satisfactorily and the organization learns from this complaint to make sure it never happens again.

Table 18.5 Customer complaints

Type of complaint	Frequency of occurrence
Authorization signature omitted	4%
Loan amount omitted	17%
Loan detail errors	12%
Arithmetic error	9%
One or more documents omitted	31%
Inappropriate documents included	2%
Payment details omitted	21%
Others	2%

16 A computer systems field repair company is considering its operations strategy for its 'quickfit' service. This is a simple service which aims to respond to customer requests in less than two hours and repair or replace the defective part of the system within half an hour of the service engineer arriving at the customer's site. A survey of customers and competitors has given the results shown in Table 18.6.

(a) Demonstrate how the company could identify its improvement priorities for this service.

(b) How would you go about improving the company's performance at delivering this service?

Table 18.6 'Quickfit' performance

Performance objective	Importance to customers	Performance against main competitors
On-time arrival	Very important	Better than most competitors
Repair/replace in half-hour	Very important	Same as competitors
Helpfulness of service	Important	Same as competitors
Range of equipment covered by service	Very important	Narrower than most competitors
Helpfulness of HQ staff when making initial contact	Only moderately important	Very much better than competitors

Notes on chapter

1 Based on Neely, A. (1993) *Performance Measurement System Design – Theory and Practice*, Manufacturing Engineering Group, Cambridge University, April.

2 *European Quality* (1999) 'How Alstom Transporte is Hot on Improvement', Vol 6, No 6.

3 Camp, C. (1989) 'Benchmarking: The Search for Best Practices Which Lead to Superior Performance – Parts 1 to 5', *Quality Progress*, Jan–May.

4 Pickering, I.M. and Chambers, S. (1991) 'Competitive Benchmarking: Progress and Future Developments', *Computer Integrated Manufacturing Systems*, Vol 4, No 2.

5 Sources: Rogers, B. (1991) 'Benchmarking as a Tool in Rank Xerox's Quality Management Strategies', *Quality Link*, Nov–Dec; and Cross, R. and Leonard, P. (1994) 'Benchmarking: A Strategic and Tactical Perspective' *in* Dale, B. (ed) *Managing Quality* (2nd edn), Prentice Hall.

6 Based on Slack, N. (1994) 'The Importance–Performance Matrix as a Determinant of Improvement Priorities', *International Journal of Operations and Production Management*, Vol 14, No 5, pp 59–75.

7 Imai, M. (1986) *Kaizen – The Key to Japan's Competitive Success*, McGraw-Hill.

8 Bessant, J. and Caffyn, S. (1997) 'High Involvement Innovation', *International Journal of Technology Management*, Vol 14, No 1.

9 Imai, M., *op. cit.*

10 Hammer, M. and Champy, J. (1993) *Re-engineering the Corporation*, Nicholas Brealey Publishing.

11 Hammer, M. (1990) 'Re-engineering Work: Don't Automate, Obliterate', *Harvard Business Review*, Vol 68, No 4.

12 Based on an example in Kruse, G. (1995) 'Fundamental Innovation', *Manufacturing Engineer*, Feb.

13 Skinner, W. (1985) *Manufacturing: The Formidable Competitive Weapon*, Wiley.

14 Source: Orly, C. (1988) 'Quality Circles in France', *The Carnell HRA Quarterly*, Nov.

Selected further reading

Armistead, C. and Roland, P. (1996) *Managing Business Processes: BPR and Beyond*, John Wiley.

Codling, S. (1992) *Best Practice Benchmarking*, Industrial Newsletter.

Dale, B.G. (ed.) (1994) *Managing Quality* (2nd edn), Prentice Hall.

DeToni, A. and Tonchia, S. (1996) 'Lean Organisation, Management by Process and Performance Measurement', *International Journal of Operations and Production Management*, Vol 16, No 2.

Evans, J.R. and Lindsay, W.M. (1993) *The Management and Control of Quality*, West.

Fitzgerald, L., Johnston, R., Brignall, S., Sylvestro, R. and Voss, C. (1991) *Performance Measurement in Service Businesses*, The Chartered Institute of Management Accountants.

Flood, R.L. (1993) *Beyond TQM*, John Wiley.

Leibfried, K.H.J. and McNair, C.J. (1992) *Benchmarking: A Tool for Continuous Improvement*, HarperCollins.

Neely, A.D., Mills, J.F., Gregory, M.J., Richards, A.H. and Platts, K.W. (1995) *Performance Measurement System Design*, University of Cambridge Manufacturing Engineering Group.

Oakland, J.S. (1993) *Total Quality Management* (2nd edn), Butterworth-Heinemann.

Introduction

Although no operation should be indifferent to failure, in some operations it is vital that products and services do not fail – aeroplanes in flight or electricity supplies to hospitals, for example. Other products and services should always be there when needed, such as car seat belts, the police service and other emergency services. In these situations dependability is not just desirable, it is essential. In less critical situations, having dependable products and services is a way organizations can gain a competitive advantage. For example, Japanese companies made great gains in market share in automobiles and electrical goods through their reputation for high product reliability.

Operations managers, who are almost always concerned with improving the dependability of their operations and the products and services which they produce, try to have strategies in place which attempt to minimize the likelihood of failure and learn from failure when it does occur. They also need to recognize, however, that failures will occur, in spite of all attempts to prevent them. What is then important is that they have plans in place which help them recover from the failures when they do occur. Figure 19.1 shows how this chapter fits into the operation's improvement activities.

Figure 19.1 Model of operations improvement showing the issues covered in this chapter

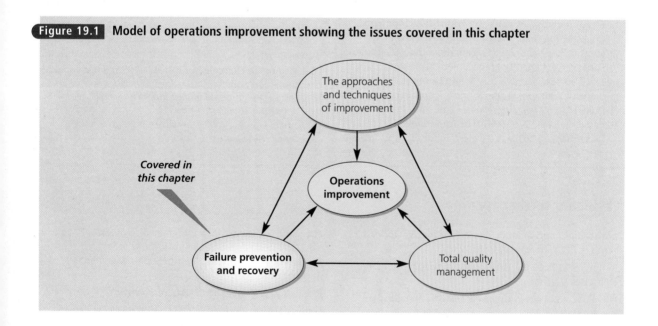

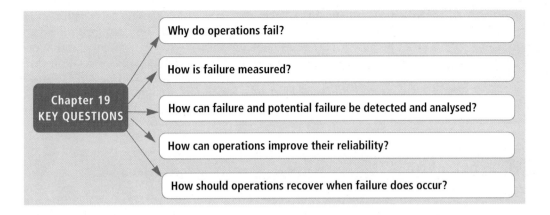

System failure

There is always a chance that in making a product or providing a service, things might go wrong. Accepting that failure will occur is not the same thing as ignoring it, however. Nor does it imply that operations cannot or should not attempt to minimize failure. Yet not all failures are equally serious. Some failures are incidental and may not be noticed. In the finale of a concert performance a violinist may play a wrong note and the effect is unlikely to have any great impact. If he or she is giving a solo performance, however, then the error may sour the whole performance. The concert, like all systems, may be more tolerant of some types and some levels of failure than others. For example, if the cigarette lighter in a car or the pen used by a police officer to write a statement fails, the effect may be irritating but not necessarily serious. Conversely, leaking hydraulics in a car or a prisoner not being informed of his or her rights can put the whole of the process at risk.

Organizations therefore need to discriminate between failures and pay particular attention to those which are critical either in their own right or because they may jeopardize the rest of the operation. To do this we need to understand why something fails and be able to measure the impact of the failure.

● Why things fail

Failure in an operation can occur for many different reasons, which can be grouped as follows:

- those which have their source inside the operation, because its overall design was faulty, or because its facilities (machines, equipment and buildings) or staff fail;
- those which are caused by faults in the material or information inputs to the operation;
- those which are caused by the actions of customers.

Design failures

In its design stage an operation might look fine on paper; only when it has to cope with real circumstances might inadequacies become evident. Some design failures occur because a characteristic of demand was overlooked or miscalculated. A production line might have been installed in a factory which in practice cannot cope with the demands placed upon it, or a theatre front-of-house layout might cause confused and jumbled customer flow at peak times. In both examples there was no unexpected demand placed on the operations; it was straightforward error in translating the requirements of demand into an adequate design. Other design-related failures occur because the circumstances under which the operation has to work are not as expected. For example, a biscuit production line might have been installed assuming a certain pack size, but then the market demands a larger pack size which causes the machine to jam occasionally. The theatre's lighting controls might have been designed for simple lighting sequences, but because it now takes bookings for shows with complex lighting needs, the control system overloads and fails. In both cases the demands placed on the operation were unexpected at the point of design, but they are still design failures (*see* box on the Socrates system below). Adequate design includes identifying the range of circumstances under which the operation has to work, and designing accordingly.

Failed philosopher[1]

Sleek, fast and smooth, the TGV trains of France's SNCF rail network look more like aircraft than the traditional train. They provide a service which carries passengers throughout Europe at speeds in excess of 175 mph. Inside, too, the trains show the influence of air travel. Seats are wide and comfortable with space for leg-stretching relaxation. The French press described the TGV as being like 'an airbus on rails'. SNCF also decided to emulate the airlines by buying a high-tech seat reservation and ticketing system which they named after the Greek philosopher Socrates. That was when their problems began. Design flaws in the booking systems software, combined with inadequate training of SNCF staff, caused chaos for months after the system was introduced. Socrates refused to believe in the existence of some places. Suddenly it refused to issue tickets for Rouen or Barcelona, insisting that neither city existed. It also failed at times to recognize the existence of several of the trains which ran between Paris and Lyon. As a result, the trains made the trip with only four passengers on board. However, these straightforward system design errors have been compounded by over-complexity of some parts of the system: the automatic ticket-vending machines often stand unused by passengers because they have given up trying to understand how to use them. The graffiti outside the Gare de Lyon station reads 'One hour from Lille to Paris ... one hour to buy a ticket!' Although the problems were eventually sorted out, the reputation of what was essentially a fast and efficient operation took longer to recover.

Questions

1 This box contrasts two micro operations which affect overall quality from a customer's point of view. What are these two micro operations and what other micro operation might affect the customer's overall perception of quality?

2 Why did the ticket-issuing and reservations system cause such chaos?

Facilities failures

All the facilities (that is, the machines, equipment, buildings and fittings) of an operation are liable to break down. The 'breakdown' may only be partial, for example a worn or marked carpet in a hotel, or a machine which can only work at half its normal rate. Alternatively, it can be what we normally regard as a 'failure' – a total and sudden cessation of operation. Either way, it is the effects of a breakdown which are important. Some breakdowns can bring a large part of the operation to a halt. For example, a computer failure in a supermarket chain could paralyse several large stores until it is repaired. Other failures might only have a significant impact if they occur at the same time as other failures. For example, *see* box on air crashes.

Staff failures

People failures come in two types: *errors* and *violations*. 'Errors' are mistakes in judgement; with hindsight, a person should have done something different. For example, if the manager of a sports shop fails to anticipate an increased demand for footballs during the World Cup, the shop will run out of stock. This is an error of judgement. 'Violations' are acts which are clearly contrary to defined operating procedure. For example, if a machine operator fails to clean and lubricate his or her machine in the prescribed manner, it is eventually likely to fail. The operator has 'violated' a set procedure.

As the number of people travelling by air has grown, the chances of suffering a fatal accident have fallen substantially. Air crashes still do happen, however. Predominantly, the reason for this is not mechanical failure but human failure such as pilot fatigue. Boeing, which dominates the commercial airline business, has calculated that over 60 per cent of all the accidents which have occurred in the past 10 years had flight crew behaviour as their 'dominant cause'.

The chances of an accident are still very small, however. One kind of accident which is known as 'controlled flight into terrain', where the aircraft appears to be under control and yet still flies into the ground, has a chance of happening only *once in two million flights*. For this type of failure to occur, a whole chain of minor failures must happen. First, the pilot at the controls has to be flying at the wrong altitude – there is only one chance in a thousand of this. Second, the co-pilot would have to fail to cross-check the altitude – only one chance in a hundred of this. The air traffic controllers would have to miss the fact that the plane was at the wrong altitude (which is not strictly part of their job) – a one-in-ten chance. Finally, the pilot would

have to ignore the ground proximity warning alarm in the aircraft (which can be prone to give false alarms) – a one-in-two chance.

Small though the chances of failure are, aircraft manufacturers and airlines are busy working on procedures which make it difficult for aircrew to make any of the mistakes which contribute to fatal crashes. For example, if the chances of the co-pilot failing to check the altitude are reduced to one in two hundred, and the chances of the pilot ignoring the ground proximity alarm are reduced to one in five, then the chances of this type of accident occurring fall dramatically to one in 10 million.

Questions

1 What are your views on the quoted probabilities of each failure described above occurring?

2 How would you try to prevent these failures occurring?

3 If the probability of each failure occurring could be reduced by a half, what would be the effect on the likelihood of this type of crash occurring?

Supplier failures

Any failure in the delivery or quality of goods and services into an operation can cause failure within the operation. The failure of the band to turn up at a concert will cause the whole event to 'fail'. Similarly, if the band does show but proves to be of dubious talent, the concert could also be regarded as a failure. The more an operation relies on suppliers of materials or services, the more it is liable to failure caused by missing or sub-standard inputs.

Customer failures

Not all failures are (directly) caused by the operation or its suppliers. Customers can misuse the products and services which the operation has created. For example, a washing machine might have been manufactured in an efficient and fail-free manner, yet the customer who buys it could overload it or misuse it in some other way which causes it to fail. The customer is not 'always right'. Customers' inattention, incompetence or lack of common sense can be the cause of failure. However, merely complaining about customers is unlikely to reduce the chances of this type of failure occurring. Most organizations will accept that they have a responsibility to educate and train customers and to design their products and services so as to minimize the chances of failure. For example, the sequence of questions at automatic teller machines is designed by banks in such a way as to make their operation as 'fail-free' as possible.

Failure as an opportunity

Notwithstanding our categorization of failure, the origin of all failures is some kind of human failure. A machine failure might have been caused by someone's poor design or

A fire in the Channel Tunnel prompted a wide-ranging accident investigation which explored the various potential causes

maintenance, a delivery failure by someone's errors in managing the supply schedules, and a customer mistake by someone's failure to provide adequate instructions. Failures are rarely the result of random chance; their root cause is usually human failure. The implications of this are, first, that failure can to some extent be controlled and, second, that organizations can learn from failure and modify their behaviour accordingly. The realization of this has led to what is sometimes called the *failure as an opportunity* concept. Rather than identifying a 'culprit' who is to be held responsible and blamed for the failure, failures are regarded as an opportunity to examine why they occurred, and to put in place procedures which eliminate or reduce the probability of them recurring. This is treated further, later in this chapter, when we examine 'failure planning'.

Measuring failure

There are three main ways of measuring failure:

- *failure rates* – how often a failure occurs;
- *reliability* – the chances of a failure occurring;
- *availability* – the amount of available useful operating time.

'Failure rate' and 'reliability' are different ways of measuring the same thing – the propensity of an operation, or part of an operation, to fail. Availability is one measure of the consequences of failure in the operation.

Failure rate

Failure rate (FR) is calculated as the number of failures over a period of time. For example, the security of an airport can be measured by the number of security breaches per year, and the failure rate of an engine can be measured in terms of the number of failures divided by its operating time. Failure rate can be measured either as a percentage of the total number of products tested or as the number of failures over time:

$$FR = \frac{\text{number of failures}}{\text{total number of products tested}} \times 100$$

or

$$FR = \frac{\text{number of failures}}{\text{operating time}}$$

A batch of 50 electronic components is tested for 2000 hours. Four of the components fail during the test as follows:

Failure 1   occurred at 1200 hours
Failure 2   occurred at 1450 hours
Failure 3   occurred at 1720 hours
Failure 4   occurred at 1905 hours

$$\text{Failure rate (as a percentage)} = \frac{\text{number of failures}}{\text{number tested}} \times 100 = \frac{4}{50} \times 10 = 8\%$$

The total time of the test = $50 \times 2000 = 100\,000$ component hours

But

one component was not operating 2000 – 1200 = 800 hours
one component was not operating 2000 – 1450 = 550 hours
one component was not operating 2000 – 1720 = 280 hours
one component was not operating 2000 – 1905 =   95 hours

Thus:

Total non-operating time = 1725 hours
Operating time = total time – non-operating time
= 100 000 – 1725 = 98 275 hours

$$\text{Failure rate (in time)} = \frac{\text{number of failures}}{\text{operating time}} = \frac{4}{98\,275}$$

$$= 0.000041$$

Failure over time – the 'bath-tub' curve

Failure, for most parts of an operation, is a function of time. At different stages during the life of anything, the probability of it failing will be different. The probability of, for example, an electric lamp failing is relatively high when it is first plugged in. Any small defect in the material from which the filament is made or in the way the lamp was assembled could cause the lamp to fail. If the lamp survives this initial stage, it could still fail at any point, but the longer it survives, the more likely its failure becomes. Most physical parts of an operation behave in a similar manner.

The curve which describes failure probability of this type is called the *bath-tub curve*. It comprises three distinct stages:

● the 'infant-mortality' or 'early-life' stage where early failures occur caused by defective parts or improper use;
● the 'normal-life' stage when the failure rate is usually low and reasonably constant, and caused by normal random factors;
● the 'wear-out' stage when the failure rate increases as the part approaches the end of its working life and failure is caused by the ageing and deterioration of parts.

Figure 19.2 illustrates two bath-tub curves with slightly different characteristics. Curve A shows a part of the operation which has a high initial infant-mortality failure but then a long, low-failure, normal life followed by the gradually increasing likelihood of failure as it approaches wear-out. Curve B has roughly the same relative infant-

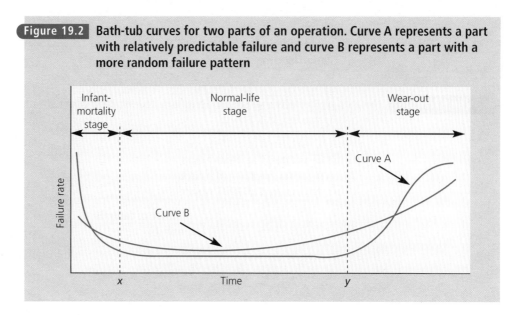

Figure 19.2 Bath-tub curves for two parts of an operation. Curve A represents a part with relatively predictable failure and curve B represents a part with a more random failure pattern

mortality, normal-life and wear-out stages. It differs markedly, however, in the predictability with which failure occurs. Curve A shows a part with very predictable failure characteristics. If it survives infant mortality (that is, past time x) it is very likely to survive at least until wear-out starts (at time y). However, after time y its chances of survival rapidly diminish. Curve B, on the other hand, shows a part which is far less predictable. The distinction between the three stages is less clear, with infant-mortality failure subsiding only slowly and a gradually increasing chance of wear-out failure.

Facilities with failure curves similar to that shown in curve B are far more difficult to maintain in a planned manner, as will be discussed later.

The failure of operations which rely more on human resources than on technology, such as some services, can follow a somewhat different curve. They may be less susceptible to component wear-out but more so to staff complacency, as the service, without review and regeneration, may become tedious and repetitive. In such a case there is an initial stage of failure reduction, equivalent to the infant-mortality stage, as problems in the service are ironed out. This may be followed by a long period of increasing failure (*see* Fig. 19.3).

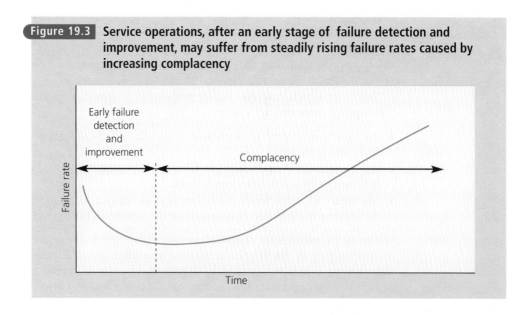

Figure 19.3 Service operations, after an early stage of failure detection and improvement, may suffer from steadily rising failure rates caused by increasing complacency

Reliability

Reliability measures the ability of a system, product or service to perform as expected over time.

The importance of any particular failure is determined partly by the effect it has on the performance of the whole operation or system. This in turn depends on the way in which the parts of the system which are liable to failure are related. If components in a system are all interdependent, a failure in any individual component will cause the whole system to fail. For example, if an interdependent system has n components each with their own reliability, $R_1, R_2 \dots R_n$, the reliability of the whole system, R_s, is given by:

$$R_s = R_1 \times R_2 \times R_2 \times \dots R_n$$

where

R_1 = reliability of component 1
R_2 = reliability of component 2
etc.

Worked example

An automated pizza-making machine in a food manufacturer's factory has five major components, with individual reliabilities (the probability of the component not failing) as follows:

Dough mixer	Reliability = 0.95
Dough roller and cutter	Reliability = 0.99
Tomato paste applicator	Reliability = 0.97
Cheese applicator	Reliability = 0.90
Oven	Reliability = 0.98

If one of these parts of the production system fails, the whole system will stop working. Thus the reliability of the whole system is:

$$R_s = 0.95 \times 0.99 \times 0.97 \times 0.90 \times 0.98$$
$$= 0.805$$

The number of components

In the example above, the reliability of the whole system was only 0.8, even though the reliability of the individual components was significantly higher. If the system had been made up of more components, then its reliability would have been even lower. The more interdependent components a system has, the lower its reliability will be. Figure 19.4 shows the reduction in system reliability as the number of components in the system increases. For a system composed of components which each have an individual reliability of 0.99, with 10 components the system reliability has shrunk to 0.9, with 50 components it is below 0.8, with 100 components it is below 0.4, and with 400 components it is down below 0.05. In other words, with a system of 400 components (not unusual in a large automated operation), even if the reliability of each individual component is 99 per cent, the whole system will be working for less than 5 per cent of its time.

Mean time between failures

An alternative (and common) measure of failure is the *mean time between failures* (MTBF) of a component or system. MTBF is the reciprocal of failure rate (in time). Thus:

$$\text{MTBF} = \frac{\text{operating hours}}{\text{number of failures}}$$

Figure 19.4 **The effect of the number of components in a system (*n*) on the reliability of the total system**

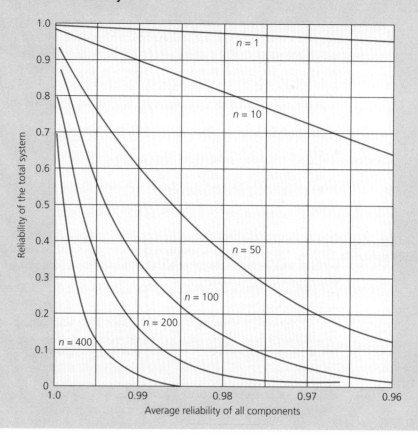

In the previous worked example which was concerned with electronic components, the failure rate (in time) of the electronic components was 0.000041. For that component:

$$\text{MTBF} = \frac{1}{0.000041} = 24\,390.24 \text{ hours}$$

That is, a failure can be expected once every 24 390.24 hours on average.

Availability

Availability is the degree to which the operation is ready to work. An operation is not available if it has either failed or is being repaired following failure.

There are several different ways of measuring availability depending on how many of the reasons for not operating are included. Lack of availability because of planned maintenance or changeovers could be included, for example. However, when 'availability' is being used to indicate the operating time excluding the consequence of failure, it is calculated as follows:

$$\text{Availability (A)} = \frac{\text{MTBF}}{\text{MTBF} + \text{MTTR}}$$

where

MTBF = the mean time between failures of the operation
MTTR = the mean time to repair, which is the average time taken to repair the operation, from the time it fails to the time it is operational again.

Worked example A company which designs and produces display posters for exhibitions and sales promotion events competes largely on the basis of its speedy delivery. One particular piece of equipment which the company uses is causing some problems. This is its large platform colour laser printer. Currently, the mean time between failures of the printer is 70 hours and its mean time to repair is six hours. Thus:

$$\text{Availability} = \frac{70}{70+6} = 0.92$$

The company has discussed its problem with the supplier of the printer who has offered two alternative service deals. One option would be to buy some preventive maintenance (*see* later for a full description of preventive maintenance) which would be carried out each weekend. This would raise the MTBF of the printer to 90 hours. The other option would be to subscribe to a faster repair service which would reduce the MTTR to four hours. Both options would cost the same amount. Which would give the company the higher availability?

With MTBF increased to 90 hours:

$$\text{Availability} = \frac{90}{90+6} = 0.938$$

With MTTR reduced to four hours:

$$\text{Availability} = \frac{70}{70+4} = 0.946$$

Availability would be greater if the company took the deal which offered the faster repair time.

● Failure prevention and recovery

In practical terms, operations managers have three sets of activities which relate to failure. The first is concerned with understanding what failures are occurring in the operation and why they are occurring. Once the nature of any failures is understood, an operations manager's second task is to examine ways of either reducing the chances of failure or minimizing the consequences of failure. The third task is to devise plans and procedures which help the operation to recover from failures when they do occur. The first of these tasks is, in effect, a prerequisite for the other two (*see* Fig. 19.5). The remainder of this chapter deals with these three tasks.

Figure 19.5 **The three tasks of failure prevention and recovery**

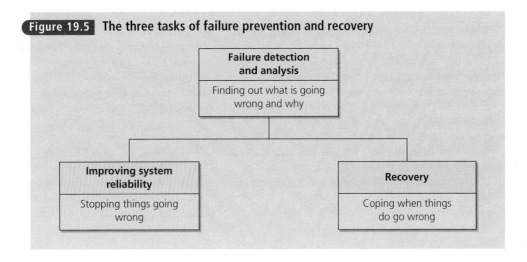

Failure detection and analysis

Given that failures will occur, operations managers must first have mechanisms in place which ensure that they are aware that a failure has occurred and, second, have procedures in place which analyse the failure to find out its root cause.

● Mechanisms to detect failure

Organizations sometimes may not be aware that the system has failed and thereby lose the opportunity both to put things right for the customer and to learn from the experience. Customers dissatisfied with the food or the service at a restaurant are very likely to 'vote with their feet' and tell all their friends about the poor experience rather than complain to the management at the time. When customers do complain about a product or a service, the situation may be dealt with on the spot but the system may not be changed to prevent such problems occurring again. This may be due to staff fearing that drawing attention to a problem might be seen to be a sign of weakness or lack of ability, or because there are inadequate failure identification systems, or a lack of managerial support or interest in making improvements.

Many mechanisms are available to seek out failures in a proactive way:

- *In-process checks.* Employees check that the service is acceptable during the process itself. This is often undertaken in restaurants, for example 'Is everything alright with your meal, madam?'
- *Machine diagnostic checks.* A machine is tested by putting it through a prescribed sequence of activities designed to expose any failures or potential failures. Computer servicing procedures often include this type of check.
- *Point-of-departure interviews.* At the end of a service, staff may formally or informally check that the service has been satisfactory and try to solicit problems as well as compliments.
- *Phone surveys.* These can be used to solicit opinions about products or services. Television rental companies, for example, may check on the installation and servicing of equipment in this way.

Web under attack

There had been examples before, but in February 2000, high-profile internet-based companies found out how internet hacker activists (the so-called hacktivists) could wreak havoc on their service reliability. These so-called 'denial-of-service' attacks affected the sites of Microsoft, Yahoo, Amazon, TimeWarneronLine and Ebay. The key difference between these attacks and normal operations failure is that hacker attacks are deliberate and planned attempts to disrupt commercial activity. Technologically this is not difficult. The hacker creates a program to attack a website which is duplicated many times and placed surreptitiously on computers all over the internet which have inadequate security. Once these are in place, the hacker triggers them by a brief command. Each one then communicates with the targeted website in a way that appears like routine traffic. However, taken together, the individual requests add up to an overwhelming attack, with the targeted computer having insufficient capacity to deal with real users.

Defensive solutions include a form of condition-based monitoring (*see* later). This uses monitoring software to detect the first signs of an attack and re-routes the offending communications to a standby computer where they can be isolated and studied, whilst saving the main site from being overwhelmed.

> **Question**
>
> What other options for preventing such denial-of-service failures do you think are open to the owners of potential victim websites?

- *Focus groups.* These are groups of customers who are brought together to focus on some aspects of a product or service. These can be used to discover either specific problems or more general attitudes towards the product or service.
- *Complaint cards or feedback sheets.* These are used by many organizations to solicit views about the products and services. The problem here is that very few people tend to complete them. It may be possible, however, to identify the respondents and so follow up on any individual problem.
- *Questionnaires.* These may generate a slightly higher response than complaint cards. They may only generate general information, however, from which it is difficult to identify specific individual complaints.

Failure analysis

One of the critical activities for an organization when failure has occurred is to understand why it occurred. This activity is called *failure analysis*. There are many different techniques and approaches which are used to uncover the root cause of failures. Some of these were described in the final part of the previous chapter. Some others are briefly described in this section.

Accident investigation

Large-scale national disasters like oil tanker spillages and aeroplane accidents are usually investigated by accident investigators specifically trained in the detailed analysis of the causes of the accident. Although the techniques they use have usually been developed to be appropriate for the particular type of accident being investigated, the common role of the accident investigators is to make recommendations to minimize or even eradicate the likelihood of any such failures occurring again.

Product liability

Many organizations (either by choice or more often because of a legal requirement) adopt 'product liability'. This ensures that all their products are traceable. Any failures can be traced back to the process which produced them, the components from which they were produced, or the suppliers who provided them. This means that any fault can be rectified and also that, if necessary, all other similar products can be recalled for checking. This is sometimes seen when car and electrical components or food items are recalled.

Complaint analysis

Complaints, just like errors, will always arise. They are increasingly seen to be a cheap and easily available source of information about errors. Complaints, and indeed compliments, need to be taken seriously as they are likely to represent only the 'tip of the iceberg' of customer attitudes. In some service operations it is believed that for every person who complains, there are another 20 who have not. Two key advantages of complaints are that they come unsolicited and also they are often very timely pieces of information that can pinpoint problems quickly within an organization. Complaint analysis also involves tracking the actual number of complaints over time, which can in itself be indicative of developing problems. The prime function of complaint analysis involves analysing the 'content' of the complaints to understand better the nature of the problem as it is perceived by the customer.

Critical incident analysis

Critical incident analysis simply requires customers to identify the elements of products or services that they found either particularly satisfying or not particularly satisfying. They are asked to write down incidents which gave them cause for dissatisfaction or satisfaction. The transcript of this anecdotal evidence is then analysed in detail for factors, traits and causes of the satisfaction and dissatisfaction. These causes can then be categorized and linked to possible causes of failure. It is a popular way of collecting information, especially in service operations. Critical incident technique (CIT) has been defined as 'essentially a procedure for gathering certain important facts concerning behaviour in defined situations'.[3] This technique has been applied to many different service industries, including hotels, banks and airlines.

Failure mode and effect analysis

The objective of failure mode and effect analysis (FMEA) is to identify the product or service features that are critical to various types of failure. It is a means of identifying failures before they happen by providing a 'checklist' procedure which is built around three key questions.

For each possible cause of failure:

- What is the likelihood that failure will occur?
- What would the consequence of the failure be?
- How likely is such a failure to be detected before it affects the customer?

Based on a quantitative evaluation of these three questions, a *risk priority number* (RPN) is calculated for each potential cause of failure. Corrective actions, aimed at preventing failure, are then applied to those causes whose RPN indicates that they warrant priority.

Worked example

Part of an FMEA exercise at a transportation company has identified three failure modes associated with the failure of 'goods arriving damaged' at the point of delivery:

- Goods not secured (failure mode 1)
- Goods incorrectly secured (failure mode 2)
- Goods incorrectly loaded (failure mode 3).

The improvement group which is investigating the failures allocates scores for the probability of the failure mode occurring, the severity of each failure mode, and the likelihood that they will be detected using the rating scales shown in Table 19.1, as follows:

Probability of occurrence
Failure mode 1	5
Failure mode 2	8
Failure mode 3	7

Severity of failure
Failure mode 1	6
Failure mode 2	4
Failure mode 3	4

Probability of detection
Failure mode 1	2
Failure mode 2	6
Failure mode 3	7

The RPN of each failure mode is calculated:

Failure mode 1 (goods not secured)	$5 \times 6 \times 2 = 60$
Failure mode 2 (goods incorrectly secured)	$8 \times 4 \times 5 = 160$
Failure mode 3 (goods incorrectly loaded)	$7 \times 4 \times 7 = 196$

Priority is therefore given to failure mode 3 (goods incorrectly loaded) when attempting to eliminate the failure.

Table 19.1 Rating scales for FMEA

A. Occurrence of failure

Description	Rating	Possible failure occurrence
Remote probability of occurrence It would be unreasonable to expect failure to occur	1	0
Low probability of occurrence Generally associated with activities similar to previous ones with a relatively low number of failures	2 3	1:20 000 1:10 000
Moderate probability of occurrence Generally associated with activities similar to previous ones which have resulted in occasional failures	4 5 6	1:2000 1:1000 1:200
High probability of occurrence Generally associated with activities similar to ones which have traditionally caused problems	7 8	1:100 1:20
Very high probability of occurrence Near certainty that major failures wil occur	9 10	1:10 1:2

B. Severity of failure

Description	Rating
Minor severity A very minor failure which would have no noticeable effect on system performance	1
Low severity A minor failure causing only slight customer annoyance	2 3
Moderate severity A failure which would cause some customer dissatisfaction, discomfort or annoyance, or would cause noticeable deterioration in performance	4 5 6
High severity A failure which would engender a high degree of customer dissatisfaction	7 8
Very high severity A failure which would affect safety	9
Catastrophic A failure which may cause damage to property, serious injury or death	10

C. Detection of failure

Description	Rating	Probability of detection
Remote probability that the defect will reach the customer (It is unlikely that such a defect would pass through inspection, test or assembly)	1	0 to 15%
Low probability that the defect will reach the customer	2 3	6 to 15% 16 to 25%
Moderate probability that the defect will reach the customer	4 5 6	26 to 35% 36 to 45% 46 to 55%
High probability that the defect will reach the customer	7 8	56 to 65% 66 to 75%
Very high probability that the defect will reach the customer	9 10	76 to 85% 86 to 100%

It is essentially a seven-step process:

Step 1   Identify all the component parts of the product or service.

Step 2   List all the possible ways in which the components could fail (the failure modes).

Step 3   Identify the possible effects of the failures (down time, safety, repair requirements, effects on customers).

Step 4   Identify all the possible causes of failure for each failure mode.

Step 5   Assess the probability of failure, the severity of the effects of failure and the likelihood of detection.

Step 6   Calculate the RPN by multiplying all three ratings together.

Step 7   Instigate corrective action which will minimize failure on failure modes that show a high RPN.

Fault-tree analysis

This is a logical procedure that starts with a failure or a potential failure and works backwards to identify all the possible causes and therefore the origins of that failure. The *fault tree* is made up of branches connected by two types of nodes: *AND nodes* and *OR nodes*. The branches below an AND node all need to occur for the event above the node to occur. Only one of the branches below an OR node needs to occur for the event above the node to occur.

Carlsberg Tetley's product recall[4]

Very few crises happen at convenient times. Carlsberg Tetley learnt of its crisis late one Friday afternoon, with a public holiday the following Monday and on the eve of the Chairman's holiday. Something appeared to have gone wrong with the 'widget' in one of its cans of beer (a widget is the device in the bottom of a can which gives some canned beer its creamy characteristic). One customer had taken a drink from a can of beer and found a piece of plastic in his mouth. He had complained to an environmental health official who had then taken it up with the company. The company's pre-planned crisis management procedure immediately swung into action. A crisis control group of 12 members, with experts on insurance, legal affairs, quality control and public relations, took control. This group always has everyone's telephone number, so any relevant person in the company can be contacted. It also has a control room at one of the company's sites with fax and telephone lines always available for the sole use of the crisis team. Over the weekend the team investigated the problem and by the following Tuesday had issued a press release, set up a hotline and taken out national advertising to announce the recall decision. Even though the problem had originated in only one of its six brands,

the company decided to recall all of them – a total of one million cans. The hotline received 500 calls during its first week of operation, and all production using the suspect widget was halted. Linda Bain, the company spokeswoman, explained,

'We were very happy with our recall procedure and the effectiveness of the control group. It all went according to plan. In terms of public relations, the coverage we got from the media was positive, factual and up-front, and indicated the company had been as honest and truthful as it possibly could'.

Questions

1   What seem to be the essential elements of this successful recovery from failure?

2   How do the advantages and disadvantages of deciding whether or not to recall products in a case such as this depend on the likelihood of another potential failure being out there in the market?

3   Relate this issue to the concept of type I and type II errors dealt with in Chapter 17.

Figure 19.6 shows a simple tree identifying the possible reasons for a hot dish being served cold in a restaurant.

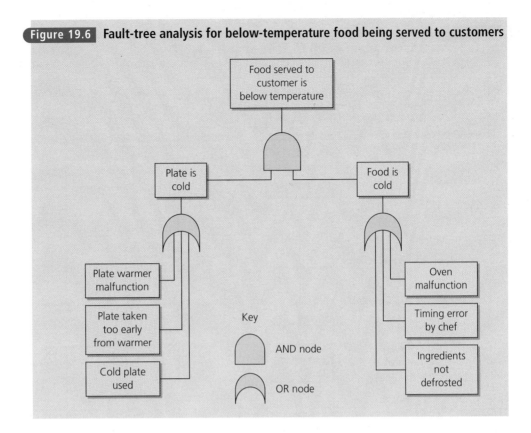

Figure 19.6 Fault-tree analysis for below-temperature food being served to customers

Improving the operation's reliability

Once a thorough understanding of the causes and effects of failure has been established, the next responsibility of operations managers is to try to prevent the failures occurring in the first place. They can do this in a number of ways:

- designing out the fail points in the operation;
- building redundancy into the operation;
- 'fail-safeing' some of the activities in the operation;
- maintenance of the physical facilities in the operation.

We will examine each of these, but especially the maintenance of physical facilities (equipment, machines and buildings) which is an important activity in all operations.

● Designing out fail points

Chapter 5 on product/service design and Chapter 17 on quality planning and control were concerned with identifying and then controlling product and service characteristics to try to prevent failures occurring. In particular, Chapter 17 described the use of process control charting to try to detect when a process was going out of control so that action could be taken before failures occurred.

All the process flow design methods described in Chapter 5 can be used to 'engineer out' the potential fail points in operations. For example, Figure 19.7 shows a flow process chart for an automobile repair process. The stages in the process which are particularly prone to failure and the stages which are critical to the success of the service have been marked. This will have been done by the staff of this operation metaphorically 'walking themselves through' the process and discussing each stage in turn.

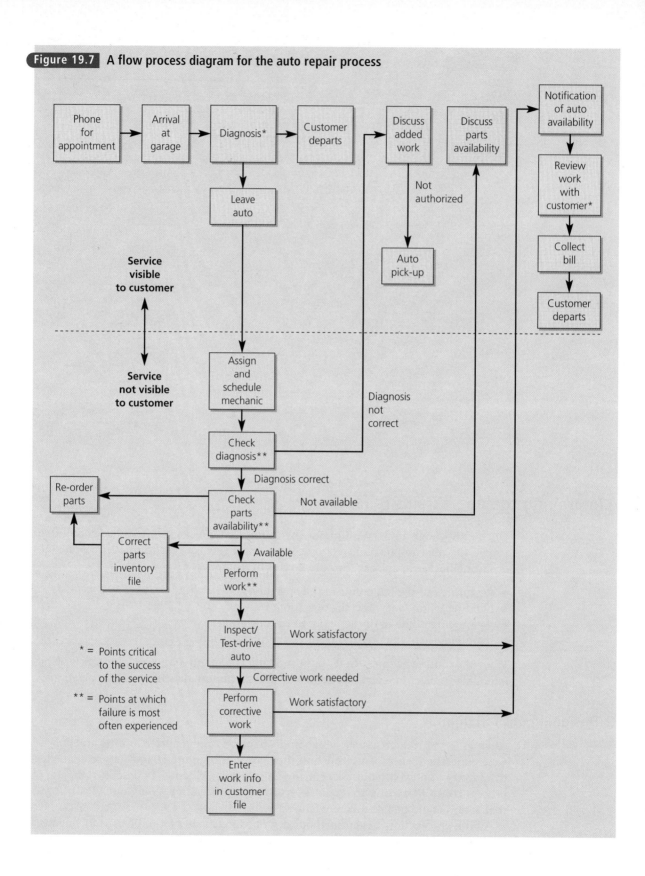

Figure 19.7 A flow process diagram for the auto repair process

Redundancy

Building in redundancy to an operation means having back-up systems or components in case of failure. It can be an expensive solution to reduce the likelihood of failure and is generally used when the breakdown could have a critical impact. Redundancy means doubling or even tripling some of the components in a system so that these 'redundant' elements can come into action when one component fails. Nuclear power stations, hospitals and other public buildings have auxiliary or back-up electricity generators ready to operate in case the main electricity supply should fail. Some organizations also have 'back-up' staff held in reserve in case someone does not turn up for work or is held up on one job and is unable to move on to the next. This is done by railways, theme parks and hospitals, for example. Spacecraft have several back-up computers on board that will not only monitor the main computer but also act as a back-up in case of failure. Rear brake lighting sets built into the back of buses and lorries contain two bulbs to reduce the likelihood of showing no red light at the rear. Human bodies contain two of some organs – kidneys and eyes, for example – both of which are used in 'normal operation' but the body can cope with a failure in one of them.

The reliability of a component together with its back-up is given by the sum of the reliability of the original component and the likelihood that the back-up component will both be needed *and* be working.

$$R_{a+b} = R_a + (R_b \times P \text{ (failure)})$$

where

R_{a+b} = reliability of component *a* with its back-up component *b*
R_a = reliability of *a* alone
R_b = reliability of back-up component *b*
P (failure) = the probability that component *a* will fail and therefore component *b* will be needed

Worked example

The food manufacturer in the earlier worked example has decided that the cheese depositor in the pizza-making machine is so unreliable that it needs a second cheese depositor to be fitted to the machine which will come into action if the first cheese depositor fails.

The two cheese depositors (each with reliability = 0.9) working together will have a reliability of:

$$0.9 + [0.9 \times (1 - 0.9)] = 0.99$$

The reliability of the whole machine is now:

$$0.95 \times 0.99 \times 0.97 \times 0.99 \times 0.98 = 0.885$$

Fail-safeing

The concept of fail-safeing has emerged since the introduction of Japanese methods of operations improvement. Called *poka-yoke* in Japan (from *yokeru* (to prevent) and *poka* (inadvertent errors)), the idea is based on the principle that human mistakes are to some extent inevitable. What is important is to prevent them becoming defects. Poka-yokes are simple (preferably inexpensive) devices or systems which are incorporated into a process to prevent inadvertent operator mistakes resulting in a defect.

Typical poka-yokes are such devices as:

● limit switches on machines which allow the machine to operate only if the part is positioned correctly;

- gauges placed on machines through which a part has to pass in order to be loaded onto, or taken off, the machine – an incorrect size or orientation stops the process;
- digital counters on machines to ensure that the correct number of cuts, passes or holes have been machined;
- checklists which have to be filled in, either in preparation for, or on completion of, an activity;
- light beams which activate an alarm if a part is positioned incorrectly.

More recently, the principle of fail-safeing has been applied to service operations. Service poka-yokes can be classified as those which 'fail-safe the server' (the creator of the service) and those which 'fail-safe the customer' (the receiver of the service).[5]

Examples of fail-safeing the server include:

- colour-coding cash register keys to prevent incorrect entry in retail operations;
- the McDonald's french-fry scoop which picks up the right quantity of fries in the right orientation to be placed in the pack;
- trays used in hospitals with indentations shaped to each item needed for a surgical procedure – any item not back in place at the end of the procedure might have been left in the patient;
- the paper strips placed round clean towels in hotels, the removal of which helps housekeepers to tell whether a towel has been used and therefore needs replacing.

Examples of fail-safeing the customer include:

- the locks on aircraft lavatory doors, which must be turned to switch the light on;
- beepers on ATMs to ensure that customers remove their cards;
- height bars on amusement rides to ensure that customers do not exceed size limitations;
- outlines drawn on the walls of a child-care centre to indicate where toys should be replaced at the end of the play period;
- tray stands strategically placed in fast-food restaurants to remind customers to clear their tables.

Photo courtesy of Severn-Trent

Maintenance is vital to utilities in order to ensure the safe and dependable supply of energy, water and other services

● Maintenance

Maintenance is the term used to cover the way in which organizations try to avoid failure by taking care of their physical facilities. It is an important part of most operations' activities, especially those whose physical facilities play a central role in creating their goods and services. In operations such as power stations, hotels, airlines and petrochemical refineries, maintenance activities will account for a significant proportion of operations management's time, attention and resources.

Keep left[6]

For over half an hour the pilot of an Airbus A320 jet with nearly 200 people on board fought to control his aircraft, which did not seem to be responding to the controls. The aircraft would not turn left no matter what the pilot tried. Eventually he managed to make a high-speed emergency landing at the second attempt. Fortunately no one was hurt, but the pilot was not pleased to find out that the cause of the near-disaster was that engineers had forgotten to reactivate four of the five spoilers on the right wing. Spoilers are the panels that help the plane to roll and hence turn. The official air accident investigation report on the incident blamed 'a complex chain of human errors', not only by the engineers but also by the pilots who had failed to notice the problem before take-off. The A320 is a 'fly-by-wire' aircraft where computer-controlled electrical impulses activate the hydraulically powered spoilers and surfaces which control the movement of the plane. When the aircraft went for repair to a damaged flap, the engineers had put the spoilers into 'maintenance mode' to block them off from the controls so that they could be worked on independently. They had then forgotten to reactivate them when the plane was needed urgently to replace another aircraft. According to the official report, the engineers were not guilty of:

'simple acts of neglect or ignorance. Their approach implied that they believed there were benefits to the organization if they could successfully circumvent problems to deliver the aircraft on time. With the introduction of aircraft such as the A320 it is no longer possible for maintenance staff to have enough information about the aircraft and its systems to understand adequately the consequences of any deviation. The avoidance of future unnecessary accidents with high-technology aircraft depends on an attitude of total compliance within the industry. If a check has previously been carried out numerous times without any fault being present, it is human nature to anticipate no fault when next the check is carried out.'

Questions

1 Why should fly-by-wire aircraft pose a more complex maintenance problem than conventional aircraft which have a physical link between the control and the flaps?

2 If you were the accident investigator, what questions would you want to ask in order to understand why this failure occurred?

The benefits of maintenance

Before examining the various approaches to maintenance, it is worth considering why operations bother to care for their facilities in a systematic manner:

- *Enhanced safety.* Well-maintained facilities are less likely to behave in an unpredictable or non-standard way, or fail outright, all of which could pose a hazard to staff.
- *Increased reliability.* This leads to less time lost while facilities are repaired, less disruption to the normal activities of the operation, and less variation in output rates.
- *Higher quality.* Badly maintained equipment is more likely to perform below standard and cause quality errors.
- *Lower operating costs.* Many pieces of process technology run more efficiently when regularly serviced: motor vehicles, for example.
- *Longer life span.* Regular care can prolong the effective life of facilities by reducing the problems in operation whose cumulative effect causes deterioration.
- *Higher end value.* Well-maintained facilities are generally easier to dispose of into the second-hand market.

The three basic approaches to maintenance

In practice an organization's maintenance activities will consist of some combination of the three basic approaches to the care of its physical facilities. These are *run to breakdown* (RTB), *preventive maintenance* (PM) and *condition-based maintenance* (CBM).

Run to breakdown (RTB)

As its name implies, this approach involves allowing the facilities to continue operating until they fail. Maintenance work is performed only after failure has taken place. For example, the televisions, bathroom equipment and telephones in a hotel's guest rooms will probably only be repaired when they fail. The hotel will keep some spare parts and the staff available to make any repairs when needed. Failure in these circumstances is neither catastrophic (although perhaps irritating to the guest) nor so frequent as to make regular checking of the facilities appropriate.

Preventive maintenance (PM)

Preventive maintenance attempts to eliminate or reduce the chances of failure by servicing (cleaning, lubricating, replacing and checking) the facilities at pre-planned intervals. For example, the engines of passenger aircraft are checked, cleaned and calibrated according to a regular schedule after a set number of flying hours. Taking aircraft away from their regular duties for preventive maintenance is clearly an expensive option for any airline. The consequences of failure while in service are considerably more serious, however. The principle is also applied to facilities with less catastrophic consequences of failure. The regular cleaning and lubricating of machines, even the periodic painting of a building, could be considered preventive maintenance.

Condition-based maintenance (CBM)

Condition-based maintenance attempts to perform maintenance only when the facilities require it. For example, continuous process equipment, such as that used in coating photographic paper, is run for long periods in order to achieve the high utilization necessary for cost-effective production. Stopping the machine to change, say, a bearing

The state of equipment such as this can be assessed through the use of condition-based monitoring

when it is not strictly necessary to do so would take it out of action for long periods and reduce its utilization. Here condition-based maintenance might involve continuously monitoring the vibrations, for example, or some other characteristic of the line. The results of this monitoring would then be used to decide whether the line should be stopped and the bearings replaced.

Mixed maintenance strategies

Each approach to maintaining facilities is appropriate for different circumstances. RTB is often used where repair is relatively straightforward (so the consequence of failure is small), where regular maintenance is very costly (making PM expensive), or where failure is not at all predictable (so there is no advantage in PM because failure is just as likely to occur after repair as before). PM is used where the cost of unplanned failure is high (because of disruption to normal operations) and where failure is not totally random (so the maintenance time can be scheduled before failure becomes very likely). CBM is used where the maintenance activity is expensive, either because of the cost of providing the maintenance itself, or because of the disruption which the maintenance activity causes to the operation.

Most operations adopt a mixture of these approaches because different elements of their facilities have different characteristics. Even a motor car uses all three approaches (*see* Fig. 19.8). Some parts of the car are normally replaced only when they fail: light bulbs and fuses, for example. A wise motorist might carry spares and some cars have warning systems to tell the driver when a light bulb has failed, so the failure can be identified and repaired immediately. More fundamental parts of the car should not be run to breakdown, however. The engine oil would be subject to preventive maintenance at the car's regular service. At the service other parts of the car would also be checked and replaced as necessary. Finally, most drivers would also monitor the condition of the car. Some monitoring would be done informally, by listening to the engine noise when driving. Other monitoring might be done regularly, such as measuring the amount of tread on the tyre.

Breakdown *versus* preventive maintenance

Most operations plan their maintenance to include a level of regular preventive maintenance which gives a reasonably low but finite chance of breakdown. Usually the more frequent the preventive maintenance episodes, the less are the chances of a breakdown. The balance between preventive and breakdown maintenance is set to minimize the total cost of breakdown. Infrequent preventive maintenance will cost little to provide but will

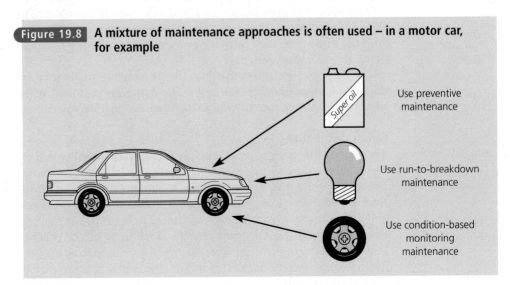

Figure 19.8 A mixture of maintenance approaches is often used – in a motor car, for example

Use preventive maintenance

Use run-to-breakdown maintenance

Use condition-based monitoring maintenance

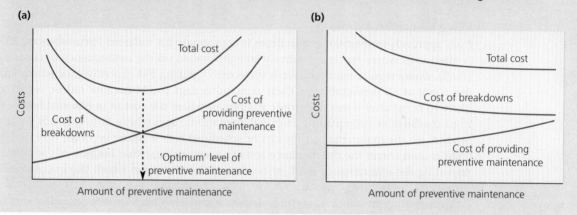

Figure 19.9 Two views of maintenance costs. (a) One model of the costs associated with preventive maintenance shows an optimum level of maintenance effort. (b) If routine preventive maintenance tasks are carried out by operators and if the real cost of breakdowns is considered, the 'optimum' level of preventive maintenance shifts toward higher levels

result in a high likelihood (and therefore cost) of breakdown maintenance. Conversely, very frequent preventive maintenance will be expensive to provide but will reduce the cost of having to provide breakdown maintenance (*see* Fig. 19.9a). The total cost of maintenance appears to minimize at an 'optimum' level of preventive maintenance.

This representation of maintenance-related costs, however, although conceptually elegant, may not reflect reality. The cost of providing preventive maintenance may not increase quite so steeply as indicated in Figure 19.9(a). The curve assumes that it is carried out by a separate set of people (skilled maintenance staff) whose time is scheduled and accounted for separately from the 'operators' of the facilities. Furthermore, every time preventive maintenance takes place, the facilities cannot be used productively. This is why the slope of the curve increases, because the maintenance episodes start to interfere with the normal working of the operation. In many operations, however, at least some of the preventive maintenance can be performed by the operators themselves (which reduces the cost of providing it) and at times which are convenient for the operation (which minimizes the disruption to the operation). The cost of breakdowns could also be higher than is indicated in Figure 19.9(a). Here the argument is similar to that which we used in Chapter 2 to describe dependability and in Chapter 12 to determine optimum stock levels (and will again in the next chapter when discussing the costs of quality). Unplanned breakdowns may do more than necessitate a repair and stop the operation; they can take away stability from the operation which prevents it being able to improve itself.

Put these two ideas together and the minimizing total curve and maintenance cost curve look more like Figure 19.9(b). The emphasis is shifted more towards the use of preventive maintenance than run-to-breakdown maintenance.

Failure distributions

The shape of the failure probability distribution of a facility will also have an effect on the benefits of preventive maintenance. Figure 19.10 shows two probability curves for two machines, A and B. For machine A, the probability that it will break down before time x is relatively low. This machine will almost always break down between times x and y. If preventive maintenance was timed to occur just before point x, it could reduce the chances of breakdown substantially. Machine B, on the other hand, has a relatively high probability of breaking down at any time, although again the probability of breakdown increases after time x. This means that applying preventive maintenance at point x (or any other time) cannot bring the dramatic reduction in breakdowns possible with

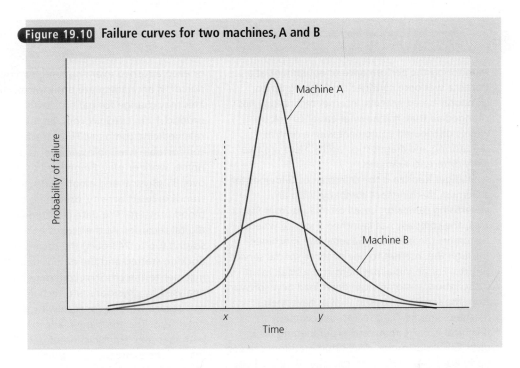

Figure 19.10 Failure curves for two machines, A and B

machine A. The implication of this is that preventive maintenance is more likely to lead to benefits when periods of high breakdown are reasonably predictable. When breakdown occurs in a relatively random manner there is less to gain from preventive maintenance because it has little effect on the chance of the machine breaking down in the future.

Total productive maintenance

Total productive maintenance (TPM) is defined as:

> *...the productive maintenance carried out by all employees through small group activities*

where productive maintenance is:

> *...maintenance management which recognizes the importance of reliability, maintenance and economic efficiency in plant design.*[7]

In Japan, where TPM originated, it is seen as a natural extension in the evolution from run-to-breakdown to preventive maintenance. TPM adopts some of the team-working and empowerment principles discussed in Chapter 9, as well as a continuous improvement approach to failure prevention as discussed in Chapter 18. It also sees maintenance as an organization-wide issue, to which staff can contribute in some way. It is analogous to the total quality management approach discussed in Chapter 20.

The five goals of TPM

TPM aims to establish good maintenance practice in operations through the pursuit of 'the five goals of TPM':[8]

1 *Improve equipment effectiveness.* Examine how the facilities are contributing to the effectiveness of the operation by examining all the losses which occur. Loss of effectiveness can be the result of down-time losses, speed losses or defect losses.
2 *Achieve autonomous maintenance.* Allow the people who operate or use the operation's equipment to take responsibility for at least some of the maintenance tasks. Also encourage maintenance staff to take responsibility for the improvement of maintenance

Long-distance monitoring[9]

Monitoring the performance of equipment at a distance was once confined to checking up on computer-based systems. Internet technology has changed all that. It is now far easier to link up widely distributed equipment with a central monitoring and diagnostics facility. Here are two (very different) examples.

Rüdiger Kapitza is the chairman of Gildemeister, a German machine tool company. With an advertising campaign based on images from *Star Trek,* the company has launched a service where customers can link their Gildemeister machines through the internet to one of three special service centres. For an initial payment and a small monthly subscription, customers can download new software from the service centres as well as have their machines checked and talk to the company's technical experts about any programming or mechanical difficulties. Given that machines can cost up to €3 million, it is important that they are kept running. Says Mr Kapitza:

'This is why customers are willing to pay extra for a service in which we can sort out their problems. In 30 per cent of cases, using the service centre concept, we can fix machine breakdowns in less than one hour.'

Doctors (the maintenance engineers of the human body) have long complained that a patient's vague description of his or her symptoms, or even a rushed examination by an overworked doctor, is an inadequate basis for proper diagnosis. This may change for patients with access to a new product from LifeShirt.com, an internet-based telemedicine company. The 'LifeShirt' is a comfortable washable garment that can be worn at home, work or play. Embedded sensors monitor over 35 physical and emotional signs derived from trends in heart activity, breathing pattern and blood pressure. The data is stored in a pocket-sized digital recorder. At the end of each monitoring session (up to 24 hours) the record is placed in a PC docking station and the data is uploaded via the internet to the LifeShirt.com data hub. It is then analysed by physicians and technicians and posted to a secure website for review by patients and their physicians. The company plans to develop products with real-time transmission of data in the near future. The company says its products enable doctors to see a 'movie' of a patient's physical signs instead of a 'snapshot'. It also allows postoperative outpatients to be monitored 24 hours a day.

Question

What are the advantages of such 'distance monitoring' to the people or operations being monitored, and to those doing the monitoring?

---

performance. Murata and Harrison, based on their work at Yuasa batteries, propose three levels at which staff take responsibility for maintenance:[10]

- *Repair level* – staff carry out instructions but do not predict the future; they simply react to problems.
- *Prevention level* – staff can predict the future by foreseeing problems, and take corrective action.
- *Improvement level* – staff can predict the future by foreseeing problems; they not only take corrective action but also propose improvements to prevent recurrence.

For example, suppose the screws on a machine become loose. Each week it jams up and is passed to maintenance to be fixed. A 'repair-level' maintenance engineer will simply repair it and hand it back to production. A 'prevention-level' maintenance engineer will spot the weekly pattern to the problem and tighten the screws in advance of their loosening. An 'improvement-level' maintenance engineer will recognize that there is a design problem and modify the machine so that the problem cannot recur.

3 *Plan maintenance.* Have a fully worked out approach to all maintenance activities. This should include the level of preventive maintenance which is required for each piece of equipment, the standards for condition-based maintenance and the respective responsibilities of operating staff and maintenance staff. Table 19.2 illustrates the respective roles of operating and maintenance staff.

Table 19.2 The roles and responsibilities of operating staff and maintenance staff in TPM

	Maintenance staff	*Operating staff*
Roles	To develop: – preventive actions – breakdown services	To take on: – ownership of facilities – care of facilities
Responsibilities	Train operators Devise maintenance practice Problem-solving Assess operating practice	Correct operation Routine preventive maintenance Routine condition-based maintenance Problem detection

4 *Train all staff in relevant maintenance skills.* The responsibilities listed in Table 19.2 require that both maintenance and operating staff have all the skills to carry out their roles. TPM places a heavy emphasis on appropriate and continuous training.

5 *Achieve early equipment management.* This goal is directed at going some way to avoiding maintenance altogether by 'maintenance prevention' (MP). MP involves considering failure causes and the maintainability of equipment during its design stage, its manufacture, its installation and its commissioning.

Reliability-centred maintenance

One of the criticisms of the total productive maintenance (TPM) approach is that it tends to recommend preventive maintenance (PM) at times when PM would be inappropriate. We have already seen in Figure 19.10 that the pattern of failure for a particular part of a process will influence how effective a PM approach can be. Reliability-centred maintenance (RCM) uses the pattern of failure for each type of failure mode of a part of a system to dictate the approach to its maintenance. For example, take the process illustrated in Figure 19.11. This is a simple shredding process which prepares vegetables prior to freezing. The most significant part of the process which requires the most maintenance attention is the cutter sub-assembly. However, there are several modes of failure which could lead to the cutters requiring attention. Sometimes they require changing simply because they have worn out through usage, sometimes they have been damaged by small stones entering the process, sometimes they have shaken loose because they were not fitted correctly. The failure patterns for these three failure modes are very different, as illustrated in Figure 19.11. Certainly, 'wear out' can be managed by timing preventive maintenance intervals just prior to the increased likelihood of failure. But this approach would not help prevent stone damage which could happen at any time with equal likelihood. The approach here would be to prevent stones getting to the cutters in the first place, perhaps through fixing a screen. The failure pattern for the cutters shaking loose is different again. If the cutters have been incorrectly fitted, it would become evident soon after the fitting. Again, preventive maintenance is unlikely to help here; rather effort should be put into ensuring that the cutters are always correctly fitted, perhaps by organizing more appropriate training of staff.

The approach of RCM is sometimes summarized as, 'If we cannot stop it from happening, we had better stop it from mattering'. In other words, if maintenance cannot either predict or even prevent failure, and the failure has important consequences, then efforts need to be directed at reducing the impact of the failure.

Figure 19.11
One part in one process can have several different failure modes, each of which requires a different approach

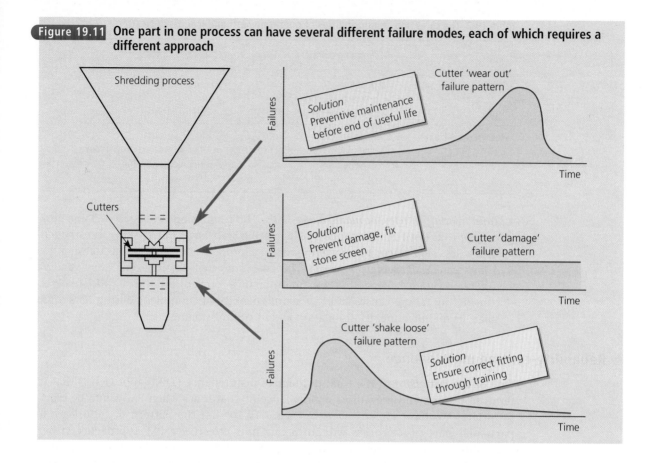

Recovery

In parallel with considering how to prevent failures occurring, operations managers need to decide what they will do when failures do occur. This activity is called *recovery* from failure. All types of operation can benefit from well-planned recovery. For example, a construction company whose mechanical digger breaks down can have plans in place to arrange a replacement from a hire company. The breakdown might be disruptive, but not as much as it might have been if the operations manager had not worked out what to do.

Recovery procedures will also shape customers' perceptions of failure. Even where the customer sees a failure, it may not necessarily lead to dissatisfaction. Indeed, in many situations, customers may well accept that things do go wrong.[11] If there is a metre of snow on the train lines, or if the restaurant is particularly popular, we may accept that the product or service does not work. It is not necessarily the failure itself that leads to dissatisfaction but often the organization's response to the breakdown. While mistakes may be inevitable, dissatisfied customers are not.

A failure may even be turned into a positive experience. If you are due to catch an aeroplane flight at midnight in a remote airport and are told that it is delayed by five hours, this is a potentially dissatisfying situation. Suppose, however, that then you are told that the aircraft was delayed taking off from its previous destination by a cyclone and that arrangements have been made for you to be taken to a local hotel for a complimentary meal with a room provided for a shower and rest, and that a telephone will be made available so that you can deal with any knock-on effects at the next destination. You might then feel that you have been dealt with well and even recommend that airline to others because you were so well looked after. A good recovery can turn angry, frustrated customers into loyal ones.

Professor Colin Armistead of Bournemouth University and Graham Clark of Cranfield University give details of investigations into customer satisfaction and customer loyalty in relation to service organizations in the USA.[12] The research used four service scenarios and examined the willingness of customers to use an organization's services again. The four scenarios quoted are:

1 The service is delivered to meet the customers' expectations and there is full satisfaction.
2 There are faults in the service delivery but the customer does not complain about them.
3 There are faults in the service delivery and the customer complains but he/she has been fobbed off or mollified. There is no real satisfaction with the service provider.
4 There are faults in the service delivery and the customer complains and feels fully satisfied with the resulting action taken by the service providers.

Customers who are fully satisfied and do not experience any problems (1) are the most loyal, followed by complaining customers whose complaints are resolved successfully (4). Customers who experience problems but don't complain (2) are in third place and last of all come customers who do complain but are left with their problems unresolved and feelings of dissatisfaction (3).

Recovery in service operations

Recovery has been developed particularly in operating services. The word 'recovery' was said to have originated from British Airways' 'Putting the Customer First Campaign'.[13] Donald Porter, the consultant involved with BA, stated:

> It had never occurred to us before in any concrete way. 'Recovery' was the term we coined to describe a very frequently repeated concern. If something goes wrong, as it often does, will anybody make special efforts to get it right? Will somebody go out of his or her way to make amends to the customer? Does anyone make an effort to offset the negative impact of a screw-up?

It has also been suggested that service recovery does not just mean 'return to a normal state' but to a state of enhanced perception.

> All breakdowns require the deliverer to jump through a few hoops to get the customer back to neutral. More hoops are required for victims to recover. [14]

Service operations managers need to recognize that all customers have recovery expectations that they want organizations to meet. Recovery needs to be a planned process. Organizations therefore need to design appropriate responses to failure, linked to the cost and the inconvenience caused by the failure to the customer, that will meet the needs and expectations of the customer. Such recovery processes need to be carried out either by empowered front-line staff or by trained personnel who are available to deal with recovery in a way which does not interfere with day-to-day service activities (*see* the discussion of 'Empowerment' in Chapter 9).

Failure planning

Identifying how organizations can recover from failure is of particular interest to service operations because they can turn failures around to minimize the effect on customers or even to turn failure into a positive experience. It is also of interest to other industries, however, especially those where the consequences of failure are particularly severe. Bulk chemical manufacturers and nuclear processors, for example, spend considerable resources in deciding how they will cope with failures. The activity of devising the procedures which allow the operation to recover from failure is called *failure planning*.

Failure planning is often represented by stage models showing the steps to be followed in the event of failure. These stage models all follow a similar pattern. One is represented in Figure 19.12. We shall follow it through from the point where failure is recognized.

Discover

The first thing any manager needs to do when faced with a failure is to discover its exact nature. Three important pieces of information are needed: first of all, what exactly has happened; second, who will be affected by the failure, and, third, why did the failure occur? This last point is not intended to be a detailed inquest into the causes of failure (that comes later) but it is often necessary to know something of the causes of failure in case it is necessary to determine what action to take.

Act

The discover stage could only take minutes or even seconds, depending on the severity of the failure. If the failure is a severe one with important consequences, we need to move on to doing something about it quickly. This means carrying out three actions, the first two of which could be carried out in reverse order, depending on the urgency of the situation. First, tell the significant people involved what you are proposing to do about the failure. In service operations this is especially important where the customers need to be kept informed, both for their peace of mind and to demonstrate that something is being done. In all operations, however, it is important to communicate what action is going to happen so that everyone can set their own recovery plans in motion. Second, the effects of the failure need to be contained in order to stop the consequences spreading and causing further failures. The precise containment actions will depend on

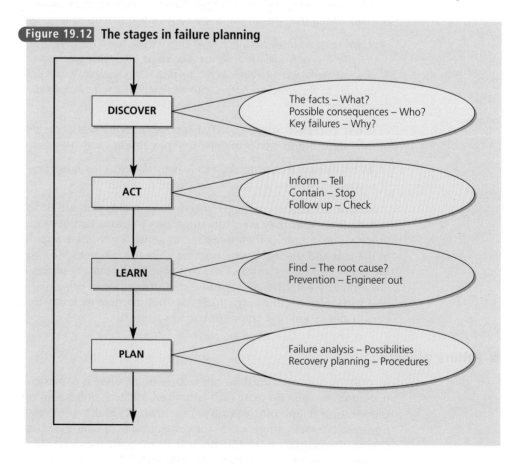

Figure 19.12 The stages in failure planning

the nature of the failure. Third, there needs to be some kind of follow-up to make sure that the containment actions really have contained the failure.

Learn

As discussed earlier in this chapter, the benefits of failure in providing learning opportunities should not be underestimated. In failure planning, learning involves revisiting the failure to find out its root cause and then engineering out the causes of the failure so that it will not happen again.

Plan

Learning the lessons from a failure is not the end of the procedure. Operations managers need formally to incorporate the lessons into their future reactions to failures. This is often done by working through 'in theory' how they would react to failures in the future. Specifically, this involves first identifying all the possible failures which might occur (in a similar way to the FMEA approach). Second, it means formally defining the procedures which the organization should follow in the case of each type of identified failure.

● Business continuity

Many of the ideas behind failure, failure prevention and recovery are incorporated in the growing field of *business continuity*. This aims to help operations avoid and recover from disasters while keeping the business going. As operations become increasingly integrated (and increasingly dependent on integrated technologies such as information technologies), critical failures can result from a series of related and unrelated events and combine to disrupt totally a company's business. These events (sometimes called *disasters*) are identified as the critical malfunctions which have the potential to interrupt normal business activity and even stop the entire company. Typically, such disasters are:

- floods, lightning, temperature extremes
- fire
- power or telecommunications failure
- corporate crime, theft, fraud, sabotage
- computer system failure
- bomb blast, bomb scare or other security alert
- key personnel leave, become ill or die
- key supplier ceases trading
- contamination of product or processes
- health and safety infringement.

The procedures adopted by business continuity experts are very similar to those described in this chapter:

- *Identify and assess risks* to determine how vulnerable the business is to various risks and to take steps to minimize or eliminate them.
- *Identify core business processes* to prioritize those that are particularly important to the business and which, if interrupted, would have to be brought back to full operation quickly.
- *Quantify recovery times* to make sure staff understand priorities (for example, get customer ordering system back into operation before the internal e-mail).
- *Determine resources needed* to make sure that resources will be available when required.
- *Communicate* to make sure that everyone in the operation knows what to do if disaster strikes.

Summary answers to key questions

Why do operations fail?

● There are three major reasons why operations fail. The first is that the goods or services which are supplied to the operation are themselves faulty. The second is that something is happening within the operation, either because there is an overall failure in its design, or because one or more of the physical facilities break down, or because there is human error. The third is that the customers themselves may cause failure through their incompetent handling of goods or services. Even so, this is the responsibility of the management of the operation.

● Remember, though, not all failures are equally serious and attention is usually directed at those which have the most impact on the operation or its customers.

How is failure measured?

● There are three ways of measuring failure. 'Failure rates' indicate how often a failure is likely to occur. 'Reliability' measures the chances of a failure occurring. 'Availability' is the amount of available and useful operating time left after taking account of failures.

● Failure over time is often represented as a failure curve. The most common form of this is the so-called 'bath-tub curve' which shows the chances of failure being greater at the beginning and end of the life of a system or part of a system.

How can failure and potential failure be detected and analysed?

● Failure detection and analysis involves putting mechanisms into place which sense that some kind of failure has occurred, and then analysing the failure to try to understand its root causes.

● Failure detection mechanisms include in-process checks, machine diagnostic checks, point-of-departure interviews, phone surveys, focus groups, complaint cards or feedback sheets, and questionnaires.

● Failure analysis mechanisms include accident investigation, product liability, complaint analysis, critical incident analysis, and failure mode and effect analysis (FMEA).

How can operations improve their reliability?

● There are four major methods of improving reliability:
– designing out the fail points in the operation;
– building redundancy into the operation;
– 'fail-safeing' some of the activities of the operation;
– maintenance of the physical facilities in the operation.

● Maintenance is the most common way operations attempt to improve their reliability.

● There are three broad approaches to maintenance. The first is running all facilities until they break down and then repairing them, the second is regularly maintaining the facilities even if they have not broken down, and the third is to monitor facilities closely to try to predict when breakdown might occur.

● Two specific approaches to maintenance have been particularly influential: total productive maintenance (TPM) and reliability-centred main-tenance (RCM).

How should operations recover when failure does occur?

● Recovery can be enhanced by a systematic approach to discovering what has happened to cause failure, acting to inform, contain and follow up the consequences of failure, learning to find the root cause of the failure and preventing it taking place again, and planning to avoid the failure occurring in the future.

● The idea of 'business continuity' planning is probably the most common form of recovery planning.

Better late and happy than just late

Fiona Rennie sat and enjoyed her coffee at Warsaw airport. Returning home to the UK after a week of energetic academic research, she was pondering her latest project – how service businesses have to be more aware of their customers' needs and, in order to compete, must be able to offer a high level of customer service, especially if the intended delivery package has been compromised in some way.

She knew that airlines, especially, had well-developed recovery procedures. In the case of failure the airline could activate various levels of preconceived and *ad hoc* customer care.

Warsaw airport was busy with passengers waiting to board the afternoon British Airways flight to London Heathrow, the anticipation growing as they passed through the scanners and walked down the aisle onto the aircraft. Safely in their seats, the 200 travellers were soon dismayed to hear from the captain that there was a slight mechanical problem and that their take-off would be delayed by approximately half an hour. This delay did not merit having to disembark and complimentary drinks were soon on the way round.

Inevitably, the half-hour delay soon blossomed into a bigger problem and an apologetic captain announced that he felt that passengers would be better placed, waiting for the repair to be completed, back in the departure lounge and please could they take all of their hand baggage off the plane with them. A few grumbles and mutters about connections at Heathrow and other missed appointments could be heard – but generally the mood was fairly genial and the airline staff went out of their way to try to accommodate passenger queries. One representative escorted a worried passenger off to the airline office to allow her to phone home and advise her family of the late departure. She had spent all of her Polish 'holiday money' and so couldn't use the standard phones in the departure area. After an hour in the departure lounge and with no definitive answer available on the estimated take-off time, the airline moved into the next stage of its 'customer-placating programme' by providing meal vouchers for everyone and directing them to the airport restaurant. As the mood quietened and passengers began to question

further just how long they were going to have to wait, the airline announced the departure time – some four hours behind schedule.

The flight itself went according to plan and the cabin crew walked up and down the aisles answering, where possible, queries on connecting flights and subsequent travel arrangements.

On arrival (finally) at Heathrow, the captain, who had been very apologetic throughout the whole process, bade the passengers farewell, expressing his concerns at the late arrival and hoping that it hadn't inconvenienced them too greatly. For some, though, the four-hour delay meant considerable problems in trying to reach their onward destinations that evening and the airline sales desk was soon busy with anxious passengers looking for help. Several were to be put up in a local hotel, courtesy of the airline, leaving them to recommence their travels, fresh, the next morning. Others did not have so far to go and to stay overnight in the UK's capital city would actually mean more inconvenience the following day. Unperturbed, the airline's Customer Service Manager quickly took it upon himself to arrange chauffeur-driven transport for these people, ensuring that the inconvenience caused by the delay was effectively minimized. The priority wasn't necessarily to deal with each customer as quickly as possible, but to ensure that each person was given a solution that suited his or her needs. No awkward questions asked – only 'How can I help you?'; 'What can I possibly do to ensure that given the choice you will fly again with our airline?'

Fiona was certainly impressed, and although very late back, glad to be safely home as planned.

Questions

1 Is Fiona a particularly tolerant person or was she right to be impressed by the way British Airways reacted?

2 Draw up a 'failure plan' for delays of this type. How could it help the airline to improve its recovery procedures further?

3 When are failure and recovery particularly important to an operation?

The Chernobyl failure[15]

At 1.24 in the early hours of Saturday morning on the 26 April 1986, the worst accident in the history of commercial nuclear power generation occurred. Two explosions in quick succession blew off the 1000-tonne concrete sealing cap of the Chernobyl–4 nuclear reactor. Molten core fragments showered down on the immediate area and fission products were released into the atmosphere. The accident cost probably hundreds of lives and contaminated vast areas of land in the Ukraine.

Many reasons probably contributed to the disaster. Certainly the design of the reactor was not new – around 30 years old at the time of the accident – and had been conceived before the days of sophisticated computer-controlled safety systems. Because of this, the reactor's emergency-handling procedures relied heavily on the skill of the operators. This type of reactor also had a tendency to run 'out of control' when operated at low power. For this reason, the operating procedures for the reactor strictly prohibited it being operated below 20 per cent of its maximum power. It was mainly a combination of circumstance and human error which caused the failure, however. Ironically, the events which led up to the disaster were designed to make the reactor safer. Tests, devised by a specialist team of engineers, were being carried out to evaluate whether the emergency core cooling system (ECCS) could be operated during the 'free-wheeling' run-down of the turbine generator, should an off-site power failure occur. Although this safety device had been tested before, it had not worked satisfactorily and new tests of the modified device were to be carried out with the reactor operating at reduced power throughout the test period. The tests were scheduled for the afternoon of Friday, 25 April 1986 and the plant power reduction began at 1.00 pm. However, just after 2.00 pm, when the reactor was operating at about half its full power, the Kiev controller requested that the reactor should continue supplying the grid with electricity. In fact it was not released from the grid until 11.10 that night. The reactor was due to be shut down for its annual maintenance on the following Tuesday and

the Kiev controller's request had in effect shrunk the 'window of opportunity' available for the tests.

The following is a chronological account of the hours up to the disaster, together with an analysis by James Reason, which was published in the *Bulletin of the British Psychological Society* the following year. Significant operator actions are italicized. These are of two kinds: *errors* (indicated by an '*E*') and *procedural violations* (marked with a '*V*').

25 April 1986

1.00 pm Power reduction started with the intention of achieving 25 per cent power for test conditions.

2.00 pm ECCS disconnected from primary circuit. (This was part of the test plan.)

2.05 pm Kiev controller asked the unit to continue supplying grid. *The ECCS was not reconnected (V).* (This particular violation is not thought to have contributed materially to the disaster; but it is indicative of a lax attitude on the part of the operators toward the observance of safety procedures.)

11.10 pm The unit was released from the grid and continued power reduction to achieve the 25 per cent power level planned for the test programme.

26 April 1986

12.28 am *Operator seriously undershot the intended power setting (E).* The power dipped to a dangerous one per cent. (The operator had switched off the 'auto-pilot' and had tried to achieve the desired level by manual control.)

1.00 am After a long struggle, the reactor power was finally stabilized at 7 per cent – well below the intended level and well into the low-power danger zone. *At this point, the experiment should have been abandoned, but it was not (E).* This was the most serious mistake (as opposed to violation): it meant that all subsequent activity would be conducted within the reactor's zone of maximum instability. This was apparently not appreciated by the operators.

1.03 am *All eight pumps were started (V).* The safety regulations limited the maximum number of pumps in use at any one time to six. This showed a profound misunderstanding of the physics of the reactor. The consequence was that the increased water flow (and reduced steam fraction) absorbed more neutrons, causing more control rods to be withdrawn to sustain even this low level of power.

1.19 am *The feedwater flow was increased threefold (V).* The operators appear to have been attempting to cope with a falling steam-drum pressure and water level. The result of their actions, however, was to further reduce the amount of steam passing through the core, causing yet more control rods to be withdrawn. *They also overrode the steam-drum automatic shut-down (V).* The effect of this was to strip the reactor of one of its automatic safety systems.

1.22 am The shift supervisor requested printout to establish how many control rods were actually in the core. The printout indicated only six to eight rods remaining. It was strictly forbidden to operate the reactor with fewer than 12 rods. *Yet the shift supervisor decided to continue with the tests (V).* This was a fatal decision: the reactor was thereafter without 'brakes'.

1.23 am *The steam line valves to No 8 turbine generator were closed (V).* The purpose of this was to establish the conditions necessary for repeated testing, but its consequence was to disconnect the automatic safety trips. This was perhaps the most serious violation of all.

1.24 am An attempt was made to 'scram' the reactor by driving in the emergency shut-off rods, but they jammed within the now warped tubes.

1.24 am Two explosions occurred in quick succession. The reactor roof was blown off and 30 fires started in the vicinity.

1.30 am Duty firemen were called out. Other units were summoned from Pripyat and Chernobyl.

5.00 am Exterior fires had been extinguished, but the graphite fire in the core continued for several days.

The subsequent investigation into the disaster highlighted a number of significant points which contributed to it:

- The test programme was poorly worked out and the section on safety measures was inadequate. Because the ECCS was shut off during the test period, the safety of the reactor was in effect substantially reduced.
- The test plan was put into effect before being approved by the design group who were responsible for the reactor.
- The operators and the technicians who were running the experiment had different and non-overlapping skills.
- The operators, although highly skilled, had probably been told that getting the test completed before the shut-down would enhance their reputation. They were proud of their ability to handle the reactor even in unusual conditions and were aware of the rapidly reducing window of opportunity within which they had to complete the test. They had also probably 'lost any feeling for the hazards involved' in operating the reactor.
- The technicians who had designed the test were electrical engineers from Moscow. Their objective was to solve a complex technical problem. In spite of having designed the test procedures, they probably would not know much about the operation of the nuclear power station itself.

Again, in the words of James Reason:

'Together, they made a dangerous mixture: a group of single-minded but non-nuclear engineers directing a team of dedicated but over-confident operators. Each group probably assumed that the other knew what it was doing. And both parties had little or no understanding of the dangers they were courting, or of the system they were abusing.'

Questions

1 What were the root causes which contributed to the ultimate failure?

2 How could failure planning have helped prevent the disaster?

Discussion questions

1 Briefly describe a time when a product you bought or a service you received failed. Identify all the different reasons why this happened and assess which you think was the most likely.

2 In what ways could customers 'fail' in their use of a bank? How might the bank's management use this information to improve its operations?

3 What do you think will be the best ways of measuring failure for:
   - a university course
   - a lift (elevator)
   - a security service
   - a home pregnancy-testing kit
   - a car?

4 A 24-hour ATM machine outside a bank was closed down between the following times during a seven-day period:
   11.00 am Monday – 2.00 pm Monday
   1.00 am Tuesday – 10.30 am Tuesday
   4.00 pm Tuesday – 10.00 am Wednesday
   3.00 pm Friday – 10.00 am Saturday

   Calculate the ATM's failure rate (in time), the mean time between failures and its availability.

5 A manufacturer has four machines which are used in sequence: stripping, steaming, buffing and polishing. The reliabilities of the individual machines are 95 per cent, 78 per cent, 45 per cent and 56 per cent, respectively. This year the Managing Director has agreed to buy one new machine to replace one of the old ones. The failure rates of the possible replacement machines are shown in Table 19.3. Which one would you recommend should be chosen to maximize the reliability of the whole process?

6 A catering company that provides catering services in people's homes for dinner parties, etc. has encountered a number of problems. From their past activities the managers have identified how many times these problems have occurred and have rated them for importance and the likelihood of detection by the customer, as shown in Table 19.4. The managers wish to try to improve their reputation for a quality service. Which area would you recommend them giving most attention to first?

7 Flow chart a service process you have recently encountered, identifying what you consider to be the key fail points. Assess any poka-yokes in evidence and explain how you might design poka-yokes to overcome the fail points you have identified.

8 Describe the difference between 'run-to-break-down', 'condition-based maintenance' and 'preventive-maintenance' approaches to maintenance. Provide examples from your own experience to illustrate your answer.

Table 19.3 Machine failure rates

Possible replacement machines	Known failure rates
Superstripper	1/10
Stripper XXXX	7/30
Steadysteam	1/20
The Steam Machine	3/40
Buffer Mark2	1/10
Buffalot	4/25
Buffalotmore	3/25
Polishoff	6/70
Superfinish*	1/5
Finishkwik*	1/6

*Note the Superfinish and Finishkwik machines will replace both the buffing and polishing machines.

Table 19.4 Catering problems

Problems encountered	Times problem occurred	Severity of failure	Probability of customer finding out
Insufficient food	1/800	5	50%
Host/hostess wants to be involved	1/25	1	10%
Food damaged in transit	1/3	7	20%
Food kept at wrong temperatures	1/30	9	70%
Breaking customers' equipment	1/90	7	90%

9 Talk to an operations manager in a car repair garage or a catering operation, for example, and find out the different ways in which the organization maintains its equipment. Assess the organization's approach to maintenance.

10 Describe a recent equipment, product or service failure that involved you. Did the organization make any attempt to recover from the situation?

If so, how? If not, what steps might have been taken to bring about a recovery?

11 Should the same approach to service recovery be used inside an operation as that which is used for external customers?

12 Sould the service recovery process for an internet-based retailer be different from that for a bricks and mortar retailer?

Notes on chapter

1 Sources: Ridding, J.(1994) 'Recession and Blunders Derail SNCF', The *Financial Times*, 28 Jan; and Jenkins, I. (1993) 'Socrates Derails French Travellers', The *Sunday Times*, 29 Aug.

2 Source: 'Air Crashes, But Surely ...', *The Economist*, 4 June 1994.

3 Flanagan, J. (1954) 'The Critical Incident Technique', *Psychological Bulletin*, Vol 51, No 4.

4 Source: 'How to Cope in a Crisis', *The Times*, 24 Aug 1995.

5 Chase, R.B. and Stewart, D.M. (1994) 'Make Your Service Fail-safe', *Sloan Management Review*, Spring, Vol 35, No 3.

6 Source: 'Mistake by Engineers left Holiday Airbus Unable to Turn Left', *The Times*, 25 Jan 1995.

7 Nakajima, S. (1988) *Total Productive Maintenance*, Productivity Press.

8 Nakajima, S., *ibid*.

9 Sources: Marsh, P. (1999) 'Germany Engineers Set Market Phases to Stun', The *Financial Times*, 16 Nov; *The Economist* (1999) 'Medical Monitoring, Web Shirts', 4 December, www.LifeShirt.com.

10 Murata, K. and Harrison, A. (1991) *How To Make Japanese Management Methods Work In The West*, Gower.

11 For a full discussion of this idea *see* Hart, C.W.L., Heskett, J.L. and Sasser, W.E. (1990) 'The Profitable Art of Service Recovery', *Harvard Business Review*, Vol 68, No 4.

12 Armistead, C.G. and Clark, G. (1992) *Customer Service and Support*, FT/Pitman Publishing.

13 Zemke, R. and Schaaf, R. (1990) *The Service Edge: 101 Companies that Profit from Customer Care*, Plume Books.

14 Zemke, R. and Bell, C.R. (1991) *Service Wisdom: Creating and Maintaining the Customer Service Edge*, Lakewood Books.

15 Based on information from Read, P.P. (1994) *Ablaze: The Story of Chernobyl*, Secker and Warburg; and Reason, J. (1987) 'The Chernobyl Errors', *Bulletin of the British Psychological Society*, Vol 4, pp 201–6.

Selected further reading

Albrecht, K. and Bradford, L.J. (1990) *The Service Advantage*, Dow Jones Irwin.

Condra, L.W. (1993) *Reliability Improvement with Design of Experiments*, Marcel Dekker, New York.

Dale, B.G. (ed) (1994) *Managing Quality* (2nd edn), Prentice Hall.

Davis, R. (1997) 'TPM and RCM: Must it be One or the Other?', *Works Management*, Vol 50, No 6

Evans, J.R. and Lindsay, W.M. (1993) *The Management and Control of Quality* (2nd edn), West.

Geraghty, T. (1996) 'Beyond TPM', *Manufacturing Engineer*, Aug.

Harrison A. (1992) *Just-in-time Manufacturing in Perspective*, Prentice Hall.

Hayes, R.H. and Clark, K.B. (1986) 'Why Some Factories are More Productive Than Others', *Harvard Business Review*, Vol 64, No 5.

Heskett, J.L., Sasser, W.E. and Hart, C.W.L. (1990) *Service Breakthroughs: Changing the Rules of the Game*, The Free Press.

HMSO (1995) *An Introduction and a Guide to Business Continuity Management*, HMSO.

Ljungberg, O. (1998) 'Measurement of Overall Equipment Effectiveness as a Basis for TPM Activities', *International Journal of Operations and Production Management*, Vol 18, No 5.

Löfsten, H. (1999) 'Management of Industrial Maintenance – Economic Evaluation of Maintenance Policies', *International Journal of Operations and Production Management*, Vol 19, No 7.

Moore, R. (1997) 'Combing TPM and Reliability-focused Maintenance', *Plant Engineering*, Vol 51, No 6.

Moubray, J. (1991) *Reliability-centred Maintenance*, Butterworth-Heinemann.

Nakajima, S. (1988) *Total Productive Maintenance*, Productivity Press.

Raouf, A., Ali, Z. and Duffuaa, S.O. (1993) 'Evaluating a Computerized Maintenance Management System', *International Journal of Operations and Production Research*, Vol 13, No 3.

Sherwin, D.J. (1990) 'Inspect or Monitor', *Engineering Costs and Production Economics*, Jan.

Total Productive Maintenance, Proceedings of the First International Conference 1992, Published by Industrial Newsletters.

20 Total quality management

Introduction

Total quality management (TQM) is arguably the most significant of the new ideas which have swept across the operations management scene over the last few years. There can be few, if any, managers in any developed economy anywhere in the world who have not heard of TQM. It certainly has had an impact on most industries which goes beyond its recent fashionability. There are two reasons for this: first, the ideas of TQM have a great intuitive attraction for many people – most of us want to be 'high quality'; second, a TQM approach to improvement can result in,

sometimes dramatic, increases in operational effectiveness. In this book we have separated the treatment of general quality planning and control (in Chapter 17) from TQM because TQM is concerned with more than quality alone. It is concerned with the improvement of *all* aspects of operations performance and particularly how improvement should be managed.

This chapter looks at TQM both as a philosophy of improvement and as an organizational process which can be used to manage the improvement effort (*see* Fig. 20.1).

Figure 20.1 Model of operations improvement showing the issues covered in this chapter

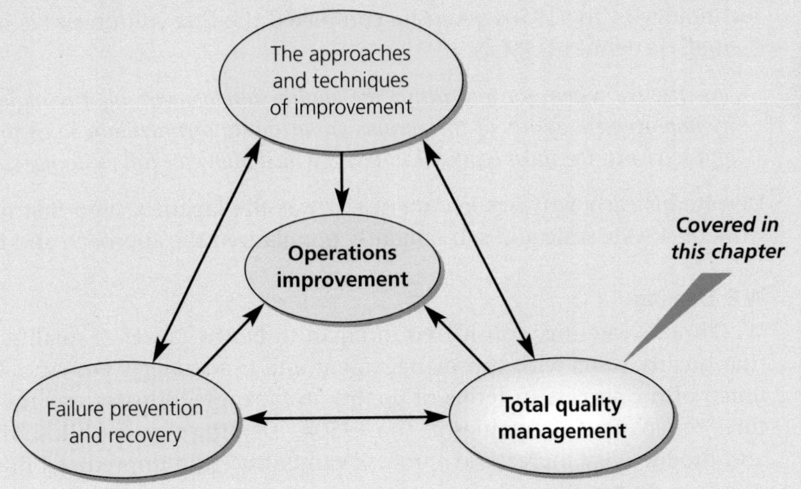

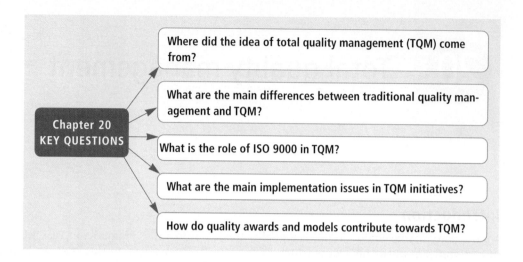

Where did the idea of total quality management (TQM) come from?

What are the main differences between traditional quality management and TQM?

What is the role of ISO 9000 in TQM?

What are the main implementation issues in TQM initiatives?

How do quality awards and models contribute towards TQM?

Chapter 20
KEY QUESTIONS

The origins of TQM

The notion of total quality management was introduced by Feigenbaum in 1957. More recently, it has been developed through a number of widely recognized approaches put forward by several 'quality gurus' such as Deming, Juran, Ishikawa, Taguchi and Crosby. Therefore, to understand the origins of TQM, it is important to understand the contributions from these quality pioneers.

The quality gurus

Feigenbaum

Armand Feigenbaum was a doctoral student at the Massachusetts Institute of Technology in the 1950s when he completed the first edition of his book *Total Quality Control*. He defines TQM as:

> 'an effective system for integrating the quality development, quality maintenance and quality improvement efforts of the various groups in an organization so as to enable production and service at the most economical levels which allow for full customer satisfaction'.[1]

Despite his early writings in America, it was the Japanese who first made the concept work on a wide scale and subsequently popularized the approach and the term 'TQM'.

W.E. Deming

W. Edwards Deming, considered in Japan to be the father of quality control, asserted that quality starts with top management and is a strategic activity.[2] It is claimed that much of the success in terms of quality in Japanese industry was the result of his lectures to Japanese companies in the 1950s.[3] Deming's basic philosophy is that quality and productivity increase as 'process variability' (the unpredictability of the process) decreases. In his *14 points for quality improvement*, he emphasizes the need for statistical control methods, participation, education, openness and purposeful improvement:

1 Create constancy of purpose.
2 Adopt new philosophy.
3 Cease dependence on inspection.
4 End awarding business on price.

5 Improve constantly the system of production and service.

6 Institute training on the job.

7 Institute leadership.

8 Drive out fear.

9 Break down barriers between departments.

10 Eliminate slogans and exhortations.

11 Eliminate quotas or work standards.

12 Give people pride in their job.

13 Institute education and a self-improvement programme.

14 Put everyone to work to accomplish it.

J.M. Juran

Joseph M. Juran tried to get organizations to move away from the traditional view of quality as 'conformance to specification' to a more user-based approach, for which he coined the phrase 'fitness for use'. He pointed out that a dangerous product could conform to specification but would not be fit to use. Juran was concerned about management responsibility for quality, but he was also concerned about the impact of individual workers and involved himself with the motivation and involvement of the workforce in quality improvement activities.[4]

K. Ishikawa

Kaoru Ishikawa has been credited with originating quality circles and cause-and-effect diagrams (*see* Chapter 18). Ishikawa[5] claimed that there had been a period of over-emphasis on statistical quality control (in Japan), and as a result people disliked quality control. They saw it as something unpleasant because they were given complex and difficult tools rather than simple ones. Furthermore, the resulting standardization of products and processes and the creation of rigid specification of standards not only made change difficult but made people feel bound by regulations. Ishikawa saw worker participation as the key to the successful implementation of TQM. Quality circles, he believed, were an important vehicle to achieve this.

G. Taguchi

Genichi Taguchi (*see also* Chapter 5) was the director of the Japanese Academy of Quality and was concerned with engineering-in quality through the optimization of product design combined with statistical methods of quality control. He encouraged interactive team meetings between workers and managers to criticize and develop product design. Taguchi's definition of quality uses the concept of the loss which is imparted by the product or service to society from the time it is created. His quality loss function (QLF, *see* Chapter 17) includes such factors as warranty costs, customer complaints and loss of customer goodwill.[6]

P.B. Crosby

Phillip B. Crosby[7] is best known for his work on the cost of quality. He suggested that many organizations do not know how much they spend on quality, either in putting it right or getting it wrong. He claimed that organizations that have measured their costs say that they equate them to about 30 per cent of sales (others suggest a smaller figure of around 10 per cent). Crosby tried to highlight the costs and benefits of implementing quality programmes through his book *Quality is Free* in which he provided a *zero defects* programme. This is summarized in his absolutes of quality management:[8]

1 Quality is conformance to requirements.

2 Prevention not appraisal.

3 The performance standard must be 'zero defects'.

4 Measure the 'price of non-conformance' (PONC).

5 There is no such thing as a quality problem.

Even from these brief summaries, it is evident that each 'guru' stressed a different set of issues from which emerged the TQM approach to operations improvement. Table 20.1 summarizes the strengths and weaknesses of each guru's approach.

Table 20.1 The relative strengths and weaknesses of some of the quality gurus[9]

Quality 'guru'	Strengths of approach	Weaknesses of approach
Feigenbaum	• Provides a total approach to quality control • Places the emphasis on the importance of management • Includes socio-technical systems thinking • Participation by all staff is promoted	• Does not discriminate between different kinds of quality context • Does not bring together the different management theories into one coherent whole
Deming	• Provides a systematic and functional logic which identifies stages in quality improvement • Stresses that management comes before technology • Leadership and motivation are recognized as important • Emphasizes role of statistical and quantitative methods • Recognizes the different contexts of Japan and North America	• Action plan and methodological principles are sometimes vague • The approach to leadership and motivation is seen by some as idiosyncratic • Does not treat situations which are political or coercive
Juran	• Emphasizes the need to move away from quality hype and slogans • Stresses the role of the customer, both internal and external • Management involvement and commitment are stressed	• Does not relate to other work on leadership and motivation • Seen by some as undervaluing the contribution of the worker by rejecting bottom-up initiatives • Seen as being stronger on control systems than the human dimension in organizations
Ishikawa	• Strong emphasis on the importance of people and participation in the problem-solving process • A blend of statistical and people-oriented techniques • Introduces the idea of quality control circles	• Some of his problem-solving methods seen as simplistic • Does not deal adequately with moving quality circles from ideas to action
Taguchi	• Approach pulls quality back to the design stage • Recognizes quality as a societal issue as well as an organizational one • Methods are developed for practising engineers rather than theoretical statisticians • Strong on process control	• Difficult to apply where performance is difficult to measure (e.g. in the service sector) • Quality is seen as primarily controlled by specialists rather than managers and workers • Regarded as generally weak on motivation and people management issues
Crosby	• Provides clear methods which are easy to follow • Worker participation is recognized as important • Strong on explaining the realities of quality and motivating people to start the quality process	• Seen by some as implying that workers are to blame for quality problems • Seen by some as emphasizing slogans and platitudes rather than recognizing genuine difficulties • Zero defects sometimes seen as risk avoidance • Insufficient stress given to statistical methods

What is TQM?

TQM can be viewed as a logical extension of the way in which quality-related practice has progressed (*see* Fig. 20.2). Originally quality was achieved by inspection – screening out defects before they were noticed by customers. The quality control (QC) concept developed a more systematic approach to not only detecting, but also treating quality problems. Quality assurance (QA) widened the responsibility for quality to include functions other than direct operations. It also made increasing use of more sophisticated statistical quality techniques. TQM included much of what went before but developed its own distinctive themes. We will use some of these themes to describe how TQM represents a clear shift from traditional approaches to quality.

On the face of it, it would appear that the quality 'gurus' provide different solutions to bringing about improvement in organizations. However, it has been suggested that 'they are all talking the same "language" but they use different dialects'.[10] In fact TQM is best thought of as a philosophy of how to approach quality management. It is a way of thinking and working in operations which lays particular stress on the following:

- meeting the needs and expectations of customers;
- covering all parts of the organization;
- including every person in the organization;
- examining all costs which are related to quality, especially failure costs;
- getting things 'right first time', i.e. designing-in quality rather than inspecting it in;
- developing the systems and procedures which support quality and improvement;
- developing a continuous process of improvement (this was treated in Chapter 18).

We shall treat each of these issues in turn.

● TQM meets the needs and expectations of the customers

In Chapter 17 we defined quality as 'consistent conformance to customers' expectations'. Yet there is little point in putting a quality system in place – calculating costs, training and motivating people, and so on – unless it meets the requirements of

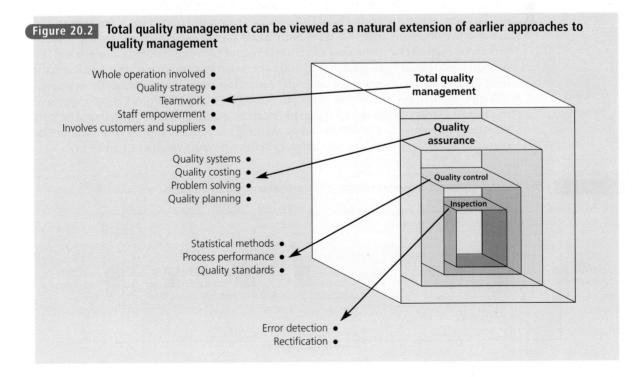

Figure 20.2 Total quality management can be viewed as a natural extension of earlier approaches to quality management

the customers. Chapter 17 explained a number of ways in which organizations can find out what customer expectations are. However, in the TQM approach, meeting the expectations of customers means more than this; it means seeing things *from a customer's point of view*. This involves the whole organization in understanding the central importance of customers to its success and even to its survival. Customers are seen not as being *external* to the organization but as the most important *part* of it.

● TQM covers all parts of the organization

For an organization to be truly effective, every single part of it, each department, each activity, and each person and each level, must work properly together, because every person and every activity affects and in turn is affected by others.[11]

One of the most powerful aspects to emerge from TQM is the concept of the internal customer and supplier. This is a recognition that everyone is a customer within the organization and consumes goods or services provided by other internal suppliers, and everyone is also an internal supplier of goods and services for other internal customers. The implication of this is that errors in the service provided within an organization will eventually affect the product or service which reaches the external customer. So one of the best ways to ensure that external customers are satisfied is to establish the idea that every part of the organization contributes to external customer satisfaction by satisfying its own internal customers. This idea was introduced in Chapter 1.

TQM utilizes this concept by stressing that each 'micro operation' has a responsibility to manage these internal customer–supplier relationships. They do this primarily by defining as clearly as possible what their own and their customers' *requirements* are. In effect this means defining what constitutes 'error-free' service – the quality, speed, dependability and flexibility required by internal customers. The exercise replicates what should be going on for the whole operation and its external customers (*see* Fig. 20.3).

The internal customer concept is useful because it impacts on the 'upstream' parts of the internal supply network. For example, in manufacturing operations the Product Design Department may make an error in the basic concept of a product. At this stage the error is relatively inexpensive to correct – maybe a little time re-researching or rethinking some issues will be required. If the error is not discovered until the detailed design stage, it can be as much as 10 times more expensive to correct, because of the many other decisions that will have been based on the original error. By the time of prototype manufacture, the cost of rethinking and re-commissioning designs for the product could easily have escalated to 100 times what it would have been had the error been discovered at concept stage. By pilot production stage, investment in process technologies, job designs, marketing plans, etc. could be up to 1000 times more expensive to change. Errors discovered in the market can be phenomenally expensive. The cost illustrated in Figure 20.4 of 10 000 times the original cost could even be an underestimate (for example, *see* the box on Carlsberg Tetley's product recall in Chapter 19).

Figure 20.3 **The internal customer–supplier relationship between micro operations**

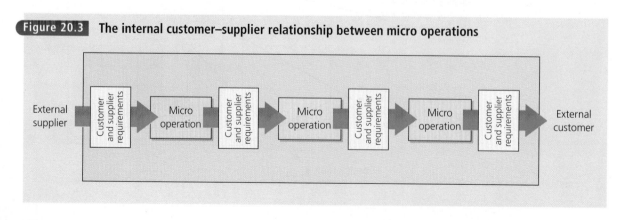

Figure 20.4 The cost of rectifying errors becomes increasingly expensive the longer the errors remain uncorrected in the development and launch process

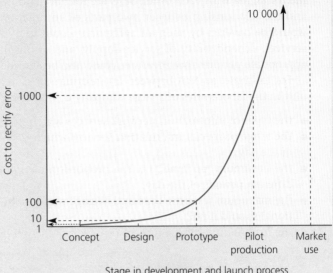

Stage in development and launch process

Hewlett-Packard's internal customer checklist[12]

The computer industry has always been at the forefront of developing and utilizing quality concepts. Quality failures of hardware, software or service are immediately obvious to customers and seriously damaging to their trust in the supplier. Hewlett-Packard, the worldwide information systems company, is no exception. It was one of the first companies to make a success of the internal-customer concept in its operations. One part of the way it used the concept was a short, but effective, checklist 'pocket guide' which came out of its South Queensferry plant in Scotland. The pocket guide was distributed throughout the company. It suggests each part of the organization should ask itself seven questions, which it regards as fundamental to the operation:

● Who are my customers?
● What do they need?
● What is my product or service?
● What are my customers' expectations and measures?
● Does my product or service meet their expectations?
● What is the process for providing my product or service?
● What action is required to improve the process?

H-P then went on to devise a problem-solving methodology, based on its seven questions, the stages for which are as follows:

● Select the quality issue.
● Write an issue statement.
● Identify the process.
● Draw a flow chart.
● Select a process performance measure.
● Conduct a cause-and-effect analysis.
● Collect and analyse the data.
● Identify the major causes of the quality issue.
● Plan for improvements.
● Take the corrective action.
● Collect and analyse the data again.
● Are the objectives met?
● If yes, document and standardize the changes.

Questions

1 What do you see as the limitations of the set of questions which comprises Hewlett-Packard's internal customer checklist?

2 Do you think anything is missing from the problem-solving methodology described above?

3 What seems to be the implied problem-solving methodology described above? How does it compare with the Plan-Do-Check-Act (PDCA) process described in Chapter 18?

Service-level agreements

Some organizations bring a degree of formality to the internal customer concept by encouraging (or requiring) different parts of the operation to agree 'service-level agreements' (SLAs) with each other. SLAs are formal definitions of the dimensions of service and the relationship between two parts of an organization. The type of issues which would be covered by such an agreement could include response times, the range of services, dependability of service supply, and so on. Boundaries of responsibility and appropriate performance measures could also be agreed.

For example, an SLA between an information systems support unit and a research unit in the laboratories of a large company could define such performance measures as:

- the types of information network services which may be provided as 'standard';
- the range of special information services which may be available at different periods of the day;
- the minimum 'up time', i.e. the proportion of time the system will be available at different periods of the day;
- the maximum response time and average response time to get the system fully operational should it fail;
- the maximum response time to provide 'special' services, and so on.

● **CRITICAL COMMENTARY**

While some see the strength of SLAs as the degree of formality they bring to customer–supplier relationships, there also some clear drawbacks. The first is that the 'pseudo-contractual' nature of the formal relationship can work against building partnerships (*see* Chapter 13). This is especially true if the SLA includes penalties for deviation from service standards. Indeed, the effect can sometimes be to inhibit rather than encourage joint improvement. The second, and related problem is that SLAs, again because of their formal documented nature, tend to emphasize the 'hard' and measurable aspects of performance rather than the 'softer' but often more important aspects. So a telephone may be answered within four rings, but how the caller is treated, in terms of 'friendliness', may be far more important.

● Every person in the organization contributes to quality

TQM is sometimes referred to as 'quality at source'. This notion stresses the impact that each individual staff member has on quality, as well as the idea that it is each person's personal responsibility to get quality right. Some staff can affect quality directly. The staff who physically make products and the staff who serve customers face to face all have the capability to make mistakes which will be immediately obvious to customers (although the effects will be noticed much sooner in high customer contact service operations). Other staff who may be less directly involved in producing goods and services can also generate problems, however – the keyboard operator who miskeys data, or the product designer who fails to investigate thoroughly the conditions under which products will be used in practice. Any person could set in motion a chain of events which customers will eventually see as poor-quality products and services.

It follows then that, if everyone has the ability to impair quality, they also have the ability to improve quality – if only by 'not making mistakes'. It is partly because of this that TQM philosophies place considerable emphasis on the contribution which the individual staff of the organization can make to quality. In TQM, however, the contribution of all individuals in the organization is expected to go beyond understanding their contribution and a commitment to 'not make mistakes'. Individuals are expected to bring something positive to the way they perform their jobs. Everyone is capable of improving the way in which they do their own jobs and practically everyone is capable of helping others in the organization to improve theirs. Therefore, neglecting this potential in staff is neglecting a powerful source of improvement. The principles of 'empowerment' (*see* Chapter 9) are frequently cited as supporting this aspect of TQM.

The shift in attitude which is needed to view employees as the most valuable intellectual and creative resource which the organization possesses can still prove difficult for some organizations. When TQM practices first began to migrate from Japan in the late 1970s, the ideas seemed even more radical. Some Japanese industrialists even thought (mistakenly) that companies in Western economies would never manage to change. Take, for example, a statement by Konosuke Matsushito which attracted considerable publicity:

> *We are going to win and the industrial West is going to lose out – there is nothing much you can do about it, because the reasons for your failure are within yourselves. For you, the essence of management is getting the ideas out of the heads of bosses into the hands of labour. For us, the core of management is precisely the art of mobilizing and pulling together the intellectual resources of all employees in the service of the firm. Only by drawing on the combined brainpower of all its employees can a firm face up to the turbulence and constraints of today's environment.*
>
> *'That is why our large companies give their employees three to four times more training than yours. This is why they foster within the firm such intensive exchange and communication. This is why they seek constantly everybody's suggestions and why they demand from the educational system increasing numbers of graduates as well as bright and well-educated generalists, because these people are the lifeblood of industry.*[13]

● **CRITICAL COMMENTARY**

Be careful of what is meant by 'empowerment' in a TQM context. In many cases, it can be little more than an increase in employee discretion over minor details of their working practice. Some industrial relations academics argue that TQM rarely affects the fundamental imbalance between managerial control and employees' influence over organizational direction. For example:

> *...there is little evidence that employee influence over corporate decisions which affect them has been, or can ever be, enhanced through contemporary configuration of involvement. In other words, whilst involvement might increase individual task discretion, or open up channels for communication, the involvement programme is not designed to offer opportunities for employees to gain or consolidate control over the broader environment in which their work is located.*[14]

● All costs of quality are considered

The costs of controlling quality may not be small, whether the responsibility lies with each individual or a dedicated quality control department. It is therefore necessary to examine all the costs and benefits associated with quality (in fact 'cost of quality' is usually taken to refer to both costs and benefits of quality). These costs of quality are usually categorized as *prevention costs, appraisal costs, internal failure costs* and *external failure costs*.

Prevention costs
Prevention costs are those costs incurred in trying to prevent problems, failures and errors from occurring in the first place. They include such things as:

- identifying potential problems and putting the process right before poor quality occurs;
- designing and improving the design of products and services and processes to reduce quality problems;

- training and development of personnel in the best way to perform their jobs;
- process control through SPC.

Appraisal costs

Appraisal costs are those costs associated with controlling quality to check to see if problems or errors have occurred during and after the creation of the product or service. They might include such things as:

- the setting up of statistical acceptance sampling plans;
- the time and effort required to inspect inputs, processes and outputs;
- obtaining processing inspection and test data;
- investigating quality problems and providing quality reports;
- conducting customer surveys and quality audits.

Eurocamp Travel

Eurocamp Travel, which provides family camping holidays, has a reputation for the high-quality of its equipment and services, and has become market leader in this rapidly growing holiday sector. In recent years, sales offices have been opened in the Netherlands and Germany, and Eurocamp's geographic coverage has been extended from its original French sites to include sites throughout Europe. As the business has become larger and more complex, the demands placed on the office systems have also become greater, reinforcing the need for functional specialization of staff, yet requiring more interdepartmental understanding and cooperation. When it became clear that Eurocamp's service package could be copied by competitors eager to attract premium customers, the company decided to reinforce quality at every stage in their process. This was, they believed, the main criterion that already differentiated Eurocamp, and this was also potentially the most difficult for lower priced competitors to follow. A consultant was brought in to facilitate a major quality improvement programme. This was conceived as a 'top-down' approach, wherby important projects were identified and tackled by trained teams, But soon it became apparent that these early projects were not achieving the anticipated sustainable improvements. It also became clear that the failure was largely the result of only involving senior managers, who could not devote the time required to projects, and did not fully understand the process concerned. Those employees who did have a very detailed understanding of the process had been excluded from problem definition, evaluation and implementation of changes. So, the company launched their quality management system (QMS) initiative. Each department established a quality

Happy campers at Eurocamp

steering committee which comprised at least one director, a trained facilitator and volunteers from every grade of employee. The emphasis at this stage was on the identification and improvement of internal processes with further emphasis on satisfying the internal customer. Early success demonstrated the validity of this approach and generated a high level of enthusiasm throughout the company.

> **Questions**
>
> 1 Why are the differences between the first 'top-down' attempt, and the second attempt at establishing a quality initiative?
>
> 2 What do you think are the main advantages and problems with the more participative approach?

Internal failure costs

Internal failure costs are failure costs associated with errors which are dealt with inside the operation. These costs might include such things as:

- the cost of scrapped parts and material;
- reworked parts and materials;
- the lost production time as a result of coping with errors;
- lack of concentration due to time spent troubleshooting rather than improvement.

External failure costs

External failure costs are those which are associated with an error going out of the operation to a customer. These costs include such things as:

- loss of customer goodwill affecting future business;
- aggrieved customers who may take up time;
- litigation (or payments to avoid litigation);
- guarantee and warranty costs;
- the cost to the company of providing excessive capability (too much coffee in the pack or too much information to a client).

The relationship between quality costs

In traditional quality management it was assumed that failure costs reduce as the money spent on appraisal and prevention increases. Furthermore, it was assumed that there is an *optimum* amount of quality effort to be applied in any situation, which minimizes the total costs of quality. The argument is that there must be a point beyond which diminishing returns set in – that is, the cost of improving quality gets larger than the benefits which it brings. Figure 20.5(a) sums up this idea. As quality effort is increased, the costs of providing the effort – through extra quality controllers, inspection procedures, and so on – increases proportionally. At the same time, however, the cost of errors, faulty products, and so on, decreases because there are fewer of them.

Criticisms of the traditional quality cost model

A 'pure' TQM approach would be to assert that this logic is flawed in a number of important respects:

1 This compromise position implies that failure and poor quality are acceptable. It recognizes that the 'optimum' point is one where there will be errors and failures. TQM challenges the whole concept of the acceptable quality level (AQL) which was

Deliberate defectives

A story which illustrates the difference in attitude between a TQM and a non-TQM company has become almost a legend among TQM proponents. It concerns a plant in Ontario, Canada, of IBM, the computer company. It ordered a batch of components from a Japanese manufacturer and specified that the batch should have an acceptable quality level (AQL) of three defective parts per thousand. When the parts arrived in Ontario they were accompanied by a letter which expressed the supplier's bewilderment at being asked to supply defective parts as well as good ones. The letter

also explained that they had found it difficult to make parts which were defective, but had indeed managed it. These three defective parts per thousand had been included and were wrapped separately for the convenience of the customer.

Question

How does this short story illustrate the essence of TQM?

Figure 20.5 **(a) The traditional cost of quality model, and (b) the traditional cost of quality model with adjustments to reflect TQM criticisms**

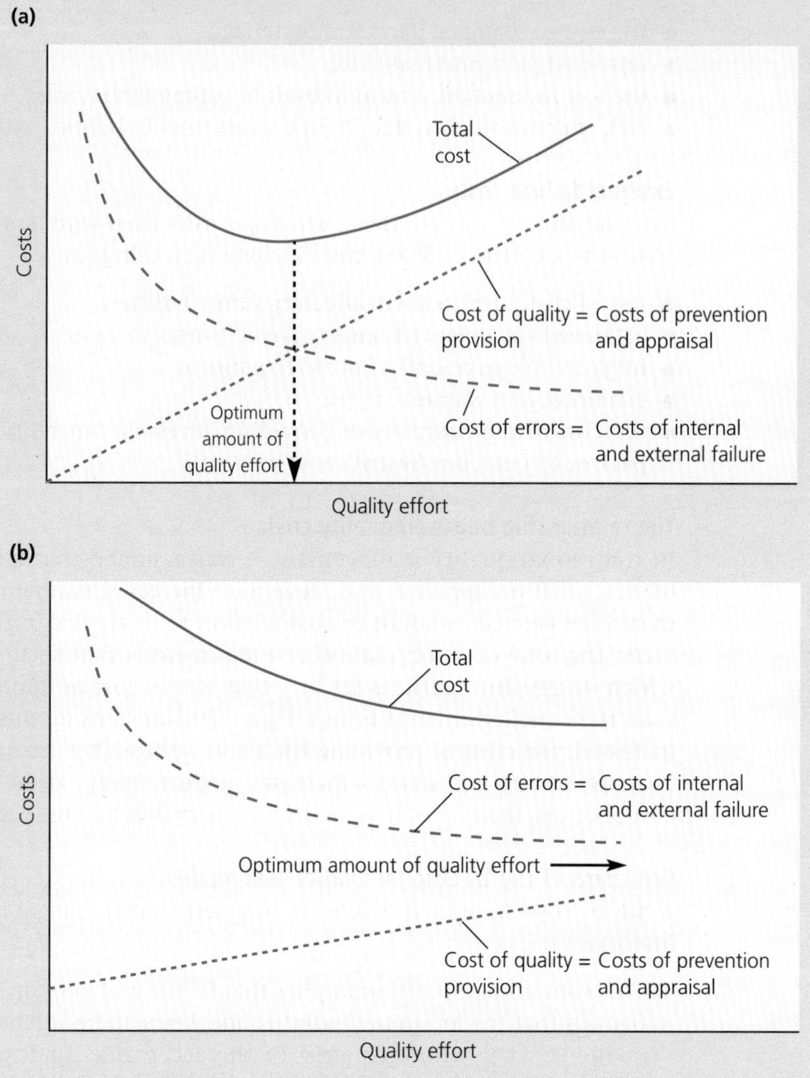
(a)
Total cost
Costs
Cost of quality = Costs of prevention provision and appraisal
Optimum amount of quality effort
Cost of errors = Costs of internal and external failure
Quality effort
(b)
Total cost
Costs
Cost of errors = Costs of internal and external failure
Optimum amount of quality effort
Cost of quality = Costs of prevention provision and appraisal
Quality effort

outlined in Chapter 17. Why, it is argued, should any operation accept the *inevitability* of errors? Some occupations seem to be able to accept a zero-defect standard (even if they do not always achieve it). No one accepts that it is inevitable that pilots will crash a certain proportion of their aircraft, or that nurses will drop a certain proportion of the babies they deliver.

2 It assumes that the costs are known and measurable. Obtaining precise costs of quality is not straightforward, however. Putting realistic figures to the quality cost categories of prevention, appraisal and failure is not a straightforward matter. One study exposes a number of difficulties, including the following:[15]
   - It is not easy to separate quality-related costs from those which are an integral part of the manufacturing operation anyway.
   - The categorization of costs into prevention, appraisal and failure is more meaningful to quality managers than operations managers.
   - Costs of activities which are part-time activities of indirect staff are particularly difficult to derive.

- Accounting systems are not designed to yield quality-related costs and different accounting practices can distort the results in different ways.
- The significance of warranty costs is difficult to gauge because they relate to earlier manufacture.

3 Failure costs in the traditional model are greatly underestimated. In practice, the failure cost is usually taken to include the cost of 'reworking' defective products, 're-serving' customers, the cost of scrapping parts and materials, and the loss of goodwill or even warranty costs if the defective part gets out to the customer. All these are important, but one of the most important costs is that associated with the disruption caused by errors. The real cost of not having quality should include all the management time wasted in organizing rework and rectification. Even more important, it should take into account the loss of concentration and the erosion of confidence between parts of the operation. If we include these, even though they are difficult costs to measure, it becomes clear that error costs can be considerably higher than traditionally thought.

4 It implies that prevention costs, the costs of getting towards zero defects, are inevitably high. The TQM approach, by stressing the importance of quality to every individual, makes quality an integral part of everyone's work. The traditional assumption is that more quality is achieved primarily by using more inspectors. For example, it is assumed that doubling the effort put into quality means, if not doubling the resources devoted to it, certainly a considerable increase in costs. This need not necessarily be so, however. At the very heart of TQM is the idea that each of us has a responsibility for his or her own quality and is capable of 'doing it right'. This may incur some costs – training, gauges, anything which helps to prevent errors occurring in the first place – but not such a steeply inclined cost curve as the 'optimum-quality' theory.

5 The 'optimum-quality level' approach, by accepting compromise, does little to challenge operations managers and staff to find ways of improving quality.

Put these corrections into the optimum-quality effort calculation and the picture looks very different (*see* Fig. 20.5b). If there is an 'optimum', it is a lot further to the right, in the direction of putting more effort (but not necessarily cost) into quality. We used a similar argument to this when describing the 'optimum' degree of preventive maintenance in Chapter 19.

Photo courtesy of Coates Thread

The costs of not 'getting it right first time' can be very large. In this laboratory process any mistakes can scrap whole batches of product

The TQM quality cost model

TQM rejects the optimum-quality level concept and strives to reduce all known and unknown failure costs by preventing errors and failure taking place. Rather than looking for 'optimum' levels of quality effort, it is more usual for TQM proponents to stress the relative balance between different types of quality cost. Of the four cost categories, two – costs of prevention and costs of appraisal – are open to managerial influence, while the other two – internal costs of failure and external costs of failure – show the consequences of changes in the first two. Of the two categories open to direct managerial influence, rather than placing most emphasis on appraisal (so that 'bad products and service don't get through to the customer') TQM emphasizes prevention (to stop errors happening in the first place).

What seems to happen is that when more effort is put into defect prevention, it has a significant, positive effect on internal failure costs, followed by reductions both in external failure costs and, once confidence has been firmly established, in appraisal costs. Eventually even prevention costs can be stepped down in absolute terms, though prevention remains a significant cost in relative terms. Figure 20.6 illustrates this idea. Initially total quality costs may rise as investment in some aspects of prevention – mainly training – is increased. However, some reduction in total costs can quickly follow.

Getting things 'right first time'

Accepting the relationships between categories of quality cost as illustrated in Figure 20.6 has a particularly important implication for how quality is managed. It shifts the emphasis from *reactive* (waiting for something to happen) to *proactive* (doing something before anything happens). This change in the view of quality costs has come about with a movement from an inspect-in (appraisal-driven) approach to a design-in (getting it right first time) approach.

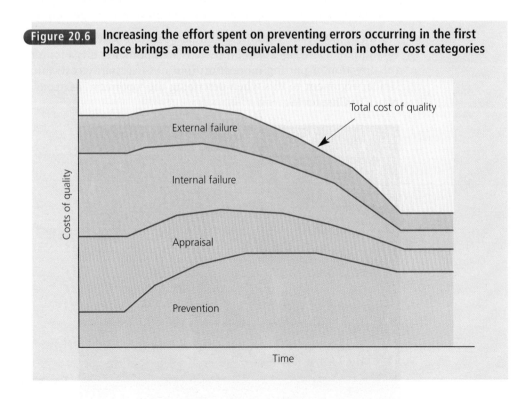

Figure 20.6 Increasing the effort spent on preventing errors occurring in the first place brings a more than equivalent reduction in other cost categories

Quality systems and procedures

Improving quality is not something that happens simply by getting everyone in an organization to 'think quality'. Very often people are prevented from making improvements by the organization's systems and procedures. Indeed, there is a belief that direct operators can only correct, at the moment, 15 per cent of quality problems; the other 85 per cent are management's responsibility because they are due to 'the system' or the lack of one.

A quality system is defined as:

the organizational structure, responsibilities, procedures, processes and resources for implementing quality management.[16]

According to Professor Barrie Dale of the University of Manchester Institute of Science and Technology:

The quality system should define and cover all facets of an organization's operation, from identifying and meeting the needs and requirements of customers, design, planning, purchasing, manufacturing, packaging, storage, delivery and service, together with all relevant activities carried out within these functions. It deals with organization, responsibilities, procedures and processes. Put simply, a quality system is good management practice.[17]

The documentation which is used in a quality system can be defined at three levels:

Level 1 *Company quality manual.* This is the fundamental document and provides a concise summary of the quality management policy and quality system along with the company objectives and its organization.

Level 2 *Procedures manual.* Describes the system functions, structure and responsibilities in each department.

Level 3 *Work instructions, specifications and detailed methods for performing work activities.*

There can also be a database (level 4) which contains all other reference documents (forms, standards, drawings, reference information, etc.).

The ISO 9000 quality system

The ISO 9000 series is a set of worldwide standards that establishes requirements for companies' quality management systems. ISO 9000 is being used worldwide to provide a framework for quality assurance. Most countries have their own quality system standards which are equivalent (usually identical) to the ISO 9000 series. Australia has AS3900, Belgium NBN X50, Denmark DS/EN 29000, Malaysia MS985, Netherlands NEN-9000, South Africa SABS 0157, Sweden SS-ISO 9000, the UK BS5750, and Germany DIN ISO 9000. By 2000, ISO 9000 had been adopted by more than a quarter of a million organizations in 143 countries

ISO 9000 registration requires a third-party assessment of a company's quality standards and procedures and regular audits are made to ensure that the systems do not deteriorate.

The ISO series provides detailed recommendations for setting up quality systems:

ISO 9000 Deals with ... 'quality management and quality assurance standards and guidelines for selection and use'.

ISO 9001 Deals with ... 'quality systems model for quality assurance in design/development, production, installation and servicing'.

ISO 9002 Deals with ... 'quality systems model for quality assurance in production and installation'.

ISO 9003 Deals with ... 'quality systems model for quality assurance in final inspection and test'.

ISO 9004 Deals with ... 'quality management and quality system elements: guidelines'.

The purpose of ISO 9000 is to provide an assurance to the purchasers of products or services that they have been produced in such a way that they meet their requirements. The best way to do this, it is argued, is to define the procedures, standards and characteristics of the management control system which governs the operation. Such a system will then help to ensure that quality is 'built into' the operation's transformation processes. This is why ISO 9000 is seen as providing benefits both to the organizations adopting it (because it gives them detailed guidance on how to design their control procedures) and especially to customers (who have the assurance of knowing that the products and services they purchase are produced by an operation working to a defined standard). The following are just some of the advantages associated with ISO 9000:

- Many operations do find that it provides a useful discipline to stick to 'sensible' procedures.
- Many operations have benefited in terms of error reduction, reduced customer complaints and reduced costs of quality.
- The ISO 9000 audit (when an organization is inspected to see if it warrants the award of the ISO, or local country, accreditation) is generally accepted and takes the place of other audits such as customer audits.
- Adopting ISO 9000 procedures can identify existing procedures which are not necessary and can be eliminated.
- Gaining the certificate demonstrates to actual and potential customers that the company takes quality seriously; it therefore has a marketing benefit.

● CRITICAL COMMENTARY

Notwithstanding its widespread adoption, ISO 9000 is not seen as beneficial by all authorities, and has been subject to some specific criticisms. These include the following:

- The emphasis on standards and procedures encourages 'management by manual' and over-systematized decision-making.

- Choosing which of the various ISO 9000 series of standards to apply for is not always easy.

- The standards are too geared to the engineering industries and some of the terms used are unfamiliar in other industries.

- The whole process of writing procedures, training staff and conducting internal audits is expensive and time-consuming.

- Similarly, the time and cost of achieving and maintaining ISO 9000 registration are excessive.

- There is little encouragement or guidance in ISO 9000 on such important issues as continuous improvement and statistical quality control.

ISO 9000 Unichema Chemie BV[18]

The original motive for companies to gain ISO 9000 certification is often pressure from customers. This was certainly one of the reasons at Unichema Chemie BV, the Netherlands chemical company. Yet once gained, it found that there were many other benefits apart from the effect it had on its customers' perceptions of the company.

For example, the company had been puzzled by the number of complaints which it received about delivery delays and errors. These always seemed to be higher in the summer, especially in July and August. This being the holiday season, the overall level of business was lower and so complaints should also have been lower. It found that the reason was that many of Unichema's staff, who were taking their holidays in the summer, were also taking their knowledge of the operation with them. The staff who were covering for them back at the plant, although they were competent at the fundamentals of the job, did not know how to cope with anything out of the ordinary. Once the company's procedures were fully documented and put down on paper (a requirement of ISO certification), people standing in for others had a far better set of guidelines which would help them cope with unusual situations. They were not having continually to improvise. However, the company is aware of some of the dangers of being too procedures-driven.

'Procedures are a support, they are not sacred,' says Mr Jan Löwik, the General Manager of Unichema, 'The whole thing about certification is that you put on paper what you are doing and then do what you put on paper. If a procedure doesn't work, however, do not, as we used to do, throw it in the corner and do it your own way. You modify the procedure instead by writing in how you think it should be done. The people who know best how to do it are my people in the plant. It is their system: they own it, they maintain it and they change it whenever they need to on a continuous basis. If you don't do that it becomes rigid; it becomes a strait-jacket. That is the big danger, and I see it happening in many companies. If the system is too rigid it becomes limiting and leads to bureaucratic behaviour. It should be dynamic.'

Questions

1 What did ISO 9000 do for the 'reserves of stored knowledge' at Unichema?

2 How does the company avoid too much bureaucracy in running ISO 9000?

Implementing TQM improvement programmes

Not all of the TQM initiatives which are launched by organizations, often with high expectations, will go on to fulfil their potential of having a major impact on performance improvement. *The Economist* magazine, reporting on some companies' disillusionment with their TQM experiences, quoted from several surveys.[19] For example:

'Of 500 US manufacturing and service companies, only a third felt their TQ programmes had significant impact on their competitiveness.'

'Only a fifth of the 100 British firms surveyed believed their quality programmes had achieved tangible results.'

'Of those quality programmes that have been in place for more than two years, two thirds simply grind to a halt because of their failure to produce hoped-for results.'

There are two broad types of failure which affect TQM implementation:

● the TQM initiative is not introduced and implemented effectively;
● after the TQM has been introduced successfully its effectiveness fades over time.

● TQM implementation

A number of factors appear to influence the eventual success of performance improvement programmes such as TQM. These are as follows.

A quality strategy

Without thinking through the overall purpose and long-term goals of a TQM programme it is difficult for any organization to know where it is going. A quality strategy is necessary to provide the goals and guidelines which help to keep the TQM programme heading in a direction which is appropriate for the organization's other strategic aims. Specifically, the quality strategy should have something to say about:

- the competitive priorities of the organization, and how the TQM programme is expected to contribute to achieving increased competitiveness;
- the roles and responsibilities of the various parts of the organization in the quality improvement;
- the resources which will be available for quality improvement;
- the general approach to, and philosophy of, quality improvement in the organization.

Top-management support

The full understanding, support and leadership of an organization's top management emerge as crucial factors in almost all the studies of TQM implementation. Table 20.2 shows one such study.

The importance of top-management support goes far beyond the allocation of resources to the programme; it sets the priorities for the whole organization. If the organization's senior managers do not understand and show commitment to the programme, it is only understandable that others will ask why they should do so. By 'top-management support', TQM proponents usually mean that senior personnel must:

- understand and believe in the link between 'doing things right' and the company's overall business;
- understand the practicalities of quality and be able to get over the principles and techniques (for example, statistical process control) to the rest of the organization;
- be able to participate in the total problem-solving process to eliminate errors;
- formulate and maintain a clear idea of what quality means for the organization.

A steering group

The task of a steering group is to plan the implementation of the programme. It could be argued that it also has a second task: that is, to make sure that, even if it does not work itself totally out of a job, its role diminishes over time. The first of these tasks involves planning the overall direction of the programme in terms of what it should achieve as it gathers pace. It also involves deciding where to start the programme and who initially to involve. Further, the group is responsible for monitoring the programme and making sure that all the learning and experience, accumulated as the programme progresses, are not lost. The second task is achieved, at least partly, by establishing self-supporting improvement groups.

Group-based improvement

No one can really know a process quite like the people who operate it. The staff who work in the operation are often the ones who know best, for example, how to stop the machines malfunctioning, or who can predict that most adjustments will be needed

Table 20.2 Quality barriers ranked in order of 'very significant' replies[20]

Top-management commitment	92%
Too narrow an understanding of quality	38%
Horizontal boundaries: functions and specialisms	31%
Vested interests	29%
Organizational politics	28%
Cynicism	28%
Organizational structure	27%
Customer expectations	26%
Speed of corporate action	24%

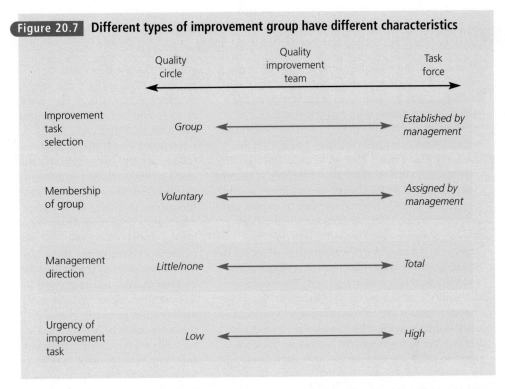

Figure 20.7 Different types of improvement group have different characteristics

after a product change. People inside the system have access to the informal as well as the formal information networks. However, working as individuals, staff cannot pool their experience or learn from one another. This is why successful TQM programmes are almost always based on teams.

The nature and composition of the team will depend on the circumstances. *Quality circles* are much used in Japan but have encountered mixed success in the West. A very different type of team is the '*task force*', or what some US companies call a 'tiger team'. Compared with quality circles, this type of group is far more management directed and focused. Most quality improvement teams are between these two extremes (*see* Fig. 20.7).

Success is recognized

Any TQM implementation needs to consider how it should respond to the efforts of the improvement teams. If quality improvement is so important, then success should be marked in some way. Recognizing success formally stresses the importance of the quality improvement process as well as rewarding effort and initiative. Participating in the development process itself (a part of their job which most managers take for granted) is also sometimes seen as rewarding by many in the organization. For example, a company making lighting products in Europe has several manufacturing sites. At one site an improvement team had developed a new cell layout with in-process gauging devices and quality charting methods. The company's management had decided to launch a similar series of quality improvement initiatives at one of its other sites. The improvement group of seven operatives together with their supervisor, production management and quality supervisor were asked to give a presentation at the other site. To quote one of the operators:

> We had a rehearsal a few days before we went and we were all nervous – remember we aren't used to doing this kind of thing. But we took photographs of the cell and generally got our act together before the visit. The presentation took place in the works canteen, and I think that we were all daunted by the sea of faces, but it seemed to go well. When they started asking us questions, it was surprising how interested they were in our answers; no one has taken that much notice of me before! At the end they all applauded! That was the best reward of all.

Unipart Industries implements a recovery[21]

At one time, the manufacturing division of Unipart, which makes such products as exhaust systems and fuel tanks, was by far the worst performer in the group. Its reputation with customers was one of poor quality, unreliable delivery and uncompetitive prices. When its largest customer, Rover, told the company that it had 13 weeks to improve its quality or it would switch to alternative suppliers, it became clear that rapid and sustained improvement would be needed. Initially, Unipart decided to inspect-out defective components, saturating the shop floor with an army of inspectors. Although quality improved, the cost of this was unsustainable; yet this action did make it clear both within the company and outside that it meant business. The company then quickly moved on to more fundamental changes. Process layout was reorganized onto a cell basis; multi-skilled flexible teams were introduced; the number of management layers was cut from seven to three; performance results were displayed to all staff; and a type of quality circle known as a 'contribution circle' was introduced.

Not all of these changes were well received, however. The company had sent a group of operators to Japan for six weeks to learn how to operate some new machinery prior to the same equipment being installed in its Oxford factory. The team discovered that the Japanese had a completely different approach to their work. They stressed quality and waste reduction. When they returned, the team were enthusiastic. An unexpected chain of events then began to unfold. The operators who had been sent to Japan by the company were ostracized by the rest of the workforce and accused of being 'management lackeys'. Feelings ran so high that some even had their tyres slashed in the car park.

When the new plant was installed in a dedicated section of the factory and operated by the Japanese-trained team, Unipart's management were surprised to find that the quality and productivity were not as good as that which had been achieved in Japan. Alarmed by these unexpected developments, management were prepared to 'get in there and sort it out'. The operators complained, however, that they were being 'checked up on' and not trusted. As for the adverse treatment from their colleagues, they would resolve that themselves. The managers then made the difficult decision not to get involved. They pulled out all inspection staff and supervisors and left the new plant solely in the hands of its operators. The production rate and quality started to improve and the fears of the rest of the workforce began to be seen as unfounded.

The members of the new section were not paid on their output, but received a salary for the job. Nor did they appear to have to work excessively hard or have to 'clock' in or out. There were no company songs or pre-shift exercises; in fact they seemed very happy with their work and, if anything, management seemed to leave them alone to get on with the job. After a while, other workers began to see some of the advantages of the new approach and attitudes began to move in favour of the new ways.

Eventually, the company introduced single status for all employees, the end of clocking in and out, team working, and salaries linked to individual performances. Far more controversially, the company also announced that it would no longer recognize trade unions as representing its 4000 workers.

Questions

1 Why did Unipart initially use inspecting as a method of improving quality? Isn't this directly opposed to the idea of TQM?

2 What do you think was the thinking behind the way Unipart implemented its new processes and system?

Training is the heart of quality improvement

It is no coincidence that so many successful programmes have a training manager as one of their prime movers. TQM is, partly at least, an attitudinal change, so the development task is fundamental to it. There are techniques for staff to learn as well, of course, but the purpose of the techniques is solely to work towards the basic objective – the elimination of errors.

● TQM loses its effectiveness

Even TQM programmes which are successfully implemented are not necessarily guaranteed to continue to bring long-term improvement. They may lose their impetus over time. This phenomenon has been variously described as *quality disillusionment*[22] and *quality droop*.[23] Figure 20.8 illustrates this loss of effectiveness.

Various researchers and consultants who have experienced quality disillusionment have put forward prescriptions which are intended to reduce the risk of it occurring. Typically, these prescriptions include the following:[24]

- Do not define 'quality' in TQM narrowly; it includes all aspects of performance (what we have called the performance objectives of operations management).
- Make all quality improvement relate to the performance objectives of the operation. TQM is not an end in itself; it is a means of improving performance.
- TQM is not a substitute for the responsibilities of normal managerial leadership. Ineffective managers are not made better simply by adopting TQM.
- TQM is not a 'bolt-on' attachment to the company – an activity which is separate from the other activities of the organization. It should be integrated with and indistinguishable from everyday activities.
- Avoid the hype. TQM has a considerable intuitive attraction for many. It is sometimes tempting to exploit the motivational 'pull' of TQM through slogans and exhortations rather than thoroughly thought-out plans.
- Adapt TQM to the circumstances of the organization. Different organizations will have different needs depending on their circumstances. This means that different aspects of TQM might become more or less important.

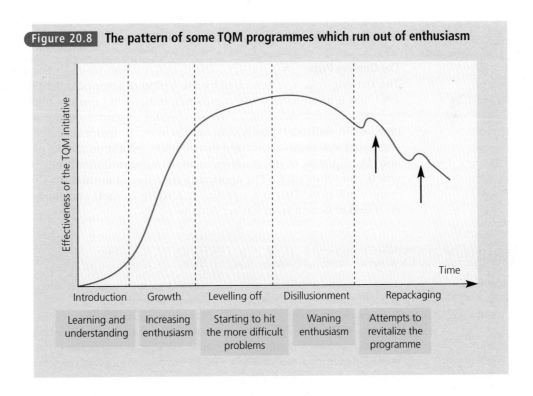

Figure 20.8 **The pattern of some TQM programmes which run out of enthusiasm**

Some companies and academics see far more fundamental flaws in the TQM philosophy than are implied by the list of implementation issues described above. The first set of criticisms is centred on the 'quality bureaucracy' which many firms find they need to manage a large-scale TQM initiative. Some companies who were in the vanguard of the TQM movement, such as Hewlett-Packard, admit that at one time they pushed quality for its own sake, and have shifted too much responsibility down to the shop floor. The second criticism is that TQM is incompatible with more radical improvement approaches such as business process re-engineering (BPR, *see* Chapter 18). Note that one of Deming's original 14 points (*see* the beginning of the chapter) concerned 'driving out fear'. In other words, staff security is important to the acceptance of change. Yet radical BPR is often accompanied by equally radical 'downsizing' of the organization. It is difficult to reconcile such job losses with the job security necessary for true TQM. The third criticism is that TQM, notwithstanding its implications of empowerment and liberal attitude toward shop-floor staff, is merely a further example of management exploiting workers. By its critics, TQM has been defined as 'management by stress'. Or, even more radically, 'TQM is like putting a vacuum cleaner next to a worker's brain and sucking out ideas. They don't want to rent your knowledge anymore, they want to own it – in the end that makes you totally replaceable.'

Quality awards

TQM has been recognized as an important integrator of many aspects of operations improvement, to the extent that various bodies have sought to stimulate quality improvement through establishing quality awards. The three best-known awards are The Deming Prize, The Malcolm Baldrige National Quality Award and the European Quality Award.

The Deming Prize

The Deming Prize was instituted by the Union of Japanese Scientists and Engineers in 1951 and is awarded to those companies, initially in Japan, but more recently opened to overseas companies, which have successfully applied 'company-wide quality control' based upon statistical quality control. There are 10 major assessment categories: policy and objectives, organization and its operation, education and its extension, assembling and disseminating of information, analysis, standardization, control, quality assurance, effects and future plans. The applicants are required to submit a detailed description of quality practices. This is a significant activity in itself and some companies claim a great deal of benefit from having done so.

Ulster carpets using the EFQM Excellence Model

Ulster Carpet Mills Limited, finalist for the European Quality Award, has doubled its share of the quality carpet sector in recent years and now holds over 10 per cent of the world market for its products. By encouraging continuous improvement through self-assessment against the EFQM Excellence Model, EQA has created the necessary drive for customer focus. The company's total quality process has graduated from 'total customer satisfaction' to 'total customer delight', to its present form – 'bridging the gap', which is effectively a 'where we are' and 'where we should be'

yardstick for the company. Developments in the warehouse are typical. The role of the manager/supervisor has been replaced by the nomination of a group leader who acts in a 'leading role', working within the team. The picture opposite shows a group leader with her team, each of whom is trained to carry out his/her main job plus five others on a rotating work rota. Fixed hours are a thing of the past, as is overtime. At peak times, such as the run-up to Christmas, the team works the required hours (be it until 10 pm at night) to dispatch orders, and at off-

Photo courtesy of Ulster Carpets

A group leader briefs her team as part of the quality process

peak times, when work is completed to the satisfaction of the group leader, the team can leave. New technology now means that dispatch labels and address labels are computer-generated and the carpets are bar-coded which reduces the possibility of human error. Each process within the warehouse has been analysed and re-engineered to answer the question, 'Do the processes meet the needs?' The company sees the use of the EFQM Excellence Model as a means of evaluation, as well as raising internal awareness of the measures necessary to meet external needs.

'The warehouse is illustrative of what is currently happening within each department of Ulster Carpet Mills. It is the EFQM Excellence Model which provides the framework to assess the "enablers" and "results" with fresh eyes, and to identify the challenges of the way forward in relation to our customer,' says Daniel McLarnon, head of quality.

Photo courtesy of Ulster Carpets

Loading carpet looms at Ulster Carpets

Questions

1 What is implied by the progression of the company's three initiatives from 'total customer satisfaction' to 'total customer delight' to 'bridging the gap'?

2 What 'enablers' are mentioned in this example, and how might they affect 'results'?

The Malcolm Baldrige National Quality Award

In the early 1980s the American Productivity and Quality Center recommended that an annual prize, similar to the Deming Prize, should be awarded in America. The award was named after the Secretary of Commerce, Malcolm Baldrige, who was killed in an accident shortly before the legislation for the award became law in 1987.

The purpose of the awards was to stimulate American companies to improve quality and productivity, to recognize achievements, to establish criteria for a wider quality effort and to provide guidance on quality improvement. The main examination categories are: leadership, information and analysis, strategic quality planning, human resource utilization, quality assurance of products and services, quality results and customer satisfaction. The process, like that of the Deming Prize, includes a detailed application and site visits.

The EFQM Excellence Model

In 1988, 14 leading Western European companies formed the European Foundation for Quality Management (EFQM). By July 1993 there were more than 300 members from most Western European countries and most business sectors. An important objective of the EFQM is to recognize quality achievement. Because of this, in 1992, it launched the European Quality Award (EQA), awarded to the most successful exponent of total quality management in Western Europe each year. European quality prizes are awarded to a number of companies that demonstrate excellence in the management of quality as their fundamental process for continuous improvement. To receive a prize, companies must demonstrate that their approach to total quality management has contributed significantly to satisfying the expectations of customers, employees and others with an interest in the company for the past few years.

In 1999, the model on which the European Quality Award was based was modified and renamed 'The EFQM Excellence Model'. The changes made were not fundamental but did attempt to reflect some new areas of management and quality thinking (for example, partnerships and innovation) and placed more emphasis on customer and market focus.

The EFQM Excellence Model is based on the idea that the outcomes of quality management in terms of what it calls 'people results', 'customer results', 'society results' and 'key performance results' are achieved through a number of 'enablers'. These enablers are leadership and constancy of purpose, policy and strategy, how the organization develops its people, partnerships and resources, and the way it organizes its processes. These ideas are incorporated in the EFQM Excellence Model as shown in Figure 20.9. The five enablers are concerned with how results are being achieved, while the four 'results' are concerned with what the company has achieved and is achieving.

The nine elements of the model are defined by the EFQM as follows:

- *Leadership* – how leaders develop and facilitate the achievement of the mission and vision, develop values required for long-term success and implement these through appropriate actions and behaviour, and are personally involved in ensuring that the organization's management system is developed and implemented.
- *Policy and strategy* – how the organization implements its mission and vision through a clear stakeholder-focused strategy, supported by relevant policies, plans, objectives, targets and processes.
- *People* – how the organization manages, develops and releases the knowledge and full potential of its people at an individual team and organization level, and how it plans these activities in order to support its policy and strategy and the effective operation of its processes.
- *Partnerships and resources* – how the organization plans and manages its external partnerships and internal resources in order to support its policy and strategy and the effective operation of its processes.

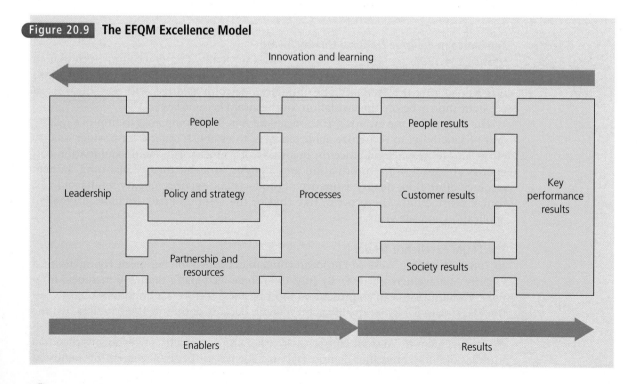

Figure 20.9 **The EFQM Excellence Model**

- *Processes* – how the organization designs, manages and improves its processes in order to support its policy and strategy and fully satisfy, and generate increasing value for, its customers and other stakeholders.
- *Customer results* – this includes customers' loyalty and their perceptions of the organization's image, product and services, sales and after-sales support.
- *People results* – this covers employees' motivation, satisfaction, performance and the services the organization provides for its people.
- *Society results* – this relates to the organization's performance as a responsible citizen, its involvement in the community in which it operates, and any recognition it might have received.
- *Key performance results* – this shows the financial and non-financial outcomes of the organization's planned performance, including such things as cash flow, profit, meeting budgets, success rates and the value of intellectual property.

Self-assessment

Increasingly, the frameworks behind awards such as the EQA are being used by operations for self-assessment purposes. The European Foundation for Quality Management (EFQM) defines self-assessment as *'a comprehensive, systematic, and regular review of an organization's activities and results referenced against a model of business excellence'*, in its case the model shown in Figure 20.9. The main advantage of using such models for self-assessment seems to be that companies find it easier to understand some of the more philosophical concepts of TQM when they are translated into specific areas, questions and percentages. Self-assessment also allows organizations to measure their progress in changing their organization and in achieving the benefits of TQM.

An important aspect of self-assessment is an organization's ability to judge the relative importance of the assessment categories to its own circumstances. So, for example, the EFQM Excellence Model originally placed emphasis on a generic set of weighting for each of its nine catagories. With the increasing importance of self-assessment, the EFQM moved to encourage organizations using its model to allocate their own weightings in a rational and systematic manner.

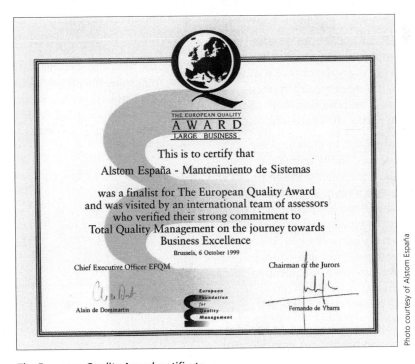

Photo courtesy of Alstom España

The European Quality Award certificate

Where did the idea of total quality management (TQM) come from?

● Although the origins of TQM go back to the 1940s and '50s, the term was first formally used in 1957 by Feigenbaum. Many authorities have contributed to the development of the idea, however. These authorities include Feigenbaum, Deming, Juran, Ishikawa, Taguchi and Crosby.

● The emphasis placed on various aspects of TQM varies among these authorities but the general thrust of their arguments is similar.

● TQM can be seen as being an extension of the traditional approach to quality – inspection-based quality control being replaced by the concept of quality assurance which in turn has been superseded by TQM.

What are the main differences between traditional quality management and TQM?

● TQM puts customers at the forefront of quality decision-making. Customers' needs and expectations are always considered first in measuring achieved quality.

● TQM takes an organization-wide perspective. It holds that all parts of the organization have the potential to make a positive contribution to quality. Central to this idea is the concept of the internal customer–supplier chain.

● TQM places considerable emphasis on the role and responsibilities of every member of staff within an organization to influence quality. It often encourages the idea of empowering individuals to improve their own part of the operation.

● The implied cost models of TQM are very different from those used in the traditional approach to quality. Traditionally, the emphasis was placed on finding an optimum amount of quality effort which minimized the costs associated with quality. By contrast, TQM emphasizes the balance between different types of quality cost. It argues that increasing the expenditure and effort on prevention will give a more-than-equivalent reduction in other costs. This idea is often summarized in the phrase 'right first time'.

● TQM also places a heavy emphasis on the ideas of problem-solving and continuous improvement dealt with in Chapter 18.

What is the role of ISO 9000 in TQM?

● ISO 9000 and associated standards are concerned with the systems and procedures which support quality. These are intended to assure purchasers of products and services that they have been produced in a way which meets customer requirements.

● ISO 9000 has received some criticism as being over-bureaucratic and inflexible.

What are the main implementation issues in TQM initiatives?

● A number of factors appear to be influential in ensuring the success of TQM. These are:
  – the existence of a fully worked-out quality strategy;
  – top-management's support;
  – a steering group to guide the initiative;
  – group-based improvements;
  – an adequate recognition and rewards scheme;
  – an emphasis on appropriate training.

How do quality awards and models contribute towards TQM?

● By providing a focused structure for organizations to assess their own quality management and improvement efforts.

● A number of organizations have attempted to encourage TQM by the awarding of prizes and certificates. The best known of these are the Deming Prize, the Malcolm Baldrige National Quality Award and, in Europe, the EFQM Excellence Model. This is based on a nine-point model which distinguishes between the 'enablers' of quality and the 'results' of quality. It is often now used as a self-certification model.

The Waterlander Hotel[25]

The previous evening's banquet for Plastix International had been a complete disaster, and Walter Hollestelle, the hotel General Manager, was still recovering from the series of telephone conversations of that morning.

First with the Vice-President of Global Marketing, Plastix International Plc:

'I had hoped that by having our annual sales conference at your renowned hotel in Amsterdam, we would be treated to an even better level of service than last year, when we were at Rotterdam; but we were to be deeply disappointed. After all the problems you have caused us over the last two days, from faulty video projection to shortages of cups at coffee breaks, I had hoped that at least the final conference dinner would run smoothly, but you let us down badly. The cocktail reception was a farce: the choice of non-alcoholic drinks that we specially ordered didn't appear until the last minute, and as the President's wife is teetotal, you can imagine the embarrassment that caused! A spilt tray of snacks was not cleared up quickly and several guests got food all over their shoes and dresses. And why did the reception drag on for so long?

'When we were finally asked into the dining room, it clearly wasn't properly prepared. Some of the tables (including ours) were without flowers, which upset my wife, who had been involved with the selection of arrangements. Even the flowers that were there were the wrong variety and looked as if they had been on the tables since yesterday.

'The meal was the worst I have ever seen! I never expect banquet food to be as good as à la carte, but this was awful! The starter was dried up and chewy, and the sweet soufflés were flat and rubbery. And we couldn't believe that anyone could mess up a simple entrée. We were served the cutlets and potatoes, but the sauce and vegetables didn't appear until I'd nearly finished mine.

'And what happened to the microphones on the top table? The photographer didn't turn up either, which is perhaps a blessing, as the tables weren't cleared completely after the sweet, and I'm sure that everyone would have looked in a bad mood after all the mess-up! I can tell you straight – we won't be paying all your exorbitant charges for this banquet and I expect a written apology for all the upset we have been caused. The President must think I am an idiot to have chosen this hotel, and I think he has a point ...'

Next, with the Manager of Aalsmeer Electronics:

'... I was told that the public address system had to be set up by 7.00 pm. We often do jobs of this type, and two hours is more than enough, so we allowed an extra half-hour and started at 4.30 pm. Your staff wouldn't let us get to the tables to wire them, and we had to wait until they cleared them off for us ...'

Then, with his own Hotel Services Manager:

'... it has always been agreed that we must wait until the cutlery has been laid before we set out the flowers, and yesterday we simply weren't given enough time to see to all the tables. As for the types of flowers, we were never told that the client wanted red and pink arrangements. I would have recommended other colours anyway, as reds would not look good against the dining room decor. Unfortunately, the electricians moved our arrangements out of the way against a heating outlet, so by the time we got to them, the flowers looked a bit beyond their best condition. I suppose that's what happens if you allow contractors to interfere with our operation.'

And, with the Conference Manager:

'We were never told that the client wanted to use the video equipment, which was scheduled for repairs next weekend. Had I known, we could have hired in another projector, but we never got the conference checklist back from the client. If we had got that, it would also have indicated that there were an extra 10 delegates here just for the morning to make some sort of presentation to the conference. These problems are all down to the client: if they don't follow our system, it's their fault if things go wrong.'

From the Head Chef:

'... I always get a detailed schedule from the head waiter. I get the fish, the sauces, the vegetables and the desserts ready according to that schedule – if things run as late as they did last night, you can expect a few problems. Cooking is an art. All the chefs know how to cook to perfection every time, but if we can't serve the food when it's ready, it will be messed up. I can tell you that if you think the customer was angry, you should have come into the kitchen. Some of the conference delegates were rude to the waiters, who came back into the kitchen and told the chefs. All the staff were really upset and Pierre, our sauce chef, refused to start on the cutlet sauce until the fish course was cleared.'

From the Head Waiter:

'... we weren't told that the electricians would have to wire the tables. They worked setting up the loudspeakers and amplifiers while we were setting the tablecloths and laying the place settings. Their foreman then told us that the tables would have to be cleared for them, so you can imagine the problems that caused. I think we did very well to put everything right in under half an hour.'

Finally, with the photographer:

'... we were booked for 10.00 pm and the Conference Manager told us that, according to the customer, we would only be needed for half an hour during the speeches. When we arrived they were still in the middle of the meal, and so I waited a bit, but we had another booking at the Concert Hall at the end of a performance at 11.00 pm, so I had to rush off. If we'd known earlier I could have arranged for a partner to come along ...'

Questions

1 Why did things go wrong at the banquet?

2 How could a TQM approach to the hotel's operations help to prevent such disasters occurring in the future?

3 How could ISO 9000 help the hotel?

Discussion questions

1 Find out more about one of the 'quality gurus'. Describe his background, his approach to quality and his key contributions to the subject.

2 Talk to an operations manager about TQM. Try to assess what TQM means for that organization and the benefits and problems that have resulted.

3 Identify some of the micro operations that might be found in a high-class restaurant operation. Describe some of the things that might go wrong in each of them and assess the impact of them on the final, external customer.

4 A university is considering creating service-level agreements for its lecturing staff. Explain what is meant by a service-level agreement and suggest some performance measures that might be used.

5 What resistance might there be in an organization to Matsushito's assertion that 'the core of management is precisely the art of mobilizing and pulling together the intellectual resources of all employees in the service of the firm'?

6 Identify the main costs of quality for the following organizations:
   – a university library
   – a washing-machine manufacturer
   – a nuclear electricity generating plant
   – a church.

7 Discuss the differences between the 'traditional' and the TQM views on the cost of quality.

8 Get hold of a copy of ISO 9000 or an equivalent and assess its potential impact on quality.

9 Ask an operations manager to describe how quality has been improved in the organization over the last few years. Compare and contrast your findings with the section in this chapter on TQM implementation.

10 Discuss the advantages and disadvantages for an organization considering applying to be assessed for a major quality award.

11 Why do you think that quality award procedures are now used predominantly as self-assessment vehicles?

12 The worldwide fast-food restaurant chain McDonalds has never actually used TQM as such. Yet their quality is renowned for being excellent throughout the world. How do you explain this?

Notes on chapter

1 Feigenbaum, A.V. (1986) *Total Quality Control*, McGraw-Hill.

2 Deming, W.E. (1982) *Quality, Productivity and Competitive Position*, MIT Center for Advanced Engineering Study.
Deming, W.E. (1986) *Out of Crisis*, MIT Center for Advanced Engineering Study.

3 Oakland, J.S. (1993) *Total Quality Management* (2nd edn), Butterworth-Heinemann.

4 Juran, J.M. (1989) *Juran on Leadership for Quality, and Executive Handbook*, The Free Press.
Juran, J.M. and Gryna, F.M. (1980) *Quality Planning and Analysis*, McGraw-Hill.
Juran, J.M., Gryna, F.M. and Bingham, R.S. (eds) (1988) *Quality Control Handbook* (4th edn), McGraw-Hill.

5 Ishikawa, K. (1972) *Guide to Quality Control*, Asian Productivity Organization.
Ishikawa, K. (1985) *What is Total Quality Control? – The Japanese Way*, Prentice Hall.

6 Taguchi, G. and Clausing, D. (1990) 'Robust Quality', *Harvard Business Review*, Vol 68, No 1, pp 65–75.

7 Crosby, P.B. (1979) *Quality is Free*, McGraw-Hill.

8 Crosby, P.B., *ibid*.

9 Based on the analysis by Flood, R.L. (1993) *Beyond TQM*, John Wiley.

10 Oakland, J.S. (1993) *op. cit.*

11 Muhlemann, A., Oakland, J. and Lockyer, K. (1992) *Production and Operations Management* (6th edn), Pitman Publishing.

12 Source: Rees, J. and Rigby, P. (1988) 'Total Quality Control – The Hewlett-Packard Way' *in* Chase, R.L. (ed) (1988) *Total Quality Management*, IFS.

13 Matsushito, K. (1985) 'Why the West will Lose', *Industrial Participation*, Spring.

14 Hyman, J. and Mason, B. (1995) *Management Employees Involvement and Participation*, Sage.

15 Source: Plunkett, J.J. and Dale, B.S. (1987) 'A Review of the Literature in Quality-Related Costs', *The International Journal of Quality and Reliability Management*, Vol 4, No 1.

16 International Standards Organization, *ISO 8402*, 1986.

17 Dale, B.G. (1994) 'Quality Management Systems' *in* Dale B.G. (ed) *Managing Quality*, Prentice Hall.

18 'Waging War on Waste' (1994) *European Quality*, Vol 1, No 2.

19 Quoted *in* Smith, S., Tranfield, D., Foster, M. and Whittle, S. (1994) 'Strategies for Managing the TQ Agenda', *International Journal of Operations and Production Management*, Vol 14, No 1.

20 Binney, G. (1992) 'Making Quality Work: Lessons from Europe's Leading Companies', The Economist Intelligence Unit, *Special Report*, No P655.

21 Mason, C. (1994) 'Unipart Industries', *Internal Warwick Business School Report*.

22 Oakland, J.S. (1993) *op. cit.*

23 Slack, N. (1991) *The Manufacturing Advantage*, Mercury Business Books.

24 Slack, N., *ibid*.

25 Based on an idea originally used by Professor Keith Lockyer.

Selected further reading

Albrecht, K. and Bradford, L.J. (1990) *The Service Advantage*, Dow Jones Irwin.

Armistead, C.G. (ed) (1994) *The Future of Services Management*, Kogan Page.

Berry, L.L. and Parasuraman, A. (1991) *Marketing Services: Competing Through Quality*, The Free Press.

Boaden, R.J., Dale, B.G. and Polding, E. (1991) 'A State-of-the-Art Survey of Total Quality Management in the Construction Industry', *A Research Report to the European Construction Institute*, Loughborough.

Bounds, G., Yorks, L., Adams, M. and Ranney, G. (1994) *Beyond Total Quality Management: Towards the Emerging Paradigm*, McGraw-Hill.

Brown, S.W., Gummesson, E., Edvardsson, B. and Gustavsson, B. (eds) (1991) *Service Quality: Multidisciplinary and Multinational Perspectives*, Lexington Books.

Crosby, P.B. (1979) *Quality is Free*, McGraw-Hill.

Crosby, P.B. (1996) *Quality is Still Free*, McGraw-Hill.

Dale, B.G. (1994) *Managing Quality* (2nd edn), Prentice Hall.

Dale, B.G. and van der Wiele, T. (1993) *Total Quality Management Directory*, The University Press, Rotterdam.

Deming, W.E. (1986) *Out of the Crisis*, MIT Press.

Feigenbaum, A.V. (1986) *Total Quality Control*, McGraw-Hill.

Garvin, D.A. (1998) *Managing Quality: The Strategic and Competitive Edge*, The Free Press.

Garvin, D.A. (1991) 'How the Baldridge Award Really Works', *Harvard Business Review*, Vol 69, No 6

Ghobadian, A. and Gallear, D. (1997) 'TQM and Organisation Size', *International Journal of Operations and Production Management*, Vol 17, No 2.

Godfrey, G., Dale, B., Marchington, M. and Wilkinson, A. (1997) 'Control: A Contested Concept in TQM Reasearch', *International Journal of Operations and Production Management*, Vol 17, No 6.

Harari, O. (1993) 'Ten Reasons Why TQM Doesn't Work', *Management Review*, Jan.

Hyman, J. and Mason, B. (1995) *Managing Employee Involvement and Participation*, Sage.

Jonker, J. (1999) 'The Future of Quality: Time for New Solutions', *European Quality*, Vol 6, No 4.

Kehoe, D.F. (1996) *The Fundamentals of Quality Management*, Chapman and Hall.

Kordupleski, R., Rust, R.T. and Zahorik, A.J. (1993) 'Why Improving Quality Doesn't Improve Quality', *Californian Management Review*, Vol 35, Spring.

Leonard-Barton, D. (1992) 'The Factory as a Learning Laboratory', *Sloan Management Review*, Vol 34, No 1.

McGoldrick, G. (1994) *The Complete Quality Manual: A Blueprint for Producing your own Quality Manual*, FT/Pitman Publishing.

Oakland, J.S.(1992) *Total Quality Management* (2nd edn), Heinemann.

Øvretveit, J. (1992) *Health Service Quality*, Blackwell.

Quaglia, G. (1999) 'Extending the Excellence Range', *European Quality*, Vol 6, No 2.

Schonberger, R.J. (1994) 'Human Resource Management Lessons from a Decade of TQM and Re-engineering', *California Management Review*, Summer.

Taguchi, G. (1986) *Introduction to Quality Engineering: Designing Quality into Products and Process*, Asian Productivity Organization.

Teboul, J. (1991) *Managing Quality Dynamics*, Prentice Hall.

Whitford, B. and Bird, R. (1996) *The Pursuit of Quality*, Prentice Hall.

Part Five

THE OPERATIONS CHALLENGE

The ultimate test for any operations manager is whether he or she can develop an operation which meets the challenges that lie ahead for the organization. This final part of the book identifies a number of key challenges which all operations managers will eventually face.

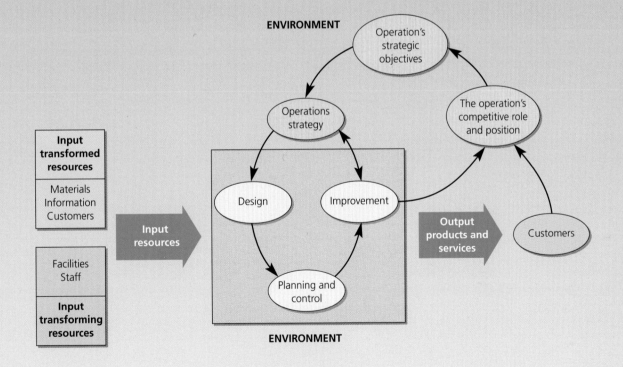

Chapter 21
The operations challenge

- What impact will globalization and an increasingly international perspective on business have on operations management?

- How does a wider view of social responsibility influence operations management?

- Why is it important for operations management to take their environmental responsibility seriously?

- What will new technologies mean for operations management?

- Does 'knowledge management' have a role in operations management?

The operations challenge

Introduction

In the preceding 20 chapters, we have outlined the nature, purpose and decisions of operations management. As a postscript we identify some of the challenges faced by all operations managers in their continuing attempts to cut through the complexity and uncertainty which characterizes most operations. Of course, this list of strategic 'challenges' could be very long, but we have identified five in particular for attention, all of which were introduced in Chapter 1:

- the impact of the *globalization* of markets, supply bases and (perhaps most important) the state-of-mind of operations managers;
- the changing view of the *social responsibility* which all types of business should show and the

role of operations managers in establishing ethical values;

- the *environmental responsibility* of businesses, especially the impact operations management decisions have on the environment and the impact environmental regulatory frameworks have on operations managers;
- the influence of increasingly rapid but difficult-to-predict *technology* developments on operations management;
- the emergence of the concept of *knowledge management* and the operations manager as a key custodian of process technology.

Figure 21.1 illustrates these issues.

Figure 21.1 Five challenges for operations managers

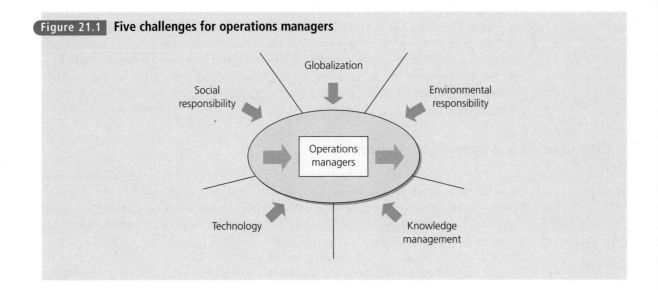

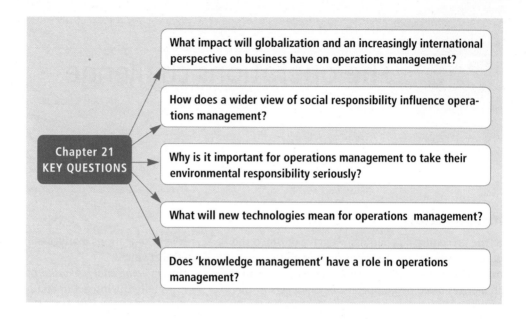

Globalization

The world is a smaller place to do business in. Even many medium-sized companies are sourcing and selling their products and services on a global basis. A well-designed website and an adventurous attitude can make even small companies into international players. Trade between widely dispersed parts of the world continues to grow, both in products and in services. Considerable opportunities have emerged for operations managers to develop both supplier and customer relationships in new parts of the world. All of which is exciting but it also poses many problems. Globalization of trade is considered by some to be the root cause of exploitation and corruption in many developing countries. Others see it as the only way of spreading the levels of prosperity enjoyed by developed countries throughout the world. What is clear is that it is an issue which cannot be ignored by the operations managers who produce products and services with, and for, increasingly global partners.

Globalization and operations decisions

Most of the decision areas we have covered in this book have an international dimension to them. Often this is simply because different parts of the world have different views on the nature of work, because of differences in culture. So, for example, highly repetitive work on an assembly line may be unpopular in parts of northern Europe, but it is welcome as a source of employment in other parts of the world. Does this mean that operations should be designed to accommodate the cultural reactions of people in different parts of the world? Probably. Does this mean that we are imposing lower standards on less wealthy parts of the world? Well, it depends on your point of view. The issue, however, is that cultural and economic differences do impact on the day-to-day activities of operations management decision-making. Some of these are included in Table 21.1.

Table 21.1 Some globalization considerations of operations management decisions

Decision area	Some globalization issues
Product/service design	Transferability of product/service design
	Adaptation of design to fit culture and legislation
Network design	Location of global network of facilities
	Ownership and capacity change legislation
Layout of facilities	Cultural reaction to work organization
Process technology	Serviceability and maintenance of technology
	Skills availability
Job design	Cost of labour
	Skills availability
	Cultural reaction to work requirements
Planning and control (including MRP, JIT and project planning and control)	Cultural reaction to necessity for planning
	Cultural reaction to need for flexibility
Capacity planning and control	Differences in seasonality and demand patterns
	Legislation part-time or temporary work contracts
	Legislation and cultural view of flexible working
Inventory planning and control	Storage conditions and climatic sensitivity
	Cost of capital and other storage cost differences
Supply chain planning and control	Real cost of transportation
	Differences in contractual arrangements
	Supplier conformance to employment standards
Quality planning and control and TQM	Cultural views of acceptable quality
	Cultural views of participation in improvement groups
	Safety
Failure prevention and recovery	Maintenance support
	Cultural attitude to risk
	Flexibility of response to failure

● The anti-globalization movement

Globalization and the international perspective on business are not just concerns for individual companies, but are also broader moral and political issues. Partly, the debate (and violence, *see* the picture) around globalization is connected to the changing status of the nation state and its retreat before the forces of globalization. What Mike Moore (Head of the World Trade Organization, WTO) calls the 2 Ts – technology and telecommunications – have helped to reduce the importance of barriers between nations. This has led, by necessity, to a broad move towards the reduction of protectionist barriers between countries and trading blocks, and a rise in trade liberalization. In turn, this has exposed a number of problems. For example, should trade liberalization be forced on nations, even if they disagree with the policies of those who wish to export to them? Should one trading block (Europe) be allowed to ban the sale of the food (beef) which another trading block (the USA) eats quite happily? Also, should the rate of liberalization of trade rules be reined in to take account of other factors – environmental protection, for example?

Thousands of anti-globalization protesters march down Sixth Avenue in downtown Seattle to disrupt the ministerial meeting of the World Trade Organization (WTO)

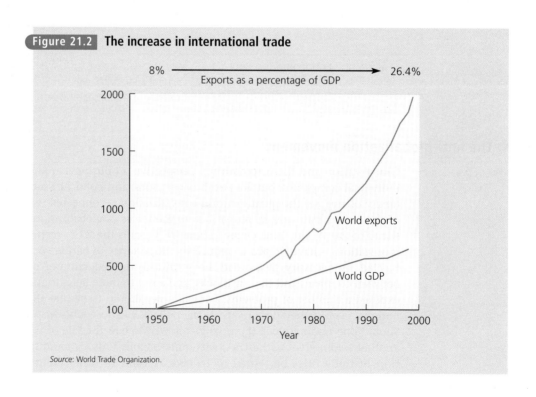

Figure 21.2   **The increase in international trade**

Source: World Trade Organization.

Certainly the world is more interdependent, as the world trade growth in Figure 21.2 shows. If all this seems at too high a level for a humble subject like operations management, revisit Table 21.1 and consider how many of these issues have an impact on day-to-day decision-making. If a company decides to import some of its components from a Third World country, where wages are substantially cheaper, is this a good or a bad thing? Local trade unions might oppose the 'export of jobs'. Shareholders would, presumably, like the higher profits. Environmentalists would want to ensure that natural resources were not harmed. Everyone with a social conscience would want to ensure that workers from a Third World country were not exploited (although one person's exploitation is another's very welcome employment opportunity). Such decisions are made every day by operations managers throughout the world.

● International location

Perhaps the longest-term operations management decision with a global impact is that of international location. The location decision has been discussed in general terms in Chapter 6 as part of the design of the overall network. Networks of operations can spread across several geographic regions. Large global companies such as Disney, with its theme parks, Mercedes-Benz, the vehicle manufacturer, or Kodak, the photographic materials company, have operations all over the world. However, not all organizations will choose to design their international networks to the same pattern. Different configurations of operations will be appropriate for different organizations. Four configuration strategies have been identified in the location behaviour of international companies:[1]

- *Home country configuration.* The simplest strategy for an organization trading around the world is not to locate plants outside its home country and to export its products to foreign markets. In effect, any organization adopting this strategy is avoiding the necessity of locating any part of the network over which it has direct control outside its own home country.
- *Regional configuration.* An alternative strategy is to divide the company's international markets into a small number of regions, for example, the European region, the Pacific region, the American region. Any company adopting this strategy might then try to make each region as self-contained as possible. So, for example, the European region's market would be served by an operation, or operations, in the European region.
- *Global coordinated configuration.* The converse of the regional strategy, for companies with worldwide locations, is termed the global coordinated configuration. Here the various operations concentrate on a narrow set of activities and products and then distribute their products to the markets around the world
- *Combined regional and global coordinated configuration.* The regional strategy has the advantage of organizational simplicity and clarity, the global coordinated strategy of well-exploited regional advantages. Firms often attempt to seek the advantages of both by adopting a compromise between them. Figure 21.3 illustrates in diagrammatic form the broad shape of each of the four configurations.

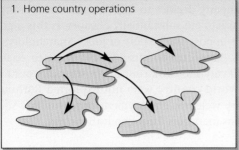

1. Home country operations

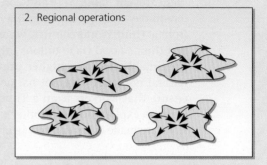

2. Regional operations

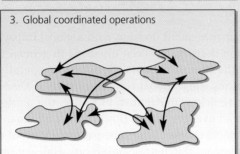

3. Global coordinated operations

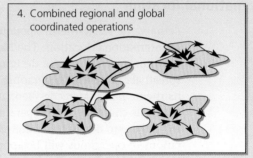

4. Combined regional and global coordinated operations

Social responsibility

Society is made up of organizations, groups and individuals. Each is more than a simple unit of economic exchange. Organizations and their operations functions have responsibility for the general well-being of society beyond short-term economic self-interest. At the level of the individual, this means devising jobs and work patterns which allow individuals to contribute their talents without undue stress. At a group level, it means recognizing and dealing honestly with employee representatives. This principle also extends beyond the boundaries of the organization. Any business has a responsibility to ensure that it does not knowingly disadvantage individuals in its suppliers or trading partners. Businesses are also a part of the larger community, often integrated into the economic and social fabric of an area. Increasingly, organizations are recognizing their responsibility to local communities by helping to promote their economic and social well-being.

The concept of social responsibility permeates operations management. Table 21.2 identifies just some of the social responsibility issues for each of the major decision areas covered in this book.

Social responsibility can be seen as the broad application of ethics in decision-making. For our purposes, ethics can be considered as the framework of moral behaviour which determines whether we judge a particular decision as being right or wrong.[2] In operations management, as in other areas of management, such judgements are not straightforward. What might be unremarkable in one country's or company's ethical framework could be regarded as highly dubious in another's. Nevertheless, there is an emerging agenda of ethical issues to which, at the very least, all operations managers should be sensitive. The first step in this sensitization process is to identify the groups to whom an ethical duty is due. These groups can be categorized as: the organization's customers, its staff, the suppliers who provide it with materials and services, the community in which the organization operates and the shareholders and owners who invest their capital in the business.

Table 21.2 Some social responsibility considerations of operations management decisions

Decision area	Some social responsibility issues
Product/service design	Customer safety Social impact of product
Network design	Employment implications of location Employment implications of plant closure Employment implications of vertical integration
Layout of facilities	Staff safety Disabled access
Process technology	Staff safety Noise damage Repetitive/alienating work
Job design	Staff safety Workplace stress Repetitive/alienating work Unsocial working hours Customer safety (in high contact operations)
Planning and control (including MRP, JIT and project planning and control)	What priority to give customers waiting to be served Unsocial staff working hours Workplace stress Restrictive organizational cultures
Capacity planning and control	'Hire and fire' employment policies Working hours fluctuations Unsocial working hours Service cover in emergencies Relationships with sub-contractors 'Dumping' of products below cost
Inventory planning and control	Price manipulation in restricted markets Warehouse safety
Supply chain planning and control	Honesty in supplier relationships Transparency of cost data Non-exploitation of developing country suppliers Prompt payment to suppliers
Quality planning and control and TQM	Customer safety Staff safety Workplace stress
Failure prevention and recovery	Customer safety Staff safety

Customers' welfare is directly affected by many of the decisions made by operations managers. The first and most obvious effect is that their safety might be compromised by poor operations management decisions. If a product is badly assembled or if the equipment used in a service (such as a rail transport system) is not maintained, customers can come to harm. But customer safety is influenced by more than good manufacturing or maintenance practice; it could also be affected by the degree to which an operation discloses the details of its activities. When should an airline admit that it has received bomb threats? At a less serious level, the ethical framework of operations decisions can affect the equity and fairness with which customers are treated. For example, should a bank discriminate between different customers in order to give priority to those from whom they can make more profit?

Staff are constantly exposed to the ethical framework of the organization throughout their working lives. Organizations have a duty to their staff to prevent their exposure to hazards at work. This means more than preventing catastrophic physical injuries; it means that organizations must take into account the longer-term threat to staff health from, say, repetitive strain injury (RSI) due to short-cycle, repetitive work motions. A more subtle ethical duty to staff is the operations responsibility to avoid undue workplace stress. Stress could be caused through not providing employees with the information which allows them to understand the rationale and consequences of operations decisions, or expecting staff to take decisions for which they are not equipped, because they do not have either the information that they need or the training to make the decision. Again, though, many staff-related ethical decisions are not straightforward. Should an operation be totally honest with its staff regarding future employment changes when doing so might provoke a labour dispute, or signal the company's intentions to its competitors?

Suppliers are always a source of ethical dilemma for the operation. Is it legitimate to put suppliers under pressure not to trade with other organizations, either to ensure that you get focused service from them or to deny competitors this source of supply? Also, do you have any right to impose your own ethical standards on your suppliers, for example, because you would not wish to exploit workers in developing countries? How much effort should you put into making sure that your suppliers are operating as you would? More significantly, would you be prepared to pay a higher price for their product or service if it meant them abandoning what you regard as unethical practice? The recent increase in the transparency expected from suppliers also poses ethical dilemmas. If you are expecting your suppliers to be totally honest and transparent in opening up their costing calculations to you, should you be equally transparent in revealing to them your own internal costings?

Photo courtesy of Howard Davies Oxfam

Some operations have social responsibility as their primary objective. Here Oxfam assists a fresh water project in Kosovo (see the case exercise on Oxfam at the end of this chapter)

The community also has a right to expect its organizations to adopt a responsible attitude. At its most obvious level, organizations have a direct impact on levels of environmental pollution in the community. All manufacturing processes have waste emissions of some sort. What, then, should be the balance between an operation's responsibility to minimize its pollution-causing activities on the one hand, and the cost of doing this on the other? Most countries have legislation which sets minimum standards for such decisions, but should an organization try to achieve a better standard if it is technically possible to do so? The ethical dilemma is similar for a company's products after they have been sold. To what extent should an organization ensure that its products are easily disposed of, or recycled, or perhaps even made so durable that they do not need replacing for a long time? Clearly this last option could have a negative effect on a company's revenues. The responsibility to the community means more than pollution and recycling. It also means sharing responsibility for other groups and organizations within the community, such as schools, hospitals, groups representing special interests, and so on. To what extent should an operation fund or take part in projects with these groups within the community?

Finally, shareholders and owners are also due some ethical duties, even though it may be obvious to state them. They are entitled to a reasonable return on their investments, although what constitutes 'reasonable', and whether the return should be judged in the short or long term are both open to interpretation.

Environmental responsibility

The pollution-causing disasters which make the headlines seem to be the result of a whole variety of causes – oil tankers run aground, nuclear waste is misclassified, chemicals leak into a river, or gas clouds drift over industrial towns. But in fact they all have something in common. They were all the result of an operational failure. Somehow operations procedures were inadequate. Less dramatic in the short term, but perhaps more important in the long-term, is the environmental impact of products which cannot by recycled and processes which consume large amounts of energy – again, both issues which are part of the operations management's broader responsibilities. The good news is that most businesses are now recognizing their environmental responsibilities, often responding to pressures from legislators, regulators, customers and local communities. The bad (or at least challenging) news is that operations managers, together with product or service designers, have to find environmentally sensitive solutions.

● Environmental balance

One way of demonstrating that operations, in a fundamental way, is at the heart of environmental management is to consider the total environmental burden (EB) created by the totality of operations activities:[3]

$$EB = P \times A \times T$$

where

P = the size of the population
A = the affluence of the population (a proxy measure for consumption)
T = technology (in its broadest sense, the way products and services are made and delivered, in other words operations management)

Achieving sustainability means reducing, or at least stabilizing, the environmental burden. Considering the above formula, this can only be done by decreasing the human population, lowering the level of affluence and therefore consumption, or

Environmental policy at 3M[4]

Although the need for organizations to have an environmental policy has become increasingly evident in the last few years, some progressive companies have been aware of their ethical, environmental responsibilities to the community for many years. Back in 1974, 3M published an official corporate environmental policy. This policy articulated the principles by which 3M aimed to solve any environmental pollution it might cause as well as addressing conservation problems. It also set itself measurable environmental goals. These have been updated regularly, so, for example, 3M's goal is to reduce emissions to air, land and water by the year 2000 to 10 per cent of its 1987 levels. One of the company's early programmes was called Pollution Prevention Pays (3P). Its aim was to reduce, or even eliminate, the sources of pollution for which 3M was responsible through its processes or products. In its first 14 years of operation, this programme cut 3M's pollution in half. However, although its original programmes are still in place (albeit updated) the company's approach to pollution control has changed. In the early period of the 3P policy, the company controlled pollution largely through 'end-of-line' control. In other words, its basic processes remained largely unchanged but any emissions and pollution were captured and controlled before they could damage the environment. This approach usually requires capital expenditure on the technology which captures,

cleans and disposes of emissions. 3M found that a cheaper and fundamentally more sound approach to its environmental management was to focus on prevention rather than containment. The concept is to stop all pollution at source, through prevention measures. The 3P programme now seeks to prevent pollution at source, as follows:

- *Product reformulation* – using different raw materials to reduce the polluting effect of products.
- *Process modifications* – physically changing the technology of manufacturing processes to reduce the creation of by-products and pollutants.
- *Equipment redesign* – changing the design of tools and equipment so that they operate more effectively under the specific manufacturing conditions where they are used.
- *Resource recovery* – the recycling of waste and by-products, either for sale to other organizations or for use in 3M products.

Questions

1 How does 3M's 3P policy differ from operations management as we have defined it in this book?

2 Do you have any suggestions for improving the 3P programme?

---

changing the technology used to create products and services. Decreasing population is not feasible. Decreasing the level of affluence would not only be somewhat unpopular, but would also make the problem worse because low levels of affluence are correlated with high levels of birth rate. The only option left is to change the way goods and services are created. Nothing could be closer to the concerns of operations managers.

● Operations decisions and environmental responsibility

Again, it is important to understand that broad issues such as environmental responsibility are intimately connected with the day-to-day decisions of operations managers. Many of these are concerned with waste. Operations management decisions in product and service design significantly affect the utilization of materials both in the short term as well as in long-term recyclability. Process design influences the proportion of energy and labour which is wasted and, again, materials wastage. Planning and control may affect material wastage (packaging being wasted by mistakes in purchasing, for example), but also affects energy and labour wastage. Improvement, of course, is dedicated largely to reducing wastage. Here environmental responsibility and the conventional concerns of operations management happily coincide. Reducing waste, in all it forms, may be environmentally sound but it also saves cost for the organization.

At other times, decisions can be more difficult. Process technologies may be efficient from the operations point of view but may cause pollution, the economic and social consequences of which are borne by society at large. Such conflicts are usually resolved through regulation and legislation. Not that such mechanisms are always effective – there is evidence that just-in-time principles applied in Japan may have produced significant economic gains for the companies which adopted them, but at the price of an overcrowded and polluted road system. Table 21.3 identifies some of the issues concerned with environmental responsibility in each of the operations management decision areas.

Table 21.3 Some environmental considerations of operations management decisions

Decision area	Some environmental issues
Product/service design	Recyclability of materials Energy consumption Waste material generation
Network design	Environmental impact of location Development of suppliers in environmental practice Reducing transport-related energy
Layout of facilities	Energy efficiency
Process technology	Waste and product disposal Noise pollution Fume and emission pollution Energy efficiency
Job design	Transportation of staff to/from work Development in environmental education
Planning and control (including MRP, JIT and project planning and control)	Material utilization and wastage Environmental impact of project management Transport pollution of frequent JIT supply
Capacity planning and control	Over-production waste of poor planning Local impact of extended operating hours
Inventory planning and control	Energy management of replenishment transportation Obsolescence and wastage
Supply chain planning and control	Minimizing energy consumption in distribution Recyclability of transportation consumables
Quality planning and control and TQM	Scrap and wastage of materials Waste in energy consumption
Failure prevention and recovery	Environmental impact of process failures Recovery to minimize impact of failures

Figure 21.4 illustrates how one set of operations managers studied the reduction in the wastage of materials and energy, as well as the external environmental impact of their packaging policies.

Figure 21.4 **Identification of waste minimization for packaging in one company**

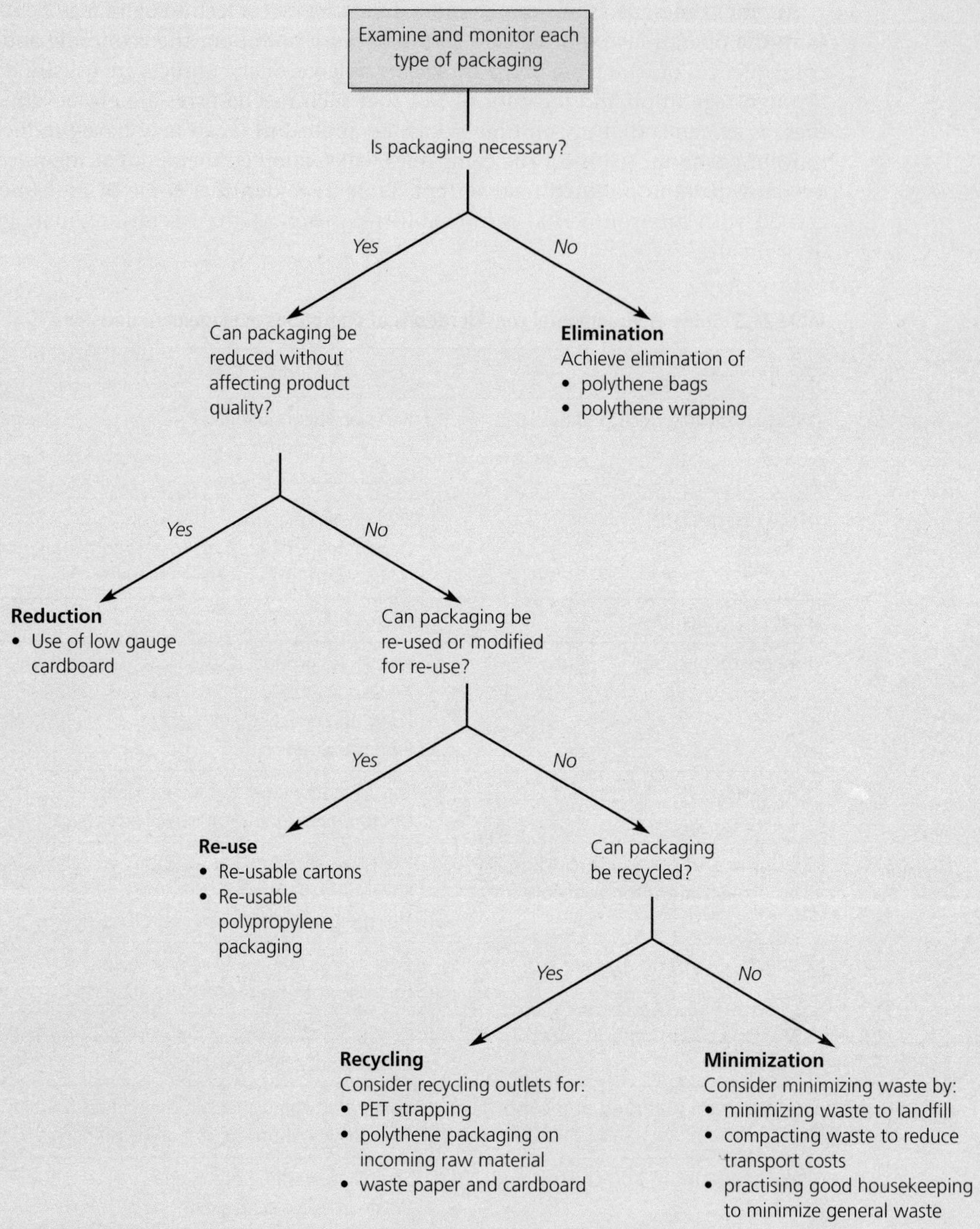

Examine and monitor each type of packaging

Is packaging necessary?

Yes → Can packaging be reduced without affecting product quality?

No → **Elimination**
Achieve elimination of
• polythene bags
• polythene wrapping

Yes → **Reduction**
• Use of low gauge cardboard

No → Can packaging be re-used or modified for re-use?

Yes → **Re-use**
• Re-usable cartons
• Re-usable polypropylene packaging

No → Can packaging be recycled?

Yes → **Recycling**
Consider recycling outlets for:
• PET strapping
• polythene packaging on incoming raw material
• waste paper and cardboard

No → **Minimization**
Consider minimizing waste by:
• minimizing waste to landfill
• compacting waste to reduce transport costs
• practising good housekeeping to minimize general waste

Source: Adapted from Maunder, A. (1999) 'Lower Costs from Reduced Packaging', *Engineering Management Journal*, June.

Ecological footprints[5]

To supply the average person's basic needs in the United States, it takes 12.2 acres of land. In the Netherlands it takes 8 acres, and in India it takes 1 acre. Calculated this way, the Dutch ecological footprint covers 15 times the area of the Netherlands. India's ecological footprint is 1.35 of its area. Most dramatically, if the entire world lived like North Americans, it would take three planet earths to support the present world population.

● Green reporting[6]

Even as late as 1990, relatively few companies around the world provided meaningful information on their environmental practices and performance. Now environmental reporting is increasingly common. One report from the accounting firm KPMG estimates that (as of 2000) around 35 per cent of the world's largest corporations publish reports on their environmental policies and performance. Partly, this may be motivated by an altruistic desire to cause less damage to the plant. However, what is also becoming accepted is that green reporting makes good business sense. There are a number of reasons for this:

● Environmental reporting motivates companies to be more analytical and disciplined in understanding the nature of their processes. This, in turn, both identifies opportunities for cost saving and enhances the degree of process knowledge within the operation. The benefits of process knowledge, as obtained through process control, were explained in Chapter 10.
● The same set of motivational factors pushes operations towards identifying potential environmental risks. This reduces the chances of operational failure resulting in environmental damage, together with all its cost implications. It also creates positive public relations for the organization.
● When talented labour is in short supply, environmental reporting can serve to differentiate socially responsible companies from the rest. In other words, it makes an operation more attractive to work for.
● For the same reasons, it also makes the company more attractive to investors and customers. The growth of 'green living' as a way of life, together with increasing use of 'ethical investment' funds, has significant implications for both the demand for products and services and a company's ability to attract investment.

The effects of operations practice can have real impact on the environment

Photo courtesy of Powerstock

The Global Reporting Initiative sponsored by the Coalition for Environmentally Responsible Economics (CERES) has published guidelines which, it is hoped, will bring some consistency to environmental reporting. Companies which have been influenced by these guidelines include Bristol-Myers Squibb, the health and personal-care company, and Royal Dutch/Shell. In the latter's case, their reporting procedure has, to some extent, been influenced by the controversy over their attempted disposal of the Brent Spar oil rig in 1995. Now all its environmental reports are submitted to external auditors for verification. Some of those who once criticized the company now applaud the reliability of its reports.

● ISO 14000

Another emerging issue in recent years has been the introduction of the ISO 14000 standard. This standard has its historical roots in two systems. The first was the British Standard BS7750 which was intended primarily for UK companies. The second was the EMAS (the Eco-Management and Audits Scheme) which is a voluntary standard introduced throughout the European Union which was incorporated into European law. In fact, both are very similar in principle, although in detail they differ slightly. Both have a three-section environmental management system recommendation which covers initial planning, implementation and objective assessment. Both also had some impact, but largely limited to Europe. The international standard of ISO 14000 allows companies throughout the world to systematically evaluate how their products, services and processes interact with the environment.

ISO 14000 makes a number of specific requirements, including the following:

- a commitment by top-level management to environmental management;
- the development and communication of an environmental policy;
- the establishment of relevant and legal and regulatory requirements;
- the setting of environmental objectives and targets;
- the establishment and updating of a specific environmental programme, or programmes, geared to achieving the objectives and targets;
- the implementation of supporting systems such as training, operational control and emergency planning;
- regular monitoring and measurement of all operational activities;
- a full audit procedure to review the working and suitability of the system.

The ISO 14000 group of standards covers the following areas:

- Environmental Management Systems (14001, 14002, 14004)
- Environmental Auditing (14010, 14011, 14012)
- Evaluation of Environmental Performance (14031)
- Environmental Labelling (14020, 14021, 14022, 14023, 14024, 14025)
- Life-cycle Assessment (14040, 14041, 14042, 14043).

● Quality management and environmental management

Although environmental management is a relatively new field, its organizational role has some parallels with that of quality management. At one time, quality management was a separate discipline from operations management, albeit often organizationally close. Furthermore, quality management was seen as primarily an operational issue rather than a strategic one. Now we can see the result of three trends. First, quality management is seen as a strategic issue which has a profound effect on the competitive success of any business. Second, it is no longer the province of a small group of technical specialists. Rather, it is of immediate concern to everyone in the business, but especially to operations managers. Third, quality is increasingly the subject of awards, self-certification and systemization – for example, the EFQM Excellence Model and ISO 9000 were described in Chapter 20. Environmental management seems to be treading the same path. It is clearly being accepted as having a strategic impact on any business, both in terms of environmental and reputational risk and in terms of identifying cost savings. Second, there are some signs that it is being accepted as an everyday responsibility of operations managers. Third, standards such as ISO 14000 are based on the quality procedures of ISO 9000.

● **CRITICAL COMMENTARY**

The similarity of ISO 14000 to the quality procedures of ISO 9000 is a bit of a giveaway. ISO 14000 can contain all the problems of ISO 9000 (management by manual, obsession with procedures rather than results, a major expense to implement it, and, at its worst, the formalization of what was bad practice in the first place). But ISO 14000 also has some further problems. The main one is that it can become a 'badge for the smug'. It can be seen as 'all there is to do to be a good environmentally sensitive company'. At least with quality standards like ISO 9000 there are real customers continually reminding the business that quality does matter. Pressures to improve environmental standards are far more diffuse. Customers are not likely to be as energetic in forcing good environmental standards on suppliers as they are in forcing the good-quality standards from which they benefit directly. Instead of this type of procedure-based system, surely the only way to influence a practice which has an effect on a societal level is through society's normal mechanism – legal regulation. If quality suffers, individuals suffer and have the sanction of not purchasing goods and services again from the offending company. With bad environmental management, we all suffer. Because of this, the only workable way to ensure environmentally sensitive business policies is by insisting that our governments protect us. Legislation, therefore, is the only safe way forward.

Technology

Technology has always been a major concern of operations managers. It is they, after all, who have a major influence on its choice, implementation and day-to-day use. So, to some extent, there is nothing new in declaring technology one of the major challenges for operations management. What makes things different now (as opposed to 20 years ago) is the sheer pace of technological change and the way in which technologies are combining (for example, computing and telecommunications technologies). This is making it far more difficult to predict the effects that technological change will have on operations management activities. Again, to some extent, this is not new. It is always amusing, for example, to look back at the technological forecasts that were made 50, 10 or sometimes even 5 years ago. Often the impact of some technologies which were confidently predicted as being in the forefront of operations (voice recognition systems, vision enabled robots, etc.) has not yet been realized, even if they are on the horizon now. Other technologies (most notably internet-based technologies) were barely envisaged 20 years ago, nor were they fully understood even a few years ago. In fact, we probably still do not have a full understanding of what such technologies will mean for operations managers.

Nonetheless, notwithstanding the difficulty of forecasting, if we do accept that the pace of technological change is accelerating then there are significant implications for operations managers. The first is that it becomes increasingly important to monitor the environment for emerging technologies. The second is that operations must be able to move quickly in order to adapt to technological change. And the third is that operations managers must develop a clearer understanding of the relationship between the, often unpredictable, potential of new technologies and the way in which they manage their operations. It is this last issue which is probably the most important.

Photo courtesy of BMW

Recyclable plastic parts in a BMW, a company which has been at the forefront of reducing the environmental impact of its products and processes

● Technology as a source of competitive advantage[7]

Technology in some form or other is starting to become a means of building competitive advantage in a wide variety of operations once largely untouched by technology. In retailing, EPOS (electronic point of sale) cash registers are one element in complex stock control systems that link customer requirements into extensive, yet lean, supply chains. Transaction-intensive financial services are increasingly reliant on volume processing equipment such as optical character recognition machines, which reduce costs through economies of scale. Sophisticated yield planning and pricing expert systems provide airlines with the cornerstone of their competitive strategies. Steel companies use small-scale but economical mini-mills to bring production closer to where it is needed. Professional service firms, such as consultants, accountants and engineers, utilize information databases in order to retain experience despite high staff turnover rates. Whatever the specific strategic intent of the firm or the exact functionality of the technology, the significant amounts of capital invested in such systems must reflect a managerial belief that they offer a response to both competitive cost pressures and customer demand for high-quality products and services. For many (if not most) operations, technology can, and indeed should, contribute to the long-term performance of companies.

Take for example the internet-based bookseller Amazon.com. It is (at the time of writing – but things can move fast in such industries) the most successful internet bookseller in the world. Amazon has created a business based on the use of interactive order forms and 'one click' ordering. This means that all customers orders are received in a standardized electronic form. Its databases enable the company to turn the customer into an employee in so much as it is the customer who is responsible for the accuracy of the order and its delivery method. Because no employee is involved in interpreting the customer's order, the improved accuracy of direct orders means that Amazon experiences a far lower return rate than its book chain competitors.

In all these examples, technology has given a competitive advantage to an organization as a result of either being *better* than its competitors or being *different* from its competitors in what it offers. So, for example:

- Technology can increase automation, which in conjunction with centralization can produce significant economies of scale. It is thus helping the company to be *better* than its competitors.
- Technology may help an organization to improve its decision-making performance. For example, one department store has put in place a video link infrastructure that permits all of its 1500 store managers to be actively involved in the central purchasing decision. Technology is again helping the company to be *better* than its competitors.
- Some internet-based music retailers allow individual music tracks to be selected from the repertoire of different artists and compiled on one conventional CD. Such customized albums are not conventionally available to customers. The technology is therefore allowing the company to offer something *different* from its competitors.
- Some technologies, most notably 'data mining' systems which allow the sophisticated manipulation of large quantities of customer-related data, will allow operations to customize the way in which they service customers and also cross-sell other products to them. In this way, the technology is allowing the organization to be both *better* than and *different* from its competitors.

Technology in the operations management decision areas

Technology issues have featured at several points in this book. Chapter 8 was devoted exclusively to issues of process technology. But there have also been technology-related issues in other chapters. Table 21.4 illustrates just some of these. The important point here is that technology has an impact of some sort in almost every area of operations management. And remember the main point here – this is a relatively recent phenomenon.

Some years ago technology was the province of the technologists. Operations managers merely had to understand it sufficiently to integrate it into their operations processes. Now technology is ubiquitous. It is also interconnected. The obvious example is enterprise resource planning (ERP), explained in Chapter 14. ERP deliberately sets out to integrate the databases of many different parts of the organization. But as technology becomes part of all of operations management, this interconnectedness will become more important as all technologies impact on each other. So the part number which is generated during its design on a computer-aided design (CAD) system becomes the 'make or buy' project reference number, which in turn is entered into the routine that plans the layout route for the part in the factory. Its characteristics will be scheduled on the planning and control system, stored and recorded by its number in the warehouse, distributed through the supply chain, and may eventually be returned if it fails, again under the same part number with its recorded characteristics and history. Thus the information and coding generated at the design stage work their way through all subsequent activities in the operation.

Table 21.4 Some technology issues in the operations management decision areas

Decision area	Some technology issues
Product/service design	Use of virtual reality in product/service design Use of virtual and rapid prototyping Common CAD systems and databases
Network design	Expert systems to help location analysis Internet technology cutting out stages in the supply network
Layout of facilities	Use of expert systems to help layout (e.g. CRAFT) Technological limitations on layout positioning
Job design	Use of communications technology to work away from work location Flexible workstations (hot-desking) General impact of technology on job design
Planning and control (including MRP, JIT and project planning and control)	Expert systems to help scheduling, loading, etc. Enterprise resource planning (ERP) systems Project management systems Monitoring and control technologies
Capacity planning and control	Computerized forecasting (including weather forecasts) to predict sales
Inventory planning and control	Automated warehouses Use of automated guided vehicles to move stocks Bar code readers Electronic point-of-sale (EPOS) technology
Supply chain planning and control	Electronic data interchange (EDI) Internet-based purchasing information Internet-based supply chain coordination
Quality planning and control and TQM	Automated quality checking Automated statistical process control of equipment
Failure prevention and recovery	Remote fault diagnostics Simulation of failure points

● The concept of disruptive technologies

One view of how technological innovation can occur is put forward by Professor Christensen of Harvard University. He divides technologies into *sustaining* and *disruptive* technologies. Sustaining technologies are those which improve the performance of established products and services along the same dimensions of performance which the majority of customers have historically valued. Disruptive technologies are those which, in the short term, cannot match the performance that customers expect from products and services. They are typically simpler, cheaper, smaller and sometimes more convenient, but they do not often provide conventionally enhanced product or service characteristics. However, all technologies, sustaining or disruptive, will improve over time. Christensen's main point is that, because technology can progress faster than the requirements of the market, disruptive technologies will eventually enter the zone of performance which *is* acceptable to the markets (*see* Fig. 21.5).

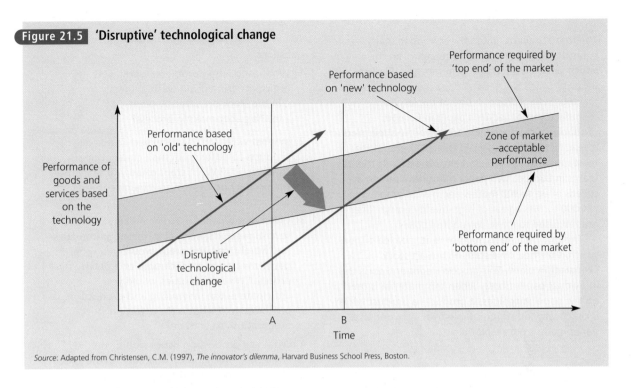

Figure 21.5 'Disruptive' technological change

Performance required by 'top end' of the market

Performance based on 'new' technology

Performance based on 'old' technology

Zone of market –acceptable performance

Performance of goods and services based on the technology

'Disruptive' technological change

Performance required by 'bottom end' of the market

A   B

Time

Source: Adapted from Christensen, C.M. (1997), *The innovator's dilemma*, Harvard Business School Press, Boston.

One example Christensen uses is that of the electric car. At the moment, no electric car can come close to the performance characteristics of internal combustion engines. In that sense, this technology is not an immediate threat to existing car or engine manufacturers (*see* the case exercise on fuel cells at the end of the chapter). However, the electric car is a disruptive technology in so much as its performance will eventually improve to the extent that it enters the lower end of the acceptable zone of performance. Perhaps initially, only customers with relatively undemanding requirements will adopt motor vehicles using this technology. Eventually, however, it could prove to be the dominant technology for all types of vehicle. The dilemma facing all organizations is how to simultaneously improve product or service performance based on sustaining technologies, whilst deciding whether and how to incorporate disruptive technologies.

Recycled St Regis

Photo courtesy of St Regis Paper

Recycled raw materials are processed and pumped through a piping system . . .

. . . to the paper-making machines

The trend towards materials recycling in many countries can have a significant impact on the way in which some products are manufactured. Perhaps the industry which has had to adjust the most is paper-making. St Regis Paper is one of the largest manufacturers of recycled paper in Europe, producing almost a million tonnes of finished product a year. Its mill in Kemsley, in the UK, is one of the most modern, efficient and environmentally friendly plants in Europe. Two paper machines running at speeds of up to 900 metres per minute each make 250 000 tonnes a year of high-quality brown 'liner grades' (used to make corrugated boxes).

The raw material is 100 per cent recycled paper, which is treated on a state-of-the-art stock preparation plant. This process cleans and sorts the individual paper fibres. When this material is used on the paper machines, it produces a product which is practically indistinguishable from conventional paper made from wood pulp.

Questions

1 What production problems would you anticipate from using waste papers
   – in the stock preparation plant
   – in the paper-making process?

2 In what ways would you expect recycled products to differ from their conventional counterparts? What steps could you take in the production process to minimize these differences?

3 Given that a paper machine is likely to make several products, each at different grammages (i.e. weight per unit area), would you regard paper-making as a continuous or a batch process? What difficulties would you anticipate in the scheduling and production processes, and what is the effect on stock preparation likely to be?

4 What key production issues would you anticipate which are associated with the speed at which paper runs through a paper machine (bearing in mind that the paper is very wet at the beginning of the process)?

Knowledge management

In Chapters 6 and 13, we discussed the way in which separate operations connect with each other to form 'supply networks'. We also indicated that the model of the supply network could apply within an operation to describe the connection between micro operations. At a more detailed and complex level of analysis, the network concept can be applied to individuals and small groups within the operation. But whereas in the inter-organizational supply network, trade is conducted in terms of products and services, at the individual level, trade or exchange is partly in terms of *knowledge*. So, one model of organization is as a network of individuals and groups exchanging knowledge within and between themselves. Although this is a somewhat simplistic model of organizations, it is useful as much as it helps us to focus on how knowledge is created and exchanged within the network of groups and individuals that constitutes the operation.

● Knowledge management is fashionable

In the world of popular management ideas, knowledge management is a current enthusiasm. Many books have been published in the last few years and management consulting firms have created a huge market for knowledge management advice. Many companies are also creating jobs with titles such as 'Chief Knowledge Manager'. As ever, this trend is partly a fad and partly based on a genuinely interesting development in management thought. The worthwhile part of the knowledge management fashion is the understanding by many companies that 'knowledge' lies at the heart of their value-adding processes. Take any product or service, whether it is a washing machine, automobile, internet flight-booking service or hospital. The way in which these products or services were created was not random. They were the product of a whole collection of decisions and actions based on an even larger collection of knowledge. One washing machine is better than another because one company has more knowledge of how to design, make, deliver or service its products. One hospital is better than another because its staff have harnessed and deployed their knowledge in such a way as to give a better service. The essential ingredient which makes a product or service what it is, is the knowledge that is embedded in it during its design, creation and delivery.

Operations management and knowledge management

If we accept that, without the application of knowledge, a washing machine is just a collection of raw materials, or a hospital just a group of staff, buildings and equipment, then the obvious question becomes: 'What is the knowledge which operations management creates and deploys to transform these input resources into products and services?' Table 21.5 identifies some of the elements of knowledge which are created and used during the operations management activities which we have described in this book. However, note that there is a difference between *data*, *information* and *knowledge*:

- Data are the objective facts independent of any context. So, in terms of understanding our staff, we could say, 'We have 15 service engineers, two managers and one technician'.
- Information is data which has been analysed or otherwise manipulated in terms of its context. So, we might say that our staff comprise 'fifteen engineers, all of whom are skilled in the maintenance of all the modern equipment likely to be used in our market; both managers are ex-engineers who understand the field engineers' job, and the technician is capable only of relatively routine testing procedures'.
- Knowledge is information which is interpreted through a process of using judgement and values. So, knowledge concerning our staff would be that although engineers are sound technically and have considerable potential, they have never been encouraged or trained to contribute to improving the service, and the best way to do this would be to encourage the two managers to devolve responsibility for customer care to the engineers. If this was successful, the technician's role would no longer be necessary.

Each of the items of knowledge in Table 21.5 may seem obvious in the sense that, from a reading of the various chapters in this book, we know that they are an integral part of decision-making in each of the activity areas. However, remember the difference between information and knowledge. The *information* which we record formally concerning (say) the sequencing and timing constraints of a particular piece of equipment may say that pale grey garments cannot be dyed immediately after dark blue garments. In fact, our *knowledge* of this equipment may be that it is possible to dye grey garments after dark blue ones provided the grey garments are one-piece items, where small colour variations are less important. This is why the concept of knowledge is so important in operations management. Knowledge is rich, interpretative and often value-laden. In very complex operations processes, it may be almost impossible to make the totality of knowledge concerning processes fully and entirely explicit.

Explicit knowledge and tacit knowledge

Much of the knowledge which we have as individuals is codified in some way. By that, we mean that it can be explained verbally, or in writing, or even in some mathematical form. This kind of knowledge is called *explicit* knowledge. It will be found around the operation in formal documents, product and process specifications, information

Table 21.5 Some knowledge requirements in the operations management decision areas

Decision area	Some key items of knowledge
Product/service design	Customer requirements and behaviour Characteristics of components of the design Constraints and capabilities of the operation which will have to produce the design
Network design	Capacity economics (e.g. economics of scale) Financial requirements of capacity change Location characteristics Supply chain capabilities
Layout of facilities	Space and resource requirements of facilities Flow patterns of materials, information and customers
Process technology	Performance characteristics of technology Integration/connectivity of equipment Development potential of technologies
Job design	Work times in reality Anthropometric requirements to perform jobs Team skills requirements and constraints
Planning and control (including MRP, JIT and project planning and control)	Information requirements and lead times Sequencing and timing constraints Capacity limits Process behaviour
Capacity planning and control	Demand sensitivity Process flexibility Performance trade-offs
Inventory planning and control	Deterioration/obsolescence rates Storage requirements Stock-out risks
Supply chain planning and control	Sourcing possibilities Supplier capabilities Relationship requirements Supply chain behaviour
Quality planning and control and TQM	Quality requirements Process behaviour Process improvement potential
Failure prevention and recovery	Failure characteristics Failure consequences Recovery procedures

systems, and on whiteboards in meeting rooms. But not everything we 'know' is written down or even verbalized. For example, much of the knowledge which enables us to drive a motor car, we have never written down, or perhaps even discussed verbally. This is not the explicit knowledge of how to change gear, how to accelerate out of a bend, and so on. This is the way we sense when to change gear to maintain momentum, or exactly how to position ourselves going into the bend to take account of the road conditions. This knowledge is built up over time and is a result of our experience driving a particular car under a wide variety of circumstances. We find it difficult to explain it in words. This type of knowledge is called *tacit* knowledge.

A part of what we put down to skill, intuition and experience is the result of tacit knowledge. Often it is difficult, or impossible, to articulate clearly. So, for example, a skilled craftsperson may not be able to explain exactly how he or she can make furniture so well, or have so much success with gardening. Tacit knowledge may be observed over time and accumulated over time. We can observe it and start to attempt to imitate it, but it will take time. In fact, the most common way of learning tacit knowledge is through some kind of 'apprentice' model. Craftspeople, consultants and doctors, for example, all go through some form of apprenticeship.

● Knowledge creation

This concept of explicit and tacit knowledge has been used to explain how knowledge is created in organizations. The idea, put forward by Nanka and Takeuchi,[8] is that individuals acquire knowledge by moving between tacit and explicit knowledge in a cycle. Figure 21.6 shows this idea and illustrates what it may mean in an operations management context.

The apprentice mode of learning which we described previously is a way of transferring tacit knowledge between individuals. This is the process which Nanka and Takeuchi call *socialization*. Learning takes place through working with, and being close to, experienced people. Thus in designing a new product, designers may work with actual users of the product or service, learning from their own, and the more experienced users', behaviour. So, for example, the designer of a new call centre may spend time working with experienced call-centre operators and supervisors observing how they handle callers. This allows the designer to develop an understanding of the operations context of any new call centre.

Moving between tacit and explicit knowledge is a process which Nanka and Takeuchi call *externalization*. It is a process of attempting to articulate experience into rules and decisions. It will never be a complete process, but at least some knowledge which was tacit may be capable of being written into formal procedures. So, for example, in the call centre, it may be noticed that particularly good staff can use the way a caller describes a problem or request to predict the type of information they will eventually require. This may lead to the concept of presenting call-centre staff with different types of information screen on their computer, depending on how they classify a caller's request for information.

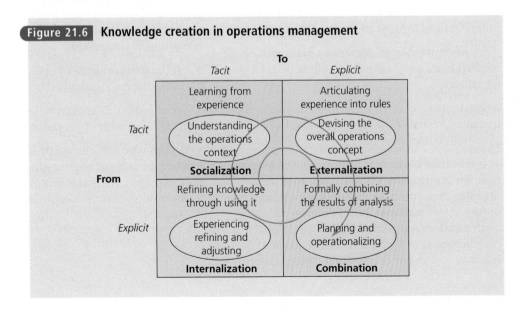

Figure 21.6 **Knowledge creation in operations management**

Different types of explicit knowledge can be brought together in what is called a *combination* process which collects related pieces of knowledge together. So, for example, in the call centre, the designer may combine his or her observations with some of the knowledge available through other call-centre managers, or by looking at some of the potential capabilities and constraints of the existing technology, or new technology which is used to present staff with their help screens.

The final part of the cycle (before going round again) is what is known as *internalization*. The information screens which have been incorporated into the call-centre design will be put into operation. Using them in practice, however, may reveal more knowledge by experiencing the interaction between the new screens and the way in which call-centre staff use them. This 'learning by doing' adds to individuals' tacit knowledge base. By observing the nuances of how this new system is used, further understandings and tacit knowledge may be generated.

● Creativity

The cyclical model described above is presented as a way of understanding how knowledge is created. It is a good point to end on. Operations managers' ultimate duty is to create knowledge, both to ensure the smooth running of their processes, and to ensure the long-term improvement of those processes.

Creativity is not always seen as being a natural attribute of operations managers. They are sometimes characterized as 'unimaginative attenders to detail'. But, hopefully, having read the book, no one could be under such a misapprehension. In reality, operations management is exciting because it calls for both the hands-on pragmatism which will keep the operation running smoothly and, at the same time, the ability to think creatively so as to devise new methods of creating and delivering products and services.

Summary answers to key questions

What impact will globalization and an increasingly international perspective on business have on operations management?

● Globalization is an emotive issue. Some see it as the best way to share wealth in the world, while others see it as the root of many of the world's ills.

● However we view it, operations managers are affected in all the decisions areas by aspects of globalization.

● Even relatively small companies, thanks to the spread and reach of the internet, could have an international dimension.

● International location is probably the biggest issue for multinational companies, who may organize their international network through one of four broad patterns: home country configuration, regional configuration, global coordinated con- figuration, and combined regional and global coordinated configuration.

How does a wider view of social responsibility influence operations management?

● Social responsibility includes understanding the effects of operations management decisions on organizations, groups and individuals. This means more than simply the economic implications of operations management.

● All the decision areas of operations management have a social responsibility dimension to them.

● Social responsibility can be seen as the broad application of ethics to decision-making.

● Groups who are affected by ethical management practice include the organization, the customers, staff, suppliers, the wider community and the organization's shareholders.

Why is it important for operations management to take their environmental responsibility seriously?

● Most of the dramatic environmental disasters are caused by operational failure.

● In a broader sense, all operations management decisions have some kind of environmental impact.

● Increasingly, companies are making formal reports and statements relating to their environmental practice. Operations managers are often responsible for providing the basic information for these reports.

● The environmental management system ISO 14000 is being adopted by a wide range of organizations. Operations managers will often have to implement these standards.

What will new technologies mean for operations management?

● It is almost impossible to say with any degree of certainty how technology will impact operations management in the future. The only thing for certain is that it will.

● It is important to understand, nevertheless, that technology has a major impact on competitive advantage. All promising technologies need to be understood in terms of their potential to make the operation either better than or different from their competitors, or both.

● As well as the obvious decisions regarding the choice of technology, a technological dimension exists for most operations management decision areas.

● The concept of disruptive technology sees future technologies as, at first, having performance levels below market requirements. But, given that technology advances faster than market requirements, these technologies eventually pass the minimum level of market acceptability.

Does 'knowledge management' have a role in operations management?

● Yes. Operations management both creates and deploys knowledge.

● Knowledge is different from information or data. Knowledge is information laden with judgement values and context.

● An important distinction is that between explicit knowledge and tacit knowledge. Explicit knowledge is codified, whereas tacit knowledge is embedded deep within individuals in the operation.

● The process of knowledge creation involves moving between tacit and explicit knowledge.

Oxfam[9]

Oxfam is a major international development, relief and campaigning organization dedicated to finding lasting solutions to poverty and suffering around the world. Oxfam GB, which is affiliated to Oxfam International, works closely with the communities it helps through a network of local partners and volunteers to provide safety, dignity and opportunity for many disadvantaged people around the world.

The Oxford Famine Relief began as one of many famine relief agencies that sprang up during the Second World War. It continued after the war and extended its remit to provide for the relief of suffering whatever the cause might be. Oxfam, as it soon became known, set up collection points for donations and opened its first charity shop in 1948. Oxfam's current network of more than 830 charity shops are run by about 22 000 volunteers and are a key source of income. The shops sell donated items and handcrafts from around the world giving small-scale producers fair prices, training, advice and funding. Orders for items can be made by mail or over the internet. Oxfam has also teamed up with Yahoo! to provide free access to the internet in the UK and at the same time raise funds. Together with legacies and donations for general use and monies raised for particular emergencies (restrictive funds), Oxfam generated a total income of around £124 million in 1998/99. Oxfam employs around 1300 staff, of whom around 700 are based in Oxford, and the others, together with about 1500 locally recruited staff, work overseas.

Oxfam is perhaps best known for its work in emergency situations providing humanitarian aid where it is needed. Oxfam has a particular expertise in providing clean water and sanitation facilities. Around 80 per cent of diseases and over one-third of deaths in the developing world are caused by contaminated water. Yet much of Oxfam's work continues out of the spotlight of disasters and the charity provides continuing help, working with poor communities through a range of programmes concerned with:

- *building livelihoods* – providing seeds and tools so people can grow their own food, helping them secure access to markets, credit and land;

- *improving health and education* – building flood prevention barriers, developing schools and providing building material so that people can rebuild homes, for example;
- *participation in processes* – providing people with some control over their lives;
- *gender issues* – for example, working to remove barriers to girls' education.

Oxfam also speaks out on behalf of disadvantaged communities, pressuring governments and decision-makers on a range of issues including pesticides, food aid, landmines, worker exploitation and Third World debt.

Whether the disasters are natural (such as earthquakes and storms) or political (such as riots and wars), they become emergencies when the people involved can no longer cope. In poor countries, disasters leave homeless and hungry people who will become ill or die within days if they do not get aid. In such situations, Oxfam, through its network of staff in local offices in 70 countries, is able to advise on the resources and help that are needed and where they are needed. Indeed, local teams are often able to provide warnings of impending disasters, giving more time to assess need and coordinate a multi-agency response.

The emergency programmes are run by Oxfam's regional and country offices. The organization's headquarters in Oxford provides advice, materials and staff, often deploying emergency support personnel (ESPs) on short-term assignments when and where their skills are required. Shelters, blankets and clothing can be flown out at short notice from the Emergencies Warehouse in Bicester. Engineers and sanitation equipment can also be provided, including water tanks, latrines, hygiene kits and containers such as the 'Oxfam bucket' which is easy to transport, has a sealable lid, is light and very useful.

Every emergency is different, with differing security situations, aid needs, logistical problems and access issues. In addition, the responses of other agencies such as governments or other relief agencies will also depend on the nature and location of the disaster. Oxfam relies on its local team to help assess each situation to decide whether the organization can make a difference. Sometimes they are unable to respond; the security situation may be too difficult, or other governments may be responding with all that is needed. Local, regional and head office managers have to weigh up all the factors to decide upon the degree and nature of response.

When an emergency is over, Oxfam continues to work with the affected communities through their local offices to help people rebuild their lives and livelihoods.

> **Question**
>
> What are the main issues facing Oxfam's operations managers in terms of:
> - globalization and international management
> - environmental management
> - social responsibility
> - technology
> - knowledge management?

CASE EXERCISE

Is the petrol engine dead?[10]

It is the usefulness of the motor car which has made it so dangerous to the environment. When it was a product affordable only by the relatively affluent in rich countries, it posed little threat. But its advantages of mobility, both for leisure and to increase earning power, made it one of the first purchases of aspiring consumers as nations around the world increased their wealth during the latter half of the twentieth century. In the most developed nations, attempts to control and reduce the environmentally damaging emissions from motor engines have centred around strengthening environmental legislation, especially in the world's largest car markets. Car makers realized that existing engine technology could, in the foreseeable future, become redundant. Even though modern engine technology has improved the emissions from car engines dramatically, many believe that conventional engines are nearing the limit of their refinement in this area.

Leading car companies around the world, especially Daimler-Chrysler, Toyota, Ford, General Motors and Honda, are all working towards the same solution – the fuel cell. Fuel cells combine hydrogen and oxygen to form water and electricity. The electricity is then used to drive an electric motor. Theoretically a fuel cell could be at least twice as efficient, in terms of fuel economy and CO_2 emissions, as internal combustion engines. Most car makers and even fuel providers agree on this. Where they disagree is on how the hydrogen needed by a fuel cell should be provided. Some manufacturers, such as Daimler-Chrysler and Ford, believe the best solution is to use methanol. This could be provided at existing filling stations and converted to hydrogen within the car's engine. However, this would require a new fuel-delivery infrastructure. It also has some health and safety problems. Others believe the best solution is to use hydrogen directly, while yet others believe that some method of extracting hydrogen from gasoline would be the better and safest way forward.

These disagreements (often likened to the disagreements between the VHS and Betamax formats in early video recorders) have led some companies to believe that the age of the fuel cell is still some years away. Hiroyuki Yoshino of Honda Motors is one of these: *'in our view, fossil fuels will continue as the primary source of energy for the next few decades.'*

Even when fuel cells do make an impact, this may not be with domestic motor cars. Trials in Washington, Vancouver and São Paulo have demonstrated that roof-mounted hydrogen cylinders can be safely and economically refuelled in the controlled environment of bus depots. With a range of 300 kilometres, fuel cells have ideal characteristics and may be a practical solution for urban buses.

> **Questions**
>
> 1. What effect do you think fuel cell technology will have on the development of further conventional internal combustion engines?
> 2. From an operations management perspective, what are the implications of hydrogen-based fuel cells for a bus company?

Discussion questions

Rather than conventional discussion questions, try debating the following points:

- Life would be considerably simpler if we went back to serving our own national markets rather than global ones.

- Anti-capitalist globalization protesters are basically conservatives who are frightened by the modern world. Throughout history there have been people like this.

- Soon all organizations will be global organizations. The internet will see to that.

- Business ethics is a contradiction in terms.

- For-profit companies have a primary responsibility to their shareholders; social responsibility therefore only makes sense when it is in the commercial interests of companies.

- The modern corporation cannot separate itself from the society in which it operates. We are entering the mature age of capitalism, where business objectives must reflect the interests of all their stakeholders.

- The only way to get firms to be environmentally responsible is by taxing them for the environmental damage they do.

- The best way to encourage firms to be environmentally responsible is by educating customers only to buy products and services from environmentally responsible companies.

- There is no point even trying to predict new technologies. The only sensible strategy is to wait and see.

- Getting first into new technology is vital, even if companies initially lose money. Only by doing this can they learn how to use the new technology. The biggest single disruptive technology in the last 100 years has been the internet.

- Knowledge management is just a fashion that will fade in a few years.

- Creation of knowledge is the ultimate responsibility of operations managers.

- How can operations managers ever be creative? To do their job well, they have to be dull, technologically obsessed and sad. They ought to get a life.

Notes on chapter

1 Du Bois, F.C. and Oliff, M.D. (1992) 'International Manufacturing Configuration and Competitive Priorities' in Voss, C.A. (ed) *Manufacturing Strategy: Process and Content*, Chapman and Hall.

2 Thompson, A. and Strickland, A.J. (1992) *Strategic Management* (6th edn), Irwin.

3 Ehrlich, P. and Commoner, B., as quoted *in* Hart, S.L. (1997), 'Strategies for a Sustainable World', *Harvard Business Review*, Jan–Feb.

4 Sources: Company information, and Hopfenbeck, W. (1992) *The Green Management Revolution: Lessons in Environmental Excellence*, Prentice Hall.

5 Meadows, D. (1996) 'Our Footprints are Treading too much Earth', *Charleston (SC) Gazette*, April 1.

6 Based on Kolk, A. (2000) *The Economics of Environmental Management*, Financial Times, Prentice Hall. Also *see* www.globalreporting.org.

7 This section is based on the work of our colleague Dr Michael Lewis.

8 Nonaka, I. and Tekeuchi, H. (1997) *The Knowledge Creating Company*, Oxford University Press, NY.

9 Our thanks to everyone at Oxfam.

10 Source: Burt, T. (1999) 'Environmental Issues Move to Centre Stage', *Financial Times Auto Survey*, 3 Dec.

Selected further reading

Andersen, B. and Fagerhaug, T. (1999) 'Green Performance Measurement', *International Journal of Business Performance Management*, Vol 1, No 2.

Azzone, G. and Noci, G. (1998) 'Identifying Effective PMSs for the Deployment of "Green" Manufacturing Strategies', *International Journal of Operations and Production Management*, Vol 18, No 4.

Flaherty, M.T. (1996) *Global Operations Management*, McGraw-Hill.

Gupta, M.C. (1995) 'Environmental Management and its Impact on the Operations Function', *International Journal of Operations and Production Management*, Vol 15, No 8.

Guth, W.D. and Tagruri, R. (1965) 'Personal Values and Corporate Strategy', *Harvard Business Review*, Vol 43, No 5.

Leonard-Barton, D. (1995) 'Wellsprings of Knowledge', *Harvard Business School Press*.

Murchison, C. and Baird, J. (1996) 'An Introduction to Green Product Development for SMEs', *Engineering Management Journal*, Dec.

Forecasting the volume of demand

Any model which describes some aspect of the behaviour of any system or phenomenon can be used to predict its future behaviour. Here, however, we are specifically concerned with some of the more common models or techniques which are used largely for the prediction of demand levels. Demand is the main determinant of volume, and volume has significant impact on design in operations.

There are several ways in which forecasting models and techniques can be classified. One classification divides techniques into:

- subjective and objective, and
- non-causal and causal.

Subjective forecasting techniques are those which involve judgement and intuition from one or more individuals, whose approach to the forecasting task is unlikely to be explicit, but will be based on experience.

Objective techniques are those which have specified and systematic procedures. This means that results produced by these methods are reproducible no matter who uses them.

Non-causal techniques are those which use the past values of a variable to predict its future values. They assume that the underlying causes of events, which have pertained in the past, will continue to shape events in exactly the same way in the future.

Causal techniques attempt to make predictions on the basis of causal relationship. If the cause–effect relationship between variables can be modelled, then predictions of the factors which influence whatever we are trying to forecast will enable a forecast to be made. The assumption of such methods is that these causal variables can be measured and projected more accurately than actual demand itself.

Some of the more common forecasting methods which we shall briefly describe are classified in Figure A1.1.

Time series analysis

Time series techniques examine the pattern of past behaviour of a phenomenon over time, and use the analysis to forecast the phenomenon's future behaviour. For example, suppose a company is attempting to predict the future sales of a product. The past three years' sales, quarter by quarter, are shown in Figure A1.2(a). This series of past sales may be analysed to indicate future sales. For instance, underlying the series might be a linear upward trend in sales. If this is taken out of the data, as in Figure A1.2(b), we are left with a cyclical seasonal variation. The mean deviation of each quarter from the trend line can now be taken out, to give the average seasonality deviation. What remains is the random variation about the trends and seasonality lines, Figure A1.2(c). Future sales may now be predicted as lying within a band about a projection of the trend, plus the seasonality. The width of the band will be a function of the degree of random variation.

Forecasting unassignable variations

The random variations which remain after taking out trend and seasonal effects are without any known or assignable cause. This does not mean that they do not have a cause, however, just that we do not know what it is. Nevertheless, some attempt can be made to forecast it, if only on the basis that future events will, in some way, be based on past events. We will examine two of the more common approaches to forecasting which are based on projecting forward from past behaviour. These are:

- moving-average forecasting;
- exponentially smoothed forecasting.

Moving-average forecasting

The moving-average approach to forecasting takes the previous *n* periods' actual demand figures, calculates

Some common forecasting techniques

	Non-causal techniques	Causal techniques
Objective techniques	Time series analysis ● Moving-average smoothing ● Exponential smoothing	Regression Economic models
Subjective techniques	Intuition	Individual expert opinion Group expert opinion (e.g. Delphi forecasting)

Figure A1.2 **Time series analysis with (a) trend, (b) seasonality and (c) random variation**

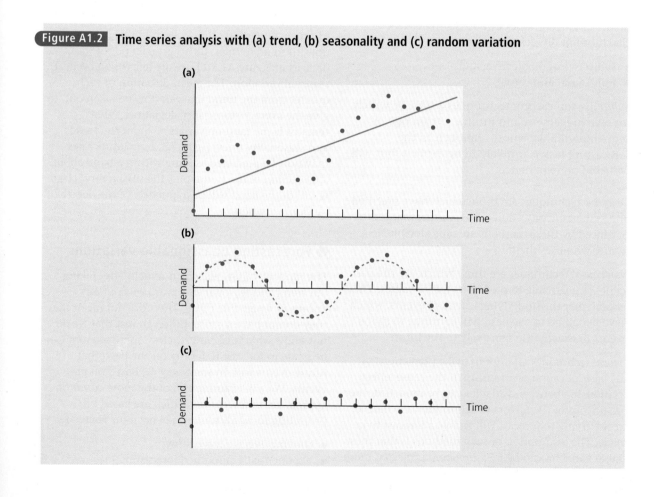

the average demand over the n periods, and uses this average as a forecast for the next period's demand. Any data older than the n periods plays no part in the next period's forecast. The value of n can be set at any level, but is usually in the range 4 to 7.

Example – Eurospeed parcels

Table A1.1 shows the weekly demand for Eurospeed, a European-wide parcel delivery company. It measures demand, on a weekly basis, in terms of the number of parcels which it is given to deliver (irrespective of the size of each parcel). Each week, the next week's demand is forecast by taking the moving average of the previous four weeks' actual demand. Thus if the forecast demand for week t is F_t and the actual demand for week t is A_t, then:

$$F_t = \frac{A_{t-1} + A_{t-2} + A_{t-3} + A_{t-4}}{4}$$

For example, the forecast for week 35:

$$F_{35} = (72.5 + 66.7 + 68.3 + 67.0)/4$$
$$= 68.8$$

Exponential smoothing

There are two significant drawbacks to the moving-average approach to forecasting. First, in its basic form, it gives equal weight to all the previous n periods which are used in the calculations (although this can be overcome by assigning different weights to each of the n periods). Second, and more important, it does not use data from beyond the n periods over which the moving average is calculated. Both these problems are overcome by *exponential smoothing*, which is also somewhat easier to calculate.

The exponential-smoothing approach forecasts demand in the next period by taking into account the actual demand in the current period and the forecast which was previously made for the current period. It does so according to the formula:

$$F_t = \alpha A_{t-1} + (1 - x) F_{t-1}$$

where α = the smoothing constant.

The smoothing constant α is, in effect, the weight which is given to the last (and therefore assumed to be most important) piece of information available to the forecaster. However, the other expression in the formula includes the forecast for the current period which included the previous period's actual demand, and so on. In this way all previous data has a (diminishing) effect on the next forecast.

Table A1.2 shows the data for Eurospeed's parcels forecasts using this exponential-smoothing method, where $\alpha = 0.2$. For example, the forecast for week 35 is:

$$F_{35} = 0.2 \times 67.0 + 0.8 \times 68.3 = 68.04$$

The value of α governs the balance between the *responsiveness* of the forecasts to changes in demand, and the *stability* of the forecasts. The closer α is to 0 the more forecasts will be dampened by previous

Table A1.1 Moving-average forecast calculated over a four-week period

Week	Actual demand (thousands)	Forecast
20	63.3	
21	62.5	
22	67.8	
23	66.0	
24	67.2	64.9
25	69.9	65.9
26	65.6	67.7
27	71.1	66.3
28	68.8	67.3
29	68.4	68.9
30	70.3	68.5
31	72.5	69.7
32	66.7	70.0
33	68.3	69.5
34	67.0	69.5
35		68.6

Table A1.2 Exponentially smoothed forecast calculated with smoothing constant $\alpha = 0.2$

Week (t)	Actual demand (thousands) (A)	Forecast $(F_t = \alpha A_{t-1} + (1-\alpha) F_{t-1})$ $(\alpha = 0.2)$
20	63.3	60.00
21	62.5	60.66
22	67.8	60.03
23	66.0	61.58
24	67.2	62.83
25	69.9	63.70
26	65.6	64.94
27	71.1	65.07
28	68.8	66.28
29	68.4	66.78
30	70.3	67.12
31	72.5	67.75
32	66.7	68.70
33	68.3	68.30
34	67.0	68.30
35		68.04

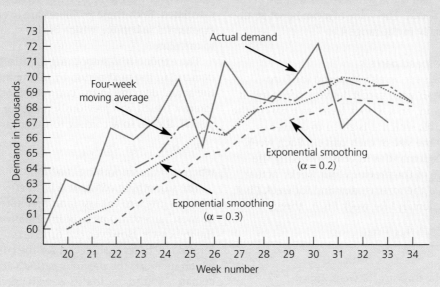

Figure A1.3 A comparison of a moving-average forecast and exponential smoothing with the smoothing constant α = 0.2 and 0.3

forecasts (not very sensitive but stable). Figure A1.3 shows the Eurospeed volume data plotted for a four-week moving average, exponential smoothing with α = 0.2 and exponential smoothing with α = 0.3.

● Regression models

Regression models use statistical techniques to determine the 'best fit' expression which describes the relationship between the variable being forecast and other variables. For example, suppose an ice-cream company is trying to forecast its future sales. After examining previous demand, it figures that the main influence on demand at the factory is the average temperature of the previous week. To understand this relationship, the company plots demand against the previous week's temperatures. This is shown in Figure A1.4. Using this graph, the company can make a reasonable prediction of demand, once the average temperature is known, provided that the other conditions prevailing in the market are reasonably stable. If they are not, then these other factors which have an influence on demand will need to be included in the regression model, which becomes increasingly complex.

● Econometric models

At very high levels of demand forecasting – examining growth rates for a whole industry sector for example – complex regression approaches are called *econometric modelling*. Econometric models

consist of a set of regression equations which describe complex cause–effect relationships. These equations are solved simultaneously, which allows a more realistic representation of the relationships within the decision. However, the cost of developing such models is usually very high.

● Individual expert judgement

Some events which we may wish to forecast cannot be expressed in a manner which allows the use of quantitative objective models. The rate of technological change in an industry, for example, might be particularly important to a company forecasting demand for its products which are bought as 'add-ons' to other manufacturers' products. The rate of technical change is not a factor which can be predicted by any objective method. Under such circumstances, decision-makers have to rely on the opinions of people who, through their experience of similar situations or familiarity with the current problem, are deemed to be 'experts'.

Sometimes, using expert judgement is partially a substitute for some more rigorous but expensive method. For example, a company wishing to predict how its sales will stand up to a well-publicized rival product, due to be launched shortly, may ask all its sales people for their opinions. The sales people will probably base their opinions partly on their perceptions of and 'feel' for the market, and partly on the comments made to them by the customers with whom they are in everyday contact. This latter

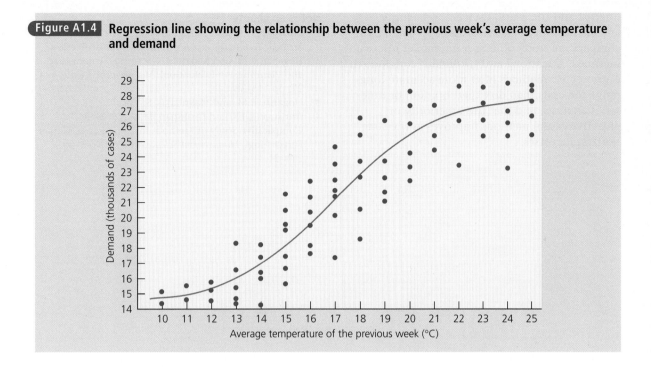

element of expert judgement could well be performed with greater accuracy by a customer survey. However, a customer survey would be more costly, would take time, and might inadvertently publicize the rival product.

● Delphi group forecasts

This technique is one of several used to bring together the opinions and forecasts of a group of experts. It has been defined as 'a method of structuring a group or communication process, so that the process is effective in allowing a group of individuals, as a whole, to deal with a complex problem'.[1] The technique seeks to obtain a group opinion through an anonymous process of controlled iterative feedback. The usual method is for a panel of experts (who are not allowed to communicate about the problem) to be interrogated through questionnaires. The information from the group is then collected together, summarized, aggregated and presented anonymously as feedback to the group. Each member of the group can then compare his or her own prediction with the group 'average'. The individual may then modify (or not as the case may be) his or her first-round prediction, and the

process is repeated. Eventually it becomes clear whether a consensus is emerging from the group.

● The performance of forecasting models

Forecasting models are widely used in management decision-making, and indeed most decisions require a forecast of some kind, yet the performance of this type of model is far from impressive. Hogarth and Makridakis,[2] in a comprehensive review of the applied management and finance literature, show that the record of forecasters using both judgement and sophisticated mathematical methods is not good. What they do suggest, however, is that certain forecasting techniques perform better under certain circumstances. In short-term forecasting there is:

> ... *considerable inertia in most economic and natural phenomena. Thus the present states of any variables are predictive of the short-term future (i.e. three months or less). Rather simple mechanistic methods, such as those used in time series forecasts, can often make accurate short-term forecasts and even outperform more theoretically elegant and elaborate approaches used in econometric forecasting'*[3]

Long-term forecasting methods, although difficult to judge because of the time lapse between the forecast and the event, do seem to be more amenable to an objective causal approach. In a comparative study of long-term market forecasting methods, Armstrong and Grohman[4] conclude that econometric methods offer more accurate long-range forecasts than do expert opinion or time series analysis, and that the superiority of objective causal methods improves as the time horizon increases.

Notes on chapter

1 Linstone, H.A. and Turoof, M. (1975) *The Delphi Method: Techniques and Applications*, Addison-Wesley.
2 Hogarth, R.M. and Makridakis, S. (1981) 'Forecasting and Planning: An Evaluation', *Management Science*, Vol 27, pp 115–38.
3 Hogarth, R.M. and Makridakis, S., *op. cit.*
4 Armstrong, J.S. and Grohman, M.C. (1972) 'A Comparative Study of Methods for Long-Range Market Forecasting', *Management Science*, Vol 19, No 2, pp 211–21.

APPENDIX

2

Time estimation – work measurement

● Time estimation

One of the most important pieces of information in the design activity of any organization is how long particular tasks will take to complete. Some estimate of a task's duration is an essential prerequisite for many key design decisions. The following list identifies some applications for time data.

Designing products, services and processes (Chapter 5)
- Evaluating alternative product designs which have different methods of assembling or manufacturing products.
- Evaluating alternative ways of designing the serving of customers in high customer contact services.

Designing the operations network (Chapter 6)
- Evaluating transportation times in location decisions.
- Evaluating whether to perform a task in-house.
- Evaluating the amount of capacity which will be needed in the operation.

Layout and flow (Chapter 7)
- Evaluating the times to perform tasks at each stage of a process.
- Evaluating alternative routings through an operation.
- Balancing the work allocated to each stage of an operation (identifying bottlenecks).

Process technology (Chapter 8)
- Evaluating alternative types of technologies.
- Evaluating alternative sizes of machines and equipment.

Job design (Chapter 9)
- Evaluating alternative work methods.
- Evaluating safety allowances.
- Evaluating remuneration schemes and 'allowed-time' schemes.

- Evaluating the performance of individuals, or groups of staff.

It is because of this wide variety of uses for time estimates that all organizations need to make some kind of estimate of the length of time which will be needed for each of the tasks which are performed. In order to get such an estimate all organizations have three options:

- they can guess;
- they can assume that the time which is taken to do a job is in fact the correct time to do it;
- they can use a measuring technique which is systematic and has reasonably predictable limits of accuracy.

It is the latter approach which we will examine in this Appendix. It involves applying systematic techniques to tasks and work-time estimation, and it is known as *work measurement*, as was outlined in Chapter 9.

● Work measurement models

Work measurement is the application of techniques designed to establish the time for a qualified worker to carry out a specified job at a defined level of performance.

Basic times
Basic times were described in Chapter 9 as the 'building blocks' of time estimation. With the basic times for a range of different tasks, an operations manager can construct a time estimate for any longer activity which is made up of the tasks. For example, suppose an operations manager of a company which erects temporary buildings needs to estimate the time which should be taken to erect a particular building. The time could be estimated by adding together the basic times for each part of the total job. This is the idea behind 'synthetic' time estimating which will be explained later.

Standard times

The standard time for each element of a job consists principally of two parts (although in some cases extra allowances may be applicable):

- Basic time: the time taken by a qualified worker, doing a specified job at standard performance.
- Relaxation allowance: the allowances which are added to the basic time to allow for rest, relaxation and personal needs.

Most of the techniques of work measurement involve the breaking down of the job to be studied into *elements*. For each of these elements, separate *standard times* are then determined. The standard time of the job as a whole is then the sum of all the standard times of its constituent elements (see Figure A2.1).

Example

Suppose a task has four elements, each of which warrants a different allowance as shown in Table A2.1.

This is shown diagrammatically in Figure A2.2.

The advantages of standard time

The standard time for any task is not necessarily the time which will be taken actually to perform it in reality. That is not a disadvantage, however, provided the operations managers who work with the information know how it has been derived. In fact the 'basic time', which is the time which a 'qualified worker, working at standard performance' would take is often a more useful piece of information at the micro level of design. Nevertheless, the standard time for a task, because it is both *normalized* to the performance of someone

Figure A2.1 The standard time for a whole job is made up of the basic times for all its elements with the addition of the allowances for each element

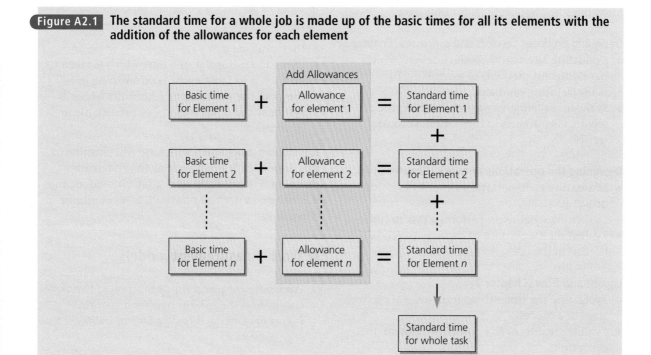

Figure A2.2 Standard time calculation for the example

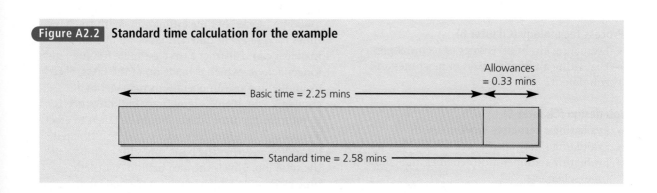

Table A2.1 Time elements of task

Element	Basic time (mins)	Relaxation allowance (%)	Relaxation allowance (mins)	Standard time (mins)
a	0.67	18	0.12	0.79
b	0.43	14	0.06	0.49
c	0.85	12	0.10	0.95
d	0.30	17	0.05	0.35
Total	2.25		0.33	2.58

working at standard performance and also contains the *allowances* which staff should be taking, can be particularly useful.

The standard time for a task is, in effect, an estimate of the total amount of *work* which is needed to perform the task. It enables all types of work to be expressed in terms of a common unit – the 'standard minute' or 'standard hour' (SM or SH). For different tasks the proportion of the standard minute or hour spent actually working and the proportion spent resting will vary, but the two parts together always add up to the common unit. Figure A2.3 illustrates this idea.

Allowances

There are several allowances which may be applied to the basic time, depending on the circumstances. The main one is *relaxation allowance*. Special allowances may also be applied such as:

- contingency allowances
- interfaces or synchronization allowances
- introductory allowances
- unusual condition allowances
- unoccupied time allowances.

Relaxation allowance is defined as:

... an addition to the basic time intended to provide the worker with the opportunity to recover from the physiological and psychological effects of carrying out specified work under specified conditions and to allow attention to personal needs. The amount of the allowance will depend on the nature of the job.

The way in which relaxation allowance is calculated, and the exact allowances given for each of the factors which determine the extent of the allowance, varies considerably between different organizations. Table A2.2 illustrates the allowance table used by one company which manufactures domestic appliances. The table shows the percentage allowance to be applied to each element of the job. All allowances are additive and a personal needs allowance of 10 per cent is added to all elements.

● The techniques of work measurement

The method of moving from the basic times for each element of a task to the standard time for the whole task is more or less the same no matter how the basic time is derived. The basic time itself can be measured or estimated by a number of techniques, however. The work measurement approach uses five techniques:

1. Time study
2. Synthesis from elemental data
3. Predetermined motion-time systems
4. Analytical estimating
5. Activity sampling

Time study was described in Chapter 9, but a brief description of the other techniques follows.

Synthesis from elemental data

A work measurement technique for building up the time for a job at a defined level of performance by totalling element times obtained previously from the studies in other jobs containing the elements concerned or from synthetic data.

Predetermined motion-time systems (PMTS)

A work measurement technique whereby times established for basic human motions (classified according to the nature of the motion and the conditions under which it is made) are used to build up the time for a job at a defined level of performance.

Figure A2.3 **Using the standard time approach to work measurement the standard unit of work remains the same, only the proportions of relaxation and working time vary**

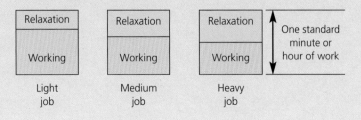

Table A2.2 An allowances table used by a domestic appliance manufacturer

Allowance factors	Example	Allowance (%)
Energy needed		
Negligible	none	0
Very light	0–3 kg	3
Light	3–10 kg	5
Medium	10–20 kg	10
Heavy	20–30 kg	15
Very heavy	Above 30 kg	15–30
Posture required		
Normal	Sitting	0
Erect	Standing	2
Continuously erect	Standing for long periods	3
Lying	On side, face or back	4
Difficult	Crouching, etc.	4–10
Visual fatigue		
Nearly continuous attention		2
Continuous attention with varying focus		3
Continuous attention with fixed focus		5
Temperature		
Very low	Below 0°C	over 10
Low	0–12°C	0–10
Normal	12–23°C	0
High	23–30°C	0–10
Very high	Above 30°C	over 10
Atmospheric conditions		
Good	Well ventilated	0
Fair	Stuffy/smelly	2
Poor	Dusty/needs filter	2–7
Bad	Needs respirator	7–12

Analytical estimating

'A work measurement technique, being a development of estimating whereby the time required to carry out the elements of a job at a defined level of performance is estimated from knowledge and experience of the elements concerned.'

Activity sampling

A technique in which a large number of instantaneous observations are made over a period of time of a group of machines, processes or workers. Each observation records what is happening at that instant and the percentage of observations recorded for a particular activity or delay is a measure of the percentage of time during which that activity or delay occurs.

The recording techniques of method study

In Chapter 9 a flow process chart was used as an illustration of one of the many techniques of work study which can be used to record the present method of doing a job. The flow process chart was chosen because it is probably the best known and most used of these techniques. Nevertheless, there are others which deserve at least a mention. Most of these techniques can be used for several purposes but tend to focus on one particular purpose – namely recording the sequence of tasks, recording the time relationships between different parts of a job, and recording the movement of staff, information or materials within the job.

Those techniques which focus primarily on determining the sequence of tasks include:

- outline process charts
- flow process charts
- two-handed process charts.

Those which concentrate primarily on the time relationships between parts of a job include:

- multiple-activity charts
- simo charts.

Those which concentrate on the movement of elements within the job include:

- memo-motion analysis
- micro-motion analysis
- flow diagrams.

Process charts

The flow process chart described in Chapter 9 used the five symbols to describe the sequence of tasks as either operations, inspections, transportations, delays or storages. In fact there are three types of process chart – outline process charts, flow process charts, and two-handed process charts. The symbols may have marginally different meanings, depending on which of these charts is being used. Process charts can be applied to the flow of materials or information through a job, or alternatively can be used to chart the sequence of activities done by the member of staff. Table A3.1 gives the meanings of each symbol for each kind of process chart.

For example, a job might need both a material (or information) flow process chart and a staff flow process chart to describe it completely. Figure A3.1 gives an example of this for the job of adjusting and packing a test meter where each meter is adjusted to a customer's particular requirements.

Outline process charts

Sometimes as a precursor to a full flow process chart, a job might be described by means of an outline process chart. An outline process chart adopts the same principles as the flow process chart but uses only the operation and inspection symbols and often aggregates several small tasks into one overall operation. Figure A3.2 shows an outline

Table A3.1 The symbols used in process charts

Symbol	Outline process chart	Flow process chart (for staff)	Flow process chart (for materials)	Two-handed process chart
●	Operation	Operation	Operation	Operation
➡	Not used	Transportation	Transportation	Transportation
▭	Not used	Delay	Delay	Delay
▪	Inspection	Inspection	Inspection	Not used
▼	Not used	Not used	Storage	Hold

Staff and materials flow process charts for an adjustment and packing task

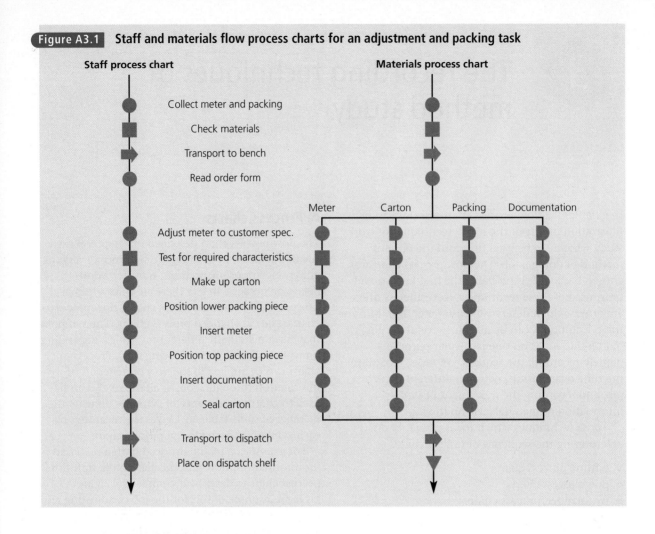

Staff process chart

- Collect meter and packing
- Check materials
- Transport to bench
- Read order form
- Adjust meter to customer spec.
- Test for required characteristics
- Make up carton
- Position lower packing piece
- Insert meter
- Position top packing piece
- Insert documentation
- Seal carton
- Transport to dispatch
- Place on dispatch shelf

Materials process chart

Meter | Carton | Packing | Documentation

Figure A3.2 **Outline process chart for adjustment and packing task**

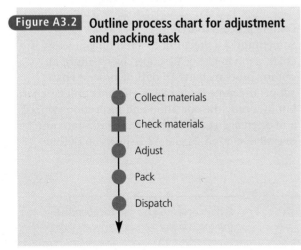

- Collect materials
- Check materials
- Adjust
- Pack
- Dispatch

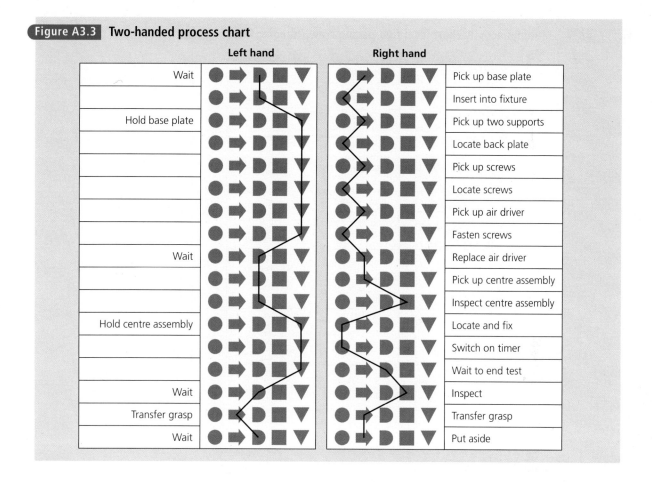

Figure A3.3 Two-handed process chart

process chart for the assembling and packing operation described previously.

Two-handed process chart

The two-handed process chart again adopts the same principles but this time on a more micro scale. The sequence of motion of each hand is charted using the same symbols as before. There are slight changes to the meaning of the symbols, however. The delay symbol is used to indicate that the hand is waiting to carry out its next task. The storage symbol is used to indicate that the hand is holding onto a piece of material or a document. Usually two-handed process charts are shown on a pre-formatted diagram similar to that shown in Figure A3.3. Here a particular assembly job is described by recording the activities of each hand during the total job. The advantage of using a pre-formatted diagram such as this is that the analysis also gives an indication of the relationship of the activities performed by each hand.

● Time relationship techniques

This idea of describing the time relationship between parts of the job is carried further with techniques such as multiple-activity charts and micro-motion analysis.

Multiple-activity charts

Often jobs involve either more than one member of staff and/or machines. It is sometimes necessary to record and understand the interrelationships between these different resources in the job. To do this, multiple-activity charts are used to record activities against the same time scale, placing the 'time map' for each resource against each other to make comparison easy. For example, Figure A3.4 shows a multiple-activity chart for two people changing and adjusting a machine used to slit paper reels into smaller reels.

Multiple-activity chart for a two-person crew changing a slitting machine

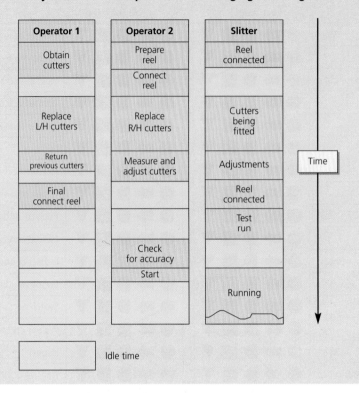

Simo chart

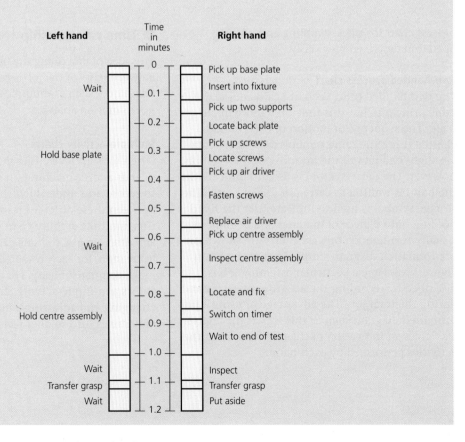

The simo chart

The principles behind the multiple-activity chart and the two-handed process chart may be combined in a simo chart. Whereas the two-handed process chart has a separate line for each element in the job, the simo chart is drawn on a time-based scale. This allows the job designer to see the relative time taken by each part of the job. Figure A3.5 shows a simo chart for the same job that was described in Figure A3.3.

● Path of movement techniques

In some jobs the path of movement of materials, information or staff is the major concern of the job designer. Work study provides a number of techniques which can be used to track the movement of resources.

Memo-motion video recording

One of the most convenient ways to record the path of movement of any aspect of a job is to record long periods of the job using video cameras. A speeded up play-back of the recording can then compress hours of activity into a few minutes. More importantly, the path of movement within the job can be recorded on charts or plans of the area of work.

Micro-motion analysis

The same principle can be used in the opposite way. For the examination of every detail of fast work (for example, the hand movements in a complicated routine assembly task) video recording of the task can be slowed down to allow the job designer to trace the exact path of movement of the hands during the job. Again, this path can be superimposed on a diagram or picture of the

Index